mr. skin's
skincyclopedia

mr. skin's
skincyclopedia

The A-to-Z Guide to Finding Your Favorite Actresses Naked

Mr. Skin

🦘 St. Martin's Griffin ✲ New York

www.stmartins.com

Library of Congress Cataloging-in-Publication Data

Skin, Mr.
    Mr. Skin's skincyclopedia: the A-to-Z guide to finding your favorite actresses
    naked / Mr. Skin.—1st U.S. ed.
       p. cm.
    ISBN 0-312-33144-4
    EAN 978-0312-33144-3
       1. Nudity in motion pictures.   2. Motion picture actors and actresses—
    Biography.   3. Actresses—Biography.   4. Motion picture actors and actresses—
    Credits.   I. Title.
    PN1995.9.N92S55 2005
    791.4302'8'0922—dc22
       [B]   2004051156

10 9 8 7 6 5 4 3 2

To London, my baby daughter.

I dread the day you figure out what Daddy actually does for a living.

Acknowledgments

Special thanks to Howard Stern for introducing your millions of listeners to me and my Web site. Without the King of All Media, I couldn't have become the King of All Naked Celebrities.

To my sister, Kristina McBride, Chieftess of Queendom at MrSkin.com, no one who worked on this book could have done so without your tireless efforts and dedication. I sure am glad your years of higher education and experience in the legitimate business world went to waste.

To my Skinployees at Skin Central who spend countless hours each day slaving over nude pictures and naked footage of the world's most beautiful women in various states of sexual abandon, thank you—wait a minute: you should thank me! But(t) seriously, thanks to: Melinda Fries, Jim "The Marinator" Mariner, Ryan McClughen, Sam Rakowski, and Matt Shadis.

To my Techies, who made it possible to convert a lifetime of obsession into convenient book form. Thanks to Bert Curtis, Derek Meklir, Scott McNulty, Dan Reed, Trey Runcie, TJ Cathey, Hank Butler, Ed Fisher, Chris Clepper, and Steve Svoboda.

Special thanks to Rob Kolson and Jim Kourlas.

To Marc Resnick at St. Martin's. Thanks for your expertise and skin-thusiasm. This beats editing romance novels, huh?

To my agents at Venture Literary, Frank Scatoni and Greg Dinkin. You guys believed in this idea for years and patiently guided it (and me) along to this beautiful skin-clusion. Drinks are on me!

To Ma and Pa Skin, who have contributed in countless ways to my career, from buying me my first VCR, to helping in the construction of this book, to always making sure you knocked before coming into my bedroom. Thanks again.

To Harry Teinowitz and Spike Manton, who were there for the creation of "Mr. Skin." Next time you get a bright idea, make sure you get a percentage of the company. Like I said: *next* time.

To Celebrity Sleuth, the man behind the magazine of which I've been a lifelong fan. You continue to be a skin-spiration.

To the radio hosts who have played such an important part in getting the word out on MrSkin.com: Steve Dahl in my hometown of Chicago; Don and Mike, Bob and Tom, Drew and Mike, The Rise Guys, Tom Leykis, Pugs and Kelly, Tom Bernard, Kirk, Mark, and Lopez, Tim and Mark, Dennis and Callahan, Jeff O'Neil, Shred and Reagan, Johnson and Tofte, Lamont and Tonelli, Wags and Elliot, The Regular Guys, Pete McMurray, and of course Lex and Terry . . .

To Mike Liuzza a.k.a. Skin Jr.: your hard work and hardcore dedication to skin-ternational pursuits make my job so much easier and MrSkin.com so much stronger. May you never become employable anyplace else. Thank you.

To Skinterns Jenny Speciale, Rosie McBride, Lindsey Butler, and Daniel "Skin Meister" Carta. Thanks.

To Mrs. Skin, Michelle: you could have married a doctor, a lawyer, a banker or anyone your heart desired. Instead, you married me. Thanks for understanding how much work it really is to be Mr. Skin and, more important, thanks for not being the jealous type.

If I forgot anybody, email me. I'll get you a free password to MrSkin.com. I promise.

—Mr. Skin

Skintroduction

Hi. I'm Mr. Skin.

I have the best job in the world.

My Web site, MrSkin.com, is the Internet's number-one outlet for celebrity movie reviews, pictures, video clips and all kinds of skinfo on actresses in the raw. So, that's right, I not only get to look at . . . and linger on . . . and think about . . . and get all kinds of involved with . . . images of naked female celebrities all day, I get paid for it.

But I'm not bragging.

I'm just reminding myself how I went from being a starstruck suburban teenager to the world's foremost authority on famous chick nudity.

It's quite an amazing tail. And, yes, I do mean "tail." Because with me, every pun is always intended.

To begin with, this is your average, garden-variety story of boy meets girls, boy wants to see girls naked, boy finds VCR, boy drops out of society. But don't worry: there's lots and lots of (female) nudity.

Ah, female nudity. It seems to be everywhere these days. But when I was growing up in the '70s—before the Internet, before home video, before cable, before I could reach the *Playboy* shelf at the newsstand—topless pygmies in *National Geographic* and the bra section of the JC Penny catalogue supplied the maximum skin available to an aspiring anatomy enthusiast such as myself.

So, let's fast-forward (a habit of mine) to Fall 1980. I was a high school senior in the suburbs of Chicago. Cable television came to my neighborhood the same month my dad bought a VCR. It was a momentous intersection of opportunity, technology, and youthful . . . *skin-thusiasm*. All of a sudden, there were nude women on my television. I taped every movie I could. I was fascinated by the nude scenes and realized I had a knack for remembering who showed what, who did what (and who), and in which films.

Soon I was popping movies in the VCR just to fast-forward to "the good parts." Then I took to creating my own nude-scene compilation tapes. In time, my knowledge grew along with my VHS library and although I (eventually) went on dates with real, live girls, I never lost interest in celebrity nudity.

Let's hit the fast-forward button again. It's 1996. After a bar conversation with a local Chicago radio personality, I was invited on the air to discuss my expertise on undressed movie stars. Since the girl I was dating still believed that my immense tape collection contained hockey fights and White Sox highlights, I was reluctant to use my real name. "Mr. Skin" was suggested. It stuck. I did the interview and the rest is a naked blur. For better or worse, I am now the world's leading expert on female celebrity nudity in film.

Boy, are my parents proud.

Fast-forward to the present . . . I've probably viewed more than 20,000 movies . . . don't ask me what they were about. I just fast-forward to the good parts. Now I am a regular guest on hundreds of radio shows every year—most notably King of All Media and my personal hero Howard Stern's morning powerhouse—and I am the proud proprietor of www.MrSkin.com, the Net's most popular interactive depot of celebrity nudity. When you come to the site, you can just type in an actress's name and every nude scene she has ever done will pop up. Again: just the good parts.

I have always been interested in writing a book and even more so now with the increasing popularity of my Web site. I want to put in every man's hands an easy-to-read warehouse of the warped information I have in my head, i.e., a Skincyclopedia of celebrities that we've all watched over the years—naked of course (is there any other way?).

And, now, here you have it: an A-to-Z guide to the 2,005 sexiest actresses of all time, with complete skinfo on every nude scene each one has ever done.

You can use it to look up your favorite babes, learn about new ones, plan trips to the video store or what to record off of cable—and we've already fast-forwarded to the good parts for you.

I also hope that the book's photos, posters, quotes and Top Ten Lists will amuse, amaze, inform, and enlighten all seekers of celebrity nudity facts and (more important) figures.

The only thing to bear in mind is that, with a book, we had a cut-off date, so the skinformation contained within these pages is complete right up until September 15, 2004.

Plus, don't forget: you can always log in to MrSkin.com, where we work 'round-the-clock, adding to our collection of thousands upon thousands of nude starlets to bring you new movie reviews, bios, pictures, clips, and continually updated skinfo on naked actresses seven days a week, 365 days a year.

By the way, did I mention that I have the greatest job in the world?

—Mr. Skin

Who Wrote This Book

As with MrSkin.com, **Mr. Skin** himself served as the Editor-in-Chief, Head Writer, bottomless font of wisdom and expertise, and original source of T(itters) & A(musement).

Mike McPadden (a.k.a. **Selwyn Harris**), Editorial Director of MrSkin.com, composed the initial pitch for the *Skincyclopedia* and then labored mightily on every aspect of the book. He also assembled and oversaw a crack roster of skin skribes who brilliantly rose to the mammoth task at (one free) hand.

MrSkin.com's Editorial A-Team consists of a quartet of heroic souls who, fortunately for us, possess superhuman talent and sensibilities as sharp and twisted as their work ethic is impeccable and unstoppable: **Peter Landau, Allan MacDonell, L.A. Simington**, and **J.R. Taylor**.

No less skin-sential were the following ace wordsmiths who each composed multiple passages: Ellen Blum, Mario Grillo, Rob Hauschild, Sam Henderson, Laurence Lerman, Kimberly Martin, Jennifer Nixon, Vance Moravian, and James Hollis Smith.

The eye-popping array of celebrity quotes enlivening these pages represent the eagle-eyed efforts of Editorial Skintern Sextraordinaire, Meg McCarville.

Many of the most hilarious and best-constructed witticisms in this massive undertaking come courtesy of the brilliant Keara Shipe. Hats off to you, Funniest Woman in Show Business.

The fact that this makes kind of spellchecked and/or grammatical sense comes due to the Herculean exertions of copy editor Kara Edington. This indispensable word-wizard routinely turned the scribbles, Morse Code, and hieroglyphics foisted upon her by Mr. McPadden into the free-flowing English language lusciousness in which you're presently basking.

Finally, Mr. Skin and Mike McPadden would also like to thank Aaron Lee, Carmine Bellucci, Steve Loshivao, Blue Horizon Media, *Celebrity Skin* magazine, Michael Raso, and EI Independent Cinema, John Strausbaugh, Daria O'Neill, Peter Bagge, Linda Lofstrom, Dan Barden, Abbie Ehmann, Eric Danville, Rick Sullivan, Marcy Wallabout, Misty Mundae, Danny Peary, Michael Weldon, and, for three decades of amazement and inspiration, Howard Stern.

How to Read the Skincyclopedia

Mr. Skin's Skincyclopedia collects 2,005 actress entries, each of which contains up to eight individual components. Some actresses will have all eight. Many will not.

For a complete breakdown of what is included with each entry, use the following key and sample actress write-up.

1. Name by which she is best known (including, in some cases, nicknames).
2. Place of birth.
3. Date of birth.
4. Date of death.
5. Bio—an overview of the star's career, including facts and highlights.
6. See Her Naked In—a chronological listing of every movie and TV show in which the actress has appeared nude as of press time, beginning with the most recent and going down to her first skintastic appearance.
7. Body Parts—listing of the various parts she showed in each movie or TV show, as explained in "Mr. Skin's Guide to Essential Naked Female Celebrity Body Parts."
8. SKIN-fining Moment—The single nude appearance that I think is her most essential.

Sample actress entry:

1. **CHERYL "RAINBEAUX" SMITH**
2. Place of birth: Los Angeles, California, USA
3. Date of birth: June 6, 1955
4. Date of death: October 25, 2002
5. The late Cheryl "Rainbeaux" Smith is the definitive '70s drive-in starlet, an ethereal nymph who brought inimitable star power and A-plus class to numerous B-movie classics. The waify blonde's film career skyrocketed from her lead in the art-short *The Birth of Aphrodite* (1971) and a bit part in the same year's biopic *Evel Knievel*. Cheryl changed her name to Rainbeaux Smith over the course of appearing in more than twenty-five motion pictures, every one of which is noteworthy, before she seemingly disappeared after 1982's *Parasite*. Sadly, the reason for Cheryl's absence was an extended battle with drug addiction that led her to destitution and jail and, ultimately, contributed to her tragic death in 2002. Fortunately, Rainbeaux will shine forever through her skintastic legacy, starting with 1974's *The Swinging Cheerleaders* and continuing on through such mammariffic milestones as *Caged Heat* (1974), *Revenge of the Cheerleaders* (1975), *The Pom Pom Girls* (1976), *Massacre at Central High* (1976), *Drum* (1976), and *Cinderella* (1977), to name just a few. In the 1975 send-up *Video Vixens*, Rainbeaux sensationally displayed her comedic talents (along with her entire body) as the Twinkle Twat Girl, hawking an unabashed feminine hygiene spray. Offscreen Cheryl performed live with Cheech & Chong and often sat in as a drummer for Joan Jett. There was nothing this multitalented knockout couldn't do . . . except find happiness in a world for which she was too beautiful.
6. SKIN-fining Moment *Cinderella* (0:30) Rainbeaux glows full-frontal perfection as she's bathed by Linda Gildersleeve and Yana Nirvana.
7. **SEE HER NAKED IN**
Parasite (1982) Breasts
The Best of Sex and Violence (1981) Breasts
The Incredible Melting Man (1977) Breasts
Fantasm Comes Again (1977) Breasts
Slumber Party '57 (1977) Buns
Cinderella (1977) Breasts, buns, bush

Revenge of the Cheerleaders (1976) Breasts, buns, bush
Massacre at Central High (1976) Breasts, buns, bush
The Pom Pom Girls (1976) Breasts
Drum (1977) Breasts
Farewell, My Lovely (1975) FFN
Video Vixens (1975) FFN
The Swinging Cheerleaders (1974) Breasts
Caged Heat (1974) Caged Heat Buns

Which Actresses Got Included in the Book and Why

The *Skincyclopedia* is Mr. Skin's guide to *essential* female celebrity nudity.

And since I, Mr. Skin, am the world's foremost authority on this topic, the babes contained in this book are the 2,005 actresses that I find most *important* to the onward-and-upward development of naked starlet arts and sciences.

The primary factor in determining who made the cut (and who didn't) was an individual star's degree of fame.

A-list headline-makers who have done nude scenes on the order of Jennifer Lopez, Pamela Anderson, and Nicole Kidman were naturals, as were relatively lesser known but instantly familiar actresses such as Julianne Moore, Parker Posey, and Kim Basinger.

Historical significance and icon status were another determining

element, as in the case of Marilyn Monroe and Jayne Mansfield. Same goes for groundbreakers such as Maria Schneider, who starred in the arthouse classic *Last Tango in Paris* (1972) and Linda Lovelace, who briefly became one of the most famous women in the world due to her titular talents on display in the breakthrough theatrical X-rated movie, *Deep Throat* (1972).

Actresses who obtain notable stardom via their very nakedness also automatically ranked on the roster. By this, I mean B-flick bombshells, cult-movie beauties, *Playboy* Playmates, skinternational sirens, scream queens, softcore starlets, and direct-to-video vixens. Among the best known and least dressed of this bunch, for (s)example, are Pam Grier, Claudia Jennings, Barbi Benton, Laura Antonelli, Debbie Rochon, Shanon Tweed, and Misty Mundae.

The quality of an individual nude scene could be enough to secure a place in these pages. Rachel Miner, ex-wife of Macaulay Culkin, has appeared naked in one film as of press time, but it's the jailbait flesh-fest *Bully* (2001), where she not only goes full frontal, she serves her furburger directly to the camera and provides my (so-far) favorite teen-babe-on-a-toilet-bowl scene of all time.

Sexceptions to the Rules

A small number of actresses in the Skincyclopedia have never done

nude scenes, but were included for otherwise ultra-sexy and skin-nificant contributions.

Case in point(s): Sarah Michelle Gellar. While TV's "Buffy" has, to date, not appeared on-screen in the buff, her lap-liquefying lesbian face-suck with Selma Blair in *Cruel Intentions* (1999) more-than-handily earned her a spot in our pantheon—a very wet spot, in fact.

To overlook such a well-known and celebrated skin-chievement would render any guide to definitive skinema sexiness incomplete.

Know a Movie with Nudity But Not the Star's Name?

Head directly for the rear. Of the book, I mean.

Included in the back of the *Skincyclopedia* is an index of every film title mentioned herein and the page numbers where you can see each time it's referenced.

Any Other Questions?

Log in to www.mrskin.com for up-to-the-minute reviews, news, and other crucial tits-and-tidbits of celebrity skinfo.

You can also email me at: questions@mrskin.com

It's a great, big, boob-iful world of celebrity nudity out there and my work is never done . . . thankfully!

Mr. Skin's Guide to Naked Female Celebrity Body Parts

Body Double. = A professional naked stand-in whose stunt-privates substitute for a star who's too skingy to perform a nude scene herself. When a Body Double shows up, the babe you thought you were watching is passing off somebody else's most skintimate of areas as her own.

Breasts = Both bouncers visible in a single shot.

Buns = Buttcrack.

Bush = The pubic region, however hairy (or not).

FFN = Both breasts and bush visible in a single shot.

Nip-slip = Momentary, usually accidental incident of a milk-spout spilling into view.

Nip-slip LB = Left nip-slip.

Nip-slip RB = Right nip-slip.

LB = Left Breast.

RB = Right Breast.

Thong = Butt-cheeks visible, but(t) crack is concealed by floss-like undergarment.

mr. skin's
skincyclopedia

a

Angela Aames

Born: February 27, 1956
Pierre, South Dakota
Died: November 27, 1988
Skin-O-Meter: Great Nudity

Although Angela Aames stands atop the busty bevy of beauties who shared their bodacious bosoms with the entire world in the slew of sex comedies that defined the late '70s and '80s, she started out "innocently" enough in *Fairy Tales* (1978) as Little Bo Peep. Let's just put it this way: Little Bo Peek didn't lose her sheep . . . she lost her bra! Angela followed that up with one of the best T&A sex-comedy romps ever produced, a steamer called *H.O.T.S.* (1979). As Linda "Boom-Boom" Bang, this stupendous, sumptuous, and supple act-chest entertained the enthralled throngs of salivating teenage drive-in goers with a whole tit-load of bouncing breasts. While she may have shed her clothing in other flicks, *H.O.T.S.* remains the hottest of the hot. Angela's warmhearted, lovable quality always came through in her performances, which helped her fans see past her enormous jugs to sense the heart of gold that beat beneath. Her portrayal of the quintessential, gullible, big-boobied blonde in *All the Marbles* (1981) defined forever a very much copied stereotype. Diane Keaton may have created the mold for the strong yet vulnerable modern self-sufficient woman;

Marilyn Monroe, the conniving, helpless vamp; and Audrey Hepburn the fragile, dainty beauty; but Angela leaves us with the consummate warm-hearted, gallon-milk-sacked, naked, dumb blonde. She Aames to please.

SKIN-fining Moment:

Fairy Tales (0:14) *Angela shows her Hairy Princess while going full frontal in the woods with a Prince-Charming-type.*

See Her Naked In:

Basic Training (1985) Breasts
The Lost Empire (1983) Breasts, Buns
Famous T&A (1982) Breasts
The Best of Sex and Violence (1981) Breasts
. . . All the Marbles (1981) Breasts
Fairy Tales (1979) FFN
H.O.T.S. (1979) Breasts

Victoria Abril

Born: July 4, 1959
Madrid, Spain
Skin-O-Meter: Hall of Fame

Sultry Spanish export Victoria Abril began her career at fourteen on popular TV shows in her native country and made her movie debut in *Cambio de Sexo* (1976) as an effeminate young man who undergoes a sex change. Excellent work, doctor! Since then she has made over sixty films in Europe. Victoria is mostly known to U.S. audiences through the work of wild Spanish director Pedro Almodovar, who cast her in *Atame!* (1990),

a.k.a. *Tie Me Up! Tie Me Down!*, in which she plays a drug-addicted porn actress who is kidnapped by obsessive fan Antonio Banderas. The film was a huge hit all over the world and gave Victoria a cult following in the States. With such diverse roles as alcoholic prostitutes, sexually ambiguous housewives, and pre- and post-op transsexuals, Victoria has secured her place as one of the quirkiest actresses around—and she's round (and round and round) in all the right places!

SKIN-fining Moment:

Tie Me Up! Tie Me Down! (0:24) *An all-time aquatic skin classic! FFN from above as history's luckiest toy frogman gets his snorkel stuck as he swims inside her. Then there's a close-up on her love-lagoon as she spreads her legs even more.*

See Her Naked In:

Don't Tempt Me (2001) Breasts
101 Reykjavík (2000) FFN, Buns
Between Your Legs (1999) LB, Buns
French Twist (1996) FFN, Buns
Intruso (1993) Breasts, Buns
Lovers: A True Story (1992) Buns
High Heels (1991) Breasts
Tie Me Up, Tie Me Down! (1990) FFN, Buns
Si Te Dicen Que Caí (1989) FFN, Buns
Ada Dans la Jungle (1989) Breasts
Baton Rouge (1988) RB, Buns
Barrios Altos (1987) Breasts
After Darkness (1985) Breasts
Padre Nuestro (1985) Breasts
On the Line (1984) FFN, Buns

The Moon in the Gutter (1983) FFN, Buns
La Colmena (1982) Breasts
La Muchacha de las Bragas de Oro (1979) Breasts
Cambio de Sexo (1977) Breasts
Obsesión (1975) RB

Amy Adams

Colorado City
Skin-O-Meter: Brief Nudity

Amy Adams landed her first role onscreen as some of the eye candy in the appropriately titled *Drop Dead Gorgeous* (1999), opposite the equally stunning Kirsten Dunst. But it was her next project that made jaws drop here at Skin Central. In fact, Amy's part in the horror spoof *Psycho Beach Party* (2000) required that she drop the bottom half of her bikini, a trend that sadly hasn't been taken up by bashful bathers. She managed to hide her seaweed, but her coral reef was exposed in all its shiny-heinie delight. Amy continued teasing in the otherwise flesh-fulfilling *Cruel Intentions 2* (2000), with a nude scene that was hardly explicit thanks to the stubborn placement of a massage table. How are audiences going to massage themselves that way? Amy may also be familiar due to her work on the boob(less) tube, including guest appearances on *That '70s Show*, *Buffy the Vampire Slayer*, and *Charmed*. But it's the holiday hit *Catch Me If You Can* (2002), in which she plays a hot southern belle, that really rings our bell.

SKIN-fining Moment:

Psycho Beach Party (1:02) *Amy's bikini bottoms get pulled off on the beach. She covers her muff, but we get an ass-tonishing shot of her naked panty-apples.*

See Her Naked In:

Psycho Beach Party (2000) Buns

Brooke Adams

Born: February 8, 1949
New York, New York
Skin-O-Meter: Brief Nudity

A characteristically natural beauty of '70s cinema, Brooke Adams first grabbed Hollywood and Richard Gere by the crotch in *Days of Heaven* (1978). Often compared to super juicy French fox Genevieve Bujold, Brooke's brown-eyed girlish charm detonated some seriously devilish diddling on and off the set. (Adams and Gere dated for a brief PR-perfect moment during the movie's release). As a hard body just begging to be snatched in *Invasion of the Body Snatchers* (1978), Brooke creates more yanker fare for the wank bank, showing a brief bit of bubbly breastage, obscured behind a plant. On par with Morticia Addams, Brooke has met the macabre many times on TV, contrasting her angelic good looks against the forces of evil in *Song of the Succubus* (1975) and *Haunted* (1984). In the horrific thriller *The Unborn* (1991), Brooke bounces out a boob, much to the delight of a sinister, starving baby and a home audience full of fantasizing Brooke bonkers. Most famous to Lifetime lovers, Brooke is scorchingly sexy in the steamy melodrama *Lace* (1984) as one of the potential maternal "bitches" of dark and lovely Phoebe Cates. Ahhhh, the well from bopping to Brooke's sensuous skinematic career overfloweth.

SKIN-fining Moment:

Invasion of the Body Snatchers (1:48) *Brooke walks topless through the pod factory before pointing out Donald Sutherland's presence. Plenty of obstruction between us and her best bits. Sorry, no snatcher.*

See Her Naked In:

The Unborn (1991) RB
Key Exchange (1985) RB
Invasion of the Body Snatchers (1978) Breasts

Jane Adams

Born: April 1, 1965
Washington, D.C.
Skin-O-Meter: Great Nudity

Jane Adams studied at the famed Juilliard School of Music and now frequently shines in films where she plays second fiddle. Her sweet, doe-eyed, non-threatening looks make her a popular choice for playing meeklings in countless movies and television shows such as *Frasier*, where she guest starred as (gasp) a psychiatrist who gets on the sex couch with Frasier's brother. Playing brainiacs and having graduated from Juilliard hasn't stopped Sweet Jane from doffing her clothing. Her mini pair debuted in the Todd Solondz black comedy *Happiness* (1998). We're happy to report that those little bits of joy stayed out for *Songcatcher* (1999) and a skinny-dipping wet look in *The Anniversary Party* (2001). Jane might not have been blessed with beefy boobies, but her bite-sized, perky tits are a salivating good meal.

SKIN-fining Moment:

The Anniversary Party (1:34) *Great shot of Ms. Adams' apples as she frolics underwater with an equally topless Parker Posey.*

See Her Naked In:

The Anniversary Party (2001) Breasts
Songcatcher (1999) Breasts
Happiness (1998) Breasts

Joey Lauren Adams

Born: January 6, 1971
Little Rock, Arkansas
Skin-O-Meter: Brief Nudity

Evil-grinning, squinty-eyed angel Joey Lauren Adams burst onto the small screen as the cherry-busting vixen who took Bud Bundy's long-lived virginity on the sitcom *Married . . . with Children*. She then cut her teeth on indie films like *Dazed and Confused* (1993) and *S.F.W.* (1994) but soon graduated to a slightly larger role in director Kevin Smith's *Mallrats* (1995), in which she tries on the top half of her birthday suit, and—what do you know—it's just her size! The fact that she was dating Smith at the time may have played a role in her starring in his next offering *Chasing Amy* (1997). Joey plays Ben Affleck's dream girl. Okay, one problem, she's a lesbian. But wouldn't we all try to make her trade her donut-bumping for cruller-humping? Once on the Hollywood map, Joey hasn't looked back, most recently playing big mommy to Adam Sandler's *Big Daddy* (1999). She remains, without a doubt, the sexiest Joey since Buttafuoco!

SKIN-fining Moment:

Mallrats (0:29) *Joey bares her juicy little joy-bags in a dressing room before a guy's head comes crashing through the wall. Can't blame him.*

See Her Naked In:

On the Edge (2001) Breasts
A Cool, Dry Place (1998) RB
Mallrats (1995) Breasts
S.F.W. (1994) LB

Lynne Adams

Born: 1968
Canada
Skin-O-Meter: Brief Nudity

Don't hate Lynne Adams just because she's beautiful. She's had a hard time lifting herself from the ghetto of B-moviedom. After a few TV movies and failed series, she turned her curvaceous figure to film, taking roles in *Wild Thing* (1987), *Street Smart* (1987), and *Cruising Bar* (1989), which is also known as *Meet Market* and *Meat Bar*. The promise of that latter film was

sadly unfulfilled, as was the entire decade for poor Lynne. She ran to French TV in the early '90s to escape what was turning out to be obscurity in Hollywood—with no worthy skin to even recommend it. But things started to change upon her return to the good old USA with a bit part in the hit Keanu Reeves action-thriller *Johnny Mnemonic* (1995), in which she played a yakuza with a rocket launcher. But more important than her return home was her first skin in *Silent Hunter* (1995), with a brief breast shot. She followed that with *Habitat* (1996), which featured her as a half-naked space hippie. Lynne continues to work to this day, so it's likely she'll be adding to the Adams family of flesh.

SKIN-fining Moment:

Habitat (1:30) *Desperate to get nude in a film, Lynne has her shirt blown off in an explosion . . . but just the parts that cover her tits!*

See Her Naked In:

Habitat (1997) Breasts
Silent Hunter (1995) LB
Forbidden Love: The Unashamed Stories of Lesbian Lives (1992) Breasts

Maud Adams

Born: February 12, 1945
Luleå, Norrbottens län, Sweden
Skin-O-Meter: Great Nudity

There are Ursula, Brit, Diane, Jill . . . and then there's Maud. With a knack for playing skinister agents, Maud Adams is most famous for her performances in the James Bond series. The only of the Bond bombshells to appear in more than two of the 007 flicks, Maud headlined in *The Man with the Golden Gun* (1974) and *Octopussy* (1983) and made a brief appearance as an extra in a crowd scene in *A View to a Kill* (1985). In *The Man with the*

TATTOO: THIS POSTER'S POTENT COMBO OF SKIN AND INK WAS BOUND TO CAUSE CON- TROVERSY (AND DID), AND THAT WAS BEFORE AUDIENCES EVEN GOT TO FULLY FEAST THEIR EYES ON MAUD ADAMS'S COLORFUL TURN AS THE ILLUSTRATED MAMS.

Golden Gun, Roger Moore's wanking weapon is cocked and ready to fire at his curvaceous costar as she reveals just a bit of boob and slip of a nip peeking out of the shower. Although less skinful, Maud is deliciously juicy in *Octopussy*, featuring a flash of back flesh and her palatable, sweet, Swedish seat before wrapping herself in a towel after a sensuous swim. In between bonding with Roger Moore, Adams gave Bruce Dern a turn in the colorfully erotic *Tattoo* (1981). Maud's *Adams* and *Eve* are in full view as turned-on tattoo artist Bruce erotically paints her entire length of loveliness. Her tats are fantastic. Her rear will endear. But Maud's monstrous mound steals the show with its beautiful, bushy bounty. Before all the *Bondage* and body modification, miss Maud debuted her shapely two in *The Girl in Blue* (1973). Today, Maud continues to court her career as a Bond girl, attending autograph conventions like Spy Fest annually.

With a flick of her pen and flash of her smile, Maud still knows how to load a man's gun.

SKIN-fining Moment:

Tattoo (1:32) *Bruce Dern removes Maud's robe and reveals that her naked body is ALMOST completely covered with tattoos—thankfully, he didn't ink up her nipples, muff, and buns, which we enjoy in all their natural glory.*

See Her Naked In:

Octopussy (1983) Buns
Tattoo (1981) FFN, Buns
The Man with the Golden Gun (1974) LB
The Girl in Blue (1973) RB

Amanda Aday

Born: January 21, 1981
New York, New York
Skin-O-Meter: Great Nudity

Amanda Aday is a serious act-chest. She knew she wanted to be in the business of show from an early age. She attended Stagedoor Manor Performing Arts Training Center in 1990, was a theater major at California Institute of the Arts, and is a resident member of the Blue Sphere Alliance, which was founded by Neve Campbell. OK, but did you see her on HBO's *Carnivàle*? She exposes her chops on this skinful series, all right. In one episode Amanda and Carla Gallo work the crowd as fat-and-skinny peepshow girls. But full-bodied Amanda really drives the customers wild when she has the stage to herself. She takes it all off, and her big boobs fall all over the place when she shakes her wide hips, stands on her head, and splits that beaver open. Damn, that's good.

SKIN-fining Moment:

Carnivàle, "Babylon" (2003) *Amanda bares it all—T,B,A—as she does a handstand and swings her legs open, the crowd goes wild, she falls, and they rough her up.*

TeleVisions:

Carnivàle Breasts, Bush, Buns

Isabelle Adjani

Born: June 27, 1955
Paris, France
Skin-O-Meter: Great Nudity

Beautiful, dark-haired, French pastry Isabelle Adjani made her film debut at fourteen in *Le Petit Bougnat* (1970) while on summer vacation from high school. This kicked off a string of Euro releases for Isabelle, but her breakthrough role came when director François Truffaut cast her as Victor Hugo's daughter in *L'Histoire d'Adèle H.*, a.k.a. *The Story of Adele H.*, which earned her an Oscar nomination and worldwide acclaim. In 1981 Isabelle won the Best Actress award at the Cannes Film Festival for her performances in *Possession* (1981) and *Quartet* (1981). Isabelle is at her best in *One Deadly Summer* (1984), in which she comes in and out of a barn, giving us both full-frontal and full-backside treats that are *magnifique* in any language! The diabolically sexy Isabelle was last seen in the Hollywood remake of *Diabolique* (1996).

SKIN-fining Moment:

Possession (0:56) *Bare boobs in bed as Isabelle chats with Sam Neill, delivering some super-succulent nipple shots in the process!*

See Her Naked In:

Diabolique (1996) Breasts, Bush, Buns
Queen Margot (1994) FFN
Ishtar (1987) LB
One Deadly Summer (1984) FFN, Buns
Mortelle randonnée (1983) Breasts
Possession (1981) Breasts
Quartet (1981) Breasts
Next Year if All Goes Well (1981) RB

Suzanne Ager

Skin-O-Meter: Great Nudity

In the world of scream queen royalty, Suzanne Ager is up there with the breast of them, which includes yummies like Linnea Quigley. She debuted in *Evil Spawn* (1987), but that appearance spawned something sexy rather than corrupt. Since then she has created a steamy body of work, sharing her hot body in such tempting titles as *Inner Sanctum* (1991), *Camp Fear* (1991), *Shock 'Em Dead* (1991), *Evil Toons* (1992), *Smoothtalker* (1992), and *Buford's Beach Bunnies* (1993). To give you an idea of what to expect when Suzanne is onscreen, in the latter movie her character was called Boopsie Underall. What's in a name . . . everything skinful! Some of her more notable nudes are from *The Bikini Carwash Company* (1992), *Beach Bunnies*, and *Fatal Justice* (1993). Suzanne usually sticks to topless turns, so don't expect a whole lot more than that. But judging by the size of Suzanne's funbags, that's a lot of fun!

SKIN-fining Moment:

Evil Toons (0:31) *Suzanne peels to a thong while slipping into her PJs.*

See Her Naked In:

Witch Academy (1993) Breasts
Angel Eyes (1993) Breasts, Thong
Fatal Justice (1993) Breasts, Thong
Smooth Talker (1992) LB, Thong
Buford's Beach Bunnies (1992) Breasts, Buns
The Bikini Carwash Company (1992) Breasts, Thong
Evil Toons (1991) Breasts, Thong

Janet Agren

Born: April 6, 1949
Landskrona, Sweden
Skin-O-Meter: Great Nudity

Janet Agren first got bitten by the entertainment bug with a bit role in the Italian production *I Due corciati* (1968). Although the better part of her career has been spent in Italy, Janet is quite the world traveler, racking up credits (and showing her rack) in such far-flung destinations as Brazil, France, Germany, and Britain. Regardless of her status as a global starlet, she doesn't let a little thing like clothing restrain her career. Consider her topless turn in *Eaten Alive* (1980), in which her golden gals are literally painted gold and are more than good enough to eat. Janet flashed her fine, full flappers again in *Aragosta a colazione* (1982). She has done quite a bit of nudity in her career, particularly back in the sexy '70s; trouble is, too many of her films have fallen off the cinema/video map. With hope, the DVD revolution will find the re-release of her skin classics. The revolution will be televised . . . and titillating.

SKIN-fining Moment:

Fiorina la vacca (0:55) *Janet takes the Skinful cake by baring her breast in bed, then flashing full-frontal flesh when she gets out of bed to grab her clothes. Furry fun for everyone!*

See Her Naked In:

La Gatta da Pelare (1987) Breasts, Buns
Aragosta a Colazione (1982) Breasts
L'Onorevole con l'Amante Sotto il Letto (1981) FFN, Buns
Prestami tua Moglie (1980) Breasts
Eaten Alive (1980) Breasts
A Chi Tocca, Tocca . . . ! (1978) Breasts
Tecnica di un Amore (1973) FFN, Buns
Ingrid Sulla Strada (1973) Breasts, Buns
La Più Bella Serata Della mia Vita (1972) LB, Buns
Fiorina la Vacca (1972) FFN, Buns

Christina Aguilera

Born: December 18, 1980
Staten Island, New York
Skin-O-Meter: Brief Nudity

Since starting her career on *The Mickey Mouse Club* in 1992, Christina Aguilera wasted no time once she grew up to shed her ears and sex up her image. In an ongoing who's-hotter competition with fellow post-pubescent pop princess (and ex-Mouskatease) Britney Spears, Christina accidentally let loose a wayward areola on MTV's *Diary*, and she continues to wow the pubic-hopeful public with an assortment of rump-shaking music videos such as "Dirrty" and her evermore scantily attired live appearances.

SKIN-fining Moment:

Diary (2001) *Christina gets "Dirrty" during a topless photo shoot when the hair covering her right-side pop-tart slides aside and reveals her nipple-ringed plastic pontoon.*

TeleVisions:

Diary Nip Slip RB

Jenny Agutter

Born: December 20, 1952
Taunton, Somerset, England, UK
Skin-O-Meter: Great Nudity

Celluloid celebrators got their first glimpse of feline-featured and enticingly engineered Jenny Agutter in the quickie *East of Sudan* (1964), followed by the kind of roles that befit an adorable child actress. It was filmmaker Nicolas Roeg who first realized her skintential in *Walkabout* (1971), a cult favorite set in the Australian outback that features aborigines, social commentary, and a healthy heap of Jenny, whose features include skinny-dipping and some full-frontal flashing. Jenny moved to L.A. in her late twenties, and Tinseltown augmented the Agutter alert by having her shed her skivvies in *Logan's Run* (1976), *Equus* (1977), and *An American Werewolf in London* (1981), in which she nurses a lycanthropy-infected David Naughton back to health via a slippery skintastic shower sequence set to Van Morrison's "Moondance." Jenny's worked steadily ever since, though it must be noted that the final years of the last millennium and first several of the new one have found her involved in a slew of British-made TV films and mini-series, none of which have offered Jenny any opportunities to let loose the skin that kept Logan out of breath a quarter-century ago when he was running and running and running.

SKIN-fining Moment:

Walkabout (0:57) *Jenny skinny dips in a river while her Aboriginal boyfriend hunts for wild game. Great boobs, buns, and even a look at her wondrous Down Under.*

See Her Naked In:

An American Werewolf in London (1981) RB
Sweet William (1980) Breasts, Buns
China 9, Liberty 37 (1978) FFN, Buns
Equus (1977) FFN, Buns
Logan's Run (1976) Breasts, Buns
Walkabout (1971) FFN, Buns

Anouk Aimée

Born: April 27, 1932
Paris, France
Skin-O-Meter: Great Nudity

With her regal manner, visible intelligence and breathtaking beauty, Anouk Aimée is the epitome of French sophistication. Best known for her role as the jaded socialite in *La Dolce Vita* (1960) or the well-bred widow in *A Man and a Woman* (1969), Anouk is always impeccable, oozing the sexy, detached air of the elite. Madame Aimée seems all the more skinful when she drops these trappings, along with her couture clothing, and is instantly transformed into a full-on flesh-and-blood bone maker. Anouk's naked perfection will annihilate you in *Justine* (1969). After a proper stint of horseback riding, this thoroughbred drops trou for a little skinny-dipping in the ocean, exposing her warm and wonderful baguettes, as well as a bit of backside and tracings of le bush. To see Anouk's can-cans at their ripest, Mr. Skin recommends *Les Amants de Vérone* (1949). At the tender age of seventeen, Anouk indulges in some mindless moshing about in a lake, her perky pastries soaking up the sunshine. Like fine French wine, Anouk improves with age. Surprisingly stunning in the sequel *A Man and a Woman: Twenty Years Later* (1986), she is even niftier in her fifties, proving to be a timeless classic beauty, with an even classier rear chassis.

SKIN-fining Moment:

Justine (0:36) *Anouk rides to the beach and drops her duds to do some skinny-dipping in the ocean. Once she's done, she walks naked with a horse, showing boobage and bunnage. Not bad at all for a PG movie!*

See Her Naked In:

Justine (1969) Breasts, Buns
Les Amants de Vérone (1949) Breasts, Buns

Lucy Akhurst

Born: November 18, 1975
London, England, UK
Skin-O-Meter: Brief Nudity

Lucy Akhurst hated school, so she left the drama department when she was discovered by the BBC. She was pegged to play the lead in the convention-breaking drama *All Quiet on the Preston Front*. Life is easy when you're beautiful. And Lucy is lovely: a small-breasted beauty with that English stiff upper lip that gets guys stiff a bit further south. With a body like that, Lucy has been able to find ample work for her perky talents on TV and in films such as *The Land Girls* (1998). Lucy is probably most known to those Stateside for her very brief role as a policewoman in *The Saint* (1997). But in the film *Trinity* (2001), Lucy opens a new door in her career—one that catches her without her clothes on. It's likely with this new development that Lucy's found the key to success.

SKIN-fining Moment:

Trinity (0:02) *Tight, blue-tinted buns then nice full-frontal view of her awesomely taut body as she exits the shower. Wow!*

See Her Naked In:

Trinity (2001) FFN, Buns

Jessica Alba

Born: April 28, 1981
Pomona, California
Skin-O-Meter: Never Nude

An illuminating olive-skinned vision of pouty-lipped perfection, Jessica Alba is truly a heavenly creature. Half French Canadian, half Mexican, this magnetic mamacita is a natural as the genetically engineered, Harley-humping hell raiser on the sci-fi series *Dark Angel*, producing an abundance of boners during the show's limited run. Before Jess became super human, she was super fine as a wet and wild lifeguard on the TV series *Flipper* and as the snotty little hottie in *Never Been Kissed* (1999). Alba admirers can't help but keep their fingers otherwise occupied while watching *Idle Hands* (1999), Jessica's juiciest role to date. This luscious Latina flaunts her finely tanned flesh in a skimpy lace bra and panties. Aye chihuahua-wow! Skinematically speaking, Jessica can be seen in all her beautiful bareness only in your dreams. Sadly, her sexcapades in *The Sleeping Dictionary* (2002) were performed by a sexy stand-in. Webster's defines this act of trickery as a RIP OFF EXTRAORDINAIRE.

SKIN-fining Moment:

Idle Hands (1:22) *Jessica's dark angelcakes look heavenly in a pair of wedgieriffic white panties while making out with her guy. Nice gauzy bra, too, but it's the cheek peekage that's truly to be cherished.*

See Her Naked In:

The Sleeping Dictionary (2002) Body Double—Breasts

Laura Albert

Skin-O-Meter: Great Nudity

Laura Albert began her career as an actress with a bit part in *Overdose* (1987) but soon took her hard body to the more bang-up position of stuntwoman. She brought home the bacon by sacrificing her frame in such films as *Starship Troopers* (1997), *The Lost World: Jurassic Park* (1997), and *Charlie's Angels* (2000), among a host of others. But she's too much of an exhibitionist to keep her large lovelies undercover. Catch Laura in all her topless glory in such films as *Doctor Alien* (1998), *Angel III: The Final Chapter* (1988), and *Roadhouse* (1989) as well as on various episodes of *Dream On* and *Tales from the Crypt*. Laura works primarily as a stuntwoman. Hope she doesn't hurt those huge hooters.

SKIN-fining Moment:

Dr. Caligari (0:10) *Laura loses her orange bra, then treats us to her pinknosed pups as she lies back and diddles her cliddle.*

See Her Naked In:

Stone Cold (1991) RB, Buns
Road House (1989) Breasts, Thong
Dr. Caligari (1989) Breasts
The Jigsaw Murders (1989) Breasts, Thong

Party Plane (1988) Breasts
Angel III: The Final Chapter (1988) Breasts, Thong
Dr. Alien (1988) Breasts
Glitch! (1988) Breasts
The Unnamable (1988) LB, Buns
Death by Dialogue (1988) Breasts
Bloodstone (1988) LB

TeleVisions:

Dream On Breasts
Tales from the Crypt Breasts

Rutanya Alda

Riga, Latvia
Skin-O-Meter: Brief Nudity

Born in Riga, Latvia, Rutanya Alda first stole moviegoers' heart-ons in her debut as Linda the Shoplifter in *Greetings* (1968). She continued working her swinging stuff in bizarre films of the times such as *Hi, Mom!* (1970), a.k.a. *Confessions of a Peeping John*, but it wasn't until the gritty film *The Panic in Needle Park* (1971) and Robert Altman's *The Long Goodbye* (1973) that Hollywood stood up and took notice. Pants stood up with her sole nude scene onscreen in *Pat Garrett and Billy the Kid* (1973). She played a topless hooker who made Old West crusty stars James Coburn and Kris Kristofferson buck their broncos. She even corralled a bit of bush for the cowboys. She's gone on to a strong supporting, although skinless, career. She was a dear in *The Deer Hunter* (1978), she was hot stuff in *The Stuff* (1985), she was quite a ride in *Last Exit to Brooklyn* (1989), and she was out of bounds in *The Ref* (1994). She continues to work, and, as long as she's warm, there's always opportunity to heat up the screen again.

SKIN-fining Moment:

Pat Garrett and Billy the Kid (1:35) *Rutty bares her rack while canoodling in the sack with James Coburn.*

See Her Naked In:

Pat Garrett and Billy the Kid (1973) Breasts

Toni Alessandrini

Skin-O-Meter: Great Nudity

Toni Alessandrini is a dreamboat. She certainly floated audiences' boats as the donkey-riding stripper Desiree in the classic Tom Hanks comedy *Bachelor Party* (1984). That kinky scene, however, is nothing compared to her carnal career. Toni has showed off more hootage than you can shake your stick at (but I recommend you try). There's *Pleasure in Paradise* (1992), *Mind, Body & Soul* (1992), and *Vice Academy 2* (1990) and *3* (1991). In such a skintacular career, her crowning achievement remains *The Sex and Violence Family Hour* (1983). Toni's ratings raiser is a full-frontal scene that doesn't leave a dry seat in the house. That's family viewing we can all get behind.

SKIN-fining Moment:

The Sex and Violence Family Hour (1:05) *Toni goes from thonged buttage in a leotard to showing her yoni when she full-frontally takes it off.*

See Her Naked In:

Pleasure in Paradise (1992) Breasts, Thong
Mind, Body & Soul (1992) Breasts
Vice Academy Part 3 (1991) Breasts, Thong
Vice Academy Part 2 (1990) Breasts, Thong
Marked for Murder (1989) Breasts, Thong
Bachelor Party (1984) Thong
The Sex and Violence Family Hour (1983) FFN, Thong

Erika Alexander

Born: November 19, 1969
Winslow, Arizona
Skin-O-Meter: Great Nudity

Cocoa-hued beauty Erika Alexander's star has been on the rise since her first foray into film, a supporting role in *My Little Girl* (1986). She's since appeared in several flicks, from *The Long Walk Home* (1990) to the disco drama *54* (1998). Erika is best known, however, for her appearances on the small screen. She spent three seasons as Phylicia Rashad's poor relation on *The Cosby Show* and five years as Maxine Shaw, Attorney at Law, on the Fox comedy *Living Single*. She then graduated to cable TV, landing a recurring role on the Showtime series *Street Time*, which gave her the chance to flash her not-inconsiderable chest charms on more than one occasion. Check local listings and keep your remote at the ready.

SKIN-fining Moment:

Street Time "The Whole Truth" (2003) *Breasts and thong-a-thong-thong-thonged bunnage as she bang-a-bang-bang-bangs Scott Cohen in bed.*

TeleVisions:

Street Time Breasts, Buns

Jane Alexander

Born: October 28, 1939
Boston, Massachusetts
Skin-O-Meter: Brief Nudity

Jane Alexander first made a colorful splash in her Broadway debut *The Great White Hope*. She played the boxer's lover, which must have been frustrating for the pugilist, as most trainers have chumps refrain from sex before a fight. She won a Tony award but gave Mr. Skin a woody. Her move to film was equally receptive, with Oscar nominations for her roles in *All the President's Men* (1976) and *Kramer vs. Kramer* (1979). But it's the less celebrated and more carnal roles we praise here at Skin Central. In *A Gunfight* (1971), her bare-ass bedroom scene is sure to make viewers shoot their loads. And *Sweet County* (1986) proved that a mature mam is still as sweet. Jane is truly an Alexander the Great.

SKIN-fining Moment:

A Gunfight Jane shows a bit of her Al-ass-zander in bed with Kirk Douglas.

See Her Naked In:

Sweet Country (1986) LB
A Gunfight (1971) Buns

Sarah Alexander

Born: 1971
London, England, UK
Skin-O-Meter: Brief Nudity

The general perception among forward-thinking Americans is that the British are staid, stuffy, sexless stuffed shirts who are afraid to show as much as a smidgen of skin lest it threaten to stiffen an organ other than their upper lips. How, then, to account for the BBC? It's not even HBO, and the English, government-run broadcasting corporation beams out high beams, broad bums, and even bushy beavers, all of which are revealed by bunny-face Sarah Alexander during her onscreen duties in the Limey sketch-comedy show *Armstrong and Miller*. Imagine *Saturday Night Live* with a trim-butt blonde with high, firm, round boobies and a moderate, light-brown thatch cracking jokes with all her sweet bits hanging out. Blimey!

SKIN-fining Moment:

Armstrong and Miller "Episode 3" (1997) *Sarah brings everything she's got to the table, dishing out delicious full frontal at a breakfast table that—be warned—is also surrounded by bare-penised bozos, to boot.*

TeleVisions:

Armstrong and Miller FFN, Buns

Charlotte Alexandra

France
Skin-O-Meter: Great Nudity

In her small yet intensely skintimate career, Charlotte Alexandra stunned and electrified audiences with her naturally bare beauty and knack for kink. Diving directly into skin in *Immoral Tales* (1974), sweet Charlotte showed every inch of her pale perfection while dabbling in a little in-and-out vegetarianism with a cucumber. In *Good-bye Emmanuelle* (1977), say hello again to Alexandra's ample, pink-nipped erectiles, tantalizing tail, and bold, thatchy patch during a long, leisurely indoor walk of wanton nudity. Charlotte's wide-eyed innocence and booming body in *A Real Young Girl* (1976) will make you giddy in the groin. This pleasantly perverse film shows the story of "Alice," a nubile farm girl getting in touch with natural drives in very unnatural ways. Obsessed with exhibitionism, this youngster likes men to watch her pee and is mostly sans panties, frequently flashing bottom and bush. Your own bicycle will be ready for a ride, watching her wiggling and cycling bottomless, her bare buns bouncing in the breeze. Then there are the wicked widgets that "Alice" likes to diddle in her wonderland of holes, including three wiggling worms and numerous fingers in her ya-ya and a bottle and flock of feathers up her backdoor, all slowly inserted in close-up focus. Warning: Those with heart conditions will sadly have to skip Charlotte's kinkerific, skinematic works completely, or else die happily of shock.

SKIN-fining Moment:

A Real Young Girl (0:40) *Close-up shots of Charlotte's spread-eagled beaver are—let's say—"enhanced" by her boyfriend's habit of jamming*

earthworms into her orifice. Beats the shit out of Fear Factor!

See Her Naked In:

Good-bye, Emmanuelle (1977) FFN, Buns
A Real Young Girl (1976) Breasts, Bush, Buns
Immoral Tales (1974) FFN, Buns

Kristian Alfonso

Born: September 5, 1964
Brockton, Massachusetts
Skin-O-Meter: Brief Nudity

Kristian Alfonso started her acting career appropriately enough as the host of the TV series *Love Stories*, and everybody fell in love with her. She then took a role in *The Star Maker* (1981), but it was still a while before this brunette beauty made it to stardom herself. In 1988, after appearing in guest spots on such series as *Amazing Stories*, *Who's the Boss?*, and *MacGuyver*, Kristian landed a role on the hit nighttime soap opera *Falcon Crest*, where she stayed until the end of the go-go decade. Next, Kristian returned to guest spots until she landed another TV gig on the hit series *Melrose Place* in 1993. It pays to be hot. She tried her supple hand at film, where she appeared in *Joshua Tree* (1993) and *In the Kingdom of the Blind, the Man with One Eye Is King* (1995). What about the girl with two boobs? That question was never answered. Kristian next ventured to the torrid world of daytime soaps in the '90s with a role on *Days of Our Lives*. Sadly, she has not showed the world much skin, although she appeared in a sexy bra- and pantie-clad bedroom scene in *Army of One* (1993). She shows off her G-string-holstered butt, which engages Mr. Skin's army of one.

SKIN-fining Moment:

Army of One (0:35) *Kristian's body douoble de-bras, showing us her Army of*

Two, followed by a bottomless shot of the real Kristian's Army of Buns.

See Her Naked In:

Army of One (1993) Body Double—Breasts, Thong

Valerie Allain

Skin-O-Meter: Great Nudity

Eurolovely Valerie Allain got her start in the gritty cop drama *Le Cowboy* (1984), but it wasn't until 1987 that her career took a turn for the skinful. She cranked out three films that year and, to the delight of skin-starved Francophiles everywhere, exposed her bouncy bon-bons in each one. *Les Nouveaux Tricheurs* (1987) and *Club de Recontres* (1987) both feature brief, dimly-lit but much-appreciated views of her boobettes and buns, while she goes mercifully full frontal in a substantially skintastic scene in the opera-themed directorial wankfest *Aria* (1987). Her segment—directed by arthouse fave Jean-Luc Godard—features a bare-tittied gymnasium romp with fellow Frenchie Marion Peterson. The girls show all, including their fantastically fuzzy croissants. Vixenish Val continued to work not-too-steadily until 1997, after which she plunged into full-time mommying. Mr. Skin, for one, would love to see what motherhood has done to those heavenly hips of hers.

SKIN-fining Moment:

Aria (0:22) Valerie joins Marion Peterson on a quest to entertain some body-builders by dancing around bare-assed naked while they try to work out. *Works for me.*

See Her Naked In:

Club de rencontres (1987) Breasts, Buns
Les Nouveaux tricheurs (1987) Breasts, Buns
Aria (1987) FFN, Buns

Ginger Lynn Allen

Born: December 14, 1962
Rockford, Illinois
Skin-O-Meter: Great Nudity

Ginger Lynn Allen earned her status as veteran video vixen through hands-on training and hard work. Known for her extreme enthusiasm and genuine love of all onscreen sexcapades, this perfectly proportioned bubbly blonde propelled to the top of the adult entertainment industry in the mid 80s. As a premiere Vivid Video Girl, her gorgeous grooves made Vivid into a million dollar company. For all her obvious love of the old in and out, Ginger meandered in and out of the bumping business. Between 1983 and 1986 she produced 69 steamy films including classic yanker fare *Surrender in Paradise* (1984) and *Trashy Lady* (1985) and then went on a fourteen-year hump hiatus. During time off from getting off, she kicked a much publicized cocaine addiction and gave Hollywood a go (with much less skinthusiasm), appearing on an episode of *NYPD Blue* and a string of B-movies like *Dr. Alien* (1988). Forever the porn pioneer, Miss Lynn returned in 1999 creating new classics like *Torn* (1999) and the futuristic *Fantasex* (2003), the first interactive, voice activated DVD porno. Here's hoping this spicy sexpot stays in for many years to come.

SKIN-fining Moment:

Dr. Alien (0:21) Ginger gets topless and shows her porn-star pom-poms while partying with a pair of rock chicks.

See Her Naked In:

Trouble Bound (1992) Breasts
Mind, Body & Soul (1992) Breasts
Bound and Gagged: A Love Story (1992) Breasts
Leather Jackets (1991) Breasts, Thong
Buried Alive (1990) LB
Vice Academy Part 2 (1990) Breasts, Thong
Wild Man (1989) Breasts
Cleo/Leo (1989) FFN
Hollywood Boulevard II (1989) Breasts
Dr. Alien (1988) Breasts
Vice Academy (1988) Buns, Breasts, Thong
Numerous Adult Movies

India Allen

Born: June 1, 1965
Portsmouth, Virginia
Skin-O-Meter: Great Nudity

They say Virginia is for lovers. If native daughter India Allen is any indication of the caliber of super-stacked chickadee produced down in ole Virginee, then they were understating the case. Dark-haired India burst upon the national consciousness by overflowing the centerfold pages of the December 1987 issue of *Playboy*. The magazine expanded India's role and made her Playmate of the Year for 1988, but much like the cup size of her bra during her developing years, no reasonable expansion could hope to hold her for long. Aside from her cover girl face, cute, camera-hogging beaver, and sex-happy attitude, India's secrets for success are obvious. Those gigantic, natural knockers will not be held back! Feel the force in almost every straight-to-obsession video India has appeared in. Extra strong are *Wild Cactus* (1993) and *Seduce Me: Pamela Principle 2* (1994).

SKIN-fining Moment:

Seduce Me: Pamela Principle 2 (1:25) India scrubs up in the shower with her loverman while her hubby watches. Bombers and buns abound.

See Her Naked In:

Silk Degrees (1994) Breasts
Seduce Me: Pamela Principle 2 (1994) FFN, Buns
Almost Hollywood (1994) Breasts, Buns
Wild Cactus (1993) FFN, Buns
Numerous Playboy Videos

Joan Allen

Born: August 20, 1956
Rochelle, Illinois
Skin-O-Meter: Great Nudity

"I was a very good girl for a long time, that's what really drew me to acting. The stage was the perfect place to be outrageous, to be sad, to be angry, to be all these different things," says Joan Allen. No surprise then, that the Rochelle, Illinois, native was a founding member of Chicago's famous Steppenwolf theater company. The stage was good to Joan, and she won a Tony award for her New York Broadway debut in Lanford Wilson's *Burn This*, which is sadly not about her bra. Cinema was a greater challenge. She was the secondary character in such films as *Compromising Positions* (1985), *Peggy Sue Got Married* (1986), *Tucker: The Man and His Dream* (1988), and *Searching for Bobby Fischer* (1993). Her breakthrough role was as the long-suffering Pat Nixon in Oliver Stone's *Nixon* (1995). That led to well-received movies such as *The Crucible* (1996), *The Ice Storm* (1997), and *Pleasantville* (1998). Sadly, Joan's characters rarely exhibit very much of their sex lives onscreen. Or at least that was the case until *Off the Map* (2003), in which Joan was off the hook with skin.

SKIN-fining Moment:

Off the Map It's Off the Clothes, as Joan provides a map with her completely bare body, doing a boobs-bush-and-bun-baring 360-degree twirl in her garden. Oh, how her lovelies are in bloom!

See Her Naked In:

Off the Map (2003) FFN

Karen Allen

Born: October 5, 1951
Carrollton, Illinois
Skin-O-Meter: Great Nudity

Though she derives the most professional satisfaction from her extensive work in live theater and is acclaimed as a gutsy, risk-taking actress, slinky brunette minx Karen Allen will forever be most widely known as the cheating sweetheart of *Animal House* (1978). Who can forget those big, flashing green eyes, so innocent and easy to trust? And the smile, slightly crooked, totally endearing, flashing like a promise of never-ending delights. And then the full view of her ass, its smile every inch as winning as the one on her face. Who cares if she smiles exactly the same way at a ton of other guys? At least one time, however long ago, she smiled that smile just for you. Six years after *Animal House*, Karen was back smiling harder than ever in *Until September* (1984). Her eyes are still big, and her boobies are still mobile and high as she straddles her man in a girl-on-top tussle. Bask in the warmth of her grinning buns as she lounges belly down in bed, then walks her happy-face rear across the room.

SKIN-fining Moment:

Animal House (1:21) Karen pulls on a shirt and showcases her bare can-can while walking into the kitchen and getting surprised by Peter Riegert. Sweet animal haunches!

SEE YOU (NAKED) IN SEPTEMBER: KAREN ALLEN IN *UNTIL SEPTEMBER*.

See Her Naked In:

Backfire! (1995) Breasts, Buns
Until September (1984) Breasts, Buns
A Small Circle of Friends (1980) Breasts
Animal House (1978) Buns

Krista Allen

Born: April 5, 1972
Ventura, California
Skin-O-Meter: Great Nudity

A rocking body, a rock-solid rack, a face like a feline sex sorceress, bewitching brunette Krista Allen qualifies as a skin icon on the basis of her TV work alone. True, nothing beyond bikinis and bed-me looks flashed when Krista pranced and pouted upon the sets of *The Bold and the Beautiful*, *Days of Our Lives*, and *Baywatch*. Still, the concentrated essence of Allen's erotic firepower blazed at every curl of her snaky lips. Try to imagine such a creature of camera-friendly carnality in a series of quality films distinguished by extensive nudity and exclusively sexual themes. Can't picture it? Then look into the *Emmanuelle* flicks, numbers 2 through 8. Krista stars as the titular temptress in each of them. Particularly awe-inspiring is *Emmanuelle 8: There's More to Love than Sex* (1994). There's a hell of a lot of sex as well.

SKIN-fining Moment:

Haunted Sea (0:03) Seat and sacks as Krista gets sexily sudsy in the shower.

See Her Naked In:

Totally Blonde (2001) Thong
Emmanuelle: First Contact (2000) Breasts, Buns
Raven (1997) Breasts
Haunted Sea (1997) FFN, Buns

TeleVisions:

Emmanuelle in Space FFN, Buns

Nancy Allen

Born: June 24, 1950
New York, New York
Skin-O-Meter: Great Nudity

Marriage can be good for a woman, especially if her husband has the means and desire to show off his wife's physical allures. Such was the happy scenario when waifish Nancy Allen caught the fancy of often skinteresting director Brian De Palma. Nancy showed her sprightly pair and the dark-haired delta below when she stood front and center in the crowded all-girl shower scene of De Palma's *Carrie* (1976). Director and starlet were soon married. After the wedding, De Palma threw his bride a shower in *Dressed to Kill* (1980), a splashy soiree that wet down the little lady's buoyant buns and baubles. Nancy flashed nip for the old man one more time, in *Blow Out* (1981), before the two divorced. There is a sweet sighting of Nancy as the menaced, middle-aged mistress filling out black lace and lingerie in *Out of Sight* (1998).

SKIN-fining Moment:

Carrie (0:02) *Nancy struts naked out of the shower and into the girls' locker room, supplying sweet full-frontalosity in the process.*

See Her Naked In:

Blow Out (1981) Breasts
Dressed to Kill (1980) Breasts, Buns
Home Movies (1979) LB
Carrie (1976) FFN

Rosalind Allen

Born: September 23, 1963
New Zealand
Skin-O-Meter: Brief Nudity

Rosalind Allen, like fellow New Zealander Lucy Lawless, found her acting successes here in America, starting with her debut on an episode of *Riptide* in 1984. After

that, Rosalind started landing bit parts in more cinematic fare such as *Perfect* (1985), *8 Million Ways to Die* (1986), and *Dangerously Close* (1986)—if only there were eight million ways to get dangerously close to the perfect Rosalind. She continued milking a TV career, with more guest spots on series such as *T.J. Hooker*, *Knight Rider*, and *St. Elsewhere*, before finally landing a gig of note on *All My Children* in 1987. Rosalind has found limited success in series work such as *SeaQuest DSV* and *Santa Barbara*. But most of her cinematic work has fallen into the more skin-friendly realm of horror, such as infesting *Ticks* (1993), biting into *Children of the Corn II: The Final Sacrifice* (1993), and lighting up *Son of Darkness: To Die For II* (1991). The latter is of note for the first-ever appearance of Rosalind's rosebud breasts. She showed off some skin again in *Pinocchio's Revenge* (1996). Mr. Skin is keeping his pants peeled for some other meat-rising performances.

SKIN-fining Moment:

Son of Darkness: To Die for II (0:37) *Ros bares her topless suckables while bedding Mr. Vampire.*

See Her Naked In:

Pinocchio's Revenge (1996) Breasts
Son of Darkness: To Die for II (1991) Breasts

Kirstie Alley

Born: January 15, 1951
Wichita, Kansas
Skin-O-Meter: Brief Nudity

Kirstie Alley studied drama in her native Kansas and then became an interior decorator, where she must have made her male clients go Feng Shwing! Kirstie's first breaths on television were held as a contestant on the game shows *Match Game PM* and *Password Plus*. "The password is . . . hottie." Kirstie's big movie debut was as Lieutenant Saavik in

Star Trek: The Wrath of Khan (1982), where Kirstie made audience members' pants as pointy as her Vulcan ears. In *Blind Date* (1984), we got the only nip slip in Kirstie's career. And while playing one-time Playboy Club bunny Gloria Steinem in the TV movie *A Bunny's Tale* (1985), Kirstie stuffed her voluptuous curves into a wonderfully tight, cotton-tailed, satin bunny outfit. From 1987 to 1993 Kirstie owned the most delicious pair of kegs on *Cheers* as Rebecca Howe. Alley had her first box-office hit with *Look Who's Talking* (1989), opposite triple-threat sweathog John Travolta. Kirstie returned to TV on the NBC sitcom *Veronica's Closet*, and her sexy sneer and bountiful booty are right up Mr. Skin's Alley.

SKIN-fining Moment:

Blind Date (0:26) *Kirstie unleashes her casabas in a slightly too-dark sex scene with Joseph Bottoms. Nice Pier One . . . and Two!*

See Her Naked In:

Blind Date (1984) Breasts

Susan Almgren

Canada
Skin-O-Meter: Great Nudity

Some call them B-movies, but Mr. Skin says they're the life's blood of sinema. And one of the red-hot mamas who circulates through this steamy vein of filmdom is Susan Almgren. She made her big-screen debut in *Separate Vacations* (1986), which offered her first, albeit from afar, nude view. She then took on roles in films such as the skinful *Shades of Love: Lilac Dream* (1987), *Champagne Charlie* (1989), and *Malarek* (1989). Another reason to relish the B-movie genre is that, rather than Grade-B, the B often stands for boobs. And Susan likes to show off her towering twins, as in the erotic thriller *Deadly Surveillance* (1991). To add that little extra, she did a little romp in the shower with Christopher Bondy. Susan looked as if she were moving up to mainstream arthouse fare when she landed a role opposite Nick Nolte in *Affliction* (1997). That same year she continued this disturbing trend; she scored the lead role in the short-lived reprise of the hit series *Lassie*. But Susan can't escape her exploitation roots. Let's hope they're always showing.

SKIN-fining Moment:

Deadly Surveillance (0:54) *Susan gives Michael Ironside an iron-front when she peels to bra and panties, then loses the bra.*

See Her Naked In:

Twin Sisters (1992) Breasts, Buns
Deadly Surveillance (1991) Breasts
Shades of Love: Lilac Dream (1987) LB
Separate Vacations (1986) Breasts, Thong

Maria Conchita Alonso

Born: June 29, 1957
Cienfuegos, Cuba
Skin-O-Meter: Great Nudity

Maria Conchita Alonso has been driving men bananas for years. Cuban born but raised in Venezuela, adorable mamacita Maria appeared in commercials while a child. At fourteen she was crowned Miss Teenager of the World, and at nineteen she took the Miss Venezuela title. It wasn't long before a modeling career led to movies, and her English-speaking movie debut came in Abel Ferrara's *Fear City* (1984). This led to a breakthrough turn as Robin Williams's girlfriend in *Moscow on the Hudson* (1986). More work came in films such as *Running Man* (1987), *House of the Spirits* (1993), and *Caught* (1995), but Maria also

became a top-selling music artist in South America.

SKIN-fining Moment:

Moscow on the Hudson (1:18) *Maria Conchita shows her topless tamales in the bathtub as she entwines herself with Robin Williams, who's going to give her some Dork from Ork.*

See Her Naked In:

Blackheart (2001) Breasts
Blind Heat (2000) Breasts
El Grito en el Cielo (1997) Breasts
Caught (1996) Breasts, Buns
The House of the Spirits (1994) Breasts, Buns
Vampire's Kiss (1989)
Colors (1988) LB
Con el Corazon en la Mano (1988) Breasts
Extreme Prejudice (1987) Breasts
Blood Ties (1986) Breasts
Moscow on the Hudson (1984) Breasts

TeleVisions:

Kingpin Breasts
Women: Stories of Passion Breasts

Carol Alt

Born: December 1, 1960
Long Island, New York
Skin-O-Meter: Brief Nudity

If the site of legendary supermodel Carol Alt doesn't make you halt in the name of lust, pinch yourself, because you are having a gay nightmare. She's known as "The Face" for modeling her magnificent mug on countless magazine covers, but her bodacious bod is what randy men recognize. *Playboy* named her The Most Beautiful Woman in the World, and *Sports Illustrated* featured her twice on the cover of the coveted Swimsuit Edition. With her electrifying good looks, no wonder she gave Howard Stern's jock a shock just sitting next to him on an airplane in *Private Parts* (1997). This magnificent mannequin has yet to be stripped

onscreen, but her svelte sweetness gave Mr. Skin's tootsie roll a tease in *Bye Bye Baby* (1989).

SKIN-fining Moment:

A Family Matter (1:08) *Panty-clad Carol shows the side of her supermodel mammary in bed with Eric Roberts.*

See Her Naked In:

Deadly Past (1995) Breasts
Millions (1991) Body Double—Buns
A Family Matter (1990) LB
Bye Bye Baby (1989) LB
My Wonderful Life (1987) Breasts, Buns
Portfolio (1983) RB

Summer Altice

Born: December 23, 1979
Fountain Valley, California
Skin-O-Meter: Great Nudity

Five-foot-ten-inch, stunning Summer Altice has a body honed from hours of volleyball—hopefully, she plays with other balls too. She was on the team in high school and again at San Diego State, where she studied communications. Her fit figure certainly gives guys a lot to talk about. She transferred to UCLA in 2000 to continue her studies and further pursue her modeling career. In 1995, Summer won *YM*'s cover girl contest and later signed with Elite modeling agency. That led to her undressing for *Playboy* as its Playmate of the Month for August 2000. She went on to star in several straight-to-video skintaculars such as *Playboy's California Girls* (2000) and *Playboy's Wet & Wild: Slippery When Wet* (2000). Those might be her moist visible roles, but she got some real exposure on the big screen as Kai, one of the warrior women in *The Scorpion King* (2002). She also stars in the Showtime series *ChromiumBlue.com*, which is like a kinky *Fantasy Island*, with Summer a sexier Tattoo. 'Tis the season . . .

SKIN-fining Moment:

Chromiumblue.com (0:25) *Get out your beach balls; it's time for Summer fun! The clip is blue-tinged and arty, but you get a few great views of her topless sandcastles.*

See Her Naked In:

Chromiumblue.com (2003) Breasts, Buns
Numerous Playboy Videos

Anicée Alvina

Born: January 28, 1954
Boulogne-sur-Seine, France
Skin-O-Meter: Great Nudity

Anicée Alvina embodies everything to love about French cinema. It's not the dialogue or the scenery. Guess what? It's the skin! French cinema pioneered onscreen nudity and should be considered as great as Lewis and Clark opening up the wild skin territories. And if any one French actress personifies that adventuresome spirit, it's Anicée. After debuting as Pregnant Teenager on TV in *Elle boit pas, elle fume pas, elle drague pas, mais . . . elle cause!* (1970) (translation: *She Does Not Drink, Smoke or Flirt But . . . She Talks!*), Anicée landed a role in the British production *Friends* (1971), which featured her very first nude scenes, in which she showed off her young and petite pair—how friendly. It is her roles in *Glissements progressifs du plaisir* (1973) and *Le Jeu avec le feu* (1975) that feature the best nudity of Anicée's arousing career. In both she strips down to her fois gras—bon appetite!

SKIN-fining Moment:

Friends (0:45) *Alvina takes off all her clothes before climbing into the tub. Nice knockers, plus some dark crotch and caboose.*

See Her Naked In:

Anima persa (1977) Breasts, Buns
Le Jeu avec le feu (1975) FFN, Buns

Glissements progressifs du plaisir (1973) FFN, Buns
Friends (1971) FFN, Buns

Caroline Ambrose

Skin-O-Meter: Great Nudity

Caroline Ambrose may not be a household name yet, but in the business of show she's done a lot to expose herself. She started her career in *Lost at Sea* (1995), and the beautiful brunette quickly took her buxom bundles to the boob tube with a run of guest spots on such sexy series as *Silk Stalkings* and *High Tide*. Caroline landed her most impressive role to date in *Allyson Is Watching* (1997), and everyone should watch her in this erotically charged performance. Between Caroline and co-star Jennifer Hammon, it's a good thing you have two eyes, because you won't want to take one off of either. Yes, they're nude, but there's so much more, including some pretty serious "simulated" sex. To add spice, the two ladies join up for some taco-munching fun. Since then, Caroline has added more spice to such films as *Deuce Bigalow: Male Gigolo* (1999) as well as a gig on the Cinemax series *Passion Cove*. She's yet to surpass *Allyson Is Watching*, but Mr. Skin will keep looking.

SKIN-fining Moment:

Allyson Is Watching (1:03) *Out-of-the-closet Caroline can no longer hide her attraction and starts having some seriously erotic sex with Jennifer Hammon. Excellent naked lesbotronics!*

See Her Naked In:

Allyson Is Watching (1997) Breasts, Bush, Buns

Tangie Ambrose

Skin-O-Meter: Brief Nudity

Tangie Ambrose owes her career to Martin Lawrence. She got her big

break on a few episodes of his series *Martin* and subsequently made her silver-screen debut in his sleeper *A Thin Line Between Love and Hate* (1996). So Lawrence is not so crazy after all. At least he knows a fine black beauty when she's rubbing her teacups against him. Since her debut, she's made a name for herself as a supporting actress with bit parts in such films as *Men Seeking Women* (1997), *Jackie Brown* (1997), and *I Got the Hook Up* (1998), as well as a spot on the short-lived series *Brutally Normal*. Tangie finally got around to showing off some of her savory body in the straight-to-video release *Diary of a Sex Addict* (2001). Although the title would have you believe it's a flesh romp to cruise through with one hand on your joystick, the flick only offers brief looks at several actresses' breasts, Tangie's included. Tangie's are tasty, though.

SKIN-fining Moment:

Diary of a Sex Addict (0:38) *Streetwalkin' Tangie picks up trick Michael Des Barres and her plump brown right tangelo pops out of her shirt in the process.*

See Her Naked In:

Diary of a Sex Addict (2001) RB

Cindy Ambuehl

Born: January 31, 1965
Skin-O-Meter: Brief Nudity

"We couldn't believe we found a girl this witty and smart in Los Angeles," said funnyman Jerry Seinfeld about possibly the sexiest business-school graduate ever, Cindy Ambuehl. While studying business and marketing, Cindy made ends meet flaunting her good looks as a model before leaving the catwalk for the Walk of Fame in Hollywood. She ended up playing the original Kimberly on the show whose name could be describing her, the hit daytime soap *The Bold and the Beautiful*. She tried her hand on the big screen, first as Miss Italy in *The Naked Truth* (1992) and then with bit parts in *Phantasm III: Lord of the Dead* (1994) and *Codename: Silencer* (1995), which offered a sexy look at the pretty blonde. But her breast performance was opposite Rodney Dangerfield in *Meet Wally Sparks* (1997), in which her big mamas definitely made sparks. She's returned to the boob(less) tube for a recurring role on *JAG* as David James Elliot's love interest, but it looks like she's holstered her hooters . . . at least for now. Here's to seeing the big guns fire their pink nipples again soon!

SKIN-fining Moment:

Meet Wally Sparks (1:10) *Very brief breastage in a fax that freaks out David Ogden Stiers.*

See Her Naked In:

Meet Wally Sparks (1996) Breasts

> "I don't think I could be a man. I like being a women too much. I'd probably be a transvestite."
>
> —MÄDCHEN AMICK

Mädchen Amick

Born: December 12, 1970
Reno, Nevada
Skin-O-Meter: Great Nudity

Mädchen Amick burst onto the entertainment scene in 1989 with a number of TV gigs, including a one-episode appearance on *Baywatch*—too bad she didn't burst out of her bathing suit—as well as a two-episode stint on *Star Trek: The Next Generation*. She made an impression on visionary weirdo David Lynch,

MUNCHIN' AMICK: MÄDCHEN CREAMS LOVER JAMES SPADER IN *DREAM LOVER.*

who cast young Mädchen in his surreal soap *Twin Peaks*. The role never gave Mädchen a chance to show off her twin peaks, nor did follow-up TV gigs on shows like *Central Park West* and *Fantasy Island*. For a real fantasy come true, though, take a gander at *Love, Cheat & Steal* (1993), which featured a half-a-second-long glimpse of Mädchen's mams. Ooh. Aah. The same goes for *Bombshell* (1996), but if you want a good . . . long . . . hard look at Mädchen's hootalage, cabooseage, and bushish, then your go-to flick is *Dream Lover* (1994). Oh, we'll dream . . . wet dreams!

SKIN-fining Moment:

Dream Lover (0:29) *Nice look at Madchen's mam-chens in bed with James Spader, then a top-notch ass and bush shot when she's walking into the bedroom.*

See Her Naked In:

Bombshell (1996) RB
Dream Lover (1994) FFN, Buns
Love, Cheat & Steal (1993) RB, Buns

Suzy Amis

Born: January 5, 1962
Oklahoma City, Oklahoma
Skin-O-Meter: Great Nudity

Suzy Amis first strutted her stuff as a Ford Agency model. Yes, she's built Ford tough, but she's tender, too. She was dubbed the Face of the '80s, and she can sit on Mr. Skin's kisser any

year. Her transition from mannequin to movie star was as smooth as her pale white skin. She debuted in *Fandingo* (1985), but fans probably remember her from the smash hits *Twister* (1990), *The Usual Suspects* (1995), and director hubby James Cameron's *Titanic* (1997). For a look at Suzy's Qs, check out her striptease down to her bee-stung boobage and some self-induced pleasure in *Two Small Bodies* (1993). Her breasts may not be *Titanic*, but the *Two Small Bodies* will give a rise to *The Usual Suspects*. Nothing Amis about that!

SKIN-fining Moment:

The Ballad of Little Jo (1:16) *Suzy shows her topless chupa-chups in bed with David Chung.*

See Her Naked In:

The Ex (1997) LB
The Ballad of Little Jo (1993) Breasts, Buns
Where the Heart Is (1990) Breasts
The Big Town (1987) RB

Elena Anaya

Born: July 18, 1975
Palencia, Castilla y León, Spain
Skin-O-Meter: Great Nudity

Elena Anaya's giant hazel eyes are wide in a continual state of awe, as if she is forever discovering the first joys of orgasm. As the pleasure waves crash upon the spritely Spanish starlet, her luscious mouth smiles in the delight of a child who has just tasted a brand-new favorite candy. Elena grew up in the limelight, and her maturation can be tracked through the progression of her skinematic achievements. Look for the demure exposure of *Africa* (1996), where young Elena appears slightly tense at being seen fully naked, but thrilled too. By the time of *Where the World Ends* (1998), the blossoming beauty is avidly flailing her luscious chest melons while engaging in simulated sex.

Once *Sex and Lucia* (2001) rolls around, intoxicating Elena has become a brazen sexual icon, modeling a corset and leaning forward to check her self-spreading butt loaves in a full-length mirror. Sizzling senorita Anaya is growing up! And her ass is still as fresh as the day she first flashed it.

SKIN-fining Moment:

Sex and Lucia (0:58) *Big bouncing boobers and a hint of the fuzz as Elena sexily masturbates to some video porn.*

See Her Naked In:

Rencor (2002) Breasts
Talk to Her (2002) FFN, Buns
Sex and Lucia (2001) FFN, Buns
El Invierno de las Anjanas (2000) FFN, Buns
Where the World Ends (1998) Breasts, Bush
Lágrimas Negras (1998) Breasts, Buns
África (1996) Breasts

Avalon Anders

Sweden
Skin-O-Meter: Great Nudity

The legacy of the Swedish sex siren raises expectations of a high-quality skin sensation. When we dream of a new object of fixation emerging from Scandinavia, we envision a specific honeyed, spun-sugar blondeness. We picture a snowy, powder-soft terrain of mountainous mammary curves and lush flesh valleys. We imagine a face glowing with the cool heat of guilt-free, shamelessly open sexuality. All of these hopes and dreams come alive, embodied by Avalon Anders, a founding member of the illustrious Swedish Bikini Team. Avalon left her teammates to pursue an acting career. Many a man has seen hints of heavenly Avalon on *Silk Stalkings* or *Married . . . with Children*. Look for the double-paired paradise of her masterfully formed breasts and her bulbous, balanced buns in *Wish*

Me Luck (1995), *Die Watching* (1993), and *Rebecca's Secret* (1997).

SKIN-fining Moment:

Die Watching (0:40) *Avalon peels out of a pink get-up and shakes her lung-balloons for striptease recipient Christopher Atkins.*

See Her Naked In:

Alien Files (1999) Breasts, Thong
Portrait of the Soul (1999) FFN
Beverly Hills Bordello (1997) Breasts, Bush, Buns
Rebecca's Secret (1997) Breasts, Thong
Wish Me Luck (1995) Breasts
The Great Bikini Off-Road Adventure (1994) Breasts
Die Watching (1993) Breasts
Bikini Summer II (1992) Breasts, Buns

TeleVisions:

Beverly Hills Bordello Breasts, Bush, Buns
Red Shoe Diaries Breasts, Thong

Bibí Andersen

Born: February 13, 1954
Manolo, Spain
Skin-O-Meter: Great Nudity

Bibí Andersen started out as Bibí Mandersen! Indeed, it was only after Bibí had his b.b.'s removed during a sex change operation that he became a starlet opposite perennial Spanish hottie Victoria Abril in *Cambio de sexo* (1977). Since then, Bibí's played second-fiddle to the sultry vixen in such films as *La Noche Más Hermosa* (1984), *Tacones lejanos* (1991), and *Kika* (1993). While Bibí is more than willing to let Victoria steal the show when they show up on the same set together, she has made quite a few lasting impressions in her own star vehicles, including *Remando al viento* (1988), *Matador* (1986), and *Una Estacion de paso* (1992). Of course, the most impressive impression that Bibí has left on us was in *Not Love, Just Frenzy* (1996), in which the lovely not-really-blonde actress bares

it all for the camera. The curtains don't match the carpet, but she's well worth a shag.

ForeSKIN-fining Moment:

Cambio de Sexo (0:19) *Bibi prances about on stage, alluring a strip-club audience with her red cape and ripe casabas before finally flashing her pre-sex-change-operation crotch at the surprised customers. That's one fully loaded Bibi-gun!*

See Her Naked In:

Not Love, Just Frenzy (1996) FFN
Kika (1993) FFN, Buns
Cambio de Sexo (1977) Breasts, Buns

Erika Anderson

Born: 1965
Tulsa, Oklahoma
Skin-O-Meter: Great Nudity

Long and limber Erika Anderson deserves to be a household name. The searing brunette native of Tulsa, Oklahoma, had a recurring part on *Twin Peaks*, a cult favorite that often had its audience asking, "What the hell is going on here?" Two bigger questions are: How were so many views of Erika Anderson's sinfully scintillating body crammed into one movie, *Zandalee* (1991), and why isn't Erika a superstar after that super exposure? The angel-faced starlet's perfect, pointed tits, like small, nipple-peaked cones, and her pitch-dark pubes steal the show from costars Nicolas Cage and Judge Reinhold. She stands fully naked in front of a full-length mirror, allowing for simultaneous contemplation of her rear mysteries and her frontal ecstasies. Her nipples pop up like they are shooting straight from the toaster. In bed, she is pliable, malleable, ballable. Her name should be top-billing marketable.

SKIN-fining Moment:

Zandalee (0:51) *Full-frontal skinitude banging Nic Cage then a nice butt shot* when he gives her an oil and cocaine massage. Now that's a picker-upper!

See Her Naked In:

Object of Obsession (1994) Breasts, Buns
Quake (1993) Breasts
Zandalee (1991) FFN, Buns

TeleVisions:

Red Shoe Diaries Breasts, Bush

Gillian Anderson

Born: August 9, 1968
Chicago, Illinois
Skin-O-Meter: Brief Nudity

Gillian Anderson is best known as the hot FBI agent on the prowl for alien booty on the Fox smash *The X Files*. Weirdly, she hasn't made a similarly sizable splash on the silver screen. She appeared in *Chicago Cab* (1998), *The Mighty* (1998), and *Playing By Heart* (1998), which didn't play by the skin as we might have hoped. For a more revealing look at Gillian's supernatural beauty, rent a copy of *The Turning* (1992), which has recently been reissued due to the *X File* getting close to the *XXX Files*, letting her flesh saucers fly out of her lacy bra for a sighting. Make sure to get your meat-beaters on a copy. The skin is out there.

SKIN-fining Moment:

The Turning (0:47) Brief revelation of Gillian's sextraterrestrials when her bra gets pulled off in the kitchen. File under X-citing!

See Her Naked In:

The Turning (1997) Breasts

Juliet Anderson

Born: July 23, 1938
Burbank, California
Skin-O-Meter: Great Nudity

Juliet, where for art thou? Well, Juliet Anderson started her adult life as an English teacher in Japan, as well as a few other foreign countries, before returning to the U.S. in the late '70s to become a porno actress. That is where it's at! When she debuted in the blue-movie world with *Pretty Peaches* (1978), no one seemed to mind that she was already in her forties. Most of her movies became runaway hits, most notably her *Aunt Peg* series, as well as the classic *Taboo* (1980), which also starred sexy Kay Parker. Known for her bob haircut and for always wearing nylons and a garter belt in her films, Juliet continued appearing in hardcore sex flicks until the late '90s, racking up well over fifty credits to her name. Now in her sixties, this sexagenarian keeps her motor running making sex videos for the nursing home set. It keeps her vehicle well lubed.

SKIN-fining Moment:

Aunt Peg (1:05) After endless incesticilious teasing, Aunt Juliet lunches on the loins of nifty niece Sharon Kane in the back of a limo.

See Her Naked In:

Taboo (1980) FFN
Aunt Peg (1980) FFN, Buns
Numerous Adult Movies

Loni Anderson

Born: August 5, 1946
St. Paul, Minnesota
Skin-O-Meter: Never Nude

During the jiggle decade on TV, when no brassiere was left latched and bounce was more than just a laundry detergent, Loni Anderson was at the top of the top-heavy batch. She auditioned for the breast show of its time, *Three's Company*, and somehow didn't get the gig (perhaps she had *too* much talent). But Loni finally caught fire as the hot secretary with the cleavage that made the DJs on *WKRP in Cincinnati* spin. The 38-E act-chest was born to play the lead in the made-for-TV movie *The Jayne Mansfield Story* (1980) and help Bob Hope keep the troops' spirits (among other things) up on USO tours. Sadly, she's always stopped just short of skin. The closest viewers have come to feasting their eyes on her bountiful boobs was opposite then-husband Burt Reynolds when she stripped to her bra and panties in *Stroker Ace* (1983). She kept on teasing, though, playing a sexy mom in *A Night at the Roxbury* (1998) and on TV's *The Mullets*. Still, it's never too late to unleash Loni's lungs.

SKIN-fining Moment:

Stroker Ace (0:59) Burt Reynolds undoes Loni's lingerie, revealing her packed white bra and pretty panties, then he passes on going for more when he realizes that she's passed out. Come on! Stroke her, Ace!

Melissa Sue Anderson

Born: September 26, 1962
Berkeley, California
Skin-O-Meter: Never Nude

Melissa Sue Anderson was born a shy, bookish girl in Berkeley, California. She had no intention of becoming a star and turning men on with her innocent good looks. But that's just what happened when her dance teacher urged her parents to find Melissa an agent. Soon the blue-eyed beauty was making TV commercials. Then in 1974 Melissa landed the role that would come to define her. She started playing Mary on the long-running hit series *Little House on the Prairie*. And that's where she stayed. Outside of some guest spots on other TV shows such as *The Brady Bunch* and *The Love Boat*, Melissa remained the chaste girl, like a rose cursed to bloom unseen in a desert. After the show went off the air, frustrated viewers waited with bated pants for her transition to the big screen. Sadly, with equally family-oriented fare such as *Skatetown, U.S.A.* (1979) and *Chattanooga Choo Choo* (1984), the potential unveiling of the century wasn't to be. But there is one lost gem, which is why you come to Mr. Skin, the best in the breast business, right? No, Melissa isn't nude, but she does expose her bounty bound in a bra. It's *Happy Birthday to Me* (1981), and it's a gift worth unwrapping.

SKIN-fining Moment:

Happy Birthday to Me (0:22) *Melissa Sue keeps her Little Houses (and Prairie) covered as she changes clothes in her bedroom. Nice white bra, though.*

Pamela Anderson

Born: July 1, 1967
Ladysmith, British Columbia, Canada
Skin-O-Meter: Hall of Fame

MR. SKIN'S TOP TEN

Blondes Who've Done Great Nudity
. . . When it comes to nudity, they're not "yellow"

10. Kim Basinger
9. Barbara Bouchet
8. Heather Graham
7. Candice Rialson
6. Charlize Theron
5. Natasha Henstridge
4. Cheryl "Rainbeaux" Smith
3. Shannon Tweed
2. Gloria Guida
1. Pamela Anderson

Fantastically, bombastically protuberant Pamela Anderson rose from LaBatt's Beer spokes-hottie to *Playboy*'s all-time hottest cover model to Tool Time Girl on the sitcom *Home Improvement* to being no less than the Ultimate Blonde Bombshell of the 1990s. Pam truly ballooned to superstar proportions on TV's *Baywatch* from 1992 to 1997. She also blew fans away in B-thrillers like *Snapdragon* (1993) and *Raw Justice* (1995) and at theaters in *Barb Wire* (1996). Back on the boob tube, Pam led a crack cadre of muffragettes on the syndicated action series *V.I.P.* and developed a cartoon titled *Stripperella* for the men's network Spike TV. And speaking of which, Mr. Skin's always got a high, hard one for this libidinally legendary honey.

SKIN-fining Moment:

Pam & Tommy Lee: Stolen Honeymoon (0:24) *Honeymooner Pam eases back on a boat, cracks a (vertical) smile, and parts the floodgates that lead to her wide-open honeypot. It's gynoriffic!*

See Her Naked In:

Scary Movie 3 (2003) Breasts
Baywatch: Hawaiian Wedding (2003) Thong
Pam & Tommy Lee: Stolen Honeymoon (1998) Breasts, Bush, Buns
Naked Souls (1995) Breasts, Buns
Barb Wire (1995) Breasts
Raw Justice (1994) Breasts
Snapdragon (1993) Breasts, Buns
Pamela Anderson and Brett Michaels Home Video FFN, Buns
Numerous Playboy Videos

Bibi Andersson

Born: November 11, 1935
Stockholm, Sweden
Skin-O-Meter: Great Nudity

Bibi Andersson is one Swedish dish sure to cook your meatballs. She

was plucked from film obscurity by arthouse fave Ingmar Bergman in the mid '50s, and the director put her in all his head-scratching best, such as *Persona* (1966) and *Scenes from a Marriage* (1973). But you'll be scratching your little head watching her in the maestro's mam-sterpiece *The Touch* (1971). Audiences are recommended to touch themselves while watching. But that wasn't the Swedish fish's first swim into onscreen skin. That boobtiful day was in *Flickorna* (1968), in which she stripped out of her black-lace bra and let her treasured chest finally take the spotlight. She got into sexual experimentation in the les-a-thon *Twice a Woman* (1979), which, suffice it to say, is true to its title in terms of twice the naked female flesh. Outside of some forays into mainstream Hollywood fare such as *Concorde: Airport '79* (1979), Bibi remains an arty Euro girl at heart. But as long as she keeps showing her Bibi's, you won't hear Mr. Skin complaining.

SKIN-fining Moment:

The Touch (0:56) *Ms. Andersson bares her bibis while smooching Elliot Gould.*

See Her Naked In:

Twice a Woman (1979) Breasts
The Touch (1971) Breasts
Flickorna (1968) Breasts

Starr Andreeff

Born: February 29, 1964
Hamilton, Ontario, Canada
Skin-O-Meter: Brief Nudity

Starr Andreeff spends her time nowadays hanging out with teenage boys whom she grooms for rock stardom as an executive at Smash Music. But when she was not that far from those wonder years herself, Starr was a staple of the horror genre, a scream queen. The

URSULA ANDRESS BRINGS HER PERFECT
EVERYTHING TO *PERFECT FRIDAY.*

Canadian-born hottie was a cheerleader back home before making the pilgrimage to L.A., where she hit the back lots struggling for work with the town's overpopulation of young beauties. She made her debut in *Skullduggery* (1983) then pretty much stuck to scare fare like *The Terror Within* (1989) and *Out of the Dark* (1989), excepting, of course, her three-season stint on *General Hospital* in the early '90s. So many B-movie horror-flick roles should have given Starr ample opportunity to show off the gifts that God gave her, but, alas, she wasn't that skinful. She did manage to show off some hootage a few times, first in the vampire-in-a-strip-club flick *Dance of the Damned* (1988) and later in the vampire-in-a-club-again flick *Club Vampire* (1997). When this scream queen stopped screaming, pants across America were collectively looser.

SKIN-fining Moment:

Dance of the Damned (0:03) *Bare-breasted, dancing in black bikini bottoms onstage in a club.*

See Her Naked In:

Club Vampire (1997) RB
Dance of the Damned (1988) Breasts

MR. SKIN'S TOP TEN

Naughty Nurses
. . . Florence Nude-ingales

10. **Kristin Scott Thomas**
    —*The English Patient* 1996

9. **Traci Lind**
    —*The Road to Wellville* 1994

8. **Sally Kellerman**
    —*M*A*S*H* 1970

7. **Veronica Hart**
    —*Young Nurses in Love* 1986

6. **Felicity Devonshire**
    —*What's Up Nurses!* 1977

5. **Barbara Leigh**
    —*The Student Nurses* 1970

4. **Alana Stewart**
    —*Night Call Nurses* 1972

3. **Carol Connors**
    —*Deep Throat* 1972

2. **Candice Rialson**
    —*Candy Stripe Nurses* 1974

1. **Ursula Andress**
    —*The Sensuous Nurse* 1975

Ursula Andress

Born: March 19, 1936
Berne, Switzerland
Skin-O-Meter: Hall of Fame

Born in Switzerland to German parents and more curvy than the Swiss Alps, Ursula Andress first sought out film work while on a holiday in Rome, where she made a series of cheap films (cheap and hot, of course). It wasn't long before a producer brought Ursula to the U.S. and was billing her as the new Marlene Dietrich. In 1957 Andress married American actor John Derek, whose many romantic conquests suggest he may have been a true master of Jedi mind tricks. Derek supervised every aspect of Ursie's

career in much the same way that he'd later mold Bo Derek. The marriage ended unhappily, but the couple remained friends. Ursula became an international sensation with her bikini-clad sashay out of the surf as Honey Rider in the first James Bond movie *Dr. No* (1962), a role for which she was paid $10,000. Within a year, Andress was sharing the screen with ring-a-ding-ding dongs Frank Sinatra and Dean Martin in *Four for Texas* (1963) and the swiveling hips of Elvis Presley in *Fun in Acapulco* (1963). When Ursula posed for a nude layout in *Playboy*, it seemed to mark the high point of her career. She then began making lower-profile but more skineriffic flicks like *Perfect Friday* (1970) and *The Sensuous Nurse* (1975). Blonde goddess Ursula is her most divine in *The Slave of the Cannibal God* (1979), where her bronze bod is strapped to a stake, stripped completely naked, and painted orange. That's a good base coat, Ursula. Now let Mr. Skin finish the job.

SKIN-fining Moment:

The Sensuous Nurse (0:51) *Ursula's flawless full-frontal form is on frequent display as she does a slow striptease and tries to seduce some lucky stiff.*

See Her Naked In:

Famous T&A (1982) FFN
Campanas Rojas (1982) Breasts, Bush, Buns
The Mountain of the Cannibal God (1979)
    FFN, Buns
The Fifth Musketeer (1979) FFN
Tigers in Lipstick (1979) Breasts
Spogliamoci cos Senza Pudor (1976) Breasts
The Sensuous Nurse (1975) FFN, Buns
Loaded Guns (1975) FFN, Buns
Stateline Motel (1975) Breasts
Soleil Rouge (1971) Breasts
Perfect Friday (1970) Breasts, Buns
The Southern Star (1969) Breasts, Buns
Casino Royale (1967) RB
The Blue Max (1966) Breasts
Les Tribulations d'un Chinois en Chine
    (1965) Breasts

MR. SKIN'S TOP TEN

Movie Stars I Can't Believe Got Naked
. . . Goody two shows

10. Sandra Bullock
 9. Olympia Dukakis
 8. Cloris Leachman
 7. Anne Hathaway
 6. Teri Garr
 5. Deborah Kerr
 4. Liza Minnelli
 3. Reese Witherspoon
 2. Molly Ringwald
 1. Julie Andrews

Julie Andrews

**Born: October 1, 1935
Walton-on-Thames, Surrey, England, UK
Skin-O-Meter: Great Nudity**

Julie Andrews made a career out of being as sweet as a spoonful of sugar. Blessed with a stunningly silky voice, she sang and smiled her way straight to stardom. Starting on Broadway as cockney cutie Eliza Doolittle in *My Fair Lady*, she soon transitioned to film. Her Oscar-winning portrayal of the magical nanny of every child's dreams in *Mary Poppins* (1964) and her role as a singing nun in *The Sound of Music* (1965) cemented her good-girl image, making dramatic roles hard to come by. How do you solve an image problem like Ms. Andrews? Julie turned miss goody-two-shoes into miss-nudie-two-boobs by giving thoroughly grown up performances as a saucy singer in the Dudley Moore comedy *10* (1979) and the gender-bending heroine in *Victor/Victoria* (1983). She was the most

supercalisexpealadocious in husband Blake Edwards's film *S.O.B.* (1981). Jules replaced nanny with naughty by giving a tour of her rolling hills in an astonishing scene where she triumphantly rips off her top. Her new public persona was equally likeable and looked deliciously lickable, and she followed up with more funbaggage in *Duet for One* (1986).

SKIN-fining Moment:

S.O.B. (1:19) *Julie pulls her Poppins out of her dress, much to the collective joy (and stunned surprise) of everyone on the set. Those hills are alive!*

See Her Naked In:

Duet for One (1986) Breasts, Buns
S.O.B. (1981) Breasts
Darling Lili (1970) LB

Vanessa Angel

**Born: November 10, 1966
London, England, UK
Skin-O-Meter: Brief Nudity**

London-born Vanessa Angel started her career as a model and made the jump to film when cast as the amorous Russian rocket-crew member in the comedy *Spies Like Us* (1985). Since then Vanessa has appeared in such notable films as *Another Chance* (1989), *King of New York* (1990), and *Kingpin* (1996), as well as steaming up the already hot series *Melrose Place* and *Baywatch*. With a career path as decidedly hot as Vanessa's, it's no surprise that she's flashed her mountainous mammaries a few times on film. Their moist notable appearance was in *Homicidal Impulse* (1992), and there's another chance to ogle in *Another Chance* (1989), but, alas, they were all but concealed under the bubbling water of a Jacuzzi. Vanessa, let's see those fallen Angels again soon!

SKIN-fining Moment:

Homicidal Impulse (0:25) *Vanessa peels down to bra and panties, then keeps going to show us her angelic orbs and ass while getting sexed up in the sack.*

See Her Naked In:

Homicidal Impulse (1992) Breasts, Buns
Another Chance (1989) RB

Jennifer Aniston

**Born: February 11, 1969
Sherman Oaks, California
Skin-O-Meter: Brief Nudity**

Long known as the best body on NBC's *Friends*, it's hard to believe that just one year before being cast as Rachel on that runaway-hit series Jennifer Aniston was thanking her lucky charms for a part in the horror flick *Leprechaun* (1992). She famously married movie star Brad Pitt in 2000, but acting is in Jen's genes, too. Her dad, John Aniston, made his bones on *Days of Our Lives*, and her godfather was Telly Savalas, the legendary chrome-domed, lollipop-sucking, bad-ass NYPD dick of TV's *Kojak*. Who loves ya, baby?

SKIN-fining Moment:

The Good Girl (0:25) *After teasing us for years on TV, Jennifer finally flashes just a bit of boob in bed with Jake Gyllenhaal. They must be FRIENDS . . .*

See Her Naked In:

The Good Girl (2002) Breasts

Amina Annabi

**Born: March 5, 1962
Carthage, Tunisia
Skin-O-Meter: Great Nudity**

Tunisian tart Amina Annabi launched her skinternational acting career with a leading role in the French flick *Maman* (1990). Since then American audiences have been most familiar with amorous Amina in such productions as *The Advocate* (1993)—Mr. Skin advocates the movie for Amina's exotic skin scenes—and the made-for-TV movie *Cleopatra* (1999). But it's Amina's role in *The Sheltering Sky* (1990), opposite John Malkovich and Debra Winger, that breast shows off her globe-sized goodies. Debra dazzles with a moist look at her fluffy muff, but Amina very nearly steals the whole movie with her one mamorable scene as a North African prostitute. Malkovich invests his hard-earned cash in a roll in the hay with the hard-nipped, bursting-bosomed babe. Judging from the look on his face, her body is more than worth the price of admission.

SKIN-fining Moment:

The Sheltering Sky (0:20) *Amina unwraps her buoyant bazongas for John Malkovich. Wish I could be him.*

See Her Naked In:

The Advocate (1993) Breasts
The Sheltering Sky (1990) Breasts

Glory Annen

Born: September 5, 1952
Kenora, Ontario, Canada
Skin-O-Meter: Great Nudity

Canadian-born Glory Annen wanted out of the frozen tundra wasteland of her home and immigrated to England at the tender age of seventeen to pursue an acting career. But it took a few years to break into the business. Glory finally made the grade as a prostitute in *Cruel Passion* (1977). She moved up the billing in the British horror flick *Alien Prey* (1978), starring as half of a lesbian couple with Sally Faulkner. In *Spaced Out* (1979), she defines the era's roller girl, skating topless for much of the movie. While Glory continued showing off her gorgeous body in its nude splendor, she hit the paramount of perversity in

Felicity (1979). This softcore coming-of-age sex film stars Glory in the title role. She engages in lesbian shower antics and an Asian trip where she's on the poo-poo platter for an explicit kinktacular. Sadly, for an actress of Glory's fearlessness in the face of nudity, her biggest hit was a bit part in *Supergirl* (1984). After another bit role as a hostess in *Water* (1985), Glory faded. Then, surprisingly, she showed up in *True Files* (2002) and was back in all her hot Glory. You can't keep a bad girl down.

SKIN-fining Moment:

Alien Prey (0:36) *Plentiful T&A during this lengthy lesbianic romp between Glory and sumptuous Sally Faulkner.*

See Her Naked In:

The Lonely Lady (1983) LB
Spaced Out (1979) Breasts
Felicity (1979) FFN, Buns
Alien Prey (1978) Breasts, Buns

Francesca Annis

Born: May 14, 1944
London, England, UK
Skin-O-Meter: Brief Nudity

Francesca Annis is a classically trained British actress, star of stage and screen. You may recall her from *Dune* (1984), where she made that desert planet even hotter! Sadly, she has rarely appeared naked to show off her real assets. But there is a brief but tempting naked shot of her in *Macbeth* (1971). If you watch carefully and can "split hairs," you'll be rewarded with glimpses of her well-proportioned, pear-shaped breasts, small nipples, and large, round, pink areolas. Unfortunately, for most of this famous nude-sleepwalking scene, her long hair obscures all the best parts. To paraphrase the Bard, "Out, out damn hair!" Francesca does have a

very nice ass that can be seen clearly in several shots, so it's not a complete tragedy. A quick glimpse of her pubes can even be seen when she is ushered out of a room. It's enough to have you reconsidering the worth of the classics.

SKIN-fining Moment:

Macbeth (1:41) *Francesca walks into the room nude, showing her beautiful boobicles, then she sits down to reveal her Macbuns.*

See Her Naked In:

Macbeth (1971) LB, Buns

Ann-Margret

Born: April 28, 1941
Valsjöbyn, Jämtland, Sweden
Skin-O-Meter: Great Nudity

Discovered by George Burns in the late '50s—who put her into his club act because he enjoyed her singing, dancing, and unbelievably large and lively chest—Ann-Margret is one Scandinavian import who was all too aware of the power she could wield with her glowing Northern Lights. It wasn't too long before Georgie's girl found her way to the silver screen, debuting in *Pocketful of Miracles* (1961) and becoming a household name several years later when she poured herself into a pair of capris in *Bye Bye Birdie* (1963) and a jet-black bathing suit opposite Elvis Presley in *Viva Las Vegas* (1964). A sexy, skin-worthy turn in *Tiger and the Pussycat* (1967) whet the world's appetite, but it wasn't until she was in her thirties that Ann-Margret fully revealed Skindinavia's finest assets in *Carnal Knowledge* (1971). Her turn as the nymphomaniacal Bobbie garnered her a Golden Globe and also celebrated the long-awaited unleashing of her own legendary globes. Sexiness and allure befitting a legendary sex kitten have underlaid Ann-Margret's career ever since, the last several years finding her playing an older and wiser but still damn sexy dame in such projects as *Grumpier Old Men* (1995) and the TV mini-series *The 10th Kingdom* (2000). There's no denying that, at any age, she's a kitten turned fully mature lioness who continues to bring pride to the pride.

SKIN-fining Moment:

Carnal Knowledge (0:49) *A-M bares her legendary mams in bed, then lights up the screen with her magnificent seat-meat as she rises to join Jack Nicholson in the shower.*

See Her Naked In:

A Tiger's Tale (1988) Body Double—Breasts, Buns
Magic (1978) RB
Carnal Knowledge (1971) Breasts, Buns
R.P.M. (1970) LB, Buns
C.C. and Company (1970) Breasts, Buns
Tiger and the Pussycat (1967) LB

Susan Anspach

**Born: November 13, 1942
New York, New York
Skin-O-Meter: Brief Nudity**

You might not remember Susan Anspach from her debut, a bit part in the made-for-TV movie *Journey of the Fifth Horse* (1966). She followed in some far-out dramas from the dope decade, like *The Landlord* (1970). But it wasn't until starring with Jack Nicholson in *Five Easy Pieces* (1970) that Susan made the big time. Her film career includes memorable roles in *Play it Again, Sam* (1972), *Blume in Love* (1973), and *The Devil and Max Devlin* (1981), but by the mid '80s she'd fallen from A-list to B-movie stardom. The drop meant a sharp rise in skin for fans to savor. She appeared in all her full-frontal glory in *Montenegro* (1981). It also happened to feature

one of her fans' favorite scenes of all time, centered on a tank-mounted dildo. She later flashed out her fun bags in *Into the Fire* (1987). Talk about hot!

SKIN-fining Moment:

Montenegro (1:08) *Furry full-frontal shower action. Rub-a-dub-do!*

See Her Naked In:

Into the Fire (1987) Breasts
Montenegro (1981) FFN

Lysette Anthony

**Born: September 26, 1963
London, England, UK
Skin-O-Meter: Hall of Fame**

Lysette Anthony has acting in her blood—literally. She is the fruit of a union between noted British actors Michael Anthony and Bernadette Milnes and started her career just about when she learned to walk, appearing in various productions with her parents on both stage and screen. She made her first "major" big-screen performance in the

SAY CELLO TO HER NOT-SO-LITTLE FRIENDS LAURA ANTONELLI IN *SECRET FANTASY*.

classic fantasy/adventure flick *Krull* (1983), which made everyone who saw it want to play with their swords. Lysette has since gone on to appear in such varied productions as *Husbands and Wives* (1992), *Dracula: Dead and Loving It* (1995), and *Robinson Crusoe* (1997), as well as on series such as *Dark Shadows*. A great actress, Lysette uses every part of her body to get the job done . . . and done right. When a character must be nude, she strips without hesitation—bless her round rump and melon-sized sweater mamas. Whether it's *Looking for Eileen* (1988) and its full-frontal, juicy furburger, or her wet goodies bouncing delightfully in *Switch* (1991) and *Save Me* (1993), Lysette is a carnal craftsman. If only all actresses were as dedicated to the art of the tart.

SKIN-fining Moment:

Save Me (0:42) *Alluring Ms. Anthony delivers all of the goods (including a few peeks at the bush!) during a languid lovemaking session with Harry Hamlin.*

See Her Naked In:

Affair Play (1995) Breasts, Buns
The Hard Truth (1994) Breasts
A Brilliant Disguise (1994) Breasts, Buns
Save Me (1993) Breasts, Bush, Buns
The Advocate (1993) FFN
Pleasure Principle (1991) Breasts
Switch (1991) Breasts
Looking for Eileen (1988) FFN, Buns

TeleVisions:

Tales from the Crypt Breasts

Laura Antonelli

**Born: November 28, 1941
Pola, Italy
Skin-O-Meter: Hall of Fame**

Laura Antonelli, all 34C-23-35 of her boobaciousness, was set to be the next Sophia Loren. Sadly, she never made it to that level of instant

---

MR. SKIN'S TOP TEN

Naked Italian Stars
. . . Nice pizza ass

10. Chiara Caselli
 9. Gina Lollobrigida
 8. Sabrina Ferilli
 7. Ornella Muti
 6. Stefania Sandrelli
 5. Asia Argento
 4. Sophia Loren
 3. Gloria Guida
 2. Monica Bellucci
 1. **Laura Antonelli**

---

worldwide recognition, but to Mr. Skin she towers forever near the top of the list of history's all-time most scorching flesh-bombs. The '70s were sheer heaven for lovers of Laura's big girls, as she starred in a string of skin-powered international smashes that included *A Man Called Sledge* (1970), *Malicious* (1973), *Till Marriage Do Us Part* (1974), and *The Divine Nymph* (1976). Her forte was the Italian sex comedy, and she brought stacked star power to classics of the genre such as *Dr. Goldfoot and the Sex Bombs* (1966), *Dr. Popaul* (1972), *Senator Likes Women* (1975), and *Secret Fantasy* (1981). If you can't find a flick with Laura nude, then you're not looking hard enough. Why not begin your search with *Devil in the Flesh* (1969)? Then you'll be hard soon enough.

SKIN-fining Moment:

Venus in Furs (0:00) *Now this is the way to open a movie—buns and breastplay behind the opening credits.*

See Her Naked In:

La Gabbia (1986) RB, Bush
The Venetian Woman (1986) Breasts, Bush, Buns

Porca Vacca (1982) FFN
Secret Fantasy (1981) FFN, Buns
Chaste and Pure (1981) Breasts, Bush
Passione d'Amore (1981) RB
Mi faccio la Barca (1980) Breasts
The Divine Nymph (1977) FFN
The Innocent (1976) Breasts, Bush, Buns
Simona (1975) LB, Bush, Buns
Till Marriage Do Us Part (1974) FFN, Buns
Malizia (1973) FFN, Buns
Sessomatto (1973) Breasts, Buns
Docteur Popaul (1972) FFN, Buns
The Eroticist (1972) Breasts, Buns
Venus in Furs (1969) Breasts, Bush, Buns
La Rivoluzione Sessuale (1968) Buns

"I may as well have been a big rubber doll with a hole strategically placed."

—GABRIELLE ANWAR on her character in *Things to Do in Denver When You're Dead* (1995)

Gabrielle Anwar

Born: February 4, 1970
Laleham, Middlesex, England, UK
Skin-O-Meter: Great Nudity

Waif-like Gabrielle Anwar first caught men's fancies with a one-episode gig on the British series *The Storyteller* (1987). The English strumpet spent the next few years mired in bit parts in European television productions before making her American film debut in *If Looks Could Kill* (1991). Her looks certainly could slay, but stardom was more elusive. Her performances in *Wild Hearts Can't Be Broken* (1991) and *The Three Musketeers* (1993) should have made her a blockbuster. They didn't, but she's still a knockout. From her role as Al Pacino's tango partner in that ever-memorable scene in *Scent of a Woman* (1992) to Abel Ferrara's gruesome remake of *Body Snatchers* (1994), Gabrielle has

the goods. Her titty turn in *Body Snatchers* showed off her puffy nippers in two more-than-worthy scenes, including a nice bubble bath that is unfortunately interrupted by a "pod person." What a pud.

SKIN-fining Moment:

Body Snatchers (1:13) *Great view of her little ta-tas waking up on a stretcher. Nice.*

See Her Naked In:

Body Snatchers (1994) Breasts

Apollonia

Born: August 2, 1959
Santa Monica, California
Skin-O-Meter: Great Nudity

Born Patty Kotero and re-christened Apollonia, this Latino lover is as mouth-wateringly delicious as a ripe apple—and every bit as sinful! The honey-skinned hottie began a spicy relationship with the big screen as Girl in the Bikini in *La Mafia de la frontera* (1979) and went on to star (and undress) in *Amor Ciego* (1980), a.k.a. *Sex Beach*. The latter remains one of her crowning achievements, exposing her ripe boobables, which makes audiences cry for her dark, soothing nipple. Apollonia entered the go-go '80s running and never stopped, enlisting her talented body for a singing and acting career that saw her raise nightsticks on the TV series *CHiPs* and bust organs in the movie *Heartbreaker* (1983). But the voluptuous vamp was barely a blip on the booty radar until R&B imp Prince cast her as his topless love interest in his semi-autobiographical blockbuster *Purple Rain* (1984). After that, she was sexy nighttime soap fodder on *Falcon Crest* but lost her big momentum by the end of the decade. Still, you can't keep a sly fox down (or clothed), and Appie returned to the silver screen as Hot Tub Lady in the skinful flick *Anarchy TV* (1997), followed by a part in *Vampirates* (2001). Do we at Skin Central dare say a comeback is in the making? We can think of two lovely reasons why we hope that's true!

SKIN-fining Moment:

Purple Rain (0:20) *Apollonia "purifies" herself in greasy Lake Minnetonka as Prince turns purple while getting a great view of her apolloulies.*

See Her Naked In:

Black Magic Woman (1991) LB
Purple Rain (1984) Breasts
Amor Ciego (1980) Breasts, Buns

Christina Applegate

Born: November 25, 1971
Hollywood, California
Skin-O-Meter: Never Nude

Christina Applegate broke into the business as a baby in diapers, selling product on TV commercials. Then she landed in the *Jaws of Satan* (1981), which isn't a fanciful way of referencing Hollywood, really, but rather her film debut at the age of ten. Then it was back to TV and various appearances on series like *Mama's Family*, *Quincy*, and *Charles in Charge*. But it was one series in particular that offered the now-buxom blonde her breakout part (if not bra-busting performances). That was, of course, her iconic role as hot Kelly Bundy on the smash hit *Married . . . with Children*. The show made her a star, and she parlayed that attention into more cinematic pursuits such as *Don't Tell Mom the Babysitter's Dead* (1991) and *Mars Attacks!* (1996). But by 1998, Christina's star was descending. Then she landed the title role on the surprise hit series

Jesse, but even that was cancelled after a three-year run. She's not down yet, though, coming up in such notable pictures as the female gross-out comedy *The Sweetest Thing* (2002) and the John Holmes biopic *Wonderland* (2003). Unfortunately, in spite of her slutty ways on *Married . . . with Children*, Christina has somehow avoided any real onscreen skinage. She did appear topless in *Streets* (1990), but the incredibly lucky David Mendenhall had his hand on her breasts the entire time, making it impossible to see anything more than what she showed off in her TV work. Forget Watergate, this Applegate is the greatest scandal of our time!

SKIN-fining Moment:

Streets (1:09) *Kelly Bundy toplessly tongue-kisses a dude whose damn hands cup her naked casabas and thereby conceal them from the rest of us. Can't say I blame him.*

Natalie Appleton

Born: May 14, 1973
Mississauga, Ontario, Canada
Skin-O-Meter: Brief Nudity

Canadian-born Natalie Appleton is one half of a beautiful pair. Aside from her meaty boobs, there's her sister Nicole Appleton, together with whom she was a member of the popular British pop sensation All Saints. Sadly, that success has kept Natalie (and her hot-ass sister) out of the acting realm for the most part. The good news is that they did do a movie together, *Honest* (2000), and both sisters show off some skin . . . honest. While Nicole definitely spends a lot more time with her breasts bared onscreen, Natalie does her best to keep up, baring her breasts as well as her incredible ass. You just have to love sibling rivalry.

SKIN-fining Moment:

Honest (0:13) *Very slight ass-crackal when pulling down jeans to show off a tattoo on her backal.*

See Her Naked In:

Honest (2000) Breasts, Buns

Nicole Appleton

Born: December 7, 1974
Hamilton, Ontario, Canada
Skin-O-Meter: Great Nudity

Every randy sinner will be clamoring to get into heaven if word ever filters down to hell that paradise is populated with pixie blonde tempt treats such as sweet teats Nicole Appleton, saucy singer and booty flinger of the dancing-girl Brit band All Saints. A lissome and lovely blonde lass in the tradition of Rolling Stones pop tart Marianne Faithfull, apple-cheeked Appleton mixes her rock career with chart-topping romance, being the bedmate and baby mama to Liam Gallagher of the loads-famous lad band Oasis. For a peek at the perky nips that treat the lips of Liam, latch the eyes to Nicole's truly topless turvy in *Honest* (2000).

SKIN-fining Moment:

Honest (1:34) *Fine, sizable bare funbaggage as a guy removes her dress and gives it to her all-natural-style outside in a garden.*

See Her Naked In:

Honest (2000) Breasts

Anne Archer

Born: August 25, 1947
Los Angeles, California
Skin-O-Meter: Brief Nudity

Anne Archer was born into acting. The daughter of John Archer and Marjorie Lord, she got her career started in the '70s on an episode of

Hawaii Five-O. McGarrett may have said, "Book 'em, Danno," but the audience wanted to bed 'em when it came to Anne's brunette beauty and her big kahunas. She went on to the hit series *Falcon Crest* and the silver screen opposite Jon Voight in *The All-American Boy* (1973), but fame eluded her. That is, until she played the hot wife whom Michael Douglas inexplicably cheats on in *Fatal Attraction* (1987). Anne went on to star as another perfect accessory for a grumbling old man, this time Harrison Ford in *Patriot Games* (1992) and *Clear and Present Danger* (1994). But if you think you've seen Anne's assets in *Nails* (1992), *Body of Evidence* (1993), or *The Man in the Attic* (1995), think again; those were body doubles. For the true skinophile, check out *Lifeguard* (1975) for some nipple slippage about an hour into the film when Anne's making out with Sam Elliott. And *Short Cuts* (1993) has a short cut of Anne's ass. It's as close to an Archer bull's eye that we've got.

SKIN-fining Moment:

Fatal Attraction (0:02) *Anne brushes her teeth and bares her bitable belly, wearing a tiny T-shirt and sheer white panties in the bathroom. I'd like to give her something to floss with!*

See Her Naked In:

The Man in the Attic (1995) Body Double—Breasts
Short Cuts (1993) Buns
Body of Evidence (1993) Body Double—Breasts, Buns
Nails (1992) Body Double—Breasts, Buns
Lifeguard (1976) LB

Manuela Arcuri

Born: January 8, 1977
Latina, Italy
Skin-O-Meter: Great Nudity

Life is good in Italy. They have three-hour lunches, wash them down with wine, and sweeten things up with cool gelato. No wonder so many of their women end up with meaty curves. That still does little to explain the full-figured fineness of Manuela Arcuri, perhaps the sleekest sexport from that country since the Ferrari. And she's just as fast to lose her clothes onscreen. She debuted in *I Buchi neri* (1995), which has also been billed as *Black Holes*, but Manuela didn't start flashing her holes until *Alla ricerca di Sherazade* (1999). It was a role that called for very few visits to the costume shop. She exposed every inch of her round and firm beauty. And she continues to do so in films like *Mad Love* (2001). Abbondanza!

SKIN-fining Moment:

Mad Love (0:54) *Muff and mammary in bed with her hard-pumping man-friend.*

See Her Naked In:

Cosa de Brujas (2003) Breasts, Thong
Mad Love (2001) FFN, Buns
Alla Ricerca di Sherazade (1999) Breasts, Buns

Fanny Ardant

Born: March 22, 1949
Saumur, Maine-et-Loire, France
Skin-O-Meter: Great Nudity

Not your run-of-the-mill French pastry, Fanny Ardant has that certain tart sweetness that can only be called pure sex appeal. With her very long legs, extended body, taut tits, and striking, rectangular face, she is both alluring and terrifically attractive. Fanny grew up keeping company with royalty in Monaco, where her father was posted as a calvary officer. Her air of sophistication makes her the type of woman least likely to get nude or engage in erotic activities. For that reason Mr. Skin can't stop watching everything she does, and, luckily, nearly everything she does will at some point display her delectable desirables! Enjoy her flashes of nudity in *Beyond the Clouds* (1995) and a longer, yet all too brief, exposure in *Elizabeth* (1998). In *The Woman Next Door* (1981), she twirls about in a high-slit dress that exposes her pink slit and gives audiences a hairy eyeful. Americans know her best for *Swann in Love* (1984), co-starring Jeremy Irons. French and international audiences relish her in *Ridicule* (1996). But everyone loves Ardant best for her Fanny!

SKIN-fining Moment:

The Woman Next Door (0:35) *Thanks to an unbuttoned shirt, Fan-tastic Fanny flashes itty bitty nippy slippies.*

See Her Naked In:

Ridicule (1996) Body Double—Buns
Australia (1989) Breasts
The Woman Next Door (1981) RB, Bush

Asia Argento

Born: September 20, 1975
Rome, Italy
Skin-O-Meter: Hall of Fame

Compelling evidence exists that daring and depravity are passed along bloodlines, along with a penchant for tit-out sensual exploitation. How else to explain the willfully wanton excesses of cinema seductress Asia Argento? The daughter of famed and revered Italian skin-and-blood maestro Dario Argento, brunette breast spectacle Asia burst out of her bra and onto the American film scene as a topless seventeen-year-old in *Trauma* (1993), a baring and daring performance assayed under the direction of her father. Daddy Argento would call for his offspring to spring into breast-quivering action again in his *Phantom of the Opera* (1998). As forthcoming as Asia is with her unclothed charms in Papa's productions, the prettiest Argento saves her unveiled muff for when Daddy is not around. Catch the beaver that the old guy missed in *B. Monkey* (1998) and *Scarlet Diva* (2000), the latter of which Asia wrote and directed as well as fleshed out.

SKIN-fining Moment:

Scarlet Diva (0:34) *Asia understands it's easier to shave one's pits when totally naked, so we're treated to a bush and breasts double feature!*

See Her Naked In:

The Heart Is Deceitful Above All Things (2004) Breasts, Buns
The Keeper (2003) Breasts, Buns
XXX (2002) Nip Slip RB

Les Morsures de l'Aube (2001) Buns
Scarlet Diva (2000) FFN, Buns
New Rose Hotel (1998) Breasts
B. Monkey (1998) Breasts, Bush
Phantom of the Opera (1998) Body Double—Buns / Her—LB
Viola Bacia Tutti (1997) Buns
La Sindrome di Stendhal (1996) LB
Queen Margot (1994) Bush
Trauma (1993) Breasts

Alison Armitage

Born: February 26, 1965
London, England, UK
Skin-O-Meter: Great Nudity

Alison Armitage started her career on the pages of *Playboy* magazine as Brittany York in October 1990. She says the spread was mainly to get back at an unfaithful ex-boyfriend. "I did it right after we split up," she smirks. "I wanted to show him 'This is what you had, and this is what you've lost.'" He got an even bigger eyeful (and another reason to put his foolish head in a noose) with Alison's turn in *I Posed for Playboy* (1991). Sure, the role wasn't that much of a stretch, although she did some rather intriguing stretching in the production itself. Her modeling exposure quickly led to several TV guest appearances—including a memorable role as a sexy dental hygienist on *Seinfeld*. Then came *Acapulco H.E.A.T.*, a cult TV show for guys who like eye candy without much of a wrapper. Alison has since shown off skinage in pictures such as *Miracle Beach* (1992), as well as in a multitude of *Playboy* video productions, including *Wet & Wild IV* (1992) and *Playboy Video Playmate Calendar* (1991). Unfortunately, Alison has since been reduced to roles such as Girlfriend and Former Girlfriend in such films as *Driven* (2001) and *Jerry Maguire* (1996), respectively. Maybe it's time for another *Playboy* spread to open doors for this hottie.

SKIN-fining Moment:

Miracle Beach (0:14) *Alison's apples are in full ripeness when she wakes up in a bed on the beach. It's a miracle!*

See Her Naked In:

I Posed for Playboy (1991) Breasts
Miracle Beach (1991) Breasts
Numerous *Playboy* Videos

Bess Armstrong

Born: December 11, 1953
Baltimore, Maryland
Skin-O-Meter: Brief Nudity

If it takes a more mature, matronly great dame to get your blood going, then take a gander at the comely but common beauty of Bess Armstrong. Since her debut on the not-quite-a-hit series *On Our Own* (1977), Bess has been making plain Janes sexy. She's spent the better part of her career on the small screen in such made-for-TV fare as *How to Pick Up Girls!* (1978) and *Christmas Every Day* (1996), as well as some theatrical teasers such as *Jaws 3-D* (1983) and *That Darn Cat* (1997). But she's best remembered as Claire Danes's tempting mom on the short-lived series *My So-Called Life*. Of course, there was a time when Bess was still an aspiring young actress willing to do anything to make it big. She made Mr. Skin big when she appeared in *The House of God* (1984), offering a lingering look at her love buds whilst bathed in examination-room fluorescent light. Other than that, there's some brief bunnage in *The Four Seasons* (1981). Bess makes more than just our Armstrong.

SKIN-fining Moment:

The House of God (1:02) *Dr. Bess drops her scrubs, showing us her pert li'l love-pillows.*

See Her Naked In:

The House of God (1984) Breasts
The Four Seasons (1981) Buns

Kerry Armstrong

Born: 1958
Sydney, New South Wales, Australia
Skin-O-Meter: Brief Nudity

Hot redhead Kerry Armstrong started her career in her native Australia in 1974 with a role on the series *Marion*. After spending several years doing TV work on such local series as *The Sullivans*, *Prisoner*, and *Skyways*, she took to the skyways for the greener pastures of America and a role on the hit nighttime soap opera *Dynasty*. After spending a few years Stateside, including gigs in *Key Exchange* (1985) and the made-for-TV movie *Dadah Is Death* (1988), Kerry retreated to The Land Down Under for the homegrown made-for-TV movie *Come in Spinner* (1990). Then Kerry took on her most daring, and skinful, role to date in *Hunting* (1991) opposite John Savage. In it, she showcased her shock absorbers several times, but, sadly, Kerry's been a bit skingy since. There's always a chance for a re-teat performance, though.

SKIN-fining Moment:

Hunting (0:35) *Topless Kerry's kaboobles bobble in bed with John Savage.*

See Her Naked In:

Hunting (1991) Breasts, Buns

Melinda Armstrong

Born: 1958
Skin-O-Meter: Great Nudity

Mega-mammed Melinda Armstrong has been swimmingly suck-cessful in skinema. Her booby and bunular baring in fun-in-the-sun flicks such as *Bikini Summer* (1991) and *Bikini Summer II* (1992) put Mel on the map of happening beach bunnies throughout the '90s. Although Melinda got off to a frigid start in films like *In the Cold of the Night*

(1989), she moved on to more memorable mammoriffic performances, sizzling onscreen in totem ticklers like *Teasers* (1993), *Alien Intruder* (1992) and, most recently, *Heavenly Hooters* (2003). While it's true that this angel's honkable halos are out of this world in the latter, any of Melinda's naked offerings are guaranteed to make your *Armstrong* in response to frequent, repeated motion.

SKIN-fining Moment:

Bikini Summer (0:35) *Melinda takes a dip in a pool and shows off all points of her taut, tan body from tits to tail to tightly trimmed tuft.*

See Her Naked In:

Heavenly Hooters (2003) Breasts, Bush, Thong
Deep Down (1994) FFN
Jailbait (1994) Breasts, Thong
Raw Adventures (1994) FFN, Buns
Nude Daydreams (1993) FFN
Teasers (1993) Breasts, Buns
Alien Intruder (1992) Breasts, Buns
Bikini Summer II (1992) Breast, Buns
Bikini Summer (1991) FFN, Thong

Rebekka Armstrong

Born: February 20, 1967
Bakersfield, California
Skin-O-Meter: Great Nudity

Rebekka Armstrong first shook the skin world to its bedrock in 1986 as a much-revered *Playboy* Playmate of the Month. Not surprisingly, she subsequently shed her threads in a number of the Bunny's videos, including *Sexy Lingerie* (1988), *Playmates at Play* (1990), and *Wet & Wild III* (1991). If plotless and poonful isn't enough, then consider her torrid turns in such films as *Hider in the House* (1989), *The Immortalizer* (1991), and *Angel 4: Undercover* (1993), all of which featured her naked breasts front and center. Sadly, Rebekka gave up the entertainment industry in 1994,

focusing her life on the pursuit of a cure for HIV/AIDS, with which she was diagnosed that year. Let's pray for a cure, because Rebekka's short time onscreen has cured Mr. Skin's problem of getting it up.

SKIN-fining Moment:

The Immortalizer (0:29) *A perv opens Rebekka's top and gropes her chest-strongs while she's dozing.*

See Her Naked In:

Hellcats in High Heels 3 (2002) FFN, Thong
Angel 4: Undercover (1993) Breasts
The Immortalizer (1991) Breasts
Hider in the House (1989) Breasts
Numerous Playboy Videos

Judie Aronson

Born: June 7, 1964
Panorama City, California
Skin-O-Meter: Great Nudity

All-nerd alert: Judie Aronson first came to the attention of the horror-geek set with her supporting role as Wyatt's love interest Hilly in the sci-fi/comedy classic *Weird Science* (1985). But her debut was a bit earlier, in the ongoing gore series *Friday the 13th: The Final Chapter* (1984), which distinguished itself from the pack thanks to cutie Judie skinny dipping not once but twice in Crystal Lake. You can't keep a good girl clothed, as Judie proved when she flashed some hoot again whilst atop Woody Harrelson in *Cool Blue* (1988). She pulled her big pair out yet again in *The Sleeping Car* (1990). Since then, Judie's been keeping her talents covered. She last appeared in a bit part as a reporter in *Hannibal* (2001). Why the cannibal didn't want to have her breasts with a nice bottle of Chianti is the riddle of the ages.

SKIN-fining Moment:

Friday the 13th: The Final Chapter (0:41) *Caboose and cup-cakes when she strips for a doomed dip in Crystal Lake.*

The Sleeping Car (1990) Breasts
Cool Blue (1988) Breasts
Friday the 13th: The Final Chapter (1984)
   Breasts, Buns

Patricia Arquette

**Born: April 8, 1968
Chicago, Illinois
Skin-O-Meter: Great Nudity**

The younger sister of Rosanna
Arquette, Patricia Arquette happily
followed in big sis's bra-cups,
showing her teats in Hollywood
treats. Patricia's breakthrough role
was as Alabama, Christian Slater's
hooker-cum-bride in the rock-'em-
sock-'em-almost-show-'em movie
True Romance (1993). She keeps her
monumental mams in an Alabama-
slammer of a push-up bustier
through most of the pic, but you're
still granted a wet peek in a
bathtub scene. *Human Nature*
(2001) is Patricia's latest and (kind
of) greatest nude appearance to
date. There's a catch, see: her
character is covered in thick hair!
Still, she looks great, and there's
no problem a little Nair won't
solve. If you're talking hairless
hooters, though, it's hard to beat
her top-notch toplessness in *Lost
Highway* (1997).

SKIN-fining Moment:

Lost Highway (1:30) *Patricia
doffs the black bra and shows off
her beautiful bags of fun when she's
forced to strip in front of Robert
Loggia.*

See Her Naked In:

The Badge (2002) Thong
Human Nature (2001) FFN, Buns
Stigmata (1999) Breasts, Buns
Lost Highway (1997) Breasts, Buns
True Romance (1993) Breasts
Wildflower (1991) RB

MR. SKIN'S TOP TEN

**Naked Sisters
. . . Sibling ribaldry**

10. Mia Farrow and Tisa Farrow

9. Michelle Pfeiffer and Dedee
   Pfeiffer

8. Heather Graham and Aimee
   Graham

7. Alicia Loren and Annie Sorell

6. Melanie Griffith and Tracy
   Griffith

5. Madeleine Collinson and Mary
   Collinson

4. Shannon Tweed and Tracy
   Tweed

3. Margeaux Hemingway and
   Mariel Hemingway

2. Jennifer Tilly and Meg Tilly

1. **Rosanna Arquette and
   Patricia Arquette**

Rosanna Arquette

**Born: August 10, 1959
New York, New York
Skin-O-Meter: Hall of Fame**

The elder of the rackadocious
Rosanna and Patricia Arquette
sister duo, lusciously rotund in the
upper torso, Rose has set a
tremendous example for li'l sis
with a full twenty years of fine
acting and phenomenal flesh
flashing. Rosanna first appeared
nude in *S.O.B.* back in 1981 and let
her nips slip as recently as *Diary of
a Sex Addict* in 2001. In between,
she put together an awesome array
of skin and scantily clad scenes,
somehow maintaining her
superhuman sexiness and those
gravity-mocking gazongas along
the way.

SKIN-fining Moment:

The Wrong Man (1:15) *Rosanna's
remarkable rack steals the show in this
incredible, super-long topless tabletop
dancing sequence. A crowning moment
in her udderly awesome body of work.*

See Her Naked In:

Diary of a Sex Addict (2001) Nip Slip LB
Too Much Flesh (2000) Breasts
Sugar Town (1999) Thong
Voodoo Dawn (1998) Breasts
I'm Losing You (1998) LB, Buns
Hell's Kitchen (1998) Breasts
Floating Away (1998) Breasts
Trading Favors (1997) Breasts
Crash (1996) LB
Nowhere to Run (1993) FFN, Buns
The Wrong Man (1993) Breasts, Thong
Black Rainbow (1990) Breasts
The Big Blue (1988) LB
Desperately Seeking Susan (1985) Breasts
Baby It's You (1983) LB
The Executioner's Song (1982) Breasts, Buns
S.O.B. (1981) Breasts

Karina Arroyave

**Born: July 16, 1969
Colombia
Skin-O-Meter: Brief Nudity**

Karina Arroyave is a graduate of
the famous LaGuardia High School
of Music and the Arts in New
York, where she honed her craft
and blossomed into the dark
beauty she is today. After a stint
on Broadway, she left the
footlights for the bright lights of
Hollywood but was sidetracked by
a long starring run on the hit soap
As the World Turns, which films in
New York. After several years on
the tawdry treadmill of daytime
TV, Karina headed to Hollywood,
where she landed guest spots on
various TV shows such as *NYPD
Blue*, *Law & Order*, and *Touched by
an Angel*. But it was her role as
Jamie Farrell on Fox's smash *24*
that made Karina a household
name. As for being a Skin Central

name, it was her scene in the crime drama *One Eight Seven* (1997). She's buck-ass naked on a couch, which for all you couch potatoes is fantasy made flesh. Karina doesn't show more than a side of yummy bum and her meaty breasts, so we'll just wait until she gets off that couch.

SKIN-fining Moment:

One Eight Seven (0:52) *Quick right tittable as she's sprawled nude on Samuel L. Jackson's sofa.*

See Her Naked In:

One Eight Seven (1997) Breasts

Lisa Arturo

Skin-O-Meter: Brief Nudity

Blonde bitsy booby Lisa Arturo has got gams and she knows how to use them. She debuted kicking those long luscious ones as a chorus-line dancer in *Bullets Over Broadway* (1994). Stardom was elusive in one indie-flick after another, such as *Border to Border* (1998) and the low-budget Angie Everhart action picture *Running Red* (1999), as well as in one-episode bit parts on such scandalous series as *Married with Children*, *Katie Joplin*, and *Walker, Texas Ranger*. Don't fall asleep . . . all that time in the Hollywood trenches paid off with a hot role in *American Pie 2* (2001). Lisa and movie roomie Denise Faye provided the movie's most impressive skin show, as well as a fairly erotic lesbianic kiss. Sweet!

SKIN-fining Moment:

American Pie 2 (0:47) *Titties in the bedroom as Lisa and Denise Faye change clothes, followed by some brief thonged-buttage as they leave the room.*

See Her Naked In:

American Pie 2 (2001) Breasts, Thong

Dena Ashbaugh

Canada
Skin-O-Meter: Great Nudity

There's this guy called The Naked Chef. Talk about a rip-off. He may be a good cook, but the man is fully dressed! Now for more truth in advertising, check out Canada's CityTV's *Barely Cooking*, in which the hosts cook in the buff, save for aprons. One of the more alluring dishes on the show is Dena Ashbaugh, who exposes special recipes that can be applied to the body and then licked off. Yummy. Dena is also an actress and model who got a taste for Asian cuisine when working as a teen model in the Far East. Although she's worked in commercials and shows up in some independent film productions such as *The Bed* (2002), this is a girl who definitely belongs in the kitchen cooking up hot stuff. Her rump roast is divine, but how about a helping of those spicy meatballs!

SKIN-fining Moment:

Barely Cooking "Body Painting with Food" (2003) *Yummy bunnage as chef Dena enters the kitchen clad only in a backless apron.*

TeleVisions:

Barely Cooking Buns

Daphne Ashbrook

Born: January 30, 1966
Long Beach, California
Skin-O-Meter: Brief Nudity

Daphne Ashbrook had guts, and more specifically tits, in her debut as one of the many exceptionally hot cheerleaders in *Gimme an "F"* (1984), the unfortunately not-quite-as-skinful follow-up to the classic *H.O.T.S.* (1979). Even more unfortunate, Daphne remained clothed throughout the flick and shortly thereafter turned to the

boob tube, a notoriously non-naked medium, though she looked hot on her stint on *Falcon Crest*. Thankfully, she took on a more cinematic gig opposite Michael Paré in *Sunset Heat* (1991), and although she played second fiddle to Tracy Tweed, Daphne made a run at the most mamorable scene by baring her breasts during a sex scene. Sadly, she's been a bit skingy since, landing on the hit series *JAG*. But flesh may be in her future after leaving the show and failing to hit the big time, which usually means big-time nudity!

SKIN-fining Moment:

Sunset Heat (1:07) *Daphne bares her pair while making it with Michael Paré.*

See Her Naked In:

Sunset Heat (1991) Breasts

Danni Ashe

Born: January 16, 1968
Beaufort, South Carolina
Skin-O-Meter: Hall of Fame

Beautiful, bodacious, superhumanly buxom, awesomely all-natural mega-mammary queen Danni Ashe has been certified by the *Guinness Book of World Records* as the most-downloaded woman on the Internet, and there are two reasons why: Her left breast and her right breast. She's also whip-smart, devastatingly gorgeous, and imbued with nuclear-strength star power. A former nude model turned stripper, turned porn star, turned girl-only porn star, turned Internet media mogul, Danni is as unstoppable as her gigantic chest. Her gloriously strained bra cups runneth over with success, as evident on her phenomenally pop-ular Web site *Danni's Hard Drive*. In addition to Danni's dairy-based dominance online, she's also appeared in numerous knocker-heavy videos. Just take a ride on *Boob Cruise '95* (1995) and watch Danni jiggle more than the waves on the ocean. Her work in *Tit to Tit 4* (1996) leaves nothing to the imagination, and Danni is just one of the many virtual hookers in *Killer Sex Queens from Cyberspace* (1998). This gal really gets around, as evidenced by *Busty Bangkok Bangers* (1996). Gee, do you think they really went to Bangkok? No matter if it is just Silicon Valley chicanery. I defy you to watch *Wild Desire* (1999) and not go wild with desire!

SKIN-fining Moment:

Soft Bodies: Double Exposure (1990) Danni kicks things off by taking off her blue bra and panties, unleashing her superhuman, all-natural wonder-whoppers, lush bush, and rockin' round rumpus.

See Her Naked In:

Cybervampz 2001: A Nude Odyssey (2001) FFN, Buns
WildWebGirls.Com (1999) FFN, Buns
All Nude Glamour (1995) FFN, Buns
Soft Bodies: Double Exposure (1990) FFN, Buns
Numerous Adult Movies

Jane Asher

Born: April 5, 1946
London, England, UK
Skin-O-Meter: Great Nudity

Redhead Jane Asher was already aflame with her career by the tender age of five, when she made her big screen debut in *Mandy* (1952). By the time she was fifteen, Jane had appeared in eight films, made nine TV appearances, over one hundred radio appearances, and was in five plays—but the breast was yet to come (as were audiences lucky enough to follow her carnal career). Jane's father taught music, and her older brother is the former in the '60s pop group

Peter and Gordon. But Jane went directly to the top of the pops when she spent five years as Paul McCartney's girlfriend during the heady days of The Beatles. The rocker was rocked by the "rave London bird," and many of his famous songs were inspired by Jane, including "We Can Work It Out." Sadly, they couldn't work it out, not when Jane caught Paul in bed with another bird in 1968. After that heartache, Jane began to share with the world what had till then been solely McCartney's. In *Dead End* (1970), where she takes one last skinny dip before dying, and *Closing Numbers* (1994), Jane proved that she was more than just a one-tit wonder. Nowadays, she's sort of the English Martha Stewart, only with nicer tits.

SKIN-fining Moment:

Deep End (1:19) Jane's totally nude with Psycho-Boy in a swimming pool. The good news: We see lots of her pale buns and pink-nipped tittables. The bad news: The kid just brained her and she's bleeding to death.

See Her Naked In:

Closing Numbers (1994) Breasts
Deep End (1970) Breasts, Bush, Buns

Elizabeth Ashley

Born: August 30, 1939
Ocala, Florida
Skin-O-Meter: Great Nudity

Although better known for her stage and TV work, Elizabeth Ashley pocketed Hollywood with her debut *The Carpetbaggers* (1964) and followed that up with another critical success, *Ship of Fools* (1965). Despite some classic cinematic outings—*Coma* (1978), *Vampire's Kiss* (1989), and *Happiness* (1998)—she has spent the better part of her career on the small screen. Audiences got to enjoy the soft-breasted brunette known for her

catty roles in TV fare like *Another World* and *Evening Shade*. But TV can be restricting, especially for a free spirit like Elizabeth. Back onscreen she was able to expose her true talents with a nipple flash in *The Marriage of a Young Stockbroker* (1971) and the whole she-bang in *Paperback Hero* (1973). Elizabeth shares a lengthy shower scene with Keir Dullea, culminating in a full-frontal mounting of the lucky fella. Hopefully, Elizabeth will come clean again soon.

SKIN-fining Moment:

Paperback Hero (0:37) Ashley spends a lot of time entirely nude in the shower with costar Keir Dullea before hopping atop him for a little ride.

See Her Naked In:

Paperback Hero (1973) FFN, Buns
The Marriage of a Young Stockbroker (1971) RB

Juli Ashton

Born: October 5, 1969
Colorado
Skin-O-Meter: Great Nudity

Juli Ashton first smiled (vertically) for the hardcore camera in *The Dinner Party* (1994). Audiences liked what was on the menu, ate it up, and asked for sloppy seconds. Since then, Juli has appeared in such films as *The Butt Detective* (1994), *Smells Like . . . Sex* (1995), the aptly titled *Wide Open Spaces* (1995), and the classic *Devil in Miss Jones 5: The Inferno* (1995), which boasts the single greatest screenplay in the history of sex films. Honest! Juli also took the onscreen virginity of squidgy-looking Scotty Schwartz, star of the Richard Pryor comedy *The Toy* (1982) and Flick from *A Christmas Story* (1983) in *Scotty's X-Rated Adventure* (1997). If adult flicks aren't your cup of T&A, check out *Orgazmo* (1997), in which Juli provides the film's only nudity in the form of an exceptionally brief, distant tit shot. Still, for all her movie work, Juli is best known and lusted after as the co-host of Playboy TV's *Night Calls*, on which, along with redheaded fireball Tiffany Granath, she injects some amazing oral electricity into the traditional concept of a talk show.

SKIN-fining Moment:

Night Calls: The Movie, Part 2 (0:10) *Nice views of Juli's sacred goods as she and Doria Rone enter a monk's holy land.*

See Her Naked In:

Night Calls: The Movie, Part 2 (1999) FFN, Buns
Orgazmo (1997) Breasts
The Dinner Party (1994) FFN, buns
Numerous Adult Movies

Jennifer Aspen

**Born: October 9, 1973
Richmond, Virginia
Skin-O-Meter: Brief Nudity**

She may not be the most famous member of the hit drama *Party of Five*, but Jennifer Aspen has a sexy quality all her own, even competing against such mega-hotties as Jennifer Love Hewitt and Neve Campbell. Whenever Jennifer's blonde sweetness filled the screen, there was a party of five in Mr. Skin's pants—and things got messy. But before TV fame, Jennifer debuted in *A Very Brady Sequel* (1996). She followed that up with her first brief nude scene in *Sometimes They Come Back . . . Again* (1996). Come back to the skin side . . . again and again, Jennifer! After the success of *Party of Five*, Jennifer appeared in bit parts on TV, such as *Married . . . with Children*, *Friends*, and *Beverly Hills, 90210*, and in films such as *Vanilla Sky* (2001), although she was uncredited.

SKIN-fining Moment:

Sometimes They Come Back . . . Again (1:13) *Jen lets free her left jug when losing her blouse to get with a guy.*

See Her Naked In:

Sometimes They Come Back . . . Again (1996) LB

TeleVisions:

The Ranch Breasts

Stéphane Audran

**Born: November 2, 1932
Versailles, Yvelines, France
Skin-O-Meter: Great Nudity**

Stéphane Audran came into the limelight with her starring role in *Les Bitches* (1968). In that bust-out performance, Stéphane plays a rich lesbian who finds herself involved in a threesome. You've got to love French sinema. An international institution for over fifty years, she was first married to famous French actor of the '50s and '60s Jean-Louis Trintignant. But she gave him no encore and soon moved on to her second husband, director Claude Chabrol, who used Stéphane in many of his films. He fully utilized her onscreen, icy sensuality in such films as *Les Bonnes Femmes* (1960), *Bluebeard* (1962), and *The Tiger Likes Fresh Blood* (1964), among others. It led to even sexier roles in *La Femme Infidèle* (1969), *Le Boucher* (1970), *Juste avant la nuit* (1971), and the very sensual *Les Noces rouges* (1973). She is sexy in all her early works, whether she's lying covered in bed, exposing cleavage, or just swishing her skirt while walking down a street; Stéphane could make a man's pants stir with a just a look! You can see her more exposed in *The Folies Bourgeoises* (1976) and completely exposed, though briefly, in a nude sun-tanning scene in *Comment Réussir . . . Quand on est con et Pleurnichard* (1974) or *How to Make Good When One Is a Jerk and a Crybaby*. That's the story of Mr. Skin's life.

SKIN-fining Moment:

Folies bourgeoises (0:18) *Top of her fine ass when she moves on the bed . . . then very brief partial right tit.*

See Her Naked In:

Folies bourgeoises (1975) RB, Buns
Comment Réussir . . . Quand on est con et Pleurnichard (1974) Breasts

Claudine Auger

**Born: April 26, 1942
Paris, France
Skin-O-Meter: Brief Nudity**

Five-foot-eight-inch voluptuous 36-23-37 beauty Claudine Auger came into prominence at the age of fifteen when she won the title of Miss France in 1958. An alumna of the Paris Drama Conservatory, she went on to play small, eye-candy parts in films with people such as Yul Brynner, Charles Aznavour, Brigitte Bardot, and even artist Pablo Picasso. She suddenly emerged from the background in the role of Domino in the James Bond epic *Thunderball* (1965)—and balls have been thundering ever since. In the whirlwind of overnight fame, Claudine went on to do a *Playboy* spread and then appeared on American national TV in a special starring Bob Hope and Danny Thomas. She went on to make some fine European films, such as *Triple Cross* (1966), *The Killing Game* (1968), and *The Bay of Blood* (1972), before settling back into being French dressing. She played the role of sexy scenic conquest to a T—and A—in such celluloid dross as *Twitch of the Death Nerve* (1971) and *Black Belly of the Tarantula* (1972). A French reviewer once observed, "She was born to fill a multitude of alluring bikinis!" Today Claudine is primarily making French TV commercials, most notably for the Concorde. Perhaps they figure if all else fails, Claudine can still get it up!

SKIN-fining Moment:

A Few Hours of Sunlight (1:11) *Claudine appears completely naked in bed with her fella, giving up a glaring glance at her Gluteus Maximus.*

See Her Naked In:

A Few Hours of Sunlight (1971) Breasts, Buns
Thunderball (1965) Nip Slip LB

Ewa Aulin

Born: February 13, 1950
Landskrona, Skåne, Sweden
Skin-O-Meter: Great Nudity

The typical Scandinavian teen fantasy of every man's dreams, Ewa Aulin created a big surge of wankie spankings around the globe in her short but skintastic career. This blue-eyed blonde boober-madchen won Miss Teen Sweden in 1965, followed by Miss Teen International in 1966. Her exposure caught the eyes (and flys) of Italians, who cast her in several obscure movies, such as *Death Laid an Egg* (1967) alongside the boobtastic Gina Lollobrigida. At the tender age of twenty, this sweetish sexpot threw the yanks a bone with her mouth-watering appearance in *Candy* (1968) by having sex with virtually everyone in the flick (including her pop). Ewa played a naked naïf eager to give lusty lads like Marlon Brando, Richard Burton, and Ringo Starr a peek at her ass-sets. Mr. Skin couldn't help fallin' for Aulin's ample, swollen-nipped Swedish meatballs, just begging for a bite.

SKIN-fining Moment:

Candy (0:43) *Ewa dishes up her own candy in this typically '60s madcap scene. She strips right down to some*

sweet sticky buns and side right gumdrop.

See Her Naked In:

Il Tuo Piacere è il Mio (1973) Buns
Una Vita Lungo un Giorno (1973) Breasts
The Legend of Blood Castle (1973) LB
Quando l'Amore è Sensualità (1973) RB, Buns
Fiorina la Vacca (1972) Buns
Rosina Fumo Viene in Città . . . per Farsi il Corredo (1972) Breasts
The Double (1971) Breasts, Buns
La Controfigura (1971) LB, Buns
Start the Revolution Without Me (1970) LB
Candy (1968) Breasts, Buns

Teri Austin

Born: April 17, 1959
Toronto, Ontario, Canada
Skin-O-Meter: Brief Nudity

Things were looking up right from the start for Teri Austin, the Canadian with the bright brown eyes. She got a role in the straight-to-video cult classic *The Sex and Violence Family Hour* (1983) and by 1985 secured the recurring role of Jill Bennett on the hit series *Knots Landing*. That success didn't stop tawdry Teri from exploring less-traditional parts (and exposing her more-hidden parts). She appeared in *Terminal Choice* (1985), which features Teri in all her full-frontal glory, although she is "dying" and subsequently "dead" and covered in blood during the sequence in question. Then came *Vindicator* (1986), again with her hooters and high-rise hootenanny, albeit from a distance whilst covered in bubbles from a bath. Sadly, after her stint on *Knots Landing* came to an end in 1989, Teri took on a part in the singing police TV drama and butt of a million jokes *Cop Rock*. Teri has trudged on, though, appearing in various made-for-TV movies and series, as well as in cinematic productions such as *Raising Cain* (1992), and she flashed more of her

fine material on the Showtime series *Bedtime* (1996). Teri's star may not be as bright as it once was, but she's still out-of-this-world hot and a real Austin power.

SKIN-fining Moment:

Terminal Choice (0:14) *Skingoria! Teri shows tits and tuft on an operating table. And, oh yeah, she's covered in blood.*

See Her Naked In:

The Vindicator (1986) LB, Buns
Terminal Choice (1985) FFN

TeleVisions:

Bedtime Breasts

Margaret Avery

Magnum, Oklahoma
Skin-O-Meter: Brief Nudity

Margaret Avery started her career with a groovalicious role in *Cool Breeze* (1972). Sexy as that performance was, Margaret, unlike many black actresses in the '70s, didn't get pigeonholed into one blaxploitation gig after another—not that being a proud ebony warrior is a bad thing. One of her most stellar performances, however, if for no other reason than she flashed her perky tits, was in the decidedly blaxploitative *Hell Up in Harlem* (1973). Shortly after that skinful gig, Margaret went on to what has become quite the successful career, with movies such as *Scott Joplin* (1977), the made-for-TV sci-fi cult classic *The Lathe of Heaven* (1980), *The Color Purple* (1985), featuring her infamous lesbian kiss with Whoopi Goldberg, and *Lightning in a Bottle* (1993) under her belt. And Margaret's belt is Avery sexy one.

SKIN-fining Moment:

Hell Up in Harlem (0:42) *Maggie shows her hooters while getting pounded in bed by Fred "The Hammer" Williamson.*

See Her Naked In:

Hell Up in Harlem (1973) Breasts

Mili Avital

Born: March 30, 1972
Jerusalem, Israel
Skin-O-Meter: Brief Nudity

Born in Jerusalem and raised near Tel Aviv, Israel, the now five-foot-four-inch shapely beauty has grown up to be quite the stunner. Best known for her movie roles in *Stargate* (1994), Jim Jarmusch's *Dead Man* (1995), *The End of Violence* (1997), and *Polish Wedding* (1998), Mili is cute, popular, determined, a bit extravagant, and someone to whom attention will be paid. *Sci-Fi Universe* magazine recognized that back in 1995 when their readers voted her Best Supporting Actress in a Genre Motion Picture for *Stargate*. Although she won the Israeli Academy Award in 1991 for Best Supporting Actress for her feature debut in *Over the Ocean* (1992) and later was nominated for Best Actress for her role in *Groupie* (1993), she left home in 1993, for America, to make it big in film. She entered the tried and true flight path to that end: she began working as a waitress in New York City. Sure enough, she was discovered by a talent agent who didn't think it mattered that she barely spoke English and got her cast in *Stargate*. Mili has sadly not been naked very often. There're some brief topless shots in *After the Storm* (2001), and she looks hot in bra and panties and then naked beneath the sheets in love scenes from *Kissing a Fool* (1998), David Schwimmer being the lucky fool—in the movie that is! In 2002, *Vanity Fair* described Mili as one of the five most promising actresses in Hollywood today. Hope that means she's going to show off her itty-bitty talents.

SKIN-fining Moment:

After the Storm (0:55) *Benjamin Bratt removes Mili's top and all that comes between us and her naked Vanillis is some sheer mosquito netting.*

See Her Naked In:

After the Storm (2001) Breasts

Charlotte Ayanna

Born: September 25, 1976
San Juan, Puerto Rico
Skin-O-Meter: Great Nudity

Charlotte Ayanna was discovered by Latino lothario Ricky Martin, who picked her to star in his romantic video "She's All I Ever Had." Martin wasn't all this spicy senorita had going for her, though. She had already made appearances on series such as *Weird Science* and *Beverly Hills, 90210* in the mid '90s. But after flirting with ambiguous pop star Martin on video, Charlotte hit the big time. She added an exotic, erotic edge to *Jawbreaker* (1999), *The Rage: Carrie 2* (1999), *Training Day* (2001), *Kate & Leopold* (2001), and the drugtastic downer *Spun* (2002). But it's her pole-spinning, head-turning role as a stripper in the skintacular *Dancing at the Blue Iguana* (2000) that caught audiences in Charlotte's web. In it, Charlotte, along with sexy sirens Darryl Hannah and Jennifer Tilly, sheds her threads on the stage of the mythical Blue Iguana bump and grind, finally showing off those incredible hooters onscreen, giving that iguana no reason to be blue anymore.

SKIN-fining Moment:

Dancing at the Blue Iguana (0:23) *Charlotte strips to just a thong and dances long and toplessly onstage at the nudie club. Killer body, completely killer scene.*

See Her Naked In:

Love the Hard Way (2001) Breasts
Dancing at the Blue Iguana (2000) Breasts, Thong

TeleVisions:

Entourage Buns

Leah Ayres

Born: May 28, 1957
Baltimore, Maryland
Skin-O-Meter: Brief Nudity

Sizzling blonde Leah Ayres first made her appearance known in the hot blockbuster *All That Jazz* (1979). It's a movie famous for its racy dance numbers, same-sex couplings, and oodles of skin, which Leah sadly didn't share in. She is better known for her stints on such TV series as *The Edge of Night*, *9 to 5*, *St. Elsewhere*, and *1st and Ten*. That isn't to say that Leah didn't return to the bright lights of the big screen—and the promise of flesh flashes therein. She landed parts in such films as *The Burning* (1981), *Dead Ringer* (1981), and *The Player* (1992). Again, no nudity! But that finally changed with Leah's role in *Hot Child in the City* (1987). She was the hot child who happened to expose some brief breastitude. But that's all the skin that loose Leah leaves us with. Not to be a bummer, but with Leah staying mostly in TV land, the chances of a re-teat performance are slim.

SKIN-fining Moment:

Hot Child in the City (1:12) *Just a slight hint of the hoots as she showers with a fella who, presumably, has a better view than this long shot.*

See Her Naked In:

Hot Child in the City (1987) Breasts

Oksana Babiy

Born: 1976
Ivano-Frankovsk, Ukraine
Skin-O-Meter: Great Nudity

Talk about from Russia with love, Oksana Babiy emigrated to the U.S. from the Ukraine and it's been a hot affair with her adopted country ever since. She hails from a Ukrainian town called Ivano-Frankovsk, which sounds like some taboo sex practice with which Cossacks ravaged peasants. Americans know her best as Irina, Tony Soprano's ex-mistress on the hit HBO series *The Sopranos*. And they know her breast from a seemingly endless topless scene in episode six of the first season, in which she tantalizes the impotent Tony to no avail. She stops just short of a full-frontal credit, remaining in her black undies, but Mr. Skin is hopeful, almost sure in fact, that those spankies will be coming off onscreen before too awful long. Oh, Babiy!

SKIN-fining Moment:

The Sopranos "Pax Soprano" **(1999)** *Oksana drops her top and shows off her Babiys while in bed on Tony Soprano's boat. Mams ho!*

TeleVisions:

The Sopranos Breasts

Joanna Bacalso

Philippines
Skin-O-Meter: Great Nudity

Although Joanna Bacalso finally achieved some notoriety as Barb in the Cuba Gooding Jr. picture *Snow Dogs* (2002), she had been working since her debut as Beautiful Young Woman in *Car 54, Where Are You?* (1994). It was the part this Philippines-born, Canadian-raised exotic treat was born to play. Joanna's tenacity, talent, and dedication to the craft of looking pretty on camera, albeit in small parts such as Henchwoman in *Half Baked* (1998), Stunning Woman in *Woo* (1998), Clubgoer in *Bedazzled* (2000), and Bartender in *Dude, Where's My Car?* (2000), finally paid off. In spite of her Hollywood calling, Joanna had to go offshore to reveal her all-over tan in *Das Traumschiff: Tahiti* (2001). In her first, but hopefully not last, skin scene, Joanna reveals her perky play toys for the viewing audience. Is it hot in here, or is it just Tahiti?

SKIN-fining Moment:

Das Traumschiff: Tahiti *Joanna airs out her cremora coconuts on the beach next to some lucky bum.*

See Her Naked In:

Das Traumschiff: Tahiti **(1999)** Breasts

Barbara Bach

Born: August 27, 1947
New York, New York
Skin-O-Meter: Great Nudity

Barbara Bach may be better known as the wife of Ringo Starr, whom she met, wooed, and finally married after starring with him in *Caveman* (1981). Babs wowed Italian audiences in a number of sultry roles that never quite made it to the States (perhaps they are lost somewhere in the Bermuda Triangle?). It was her role as Major Anya Amasova in *The Spy Who Loved Me* (1977), complete with a quick flash of her right breast in the shower, which put her on the skin map here in America. In *Force 10 From Navarone* (1978), we get a luscious look at her Force Two From Her Chest, and in the extremely rare *Ecco Noi Per Esempio* (1977), we're treated to her untrimmed "strawberry field." Baby's got Bach!

SKIN-fining Moment:

Ecco Noi Per Esempio **(0:11)** *Babs drops her clothes and BAM! Awesome full-frontal nudity by Mrs. Ringo Starr. The scene is a bit dark, but what are you gonna do—complain? That's rock star wife bush, man!*

See Her Naked In:

Ecco Noi Per Esempio **(1980)** FFN
Force 10 From Navarone **(1978)** Breasts
The Spy Who Loved Me **(1977)** RB

Catherine Bach

Born: March 1, 1954
Warren, Ohio
Skin-O-Meter: Brief Nudity

Curvaceous Catherine Bach's cheeky performance as Daisy Duke on TV's *Dukes of Hazzard*—bodaciously slipping out of halter tops and cutoff jeans—made an entire generation's south rise again. *Dukes* was the perfect vehicle for this buxom belle, who had previously scorched the big screen in features such as *Thunderbolt and Lightfoot* (1974) and *Cannonball Run II* (1984). The ultra-obscure *Nicole* (1978) showcased Catherine's bare casabas and even subjected them to a sweet (if too brief) lezzie-ish rub-

down from Leslie Caron. Baby's got Bach—and a nice pair of jugs, too. Yee-ha!

SKIN-fining Moment:

Nicole (1:01) *Daisy dares to bare her pre-Hazzard Dukes as she changes out of her nightgown. Uncle Jesse would be so proud!*

See Her Naked In:

Nicole (1978) Breasts

Pamela Bach

Born: October 16, 1963
Tulsa, Oklahoma
Skin-O-Meter: Brief Nudity

Some woman are born beautiful and others marry rich, but Pamela Bach has got the breast of both worlds. She is a hot blonde bombshell who landed David Hasselhoff, already a successful hunk. Better still, Hasselhoff was able to put Pamela's assets into a tight red bathing suit on his hit TV show *Baywatch* and launch her career as well as audiences' boners. TV has been very good to her, with her resumé littered with guest spots on shows such as *TJ Hooker*, *Cheers*, *Sirens*, and *Vipers*. She even landed a stint on the daytime soap *The Young and the Restless*, which made those lucky enough to stay home from work *hung* and restless. On the big screen, where she might finally unleash her big boobs, her rise hasn't been as swift. But she did land a role in the horror flick *Appointment with Fear* (1988). And there's nothing scary about the bedroom hootage she flashes. Let's just hope she gets Bach in the sexy saddle again soon!

SKIN-fining Moment:

Appointment with Fear (0:56) *Pam slips into a spa and you can sort of see her chest bubbles from a distance.*

See Her Naked In:

Appointment with Fear (1988) Breasts

Susan Backlinie

Born: September 1, 1947
Ventura, California
Skin-O-Meter: Brief Nudity

Susan Backlinie made quite an impression skinny dipping at the beginning of Steven Spielberg's smash-hit *Jaws* (1975) and offering up quite the tasty morsel for Bruce the Shark. Who could resist that meal? That was Susan's debut and typecast her as a grisly treat for ravenous beasts. She was the first victim in the *Jaws*-on-land rip-off *Grizzly* (1976) and followed that with a role in the revolting creature thriller *Day of the Animals* (1977). Susan was good at opening films but leaving them far too soon, as she tended to be killed off in the opening moments. Things changed when Spielberg cast her in his comedy *1941* (1979) to parody the role that made her famous. Again, she appears nude whilst dipping in the skinny, but this time, instead of being eaten by a shark or a bear, she encounters a Japanese submarine that nearly impregnates her with its hard periscope. After that role, Susan appeared in bit parts here and there and then retired to Ventura, California, where she is a computer accountant. She should come back and open some new blockbuster wearing those skintastic swimsuits for which we remember her so fondle-ly.

SKIN-fining Moment:

Jaws (0:02) *Silhouetted side breastage and some underlit bunnage as Susie Sharkfood heads for the water for some skinny dipping, then the faintest indication of bush from the shark's point of view.*

See Her Naked In:

Terror in the Aisles (1984) Breasts
1941 (1979) Breasts, Buns
Jaws (1975) FFN, Buns

Jane Badler

Born: December 31, 1953
Brooklyn, New York
Skin-O-Meter: Brief Nudity

Jane Badler is a soap opera queen, prettifying such dramatic passions as *One Life to Live*, *The Doctors*, and *Falcon Crest*. Since her TV days, she has appeared in several movies, although none of them have broken loose at the box office yet. Her killer looks and curvaceous body got her an audition for the female lead on *The A-Team*, but producers cast her instead as the head of an invading army of aliens on the hit TV mini-series *V*. Already primed at playing bitches from her soap-opera work, she took that sexy evilness to a new level when she ate a rat on camera! For a more alluring portrait of the pleasing Jane, check out her nice nibble-y knobs during a roll in the sack with Frank Stallone in *Easy Kill* (1989). It easily kills millions of sperm every time it's aired.

SKIN-fining Moment:

Easy Kill (0:35) *Skingoria! After Jane settles into a tub with slit wrists, we first see her boobies and then a quick flash of fuzz when Frank Stallone comes to her rescue.*

See Her Naked In:

Easy Kill (1989) Breasts, Bush

Carol Bagdasarian

Born:
City
Skin-O-Meter: Brief Nudity

Carol Bagdasarian began her career back in 1969 with a small appearance as a teller on an episode of the hit TV series *Mannix*. Someone was watching, because she soon landed a more noteworthy role in *The Strawberry Statement* (1970). Nevertheless, Carol spent

the next few years languishing on TV, taking single-episode parts on many of the major shows of that time, such as *Lou Grant* and *Dynasty*. More intriguing was her role in the made-for-TV movie *The Great American Beauty Contest* (1973). The looker returned to film sometime later and graced audiences with her sole skin in *The Octagon* (1980). She briefly flashed some hooterage whilst sitting on a bed with Chuck Norris, who decided for once not to kick ass but love it. Shortly after that, Carol returned to TV with a one-season stint on *General Hospital*. But after appearances in the theatrically released *The Aurora Encounter* (1986) and the made-for-TV movie *Seasons in the Sun* (1986), Carol dropped off the skin-o-meter. The poor little thing hasn't been the same since.

SKIN-fining Moment:

The Octagon (1:11) *Chatting up Chuck Norris, Carol slips off her shirt and shows us her right cantaloup.*

See Her Naked In:

The Octagon (1980) RB

Lorri Bagley

Born: August 5, 1973
Dallas, Texas
Skin-O-Meter: Great Nudity

Statuesque at five-feet-ten-inches tall, lovely Lorri Bagley has been credited as Beautiful Dancer, One-a-Day Girl, and Sofa Girl, which gives an idea of the talents of this 34-25-26 hot thing. She debuted on a 1982 *Late Night with David Letterman* skit opposite Larry "Bud" Melman. Audiences can be excused for not noticing until she was cast as the Naked Woman at the Pool who gave David Spade the urge to watch spank-o-vision in the comedy hit *Tommy Boy* (1995). She's gone on to appear in such films as *Kingpin*

(1996), *54* (1998), and *Celebrity* (1998) but didn't show off her blonde goodness again until *Trick* (1999), which offers the treat of staring wide-eyed at her giant funbags. She also had a part in the pants-pleasing sitcom about a modeling agency *Veronica's Closet* and can be seen as one of the perfectly designed better halves in the sexy remake of *The Stepford Wives* (2004). Lorri is no Bagley lady, but we'd sure like to see her in the sack!

SKIN-fining Moment:

Trick (1:03) *Long look at Lorri's FUN bagley's while on the bed and some more when leaving the apartment.*

See Her Naked In:

Trick (1999) Breasts
Tommy Boy (1995) FFN, Buns

Maxine Bahns

Born: February 28, 1971
Stowe, Vermont
Skin-O-Meter: Brief Nudity

Maxine Bahns was the high school sweetheart of actor/director Edward Burns, which was a wise career choice for the admittedly bookish beauty. Burns ended up casting her in his first movie, *The Brothers McMullen* (1995), and keeping her on as his *paramour du jour*. Unfortunately, their relationship dissolved after Maxine's next movie, a role in *She's the One* (1996), again under the tutelage of brow-beater Burns. Since then, she's appeared in a number of low-budget flicks like *Chick Flick* (1998) and *Spin Cycle* (2000). It is noteworthy that one of those outings, *Cutaway* (2000), offers up Maxine's only skinage onscreen by way of a flash of ass. And by "flash," we mean "exceptionally brief." Maxine hasn't worked since the dawn of the new millennium, but she made Mr. Skin whack to the Max!

SKIN-fining Moment:

Cutaway (0:48) *Don't let your eyes cutaway from the screen, lest you miss Maxine's hot dog Bahns as she lay in bed.*

See Her Naked In:

Cutaway (2000) Buns

Ling Bai

Born: October 10, 1970
Chengdu, China
Skin-O-Meter: Brief Nudity

Ling Bai started life in the People's Republic of China, but there's not much chance of a skinful career in commie cinema. Ling tried. At fourteen, she enlisted in the Chinese People's Liberation Army and spent a few years performing for the lucky troops stationed in Tibet. But she gave up civic duty for something more carnal, and her showy work in Beijing theater eventually led to her involvement in the famous pro-democracy protests in Tiananmen Square in 1989. That led to high-tailing her high tail out of Red China for the safer shores of Hollywood. Ling's first major film role, in *The Crow* (1994), also happens to be one of her sexiest, with lots of nice butt shots. She has since gone on to *Wild Wild West* (1999), in which she exposed that lovely tush once more, and *Star Wars: Episode III* (2005). She's also on the WB hit *Angel*: "I am Princess Shiera. She kicks ass!" Show some too, why don't you? She does again in *The Breed* (2001) and flashes more flesh in *Paris* (2003). Here's to hoping there'll be even more of Ling to linger on in the near future.

SKIN-fining Moment:

The Crow (0:23) *Ling wows us with beautiful buns as she washes up in the shower. Sexy!*

See Her Naked In:

Paris (2003) Breasts
The Breed (2001) Buns
Wild Wild West (1999) Thong
The Crow (1994) Buns

Carroll Baker

Born: May 28, 1931
Johnstown, Pennsylvania
Skin-O-Meter: Great Nudity

The bare fact about buxom blonde film star Carroll Baker is that she was simply too sexy for America. A talented and nuanced actress along with being a sugar-pie sexpot, at the outset of Carroll's career in the late 1950s, she was touted as becoming the next Marilyn Monroe. Baker chased the blonde-goddess star opposite James Dean in *Giant* (1956) and as the titular underage-but-awfully-ripe *Baby Doll* (1956). Carroll showed all the acting skills that Monroe had despaired of ever having, but something about Baker's sensuality was too sizzling for the Hollywood studio system. They didn't dare create the roles she deserved, and in 1968 Carroll moved to Italy. Over the next two decades, she made roughly two dozen European films including *Private Lesson* (1975) and *My Father's Wife* (1976), flashing all the enticing best bits of her flesh in at

PRIVATE LESSON: OBVIOUSLY, EVERYONE'S STUDYING ANATOMY. THIS CAMPY LOBBY CARD CONVEYS THE SCAMPY ERA OF '70S EUROPEAN SEX COMEDIES AND PROVES THAT CARROLL BAKER HAD COME A LONG WAY, BABY (DOLL).

least eight of them. Bite into the witchy-vampy horror concoction *Baba Yaga* (1973) and become a babbling fan.

SKIN-fining Moment:

Private Lesson (1:24) *Ms. Baker gives a young student a private lesson in Phys. Ed, showing boobs and a bit of bush in the process.*

See Her Naked In:

The World is Full of Married Men (1979) LB
Sky Is Falling (1979) Buns
My Father's Wife (1976) Breasts
Private Lesson (1975) FFN, Buns
La Moglie Vergine (1975) LB
The Body (1974) LB, Buns
Baba Yaga (1973) FFN
Paranoia (1969) Breasts, Buns
The Sweet Body of Deborah (1968) Breasts
L'Harem (1967) RB, Buns

Cheryl Baker

Skin-O-Meter: Brief Nudity

Being a tall blonde with a fetching, pale face and round pair of plush chest mounds can result in a certain amount of stereotyping. Take the typical and inspiring case of flaxen-haired and chesty sugar puss Cheryl Baker. Bubbly Baker's attributes can be summed up as sex appeal on a sweetly padded stick, and her talents were not lost upon Hollywood casting directors. Cheryl stepped into the role of Well-Endowed Wife in *Roadhouse* (1989) as easily as she would step into a shower, which she had stepped into as Girl in Shower #1 in *Lethal Weapon* (1987). Baker's most skinteresting stereotyping came as Body Flash Dancer in *The Sex and Violence Family Hour* (1983) and Woman in *Die Hard* (1988).

SKIN-fining Moment:

L.A. Story (0:18) *Steve Martin gets an eyeful of Cheryl Baker's bazooms as she changes in the dressing room. Well ex-cuuuuuse me!*

See Her Naked In:

L.A. Story (1991) Breasts
Die Hard (1988) FFN
The Sex and Violence Family Hour (1983) FFN

Kitana Baker

Born: July 15, 1977
Anaheim, California
Skin-O-Meter: Great Nudity

Yes, the 34D-26-37 figure that Kitana Baker loves to expose has been augmented, and in this case more is more! She started her career opposite *Home Improvement* kid Zachery Ty Bryan in the sleeper *Slammed* (2002). She followed that up with the straight-to-video release *The Model Solution* (2002), in which Kitana's solution was to strut her naked stuff for the majority of her time onscreen, even going so far as to bare her flying V for a lesbianic action sequence. Keeping the sexy coming, she flashed her mammoth mams for Greg Kinnear in the swinging *Auto Focus* (2002). Most famously, Kit filmed a commercial for Miller Lite in which she and another bodacious babe got into a wrestling match in a fountain, followed by some mud-covered grappling, all while two beer-swilling fellas wonder aloud, "Now who wouldn't want to watch a commercial like that?" This Baker makes the candlestick maker hard.

SKIN-fining Moment:

Auto Focus (0:47) *Kitana briefly bares her breasts for Greg Kinnear, who seems genuinely impressed. And so are we!*

See Her Naked In:

Auto Focus (2002) Breasts
The Model Solution (2002) FFN, Buns

Penny Baker

Born: October 5, 1965
Buffalo, New York
Skin-O-Meter: Great Nudity

The year 1984 marked a huge milestone for the *Playboy* publishing empire: thirty years of placing unattainable female perfection within the hands of any regular Joe. The occasion called for a special commemoration, and that unique celebratory feature was provided by the party favors of Miss January 1984 Penny Baker. Less than twenty years old at the time of her historic appearance, Penny exuded an all-embracing warmth made up of blondeness and bustiness. Fresh-faced, with a body that still clung to some of the softness of adolescence, smiling like a high schooler campaigning for head cheerleader, Penny lay like an offering to the Gods of Eros, and the readers baked.

SKIN-fining Moment:

The Men's Club (1:13) *Penny for your thoughts? Look at the huge, luscious, roly-poly melons on Penny Baker as she lies in bed talking with Treat Williams!*

See Her Naked In:

The Men's Club (1986) Breasts
Numerous *Playboy* Videos

Brenda Bakke

Born: May 15, 1963
Klamath Falls, Oregon
Skin-O-Meter: Great Nudity

Brenda Bakke fought her way from the mean streets of rural Oregon to get her big break in movies, debuting in *Last Resort* (1986) and following it up with steamy performances in *Hardbodies 2* (1986) and *Death Spa* (1988), in which she doffed her clothing in an attempt to make the big time. In more-clothed roles, she had a hilarious cameo in

L.A. Confidential (1997) as Lana Turner. Thankfully, Brenda hasn't forgotten her nudie roots, nor has she become any tamer or less shapely since those heady days of the '80s. Check out *Demon Knight* (1995) for a wonderful scene in which she, as the hooker Cordelia, gives a john the ride of his lifeline. *Shelter* (1997) is also a great flick to watch if you want to see this blonde beaut's bodacious breasts, but *Twogether* (1994) is this pretty's peak, with a peek at her moist bits, yes, full-frontal furtastic. That's Brenda's Bakke sale!

SKIN-fining Moment:

Twogether (0:24) *An artist sketches Brenda as she poses wearing just a bra, with her full-grown crotch-Bakke beautifully in view.*

See Her Naked In:

The Fixer (1998) LB
Shelter (1997) Breasts
Demon Knight (1995) LB
Twogether (1994) Breasts, Bush, Buns
Death Spa (1988) Breasts, Bush, Buns
Hardbodies 2 (1986) Breasts, Buns
Last Resort (1986) Breasts

Brigitte Bako

Born: May 15, 1967
Montreal, Quebec, Canada
Skin-O-Meter: Great Nudity

A brunette beauty with bone structure as delicate as a quail's and breasts as full and round as a marquee stripper's, Brigitte Bako spends a large portion of her on-air time completely offscreen. As the voice of Angela on the popular animated series *Gargoyles* and its subsequent spinoffs, Brigitte's intriguing tones and line delivery have caused more than one cartoon fan to muse, "Geez, I wonder what that voice would look like naked." No need to speculate, simply dip into *Dark Tide* (1993). There's the voice of Angela fully embodied in a spread-legged, dark stunner sitting knockers-up in a bathtub. An impertinently phallic water snake slithers up between her heaving breasts. The reality of Brigitte Bako is better than any cartoon boy could have imagined.

SKIN-fining Moment:

Dark Tide (1:05) *Brigitte bares her top in a bathtub while a snake slithers up between her two Bakos.*

See Her Naked In:

The Escape (1997) Breasts
Strange Days (1995) FFN
Dark Tide (1993) Breasts
Red Shoe Diaries (1992) Breasts, Buns

TeleVisions:

Red Shoe Diaries Breasts, Buns

Rebecca Balding

Born: September 21, 1955
Little Rock, Arkansas
Skin-O-Meter: Brief Nudity

Rebecca Balding worked on the gritty newsy drama *Lou Grant* in 1977 but moved on after a year for the more humorous confines of the hit TV comedy *Soap*. As Carol David, the brunette found her calling as a sexy comedienne. Soon Rebecca turned to more cinematic endeavors, including a little horror movie called *The Boogens* (1981). It is Rebecca's best skin onscreen, a nice shot of her naked ass and then a brief bit of breast for good measure—nothing scary about that. She also offered some flesh in *Silent Scream* (1980). Since then, Rebecca has made some cameo TV appearances, but nothing too lasting. Wish she'd bring back that body of work from *The Boogens*; it's likely that it has matured nicely.

SKIN-fining Moment:

The Boogens (0:31) *Buns in an open towel as a snoop sneaks up on her.*

See Her Naked In:

The Boogens (1981) Breasts, Buns
Silent Scream (1980) RB

Judith Baldwin

Born: March 26, 1946
Washington, D.C.
Skin-O-Meter: Brief Nudity

Miss New Mexico Judith Baldwin got her big break by replacing Tina Louise on the made-for-TV reunion movie *Rescue from Gilligan's Island* (1978) and the follow-up *The Castaways on Gilligan's Island* (1979). But all the work she could find after that was in bit parts playing roles such as Saloon Girl and Luckup Hostess #1 in the movies *Tales of the Apple Dumpling Gang* (1982) and *Deal of the Century* (1983), respectively. She did land a one-season stint on the soap *The Bold and the Beautiful*, but that's not why Judith is a hit at Skin Central. Although the bulk of her career has been on the boob tube and thus rather skingy, Judith managed to unleash her massive mammaries once in the film *No Small Affair* (1984) opposite Jon Cryer. It was no small affair, indeed, and must have left the young actor crying for more.

SKIN-fining Moment:

No Small Affair (0:36) *Titties in the moonlight as Judy tries to seduce a chicken-chested Jon Cryer.*

See Her Naked In:

No Small Affair (1984) Breasts

Fairuza Balk

Born: May 21, 1974
Point Reyes Station, California
Skin-O-Meter: Brief Nudity

A child actress grown up (and out) in mysteriously sexy ways, Fairuza Balk started her screen career at eleven, starring as Dorothy in *Return to Oz* (1985). Fairuza means *turquoise* in Persian, and she gave her fans turquoise balls while playing a loose convent girl in Milos Forman's *Valmont* (1989). But Fairuza showed her true colors as Shade, the sensitive girl in *Gas, Food, Lodging* (1992). She snared further cult status with her starring role as a psychotic goth-girl witch in *The Craft* (1996). Fairuza went mainstream playing the girlfriend of Adam Sandler in the smash comedy *The Waterboy* (1998) and the girlfriend of neo-Nazi Edward Norton in *American History X* (1998). And she made us all sticky as a band-aid in the seventies cock-rock epic *Almost Famous* (2000). Fairuza is at her fairiskiest in *American History X* (1998) showing her white-power*ful* body in an intense sex scene. Sieg, hottie!

SKIN-fining Moment:

American History X (0:03) *Brief bouncing chest-bitables as Balk gets balled boisterously.*

See Her Naked In:

American History X (1998) Breasts
Tollbooth (1994) Breasts
Valmont (1989) Body Double—Buns

Talia Balsam

Born: January 1, 1960
New York, New York
Skin-O-Meter: Brief Nudity

Brunette beauty Talia Balsam is famous as the one George Clooney let get away. Before he was a superstar Clooney was still a superstud and briefly married Talia. But the two divorced in 1993. While Clooney has remained the dedicated bachelor, Talia's tail is too fine, and many a genital-man caller has knocked on her delicious door. But it was actor John

Slattery, last seen peeing in the shower with Sarah Jessica Parker on *Sex and the City*, who got her pregnant and captured her with a band of gold. Talia made her acting name on the boob tube with recurring roles on *Happy Days* and *Taxi*, moving on to *Family Ties* and *Law & Order*. But it was on the big screen where her breast work was exposed, with her moist nude-worthy film being *Trust Me* (1989). Adam Ant stars as an art dealer who realizes his clients' works would be more valuable if the artists were dead, but the finest piece of art in the picture belongs to Talia's glimpse of skin. What a frame!

SKIN-fining Moment:

Trust Me (0:42) *Talia rises from the sack and somebody's seat shows up on screen. Despite the movie's title, we can't trust that this isn't a Body Double!*

See Her Naked In:

Trust Me (1989) Body Double—Buns

Anne Bancroft

Born: September 17, 1931
The Bronx, New York
Skin-O-Meter: Never Nude

Anne Bancroft made it sexy to be middle-aged, and with her spanking body it's easy to see why maturity has its pluses. Those assets were front and center in her most famous role as the sexual dynamo Mrs. Robinson in *The Graduate* (1967). That movie also marks her sole skin onscreen. Seducing her daughter's beau, played by Dustin Hoffman, she flashes shocking breastage, as well as the famous, albeit stocking-clad, shot with Hoffman in the background, mouth agape. No wonder this hot mama was previously best known for her role in *The Miracle Worker* (1962)—she

makes a miracle happen in every man's pants. But only funnyman Mel Brooks gets to enjoy Anne's shapely charms; they've been married since 1964. Who's laughing now?

SKIN-fining Moment:

The Graduate (0:16) *Fleeting glimpses of sombody's milksacks. Most likely a Body Double.*

See Her Naked In:

The Graduate (1967) Body Double—LB, Buns

Vaitiare Bandera

Skin-O-Meter: Brief Nudity

Vaitiare Bandera, a black-haired, brown-eyed beauty, started her career in 1993 with a one-episode gig on the hit series *Acapulco H.E.A.T.* It took a few years, but she finally landed her breakthrough role on the series *Pacific Blue*, pedaling her way into the syndicated hearts and minds of millions. She ended up cast on the popular cable series *Stargate SG-1* opposite her then-love-squeeze Michael Shanks. This series was made in Canada where the cable version of nearly every show must be required to include nudity . . . wonder if they do a nude version of the national news for cable distribution? Although Vaitiare made it onto the silver screen in *U.S. Marshals* (1998), it was in *Stargate* where she finally shed her threads . . . every last one of them. Unfortunately, none of her good parts are visible in the syndicated repeats on network affiliates, but if one is lucky enough to catch it on Showtime, then you're in for a real show. Keep your eyes peeled for Bandera's big bubbles, and keep your eyes wide open to stuff all the good parts in!

SKIN-fining Moment:

Stargate SG-1 "Children of the Gods" (1997) *Vaitiare gets an all points probe by an alien, and we get to see her full-frontal form as the spaceman takes control of her body.*

TeleVisions:

Stargate SG-1 FFN

Lisa Banes

Born: July 9, 1955
Chagrin Falls, Ohio
Skin-O-Meter: Brief Nudity

Lisa Banes is the only honey on Howard Stern's *Son of the Beach* who doesn't threaten to burst from a bathing suit. Sometimes, when all you have to choose from is steak, hamburger makes a nice change—especially when it sports buns as firm as Lisa's. But before Anita Massengill, Lisa was already a recognizable character actress in TV and cinema, having appeared in over twenty roles in mini-series such as *Kane & Abel* (1985) and *Hemingway* (1988), as well as loads of movies such as *The Hotel New Hampshire* (1984). She had a meatier role in *Cocktail* (1988), but she was overshadowed by the brief breastage of Elisabeth Shue. Her only onscreen nudity occurred in the Brat Pack Billy the Kid flick *Young Guns* (1988). In it, she played the hooker-with-a-heart-of-gold whom the gang sends to Casey Siemaszko in order to cure his "virginity problem." Problem is, Casey didn't want to screw, for some unbelievable reason, and they end up cuddling in perhaps the most cock-teasing scene in cinematic history. There is a brief hint of breast before he approaches Lisa, but it is a letdown, seeing as how he could have and should have been having some prairie-flatten sex with her. Poor Lisa, it's the Banes of her existence.

SKIN-fining Moment:

Young Guns (1:08) *Lisa's left gun pokes out as she talks to cowpoke Casey Siemaszko.*

See Her Naked In:

Young Guns (1988) LB

Joy Bang

Born: 1947
Skin-O-Meter: Brief Nudity

How could a woman named Joy Bang not be destined to bring a kicker of happiness to all skin folk who revel in her presence? Unfortunately, Joy's euphoric burst was here and gone as quickly as the pop of a small firecracker. The mop-top blonde with the sweet tomboy face started out as background candy in 1960s drive-in fodder but blew into the '70s with a shot at something bolder. Supporting Rock Hudson in *Pretty Maids all in a Row* (1971), Bang's banging bottom pops up in pantie-clad glory as she lies topless, face down, and butt up. The camera moves in and lingers on the felicitous fissure hidden beneath Joy's pantie shield. The briefest glimpse of joyful nip occurs during a bang-up three-way with Kris Kristofferson and Viva in *Cisco Pike* (1972). Why has there not been more Joy to the world?

SKIN-fining Moment:

Pretty Maids All in a Row (0:59) *Quick breast shot as Joy disrobes in the front seat of a car with Rock Hudson. Pay attention, because he sure wasn't.*

See Her Naked In:

Cisco Pike (1972) RB
Night of the Cobra Woman (1972) Breasts
Pretty Maids All in a Row (1971) Breasts, Buns

Adrienne Barbeau

Born: June 11, 1945
Sacramento, California
Skin-O-Meter: Great Nudity

Forget *Maude*—and then came *everyone* when Adrienne Barbeau's barbells could hardly be contained by the small screen on the popular '70s sitcom. Director John Carpenter got to stick his woodie in Adrienne's softies when he had the good sense to marry her. He directed her in *The Fog* (1980) and *Escape from New York* (1981), which may have been cool movies, but they contained no skin. That all changed once Adrienne and her girls filed for divorce. The ladies needed to get out and dirty, and what better place than the steamy bayou in *Swamp Thing* (1982)? Swampy's thing gives Adrienne's areolas a stiff green salute as she bathes topless outdoors, but don't worry if you don't remember her boggy bazooms: the scene was edited from the original cut of the film, but, thankfully, it appears as a sexy extra on the 2002 DVD release. She followed that wet treat with another top-of-the-tits performance in *Open House* (1987). But since then, the doors to Adrienne's chestiness have been closed. It's a shame. As Adrienne matures, the more must-see her body gets. It's a package worth opening again.

SKIN-fining Moment:

Swamp Thing (0:00) *A lusty, lingering look at Adrienne's D-cup Swamp Things as she takes a dip in a bog in this DVD-only scene.*

See Her Naked In:

Open House (1987) Breasts
Swamp Thing (1982) Breasts

TeleVisions:

Carnivàle RB

Frances Barber

Born: May 13, 1958
Staffordshire, England, UK
Skin-O-Meter: Great Nudity

Frances Barber is a British actress who made nude chubbiness hip before Kate Winslet beached her whales onscreen. After her debut in the made-for-BBC movie *Home Sweet Home* (1982), Frances packed her funbags for a film career and landed bit parts in *The Missionary* (1982) and *Prick Up Your Ears* (1987). She started landing some choice parts in pictures such as *Sammy and Rosie Get Laid* (1987) and *Castaway* (1987), which features some of Amanda Donohoe's best skin scenes, although it lacks any from Frances. In *A Zed & Two Noughts* (1985) she played some sort of prostitute—at least she was naked through much of her role. She showed off the entire typography of her terrific form, from the peaks of her voluptuous mountains to the valley of her moist swamplands. Nothing like getting a good trim from a Barber.

SKIN-fining Moment:

A Zed & Two Noughts (0:22) *Bare bombers as she sits on the edge of a bed with a guy, followed by bushy full frontal and sweet rump-cakes as she frolics with the dude. Nice!*

See Her Naked In:

Warrior Queen (2003) Breasts
Flyfishing (2002) Breasts
eSTheR KaHN (2000) FFN
Real Women (1998) Breasts
Orchid House (1991) Breasts
Sammy and Rosie Get Laid (1987) Breasts
A Zed & Two Noughts (1985) FFN, Buns

Paula Barbieri

Born: December 31, 1966
Panama City, Florida
Skin-O-Meter: Great Nudity

Dark-haired dish Paula Barbieri first offered herself to the prying eyes of men as a fashion model. Paula took a stab at superstardom after achieving notoriety during the trial of the (last) century, as OJ Simpson's main squeeze. She posed for *Playboy* and flaunted her perfect 34-24-34 frame on the boob tube on the cable series *The Red Shoe Diaries* and in low budget wonders such as *The Dangerous* (1994) and *Night Eyes 4: Fatal Passion* (1995). Paula was born to be in the B-movie business. Regardless of title or plot, all of Ms. B's flicks are guaranteed to have bountiful *boobage*, *bush*, and *backside!*

SKIN-fining Moment:

Night Eyes 4 . . . Fatal Passion (0:01) *The ex of O.J. shows some nifty T&A in a shower scene . . . that sets up the softcore proceedings.*

See Her Naked In:

Night Eyes 4 . . . Fatal Passion (1995) Breasts, Buns

TeleVisions:

Red Shoe Diaries Breasts, Bush, Buns

Lisa Barbuscia

Born: June 18, 1971
Brooklyn, New York
Skin-O-Meter: Great Nudity

Part Puerto Rican, Italian, and Irish and all hot, Lisa Barbuscia was already using her dark, exotic looks to get ahead at the tender age of fifteen. Whether she actually gave head is up for debate, but once the catwalks of European fashion meccas caught a glimpse of the tall and willowy drink of water mouths were agape. Soon she was pleasing trouser snakes everywhere with her debut in *Serpent's Lair* (1995), which also found her slithering skin exposed for the first time onscreen. But she really busted out (of her bra) with a role opposite

Matthew Perry and Chris Farley in *Almost Heroes* (1998). She almost wore clothes throughout the product, almost but not quite, and offered up some heroic nudity. And things just kept getting better. In what's billed as the final installment of the never-ending series *Highlander: Endgame* (2000), Lisa was more than game to show off her end and then some, getting completely nude. She turned another page in the carnal career with a sexy cameo in *Bridget Jones's Diary* (2001). About forty minutes into the film Renée Zellweger, bulging out of a tight Playboy Bunny suit, walked in on Lisa during a bathtub soak. As "Lisa B," she has also taken over the music world, and with those lungs there's no stopping her.

SKIN-fining Moment:

Serpent's Lair (1:03) *Lisa's furburger makes an appearance (albeit from a distance) as she goes full frontal for a tryst with Jeff Fahey.*

See Her Naked In:

Highlander: Endgame (2000) Breasts, Buns
Almost Heroes (1998) Buns
Serpent's Lair (1995) FFN, Buns

Brigitte Bardot

Born: September 28, 1934
Paris, France
Skin-O-Meter: Hall of Fame

When divine Brigitte Bardot took the world by storm in the landmark French flick . . . *And God Created Woman* (1957), nobody was about to argue with the title. This perfect Parisian pastry was best served au natural—no makeup, no clothing, just that hourglass figure, with a shelf of meaty jugs and that smiling, heart-shaped ass soaring like a full moon over her long and shapely legs. Brigitte was already

raising baguettes in the early '50s in films such as the suggestively titled *While Plucking the Daisy* (1956), thus giving inquisitive Americans a reason to frequent foreign-film houses. She even made the cool New Wave director Jean-Luc Goddard heat up his film *Contempt* (1963) with a lingering opening on Brigitte's backside. Brigitte retired from the sexy screen in 1973, her swan song being *Ms. Don Juan*. It was a nice way to go out, just as she came in—naked as the day she was boned.

SKIN-fining Moment:

Contempt (0:02) *Brigitte opens the flick with a side-shot of her beautiful butt while lying in bed.*

See Her Naked In:

Electric Blue (TV Magazine) (1983) FFN
Famous T&A (1982) Breasts
Ms. Don Juan (1973) FFN, Buns
L'Histoire Très Bonne et Très Joyeuse de Colinot Trousse-Chemise (1973) Buns
Les Pétroleuses (1971) Buns
Les Femmes (1969) Buns
Contempt (1963) Buns
Please Not Now! (1961) LB, Buns

Amours Célèbres (1961) Buns
Love Is My Profession (1958) Breasts, Buns
The Night Heaven Fell (1958) Breasts, Buns
And God Created Woman (1957) RB, Buns
La Lumière d'en Face (1955) LB
Manina, La Fille Sans Voile (1952) LB

Ellen Barkin

Born: April 16, 1954
New York, New York
Skin-O-Meter: Great Nudity

Long, cool, tall-drink-of-firewater Ellen Barkin looks equally capable of kicking your ass and rocking your sexual world—at the same time! Ellen debuted onstage in *Irish Coffee* in 1980, and her theater work led to a role the following year on the soap opera *Search for Tomorrow*. Ellen broke into film as the neglected wife of a record-collecting freak who takes up an affair with Mickey Rourke in Barry Levinson's *Diner* (1982). She then played Robert Duvall's troubled daughter in *Tender Mercies* (1983). Fans fell in love with Ellen in the romantic thriller *The Big Easy* (1987), as she came across as neither big nor easy. Ellen is one of the most versatile actresses in Hollywood and even ambisexually took on TV's *La Femme Nikita*, Peta Wilson, for a hot, Sapphic showdown in *Mercy* (1999). But Ellen shows us she knows how to lead no matter who the love scene is with in *Sea of Love* (1989), when murder-suspect Ellen takes Al Pacino up against a wall and gives him his first reach-around since *Cruising* (1980)!

SKIN-fining Moment:

Siesta (0:03) *Ellen opens the movie properly: by peeling off a red dress and lying down completely naked outside. Breasts, buns and a womb-view so nice you'll wonder if the camera Fell In Barkin.*

See Her Naked In:

Bad Company (1995) Bush
Wild Bill (1995) Buns

Sea of Love (1989) Body Double—Breasts, Buns / Her—Buns 2nd Scene
Siesta (1987) FFN, Buns
The Big Easy (1987) Buns

Priscilla Barnes

Born: December 7, 1955
Fort Dix, New Jersey
Skin-O-Meter: Hall of Fame

Priscilla Barnes played a bit role on a 1976 *Columbo* episode, which led to a co-starring role on the short-lived series *American Girls*. She soon nailed down a supporting part opposite super-Brit Michael Caine in *Sunday Lovers* (1980). Priscilla is of course, best known as the replacement for pinup goddess Suzanne Somers, playing nurse Teri Alden on the popular ABC jiggle-com *Three's Company*. Priscilla popped up from time to time on different TV series, but she gave her fans a triple treat in the indie film *Mallrats* (1995), where she played a highly-handicapable babe with three nipples. Apparently, she was re-imagining her nursing role! *Three's Company* never delivered Priscilla like we wished, but that's taken care of in the arty and skintastic *Erotique* (1994), in which Priscilla throws open her Barnes doors in a lusty lesbian scene with young sexpot Camilla Søeberg. If only Janet and Jack could have joined in!

SKIN-fining Moment:

Texas Detour (1:03) *Two's company when Priscilla changes clothes in her bedroom and frees her perfectly round rubbables.*

See Her Naked In:

Divorce: A Contemporary Western (1998) Breasts, Buns
Implicated (1998) RB
The Crossing Guard (1995) Breasts
Mallrats (1995) Breasts
Erotique (1994) Breasts, Buns
The Seniors (1978) Breasts

Texas Detour (1977) Breasts
Tintorera (1977) Breasts
Delta Fox (1977) Breasts

Elizabeth Barondes

Skin-O-Meter: Great Nudity

Before she flew into the mainstream as Teri Hatcher's sister Lucy Lane on the hit TV series *Lois & Clark: The New Adventures of Superman*, Elizabeth Barondes was just another busty brunette in the background of forgettable films. Her stint as one of the ladies who makes the Man of Steel hard lasted only a year, which meant a return to celluloid, if not anonymity, thanks to a wise career decision to go "blue." The red light first illuminated her svelte form in the horror flick *Not of This Earth* (1995), which is certainly enlivened by her topless sunbathing. But that was only a perverted prelude to the paramount of prurient production, the jugtacular *Full Body Massage* (1995). Most can be forgiven for not noticing Elizabeth, who played in the shadow of the huge hooters of Mimi Rogers in the breast movie for breast lovers. Elizabeth provides her breasts like cool sherbet to cleanse the palette during a banquet. Eat up!

SKIN-fining Moment:

Full Body Massage (1:08) *A nice look at Elizabeth's breasts as she meddles in a muddy pond with Bryan "Luckist Two Hands in the World" Brown.*

See Her Naked In:

Not of This Earth (1995) Breasts
Full Body Massage (1995) Breasts, Buns

Katherine Barrese

Born: May 24, 1965
California
Skin-O-Meter: Great Nudity

Every now and then a bold beauty will appear onscreen like Katherine

Barrese. She first made an impression in the little-seen film *Homer & Eddie* (1989), in which she has the little-seen part of Waitress. But her next shot at big-screen success was far more interesting. Katherine co-starred with Malcolm McDowell in *Jezebel's Kiss* (1990). It was not a blockbuster at the box office, but it was a pants-buster, and even the critics loved it. No wonder—Katherine reveals everything she's got, and she's got a lot of what we like to call the moist. That includes two of the biggest natural breasts ever seen, even by the team at Skin Central. To add to this bounty, Katherine shows off her riotous rump and even a healthy spread of her dark carpet. It's a munchable treat. Then Katherine was absent from the screen, appearing only as Woman in Prison in *Payback* (1995). Hopefully, Katherine will get out of prison soon and pay us back with more of her unbelievable body.

SKIN-fining Moment:

Jezebel's Kiss (0:36) *A rather frantic looking Katherine shows her bazooms and then her brillo pad as she takes off all her clothes and washes herself.*

See Her Naked In:

Jezebel's Kiss (1990) FFN, Buns

Alice Barrett

Born: December 19, 1956
New York, New York
Skin-O-Meter: Brief Nudity

The windmills of Alice Barrett's mind were really spinning after she caught a performance of *Man of La Mancha* in her hometown of New York City at the tender age of ten. She grew up to love old Broadway and tripped the light fantastic on its stages. But how many people can afford a trip to the Big Apple and the financial bite of attending

theater on the Great White Way? Thankfully, Alice doesn't live there anymore. She's warmed to the tropical climate of Hollywood and with it has shed some of those trendy Manhattan threads. At least, Alice was quite skinful in her movie debut *Incoming Freshman* (1979). She plays a boxing student and doesn't hold back any punches or tits. After such a splendid start, her career became suddenly skingy. She continued to cut a sexy figure through TV and films, especially on the daytime soap *Another World*, but her days of sharing were over. Doesn't she know it's nice to share?

SKIN-fining Moment:

Incoming Freshman (0:43) *Alice pops up topless and answers questions during the sexy fantasy of her nutty professor.*

See Her Naked In:

Incoming Freshman (1979) Breasts

Jacinda Barrett

Born: August 2, 1972
Melbourne, Australia
Skin-O-Meter: Brief Nudity

Australian-born Jacinda Barrett is still an all-American beauty. She's tall, svelte, and has the long honey-blonde hair that drives us wild Stateside. Her dad is an airport fireman, and she has earned a license to fly, which makes sense, because she sure sweeps Mr. Skin off his feet. Jacinda caught the attention of the execs at MTV, who cast her in *The Real World: London*. Jacinda made her stint on the proto-reality show mamorable thanks to a late-night streak with one of her suitemates . . . sweet. Hollywood called, and she went from the reality-based TV world to the surreal shine of Tinseltown. Landing a role in *Urban Legends: Final Cut* (2000), she was working her way up the starlet ladder when

the plum role of Steena Paulsson in Philip Roth's *The Human Stain* (2003) landed in her lap. That lap danced a striptease that revealed every inch of Jacinda's young body, from her pert pair to her moist garden patch, and rivaled Nicole Kidman's equally erotic moment onscreen. Co-starring in *Bridget Jones: The Edge of Reason* (2004), the sky's the limit for the former model and pilot.

SKIN-fining Moment:

The Human Stain (1:03) *Jacinda dances around in granny panties and a terrifying-looking bra, but fret not— they don't stay on for long. As she peels off her underthings, we get to see a bit o' the butt and a cute full frontal.*

See Her Naked In:

The Human Stain (2003) FFN, Buns

Pat Barrington

Born: 1941
Skin-O-Meter: Great Nudity

Pat Barrington reigned at the top of the short-lived erotic film revolution in the late '60s. And what a top she had! Better still was that she usually didn't wear a top, giving us a fine view of the Barrington Behemoths. Sadly, when the hot nudie movement ran its course, Pat was spat out, discarded and has rarely been heard from since. For about four wild and wonderful years, though, she made a decent living taking her enormous breasts out of their packaging for the cameras in films like her debut *Orgy of the Dead* (1965), *The Agony of Love* (1965), *Psychedelic Sexualis* (1966), and *Mondo Topless* (1966), which is a good description of this act-chest. Many of her psychedelic outings were rated X or received no rating at all due to their "explicit" nature. Though tame by today's gonzo standards, few can compare with Pat's pair. They're more than a mouthful.

SKIN-fining Moment:

Mondo Topless Pat ain't flat, and she proves it by swinging her towers of power at the base of an electrical plant.

See Her Naked In:

Mantis in Lace **(1968)** Breasts
Mondo Topless **(1966)** Breasts
Psychedelic Sexualis **(1966)** Breasts
The Agony of Love **(1965)** Breasts, Buns

Dana Barron

Born: April 22, 1968
New York, New York
Skin-O-Meter: Brief Nudity

Dana Barron made her debut in *He Knows You're Alone* (1980). And if he knew that it was Dana alone with him, it would have been rewritten as a sexploitation rather than a horror thriller. Of course the cute brunette was a bit too young for such an adventure, but she managed to be hot and funny in her next outing, *National Lampoon's Vacation* (1983), and it made her a star. While Juliette Lewis went on to reprise the role of "Audrey Griswold," there's still a soft spot in our hearts and a hard-on in our pants for Dana's original perfor-mance. She followed her fame to the boob tube, being cast on the daytime soap *One Life to Live* and a one-year stint on *Beverly Hills, 90210*. But she wasn't about to leave film behind. In fact, in *City of Industry* (1997) Dana flashed her well-rounded tush. It was overshadowed, however, by Lucy Liu's small wonders as a topless dancer. But in the Barron book of quotes, Dana's cheeky turn is a real mouthful.

SKIN-fining Moment:

City of Industry (0:30) *Bra-clad Dana gets her shorts yanked off by an eager fella. Very brief buns.*

See Her Naked In:

City of Industry **(1997)** Buns

Drew Barrymore

Born: February 22, 1975
Culver City, California
Skin-O-Meter: Great Nudity

Born into acting's legendary Barrymore clan, Drew's thespian future was already mapped out for her; the jug-bearing and erotically outrageous public behavior have been her own doing. Darling Drew initially won the world over as seven-year-old Gertie in *E.T. the Extra-Terrestrial* (1982). But it wasn't until party-girl-in-waiting Drew grew up (and out) in all the right places that she really snagged viewers by the zipper. Barrymore dared to bare in *Boys on the Side* (1995), *Bad Girls* (1994), and *Doppelganger* (1993). Drew wore a producer's hat in both *Charlie's Angels* adventures, which, sexy as she is in the flicks, have continued a disturbing trend of clothes wearing.

SKIN-fining Moment:

Doppelganger: The Evil Within (0:23) *A nice gander at Drew's pre-breast reduction, udderly gargantuan globes in the shower when, quite naturally, the water turns into blood and complicates all our fun.*

See Her Naked In:

Bad Girls **(1994)** RB
Boys on the Side **(1994)** Breasts
Doppelganger: The Evil Within **(1993)** Breasts
The Amy Fisher Story **(1993)** Body Double—
    LB, Bush, Buns
Guncrazy **(1992)** Body Double—Buns
Poison Ivy **(1992)** Nip Slip LB

Jaid Barrymore

Born: May 8, 1946
Brannenburg, West Germany
Skin-O-Meter: Great Nudity

If all she had done was provide the genetic source for Drew Barrymore's tits, hot mama Jaid Barrymore would be deserving of all of our respect and awe. But Jaid is a giant-jugged exhibitionist whose mammaries were destined for a role greater than that played in maternity. Plus, her thick, dark bush wanted to be part of the show. Jaid played a part in *Night Shift* (1982), a movie about hookers, but her clothes didn't fall to the wayside until *The Last Days of Disco* (1998). Look for the fully mature, fully fruitful (think firm melons of flesh) woman strolling fully nude and fully frontal through the fully clothed throng of a disco dance floor. The naked one is Jaid. She's impossible to miss.

SKIN-fining Moment:

The Last Days of Disco (1:36) *See the sacks that suckled Drew (only since enhanced by plastic) as Jaid reclines topless on a couch at the disco.*

See Her Naked In:

The Last Days of Disco **(1998)** FFN

Cheryl Bartel

Skin-O-Meter: Great Nudity

Cheryl Bartel is blonde and big in the boobs. So, it's no wonder that she made a name for herself (and her chest) in a series of guest spots on some of the most skintalating shows on TV. In the mid '90s, Cheryl's bountiful beauty first appeared on *Renegade*, and she followed that up with sexy appearances on *Baywatch* as Pretty Girl and *Baywatch Nights* as Bystander. It wasn't long afterwards that the clothes came off and no holes were barred in Cheryl's carnal career. She played Beautiful Woman in *Sawbones* (1995), a cable production that insured Cheryl wouldn't have to hold back on any of her fleshy charms. She continued the sensual streak with the role of Billie in *Centerfold* (1996), a.k.a. *Naked Ambition*, and lived up to the title . . . and how! Her highest profile part to date was as one of the murderously mamnificant Fembots in *Austin Powers: International Man of Mystery* (1997). But it's no mystery as to why Cheryl is so hot.

SKIN-fining Moment:

Centerfold (0:33) *Cheryl mounts her man in a massage room, providing plenty for him to rub in the form of her naked rack and rump.*

See Her Naked In:

Centerfold (1996) Breasts, Buns
Sawbones (1995) Breasts

TeleVisions:

Rude Awakening Breasts
Women: Stories of Passion Breasts, Thong

Erinn Bartlett

Longmeadow, Massachusetts
Skin-O-Meter: Brief Nudity

Erinn Bartlett debuted as Girl #1 in *Deep Blue Sea* (1999), and Mr. Skin defies anyone to argue with that ranking! Her dreamboat-next-door heat made her a busy actress in a hurry. She made *The In Crowd* (2000) with fellow heartbreaker and pants-acher Susan Ward and appeared in *Little Nicky* (2000) with the king-of-giving-hope-that-funny-guys-can-get-hot-chicks Adam Sandler. Although she went sans top in *The In Crowd*, she wasn't sans *sand*, which killed our view! Faithful viewers had only to wait until *100 Women* (2002) to witness the first unveiling of Bartlett's pears! They're cans, and yet they're bursting with farm-fresh goodness! She continued to

tease and please with a breastation period in *Pumpkin* (2000), providing a side view of her own pumpkins.

SKIN-fining Moment:

Pumpkin (1:13) *Erinn bucks her guy's crotch-bronco in bed and we get a bouncy gander at her left chest Pumpkin.*

See Her Naked In:

Pumpkin (2002) LB
100 Women (2002) Breasts

Diana Barton

Palm Springs, California
Skin-O-Meter: Great Nudity

Diana Barton made her entertainment debut on the hit sitcom *Charles in Charge*. When Charles got a load of this beautiful brunette with the medium cup-sized breasts, he was certainly charged up. She continued to make viewers' pants tight with guest appearances on *Baywatch* and *Silk Stalkings*. But she found her greatest success as one of daytime's grandest bitches on *The Young and the Restless*. After her character lost her mind and slipped from the papers of the script into soap-opera oblivion, Diana worked the big screen, and to fine effect, with her sole nude onscreen role in *Sexual Malice* (1994). She may have only this on her skin resumé, but it's a bang-up job that will have audiences banging their fists onto their stiff joints. She does the obligatory shower scene but makes it all her own by flashing not only her petite pair but her moist muff as well. Later in the film, she gets kinky with another actress who ties her up, blindfolds her, and exposes her hard nipples. She returned to the short-lived TV series *Air America* and a part in the

movie *Dead Man's Run* (2001) before disappearing from the scene. Come back, Diana, and show us more of that luscious backside of yours.

SKIN-fining Moment:

Sexual Malice (0:32) *Diana scrubs her perky torso pups in the shower, then shows off her snazzy shag when she steps out to towel off.*

See Her Naked In:

Sexual Malice (1994) FFN, Buns

Toni Basil

Born: September 22, 1943
Philadelphia, Pennsylvania
Skin-O-Meter: Brief Nudity

Oh, Toni Basil / You're so fine / You're so fine / You blow my mind / Hey Toni! / Hey Toni! She may have become a one-hit wonder with "Micky" in the '80s—which made it cool for chicks to shake their pom-poms as cheerleaders—but Toni actually had quite the cinematic career before her pop stardom. She had been active as an actress, dancer, singer, songwriter, and choreographer since the mid '60s, first appearing in *Pajama Party* (1964). Toni in her PJs? That's a party! She went on to go-go dance on film until her big break as the New Orleans prostitute whom groovy Peter Fonda picks up in the groovier cult classic *Easy Rider* (1969). In a romp in the famous St. Louis Cemetery, Toni shows off some nice hootage, as well as some brief lower-frontal nudity. (It may be brief, but you can't miss that enormous, untrimmed bush.) Her only other skin scenes appeared in another cult classic, *Greaser's Palace* (1972), in which she appeared as the oft-topless Indian Girl. Hope this Indian is a giver with more swinging shots of her swinging udders to come.

SKIN-fining Moment:

Easy Rider (1:25) *Toni shows her "Hey-Mickeys" and a glimpse of Basil brush as she strips out of her clothes, which is followed by a few quick shots of her ass during a wacked-out freak sequence.*

See Her Naked In:

Greaser's Palace (1972) Breasts
Easy Rider (1969) FFN, Buns

Kim Basinger

Born: December 8, 1953
Athens, Georgia
Skin-O-Meter: Hall of Fame

Kim Basinger knocked men out as Domino in the "unofficial" James Bond flick *Never Say Never Again* (1983). And it wasn't just her breakout performance onscreen; she promoted the movie with a *Playboy* pictorial that introduced the world to her thick, pink, meaty, and ultra-mouthable super-nipples. Kim's star rose throughout the '80s, culminating in the kink classic *9½ Weeks* (1986). She continued to make groins ache in *Batman* (1989) and specifically got Alec Baldwin so worked up that he married her in 1993. Kim and Alec then turned the remake *The Getaway* (1994) into a voyeuristic venture with a scorching sex scene between the real-life husband and wife, punctuated by Kim's meaty pointers.

SKIN-fining Moment:

9½ Weeks (1:11) *Kim gets kinky in an outdoor stairwell with Mickey Rourke. Her undies are soaked from the rain and then she busts out her award-caliber nipples as they get around to getting it on.*

See Her Naked In:

The Door in the Floor (2004) Breasts
8 Mile (2002) Buns
The Getaway (1994) Breasts, Bush, Buns

Final Analysis (1992) Breasts
9½ Weeks (1986) Breasts, Buns

Marianne Basler

Born: March 9, 1964
Brussels, Belgium
Skin-O-Meter: Great Nudity

Sweet as Belgian chocolate and sure to make your Swedish meatballs tingle, Marianne Basler is the Euro-mix minx who drives skin hunters to arthouse theaters. She's barely a blip on the American cinema radar, but in France—where the girls often wear no underpants—she's no UFO (that is Unidentified Fine Object). She first appeared on the scene in 1980, but it wasn't until *L'Amour propre ne le reste jamais très longtemps* (1985) that she became eligible for filmdom's sex scene. In that movie she only flashed some floppers, but where there's such a smoking-hot actress, there's fleshy fire. She ignited the screen and pants across this great globe of ours when she abandoned all flammable clothing for some sizzling full-frontal shots in flicks such as *Rosa la rose, fille publique* (1986) and *Contrainte par corps* (1987). Marianne's only Stateside release was *A Soldier's Tale* (1988), opposite Gabriel Byrne. She really Byrnes that soldier up by showing her tail and even some of her upper front. Talk about a Stateside release; there wasn't a dry seat in the house!

SKIN-fining Moment:

Contrainte par Corps (0:30) *Brief buns and breasts walking over to a guard for a cavity search.*

See Her Naked In:

On n'a qu'une Vie (2000) Breasts
La Femme de Plume (1999) Breasts
Le Danger d'Aimer (1998) RB
Vidange (1998) RB

A Soldier's Tale (1988) Breasts, Buns
Le Beauf (1987) Breasts
Contrainte par Corps (1987) Breasts, Bush, Buns
Rosa la Rose, Fille Publique (1986) Breasts, Bush, Buns
L'Amour Propre ne le Reste Jamais Très Longtemps (1985) Breasts

Angela Bassett

Born: August 16, 1958
New York, New York
Skin-O-Meter: Brief Nudity

Equally adept at stage, screen, and television—and scorchingly hot wherever she goes—Angela Bassett honed her considerable acting chops in productions at Yale University, where the brainiac beauty earned a scholarship. Angela made her screen debut in the cult favorite *F/X* (1986) and broke through to critical (and horndog) acclaim in John Singleton's *Boyz N the Hood* (1991). She got to play wacko Jacko's mother in the made-for-TV movie *The Jacksons: An American Dream* (1993). Angela's star-making breakthrough came as Tina Turner in *What's Love Got to Do with It?* (1993), a performance which earned her a Best Actress Oscar nomination and a Golden Globe. She starred as the title character in *How Stella Got Her Groove Back* (1998), playing a divorcée who gets her freak on with a twenty-year-old hunk.

SKIN-fining Moment:

City of Hope (1:20) *What's love got to do with tits? Everything here, as Angie's bare-bosomed in bed with Joe Morton.*

See Her Naked In:

Supernova (2000) Body Double—Breasts, Buns
Critters 4 (1991) Body Double—Buns
City of Hope (1991) Breasts

Tamara LaSeon Bass

Born: March 23, 1978
Syracuse, New York
Skin-O-Meter: Brief Nudity

Tamara LaSeon Bass slid into the world of professional acting on the one-time hit series *Sliders*. That was just the start, of course, and soon this dark ebony princess found herself on the big screen in *Bellyfruit* (1999). While she didn't show any of her bellyfruit or any other sweet, juicy things, her career was off and running. Audiences got another taste of her ripe freshness opposite Judge Reinhold in *Redemption High* (1999), but Tamara remained glued to the boob tube and its boobless entertainment. She jumped around in guest spots on *Moesha* and *The Fugitive*, and it appeared that viewers' chances of catching the bouncing bounty of blackness that Tamara kept hidden behind her shirt was null and void. Well, don't worry, people, you can void your balls watching Tamara in John Singleton's *Baby Boy* (2001), where we get a nice shot of her sacks wet from the shower. Most recently, Tamara has been a regular on the Fox drama *Boston Public*, but she's yet to show her pubic. She needs to get back to sex school!

SKIN-fining Moment:

Baby Boy (0:04) *Nicely lit shot of Tamara's titties when Tyrese surprises her in the shower.*

See Her Naked In:

Baby Boy (2001) Breasts

Justine Bateman

Born: February 19, 1966
Rye, New York
Skin-O-Meter: Brief Nudity

Justine Bateman reigned as TV's teen-queen supreme in the early to mid '80s playing Michael J. Fox's sister Mallory on the NBC sitcom *Family Ties*. Whether tempting next-door-horndog Skippy or sneaking out with her muscle-headed artist boyfriend Nick, tight-package Justine potently provided a generation's link between Maureen McCormick on *The Brady Bunch* and Alyssa Milano on *Who's the Boss?* Her big-screen debut, *Satisfaction* (1988), didn't provide much of its title element, as neither Justine nor breakout co-star Julia Roberts showed any skin in the goofball saga of an all-girl rock band. In fact, it took Justine fifteen more years before she blessed us with bare breasts. Their dairylicious debut occured on a June 2003 episode of the Showtime series *Out of Order*. So now that Mallory's shown her mammaries, will it be long before she visibly parts her Family *Thighs*?

SKIN-fining Moment:

Out of Order "Follow the Rat" (2003) *Mallory shows her mammaries! She pops her nifty nips out of a towel in a sauna while Eric Stoltz and Felicity Huffman praise their pertness.*

TeleVisions:

Out of Order Breasts

Kathy Bates

Born: June 28, 1948
Memphis, Tennessee
Skin-O-Meter: Great Nudity

Some like 'em hot, some like 'em fat; Kathy Bates brings the two camps together scandalously. Although primarily known as a stage actress, comfy Kathy is big enough to fill the silver screen. She plays off-beat roles that you can still beat off to in odd-ball movies that you can ball odd to. Kathy won an Oscar for her crazed-fan role in the film version of Stephen King's classic *Misery* (1990), although she has been appearing in cinema since the late '70s. And she ain't shy about showing off her formidable form. In *At Play in the Fields of the Lord* (1991), you can see a mud-plastered Kathy hysterically romping through a crowd in little more than her birthday suit, some thatch, and a fury snatch! Then in *About Schmidt* (2002), she made a hot tub even hotter for Jack Nicholson. Big and bountiful, Kathy is one master Bates.

SKIN-fining Moment:

About Schmidt (1:39) *Those who prefer flesh fully ripened (and a bit curdled) like a fine cheese will enjoy Kathy Bates's drippy droopers and flaccid fanny splashing down in a hot tub. But the question remains: Who has bigger boobs, Kathy or her tub-mate, Jack Nicholson?*

See Her Naked In:

About Schmidt (2002) Breasts, Buns
At Play in the Fields of the Lord (1991) FFN, Buns

Jaime Lyn Bauer

Born: March 9, 1949
Phoenix, Arizona
Skin-O-Meter: Great Nudity

Jaime Lyn Bauer is most famous for her long-running role as the sexy wild child Lauralee Brooks on the daytime soap *The Young and the Restless*. She owned the part from 1973 through 1982. When she left the show, the producers fired everyone in her story line and took the program in a new direction. She recently returned to the show after a stint as Dr. Laura Horton on *Days of Our Lives*, but the now devoutly Christian woman's wild days are behind her. Speaking of those days, she appeared naked with Jennifer Ashley, Tiffany Bolling, Teda Bracci, and Ruthy Ross in the cult classic

The Centerfold Girls (1974). The movie tells the tale of a depraved religious fanatic who tortures the immoral women who showed their skin in a men's magazine. Hopefully, Jaime Lyn is less into the avenging God and prefers the forgiving God. Maybe she'll even return to a life of skin. Hey, Eve is technically the first pinup in the erotic club that is the Garden of Eden.

SKIN-fining Moment:

The Centerfold Girls (0:14) *Jamie Lyn busts out her Bauers when taking off her shirt in a bathroom.*

See Her Naked In:

The Centerfold Girls (1974) Breasts, Buns

Kristin Bauer

Born: November 26, 1973
Racine, Wisconsin
Skin-O-Meter: Great Nudity

If you are a slave to the boob tube, you've probably cranked your yanker to thoughts of Kristin Bauer. This bubbly blonde with mammoth jigglies has made appearances on *Everybody Loves Raymond, Seinfeld, Dark Angel,* and *Hidden Hills.* Her repeat performance as the giggling bimbo ex-wife of George Segal on *Just Shoot Me* had viewers cocked, loaded, and ready for action. Kristin aimed her bare bullets at the big screen in a pointed performance in *Dancing at the Blue Iguana* (2000). Stripping among pros like Daryl Hannah and Jennifer Tilly, Kris held her own (and other dancer's as well), showing boobage in abundance, generous amounts of G-stringed crack, and full-frontal beaver to boot.

SKIN-fining Moment:

Dancing at the Blue Iguana (1:38) *Ms. Bauer barrells onto a strip-club stage in a blue corset. She unzips and busts out her bodacious bo-bo's.*

See Her Naked In:

Dancing at the Blue Iguana (2000) FFN, Thong
Glory Daze (1996) Breasts

Michelle Bauer

Born: October 1, 1958
Los Angeles, California
Skin-O-Meter: Hall of Fame

Former Penthouse Pet Michelle Bauer jumped from the pages of early-'80s men's mags to the wild celluloid of mid-'80s horror flicks. This gal works all the time and has played everything from hookers to holy women, but all her characters share one trait: an apparent (and glorious) aversion to clothing. Michelle's not shy about showing skin, and you can catch all kinds of fresh—or sometimes rotting—flesh in such exploitation masterpieces as *Hollywood Chainsaw Hookers* (1988), *Sorority Babes in the Slimeball Bowl-O-Rama* (1988), and *Dr. Alien* (1988). There are many shower scenes in many caged-women films, but Michelle's shower scene in the genre defining *Reform School Girls* (1986) ranks among the most raucous (and hot)! And don't miss *Spirits* (1990) for Michelle's nun with one habit—okay, two habits, the one on her head and the fact that she's got to bare her jugs! Michelle stripped right into the '90s with her top-dropping turn in the vampire-escort-agency straight-to-tape flick *Morgana* (1995), featuring fellow scream queen Julie Strain.

SKIN-fining Moment:

Nightmare Sisters (0:43) *While a gaggle of Porky's-type goofs peeps on them, Michelle scrubs in a tub with T&A-baring Linena Quigley and Brinke Stevens. Michelle's the last girl featured in the clip and shows some muff to go with her mams.*

See Her Naked In:

Timegate: Tales of the Saddle Tramps (1999) LB, Buns
Shame, Shame, Shame (1998) FFN
Mari-Cookie and the Killer Tarantula (1998) Breasts
Jewel Naked Around the World (1995) Breasts, Buns
Red Lips (1995) FFN, Buns
Blonde Heaven (1995) FFN, Buns
Bikini Drive-In (1995) Breasts, Thong
Vampire Vixens from Venus (1995) Breasts
Dinosaur Island (1994) Breasts
If I'm So Famous, How Come Nobody's Ever Heard of Me? (1994) Breasts
Witch Academy (1993) Breasts, Buns
One Million Heels B.C. (1993) FFN, Buns
Heavy Petting Detective (1993) Breasts
Naked Instinct (1993) FFN, Buns
Hellroller (1992) Breasts
Chickboxer (1992) FFN
Inner Sanctum (1991) Breasts, Buns
Puppet Master III: Toulon's Revenge (1991) Breasts
Scream Queen Hot Tub Party (1991) FFN, Buns
The Dwelling (1991) Breasts
Evil Toons (1991) Breasts, Thong
Naked Obsession (1990) Breasts
Murder Weapon (1990) LB
Spirits (1990) Breasts, Bush, Buns
The Jigsaw Murders (1989) Breasts, Buns
Wild Man (1989) Breasts, Bush, Buns
Lady Avenger (1989) Breasts
Assault of the Party Nerds (1989) Breasts
Deadly Embrace (1989) Breasts, Buns
Dr. Alien (1988) Breasts
Warlords (1988) Breasts
Demonwarp (1988) Breasts
Beverly Hills Vamp (1988) Breasts, Buns
Hollywood Chainsaw Hookers (1988) FFN, Buns
Sorority Babes in the Slimeball Bowl-O-Rama (1988) FFN
Night of the Living Babes (1987) Breasts
Cyclone (1987) LB, Buns
Nightmare Sisters (1987) FFN
The Phantom Empire (1987) Breasts
Lust for Freedom (1987) Breasts, Bush
Beverly Hills Girls (1986)
Candid Candid Camera, volume 5 (1986) Buns
Centerfold Screen Test, Take 2 (1986) FFN

Armed Response (1986) Breasts
Reform School Girls (1986) Breasts
In Search of the Perfect 10 (1986) Breasts,
    Thong
Roller Blade (1985) FFN, Buns
Candid Candid Camera, volume 4 (1985)
    FFN, Buns
Tomboy (1985) Breasts
Cave Girl (1985) Breasts
Screen Test (1985) FFN
Monaco Forever (1984) Breasts
Best Chest in the West (1984) Breasts, Buns
Bad Girls II (1984) FFN, Buns
Love Skills: A Guide to the Pleasures of Sex
    (1984) FFN
Nudes in Limbo (1983) FFN
The Man Who Wasn't There (1983) Breasts,
    Buns
Homework (1982) Breasts
Café Flesh (1982) Breasts, Bush, Buns
Bad Girls (1981) FFN, Buns
Numerous Adult Movies

Lisa Baur

Skin-O-Meter: Brief Nudity

Before she made it big in the hit
comedy *Animal House* (1978), Lisa
Baur was already making a name
for herself—or at least for her
boobs—on such jiggle-friendly
entertainment as *Charlie's Angels*.
On a 1977 episode entitled "Pretty
Angels All in a Row," Lisa played a
"Contestant." And she could have
been a contender after her backseat
mam handle from Tim Matheson in
Animal House. Lisa's bust looked
outstanding in her tight gray
sweater and even better outstanding in Matheson's hands
when he convinced her that he
needed some "comfort." Sadly, this
nude debut was followed by
nothing. Lisa just disappeared from
show business and never showed
again. But somewhere out there a
lucky fellow gets to reenact her
scene from *Animal House* in the
privacy of the martial bedroom.
Lucky beast.

SKIN-fining Moment:

Animal House (1:16) *Enjoy Lisa's
sultry sackage as she fools around with
Tim Matheson in the back of the Delta
car.*

See Her Naked In:

Animal House (1978) Breasts

Kylie Bax

Born: January 5, 1975
Thames, New Zealand
Skin-O-Meter: Never Nude

Standing five-feet-eleven-inches
tall, naturally blonde and busty
New Zealander Kylie Bax is a
towering skinferno who made
huge waves of tsunami-like sex
appeal in the swimsuit edition of
Sports Illustrated. Hollywood came
calling, and Kylie began popping
up in vids like *Jill the Ripper*
(2000). Kylie didn't get a chance to
show off her range playing
"supermodel" in the comedy *Boys
and Girls* (2000), but she soon
appeared in *Get Over It* (2001)
opposite the quickly maturing
curvature of Kirsten Dunst and
staked out some fleshy firmament
of her own by dropping her duds
and showing the bulk of her
bombastic buds while frolicking
topless on the beach. When Kylie
launches into a topless somersault,
the flying funbags actually belong
to an acrobactic stand-in, but it's
only a matter of time before this
beauty comes clean again. And
only fools will turn their backs on
this Bax!

SKIN-fining Moment:

Get Over It (0:31) *Kylie launches into
a topless somersault on the beach. She
looks awesome, even if the naked
upside-down udders belong to a stunt
double.*

See Her Naked In:

Get Over It (2001) Body Double—Breasts

Helen Baxendale

Born: February 14, 1969
Lichfield, Staffordshire, England,
UK
Skin-O-Meter: Great Nudity

Why is England so stingy with its
homegrown beauties? Take Helen
Baxendale . . . please! The dark-
haired temptress spends the
majority of her carnal career making
Limeys squeeze their lemons until
the juice runs down their thighs.
She has crossed the pond to let
Ross of *Friends* fame soak in her
womanly charms. But as his British
girlfriend Emily, we're not likely to
see her moist bits. Her breast performances are saved for the old
country, where she performed as
Lady Macbeth in the latest
incarnation of the classic
Shakespearean play, as well as in
several other TV series and mini-
dramas, like the popular *Cardiac
Arrest*. Helen is like her namesake
from Troy but has launched a
thousand erections rather than
ships. She pulled out all the stops,
as well as her incredible (wish they
were edible) boobs, for her role in
Truth or Dare (1996), which had
nothing to do with Madonna and
features way more nudity than the
pop singer's black-and-white
documentary. Her hottest role has
to be *The Investigator* (1997),
however, in which Helen portrays
an agent for the British Armed
Forces whose sole purpose is to
track down lesbians in the army.
She goes deep under the covers at
some hot spots, including one
topless encounter that will leave
even the coolest of men sweating
from the tips of their fingernails to
the soles of their feet. God save this
queen!

SKIN-fining Moment:

Truth or Dare *Truth or bare: Helen sits
up topless in bed and we see her naked
Raxendale.*

See Her Naked In:

The Investigator—BBC TV Drama (1997) Breasts

TeleVisions:

Truth or Dare Breasts

Amy Lynn Baxter

Born: September 6, 1967
Plymouth, Massachusetts
Skin-O-Meter: Great Nudity

Amy Lynn Baxter and cinematic skin go together like blonde and bombshell. This busty supernova got her start as a Penthouse Pet. What a perfect, pert, not-so-little pet to have. Who wouldn't want to come home and give Amy Lynn's honey-sweet hooters a good stroking after a hard day's work? It's easy to take a load off with any of Amy Lynn's movies, since she is nude in every role. In the nut busting *Golf Balls!* (1999), Amy Lynn gives her rosy reds some much-needed water in a car wash. In *Desire* (1997), she goes all the way, showing boobies, tan and taut booty, and her very own little hairy pet. Newsflash: Amy is at her most boobastic in *Broadcast Bombshells* (1995). The site of her fantastic rack, shown along with gal pals Debbie Rochon and Elizabeth Heyman, may cause an immediate release of bodily fluids, so keep some tissue handy.

SKIN-fining Moment:

Broadcast Bombshells (0:44) *Amy Lynn flashes some fantastic topless flesh with Debbie Rochon and pink-pantied Elizabeth Heyman in this scene. Warning: Watching this clip may cause an overdose of boobage . . .*

See Her Naked In:

Smokin' Stogies (2001) Breasts
Golf Balls! (1999) Breasts
Desire (1997) FFN, Buns
Absolute Aggression (1996) Breasts

Cyber Vengeance (1995) Breasts
Broadcast Bombshells (1995) FFN, Buns
In the Flesh (1995) Breasts, Thong
Bikini Bistro (1995) FFN, Buns
Affairs of the Heart (1992) Breasts, Thong
Summer Job (1989) Breasts, Thong
Wet Water T's (1987) Breasts, Thong
Summer's Games (1987) Breasts

Meredith Baxter

Born: June 21, 1947
South Pasadena, California
Skin-O-Meter: Great Nudity

As a TV premise, it sounds like no big deal now—a nice Jewish boy goes ga-ga for a gorgeous goy chick—but in its day, the sitcom *Bridget Loves Bernie* was as controversial as bestiality. It was also Meredith Baxter's introduction to the world of stardom. TV audiences were smitten by her kittens, even if they were hardly evident behind all that '70s polyester. Later, she matured as the sexy mom on NBC's *Family Ties*, and who didn't want to tie down that matriarch for some nasty relations? You'd never know how large and in charge Meredith's mammaries are from her memorable but milk-jugless movies, such as *Ben* (1972) and *All the President's Men* (1976). That's why Mr. Skin is grateful for women's-health issues (this one time). The breakthrough NBC TV movie *My Breast* (1994) showcases the title object, Meredith's mouth-wateringly mammoth left mammary, in a scene where a doctor probes her during a medical exam. There was no need to ask what was up on *that* doc!

SKIN-fining Moment:

My Breast (0:41) *Meredith manifests her magnificently massive left melon for the doctor, who gives it a nice rubdown in the name of "science."*

See Her Naked In:

My Breast (1994) LB

Nathalie Baye

Born: July 6, 1948
Mainneville, France
Skin-O-Meter: Great Nudity

Nathalie Baye started her career as a dancer, so her body was primed for her dramatic leap to more skinematic pursuits. That mammanimous occasion began with *Day for Night* (1973), but nasty Nathalie was just getting started. Since then, she's found considerable success in both French and international cinema, appearing in such films as *The Last Woman* (1976), *Beethoven's Nephew* (1985), *The Man Inside* (1990), and *Catch Me If You Can* (2002), opposite Leonardo DiCaprio. But Nathalie's breast performances are saved for her beret-spinning native land. In films such as *La Gueule ouverte* (1974), *Mado* (1976), and *Rive droite, rive gauche* (1984), Nathalie shows off every moist bit of her young, slim, and seductively charming self. Naturally, a hottie like this doesn't let maturity slow her down (either in terms of getting naked or of keeping her body in whacktastic shape). *En toute innocence* (1987), *De guerre lasse* (1987), *Si je t'aime, prends garde à toi* (1998), and even *Une liaison pornographique* (1999) expose why, like wine, French broads get better with age.

SKIN-fining Moment:

La Gueule Ouverte (0:35) *Nice view of her le titlets as she gets topless in bed with a guy.*

See Her Naked In:

An Affair of Love (1999) Breasts
Une Liaison Pornographique (1999) Breasts
Si je t'Aime, Prends Garde à Toi (1998) Breasts
De Guerre Lasse (1987) Breasts, Buns
En Toute Innocence (1987) Breasts, Buns
Rive Droite, Rive Gauche (1984) Breasts
La Balance (1982) Breasts

Une Semaine de Vacances (1980) Breasts
Je Vais Craquer!!! (1980) Breasts
Mado (1976) Breasts
La Gueule Ouverte (1974) Breasts, Buns

Stephanie Beacham

Born: February 28, 1947
Casablanca, Morocco
Skin-O-Meter: Great Nudity

Imperious and with a great ass, Moroccan-born actress Stephanie Beacham created the template for the achingly hot network-TV bitch. From the years 1985 through 1989, blonde and buxom Beacham inhabited Sable Colby on the prime-time soaps *The Colbys* and *Dynasty*. Stephanie's sugar-glazed sneer, rock-candy eyes, and alpha-female physique made her one of the most alluring bitch characters in the history of women who snarl. She'd had many years of practice in the role, to judge from her title turn in *Super Bitch* (1973). This Italian production relied as much upon Beacham's bod as it did her mean demeanor. Youthful and blonde, Stephanie cracks a butt smile during a bed-top romp, lounges on her back with her billowing breasts to the air, squirms on her belly with her butt up, then swings her knockers and scrubs her muff in a steamy shower sequence. A clean bitch is a godly bitch.

SKIN-fining Moment:

The Nightcomers (0:30) *Beacham's bare bazooms gets roughly manhandled by a sweaty Marlon Brando as some horny kid peeps through the keyhole.*

See Her Naked In:

Super Bitch (1973) FFN, Buns
The Nightcomers (1972) Breasts

Jennifer Beals

Born: December 19, 1963
Chicago, Illinois
Skin-O-Meter: Brief Nudity

Beautiful Jennifer Beals, a model-cum-actress, burst onto the cinema landscape as a welder-cum-dancer in *Flashdance* (1983). Who knew she could dance? Well, she couldn't, which is why a body double was used—at least for the more advanced dance moves. What do you do for a follow-up film when the whole world's waiting for another dance film? Well, you play the bride of a man with two left feet, of course. Jennifer was the unlucky gal betrothed to the monster in the remake of *The Bride of Frankenstein* titled *The Bride* (1985). The movie teamed Jennifer with rock singer Sting, and Jennifer wouldn't need a body double for her wedding night, although she did use a stunt nude for the movie. One of the hardest-working actresses around, Jennifer spent the '90s turning up in all sorts of odd places, such as direct-to-video quickies such as *Terror Stalks the Class Reunion* (1992) and indie successes such as *In the Soup* (1992) and *Roger Dodger* (2002). Perpetually reinventing her persona the way she once shredded sweatshirt sleeves, Jennifer added the boldest move yet to her repertoire on the Showtime series *The L Word*. Playing the biracial lesbian lover of luscious Laurel Holloman, Jennifer throws herself into their mound-on-mound mountings with erotic abandon and more heat than her famous *Flashdance* welder's torch ever sparked up. And since she's yet to flash complete flesh on the show, let's invoke the immortal and never-more-appropriate words of Ms. Irene Cara: "Take your passion and *make it* happen!"

SKIN-fining Moment:

Club Extinction (1:17) *Jen flashdances in the sack with a fella and flashes her dancing dairy puffs at us a couple of times while they go at it.*

See Her Naked In:

The Spree (1998) Body Double—Breasts, Buns
The Prophecy II (1997) Breasts, Buns
Blood and Concrete (1991) Body Double—LB, Buns
Club Extinction (1990) Breasts

Emmanuelle Beart

Born: August 14, 1965
St. Tropez, France
Skin-O-Meter: Hall of Fame

Director Robert Altman met Emmanuelle Beart when she was a nanny. He encouraged the fresh-faced beauty with the gorgeous Gallic figure to become an actress. Since then, this former au pair has shown her oh-so-lovely pair in a multitude of French films, becoming one of France's greatest stars. Mademoiselle Beart debuted her bouncing boobies, booming backside, and lush bush in *Premiers désirs* (1983). Her bare beauty continued to flow freely in *Manon of the Spring* (1987), as she danced naked in a field surrounded by horny goats. In *La Belle Noiseuse* (1992), Emmy emphasized her Euro skin from beginning to end as an artist's model, displaying her puff pastries, fluffy muff, and bountiful booty. In *8 Femmes* (2002), as a traditional French maid, Emmanuelle will clean your clock. The Yanks finally added Emmanuelle to their collective spank bank in 1996, when she appeared in *Mission Impossible* with Tom Cruise. Although completely clothed, it's not impossible to notice that this fine French filly is the crème de la crème.

SKIN-fining Moment:

La Belle Noiseuse (1:58) *Boobs! Bush! Oh, you won't see this much of an Emmanuelle outside of . . . well, an Emmanuelle flick!*

See Her Naked In:

Histoire de Marie et Julien (2003) Breasts,
   Buns
Nathalie . . . (2003) Breasts
Les Égarés (2003) Breasts, Buns
La Répétition (2001) LB
Voleur de Vie (1998) LB
La Belle Noiseuse (1992) FFN, Buns
Il Viaggio di Capitan Fracassa (1991) Breasts
J'embrasse Pas (1991) Breasts, Buns
Divertimento (1991) FFN, Buns
Les Enfants du Desordre (1989) FFN, Buns
A Gauche en Sortant de l'Ascenseur (1988)
   FFN
Manon of the Spring (1986) FFN, Buns
L'Amour en Douce (1985) RB, Buns
Un Amour Interdit (1984) Breasts
Premiers Désirs (1983) FFN, Buns

Michelle Beaudoin

Born: August 25, 1975
Edmonton, Alberta, Canada
Skin-O-Meter: Brief Nudity

Canadian-born Michelle Beaudoin
is a young up-and-comer perhaps
best known for her wild helmet of
kinky red hair. So much so that she
was cast in *Sunset Strip* (2000) as
The Girl with Frizzy Red Hair. But
cute Michelle is so much more
than a mere 'fro. She studied acting
in New York at Circle in the
Square, which must have gotten
her used to exposing herself
onstage, because she did a
wonderful job of revealing her little
pink nerps in her movie debut *Bad
Company* (1995). It was hard not to
notice a completely nude Michelle
doing it doggy-style for an
audience, but fans didn't catch on
to the frisky female until she
landed a coveted role on the hit TV
show *Sabrina, the Teenage Witch.*
Since then, Michelle has returned
to relative obscurity, popping up in
films such as *Waydowntown* (2000),
which, sadly, has nothing to do
with the oral sex implied by its
title. Mr. Skin waits patiently for a
return of the redheaded stranger.

SKIN-fining Moment:

Bad Company (0:10) *Brief breastage
as Michelle's getting nakedly banged by
her uncle when Larry Fishburne and
Ellen Barkin interrupt their
incestilicious fun.*

See Her Naked In:

Bad Company (1995) RB

Garcelle Beauvais

Born: November 26, 1966
St. Marc, Haiti
Skin-O-Meter: Never Nude

Garcelle Beauvais was introduced to
moviegoers in *Manhunter* (1986),
the movie which also debuted the
diabolical Dr. Hannibal Lecter.
Hannibal the Cannibal was new to
the scene and perhaps a bit unsure
of his sinister steps, so he can be
forgiven for not dining on the
delectable dark meat of Garcelle.
She, on the other hand, was already
a working stiff making TV
audiences wanking stiff from her
appearances on *Miami Vice.* Garcelle
started making a name for herself
opposite Eddie Murphy in *Coming to
America* (1988), and all red-blooded
American males were coming after
her. Aaron Spelling was so smitten
that he cast her in his short-lived
TV series *Models, Inc.,* but it was a
role on *NYPD Blue* that made
Garcelle a star. As sexy as she is, it's
surprising that the producers of
that decidedly dirty show didn't
have Garcelle peel for the camera.
The closest she's come to flashing
her finery was doing Will Smith in
Wild Wild West (1999). She's naked
but manages to hide her good bits.
If she had only exposed some of
that sweetness, then the movie
could have added another Wild to
its title.

SKIN-fining Moment:

NYPD Blue "Baby Love" (2001)
Garcelle strips down to her bra and pan-
ties for Henry Simmons. And the bra
and panties sure are nice.

Kimberly Beck

Born: January 9, 1956
Glendale, California
Skin-O-Meter: Brief Nudity

Unfamiliar with comely Kimberly
Beck? Time to get acquainted! This
very fine-looking act-chest (check
out that meat rack!) has appeared
in guest spots on more than twenty
TV series, as well as in recurring
roles on shows like *Peyton Place,
Lucas Tanner, Westwind, General
Hospital, Fantasy Island, Dynasty,* and
Capitol. Sadly, these outings did
very little to further her career, so
she continues to take on bit parts
in TV and cinema. You can ogle her
beauty in such films as *Killing Zoe*
(1994) and *Independence Day*
(1996). In Hollywood terms, no,
Kimberly is not a star. Here at Skin
Central, however, she's reached the
highest pinnacle of delight with
her contribution to *Massacre at
Central High* (1976). She reveals
her bodacious bosom for the only
time in her long, supporting-parts
career. It certainly gets our
supporting parts taking notice.
Besides her ample breasts,
Kimberly goes for the prerequisite
skinny dip and shows off the kind
of tush that is hypnotic in its juicy
charms. The only massacre in that
movie is the millions of dead
sperm dried up on the theater
floor.

SKIN-fining Moment:

Massacre at Central High (0:42)
*Nice looks at Kimberly's cannons as she
engages in a little intercourse with
Andrew Stevens on the beach. No wet
spot issues here!*

See Her Naked In:

Massacre at Central High (1976) FFN,
   Buns

Kate Beckinsale

Born: July 26, 1973
London, England, UK
Skin-O-Meter: Great Nudity

After dropping out of Oxford University, British crumpet Kate Beckinsale landed a key role in Kenneth Branagh's *Much Ado About Nothing* (1993), and suddenly much was ado with this milky-skinned, sweetly bitty-boobied beauty's career. After several years of starring in tony English productions, Kate was cast in the indie hit *The Last Days of Disco* (1998) and caught the attention of Hollywood. Kate demanded a body double for *Haunted* (1995), but the nude scenes in *Uncovered* (1994) are the real deal. Her most high-profile flick to date was *Pearl Harbor* (2001), but she kept her own bombs covered. Come on, Kate, let those Limey lickables loose!

SKIN-fining Moment:

Uncovered (0:39) *Kate walks around in white bra and panties, then busts out her deliciously demure tittables while checking out a Chinese painting. Really nice.*

See Her Naked In:

Haunted (1995) Body Double—FFN, Buns
Uncovered (1994) Breasts

Bonnie Bedelia

Born: March 25, 1952
New York, New York
Skin-O-Meter: Great Nudity

A bountifully chest-blessed frosted brunette, Bonnie Bedelia has been stealing scenes since the 1960s. She reached her widest audience playing the hard-nosed, soft-sweatered wife of Bruce Willis in the first two *Die Hard* (1988 and 1990) movies, but her biggest claim to tabloid fame might be that she is the aunt of lapsed child actor Macaulay Culkin. Not only is Bonnie every bit as pretty as Macaulay was in his prime, but she carries herself with a tremendous thrust of frontal shelf. A brief profile glimpse of the balcony occurs in *The Gypsy Moths* (1969) when Bonnie attempts and fails to wrap the protrusions in a robe. To sample Bedelia's crinkled nipples, make friends with the black-and-white flashbacks in *The Stranger* (1986).

SKIN-fining Moment:

The Stranger (0:38) *Black-and-white action starring topless Bonnie's right bo-bo as she bangs a dude in bed.*

See Her Naked In:

Judicial Consent (1994) Body Double—LB
The Stranger (1986) Breasts
Lovers and Other Strangers (1970) Breasts
The Gypsy Moths (1969) RB
Then Came Bronson (1969) Breasts

Leslie Bega

Born: April 17, 1967
Los Angeles, California
Skin-O-Meter: Great Nudity

TV viewers may remember Leslie Bega as the grade-obsessed high-school student Maria Borges on ABC's *Head of the Class* in the late '80s. She holds a special place in our heart-ons here at Skin Central for *Time of Her Time* (1999), based on a book by infamous sleaze writer Norman Mailer. It's a hoot of a performance, with Leslie's hooters flopping all over the place, her perfect posterior, and even a fleeting flash of fur. But that was only an appetizer for her kinky main dish on *The Sopranos* as Valentina La Paz, the mistress of Ralph Cifaretto (Joe Pantoliano) whom Tony Soprano (James Gandolfini) steals away. Leslie worked with Pantoliano to create the perverted backstory for their characters' S&M relationship. "We sat down, and the stuff that came out of this man's imagination was so outlandish," she says. "I couldn't even tell you if I wanted to because I don't think you can legally print it." Hopefully, that hot stuff will make it onto the extras track of the DVD.

SKIN-fining Moment:

Time of Her Time (1:20) *Leslie shows off those bouncing boobs and some more of that perfect posterior when she takes another ride on The Baloney Pony . . . Yee-hah!*

See Her Naked In:

Time of Her Time (1999) FFN, Buns
Uncaged (1991) Breasts

TeleVisions:

The Sopranos Breasts, Bush

Bérénice Bejo

Skin-O-Meter: Great Nudity

When *A Knight's Tale* (2001) came out, who would have thought that the medieval action flick would be introducing audiences to some of the hottest unknowns in the business? As hypnotic as Shannyn Sossamon is, viewers were transfixed by the darkly charming B-cupped beauty of Bérénice Bejo. But what most didn't know was that she was already a star in France, with seven movies under her svelte belt as well as three TV series. The Argentinean-born sexpot traveled to France, and the rest is her-story. She's been flashing her finery since *Histoire d'hommes* (1996), but Skin Central really got up and took notice (in our pants) with the release (and our wet release) of *Meilleur espoir feminin* (2000). In a movie-within-a-movie scene, Bérénice is seen completely naked from behind—and what a perfect ass she has. There's also a glimpse at her small wonders, which are wonderful. Don't take our word for it, though. The role earned her a French Cesar nomination as Most Promising Actress, which is ironic as that's the translation of the film's title into English. Talk about direct marketing.

SKIN-fining Moment:

Meilleur Espoir Féminin (0:41) *A nice look at Bérénice's beautiful backside (and some brief right breast) as she drops her towel while filming a nude scene.*

See Her Naked In:

24 Heures de la Vie d'une Femme (2002) Breasts, Buns
Meilleur Espoir Féminin (2000) RB, Buns
Histoire d'Hommes (1996) Breasts

Ana Belén

Born: May 26, 1951
Madrid, Spain
Skin-O-Meter: Great Nudity

Ana Belén is one of the most famous women in Spain. Just gander at her glandular deposits: firm, round, and high-rising orbs that hypnotize and seduce more powerfully than Spanish Fly. Isn't it about time for America to embrace the exotic beauty of Ana? This feisty brunette has the casual Mediterranean charm that will smile at a stranger just as easily as strip for him. While she's been working in her native land's film industry since *Zampo and Me* (1966), she didn't reveal her true talents until *El Amor del Capitán Brando* (1974). After that all bets were off, as were most of her clothes. With more than a decade of decadent skin exposure—let's not beat around the bush—her muff-see perv-formance has to be in *Divinas Palabras* (1987). It's a classic pretentious foreign flick, with all the familiar trappings,

thankfully including full-frontal nudity by Ana. Talk about bushwhacked—the audience will surely be whacking to Ana's bush!

SKIN-fining Moment:

Divinas palabras (1:38) *Ana flashes a bunch of eager fellers some fluffy full frontal followed by a fleeting bit of fanny when she turns around and walks back inside.*

See Her Naked In:

La pasión turca (1994)
The Perfect Husband (1993) Breasts, Buns
Rosa Rosae (1993)
Divinas palabras (1987) FFN, Buns
La Colmena (1982) Breasts
Cuentos eróticos (1979)
The Creature (1977) FFN, Buns
La oscura historia de la prima Montse (1977)
Emilia, parada y fonda (1976) RB, Buns
La Petición (1976)
Jo, papá (1975)
El Amor del Capitán Brando (1974)

Catherine Bell

Born: August 14, 1968
London, England, UK
Skin-O-Meter: Hall of Fame

Exotically stacked brunette Catherine Bell can thank her hybrid heritage for the sweet blend of satiny mocha-cream concupiscence that accounts for her overwhelming appeal. Born of an Iranian mother in London, England, but raised primarily in Los Angeles, a place that is a finishing school for far-flung foxes, uniquely compelling Catherine's modeling career took her all the way to Japan, and the acting bug brought her back to L.A. Best known for her role as no-nonsense, sultry Sarah MacKenzie on the criminally successful *JAG*, the bottom line on Catherine is an uncredited appearance as Isabella Rossellini's bum-baring body double in *Death Becomes Her* (1992).

SKIN-fining Moment:

Death Becomes Her (1:20) *Catherine bares that bad-ass butt and just a bit of the side of her right bobbler standing in for Isabella Rossellini during this nice little skinny-dipping sequence . . .*

See Her Naked In:

Death Becomes Her (1992) Buns

TeleVisions:

Dream On Breasts
Hot Line Breasts, Buns

Jeannie Bell

Born: November 23, 1944
St. Louis, Missouri
Skin-O-Meter: Great Nudity

Jeannie Bell was one of the great bodies of the early '70s, when the time was right for hourglass figures. Her first gig, oddly enough, was as Slavegirl Secretary Sugar Jean Bell on the white-trash sitcom *The Beverly Hillbillies*. Shortly thereafter, due to good looks and her apparent willingness to toss clothes as quickly as a laundromat, Jeannie found herself in several blaxploitation pictures, from *Black Gunn* (1972) to *Three the Hard Way* (1974)—and black guns were always hard when Jeannie was onscreen. Stressing the "ploitation" suffix of the genre, Jeannie found many opportunities to show off her amazing rack to the movie-going crowd. Although she appeared topless in some of her earlier works such as *Mean Streets* (1973), her go-to movie for nudity would have to be *Sex on the Run* (1979). Jeannie shows off her ebony charms, and there is also oodles of skin from the fairer sex too, like Britt Ekland. Now that rings Mr. Skin's Bell!

SKIN-fining Moment:

T.N.T. Jackson (0:43) *Ms. Bell's brown-sugar-sacks slip out of her open dress while she's being threatened with a cigar burn. Then they bounce all over as she kicks some ass.*

See Her Naked In:

Body Waves (1991) Breasts
Bloodfist III: Forced to Fight (1991) Breasts
Sex on the Run (1979) Breasts
The Muthers (1976) Breasts
T.N.T. Jackson (1975) Breasts
Policewomen (1974) Breasts, Buns
Mean Streets (1973) Breasts

Kathleen Beller

**Born: February 19, 1956
Westchester, New York
Skin-O-Meter: Great Nudity**

Kathleen Beller turned pro with a four-season stint on the popular daytime soap *Search for Tomorrow*.

BLUEBEARD: SO MANY WOMEN, SO LITTLE TIME. TO KILL. SOME POSTERS PERFECTLY CAPTURE A MOVIE'S MOOD. THIS S(L)ICK, SLEAZY, SUPER-'70S ONE-SHEET NAILS *BLUEBEARD* AND ITS BYGONE BEAUTIES DEAD-ON.

She quickly moved up the Hollywood ladder, landing roles in such notable films as *The Godfather: Part II* (1974) and the comic send-up *Movie Movie* (1978). She gained major recognition for her part on *Dynasty* as Kirby Colby, but the curious who dig deeper will be amply rewarded. Once the undisputed queen of TV, she deserves a more carnal crown for her work in *The Betsy* (1978), in which she appeared topless for a wonderfully skintabulous love scene. Kathleen also goes completely full frontal for a long walk into a swimming pool that should have boiled the tepid waters because she's just that hot. You can also catch her greased ass getting rubbed down in a sleazy moment from *The Sword and the Sorcerer* (1982). Sadly, since then she's left skin behind. But we still have *The Betsy*, which is enough to keep thingies hard for ages.

SKIN-fining Moment:

***The Betsy* (0:13)** *The skinny that out-dips all others! Kathleen gets completely*

bare-assed naked and wades into a pool while Tommy Lee Jones gets an eyeful of her bulbais, bouncing Betsies and beautifully furiffic lap-lushness.

See Her Naked In:

The Sword and the Sorcerer (1982) Buns
Surfacing (1981) Breasts, Buns
The Betsy (1978) FFN

Agostina Belli

**Born: April 13, 1949
Milan, Italy
Skin-O-Meter: Hall of Fame**

Italian eyeful Agostina Belli's last name should be *Bella* in honor of her breathtaking, well-built beauty. Like most other European actresses, this Milanese mama revealed her magnificent mams, curvy caboose, and/or fuzzy furburgarage in a myriad of skintastic films in the '70s, including *The Seduction of Mimi* (1972), *The Purple Taxi* (1977), and *The Sex Machine* (1975). Although Agostina was sucksexfully tasty in her super-curvy contributions to English-language films such as *Bluebeard* (1972), opposite a randy Richard Burton, and *Holocaust 2000* (1977), with a devil-demolishing Kirk Douglas, this Italian dish is most delish when shedding her spread in her native tongue. Take a bite of bella Belli's best undressed offerings today.

SKIN-fining Moment:

***Bluebeard* (1:38)** *Adorable chest-orbs as she peels off her top and spreads out on a couch for Richard Burton before a bad birdie swoops in to pick her berries.*

See Her Naked In:

Manaos (1978) Breasts
Holocaust 2000 (1977) Breasts, Buns
The Purple Taxi (1977) FFN
Il Piatto Piange (1975) Breasts, Buns
The Sex Machine (1975) Breasts, Buns
Virilità (1974) Breasts, Buns

Scent of a Woman (1974) Breasts, Buns
Sepolta Viva (1973) Breasts, Buns
Revolver (1973) Breasts
Quando l'Amore è Sensualità (1973) Breasts, Buns
Bluebeard (1972) Breasts
La Calandria (1972) Breasts, Buns
The Seduction of Mimi (1972) RB, Buns
Cran d'Arrêt (1970)

Lynda Bellingham

Born: May 31, 1948
Montreal, Quebec, Canada
Skin-O-Meter: Great Nudity

Although Lynda Bellingham started her career here in the good old USA with a part on the hit soap opera *General Hospital*, this comely Canuck soon ventured to England, where she would find her greatest successes. Lynda is definitely a TV piece of ass, appearing in such Brit series as *Tell Tarby, The Fuzz, The Pink Medicine Show, Mackenzie, All Creatures Great and Small*, and *Second Thoughts*. Much of her work was confined to the boob tube, but Lynda did find time to show off her massive mams in more cinematic endeavors. Her first skintastic outing was in the hilarious English production *Confessions of a Driving Instructor* (1976), in which she briefly flashed one of her titanic tits with a bit of assistance from one of her (lucky) male costars. However, it was her completely buff bit in *Sweeney!* (1977) that truly tented trousers. Lynda appeared topless in a few scenes, but the coup de gras occurred when she appeared completely nude, lying prostrate on a bed. Sadly, there is nary a hint of lower frontal nudity; even sadder, she's dead. But even stiff she gives her good audience a stiffy.

SKIN-fining Moment:

Sweeney! (0:06) *Rigor mor-tits and a side of deceased ass as two guys find Lynda dead in bed.*

See Her Naked In:

Sweeney! (1977) Breasts
Confessions of a Driving Instructor (1976) LB

Cynthia Belliveau

Skin-O-Meter: Great Nudity

Cynthia Belliveau wanted to be a journalist and was going to school to earn such a degree when, as she puts it, she was "bitten by the bug . . . hard." Well, stop the presses! Mr. Skin was hard, too, when this buxom brunette decided to share her charms with the viewing public. Better to see her fine lines than read her deadlines. She started doing voiceovers and TV productions such as *Alfred Hitchcock Presents, The Twilight Zone*, and *Kung Fu: The Legend Continues*. Her jump to the big screen was taken without the company of her clothing in *Loose Screws* (1985). She performed a striptease onstage that loosened our screws. Following through with the trend of silly film names, she next flashed her finery in *Goofballs* (1987). But *The Dark* (1994) was Cynthia's last skin stand. She returned to TV for a couple of seasons on the series *Wind at My Back*, but that wind is foul without Cynthia exposing her big backside.

SKIN-fining Moment:

Loose Screws (1: 24) Cynthia struts around on a strip-club stage, all burlesque n' stuff, then ditches her top to show those sweet, country-fresh-flavored tater-ta-ta's.

See Her Naked In:

The Dark (1994) Breasts
Night Friend (1987)
Goofballs (1987) LB, Buns
Loose Screws (1985) Breasts

Maria Bello

Born: April 18, 1967
Norristown, Pennsylvania
Skin-O-Meter: Great Nudity

It's no surprise that men want to scream out Maria Bello's name. It's natural, considering her suggestive moniker and breathtakingly boobilicious blonde beauty. Nobody would possibly chew off a paw to get away from the magnificent Maria in *Coyote Ugly* (2000). She's quite the pretty bitch as the canine-named club's proprietress. Mar debuted her addictive sac smack as a former junky in *Permanent Midnight* (1998) with Ben Stiller and followed up by baring her pointy pair again as a karaoke-addicted cutie in *Duets* (2000). Maria gives a most titillating performance as the swinging sex goddess of Bob Crane's dreams in *Auto Focus* (2000). Her character, Sigrid Valdis (best known as the hard-on-inducing, bosom-heaving Hilda of *Hogan's Heroes* fame), gets kinky with Colonel Klink and Sergeant Schultz, begging to be ravaged in a red bustier and garter-belted stockings. A tender flash of Maria's tasty pink nip is the cherry topper on this nasty Nazi fantasy sequence. In addition, Maria brings naked heat to *The Cooler* (2003), a high-stakes gambling drama wherein she rewards dice-thrower William H. Macy with a bedroom tumble featuring a jackpot of T&A. If Maria's skinematic career doesn't make you want to scream out by now, please go to your nearest emergency room. We recommend a thorough dose of this sexy doctress in reruns of *ER*, where Dr. M is guaranteed to infect a multitude of dirty minds in need of a thorough sponge bath. In a particularly prickly episode, her much-talked-about tan tush is on full display, receiving an injection from young Dr. Carter. Who hasn't imagined playing doctor with this delicious dish at some point in her career?

SKIN-fining Moment:

The Cooler (0:40) *Maria bares both her Bellos and even what's down below in a ferociously sexy full-frontal love tussle with William H. Macy.*

See Her Naked In:

The Cooler (2003) FFN, Buns
Auto Focus (2002) Breasts
Duets (2000) Breasts, Thong
Permanent Midnight (1998) Breasts

> "One reason that I'm comfortable with nudity is because I come from Europe and I have a good relation with my body. Nudity is pure; if not, why were Michaelangelo and Raffaello so interested in it? Nudity is something magic."
>
> —MONICA BELLUCCI

Monica Bellucci

Born: September 30, 1964
Città di Castello, Perugia, Italy
Skin-O-Meter: Hall of Fame

Millions of unsuspecting adolescent fanboys flocked to see *The Matrix Reloaded* (2003) and came away with a whole new obsession: that sultry and shapely apparition of brunette feminine fire who played the beguiling Persephone. The passion-flushed supermodel face. The fleshy bombshell bust. The mesmerizing curves of twisting seat meat. Her name is Monica Bellucci; she is from Italy; she has been stunning European audiences since the early 1990s. When *The Matrix* kids grow up, they will seek out *La Riffa* (1991) and *L'Ultimo capodanno* (1998). They will lose themselves in Monica's deep, syrup-colored crevices of cleavage and ass crack. They will find a taste of nirvana in her thick and natural bush.

SKIN-fining Moment:

L'Ultimo Capodanno (11:00) *First we see Monica's massive breasts as she puts on a bra. Then she pulls off her panties and runs around her apartment bottomless, showing off her super-fluffy muff and awesome ass galore.*

See Her Naked In:

Agents Secrets (2004) Breasts
Astérix & Obélix: Mission Cléopâtre (2002) LB, Buns
Irréversible (2002) FFN, Buns
The Brotherhood of the Wolf (2001) Breasts, Buns
Under Suspicion (2000) Breasts, Buns
Malèna (2000) Breasts, Buns
L'Ultimo Capodanno (1998) Breasts, Bush, Buns
Mauvais Genre (1997) Breasts
Dracula (1992) Breasts
Ostinato Destino (1992) Breasts
La Riffa (1991) Breasts, Buns

Brenda Benet

Born: August 14, 1945
Hollywood, California
Died: April 7, 1982
Skin-O-Meter: Brief Nudity

Brenda Benet was born in Hollywood and lived a Tinseltown tragedy that had her reach the greatest peaks and fall to the deepest valleys before she ended her life in 1982. She always knew she wanted to be a performer, and her mom helped her pay for dance lessons at an early age by taking on extra work. The lessons paid off, because Brenda fox-trotted into the business with some of the shapeliest gams in town. At the beginning of her career, she played bouffant-brunette beauties, nice girls, but she is best known for her villainous portrayal of Lee Dumonde on the daytime soap *Days of Our Lives*. But at Skin Central she is fondle-y remembered for her part in the first installment of the *Walking Tall*

(1973) series. Brenda played the stereotypical hooker-with-a-heart-of-gold character, and, like many mams before her, she flashed her set in front of a trailer home. Home is where the heart-on is. But years later, after a painful divorce and losing her only son at an early age to a mysterious illness, Brenda had about all she could take and took her own life.

SKIN-fining Moment:

Walking Tall (1:27) *Brenda bares a fleeting hint of tit when she comes a-runnin' out of her trailer. Wheeeee!*

See Her Naked In:

Walking Tall (1973) Breasts

Annette Bening

Born: May 29, 1958
Topeka, Kansas
Skin-O-Meter: Great Nudity

It took a special woman to wrap the bonds of matrimony around über-bachelor Warren Beatty. It took a fearless woman of tough intelligence and erotic-fueled radiance. It took a million-dollar mug and a priceless, matched set of tits and ass. It took Annette Bening, and in the process of taking Beatty, Annette took the rest of us too. A brief glimpse of Warren's future seat of affections was afforded as Annette squirmed ass-out across a bed in the costume drama *Valmont* (1989). The true preview of Bening's muy bien body of work came during *The Grifters* (1990). Often wearing nothing more than a crazy gleam in her eyes, Annette indulged in more bed-top squirming, was carried like a sack of stripped potatoes, posed totally reviewed from the standing rear, and dared to reveal that the carpet did not match the drapes. Annette takes the cake, wedding or otherwise.

SKIN-fining Moment:

The Grifters (0:36) *In bed, Ms. Bening bares the body—with boobs, bum, and a touch of dark, dimly lit bush to boot—that finally bested Warren Beatty.*

See Her Naked In:

The Grifters (1990) FFN, Buns
Valmont (1989) Buns

Wendy Benson-Landes

Born: July 13, 1975
Scotland, UK
Skin-O-Meter: Brief Nudity

Like so many pretty girls before her, Wendy Benson-Landes first hooked audiences through guest spots on TV shows such as *Beverly Hills, 90210*. She then made a predictable move into the world of daytime soaps on *As the World Turns*, where the women are sexy but skinless. The small-breasted cutie remained a staple of forgettable boob-tube ventures such as *Muscle*, *Secret Service Guy*, and the *Married . . . with Children* rip-off *Unhappily Ever After*. When none of those sent her into the superstar realm, she had time to test the waters on the big screen. Here her success rate is not much higher, unless you factor in nudity. In *Luck of the Draw* (2000), Wendy fulfilled the promise that her little tits only teased at on TV. She starred opposite Dennis Hopper and Michael Madsen and in a brief scene reveals a part of her petite pair. Why is it that old crusts like these guys always get the hotties to undress for them?

SKIN-fining Moment:

Luck of the Draw (1:01) *Wendy gets it on with James Marshall and we all get a gander at her left Benson.*

See Her Naked In:

Luck of the Draw (2000) LB

Barbi Benton

Born: January 28, 1950
Sacramento, California
Skin-O-Meter: Great Nudity

Born Barbara Klein, bodacious Barbi Benton—not to be confused with Robbie Benson—famously lived with *Playboy* publisher Hugh Hefner from 1969 to 1976. Those swinging years must have well prepared her for the damsel-in-kinky-distress role of Codille in the noble-yet-horny savage classic *Deathstalker* (1984). Barbi plays a fallen princess who resorts to turning tricks to regain her rightful place on the throne. In real life, she'd probably only have to give Hef a call. Not just another pretty chest—uh, I mean face—Barbi recorded over a dozen albums of original music in the '70s and regularly had hits on the country charts.

SKIN-fining Moment:

Hospital Massacre (0:32) *Topless Barbi shows her up-top doll parts while being examined by a doctor.*

See Her Naked In:

Deathstalker (1984) Breasts
Hospital Massacre (1981) Breasts

Jayne Bentzen

Born: August 8, 1955
Evansville, Indiana
Skin-O-Meter: Brief Nudity

Native Hoosier Jayne Bentzen has hooters to howl at, and she knows how to use them. The pretty brunette had a handful of sweater getters that helped get her noticed on the boob tube. She began her career with a sexy stint in the soaps, first on *One Life to Live* and then a longer turn on *The Edge of Night*. She took her bulbous pair to the big screen in *Blood Rage* (1983) but never got Mr. Skin's blood up due to her non-skin

scenes. But that was to change, and with a bang, in her next role on the silver screen. In *A Breed Apart* (1984), she certainly was. Not only are her flopping floppers out for some play, but she even flashes her dark, entangled secret garden while in bed with some lucky fellow. Sadly, it was her one and only shot at nudity and her last appearance in filmdom. Where are you, sweet Jayne?

SKIN-fining Moment:

A Breed Apart (0:56) *Breasts and side nudity talking in bed with Powers Boothe then a full-frontal view when she gets up to get dressed.*

See Her Naked In:

A Breed Apart (1984) FFN

Julie Benz

Born: May 1, 1975
Pittsburgh, Pennsylvania
Skin-O-Meter: Great Nudity

Juicy Julie Benz started ice skating at age three and even competed in the 1988 U.S. Championships in junior ice dancing. So the mystery of where she got those killer legs is solved. When a bad stress fracture ended her ice-skating career at fourteen, Julie threw herself into acting—and landed a triple Lutz in the heat department. Her first speaking role came in the Dario Argento/George Romero co-directed horror flick *Due Occhi Diabolici* (1990) playing opposite Harvey Kietel. A year later she turned up on the short-lived sitcom *Hi Honey, I'm Home*—a phrase every man would love to utter looking into Julie's, uh, face after a hard day of, uh, work. Julie auditioned for the lead in the series *Buffy the Vampire Slayer* (1997). She didn't get the part, but she was cast as Buffy's mortal enemy, Darla, and even reprised the role on the *Angel* spinoff. The undead never tasted so good! On the big screen, Julie was foxy as Marcie "Foxy" Fox in *Jawbreaker* (1999) opposite fellow homicidal hottie Rose McGowan, but for the best of this Benz's hood ornaments, don't miss her sweat-soaked gear-shift ride in *Darkdrive* (1996).

SKIN-fining Moment:

Darkdrive (1:08) *Breasts and buns while she's shagging Matthew Stolopin.*

See Her Naked In:

Darkdrive (1996) Breasts, Buns

Marisa Berenson

Born: February 15, 1946
New York, New York
Skin-O-Meter: Great Nudity

After several years strutting down the catwalk, lissome, green-eyed Marisa Berenson, like so many other internationally famous models, decided to immortalize her luscious figure on the celluloid frames of cinematic reels. After her debut in the Italian picture *Morte a Venezia* (1971), she landed her big break as the prime foil to Liza Minnelli in *Cabaret* (1972). Sadly, in a tale of Berlin at its most de-cadent, Marisa remained fully clothed. That would change. Marisa's first skinful turn was in Stanley Kubrick's period drama *Barry Lyndon* (1975), in which she soaks her furriness in an old-fashioned tub with very transparent water. She was covered by a frilly, lightweight nightie, but it did little to conceal what was submerged— and even her titty-bitties peeked out. Those small wonders also made a splash in *Sex on the Run* (1979). She has since gone on to show those little lovelies again in *S.O.B.* (1981), *Tête dans le sac* (1984), and *Hemingway* (1988), though the scenes are brief. Small exposure of her petite pleasure equals a big-time turn on!

SKIN-fining Moment:

S.O.B. (1:20) *You'll enjoy this lengthy visit with Berenson's B-cups as she kicks back in bed.*

See Her Naked In:

Tête dans le sac (1984) Breasts
S.O.B. (1981) Breasts
Sex on the Run (1979) RB
Barry Lyndon (1975) Bush

TeleVisions:

Hemingway RB

Candice Bergen

Born: May 9, 1946
Beverly Hills, California
Skin-O-Meter: Great Nudity

Although she spent her formative years overshadowed by a wooden dummy, Candice Bergen's star has risen to outshine both that of her father, ventriloquist Edgar Bergen, and his lacquered collaborator, Charlie McCarthy. Her fair Irish complexion and innate sense of grace seem distinctly European, but Candice was born in the USA's own little Beverly Hills. Considering her hometown, her father's profession, her regally borne beauty, and her seemingly effortless mastery of the acting craft, it was inevitable that young Ms. Bergen should gravitate toward show business. The future Oscar nominee and *Murphy Brown*-to-be showed the most of her breast business in *A Night Full of Rain* (1978). How is it possible that her bed-sharing costar is asleep there beside her? Is he made out of wood like Charlie McCarthy?

SKIN-fining Moment:

A Night Full of Rain (1:04) *Candice shows her right headlight in a car with Giancarlo Giannini*

See Her Naked In:

Starting Over (1979) LB
A Night Full of Rain (1978) RB

Soldier Blue (1970) Buns
The Magus (1968) Body Double—LB

Senta Berger

Born: May 13, 1941
Vienna, Austria
Skin-O-Meter: Hall of Fame

A big, brassy blonde with big, classy breasts, Senta Berger has been a naked treasure of European skinema since 1957. Austrian-born Senta seems to have been bred specifically for a long career as a sex goddess. From her earliest appearances on the big screen, the amazing Berger exuded the stunningly naïve and natural sensuality of a young Brigitte Bardot. As Senta aged, her appeal matured right along with her, rivaling that of Sophia Loren. It's not often that a heart-rending nymph grows to be such a loin-stirring matron. In *Scharf aufs Leben* (2000), Berger's fifty-nine-year-old flotation devices steam a bathtub scene by bobbing at the waterline and hinting at what lies beneath the surface. Take a trip to the foreign-film aisle and dive into any one of Senta's many revealing roles. Her buns in particular are a deep-dish asset.

SKIN-fining Moment:

When Women Had Tails (0:22) *A glimpse of tit and some nice shots of Senta's seatage when the Neanderthal thugs remove her from a trap and carry her home. Naturally, they want to eat her . . . But not in the way you'll want to.*

See Her Naked In:

Scharf aufs Leben (2000) Breasts
Una Donna di Seconda Mano (1977)
Cross of Iron (1977) Buns
Ritratto di Borghesia in Nero (1977) RB
MitGift (1976) Buns
La Padrona è Servita (1976) Breasts, Buns
L'Uomo Senza Memoria (1974) RB, Buns

Di Mamma non ce n'è una Sola (1974)
Breasts, Buns
L'Amante Dell'orsa Maggiore (1972) Bush,
Buns
When Women Lost Their Tails (1971) Buns
Roma Bene (1971) Buns
When Women Had Tails (1970) Breasts, Buns

TeleVisions:

Die Schnelle Gerdi RB

Emily Bergl

Born: April 25, 1975
Milton Keynes, Buckinghamshire,
England, UK
Skin-O-Meter: Brief Nudity

Although Emily Bergl was born in England, this British Tea & A was raised in the Chicago suburb of Glenview, which is why American audiences have gotten to ogle the pixie darling in homegrown productions. She debuted with a bang, taking the lead as the feisty little redhead in *The Rage: Carrie 2* (1999). As Rachel, she had telekinetic powers and an earthbound beauty that was riveting to watch. The movie garnered attention for the young actress, and she subsequently landed a part opposite Jeff Daniels in *Chasing Sleep* (2000), which featured her first ever foray into the wonderful world of skin. In it, she appeared topless during a scene with the older actor, who must have a very good agent to land such a lucky role. She's since appeared on TV's *Gilmore Girls* and Steven Spielberg's Sci-Fi Channel mini-series *Taken* (2002), which has the lithe cutie naked once more, though all her good parts are tastefully obscured. Here's to dining on Emily's moist bits in all their juicy glory soon.

SKIN-fining Moment:

Chasing Sleep (1:20) *Jeff Daniels assists Emily in the removal of her bra, freeing up both of her bare Bergls.*

See Her Naked In:

Chasing Sleep (2000) Breasts

Jaime Bergman

Born: September 23, 1975
Salt Lake City, Utah
Skin-O-Meter: Brief Nudity

Blonde Jaime Bergman first raised eyebrows (and other appendages) when she graced the pages of *Playboy* as the mag's 45th Anniversary Playmate. She went on to star in several skintillating videos for the Bunny, such as *Playboy: Club Lingerie*, in which the blessed Bergman boobs stood out front and center. Mainstream filmdom has not been as titillating. There's not a bit of skin in her bit parts in *Any Given Sunday* (1999) or *Gone in 60 Seconds* (2000). But Jaime is arousing as the bouncing B.J. Cummings on the Howard Stern-produced must-sleaze TV *Son of the Beach*. Finally, in *DarkWolf* (2003), we get to howl at her hooters, although they're in a dark scene.

SKIN-fining Moment:

DarkWolf (0:39) *Brief bloody boob as she gets mauled by a werewolf.*

See Her Naked In:

DarkWolf (2003) Breasts
Numerous Playboy Videos

Sandahl Bergman

Born: November 14, 1951
Kansas City, Missouri
Skin-O-Meter: Great Nudity

Statuesque, Nordically striking blonde Sandahl Bergman almost looks like the athletic, kick-ass-now, take-names-later little sister of the St. Pauli Girl. She started out as a Broadway dancer whom Bob Fosse cast as Cassie in the original production of *A Chorus Line*. Fosse later put his spotlights on her

headlights in the legendary "topless" number in the big-screen production of *All That Jazz* (1979). From that point on, Sandahl went mythological on our ass. She took film roles such as Muse 1 in *Xanadu* (1980), Valeria in *Conan the Barbarian* (1982), Queen Gedren in *Red Sonja* (1985), the title character in the remake of *She* (1985), and Valkyrie in the made-for-TV William Shatner-sci-fi-psycho-shoot-'em-up *TekWar: TekJustice* (1994). Sandahl is at her best whenever she gets to kick some ass, as she does in the greensploitation flick *Hell Comes to Frogtown* (1987).

SKIN-fining Moment:

All That Jazz (0:49) *Sandahl shows some shirt-free skinbags while performing a dairylicious dance number on a scaffold.*

See Her Naked In:

Lipstick Camera (1994) Buns
Possessed By the Night (1994) Breasts, Buns
Loving Lulu (1993) Breasts, Buns
She (1985) Breasts
Conan the Barbarian (1982) LB
All That Jazz (1979) Breasts, Thong

Elizabeth Berkley

Born: July 28, 1972
Farmington Hills, Michigan
Skin-O-Meter: Hall of Fame

Hollywood has been unkind to lithe and lissome Elizabeth Berkley. The movie industry's seeming indifference to this mesmerizing, sexy creature can be the result of nothing other than blind jealousy. How else can the industry fail to see the dedication to craft and character exhibited by Elizabeth in the seminal stripper-noir masterpiece *Showgirls* (1995)? It's not like Berkley hid anything from view. She exposed her all, engaging in rampant lesbianism, hot-tub trysts, floor dances, table dances,

YOU GO, GIRL! ELIZABETH BERKLEY IN *SHOWGIRLS.*

pole dances, and lap dances, all in an almost perfect state of muff-thrusting undress. Her entire wardrobe must have cost about sixteen dollars, but the results were worth millions of bucks. Elizabeth had been a steady-working actress prior to *Showgirls*, putting in four years on *Saved by the Bell*, for Christ's sake. Afterward? Precious little, although she did reappear front and rear in Oliver Stone's *Any Given Sunday* (1999). Why only one day of Berkley fun, eh?

SKIN-fining Moment:

Showgirls (0:26) *The Mother of All Lapdance Scenes! Elizabeth rides the zipper of Kyle MacLachlan while Gina Gershon grabs an eyeful nearby. We see Liz's luscious little titlets, taut tail, and even her bleached-blonde bush as she grinds a geyser out of Kyle's clothed crotch.*

See Her Naked In:

Any Given Sunday (1999) Breasts, Thong
Showgirls (1995) FFN, Buns

Crystal Bernard

Born: September 30, 1961
Garland, Texas
Skin-O-Meter: Never Nude

Shaggy from *Scooby Doo*—not hot. Shaggy-haired hottie behind the Sandpiper Air lunch counter—smokin'. Crystal Bernard made her show-biz debut singing at religious revivals with her daddy dearest in the '70s, but it was her role as a bikini babe in *Slumber Party Massacre II* (1987) that has us shouting hallelujah! While this box-office bomb didn't play out on the big screen, Crystal's teeny-weeny pink bikini makes it a worthy $1.99 rental. It was her eight-year gig as the spitfire cellist/counter queen on the airport sitcom *Wings*, however, that made her career take flight. And while cutie Crystal has yet to flash us the flesh, with *Wings* no longer in the late-night rerun circuit, we're hoping she makes a skintillating return to acting tout suite.

SKIN-fining Moment:

Slumber Party Massacre II (0:32) *You'll burn hard as Ms. Bernard displays her bikini-clad water-Wings during a poolside romp.*

Sue Bernard

Born: February 11, 1948
Los Angeles, California
Skin-O-Meter: Brief Nudity

Sue Bernard was almost lost to us because of the carnage of WWII. No, she isn't that old, but her father was a Nazi Holocaust survivor. He, Bruno Bernard, made a pretty big name for himself in Hollywood as a famous glamour photographer to the stars. Sue's mom, Ruth Brand, was a stage actress and director. In other words, Sue was genetically predisposed to be a precocious talent. And, oh, she is. Russ Meyer certainly thought she had the goods (and a goodly pair they are) to be in his *Faster Pussycat, Kill! Kill!* (1966). Instead of following Meyer's mam muse, Sue landed a role on the more staid but sexy-in-its-own-way soap opera *General Hospital*. She's certainly good for what ails you, but she was even better when she returned to the silver screen to sever her ties with her top. That first exposure occurred in *The Witching* (1972), in which she talks on the phone with her boobs on the line. That's a nice connection. Sue followed that up with *The Killing Kind* (1973), and her body is a killer. But after *Teenager* (1974), which showed no adolescent buds, she retired to handle her father's legacy . . . lucky guy.

SKIN-fining Moment:

The Killing Kind (0:00) *Sue's yaboos spill into view as some baddies decide to throw a surprise gang-bang.*

See Her Naked In:

The Killing Kind (1973) Breasts
The Witching (1972) Breasts

Sandra Bernhard

Born: June 6, 1955
Flint, Michigan
Skin-O-Meter: Great Nudity

Sandra Bernhard debuted as Girl Nut in *Cheech & Chong's Nice Dreams* (1981), but she became famous by appearing in a pair of grandma panties and a big white bra with Jerry Lewis in *The King of Comedy* (1983). She's got a nose that can open a bottle but a body that opens the mind to the dirtiest booty-pleasing fantasies. All slinky, with little, pointy tits and a round, juicy bubble of a butt, Sandra's comedy, her short and ugly stint as Madonna's girl-toy, and a taste for lesbianism have made her an icon to straight and gay males alike. She's not shy about her body, as evident in *Sandra After Dark* (1992) and *Dallas Doll* (1995). But to really rev up your motor, check out her tasseled pasties and American-flag G-string bump-and-grind to Prince's "Little Red Corvette" in *Without You I'm Nothing* (1990).

SKIN-fining Moment:

Without You I'm Nothing (1:20)
Sandra bumps and grinds on a nightclub stage in a pair of pasties and microscopic thong. Guaranteed to tickle your funny baner.

See Her Naked In:

Dallas Doll (1994) Breasts
Sandra After Dark (1992) Breasts, Buns
Without You I'm Nothing (1990) Thong

Elizabeth Berridge

Born: May 2, 1962
Westchester, New York
Skin-O-Meter: Great Nudity

Elizabeth Berridge couldn't get arrested until she holstered her big guns as a frumpy, no-nonsense police officer on the one-time hit *The John Larroquette Show*. But underneath that very non-sexy uniform lies one hot mama. Since her acting debut in *Natural Enemies* (1979), Elizabeth has been one busy beaver. She has worked pretty much nonstop, landing a recurring role on the hit TV series *Texas* and roles in made-for-TV movies such as *Silence of the Heart* (1984). But it's her theatrical endeavors that make Elizabeth famous at Skin Central, like her supporting role in *Amadeus* (1984). In the Director's Cut, she scampers about in nothing but a powdered wig and skirt, with her huge hooters beating her chest like kettledrums. Rock me, Amadeus! That wasn't the first time she pulled out her funbags. Check out *The Funhouse* (1981) for an eyeful of Elizabeth's oversized talents. She's been relatively quiet as of late, her biggest role being an uncredited Hooter in Bar from *Payback* (1999). To Mr. Skin, though, that's a step in the right direction.

SKIN-fining Moment:

The Funhouse (0:05) *Nude floppers bopping, Liz eases in the shower and gets assualted with a long appendage. OK, it's just a fake knife, but still.*

See Her Naked In:

Amadeus (1984) Breasts
The Funhouse (1981) Breasts

Halle Berry

Born: August 14, 1966
Cleveland, Ohio
Skin-O-Meter: Great Nudity

Halle Berry started out on the beauty pageant circuit, representing

---

MR. SKIN'S TOP TEN

Best Nudity by an Academy Award Winner
. . . I'd like to thank the Anatomy

10. **Maggie Smith**
    —*California Suite* 1978

9. **Helen Hunt**
   —*As Good as it Gets* 1997

8. **Faye Dunaway**
   —*Network* 1976

7. **Jessica Lange**
   —*Blue Sky* 1994

6. **Charlize Theron**
   —*Monster* 2003

5. **Glenda Jackson**
   —*A Woman in Love* 1970

4. **Jane Fonda**
   —*Klute* 1971/*Coming Home* 1978

3. **Mary Steenburgen**
   —*Melvin and Howard* 1980

2. **Holly Hunter**
   —*The Piano* 1993

1. **Halle Berry**
   —*Monster's Ball* 2001

Ohio in the Miss USA contest. She may have been runner-up in that contest, but Mother Nature blessed her with some incredibly winning booby prizes. Halle portrayed weather-controlling mutant Storm in *X-Men* (2000) and *X2* (2003), in which she lives up to her billing as every meteorologist's worst nightmare—and Mr. Skin's wettest dream! She scored an Oscar for her performance in *Monster's Ball* (2001), which included an all-time award-worthy sex scene wherein Billy Bob Thornton's character did a racist 180 once he got a taste of Halle's soul food. Halle had fans polishing their own trophies that same year when she tanned topless in *Swordfish* (2001).

SKIN-fining Moment:

Swordfish (0:38) *Halle Berry got herself a massive bonus paycheck by delivering her dark chest-berries for six sexy seconds here. And they were worth every cent.*

See Her Naked In:

Swordfish (2001) Breasts
Monster's Ball (2001) Breasts, Bush, Buns
Introducing Dorothy Dandridge (1999) Nip Slip RB, Buns

Bibi Besch

Born: February 1, 1942
Vienna, Austria
Died: September 7, 1996
Skin-O-Meter: Brief Nudity

Bibi Besch, who is the progeny of noted Austrian actress Gusti Huber, started her career far from her native land. In 1966 Americans got to drool over beautiful Bibi when she moved to the hallowed hills of Hollywood for a role on the hit series *The Secret Storm*. She subsequently became one of TV's most recognizable character actresses with recurring parts on such series as *Falcon Crest*, *Somerset*, and *Love is a Many Splendored Thing*.

You can catch the blonde bombshell on many guest spots on series ranging from *ER* to *Coach*. All that TV work doesn't leave much time for more skinematic endeavors, but Bibi still managed to pull a part as William Shatner's squeeze in *Star Trek II: The Wrath of Khan* (1982), as well as roles in *Steel Magnolias* (1989) and *Tremors* (1990). The horror flick *The Beast Within* (1982) starts off great, with Bibi putting her boobies on full display whilst being raped by the "beast." Judging by her incredibly erect meat bullets, it was either incredibly cold on the set, or Bibi had a serious thing for bestiality.

SKIN-fining Moment:

The Beast Within (0:06) *The Beast is one horny devil, and he shreds Ms. Besch's shirt so we can see her Bibis.*

See Her Naked In:

The Beast Within (1982) Breasts

Martine Beswicke

Born: September 26, 1941
Port Antonio, Jamaica
Skin-O-Meter: Great Nudity

Martine Beswicke used her natural talents to stir James Bond's martini. She debuted as one of the dancing girls in the credits of *Dr. No* (1962), followed that with an actual role in *From Russia with Love* (1963), and continued on to *Thunderball* (1965). From secret agents the buxom brunette beauty went primeval with roles in *One Million Years B.C.* (1966) and *Prehistoric Women* (1967). That led to B-movie obscurity until the late '80s, when Martine landed roles on both *Days of Our Lives* and the prime-time soap *Falcon Crest*. Magnificent Martine has been absent from the entertainment industry since 1995, but she left us with some great mammaries. Martine took what may have been the most important role of the '80s as Xaviera Hollander herself in *The Happy Hooker Goes Hollywood* (1980), which called for a great deal of boobage, and Martine delivered with glee. It wasn't her sole skin, of course. You can catch Martine feeling herself up in *Dr. Jekyll and Sister Hyde* (1971). It's what any brainiac nerd-boy scientist would do if suddenly blessed with Martine's luscious rack.

SKIN-fining Moment:

The Happy Hooker Goes Hollywood (0:25) *Buns jumping in pool then breasts while rubbing oil on Adam West . . . Adam West?!?!*

See Her Naked In:

The Happy Hooker Goes Hollywood (1980) Breasts, Buns
Ultimo Tango a Zagarolo (1973) Breasts
Dr. Jekyll and Sister Hyde (1971) Breasts, Buns

Frida Betrani

Canada
Skin-O-Meter: Brief Nudity

Brunette cutie Frida Betrani, with the flip hairdo that makes guys flip, is yet another hottie out of Canada who threatens to melt its frozen tundra. She first heated up the screen in the early '90s starring on the Great White North TV series *Northwood*, which left viewers with some wood down south. After that Hollywood called and Frida came— as did audiences who caught her carnal delights in the made-for-TV movie *Aftershock: Earthquake in New York* (1999), in which she made the earth move, and the feature *Prozac Nation* (2001), featuring a bust-out performance by Christina Ricci. Frida came in from the cold and took off her top in *Last Wedding* (2001). She made it a lust wedding while trying on her gown and exposing her nuptials. Forget the bride, here comes the wedding party!

SKIN-fining Moment:

Last Wedding (0:23) *Mouth-watering matrimonial mams as she drops the top of her wedding dress, then stuffs her lusciousness into a bra.*

See Her Naked In:

Last Wedding (2001) Breasts

Angela Bettis

Born: January 9, 1975
Austin, Texas
Skin-O-Meter: Brief Nudity

It took the nuthouse sleeper *Girl, Interrupted* (1999) to bring the kooky come-on Angela Bettis to sinema fans' attention. But Mr. Skin has been following the svelte sway of arousing Angela since the mid '90s when she first bloomed in TV guest spots on *Sliders* and *Touched By an Angel*. Angela is definitely touched, but in a way that makes men everywhere want to touch her. Her strange star is rising in the new millennium, both on TV with the remake of *Carrie* (2002) and in theatricals such as *Bless the Child* (2000), *Perfume* (2001), and *May* (2002), which is like Frankenstein from a cracked-chick's perspective. It's a safe Bettis that Angela's stellar rise will continue—and Mr. Skin will be raising his flesh telescope to watch.

SKIN-fining Moment:

The Last Best Sunday (1:10) *Ample nubbins and side nudity when Angela removes her top and pops onto her guy. Ooh yeah, she likes that. Mmm-hmm.*

See Her Naked In:

The Last Best Sunday (1999) Breasts

Leslie Bibb

Born: November 17, 1974
Bismarck, North Dakota
Skin-O-Meter: Never Nude

Leslie Bibb got her start from the wholesome Oprah Winfrey by winning a model search on the famous host's talk show, which was judged by John Casablanca, Naomi Campbell, Linda Evangelista, and Iman, and worked for Elite Models. Oprah has compelled the young actress to remain chaste as far as her skin is concerned. Although she appeared in *Private Parts* (1997) and *Touch Me* (1997), which both imply something nasty, she kept hers covered. She's since appeared on the hit TV series *Popular* and *ER*. Is there a doctor in the house? Because Mr. Skin is going to have a heart-on attack if Leslie doesn't drop her Bibb soon.

SKIN-fining Moment:

Line of Fire "Undercover Angel" (2003) *Les is more as she takes off her shirt and entices a scary old prick in a hotel room with her taut, black-bra-clad physique.*

Jessica Biel

Born: March 3, 1982
Ely, Minnesota
Skin-O-Meter: Never Nude

Ever fall under the spell of a girl who is so hot that even standing hip cocked in an old T-shirt and cut-off blue jeans her exquisitely formed chair cheeks and her perfectly thrusting, ever-so-slightly swaying top tier are impossible to look away from? Even when busted for staring too hard by her sly, knowing eyes and given the brush off by her curling, sex-imp nose and grin, still it is impossible to look away. She is a torturer, and she knows she causes pain, and she takes pleasure in the erotic distress that dogs her every movement. She is Jessica Biel, and to glimpse her is the first step on the road to agony and madness. Knowing all of this, aware also that she has never gone more bare than bikini or underwear, still she must be loved. Why is it that we are so weak, and that it feels so good to be that way?

SKIN-fining Moment:

Summer Catch (0:08) *Jessica rises up out of a swimming pool and proves how powerfully she fills up a bikini to the slackjawed awe of Freddy Prinze Jr. For once you'll wish you were him.*

Jennifer Billingsley

Honolulu, Hawaii
Skin-O-Meter: Brief Nudity

The 1960s were a groovy time for cool chicks who could hang loose and not freak out. Few came cooler and hung looser than hippie-dippy blonde sex kitty Jennifer Billingsley. Relying on little more than a vixen-next-door face, a wild mane of streaky blonde hair, a hip and with-it swagger to the swivel of her hips whenever she walked or simply stood still, and a pair of publicly displayed love lumps, Jennifer coasted to the forefront of the counterculture. After warm-up appearances in *Lady in a Cage* (1964), *The Young Lovers* (1964), and *The Spy with My Face* (1965), boss babe Billingsley found herself on the back of a motorcycle, clutching the waist of football hipster Joe Namath. The movie is *C.C. and Company* (1970). The attractions are chi-chis and skinny dipping.

SKIN-fining Moment

C.C. and Company (0:14) *Joe Namath and his biker buddies take in the topless show Jennifer's putting on in a pond.*

See Her Naked In:

C.C. and Company (1970) Breasts

Traci Bingham

Born: January 13, 1968
Cambridge, Massachusettes
Skin-O-Meter: Great Nudity

Traci Bingham, like so many other pinup queens of the '90s, rode the tidal wave known as *Baywatch* toward a sunny career as a 21st-century sex goddess. So far, Traci's stairway to hottie heaven has led to a gig as a faux reporter on the Comedy Central series *BattleBots*, but there are bigger things in store for this ebony beauty. Two of those bigger things appeared on the HBO series *Dream On*, which offered the first (but not last!) peek at those tasty chocolate milk sacks. She followed up her tawdry TV appearance with a bit part as a stripper in the horror flick *Demon Knight* (1995). But Traci's tops are topped in her incredible full-frontal scenes in the plotless, purely-for-skintertainment-value video *Exposed Girls of Baywatch* (1996). The 36-22-32 bosomy knockout proves that black is indeed beautiful.

SKIN-fining Moment:

Demon Knight (1:02) *Good ol' Traci. Never lets ya down. In this boobiful dream sequence, she's wearing yellow bikini bottoms and says, "Long hard one." Indeed, Traci.*

See Her Naked In:

Exposed Girls of Baywatch (1996) Breasts, Bush, Buns
The Darker Image Swimsuit Calendar (1996) Thong
Demon Knight (1995) Breasts

Juliette Binoche

Born: March 9, 1964
Paris, France
Skin-O-Meter: Hall of Fame

Credit is due to the French for their "laissez-faire" attitude, which distinguished by her refined surface perfection and smoldering erotic core. A natural magnet for the eyes of any man with a pulse, Bisset was typecast as the mesmerizing knockout Miss Goodthighs in the James Bond parody *Casino Royale* (1967). Bisset's piercing sea-green eyes and popping now-you-see-me nipples caused their most-widespread stir in the oceangoing thriller *The Deep* (1977). Jacqueline spends almost the entire movie underwater or just out of the drink, her torso encased in a flimsy, clinging white T-shirt. The dramatic tension of the film derives from the constant threat of the male divers becoming so distracted by the

Bisset high beams that they unwittingly take several deep breaths of saltwater and die.

SKIN-fining Moment:

The Deep (0:01) *All wet T-shirt scenes answer to this! Jackie emerges from the deep blue see and fills the screen with her sopping-wet, see-through tee. Deeply delicious!*

See Her Naked In:

High Season (1987) Breasts
Famous T&A (1982) Breasts
La Donna della domenica (1976) Breasts, Buns
The Mephisto Waltz (1971) Breasts
Secrets (1971) Breasts, Bush, Buns
The Grasshopper (1970) Thong
The First Time (1969) RB

Josie Bissett

Born: October 5, 1970
Seattle, Washington
Skin-O-Meter: Great Nudity

One of the great things about TV shows like *Melrose Place* is that the viewer can satisfy his girlfriend by agreeing to sit quietly through them and satisfy himself by scouting out sweet-faced, ripe-bodied, lower-tier actresses who might have flashes of skin fame in their futures or pasts. One such scoutable sexpot is finely featured, subtly carnal creature Josie Bissett, who played the vulnerable and alluring Jane Mancini on *Melrose* from 1992 to 1999. Something about Bissett's air of bruised sensuality hinted at a brush with wanton exhibitionism in years gone by. A little skin search and the hunch pays off. On the home front, *Hitcher in the Dark* (1989) sheds all manner of light on Bissett's cupcake breasts and full-bodied nudity, front and rear end. *Hitcher*'s only disappointment is no pubic access. For that treat, track down the Italian *Desideri* (1990). "Josie" is Latin for desire.

SKIN-fining Moment:

Desideri (0:28) *Josie shows her chest-posies and blooming buttocks in a long bedroom love scene.*

See Her Naked In:

All-American Murder (1992) Breasts, Buns
Desideri (1990) Breasts, Buns
Hitcher in the Dark (1989) Breasts, Buns

Karen Black

Born: July 1, 1942
Park Ridge, Illinois
Skin-O-Meter: Great Nudity

The 1960s was a revolutionary decade led by brave, freaky-deaky hippie chicks who waved their lung flesh, their bushes, and their peace-loving buttocks from drive-in screens nationwide. Brunette with a boldly sexual face and fiercely dedicated to liberating her breasts and ass from bra and panties, Karen Black started out at the top of the countercultural muff heap. She first stroked the Zeitgeist as a spacy party chick in the seminal *Easy Rider* (1969). Karen played one of Jack Nicholson's simpler pieces in *Five Easy Pieces* (1970), a film in which Black seemed to be always crouched atop a bathroom sink while in various negligees. Karen's unadulterated nips started popping out in *Drive, He Said* (1972) and *Cisco Pike* (1972). By the time *Killing Heat* (1981) rolled around, the life-long bohemian had advanced to standing with her bush pushed forward while she poured water over her head. The '60s may be gone, but the revolution lingers on.

SKIN-fining Moment:

Killing Heat (0:42) *Karen's so hot, she can't help but dump cold water all over her fiery full-frontal nudity.*

See Her Naked In:

Miss Right (1987) Breasts
Can She Bake a Cherry Pie? (1983) LB

Killing Heat (1981) FFN
Separate Ways (1981) Breasts
In Praise of Older Women (1978) Breasts
The Day of the Locust (1975) RB, Bush
The Pyx (1973) Body Double—Buns
Drive, He Said (1972) Breasts
Cisco Pike (1972) Breasts

Honor Blackman

Born: December 12, 1927
London, England, UK
Skin-O-Meter: Great Nudity

Honor Blackman is a top-heavy English tart who has made a career dominating men—and we love it! She's best known as the provocatively named Pussy Galore in *Goldfinger* (1964) and as ass-beating, leather-bound,

---

MR. SKIN'S TOP TEN

Best Nudity Over 50
. . . Senior titi-zens

10. Mamie Van Doren
    —*Slackers* 2002

9. Brenda Vaccaro
   —*Sonny* 2002

8. Patti Lupone
   —*Summer of Sam* 1999

7. Helen Mirren
   —*The Roman Spring of Mrs. Stone* 2003

6. Barbara Hershey
   —*Drowning on Dry Land* 1999

5. Diane Keaton
   —*Something's Gotta Give* 2003

4. Ellen Burstyn
   —*The Ambassador* 1984

3. Deanna Lund
   —*Roots of Evil* 1992

2. Catherine Deneuve
   —*Pola X* 1999

1. **Honor Blackman**
   —*Age of Innocence* 1977

---

boobalicious Cathy Gale on the ever-popular series *The Avengers*. Age hasn't slowed down this big mammy; her scene-stealing role in *Bridget Jones's Diary* (2001) made audiences almost forget the curvaceous treats offered by a weighty Renée Zellweger. Perhaps the most notable facet of Honor's career, though, is that even as an A-list act-chest, she still took revolutionary roles that required a bit of skin. OK, they're tame by our jaded standards, but at the time they were torrid and risky for an established hottie. Honor scoffed at uptight mores and pulled out her enormous ta-tas for films such as *Kampf um Rom I* (1968) and *The Virgin and the Gypsy* (1970). Her best flesh was as a mature piece of ass in *Age of Innocence* (1977). She was fifty years old, and her funbags swung low like sweet chariots. But word of Honor, she's still got it.

SKIN-fining Moment:

Age of Innocence (0:15) *Ms. Blackman honors us with a lovely look at her amazingly ample (and fifty-year-old) hooters as she dances around her bedroom.*

See Her Naked In:

Age of Innocence (1977) Breasts
The Virgin and the Gypsy (1970) Buns
Kampf um Rom I (1968) Breasts

Linda Blair

Born: January 22, 1959
St. Louis, Missouri
Skin-O-Meter: Hall of Fame

After a literally head-turning theatrical debut as the Satan-filled Regan in *The Exorcist* (1973), Linda Blair became a staple of deliciously sleazy '70s TV movies such as *Sweet Hostage* (1975) and *Born Innocent* (1974) then went on to put the boob in '80s B-pictures. She jiggled her juggles with the best of them in trash classics such as *Chained Heat*

(1983), her first but not last titty flash. The breast of times followed in *Savage Streets* (1984), *Night Patrol* (1984), *Bedroom Eyes II* (1990), and *Fatal Bond* (1992). All that hard work makes a girl need to hit the showers: Check out Linda's and her friend's wet jugs in *Red Heat* (1985). As the rock band Redd Kross sing in their tribute song, "Kidnapped, raped, and possessed, Linda you're the best!" Mr. Skin agrees.

SKIN-fining Moment:

Chained Heat (0:31) *Linda shows off her head-spinningly delecatable dairy-mounds in the prison shower and then Sybill Danning takes control. Heat? Oh, yes!*

See Her Naked In:

Fatal Bond (1992) RB
Bedroom Eyes II (1990) LB, Buns
Red Heat (1985) Breasts
Savage Streets (1984) Breasts
Night Patrol (1984) LB
Chained Heat (1983) Breasts

Selma Blair

Born: June 23, 1972
Southfield, Michigan
Skin-O-Meter: Great Nudity

Brunette box-office sensation Selma Blair is naked proof that sometimes dreams do come true. Defying all expectations, the post-teenage waif shed every last vestige of clothing to stand fully naked and engage in rough interracial sex in *Storytelling* (2002). Blair had long been blasting every other shooting starlet off the skin radar. With the face of a recently fallen angel and the flitting form of a girl who has become just a little too feminine to remain a ballerina, Selma kept her sports bra and jockeys on while assaying a variety of roles that called for hot blasts of her overwhelming sex appeal. Her hearty lesbo tongue swabbing in *Cruel Intentions* (1999) caused all skinthusiasts who saw it to exult and mourn simultaneously. She was an aching joy to watch in action, but she was making so much money. She would never show anything. And then the miracle of *Storytelling*: Selma's pink-white complexion glowing from head to toe, her slight and satin-smooth ass arched for entry, the big black guy pretending to dog her from behind. God lives.

SKIN-fining Moment:

Storytelling (0:16) *Teeny-framed Selma strips to show her deliciously flat-tastic nibblers and stupendous seat just before her huge, African-American*

professor presses her against the wall and educates her in dirty-mouthed sex.

See Her Naked In:

Highway (2001) RB
Storytelling (2001) Breasts, Buns
Strong Island Boys (1997) RB

Rachel Blakely

Born: July 28, 1968
Borneo, Malaysia
Skin-O-Meter: Brief Nudity

Rachel Blakely began her ascent to stardom with a sepia-toned Nissan commercial. What a vehicle; Mr. Skin would sure like to see how the pretty brunette handles with such dangerous curves. Mostly, the Down Under honey sticks to her native Australia for her acting gigs, although she has appeared on American TV in *Xena: Warrior Princess* and *The Lost World*. Rachel has appeared in several cinematic endeavors, including *Love Until* (1995) and *Mr. Nice Guy* (1997), opposite perennial good guy Jackie Chan, but she could use some more exposure Stateside. Thankfully, though, she has been kind enough to show us some skin, albeit briefly, in the Australian mini-series *Tribe*. She appeared topless in a dimly lit scene, and her tom-toms are sure beatable. It's no Nissan commercial, but we recommend taking it for a spin.

SKIN-fining Moment:

Tribe mini-series (1999) *Rachel goes native as she turns over topless in a jungle hut. Makes you want to beat your drum!*

TeleVisions:

Tribe Breasts

Susan Blakely

Born: September 7, 1952
Frankfurt, Germany
Skin-O-Meter: Great Nudity

Susan Blakely debuted in *The Way We Were* (1973) and followed that up with another high-profile hit on the TV mini-series *Rich Man, Poor Man* (1976), but then her career mysteriously ran out of steam. But her body of work stayed boiling hot . . . and how. How exactly, you ask? Susan streaked in *Report to the Commissioner* (1975) and let her Blakely beauties out to play on *The Hitchhiker: Remembering Melody*. But Susan deserves the booby prize for her groundbreaking (and leg-spreading) performance in *Capone* (1976). Long before Sharon Stone made history by flashing her sugar walls and bleached muff in the mainstream picture *Basic Instinct* (1992), Susan broke the bush barrier in the aforementioned gangland epic. As one of Al's conquests, Susan appears quite nude, several times, including the scene in question, where she is full frontal on a bed and quite nonchalantly throws a leg over to reveal the Gates of Venus to Mr. Camera. And everyone thinks Sharon Stone did it first . . . pshaw.

SKIN-fining Moment:

Capone (1:15) *Susan shows it all off in this infamous sequence, including a glimpse at The Gates of Venus when she swings her legs to gets up out of bed. Great gyno!*

See Her Naked In:

Report to the Commissioner (1975) Breasts, Buns
Capone (1975) FFN, Buns

TeleVisions:

The Hitchhiker Breasts

Jolene Blalock

Born: March 5, 1975
San Diego, California
Skin-O-Meter: Brief Nudity

The future looks good, at least prophesized by the *Star Trek* franchise. From micro-minis on the original starship to the skintight lust-o-tards of the latest installment of the star opera, *Enterprise*, starring lungy Jolene Blalock. With a name like Blalock, she's got to be good, and she is, all short Blalocks, super-size Blaboobs, and a sweet Blabutt. Jolene's jo-jugs have remain corked thus far, but eventually that champagne chest will pop out. A good indicator is that in February 2004, fans North of the Border had reason to celebrate when they got a sweet view of the south of Jolene's border. In the version of the *Enterprise* episode "Harbinger" that aired in Canada, Jolene stripped nude in front of a dude and the camera pulled back to reveal almost all of her right breast, followed by a universe-bendingly hot shot of her ass-teroid. Beam me up, Scotty; I need a Kleenex!

SKIN-fining Moment:

Star Trek: Enterprise "Harbinger" **(2004)** *In a scene that aired in Canada, we see the tip of Jolene's right jug and a fast blast of her awesome ass-teroid as she leans in for some loving with an Earth dude.*

See Her Naked In:

TeleVisions:

Diamond Hunters mini series (2001) Breasts
Star Trek: Enterprise RB, Buns

Cate Blanchett

Born: May 14, 1969
Melbourne, Australia
Skin-O-Meter: Brief Nudity

Cate Blanchett is a respected actress, but that doesn't mean that men are oblivious to her sleek body of work. Yes, she moves seamlessly from one role to the next, but her alluring figure, small-breasted sexiness, and chiseled features can't be ignored. Cate debuted in *Police Rescue* (1994) and has gone

on to wow in *Paradise Road* (1997), *An Ideal Husband* (1999), *The Talented Mr. Ripley* (1999), and *The Gift* (2000). But it's her turn as a cherry that really straightens our stem. In *Elizabeth* (1998), as horny Queen Elizabeth, Cate shows off her crates in a half-second shot of her left breast. Sadly, this represents the bulk of her skin onscreen, although we're still holding out for an encore performance. When you're as hot as Cate, you get carte Blanchett.

SKIN-fining Moment:

Elizabeth **(0:39)** *Cate gives up a very brief shot of left breast while making love in bed. Virgin Queen no more!*

See Her Naked In:

The Shipping News (2001) Thong
Elizabeth (1998) LB

TeleVisions:

Bordertown Breasts, Bush

Rosa Blasi

Born: December 19, 1972
Chicago, Illinois
Skin-O-Meter: Brief Nudity

Ravishing Rosa Blasi, a former Miss Chicago, had been featured in mere supporting roles on such shows as *Married . . . with Children*, *High Tide*, and *Caroline in the City* until she scored a starring gig opposite Janine Turner on the cable series *Strong Medicine*. For an even stronger (double) dose of Rosa, check out the Showtime film *Noriega: God's Favorite* (2000) and get blasted by her free-swingin' torso torpedoes. Bra-free milk balloons are Mr. Skin's favorite, and, Rosa, your adoring public hungers for another two portions.

SKIN-fining Moment:

Noriega: God's Favorite **(0:02)** *Rosa plays around with pock-marked Bob*

Hoskins, showing off some sweet nip-meat through her silky robe.

See Her Naked In:

Noriega: God's Favorite (2000) Breasts

Debra Blee

Born: June 8, 1961
Orange County, California
Skin-O-Meter: Great Nudity

Debra Blee made her debut on the boob tube on an episode of *T.J. Hooker*. Sadly, this was a cop drama starring William Shatner and not the tale of a streetwalker named T.J. Debra was perhaps confused and took her talented top, very large and very real, to the big screen, where jugs are appreciated in their natural state. Her first film was *The Beach Girls* (1982), and it also marked the

Crown International Pictures Presents
THE BEACH GIRLS

CROWN INTERNATIONAL PICTURES Presents "THE BEACH GIRLS" Starring DEBRA BLEE • VAL KLINE • JEANA TOMASINA • JAMES DAUGHTON And ADAM ROARKE • Produced By MARILYN J. TENSER • Co-Producer MICHAEL D. CASTLE • Directed By PAT TOWNSEND Screenplay By PATRICK DUNCAN • Director Of Photography MICHAEL MURPHY • Music Performed by ARSENAL • Edited By GEORGE BOWERS • A MARIMARK Production • COLOR BY DELUXE A CROWN INTERNATIONAL PICTURES RELEASE

THE BEACH GIRLS: FUN IN THE SUN. PLUS A NUN. EVEN AS DRIVE-INS AND GRINDHOUSES WANED WITH THE ADVENT OF THE VCR IN THE '80S, A BIKINI-PACKED POSTER LIKE THIS COULD STILL PUT BUTTS IN THE STICKY SEATS.

start of a beautiful skin career. In one scene, Debra undoes her bikini top and out flop her massive mams. It's a sight for sore eyes and sure to make your joint sore too, from all that yanking and wanking. She followed that spectacular performance with a skinless part in *Savage Streets* (1984) and a role in *Sloane* (1984), in which her shirt gets ripped off. Ironically, in the meaty *Hamburger . . . the Motion Picture* (1986), in which lots of girls showed off their buns and much more, Debra stopped just short of skin. Then she returned to the beach that had been so good to her for one last hooray in *Beach Fever* (1987). After that, her sandy footprints disappear in the coming tide. We hate to think that Debra's all washed up.

SKIN-fining Moment:

The Beach Girls **(1:18)** *Brunette beach bunny Blee hulas in bikini, and then pops the top for a quick look at her buxom buoys.*

See Her Naked In:

Sloane (1984) Breasts
The Beach Girls (1982) Breasts

"The first hickey I ever got was from a girlfriend."

—YASMINE BLEETH

Yasmine Bleeth

Born: June 14, 1968
New York, New York
Skin-O-Meter: Never Nude

Even though she began modeling at six months old, Yasmine Bleeth has yet to say, "Yes, man!" to on-camera nudity. The brunette hardbody's ya-yas did get a nice workout as one of *Baywatch*'s first luscious lifeguards, though, where she rose to stardom opposite some of the most eager-to-unveil-themselves flotation devices ever filmed. She later starred on the short-lived nighttime soap *Titans* and then made headlines in 2001 for some messy behavior that led to drug rehab. Wouldn't a great nude scene be an awesome way to begin your new life, Yaz?

SKIN-fining Moment:

Baywatch "The Red Knights" **(1994)** *Yasmine charges the beach in her first-ever appearance wearing the trademark Baywatch red swimsuit. Nice dunes!*

Boti Bliss

Colorado
Skin-O-Meter: Brief Nudity

Roadracers (1994) was the vehicle that introduced Boti Bliss to the world. But the willowy brunette made a bigger impression on the boob tube, with appearances on *Pacific Blue*, *Charmed*, and the hit series *CSI: Miami*, on which she has a recurring role. She hasn't given up her big-screen ambitions, though skinless supporting roles in straight-to-video features such as *Warlock III: The End of Innocence* (1999) don't help. Boti balked at being bawdy until she landed in the controversial biopic *Ted Bundy* (2002), directed by Matthew Bright, who helmed the two great *Freeway* movies. Bright was able to get Boti to finally flash her bulbous bounty in a scene where she boffs the serial killer. This time Bundy was only killing semen, and viewers are recommended to do the same.

SKIN-fining Moment:

Ted Bundy **(0:18)** *As her serial-killer boyfriend boffs away atop her in bed, we get Blissful news of both of her Botis.*

See Her Naked In:

National Lampoon's Dorm Daze (2003) Body Double—Breasts
Ted Bundy (2002) Breasts

Claire Bloom

Born: February 15, 1931
London, England, UK
Skin-O-Meter: Brief Nudity

English strumpet Claire Bloom is a classic brunette beauty, and while she may not be a bombshell, she is the reason the Brits have more than a stiff upper lip. She made her stage debut in 1947, but it was Charlie Chaplin who was tramping around and discovered the svelte sexpot. He cast her as the female lead ballerina in his *Limelight* (1952), only her second role onscreen. Her first role came in *Blind Goddess* (1948), and it would take a sightless sap not to realize that Claire is a goddess. Laurence Olivier and Richard Burton could see what was hot about Claire and cast her for their film and theater joints. Claire even married lucky actor Rod Steiger, who got to see Bloom's pedals up close and personal. Throughout her long movie career, starring in such productions as *The Spy Who Came in from the Cold* (1965) and *Clash of the Titans* (1981), Claire only graced her devoted audience with one fleeting shot of her bouquet. It was in *A Severed Head* (1970), which is not a horror movie but a screwball romance. The emphasis is on the screw.

SKIN-fining Moment:

A Severed Head **(1:10)** *Claire's bare boobies Bloom when she's in bed with Richard Attenborough.*

See Her Naked In:

A Severed Head (1970) Breasts

Lindsay Bloom

Born: 1952
Omaha, Nebraska
Skin-O-Meter: Great Nudity

Being Miss USA is a lot like being a stewardess: It used to be a lot more glamorous. Still, back in 1972 a farm-fresh Nebraska blonde like Lindsay Bloom could parlay her Miss USA crown, along with her pageant-winning face, showgirl rack, and sense of adventure, into a shot at bright-light stardom. Lindsay leapt from the swimsuit competition to *The Dean Martin Show*, where she enlivened the variety series as one of Dean's darling decolletage-baring Ding-a-Ling Sisters. From this humble beginning, Bloom blossomed into a full-on B-level actress, which landed her roles on *Dallas* and *Mickey Spillane's Mike Hammer*. The beauty queen's most indelible mark was left upon the breast epics *Cover Girl Models* (1975) and *H.O.T.S.* (1979). With entertainment success stories like Miss USA Lindsay's, everyone comes out a winner.

SKIN-fining Moment:

Cover Girl Models (0:11) *Lindsay takes down one side of her bathing suit during a photo session and lets her right chest flower Bloom.*

See Her Naked In:

H.O.T.S. (1979) Breasts
Cover Girl Models (1975) Breasts

Lisa Blount

Born: July 1, 1957
Fayetteville, Arkansas
Skin-O-Meter: Brief Nudity

Blonde and doll-faced, with wide shoulders built to carry a heavy load of breast fodder, film personality Lisa Blount has been afforded every opportunity to tantalize and titillate the skin-fixated masses, but to little avail. She has spent many years laboring in marginal big-screen productions, an environment that generally encourages sultry-eyed actresses of Lisa's sexually engaging ilk to pull out the udders. Lisa's reaction, basically, can be summed up by her mooning the camera from a bouncing speedboat in *An Officer and a Gentleman* (1982). We can kiss her ass! This attitude despite the fact that she had given up toothy views in the horror and skin cheapo *Dead & Buried* (1981) a year earlier! Surely, Lisa jests, and more chest is to come? Not if her bra-and-gone stalk through *Out Cold* (1989) is any indication.

SKIN-fining Moment:

An Officer and a Gentleman (1:03) *Lisa bends over on a speedboat and shoots her moon toward someone very fortunate on the shore.*

See Her Naked In:

Chrystal (2004) Breasts
An Officer and a Gentleman (1982) Buns
Dead & Buried (1981) Breasts

Catherine Blythe

Skin-O-Meter: Brief Nudity

Catherine Blythe made her movie debut in *Where the Heart Is* (1990) before moving on to the sadly skinless world of made-for-TV dramas. Catherine moved back to the more potentially fleshy world of film in such ventures as *Terminal Justice* (1995), *The Legend of Gator Face* (1996), and *Papertrail* (1997). Obscure titles all, which is good for Skin Central, because with such B-movie fare, Catherine is on a career path where all roads lead to nudity! *The Second Arrival* (1998) is the first arrival of Catherine's carnal charms. And what a package! She shows her lithe figure in all of its fit glory, from her mini-cans to her furry bush. She also appeared nude in *The List* (2000), and let's hope her skin list goes on and on.

SKIN-fining Moment:

The Second Arrival (0:15) *Blistering full-frontal beauty as Ms. Blythe stands naked in a doorway.*

See Her Naked In:

The List (2000) Breasts, Buns
The Second Arrival (1998) FFN

Tina Bockrath

Born: June 30, 1967
Dayton, Ohio
Skin-O-Meter: Great Nudity

Tina Bockrath comes from Dayton, Ohio, and anyone lucky enough to be dating this delectable darling is in for a treat. A statuesque five-foot-eight-inch tall yummy, with a head full of thick, flowing blonde hair, Tina is the all-American (wet) dream girl. And what sweet dreams this leggy beauty conjures. Unlike the manufactured glamour girls of Hollywood, Tina is the real deal. Her full melons are not only juicy, they have not been tampered with by medical science. There's no need. Those upright ladies are fresh, fine, and a formidable handful. Her stomach is taut, flat, and toned to perfection. Her legs go for curvy miles and meet at the intersection of seat and meat. And to gaze on her glazed-sugar treat between those legs is a just dessert for any hungry he-man. Yet, Tina has not graced the screens of Tinseltown with her shining sexuality, except on the cable series *Tales from the Crypt*. But she made her one-shot a sure shot in the pants. She played a naked cadaver that will have viewers stiff with pleasure, especially when she suddenly rose from the cold morgue slab and exposed her hot spot. She certainly puts her all in translates to *we all go bare* in cinematic skinspeak. Case in point: Juliette Binoche. She's your typical French femme, consistently going au naturel with mouth-watering results. La Binoche unveiled her sweet teats at the tender age of twenty-three in *The Unbearable Lightness of Being* (1988). Ahhh . . . to munch on Juliette's tiny mounds of vanilla, topped with circular rosy-brown dollops of frosting. Tongues were wagging for those tender tartlets in *Damage* (1992) and *The English Patient* (1996). For a slice of Binoche's hairy brioche, rent *Rendez-vous* (1985). This Gallic gal shows bountiful bush, baby baguettes, and bare ass to boot, making Mr. Skin want to cum and rent it repeatedly.

SKIN-fining Moment:

Rendez-vous (0:24) *It's a nice rendez-view as Juliette offers a feast of her nude body to her lover in a kitchen. First she's topless, then she shows bush when sitting on a table, and finally she offers up her ass on the floor. Bon(er) apetit!*

See Her Naked In:

Jet Lag (2002) RB, Buns
La Veuve de Saint-Pierre (2000) RB
The English Patient (1996) LB
The Horseman on the Roof (1995) Body Double—Breasts
Damage (1992) Breasts, Bush
Les Amants du Pont-Neuf (1991) FFN
The Unbearable Lightness of Being (1988) Breasts, Bush, Buns
Rendez-vous (1985) FFN, Buns
La Vie de Famille (1985) Breasts

Thora Birch

Born: March 11, 1982
Los Angeles, California
Skin-O-Meter: Brief Nudity

Young in years but gargantuan in the gazongas, Thora Birch debuted on the TV show *Day by Day* as a tot in 1988. She quickly found fame on the big screen as the daughter in the Jack Ryan series, appearing in *Patriot Games* (1992) and *Clear and Present Danger* (1994). We watched her grow up, and, mam-oh-mam, did she grow. Still a teen as stardom called, Thora showed audiences how miraculously she had matured in the milkers during her lap-liquefying topless scene in *American Beauty* (1999). According to the tabloid *The Sun*, Thora's mom, Carol Connors, is an ex-porno star who played the naughty nurse in *Deep Throat* (1972). Named after the Norse god Thor, there is no doubt that this girl's got two mighty hammers—she's the golden goddess of thundering udders.

SKIN-fining Moment:

American Beauty (1:10) *Torpedo-torso'd Thora is aware she's being watched in her bedroom by her boyfriend next door, so she gives him something to look at. She takes her time and slowly undresses to reveal her American Beauties. They're huge!*

See Her Naked In:

American Beauty (1999) Breasts

Jane Birkin

Born: December 14, 1946
London, England, UK
Skin-O-Meter: Hall of Fame

Jane Birkin debuted in Richard Lester's *The Knack, And How to Get It* (1965). Oh, she got it, appearing next as one of the nude dancing models who romp with David Hemmings in Michelangelo Antonioni's '60s sextacular *Blowup* (1966), which marked the beginning of her carnal career in international nude acting. Since then, she has appeared in some state of undress in at least fifteen films and continues to do so to this day, albeit generally in French cinema, where the living is sleazy.

For some highlights from her sweet body of work, as well as to gawk at her savory, waif-like body, check her out in *Slogan* (1969), as Brigitte Bardot's lover in *Ms. Don Juan* (1973), and *Je t'aime moi non plus* (1976), in which she plays an androgynous bartender. For the breast of this small-breasted one, there's *Le Mouton enrage* (1974), featuring Jane in some seriously hot full-frontal scenes. Bon appetitties!

SKIN-fining Moment:

Blowup (1:14) *Jane and Gillian Hills romp amongst piles of paper completely nude. One of the first instances of bush on the big screen.*

See Her Naked In:

Ceci est mon Corps (2001)
Comédie! (1987) Breasts, Buns
La Femme de ma Vie (1986) Buns
Dust (1985) Breasts, Buns
La Pirate (1984) Breasts, Bush, Buns
Je t'aime, moi non plus (1976) FFN, Buns
Bruciati da Cocente Passione (1976) Buns
Catherine and Company (1975) Breasts, Buns
Love at the Top (1974) FFN, Buns
La Moutarde me Monte au Nez (1974) FFN, Buns
Sérieux Comme le Plaisir (1974) Breasts, Buns
Projection Privée (1973) FFN, Buns
Ms. Don Juan (1973) FFN
Trop Jolies pour Être Honnêtes (1972)
May Morning (1970) Breasts
Les Chemins de Katmandou (1969) Breasts
Cannabis (1969) FFN, Buns
Slogan (1969) LB, Buns
Blowup (1966) Breasts, Bush, Buns

Jacqueline Bisset

Born: September 13, 1944
Weybridge, Surrey, England, UK
Skin-O-Meter: Hall of Fame

Born of a French mother and a British father, elegantly beautiful actress Jacquline Bisset is this singular performance. And Mr. Skin would like to put his all in her.

SKIN-fining Moment:

Tales from the Crypt "Abra Cadaver" (1991) *Night of the Living FFN! In B&W! Tina rises completely naked from a morge slab and strangles Beau Bridges. When it's revealed to be only a movie, she slaps on a lab coat and sexily fails to cover her lap fur.*

See Her Naked In:

Numerous Playboy Videos

TeleVisions:

Tales from the Crypt FFN

Corinne Bohrer

Born: October 18, 1959
Camp Lejeune, North Carolina
Skin-O-Meter: Great Nudity

To date, Corinne Bohrer's career highlight remains *Police Academy 4: Citizens on Patrol* (1987), but what she lacks in box-office boffo she more than makes up for with being in the buff. Not that Corinne is a nudie star, but she's been free with her assets at least once—and it was a humdinger! Corinne scored memorable roles in the teen T&A classic *Joysticks* (1983), the Martin-Short-shows-his-ass flop *Cross My Heart* (1987), and on the series *E/R*. No, not NBC's famous, long-running *ER*; this was a short-lived CBS comedy set in the emergency room also starring a pre-fame George Clooney, Jason Alexander, and post-superstardom Elliot Gould. Now back to that skinful performance, which comes in the HBO golf romp *Dead Solid Perfect* (1988). Corinne exposes every inch of her impressive frame, from tits to full frontal to an impressive shot of her love cave from between her legs as Randy Quaid hoists her up in a hotel hallway. It's a hole-in-one

muff-see wherein it's leading lady more than lives up to the title.

SKIN-fining Moment:

Dead Solid Perfect (0:33) Corrine struts completely naked down a hotel hallway in search of the ice machine. Her outstanding boobs, pubes, and cheeks are bound to melt the whole room when she finds it.

See Her Naked In:

The Coriolis Effect (1994) Breasts
Dead Solid Perfect (1988) FFN, Buns

Romane Bohringer

Born: August 14, 1973
Pont-Sainte-Maxence, Oise, France
Skin-O-Meter: Great Nudity

It's not totally gay to say that Leonardo DiCaprio cuts a fine figure as the nude poet in *Total Eclipse* (1995). But it would be queer if you passed over Romane Bohringer, that French act-chest with the mammoth mammalian mounds hanging all over David Thewlis in the same movie. Since her debut as a teen in *Kamikaze* (1986), Romane has pretty much worked her hot little ass off in her native land of cork-popping cinema. While her best skin movie would have to be the aforementioned title, she has not been shy about showing off her ample figure. *Savage Nights* (1992), *L'Appartement* (1996), and *Rembrandt* (1999) all offer the baguette-raising temptress and her titanic tits. There's something about the French that we like . . . oh, yeah, their women are horny, naked sluts!

SKIN-fining Moment:

Total Eclipse (0:52) Awesome ass as she lies in bed. A guy enters, she jumps up, showing more seatage, then some full frontal and, finally, several unbelievably amazing looks at her udderly magnificent, mammothly mountainous super-mams. Breastacular!

See Her Naked In:

Aurélien (2003) Breasts
Rembrandt (1999) RB
Vigo (1998) LB, Buns
L'Appartement (1996) Breasts
Total Eclipse (1995) FFN, Buns
Savage Nights (1992) FFN

Florinda Bolkan

Born: February 15, 1941
Ceara, Brazil
Skin-O-Meter: Great Nudity

With long, jet-black hair and a darkly arousing body, one look at Florinda Bolkan and it's obvious this girl is from south of the border—and she loves to expose her southern views. Though raised in the hot climate of Brazil, Florinda found fame and fortune onscreen in the cinemas of Europe and America, which makes it much easier for everybody to appreciate her carnal charms. Her debut was in the Italian John Cassavetes picture *Machine Gun McCain* (1968). She didn't show off her big guns, but it's still a banging performance. Since then, Florinda has appeared in over forty films, TV series, and made-for-TV movies, including the noteworthy productions *Candy* (1968), *The Last Valley* (1971), *Royal Flash* (1975), *The Word* (1978), *Some Girls* (1988), and the hit Italian series *La Piovra*. This exotic seductress's more nude-worthy ventures began early in her career with *Le Voleur de crimes* (1968). It stands (and so will audiences . . . in their pants) as one of her skinfully moist explicit entries. But she's gone on to a rich and varied career in nudity, such as *Una Ragazza piuttosto complicata* (1968), *Incontro* (1971), *Flavia, la monaca musulmana* (1974), and *La Settima donna* (1978). She hasn't done a whole lot of thread shedding since the sexy days of the '70s. That shouldn't stop the mature matron of mams, as sensual stock like hers only appreciates in value with age.

SKIN-fining Moment:

Le Voleur de Crimes (0:42) *In the distance, through a window, you see her ass while she gets a massage.*

See Her Naked In:

La Settima Donna (1978) Breasts
Flavia, la Monaca Musulmana (1974) RB, Buns
Una Lucertola con la Pelle di Donna (1971) Breasts, Buns
Incontro (1971) LB
Una Ragazza Piuttosto Complicata (1968) RB
Le Voleur de Crimes (1968) Buns

Tiffany Bolling

Born: February 6, 1946
Santa Monica, California
Skin-O-Meter: Great Nudity

A renaissance woman who has exuded prototypical California-girl sexuality in the realms of modeling, TV, film, and song, dirty-blonde beach nymph Tiffany Bolling's career as an object of desire ran from the 1960s through the 1980s. The tawny temptress first pranced and preened on the big screen as an oversexed model in *Tony Rome* (1967). Bolling's effervescent smile and sparkling assets were tapped to light up Rod Serling's ahead-of-its-time *Survivor* presager *The New People* in 1969. From there on out, Tiffany let it all hang out in a string of nudie-cutie and skingoria flicks such as *The Centerfold Girls* (1974) and *Kingdom of the Spiders* (1977).

SKIN-fining Moment:

Love Scenes (0:06) *Topless Tiff bares her Bolling balls for photog Britt Ekland.*

See Her Naked In:

Love Scenes (1984) FFN
Kingdom of the Spiders (1977) Breasts
The Centerfold Girls (1974) Breasts
Bonnie's Kids (1973) Breasts

Tiffany Bolton

Houston, Texas
Skin-O-Meter: Brief Nudity

Big things come from Texas, like buxom Tiffany Bolton, a tall brunette with a chest as large as the vast prairie but far more hospitable. Tiffany is best known for her gig as cohost of the regular-people-versus-super-intelligent-trivia-whizzes game show *Beat the Geeks*, where her eye candy was a sweet distraction for the guests. She's obviously the hostess with the moistest, which is why she was cast on the *Candid Camera* rip-off *Spy TV*. But for those who'd like to really spy what Tiffany has to offer and beat off the geek in their pants, Mr. Skin recommends taking a look at her straight-to-video debut in the Shannon Tweed steamer *Scandalous Behavior* (2000), a.k.a. *Singapore Sling*. Her scene appears early in the film, when she shows off her big breasts with equally topless blonde Rena Riffel as they tease a bound and ga-ga guy in bed. Most recently, she's been seen in the short trailer spoof *12 Hot Women* (2003), featuring no plot and 12 hot women. It's a role she was born to play.

SKIN-fining Moment:

Scandalous Behavior (0:05) *Tiffany and Rena Riffel show off their racks while seducing a dude in the sack.*

See Her Naked In:

Scandalous Behavior (1998) Breasts

TeleVisions:

Black Tie Nights Breasts, Buns

Gretchen Bonaduce

Skin-O-Meter: Brief Nudity

If fame is a bitch, at least she has the decency to show her tits. Tidy straw blonde Gretchen Bonaduce has given no indication that she desires to be in the limelight, other than her marriage to former kid actor and punchy celebrity boxer Danny Bonaduce. If pale, pretty Gretchen had not taken vows with the one-time *Partridge Family* runt, she probably would not have co-starred as his wife in the no-budget amateur like flick *America's Deadliest Home Video* (1993). But in fact, Gretchen did say I do, and as a result her conical hooters were caught swaying in the momentary blink of renown as she portrayed a woman in the throes of an adulterous embrace. These sweet, compact boobies must be the secret to why Danny is always smiling.

SKIN-fining Moment:

America's Deadliest Home Video *Mrs. Danny Partridge lets her pair free while riding a guy in bed the way her hubby's old group rode the top of the pop charts.*

See Her Naked In:

America's Deadliest Home Video (1993) Breasts

Rene Bond

Born: October 11, 1950
San Diego, California
Died: June 2, 1996
Skin-O-Meter: Great Nudity

It was because of women like Rene Bond that there was such a thing as a golden age of porn. Rene was known for her waves of amber hair, her structurally perfect, billowing breasts (when she started out in 1970, they were bite-sized tit bits, but our girl Bond evolved with the times), and the sudden swelling of a big, round ass that ballooned out from a baby-fat frame that was forever plush and young. With her big, pouting eyes, button nose, and toothy grin, Rene retained the air of a little girl licking a lollipop throughout her long and eventful career. Although she appeared in a number of non-X projects (including savant Ed Wood's lost swan song *Necromania* [1971]), Bond is best savored in her native porn land.

SKIN-fining Moment:

Country Cuzzins (0:06) *Farmgirl Rene steps outside and bares all three B's before (and during and after) she hoses off her country fuzzing.*

See Her Naked In:

The Adult Version of Jekyll & Hyde (1972) FFN, Buns
Please Don't Eat My Mother (1972) FFN, Buns
Below the Belt (1971) FFN, Buns
Country Cuzzins (1970) FFN, Buns
Numerous Adult Movies

Lisa Bonet

Born: November 16, 1967
San Francisco, California
Skin-O-Meter: Great Nudity

Lisa Bonet was voted the most likely *Cosby Show* cast member to give audiences a boner, at least by Mr. Skin. The hussy Huxtable decided to leave her uplift-the-peeps sitcom for an uplift-the-penis movie debut in *Angel Heart* (1987). Soon after, Lisa married then-unknown guitar-slinger Lenny Kravitz. Fame followed, and Lisa's wedding band was flicked off the rocker's finger in a hurry. Since the late-'80s, Lisa has been a straight-to-video vixen and yet has never matched the nudity of her debut. But check out 1993's *Bank Robber* for a stealing glance at her silver-dollar-shaped nipples.

SKIN-fining Moment:

Angel Heart (1:27) *Lisa shares a supremely steamy sex scene with Mickey Rourke, and judging by the rather erect status of her nipples, I'd say she was really enjoying it.*

See Her Naked In:

New Eden (1994) LB
Dead Connection (1994) Breasts
Bank Robber (1993) Breasts, Buns
Angel Heart (1987) Breasts

Helena Bonham Carter

Born: May 26, 1966
Golders Green, London, England, UK
Skin-O-Meter: Hall of Fame

Helena Bonham Carter gave up higher education for a higher calling: turning on men of the world with her five-foot-three-inch pixie perfection as an actress. At seventeen, she made a splash debuting in the made-for-BBC movie *A Pattern of Roses* (1983), where she got her period . . . period piece, that is, and a reputation for corset-wearing carnality. Her costume (and out-of-costume) performances continued with *Lady Jane* (1986), which debuted her pale skin—although it would pale in comparison to her later lustrous works. In *Getting It Right* (1989), she flashed her petite pair; *Margaret's Museum* (1995) offered a wet and wild shower schtup; and *The Wings of the Dove* (1997) spread Helena's wings for a fully nude and noteworthy back view of her heart-shaped tush and even a dark patch of behind-the-scenes bush. But you don't have to dwell in the past; *Fight Club* (1999) and *Novocaine* (2001) proved Helena is just as frisky in the here and now—and how.

SKIN-fining Moment:

The Wings of the Dove (1:30) *During a long lovemaking session, you can enjoy Helena's hoots and hairpie from various vantage points.*

See Her Naked In:

The Heart of Me (2002) Breasts
Till Human Voices Wake Us (2001) RB
Novocaine (2001) Breasts
Fight Club (1999) Breasts, Buns
The Wings of the Dove (1997) FFN, Buns
Margaret's Museum (1995) Breasts
Dancing Queen (1993) Breasts
Getting it Right (1989) Breasts
La Maschera (1988) Buns
Lady Jane (1986) Breasts

Sandrine Bonnaire

Born: May 31, 1967
Clermont-Ferrand, France
Skin-O-Meter: Great Nudity

A funny thing happens when you watch *Police* (1985). No, not the TV reality show *Cops* or the new wave band, but the French film starring Sophie Marceau. What occurs is udder disappointment because sexy Sophie for once doesn't flash her floppers. But sometimes victory is snatched from the jaws of defeat, and in this case that snatch belongs to the nakedly ambitious Sandrine Bonnaire. It is in every American's breast interest to get to know this usually naked and never-trimmed, full-frontal Parisian pretty. She first came on the scene after rising to the top from the flood of adolescent hopefuls looking for a role in *À nos amours* (1983). And viewers came creamy buckets thanks to her ample skin. She won a César, which is the French version of the Oscar. But with nude-worthy performances in such films as *Tir à vue* (1984), *Le Milleur de la vie* (1985), and *La Peste* (1992), it's obvious this baguette-pleaser deserves the booby prize.

SKIN-fining Moment:

Le Meilleur de la Vie (0:36) *Stark naked Sandrine walks into the kitchen and gets a bowl of cereal. Thanks, but I'll have that fluffy croissant between her thighs . . .*

See Her Naked In:

La Peste (1992) Breasts
Police (1985) FFN

Le Meilleur de la Vie (1985) FFN, Buns
Tir à Vue (1984) Breasts
À nos Amours (1983) Breasts, Bush, Buns

Céline Bonnier

Born: August 31, 1965
Lévis, Quebec, Canada
Skin-O-Meter: Great Nudity

The earth moved with Céline Bonnier's film debut in *Tectonic Plates* (1992). The publicity-shy, dark-haired, svelte Canadian made such an impression that viewers wanted to see more. And they'd soon be rewarded by the adventuresome act-chest. Born into a family of eight children and raised in a convent school in Quebec City, Céline may be a good Catholic girl, but she still stands out. And audiences' pants stood out too, especially when they caught her first flesh in *Le Vent du Wyoming* (1994). What a way to show it off. She's completely naked in a boxing ring, biting the ropes in some rough sex that climaxes with a knee in her lover's groin. Ouch. But this frisky kitten purrs in more than the French-Canadian niche. She appeared in the made-for-TV movie *Million Dollar Babies* (1994) and the hit film *The Assignment* (1997). Audiences didn't fill the seats to see stars Aidan Quinn or Donald Sutherland, but rather filled their seats watching Céline's cups runneth over. Yet it's on cable that this minx is moist alluring. On the series *The Hunger*, she has a fairly convincing sex scene, which also exposes a trilogy of lusty parts, and it's quite the meal. Eat up!

SKIN-fining Moment:

Le Vent du Wyoming (0:45) *Completely nude Celine tackles and mounts the tool of a tuxedo-clad gent in a boxing ring. Breasts, buns, and beav.*

See Her Naked In:

The Assignment (1997) Breasts
Caboose (1996) Breasts
Le Sphinx (1995) RB, Buns
Le Vent du Wyoming (1994) FFN, Buns

TeleVisions:

The Hunger FFN

Katrine Boorman

Born: 1958
London, England, UK
Skin-O-Meter: Brief Nudity

Katrine Boorman is the daughter of legendary director John Boorman, who brought us such films as *Hell in the Pacific* (1968) and *Deliverance* (1972). No surprise then that she got her start in the acting arena with a bit part in daddy's film *Zardoz* (1974), which starred Sean Connery. After taking some time to finish puberty, Katrine returned to the silver screen in another one of her papa's masterpieces, *Excalibur* (1981), opposite then-unknowns Gabriel Byrne, Patrick Stewart, and Liam Neeson. In the brief time that she was onscreen, pop saw fit to show the world exactly what the fruit of his loins looked like under all those period costumes, directing her in an eye-popping scene. Katrine goes under Byrne's flesh sword while he's dressed in full armor—talk about safe sex. She's gone on to a career beyond her father's camera but, thankfully, without giving up his influence. Katrine must have made Big Daddy Boorman proud with her sexy topless scene in *Le Bonheur est un mensonge* (1996). Katrine may be a Boorman, but she's never a bore, man.

SKIN-fining Moment:

Excalibur (0:14) *Kat gets duped by a horny dude and bares her breasts as they*

bone by a fireplace. Hot stuff—especially considering that Kat's dad was the director!

See Her Naked In:

Le Bonheur est un Mensonge (1996) Breasts
Excalibur (1981) Breasts

Connie Booth

Born: 1944
Indianapolis, Indiana
Skin-O-Meter: Great Nudity

It would be hard to guess the truth about trim bit of hot blonde stuff Connie Booth. Married to British comedian John Cleese soon after appearing with him in the film *How to Irritate People* (1968), Connie went on to accompany her husband by playing various characters on the definitively English comedy series *Monty Python's Flying Circus*. Who would have guessed that rather than being a lissome Limey lass Connie was actually a corn-fed filly from Indianapolis, Indiana? As Polly Sherman, the house maid on Cleese's comedy of uptight manners *Fawlty Towers*, Connie bustled with a prim self-containment that was all the more sexually alluring for its almost complete absence of overt eroticism. Who would have guessed that Booth had gone fully buff, with beaver and all the trimmings, in *Romance with a Double Bass* (1974)? Mr. Skin would have guessed, that's who.

SKIN-fining Moment:

Romance with a Double Bass (0:09) *The former Mrs. Cleese full frontally skinny dips and some schemer steals her clothes. We see Connie's buns, not-so-Faulty Towers, and even her Hairy Grail.*

See Her Naked In:

Romance with a Double Bass (1974) FFN, Buns

Emily Booth

Born: April 26, 1976
Chester, England, UK
Skin-O-Meter: Great Nudity

Emily Booth was born in Chester, England, which is very appropriate because she's got one of the best chests in the UK. She's used her prize boobies to skyrocket to the top of the steamy heap of British B-movies. Her debut and best skinage is *Pervirella* (1997), in which she shows off her monstrously bountiful bosom in several well-lit, quite-entertaining scenes. Emily went on to play frisky in such films as *Witchcraft X: Mistress of the Craft* (1998), *Sacred Flesh* (2000), and *Cradle of Fear* (2001). Although she has appeared on several television series, including *Threesome*, *Bits*, and *Shock Movie Massacre*, Emily's bread and butter (and audiences' delight) continues to be those cult-favorite straight-to-video flicks. Therefore, it isn't all that difficult to locate a production or two with Emily's girls coming out of the Booth—talk about a peep Booth.

SKIN-fining Moment:

Pervirella (0:46) *Big breastages as Emily splashes cold water on her naked chest, plus a few thong shots as Mr. Skin beats off behind her.*

See Her Naked In:

Cradle of Fear (2001) Breasts, Buns
Pervirella (1997) Breasts, Buns

Lindy Booth

Born: April 2, 1979
Oakville, Ontario, Canada
Skin-O-Meter: Brief Nudity

Lindy Booth is a cold Canadian who has been a bit too skingy throughout her career. But with those perky upturned tits and a face that was born to bob for meat sausage, it's hard to stay mad at the Northern pretty. Lindy certainly has had ample opportunity to flash her ample charms in such B-movies as *Teenage Space Vampires* (1998). The problem seems to be that she's spent most of her time on TV, most notably on the hit series *Relic Hunter*, which doesn't exactly lend itself to gratuitous nudity. Nevertheless, Lindy was kind enough to flash her hella-hooters and even her heavenly heinie in *Century Hotel* (2001). It's enough to make Mr. Skin do the Lindy hop . . . in his pants!

SKIN-fining Moment:

Century Hotel (1:29) *Tits as she sits atop a guy and wields a gun. We get two clear looks, then some annoying darkness.*

See Her Naked In:

Century Hotel (2001) Breasts, Buns

Lynn Borden

Born: March 24, 1939
Detroit, Michigan
Skin-O-Meter: Great Nudity

Born in Detroit, Michigan, Lynn Borden really gets our motors running here at Skin Central. A beautiful blonde with ample apples and a ripe rump, Lynn took her body to Hollywood and began getting uncredited roles in such films as *The Days of Wine and Roses* (1962). It was a sobering experience for her, but Lynn didn't give up. She landed a starring role on the hit series *Hazel* and made audiences see why Mr. B was such a happy provider. Back in film, she appeared in the swinging hit *Bob & Carol & Ted & Alice* (1969), but it wasn't until the sexy '70s that Lynn really began to show us what she's got. That began in a skinless but still mamorable part in the naked-girls-in-prison flick *Black Mama, White Mama* (1972), exploitation's stab at racial equality. Next came the cult horror classic *Frogs* (1972). But it wasn't until the carry-a-big-stick action flick *Walking Tall* (1973) that Lynn really gave viewers a big stick. She played her part fully nude on a bed, on her stomach and getting her tush smacked. Lynn even sat up briefly to give a glimpse of boob. It was her sole skin onscreen, but Lynn continued to appear in some hot productions such as *Dirty Mary Crazy Larry* (1974). But by *Hellhole* (1985), Lynn was on her way out. We'll always have her seat-meat, though.

SKIN-fining Moment:

Walking Tall (1:31) *Lynn bares her butt and a bit of breast whilst receiving an ass-whipping in bed.*

See Her Naked In:

Walking Tall (1973) LB, Buns

Angel Boris

Born: August 2, 1974
Fort Lauderdale, Florida
Skin-O-Meter: Great Nudity

You don't know heaven until you've seen Angel Boris in a swimsuit. Only a lucky few got to see the svelte redhead win a *Hawaiian Tropic* bikini contest, but everybody got to enjoy her shapely display when *Playboy* published its feature "Girls of Hawaiian Tropic" in April 1995. The Bunny must have been shaking its tail, because for the July 1996 issue Angel became a coveted Playmate. Around the same time, she made her screen and skin debut as an erotic dancer in *Exit* (1996). Her scene was brief, but nobody was heading for the exit when Angel was shaking her cute cupfuls. She hit the big time with a role on the boob-tube hit *Beverly Hills, 90210* but left the show after a season. No loss, as Angel's assets are breast seen in the more nude-friendly confines of the sinema. Her topless spell in *Warlock III: The End of Innocence* (1999) is bewitching, and she's to die for in *Suicide Blonde* (1999). But it's her eye-popping videos for Hugh Hefner that are moist revealing, such as *Playboy Prime Time Playmates* (2002). It's nice to see Angel without a staple in her belly.

SKIN-fining Moment:

Suicide Blonde (1:03) *Right breast as she sits up in bed talking to a guy. The sheet falls and she shows the complete set. It's great when that happens.*

See Her Naked In:

Boa vs. Python (2004) FFN, Breasts
Dragon Storm (2004) LB
Suicide Blonde (1999) Breasts, Buns
Warlock III: The End of Innocence (1999) Breasts, Thong
Exit (1996) Breasts, Thong
Numerous Playboy Videos

Katherine Borowitz

Chicago, Illinois
Skin-O-Meter: Brief Nudity

Katherine Borowitz has made a career of playing bit parts, while audiences anxiously wait for when she'll show her luscious bit parts. After her debut in the star-studded *The World According to Garp* (1982), Katherine's career looked like it was on an upswing. She landed roles in *Harry and Son* (1984), *Seize the Day* (1986), and the mini-series *Evergreen* (1985) before falling back into the supporting-role gig with a bit part in *Baby Boom* (1987). Then prayers were answered when John Turturro picked Katherine for his farcical *Illuminata* (1998) and directed her only skin to date. It's a brief, open-dress shot of her small wonders, but it's truly illuminating. That's one small breast for Katherine, one giant leap for mankind.

SKIN-fining Moment:

Illuminata (0:35) *Long shot of Katherine's skinny shanks on stage. Little, but lovely!*

See Her Naked In:

Illuminata (1998) LB

Barbara Bouchet

Born: August 15, 1943
Reichenberg, Sudetenland, Germany
Skin-O-Meter: Hall of Fame

This gorgeous model chucked Czechoslovakia to conquer America with her sexy bod in the 1960s. In the process, Barbara Bouchet became a naval pioneer, flashing her midriff at any opportunity. She made Pearl Harbor a happy place while flaunting one of her twin missiles in *In Harm's Way* (1965), while her sexy turns in the spy spoofs *Agent for H.A.R.M.* (1966) and *Casino Royale* (1967) would dent even Austin Powers's mojo. Barbara then kept the '70s swinging with nude work in European epics such as *Don't Torture A Duckling* (1972), *Vertiges* (1975), and *Sex with a Smile* (1976). She's still a hottie, too, as seen when Barbara returned to the screen—after a nineteen-year absence—in the *Gangs of New York* (2002).

SKIN-fining Moment:

Una Cavalla tutta nuda (0:32) *Bare-butted Babs kneels down in a barn and sticks her boo-yah in the air before rolling over to treat us to a long, viscious, no-holes-barred view of her full-frontal mammarial-and-muffilicious magnificence.*

See Her Naked In:

Per Favore, Occupati di Amelia (1982) Buns
Come Perdere una Moglie e Trovare un'Amante (1978) FFN, Buns
Con la Rabbia Agli Occhi (1976) FFN
Sex with a Smile (1976) Breasts
The Rogue (1976) FFN
To Agistri (1976) Breasts, Buns
Amore Vuol dir Gelosia (1975) Breasts, Buns
Vertiges (1975) FFN
Cry of a Prostitute (1974) Breasts
La Badessa di Castro (1974) Breasts, Buns
Il Tuo Piacere è il Mio (1973) Breasts, Buns
The Sexy Virgin (1973) Breasts
La Dama Rossa Uccide Sette Volte (1972) Breasts
Black Belly of the Tarantula (1972) FFN, Buns
Finalmente . . . le Mille e una Notte (1972)
Alla Ricerca del Piacere (1972) LB, Bush, Buns
Don't Torture a Duckling (1972) FFN, Buns
Una Cavalla Tutta Nuda (1972) FFN, Buns
Milano Calibro 9 (1971) Breasts
Non Commettere Atti Impuri (1971) Breasts, Buns
Surabaya Conspiracy (1969) RB
In Harm's Way (1965) RB

Élodie Bouchez

Born: April 5, 1973
Montreuil-sous-Bois, France
Skin-O-Meter: Hall of Fame

The baguette-raising, beret-twirling charms of the French are well documented. But even in the realm of the randy French actresses, Élodie Bouchez manages to stand legs apart from the rest. Like the dark bouquet of rich French wine and as tasty as any classic French dish, Élodie's deep chocolate eyes and her two dollops of whipped-cream C-cups make her the ultimate French tart. American audiences know her best from the *Barbarella* (1968) homage *CQ* (2001), in which she's stark raving nude, complete with le bush. But outside of some indie exposure in the States, like *Shooting Vegetarians* (2000), this is one French treat best enjoyed in her native land. Élodie may have a succulent ass good enough to eat with a fork, but Mr. Skin suggests using a spoon to slurp up all her juicy goodness in such French skin classics as *Le Plus bel age* (1995),

Zonzon (1998), and *Too Much Flesh* (2000). Viva Élodie!

SKIN-fining Moment:

Too Much Flesh (1:10) *Elodie reclines on a couch—flappers flopping, muff fluffed—while Artie Buocco from* The Sopranos *paints her toenails.*

See Her Naked In:

La Guerre à Paris (2002) RB
La Faute à Voltaire (2001) Breasts, Bush, Buns
CQ (2001) RB, Bush, Buns
Too Much Flesh (2000) FFN
Lovers (1999) Breasts, Bush
Zonzon (1998) Breasts
Don't Let Me Die On a Sunday (1998) FFN
Les Kidnappeurs (1998) RB
Louise (Take 2) (1998) LB
Flammen im Paradies (1997) LB
Les Brouches (1996) Breasts, Buns
À Toute Vitesse (1996) Breasts, Bush, Buns
Le Plus Bel Âge . . . (1995) FFN, Buns
The Wild Reeds (1994) Breasts
Le Cahier Vole (1992) Breasts

Carole Bouquet

Born: August 18, 1957
Nevilly-sur-seine, France
Skin-O-Meter: Great Nudity

Many men developed an interest in French films after Carole Bouquet appeared as the title knockout in *That Obscure Object of Desire* (1977). Sharing the role with another actress, Carole's objects got a lot less obscure when she appeared in the James Bond hit *For Your Eyes Only* (1981). She preferred to flaunt her French finery, however, in foreign films that you can still enjoy without speaking the language. The ever-blooming Bouquet then went on to spend the '90s as a Chanel spokeswoman but graced us (and costar Christopher Walken) with some impressive older nudity in *A Business Affair* (1994).

SKIN-fining Moment:

Tag Der Idioten (0:02) *Carole goes full frontal while looking for something in the bedroom. If it's pubic hair, I know where she can find it.*

See Her Naked In:

A Business Affair (1994) RB, Buns
Dagobert (1984) Buns
Tag Der Idioten (1982) FFN, Buns
Il Cappotto di Astrakan (1979) Breasts
That Obscure Object of Desire (1977) Breasts

Clara Bow

Born: July 29, 1905
Brooklyn, New York
Died: September 27, 1965
Skin-O-Meter: Brief Nudity

The original "It Girl," milky-skinned brunette sexpot Clara Bow led the way for every celluloid sex symbol who followed. Born in Brooklyn, New York, in 1905, Bow's meteoric rise to national fantasy fodder coincided with the incredible burgeoning of the motion picture industry. She appeared in fifty-nine silent films, including the aptly if euphemistically named *It* (1927), in just over eleven years. Clara Bow established herself as the embodiment of lustful hopes and dreams cherished by a nation on an unprecedented growth spurt. Without a word, her sex-brimming eyes and the sinuous eroticism of her slightest movement filled the screen with the crackling potential of spontaneous combustion. With the advent of talkies, Bow became self-conscious of her honking Brooklyn accent and retired at the age of twenty-seven. The onset of the Great Depression may have been a simple sign of mourning over all of Clara's squandered, middle-aged opportunities.

SKIN-fining Moment:

Wings (1:22) *Clara stands in front of a mirror and we get a glimpse of her bare left Bow-Bow.*

See Her Naked In:

Call Her Savage (1932) Nip Slip—LB
Wings (1927) Breasts

Judi Bowker

Born: April 6, 1954
Shawford, Hants, England, UK
Skin-O-Meter: Never Nude

It's hard to find a sexier aristocrat than Judi Bowker, whose British boobies have driven us bonkers in all kinds of period outfits. The former ballerina got her first break starring on the UK TV series *Black Beauty* before making her big-screen debut in *Brother Sun, Sister Moon* (1973). Unfortunately, Bowker's own beauties stayed clothed in the film, and she then concentrated on a TV career overseas. Her role as Princess Andromeda in *Clash of the Titans* (1981) finally brought a glimpse of a titanic titty, although it's strictly a side view—and there's certainly some chance we're looking at an exceptionally accurate body double. Then it was back to classy (and chaste) TV roles for Bowker, with the actress pretty much bowking out by the end of the '80s.

SKIN-fining Moment:

Clash of the Titans (1:41) *Judi's Body Double rises from the tub and supplies us with Titan-ic tush, plus some side right boobage.*

See Her Naked In:

Clash of the Titans (1981) Body Double—RB, Buns

Tanya Boyd

Born: March 20, 1951
Detroit, Michigan
Skin-O-Meter: Brief Nudity

Black is beautiful, but Tanya Boyd is hot. She proved that sexy was separate but not equal when she made her debut in *Black Heat* (1975). Her Nubian booty and boobies were steaming. Coming out of the gate, this skinful flick made the black stallion a sure winner. She followed it up with *Black Shampoo* (1976), in which she let her afro down again for some nakedness, and some righteous boob-tube appearances in the mini-series *Roots* and the sitcoms *What's Happening!!* and *Good Times*. But the real good times began when Tanya was cast in the sexploitation classic *Ilsa, Harem Keeper of the Oil Sheiks* (1976). She played "Satin," and her skin scenes were smooth as silk. By the '80s Tanya's tawdriness was coming, sadly, to an end. In 1994 she ended up where all sweet, not-so-young things land, on a daytime soap, *Days of Our Lives* to be precise. There's still life in the old girl, though, as she strutted her stuff in the comedy *For da Love of Money* (2002) wearing little more than a G-string and bra. You can take the girl out of the ghetto, but you can't take the ghetto out of the girl . . . thank the G-Man!

SKIN-fining Moment:

Black Heat (0:42) *Tanya flashes her left tit for Jim Brown to suck on, then proceeds to offer up an incredible ass-shot, a flash of fur, and a full-on rack-baring to cap the whole thing off!*

See Her Naked In:

The Happy Hooker Goes Hollywood (1980) Breasts
Ilsa, Harem Keeper of the Oil Sheiks (1976) Breasts, Thong
Black Shampoo (1976) FFN, Buns
Black Heat (1975) Breasts, Bush, Buns

Lara Flynn Boyle

Born: March 24, 1970
Davenport, Iowa
Skin-O-Meter: Hall of Fame

So much has been said about the presumed dieting habits of searing brunette vixen Lara Flynn Boyle that the wholly eroticized thespian's massive body of nude work is often overlooked. Equally comfortable in the role of a femme fatale or a simply killer-hot chick,

Lara employs her delicately and deliciously chiseled jaw, cheeks, and chin; her flashing, flamethrower eyes; and the voraciously sexual workings of her lips to create a patently ravishing being. And then she takes her clothes off a lot. See her as the skin-sandwich filler between two naked dudes in *Threesome* (1994). Bask in the warmth of her hot-tub boobies in *Afterglow* (1997). Come to grips with the clothes-free groping and grappling of *Since You've Been Gone* (1998). Talk about the titty tweaking in *Speaking of Sex* (2001). You have only scratched the surface.

SKIN-fining Moment:

The Road to Wellville (1:07) *A wonderfully long visit with Lara Flynn's Bubbles as she lies topless on a bed while talking to a horny Matthew Broderick.*

See Her Naked In:

Speaking of Sex (2001) Breasts
Susan's Plan (1998) Breasts
Since You've Been Gone (1998) RB
Afterglow (1997) Breasts
Farmer and Chase (1997) RB
The Big Squeeze (1996) RB
Cafe Society (1995) RB
Threesome (1994) Buns
Past Tense (1994) Breasts, Buns
The Road to Wellville (1994) Breasts
Mobsters (1991) RB

Lisa Boyle

Born: August 6, 1968
Chicago, Illinois
Skin-O-Meter: Great Nudity

Brown-haired butt tosser Lisa Boyle is the ultimate fun girl. She has plump, juicy lips, impish eyes like dark liquid M&Ms, a smile that is eager to tease or be teased, showgirl struts, a neatly coiffed trim, and a top-of-the-line sweater shelf. Combine these happy attributes with a track record of

showing them off in twenty or so movies, and out pops the world's sexiest play date. Lisa's best trick is that she's not just naked: she's naked and active. Although she occasionally coasts through flossy parts in big-budget fare such as *Bad Boys* (1995) or *The Nutty Professor* (1996), Boyle's specialty is the hot humping seductress in productions where the budget is as stripped as she is. *I Like to Play Games* (1995) sums up Lisa's style: rocking the bed in a bondage-harness bang, opening her legs for the close-up crotch shot, fast-fingering her little man in the boat. Lisa puts the fun in games.

SKIN-fining Moment:

I Like to Play Games (0:35) *Kinked-up Lisa dons a leather outfit that showcases her boomers and bumcakes while she drips hot wax on her man-friend.*

See Her Naked In:

Pray for Power (2000) FFN
Let the Devil Wear Black (1999) Breasts, Thong
Sheer Passion (1998) FFN, Buns
Lost Highway (1997) Breasts
The Night That Never Happened (1997) FFN, Buns
Leaving Scars (1997) Breasts, Buns
Dreammaster: The Erotic Invader (1996) Breasts, Buns
Intimate Deception (1996) FFN, Buns
Alien Terminator (1995) Breasts
When the Bullet Hits the Bone (1995) Breasts
I Like to Play Games (1995) FFN, Buns
Friend of the Family (1995) Breasts, Buns
Caged Heat 3000 (1995) Breasts, Buns
Concealed Weapon (1994) Breasts
Midnight Tease (1994) FFN, Buns
Starquest (1994) Breasts
Midnight Witness (1992) FFN, Thong, Buns

TeleVisions:

Dream On Breasts, Buns
Love Street FFN
Red Shoe Diaries Breasts, Thong

Ivana Bozilovic

Born: September 28, 1980
Belgrade, Yugoslavia
Skin-O-Meter: Great Nudity

Ivana Bozilovic, which if you say it fast sounds kind of like "I wanna blow this," made her big-screen debut in *100 Girls* (2000) as Rene, the breast cheater. She wasn't nude but was seen scribbling on the fleshly overrun from her lacy bra. No chest charlatan, the Yugoslavian yummy pie packs a walloping pair of Eastern European eyefuls. She went on to play an uncredited role in *Charlie's Angels* (2000) as a female rock climber. She sure gets Mr. Skin's rocks off. And speaking of rocks, check out the boulders Ivana shares in the carnal college comedy *National Lampoon's Van Wilder* (2002). She definitely provides the wild in Van's moniker.

SKIN-fining Moment:

Van Wilder (0:50) *Great look at Ivana's yugos while she strips for an oil massage.*

See Her Naked In:

Van Wilder (2002) Breasts

Lorraine Bracco

Born: October 2, 1955
New York, New York
Skin-O-Meter: Great Nudity

Do you want to get whacked or wanked? Lorraine Bracco can do both. From the Italian beauty who bared almost all in her first film performance *Duos sur canapé* (1979), to her most memorable recurring role as Tony Soprano's arousing analyst on HBO's mob hit *The Sopranos*, Lorraine flirts with death and sex in every performance. Her Mediterranean good looks make her a natural for the slew of Mafia pictures coming out of

Hollywood—*The Pick-Up Artist* (1987), *Goodfellas* (1990), and *Getting Gotti* (1994). Sadly, besides her debut, Lorraine's skin hits have been wiped out, with fans getting merely a glimpse of her rosy nips in a transparent bra in *Medicine Man* (1992). Even a sexy shower scene on *The Sopranos* featured the wet charms of a body double. But the observant Lorraine-looker can catch a quick glimpse of her muff from *Even Cowgirls Get the Blues* (1994). Lorraine should go west and show south more often.

SKIN-fining Moment:

Duos Sur Canapé (0.55) *Shazzam! Nude in the bedroom changing clothes, rear view. (Nice buns!) Then breasts sitting on the bed. This will frazzle your French fries!*

See Her Naked In:

Even Cowgirls Get the Blues (1994) Bush
Traces of Red (1992) RB
Goodfellas (1990) LB
Duos sur Canapé (1979) Breasts, Buns

TeleVisions:

The Sopranos Body Double—Buns / Her—
  Breasts

Orla Brady

Born: March 28, 1963
Dublin, Ireland
Skin-O-Meter: Brief Nudity

Raised by nuns, this Irish beauty says she's an atheist. But one look at Orla Brady is proof of the existence of God. She's a familiar face on the telly in the UK, with appearances in made-for-TV movies such as *The Rector's Wife* (1993) (damn near killed him). Orla made her film debut in *Words upon the Window Pane* (1994), which is based on a play by W.B. Yates about seances and Jonathan Swift. When it comes to skin, though, this lassie removes her

collar on the little screen, where she exposed her little screams in *The Heart Surgeon* (1997). Orla is getting dicked by a doctor who ends up operating on her husband, too— well, in the operating theater, while she gets his instrument in bed. Not much of a name Stateside, though she did star with lucky American Luke Perry in *Fogbound* (2002), let's hope Orla makes it past the fog and clearly into the sights of skin-watching US of Aers.

SKIN-fining Moment:

The Heart Surgeon *Orla mounts her man and we see her Brady butt and Brady boobs.*

See Her Naked In:

The Heart Surgeon (1997) RB, Buns

Sonia Braga

Born: June 16, 1951
Maringa, Parana, Brazil
Skin-O-Meter: Hall of Fame

A Brazilian bombshell with a bottom that defines rumptastic, Sonia Braga remains the sexiest thing to come from that South American country since the thong. It was the seriously weird threesome flick *Dona Flor and Her Two Husbands* (1978), one of whom was a ghost, that put the butt-length-ebony-haired, dark-skinned beauty on the map—chart a course for carnal adventure! Sonia had been driving Brazilians wild with her kinky soap operas, but American audiences had to wait until *Kiss of the Spider Woman* (1985) to learn of her feminine charms. She's since become a staple of Americans' libidos, especially her stint on *Sex and the City* as Kim Cattrall's lesbian lover. To see Sonia hetero, check out *I Love You* (1982), one her most erotic performances. It features every inch of Sonia's talent—her gravity-defying Hershey's Kisses, barrels of booming booty, and even her darkly entangled Brazilian rain forest. It's a body of work to Braga about.

SKIN-fining Moment:

I Love You (0:54) Sonia makes balletic hoo-hah with her Brazilian boyfriend, baring her supple suckables and nifty nether-curls. Sonia, I love you too!

See Her Naked In:

Tieta do Agreste (1996) Breasts
Two Deaths (1995) Breasts
Roosters (1993) RB, Bush
Gabriela (1983) FFN, Buns
I Love You (1981) FFN, Buns
Lady on the Bus (1978) FFN, Buns
Dona Flor and Her Two Husbands (1977) Breasts, Buns

TeleVisions:

Tales from the Crypt Breasts

Laura Branigan

Born: July 3, 1957
Brewster, New York
Died: August 26, 2004
Skin-O-Meter: Brief Nudity

A chart-topping pop singer whose smash hit "Gloria" remains a remixed standard in the dance clubs of today, lovely Laura Branigan did a bit of dabbling in the acting game, bringing a smile to small spots in the movie *Delta Pi* (1985) and the TV show *ChiPs*. The most skinsational moment in her acting career was undoubtedly when she portrayed an American pop singer yearning to become an actress in the Aussie chick flick *Backstage* (1988). The film offered a love scene with Laura where she disposed of her top and revealed her musical mams in all their "Gloria!" Sadly, a fatal brain aneurysm took this chart-topper from us in August 2004.

SKIN-fining Moment:

Backstage (0:44) Just a touch of the "Gloria" singer's left globe-ia while she reclines topless in bed with her bang buddy.

See Her Naked In:

Backstage (1988) LB

Julia Brendler

Born: February 26, 1975
Schwedt, Germany
Skin-O-Meter: Hall of Fame

Those beguiling eyes make Julia Brendler seem like a German Christina Ricci, and her lucky countrymen got to watch the former child actress grow up, out, and naked. This indie queen was quick to flaunt her barely legal beauty, too. She started by frolicking in the rain in *Verbotene Liebe* (1989) then only got wetter in *Reise in die Nacht* (1998). Her aquatic antics culminate in some full-frontal frolicking with *Dolphins* (1999). Always in demand, Julia's now begun to work in English-language productions. Fortunately, you don't need to speak German to appreciate every inch of Julia's talent.

SKIN-fining Moment:

Verbotene Liebe (0:24) Julia joins a horned-up farmhand for some boinking in the barn. She strips down, they get it on, and everybody can see her happy-sacks, hairpie, and heinie.

See Her Naked In:

Deeply (2000) RB
Dolphins (1999) FFN, Buns
Sawdust Tales (1998) Breasts
Blutjunge Liebe—und Keiner Darf es Wissen (1998) FFN
Reise in die Nacht (1998) FFN
Leben in Angst (1997) Breasts
Tatort—Der Tod Spielt mit (1997) FFN, Buns
2½ Minuten (1996) FFN
Moondance (1995) Breasts, Bush
Verbotene Liebe (1989) FFN, Buns

TeleVisions:

Auf Eigene Gefahr Buns
Der Letzte Zeuge FFN

Eileen Brennan

Born: September 3, 1935
Los Angeles, California
Skin-O-Meter: Brief Nudity

Eileen Brennan is probably most famous for her Oscar-nominated role in *Private Benjamin* (1980), and she's the kind of sergeant anyone would like to drill in the booty camp. Not that Eileen has exposed her private benjamins much onscreen. In fact, that happened only once, but it's well worth seeking out. She appeared opposite Gene Hackman and Al Pacino in *The Scarecrow* (1973), another one of that decade's alienated buddy pictures. Eileen's scene won't scare any crows away, but it's not for the birds—it's for the hawks out there who like to circle around some choice skin. Eileen is a funny lady, and she was a regular on the boob-tube comedy *Rowan & Martin's Laugh-In*. But when she takes it all off, that's no laughing matter—it's a lustful one.

SKIN-fining Moment:

Scarecrow (0:27) Gene Hackman reaches over in bed, removes Eileen's bra, and grabs a mittful of her bare Brennans.

See Her Naked In:

Scarecrow (1973) Breasts

Amy Brenneman

Born: June 22, 1964
Glastonbury, Connecticut
Skin-O-Meter: Brief Nudity

Before you judge Amy Brenneman, the star of the hit TV drama *Judging*

Amy, don't forget her case was first opened on the notoriously skin-friendly *NYPD Blue.* And she didn't disappoint, dropping her briefs for a brief shot of her bottom as it writhed on a fellow precinct dick. Her big-screen career has been less skintacular in *Heat* (1995), *Fear* (1996), and *Daylight* (1996). She continued with the one-word titles with *Nevada* (1997), but at least offered a sexy glimpse at her titillating talents in bra and panting panties. As the movie titles lengthened, conversely her clothing shortened, until, in *Your Friends and Neighbors* (1998), she was not only topless but bottomless. Now that's what Mr. Skin calls a friendly neighbor.

SKIN-fining Moment:

Your Friends and Neighbors **(1:34)** *Amy lies on her side in bed in front of Jason Patric. Her bare right Brenneman is visible and she's bottomless, so if you tweak the lighting—you've got bush!*

See Her Naked In:

Your Friends and Neighbors **(1998)** RB, Bush
Nevada **(1997)** Body Double—Buns

TeleVisions:

NYPD Blue Breasts, Buns

Bobbie Bresee

Born: 1950
San Diego, California
Skin-O-Meter: Great Nudity

Blonde and *beautiful . . . a buxom, bootilicious body . . . bountiful bare skinematic moments . . . Bobbie Bresee* has every right to claim the title of *B* movie bombshell. Starring in classic camp fare such as *Surf Nazis Must Die* (1987) and *Ghoulies* (1985), this stacked starlet became a favorite scream queen

among the late-night feature seekers and drive-in set. This horror hottie's kicking and screaming caused lots of wet dreaming in *Mausoleum* (1983). As a cursed young housewife turned sexual predator, it's easy to envy Bresee's next victim. Shots of her incredibly luscious, round ass are mesmerizing, as she stands naked pondering her padded perfection in a mirror. *Evil Spawn* (1987) might cause an urge for a medieval spank, as glimpses of Bobbie's bobbling boobies are in abundance. Regardless of the title you choose, it's easy to be swept away by Bresee's "I know you want to squeeze me" attitude in all of her films.

SKIN-fining Moment:

Mausoleum **(0:25)** *Bobbie busts out the Bresees and backside while wrapping a towel around her nude niceness.*

See Her Naked In:

Evil Spawn **(1987)** Breasts
Mausoleum **(1983)** Breasts, Buns

Jordana Brewster

Born: April 26, 1980
Panama City, Panama
Skin-O-Meter: Brief Nudity

At fifteen Jordana Brewster broke into show business in the lurid world of soap operas. She ventured into movies in the horror film *The Faculty* (1998), although not with any of that genre's gratuitous nudity. Damn. Jordana played a hippie in the TV mini-series *The '60s,* only this flower girl kept her petals on. Stardom followed the surprising success of the cars-and-cuties blockbuster *The Fast and the Furious* (2001). It's one sexy vehicle, but juggy Jordana stalled at going topless. Those ripe, sweet, gravity-

defying, young melons fell ripe and juicy from her shirt at last in *The Invisible Circus* (2001). The brief scene is enough to pitch Mr. Skin's tent.

SKIN-fining Moment:

The Invisible Circus **(1:04)** *Jordana drops her dress and reveals her rack and temporarily turns the movie into The Visible (Two-Ring) Circus.*

See Her Naked In:

The Invisible Circus **(2001)** Breasts

Angelica Bridges

Born: November 20, 1973
Harrisonville, Missouri
Skin-O-Meter: Brief Nudity

Angelica Bridges reached out from TV as one of the big-busted beauties on *Baywatch.* She was already a staple of sexy broadcasting, having guest starred on various scandalizing shows such as *Silk Stalkings, NYPD Blue, Mortal Kombat: Conquest,* and Howard Stern's *Son of the Beach.* Angelica even had daytime panting with her stint on the soap opera *Days of Our Lives.* Her film work is less stellar, but she did appear in one nude-worthy feature called *California Heat* (1995). She's taking a shower, as all hot mamas like to do onscreen, and, being a multi-tasker, is banging her boyfriend too. It's her sole skin on camera, and those heaving hooters are put to good use, though they're a bit too closely squeezed onto her lover's chest for Skin Central's enjoyment. Thankfully, in 2001 Angelica proved herself a real angel when she posed completely nude, without any man-meat to mess it up, on the prurient pages of *Playboy.* Angelica is a Bridges too far out!

SKIN-fining Moment:

California Heat Ms. Bridges opens her tunnel for a man in the sack, Bombers and thonged buns.

See Her Naked In:

California Heat (1996) Breasts

Cynthia Brimhall

Born: March 10, 1964
Ogden, Utah
Skin-O-Meter: Great Nudity

If you want to star in a bikini-action epic from director Andy Sidaris, it helps to be a *Playboy* Playmate (or a has-been '70s male star). Cynthia Brimhall met her qualifications back when she was Miss October 1985. Now she's a proud veteran of productions such as *Hard Ticket to Hawaii* (1987) and *Hard Hunted* (1992), in which her naked hardbody prompts plenty of hard . . . well, you get the idea. Don't forget to check out her fine work with the *Playboy* line of videos, either. You can also find Brimhall brimming out of sexy outfits in Las Vegas, where she's one of the city's most respected showgirls.

SKIN-fining Moment:

Do or Die (0:36) Funbaggables and fanny-cakes as she gets hot with her boyfriend by the fireplace.

See Her Naked In:

Fit to Kill (1993) Breasts
Hard Hunted (1992) Breasts
Do or Die (1991) Breasts, Buns
Guns (1990) Breasts, Thong
Picasso Trigger (1989) Breasts
Hard Ticket to Hawaii (1987) Breasts
Numerous Playboy Videos

Christie Brinkley

Born: February 2, 1954
Malibu, California
Skin-O-Meter: Never Nude

The '70s had Cheryl Tiegs in a mesh bathing suit. The '80s had Christie Brinkley in . . . well, everything. Christie actually scored her first *Sports Illustrated* cover back in 1979, but that only primed the '80s for college dorms wallpapered in the poster form of Christie (not to mention two more *SI* covers). And, of course, Christie was perfectly cast as Chevy Chase's skinny dipping lust object in *National Lampoon's Vacation* (1983). She reprised the role in *Vegas Vacation* (1997), while her modeling career still has her providing masturbatory fodder for new generations.

SKIN-fining Moment:

Vacation (1:13) Dreamgirl Christie proves she's all real by peeling to her bra-and-panties and plunging into a hotel pool for potential canoodling with super-stud Chevy Chase.

Danielle Brisebois

Born: June 28, 1969
Brooklyn, New York
Skin-O-Meter: Great Nudity

As Archie Bunker's cute little sidekick in the final days of *All in the Family*, Danielle Brisebois couldn't quite revive a fading sitcom (or save the short-lived spinoff *Archie Bunker's Place*). Danielle, however, sure kept us feeling fresh while establishing herself as a sexy young woman. Her first nudity kept things all in the family with *Big Bad Mama II* (1987), as her outlaw character frolicked under a waterfall with her sister in crime. Danielle's twin guns then kept blazing in a stunning scene in *Kill Crazy* (1989). Unfortunately, Danielle decided to concentrate on being a singer and songwriter, although her stalled career will hopefully get those Brisbees flying back onto the big screen.

SKIN-fining Moment:

Big Bad Mama II (0:12) Archie's Little Girl shows her not-so-little love balloons while frolicking topless in a pond with (the shorter-haired) Julie McCullough.

See Her Naked In:

Kill Crazy (1990) Breasts, Buns
Big Bad Mama II (1987) Breasts

Anne Brochet

Born: November 22, 1966
Amiens, Somme, France
Skin-O-Meter: Great Nudity

A facile and fetching French actress, google-eyed brunette Anne Brochet has been a star in her native land due to the light and accessible nature of her airy beauty. She has been a fixation among Stateside cognoscenti due to the plethora of well-lit, accessible shots that show off her airy boobies, hairy beav, and bouncing booty. Fans of foreign family entertainment may have registered a flicker of skinterest watching playful Brochet teasing Gerard Depardieu in the French version of *Cyrano de Bergerac* (1990). Further skinvestigation would lead the pointedly curious skinvestigator to *Tous les matins du monde* (1991) and reward him with mouth-watering close-ups of Anne's actively rising nipples and a shot from further back of the Brochet beaver being gracefully hung.

SKIN-fining Moment:

Dust (1:18) Skinny-dipping Anne emerges from a lake, treating us to a booby view followed by some nice buttage.

See Her Naked In:

Dust (2001) Breasts, Buns
30 ans (1999) LB
Une journée de merde! (1999) Breasts, Buns
Driftwood (1996) Breasts, Buns

Consentement mutuel (1994) FFN, Buns
Tous les matins du monde (1991) FFN,
  Buns

Beth Broderick

Born: February 24, 1959
Falmouth, Kentucky
Skin-O-Meter: Great Nudity

Sabrina, the Teenage Witch cast a
spell on a lot of men, many of
whom fantasized that Sabrina's
Aunt Zelda and Aunt Hilda had a
relationship that was more than
sisterly. Zelda—as played by
stunning blonde Beth Broderick—
also had plenty of guys dreaming of
her riding their broomsticks. Beth
is more than just a sitcom goddess,
though. She's also a respected
stage actress, writer, and director.
Fortunately, her late-blooming
career has also shown Beth to be a
fearless presence onscreen,
displaying her well-aged assets in
sexy scenes from the cable-TV
series *Women: Stories of Passion*
(1997).

SKIN-fining Moment:

The Bonfire of the Vanities (1:31)
*Panties and ass shot as she photocopies
her derrière. Pretty kinko.*

See Her Naked In:

Breast Men (1997) Breasts
The Bonfire of the Vanities (1990) Buns

TeleVisions:

Women: Stories of Passion Breasts

Jayne Brook

Born: September 16, 1962
Northbrook, Illinois
Skin-O-Meter: Brief Nudity

When your first role onscreen is
that of a schoolteacher, even if it's
in the action-packed *Superman IV:
The Quest for Peace* (1987), it's
unlikely you're a piece of ass. But

despite her family-oriented career
path, Jayne Brook is the kind of girl-
next-door that gets guys babbling.
She continued on to the hilarious
but very un-skin-friendly
Kindergarten Cop (1990). Since then,
she's made a nice life for herself in
films such as *Don't Tell Mom the
Babysitter's Dead* (1991) and *Gattaca*
(1997), as well as TV shows such as
Chicago Hope and *The District*. But fear
not, this plain Jayne is not as skingy
as she may first appear. She finds a
way into viewer's heart-ons with the
flick *Into My Heart* (1998). In it, she
lets her boobs out briefly in bed with
Rob Morrow and again in the
classic-nudity-onscreen shower
scene. Let's hope Jayne lets
audiences take another dip in the
Brook soon.

SKIN-fining Moment:

Into My Heart It's a boobling Brook as
we see Jayne's jugalos through a semi-
steamy glass shower door.

See Her Naked In:

Into My Heart (1998) Breasts

Kelly Brook

Born: November 23, 1979
Rochester, Kent, UK
Skin-O-Meter: Brief Nudity

Bigger is better, and Great Britain is
leading the pack in this fleshy
female trend with buxom beauties
such as Kate Winslet, Elisabeth
Hurley, and the most stacked
English tart of them all, Kelly
Brook. She first came to attention
as a real stiff pick-me-up on the hit
British morning TV program *The
Big Breakfast*. Forget coffee or tea;
Kelly's cups are the real eye-
opener! But the boob tube was
simply too small to contain the
bountiful gifts Kelly had to share,
and soon the top-heavy teabag was
being seen on the big screen.
Despite starring in provocative

titles such as *Sorted* (2000), *Ripper:
Letters from Hell* (2001), and *The
Italian Job* (2003), the one job
requirement this busty babe won't
fill is nudity onscreen. She has been
seen in America in a recurring role
on *Smallville*, and Mr. Skin will
remain small indeed until this
heavenly body exposes her milky
ways. The bikini tease on one
episode of MTV's *Select* just doesn't
cut it. But maybe her upcoming
role in *School for Seduction* (2004)
will teach us something nude.

SKIN-fining Moment:

Three In *Three*, *Kelly shows off her
one—specifically, her right one, when
her nip slips free of its bikini casing
while she sucks face seaside with her
dude.*

See Her Naked In:

Three (2004) RB

Deanna Brooks

Born: April 30, 1974
Boulder City, Nevada
Skin-O-Meter: Great Nudity

Former Playmate Deanna Brooks
had men babbling over her
bubbliness after a skinful
appearance in *Playboy* in May of
1998. Her booby baring led to a
stint in softcore sinema, displaying
the full force of her glamour-girl
giggliness in *Playboy* video flicks
such as *California Girls* (2000) and
Playmates in Bed (2002). For Brooks
at her best undressed, check out the
flesh flick *The Rowdy Girls* (2000).
At her randiest and rowdiest,
Deanna is quite the teaser and
crowd pleaser.

SKIN-fining Moment:

Boat Trip (0:00) *From maybe the
greatest DVD menu of all time: Jami
Ferrell, Natalia Sokolova, and Deanna
(left to right) sprawl out topless and
offer you some beautiful choices.*

See Her Naked In:

Boat Trip (2002) Breasts
Numerous Playboy Videos

TeleVisions:

Weekend Flash FFN, Buns

Elisabeth Brooks

Born: July 2, 1951
Toronto, Ontario, Canada
Died: September 7, 1997
Skin-O-Meter: Great Nudity

She didn't have many lines—or even much screen time—but Elisabeth Brooks still became a horror legend for her role as a sniff-worthy seductress in the classic werewolf film *The Howling* (1981). Hollywood didn't appreciate her lupine wiles, though, and Elisabeth only appeared in a few more low-budget films before her untimely death from cancer in 1997. She'll still always be remembered by legions of horror geeks, in addition to the many actors who benefited from Elisabeth's later work as an acting coach.

SKIN-fining Moment:

The Howling (0:48) *Full-frontal stripping by the fire. Then more nudity making love. It burns! It burrrns!*

See Her Naked In:

The Howling (1981) FFN, Buns

Randi Brooks

Born: November 8, 1956
New York, New York
Skin-O-Meter: Great Nudity

After the death of the great Carol Wayne, Randi Brooks stepped in as Hollywood's sexiest ditz. This brilliant comic actress used her huge knockers and squeaky voice to steal any number of scenes. It took someone with the genius of *The Man with Two Brains* (1983) to finally get her naked, but it's impossible for

Randi to ever downplay her sex appeal. Her turn as a dot-brained swinger in *TerrorVision* (1986) is more riveting than the film's monster, while Randi's orgasmic restaurant scene in *Hamburger . . . The Motion Picture* (1986) leaves Meg Ryan sounding like Shirley Temple. Randi's randiness has been missing in action since her role on the 1989 series *Mancuso, FBI* (where she was billed as Randi Brazen), but her unique presence will always be appreciated—even with the sound off on our TV sets.

SKIN-fining Moment:

The Man with Two Brains (1:11) *Randi bares her rack to Steve Martin outside a hotel then flashes fanny as she changes clothes once they check in. Finally, she wears one wild-and-crazy black see-through negligee.*

See Her Naked In:

Hamburger . . . The Motion Picture (1986) Breasts
Tightrope (1984) Breasts, Buns
The Man with Two Brains (1983) Breasts, Thong

Blair Brown

Born: April 23, 1946
Washington, D.C.
Skin-O-Meter: Great Nudity

A busy, New York-based actress who appears comfortable on screens big and small (not to mention the stage), Blair Brown is most fondly remembered by women for her title role on TV's *The Days and Nights of Molly Dodd*, amongst numerous other boob-tube credits. Her true skin was revealed in 1980's mind-tripping psycho-drama *Altered States*, where Blair portrayed an Ivy League-trained anthropologist who takes the most primal of amazing, effects-filled journeys alongside fellow brain-drainer William Hurt. It's he (and we!) who gets a good glimpse of some Brown boobage and bum as

they engage in some co-ed coitus. She's also the subject of a handful of heady hallucinations experienced by Hurt, who's at least intelligent enough to imagine what Blair looks like when she's naked! Keep your eyes open for a shot or two of Blair's hairy armpits, something that can no doubt be chalked up to a little funky Method acting from the lady who lets her inner animal loose.

SKIN-fining Moment:

Altered States (0:34) *Blair Brown shows pink-buds during William Hurt's mushroom-induced hallucination.*

See Her Naked In:

A Flash of Green (1984) RB
Altered States (1980) Breasts, Buns

Bobbie Brown

Born: October 7, 1969
Baton Rouge, Louisiana
Skin-O-Meter: Great Nudity

She won the spokesmodel competition on *Star Search* a record thirteen times, but Bobbie Brown was meant for bigger things. Or, rather, her bigger things were meant for exposure on shows such as *Married . . . with Children* and fantasy films ranging from *Flash Gordon* (1980) to *The Last Action Hero* (1993). Bobbie also stayed busy as a model for Budweiser before making our chubs rise with a sexy turn in *Kounterfeit* (1996). And don't forget Bobbie's important contribution to rock 'n' roll, cavorting with her former husband Jani Lane in the "Cherry Pie" video for his band Warrant.

SKIN-fining Moment:

Betrayal of the Dove (1:03) *Thonged buttage backed up by booming bazookas when Bobbie boogies on stage at a club.*

See Her Naked In:

Betrayal of the Dove (1992) Breasts

Judith M. Brown

Born: October 1, 1956
Skin-O-Meter: Great Nudity

Crimson-tressed and cuddly, Judith M. Brown made her bones—and inspired a good number of them amongst skinophiles—as an actress in a string of '70s exploitation flicks. Most notably, she ignited a pair of the era's quintessential Roger Corman-produced babes-behind-bars classics. First up, Judy did a spin as a not-to-be-trusted junkie in *Women in Cages* (1971), which also starred such genre mainstays as Pam Grier and Roberta Collins. Immediately thereafter, she could be seen (along with her fellow incarcerated friskies Pam and Roberta) as the new girl on the block in *The Big Doll House* (1971). Both films featured a moderate serving of juicy Judy's jigglers as she got prodded, probed, groped, and gang-raped as only they could in a women in prison quickie. The next ten years found Judy popping up in a handful of similarly exploitative fare, sans skin. And by the early '80s, Judy was apparently paroled from acting, as she hasn't appeared in a film since.

SKIN-fining Moment:

Slaughter's Big Rip-off **(0:31)** *Judy, Judy, Judy! Ms. Brown full-frontally bares her bitable meat bullets and plush plume while approaching the camera.*

See Her Naked In:

Slaughter's Big Rip-off (1973) FFN
The Manhandlers (1973) Breasts
Big Doll House (1971) Breasts
Women in Cages (1971) Breasts

Julie Brown

Born: August 31, 1958
Van Nuys, California
Skin-O-Meter: Great Nudity

Not to be confused with the ebony sweets of "Downtown" Julie Brown, this Julie Brown was another MTV hostess with the moistess. Never has a comedienne been as busty in body and gut-busting in humor. The booby prize of comedy, Julie has cut a seductive figure on TV as well as in such heinie-slappers as *The Incredible Shrinking Woman* (1981), *Police Academy 2: Their First Assignment* (1985), *Earth Girls Are Easy* (1988), and *Shakes the Clown* (1992). But Mr. Skin thinks her best role is the nearly forgotten horror B-movie *Bloody Birthday* (1981). At a young age, this prime USDA grade piece of meat stripped down naked as a peeping tom leered. Those ripe hooters were never juicier as she bounced about in her birthday suit. No bush, but that bottom is buttlicious.

SKIN-fining Moment:

Bloody Birthday **(0:14)** *MTV's white July Brown shows the pink tips of her great gazongas followed by a potent peek at her posterior.*

See Her Naked In:

Bloody Birthday (1981) Breasts, Buns

Joy Bryant

Born: 1976
The Bronx, New York
Skin-O-Meter: Brief Nudity

Joy Bryant first spread Joy to the world with her dusky deliciousness as a model for Tommy Hilfiger. Her lovely lungs and long-legged looks soon landed her a part in *MTV*'s *Carmen: A Hip Hopera* (2001) and a supporting role with Denzel Washington in *Antwone Fisher* (2002). It's impossible not to take a nibble when someone as juicy as Joy is offered as bait. Her super flyness will snag you in the shorts in the *Flashdance*-esque flick *Honey* (2003) with Jessica Alba. A dark angel all her own, with acting abilities to rival blacktress Halle Berry, in all likelihood Bryant should be flying toward stardom soon.

SKIN-fining Moment:

3-Way **(0:14)** *Bryant gives much Joy when she flashes her bare boobies during a shower schtup with her tattooed boytoy.*

See Her Naked In:

3-Way (2004) Breasts, Buns

Pamela Jean Bryant

Born: February 8, 1959
Indianapolis, Indiana
Skin-O-Meter: Great Nudity

Five-feet-five-inches tall, eyes of deep blue, with a mane of striking blonde hair, and a perfect 35-24-35 figure, Pamela Jean Bryant seems almost genetically composed to make guys pop off. Mission accomplished. Pamela is a generous lass, and she shared her charms first on TV, guest starring on episodes of the provocative *Fantasy Island*, the steamy *The Dukes of Hazzard*, and the amorous *The Love Boat*. And then she exposed her real talents onscreen. From the moment she took it off in *H.O.T.S.* (1979), it was clear that Pamela was on the fast track to T&A stardom. She continued to add that flash of skin that movies such as *Lunch Wagon* (1980) and *Private Lessons* (1981) needed to keep audiences' attention (among other things) riveted. But it wasn't until *Trapped* (1994) that Pamela went fully frontal. It's worth getting ensnarled in all that goodness.

SKIN-fining Moment:

H.O.T.S. **(1:33)** *Rah-rah-raw! Pamela's funbags are just two highlights of the flick's climactic strip football game.*

See Her Naked In:

Trapped (1994) FFN, Buns
Private Lessons (1981) RB
Lunch Wagon (1980) Breasts
Don't Answer the Phone! (1980) Breasts
H.O.T.S. (1979) Breasts

Ursula Buchfellner

Born: June 8, 1961
Munich, Germany
Skin-O-Meter: Great Nudity

Blonde, blue-eyed, five-feet-six-inches tall, with large and natural tits—this sort of über-bitch can only come from one place. Yes, Ursula Buchfellner is one of the masturbator race from Munich, Germany. Ursula knew she was built for one thing, sex, and was not shy about it. She began her career early and well exposed in her first nude revue *Popcorn und Himbeereis* (1978), which translates as *Popcorn and Ice Cream*—what a treat to eat . . . Ursula. She continued the carnal course with *Der Kurpfuscher und seine fixen Töchter* (1980) and *Il Cacciatore di uomini* (1980), better known by its American release title *Sexo Cannibal*. Yum, yum—eat her up! She followed that up with *L' Ultimo harem* (1981) and the indescribable *Sadomania-Hölle der Lust* (1981). The banned-in-the-UK, Jesus Franco-helmed shocker has a transsexual, fifty naked female extras, and bestiality. Ursula's role is not quite that extreme. She has a lesbian love affair and is sold to a brothel as a sex slave, where a john bites her boob and infects her with VD that kills her. In a few years the spotlight would fade on the alluring Ursula, but the movies live on. And what a turn-on they are!

SKIN-fining Moment:

L'Ultimo Harem (1:17) *Ursula lies back for an awe-insipring lesboid tongue-bath from Adriana Vega.*

See Her Naked In:

L'Ultimo Harem (1981) FFN, Buns
Sadomania-Hölle der Lust (1981) FFN
Naked Super Witches of the Rio Amore (1981) FFN, Buns

MR. SKIN'S TOP TEN

Money Honeys
. . . Fine-ancial figures

10. Brenda Price
9. Kristy McNichol
8. Meta Golding
7. Constance Money
6. Rosalind Cash
5. Rene Bond
4. Jewel Kilcher
3. Penny Baker
2. Alicia Silverstone
1. **Tara Buckman**

Der Kurpfuscher und Seine Fixen Töchter (1980) FFN, Buns
Il Cacciatore di Uomini (1980) FFN
Elles Font Tout (1978) FFN, Buns
Popcorn und Himbeereis (1978) FFN, Buns

Tara Buckman

Los Angeles, California
Skin-O-Meter: Great Nudity

Tara Buckman is one of those big-breasted beauties who populate daytime TV. She made viewers want to call in sick to work so they could stay home and wank watching her on the soap opera *Days of Our Lives*. For those who need the paycheck, Tara rewarded their responsibility by spicing up the prime-time sitcom *The Misadventures of Sheriff Lobo*. And for those adventuresome theatergoers, Tara added eye candy to the big-screen comedy *The Cannonball Run* (1981). But it wasn't until she entered the horror genre that things got really scary, at least for semen. That's because when Tara's naked titans debuted in *Silent Night, Deadly Night* (1984), everybody was filled with good cheer (and sticky crotches). She made candy canes stiffen again, returning to make *Silent Night, Deadly Night Part 2* (1986), a skin stocking stuffer. But that was only a prelude to the skin classic *Objects of Desire* (1989), in which Tara's three Bs were too good. *The Loves of a Wall Street Woman* (1989) continued to make her stock rise, and *The Marilyn Diaries* (1990) was a real page turner. But since then, Tara's been skinless, and after playing a non-nude Barmaid in *Blindfold: Acts of Obsession* (1994), she fell off the radar. Let's hope we pick up her heavenly body again soon.

SKIN-fining Moment:

Object of Desire (1:09) *A grab bag of full-frontal goodies as Tara poses for a skintastic photo shoot.*

See Her Naked In:

The Marilyn Diaries (1990) FFN, Buns
Object of Desire (1989) FFN, Buns
The Loves of a Wall Street Woman (1989) Breasts
Silent Night, Deadly Night: Part 2 (1986) Breasts
Silent Night, Deadly Night (1984) Breasts

Geneviève Bujold

Born: July 1, 1942
Montreal, Quebec, Canada
Skin-O-Meter: Great Nudity

A combination of many alluring elements is at play in the impetuous ingénue that is Geneviève Bujold. A convent-school dropout from Montreal, Quebec, this French Canadian delicacy began her filmic sexploits in the art-tinged skinema of late-1960s Paris. American producers were soon drawn to the impish allure, both sophisticated and childlike, of dear, sweet Geneviève. Cute accent. Naïve earnestness. Pixie-seductress eyes and lips. It's no wonder that *Coma* (1978) is remembered not for Bujold's gripping portrayal of a doctor who discovers a plot to murder patients and harvest their organs, but for a hot and humid shower scene that steams Geneviève straight down to her clam. Extraordinary shots of Bujold's pert-nipped parts also pop up in *Alex and the Gypsy* (1976) and *Monsignor* (1982).

SKIN-fining Moment:

Monsignor (1:05) *Miss Bujold gives us her breasts to behold as she tosses off her top and hops in the sack with Christopher Reeve.*

See Her Naked In:

Dead Ringers (1988) Breasts
Monsignor (1982) Breasts
Coma (1978) Breasts
Alex and the Gypsy (1976) FFN, Buns
Swashbuckler (1976) Body Double-FFN, Buns
Kamouraska (1973) Breasts

Sandra Bullock

Born: July 26, 1964
Arlington, Virginia
Skin-O-Meter: Brief Nudity

At this point, maybe Sandra Bullock should change her name to Sandra Blueballs! A super-sexy and slinky brunette whom men would love to screw *and* bring home to Mom, this merciless tease has done everything *but* show off that hot bod from day one onscreen. It's not like she hasn't come *this close* to delivering her good-girl goods. In *Who Shot Patakango?* (1990), Sandra stripped, but all we got was a brief shot of the top of her butt crack. Then came the steaming jungle sex scene in *Fire in the Amazon* (1993), wherein Sandra, completely nude,

straddles her boy-toy and goes wild, but without one nip or pubic hair out of place. In fact, she taped down her little girls to insure they didn't stray. Ouch! It hurts Mr. Skin, Sandy, more than it hurts you.

SKIN-fining Moment:

Fire on the Amazon (0:50) *Sandra is completely nude during sex, but the camera angles don't allow a clear shot of the important parts.*

See Her Naked In:

Fire on the Amazon (1993) Breasts
Who Shot Patakango? (1990) Buns

Brooke Burke

Born: September 8, 1971
Hartford, Connecticut
Skin-O-Meter: Never Nude

Brooke Burke majored in journalism in college. Here's a story for you, newsy: Why haven't you revealed your sources? The big-breasted host of E!'s *Wild On . . .* and *Rank* has yet to grace us with a moving picture of her moist picks, while remaining very generous in various states of undress for many of the lustrous lady mags. The former Frederick's of Hollywood and swimsuit model has got a body to die for, and Mr. Skin will kill himself if she doesn't share it on the big screen soon. Of course, she's yet to appear in film. Although that's about to change with the release of *The Hazing* (2004), which will hopefully get Brooke out of her bikini and into something a little more comfortable—Mr. Skin's lap! In the meantime, Brooke did go totally nude in the pages of *Playboy*. Read it and wank.

SKIN-fining Moment:

E! Wild On . . . "Amazon Education" (2002) *Brooke's initial swimsuit-clad entrance as this sex-soaked show's*

hostess practically rewrote the possibilities for (barely) wearing a bikini!

Michelle Burke

Born: November 30, 1970
Defiance, Ohio
Skin-O-Meter: Brief Nudity

Plenty of cones sprouted in trousers when Michelle Burke made her debut as Connie Conehead in the big-screen version of *The Coneheads* (1993). This was followed by a sexy turn as Jodi Kramer in the same year's acclaimed high-school comedy *Dazed and Confused* (1993). Michelle's projects then took a much lower profile, despite her raising our crotches with a topless strip routine in *The Last Word* (1994). Michelle began performing as Michelle Rene Thomas after her marriage and seems to have firmly retired from the screen since 1998.

SKIN-fining Moment:

The Last Word (0:10) *Boobiful bare breasts and nifty thongage as Michelle dances on a nudie-club stage.*

See Her Naked In:

The Last Word (1995) Breasts, Thong

Carol Burnett

Born: April 26, 1933
San Antonio, Texas
Skin-O-Meter: Never Nude

Television's grande dame of sketch comedy—who doesn't love *The Carol Burnett Show?*—is a subtly sexy comedienne who's appeared in a whole slew of TV projects, movies, and stage shows. That Carol Burnett has never appeared nude on film is no joke, though, and for years fans have had to settle for only a slight hint at the goods that this funny lady is packaging. The closest Carol ever came was in the 1972 dramedy *Pete 'n' Tillie*, wherein she removes her top and skirt to reveal a dimly lit shot of her bra-covered boobs and rather-matronly panties. The real shock in the sequence is that she's getting undone in preparation for a night of lovemaking with (gasp!) Walter Matthau!

SKIN-fining Moment:

Pete 'n' Tillie (0:28) *Carol lifts her shirt and offers up her bra-clad sad sacks to Walter Matthau.*

Hedy Burress

Born: October 3, 1973
Edwardsville, Illinois
Skin-O-Meter: Great Nudity

Trained as a stage actress as a young teen in the small town of Edwardsville, Illinois, noteworthy and nubile Hedy Burress stripped down to her skin in her very first cinematic outing, that opus of young female empowerment *Foxfire* (1996). The popular indie offering featured Hedy engaging in some skinsual lesbian overtures opposite Angelina Jolie. She took it to the next level a couple of years later in the foreign-produced, rowdy student comedy *Los Años Bárbaros* (1998), flashing nice Burress bush during a skintillating skinny-dipping sequence. Half a decade and twice as many features later (not to mention a handful of TV appearances), Hedy has yet to follow up on her daily double, but the chance of a titillating trifecta is a distinct possibility.

SKIN-fining Moment:

Foxfire (0:40) *Nice look at Hedy's hogans while she gets a tattoo from Angelina.*

See Her Naked In:

Los Años Bárbaros (1998) FFN, Buns
Foxfire (1996) Breasts

Saffron Burrows

Born: January 1, 1973
London, England, UK
Skin-O-Meter: Brief Nudity

Those flaring nostrils give Saffron Burrows away. Gazing out from big, blameless, insolent eyes, she may present herself as a proper English lady, but a scent of sex wafts by, and by God if it hasn't emanated from our own dear Ms. Burrows. Suddenly the stiff-lipped resolve of the mouth—stiff but plump and juicy—quivers in a sensualist's gasp. The eyes dart like those of a furry, wild thing. Has anyone noticed that within this prim fox is a ravening minx? Only everyone who laid eyes on *The Loss of Sexual Innocence* (1999), in which subtle spice Saffron plays identical twins, one of whom stands fully naked in the bath, presenting the ready-to-be-randy Burrows bum in its entirety, a posterior to slaver over for all posterity.

SKIN-fining Moment:

The Loss of Sexual Innocence (0:49) *Saffy strips, showing her chunky buns and the side of her sacks as she steps into the shower.*

See Her Naked In:

Enigma (2001) RB, Buns
Tempted (2001) LB, Buns
The Loss of Sexual Innocence (1999) LB, Buns

Ellen Burstyn

Born: December 7, 1932
Detroit, Michigan
Skin-O-Meter: Hall of Fame

Burstin' with round-bottom goodness and up-top appeal, veteran eye pleaser (and critically acclaimed thespian) Ellen Burstyn is now old enough to be a hot chick's grandma, but don't be fooled by the tricks of time. The Detroit native hails from an era when being a serious actress meant showing your muff. Ellen's melons and furry slice shot to pubic acclaim in the skinematic adaptation of Henry Miller's banned sexual memoir *Tropic of Cancer* (1970). Lolling in full nubile nudity atop a set of rumpled sheets, Ellen was the primary source of *Tropic*'s heat. Bouncy Burstyn jumped out of bed and straight into more rack-swinging roles. Titty-stingy actresses of today should check out *Alex in Wonderland* (1970), *King of Marvin Gardens* (1972), and *The Ambassador* (1984) for tips on how a real artist displays her instrument.

SKIN-fining Moment:

Tropic of Cancer (0:03) *Ellen's body is Burstyn out all over as she relaxes in bed, then jumps up. Nice nerps and nether-hair.*

See Her Naked In:

The Ambassador (1984) Breasts
King of Marvin Gardens (1972) Breasts
Tropic of Cancer (1970) FFN
Alex In Wonderland (1970) Breasts

Jennifer Burton

Skin-O-Meter: Great Nudity

Graced with a stunningly sexy body, Jennifer Burton has been happy to relieve herself of the burden of her clothing in many flesh-packed films. As a wee little-bit she appeared in the thriller *Invisible Strangler* (1976), but Jennifer waited for puberty to fully strangle pants serpents, debuting her bouncy breasties in the sinematic flick *Desire* (1993). Then Jen's own desirous yin for skin hit full tit. Since *Desire* she has appeared naked in over fifteen flicks with naughty names such as *Play Time* (1994), *Mischievous* (1996), and *Watch Me* (1996). You can't help but keep your eyes on Jennifer's prize. She steals the scene in every skindeavor.

SKIN-fining Moment:

Play Time (0:42) *Jenny's jugs jiggle as she enjoys a hot-tub menage with Monique Parent and a some lucky meathead.*

See Her Naked In:

Sex, Lies, & Politics (2003) FFN, Buns
Emmanuelle: First Contact (2000)
Night Shade (1997) FFN, Buns
Watch Me (1996) FFN, Buns
Dead of Night (1996) Breasts
Mischievous (1996) FFN, Buns
Call Girl (1995) FFN, Buns
I Like to Play Games (1995) FFN, Buns
Killing for Love (1995) FFN
Play Time (1994) FFN, Buns
Desire (1993) Breasts

TeleVisions:

Beverly Hills Bordello FFN, Buns
Butterscotch Breasts
The Click Breasts
Emmanuelle in Space Breasts, Buns
Erotic Confessions FFN, Buns
Red Shoe Diaries Breasts

Pascale Bussières

Born: June 27, 1968
Montréal, Quebec, Canada
Skin-O-Meter: Great Nudity

Our neighbors to the north are surprisingly skinful, considering that they spend their time shivering in igloos and feeding their pet moose. It must be the French part of the Canadian identity that explains the love of letting it all hang out. And when you look as sultry as Pascale Bussières, why not flaunt it? Though she's relatively unknown south of the border, those who want to check out the view south of her border need do little more than savor her career. Her first fleshy venture onscreen was in *La Vie fantôme* (1992). It was only her third film but exposed her as a nude-comer worth keeping a randy eye on. She also appeared clothes-less in *When Night Is Falling* (1995), and viewers got to

see night falling over her love patch. She continues to strut her stuff in various foreign-language sizzlers, but Americans may recall that she wooed Stephen Baldwin in *X Change* (2000), which featured some extreme close-ups of her ski slopes. And Pascale just gets better with age, like a fine Canuck beer. Her moist skinful appearance is in *La Turbulence des fluides* (2002), where she runs completely naked through the surf during an earthquake. She'll make the earth move under your feet!

SKIN-fining Moment:

When Night Is Falling (0:56) *Bussières and Rachael Crawford rub rugs and nibble nips—naked all the way—in a great Sapphic suck-down.*

See Her Naked In:

La Turbulence des Fluides (2002) FFN, Buns
Between the Moon and Montevideo (2001) Breasts
La Répétition (2001) Breasts, Bush
X Change (2000) Breasts
Twilight of the Ice Nymphs (1997) Buns
Thunder Point (1996) Breasts, Buns
When Night Is Falling (1995) Breasts, Buns
La Vie Fantôme (1992) Breasts, Buns

Yancy Butler

Born: July 2, 1970
New York, New York
Skin-O-Meter: Brief Nudity

Yancy Butler served her time on TV but made her big-screen debut as a nine-year-old in *Savage Weekend* (1979). Her hot, husky voice and intense eyes made her a must-see on the tube on episodes of *Law & Order* and the short-lived series *Mann & Machine*. Returning to movies, she made a lusty bull's-eye in John Woo's *Hard Target* (1993). But it's her skin debut that really hit the mark in *The Hit List* (1993). Yancy seems to treat us to a side of teat with a schmear of moist muff in *The Hit List*, but,

alas, those parts actually belong to a body double (and if this throaty beauty weren't so smokin' hot, that sort of transgression might have landed her on something that rhymes with *Hit List*.) Yancy's only true nudity comes in *The Ex* (1997)—nice ass, terrific tits, but don't blink or you'll miss the skin show. It's been some time since Yancy's fancies appeared onscreen. The Butler did it; let's hope she does it again!

SKIN-fining Moment:

The Ex (1:02) *As Suzy Amis watches from another building, Yancy shows her bare Butler and right-side cancy while loving it up with Nick Mancuso.*

See Her Naked In:

The Ex (1997) RB, Buns
The Hit List (1993) Body Double—Buns

Sarah Buxton

Born: March 23, 1965
Brentwood, California
Skin-O-Meter: Brief Nudity

A message to young hot teen girls everywhere: Fight with your parents, anywhere and anytime. That's how sultry Sarah Buxton got discovered. She was in the midst of a knockdown, drag-out argument with Mom in the supermarket when her future agent passed her business card to the immature knockout. That led to TV commercials and a film and TV career that's still percolating to this day. From a mid-'80s stint on the TV series *Rags to Riches* to a bit part in the Brat Pack movie *Less Than Zero* (1987), this brat was on her way. She parlayed that into a string of B-movies, such as *Nightmare Beach* (1988) and *Rock 'n' Roll High School Forever* (1990), which only makes her more dear to Mr. Skin's heart-on. Sarah kept getting hotter, landing bigger roles in movies such as *Don't Tell Mom the Babysitter's Dead* (1991), and then returned to TV as one of the sexy bitches on the hit series *Sunset Beach* and *The Bold and the Beautiful*. But what's really bold about this beauty is her sole skin in *The Climb* (1997), in which she flashes her boobs next to a man of the cloth. You'll need a cloth, too, to clean up your sticky mess. So climb on board.

SKIN-fining Moment:

The Climb (0:29) *Brief right buxombag as Ms. Buxton undresses while a little kid watches from the closet.*

See Her Naked In:

The Climb (1998) Breasts

Rose Byrne

Born: July 24, 1979
Sydney, Australia
Skin-O-Meter: Brief Nudity

Two Hands (1999) was the hit crime comedy that made Rose Byrne a star in her native Australia. The title also describes what was necessary to handle all the boners inspired by this vibrant young actress. Rose went on to claim a horny international audience in a small role as one of Queen Amidala's handmaidens in *Star Wars: Episode II—Attack of the Clones* (2002). But before that, Rose rose more Aussie trousers with some stunning nudity in *The Goddess of 1967* (2000).

SKIN-fining Moment:

The Goddess of 1967 (1:01) *A nice, if fleeting, flash of Rose's perfect posterior in bed with a dude, followed by an encore presentation of her perky rack whilst astride the lucky fellow.*

See Her Naked In:

The Goddess of 1967 (2000) Breasts, Buns
My Mother Frank (2000) RB

C

Lisa Ann Cabasa

Skin-O-Meter: Brief Nudity

The year was 1990, and Lisa Ann Cabasa was just another hot model-turned-actress trying to break into the business. With a body built for sin, even if her top was less than Everest in size, she landed a guest spot on *Twin Peaks*. She must have made quite the impression on the bizarre sensibilities of director David Lynch, because he then cast her in his weird flick *Wild at Heart* (1990). It was her first appearance onscreen, and Lynch was able to convince her to make it her nude debut as well. And so audiences were treated to her topless routine as a Reindeer Dancer. What that is exactly, even the great minds at Skin Central can't say, but it sure fills us with cheer. That was Lisa Ann's sole skin. Though she did get a role in *One Night Stand* (1997), she left the fleshy scenes for Nastassja Kinski and Ming-Na Wen. Lisa Ann kept busy with a one-shot on *Beverly Hills, 90210* and a recurring stint on *Buffy the Vampire Slayer*. But things started looking up when she got cast on the hit series *Dark Angel*. It's also the perfect nickname for this dark angel.

SKIN-fining Moment:

Wild at Heart (0:30) *Now THIS is full-service from a stripper. Lisa busts out her lung-balloons and dances for a tux-clad dandy while he's taking a dump on a toilet.*

See Her Naked In:

Wild at Heart (1990) Breasts

Ava Cadell

Born: June 15, 1956
Budapest, Hungary
Skin-O-Meter: Great Nudity

A buxom-plus prize born in Budapest, Hungary, bare-skin superstar Ava Cadell is classically trained in the school of ultra-ultra-ultra rack actresses. Even without tits that are each bigger than her head, Ava would be a standout. Red hair frames a face both sultry and pensive, as if always musing over her most recent hot sex scene or envisioning a boisterous banging to come. And then she has that huge mouth, capable of opening wide in wonder or alarm at the slightest provocation. Perhaps she has caught sight of her jaw-dropping wasp waist, right where it burgeons into a curvy, compact bottom. Lean and long legs taper to the cheery chair cheeks. And then the tits—aerodynamically superb and bigger than her head. No wonder that Ava has given unforgettable and highly individualized turns in such generic roles as Schoolgirl and Maid.

SKIN-fining Moment:

Hard Hunted (0:38) *Ava airs out her melons in a hot tub with also-topless Becky Mullen.*

See Her Naked In:

Fit to Kill (1993) Breasts
Lunch Box (1992) Thong
Hard Hunted (1992) Breasts, Buns
Do or Die (1991) Breasts, Buns
Not of This Earth (1988) Breasts
Commando (1985) Breasts
Jungle Warriors (1984) Breasts
Golden Lady (1979) FFN, Buns
Spaced Out (1979) Breasts, Buns
The Ups and Downs of a Handyman (1975) Breasts
Confessions of a Window Cleaner (1974) FFN, Buns

Cheri Caffaro

Born: 1945
California City
Skin-O-Meter: Hall of Fame

Cheri Caffaro popped her sinema cherry with the start of a beautiful franchise, the wickedly hard-boiled detective series that starts with *Ginger* (1971). Director (and Cheri's husband) Don Schain freely shared his schwing, featuring his better half either half naked or fully nude and in some moist-compromising positions. *A Place Called Today* (1972) followed, and Cheri reprised her role as Ginger in *The Abductors* (1972), a kinky classic of taboo sex and bound pleasures. An edited version was also released, her first foray into mainstream success, taming the triple-X of previous fare down to a still-randy R rating.

With *Girls Are for Loving* (1973), Ginger remained an R-rated temptress and retired her Ginger character, giving new meaning to the term "blue movie." *Savage Sisters* (1974) and *Too Hot to Handle* (1976) closed the door on Cheri's carnal career. But in that short time, she created the bridge from the Ginger skin classics to the campy come-ons of Andy Sidaris—definitely a bridge too far out!

SKIN-fining Moment:

Ginger (1:32) *Her ass appears when Duane Tucker helps her out of her panties as she's all bound up. Then he flips her over for an outstanding full-frontal.*

See Her Naked In:

Too Hot to Handle (1976) FFN, Buns
Girls Are for Loving (1973) FFN, Buns
A Place Called Today (1972) FFN
The Abductors (1972) FFN, Buns
Ginger (1971) FFN, Buns

> "To me, sex is eighty-five percent of my thoughts—whether it's straight, sick, or twisted."
>
> —DARIAN CAINE

Darian Caine

Born: October 24, 1973
Xenia, Ohio
Skin-O-Meter: Great Nudity

Since hooking up with the Garden State geniuses at Seduction Cinema, Darian Caine has played opposite—and played with—all of the studio's signature starlets. Always up for a down-and-dirty good time, Darian can be found fully nude and necking with naughty netherworld nubiles in Seduction's *The Erotic Witch Project* (1999), *Mistress Frankenstein* (2000), and *Mummy Raider* (2001). Don't

miss delicious Darian diddling while ancient Rome burns in *Gladiator Eroticvs: The Lesbian Warriors* (2001). Her scorching Sapphic showdowns with Misty Mundae in *Play-Mate of the Apes* (2002) and *Roxanna* (2002) proved to be just warm-ups for their cooze canoodling in the elfin-magic epic *Lord of the G-Strings: The Femaleship of the String* (2003).

SKIN-fining Moment:

Lord of the G-Strings: The Femaleship of the String (1:00) *Darian dares to bare it all during a fireside four-way with AJ Khan, Misty Mundae, and Barbara Joyce. Funbags, fur-pies and fannies for all.*

See Her Naked In:

Sexy American Idle (2003) Breasts
SpiderBabe (2003) FFN, Buns
Vampire Vixens (2003) FFN
Lustful Addiction (2003) FFN
The Erotic Mirror (2002) FFN
Vampire Queen (2002) FFN
Lord of the G-Strings: The Femaleship of the String (2002) FFN, Buns
Satan's School for Lust (2002) Breasts
Roxanna (2002) Breasts, Buns
Vampire Obsession (2002) FFN
Pleasures of a Woman (2002) FFN, Buns
Play-Mate of the Apes (2002) FFN, Buns
Gladiator Eroticvs: The Lesbian Warriors (2001) FFN
Erotic Survivor (2001) FFN, Buns
Witchbabe: Erotic Witch Project 3 (2001) FFN, Buns
Mummy Raider (2001) FFN

Danone Camden

Skin-O-Meter: Brief Nudity

Disco was already on the wane, but don't tell that to dancing queen Danone Camden. She started her career tripping the light fantastic in *Can't Stop the Music* (1980). While that didn't catapult the tube-topped tramp into the limelight, it did set her up

for a successful run on the hit nighttime soap *Dallas*. Forget who shot J.R., Danone made audiences shoot off whenever she sashayed onscreen. After that show ended in 1991, so did Danone's career, and she hasn't been seen since. But she didn't leave without preserving her perfection for guys to leer at endlessly. For that, please check out *The Killer Instinct* (1982), where Danone plays a cheating wife. Of course, her affairs are explicitly documented, and so is her exquisite T&A. She begins the movie with a bang, and it's killer all the way through.

SKIN-fining Moment:

The Killer Instinct (0:13) *As Danone's doing a dude in bed, a rather irate gent interrupts. Fists, fury, and a flash of full frontal ensue.*

See Her Naked In:

The Killer Instinct (1982) Breasts, Buns

Jennifer Campbell

Skin-O-Meter: Brief Nudity

To ponder the tangy and toothsome appeal of bouncy blonde Jennifer Campbell is to raise an age-old question: Is there life after *Baywatch*, and will that life have any kind of meaning? By meaning we refer to profoundly nude revelations. A spine-tingling beauty of the tawny-skinned variety, firm but jiggleriffic Jen gave her first bikini thrill to *Baywatch* fans as a guest object of adulation in 1992. The high-toned buns and breasts made a lasting impression. Campbell and her cans were invited to perform full time for a two-year stint as a favorite *Baywatch* balloon smuggler. Aching for a peek at the peaks beneath that one-piece? Peer into the past as captured in *Dan Turner, Hollywood Detective* (1990). Then pray for a future from Jennifer that has some meaning.

SKIN-fining Moment:

Dan Turner, Hollywood Detective (1:10) *Jen's juggles make a nice appearance when she's in bed with her dude, then they're kind of fuzzy in the background.*

See Her Naked In:

Dan Turner, Hollywood Detective (1990) Breasts

Nell Campbell

Born: May 24, 1953
Sydney, Australia
Skin-O-Meter: Great Nudity

Absolutely fabulous Australian-born actress/singer/dancer Nell "Little Nell" Campbell is best known on these shores as the deliciously demented Columbia, an "associate" of Dr. Frank-N-Furter in the midnight movie classic *The Rocky Horror Picture Show* (1975), a role she created in the original 1973 London stage production. Nell's fire-engine-red mane and equally crimson nipples—which popped into view a handful of times— remain some of the film's most memorable images. As the film began to develop its legendary cult status, Nell's nipple-popping naughtiness was further exploited in such entries as *Lisztomania* (1975) opposite Roger Daltrey and *Jubilee* (1977). Roles in a handful of other movies followed, including one in *Rocky*'s quasi-sequel *Shock Treatment* (1981), but after Nell moved to the States in the early '80s, she took a stab at the nightclub business. The result was the self-named Nell's, which opened in 1987 and is still going strong today. There have been no official reports of the skintuations that have transpired behind those late-night doors.

SKIN-fining Moment:

Lisztomania (1:04) *Little Nell shows her not-so-little-nerps with Roger Daltrey and Ringo Starr. Rockin'!*

See Her Naked In:

Jubilee (1977) Breasts, Buns
Lisztomania (1975) Breasts
The Rocky Horror Picture Show (1975) Nip Slip RB
Barry McKenzie Holds His Own (1974) Breasts, Buns

Neve Campbell

Born: October 3, 1973
Guelph, Ontario, Canada
Skin-O-Meter: Brief Nudity

It just took Ontario-born Neve Campbell (whose first name means "snow" in Italian) a few forgettable TV movies and series and a couple of years of teen-catalog modeling in her native Canada to get herself noticed and cast as Julia on the long-running Stateside series *Party of Five*. Theatrical ventures quickly beckoned, leading to starring roles in *The Craft* (1996), *54* (1998) and the popular *Scream* franchise, which often featured Neve in compromising positions—whilst wearing only her bra. Neve's deskinitive moment came in the neo-noir *Wild Things* (1998), where she engaged in a three-way lust session with Matt Dillon and a very topless Denise Richards. The scene did indeed find Neve taking off her T-shirt and engaging in a sensual smooch with her curvy co-starlet, but with her back all-too-obviously turned to the camera. The still-skintillating sequence raised questions about a reported "no nudity" clause in Neve's contract, a bit of legalese that many pined to see dropped and outlawed right up until the 2004 premiere of director James Toback's *When Will I Be Love*d. Neve opens and closes *Loved* with bare-breasted shower scenes. Now that's something to *Scream* about, as Neve's knockout nerps, healthy hairpie, and Canadian backside bacon bring to mind the canned-soup brand that shares her last name: "Mmm-mmm-good!"

SKIN-fining Moment:

Wild Things (0:57) *Neve keeps her own Wild Things covered, but her tongue-swirling lesboid face-suck with Denise Richards provides the fire that makes their threeway with Matt Dillon the hottest ménage in skinema history.*

See Her Naked In:

When Will I Be Loved? (2004) Breasts, Bush, Buns
Blind Horizon (2003) Body Double—LB

Colleen Camp

Born: June 7, 1953
San Francisco, California
Skin-O-Meter: Hall of Fame

It was Colleen Camp's debut, the role she was born to play, one of the humans in *Battle for the Planet of the Apes* (1973). The uncredited performance launched this buxom blonde beauty into the fantasy life of many moaning men. Comely Colleen is best known not for driving men ape but for her carnal comic sense. Her screwball (and, oh, to screw and/or ball Colleen) antics are well documented in *Valley Girl* (1983), *Smokey and the Bandit III* (1983), and most mammorably as Sergeant Kathleen Kirkland in the randy, riotous *Police Academy* series. Mr. Skin has a busty-French-maid fetish and particularly enjoyed Colleen's cleavage-bearing role as Yvette in the whoduntit classic *Clue* (1985). Yes, this bosomy babe isn't bashful about her body. She's flashed floppers in *Cat in the Cage* (1978) and went topless as a Playmate in the reedited *Apocalypse Now Redux* (2001). If camp were like this, Mr. Skin would have pitched his tent and never left.

SKIN-fining Moment:

Death Game (0:18) *Buns getting out of hot tub with Sondra Locke, then various naked shots during a menage a trois! Tough to see because of the steam.*

See Her Naked In:

Apocalypse Now Redux (2001) Breasts
Deadly Games (1982) RB
Cat in the Cage (1978) LB
Death Game (1977) Breasts, Buns
Smile (1975) RB

Trishelle Cannatella

Born: November 4, 1979
Cut Off, Louisiana
Skin-O-Meter: Brief Nudity

When Trishelle Cannatella debuted on MTV's *The Real World: Las Vegas*, men all over the country longed to score a jackpot with this tight-topped, loose-lipped vixen. Trishelle's reality-based career continued to plump peters on *The Girl's of Reality TV*, two installments of *The Real World/Road Rules Challenge*, and most recently *The Surreal Life*. With bunk buddies such as Ron Jeremy and Tammy Faye Baker, Trishelle's tawny beauty, booming boobs, and bountiful booty were perfect for rounding out the diverse herd and adding the necessary fox factor to the flock. Surrounded by the pious and the porn proud in unusual circumstances, Trishelle remained her usual really hot, really hammered, barely clothed self.

SKIN-fining Moment:

The Surreal Life "Nude Resort" (2004) *Trishelle sits topless at a dinner table, gabbing with other guests as her naked Real World globes glow in plain sight.*

TeleVisions:

The Surreal Life Breasts

Dyan Cannon

Born: January 4, 1937
Tacoma, Wasington
Skin-O-Meter: Brief Nudity

Dyan Cannon started at the top, actually on top of husband Gary Grant. The marriage slowed her burgeoning acting career in the early '60s, but it's doubtful Grant complained about having Dyan's Cannons to himself. When they divorced in 1968, Hollywood and horny men let out a collective sigh of relief. Dyan got right into the swing of things, literally, with the wife-swapping film *Bob & Carol & Ted & Alice* (1969). The subject matter was risqué, and Dyan was displayed in all her voluptuousness, if only down to bra and panties. The golden-tressed beauty did give up her darkly tangled pubes in *Such Good Friends* (1971), although the rumors point toward body double. But those are definitely Dyan's topless damsels in that dress—well, a see-through shawl. Dyan remains one of the hottest old-school Hollywood ladies even today. She made heads spin on *Ally McBeal* and will probably continue to seduce in the retirement home.

SKIN-fining Moment:

Such Good Friends (10:26) *A great full-frontal nudity shot (via Polaroid) of Dyan. Supposedly those are not Dyan's cannon's . . . word on the street is Otto Preminger did a little photo trickery.*

See Her Naked In:

Child Under a Leaf (1974) FFN
Such Good Friends (1971) Body Double—
    FFN, Breasts—Hers

Katherine Cannon

Born: September 6, 1953
Hartford, Connecticut
Skin-O-Meter: Great Nudity

Katherine Cannon first shared her girl-next-door good looks with the viewing public when she landed the role of Sheba on Harold Robbins's *The Survivors*. She liked the little screen and bounced her buxom body in guest-starring parts on shows such as *Gunsmoke*, *The Streets of San Francisco*, and *Cannon*, no relation. That was much to William Conrad's relief, as the heavyset actor probably tried to get Katherine to play with his cannon on occasion. Everybody found out why Katherine was such a hot property when she ended up in *Private Duty Nurses* (1971), and the svelte brunette exposed her charms for the only time onscreen. She played one of a trio of naked candy stripers who found time to fight a drug ring, racism, and murder while getting it on with their happy patients. It's sure to raise your blood pressure. She followed that up with *Women in Chains* (1972), which sounds promising but was a made-for-TV movie and not skin friendly. Katherine never broke out from the clothing restraints of TV, appearing on *Baa Baa Black Sheep* but not revealing her more wolfish side. She still works, her most recent film being *Luxury of Love* (2001), and Mr. Skin hopes she'll return to her nursing days soon.

SKIN-fining Moment

Private Duty Nurses (1:12) *Katherine lies nude in bed and shows her Private Duty Nurses.*

See Her Naked In:

Private Duty Nurses (1971) Breasts

Jesse Capelli

Born: May 21, 1979
Canada Vancouver, Canada
Skin-O-Meter: Brief Nudity

Greatness is often visible from it's very first moment on the stripper pole. The spotlight had hardly settled upon tawny and trim sexual acrobat Jesse Capelli, and her special superior qualities were self-evident. First she nails you with that face—green eyes that could be mates to the serpent of Eden, jewel-cut facets to her cheeks and jaw line, a plush-lipped mouth like an advertisement for sexual enticement, all of it framed in a mane of hair streaked blonde, auburn, and red. After the grin and leer have done their damage, Jesse twirls her back to the camera, and your last vestigial defenses crumble. You'd follow her anywhere, even back to her native Canada, where she appears to have retreated. Put a watch out for her, and pray she appears again.

SKIN-fining Moment:

Van Wilder (0:19) *Brief look at her juggies when she helps the boys study their algebra. "Flash" cards, indeed!*

See Her Naked In:

Van Wilder (2002) Breasts, Thong

Deborah Caprioglio

Born: May 3, 1968
Mestre, Italy
Skin-O-Meter: Great Nudity

When Deborah Caprioglio was only a busty twenty-year-old, her sixty-two-year-old boyfriend, the wild man of German cinema Klaus Kinski, launched her career and lifelong notoriety by costarring with the dark-haired beauty in *Paganini* (1989). The film is a sex flick that is so explicit that it prompted a lawsuit from the movie's own production company because they claimed it was nearly pornographic! She took the sex down just a notch for her next film, *Paprika* (1989), a spicy softcore skin fest in which she insures her nude scenes by playing a whore. Her Italian countrymen, after playing with their sausages, hailed the top-heavy tramp as the next Sophia Loren. But then

Deborah and Klaus broke up, and, during the lull in her career, she dated government ministers and seemed on the fast track to a skinless life of bureaucratic bliss. But you can't keep tits like hers from flashing, and soon she was back in front of the camera making life a kick for the boot-shaped country. With titles like *Foxy Lady* (1992) and *Love Story with Cramps* (1995), Deborah raised the bar (among other things) in bawdy.

SKIN-fining Moment:

Paprika (0:11) *Deborah delivers full-frontal nudity from several different angles as she spends naked-time with her man.*

See Her Naked In:

The Smile of the Fox (1994) Breasts, Bush, Buns
Paganini (1989) Breasts, Buns
Paprika (1989) FFN, Buns

Kate Capshaw

Born: November 3, 1953
Fort Worth, Texas
Skin-O-Meter: Brief Nudity

'Twas a time when Kate Capshaw was considered a real comer—particularly by skin-seekers. Her delicious derriere first intrigued audiences in the minor hit *A Little Sex* (1984), while Capshaw did some bedazzling jiggling immediately thereafter in the same year's *Dreamscape* (1984). It was on the set of *Indiana Jones and the Temple of Doom* (1984) that captivating Kate met über-director Steven Spielberg, whom she later married. Spielberg was no doubt similarly captivated by his leading lady's generous swath of cleavage (which he so lovingly focused on in the production). Since becoming Mrs. Spielberg, Kate's skinquences have been noticeably few and far between, the exception being a derriere dolly-in and a frame full of floppies in the romance *The*

Love Letter (1998), though it must be noted that she gets memorably lesbianic with super-duper model Elle Macpherson in the mini-series *A Girl Thing* (2001).

SKIN-fining Moment:

A Little Sex (0:10) *Kate flashes some ass while running from Tim Matheson after stuffing a pancake down his underpants.*

See Her Naked In:

The Love Letter (1999) LB, Buns
Dreamscape (1984) RB
A Little Sex (1982) Breasts, Buns

Irene Cara

Born: March 18, 1959
New York, New York
Skin-O-Meter: Great Nudity

It would be easier to care about Irene Cara—and there might be a lot more Cara footage worth caring about—if only the Manhattan Latin had been more careless in keeping her goodies covered. A former kiddie TV star who honed her pre-teen cutie-pie chops on small-screen tease series *Love of Life* (1970) and *The Electric Company* (1971), the dusky, dimpled delight leapt to the big-screen with a skimpy leotard and a song in *Fame* (1980). The post-adolescent took home an Oscar for her singing and also deserved Most Promising Flash plaque for the classic scene in which she goes topless in front of a creepy Times Square pornographer. Sadly, Irene never lived up to her exposure potential. The hard-bodied heroine retained a bikini throughout the tropical-island prison flick *Caged in Paradiso* (1989), and her only significant appearance comes in the thriller *Certain Fury* (1985), in which a certain furry creature is shown wet and dripping in a shower scene.

SKIN-fining Moment:

Certain Fury (0:42) *Irene gets attacked by a would-be rapist, but beats him down with her bare titlets flying!*

See Her Naked In:

Certain Fury (1985) FFN, Buns
Fame (1980) Breasts

Linda Cardellini

Born: June 25, 1975
Redwood City, California
Skin-O-Meter: Brief Nudity

Don't remember the long, dark-haired beauty Linda Cardellini from her debut on the kid's TV series *Bone Chillers*? The show wasn't a hit, but Linda sure made Mr. Skin's bone chill. Her career got a boost with a supporting role in the suggestively titled *Good Burger* (1997), in which juicy Linda was good enough to eat. Too bad she was fully dressed. Linda has gone on to be the second string in a series of number-one productions, such as the critic's darling cult series *Freaks and Geeks* and the film *Legally Blonde* (2001). But it wasn't until she covered her hot body with glasses and a bulky orange sweater as Velma in the live-action hits *Scooby Doo* (2002) and *Scooby Doo 2: Monsters Unleashed* (2004) that things really took off. Of course, what Mr. Skin wants to see Linda take off is her clothing, which she did in *Strangeland* (1996). She's completely naked, though she's being tortured in a metal cage by ex-Twisted Sister and current radio DJ Dee Snider. Linda ends up dead meat, but her good burger is finally served up like we like it.

SKIN-fining Moment:

Strangeland (0:41) *Glimpses of boobs and buns and just an eensy side-peek of boosh as Linda gets sprung from a torture cage.*

See Her Naked In:

Strangeland (1998) Breasts, Bush, Buns

Claudia Cardinale

Born: April 15, 1938
Tunis, Tunisia
Skin-O-Meter: Brief Nudity

After winning a contest for the Most Beautiful Italian Girl in Tunis in 1957, Claudia Cardinale was coached by crotch-chasing creators of Italian skinema to become the next Sophia Loren. Like Loren, Claudia was coveted for her beautiful face, sultry voice, and charismatic curvature. After making a huge show with her hefty hoots in *Big Deal on Madonna Street* (1958), cantastic Claudia went on to star as the prettiest pussy in *The Pink Panther* (1964) and the sizzling sex kitten in *Blonde in Black Leather* (1975). Perk up your troubles by watching Cardinale doused in bubbles. Although she never dared to go *tutta* bare, this rare Romanesque bird's sun-tanned shoulders and quick flashes of boulders can be seen while sudsing in a tub in *Once Upon a Time in the West* (1969) and *Queen of Diamonds* (1970). Any of this royal ravisher's endeavors are guaranteed to put a bone on your throne.

SKIN-fining Moment:

The Professionals (1:24) *In the un-cut Euro version, Claudia removes her top in front of Burt Lancaster and shows him a far more mouth-watering chest than Kirk Douglas ever did.*

See Her Naked In:

The Professionals (1966) Breasts

Mary Carey

Born: June 15, 1981
Cleveland, Ohio
Skin-O-Meter: Great Nudity

Mary Carey has only been in the business for a couple of years, but she already has a slew of sex tapes circulating that are sure to get viewers' circulation pumping. She debuted in *Busty Beauties 3* (2002), and there's no need to have seen the first two installments to know that Mary is the mother of mammary. She continues to make triple-X fare such as *Asses in the Air 4* (2002), *New Wave Hookers 7* (2003), and *Thumpin Melons* (2003). If a venture into that scary, dark corner of your local video store is unappetizing, may we suggest renting the less extreme but still savory sexploitation of *Sapphire Girls* (2003). Mary plays Ruby, and her gems are dazzling. The 36DD-24-36 beauty made a name for herself beyond the world of adult entertainment and into the really wild world of politics when she announced her candidacy for governor of California in the recall election of 2003. Though she didn't win, she added some much-needed sex appeal to the staid political process. Mary got 10,316 votes, putting her in tenth place. But she's a winner at Skin Central, and we hail to her chest.

SKIN-fining Moment:

Sapphire Girls Mary shows all she's got during some hardcore swallowing, schtipping, and spewing. Breasts, buns, baby-gutter, close-up and wide-open browneye. Carey on!

See Her Naked In:

Sapphire Girls (2003) Breasts
The New Girl: A Model Agent (2003) Breasts
Numerous Adult Movies

Gia Carides

Born: June 7, 1964
Sydney, New South Wales, Australia
Skin-O-Meter: Brief Nudity

Look into those mesmerizing hazel eyes. Blankly stare at the plush, parted, sensual lips of that commanding mouth. Try not to let her catch you staring at that shelf of mammary flesh, big enough to shade an entire convention of damp skinthusiasts. Australian-bred Gia Carides is a bombshell not to be trifled with. Gia is a dangerously attractive woman. As Robin Spitz Swallows in the campy *Austin Powers: The Spy Who Shagged Me* (1999), alarmingly attractive Carides plied a menacing sex appeal without cracking so much as a butt smile. For a complete helping of cleavage with nipple garnish, order out for *Lifebreath* (1997).

SKIN-fining Moment:

Bliss (1:25) *During a nightmare, a cut appears in the center of Gia's glorious rock and thousands of cockroaches come marching out. It'll bug ya!*

See Her Naked In:

Lifebreath (1997) LB
Bliss (1985) Breasts

Karen Carlson

Born: January 15, 1945
Shreveport, Louisiana
Skin-O-Meter: Great Nudity

When Karen Carlson made her acting debut guest starring on *The Man from U.N.C.L.E.* in 1967, groins across this great land of ours cried, "Uncle!" That outburst wasn't ignored by carnal Karen, who went from TV to the big screen in *The Student Nurses* (1970), a slaphappy skin fest that's good for what ails you. The groovy candy stripers offer sweet medicine for their patients, which includes ample doses of Karen's pharmaceutical-grade T&A. Karen jumped back to the boob (less) tube with a short stint on the daytime soap *Days of Our Lives*. Sadly, she left the nudity part of her life behind—but what a behind it was. She continued to jump to the big screen in movies such as *The Candidate* (1972), opposite Robert Redford, and *Teen*

Vamp (1988), in which she played a middle-aged hottie still able to give the young tramps a run for their honey. TV remained her bread and butter as she appeared on *Dallas* and in many TV movies of the week. Well, she always had a nice spread.

SKIN-fining Moment:

The Student Nurses (0:48) *Karen airs out her lusciously cumbersome casabas, then treats us to caboose, too.*

See Her Naked In:

The Student Nurses (1970) Breasts, Buns

Kelly Carlson

Minneapolis, Minnesota
Skin-O-Meter: Brief Nudity

Kelly Carlson was certainly well cast to kick alien ass in *Starship Troopers 2* (2004), because we can't think of a more fearless actress working today. First, the gorgeous blonde was actually believable as a biker in *3000 Miles to Graceland* (2001). Then, Kelly became a true overnight star after the debut episode of FX's *Nip/Tuck*. Playing a model picked up by a decadent plastic surgeon, Kelly performed the wildest simulated sex to ever grace a basic-cable network. She was even pretty impressive in the role before she started doing it doggy style. Naturally, the smart *Nip/Tuck* producers are already talking to Kelly about returning for another episode.

SKIN-fining Moment:

Starship Troopers 2: Hero of the Federation (0:42) *She's onstage, singing shlocky '90s hits to a trio of judges—oh wait, I'm thinking of Kelly CLARKSON. OK, Kelly CARLSON walks around naked talking to various people, showing some spectacular T&A. Much more interesting.*

See Her Naked In:

Starship Troopers 2: Hero of the Federation (2004) Breasts, Buns

TeleVisions:

Nip/Tuck LB

Hope Marie Carlton

Born: March 3, 1966
Riverhead, New York
Skin-O-Meter: Great Nudity

Hope is both a blessing and a mystery, no more so than as embodied by Hope Marie Carlton. During the second half of the 1980s, Skin watchers were blessed with repeated sightings of naturally endowed Marie Carlton's hope chest, most particularly in three Andy Sidaris naked-chick spy flicks. *Hard Ticket to Hawaii* (1987) bestowed the uplifting presence of Hope's boobs and buns; *Savage Beach* (1989) was soothed by the influence of Hope's heavenly on-highs; and *Picasso Trigger* (1989) transcended despair with a visitation from the ass of Hope. After featured spots on *Baywatch* and *Married . . . With Children*, Hope Marie was set for TV immortality, but she turned down a recurring role on *The Guiding Light* in favor of marriage. The mystery of why she has abandoned us will forever perplex Hope's legions of devotees.

SKIN-fining Moment:

Hard Ticket to Hawaii (0:23) *Hope chest! Her bare globes glow while checking out diamonds with Donna Speir.*

See Her Naked In:

Round Numbers (1992) LB
Ghoulies 3: Ghoulies Go to College (1991) Breasts, Buns
Picasso Trigger (1989) Breasts, Buns
Savage Beach (1989) FFN

Terminal Exposure (1988) Breasts,
   Buns
A Nightmare on Elm Street 4: The Dream Master (1988) Breasts
Slaughterhouse Rock (1988) Breasts
Hard Ticket to Hawaii (1987) Breasts,
   Thong
Numerous *Playboy* Videos

Rebekah Carlton-Luff

Auckland, New Zealand
Skin-O-Meter: Brief Nudity

Rebekah Carlton-Luff was discovered when she was just a precocious schoolgirl during the shooting of a Coke commercial at her Sydney, Australia, school. It was obvious even at a young age that she was the real thing. But it wasn't until she moved to the United States that Hollywood really popped for her effervescent talents. The boob tube called, and Rebekah answered with a recurring role on the jiggle fest *Baywatch*. Catching Rebekah in a skimpy bathing suit was all casting agents needed to land her guest appearances on *Acapulco H.E.A.T.*, *Charmed*, and *Beverly Hills, 90210*. Her first film venture was *Wet and Wild Summer* (1992), but she was neither wet nor wild. That would come later, with her role as the Queen of the Damned in *Leprechaun 4: In Space* (1996), where she lets her glittery boobs out for an alien version of the kiss of death. Watching Rebekah's cups is far from a bitter drink to swallow.

SKIN-fining Moment:

Leprechaun 4: In Space (1:06) *Rebekah flashes her tits to illustrate the fact that she's "The Queen of the Damned." Damned hot, that is!*

See Her Naked In:

Separate Ways (2001) Breasts, Buns
Leprechaun 4: In Space (1996) Breasts

Gabrielle Carmouche

Skin-O-Meter: Great Nudity

Gabrielle Carmouche found a respectful place as a recurring player on the highly acclaimed sitcom *The Cosby Show*, where she was known as Deirdre. With an auspicious debut like that, the sky seemed to be the limit for this ebony enchantress. It's a given that she'd be cast on the sitcom *Sister, Sister*, and the world was Gabrielle's oyster when she landed on *In the House*. But this black pearl has a dark side. Her TV credentials were tight, but it seems that her pussy is loose, and she made the jump from prime-time network broadcasts to hardcore, full-penetration pornography by the turn of the century. Her first time on the big screen (that is if you have a wide-screen TV at home) was in the straight-to-video steamer *Chillin' with Jake Steed's Freaks Whoes & Flows 18* (2000). What would Bill say? Not too much; he'd be too busy jacking off like the rest of us. Gabrielle is now a full-fledged slut, shaking her booty in productions such as *Young Muff 8* (2001), *Bootilicious: Straw Berries* (2001), and *Black on Black #1* (2002). Skin Central applauds Gabrielle's career move—it's sure moved us.

SKIN-fining Moment:

Young Muff 8 *Gabby gobbles man-groin, then parts her brown thighs to expose her pink parts which shortly thereafter are plied by a throbbing pole. Hardcore heat, nothing left to the imagination (but lots of stuff left on Gabrielle's face at the end).*

See Her Naked In:

Black on Black #1 (2002) FFN, Buns
Young Muff 8 (2001) FFN, Buns
Bootilicious: Straw Berries (2001) FFN, Buns
Chillin' with Jake Steed's Freaks Whoes & Flows 18 (2000) FFN, Buns

Jean Carol

Hillsdale, New Jersey
Skin-O-Meter: Great Nudity

Few actresses have made a debut like Jean Carol, whose villainess in the T&A classic *Vice Academy* (1988) certainly had us arrested. Her Batman-style antics as Queen Bee (with her bevy of sexy B-girls) got plenty of crotches buzzing. Then fans were opening their zippers while Jean opened her robe in the crime thriller *Payback* (1988). Jean followed that by going legit with mainstream roles and a long soap opera stint on *The Guiding Light*. To us, though, she'll always be a platinum-primping, honey-sucking pimp.

SKIN-fining Moment:

Payback (0:24) *Jean opens her pink robe for a dude, and we all get a gander at the globular glories contained therein.*

See Her Naked In:

Payback (1988) Breasts

TeleVisions:

Arli$$ Breasts

Leslie Caron

Born: July 1, 1931
Boulogne-Billancourt, Paris, France
Skin-O-Meter: Brief Nudity

Fans of Leslie Caron can thank the fancy footwork of Gene Kelly for discovering the French tart. He was scouting for a female lead in his upcoming *An American in Paris* (1951), and, after seeing Leslie shake her moneymaker in a ballet production, the American soft shoe got hard for the Parisian pussycat. The movie made Leslie an international star and set her up with a sweet contract at MGM that had her starring in features such as *Gigi* (1958). But Leslie is too great of a talent just to trip the light fantastic. She's moved on to non-dancing roles that often find her in a blue mood—and we're not talking about sad. Leslie let audiences have a peek at what's beneath her leotard in *The Head of the Family* (1967). OK, she's breastfeeding in the scene, but it's still a nourishing look-see. The only other glance at her dancer's tight body was in *Madron* (1970), in which she played a nun who gets her shirt ripped off by the bad guys. Too bad she didn't make a habit of it. Lately, Leslie is experiencing a bit of a renaissance, having appeared in *The Last of the Blonde Bombshells* (2000), *Chocolat* (2000), and *Le Divorce* (2003). Let's hope her hooters make a resurgence as well.

SKIN-fining Moment:

Madron (0:46) *Leslie has her top ripped open by bad guys, briefly revealing her right ta-ta.*

See Her Naked In:

Madron (1970) RB

Barbara Carrera

Born: December 31, 1951
Managua, Nicaragua
Skin-O-Meter: Great Nudity

This exotic treat from Nicaragua easily stood out from the California girls who dominated the '70s modeling scene. Barbara Carrera was soon in demand to play some sexy, shady characters, though her breasts came to light as Rock Hudson's lovely lab experiment in *Embryo* (1976). Barbara also helped fuel the VHS revolution when she doffed her top exclusively in the videotape version of the 1981 TV mini-series *Masada*. Then Carrera really got carried away with some hammering from Mike Hammer in the feature film *I, The Jury* (1982), followed by her vixenous turn as Fatima Blush in the James Bond film *Never Say Never Again* (1983). There's also a slip of

PIE, THE FURRY: BARBARA CARRERA LOSES HER SUIT IN *I, THE JURY*.

the nip in *Wicked Stepmother* (1989), a sexy love scene in *Tryst* (1994), and her fabulous ass in *Sawbones* (1995). And your trousers will be making a point of their own once you catch Barbara's wild pool scene in *Point of Impact* (1993).

SKIN-fining Moment:

I, the Jury (1:02) *Full-frontal skinitude as Barb undresses, lays on a bed and launches herself on the loin of Armand Assante.*

See Her Naked In:

Sawbones (1995) Body Double—Buns
Tryst (1994) LB
Point of Impact (1993) Breasts, Thong
Wild Geese II (1985) LB
I, the Jury (1982) FFN, Buns
Embryo (1976) Breasts, Buns

TeleVisions:

Masada Breasts

Tia Carrere

Born: January 2, 1965
Honolulu, Hawaii
Skin-O-Meter: Never Nude

Tease Tia Carrere has got the exotic goods, and Mr. Skin is awaiting the

delivery. She's got a real large pair of ta-tas that have been all but exposed in bra and bikini in many roles as the pretty hot thing, including *Wayne's World* (1992) and *Wayne's World 2* (1993). Criminally, Mike Myers flashes tush, but Tia remains clothed. She's also appeared in *True Lies* (1994), *Kull the Conqueror* (1997), and vocally in the cartoon hit *Lilo & Stitch* (2002), where the opportunity to animate her bare hooters was sadly lost. Then in the January 2003 U.S. edition of *Playboy*, Tia's treasures were at last revealed. A ten-page pictorial left nothing to the imagination—all busty bounty, reddish-brown nips, and bulbous butt. There's even a glimpse at her sweetie pie, which Tia trims, or as she likes to say: "I've cleared the way to the Promised Land." Now let Mr. Skin into that Promised Land, and get thee holy in filmdom.

SKIN-fining Moment:

Showdown in Little Tokyo (0:50) *BODY DOUBLE! Tera Tabrizi strips down in place of Tia and shows boobs, butt, and brief side bush as she gets into a hot tub with Dolph Lundgren.*

See Her Naked In:

Showdown in Little Tokyo (1991) Body Double—LB, Bush, Buns

Diahann Carroll

Born: July 17, 1935
The Bronx, New York
Skin-O-Meter: Brief Nudity

A chocolaty sweet reprieve from the lily-white face of mid-twentieth-century Hollywood, Diahann Carroll crushed color barriers, pioneering a proper path for future blacktresses. Di made her soulful debut in the all-colorful cast of *Carmen Jones* (1954), working with the delightfully dusky Dorothy Dandridge. Putting her lovely lungs and lively, long legs to good use, Carroll sang and danced in musical greats such as *Porgy and Bess* (1959) and *Paris Blues* (1961) alongside African American then-up-and-comer Sidney Poitier, who must have been *Diahann* to get his hands on her curvaceous caboose throughout both productions. At the end of the swinging '60s, foxy lady Di's deliciousness was so palatable, she was chosen as the first cutie of color to star in her own TV series, *Julia*, re-creating the trials and tribulations of a sultry, single black mother with dignity and a delectable aura of grace. In her one and only peek of skinematic perfection, Diahann debuted a fine flash of coffee-caramel flesh, unwrapping one of her Hershey-kissed floaters in a bathtub scene in *Claudine* (1974). What a bitingly bittersweet performance and career, full of remarkably fresh choices and powerful, color-blinding beauty.

SKIN-fining Moment:

Claudine (0:16) *Diane's left-side chest-bauble peeks through the bubbles as she relaxes in a hot bath.*

See Her Naked In:

Claudine (1974) LB

Patricia Carr

Skin-O-Meter: Brief Nudity

Success can have its downside. Take the full and frenzied career of regal blonde Patricia Carr. Once an erotically charged leading presence in Italian films that have since been allowed to lapse from her resumé, sublimely Limey Carr had reached that juncture in her performing career that leads many ambitious actresses down the avenue of naked emoting. Rather than take the path to skinmortality, Patricia refastened her bra and stepped behind the camera. In one production capacity or another, she has helped bring more than one hundred films to the screen. Comely Carr had a lovely hand in *Superman* (1978), *Star Wars* (1977), *Day of the Jackal* (1973), *The Empire Strikes Back* (1980), and *Raiders of the Lost Ark* (1980). Too bad she's so good at what she does.

SKIN-fining Moment:

American Gigolo (0:19) *Quick nippage as Richard Gere provides Patty with a little rubdown.*

See Her Naked In:

American Gigolo (1980) RB

Finn Carter

Skin-O-Meter: Brief Nudity

Despite a recurring role on the TV series *China Beach*, most guys first saw Finn Carter as a sexy geologist—with, er, sunblock on her nose—taking on giant worms in *Tremors* (1990). That role should've launched Finn's career, but this incredibly cute gal has since been criminally underused. Horny guys, however, have made use of her pool scene in *Sweet Justice* (1992), in which Finn shows off her adorable, tiny titties. Don't forget Finn's big contribution to sci-fi, either, flashing her left breast while bedding Michael O'Keefe on a 1995 episode of cable's *The Outer Limits*.

SKIN-fining Moment:

Sweet Justice (0:52) *Submerged skinbaggies as Finn stews in a hot tub with a few equally topless girlfriends.*

See Her Naked In:

Sweet Justice (1992) Breasts

TeleVisions:

Outer Limits LB

Lynda Carter

Born: July 24, 1951
Phoenix, Arizona
Skin-O-Meter: Great Nudity

> **MR. SKIN'S TOP TEN**
>
> **'70's TV Stars Who Got Naked**
> **. . . Those '70s Show-ers**
>
> 10. **Sally Struthers**
>   —(Gloria) *All in the Family*
>
> 9. **Susan Dey**
>   —(Laurie) *The Partridge Family*
>
> 8. **Lindsay Wagner**
>   —(Jaime Sommers) *The Bionic Woman*
>
> 7. **Pamela Sue Martin**
>   —(Nancy Drew) *Nancy Drew Mysteries*
>
> 6. **Suzanne Somers**
>   —(Chrissy Snow) *Three's Company*
>
> 5. **Jaye P. Morgan**
>   —*The Gong Show*
>
> 4. **Farrah Fawcett**
>   —(Jill Munroe) *Charlie's Angels*
>
> 3. **Adrienne Barbeau**
>   —(Carol Trainer) *Maude*
>
> 2. **Angie Dickinson**
>   —(Sgt. Pepper Anderson) *Police Woman*
>
> 1. **Lynda Carter**
>   —*Wonder Woman*

Lynda Carter busted out with a boom-boom in 1976 as TV's super-chesty superhero *Wonder Woman*. Fans were instantly lassoed by the way Lynda overflowed from the front of her ultra-tight patriotic costume with her long legs and athletic build. But when Lynda retired *Wonder Woman*'s eagle-adorned bustier (oh, how those wings flapped), audiences grabbed their remotes for more jiggle action. Sharp-eyed Lynda lovers sought out her obscure drive-in flick *Bobbie Jo and the Outlaw* (1976) (filmed the year before she became Wonder Woman), a shoot-'em-up featuring three shots of Lynda's big guns. Technically, *Bobbie Jo* boasts only brief nudity, but how brief can anything be when it involves the awesome amplitude of Lynda's love pillows?

SKIN-fining Moment:

Bobbie Jo and the Outlaw (0:18) *A wondrous look at Lynda's left whopper while she's making whoopee with Marjoe Gortner. Have mercy!*

See Her Naked In:

Bobbie Jo and the Outlaw (1976) LB

Katrin Cartlidge

Born: May 15, 1961
London, England, UK
Died: September 7, 2002
Skin-O-Meter: Great Nudity

Revered in dramatic circles for her ability to bring humanity and dignity to a range of tough, compromised female characters, striking British actress Katrin Cartlidge is also revered among skinthusiasts for her ability to bring to light the vulnerable, unclothed undersides of those same female characters. For most U.S. flesh seekers, Katrin came to the eye first and most memorably as the conflicted and slightly crusty punk-rock chick Sophie in English director Mike Leigh's *Naked* (1993). A gritty drama of scraping by and making do, *Naked* showcased Katrin in a pair of scrappy, gritty sex scenes that more than make do in the department of nude.

SKIN-fining Moment:

Naked (0:16) *Katrin makes good on the movie's title from the waist up with David Thewlis.*

See Her Naked In:

Claire Dolan (1998) Breasts, Buns
Career Girls (1997) Breasts
3 Steps to Heaven (1995) Breasts, Bush
Before the Rain (1994) Breasts
Naked (1993) Breasts

Nancy Cartwright

Born: October 25, 1959
Kettering, Dayton, Ohio
Skin-O-Meter: Brief Nudity

What do the animated television series *Richie Rich*, *Rugrats*, *The Shirt Tales*, *The Snorks*, *Pound Puppies*, *Goof Troop*, and *The Twisted Adventures of Felix the Cat* all have in common? Each of them has a voice played by big-boobed blonde cast member Nancy Cartwright. Nancy made her in-front-of-the-camera debut in the made-for-TV movie *Skokie* (1981) and has continued to spend time onscreen since then, including a small part in *Godzilla* (1998). No matter how much work Nancy finds flashing her beaming face and bubble-butt flesh on the tube or the silver screen, she will never be anywhere as well known as her most famous character. Nancy is the voice of Bart Simpson of *The Simpsons*, and she will probably never step out from under the ten-year-old's shadow.

SKIN-fining Moment:

Flesh & Blood (0:29) *Ay caramba, it's Bart Simpson's have-a-cow udders!*

See Her Naked In:

Flesh & Blood (1985) Breasts

Veronica Cartwright

Born: April 20, 1950
Bristol, England, UK
Skin-O-Meter: Great Nudity

Life on the Ponderosa would have been a lot more skinteresting if sprightly British import Veronica Cartwright had joined the four Cartwright bozos and been allowed to put the "bone" in *Bonanza*. A performing prodigy, Veronica made her big-screen debut at eight in *Love and War* (1958), although her acting cherry had been lost earlier to TV's *Leave It to Beaver*. Beaver is exactly what Veronica left it to when she bared all playing a porno chick in

Inserts (1973), an ahead-of-its-time full-frontal story of head and orgies that broke ground that mainstream films have seldom dared take since. Aside from showing up in gratuitous material such as *Alien* (1979) and *The Witches of Eastwick* (1987), Cartwright spun revealing topless turns in *My Man Adam* (1986) and *Valentino Returns* (1988).

SKIN-fining Moment:

Inserts (0:31) *Make room for mammies—and one hair-ay muff—as Veronica lies back completely bare on a porn movie set.*

See Her Naked In:

Valentino Returns (1989) Breasts
My Man Adam (1986) RB
Inserts (1975) FFN, Buns

Amira Casar

Born: July 1, 1971
Skin-O-Meter: Great Nudity

We wouldn't let our sixteen-year-old daughter go to work for a noted kinky photographer. We're grateful to the liberated French parents of Amira Casar, however, who were happy to let Helmut Newton use their little darling as a model. Amira took her other pursuits seriously, too, studying drama at the Paris Conservatoire. All of these fine arts eventually led to her appearance in *Ainsi Soient-Elles* (1995), where the gorgeous young lady doffed her top (and bottom) while being covered in paint. Fortunately, the artist took his time covering the best parts. Amira is still one of Europe's hottest talents, and we can't wait until America finally taps this hot, young import.

SKIN-fining Moment:

Anatomie de L'enfer *Hail, Casar! Amira shows FFN and buns while carnally cavorting with prosciutto-schlonde porn legend Rocco Siffredi.*

See Her Naked In:

Anatomie de L'enfer (2003) FFN
Ainsi Soient-Elles (1995) Breasts, Buns

Chiara Caselli

Born: 1967
Bologna, Italy
Skin-O-Meter: Hall of Fame

She's an Italian film star, but we're happy to say that America hasn't missed out on Chiara Caselli. Right after Chiara's breasts made their debut in a sex-and-sunning scene in *L' Année de l'Éveil* (1991), director Gus Van Sant brought this stunning actress over for a bizarre sex scene with Keanu Reeves in *My Own Private Idaho* (1991). Too bad, though, about all the quick cuts in the editing. Fortunately, Chiara returned overseas for a leisurely bathing scene in *Senso* (1993). This was followed by a woodsy love scene that made more than noses grow in *OcchioPinocchio* (1994). There's also a very hot full-frontal sex scene in *Beyond the Clouds* (1996), and don't miss her beauty among the beastly slayings in the Dario Argento thriller *Sleepless* (2001).

SKIN-fining Moment:

Beyond the Clouds (1:05) *Peter Weller helps Chiara out of her dress and gives her completely naked body a good tongue-lashing. FFN, bootay.*

See Her Naked In:

Waiting for the Messiah (2000) Breasts, Buns
The Vivero Letter (1998) Breasts
Oui (1996) Buns
Beyond the Clouds (1995) FFN
OcchioPinocchio (1994) FFN
Senso (1993) FFN, Buns
Zuppa di Pesce (1992) FFN, Buns
La Domenica Specialmente (1991) Breasts
My Own Private Idaho (1991) Breasts, Buns
L'Année de l'Éveil (1991) FFN, Buns

Rosalind Cash

Born: December 31, 1938
Atlantic City, New Jersey
Died: October 31, 1995
Skin-O-Meter: Brief Nudity

Most comfortable playing a hard-assed sister who don't take no mess, soulful thespian Rosalind Cash had a soft side as well. Her front bumpers were like rising bullets and the shapely cushions of her behind had a way of negating her adamantine attitude. Still, with the trademark 'fro and inimitable scowl, Rosalind was a fixture playing cops or street tramps on TV shows such as *Police Story*, *Cagney & Lacey*, *Barney Miller*, *Starsky and Hutch*, *Kojak*, and *Hill Street Blues*. Cash also added value to the feature films *Monkey Hustle* (1976), *Wrong Is Right* (1982), and *Tales from the Hood* (1995). Unfortunately, the screen will not be graced with Rosalind anymore, as she was sadly claimed by cancer in October 1995.

SKIN-fining Moment:

The Omega Man (0:49) *Awesome cocoa-colored boobs and buns as Rosalind closes the curtains and sits on the bed awaiting Chuck Heston's big gun.*

See Her Naked In:

The Omega Man (1971) Breasts, Buns

Crystal Cass

Born: December 1, 1976
Vancouver, British Columbia, Canada
Skin-O-Meter: Brief Nudity

Crystal Cass started her career in a few episodes of the hit cable series *The Outer Limits* in the late '90s, which first gave viewers a look at her outer limits. That led Crystal to her silver screen debut in the martial arts action flick *American Dragons* (1998). Although she played a call girl, Crystal never really got around to showing off any

skin until her follow-up film *Disturbing Behavior* (1998). She had a bit part in the movie (at least compared to Katie Holmes) but made the most of it, showing off her perky bit parts for a nice, long scene which unfortunately ends with her character's death. Or does it? You'll just have to check it out to find out for yourselves. Nothing is Crystal clear except that Cass is a stone fox.

SKIN-fining Moment:

Disturbing Behavior (0:46) *Fleeting left funbag on her way out of the bathroom.*

See Her Naked In:

Disturbing Behavior (1998) Breasts

TeleVisions:

Dead Man's Gun Breasts
Outer Limits Breasts

Joanna Cassidy

Born: August 2, 1944
Camden, New Jersey
Skin-O-Meter: Great Nudity

Redheads have a way of seeming like they come from a planet where the women are just slightly more beautiful than is possible on Earth. Who would not have liked to be at the airport when the spaceship that carried Joanna Cassidy came in? Perhaps because her own high-caliber projectiles were so cinematically smashing, copper top Cassidy broke her film cherry in *Bullitt* (1968). With green eyes that flash from warm to scalding and a versatile smile that can spread in a sneer of eroticized challenge or spread in open and convivial welcome, Joanna has left her mark in the TV archives, recurring on at least a dozen series, from *Dallas* to *Six Feet Under*. Her more adventurous roles, those that required her entire naked instrument, are typified by the stupendous butt shot of *Night Games* (1980). Joanna lies supine on a blow-up mattress, her puffy butt cushions looking better inflated than the rubber pillow. Cassidy's signature scene is a topless turn in *Blade Runner* (1982). Her exquisite rack allows her to portray a machine that has been modeled on feminine perfection.

SKIN-fining Moment:

Blade Runner (0:54) *After a long, torturous teasing with her breasts just below the frame, the camera finally pans downs and we see Joanna's glorious grapefruits.*

See Her Naked In:

The Fourth Protocol (1987) LB
Blade Runner (1982) Breasts
Night Games (1980) FFN, Buns
The Cursed Medallion (1975) RB

Laetitia Casta

Born: May 11, 1978
Pont-Audemer, France
Skin-O-Meter: Great Nudity

High fashion's Twiggy-like mannequins snapped like brittle sticks when buxom and curvaceous Laetitia Casta exploded on the scene. This French model sports an ample 35-24-35 frame and is built for sex with a beret-twirling backside and a pair of heavy breasts that will erect any man's Eiffel Tower. Laetitia is no stranger to the nude routine of a fashion spread, but it wasn't until the end of the millennium that the saucy French dish exposed her talents on the motion-picture screen. She let some nips slip opposite fat French freak Gerard Depardieu in the comic-book comedy *Astérix & Obélix: contre César* (1999). In the made-for-TV movie *La Bicyclette Bleue* (2000), Laetitia busts out her big, round bubbliciousness and even flashes some smooth white ass. Now if

she'd only let Mr. Skin smell the bicycle seat.

SKIN-fining Moment:

Gitano (0:41) *Long, sexy love scene featuring Laetitia's awesome torso-orbs as she's getting bonked in bed.*

See Her Naked In:

La Bicyclette bleue (2000) Breasts, Bush, Buns
Gitano (2000) FFN, Thong

TeleVisions:

Luisa Sanfelice Buns

Georgina Cates

Born: 1975
Essex, UK
Skin-O-Meter: Great Nudity

Although she has played wiggy brunettes and carried long, blonde hair as though it were her own, British film actress Georgina Cates is a redhead by birth and inclination. Fiery, intense, and risqué, Georgina is a girl who knows how to play naked. Unveiling her bounty in *An Awfully Big Adventure* (1995), Cates sits all nips up in bed, portraying the star-struck jail bait inamorata of Alan Rickman (playing an aging ham). With her red hair in an adolescent bob and her adolescent titties bobbing upward, Cates steals the scene, the movie, and our hearts. We will follow her to America and worship her milky skin and rose-petal nipples in *Illuminata* (1998). We will twitch with desire as she flings her head back and thrusts out a breast in a sex video within the film of *Clay Pigeons* (1998). We will attempt to transport ourselves into the apartment that she so casually and so nakedly strolls through in *Big City Blues* (1999). We are hooked.

SKIN-fining Moment:

Illuminata (0:27) *Great view of Georgina's left love pillow, while an amorous artiste paints her nipple.*

See Her Naked In:

Big City Blues (1999) Breasts, Buns
Clay Pigeons (1998) LB
Illuminata (1998) Breasts
An Awfully Big Adventure (1995) Breasts
Frankie Starlight (1995) RB

Phoebe Cates

Born: July 16, 1963
Manhattan, New York
Skin-O-Meter: Hall of Fame

Eyes brimming with dark mischief; a smirking and smiling pair of chew-toy lips; a fetching brunette shag; slim, contoured legs; tiny, trim chair cheeks; a pair of perky delights up top—erotic imp Phoebe

---

MR. SKIN'S TOP TEN

Favorite Celeb Nude Scenes
. . . Best of the breast

10. **Jayne Mansfield**
    —*Promises! Promises!* 1963 (0:04)

9. **Meredith Baxter**
    —*My Breast* 1994 (0:41)

8. **Phyllis Davis**
    —*Terminal Island* 1973 (0:39)

7. **Ann-Margret**
    —*Carnal Knowledge* 1971 (0:49)

6. **Pam Grier**
    —*Coffy* 1973 (0:38)

5. **Kelly Preston**
    —*Mischief* 1985 (0:59)

4. **Jennifer Connelly**
    —*The Hot Spot* 1990 (1:27)

3. **Uschi Digard**
    —*Prison Girls* 1972 (0:02)

2. **Mimi Rogers**
    —*Full Body Massage* 1995 (1:11)

1. **Phoebe Cates**
    —*Fast Times at Ridgemont High* **1982 (0:51)**

PRIVATE SCHOOL: AFTER GRADUATING FROM RIDGEMONT HIGH, PHOEBE CATES TOOK HER PUBLIC PARTS TO *PRIVATE SCHOOL* WHERE, AS THE LOBBY CARD MAKES CLEAR, THEIR GYM CLASS IS OUR SEX EDUCATION.

Cates reigns as one of the sexiest young creatures ever to disrobe onscreen in the early 1980s. The runaway success and lasting impact of *Fast Times at Ridgemont High* (1982) can be ascribed to many contributing factors, two of which jutted out from the breastplate of Phoebe Cates. Her bikini-popping revelation in the fantasy of self-flagellating Judge Rheinhold remains the celebrity nude scene to which all previous high-profile exposures led, and from whence all subsequent starlet skin-shows have proceeded. The skintelligentsia bow down before Phoebe's *Fast Times* feat, even as we are armed with the knowledge that superior views of Cates's posterior, pubes, and puff-tipped prizes existed already on the island of *Paradise* (1982), an Eden on earth where Phoebe floated muff first through clear-blue waters of warm regard. Phoebe's parting shot from the realm of fleshly revelations occurs with a flash of ass in *Private School* (1983), her *Fast Times* follow-up and, so far, her farewell to nude scenes. But what a run it was. And is. And shall forever be. Amen.

SKIN-fining Moment:

Fast Times at Ridgemont High (0:51) *All previous celebrity nude scenes lead to this moment; all subsequent ones emanate in its wake. In a slow-motion daydream set to The Cars' "Moving in Stereo," fantasy figure Phoebe emerges* from a swimming pool and pops open her bikini top to reveal cinema's most perfect pair to Judge Rhein hold as he bangs his gavel. My all-time favorite skin scene.

See Her Naked In:

Private School (1983) Buns
Fast Times at Ridgemont High (1982) Breasts
Paradise (1982) FFN, Buns

Kim Cattrall

Born: August 21, 1956
Liverpool, England, UK
Skin-O-Meter: Hall of Fame

Half-a-century in, the sultry Kim Cattrall continues to keep it real. Real hot, that is, thanks to her frequently naked appearances as the nymphomaniacal Samantha on HBO's *Sex and the City*. Still, for all that series' metropolitan sass and class, Kim's howlingly hilarious breakthrough as the loudly orgasming Lassie in *Porky's* (1982) remains a fan favorite and a masterpiece of muffshish. Alas, Kim sought to end her stint on *Sex* in muff the same fashion that we first got to know her—going fantastically full frontal on the show's final episode. For Kim, fifty sure looks nifty.

SKIN-fining Moment:

Porky's (0:58) *Kim shows her caboose and flashes fluff while getting banged by a gym-coach colleague in the boy's locker room.*

See Her Naked In:

36 Hours to Die (1999) Body Double—Buns
Live Nude Girls (1995) RB, Thong
Above Suspicion (1995) Breasts, Buns
Breaking Point (1993) Breasts, Thong
Split Second (1992) Breasts
Smoke Screen (1988) Breasts
Masquerade (1988) Breasts
Midnight Crossing (1988) Body Double—RB
City Limits (1985) RB
Porky's (1981) Bush, Buns
The Bastard (1978) RB
Rosebud (1975) Buns

MR. SKIN'S TOP TEN

Nake Women of HBO
. . . Home babe office

10. **Sandra Oh**
    —*Arli$$*

9. **Wendie Malick**
   —*Dream On*

8. **Rita Moreno**
   —*Oz*

7. **Sonya Walger**
   —*The Mind of the Married Man*

6. **Paula Malcolmson**
   —*Deadwood*

5. **Kristin Davis**
   —*Sex and the City*

4. **Lorraine Bracco**
   —*The Sopranos*

3. **Sonja Sohn**
   —*The Wire*

2. **Rachel Griffiths**
   —*Six Feet Under*

1. **Kim Cattrall**
   —*Sex and the City*

TeleVisions:

The Bastard Nip Slip RB
Sex and the City FFN, Buns

María Celedonio

Skin-O-Meter: Brief Nudity

With her debut in the laughably cheap *One Man Force* (1989), luscious Latina María Celedonio thoughtfully put the "B" in B-movie by flashing her young boobies. María then toiled away in low-budget projects until someone noticed her stealing every scene. But despite the occasional A-list project—such as *How to Make an American Quilt* (1995)—María's charisma remained untapped until the amazing *Freeway II: Confessions of a Trickbaby* (1999), where she joined in the film's wild spirit by going native and going topless, exposing a perfect pair of tits that had guys masturbating way past the legal limit.

SKIN-fining Moment:

Freeway II: Confessions of a Trickbaby (0:25) *Skingoria! After bare-mammaried serial killer María offs a pair of victims, she confabs while covered in blood with her lezzie lover, Natasha Lyonne.*

See Her Naked In:

Freeway II: Confessions of a Trickbaby (1999) Breasts
One Man Force (1989) Breasts

June Chadwick

Born: November 30, 1951
Warwickshire, England, UK
Skin-O-Meter: Great Nudity

Cool, calm, composed, archetypally English, and able to play any type of crank or space alien, imperious blonde June Chadwick defies categorization as anything beyond a crafty actress who can bring a vast array of characters to life. Chadwick made her bones as a bossy, know-it-all nitwit in the hilarious true-life rockumentary *This Is Spiñal Tap* (1984) and from there was able to pick and choose whatever else she wanted to do. Ultimately, June chose to become an object of sci-fi veneration by taking a role on the spacey series *V*. Some skin purists would prefer if she had chosen to appear in more films of the caliber of *Forbidden World* (1982), an alternate universe that is populated by the orbiting chest planets of otherworldly June Chadwick.

SKIN-fining Moment:

Forbidden World (0:54) *A slightly dark but decent look at June's balloons in the shower with Dawn Dunlap.*

See Her Naked In:

The Evil Below (1991) LB
Forbidden World (1982) Breasts, Buns

Sarah Chalke

Born: August 27, 1977
Ottawa, Ontario, Canada
Skin-O-Meter: Never Nude

A soft and compassionate quality inhabits the friendly and sexy blondeness of Canadian actress Sarah Chalke. A staple on American television for a decade, Sarah has most recently been seen as an often-harried, slightly disheveled young doctor on the hit series *Scrubs*. Her smile and eyes are concerned and comforting, hinting at a depth of feeling that can only be plumbed with an erotic probe. Chalke left her first marks on viewers brainpans as one of the cute, sassy, fundamentally sweet Conner daughters on *Roseanne*. She retains all these qualities on *Scrubs*, plus she is shown stripped down to a lace bra in the locker room between shifts.

SKIN-fining Moment:

Scrubs "My Clean Break" (2004) *Sarah strips to a bra in a hospital locker room. Call the doctor!*

Marilyn Chambers

Born: April 22, 1952
Westport, Connecticut
Skin-O-Meter: Hall of Fame

From Ivory Soap girl to the second-most famous starlet of porno's 1970s Golden Age to sci-fi scream-screen queen, Marilyn Chambers's career has had more ins and outs than the gullet of her chief XXX rival Linda "Deep Throat" Lovelace. Turned off by the casting couch mentality of Hollywood, bushy-tailed Chambers retreated to San Francisco and auditioned for Jim and Artie Mitchell, two sibling

pornographers with no hidden agenda. The resultant *Behind the Green Door* (1972) catapulted Marilyn to the apex of blue-screen adulation, from which height she attempted the leap into mainstream shock and schlock flicks. Her crowning hard-R moment was in director David Cronenberg's *Rabid* (1977), a horrific look at sexual illnesses gone awry in bizarre, sci-fi fashion. Marilyn spends a portion of the proceedings with her tits flailing openly. She is also equipped with a penis that protrudes from a vagina that grows under her arm. The actress soon reverted to hardcore work, and it is no hard feat to find examples of penises invading every other nook and cranny of Marilyn Chambers's anatomy.

SKIN-fining Moment:

Behind the Green Door (1:01) *Marilyn Caps her travels through the movie's sexual circus by performing on a trapeze, satisfying five different male performer's tent-poles as she swings.*

See Her Naked In:

The Naked Feminist (2004)
Desire (1997) FFN, Buns
Bikini Bistro (1995) FFN, Buns
New York Nights (1994) Breasts, Buns
Marilyn Chambers' Bedtime Stories (1993) Breasts
Breakfast in Bed (1990) FFN
The Marilyn Diaries (1990) Breasts
Party Girls (1989) Breasts
My Therapist (1984) FFN, Buns
Up 'n' Coming (1983) FFN
Deadly Force (1983) Breasts
Electric Blue (TV Magazine) (1983) FFN
Angel of H.E.A.T. (1982) FFN
Rabid (1977) Breasts
Behind the Green Door (1972) FFN, Buns
Numerous Adult Movies

Stockard Channing

Born: February 13, 1944
New York, New York
Skin-O-Meter: Brief Nudity

Since her uncredited part in *The Hospital* (1971), Stockard Channing has been wowing men with her unconventional good looks. She's also an acting icon, due to her incredible versatility as an actress and her ability to play quite a wide range of roles. She played a murderer in *The Girl Most Likely to . . .* (1973), an heiress in *The Fortune* (1975), and most recently the First Lady on the hit TV series *The West Wing*. She will, however, forever be remembered as "Rizzo," the girl who pounced on bed in her skivvies singing "Look at me, I'm Sandra Dee," in the smash-hit musical *Grease* (1978), opposite John Travolta. Sadly, even in her more youthful years, the fetching Stockard was quite a skingy lass. The only time that she ever revealed her luscious flesh onscreen was in *Sweet Revenge* (1977), in which she drops a robe whilst walking away from the camera. The movie is really difficult to find, but there is a nice look at her booty, as well as a brief glimpse at the side of her breast. That's film Stockard worth searching out.

SKIN-fining Moment:

Sweet Revenge (0:17) *Quick side-hootage and hinder as Stockard drops her robe and heads into the bathroom.*

See Her Naked In:

Sweet Revenge (1977) Buns

Geraldine Chaplin

Born: July 31, 1944
Santa Monica, California
Skin-O-Meter: Great Nudity

What does a girl do for attention when her father's profile is one of the most recognizable images in the history of film? Well, if she's lean, ethereal brunette Geraldine Chaplin,

she stands naked to the world, proudly thrusting out her low, fluffy muff. In fairness, Geraldine's delicate, exquisitely expressive face and ballerina's body control have given her the raw materials that she has wielded to become an accomplished actress. She has held her own fully costumed in such respected pictures as *Dr. Zhivago* (1965) and *Nashville* (1975). She has more than held her own fully uncostumed in *Welcome to L.A.* (1977) and *Le Voyage en Douce* (1980). Both pictures are blessed with Geraldine standing stripped to the bush, facing the camera bold and bare and every inch as memorable as her iconic father.

SKIN-fining Moment:

Welcome to L.A. (1:31) *Whoa! Stark raving nude standing in front of Keith Carradine. Nice FFN.*

See Her Naked In:

Le Voyage en Douce (1980) FFN
Remember My Name (1978) Breasts
Welcome to L.A. (1977) FFN

Patricia Charbonneau

Born: 1959
Valley Stream, Long Island, New York
Skin-O-Meter: Great Nudity

Patricia Charbonneau has become an icon for the "ladies who munch" based on her Sapphic skinematic performance in *Desert Hearts* (1986). Playing a bi-curious beauty who meets society dame Helen Shaver, she engages in a friendly game of tit-a-tit onscreen. Temperatures rise as these lusty ladies writhe around bumping boobies in tangled, sticky sheets. The sight of Patricia tasting Helen's over-heated hooter spouts is particularly delicious. Precious Pat has gone on to have small skinematic moments in *Call Me* (1988), *Brain Dead* (1990), and *Kiss the Sky* (1999), but none of those

performances come close to the sweet depths she sunk to with Helen Shaver in *Desert Hearts*.

SKIN-fining Moment:

Desert Hearts (1:10) *Patricia's pert pair jiggle juicily as she grind groins leztastically Helen Shaver. Hot!*

See Her Naked In:

Brain Dead (1990) Buns
Call Me (1988) Breasts
Desert Hearts (1985) Breasts

Joan Chen

Born: April 26, 1961
Shanghai, China
Skin-O-Meter: Hall of Fame

Mr. Skin has a yen for Joan Chen. The Chinese-born actress made a few films in her native land before becoming a hot sexport to Hollywood and landing a part in *Dim Sum: A Little Bit of the Heart* (1984). But it was in *Tai-Pan* (1986), with Joan's jugs slipping through her transparent silk top, that the Chinese dish became a sizzling platter. The Asian arouser is no one-trick horny, making weird and wanton choices like her stint on the cult TV show *Twin Peaks*. Joan's twin peaks were never hotter than in *The Wild Side* (1995), in which she gets it on with legendary labia-licker Anne Heche in a lesbo scene so real there was no need to yell "Action!" For a reary good view of Joan's assets, check out *Turtle Beach* (1992). If you like them hairless, watch bald Joan get bold in a topless scene from *Temptation of a Monk* (1993)—and watch out for those nipples, they can take an eye out! But what a way for it to go!

SKIN-fining Moment:

Wild Side (0:40) *Joan flashes that fantastic rack as she chows down on Anne Heche in this all-time classic girl-girl grapple.*

See Her Naked In:

Wild Side (1995) Breasts
The Hunted (1995) RB
Temptation of a Monk (1993) Breasts
Turtle Beach (1992) Buns
Tai-Pan (1986) LB, Nip-Slip RB

TeleVisions:

Strangers Breasts

Cher

Born: May 20, 1946
El Centro, California
Skin-O-Meter: Never nude

Big of hair and talent, little of skirt and tact, Cher's charisma and cojones propelled a career that's spanned four decades and counting. Denounced by obvious female haters as one of the "worst dressed" celebrities for her sexed-up slut wear and tattoos, as well as being criticized for her acid tongue and lusty taste for bad boys such as Gene Simmons, this dark lady has ultimately had the last laugh. Known as "She Who Sings for Bathhouse Boys" to a tribe of *Will & Grace* lovers, Cher is most beloved and imitated for her lustful lungs and ostentatious nature. She continues to make wampum from singles during her Sonny Bono co-singing days, and in a day where teeny queens rule, this seasoned squaw has stayed on the warpath to success with mega hits such as "If I Could Turn Back Time" and "Believe." Then there's that little gold statue she won for Best Actress in *Moonstruck* (1987). If you really want to be dumbstruck, find Cher's first flick, *Chastity* (1969). This digger of wigs shows her budding teepees prior to surgical scalping.

SKIN-fining Moment:

Chastity (0:27) *We don't got Cher, babe. Her body double walks out of a bathtub and shows her Sonny Butto and left Sonny Boobo.*

See Her Naked In:

Chastity (1969) Body Double—Breasts, Buns

Lois Chiles

Born: April 15, 1947
Alice, Texas
Skin-O-Meter: Brief Nudity

Lois Chiles is an auburn-haired Texan best known for her portrayals of two Hollys. The svelte and captivating Chiles used all her comely wiles to inhabit the character Holly Harwood on the nighttime soap *Dallas* during the 1982 and 1983 seasons of the show. Perhaps playing a femme fatale named Holly came easy to her since she had dazzled skinema-goers a few years prior as Dr. Holly Goodhead in the James Bond thriller *Moonraker* (1979). Aside from these two high points, Lois has had her way in acclaimed productions from *The Way We Were* (1973) to *The Great Gatsby* (1974) to *Broadcast News* (1987).

SKIN-fining Moment:

Creepshow 2 (0:59) *Lois leaps out of her fella's bed and bares her chest Chiles while pulling on some clothes. Nothing Creepy about that Show!*

See Her Naked In:

Creepshow 2 (1987) Breasts

Rae Dawn Chong

Born: February 28, 1962
Vancouver, British Columbia, Canada
Skin-O-Meter: Hall of Fame

Rae Dawn Chong was one of many struggling actresses in the mid '70s, then came *Quest for Fire* (1981), and a heap of horny men came too, after watching the film so hot it didn't even need dialogue. This cavemen-in-love movie featured the always nude Rae with young, perky jugs enlivening her every scene. No boob, Rae knew what the public wanted and gave it to them in pairs: *Fear City* (1984), *Tales from the Darkside: The Movie* (1990), *Boulevard* (1994), *Boca* (1994), *Power of Attorney* (1995), and *Valentine's Day* (1997) all reveal Rae's melons—and they're sweet and juicy. And she's even lent her form to the girls-behind-bars genre in the made-for-cable steamer *Prison Stories: Women on the Inside* (1990). Talk about a Rae of sunshine.

SKIN-fining Moment:

Fear City (0:26) *Tommy's daughter fires up her chest-bongs and buttables on stage at a strip club.*

See Her Naked In:

Small Time (1998) Thong
Valentine's Day (1998) Breasts
Power of Attorney (1995) Breasts
Boca (1994) Breasts, Buns
Boulevard (1994) Breasts
When the Party's Over (1992) Buns
Tales From the Darkside: The Movie (1990) LB
Prison Stories: Women on the Inside (1990) RB
Running Out of Luck (1986) Breasts, Buns
Fear City (1984) Breasts, Thong
Quest for Fire (1981) FFN, Buns

Robbi Chong

Born: May 28, 1965
Vancouver, British Columbia, Canada
Skin-O-Meter: Great Nudity

It certainly makes sense that she's Tommy Chong's daughter. We'd get stoned, too, if our daughter got ogled as much as Robbi Chong. Standing five feet ten inches, this luscious lovely started her career modeling around the world. Her film career has been overshadowed by half-sister Rae Dawn, but Robbi did pretty well once she freed herself from being in Dad's films. She scared up plenty of chubbies on the TV series *Poltergeist: The Legacy* then taught some Nudity 101 as a professor on a 1992 episode of *Red Shoe Diaries*. She outdoes her dad in that one, going full-frontal and getting our crotches smoking.

SKIN-fining Moment:

Red Shoe Diaries "Written Word" **(1992)** *Robbi busts out her chang-bangs while topless in bed with her loverman. Smokin'!*

TeleVisions:

Red Shoe Diaries FFN

Sarita Choudhury

Born: 1966
London, England, UK
Skin-O-Meter: Great Nudity

One passing glance at the inky black hair, sweet and deep chocolate eyes, and skin like burnished copper is enough to know that Sarita Choudhury is a truly exotic woman, but her looks are only half of it. Sarita's unique perspective and presentation must in part result from her unusual background—she was born half-Indian, half-English in London, raised in Jamaica, Mexico, and Italy and studied economics at Queens College in Ontario, Canada. Her first film role was as an Indian immigrant to the American South in *Mississippi Masala* (1992). Sarita, through long exposure to multi-culturalism, quickly picked up the American custom of allowing her breast to pop into focus during a naked love scene with her clenching costar. Choudhury returned to her Indian roots as an object of sexual veneration in *Kama Sutra: A Tale of Love* (1996). All the dark mystery and musky allure of the Indian continent are revealed. But why did the ancients of that land need to write a sex manual? One passing glance at the inky depths of cleavage, butt crack, and bush, and

any half-attentive skinthusiast would know exactly what to do.

SKIN-fining Moment:

Kama Sutra: A Tale of Love **(0:26)** *Looky! Looky! Boobs on rookie! We see Sarita's sacks during her awkward first crack at sex.*

See Her Naked In:

Kama Sutra: A Tale of Love (1996) FFN, Buns
The House of the Spirits (1994) Breasts
Mississippi Masala (1992) RB

Claudia Christian

Born: August 10, 1965
Glendale, California
Skin-O-Meter: Brief Nudity

Claudia Christian is a chameleon. You just never know what you might expect to see this gorgeous creature blending into next. Tune into late-night TV to catch Claudia sinking her claws into horror camp such as *The Hidden* (1987) and *The Haunting of Hell House* (1999) or on reruns of *Mad About You* and *Freaks and Geeks*. Christian has even done something wholesome for the kiddies, loaning her lungs to Disney's *Atlantis: The Lost Empire* (2001). In her colorful career, fans are at their most fanatical watching Claudia in all her sci-fi glory as "Susan Ivanova" on the *Babylon 5* series. Mr. Skin likes sister Christian best when she's blending into something bare. For a glimpse of Claudia's curvaceous chestal cavity, rent *Never on Tuesday* (1998) or *Hexed* (2000). Both flicks make excellent use of her extremely fine extraterrestrials. After watching any of her offerings, it's easy to *Babylon* and on about Claudia's charisma all day.

SKIN-fining Moment:

Hexed **(0:38)** *Claudia's right flapper flips out for a nice little nipple-slipple in bed with Arye Gross. Hooray for incidental nudity!*

See Her Naked In:

Hexed (1993) RB, Buns
Never on Tuesday (1988) Breasts
The Hidden (1987) Thong

Julianne Christie

Skin-O-Meter: Brief Nudity

For such a singularly sexy woman, Julianne Christie has mostly been cast as a supporting player. Julie is best recognized as the ass-tastic actress who gave Chuck Norris a tingle in his dingle on *Nash Bridges*, but this blondilicious babe's biggest role was as Gwyneth Paltrow's gal pal in the major flick *Bounce* (2000). And speaking of bouncing, Jules has quite the buoyant set of boobage. Even in tiny parts such as "Strip Club Hostess" in *It's Pat* (1994) or "Sporting Goods Clerk" in *The Nutty Professor* (1996), Christie always gives a huge shock to jocks with her skimpy attire. It's time for Hollywood to take notice and give blonde, buxom, and beautiful Julianne the juicy roles she was born to bounce in.

SKIN-fining Moment:

NYPD Blue "NYPD Lou" **(1993)** *Julianne jumps out of bed, flashes her fantastic ass crack at us, pulls on some panties, and then just barely covers her nips with her fingers while Dennis Franz asks some hard questions. This was on TV!*

TeleVisions:

NYPD Blue Breasts, Buns

Julie Christie

Born: April 14, 1941
Chabua, Assam, India
Skin-O-Meter: Great Nudity

Mod '60s bird Julie Christie let audiences know exactly where she was coming from in her naughty debut *Darling* (1965). The film follows an amoral model who uses

JULIE CHRISTIE WILL HAVE YOU SPILLING
SEED LIKE A DEMON IN *DEMON SEED*.

sex to ascend the social ladder, and it garnered Julie an Oscar, but Mr. Skin was unmoved. While provocative, the movie's best scenes were behind closed doors—without even a peep in the keyhole. Julie's juicers remained unwrapped until the mind-bending mystery *Don't Look Now* (1973), where a lengthy, nearly X-rated sex scene with Donald Sutherland finally shows off Julie's slinky bod in rumored-to-be-real action. Her fiery (topless) form also hotwires an evil hard drive in *Demon Seed* (1977), wherein she is seduced by a computer. Julie returned in 1992 to her main squeeze Sutherland for a long-shot butt view and side glance at her aging jugs in *The Railway Station Man*. She looks matronly, but, like fine wine, Julie only gets tastier with age.

SKIN-fining Moment:

Don't Look Now (0:29) *A nice shot of Julie's bush when Donald Sutherland proves that he is, indeed, a cunning linguist.*

See Her Naked In:

The Railway Station Man (1992) Buns
Demon Seed (1977) Breasts, Buns
Don't Look Now (1973) FFN, Buns
Darling (1965) Breasts, Buns

Christy Chung

Born: September 17, 1970
Montreal, Quebec, Canada
Skin-O-Meter: Great Nudity

She's been voted the Sexiest Woman in Asia by *FHM* readers, so don't tell them that Christy Chung actually went to high school in Canada. She flew to Hong Kong to start her career, though, winning the Miss China International beauty pageant and starring as Moon in the classic *Bride with White Hair 2* (1993). That got us mooning for Christy, although she didn't show her Chung queens until an adorable turn in *Jan Dara* (2001). This was followed by her sizzling star turn in *The Samsara* (2001). Christy puts her all into sex scenes that suggest she's having it all put into her. Despite a recent high-profile role in the Jackie Chan film *The Medallion* (2003), Christy's become more daring in her native land. *Feel: Christy Chung* (2001) features Christy in a series of sexual settings, including bizarre outfits and S&M antics.

SKIN-fining Moment:

Samsara (1:04) *Christy's cannage is presented in a variety of angles, as much sex is had.*

See Her Naked In:

Feel: Christy Chung (2001) Buns
Jan Dara (2001) Breasts, Buns
Samsara (2001) Breasts

Julie Cialini

Born: November 14, 1970
Rochester, New York
Skin-O-Meter: Great Nudity

Dangerously stacked Julie Cialini is what is known as a killer blonde. The signs of her lethal appeal are in the taunting sexual contents of her glaring green eyes and in the daunting all-natural contents of her worked-to-death bra. Cialini exposed her secret weapons as the centerfold Playmate of the February 1994 issue of *Playboy* and promptly knocked off (or is that knockered off?) all competition on her way to being proclaimed Playmate of the Year for 1995. TV stints followed as a matter of course, including a stint on *The Price Is Right*, on which the Cialini couple choked off attention from any other living thing in the camera frame. Feel like risky living? Take a chance on surviving the big, bulging expanses of chest slope, the sleek landing-strip muff, and round mound of butt meat in *Wolfhound* (2002). *Wolfhound*'s lighting is generally obscured by steam, shadowy or blue-tinged, which is why most who view Julie can survive the experience.

SKIN-fining Moment:

Wolfhound (0:35) *Bouncing butt and boobs doing her Ride-'em-Cowboy impression on a lucky feller's boloney pony.*

See Her Naked In:

Watchful Eye (2002) FFN, Thong
Wolfhound (2002) FFN, Buns
Numerous *Playboy* Videos

Candy Clark

Born: June 20, 1947
Fort Worth, Texas
Skin-O-Meter: Great Nudity

Best remembered for a bed-wetting episode while loving the alien David Bowie in *The Man Who Fell to Earth* (1976), Candy Clark is a tidbit-topped Texas tornado who almost won an Academy Award for her perky performance in *American Graffiti* (1973). A performance even more winning is that of her perky nipples in the aforementioned *Man Who Fell*, a science-friction sextravaganza that puts Candy's bush, draperies, and buttocks to good use along with her bite-size breasts. Clark continued her theme of casual full disclosure in *The Big Sleep* (1978); be sure to stay awake for willowy Candy's reprise of unfettered frontal nudity. Nowadays, Clark keeps busy in maternal roles and at *American Graffiti* reunions, but her past bare glory will forever provide a beacon to lonely space invaders.

SKIN-fining Moment:

When Ya Comin' Back, Red Ryder? (0:01) *Candy's casabas, coochie, and can all come out while she cleans up in the river . . . Spectacular!*

See Her Naked In:

When Ya Comin' Back, Red Ryder? (1979) FFN, Buns
The Big Sleep (1978) FFN
The Man Who Fell to Earth (1976) FFN, Buns

Marlene Clark

Skin-O-Meter: Great Nudity

Black and bootyful Marlene Clark beamed into America's living rooms weekly as the trash-talking Janet Lawson, serving as a foil to lecherous and conniving Redd Foxx on the classic television comedy of manners *Sanford and Son*. How many *Sanford* viewers would have guessed that lippy Janet had a past as a revolutionary performer in such ethnically fueled productions as *Switchblade Sisters* (1975), *Black Werewolf* (1972), *Black Mamba* (1974), and *Night of the Cobra Woman* (1973)? And how many would have been pleasantly shocked to view clips of Clark's bountiful, proudly hanging bosom and unabashedly protruding butt cushions in *Clay Pigeons* (1971), *Slaughter* (1972), or *Ganja & Hess* (1972)? But honestly, how many of you *Sanford* fans knew about Marlene's past all along?

SKIN-fining Moment:

Slaughter (0:12) *Marlene briefly bares some boobage and butt when Big Jim Brown kicks her groupie ass out of his hotel room.*

See Her Naked In:

Slaughter (1972) RB, Buns
Ganja & Hess (1972) Breasts
Night of the Cobra Woman (1972) Breasts
Clay Pigeon (1971) Breasts

Susan Clark

Born: March 8, 1940
Sarnia, Ontario, Canada
Skin-O-Meter: Great Nudity

Some combinations are always winners. Flaming red hair, glaring green eyes, a freckled chest, and skin the color of strawberry-rinsed cream, such is the classic mix that has served Susan Clark well. The Canadian import has been putting the pizzazz in color TV since 1967 and also lit up the big screen in such high-toned pictures as *Coogan's Bluff* (1968) and *The Skin Game* (1971). Skin had more to do with racial politics than epidermal delights, but Susan peeled the covers off her strawberry-cream funsacks in at least three instances. Although some skinthusiasts prefer the quick glimpses of copper-top tit pop in *Deadly Companion* (1980), old-school voyeurs swear by the classic lady-on-top sex bop with tittie flop in *Night Moves* (1975).

SKIN-fining Moment:

Night Moves (1:09) *A fast look at Susan's yabbos as she chit-chats in bed with Gene Hackman.*

See Her Naked In:

Deadly Companion (1980) Breasts
Night Moves (1975) Breasts
Tell Them Willie Boy is Here (1969) Buns

Mindy Clarke

Born: April 24, 1969
Dana Point, California
Skin-O-Meter: Great Nudity

How did an auburn beach bunny from Dana Point, California, grow up to become the ultimate icon of goth-chick excess? Was Mindy Clarke's transformation from a sweet-faced nymphet with billowy, real-flesh tits into the self-mutilating zombie slut of *Return of the Living Dead 3* (1993) the result of rebellion against the cultural aspirations of her soap-actor father and her ballet-dancer mom? Whatever. Why ask how come when you can enjoy the BD/SM overtones of a fitfully clothed zombie broad feverishly piercing her nipples, ears, cheeks, and stomach? Later, she's gagged and suspended in a harness from the ceiling of a cage. Fans of traditional skin sightings may prefer *Return to Two Moon Junction* (1993), where the two halves of Mindy's moon junction are repeatedly turned to the camera. Sensing it could never be as much fun as the filming of *Living Dead 3*, Mindy turned down the Rose McGowan part in *Scream* (1996). Since then, she's become one of TV's premiere bad asses, with guest spots on *Xena: Warrior Princess* and *Charmed* and eventually landing in the incandescent role as ultimate rich bitch "Julie Cooper" (the mom of Mischa Barton's character) on the smash Fox soap *The O.C.*

SKIN-fining Moment:

Return of the Living Dead Part III (1:07) *Turning half-zombie/half-pincushion, Mindy displays her hooters in all their spiked, pierced, and gory glory. You won't believe it's the M.I.L.F. from The O.C.*

See Her Naked In:

Return to Two Moon Junction (1994) Breasts, Buns
Return of the Living Dead Part III (1993) Breasts

Lana Clarkson

Born: April 5, 1962
Los Angeles, California
Died: February 3, 2003
Skin-O-Meter: Great Nudity

In a better world, statuesque and buxom California blonde Lana Clarkson would be remembered as the star attraction of five Roger Corman bare-breasted warrior-princess films that provided an inspiration and prototype for television's *Xena*. In this better world, the skin fanatic could spend an afternoon fixating purely upon Lana's unleashed mammaries in *The Haunting of Morella* (1990), *Blind Date* (1984), *Death Stalker* (1984), and *Vice Girls* (1996), all of which are graced with generous helpings of breasts so large and beckoning that they are the visual equivalent of comfort food. How then, in the world in which we live, do we digest the fact that Lana Clarkson will forever be remembered as the girl who was shot to death in record producer Phil Spector's Alhambra, California, house?

SKIN-fining Moment:

Barbarian Queen (0:43) *Bouncin' Barbarian Boobies as Lana is lashed to a rack in the lab of mad, horny scientist.*

See Her Naked In:

Vice Girls (1996) Breasts
The Haunting of Morella (1990) Breasts
Barbarian Queen II: The Empress Strikes Back (1989) Breasts
Barbarian Queen (1985) Breasts
Deathstalker (1984) Breasts
Blind Date (1984) Breasts

Patricia Clarkson

Born: December 29, 1959
New Orleans, Louisiana
Skin-O-Meter: Brief Nudity

Patricia Clarkson's tender fragility of face results from the combined effects of unconditionally loving green eyes, high cheeks with a touch of rose, and an inviting, expectant, light, and easy smile. A TV presence who has had recurring roles on such shows as *Davis Rules*,

Murder One, and *Wonderland*, the deep-voiced alumna of Yale Drama School won an Emmy as Aunt Sarah on HBO's *Six Feet Under*. The strawberry blonde has shown her versatility by playing a cop's wife in *The Untouchables* (1987) and a strung-out doper in *High Art* (1998).

SKIN-fining Moment:

Pieces of April (0:46) *We see topless Patricia's round-and-lovely Lewis & Clarksons in a black-and-white photo.*

See Her Naked In:

Pieces of April (2003) Breasts

Tamara Clatterbuck

Seattle, Washington
Skin-O-Meter: Great Nudity

In her early days as "Tami Bakke," Tamara Clatterbuck was an '80s video vixen. Then she reclaimed her real name, wore respectable clothes in made-for-TV movies, and has become a regular fixture on several popular soap operas. But don't think that Clatterbuck sold out her early promise. She gladly showed a slip of a nip in the big-budget crime drama *Set It Off* (1996) and almost struck us all blind with her sexy turn in *Blind Side* (1993). Tamara also showed off her titanic twosome as a hooker in the sex comedy *Lewis & Clark & George* (1997). She even returned as "Tami Bakke" in a sensational appearance as "Sophisticatia" in *Vice Academy Part 6* (1998).

SKIN-fining Moment:

Blind Side (1:13) *Tamara enjoys a spa with Rutger Hauer and we all enjoy her topless Clatterbucks.*

See Her Naked In:

Lewis & Clark & George (1998) Breasts
Set It Off (1996) Breasts
Blind Side (1993) Breasts

Jill Clayburgh

Born: April 30, 1944
New York, New York
Skin-O-Meter: Great Nudity

Jill Clayburgh ended up becoming the symbol of liberated women in the '70s. The tall, busty brunette certainly liberated herself from such unimportant things as clothes in many of her more moan-inducing movies. She first started getting attention as one of the hot young things of daytime on the soap *Search for Tomorrow*, but it's her early film appearance in *The Telephone Line* (1971) that really rings our bells here at Skin Central. It's the first time this randy rebel removed her costume. That was uncredited, but she had a more substantial, if less skinful, turn in the masturbation classic *Portnoy's Complaint* (1972). By the end of the decade, she was back up to steam at her skintillatingly breast in *An Unmarried Woman* (1978). That got her an Oscar nod for Best Actress, and Mr. Skin gives her fabulous floppers the booby prize. Even on TV she was hot in *Hustling* (1975), in which she played a hooker. She rounded out the Mam Decade with some fleshy peeks of her breasts in a shower scene from *Starting Over* (1979) and a parting shot of ass in *Luna* (1979). By *It's My Turn* (1980), her funbags were flashed for the last time. Now those mature mams are still working, but it'd be nice to have them out so audiences can get wanking again.

SKIN-fining Moment:

Luna (1:09) *Jill shows her buns when she takes off her excercise tights and walks to the shower, but the real treat is a brief glimpse of Clayburgh's "Furburgh"!*

See Her Naked In:

It's My Turn (1980) LB
Starting Over (1979) Breasts
Luna (1979) FFN, Buns
An Unmarried Woman (1978) Breasts

Corinne Clery

Born: March 23, 1950
Paris, France
Skin-O-Meter: Hall of Fame

Immortality often comes in one fell swoop. The breathtaking sweep of Corinne Clery's revelatory turn in *The Story of O* (1975) would have secured the fine-boned French brunette's place in skin heaven even if she had never taken off her clothes again. Corinne could not have been any more naked in *O*. Proudly and poignantly she parades her perfectly matched set of pairs. Her subtly rounded chair cheeks taper into a waist fit for a wasp, then burgeon above the ribs to accommodate a splendidly dependent rack of perfectly paired pert and perky plea-sure sacks. And don't overlook the precisely trimmed triangle of Clery bush! The filmmakers certainly made sure to take all the parts into account, creating a whole that will live forever. Creating an embarrassment of bare-ass riches, Corinne continued to strip to the basic wondrous female essence in films for more than a decade. If

HITCH HIKE: YOU CAN SEE CLERY NOW! THIS RARE JAPANESE POSTER FOR CORINNE CLERY'S HIGH-OCTANE CLASSIC GETS A BIG THUMB'S UP. IN YOUR PANTS.

feeling poor, find a cure in *Kleinhoff Hotel* (1977) and *Hitch Hike* (1977).

SKIN-fining Moment:

The Story of O (0:18) *Full-frontal wonder as Cori is unchained from the furnace, offered a light breakfast and then molested by two horny perverts.*

See Her Naked In:

The Gamble (1988) Bush, Buns
Il Miele del Diavolo (1986) FFN
Odio le Bionde (1980) LB
Il Viaggiatori Della Sera (1979) Buns
Covert Action (1978) Breasts
Kleinhoff Hotel (1977) FFN, Buns
Hitch Hike (1977) FFN, Thong
Strip-tease (1976) FFN, Buns
Il Grande Bluff (1976) Breasts
Natale in Casa d'Appuntamento (1976) Breasts
The Story of O (1975) FFN, Buns

Karen Cliche

Born: July 22, 1976
Sept-Iles, Quebec, Canada
Skin-O-Meter: Great Nudity

She started as a gorgeous blonde model, but there's nothing clichéd about the knockout appeal of Karen Cliche (which, by the way, is pronounced "Kleesh"). This Canadian cutie helped spice up MTV's *Undressed* and then went on to lots of forgettable films and tele-vision series. Karen was always memorable, though, and became a syndicated TV favorite as Lexa in *Mutant X* and beautiful soldier of fortune Mackenzie Previn in *Adventure Inc.* Her outfits have prompted plenty of mercenary mutant fantasies, but we keep turning back to her sexy shower scene from a bizarre retelling of *Dr. Jekyll & Mr. Hyde* (1999).

SKIN-fining Moment:

Dr. Jekyll & Mr. Hyde (0:09) *Karen cozies up in bed with hairy-scary Adam Baldwin, and he gets to savor her sumptuous, milky-white little tittables.*

See Her Naked In:

Dr. Jekyll & Mr. Hyde (1999) Breasts, Buns

Glenn Close

Born: March 19, 1947
Greenwich, Connecticut
Skin-O-Meter: Great Nudity

Far and away the scariest sexual attraction in the history of skinema (aside from the homoerotic twinges pricked by watching too many episodes of *Oz*), esteemed thespian Glenn Close created the template for the psycho-bitch girlfriend with her performance in the immorality tale *Fatal Attraction* (1987). In the course of this intense unsafe-sex cautionary tale, Close bares her perfectly serviceable chest sacks, her fully adequate butt globes, and an erotic hunger that is akin to the ravening of piranhas or vampires or starved she-beasts in estrus. The Academy-acclaimed dramatist's titty treats are presented with more demure manners in *The World According to Garp* (1982), *The Big Chill* (1983), and *Jagged Edge* (1985), but skinventurers yearning to live dangerously still swear by *Fatal*.

SKIN-fining Moment:

Fatal Attraction (0:33) *Glen's cans flop out in full view as she lays in bed talking to Michael Douglas.*

See Her Naked In:

Fatal Attraction (1987) Breasts, Buns
Jagged Edge (1985) LB
The Big Chill (1983) Breasts

GLENN CLOSE (WITH MICHAEL DOUGLAS) WILL BOIL YOUR BUNNY IN *FATAL ATTRACTION.*

Michelle Clunie

Born: November 7, 1969
Portland, Oregon
Skin-O-Meter: Great Nudity

Michelle Clunie's three best breast roles taken in combination add up to the perfect composite girlfriend. First, in *Sunset Strip* (1992), the tomboyish brunette from Portland, Oregon, plays a stripper, indicating qualities of uninhibitedness and intense daddy issues. Next, on the Showtime series *Queer as Folk*, the brave performer portrays an active lesbian who is often naked and bumping bush with other sweet slits, leading to the logical assumption that she would be open to bringing home coworkers to create a special occasion. Finally, during a totally naked simulated-sex session with a dude in *Jason Goes to Hell: The Final Friday* (1993), versatile Michelle's erectile nipples indicate she's fully into doing the dirty with a man. Michelle is the ultimate date from skin heaven.

SKIN-fining Moment:

Sunset Strip (0:23) *Michelle gives good gyrations on a club stage, popping off her black bra and shimmying her thonged bunnage.*

See Her Naked In:

Erotique (1994) Breasts, Thong
Jason Goes to Hell: The Final Friday (1993) Breasts
Sunset Strip (1992) Breasts, Thong

TeleVisions:

Hotline Breasts, Buns
Queer as Folk FFN, Buns

Claudette Colbert

Born: September 13, 1903
Paris, France
Died: July 30, 1996
Skin-O-Meter: Brief Nudity

Born in France but in the United States since the age of three, screen siren Claudette Colbert's sex appeal was infused with just enough Old World cunning to make her quicken the American public's taste for danger. A man could lose his sense, his pride, and his heart to the impertinent false innocence of those giant, dark eyes. Upstanding moral resolve could only melt away when faced with the constant supercilious simper that played upon Claudette's lips. Honey would not be sweet enough for those lips. And what of the unblemished perfection of Colbert's unfairly fair complexion? It was only natural that she should be pegged to play Poppea, the seductive incarnation of cunning female evil, in Cecil B. DeMille's *Sign of the Cross* (1932). While floating her baby feeders in a milk bath, Claudette inadvertently allowed her nipplettes to pop into view, creating the climax of the film and also of the decade.

SKIN-fining Moment:

Sign of the Cross (0:21) *Claudette enjoys a milk bath and we enjoy several flashes of her floating milk bags.*

See Her Naked In:

Sign of the Cross (1932) Breasts

Toni Collette

Born: November 1, 1972
Sydney, New South Wales, Australia
Skin-O-Meter: Great Nudity

Awesome Aussie Toni Collette is one of those chameleon-like actors who can disappear into a role—but for all her many shades, she always comes up hot. Beyond playing suffering moms in *The Sixth Sense* (1999) and *About a Boy* (2002), Toni electrically embodies an Angela Bowie-esque groupie in *Velvet Goldmine* (1998) and offers a bit of sunken boobage in the tub. Go back a few years, though, and experience the whole kit-and-kabobblers. *Lilian's Story* (1995) is one we'd all like to hear more about. In the film, Toni falls asleep in the mud and wakes up without a stitch, her jugs dangling as she walks home with only her silky bush to protect her from the elements. Is there anywhere to go after muff? Yes: muffless! By 1999's *8½ Women*, Toni is a total ten as she strips nude, completely shaved from head to camel toe.

SKIN-fining Moment:

8½ Women (1:17) *Toni flashes some fabulous full-frontal flesh when she sheds her religious threads . . . Surprisingly, where there should be some muffshish, we are instead treated to a bare wood floor!*

See Her Naked In:

The Last Shot (2004) Breasts
Japanese Story (2003) Breasts, Buns
Hotel Splendide (2000) Breasts
8½ Women (1999) FFN
Velvet Goldmine (1998) Breasts, Bush, Buns
Lilian's Story (1995) FFN, Buns

Jessica Collins

Born: April 1, 1971
Schenectady, New York
Skin-O-Meter: Brief Nudity

Jessica Collins was born Jessica Lynn Capogna, and when audiences first get a look at her huge bazoombas, they shout, "Capogna!" If there's any justice in the world of linguistics, when you look up Capogna in the dictionary, you'll find a picture of Jessica's jugs. But then, that's why you subscribe to Mr. Skin. Like many a hot property before her, Jessica began her working life on the boob tube with a stint on the soaper *Loving*. Her big-screen appearances have been promising, if not for stardom then at least for skin, as she ended up in horror schlock such as *Leprechaun 4: In Space* (1996). But it was back on the little screen that her big talents were breast seen, with appearances on *Beverly Hills, 90210* and *American*

Dreams. America's dreams have finally been answered as Jessica exposes her hourglass figure on *The Ranch*, a Showtime series about a Nevada brothel. Jessica is Collins her girls, and the boys are heeding the call.

SKIN-fining Moment:

The Ranch **(0:23)** *Jessica topless sunbathes amidst some bikini-clad pals. Her jugs are massive, beautiful, all-natural, and the kind of knockout knockers you sometimes think they stopped growing in the '70s. Bless her. Bless them. Bless us, everyone!*

See Her Naked In:

The Ranch Breasts

Joan Collins

Born: May 23, 1933
London, England, UK
Skin-O-Meter: Great Nudity

The only sight more famous and lasting than the big, round, rolling eyes of television's most instantly recognizable minx, *Dynasty's* Joan Collins, is her big, round, rolling bust line. British and breathy Joan has been ravishing in the raw since her fully nude butt sauntered in front of the lenses of *L'Amore Breve* (1969), a picture that also benefited from Collins pinching her own plump nipples and pulling a sheer-black stocking top up to within a sniff of her haughty muff. The lasting magic of Joan's appeal is a facial insouciance that seems to be always communicating that she's ready for a go or has just finished with one. While indulging in the wiles of that provocative face, don't overlook the wonders of the body below, amply displayed in celluloid classics ranging from *Playing the Field* (1974) to *The Stud* (1978). Dame Joan's defining role, according to most who love her singular appeal, would be *The Bitch* (1979).

SKIN-fining Moment:

Oh, Alfie! **(1:00)** *Joan shows her deliciously lopsided love-bubbles in bed after Alan Price rolls off her. Looks like he was leaning hard on Joan's right one.*

See Her Naked In:

Homework (1982) Body Double—Breasts
The Bitch (1979) Breasts, Buns
The Stud (1978) Breasts, Buns
Fearless (1977) Breasts
The Devil Within Her (1975) Breasts, Buns
Oh, Alfie! (1975) Breasts
Playing the Field (1974) Breasts, Buns
Tales That Witness Madness (1973) Breasts, Buns
L'Amore Breve (1969) Breasts, Buns

Roberta Collins

Skin-O-Meter: Brief Nudity

Half the secret to lasting success is finding your niche, and for lean and lovely blonde Roberta Collins immortality was to be found in the women-in-prison genre of exploitation cinema. Working with her classic blue eyes and fair skin with pinkish highlights, the flighty flesh artist was first locked down in *Women in Cages* (1971). In those days, mean, vaguely dominatrix wardens sent prisoners to bed without pillows, blankets or pajamas. Roberta's bobbing boobies held up well under the severe treatment. But evidently she complained about some imagined mistreatment and ended up strapped naked to the spokes of a giant wheel. Rehabilitation seems to have come hard to Roberta. She and her cans were back in the can in *The Big Doll House* (1971) and *Caged Heat* (1974).

SKIN-fining Moment:

Big Doll House **(0:30)** *Three cheers for Roberta's tattered tunic, touting her terrific tittlage!*

See Her Naked In:

Death Race 2000 (1975) Breasts
Caged Heat (1974) Breasts
Sweet Kill (1972) Breasts
Big Doll House (1971) Breasts
Women in Cages (1971) Breasts

Tai Collins

Born: 1963
Roanake, Virginia
Skin-O-Meter: Great Nudity

Tai Collins is a true rarity amongst *Baywatch* beauties, as this coppertoned cutie made only two appearances on the actual show—plus another appearance on *Baywatch Nights*. Tai really cashed in on *Baywatch* by spending six seasons on the series' writing staff. Now you know why the show had such an impressive understanding of women's issues. And speaking of impressive, the former *Playboy* model saved her own best work for her sole film role, heating up a sauna to new temperatures in the flick *Enemy Gold* (1993). It's full frontal and fully gratuitous, proving that Tai's easygoing ways aren't limited to her breezy scripts.

SKIN-fining Moment:

Enemy Gold **(0:20)** *Tai shows her naked top, tuchus, and just a hint of trim hopping out of a sauna and into the shower.*

See Her Naked In:

Enemy Gold (1993) FFN, Buns

Madeleine Collinson

Born: July 22, 1952
Malta
Skin-O-Meter: Great Nudity

Perfection as a concept is a singular excellence, incapable of being duplicated or paralleled. Thank God that the world is a so much richer place than the arid plane of theoretical values. The rich reality is that we on this earth have at least once enjoyed double doses of perfection, one half of which is embodied by Madeleine Collinson. A simultaneously wholesome and exotic brunette, Madeleine is one half of the Collinson twins, a late 1960s and early 1970s phenomenon of mirror-image female fantasy bait, two sisters born minutes apart who enthralled legions of men around the globe with their October 1970 *Playboy* centerfold. Not ones to shy away from onscreen skin, this pair of stellar pairs can be seen dually cavorting in a string of three shocking skin relics from the Age of Aquarius. How can you tell Madeleine and sister Mary apart? Easy. Madeleine is the one who plays the vampire in the woefully misnamed *Twins of Evil* (1971).

SKIN-fining Moment:

Some Like it Sexy (0:41) *Maddy shows off an extremely fluffity muff as her kissy sissy nuzzles her na-nas. Taboolicious!*

See Her Naked In:

Up in Smoke (1978) Breasts
The Love Machine (1971) Breasts
Twins of Evil (1971) FFN
Some Like It Sexy (1969) Breasts, Bush, Buns

Mary Collinson

Born: July 22, 1952
Malta
Skin-O-Meter: Great Nudity

If God created another brunette with as splendid and airborne a rack as that sported by gorgeously grinning imp Mary Collinson, then you'd think He would keep her and her heavenly hydraulics for Himself. But the Almighty is not the greedy sex fiend that the rest of us might be if we wielded His powers, and thus Mary's twin sister Madeleine was allowed to be born along with her. As the 1960s burned out and the 1970s flowered, greedy sex

fiends found matching altars at which to worship in the laps and ledges of the Collinson twins, displayed for purposes of erotic reverence in the October 1970 issue of *Playboy* and in a trio of turn-of-the-decade filmic events. Like to see an identically paired pair of pair holders holding their peeled pairs against one another whilst sensually brushing lips and batting lashes? Bow down before the sisterly foreplay of *Some Like It Sexy* (1969).

SKIN-fining Moment:

Some Like it Sexy (0:41) *Mary bareys all three B's snagging her sister. Those crazy '60s kids and their free love!*

See Her Naked In:

Up in Smoke (1978) Breasts
Twins of Evil (1971) RB
The Love Machine (1971) Breasts
Some Like It Sexy (1969) Breasts, Bush, Buns

Holly Marie Combs

Born: December 3, 1973
San Diego, California
Skin-O-Meter: Brief Nudity

You are charmed, I'm sure, by the hair-raising hotness of Holly Marie Combs. She is spellbinding as the middle sister in a trio of white-hot witches on the supernatural, super sexy WB thriller *Charmed* (1998). Sandwiched between bewitchingly bodacious beauties Alyssa Milano and Rose McGowan, Holly adds a dash of girlish innocence to the show's potent mix. Watching these witchy women weekly increases Mr. Skin's orgasm by the power of three. Although Holly is not related to P. Diddy, she does have some mighty *puffy* nips. Though diminutive in size, her B-cups runneth over with large, inflated pegs just begging to be sucked. If you are skeptical, Holly's topless scene in *A Reason to Believe* (1995) will convince you.

With knobs like these, who wouldn't want to deck Holly's halls?

SKIN-fining Moment:

A Reason to Believe (1:06) *You'll be "charmed" to see Holly deliver a nice long look at her puffy-nipped hootage as she pulls off her top for an appreciative fella.*

See Her Naked In:

A Reason to Believe (1995) Breasts

Lisa Comshaw

Born: February 18, 1964
Akron, Ohio
Skin-O-Meter: Great Nudity

A versatile and willing nudist, immodestly stacked Lisa Comshaw has been pleasing skinthusiasts for more than a decade, turning in epidermal performances at a rate of about three a year. A natural redhead with a preternatural redhead's body of pale, plush flesh, Comshaw's skinful ways began with a trifling exposure of boobs and buns in *Almost Pregnant* (1992). However, before Lisa was able to move her ass out of frame, some guy put his face in there and bit it, infecting her with the desire to be seen in all of her skinful glory as often as possible by as many as possible. Comshaw has as many titles as professional boxing has belts. Start with *Housewife From Hell* (1993) and work up to *Teacher's Pet* (2000). They're all knockouts.

SKIN-fining Moment:

Illicit Confessions (0:33:) *Lisa's tied up and blindfolded, providing a full-frontal lez-time feast for Blake Pickett.*

See Her Naked In:

Deviant Vixens I (2002) FFN
Teacher's Pet (2000) Breasts
Casting Couch (2000) Breasts, Buns
Secret Needs (1999) FFN, Buns

Shandra: The Jungle Girl (1999) Breasts, Buns
Sexual Matrix (1999) Breasts, Buns
Devil in the Flesh (1998) Breasts
Scandalous Behavior (1998) FFN, Buns
Centerfold Fantasies (1997) FFN, Buns
La Iena (1997) FFN, Buns
Lolita 2000 (1997) FFN, Buns
Illicit Confessions (1997) FFN
Erotic Boundaries (1997) FFN
Arranged Marriage (1996) FFN, Buns
Deadly Currency (1996) Breasts
Depraved (1996) Breasts
The Killer Inside (1996) Breasts, Bush,
   Buns
Obsession Kills (1995) FFN
Midnight Confessions (1995) FFN
Raven Hawk (1995) Breasts
Portrait in Red (1995) FFN, Buns
Don Juan DeMarco (1995) RB
Babes, Bikes and Beyond (1994) FFN,
   Buns
Bikini Med School (1994) Breasts
Divorce Law (1993) FFN, Buns
Buck Naked Line Dancing (1993)
   Breasts
Love Scenes, Volume 3 (1993) Breasts
Teasers (1993) FFN, Buns
Nude Daydreams (1993) FFN, Buns
Housewife From Hell (1993) FFN, Thong
. . . And God Spoke (1993) Breasts
Almost Pregnant (1992) Buns
Numerous Adult Movies

TeleVisions:

Erotic Confessions Breasts, Bush, Buns
Pleasure Zone Breasts, Bush, Buns
Women: Stories of Passion Breasts, Bush,
   Buns

Cristi Conaway

Born: 1965
Lubbock, Texas
Skin-O-Meter: Brief Nudity

So maybe it's easy for a gorgeous
American blonde to become a
successful model in Japan. Cristi
Conaway went on to do very well
for herself in Hollywood, making us
wish some director had been able
to *con away* her clothes in a bunch
of TV movies. Instead, we're happy
to ogle Cristi as a Gotham ice

princess in *Batman Returns* (1992).
Cristi also makes our trousers grow
in *Attack of the 50 Ft. Woman*
(1993), playing a small-town hottie
who shows off some brief boobage
and bodacious butt meat. And the
kitschy outfits she wears in the rest
of the movie should please plenty
of fetishists.

SKIN-fining Moment:

Attack of the 50 Ft. Woman (0:16)
*Cristi's sweet can bares itself ever-so-
briefly as she gets out of bed and heads
for the bathroom.*

See Her Naked In:

Attack of the 50 Ft. Woman (1993)
   Buns

TeleVisions:

Tales from the Crypt Breasts, Buns

Jennifer Connelly

Born: December 12, 1970
New York, New York
Skin-O-Meter: Hall of Fame

From the *Book of Skin*, chapter one:
   "In the beginning, God created
Jennifer Connelly. Jennifer Connelly
was without form and void, and the
Spirit of God was moving over the
face of her."
   And God said, "Let there be
boobs," and there were boobs. And
God saw that the boobs were good;
and God separated the boobs from
one another.
   And God said, "Let there be ass,
and let the ass sometimes detract
thine attention from the boobs."
And God created the ass, and it was
plump and luscious and perfect in
every way, and it was good.
   And God said, "Let there be
gracious gams, protruding from the
perfect ass, and let those gams
swagger to and fro in sensuous
delight." God saw the gams, and
gasped.
   On the final day, God finished

the Jennifer Connelly, and he
spoke unto her. "Jennifer Connelly,
thou shalt go forth and bring
erections to all men, cause
jealousy in most women, and
appear nude on film, thusly nude
thou shalt appear, sharing thine
divine beauty with the world.
Thine skin shall radiate unknown
powers amongst men, causing
teeny spots upon thine pants, and
they shall go away ashamed, but
knowest thou that thine powers be
used for good. Especially in *The
Hot Spot*."
   And Jennifer Connelly said,
"'Kay."

SKIN-fining Moment:

The Hot Spot (1: 26) *Jennifer first
bares her butt from afar while
sunbathing with Debra Cole, then offers
up the best-ever look at her perfect pair
ever to be caught on film . . . What a
rack!*

See Her Naked In:

House of Sand and Fog (2003) Breasts,
   Buns
Waking the Dead (2000) Breasts
Requiem for a Dream (2000) Body Double—
   Buns / Her—Bush
Inventing the Abbotts (1997) Breasts
Mulholland Falls (1996) Breasts
Of Love and Shadows (1994) RB
The Hot Spot (1990) Breasts, Buns
Once Upon a Time in America (1984) Body
   Double—Buns

**JENNIFER CONNELLY MAKES IT A WET SPOT
IN *THE HOT SPOT*.**

Carol Connors

Skin-O-Meter: Great Nudity

What's a curvaceous blonde cutie to do? If you're Carol Connors it's got to be porno! She came on the big screen playing The Waitress in *Red Line 7000* (1965)—not much of a breakthrough for the rosy-nippled flopper. After five years of Tinseltown turndowns, Carol wisely followed her meaty breasts to where the money was: hardcore sex films. It's a career change that Mr. Skin endorses wholeheartedly. Her first adventure in the skin trade was as the title character in *Cousin Betty* (1970), which led to the money shot of all adult films, *Deep Throat* (1972), in which she played the buxom nurse. From there, the titles came like so many men: *Weekend Tail* (1972), *School Teacher's Weekend Vacation* (1973), and *The Erotic Adventures of Candy* (1978). Carnal Carol was so into the hot action she even directed a flesh feature called *Desire for Men* (1981)—a true sex auteur. According to the tabloid *The Sun*, Carol is the mother of equally well-endowed Thora Birch. It makes sense, as Carol gave up her sex stardom in 1982, around the time of Thora's birth. And looks don't deceive. They certainly have the same busty abandon.

SKIN-fining Moment:

Deep Throat (0:40) *Nurse Carol delivers huge boobs, hot buns, and the open hole from whence Thora Birch emerged as she gets reamed by Harry Reems.*

See Her Naked In:

Candy Goes to Hollywood (1979) Breasts, Buns
Deep Throat (1972) FFN, Buns
Numerous Adult Movies

Rachael Leigh Cook

Born: October 4, 1979
Minneapolis, Minnesota
Skin-O-Meter: Never Nude

A five-foot-two-inch wee wonder, Rachael Leigh Cook proves sexy things come in small packages. What she lacks in stature Rachael more than makes up in jugs—two architecturally massive structures that stick straight out like globular skyscrapers. By age ten she was modeling for the cover of Milk-Bone packaging, which made Mr. Skin want to milk his bone. She's been acting since fourteen and first hit a vein in an anti-heroin public-service announcement. The curvaceous cutie brandished a frying pan and proceeded to destroy a kitchen to symbolize the effects of drugs on the body. Considering the delectable perfection of her body, Rachael knows what she's talking about. Her big-screen debut was in *The Baby-Sitters Club* (1995), followed by *Living Out Loud* (1998) and *The Naked Man* (1998). There's been no naked woman title yet for randy Rachael, although she was hot in the hit *She's All That* (1999) and even hotter as the teenybopper rocker in *Josie and the Pussycats* (2001). Mr. Skin hopes that Rachael cooks up something spicy soon.

SKIN-fining Moment:

The Big Empty (0:17) *This curvaceous cutie-pie tugs her thumbs through the loops of her low-rise jeans for Jon Favreau and we damn near get a taste of her Rachael Leigh Cookie.*

Jennifer Cooke

Born: September 19, 1964
New York
Skin-O-Meter: Brief Nudity

Due to her role as an alien/earthling hybrid on the series *V*, Jennifer Cooke is still remembered as a sci-fi goddess—mainly to lucky young geeks who bought some of her stunning '80s pinup posters. Jennifer's brief career also included a stint on the soap opera *The Guiding Light* before she exposed her breasts for HBO's anthology series *The Hitchhiker*. Jennifer then cooked up a great moment in patriotism, bouncing her boobies while wearing nothing but small American flags as pasties in the cheerleading epic *Gimme an 'F'* (1984). She was even one of the rare females to survive a run-in with Jason, helping to (temporarily) kill off the killer in *Friday the 13th, Part VI: Jason Lives* (1986).

SKIN-fining Moment:

The Hitchhiker "Man's Best Friend" (1986) *Jen sticks out more than her thumbs as she doffs her top to take a shower. Nice booby action!*

TeleVisions:

The Hitchhiker Breasts

Rita Coolidge

Born: May 1, 1945
Nashville, Tennesee
Skin-O-Meter: Brief Nudity

Blessed with a smokingly sexy singing voice and exotic Native American allure, Rita Coolidge shot to superstardom in the '70s, wailing onstage with legends Eric Clapton, George Harrison, Joe Cocker, Bob Dylan, and Jimi Hendrix. With her sensuously unique sound, Rita made major wampum with "Higher and Higher." Lovely Rita's luscious lungs caught the flies of randy rockers such as Graham Nash, Stephen Stills, and '70s super stud Kris Kristofferson, who married Rita in 1973. This Cherokee cutie shocked Hollywood with hits such as "All Time High" for the James Bond thriller *Octopussy* (1983) and "Love Came for Me" for *Splash* (1984). Rita made her own waves premiering her tiny teepees onscreen in *Pat Garrett and Billy the Kid* (1973). While her ta-tas aren't statuesque, her pointy totem poles are worth the trip to the video store for a peek. With an undying natural beauty and over thirty years of soulful crooning, this deliciously dark lady continues to take fans to *higher and higher* levels of lust and inspiration.

SKIN-fining Moment:

Pat Garrett and Billy the Kid (1:48) *Rita's right teat-a pokes out of her shirt while she chats up Kris Kirstofferson.*

See Her Naked In:

Pat Garrett and Billy the Kid (1973) RB

Jeanne Cooper

Born: October 25, 1928
Taft, California
Skin-O-Meter: Brief Nudity

She's no superstar, but sexy Jeanne Cooper has had plenty of historical moments during her long Tinseltown career. The soap siren became news when she actually incorporated her own facelift into the storyline for her character on *The Young and the Restless*, with the show actually filming the operation. She kind of needed one, after all, since Jeanne's sex appeal has been steaming up TV shows and movies since 1951. And she was happy to keep up with the times, dropping her top in front of Henry Fonda in the 1970 western *There Was a Crooked Man . . .*

SKIN-fining Moment:

There Was a Crooked Man (0:18) *Jeanne rolls over in bed and flashes her right breast at Henry Fonda when he peeks in.*

See Her Naked In:

There Was a Crooked Man (1970) LB

Teri Copley

Born: May 10, 1961
Arcadia, California
Skin-O-Meter: Brief Nudity

Full of fluffy mane, buoyant breastage, and tantalizing tail, Teri Copley had a perfectly *maid to order* career on the boob tube in the 1980s. The bubbly buxom blondie is simply at her breast amusing and arousing us via the natural wonder of TV. And speaking of natural wonders, her marvelous mams and gregarious giggling personality are stupendously grand in friction-causing flicks such as *The Star Maker* (1981) and *I Married a Centerfold* (1984). Teri is most tempting on the syndicated series *We Got It Made* as the hotter than Hades housemaid of two randy, unbelievably lucky bastard bachelors. Vacuuming in the '80s regalia of leotards and leg warmers, Teri just begs for a vigorous one-on-one workout. Copley debuted her terrific two in *New Year's Evil* (1981), going topless during a hotsy-totsy session in the backseat. Any of this tasty twinkie's offerings will leave you with a creamy center.

SKIN-fining Moment:

Down the Drain (0:32) *Teri strips to her black bra and panties, then a bed double takes over, shows gorgeous gazongas, bent-over butt and full-frontal.*

See Her Naked In:

Down the Drain (1990) Body Double—FFN, Buns
New Year's Evil (1981) RB

Danielle Cormack

New Zealand
Skin-O-Meter: Brief Nudity

Plenty of young guys wanted to go down under with Danielle Cormack in her recurring role as Ephiny on *Xena: Warrior Princess*. This rising star from New Zealand has also stayed busy in plenty of acclaimed indie films from her own country. After making good on the provocatively

titled *Topless Women Talk About Their Lives* (1997) Danielle further milked her own twin superpowers while taking a countryside bath in *The Price of Milk* (2000).

SKIN-fining Moment:

The Price of Milk (0.08) *Danielle and her man sit in an old-fashioned bathtub outdoors, washing the dishes that float between their bare bodies. Don't ask why. Just look at her right nipple.*

See Her Naked In:

The Price of Milk (2000) RB
Topless Women Talk About Their Lives (1997) Breasts

Adrienne Corri

Born: November 13, 1933
Glasgow, Scotland, UK
Skin-O-Meter: Great Nudity

Adrienne Corri made her first screen appearance in 1949, back when nobody figured this redhead would eventually become an icon of sex in the cinema. This stunning Brit quickly established herself as a formidable presence in both classical period pieces and big-screen schlock. Stanley Kubrick cast Adrienne as the Droogs' incredibly sexy victim in the gang-rape scene in *A Clockwork Orange* (1971). People still debate whether it's okay to get turned on during Kubrick's bizarre handling of this controversial scene. However, any guy's trousers can proudly raise the big top during Corri's ravaging in *Vampire Circus* (1972). There's some bloodshed here, too, but only after Adrienne goes gloriously full frontal.

SKIN-fining Moment:

A Clockwork Orange (0:11) *Malcom MacDowell slices off Adrienne's tight red dress and attacks her while wailing "Singin' in the Rain." Rough-and-tumble full-frontal.*

See Her Naked In:

A Clockwork Orange (1971) FFN

Marion Cotillard

Born: September 30, 1975
Paris, France
Skin-O-Meter: Great Nudity

Americans think of it as a '70s sitcom, but Europe knows *Taxi* (1998) as the title of one of France's most popular films—with the popularity fueled by Marion Cotillard's full-frontal nudity. This stunning young Parisian kept her pussy covered for *Taxi 2* (2000), but she had our meters running with her bizarre sex scene in *Les Jolies choses* (2001). If you really need a reason to unfasten your seatbelt, though, check out Marion's amazing sex scene in *Une Affaire Privée* (2002).

SKIN-fining Moment:

Une Affaire privée (0:51) *It's sort of dark (and there's a bit of man-meat in the shot) but Marion manages to manifest her mammaries, muff, and even a bit of butt in this extra-long skin sequence.*

See Her Naked In:

Une Affaire Privée (2002) FFN, Buns
Les Jolies Choses (2001) FFN
Furia (2000) Breasts, Bush
La Guerre dans le Haut Pays (1998) FFN, Buns
Taxi (1998) FFN
My Sex Life . . . Or How I Got Into An Argument (1996) Breasts

Clotilde Courau

Born: April 3, 1969
Levallois-Perret, Hauts-de-Seine, France
Skin-O-Meter: Great Nudity

This French filly started her career in her native France, but Clotilde Courau came to America to flash her breasts in the bizarre indie film *The Pickle* (1993). Then Clotilde displayed those charming little titties in *Le Poulpe* (1998), throwing in a shot of full-frontal furburgerage. But that was all just a tease for the glory of *Promenons-nous dans les Bois* (2000). Clotilde has spent the years keeping her precious pussy safe from any kind of razor, showing a full bush amidst some sizzling sex scenes.

SKIN-fining Moment:

Le Poulpe (1:21) *Nice view of her beehive and breasts as Courau waves a gun around in her birthday suit.*

See Her Naked In:

Un Monde Presque Paisible (2002) Bush
En Face (2000) Breasts, Buns
Promenons-nous dans les Bois (2000) FFN, Buns
La Parenthèse Enchantée (2000) Breasts
Milk (1999) Breasts, Buns
Le Poulpe (1998) FFN, Buns
Fred (1997) Breasts, Buns
Marthe ou la Promesse du Jour (1997) Breasts, Buns

Christina Cox

Toronto, Canada
Skin-O-Meter: Great Nudity

Oh, Canada, thank you for giving us wonderful things like the tastiest bacon, rich maple syrup, and hockey, but what moves men to whack their sticks most are your lovely actresses like Christina Cox. Chris had it tough growing up with a last name like *Cox*, and it's ironic that she's inspired so many stiff ones in her skinful career. Christina isn't exactly hard pressed to find fans, attracting attention with her blonde beauty and bountiful breasts on Canadian television in *A Brother's Promise: The Dan Jansen Story* (1996), *Sins of Silence* (1996), and *F/X: The Series*. Cox is a prick tease onscreen in *Street Law* (1995) and *The Donor* (1997), forcing fans to believe she's baring her own magnificent mams and buoyant bottom. After repeated viewings of both flicks, we at Skin Central determined that we were giving our squirty specimens to someone other than Christina. All is forgiven thanks to Christina's skinsational Sapphic turn in *Better Than Chocolate* (1999). In an erotic body-painting session with costar cutie Karyn Dwyer, Chris uses delicate breast strokes to make a deliciously delightful piece and debuts her own work of art: her bouncy boobies and acrylic-covered coochie. Christina, you are truly one of Canada's finest national treasures.

SKIN-fining Moment:

Better Than Chocolate (0:17) *Lesboliciously colorful breasts and buns as blonde Christina and dark-maned Karyn Dwyer cover each other in body paint and then roll around on canvas.*

See Her Naked In:

Better Than Chocolate (1999) Breasts, Buns
Street Law (1995) Body Double—Breasts, Buns
The Donor (1994) Buns

Courteney Cox

Born: June 15, 1964
Birmingham, Alabama
Skin-O-Meter: Brief Nudity

Brunette lust bomb Courteney Cox first turned on TV fans on the soap *As the World Turns* and boogieing with The Boss in Bruce Springsteen's "Dancing in the Dark" music video. In 1993, she exploded into small-screen superstardom as ultra-competitive Monica on NBC's *Friends*, but her sizzling screen roles will leave you longing to be more than just friends. In *The Runner* (1999), the teasing shots of Courteney's luscious but covered love mounds leave you believing that her cleavage could be one of the characters. Courteney proves that she is both bright eyed and bushy tailed, however, in *3000 Miles to*

Graceland (2001), playing a trailer-trash trollop with a tush that would have left Elvis drooling all over his peanut butter and banana sandwich.

SKIN-fining Moment:

Blue Desert (0:53) *Left breast, in bed lying under D. B. Sweeney. Little hard to see her face, but it is her.*

See Her Naked In:

3000 Miles to Graceland (2001) Buns
Commandments (1997) LB
Blue Desert (1991) LB

Nikki Cox

Born: June 2, 1978
Los Angeles, California
Skin-O-Meter: Never Nude

Durable Fox television fixation *Married . . . with Children* naturally spawned crass imitations, the brassiest of which was *Unhappily Ever After*, a Bundy-lite sass-and-ass-fest that enjoyed a five-year run on the large strengths of bimbo-bright brunette bombshell Nikki Cox's knockout knockers. Nikki instantly became a fixture upon the walls of adolescent boys all across America and within the brain pans of their dads. Cox's overnight success was years in the making, her climb to mass infatuation beginning as a ten-year-old with a guest spot on *Mama's Family*. The former dance student never looked back, although every man she passed paused to look back at her behind. Cox's imposing presence on *Unhappily* won her a short-lived, cleavage-baring series of her own, *Nikki*, and a marriage to comedian Bobcat Goldthwait, alternately known as Mr. Floppy, which lasted a few years longer.

SKIN-fining Moment:

Run Ronnie Run! (0:47) *Nikki paddles around in the world's luckiest swimming pool, and you'll marvel at how she somehow packed those*

stupendous knockers into a hard-working red bikini top. Then she climbs out of the water and there's a devastatingly hot shot of her sumptuously sizable seat. Nikki rox!

Ria Coyne

Born: February 20, 1962
Scranton, Pennsylvania
Skin-O-Meter: Great Nudity

Ria Coyne has already shown her gorgeous all in *Playboy*, and her acting skills are more of a shock than her nudity in *Corporate Affairs* (1990). But we've certainly gotten obsessed over her stealth appearance in *Naked Obsession* (1990). Take a look in the background, and there's Ria shaking her titties and shaking us up as a topless dancer. She's a Mr. Skin favorite, and the rest of the world still has a chance to catch on.

SKIN-fining Moment:

Corporate Affairs (0:10) *Several flashes of Ria's left headlight in the backseat of a car.*

See Her Naked In:

Corporate Affairs (1990) LB
Naked Obsession (1990) Breasts, Buns

TeleVisions:

Tales from the Crypt Breasts

Barbara Crampton

Born: December 27, 1962
Levittown, Long Island, New York
Skin-O-Meter: Great Nudity

Watching soap operas is always a combination of gratification and frustration. The female characters on the daytime dramas are generally so overtly erotic that to watch an episode is almost always a sexually actualizing experience. The frustration comes in when the impossible-to-satisfy skinthusiast wonders why on earth he never has

the opportunity to see any of these soap vixens fully nude in a halfway-explicit sexual situation. Well, complete satisfaction exists, and her name is Barbara Crampton. A striking blonde with a large, savory mouth and blue-green eyes that open as big as the whole wide world in sexy wonder, Barbara has been pursuing parallel careers in A-list soaps and hard-R B-movies. You may have seen her daytime highlights on *Days of Our Lives*, *The Young and the Restless*, and *The Bold and the Beautiful*. You can see her R-rated hijinks in bun- and boob-baring outings from *Re-Animator* (1985) to *Poison* (2000), with a ton of titty satisfaction in between.

MR. SKIN'S TOP TEN

Skingoria Scenes
. . . A cut above the breast!

10. **Kate Fallon**
    —*Rock n' Roll Frankenstein* 1999 (0:54)

9. **Tawny Kitaen**
   —*Crystal Heart* 1985 (0:53)

8. **Izabello Miko**
   —*The Forsaken* 2001 (0:01)

7. **Ashley Judd**
   —*Normal Life* 1996 (0:39)

6. **Emily Haack**
   —*Scrapbook* 2000 (0:16)

5. **Peta Wilson**
   —*Mercy* 2000 (0:46)

4. **Drew Barrymore**
   —*Doppelganger: The Evil Within* 1993 (0:23)

3. **Julia Ormond**
   —*The Baby of Mâcon* 1993 (1:05)

2. **Michelle Bauer**
   —*Hollywood Chainsaw Hookers* (0:09)

1. **Barbara Crampton**
   —*Re-Animator 1985* (1:10)

SKIN-fining Moment:

Re-Animator (1:10) *A great moment in Skingoria: Barbara's full-frontally nude (with heaving hooters everywhere) as Dr. Hill's re-animated head makes some . . . amorous advances.*

See Her Naked In:

Poison (2000) Body Double—Breasts, Buns
Castle Freak (1995) LB
Chopping Mall (1986) Breasts
Kidnapped (1986) Breasts
From Beyond (1986) Breasts, Thong
Prince of Bel Air (1986) Breasts
Re-Animator (1985) FFN, Buns
Fraternity Vacation (1985) FFN, Buns
Body Double (1984) Breasts

Cindy Crawford

Born: February 20, 1966
Dekalb, Illinois
Skin-O-Meter: Great Nudity

Is there a man alive who has not salivated over some image of Cindy Crawford? This tall, auburn-tinged brunette with the creamy-tan complexion has been on the mass skinconsciousness for so long, it's hard to imagine a time when her sly, seductive, toothy grin; twinkling, teasing eyes; multimillion-dollar body; and singular mole beside the mouth were not listed among the nation's top five accessed images for bedtime fantasy fodder. Although she'd already become the ultimate dream date for any straight guy who'd ever looked at a single fashion magazine, scintillating Cindy's extended stint on MTV's *House of Style* alerted the fashion deprived to what they had been missing. Exactly how hot is Cindy Crawford? The mere mention of her name managed to launch the career of comedian Denis Leary.

SKIN-fining Moment:

Fair Game (1:09) *Fast toplessness as she takes man-pipe from William*

Baldwin on a train. It's quick but those are supermodel maw-maws.

See Her Naked In:

The Simian Line (2000) Breasts
Fair Game (1995) Breasts

Rachael Crawford

Born: 1969
Toronto, Ontario, Canada
Skin-O-Meter: Brief Nudity

After years of gracing Canadian television with her beauty, Rachael Crawford finally made the kind of big-screen debut men like—specifically, playing a lesbian circus performer seducing a female college professor in *When Night Is Falling* (1995). That was a long way from Rachael's days as a cute kid costarring with Mr. T on the series *T. and T.* Rachael followed up her Sapphic turn with some heterosexual under-the-sheets sex in *Rude* (1995). This Canadian cutie still works steadily in her homeland, but Hollywood could sure stand to see more of Rachael's great white somethings.

SKIN-fining Moment:

When Night Is Falling (0:59) *Nice look at Rachael's rack as she sapphos it up between the sheets with Pascale Bussières.*

See Her Naked In:

When Night Is Falling (1995) Breasts
Rude (1995) Buns

Sophia Crawford

Born: May 19, 1966
Battersea, England, UK
Skin-O-Meter: Great Nudity

It's not totally far-fetched that delectable Sophia Crawford should end up playing a live-action cartoon character. The sizzling scene stealer

has fashioned herself into a heightened version of the alluring female prototype. The blonde-streaked brunette has a perky, pretty, pointy, ski-jump nose; protruding lips shaped like an animator's realization of pouting sexuality; and eyes that are every iota as big but not one whit as innocent as Betty Boop's. Add to that the toned, tight body of a martial arts expert, and you have a winning candidate for *Mighty Morphin' Power Rangers*. Sophia came by that powerful, lean body the honest way: She bared it in Chinese-produced karate pics such as *Escape from the Brothel* (1992). While fleeing the cathouse, Crawford engaged in an ass-out kung-fu-fighting scene, a bout of naked kick boxing that focused on her hairy box.

SKIN-fining Moment:

Escape from the Brothel (0:13) *Amazing! Sophia does a little Cunt-Fu fighting with Alex Fong, while totally in the buff. Watch the fur fly!*

See Her Naked In:

Sword of Honor (1994) RB, Buns
Miao Tan Shuang Jiao (1992) Breasts, Buns
Escape from the Brothel (1992) FFN, Buns

Wendy Crewson

Born: May 9, 1956
Hamilton, Ontario, Canada
Skin-O-Meter: Brief Nudity

A calm and steady professional, Canadian actress Wendy Crewson has been working almost constantly since her debut in the CBS TV movie *War Brides* (1979). Brunette, with softly sculpted features, a heart-winning smile and pulse-quickening curves, Crewson exudes the kind of matured, vital sexuality that Hollywood likes to downplay slightly in roles as hot mothers. This industry tendency accounts for Wendy's matronly spins in *The Good Son* (1993) and *Air Force One* (1997). Wendy's mama-lovin' body inspires the desire to make babies as she writhes and lolls wearing a gray sports bra and panties upon a chaise in *Mercy* (1999). The film also captures the part in Crewson's downstairs crewcut, but by then her character has been killed off, so prepare to be satisfied with the lingerie tease.

SKIN-fining Moment:

Mercy (0:04) *Wendy's on a bed. She's full-frontal naked, but she's also dead.*

See Her Naked In:

Suddenly Naked (2001) Breasts, Buns
Mercy (2000) FFN
Getting Married in Buffalo Jump (1990) Breasts, Buns

Cathy Lee Crosby

Born: December 2, 1944
Los Angeles, California
Skin-O-Meter: Brief Nudity

Cathy Lee Crosby boasts a remarkably skintastic career. This tall blonde beauty first garnered groin coinage by displaying her gorgeous gams weekly on *Dean Martin Presents the Golddiggers* in the late '60s. Her statuesque sex appeal and athletically enticing body are definitely diggable. She shows it off best in the *Circus of the Stars* series, proving her prowess as a performer under the watchful eyes and bulging flies of randy ring masters Sammy Davis Jr. and Jerry Lewis—a performance worthy of the big tent. Cathy's amazing allure is in perfect form on the reality show *That's Incredible!* Her sweet presence among the wacky world of human lightning rods, expert axe throwers, and dancing chipmunks is not easy to forget.

On *That's Incredible: The Reunion* (2002), former frequent guest beekeeper Dr. Gary asked Cathy Lee to let one of his drones sting her. He isn't alone in his appreciation of this honey's appeal. The show was rated in the top ten for six years and is in worldwide syndication. Cathy Lee had her one and only skinful moment as an Olympic gold medalist turned high-school manager of a boys basketball team in *Coach* (1978). Imagine the sixteen-year-old kid's horny surprise of catching his cunningly curvy coach mid dress. You don't have to. The reality of Cathy Lee's naked cupfuls is right there. Onscreen or off, Cathy Lee will always be skincredible!

SKIN-fining Moment:

Coach (0:31) *Very brief side view of her left love-lump when one of her players walks in on her.*

See Her Naked In:

Coach (1978) Breasts

Denise Crosby

Born: November 24, 1957
Hollywood, California
Skin-O-Meter: Great Nudity

The granddaughter of crooner Bing Crosby, Denise Crosby had an automatic leg up getting into Hollywood. Her famous name, blonde mane, and bubbling personality helped her land parts in the Dudley Moore classic *10* (1979) and *Trail of the Pink Panther* (1982), as well as starring roles on series such as *Days of Our Lives* and *Star Trek: The Next Generation.* Thankfully, Crosby was considerate enough to throw the rest of her body into her career as well. Denise's first titillating performance in *48 Hrs.* (1982) presented

the pretty petite lady in all her bra-less brilliance, nips standing straight at attention from either the honor of working with Eddie Murphy or a very cold set. You decide. Denise happily removes herself from her soggy shirt in *Eliminators* (1986) after a sexy swim in a lake. (You too will need to dry off after peering at her perky pair.) Den shows skin again in *Arizona Heat* (1988), her taut tits warming your heart-on. Delightfully dominating in *Red Shoe Diaries 2: Double Dare*, Denise radiates authority as a copulative cop playing games with a perp by tying him to a chair, stripping down to a tiny G-string, and having her way with him. The opening sequence in *Dream Man* (1995) might just cause you to have a wet one of your own. A blindfolded Denise is delightfully stripped bare by a mysterious masked man. Famous for *Der Bingle* or not, this skintastic beauty still makes Mr. Skin swoon.

SKIN-fining Moment:

48 Hrs. (0:17) *Glimpse of left breast while threatening Eddie Murphy with a bat.*

See Her Naked In:

Dream Man (1995) Breasts
Red Shoe Diaries 2: Double Dare (1993) Breasts, Thong
Arizona Heat (1988) LB
48 Hrs. (1982) Breasts

TeleVisions:

Red Shoe Diaries Breasts, Buns

Mary Crosby

Born: September 14, 1959
Los Angeles, California
Skin-O-Meter: Brief Nudity

The same woman who shot J.R. already had our own crotches firing as sexy ex-hooker Kristin Shepard on the TV series *Dallas*. The role made Mary Crosby a cultural icon and perpetual answer to a trivia question. Sadly, it didn't make Bing Crosby's sexy daughter into a proper star. Mary still works steadily, but she's mainly got us worked up over her role in *Deadly Innocents* (1990), where an accommodating nightgown provides some fine slips of the nips.

SKIN-fining Moment:

Deadly Innocents (0:01) *Mary's right mammary pops out of her nightgown as she's thwarted from blasting some bastard the way she handled J.R. Ewing.*

See Her Naked In:

Deadly Innocents (1990) RB

Marcia Cross

Born: January 1, 1961
Marlborough, Massachusettes
Skin-O-Meter: Brief Nudity

Television is a realm of promise. The boob tube is not called that for nothing. Often a soon-to-be coveted rack is first spotted as it jiggles across the small screen. Perhaps a promising pair is tracked as it progresses through the ranks of soap operas to night-time melodramas to prime-time series. One such route a rack might take is from *The Edge of Night* to *Another World* to *One Life to Live* to *Knots Landing* to *Melrose Place* to *Boy Meets World*. Such is the ascension of the large and buoyantly lovely chest globes of seriously attractive redhead Marcia Cross. Only one more step is needed to perfect the rising career projection of the Cross treasure chest—a leap into the realm of the topless.

SKIN-fining Moment:

Female Perversions (1:33) *Maria's mounds peek out from her open nightgown while she's on an old man's lap. Then she draws a circle around her upturned tittie. Now that's art!*

See Her Naked In:

Female Perversions (1997) Breasts

Lindsay Crouse

Born: May 12, 1948
New York, New York
Skin-O-Meter: Brief Nudity

Brunette beauty Lindsay Crouse is a widely used, highly capable actress who has amassed a great body of work without showing much of her body (much to Mr. Skin's chagrin). Bare bottom or no, Crouse has proven herself a magnetic screen presence—she garnered an Oscar nom for her role in the Sally Field dustbowl drama *Places in the Heart* (1984)—who brings a brainy, wry-tongued charm to her performances. She's starred in a score of well-received flicks spanning many a genre, from *Slap Shot* (1981) to *Communion* (1990) to *The Insider* (1999). She garnered her best reviews for her lead role in the noir-ish thriller *House of Games* (1987), written by her then-husband David Mamet. More recently, she inspired chills and thrills as power-mad military scientist Professor Maggie Walsh on the popular cult TV series *Buffy the Vampire Slayer*. Fans loved to hate Lindsay and her dominatrix-like demeanor, but the cruelest cut of all was never seeing what she hid beneath her lab coat.

SKIN-fining Moment:

Parallel Lives (0:12) *Very, very brief right breast in gaping dress bending over to make her bed on the sofa. How sick are we?*

See Her Naked In:

Parallel Lives (1994) RB

Marie-Josée Croze

Born: February 23, 1970
Montréal, Québec, Canada
Skin-O-Meter: Great Nudity

Her filmography—and her sex scenes—may suggest that Marie-Josée Croze is a fine French find. Instead, she comes to us from our bilingual friends in Canada. Fortunately, Marie-Josée broke the language barrier at the same time that she stripped for the camera, making love to Esai Morales on the cable-TV anthology series *The Hunger*. This was followed by some fine simulated sex in *Maelstrom* (2000), in which Marie-Josée's natural breasts threatened to melt the frozen North. Marie-Josée isn't just getting by on her looks, though, as she contributed a critically acclaimed performance to *The Barbarian Invasions* (2003).

SKIN-fining Moment:

Maelström (0:33) *A fantastic look at Marie-Josée's jet black muffalotta as she messes about in the sack. Tres fuzzee!*

See Her Naked In:

Ararat (2002) Breasts, Buns
Des Chiens dans la Neige (2002) Breasts
Maelström (2000) FFN, Buns
Captive (1998) RB

TeleVisions:

The Hunger Breasts, Buns

Penélope Cruz

Born: April 28, 1974
Madrid, Spain
Skin-O-Meter: Hall of Fame

Formerly known as "The Madonna of Madrid," Penélope Cruz turned from beautiful ballerina to buxom film star in the Spanish-lensed international arthouse smash *Jamón, jamón* (1992). Other Europe-an hits followed, and Pen made the leap to Hollywood with *Woman on Top* (2000), followed by *All the Pretty Horses* (2000) and *Captain Corelli's Mandolin* (2001). *Vanilla Sky* (2001) is director Cameron Crowe's remake of the Spanish sci-fi mind and wad blower *Abre los ojos* (1997). Penélope starred in both versions, but she took up with *Vanilla* guy Tom Cruise in one of the least-wondered about Hollywood couplings in recent years.

SKIN-fining Moment:

Jamón, Jamón (0:11) *Okay, you're in the desert and Penelope Cruz is letting you suck her glorious breasties . . . and you stop to answer your cell phone? The dude does here.*

See Her Naked In:

Head in the Clouds (2004) Buns
Captain Corelli's Mandolin (2001) Breasts
Vanilla Sky (2001) Breasts
All the Pretty Horses (2000) LB
Woman on Top (2000) Buns
Volavérunt (1999) Breasts
La Niña de Tus Ojos (1998) Breasts
Open Your Eyes (1997) Breasts
Jamón, Jamón (1992) Breasts

TeleVisions

Série Rose (1990) Breasts

Suzanne Cryer

Born: August 5, 1978
New York, New York
Skin-O-Meter: Brief Nudity

After she got her master's degree from Yale, Suzanne Cryer headed for the bright lights of Broadway, where she's made quite a career for herself on the stage. Although that doesn't leave much time for more skinematic efforts, at least the kind that can be recorded and shared, Suzanne's been kind enough to appear on film from

time to time. She landed her first gig in the short film *Some Folks Call it a Sling Blade* (1994), opposite Billy Bob Thornton. Unfortunately, she didn't land a part in the feature-length film based on the same story that garnered such attention a few years later. Since then, Suzanne's spent the better part of her career on the silver screen in background parts, albeit in films such as *Wag the Dog* (1997) and *Office Space* (1999). She wasn't remanded to the background of *Friends & Lovers* (1999), though! Suzanne provides some much-appreciated gratuitous nudity in the film, baring a breast following some sex in a cabin in the woods. It's hooterific—and gets our wood up!

SKIN-fining Moment:

Friends & Lovers (1:31) *A brief flash of Suzanne's left tit, followed by a close-up of her pregnant body-double's left hooter, all of which is capped off by a nice look at her right boob when she sits up.*

See Her Naked In:

Friends & Lovers (1999) Breasts

Sondra Currie

Skin-O-Meter: Great Nudity

Does she have a sister? Oh, yeah. Sondra Currie's got a sexy set of twins in Cherie and Marie, who were briefly a rock duo after Cherie's time fronting The Runaways. Sondra's a trashy icon herself, making her debut on a 1967 episode of *Mannix* and then becoming a '70s drive-in icon in the title role of *Teenage Seductress* (1971). Her hot young bod got exposed again in *Policewoman* (1974), in which Sondra got our nightsticks standing at attention.

Her bountiful breasts made another appearance in *Jessi's Girls* (1975). Then Sondra settled into more serious roles, ending her hedonistic heyday by stripping in front of George Segal and Natalie Wood in *The Last Married Couple in America* (1980).

SKIN-fining Moment:

Policewomen (0:51) *Great, gravity-defying breasts and a heart-shaped heinie as Sondra drops her robe and gets in bed with a guy, followed by some more flashes of those magic mams as they mate.*

See Her Naked In:

The Last Married Couple in America (1980) FFN, Buns
Jessi's Girls (1975) FFN, Buns
Policewomen (1974) Breasts, Buns
Teenage Seductress (1971) Breasts, Buns

Allegra Curtis

Born: July 12, 1966
Los Angeles, California
Skin-O-Meter: Great Nudity

Who knew Jamie Lee Curtis had a half-sister—much less one as sexy as babetastic brunette Allegra Curtis? Long legs and striking faces aren't the only things they share—they both call acclaimed actor Tony Curtis Dad. Allegra's mom is German film star Christine Kaufmann, and with a pedigree like that, it was only a matter of time before she hit the silver screen. Unfortunate for skinophiles, her work has mostly been limited to appearances in tame and tepid German B-movies such as *Das Gold der Liebe* (1983) and *Gluck auf Raten* (1995). Despite her good looks, genetic advantages and multilingual capabilities (she speaks German, English, and French), Allegra never really took the acting world by storm, and her filmic output has slowed to a crawl. Sporadic career or no, at least she graced us with a brazen look at her petite chest pups, bush, and tush in the Frank Stallone/Morgan Fairchild crime flick *Midnight Cop* (1988).

SKIN-fining Moment:

Midnight Cop (0:16) *Allegra takes off her top, showing her front saddlebags, and lies back awaiting her smack injection. According to reports, Courtney Love auditioned for this role.*

See Her Naked In:

Kabel und Liebe (1995) FFN
Midnight Cop (1988) FFN, Buns

"My breasts are beautiful, and I've got to tell you, they've gotten a lot of attention for what is relatively short screen time."

—JAMIE LEE CURTIS

Jamie Lee Curtis

Born: November 22, 1958
Los Angeles, California
Skin-O-Meter: Hall of Fame

Jamie Lee Curtis inherited her good looks from both her mom Janet Leigh and her dad Tony Curtis. She's like some mad scientist's experiment in sexy-made-flesh. What's better, Jamie's got good taste and started off her career in the realm of the gory slasher film. She defined the genre in classics such as *Halloween* (1978), *Prom Night* (1980), and *The Fog* (1980). Then she took an about face in her career, pursuing lighter, comedic roles. She starred with Eddie Murphy and Dan Aykroyd in *Trading Places* (1983), playing a hooker with a heart of

gold and jugs like gallons of lush ice cream when she goes topless. She followed that up with some nice bra-and-pantie teases in *A Fish Called Wanda* (1988) and *True Lies* (1994), which features Jamie's other asset, her meaty ass, dancing about in a G-string. But mostly Jamie takes it all off. She was something to write home about in *Love Letters* (1983), offered a grand view in *Grandview U.S.A.* (1984), and was a perfect ten in *Perfect* (1985). *The Tailor of Panama* (2001) shows the world that "they" have only gotten better with age.

MR. SKIN'S TOP TEN

Naked Babes in C. Thomas Howell Movies
. . . See Thomas Howl!

10. Kimberley Kates
    —*First Degree* 1998 (0:09)

9. Melinda Armstrong
    —*Jailbait* 1993 (0:43)

8. Brandy Ledford
    —*Separate Ways* 2001 (0:55)

7. Randi Ingerman
    —*Treacherous* 1994 (0:54)

6. Joan Severance
    —*Payback* 1995 (0:51)

5. Heidi Sorenson
    —*Suspect Device* 1995 (0:05)

4. Amber Smith
    —*Laws of Deception* 1997 (0:15)

3. Elizabeth Hurley
    —*Shameless* 1997 (0:35)

2. Kelly Preston
    —*Secret Admirer* 1985 (1:18)

1. **Jamie Lee Curtis**
    —*Grandview USA* **1984 (1:02)**

SKIN-fining Moment:

Trading Places (0:59) *In front of a mirror (and Dan Aykroyd), hooker-with-a-chest-of-gold Jamie Lee doffs her top and lets loose her mam-nificent money-markers in one of history's all-time hottest topless scenes.*

See Her Naked In:

The Tailor of Panama (2001) Breasts
True Lies (1999) Thong
Mother's Boys (1994) LB, Buns
Blue Steel (1990) Buns
Perfect (1985) LB, Buns
Grandview, U.S.A. (1984) LB
Love Letters (1984) Breasts, Buns
Trading Places (1983) Breasts

Elisha Cuthbert

Born: November 30, 1982
Calgary, Alberta, Canada
Skin-O-Meter: Brief Nudity

With her knockout North American looks, Elisha Cuthbert has all the right equipment to be a skinsation. Canadian network execs took one look at this boobilicious blonde beauty and said, "What a perfect hostess for children's television. Let's debut her as the star of *Popular Mechanics for Kids*!" Having once been a young lad himself, Mr. Skin applauds this decision. After all, growing boys crave eye candy too. Elisha is also quite an eyeful in the made-for-Canadian-TV movie *Lucky Girl* (2001). She certainly is lucky, and so are we for her presence on this earth. Thankfully, God does bless the beasts and the children, and Cuthbert's appealing girly girth is properly positioned as Kiefer Sutherland's troubled daughter on the hit action series *24*. Talk about your skincest fantasies! Elisha can also be seen bouncing around with Luke Wilson in *Old School* (2003) and comes teasingly close to breaking the skin barrier in *The Girl Next Door* (2004). Playing a down-home porn star, Elisha peels to a thong and provides awesome side-boobage early on and appears in undies and various other sexy get-ups throughout the rest of the flick. Next, I'd love to knock on this girl's *back* door. . . .

SKIN-fining Moment:

The Girl Next Door (0:12) *Changing clothes by a window, Elisha unleashes that superhuman caboose that was so tempting in pink panties in Old School. Now that she's moved next door, the undies are now a mere red thong and the gluteus is even more beauteous!*

See Her Naked In:

The Girl Next Door (2004) Thong

d

Maryam d'Abo

Born: December 27, 1960
London, England, UK
Skin-O-Meter: Great Nudity

British blondie Maryam d'Abo is the skintastic cousin of Olivia d'Abo (hottie hippie chick of *The Wonder Years* fame). Beauty is obviously in the d'Abo genes—and jeans! The family name d'Abo, loosely skinterpreted, means one who happily indulges in gratuitous nudity onscreen. True to interpretation, Maryam makes a full-frontal assault of the senses in her nudie debut in the *Red Shoe Diaries: Another Woman's Lipstick*. Not only do you see her bountiful breasts, but, she offers up a long and tasty view of her English muffin. d'Elicious! She continues this pussy-pushing trend in *Tomcat: Dangerous Desires* (1993), baring her furry patch to the equally fuzzy Richard Grieco. Meooooow wow wow! Mary merrily offers a taste of her breakfast biscuits in *An American Affair* (1997) and *The Point Men* (2001). With Maryam, it's T (and A) time most every time, making all things d'Abo a d'Elight.

SKIN-fining Moment:

Xtro (0:24) *Full-frontal skinitude getting up after banging her boyfriend.*

See Her Naked In:

The Point Men (2001) Breasts
An American Affair (1997) LB

Tomcat: Dangerous Desires (1993) Breasts, Bush
Tropical Heat (1993) Breasts
Double Obsession (1993) Breasts
Xtro (1983) FFN

TeleVisions:

Red Shoe Diaries Breasts, Bush

Olivia d'Abo

Born: January 22, 1967
London, England, UK
Skin-O-Meter: Great Nudity

Over-bitten beauty Olivia d'Abo seemed destined to be a free spirit. Sired by '60s model Maggie London and Mike d'Abo, lead vocalist of the cosmic rockers *Manfred Mann's Earth Band*, Olivia grew up in a gorgeous and groovy environment. Her real-life training in psychedelia made her all the more adorable as the hippie-chick hottie on the super '70s flashback series *The Wonder Years*. Like every grown-up flower child worth her weight in wheat germ, Olivia embraces the concept of nudity and free love. Her first run-in with skin was a perfect ten. In *Bolero* (1984), Olivia is lustfully bathed by the braided beauty Bo Derek herself, showing off her fantastic ass, tender tits, and English muffin in the process. d'Ole! Sapphic sophisticates remember Olivia as Neve Campbell's foxy female love interest on *Party of Five* (now that's a party of two EVERYONE would enjoy) and in

Live Nude Girls (1995), getting her pointy pudding bags licked by Lora Zane. d'Yummy! Livi is all washed up again in *Into the Fire* (1987), lounging in a bubble bath, her sudsy crumpets coming up for air, and in *The Last Good Time* (1994) toweling her ta-tas after a shower. d'Lightful! d'Licious! d'Abo!

SKIN-fining Moment:

Live Nude Girls (0:46) *Olivia d'Abo feeds her sizable y'Abos to Lora Zane in a black-and-white lesboid love session.*

See Her Naked In:

Dad's Week Off (1997) RB
Live Nude Girls (1995) Breasts
The Last Good Time (1994) Breasts
Bank Robber (1993) Breasts
Into the Fire (1987) Breasts
Bolero (1984) Breasts, Bush, Buns

Arlene Dahl

Born: August 11, 1928
Minneapolis, Minnesota
Skin-O-Meter: Brief Nudity

Back in the '40s, Arlene Dahl was working as a model for department stores. In its time, that was the equivalent of posing for the Victoria's Secret catalogue, so you know this broad was hot enough to stick pages together. Then she took Hollywood by storm with her debut in *My Wild Irish Rose* (1947), where she flaunted her fabulous stuff in some lingerie, which was akin to hardcore pornography back in the day. Soon Arlene was on her way to stardom as the era's hottest glamour girl. But this beauty has brains and prepared herself for when the tits would start to sag by launching Arlene Dahl Enterprises marketing lingerie and cosmetics, so that every woman could look as sexy as she does. Arlene loves life and was never content to settle down with just one man. One of her many husbands was Fernando Lamas, with whom she spawned this generation's favorite cocksmith Lorenzo Lamas. Mother and son even appeared together in *Night of the Warrior* (1991). But for a more revealing peek at mommy dearest, check out *Land Raiders* (1970). Keep your eyes peeled, because Arlene only peels off her shirt for a very brief nipple exposure. But it's the top of the tits for this act-chest.

SKIN-fining Moment:

Land Raiders (0:59) *Arlene's right-side dairy-Dahl spills into view as she wrestles in bed with a badguy.*

See Her Naked In:

Land Raiders (1969) RB

Elizabeth Daily

Born: September 11, 1962
Los Angeles, California
Skin-O-Meter: Great Nudity

Is there a cartoon character out there Elizabeth Daily hasn't lent her squeaky-yet-raspy voice to? The vivacious blonde has brought many a character to life, giving spark to creatures from *Rugrats* and *The Powerpuff Girls* and to Hollywood's fave porker *Babe: Pig in the City* (1998). She's one of the top voice talents in Hollywood, and it's a sure bet you've heard her work. Problem is, since she spends most of her time in a recording booth and not in front of the

---

MR. SKIN'S TOP TEN

Naked Babes who do Cartoon Voices
. . . Spongebob Tight Pants

10. **Nancy Cartwright**
    —(Bart Simpson) *The Simpsons*

9. **Kathy Nijimy**
   —(Peggy Hill) *King of the Hill*

8. **Yeardley Smith**
   —(Lisa Simpsons) *The Simpsons*

7. **Ashley Gardner**
   —(Nancy Gribble) *King of the Hill*

6. **Ellen DeGeneres**
   —(Dory) *Finding Nemo*

5. **Nancy Travis**
   —(Bernice/Beverly/Beatrice) *Duckman*

4. **Kimmy Robertson**
   —(Dot/Mrs. Dinosaur/Mell/Minda) *The Tick*

3. **Cameron Diaz**
   —(Princess Fiona) *Shrek*

2. **Pamela Segall**
   —(Bobby Hill) *King of the Hill*

1. **Elizabeth Daily**
   —(Babe the Pig) *Babe*

---

camera, her corporeal talents are going way unnoticed. It's a damn shame, since the puffy-lipped sexpot personifies "cute" from her long, silky hair to her teeny, sandal-clad feet. Thankfully, the diminutive darling hasn't always been out of the picture—early on, she made appearances on the TV shows *Laverne and Shirley* and *Fame* and had roles in films such as *Streets of Fire* (1984) and *Better Off Dead* (1985). And if you're really jonesing to see her shuck her clothes, you're in luck. She's done so twice, once in the little-seen *Street Music* (1981) and once opposite Nicolas Cage in the cult fave *Valley Girl* (1985), revealing a

---

butt as bubbly as the voice that made her famous.

SKIN-fining Moment:

Valley Girl (0:18) *The voice of Babe the Pig bares her adorable oinkers as a dude paws her in the sack.*

See Her Naked In:

Valley Girl (1983) Breasts
Street Music (1981) Breasts, Bush

Cynthia Dale

Born: 1961
Toronto, Ontario, Canada
Skin-O-Meter: Brief Nudity

Cynthia Dale is a product of the Great White North and seems as cold as the Canadian climate she calls home. But don't be put off by her old-fashioned demeanor; this dancer has a toned and tight body that's worth cutting the rug with. For one thing, she made her debut in the classic slasher flick *My Bloody Valentine* (1981), but only with a supporting role that didn't show off her sweet jellyroll. Then came her breakthrough (and bra-busting) appearance in *Heavenly Bodies* (1984), which exposed the era's "dancercize" craze along with Cynthia's heavenly body, specifically her pert pair. It took several years before Cynthia let the girls out of the dale again, this time in *The Boy in Blue* (1986). Don't worry about blue balls, this is Cynthia's crowning moment of onscreen nudity. Sadly, after this they went back in the ice chest, and she hasn't thawed her sweet dishes since. She's continued to shine on the boob tube, especially in the mini-series *P.T. Barnum* (1999), in which she played Charity. If Cynthia were really generous, though, she'd bring out her sideshow attractions again. Because there's a sucker born every minute, and Mr. Skin would sure love to suck hers.

SKIN-fining Moment:

The Boy in Blue (1:15) *Topless Cynthia gets nippleous while making out with Nicholas Cage in a loft.*

See Her Naked In:

The Boy in Blue (1986) Breasts
Heavenly Bodies (1984) Breasts

Jennifer Dale

**Born: January 15, 1956
Toronto, Ontario, Canada
Skin-O-Meter: Great Nudity**

A stormy brunette with tempestuous eyes and the passions of a typhoon, acclaimed Canadian actress Jennifer Dale has a list of credits in Great-White film and TV as long as her tapered, great-white pegs. Dale often portrays women

JENNIFER DALE IN SUZANNE: OVER HILLS! OVER DALE! SOME PICTURES ARE WORTH A THOUSAND WORDS. THIS BARE-BONES, UP-FRONT POSTER IS WORTH ONLY TWO— JENNIFER'S JUGS—BUT WHAT A MOUTHFUL THEY MAKE!

whose bosoms heave with gale-force velocity as her lovers puff like hurricanes. Put a weather watch on *Suzanne* (1980), *Your Ticket Is No Longer Valid* (1981), and *Separate Vacations* (1996). The incredibly strong gusts of Jennifer's twin tornado titties spin out of control in *Stone Cold Dead* (1979).

SKIN-fining Moment:

Stone Cold Dead (0:16) *Jennifer slings up several magnificent mammaric manifestations while stripping on stage to Bob Seger's "Fire Down Below." That's where you'll feel it too.*

See Her Naked In:

Whale Music (1994) LB
Cadillac Girls (1993) Breasts
The Adjuster (1991) Breasts
Separate Vacations (1986) Breasts
Your Ticket Is No Longer Valid (1981) Breasts
Suzanne (1980) Breasts, Bush
Stone Cold Dead (1979) Breasts

Béatrice Dalle

**Born: December 19, 1964
Brest, France
Skin-O-Meter: Hall of Fame**

Hair tussled high above expansive, expressive eyes, luscious bee-stung lips, boobage bubbling over the confines of a bra, balanced by a shapely seat and wide-swinging hips, everything about Beatrice Dalle is BIG, BIG, BIG! Her grandiose gorgeousity makes her a huge star in her native France and a skinematic marvel. This top-heavy, hazel-eyed harlot (appropriately born in Brest, France) is breast known as the slightly psychotic, largely naked *Betty Blue* (1986). In between throwing furniture and fits, Dalle divvies out detailed looks at her fine flesh. In one hair-raising scene, Beatrice flashes her thickly patched French furburger to a pesky next-door neighbor. (Who wouldn't

DALLE PARTS: BEATRICE DALLE ERECTS HER EYEFUL TOWERS IN *BETTY BLUE.*

want to come over for a big cup of Beatrice's sugar?) This man-eater best used her big mouth as the carnal cannibal in *Trouble Every Day* (2001). After having mouth-watering, manic sex with four men, she slays and devours each one whole. Deadly yet delicious! Showing le maximum boobage, bush, and buns in almost every endeavor, this Queen Bea is guaranteed to give you a buzz.

SKIN-fining Moment:

Betty Blue (0:01) *You won't have Betty Blue Balls when Beatrice opens up the movie with her topless French pastries getting pawed by her loverman.*

See Her Naked In:

Trouble Everyday (2001) Breasts, Bush
The Blackout (1997) Breasts
À la Folie (1994) FFN
Les Bois Noirs (1989) Breasts
The Sabbath (1988) Breasts
Betty Blue (1986) FFN, Buns

Tyne Daly

**Born: February 21, 1946
Madison, Wisconsin
Skin-O-Meter: Brief Nudity**

In the age-old "who would you rather date" debate of Ginger vs. Mary Ann, Samantha vs. Jeannie, why not add Cagney vs. Lacey to the list? As Detective Mary Beth Lacey on the hit series *Cagney & Lacey*, Tyne Daly's portrayal of a hard-boiled yet soft-hearted cop cutie is sexier at second glance. Although less noticeable than her blonder, taller partner in anti-crime, Sergeant Christine Cagney (played by buxom Sharon Gless), Lacey has a tender vulnerability just below her tough skin that, in showing, glowingly garners almost as many bones as the site of Cagney's caboose. Lacey also has that sexier, Brooklynesque, bad-girl voice to her credit. But the topper to the Cagney vs. Lacey debate . . . if Mary Beth Lacey is good enough for TV hubby Harv, than she's definitely good enough for Mr. Skin. Before *Cagney & Lacey* the show, there was *Cagney & Lacey* the movie. Darling Daly also stars in the previous version with the ever sMASHing Loretta Swit, giving the polished performance that earned her the series. Before all things *Cagney & Lacey* there was (best of all) *The Adulteress* (1973). Tyne's tiny titties can be seen in their one and only sweet skinematic appearance. Talk about perky! Now Mr. Skin really knows what Harv was always making such a loud fuss about.

SKIN-fining Moment:

The Adultress (0:53) *Tyne's teeny tatas get some screen time as she sits atop a horse with her cowboy friend.*

See Her Naked In:

The Adultress (1973) Breasts

Claire Danes

Born: April 12, 1979
New York, New York
Skin-O-Meter: Brief Nudity

Reddish blonde hair, an active, intelligent face that appealingly blends eager sexual curiosity with an air of expertise, little tittle Claire Danes was at one time being hailed as the greatest actress of her generation. Her subsequent roles in underachieving productions

such as *The Mod Squad* (1999) and blockbusters like *Terminator 3* (2003) have dulled the anticipation of Oscars to come, but an apparently accidental slip of nip in *Polish Wedding* (1988) has raised hopes for a skintastic future. Although Claire's chest bumps are more dainty than great danes, the nipples are quite outstanding. The right-hand-side one protrudes in a three-quarters rear profile so that it sticks out as clear as a weather vane. The wind is blowing toward less clothing.

SKIN-fining Moment:

To Gillian on Her 37th Birthday (0:04) *Thong-bikini-clad Clare nearly bares her entirely detectable derriere as she strolls on the beach alongside similarly skimpy-suited Laurie Fortier.*

See Her Naked In:

Stage Beauty (2004) Breasts
Polish Wedding (1998) Nip Slip RB
To Gillian on Her 37th Birthday (1996) Thong

Beverly D'Angelo

Born: November 15, 1951
Columbus, Ohio
Skin-O-Meter: Hall of Fame

Bodaciously bountiful blonde Beverly D'Angelo presents more than one pleasant mystery. It makes no sense that a woman of D'Angelo's angelic bra caliber would be strapped down to a bumbler such as played by Chevy Chase in all those farcical *Vacation* movies. The fact that she remains saddled to him and shares her bed and dressing rituals with him is an inspiration and shot of hope to all men who have pratfallen. The other thing that's hard to figure out and fun to think about is why an actress of Beverly's stature has left so much of her big boobs on the silver screen. She's fished the beauties out at least nine times and

still counting. Is her eagerness to expose rooted in physical pride? It certainly would be pride well placed.

SKIN-fining Moment:

Vacation (0:19) *A spectacular shot of Beverly's bouncing boobs in the shower when Chevy Chase sneaks up on her Psycho-style . . .*

See Her Naked In:

Women in Film (2001) Breasts
Widow's Kiss (1994) RB
Pacific Heights (1990) RB
Slow Burn (1986) Breasts
Vacation (1983) Breasts
Lonely Hearts (1982) Breasts, Buns
Hair (1979) Breasts
The Sentinel (1977) FFN
First Love (1977) Breasts

Brittany Daniel

Born: March 17, 1976
Gainesville, Florida
Skin-O-Meter: Brief Nudity

TV shows that focus on teenage angst are a guilty pleasure, with the pleasure—thanks to strumpet-lite starlets such as athletically toned, tanned imp Brittany Daniel—far outweighing the guilt. Adolescent conflict, at least during network prime time, generally stems from erotic awakening. There is no more effective erotic wake-up call than Brittany's nymph nuggets squeezed tightly into a bra or bikini top. Actually, a bare breast of Daniel might be more effective, but for years we were all shook up over her girlie globes of puffy chest flesh splendidly laid out in a black push-up bra in The *Basketball Diaries* (1995). And she has the distinction of being the only hottie in *Club Dread* (2004) to not take off her clothes. But all that's changed. Because if there's one thing Mr. Skin knows it's that eventually they all come to the skin side. Brittany's bounty is finally and copiously revealed in *The Hillside Strangler* (2004). Within five minutes she's topless at a swinger's party and by the mid-point in the movie is going down the threeway with Michelle Barth for a ride no one will soon forget. It took a while to leave the innocence of Dawson's Creek behind, but judging by that naked round ass she moons after engaging in group sex, Brittany is ready for her carnal close-up.

SKIN-fining Moment:

The Hillside Strangler (0:44) *Brittany shows her tittanys throughout a threesome with her boyfriend and Michelle Borth, then adds a splash of A to all that T by getting out of bed and taking a nude stroll through the house.*

See Her Naked In:

The Hillside Strangler (2004) Breasts, Buns

Erin Daniels

St. Louis, Missouri
Skin-O-Meter: Great Nudity

Justice prevailed when Erin Daniels debuted her wholesome looks on a 1996 episode of *Law & Order*. She's since showcased her Irish American charms on TV series such as *Jack and Jill* and *Philly*. Erin made some interesting developments in her career in *One Hour Photo* (2002). She removed her *Erin Go Braugh* and donned an open robe, exposing her wee blarney stones and bonny bush. Although her back is to the camera for most of the scene, you can thank your lucky stars that this lass's bare bottom is in booming view.

SKIN-fining Moment:

One Hour Photo (1:12) *Short, sweet glimpses at Erin's fuzzbox as she's threatened by a knife-wielding Robin Williams.*

See Her Naked In:

One Hour Photo (2002) RB, Bush, Buns

TeleVisions:

The L Word Breasts

Blythe Danner

Born: February 3, 1943
Philadelphia, Pennsylvania
Skin-O-Meter: Great Nudity

To see her holding steady as an attractive, slightly uptight, middle-aged married lady in *Meet the Parents* (2000), it's easy to forget that Blythe Danner has not always been old enough to be Gwyneth Paltrow's mother. Go back to the dawn of the '70s, a time of innocent exploration in skinema, before the anorexic standard had been applied. Seek out *To Kill a Clown* (1971). Marvel at the young, blonde, big-eyed Blythe. She wears the placid expression so often seen on the face of her famous daughter, but she wears nothing else. She stands full-backside nude, revealing a cottontail contrasting with bikini tan as she cocks her plush buttocks while standing in a doorway. Fast-forward a few years and pause at *Lovin' Molly* (1974). They've packed on a pound or two, but Blythe is prouder than ever of those buns, and justifiably so. The pillows are fuller now, augmented by clear tit views and a camera pan that follows the bottom motion as Danner trots and dances.

SKIN-fining Moment:

To Kill a Clown (1:10) *Brief left breast on the bed with Alan Alda then a great white butt-shot when she gets up and runs outside.*

See Her Naked In:

Lovin' Molly (1974) Breasts, Buns
To Kill a Clown (1971) LB, Buns

SYBIL DANNING BURNS UP A BIKINI IN *THEY'RE PLAYING WITH FIRE.*

Sybil Danning

Born: May 4, 1952
Salzburg, Austria
Skin-O-Meter: Hall of Fame

Entertainment Tonight proclaimed Sybil Danning to be The World's Number One Female Action Star, but her success was measured in videotape rentals. Thankfully, this Austrian beauty bared as much ass as she kicked. Sybil started out in classic international sexploitation such as *Housewives Report* (1971). She became semi-respectable, however, while providing full-on erections as Richard Burton's bisexual wife in *Bluebeard* (1972). Then it was back to European delights such as *Naughty Nymphs* (1972) before Sybil broke through as a mighty warrior in a mighty-skimpy outfit in *Battle Beyond the Stars* (1980). Fans adore her naked scenes in a wide variety of vintage B-movies, and it's hard to choose a favorite—although many people consider *Chained Heat* (1983) to be the definitive women's prison movie, in large part due to large Sybil's domineering shower scene with Linda Blair. In addition, fans of teen-sex comedies rank Sybil's bizarre May-December romance *They're Playing With Fire* (1984) as one of the weirdest entries in the genre (the flick combines typical hormone-farce antics with slasher movie elements and, of course, Sybil's sumptuous sacks). Crossover success never came for her, though—despite talk of Bond films and *Terminator* sequels—and Sybil retired in 1986 as a true icon of low-budget sexuality.

SKIN-fining Moment:

They're Playing with Fire (0:08) *Robust rackage and righteous rear as Sybill sizzles atop her man-mate.*

See Her Naked In:

Young Lady Chatterley II (1985) Breasts
Malibu Express (1985) Breasts
Howling II (1985) Breasts, Thong
Jungle Warriors (1984) Buns
They're Playing with Fire (1984) Breasts, Buns
Chained Heat (1983) Breasts
Daughter of Death (1982) Breasts
Famous T&A (1982) LB, Buns
S.A.S. Malko—Im Auftrag des Pentagon (1982) LB
The Day of the Cobra (1980) RB, Buns
Cat in the Cage (1978) FFN, Buns
God's Gun (1976) RB
Albino (1976) FFN
Folies Bourgeoises (1975) Breasts
Naughty Nymphs (1972) FFN, Buns
Bluebeard (1972) Breasts
The Loves of a French Pussycat (1972) Breasts, Buns
La Dama Rossa Uccide Sette Volte (1972) Breasts
The Erotic Adventures of Siegfried (1971) FFN, Buns

TeleVisions:

The Hitchhiker RB

Leslie Danon

Skin-O-Meter: Brief Nudity

How great of a young actress is Leslie Danon? Enough that her career survived the awful mid-'90s series *Tattooed Teenage Alien Fighters From Beverly Hills*. Of course, that kind of role also inspired the former child actress to start showing us how she has all grown up. That's why we always come back to *Sometimes They Come Back . . . Again* (1996). This sequel to a lame TV movie offers something the original couldn't—mainly, Leslie doffing her top and getting us to come back again and again while whipping up some Danon yogurt. And while Hollywood's portrayed as a real sleaze pit in *Burning Down the House* (2001), Leslie makes the place seem like paradise as she lounges around in bikinis and underwear.

SKIN-fining Moment:

Beach Balls (1:06) *Leslie gets auto-erotic when she tosses her bra and out bounce her own beach-balls.*

See Her Naked In:

Blood Thirsty (1998)
Sometimes They Come Back . . . Again (1996) Breasts
Beach Balls (1988) Breasts

Patti D'Arbanville

Born: May 25, 1951
New York, New York
Skin-O-Meter: Great Nudity

Kids start out wild, but they usually settle down and never again do the crazy stuff they did back when their buns were tightly creased and cheese-free and their nibble-bit titties were foes of gravity. This growing-up process of eliminating exhibitionistic behavior would be tragic in the case of stoner-eyed blonde Patti D'Arbanville, except that the cameras were rolling. Discovered at age fourteen by master exploiter Andy Warhol and waxing lesbianic in his movie *Flesh* (1968) three years later, Patti was on the highway to skinville. *Rancho Deluxe* (1975) features D'Arbanville top and bottom but in shadows and from a distance. Hold out for *Bilitis* (1977), a well-lit depiction of lesbo awakening. Even though Patti is in her mid-twenties, her popping nipples, clenching buns, and fuzzy pubic thatch have retained the nymphlike qualities of youth. Later, she would grow up.

SKIN-fining Moment:

Bilitis (0:31) *Patti loses her swimsuit alongside Catherine Leprince, treating us to her retro-ruggage and world-class mega-nipples.*

See Her Naked In:

Modern Problems (1981) RB
Bilitis (1977) FFN, Buns
Rancho Deluxe (1975) Breasts

TeleVisions:

The Sopranos FFN, Buns

Stacey Dash

Born: January 20, 1966
The Bronx, New York
Skin-O-Meter: Great Nudity

Best known for her titillating performance as bronze-hued Beverly Hills beauty Dionne in both *Clueless* (1995), the classic teen comedy, and it's long-running TV spinoff, Stacey Dash has had a skinfully spicy career. This green-eyed, raven-maned honey played a hitchhiker that no man could resist picking up in *Tennessee Nights* (1989), baring just a bit of bunnage in sexy shorts. Stacey also showed a dash of ass and a pinch of tit in *Illegal in Blue* (1995). The dusky darling just begs to be cuffed and frisked in this erotic thriller as the delicious and deranged dish accused of killing her husband.

SKIN-fining Moment:

Illegal in Blue (0:47) *Mouth-watering close-up of Stacey's cocoa nip-neat while she's doing Dan Gauthier.*

See Her Naked In:

Illegal in Blue (1995) Breasts
Black Water (1989) Breasts, Buns

Alexa Davalos

Skin-O-Meter: Brief Nudity

Alexa Davalos first caught the carnal eye of skin watchers with a guest-starring appearance on *Undeclared*. The dark-haired beauty with the hand-sized boobs and shapely legs raised more than our attention. She followed that up with a recurring role on the hit series *Angel*. Her character Gwen Raiden was introduced in season four. She has the gift of channeling electricity with her touch, which is understandable, as Alexa is shockingly seductive. In character, she jump-started Angel's heart and viewers' heart-ons. Alexa has tested the waters of theatrical releases, in the short *The Ghosts of F. Scott Fitzgerald* (2002) and in the sequel to *Pitch Black* (2000), *The Chronicles of Riddick* (2004), in which she revved Vin Diesel's motor. But Alexa really started our engine in *And Starring Pancho Villa as Himself* (2003), which was her first and as yet only skin scene onscreen. She got booby with some lucky hombre. Viva la nudity!

SKIN-fining Moment:

And Starring Pancho Villa as Himself (1:08) *Brief chest-burritos during a darkish sex scene in bed with a lucky caballero.*

See Her Naked In:

And Starring Pancho Villa as Himself (2003) Breasts

Lolita Davidovich

Born: July 15, 1961
Toronto, Ontario, Canada
Skin-O-Meter: Great Nudity

The leggy, ever lovely Lolita Davidovich has one skinsationally sweet career. Lolly will make you pop as the sizzling sexpot stripper in *Blaze* (1989). In one delectable scene, co-star Paul Newman alternates between snacking on a watermelon and Lol's own mouth-watering suckables. What tasty teats! Lolita is at her breast when enlisting in a little topless fun in *Recruits* (1996). The thought of her magnificent melons meandering in the breeze should be enough to twist your arm into seeing it. Davidovich's delicious dewdrops are also ripe for the sucking in *Intersection* (1994) and *Cobb* (1994). Equally succulent, any of Lolita's appearances are guaranteed to give you a sugary rush.

SKIN-fining Moment:

Blaze (0:48) *Lolita offers up the massive mammos as she rides Paul Newman. They also enjoy a watermelon.*

See Her Naked In:

Four Days (1999) Body Double—RB
Cobb (1994) Breasts
Intersection (1994) Breasts
Blaze (1989) Breasts
Blindside (1988) Breasts, Thong
Recruits (1986) Breasts, Bush

TeleVisions:

Perversions of Science Breasts

Eileen Davidson

Born: June 15, 1959
Artesia, California
Skin-O-Meter: Great Nudity

Soap-opera stardom is a fox-eat-fox business. The average ravishing vixen is chewed up and spat out after half a season, never to be drooled over again. Slinky-soft sensual manipulator Eileen Davidson has purred and growled and snake-hipped herself to the top of the fox pile. Eileen's record of

doing it foxy style on top-ranked soaps extends for almost twenty years; she has been an eye-catching danger to hens and male chickens on *The Young and the Restless*, *Days of Our Lives*, and *Santa Barbara*. But all that sexually predatory prowling takes its toll on a girl. Sometimes she just needs to relax. Which explains her shy smile, endearing sidelong glance, and proudly displayed chest puffies in *The House on Sorority Row* (1983).

SKIN-fining Moment:

Goin' All the Way (0:12) *Surrounded by other very-'80s-looking lovelies, Eileen gets topless and shows her Dexy's Midnight Gunners in a girls' locker room.*

See Her Naked In:

Eternity (1989) Breasts, Buns
The House on Sorority Row (1983) Breasts, Buns
Goin' All the Way (1982) Breasts

Embeth Davidtz

Born: January 1, 1966
Trenton, New Jersey
Skin-O-Meter: Great Nudity

Starkly stunning Embeth Davidtz is a brunette vision of intensity, depth, and passion. Valued for acting performances that emanate from her deepest core, Embeth is also blessed with a flawless surface. The planes of her high-boned, angular face have been honed so exquisitely as to seduce the Master Craftsman above. Her dark eyes communicate a soul-felt longing. The legs are like tapered lengths of the palest, purest, smoothest marble made flesh. Small, fully functional breasts, a trim and tidy bush. All of it on display in the dramatic thriller *The Gingerbread Man* (1998). Embeth Davidtz stands behind a translucent curtain, naked from her core to her flawless surface, and it is as if she has removed all barriers between herself and her rapt audience. Now that's acting.

SKIN-fining Moment:

The Gingerbread Man (0:17) *Full frontal nudity when she strips down in her room, then Kenneth Branagh walks in.*

See Her Naked In:

The Gingerbread Man (1998) FFN
Schindler's List (1993) FFN
Army of Darkness (1993) Breasts
Till Death Do Us Part (1991)

Geena Davis

Born: January 21, 1957
Wareham, Massachusetts
Skin-O-Meter: Brief Nudity

A tall and toothy beauty whose wide smile is complemented by wide hips and a broad-shouldered bust, towering auburn inferno Geena Davis has flashed more skin while stalking the red carpet and while preening on talk shows than many divas do in the privacy of their own homes. Geena's slinky, skintight or dangerously loose attire has been the delight of award-show watchers and fans of tabloid fashion for more than a decade. Odd then, that only one silver-screen sighting of Davis's delightful derriere has so far been reported. In the oft-cited *Thelma & Louise* (1991), Davis's buns are seen from behind and below, slightly parted, as she stands with her pudenda perched above the eager face of young Brad Pitt. As for Geena nip, we have no nip to speak of.

SKIN-fining Moment:

Thelma & Louise A nice little bit of deleted footage that displays Ms. Davis's derriere, albeit in some rather poor lighting . . .

See Her Naked In:

Thelma & Louise (1991) Buns

Josie Davis

Born: January 16, 1973
Los Angeles, California
Skin-O-Meter: Great Nudity

If there is ever any doubt that extensive television exposure as a child has a positive effect on the growth process of a budding female's personality, let those doubts be assuaged by the slender but enticingly padded maturity of blonde boob-tube tartlet Josie Davis. Flaxen tressed, blue eyed, with a smile flashing along the range of imp to vamp, Josie Davis's network run began in the late 1980s as perky, dimpled Sara Powell on *Charles in Charge* and climaxed in 2000 as sultry, dimpled Camille Desmond on *Beverly Hills, 90210*. The proof of Josie's grown-up-right pudding is in the splendidly split but still unified butt shot as she gracefully and nakedly sits on the camera lens in *Sonny* (2002). More kid chicks should look up to Josie Davis's example.

SKIN-fining Moment:

Sonny (0:37) *We get some bare boobage as Josie satisfies her cough syrup addiction, followed by a brief peek at the puss when James Franco tosses her to the floor.*

See Her Naked In:

Sonny (2002) Breasts, Bush, Buns

Judy Davis

Born: April 23, 1955
Perth, Western Australia, Australia
Skin-O-Meter: Brief Nudity

Brunette Aussie serious dramatist Judy Davis splashed into the world's attention at age twenty-four as the leading lady in *My Brilliant Career* (1978). A big hit from Down Under, *Brilliant* gave Davis the chance to be picky about her roles, and she has often chosen to star in projects that are more

literary than Hollywood, such as *Naked Lunch* (1991), an adaptation of the William S. Burroughs novel, and the Woody Allen word fests *Alice* (1989), *Husbands and Wives* (1992), *Deconstructing Harry* (1997), and *Celebrity* (1998). Like any good writer, Judy realizes that sex appeal keeps the readers glued to the page. She lies shirtless on her back in bed in the shadows of *Husbands and Wives*, and her nipple reaches out toward the light. Her muff does the same thing in *On My Own* (1992).

SKIN-fining Moment:

On My Own (0:29) *Judy gives us a fleeting glimpse at her entire full-frontal package as she strips and hops into bed.*

See Her Naked In:

On My Own (1992) FFN
Husbands and Wives (1992) Breasts
Heatwave (1982) RB
Winter of Our Dreams (1981) Breasts

Julie Davis

Born: 1969
Miami Beach, Florida
Skin-O-Meter: Brief Nudity

With her wavy, rusty-blonde hair, earnest hazel eyes straining for a deeper focus, bemused smile stretched across a yearning mouth, and her skin taut over muscles and nerves tense with anticipatory satisfaction, actress Julie Davis looks like a woman whose time is about to come. Though primarily a director/screenwriter, Dartmouth grad Julie is as multitalented as she is multi-attractive. The brainy babe is screenwriter, star, editor, director, and producer of *Amy's Orgasm* (2002). The story of a self-help author sharing the covers with a radio shock jock, it can be no accident when Julie's jug jostles loose for a full side view.

SKIN-fining Moment:

Amy's O (0:41) *Julie bares a brief right juggle while the real action goes down beneath the sheets.*

See Her Naked In:

Amy's O (2001) Breasts

Julienne Davis

Born: 1975
La Canada, California
Skin-O-Meter: Great Nudity

Intelligent life is sometimes found in the most unlikely places. Statuesque blonde Julienne Davis's billowing breasts and neatly coiffed bush are burned into the memory of any skin-conscious male who kept his eyes wide open during Stanley Kubrick's *Eyes Wide Shut* (1999). Davis is the dramatically stacked doll who lay OD'd and undressed in a chair and later showed up full-frontally nude on a morgue slab. Julienne is proof that life continues after skinematic death and that some amount of brainpower informs that existence. Though born in the Los Angeles suburbs, Davis is playing out her existence in England, acting on TV series such as *Too Much Sun*, posing for MandPmodels of London, and singing and writing for the band Sophisticated Savage.

SKIN-fining Moment:

Eyes Wide Shut (0:13) *Julienne flashes some serious full-frontal fleshitudity whilst passed out in a chair when Tom Cruise comes over to check her out.*

See Her Naked In:

Come Together (2002) Breasts
Eyes Wide Shut (1999) FFN, Thong

Kristin Davis

Born: February 24, 1965
Boulder, Colorado
Skin-O-Meter: Brief Nudity

The toughest thing for skin-watching fans of HBO's monster hit *Sex and the City* is trying to decide which of the fabulous four babes has the hottest and most-coveted bod. A strong case can be made for squeaky-clean sex machine Charlotte as played by Kristin Davis. The bubbly brunette with the goo-goo eyes and go-go boobies hasn't been the most nude gal in *the City*, but she's far more giving of the mammary glimpses than her prudish demeanor might indicate. Anyone who missed the shenanigans the first time around should keep an eye open for reruns of Kristin's darling little creations bouncing and erect and full of fun. Davis also doubles as an underwear model in *Blacktop* (2000).

SKIN-fining Moment:

Sex and the City "Frenemies" (2000) *Kristin strips for Kyle McLaughlin and shows us her (sex and the) titties.*

TeleVisions:

Sex and the City Breasts

Neriah Davis

Born: October 12, 1972
Los Angeles, California
Skin-O-Meter: Great Nudity

A child of agrarian hippie parents, boob-blessed blonde Neriah Davis ran away from the organic farm at the age of eighteen and sought her fame and fortune in Los Angeles. Unlike the typical outrageously pretty, fresh-faced sexpot, daring and darling Davis established her motion-picture resumé *before* reigning as *Playboy* Playmate of the Month for March 1994. Keen-eyed Lords of the Bunny recalled seeing those cheery nipples somewhere before. To be precise, the Davis dependants had perked up in *Meatballs 4* (1992), *The Bikini Carwash Company* (1992), and *The*

Bikini Carwash Company II (1993). The major plot twist of the first *Bikini Carwash* movie seems to hinge upon Neriah's innovative attempt to wash cars without wearing any bikini at all.

SKIN-fining Moment:

The Bikini Carwash Company (0:15) *Neriah unbinds her naked knockers when she offers her bikini top for a fisherman to use as bait. I'm hooked!*

See Her Naked In:

The Bikini Carwash Company II (1993) Breasts, Buns
The Bikini Carwash Company (1992) Breasts, Buns
Meatballs 4 (1992) Buns
Numerous Playboy *Videos*

Patti Davis

Born: October 22, 1952
Los Angeles County, California
Skin-O-Meter: Great Nudity

When your dad is the widely beloved President of the United States and you've grown up in Governor's mansions and the Hollywood heights, then you will have walked in the shoes of California-cool brunette Patti Davis. Hopefully, you will toss your shoes off as Patti did and shed your clothes too and be one among the naked mass of humanity. As an actress, Davis's success was limited to one-shot stints on shows such as *The Edge of Night*, *Trapper John, M.D.*, and *Vega$*. Her skin rebellion was played out in the pages of a 1994 *Playboy* spread, with the accompanying video *Playboy Celebrity Centerfold: Patti Davis* (1994).

SKIN-fining Moment:

Playboy *Celebrity Centerfold: Patti Davis* (0:02) *The former First Daughter poses full-frontally nude on a rock, offering up both her Bonzos and Gipper.*

Playboy Celebrity Centerfold: Patti Davis
(1994) FFN, Buns

Phyllis Davis

Born: July 17, 1947
Port Arthur, Texas
Skin-O-Meter: Hall of Fame

Legtastic and boobulous, with a
face that could stop or start a riot,
showgirl-quality Phyllis Davis
began her ascent to skin stardom
with her standout parts pushed
forward in such roles as Bit Girl,
Model #10, and 2nd Secretary in a
string of Elvis Presley movies. Davis
had a moving way of moving
herself, and she moved right into a
recurring spot on the TV sitcom
Love, American Style, a gig that
stretched from 1970 to 1974. Also
in those years, Phyllis strayed into

MEN AND
WOMEN...
BLACK AND
WHITE.
TAKEN FROM
DEATH ROW -
CONDEMNED
TO DEVILS
ISLAND, U.S.A.
WHERE LIVING
IS WORSE
THAN DYING!

TERMINAL ISLAND: LIKE TV'S *SURVIVOR*, BUT
WITH *MAGNUM, P.I.* AND BOOBS. SAVAGE '70S
EXPLOITATION POSTERS ACTUALLY COULD BE
MORE TAWDRY AND ILLICIT THAN THIS ONE
BUT, STILL, THIS *TERMINAL ISLAND* ONE-
SHEET IS KILLER!

risqué territory. She held the title
role in chick prison flick *Sweet Sugar*
(1972). No one ever lost any money
betting that there would be a
steamy girl-on-girl shower soap up
in *Sugar*. And no one ever lost any
time blinking at Phyllis's truck-
stopping mammary shelf as an
open-shirted hitchhiker in *Terminal
Island* (1973). *Famous T&A* (1982)
illustrates the Davis ability to play
both blonde and brunette, although
she is consistently brunette on the
bottom half.

SKIN-fining Moment:

***Terminal Island* (0:41)** *Terrific taits
and tail as Phyllis bathes in a pond,
then puts her clothes back on.*

See Her Naked In:

Famous T&A (1982) FFN
The Best of Sex and Violence (1981) Breasts,
Buns
Terminal Island (1973) FFN, Buns
Sweet Sugar (1972) Breasts
Beyond the Valley of the Dolls (1970) Breasts

Sammi Davis-Voss

Born: June 21, 1964
Kidderminster, England, UK
Skin-O-Meter: Great Nudity

With kinky, blonde hair and a kinky,
bold flair, British dish Sammi Davis-
Voss has everything the world looks
for in a classically trained English
dramatist: A plush bum that creases
at the bottom with just a hint of
cheese, skin the color of milk in the
predawn, a curvy torso shaped like
the solid-body clouds of a sensual
heaven, boobies that are raised and
perpendicular, and—most
importantly—the overpowering
desire to traipse about fully naked
hand-in-hand with another
classically trained English female
dramatist who exhibits all the same
sterling qualities! Don't trust us.
Rent *The Rainbow* (1989) and try to
believe the extent and quality of
Limey lady flesh on display. Frontals,

backsides, tops, and bottoms;
standing, sitting, running up a hill.
It's like these female English
dramatists can never get their fill.

SKIN-fining Moment:

***The Rainbow* (0:21)** *Sammi and
galpal Amanda Donohue enjoy quality
Naked Time, from prancing through the
forest to massage therapy in front of the
fireplace. Bush, boobs, and butt aplenty!*

See Her Naked In:

Four Rooms (1995) Breasts
The Rainbow (1989) FFN, Buns

Kim Dawson

Born: December 8, 1963
Tifton, Georgia
Skin-O-Meter: Great Nudity

Kim Dawson's dad was a palm
reader. Think he could tell that his
daughter would grow up to make so
many hairy-palm pumpers happy?
The southern belle made her film
debut in *Not of this Earth* (1988),
and the title is certainly fitting for
the out-of-this-world, big-breasted
blonde bombshell. It took a number
of years before she finally parted
ways with all that cumbersome
clothing that obscures her breast
view. Her first skinful onscreen
appearance was in *Buck Naked Line
Dancing* (1993), which pretty much
says it all. Since then it's been one
long, hard, and hot career of
carnality. From the life's-a-beach
flicks *Surf, Sand, and Sex* (1994) and
Bikini Med School (1994) to her pole
work in *Lap Dancing* (1995) and
Stripteaser 2 (1997), Kim has been
synonymous with sin. If Mr. Skin
had to choose a favorite from this
frisky filly's filthy freakfest of a film
life it would have to be *Voyeur*
(1995), only because there's more
peeping for the peepers. Kim
continues to rally around the ribald
flag, and she's just as hot in *The
Erotic Misadventures of the Invisible*

Man (2003) as when audiences first laid eyes on her. Now if only we could actually lay her.

SKIN-fining Moment:

Lawful Entry **(0:55)** *A judge gives it to Kim right up her Dawson's Creek, showing us her top flight rack and a tiny touch of booshish. No objections here, your honor.*

See Her Naked In:

The Erotic Misadventures of the Invisible Man (2003) Breasts
15 minutes of Fame (2001) FFN, Buns
Sin in the City (2001) Breasts, Bush, Buns
Bedtime Stories: The Perfect Man (2000) Breasts
Lawful Entry (2000) FFN
Sexual Intrigue (2000) FFN
Scandal: The Big Turn On (2000) Breasts, Buns
Hollywood Sins (2000) Breasts, Buns
Surrender (1999) Breasts
Lethal Target (1999) Breasts, Buns
The Big Hustle (1999) FFN, Buns
Sex@Students.edu (1999) FFN
Hidden Passion (1999) FFN, Buns
Sensual Friends (1999) FFN
The Sexperiment (1998) FFN, Buns
I Like to Play Games Too (1998) Breasts
Dreamboat (1997) Breasts
Hot Lust (1997) FFN, Buns
Sex, Lies, & Politics (1997) Breasts
Legally Exposed (1997) FFN, Buns
Stripteaser 2 (1997) Breasts
Maui Heat (1996) FFN
Voyeur (1995) FFN, Buns
Lap Dancing (1995) FFN
Lurid Tales: The Castle Queen (1995) Breasts
Bad Blood (1994) Breasts, Bush
Bikini Med School (1994) Breasts
Sexual Outlaws (1994) FFN, Buns
Surf, Sand, and Sex (1994) FFN
Buck Naked Line Dancing (1993) Breasts

TeleVisions:

Erotic Confessions Breasts
Love Street Breasts, Buns
Nightcap FFN, Buns
Pleasure Zone Breasts, Bush, Buns

Portia Dawson

Skin-O-Meter: Brief Nudity

A girl in a bikini can monopolize male attention wherever she goes. Especially if she is tawny, taut, and tan; an indeterminately ethnic brunette with sleek and sinuous curves of hip and breast; with long legs tapering up to a coy, cozy crevice; and a face that could launch a multitude of lust-touched reveries when its flashing eyes and gleaming teeth are held in a television close-up. All these aforementioned attributes are bundled together in the proudly prurient package that is Portia Dawson. One of the few ways to improve upon the visual paradise of Portia in a bikini, as seen on the beach in surfer-and-sand epic *Boardheads* (1998), is to have her dispense with the top half of her bathing suit and play hide-and-peep with her perky nips, as also seen in *Boardheads*.

SKIN-fining Moment:

Boardheads **(0:57)** *Seaside nipple-slipple as Portia tries to cover her bare chest during an oceanside photo shoot.*

See Her Naked In:

Boardheads (1998) Nip-Slip RB

Rosario Dawson

Born: May 9, 1979
New York, New York
Skin-O-Meter: Brief Nudity

Mocha-skinned Manhattan Latin Rosario Dawson, with her fast-rapping diction and super-salsa-saucy smirk and smile, burst upon the world as a bold-talking boy expert in director/photographer Larry Clark's no-budget indie flick *Kids* (1995). Though she kept thoroughly covered, Rosario's lush lips and big, round cheekbones hinted of orbicular delights below her clothed surface. Director Spike

Lee brought the dark, hidden delights to light in *He Got Game* (1998). Aside from game, the titular He also got his paws all over the hanging breast heaven of Dawson's chest cheeks. There appears to be plenty more where those came from.

SKIN-fining Moment:

He Got Game **(1:52)** *Rosario busts out her fantastic flotation devices while getting it on with her guy under a seaside pier. She got game enough for two players!*

See Her Naked In:

He Got Game (1998) Breasts

Taylor Dayne

Born: March 7, 1963
Long Island, New York
Skin-O-Meter: Brief Nudity

Throughout the late 1980s and early 1990s, porn-star-quality blonde Taylor Dayne had a string of pop-lite hit songs, including the suggestively titled "Prove Your Love." Considering that even her name would look right at home on a Vivid Video box cover, Taylor took her shot at scratching the acting itch. Unfortunately, her sensibilities were much more PG-13 than hard-R. The sultry songbird's sexiest and most revealing screen time was logged during *Stag* (1997). Clad in a cheek-invading G-string and a bra that might be tinfoil, Taylor bumps and grinds through a sizzling lap dance and mock oral-sex scene. Stardom might not be so far away; it might only be awaiting a glimpse of the real things.

SKIN-fining Moment:

Stag **(0:16)** *Discodiva Taylor shakes her groove things and peels to a thong as a bachelor-party stripper.*

See Her Naked In:

Stag (1997) Thong

Amanda De Cadenet

Born: May 19, 1972
England, UK
Skin-O-Meter: Great Nudity

British temptress Amanda De Cadenet comes from that full-lipped, dirty-blonde school of princess tarts who stare out with their falsely innocent eyes in some sort of unblinking challenge, daring the viewer to decide whether she wants to be sexed up or slapped up. A highly provocative beauty, alternately infuriating and exhilarating, De Cadenet is almost as well known for being a rock star-wife (of the ex-variety) and world-class partygoer as she is for her cinematic achievements. In the world of skinema, however, Amanda's place is clear: Start at the top with *Mascara* (1999). Playing some sort of "difficult," high-end trollop, amazing Amanda stands lounging and lazy for a few full moments of full nudity, flexing her full butt, then squatting in the shower to eat a plate of meatballs, using her full shelf as a spill tray. If grudge love did not exist, we might have to invent it for this luscious lump.

SKIN-fining Moment:

Mascara (0:32) *Delicious view of Amanda's dairy-guns as sits in the shower and . . . uh . . . eats meatballs.*

See Her Naked In:

Mascara (1999) Breasts, Buns
Fall (1997) RB

TeleVisions:

The Hunger Breasts

Raven De La Croix

Born: August 24, 1947
Manhattan, New York
Skin-O-Meter: Great Nudity

There's something to be said about doing things the classy way. The theory of top-shelf sex appeal can be summed up in four words or less, depending on who's doing the spelling: Raven De La Croix. Incredibly fantastic is an understatement when applied to her under-wire-defying, miraculously buoyant tits. Take a look at Russ Meyer's *Up!* (1976). Raven's bra busters are each bigger than a hog's head. They are impossible to look at without mentally hearing the sound of snuffling. Who would not give up their place in the manor to root and slobber between those two cushiony boulders of earthy nirvana? And with the face, pelvis, legs, and backside to match, Raven De La Croix is one of the most stacked classy chassis in history.

SKIN-fining Moment:

Up! (1:11) *Naked Janet Wood stands in a river with a sword, then slashes the also-nood Raven. Boobs, bush, and buns galore, with a sprinkle of Skingoria, to boot.*

See Her Naked In:

Screwballs (1983) Breasts
The Lost Empire (1983) Breasts
The Happy Hooker Goes to Washington (1977) Breasts, Buns
Up! (1976) FFN, Buns

Drea de Matteo

Born: January 17, 1973
Queens, New York, New York
Skin-O-Meter: Never Nude

A not-quite-reformed rocker chick whose past is evident in every snap of her gum, bad-girl prototype Drea de Matteo has survived in a world where people go missing every episode. Drea's character Adrianna, young Christopher's long-suffering fiancée on the HBO mob hit *The Sopranos*, was only intended to make one appearance and then be out. All hail Drea's survival instincts and also her intuitive understanding that Adrianna should spend as much time as possible in her underwear. Panties and bra come as naturally to de Matteo's hard-broad, high, hard cones and elevated rump as wishing she'd take those bras and panties off comes to the rest of us.

SKIN-fining Moment:

The Sopranos "Mr. Ruggerio's Neighborhood" (2001) *Drea models her cheetah-print panties on a tennis court. Love! Set! Thatch!*

Maria de Medeiros

Born: August 19, 1965
Lisbon, Portugal
Skin-O-Meter: Great Nudity

Those big, wide, woebegone waif's eyes; the high, round cheeks puffed out like a sexy humanized squirrel; the long quivering nose; the tightly controlled lips that suddenly break into a giant shining smile, Portuguese-born Maria de Medeiros's face of spritely innocence may have made her an unlikely supermodel, but her unfettered expressiveness served her well once she'd made the jump to the actress game. The gorgeous gamine's unfettered nymphet breasts and exploratory sexuality also served her well, particularly in the sensually charged skinema of *Henry and June* (1990). The story of libertine writer Henry Miller and his do-anything wife, *Henry & June*'s crowning glory is a naked *tit-a-tete* tussle between Maria and the blooming Uma Thurman. The Sapphic emoting was so scorching that a new rating had to be invented before the film was released to avoid an X: thus, NC-17.

SKIN-fining Moment:

Henry & June (1:28) *Maria sits bare-breasted in bed with smokin' blonde*

Brigitte Lahaie before they get to lez-canoodling.

See Her Naked In:

Huevos de Oro (1993) Breasts
The Man of My Life (1992) Breasts
Henry & June (1990) Breasts, Buns

Rebecca De Mornay

Born: August 29, 1961
Santa Rosa, California
Skin-O-Meter: Hall of Fame

Golden-haired, milky-bodied Rebecca De Mornay, the daughter of hotheaded right-wing TV talker Wally George, debuted as a hooker with a heart-on in *Risky Business* (1983), scorching the classic (and classy) sex satire so incandescently that even headliner Tom Cruise looked like he was genuinely digging her steamy sex act. In *And God Created Woman* (1988), a remake of the movie that made Brigitte Bardot a universal synonym for heat, Rebecca did the French tart one better with zipper-popping skin. *The Hand that Rocks the Cradle* (1992) rocked the crotch, too. *Blind Side* (1993) offers a tempting peek at Rebecca's boob side. *Never Talk to Strangers* (1995) screams with a kinky sex scene. And the title of *Wicked Ways* (1999) says it all.

SKIN-fining Mornent:

Risky Business (0:28) *Rebecca gets Risky with Tom Cruise, baring her boobs, butt, and bush as they get to Business.*

See Her Naked In:

Wicked Ways (1999) Breasts
Never Talk to Strangers (1995) Breasts
Blind Side (1993) RB
The Hand that Rocks the Cradle (1992) RB
And God Created Woman (1988) Breasts, Bush, Buns
Risky Business (1983) FFN, Buns

Barbara De Rossi

Born: August 9, 1960
Rome, Italy
Skin-O-Meter: Great Nudity

Though she is Italian by birth, no borders can contain the allure of tawny-skinned blonde Barbara De Rossi. The soul-gripping gaze of her hazel eyes and the pristine planes of her divinely sculpted face defy containment and have helped to establish her as an international fixation. She has worked in American TV. She has worked in German TV. She has worked in the nude. For examples of that last lovely labor, work out a way to see *Angela Come Te* (1988) for inspiring views of De Rossi naked on a beach toweling off with another gal in the same condition, exhibiting breasts, beav, and the breeze-way between her thighs. *Quiet Days in Clichy* (1990) treats the viewer to tranquilizing studies of Barbara's naturally holding chest fruit and her firm and twisting bum.

SKIN-fining Moment:

La Cicala (0:40) *Barbara is the light-haired siren swimming nude with Clio Goldsmith under a waterfall. FFN, buttables.*

See Her Naked In:

Jours Tranquilles a Clichy (1990) Breasts, Buns
Angela Come Te (1988) FFN, Buns
Paladini—Storia d'Armi e d'Amori, I (1983) Breasts, Thong
La Cicala (1980) FFN, Buns

TeleVisions:

Verwirrung des Herzens LB

Portia de Rossi

Born: January 31, 1973
Melbourne, Victoria, Australia
Skin-O-Meter: Great Nudity

Australian platinum blonde Portia de Rossi cemented her position in the libidinal subconscious of the American male the first time she let her hair down as lawyer Nelle Porter on the Fox TV fox preserve *Ally McBeal*. When Portia's heavy lengths of shimmering tresses tumble across her shoulders and fall from her face as she tosses back her shoulders, the imagination reels, stumbling into Portia's bedroom, where she is preparing for a night between the sheets. We can all picture what drops after the hair. That picture became even clearer when tabloids snapped Portia in what appeared to be a lip-locked bout of passion with an apparently very close gal pal, which caused the genital public's imagination to reel anew. For a clear view of the private Portia parts, imagine squinting into *Sirens* (1994), a comedy of manners from Down Under that displays all manner of de Rossi, from her tuft to her titties. Once you've seen the real skinny, your imagination is free to roam to more challenging material.

SKIN-fining Moment:

Sirens (1:15) *Portia and her picture-perfect pals pose for a painting, the subject of which seems to be impossibly hot chicks who show rack, rug, and rear.*

See Her Naked In:

Women in Film (2001) FFN, Buns
Sirens (1994) FFN, Buns

Danyi Deats

Skin-O-Meter: Great Nudity

Danyi Deats has got a fine pair of teats. Oh, sure, they're a bit cold, but with some imagination a viewer can warm up to them. She made her debut getting chilly by the *River's Edge* (1987) in little more than a pair of cloudy contact lenses to make her eyes look lifeless. Yes, Danyi played the corpse that everyone wanted to

MR. SKIN'S TOP TEN

Naked and Dead
. . . The cold and the beautiful or
Blue is the color of my true love's tits

10. Amber Smith
    —*L.A. Confidential* 1997 (0:35)

9. Catherine Sutherland
   —*The Cell* 2000 (0:13)

8. Keira Knightley
   —*The Hole* 2001 (1:19)

7. Wendy Crewson
   —*Mercy* 2000 (0:04)

6. Joanna Cassidy
   —*The Fourth Protocol* 1987 (1:39)

5. Julienne Davis
   —*Eyes Wide Shut* 1999 (2:07)

4. Debralee Scott
   —*Dirty Harry* 1971 (1:10)

3. Lisa Niemi
   —*Slam Dance* 1987 (0:59)

2. Randi Brooks
   —*Tightrope* 1984 (0:24)

1. **Danyi Deats**
   —*River's Edge* **1986 (0:15)**

poke with their stick. Considering she's dead throughout the movie, she's more skinful than a packed house of lap dancers. The deadly Danyi exposed every inch of her fine young form, from those aforementioned tits to her unmentionables. She even got turned around for a rear view. Forget about robbing the cradle; go to the cemetery for some real action. Sadly, this was the beginning of the end of Danyi's career. She did follow up *River's Edge* with a small part as a junkie in *The Allnighter* (1987), but then it was good night, sweet piece. Wish

there were more of Deats's treats to sample onscreen.

SKIN-fining Moment:

River's Edge (0:15) *Danyi lays dead in a field with her nipples and nether-hair in excellent view as Crispin Glover and a gaggle of burn-outs investigate.*

See Her Naked In:

River's Edge (1986) FFN, Buns

Kristine DeBell

Born: 1954
New York, New York
Skin-O-Meter: Great Nudity

The hypocrisy of our sex-obsessed but image-conscious society would seem to have cast an unjust cloud upon the sunny horizons that were the future career of comic, cuddly, blonde, and boldly bare actress Kristine DeBell. But, hey, she got famous in the '70s. So although Kristine may be less well known (today) than the likes of Traci Lords or Ginger Lynn, she remains, to date, the most successful starlet to cross over from X-rated entertainment to the Hollywood mainstream. The bubbly, boobular, multi-talented New York City native broke into showbiz at a time of great erotic experimentation and exploitation, landing a leading role in the hardcore fantasy musical *Alice in Wonderland* (1976). Kristine's versatility extended beyond merely singing and dancing—her XXX prowess encompassed activities as disparate as eating man and eating clam. A few years later, when Kristine popped up as the wacky but whack-worthy A.L. in the camp comedy *Meatballs* (1979), she was already familiar to late-'70s TV fans from regular appearances on network fare such as *Eight is Enough*, *Fantasy Island*, and *BJ and the Bear*. That's no small feat for a

screen beauty who just a short time earlier was best known for giving bj's *while* bare.

SKIN-fining Moment:

Alice in Wonderland (0:22) *Alice discovers that her own body is a Wonderland, petting her Cheshire pussy and pinching Tweedle-Nip and Tweedle Nerp by a river.*

See Her Naked In:

The Big Brawl (1980) Breasts
Willie and Phil (1980) Breasts
Alice in Wonderland (1976) FFN, Buns

Sandra Dee

Born: April 23, 1944
Bayonne, New Jersey
Skin-O-Meter: Brief Nudity

The late 1950s and early 1960s were times when Americans liked things to be big, pointy, and protruding, whether it was the tail fins of our automobiles or the breasts of our teen idols. Sandra Dee had many claims to fame. A perky insouciance that was pointless to resist. A face of eager innocence and willingness to please. A work ethic that had her creating postadolescent prototypes at a dazzling rate—one day Gidget, the next day Tammy Tyree. Blondeness, of course. A mane of flaxen tresses never hurts. And to top it off, in her pursuit of national veneration, Sandra Dee has the lung balloons of a full-grown burlesque queen, lurking only a fraction of an inch beneath her mohair cardigan. Oh, how the boys ached imagining the fleshly delights beneath her thick, old-school bra. And how the boys ached when they grew into men, and Sandra became a woman, and all she ever showed was a blink of nipple in the bad lighting of *The Dunwich Horror* (1970). Who ever thought that Gidget would be a parable of wasted potential?

SKIN-fining Moment:

The Dunwich Horror (0:47) *Extremely brief glimpse of Sandra's left gidget. Her nip pops out when Dean Stockwell's fondling her.*

See Her Naked In:

The Dunwich Horror (1970) LB

Heather Deeley

Born: 1956
Suffolk, England, UK
Skin-O-Meter: Great Nudity

Although the film career of auburn-tressed Heather Deeley, she of the slightly cross-eyed gleam of passion and petulant, pouting mouth, lasted from only 1975 through 1977, those two years gave her enough time to light up the life in pictures such as *Girls Come First* (1975), *It's Getting Harder all the Time* (1975), *Erotic Inferno* (1975), *Sex Express* (1975), and *I'm not Feeling Myself Tonight* (1976). In the repressive times of their production, these farcical masterpieces were saddled with X ratings, although they would be hard pressed to earn a hard-R by today's advanced standards. Still, by any measure, Heather is a great Deeley of fun, thanks in large part to her playfully perfect chest protrusions. Meaty and sweet to the eye, Heather's very nice tits make a very nice appearance in *Hardcore* (1977). The twins descend in a full, rounded, gradual slope and are upturned at the tips, just the right steepness and pitch to launch a skinthusiast into an orbit of happiness.

SKIN-fining Moment:

Intimate Games (0:34) *Ms. Deeley gets all kinds of touchy-feely with Suzy Mandel during an all-points nudity lesbo munch-fest.*

See Her Naked In:

Hardcore (1977) Breasts, Buns
Intimate Games (1976) FFN, Buns

Ellen DeGeneres

Born: January 26, 1958
New Orleans, Louisiana
Skin-O-Meter: Brief Nudity

Despite the fact that she's as deep into chicks as any guy is, or maybe because of that fact, television personality Ellen DeGeneres seems like she'd be a great chick to hang out with. She's funny, easy-going, rich, blonde, happy in the face, and fully functional in the body. Who knows? After a few nights cruising at the strip bar, maybe she'd come back to the pad and mimic the various dancers. The fun could get out of hand, and this wise-cracking best buddy might turn into a bed buddy after all. What kind of freaky scene would the two of you be getting into? Well, if Ellen's topless bed lolling in *If These Walls Could Talk 2* (2000) is any indication, things might not be so bad. The boobs are good; they are really quite good.

SKIN-fining Moment:

If These Walls Could Talk 2 (1:19) *Brief look at her right breast while she and Sharon Stone enjoy a little sisterly love. Anne Heche must have been fuming.*

See Her Naked In:

If These Walls Could Talk 2 (2000) RB

Maria Del Mar

Born: June 27, 1964
Madrid, Spain
Skin-O-Meter: Brief Nudity

Born of Venezuelan parents in Madrid, Spain, the exotic and refined sensualist Maria Del Mar has become a heart-grabbing presence on Canadian television and in American films due to a tragedy of her youth. Maria's father was a diplomat on assignment in Canada, and when he unexpectedly died, the family

voted to stay on living in Ottawa. Young Maria's dramatic flair and deep well of emotional experience, coupled with her striking cheekbones and flaring, dark eyes, won her a high-temperature guest spot on *Night Heat*, a north-of-the-border cathode thriller, which led to recurring hot spots on *Street Legal*, *TekWar*, and *Mercy Point*. Maria burns brightest as Inspector Victoria Castillo on the Gemini-winning (read: Emmy-caliber) *Blue Murder*.

SKIN-fining Moment:

Cold Sweat (0:35) *Two looks at her torso-tarts as she opens her robe and sits on a couch.*

See Her Naked In:

Moonshine Highway (1996) Breasts
Cold Sweat (1993) Breasts

Kim Delaney

Born: November 29, 1961
Philadelphia, Pennsylvania
Skin-O-Meter: Great Nudity

Best remembered as a deliciously dark-haired detective on *NYPD Blue*, Kim Delaney has a knack for arresting men with her intoxicating beauty. Like her buoyant B-cups, Kim has done a lot of bouncing in her career, from law to order and back again. Delaney enhanced the law with her foxy frame on *Law & Order* and *Philly* and upheld the peace as the finest piece in the east on *NYPD Blue* and the short-lived *CSI: Miami*. Kim's stint as a perky-topped cop wasn't her first run-in with the blue. To see Kim's own acts of indecent exposure, check out her tantalizing top knots in *Temptress* (1994) and *The Drifter* (1998). David Caruso may find Kim to be objectionable, but with bullets as sharp as hers, Mr. Skin will always be gunning for Kimmy.

SKIN-fining Moment:

The Drifter (0:21) *Nice look at her party hats in bed talking to Timothy Bottoms.*

See Her Naked In:

Temptress (1994) Breasts, Buns
The Drifter (1988) Breasts

TeleVisions:

NYPD Blue Breasts, Buns

Dana Delany

Born: March 13, 1956
New York, New York
Skin-O-Meter: Great Nudity

Most audiences first got bombarded by Dana Delany's sexy two-gun assault on the ABC drama *China Beach*, on which she played a nurse on the frontlines during the Vietnam war. Bringing her big talents to the big screen, Dana supplied a brief but jaw-dropping glimpse of her perfectly formed right breast in *Light Sleeper* (1991). It was *hard* to sleep after catching a taste of the Dana dish. Then in 1995, Dana turned up in *Live Nude Girls*. Good title. The movie also starred skin queen Kim Catrall. Intriguing? No, misleading: there was only one short shot of Dana's delightful derriere. All this teasing finally came to a head in the inexplicable S&M comedy *Exit to Eden* (1994). Now this was the Dana we all dreamed of, coming fully nude and wet from a pool and delivering bobbling bare breastaciousness and sopping bush for our drooling eyes. Hurt me! Hurt me!

SKIN-fining Moment:

Exit to Eden (0:37) *Dana flashes some seriously furry full-frontal flesh climbing out of the pool so her equally naked assisstant can help her into her robe.*

See Her Naked In:

Live Nude Girls (1995) Buns
Exit to Eden (1994) FFN, Buns
Light Sleeper (1992) RB, Bush

Idalis DeLeon

Born: June 15, 1966
New York, New York
Skin-O-Meter: Brief Nudity

Television is a medium that both promises and rewards. As the devoted viewer faithfully sits in front of his set, soaking up the quick-cut images of sexually alluring women and funky dances they do, occasionally a particularly hot strumpet will come into view. Such is the case with mocha-skinned Manhattan Latin Idalis DeLeon. Always sporting a lascivious grin and several pounds of bra ballast that threatened to burst out of their holster, Idalis became a prominent fixation while veejaying and as a special correspondent on the booty-rockin' MTV. Her every appearance seemed to promise that next time those bangin' boobs might just bump into view. A few years later, the devoted fan is still faithful at his set, and *boom!* There's Idalis, playing a titty-bar dancer on *Six Feet Under*. The jugs float out on their own, and the camera zeros in on the DeLeon derriere while Idalis squats to the floor in sparkling Lucite spiked heels. Only the skimpiest of G-strings keeps the brown beauty's brown eye from winking out at the camera. Reward!

SKIN-fining Moment:

Six Feet Under "*I'm Sorry, I'm Lost*" (2003) *Quick robo-hootage as she dances at a strip club in a bikini and loses the top.*

TeleVisions:

Six Feet Under Breasts, Thong

Nathalie Delon

Born: August 1, 1941
Oujda, Morocco
Skin-O-Meter: Great Nudity

Feline French brunette Nathalie Delon took her first step toward iconic stature with a pivotal appearance in the cult classic *La Samourai* (1967). The groundbreaking and highly influential picture made the best use of Nathalie's delicate strawberry blondeness. Delon's fiery eyes, pale-blood lips, and puffy, girly nips were drafted into the service of *Le Sorelle* (1969), but the breathy and breathtaking beauty didn't make the big splash until her scandalous shenanigans in Richard Burton's *Bluebeard* (1972). Not only does Delon have the audacity to strip down to a fetchingly clinging pair of black panties in *Bluebeard*, she has the gall to grapple on the carpet in a girl-girl ball with young and blonde Sybil Danning, future doyenne of so many women-in-prison movies.

SKIN-fining Moment:

Bluebeard (1:07) *Nat peels down her nightie and bares her neat little knockers while squirming atop Richard Burton in bed.*

See Her Naked In:

Vous Intéressez-vous à la Chose? (1973) Breasts
Bluebeard (1972) Breasts
Le Sorelle (1969) Breasts

Julie Delpy

Born: December 21, 1969
Paris, France
Skin-O-Meter: Great Nudity

Big, fragile eyes, lush lips, and the intriguing hint of an overbite, delicate, fair-skinned Julie Delpy is a French treasure who has been enriching skin lives worldwide since her debut at age seven in *Guerres Civiles en France* (1976). Julie's charming, girlish tits have been pale but powerful presences in at least eight major films, evenly split between English language and the tongue of the Gauls. Delpy's ethereal, always sensual and refined eroticism is revealed to near mystical effect in such overseas celluloid dreams as *La Noche Oscura* (1989), *Warszawa* (1992), and *Les Mille Merveilles de l'Univers* (1997). The perfect expression of Julie Delpy emanates from *The Passion of Beatrice* (1998). Heavenly Julie displays a passion for fully nude, full-frontal jogging and for standing with her beaver in the wind behind a tub of steaming water. If paradise could be contained within a single body, we would all be praying to Delpy.

SKIN-fining Moment:

The Passion of Beatrice (1:13) *Enjoy an extended gander at Julie's full-frontal loveliness as she burns her clothes in a barbecue pit.*

See Her Naked In:

Investigating Sex (2001) Breasts
Les Mille Merveilles de l'Univers (1997) Breasts
An American Werewolf in Paris (1997) Breasts
Tykho Moon (1996) Breasts
Killing Zoe (1994) Breasts
Warszawa (1992) Breasts
La Noche oscura (1989) FFN
The Passion of Beatrice (1988) FFN, Buns

Judi Dench

Born: December 9, 1934
York, England, UK
Skin-O-Meter: Brief Nudity

Judi Dench is, of course, best known for her portrayal of "M" in the James Bond films *Goldeneye* (1995), *Tomorrow Never Dies* (1997), *The World Is Not Enough* (2000), *Die Another Day* (2002), and *Everything or Nothing* (2004). But she has been quite active in cinema since her debut in *The Third Secret* (1964). However, by the time she appeared in that film, she had become quite well known as a theatrical actress in London, most notably for The Royal Shakespeare Company. Having that experience hasn't hurt her career in the slightest, either, seeing as she has appeared in basically every screen adaptation of the Bard's works since the late '60s. One such film, the made-for-TV version of *A Midsummer Night's Dream* (1968), also happens to feature Dame Judi's first skin scenes. In it, as the busty Titania, Judi bares her breasts, albeit through green makeup, much to the delight of mammarian moviegoers worldwide. Unfortunately, that is the only flesh she has ever bared. But a mature Judi shouldn't sit out her naked second act on the Dench.

SKIN-fining Moment:

A Midsummer Night's Dream (0:21) *Very brief view of Dench's devil's dumplings while she runs around in the woods, and then more of her lovely jubblies as she recites some long monologue. She had quite the rack in her time, the old bird.*

See Her Naked In:

Langrishe Go Down (1978) FFN, Buns
A Midsummer Night's Dream (1969) Breasts

Catherine Deneuve

Born: October 22, 1943
Paris, France
Skin-O-Meter: Hall of Fame

An international sex symbol since her harrowing portrayal of a beauty gone mad in Roman Polanski's *Repulsion* (1965), willow-thin blonde Catherine Deneuve has a face and figure so perfectly angelic they would make the Devil himself regret having turned in his wings. As an ageless bloodsucker in *The Hunger* (1983), Catherine made falling under the spell of a vampire seem like a sweet way to go, especially when she went nipple-to-nipple with the plush bosom of victim Susan Sarandon. Deneuve's histoire du nuditie stretches all the way back to the shadowy black-and-white swell of bust in *Chateau en Suede* (1963). The protrusion-to-droop ratio of the Deneuve shelf is still marvelously stellar thirty-six years later in *Pola X* (1999). Perhaps this ageless beauty really is a vampire.

SKIN-fining Moment:

Belle de Jour (0:52) *Catherine flashes her left belle, then shows buns du jour poking out from under black fabric as she strolls around her house.*

See Her Naked In:

Pola X (1999) Breasts
The Hunger (1983) Breasts, Buns
Le Sauvage (1975) Breasts
La Femme aux Bottes Rouges (1974) RB
Liza (1972) Breasts
Mississippi Mermaid (1969) Breasts
Belle de Jour (1967) Buns, LB
Château en Suède (1963) RB

Marianne Denicourt

Born: May 14, 1966
Paris, France
Skin-O-Meter: Great Nudity

With eyes like two star-filled night skies contained in a face as pale and perfectly round as the clouds of heaven, it is no wonder that the French revere their native daughter Marianne Denicourt as a living, breathing, sensual muse of Eros. No mere symbol of the spiritually freeing aspects of physical love, the thin and dainty brunette Denicourt has put her skin where her heart is on many occasions. *My Sex Life... Or How I Got Into An Argument* (1996), for instance, is elevated by the freely given gift of Marianne's lovely breasts and frilly bush as she unself-consciously sits grinning and impish or sprawls on a hardwood floor playing strip twiddlesticks. This is a performance for Eros and everyman alike to muse over.

SKIN-fining Moment:

Le Jour et la nuit (0:11) *Great look at Marianne's seat and milk-sacks while she gets very believably boinked in her villa's bedroom.*

See Her Naked In:

Me Without You (2001) LB
Sade (2000) Breasts
The Lost Son (1999) Buns
Le Jour et la nuit (1997) FFN, Buns
My Sex Life . . . Or How I Got Into An Argument (1996) FFN, Buns
Le Bel été 1914 (1996) Breasts
La Vie des Morts (1991) Breasts

Lydie Denier

Born: April 15, 1964
Saint Nazaire, France
Skin-O-Meter: Great Nudity

With her flashing gray eyes giving off glittering reflections of any color of the rainbow, her tasty little mouth forever twisting into a teasing, attainable smirk, and her long, brunette locks casting about for a pillow to thrash on, French-born American actress Lydie Denier had us before she even popped open a button on her blouse. Her TV roles alone, in such fare as *General Hospital*, *Tarzan*, and *Acapulco H.E.A.T.*, are winningly eroticized, an effect magnified once light is cast upon her cleavage and crevices. A lean and ready-to-ride robustness makes Lydie's sensuality seem like the most natural thing in the world when she flashes flesh. The first exposure came in *The Night Stalker* (1987), and lissome Lydie has shown a bit in almost every role ever since.

SKIN-fining Moment:

Satan's Princess (0:31) *Boobs and bush aplenty before Lydie engages in some hot lesbotronic action with Leslie Huntly.*

See Her Naked In:

Perfect Alibi (1995) LB, Buns
Mardi Gras for the Devil (1993) Breasts
No Place to Hide (1993) Breasts
Invasion of Privacy (1992) Breasts
Wild Orchid II (1992) Breasts
Satan's Princess (1990) FFN, Buns
Red Blooded American Girl (1990) Breasts, Thong
Bulletproof (1988) Breasts, Buns
Blood Relations (1988) FFN
The Night Stalker (1987) Breasts

TeleVisions:

Red Shoe Diaries Breasts, Buns

Julie Depardieu

Born: June 5, 1973
France
Skin-O-Meter: Great Nudity

Julie Depardieu is the very best-case scenario of what a girl is to do when she inherits her country's most famous and far-reaching nose from her father. Lissome, lovely Julie calls Gerard Depardieu dad, he whose nose gives him the most recognizable profile in French cinema. A more feminine version of the same proboscis graces the green-eyed face of blonde fille Julie, but her profile is dominated by a pair of outgoing chest protrusions, which she seems to have sprouted for the sole purpose of surpassing the schnoz. Aside from a dominating facial feature, Daddy made sure to pass down parts for his girl in films of his such as *La Machine* (1994), *Le Colonel Chabert* (1999), and *Le Comte de Monte Cristo* (1999). It's in her films free from parental supervision, *Le Passion de Docteur Bergh* (1996) and *L'Examen de Minuit* (1998), that Julie shows

moves and curves all her own, posing the slopes of her girlish chest so that all remnants of her father are blown away.

SKIN-fining Moment:

L'Examen de Minuit (0:33) *L'examen Julie's full-on frontal nudity after she escapes her nightgown. Great Gallic fur baguettes and fluffy croissant.*

See Her Naked In:

L'Examen de Minuit (1998) FFN, Buns
La Passion de Docteur Bergh (1996) Breasts

Bo Derek

Born: November 20, 1956
Long Beach, California
Skin-O-Meter: Hall of Fame

Udderly bountiful, naturally dazzling Bo Derek debuted opposite a killer whale in *Orca* (1977) and quickly shot to enduring sex-symbol superstardom opposite a comic shrimp—Dudley Moore—in the skintacular comedy classic *10* (1979). As the titular figure, Bo came to immediately represent carnal perfection and she seemed more than happy to expose her head-to-toe flawlessness. And Mr. Skin is always happy to watch her do it. Bo goes full frontal in *Tarzan the Ape Man* (1981), *Bolero* (1984), and *Ghosts Can't Do It* (1989), all of which were directed by her husband/mentor John Derek, who died of a heart attack in 1998, perhaps finally realizing how lucky he was. The non-John-helmed *Woman of Desire* (1993) features Bo at her all-time most bare, still looking every inch the Perfect 10 as 40 approached.

SKIN-fining Moment:

10 (1:31) *Bo bares her perfect-10 posterior while walking into the bathroom, followed by a bit of far-off tit in a mirror while Dudley Moore looks on . . .*

"10"

A temptingly tasteful comedy for adults who count.

ANY THEATER LOBBY THAT DARED TO EXHIBIT THIS ULTRA RARE POSTER FOR THE COMEDY CLASSIC MUST HAVE HAD MALE AUDIENCE MEMBERS POPPING INSTANT BO-NERS.

See Her Naked In:

Shattered Image (made for TV) (1993) Breasts, Buns
Woman of Desire (1993) FFN, Buns
Hot Chocolate (1992) RB
Ghosts Can't Do It (1989) FFN, Buns
Bolero (1984) Breasts
Tarzan, The Ape Man (1981) FFN, Buns
A Change of Seasons (1980) Breasts
10 (1979) Breasts, Buns
Fantasies (1974) FFN, Buns

Lisa Dergan

Born: August 10, 1970
Corpus Christi, Texas
Skin-O-Meter: Great Nudity

For having started out as an interior decorator for the *Chili's* chain of restaurants, deeply tanned Texas blonde Lisa Dergan sure has done herself proud. All it took was one bounce on the *Playboy* trampoline, and Miss July 1998 was flying to the vicinity of her wildest dreams. First, the saucy smiler became a movie star, portraying a female gladiator in *The Arena* (2001). Embattled Lisa engages in a girl fight with another blonde of her caliber, which results in her tunic being torn from her pugilistic boobies and her nipples standing at pink alert. Dynamic Dergan's eye-popping protrusions did not go unnoticed, and soon she was established as a newsreader on *The Best Damn Sports Show Period*. Guys who don't know a birdie from a puck watch that show for Lisa Dergan.

SKIN-fining Moment:

The Arena (0:37) *An assortment of titty-shots as Lisa enjoys the meat of a muscle-bound mook.*

See Her Naked In:

The Arena (2001) Breasts
Numerous *Playboy* Videos

Laura Dern

Born: February 10, 1967
Los Angeles, California
Skin-O-Meter: Great Nudity

Tall, blonde, blue-eyed Laura Dern is a gangly dream come true for girl-next-door connoisseurs everywhere. Her parents, Bruce Dern and Diane Ladd, are both successful actors, and after her parents divorced, Laura made her film debut at the age of six in *White Lightning* (1973). Her first major role was in director Adrian Lyne's aptly named *Foxes* (1981). She went on to star as a blond bombshell in *Mask* (1985). Dern joined the David Lynch whack pack in *Blue Velvet* (1986) and *Wild at Heart* (1990) and later became a big star portraying a brainy botanist in the Steven Spielberg blockbuster *Jurassic Park* (1993). In 1997, Laura hit the small screen with her Emmy-nominated portrayal of a lesbian on a landmark episode of the sitcom *Ellen* in which star rug-rubber Ellen DeGeneres finally came out of the closet. We don't blame her.

SKIN-fining Moment:

Wild at Heart (0:07) *Laura loses her bra before bedding Nic Cage. Dern, her hoots are hot!*

See Her Naked In:

Down Came a Blackbird (1995) Breasts
Rambling Rose (1990) RB
Wild at Heart (1990) Breasts, Bush

Donna D'Errico

Born: March 30, 1968
Dothan, Alabama
Skin-O-Meter: Great Nudity

Taken together, *Playboy* magazine and the bouncing-bikini TV series *Baywatch* have launched the careers of at least half of the most important and influential blonde boob jugglers of the past quarter century. A veteran and beneficiary of both of those esteemed launching pads, flaxen-tressed breast rack Donna D'Errico can take a deep breath and puff out her chest as good as any set of Oscar-worthy knockers since Pamela Anderson. Just watch beater-T-clad Donna inhale and hold it in *Candyman 3: The Day of the Dead* (1999). Then exhale and slip in the revelatory *Playboy* video *Playboy's Celebrities* (1999).

SKIN-fining Moment:

Baywatch "The Incident" (1996) *Donna's chest dunes shimmy in slow-mo with the best of them as she debuts in the* Baywatch *red swimsuit.*

See Her Naked in:

Playboy's *Celebrities* (1999) FFN, buns
Numerous *Playboy* Videos

Pamela Des Barres

Born: September 9, 1948
Reseda, California
Skin-O-Meter: Brief Nudity

Groupie's groupie Pamela Des Barres made her name in the heady days of late-1960s rock music by making (and getting heady with) the biggest names in late-1960s rock music. After scoring a gig as the nanny of Frank Zappa's famously odd-named brood, Pamela's mustachioed crackpot boss made her the centerpiece of his all-female pop experiment The GTO's (Girls Together Outrageously). Pam's eclectic (and electric) glam-slamming about the glitter-era Sunset-Strip led to her being squired about by the saturnine, arena-packingly regal r-&-r likes of Mick Jagger, Jimmy Page, Alice Cooper, Keith Moon, and numerous other hip-swinging, fist-pumping, Rolling-Stone-cover-adorning notables. Ultimately Pam married (and later divorced) heavy-metal crooner Michael Des Barres and turned her adventures in the bedrooms and backstage areas of rockdom's hottest and horniest into the best-selling 1987 memoir *Confessions of a Groupie: I'm With the Band*. On the big screen, Pam bared her adorable tweeters (but no woofer) as a dancing girl in the blaxploitation face-stomper *Slaughter's Big Rip-Off* (1973). The following year she played Amy Kaslo #1 on the TV soap *Search for Tomorrow*. Pam will always be the #1 in the hearts (and even harder places) of classic rockers and their generations of audiences who salivate at the prospect of

someday sniffing their idol's facial hair.

SKIN-fining Moment:

Slaughter's Big Rip-Off (0:43) *Des Barres looks killer dancing for a couple of dudes in bikini bottoms and a halter top, and then she doffs the top to add some spice to her routine. Wham, bam, thank you Pam!*

See Her Naked In:

Slaughter's Big Rip-Off (1973) Breasts

Amanda Detmer

Born: September 27, 1971
Chico, California
Skin-O-Meter: Brief Nudity

Not all blondes are more fun, but those with tight buns, high, heaving chest cushions, a sweet-lipped smile, lovey-dovey blue eyes, and lank, curly falls of the blonde stuff sure are. The proof is in Amanda Detmer. Not only is Amanda seriously sexy, she's also willing to play a shirtless goof. Looking closely you will catch delightful Detmer in the aptly named *Drop Dead Gorgeous* (1999) and *Final Destination* (2000). Is Amanda not any man's ultimate point of arrival? Comedic relationship romp *Saving Silverman* (2001) earned its bones with the up-skirt, spread-crotch pantie shots and bare ass close-ups purportedly provided by the Detmer derriere. While these cut-ins may in fact be of a body double, the unclothed breasts that Amanda casually squeezes and half covers with her arm are definitely all her own. Ain't she got fun?

SKIN-fining Moment:

Saving Silverman (0:54) *Brief beautiful buns as Amanda pulls on some panties in the laundromat.*

See Her Naked In:

Saving Silverman (2001) Buns

Maruschka Detmers

Born: December 16, 1962
Schoonebeck, Netherlands
Skin-O-Meter: Hall of Fame

A slim-line brunette with tits that are not overly large but full and firm, with ass cheeks to match, waifish Continental sex siren Maruschka Detmers is a screen gem who has left nothing to hide. This Netherlander's delectable hide has been shown from head to toe, front view and back, in a half-dozen foreign-language flicks. Marvelous Maruschka's full-contact nipples have popped up on U.S. shores in *The Mambo Kings* (1992) and *Hidden Assassin* (1995), standing erect and at attention. To see what a fine match her thick eyebrows are for her thick bush, comb through overseas fare such as *First Name Carmen* (1983), in which the bubble-bun babe's middle name must be Beaver, or *Te Quiero* (2001), a title that loosely translates to "Maruschka shows it." And you want it.

SKIN-fining Moment:

Devil in the Flesh (1:21) *Devil in the Flesh? More like Dong in the Mouth! Maruschka gives her guy a very naked, very real blowjob on-camera.*

See Her Naked In:

Mère, Fille: Mode d'Emploi (2002) Breasts, Buns
Te Quiero (2001) FFN, Buns
Hidden Assassin (1995) Breasts
The Mambo Kings (1992) Breasts
Devil in the Flesh (1986) FFN, Buns
Via Mala (1985) FFN
La Pirate (1984) FFN
Vengeance du Serpent a Plumes (1984) Breasts, Buns
First Name Carmen (1983) FFN, Buns

Devin DeVasquez

Born: June 25, 1963
Baton Rouge, Louisiana
Skin-O-Meter: Great Nudity

Lovely Latina Devin DeVasquez is an open invitation to senorita fever. Whether her sparking, dark eyes and full, sensual lips have conspired in a smile or a sneer, the result is the same. Blood boils, and blood-pumping organs, such as the heart, throb with a desire to be closer to that heat. With flawless, sky-high, browned buttocks and boobs as thrillingly pronounced as this fast-talking sexpot's Rs, it was predestined that DeVasquez should go clothesless as the designated Playmate for the June 1985 issue of *Playboy*. Also predestined is Devin's dangling and dazzling effectiveness in a string of fully revealing skinematic classics from *Society* (1989) to *Hard Time* (1996). Start with *Guns* (1996), and then try to quit her. You will succumb. It is predestined.

SKIN-fining Moment:

Society (0:37) *Devin's dirigibles are nakedly delectable while she makes incestilicious love with her movie brother.*

See Her Naked In:

A Passion (2001) FFN, Buns
Hard Time (1996) Breasts, Buns
Busted (1996) Breasts, Buns
Guns (1990) FFN, Buns
Society (1989) Breasts
Numerous *Playboy* Videos

Felicity Devonshire

Skin-O-Meter: Great Nudity

Felicity Devonshire burst onto the English sex scene of the early '70s as fresh as the day she was born. In fact, besides being a bit more mature, she has looked just as she did at birth, playing Nude Girl in *The Magnificent Seven Deadly Sins* (1971). Sin is the operative word in describing Felicity's carnal career on camera. She was certainly enjoyed in a progression of pervy

productions such as *Four Dimensions of Greta* (1972), *Secrets of a Door-to-Door Salesman* (1973), and *What's Up Nurse!* (1977). Her time in the public eye, with the public's eye on her pubic, was short and ended with *Sex and the Other Woman* (1979), but what a ride it was. Felicity's name means pleasure, joy, and ecstasy, and she's given men all that and more over her brief exposure.

SKIN-fining Moment:

La Fine dell'Innocenza (0:21) *Bare boobs while talking on the phone in the pool, then luscious full frontal as she emerges and walks over to the breakfast table.*

See Her Naked In:

Sex and the Other Woman (1980) FFN, Buns
What's Up Nurse! (1977) FFN, Buns
Intimate Games (1976) FFN
La Fine dell'innocenza (1975) FFN, Buns
Secrets of a Door-to-Door Salesman (1973) FFN
Four Dimensions of Greta (1972) FFN

Susan Dey

Born: December 10, 1952
Pekin, Illinois
Skin-O-Meter: Great Nudity

In 1970 Susan Dey was only sixteen years old when she auditioned for *The Partridge Family*, won the part, and moved to L.A. The story of the family that plays together made her an overnight sensation, and viewers wanted Susan to play their organ for a one-hit wonder. After the series ended in 1974 and she tried her hand at several made-for-TV movies, Susan decided to shed her "wholesome" girl-next-door image with a few "naughty" parts, which we can all be thankful for. She went topless as the "older woman" in *First Love* (1977), showing off her plump boobies for a nice, long stare. Later

on, she would again show off some skinage in *Looker* (1981), in which she plays some sort of killer model or something. In any case, she shows off both her luscious rack and meaty buns for a fully erotic set piece. Susan got critical kudos for *Echo Park* (1986) and woo-hoos from Mr. Skin for her bustier-busting scene. Sadly, the remainder of her career, much of it spent on TV on series such as *L.A. Law*, *Love & War*, and *Loves Me, Loves Me Not*, has been pretty scarce in the nudity department. Hopefully, Susan will let her skin see the light of Dey again soon.

SKIN-fining Moment:

First Love (0:34) *An incredible lingering look at Dey's Double Bubbles during a game of Hide the Hot Dog with William Katt . . . Come on, get horny!!!*

See Her Naked In:

Echo Park (1986) RB
Looker (1981) Breasts, Buns
First Love (1977) Breasts

Cameron Diaz

Born: August 30, 1972
San Diego, California
Skin-O-Meter: Brief Nudity

Blonde, long-legged, lovely-in-every-way Cameron Diaz has had men longing to taxi down her runway since she took to prowling the catwalk as a model at age fifteen. Her big-time breakthrough came in *The Mask* (1994), opposite rubberface Jim Carrey, and her gorgeous mug has lit up movie screens ever since. Thanks to Cameron's bubbly persona, blue saucer eyes, and miles of glowing white skin, chicks have no trouble dragging their men to flicks such as *My Best Friend's Wedding* (1997) and *The Sweetest Thing* (2002). Cameron's tight bod launched a thousand gallons of . . . hair gel in

There's Something About Mary
(1998). But her tastiest endeavor
to date was in *Vanilla Sky* (2001),
in which Cameron exposed her
creamy flesh to the max and
offered a tasty little nip slip to her
eager viewers. There's also quick
nip slippage during a love scene in
Gangs of New York (2002). Thanks,
Leo!

SKIN-fining Moment:

There's Something About Mary
(0:31) Cameron peels off her shirt and
packs herself into a beautifully too-tight,
pretty-much see-through tank-top in an
open window as Matt Dillon spies from
the street.

See Her Naked In:

Gangs of New York (2002) Nip-Slip RB
Vanilla Sky (2001) Nip-Slip LB

Kim Dickens

Born: June 18, 1965
Huntsville, Alabama
Skin-O-Meter: Great Nudity

It's impossible to look into the
soft, loving eyes and all-American
smile flashing from the face of
blonde daughter of Dixie Kim
Dickens and not think, "Boy, I'd
like to see this honey's rib cakes.
And I'd trade my tractor for a peek
at her bush." Save your machinery,
Billy Bob, and ride it down to the
ol' video store. Order up a copy of
a movie called *Things Beyond the Sun*
(2001). Try to make sure no one is
home when you put it on, because
you are guaranteed to have
company. Kim is as hot as the
dickens in a scene in which she
shares a bed with a pair of dudes
(nothing gay about it; the men are
entirely separated by Kim's naked
body). One of her man friends
takes her by her ankles and makes
like her legs are a wishbone
connected at the crotch. In that
moment, everybody's wishes come
true.

SKIN-fining Moment:

Hollow Man (0:39) Invisible man
Kevin Bacon sneaks a peak and then cops
a feel of Kim's right-side visible mam.

See Her Naked In:

Things Behind the Sun (2001) Breasts, Buns
Hollow Man (2000) RB
Truth or Consequences, N.M. (1998) Breasts
Palookaville (1995) Breasts

TeleVisions:

Out Of Order Breasts, Buns

Angie Dickinson

Born: September 30, 1931
Kulm, North Dakota
Skin-O-Meter: Hall of Fame

Slinky, sultry blonde Angie
Dickinson personified the
sensually swaggering sophisticate
of the swinging 1960s. The brash
and unapologetic blondness. The
full but tight lips, usually lubed
with a pastel shade of lipstick. The
thick, dismissively batting
eyelashes. The casually flaunted
secondary sexual characteristics.
The whip-thin frame. The Rat Pack
connection from having appeared
in the original *Ocean's Eleven*
(1960). The scandalous stripped
sexuality and shadowy breast of
Point Blank (1967). The full-frontal
"fuck you" frolic of *Big Bad Mama*
(1974). And then she ends up best
remembered as Sergeant Pepper
Anderson of *Police Woman*. With a
record like hers, how did Angie

ANGIE DICKINSON, UNDRESSED TO THRILL IN
DRESSED TO KILL.

Dickinson ever become a cop?
Fortunately, after her time on the
force, Dickinson reverted to type,
shedding the plainclothes in
Dressed to Kill (1980) and *Big Bad
Mama II* (1987).

SKIN-fining Moment:

Big Bad Mama (1:18) Angie's Big
Bad Boobs, complete with a flash of fur-
burger after a roll in the hay with
William Shatner. It'll beam you up!

See Her Naked In:

Big Bad Mama II (1987) FFN
Dressed to Kill (1980) Body Double—FFN /
Her—Buns
Big Bad Mama (1974) FFN, Buns
Pretty Maids All in a Row (1971) Buns
Sam Whiskey (1969) RB
Point Blank (1967) Breasts

MR. SKIN'S TOP TEN

**TV Policewomen
Who've Been Naked
. . . Cop a feel**

10. **Callie Thorne**
    —*The Wire*

9. **Paula Trickey**
    —*Pacific Blue*

8. **Teresa Graves**
    —*Get Christie Love*

7. **Melissa Leo**
    —*Homicide: Life on the Street*

6. **Marg Helgenberger**
    —*CSI*

5. **Charlotte Ross**
    —*NYPD Blue*

4. **Elizabeth Berridge**
    —*The John Larroquette Show*

3. **Janet Gunn**
    —*Silk Stalkings*

2. **Kim Delaney**
    —*NYPD Blue*

1. **Angie Dickinson**
    —*Police Woman*

Uschi Digard

Born: August 15, 1948
Bismarck, North Dakota
Skin-O-Meter: Hall of Fame

Brunette wonder bust Uschi Digard is one of the eternal superstars of T&A skinema. Uschi started at the top, debuting her mammoth mounds of mam in the Russ Meyer big-top spectacular *Cherry, Harry and Raquel!* (1969). Throughout the 1970s, the golden decade of drive-in depravity, Uschi pulled out the prize winners in low-rent classic after low-rent classic. On top of those dirigible dependants, Digard had a sly, foxy face with big brown eyes and a slick pair of lips that could just as easily slide into a glowering vixen sneer as tremble in aroused fear or burst out in the winning grin of the goddess next door. Uschi excelled in every sub-niche of the sexploitation genre. She was a dominant attraction in a second Russ Meyer sextravaganza, *Supervixens* (1975). She whimpered and wiggled in distressed-dame pics

such as *She Devils of the SS* (1973), *Ilsa: She Wolf of the SS* (1974), and *Ilsa, Harem Keeper of the Oil Sheiks* (1976). She giggled and groped in goofball comedies that included *If You Don't Stop, You'll Go Blind* (1976) and *Kentucky Fried Movie* (1976).

SKIN-fining Moment:

The Kentucky Fried Movie **(0:09)** *Squooshy Uschi squashes her superhumanly huge milk-stacks smack against the glass shower door.*

See Her Naked In:

Famous T&A (1982) Breasts
The Best of Sex and Violence (1981) Breasts
C.B. Hustlers (1978) FFN, Buns
The Kentucky Fried Movie (1977) Breasts
If You Don't Stop It You'll Go Blind (1976) FFN
Ilsa, Harem Keeper of the Oil Sheiks (1976) FFN
Supervixens (1975) FFN, Buns
The Killer Elite (1975) RB
Ilsa, She Wolf of the S.S. (1974) Breasts
Pleasures of a Woman (1974) FFN, Buns
Truck Stop Women (1974) Breasts, Buns
Superchick (1973) Breasts, Bush, Buns
The Beauties and the Beast (1973) Breasts
She Devils of the SS (1973) FFN, Buns
Up Your Alley (1972) Breasts
Prison Girls (1972) FFN, Buns
The Dirt Gang (1972) Breasts
I, Uschi (1971) FFN, Buns
The Godson (1971) FFN, Buns
Below the Belt (1971) FFN
Roxanna (1970) FFN, Buns
Getting Into Heaven (1970) FFN, Buns
Cherry, Harry and Raquel! (1969) FFN, Buns
Numerous Adult Movies

Victoria Dillard

Born: September 20, 1969
New York, New York
Skin-O-Meter: Great Nudity

Best known for bringing an ongoing tang of "flavah" to the otherwise white-bread hit series *Spin City*, long and lean African American fantasy machine Victoria Dillard has been a force to be marveled over since taking the topless plunge in

Coming to America (1988). Playing a Nubian attendant to a princely Eddie Murphy, shapely Dillard makes a high and firm impression while wearing an elaborate headdress and relying on her organic accoutrements for chest ornamentation. The decorative set is shown to great effect in *Deep Cover* (1992) as Victoria pulls a shirt over her head and unsheaths her darling daggers.

SKIN-fining Moment:

Coming to America **(0:04)** *Victoria emerges topless from beneath the bathtub bubbles to announce that her (dirty) work is done with the classic line: "The royal penis is clean, your majesty!"*

See Her Naked In:

Out of Sync (1995) Breasts
Deep Cover (1992) Breasts
Coming to America (1988) Breasts

Melinda Dillon

Born: October 13, 1939
Hope, Arkansas
Skin-O-Meter: Great Nudity

Streaked blonde Melinda Dillon has a host of attractive qualities. Her sleepy green eyes are comforting soulful windows, and they know passion is the better part of compassion. Her wistful smile is kind, patient, slightly sly, covertly sexy. Her eyebrows and lashes of blonde corn silk are invitations to cozy bedtime nuzzles and butterfly kisses. Melinda would make a great mom to some lucky dad, which is probably why she's been given the maternal role in such family-based hits as *Close Encounters of the Third Kind* (1977), *A Christmas Story* (1983), and *Harry and the Hendersons* (1987). Of course, one essential for mothers is the mammary rack, and Melinda's is top shelf. In fact, as exquisitely displayed by the evocative lighting of a bedroom scene with Paul Newman in *Slap Shot* (1977), Dillon's gentle slope of chest and thick, protruding nipples throw a shadow across all the rest of her attractive qualities.

SKIN-fining Moment:

Slap Shot (0:30) *Awesome view of Melinda's banana boobs as she spends time in bed with Paul Newman.*

See Her Naked In:

Slap Shot (1977) Breasts

Jamie-Lynn DiScala

Born: May 15, 1981
Jericho, New York
Skin-O-Meter: Brief Nudity

Jamie-Lynn DiScala is a nice little Jewish girl of Cuban and Greek derivation who made a big, big name for herself by playing that most Italian of Italian-American young ladies, Meadow Soprano, mob boss Tony Soprano's little girl, on the sensational series *The Sopranos*. New York-born Jamie-Lynn has popped up in only a couple of projects since her debut as, you guessed it, a mobster's daughter in *A Brooklyn State of Mind* (1997), but she's yet to fully serve up her magnificent meatballs or any other dish in her tasty-looking antipasto. The tastiest treat we've received from Jamie so far, in fact, came when she played a criminal herself. In the 2004 made-for-cable movie *Call Me: The Rise & Fall of Heidi Fleiss*, her serious nudity was provided by a body double, but look close at the uncut DVD version and you'll get a peek at Meadow's peaks.

SKIN-fining Moment:

Call Me: The Rise and Fall of Heidi Fleiss (0:06) *Nip-slip as she's dancing in her panties.*

See Her Naked In:

Call Me: The Rise and Fall of Heidi Fleiss (2004) Body Double-Breasts, Buns / Her-Nip Slip LB

Shannen Doherty

Born: April 12, 1971
Memphis, Tennessee
Skin-O-Meter: Brief Nudity

You might be able to spell "bitch" without Shannen Doherty, but she might slap you silly if you tried. This hotheaded hottie is infamous for being a pain in the ass—and what an ass she has. Her debut was threefold, landing a role on the chaste TV drama *Little House on the Prairie*, appearing in the hooker comedy *Night Shift* (1982), and voicing a character in the classic animated feature *The Secret of NIMH* (1982). It wasn't until *Heathers* (1989), as one of the snotty murder victims, that Shannen came into her own. That led to Brenda, the bitch we loved to hate, on the smash Fox soap *Beverly Hills, 90210*. Four years later, the sex symbol's reputation as a snot-nose absentee and Republican got her nearly blacklisted from the business. But the small screen loves dotty Doherty, and she got a part as a sexy witch on the hit series *Charmed* in 1998—then got ousted in 2001 for the same lazy work habits. On cable Shannen truly charmed in the movie *Blindfold: Acts of Obsession* (1993). Be sure to keep both eyes wide open for her hot sex scene that stops just shy of full-frontal fun but gives up her tasty ass and ripe hooters. When bad girls go nude everyone wanks.

SKIN-fining Moment:

Blindfold: Acts of Obsession (0:10) *UNRATED VERSION: Lotsa boobies as Shannen shags with her fella. Some of the nudity in the living room is body-doubled, but it's Doherty's donuts in the shower.*

See Her Naked In:

Blindfold: Acts of Obsession (1993) Breasts

Lexa Doig

Born: June 8, 1973
Toronto, Ontario, Canada
Skin-O-Meter: Great Nudity

She's no bow-wow, Lexa Doig. The Canadian star is not as well known in the U.S. as her native tundra, but she'll throw hungry fans Stateside a bone or two. Her stint on the William Shatner-helmed sci-fi series *TekWar* made her a nerd's wet dream. She went on to play the personification of a starship on another space opera, *Andromeda*—what a ride. But her most skinful performances are on Mother Earth. Don't blink or you'll miss Lexa's rosy nip in a bathtub 'ho down in *The Tracker* (2000). For a more lewdly lingering shot of Lexa's assets, check out *No Alibi* (2000), in which she really gets the Doig on. When she's onscreen, Mr. Skin says Lexa go!

SKIN-fining Moment:

No Alibi (0:16) *Lexa's perky pillows are on full display during this violin-laden moment of lovemaking.*

See Her Naked In:

No Alibi (2000) Breasts
The Tracker (2000) Breasts

Lou Doillon

Born: September 4, 1982
Paris, France
Skin-O-Meter: Great Nudity

This scorching-hot Gallic brunette is frequently percieved to be a stunning strumpet of either Spanish or Italian distillation, but the French are no slouches in breeding raven-haired vixens capable of causing a heart seizure and a smile simultaneously. With her billowing mane of auburn-brown, her passion-fueled face, her tawny complexion, and her sex-ready, power-packed protrusions front and back, pièce-de-résistance Lou Doillon is a prime example of the Parisian firebrand. See lovely Lou sizzle as a model doing a high-impact photo shoot in *Nana* (2001). Cameras seem to make Lou hot. In *Embrassez qui Vous Voudrez* (2002), she plays a lusty Latina who straddles her boyfriend and flings her breasts about as he films the fireworks with a handheld video camera.

SKIN-fining Moment:

Nana (0:37) *Lou tries to cover the clam but a persistent photographer gets her to bare it all.*

See Her Naked In:

Embrassez qui Vous Voudrez (2002) Breasts
Nana (2001) Breasts, Bush
Mamirolle (1999) FFN

Arielle Dombasle

Born: April 27, 1955
Norwich, Connecticut
Skin-O-Meter: Great Nudity

With the bone structure of a delicate, graceful bird, lighter-than-air blonde Arielle Dombasle has soared to the heights as one of the most adored and admired women ever to drop her clothes in Europe-an cinema. Arielle's hazel eyes twinkle in a sensualist's delight; her lips are parted as if for that sudden intake of breath that comes with a first surge of pleasure; her complexion, like freshly fallen warm snow, glows red with the flush of arousal, from the tips of her breasts to the heights of her cheeks. And that's just when the delicious Dombasle is eating her cereal. For an intimate look at Arielle as a lovely love-maker making lovely love, linger over the bedtime scenes

of *Pauline at the Beach* (1983). Her sinuous gyrations and pink-tipped titties will create an appetite for more, a desire amply satisfied by the depth of Arielle's clothing-optional catalog. Perhaps because she is American at heart, Dombasle has never shown the bushy parts her European counterparts are so happy to toss around.

SKIN-fining Moment:

Les Fruits de la Passion (0:45) *Kinski dips his weinerschnitzel into Arielle while a completely naked Isabelle Illiers keeps watch.*

See Her Naked In:

Le Jour et la Nuit (1997) FFN, Buns
Les 2 Papas et la Maman (1996) Breasts
The Boss' Wife (1986) Breasts
Pauline at the Beach (1983) Breasts
Les Fruits de la Passion (1981) FFN
Numerous Adult Movies

TeleVisions:

Red Shoe Diaries Breasts, Bush, Buns

Marika Dominczyk

Born: July 7, 1980
Kielce, Poland
Skin-O-Meter: Brief Nudity

Towering, sensual, and packing a body as hard as her last name is to pronounce, dark-maned temptress Marika Dominczyk may well turn out to be the Teri Copley of the early twenty-first century. By this, I mean that not since Ms. Copley's delectable domestic of the short-lived (but never-forgotten) NBC sitcom *We Got It Maid* has a house-hold custodian ignited the boob tube as brilliantly as Marika does on the 2004-launched WB laffer *The Help*. Prior to her wanton ways with a feather duster on the fifth network, Marika showed skin in the 2001 flick *3 A.M.*, which, once witnessed, will keep you up well past that titular wee hour. With

Help like Marika, cleaning has never seemed so dirty.

SKIN-fining Moment:

3 A.M. (0:07) *Marika massages her man, mounts his meat, then drops to all fours for some doggie-style dorking. Somehow, all we see is side-skin.*

See Her Naked In:

3 A.M. (2001) RB

Camille Donatacci

Born: September 2, 1968
Newport Beach, California
Skin-O-Meter: Great Nudity

A leading blonde of the platinum-bombshell variety, long-legged Camille Donatacci is an actress with an entirely enticing list of credits. Armed with the knowledge that long, lean legs often lead up to elevated, compact chair cushions, what informed skinvestigator could resist a skinspection of Donatacci titles such as *Marilyn Chambers' Bedtime Stories* (1993), *The Naked Detective* (1996), or *Private Parts* (1997)? Camille is least revealed in *Parts*, standing shivering in the snow with her high-riding chest orbs holstered in a skimpy bikini top. The best clues to Camille's carnality are to be found in *Detective*. She plays a take-charge sexual athlete who uses bush, boobs, and buns to score a classic three-point play.

SKIN-fining Moment:

Marilyn Chambers' Bedtime Stories (0:34) *Camille shows her naked Dona-topsy and Dona-tushy while slipping into lingerie. You won't need a Frasier crane to get it up after you watch this!!!*

See Her Naked In:

The Naked Detective (1996) FFN, Buns
Marilyn Chambers' Bedtime Stories (1993)
   Breasts, Buns

Lisa Donatz

Born: October 1, 1980
Redondo Beach, California
Skin-O-Meter: Brief Nudity

Perhaps the skin-seeker has been scanning the red carpet at award shows and movie premieres, looking for a squeeze of unguarded cleavage, and the roving eye is stopped by the lecherous grin of MTV comedian Andy Dick. It's not Dick exactly that catches the eye. The sight to be seen is the blonde at his side. Sweet, young, precious, and smiling like the sunshine of love, this darling spins to show off her tight butt and budding profile up top. "Who is she?" wonders the skinvestigator. "Why is she monopolized by Andy Dick? Why can I not see more of her?" There is no need for consternation, not when *Old School* (2003) is only a video store away. See Lisa magically change herself into a pair of glazed donatz after a titties-out bout of KY wrestling with toothsome brunette Corrine Kingsbury. Should we thank Andy for allowing Lisa to show her secret chest delights or condemn him for keeping the bush and buns to himself?

SKIN-fining Moment:

Old School (1:00) *Cute blonde Lisa Donatz shows her glazed donate alongside topless brunette Corine Kingsbury in a KY jelly wrestling match.*

See Her Naked In:

Old School (2003) Breasts

Patrice Donnelly

Skin-O-Meter: Brief Nudity

Good looks can be an androgynous quality, such as in the sculpted, clear angles in the face of actress Patrice Donnelly. Is the athletically lean brunette so handsome in a womanly way that she actually exhibits a feminine prettiness beneath her butch exterior? Or does her intrinsic female comeliness shine through despite years of devoting herself to sportsmanlike pursuits? The debate is rendered moot by Donnelly's clothes-doffing, lesbianic workout in *Personal Best* (1982), a saga of female Olympic hopefuls training for some sort of special nude competition. Join the jockless jocks in the steam room. Pretty, buff Patrice cracks a quick split of beav as the all-nude centerpiece in a clutch of athletic naked chicks lounging in the sheen of a steam bath. Look for full muff in the mist.

SKIN-fining Moment:

Personal Best (0:33) *Full-frontal fun in the sauna with Patrice and a furry flock of her fellow female track athletes.*

See Her Naked In:

The Celluloid Closet (1996) Breasts, Buns
Personal Best (1982) FFN, Buns

Amanda Donohoe

Born: June 29, 1962
London, England, UK
Skin-O-Meter: Great Nudity

Amanda Donohoe is a girl's girl. From her stint as the lesbo on the hit TV series *L.A. Law* to *The Rainbow* (1989), in which she and Sammi Davis-Voss show off their juniors and everything else as Sapphic suck sisters, Amanda never met a chick she couldn't do. But even more than licking labia, Amanda loves to show off her five-foot-eight-inch, boobalicious bod. She's adorned her slender form with a wooden dildo as the Snake Goddess in kinky Ken Russell's *The Lair of the White Worm* (1988) and *Castaway* (1986) her clothing for this nudes-on-a-beach epic. As Amanda has matured, she hasn't lost any of her juvenile joy of skin. By the dawning of the new millennium, the thirty-eight-year-old sizzler was letting those scalding cupfuls overflow in *The Atlantis Conspiracy* (2000). No covert operation with Amanda, what you see is what you get—and you get a lot!

SKIN-fining Moment:

The Lair of the White Worm (1:22) *Amanda toplessly approaches tied-up Catherine Oxenberg with a large, wooden strap-on. Splinters!*

See Her Naked In:

The Atlantis Conspiracy (2000) RB
Hooded Angels (2000) Breasts
Paper Mask (1991) Breasts
Dark Obsession (1989) Breasts, Bush
The Rainbow (1989) FFN, Buns
The Lair of the White Worm (1988) FFN, Buns
An Affair in Mind (1988) Breasts
Castaway (1987) FFN, Buns
Foreign Body (1986) Breasts

Alison Doody

Born: 1965
Dublin, Ireland
Skin-O-Meter: Brief Nudity

Irish eyes must be crying every time delectable Dublin damsel Alison Doody leaves the emerald isle to come ply her trade in America. Alison is a professional heartbreaker, and she does so on a grand scale, causing mass infatuation and widespread frustration as the completely sexy but fully clothed wily females Jenny Flex in *A View to a Kill* (1985) and Dr. Elsa Schneider in *Indiana Jones and the Last Crusade* (1989). A blonde of the naturally stunning style, with a mouth that a man's mind could melt in, the Doody boody has been glimpsed only for the briefest moment, and that was from across the room in *Taffin* (1988). Don't look away when IRA bad man Pierce Brosnan puts the moves on Alison. The nip is on the way.

SKIN-fining Moment:

Taffin (0:14) Pierre Brosnan rips off Alison's shirt and we get a glimpse of her right-side Doody-booby.

See Her Naked In:

Taffin (1988) RB

Françoise Dorléac

**Born: March 21, 1942
Paris, France
Died: June 26, 1967
Skin-O-Meter: Brief Nudity**

France in the 1960s loomed brilliantly as the land of towering eyefuls. Among the most glowing Gallic beauties, of course, was Catherine Deneuve, whose greatness may have cast an unfair shadow actress Françoise Dorléac. Doe-eyed, dark-maned Françoise remains unforgettable to all who witness the way she injects Roman Polanski's black-and-white masterpiece *Cul-de-sac* (1966) with a searing palette of sexual possibilities. Alas, this Paris-born pastry may forever be overpowered by her natural status as Catherine Deneuve's older (and less skinfully prolific) sister. Nonetheless, Françoise is to be saluted for her own unique presence, explosively applied to *Cul-de-sac* via a haunting performance and groundbreaking shots of her beauteus gluteus and impossibly pert bon-bons. Here's to sibling ribaldry.

SKIN-fining Moment:

Cul-de-sac (0:40) Françoise emerges from bed and we get very sexy, black-and-white views of first her cul-de-seat and then her cul-de-sacks as she strolls into another room and puts on a robe.

See Her Naked In:

Cul-de-sac (1966) Breasts, Buns

Sarah Douglas

**Born: December 12, 1952
Stratford-on-Avon, Warwickshire, England, UK
Skin-O-Meter: Brief Nudity**

Men, even the most butch of us, even tough characters so hard and indomitable that they are raised to mythological, cartoon-book status, are susceptible to the wiles of certain members of the female gender. If her male-bashing performances as the hot and sultry anti-heroines in *Superman* (1978), *Superman II* (1980), and *Conan the Destroyer* (1984) are any indication, British-bred brunette Sarah Douglas's enticing wiles are no match for a mere mortal male. This is a lesson learned the hard way by the bonehead husband who dares to smack around (and briefly bare) Sarah's battered-but-not-beaten character in *The Brute* (1973).

SKIN-fining Moment:

The Brute (0:08) Sarah scrubs her naked Dougl-ass in the shower.

See Her Naked In:

The Brute (1973) Breasts, Buns

Robyn Douglass

**Born: June 21, 1953
Sendai, Japan
Skin-O-Meter: Brief Nudity**

A spunky brunette whose amber eyes sparkle with mischief and delight, adorable hug kitten Robyn Douglass deserved to make a bigger impression on the mass skinconsciousness than she ever did. After having strutted and preened through such second-tier productions as the TV movies *The Clone Master* (1978) and *The Girls in the Office* (1979) and the series *Galactica 1980*, Robyn seemed poised to make her move. She

landed a small but revealing part in *Partners* (1982), a cop-buddy comedy/drama, which led to playing Steve Martin's girlfriend in *The Lonely Guy* (1983). Robyn's tawny, smooth boobs and rose-petal nipples are fully shining through the flimsy fabric of see-through lingerie when Steve's character comes home to catch her in bed with another man. Sad for Robyn, nobody likes a cheat.

SKIN-fining Moment:

Partners (1:00) Robin shows her non-red-breasts sliding between the sheets with Ryan O'Neal.

See Her Naked In:

The Lonely Guy (1983) Breasts
Partners (1982) Breasts

Lesley-Anne Down

**Born: March 17, 1954
London, England, UK
Skin-O-Meter: Great Nudity**

Lesley-Anne Down, merely a decade into her young life, made a splash as a professional model and developed in stature—and structure—as her beauty blossomed before the camera's eye. The engaging Englishwoman stormed the silver screen in her native Britain by her mid-teens, with provocative titles such as *School for Unclaimed Girls* (1969), *All the Right Noises* (1969)—moan, moan—and *Countess Dracula* (1970), which raised Mr. Skin's stake. But it was on TV that Lesley-Anne got down, first with *To Lay a Ghost* (1971) and most famously in *Upstairs, Downstairs* (1971). To see Lesley-Anne's upstairs you have to wait a few years. In *The Betsy* (1978), there's a quick glimpse of her hooter handfuls in a rollicking sex scene. Then in *Hanover Street* (1979), Lesley-Anne strips out of her silky top. But her downstairs has been off limits. And with her reign as the queen of the mini-series, it's unlikely she'll be letting us down there for a view. That brings Mr. Skin down.

SKIN-fining Moment:

The Betsy (0:40) *Lesley-Anne bares about an inch of ass-crack and a fleeting flash of itty-bitty as she meets up with Tommy Lee Jones for a No-Tell Motel tryst.*

See Her Naked In:

Hanover Street (1979) Breasts
The One and Only Phyllis Dixie (1978) Breasts, Buns
The Betsy (1978) LB, Buns
The Pink Panther Strikes Again (1976) RB

Gabrielle Drake

Born: March 30, 1944
Lahore, Pakistan
Skin-O-Meter: Great Nudity

Born in Pakistan and based primarily in London, England, unusually pretty brunette Gabrielle Drake exudes a sultry reserve that is at once high class and down and dirty. Gabrielle's uncommonly wide eyes, lips plush beyond the norm, and otherworldly placidity of expression cause her to seem almost doll-like or extraterrestrial in her comely perfection. This vaguely alien allure accounts for dreamy Drake's successful and hypnotic portrayal of Lieutenant Gay Ellis on the English sci-fi series *UFO*. Gabrielle was able to combine comedy with comeliness in the Peter Sellers absurdity *There's a Girl in My Soup* (1970). In a lapse into logical behavior, Sellers drools over the taunting nipples of Gabrielle, and we the audience salivate along with him.

SKIN-fining Moment:

There's a Girl in My Soup (0:10) *Gabrielle gives a few glimpses of her left globe in bed with Peter Sellers.*

See Her Naked In:

Au Pair Girls (1972) FFN, Buns
Connecting Rooms (1972) Breasts
There's a Girl in My Soup (1970) LB

Michele Drake

Born: February 7, 1958
La Jolla, California
Skin-O-Meter: Brief Nudity

When The Beach Boys sang about wishing all the little darlings could be California girls, they were no doubt dreaming of an angelic surfside vision very much like Michele Drake. A beachfront babe with a peachy front of her own, delicious Drake hails from the seaside Southern California town of La Jolla, a Spanish name that translates to "next stop Bunnyland." Michele quite naturally made the hop and skip to *Playboy*, providing that esteemed journal of epidermal study with its May 1979 Playmate. The skinematic highlight of Drake's short-lived but eternal film career was her depiction of a cheerleader who forgot to wear panties in *Hollywood Knights* (1980), baring the whole below-the-waist bundle, from butt to mons veneris. Michele returned to her sun-kissed roots in *American Gigolo* (1980), sunning the twins on a beach-side deck.

SKIN-fining Moment:

The Hollywood Knights (0:28) *Rah-rah-raw-rump! Pom pom girl Michele puts the peep in her high school pep rally by launching into a cheerleading routine with no panties under her varsity-striped skirt. Those bouncing bare buns should earn Michele the title of "head cheekleader."*

See Her Naked In:

American Gigolo (1980) RB
The Hollywood Knights (1980) Bush, Buns

Fran Drescher

Born: September 30, 1957
Flushing, New York
Skin-O-Meter: Brief Nudity

Fran Drescher has an earthy sensuality that permeates her entire being but seems to be localized in her wide, often-grinning libertine's mouth and her wide, all-enveloping, ass-man's dream of a rear end. She also boasts a pair of eyes that are a perpetual sexual taunt. The loud and loquacious comedienne honed her chops in bit parts that generally required her to squeeze into a form-fitting skirt and twist and turn her buttock profile to such grand effect that her foghorn voice often went unnoticed. Though Fran as a whole has been most visible running a dysfunctional household as TV's *The Nanny*, she's been best viewed as a seconds-only flash of nip from beneath a tossing bed sheet in *Cadillac Man* (1990).

SKIN-fining Moment:

Cadillac Man (0:07) *The Queen of Queens is topless in bed next to Robin Williams and we get a few looks at her right-side Nanny-knob.*

See Her Naked In:

Cadillac Man (1990) RB

Griffin Drew

Born: August 18, 1968
Hazelhurst, Georgia
Skin-O-Meter: Hall of Fame

Shyness is not a quality to be listed on the resumé of clothing-optional screen star Griffin Drew. The curvy blonde stunner has a fuzzy box and she knows how to use it. Seldom is so much seen of one B-screen queen. In upwards of forty finely lit, crisply focused softcore sex flicks, Griffin exhibits everything except restraint. Her breasts are solid as real estate and twice as attractive as an investment of time.

Her sleek, slim-lined buttocks are beauties to behold, whether standing and flexed, rising from bed, squatting for inspection, or bent over a barrel and poised in perfection. With so many carnal relations in her credentials, finding a hot view of Griffin Drew is no more difficult than locating her name on a video box.

SKIN-fining Moment:

Friend of the Family (0:44) *Griffin leztastically steams up a bubble bath with Shauna O'Brien. Breasts, buns, bush, fingers, tongues, the works!*

See Her Naked In:

Erotic Obsessions (2002) FFN, Buns
Sinful Temptations (2001) FFN
Carnal Sins (2001) FFN, Buns
The Bare Wench Project 2: Scared Topless (2001) FFN, Buns
Erotic Possessions (2000) FFN
Emmanuelle 2000: Being Emmanuelle (2000) FFN, Buns
Burning Desires (2000) FFN
Phantom Love (2000) FFN, Buns
Andromina: The Pleasure Planet (2000) FFN
The Mistress Club (1999) Breasts
Ancient Desires (1999) FFN, Buns
Scandal: On the Other Side (1999) FFN
Sensual Friends (1999) FFN
Recoil (1997) Breasts
Bikini Hoe Down (1997) FFN, Buns
Kounterfeit (1996) Thong
Dinosaur Valley Girls (1996) Breasts
Subliminal Seduction (1996) Breasts, Thong
Masseuse (1996) Breasts, Buns
Busted (1996) Breasts, Buns
Midnight Tease II (1995) Breasts, Thong
Friend of the Family (1995) FFN, Buns
Indecent Behavior 3 (1995) FFN
Over the Wire (1995) FFN
Forbidden Games (1995) Breasts
Sinful Intrigue (1995) FFN, Buns
Dinosaur Island (1994) Breasts, Buns

TeleVisions:

Erotic Confessions FFN, Buns
Intimate Sessions Breasts

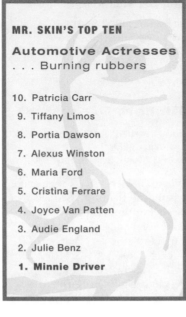

MR. SKIN'S TOP TEN

Automotive Actresses
. . . Burning rubbers

10. Patricia Carr
9. Tiffany Limos
8. Portia Dawson
7. Alexus Winston
6. Maria Ford
5. Cristina Ferrare
4. Joyce Van Patten
3. Audie England
2. Julie Benz
1. **Minnie Driver**

Minnie Driver

Born: January 31, 1970
London, England, UK
Skin-O-Meter: Great Nudity

Exotic Brit Minnie Driver grew up in Barbados and attended finishing schools in Paris and Grenoble. She looks done to me! Minnie worked as a jazz singer and guitarist all over London, but it wasn't long before she decided to scat her scales on camera. A not-so-mini Minnie packed on the pounds for her plump turn in *Circle of Friends* (1995), in which she tried to win the affections of the always strapping boy wonder Chris O'Donnell, who fell out of his Irish accent almost as much as Minnie fell out of her period costume. Minnie dieted down to her sexpot fighting weight to become a luscious Bond lady in *GoldenEye* (1995). She next starred opposite John Cusack in *Grosse Point Blank* (1997), which proved once and for all that hitmen are funny too—especially if they're titmen. Minnie brought a safe-yet-sexy sensuality to her blonde,

American-dream girl in *Big Night* (1997), but her biggest breakthrough role was as boy-genius Matt Damon's arm candy in *Good Will Hunting* (1997). Who wouldn't want to eat caramels with this curly-maned cutie?

SKIN-fining Moment:

Mr. Wroe's Virgins mini-series (1993) *Minnie goes to the max, peeling off her nightie for Jonathan Pryce and standing full frontal before the world. She should change her name to Muffy Diver!*

See Her Naked In:

The Governess (1998) Body Double—Buns / Her—LB
Cruel Train (BBC-TV) (1995) Breasts

TeleVisions:

Mr. Wroe's Virgins FFN

Caroline Ducey

Born: 1977
Paris, France
Skin-O-Meter: Great Nudity

Ooh, là-là!, the French can raise Mr. Skin's Eiffel Tower. Not only are the women hot as melted Brie cheese, but they're kinkier than a corkscrew. While Caroline Ducey launched her career in the comedy *Trop de Bonheur* (1994), the sweet French pastry, a shy-looking skinny brunette with teaspoon tits, shocked even the sexually jaded Parisians with her unabashed performance in *Romance* (1999). When her boyfriend refuses to have sex with Caroline, she takes her pussy out for a walk—and you should see what the cat drags in. From anonymous street schtups and bizarre bondage to full-penetration oral fixations, Caroline was shameless in her pursuit of perversion. Needless to add, every inch of her tight body is exposed and often probed. While it's hard to top such over-the-top hotness,

Caroline did try with *La Chambre Obscure* (2000). Her lovely lithe body and darkly tangled French garden give audiences an eyeful as she rolls out of bed. But *Romance* remains Ducey's doozy.

SKIN-fining Moment:

Romance (1:21) *A long look at Ducey's spread-eagled thatch as a series of curious gynecologists check her temperature.*

See Her Naked In:

Three Step Dancing (2003) LB
La Cage (2002) Breasts
La Chambre Obscure (2000) Breasts, Bush, Buns
Romance (1999) FFN, Buns

Denice Duff

New York, New York
Skin-O-Meter: Great Nudity

With her impish come-on grin, bold and teasing eyes, a streaky brunette mane that seems to have never fully tossed off the effects of vigorous bedtime activity, and a body that is toned and limber as if from extensive exercising in that same silk-sheeted environment, who would ever think of looking for delightful Denice Duff's special sparkle in a movie called *Meet Me at the Dog Bar* (1990)? And yet, said film marked Denice's cinematic debut. Perhaps the unlikelihood of a fox of Duff's caliber being found in a dog joint is why her initial foray went largely unnoticed. Eyes were widely opened, however, when Duff in the buff bounced back in such blood-and-boobs fare as *Warlords 3000* (1992) and *Vampire Resurrection* (2001). Think Denice's naked charms are being exploited? As well as baring her sweet vampire buns in *Vampire Resurrection*, she was also the movie's director.

SKIN-fining Moment:

Warlords 3000 (0:50) *Denice doffs her top to make it with a Mad-Max-type.*

See Her Naked In:

Vampire Resurrection (2001) RB, Thong
Phoenix (1998) Breasts
Bloodstone: Subspecies II (1993) Breasts
Warlords 3000 (1992) Breasts

TeleVisions:

Dream On Breasts

Patty Duffek

Born: August 27, 1963
Woodland Hills, California
Skin-O-Meter: Great Nudity

The Southern California suburbs that sprawl out from the hub of Los Angeles are blessed with a wealth of natural resources, the richest among them being the enormous God-crafted chest appendages of Patty Duffek. Patty and her plentiful cakes are natives of Woodland Hills, an outlying bedroom community where Bunnies are known to hop through the hillocks and glades. It came as no surprise, then, that Patty's super stack should bounce into prominence as the May 1984 Playmate in that magazine most favored by randy rabbits, *Playboy*. Next came a three-film career as an action hero among a team of gorgeous lady crime fighters. The good gals always win in *Hard Ticket to Hawaii* (1987), *Savage Beach* (1989), and *Picasso Trigger* (1989). And viewers always win too, because the ladies do their crime fighting naked.

SKIN-fining Moment:

Picasso Trigger (1:05) *Patty's perfect pair float to the surface in a steamy Jacuzzi.*

See Her Naked In:

Savage Beach (1989) Breasts
Picasso Trigger (1989) Breasts, Buns

Hard Ticket to Hawaii (1987) Breasts
Numerous *Playboy* Videos

Julia Duffy

Born: June 27, 1951
Minneapolis, Minnesota
Skin-O-Meter: Brief Nudity

For thirty years, pert and pretty Julia Duffy has been one of the cutest blonde temptations on TV. Capable of playing a fluffy bunny of love or a scheming vixen, Duffy's versatility and clean, high-cheeked features have helped her survive and thrive in small-screen projects as diverse as *One Life to Live*, *Baby Talk*, and *Social Studies*. Her most enduring creation is the prudish blonde killjoy Stephanie Vanderkellen on the long-running yuck-fest *Newhart*. Julia's forays into big-screen work are less well known but more revealing, although not fully so. In *Wacko* (1981), Julia pulls up her dress to show a long expanse of pearly white flank, broken only by a skimpy pantie line. She also shows whiter than bright arms and legs as she lay on a parade ground with her hands and feet attached to opposing lawnmowers. What's really wacko is that more does not meet the eye.

SKIN-fining Moment:

Night Warning (0:45) *A few sweet moments with Julia's jiggly jewels as she relaxes in bed, prepares for a screw, and then gets called a "slut" by Jimmy McNichol's pissed-off mama.*

See Her Naked In:

Night Warning (1981) Breasts

Karen Duffy

Born: May 23, 1961
New York, New York
Skin-O-Meter: Never Nude

A reigning glamour queen of the 1990s, long drink of brunette beauty Karen Duffy was an iconic omnipresence in her prime, holding down high-profile positions as an MTV yakker and spokesmodel for Revlon cosmetics, as well as doing simmering star turns in such generation-defining films as *Reality Bites* (1993) and *Dumb and Dumber* (1994). Then what would have been tragedy to a lesser light struck. Duffy was diagnosed with sarcoidosis of the central nervous system, a degenerative disease that caused lesions to grow in her brain and left the stunning world beater partially paralyzed. Duffy refused to lie down and suffer in obscurity. She released a book revealing her ordeal, *Model Patient: My Life as an Incurable Wise-Ass*, and dedicated her life to being an inspiration for fellow sufferers.

SKIN-fining Moment:

Memory Run (0:10) Duff does it with a dude and somebody's seat and side-boobs flash on the screen. No face equals Body Double. These things happen.

See Her Naked In:

Memory Run (1996) Body Double-Buns, LB

Olympia Dukakis

Born: June 21, 1931
Lowell, Massachusetts
Skin-O-Meter: Brief Nudity

It's always a good sign to be dating a girl who has a hot mom. If you're serious about spending any extended time—as in the years leading up to and including the rest of your life—with a female who has graduated from being a hot date to a pleasant companion who is also a hot bed mate, the mother is key. If the mom is still hot, chances are your girl is not merely going through a hot phase that is biologically programmed within her for the purposes of snaring a mate. Chances are, she will remain hot for as long as you want her to. Any male with any questions about what to look for in a hot mother should consult the template set out by Olympia Dukakis's performance as Cher's ma in *Moonstruck* (1987). Olympia's passionate, spicy delivery would win her an Academy Award, which is more than her most-famous relation, former presidential candidate Michael Dukakis, would ever take home.

SKIN-fining Moment:

Over the Hill (0:56) Topless Dukakis gets her Mount Olympias painted while prepping for a tribal dance (probably not a fertility ritual).

See Her Naked In:

Over the Hill (1992) Breasts

Patty Duke

Born: December 14, 1946
Manhattan, New York
Skin-O-Meter: Brief Nudity

The Patty Duke Show was as wholesome as anything in the early '60s, but many young men had fantasies of gleesome threesomes with Patty Duke in her dual role as identical cousins. Already an Oscar winner for *The Miracle Worker* (1962), Patty went on to one of the (literally) craziest careers in Hollywood. She fixed her clean-cut image with some sexy scenes—and a great catfight—in *Valley of the Dolls* (1967). This was followed by multiple marriages and extreme behavior, later explained by a 1982 diagnosis of manic depression. She's also kept working as an actress and activist in TV and film, even combining the two while showing her breasts in the lesbian adoption saga *By Design* (1982). Strangely, however, there aren't many lesbo love scenes, even though the film is about two lesbians trying to have a baby.

SKIN-fining Moment:

By Design (1:05) Patty pops out her identical chest-cousins in bed.

See Her Naked In:

By Design (1982) Breasts

Hayley DuMond

Born: July 12, 1978
Anchorage, Alaska
Skin-O-Meter: Great Nudity

Anchorage, Alaska, is not often thought of as a hotbed for hotties, but the ascension of white-hot Hayley DuMond should change all that. Pale from toe to tit, her taut skin the color of a bone bleached by endless hours of exposure to the midnight sun, Hayley's ethereal form first wafted into view on a 1998 episode of *Sliders*. The show raised the question, "Why can this pale vision not be seen in all her naked glory, resulting in bare butt, a flash of bush, and an exciting flaunting of those chesty tidbits?" The very next year, the answer arrived in *The Hunter's Moon* (1999).

SKIN-fining Moment:

The Hunter's Moon (0:06) Fully frontal skin as Hayley gets nude to soak in the sun and lounge in a lake.

See Her Naked In:

The Hunter's Moon (1999) FFN, Buns

Faye Dunaway

Born: January 14, 1941
Bascom, Florida
Skin-O-Meter: Great Nudity

Fair southern belle Faye Dunaway blew audiences away as the gun moll in the low-budget surprise hit *Bonnie and Clyde* (1967). The five-foot-seven-inch blonde stunner stripped down to her panties but only gave a teasing glance at her back. Her skin debut was in *The Arrangement* (1969), with a flash of her bum. She followed that up with the mother of messed-up broads in the incestuous *Chinatown* (1974), in which Jack Nicholson fondles her petite pair. And she lets William Holden in *Network* (1976). It wasn't until *Barfly* (1987), as a soused slut, that her nips peeked out again. It's been some time since Faye fanned Mr. Skin's manhood. Hopefully, she hasn't Dunaway with skin.

SKIN-fining Moment:

Network (1:13) *A brief-yet-memorable moment with Faye's flopping friends as she hurriedly gets naked for Bill Holden.*

See Her Naked In:

Barfly (1987) Breasts
Network (1976) Breasts
Chinatown (1974) RB
The Arrangement (1969) Buns

Alison Dunbar

Skin-O-Meter: Great Nudity

Fame may be fickle, fleeting, and eternally out of grasp, but a clear and lingering rack shot, even in a little-seen flick such as *Time of Her Time* (1999), will endure unto eternity. Funny, firm of fanny, full chested, and fetching with a fox-like, forward face, Alison Dunbar may be most commonly remembered as the aptly named Hedda Hummer on the short-lived and widely bereaved Comedy Central flesh-trade send-up *Strip Mall*. Dunbar makes a much more focused impression in *Time of Her Time* as the spectacle-sporting sport-baller who lounges on her back as her tantalizing twins jump out toward the camera and etch themselves forever in the memory of all who witness their vibrant presence.

SKIN-fining Moment

Time of Her Time (0:23) *Alison's perky pair appear as she addresses her guy.*

See Her Naked In:

Time of Her Time (1999) Breasts

FORBIDDEN WORLD: HEY, WHO LET THE MONSTER OUT OF MY PANTS? HE'S ABOUT TO DUNLAP DAWN! THIS POSTER IS A PRIME EXAMPLE OF EARLY '80S EXPLOITATION AT ITS MOST SKIN-MAGINATIVE.

Dawn Dunlap

Born: 1962
Austin, Texas
Skin-O-Meter: Great Nudity

A satin-skinned brunette with glittering green eyes and a soft pink croissant of a mouth set in a tender, round face, Dawn Dunlap is a study in innocence and experience. Though an American from Texas, Dawn made her film debut in the sensual French study *Laura, les Ombres de l'Été* (1979). Standing naked, Dawn is the essence of youth, her expression brimming with expectant innocence, hair as light as down, puffy lips pouting with the softness of a child, chest heaving with the billowy breasts of a teenager, which is what she was. Three years later, in the Roger Corman sci-fi and skin sextravaganza *Forbidden World* (1982), Dunlap's butt flaps retain only the merest hint of baby flesh. Her face is a canvas of adult emotion, the lips parted in grown-

up excitation. Her bush has grown in and been trimmed in an artful, tidy triangle. Her tits have filled out. The innocence is gone. Dawn is all woman from here on out.

SKIN-fining Moment:

Laura, les Ombres de l'Été (1:15) *Dawn offers her ultra-fine little body to a sculptor, whose roaming hands get her sexed up. Boobs and buns.*

See Her Naked In:

Barbarian Queen (1985) Breasts
Heartbreaker (1983) Breasts
Forbidden World (1982) FFN, Buns
Laura, les Ombres de l'Été (1979) FFN, Buns

"I just heard that this young actress who's pretty well-known got a boob job. I guess it works for some people, but my boobs are fine! They go with my body!"

—KIRSTEN DUNST

Kirsten Dunst

Born: April 30, 1982
Point Pleasant, New Jersey
Skin-O-Meter: Never Nude

Naturally blonde charm machine Kirsten Dunst warmed to the camera early as a child model for the world-famous Ford Agency. Then Tinseltown beckoned. She blossomed into instant stardom with her eerie turn in *Interview with the Vampire* (1994), in which she embodies a bloodsucker who's been trapped in the body of a pre-pubescent vampire for centuries. Since then, Kirsten has grown up— and spectacularly out—in a progressively popular (and progressively sexy) series of hits such as *Little Women* (1994), *Wag the Dog* (1998), *Drop Dead Gorgeous* (1999), and the gut busting *Dick* (1999), in which Kirsten and Michelle Williams exhibit teenage curves that would be worth getting impeached over. *Bring It On* (2000) put Kirsten immediately in the pom-pom pantheon of all-time great movie cheerleaders, while *Get Over It* (2001) solidified her as a bikini bombshell, as she cavorts poolside with Mila Kunis in itsy-bitsy swimwear. Her sopping-wet red dress and resulting prodigious pokies were also the greatest visual effects in *Spider-Man* (2002).

SKIN-fining Moment:

Spider-Man (1:20:) *During some extremely nipply weather, sopping wet Kirsten's perfectly pointed pair of pokies protrude prodigiously from her red dress as she leans in to suck some face with Mr. Web-Slinger.*

Erica Durance

Skin-O-Meter: Great Nudity

Horrowing and heavenly feral brown eyes, fine-honed cheek bones, and a perpetually pursed mouth, with two kissable lips forever containing the secret of whether the nectar-sweet tongue within has just finished licking them or is poised and ready to do so, this is the face of Erica Durance. Erica's is a visage fit for a man of steel, one capable of leaping tall bedposts and rushing to her embrace with the speed of a flying bullet, there to thrust with the power of a steaming locomotive. No wonder then that young Clark Kent's penetrating *Smallville* gaze feasts its fill on the fleshy form of Erica Durance as the young Lois Lane.

SKIN-fining Moment:

House of the Dead (0:10) *Beachy babe Erica strips down to her G-string and frolics in the surf. Tits overboard!*

See Her Naked In:

House of the Dead (2003) Breasts, Thong

Ann Dusenberry

Born: September 13, 1953
Tucson, Arizona
Skin-O-Meter: Great Nudity

Blasting in from Tucson, Arizona, like a pink-skinned, doe-eyed tornado, Ann Dusenberry and her face of unfazed blondness took Hollywood by storm at the end of the 1970s. After having been scared out of her wits by a big white shark in *Jaws 2* (1978), it was only a small step for Ann to fish out her tits in a string of memorable 1980s feature films. Ann's first flaunt of teat came in *Heart Beat* (1980), and she hit a skinful stride—more like a nude strut—the very next year in *National Lampoon Goes to the Movies* (1981). Young, lingerie heightened, chest exposed from neck to belly, Dusenberry indulges in a lounging game of couch ball that will satisfy amateur sofa athletes at home.

SKIN-fining Moment:

Heart Beat (0:41) *Full frontal nudity frolicking in the tub with Nick Nolte.*

See Her Naked In:

The Men's Club (1986) Breasts
Basic Training (1985) Breasts
Lies (1983) Breasts
National Lampoon Goes to the Movies (1981) Breasts, Buns
Heart Beat (1980) FFN

Eliza Dushku

Born: December 30, 1980
Boston, Massachusetts
Skin-O-Meter: Never Nude

Discovered as part of a talent search for the "perfect" girl to play opposite Juliette Lewis in the film *That Night* (1992), eagerly aggressive Eliza Dushku broke into the business at the tender age of twelve. A handful of notable roles in high-profile projects—opposite Robert De Niro and Leonardo

DiCaprio in *This Boy's Life* (1993) and Arnold Schwarzenegger in *True Lies* (1994)—yielded five years of teen TV titillation as the vampire-vanquishing Faith on the wildly popular series *Buffy the Vampire Slayer*. But it's Eliza's later film work that caught the attention of those not tuned into the teen-tube titles, though her roles have been sadly skin shy. But the temptation and teasing remained high for her slinky starring roles in such varied pop projects as the cheerleader opus *Bring It On* (2000), the teen horror knock-off *Soul Survivors* (2001), and the comedies *Jay and Silent Bob Strike Back* (2001) and *The New Guy* (2002), the latter of which featured an eye-opening montage of Eliza trying on a bunch of bikinis for her latest beau.

SKIN-fining Moment:

The New Guy (0:49) *Bodaciously built, ferociously fit Eliza models a stupefyingly sexy series of barely there bikinis in a department store dressing room to the head-spinning delight of DJ Qualls.*

Deborah Dutch

Born: May 17, 1967
Titusville, New Jersey
Skin-O-Meter: Great Nudity

Perhaps double-D delight Deborah Dutch harbored aspirations beyond tits-and-ass skinema when she flounced about in a flowing nightie and flimsy cotton panties during her filmic debut in *Bruce Lee Fights Back from the Grave* (1976), but she certainly has nothing to be ashamed of in the leg-ass-y she has left behind. A vulnerable-looking brunette who might seem a trifle undernourished if not for the hefty flesh deposits stockpiled upon her rib cage, Deborah's butt-tastic manner of disrobing and climbing into a bathtub in *The Haunting of*

Morella (1990) will forever reappear in the dreams of all who witness it. Durable Dutch was incredibly generous with her treats, doling out fleshly tricks in a revelatory career that spanned almost twenty years.

SKIN-fining Moment:

Jokes My Folks Never Told Me (0:33) Deborah delivers her left Dutch teat while chatting to a chick on a bed.

See Her Naked In:

Baberellas (2003) Breasts, Thong
Bikini Drive-In (1995) Breasts, Thong
Tender Loving Care (1995) Breasts
Mind Twister (1994) Breasts
Divorce Law (1993) Breasts
Death Dancers (1993) Breasts, Bush, Buns
Scream Queen Hot Tub Party (1991) Breasts
Hard To Die (1990) Breasts, Buns
The Haunting of Morella (1990) Breasts, Buns
Sorority Girls and the Creature From Hell (1990) LB
Jokes My Folks Never Told Me (1977) LB

Clea Duvall

Born: September 25, 1977
Los Angeles, California
Skin-O-Meter: Brief Nudity

Cat-eyed Clea DuVall came out of the skin gate with a score in *Little Witches* (1996), one of several sexy, supernatural teen knock-offs of the same year's *The Craft*. In her straight-to-tape but sufficiently startling version, Clea's delicious dark princess flashes a bit of Beelzeboob and a devilish dose of derriere, much to the delight of her fellow sorceresses and a league of pause-button-prone home viewers. That role more or less set the tone for Clea's subsequent film characters: that of the darkly dressed, quietly subversive outsider, which became second nature for her in striking

but sadly skinless turns in *The Faculty* (1998), *Girl* (2000), and *Wildflower* (2000). A startlingly Sapphic but so, so, so sweet turn in the lesbian-themed rah-rah indie *But I'm a Cheerleader* (1999) found Clea and co-star Natasha Lyonne sharing a deep and lingering soul kiss that undoubtedly had viewers' tongues equally a-wagging. As for any subsequent skinquences, well, let's hope that Clea has fond memories of her Season of the Witch.

SKIN-fining Moment:

Little Witches (0:35) Clea bares her rump as she takes off her undies, followed by brief breasts as she dances around during a witchy ritual.

See Her Naked In:

Wildflowers (2000) Body Double—LB
Little Witches (1996) Breasts, Buns

Shelley Duvall

Born: July 7, 1949
Houston, Texas
Skin-O-Meter: Brief Nudity

It was acclaimed filmmaker Robert Altman who gave lavishly lanky, deliciously ditzy Shelley Duvall roles in the films for which she is best known (save that of Wendy Torrance in *The Shining* [1980]): *Brewster McCloud* (1970), *McCabe and Mrs. Miller* (1971), *3 Women* (1977), and the lead to which she will be perpetually linked, that of cartoon hysteric Olive Oyl in *Popeye* (1980). And it was Altman who undoubtedly convinced the inimitably structured Duvall to engage in a skinworthy bathing scene in his *Thieves Like Us* (1974) and strip down to her shockingly sheer skivvies in his epic *Nashville* (1975).

SKIN-fining Moment:

Thieves Like Us (1:19) Shelley stands up in an old-fashioned bathtub, showing brief mini-mams and an extensive, full-on view of her petite seat.

See Her Naked In:

Thieves Like Us (1974) Breasts, Bush, Buns

Karyn Dwyer

Newfoundland, Canada
Skin-O-Meter: Brief Nudity

Canada must be missing an angel. Newfoundland native Karyn Dwyer is in danger of being co-opted by Hollywood. You will know her by her tight ringlets of red hair cascading onto her shoulders; skin pale and unblemished and smooth as an unskied slope; strong, full nose with flaring love-addict nostrils; and lippy, sensual mouth that effortlessly morphs from impish grin to the sly smile of a seductress. You want to see her as an earthy, sweetie-pie lesbian in *Better Than Chocolate* (1999). Watch her frolic naked with her girlfriend, smearing chocolate-colored paint along the soft contours of their pleasingly curvy forms. Ache for Karyn's yearning as she spreads her arms tits out in an appeal for love. Drool over the butt crack as fully naked Dwyer reclines belly down. It's enough to make a guy wish he could be a gay woman.

SKIN-fining Moment:

Better Than Chocolate (0:17) Curly-maned Karyn and flaxen Christina Cox smear each other in body paint and make lesboid love all over a canvas.

See Her Naked In:

Better Than Chocolate (1999) FFN
End of Summer (1997) Breasts
The Paper Boy (1994) Breasts

Leslie Easterbrook

Born: July 29, 1951
Nebraska
Skin-O-Meter: Great Nudity

Statuesque showstopper Leslie Easterbrook has a figure full of swooping curves, blonde hair like finely spun corn silk, and the unconsciously sensual expression of the innocent, purring, sexual feline that propelled goddesses such as Marilyn Monroe and Jayne Mansfield to the outer reaches of superstardom. Leslie also comes equipped with a bra-busting sense of humor. Her ability to serve a side dish of levity with her main course of levitating chest orbs is why the mouth-watering Easterbrook has been a recurring special on the menu of the *Police Academy* series. Leslie's breast day at the cop shop comes in *Police Academy 4* (1987). To cool off the heat caused by the friction of her hooters rubbing against one another, the law-enforcement siren plunges into a pool of cool water. Her high beamers pop up through a thin, white, soaking-wet T-shirt, and it's time for another fire drill.

SKIN-fining Moment:

Police Academy 4: Citizens on Patrol (0:34) *Leslie rises out of a pool in a sopping wet, see-through T-shirt and, for once, Steve Gutterberg and Bobcat Goldthwait aren't the two* biggest boobs in a Police Academy movie.

See Her Naked In:

Private Resort (1985) RB, Buns

Alison Eastwood

Born: May 22, 1972
Los Angeles, California
Skin-O-Meter: Great Nudity

Daughter of he-man Clint Eastwood, Alison Eastwood makes Mr. Skin's day. Breast of all, she doesn't share her daddy's grizzled skin, as evident by her luscious nudity onscreen. Sadly, they don't call him *Dirty Harry* for his perverted bent. When Eastwood cast Alison in his *Midnight in the Garden of Good and Evil* (1997), her debut celluloid sex scene was shot once and then rudely cut from the film. Papa don't preach! Once free of Eastwood's steely grip, Alison got into the swing of things with *Friends & Lovers* (1999), playing one of the lovers who had a hard time keeping her shirt on. Then in *If Only You Knew* (2000), Alison showed off her heavenly hooter handfuls in a skin rite of passage, the shower scene. Do you feel lucky, punk?

SKIN-fining Moment:

Friends & Lovers (1:13) *Alison flashes her boobs at some feller, which, quite naturally, results in some serious sexcapades.*

See Her Naked In:

The Spring (2000) LB
If You Only Knew (2000) Breasts
Friends & Lovers (1999) Breasts

Jayne Eastwood

Skin-O-Meter: Brief Nudity

A loose-featured blonde with big droopy eyes that could play sultry to menaced to menacing all with the infinitesimal adjustment of her eyelashes, Canadian actress Jayne Eastwood has won awards that most of us Stateside don't even know exist. So while being presented an Earle Grey award for her body of work might not have made Jayne a household name on the U.S. side of the border, her face and figure have been featured in a steady string of recognizable productions spanning four decades. From *Goin' Down the Road* (1970) to *Videodrome* (1983) to *The Santa Clause* (1994) to *How to Deal* (2003), with dozens of stops filling in between, Jayne Eastwood has been at home in America.

SKIN-fining Moment:

My Pleasure is My Business (1:16) *Bare-breasted Jayne wobbles her East-and-Westwoods at a guy in bed.*

See Her Naked In:

My Pleasure is My Business (1974)
Breasts

Barbara Eden

Born: August 23, 1934
Tucson, Arizona
Skin-O-Meter: Never Nude

Barbara Eden will forever be known as the hot-bottled blonde from the TV hit *I Dream of Jeannie*. On the show, she was discovered by a swinging astronaut who for some inexplicable reason played the field instead of letting Barbara make all his wishes come true. Only a spaced-out man would turn down the amorous charms of the shapely, barely dressed Arabian arouser. After the sitcom was cancelled, Barbara went on to play foils to major characters and was more or less a pretty part of the scenery. Be that as it may, she has had some unforgettable roles. Check out the film *Chattanooga Choo Choo* (1984) or her runs on the series *Dallas* and in the film and series *Harper Valley P.T.A.* (1978). Now over seventy years of age, she can still stop hearts and harden more exterior organs leaping seductively clad from a glass bottle. Unfortunately, the gorgeous 36-24-36 figure that Barbara flaunted never appeared nude on film. She did strip down to her white bra in *Harper Valley P.T.A.* (the film, not the series), but that's it. Best bet: rub your flesh bottle when Jeannie comes out of her glass one and see what comes out of your spout.

SKIN-fining Moment:

Harper Valley P.T.A. (0:24) *Barbara unbuttons her blouse and wows the bejeezus out of WKRP's bare-assed Les Nessman but she unfortunately keeps her chest-jeannies corked up in a bra.*

Barbara Edwards

Born: June 26, 1960
Albuquerque, New Mexico
Skin-O-Meter: Great Nudity

Barbara Edwards shot to fame in the early '80s as a *Playboy* Playmate of the Month for September 1983 and subsequently as the big winner of the Playmate of the Year title the following year. Needless to say, this five-foot-five-inch beauty has breasts the size of flesh trophies. Barbara, like so many other former nude models, turned to acting to lengthen her stay on top of the world. She has no inhibitions in front of the camera and it shows. Speaking of showing, check out her debut movie *Malibu Express* (1985), in which Barbara engages in one of the hottest lesbian topless shower scenes in the long and hot tradition of lesbian topless shower scenes. She has since appeared nude in almost everything, including *Terminal Entry* (1986), *Another Chance* (1989), and several *Playboy* videos. Lately she's cleaned up her act. Barbara played a news anchor in *For the Love of My Child: The Anissa Ayala Story* (1993) and a TV reporter in *Trucks* (1997). Sadly, she's not working for the all-the-nudes-that's-fit-to-print station.

SKIN-fining Moment:

Malibu Express (0:12) *Barbara flashes her mighty, perfect mammaries and an exceptionally brief bit of bush in the shower with Kimberly McArthur.*

See Her Naked In:

Another Chance (1989) Breasts, Buns
Terminal Entry (1986) Breasts
Malibu Express (1985) FFN, Buns
Numerous *Playboy* Videos

Stacy Edwards

Born: March 4, 1965
Glascow, Montana
Skin-O-Meter: Brief Nudity

Who's standing up for supercute small breasts attached to supercute small women? It's gals like the adorable Stacy Edwards—or, more specifically, her supercute titties standing up in *Relentless 3* (1993). Stacy's military family had her growing up all over the world, but she settled in Hollywood and quickly became a regular fixture in TV series and films. She even came close to breaking out big with her role as a deaf secretary being used as a plaything in the hit indie *In the Company of Men* (1997). With over fifteen years of steady work in Hollywood, the only question left about Stacy's talent and beauty is why the hell isn't she a star?

SKIN-fining Moment:

Relentless 3 *Stacy's bare buns look red hot even though, as she's playing a corpse, they're ice cold.*

See Her Naked In:

Relentless 3 (1993) Buns

Julie Ege

Born: November 12, 1943
Sandnes, Norway
Skin-O-Meter: Great Nudity

Stunning Norwegian wood-maker Julie Ege was a prisoner of her own beauty. An auburn-tinged blonde stack of long legs, high buttocks, and rising breasts, with a face dominated by Arctic Circle eyes and an icy, glacially planed bone structure, young Julie was a shoo-in for the Miss Norway title. The reigning beauty gained a worldwide audience in the classic Bond film *On Her Majesty's Secret Service* (1969), being typecast as The Scandinavian Girl. Following the success of the film, Julie became one of the first exceptionally attractive women ever to grace the pages of *Penthouse* magazine, after which she would be forever pigeonholed as the gorgeous woman who takes off her clothes. But what a wonderful hole to be pigeoned into!

SKIN-fining Moment:

Not Now Darling (0:21) *Several looks at Julie's killer keister as she hides in a coat room.*

See Her Naked In:

Not Now Darling (1973) FFN, Buns
The Mutations (1973) Breasts
Rentadick (1972) Breasts
Creatures the World Forgot (1971) Body Double—Breasts
Every Home Should Have One (1970) FFN, Buns

Samantha Eggar

Born: March 5, 1939
London, England, UK
Skin-O-Meter: Brief Nudity

The sleek silhouette of redheaded head-turner Samantha Eggar would be as fresh and contemporary if she were debuting today as when her *Vogue*-quality profile first catwalked onto the world stage in *The Wild and the Willing* (1962). Samantha was a bit of both wild and willing in the role she is best remembered for, that of a young girl held captive by a sexual misfit in the creepy thriller *The Collector* (1965). Although no nipples, pubes, or crack of bum survive in *The Collector*'s final cut, long, exquisitely lensed scenes of Eggar's captor bathing the comely hostage's nude body in a sudsy tub are erotic in a highly charged, eerie, and disturbing way. Samantha's open-view roll of breast flesh in *A Name for Evil* (1973) is pleasing in its own way, but *The Collector* is where her best and oddest sexual thrills are to be found.

SKIN-fining Moment:

A Name for Evil (0:47) *She shows a bit of butt crack as Bob Culp puts some salve on her, then she bares very brief nipplets when she rolls over.*

See Her Naked In:

The Brood (1979) RB
A Name for Evil (1973) Breasts

Nicole Eggert

Born: January 3, 1972
Glendale, California
Skin-O-Meter: Great Nudity

Quintessential California blonde Nicole Eggert went from little-girl beauty pageants to TV ads for Johnson's Baby Shampoo to classic '70s fare such as *Fantasy Island* before she even hit puberty. Fortunately, viewers got to watch that process as Nicole grew up—and out—as Alyssa Milano's best friend on *Who's the Boss?* and as petite Jamie Powell on *Charles in Charge* from 1987 to 1990. Once she was (finally!) legal, Nicole got jiggly with it as Summer Quinn on *Baywatch* from 1992 to 1994. If you wondered why the five-foot-one-inch babe's breasts were unusually boulder-like for her frame, it was because she had implants. But they were just loaners.

SKIN-fining Moment:

Blown Away (0:12) *Suberb shots of Nicole's back yard and pre-plastic palookas while getting it on against a wall with Corey Haim. Lucky Haim. Lucky wall.*

See Her Naked In:

Blown Away (1992) Breasts, Buns

Jennifer Ehle

Born: December 29, 1969
Winston-Salem, North Carolina
Skin-O-Meter: Great Nudity

What has America done to forsake Jennifer Ehle? Although born in the U.S., she has spent most of her time (on celluloid, at least) in England (no wonder they call it "Merry Old"). She mostly shares her body onstage, which is her bread and butter, and what a meal it is! Nevertheless, juggy Jennifer has found quite a bit of success in British TV productions and movies, most notably in made-for-TV movies such as *Micky Love* (1993), *The Maitlands* (1993), *Pride and Prejudice* (1995), and *Melissa* (1997). She has also appeared in more cinematic endeavors such as *Backbeat* (1993), *Wilde* (1997), and *Possession* (2002), opposite Gwyneth Paltrow, but her best skin scenes were reserved for her debut on the English TV mini-series *The Camomile Lawn* (1992), in which Jennifer's jiggling big girls were free, and she even let the dewy patch between her shapely legs come out briefly to play. The grass is always sexier when its on Jennifer.

SKIN-fining Moment:

The Camomile Lawn (mini-series) (1992) *Jen goes all-out in her living room in front of lucky man Toby Stephens. Great big boobs, sweet thick thatch.*

See Her Naked In:

Sunshine (1999) Body Double—LB, Buns

TeleVisions:

The Camomile Lawn FFN

Lisa Eichhorn

Born: February 4, 1952
Glenn Falls, New York
Skin-O-Meter: Great Nudity

With her tight ringlets of blondness, soul-probing gaze, mouth quavering with passion set in a strong chiseled chin, uncompromising emotress Lisa Eichorn would seem to be a natural for small-screen stardom. Lisa has filled recurring roles on both *All My Children* and *Feel the Heat*, but for the most part her artistic expression plays on the stage rather than in front of TV or movie cameras. When Lisa has ventured into film, she's left her shirt behind in at least a quartet of pics, starting with *Yanks* (1979). Eichorn's most striking go at being starkers was in *Opposing*

Force (1986), a military-adventure picture in which our busty heroine prepares for battle by holding her hands above her head and walking naked through a shower. Lisa's clenched butt cheeks in *Opposing Force* give a thoroughly attractive meaning to the term "hard ass."

SKIN-fining Moment:

Opposing Force (1:05) *Boobs, butt, and a hint of the hairpie as Ms. Eichorn is ordered to get naked, then smacked around by a villainous Anthony Zerbe in his jungle lair.*

See Her Naked In:

Opposing Force (1986) Breasts, Bush, Buns
The Weather in the Streets (TV) (1983) RB
Cutter's Way (1981) RB
Yanks (1979) RB

Lisa Eilbacher

Born: May 5, 1957
Dharan, Saudi Arabia
Skin-O-Meter: Brief Nudity

Lisa Eilbacher was a little girl walking down a Hollywood street with her mother when a television talent scout spotted the child-star-to-be and signed her up. It must have been her face that caught his eye. Lisa has the sort of active, highly expressive features that are ideal for the instant emoting required by the quick cuts and the fast reaction shots on TV dramas and sitcoms. Before she was even old enough to date, Lisa had been bringing home checks for her work on *Wagon Train, Laredo, Bonanza, My Three Sons,* and *The Brady Bunch.* What does such a precocious young lady do when she finally grows up? She takes a part that allows her to go boob and nipple out in a passionate love bout that takes her from bathtub to bed. The movie is called *Live Wire* (1992). Its electricity comes directly from Eilbacher.

SKIN-fining Moment:

Live Wire (1:01) *Lisa takes a bath with Pierce Brosnan before they bang in bed. Nice flashes of her funbags and fanny along the way.*

See Her Naked In:

Live Wire (1992) Breasts

Janet Eilber

Born: July 27, 1951
Detroit, Michigan
Skin-O-Meter: Great Nudity

For many a hormone-addled young man, the high-school years are a span of time to endure by any means possible. If that includes gazing rapt and slack jawed as his still-youthful English teacher pirouettes naked through the artfully lit, empty halls of his imagination, then let's hope the teacher is someone on par with Janet Eilber, the brunette, lithe, and pretty pedagogue of NBC's schooltime drama *The Best Times.* Eilber would be fleet on her toes, having been trained in the balletic arts prior to leaving her tutu behind and brightening the world with her feats upon the small and silver screens. As an aid to the fantasy scenario, we know exactly how sylphlike and nimble Janet Eilber would be dancing naked, because she does just that in *Whose Life Is It Anyway?* (1981).

SKIN-fining Moment:

Whose Life Is It Anyway? (0:29) *She shows tit, tush, and tang while ballet dancing in Dick Dreyfuss's dream.*

See Her Naked In:

Whose Life Is It Anyway? (1981) FFN, Buns

Anita Ekberg

Born: September 29, 1931
Malmö, Skåne, Sweden
Skin-O-Meter: Brief Nudity

Neither blonde bombshells nor Swedish knockouts come more stunning than the great and glorious Anita Ekberg, figure rated at 40-23-38. One of the top shelves of the 1960s, enormously blessed Anita's sultry, pensive facial perfection adorned dozens of films, many of them foreign, in a prime that lasted from the 1950s through the 1970s. In Italian director Federico Fellini's masterpiece of cosmopolitan decadence, *La Dolce Vita* (1960), Anita cavorted in the Trevi Fountain, her black dress slipping off her shoulders and clinging to her massive front. An awestruck poet among the film's cast defines Ekberg as "the first woman on the first day of creation; you are

---

MR. SKIN'S TOP TEN

Nude Nuns
. . . Bad habits

10. Florinda Bolkan
   —*Flavia, la Monaca Musulmana* 1974

9. Frankie Thorn
   —*Bad Lieutenant* 1992 (0:18)

8. Leslie Caron
   —*Madron* 1970 (0:46)

7. Olivia Pascal
   —*Behind Convent Walls* 1977 (0:23)

6. Gloria Guida
   —*La Novizia* 1975 (1:01)

5. Anne Heywood
   —*La Monaca di Monza* 1969 (0:24)

4. Toni Collette
   —*8½ Women* 1999 (1:17)

3. Laura Antonelli
   —*The Eroticist* 1972 (1:04)

2. Eleonora Giorgi
   —*Storia di una Monaca di Clausura* 1973 (0:15)

1. **Anita Ekberg** (0:37)
   —***Suor Omicidi*** 1978

mother, sister, friend, angel, devil, home; that's what you are . . . home!" When can we move in?

SKIN-fining Moment:

Suor Omicidi (0:37) *You'll need an iceberg to cool down after seeing Anita's bare ass-berg getting groped by a guy before they bang against a wall.*

See Her Naked In:

Suor Omicidi (1978) Buns

Britt Ekland

Born: October 6, 1942
Stockholm, Sweden
Skin-O-Meter: Hall of Fame

"She's a professional girlfriend and an amateur actress," said ex-hubby Peter Sellers after the lovebirds divorced. But it's thanks to her marriage to the Brit funnyman that Hollywood got a hell of a woman in Britt Ekland. Sellers took the little-known Swedish act-chest out of obscurity and cast her in several of his films, most notably the Neil Simon-penned comedy *After the Fox* (1966). Oddly, it was Sellers who played the Fox of the title. But Britt faired better without her lesser half. She played the girl who invented the striptease in *The Night They Raided Minsky's* (1968). By the '70s, Britt came into her own, and Mr. Skin came into his hands watching her jugs jangle in *Percy* (1970) and *Get Carter* (1971). She continued the torrid trend in *What the Peeper Saw* (1972) and the cult classic *The Wicker Man* (1973). She even played a Bond girl, Mary Goodnight, in *The Man with the Golden Gun* (1974). Britt's got a bod that won't call it quits, and, even as a middle-aged matron of the mams, she could stiffen the crowd when she took off her blouse in *Scandal* (1989). If she's in the film, the skin will be a perfect Britt.

SKIN-fining Moment:

The Wicker Man (0:18) *This golden-tressed goddess croons a pretty tune dancing around her apartment starkers. She bares quite a bit of Britt tit, but the buns? They ain't hers!*

See Her Naked In:

Scandal (1989) Breasts
Erotic Images (1983) Breasts
Dr. Yes: Hyannis Affair (1983) Breasts
Sex on the Run (1979) LB
Slavers (1976) Breasts
The Wicker Man (1973) Body Double—Buns / Her—Breasts
Get Carter (1971) Breasts
Endless Night (1971) Breasts
Percy (1970) RB
The Night They Raided Minsky's (1968) Body Double—Breasts

> "I was watching an HBO special the other night on real-life maximum-security-prison guys. I glanced up and my poster was in quite a few cells. I was screaming, 'Oh, no!'"
>
> —CARMEN ELECTRA

Carmen Electra

Born: April 20, 1972
Cincinnati, Ohio
Skin-O-Meter: Great Nudity

Electrifying Carmen Electra was discovered by Prince (a.k.a. the Artist Formerly in Contact with Reality). Her early, Prince-produced pop album didn't exactly set her music career on fire, so, lucky for us, she soon shifted into more visual arts. She was the boobilicious cohost on MTV's *Singled Out*, replacing bubbling blonde Jenny McCarthy. On *Baywatch*, she took the place of another flaxen ultra-vixen, Pamela Anderson. Whereas Anderson's honeydews have succumbed to the melonballer, Carmen Electra's phony minestrones are mammoth as ever.

Unfortunately, you won't be able to see them in the 1998 direct-to-video flick *The Chosen One*, which features an indecipherable plot and a pair of body-double breasts that hardly pass as Electra's fun-filled falsies. Do they really think they can fool Mr. Skin? Fortunately, Carmen's luscious robo-casabas play a pivotal role (and roll) in *The Mating Habits of the Earthbound Human* (1999).

SKIN-fining Moment:

My Boss's Daughter (0:37) *Carmen emerges from a hot tub in a sopping-wet, udderly see-through T-shirt that shows off her super-sized casabas most mouth-wateringly.*

See Her Naked In:

The Mating Habits of the Earthbound Human (1999) Breasts
The Chosen One: Legend of the Raven (1998) Body Double—Breasts, Buns

TeleVisions:

Erotic Confessions Thong

Erika Eleniak

Born: September 29, 1969
Glendale, California
Skin-O-Meter: Great Nudity

Fair haired and full of form, Erika Eleniak puckered her way into history at twelve, playing the dreamgirl who gets kissed by Henry Thomas during the frog-releasing scene in *E.T. The Extra-Terrestrial* (1982). Bit roles continued as she grew up on camera, and before long, Hugh Hefner was calling to make her a *Playboy* Playmate in July 1989. Erika was able to parlay her centerfold spread into a role as ravishing rookie lifeguard Shauni McClain Kramer on *Baywatch* from 1989 to 1992, figuring as that ultimate skin series' first bust-out starlet. Erika bounced along on the beach and left men drowning in drool, aided, like so many other

Baywatch babes, by the breast investment she ever made: a 1988 enlargement of her flotation devices. This boobilicious blonde couldn't have been any tastier than in the Steven Seagal *Die-Hard*-on-a-boat smash *Under Siege* (1992), when she jumped out of a cake topless. Talk about two scoops of the sweet stuff! Still her most skintastic turn to date came in *Chasers* (1994), in which she is bound to a bed and freed from her bra.

SKIN-fining Moment:

Chasers (1:04) *We see Erika's ogle-orbs while she's handcuffed to the bed. Then buns and more breasts when William McNamara goes for it. Nice!*

See Her Naked In:

The Opponent (2000) LB
Chasers (1994) Breasts, Buns
Under Siege (1992) Breasts, Thong
Numerous *Playboy* Videos

> "It looks like I have huge breasts, but I really don't."
>
> —SHANNON ELIZABETH

Shannon Elizabeth

Born: September 7, 1973
Houston, Texas
Skin-O-Meter: Great Nudity

Tall drink of Texas sweet-water Shannon Elizabeth made her skin debut in the killer snowman howler *Jack Frost* (1997), but it was only after she augmented her upper assets that Shannon truly emerged from the pack. Shannon's long, lithe body added a touch of "Holy FUCK!" to the teen sex comedy classic *American Pie* (1999), where, as foreign-exchange student Nadia, she gave Jason Biggs's character all the Web-worthy hits he could handle. Made before *Pie*, but released on DVD afterward, *Dish Dogs*

SHANNON ELIZABETH SERVES UP HER SWEETS FOR JASON BIGGS IN *AMERICAN PIE.*

(1998) showcased Shannon as poetry in motion on a strip-club stage. The disc also features deleted scenes of, you guessed it, Shannon naked. More stripping, dancing, and trying on bras. Mr. Skin gets misty over this modern technology— misty all over!

SKIN-fining Moment:

American Pie (0:44) *Shannon sheds her threads while the fellers watch via the Internet, and then provides another peek at her poppers while she paddles her pink canoe in bed.*

See Her Naked In:

American Pie (1999) Breasts
Dish Dogs (1998) Breasts, Thong
Jack Frost (1997) Buns

Alison Elliott

Born: May 19, 1970
San Francisco, California
Skin-O-Meter: Brief Nudity

The show-stopping highlights of magic-eyed brunette Alison Elliott were discovered early on. At fourteen the wiry, San Francisco-born beauty was already modeling, and before she was twenty she'd been typecast as a world-class teen model on the ABC comedy drama *Living Dolls*. Alison toiled toward adulthood within the medium of the cathode box, but with maturity she burst into bigger-than-life drama as the lead in *The Spitfire Grill* (1996). Alison's gritty, gutsy,

and still somehow gonadally intriguing performance as a young lady ex-con who has been paroled from prison and takes a job at a grungy diner in a rural outpost of Maine earned her critical acclaim and the respect of industry peers. The previous year, she had earned a boner by slipping out of her underthings in Steven Soderbergh's *The Underneath* (1995).

SKIN-fining Moment:

The Underneath (0:39) *Ali rolls over in bed with Peter Gallagher and we glimpse her glutes. Nice buns, but the shot is almost as dark as his eyebrows.*

See Her Naked In:

The Underneath (1995) Buns

Elvira

Born: September 17, 1951
Manhattan, Kansas
Skin-O-Meter: Great Nudity

Born Cassandra Peterson, this raven-wigged maven drew the

MR. SKIN'S TOP TEN

Naked One Name Wonders
. . . Sylla-belles: no surname in her name

10. Nena
9. Haji
8. Lio
7. Zabou
6. Nico
5. Sable
4. Morganna
3. Apollonia
2. Vanity
1. **Elvira**

infamous name Elvira from a coffee can just before premiering as host of *Movie Macabre*. The rest is horror-show history. The term "boob tube" was never more apropos than when the curvaceous Cassandra flaunted her monstrous cleavage for late-night TV. Viewers sat through schlocky spookers in hope of catching a glimpse of her beaming bosom. Cassandra's cazoongas were larger than life on the silver screen in *Elvira, Mistress of the Dark* (1988). Most recently, she flaunted her peaks and valleys in *Elvira's Haunted Hills* (2001). As a young featured creature of the night, Cassie gave a performance to rival Bettie Page as an old-fashioned stripper in *The Working Girls* (1973).

SKIN-fining Moment:

The Working Girls (0:20) *An awesome, lengthy, beautifully lit strip-club scene featuring Elvira getting topless. Great pumpkins!*

See Her Naked In:

Elvira, Mistress of the Dark (1988) Nip-Slip RB
Jekyll & Hyde . . . Together Again (1982) RB
Famous T&A (1982) Breasts, Thong
The Best of Sex and Violence (1981) Breasts
The Working Girls (1973) Breasts, Thong

Audie England

Born: October 9, 1972
Los Angeles, California
Skin-O-Meter: Great Nudity

Audie England is not English, but who wouldn't want to have Tea & A with her? She was born and raised in Southern California and went to UCLA with the intent of becoming a cinematographer. But after meeting Zalman King, the legendary nudie producer/director of such classics as *The Delta of Venus* (1995) and *The Red Shoe Diaries*—both featuring Audie in some stage of undress—she was convinced that her calling was in front of the camera. Audie has appeared in many nude-worthy

roles, such as *Miami Hustle* (1996), *Venus Rising* (1995), and *Love and Happiness* (1995). But her most skinful turns have been in Zalman's movies, most notably in his *Shame, Shame, Shame* (1998), in which she appears in full-frontal glory and for longer than a fleeting moment. She has been naked in the greater part of her credits, so if you see her on a video box, chances are that she will be naked in the movie. Let's hope the sun never sets on the England empire.

SKIN-fining Moment:

Delta of Venus (0:29) *Full frontal in an open robe offering herself to an understandably horny dude, followed by funbaggage as he makes her happy on the floor.*

See Her Naked In:

Free Enterprise (1998) Breasts
Miami Hustle (1996) RB, Thong
One Good Turn (1996) Breasts
Delta of Venus (1995) FFN, Buns
Venus Rising (1995) Breasts

TeleVisions:

Red Shoe Diaries Breasts, Buns

Kathryn Erbe

Born: July 5, 1966
Newton, Massachusetts
Skin-O-Meter: Great Nudity

Brunette, with her bangs often hanging down into her eyes, busty broad Kathryn Erbe exudes vulnerable tough-chick appeal that makes her an excellent choice for any role that requires a bad girl to have a heart of stone and the naturally overflowing tits of an old-school stripper. Although Kathryn has played her share of sympathetic roles in mainstream fare such as *D2: The Mighty Ducks* (1994), she excels as the cohort of hoods and losers. Her cascading avalanches of tit flesh and big, flat-bread nipples are the primary special effect of

Dream with the Fishes (1997), a gritty tale of no-future f-ups and the ripe-hipped woman who gives them home-delivery lap dances. Erbe's perfectly cracked ass is a haunting reminder of death and sexual trysts past in *Stir of Echoes* (1999). Kathryn's tough roles are hard to forget, and why would you want to?

SKIN-fining Moment:

Oz "Losing You" (1998) *Pantiless Kat lifts her prison smock up past her waist to tempt a male inmate with a naked view of her lovely, full-grown Erbe-garden.*

See Her Naked In:

Stir of Echoes (1999) RB, Buns
Dream with the Fishes (1997) Breasts

TeleVisions:

Oz Bush

Krista Errickson

Born: May 8, 1964
Abington, Pennsylvania
Skin-O-Meter: Brief Nudity

Charismatic cutie Krista Errickson was a frequent fresh face on '80s television. Cute as a button, with a girl-next-door glow, Krista was the perfect Miss Priss on episodes of *Diff'rent Strokes*, *Fame*, and *Mr. Belvedere*, as well as in the teeny comedy *Little Darlings* (1980). After playing the underappreciated ingénue in a string of forgettable films such as *Jekyll & Hyde . . . Together Again* (1982) and *The First Time* (1982), Krista left darling for devilish, brazenly baring her boobies in *Mortal Passions* (1989) and *Jailbait* (1994). With the huge-nipped horns on her form, Mr. Skin prefers the sinfully skinful Errickson every time.

SKIN-fining Moment:

Mortal Passions (0:40) *Krista drops her sheet and shows off her sugar-heaps to the man who then bones her.*

See Her Naked In:

Jailbait (1994) Breasts
Mortal Passions (1990) Breasts

Jennifer Esposito

Born: April 11, 1973
New York, New York
Skin-O-Meter: Brief Nudity

Jennifer Esposito spun a role on the TV series *The City* into several seasons on *Spin City* as a sexy bridge-and-tunnel hottie—and what a pair of bridges she has hanging over her tunnel. She also shows up in *A Brother's Kiss* (1997), *Kiss Me Guido* (1997), *Just One Time* (1997), and *A Brooklyn State of Mind* (1997)—a good year, but not for nudity lovers, as Jennifer remained clothed throughout. In 1998 she took a role on the hit soap opera *All My Children* but only stayed for a year. Then she rode Spike Lee's Joint in *He Got Game* (1998), albeit briefly, but returned for a spicier turn in Lee's *Summer of Sam* (1999) as a punk-rock vixen. She has also lent her fine figure to *I Still Know What You Did Last Summer* (1998), *The Bachelor* (1999), and *Dracula 2000* (2000), which offers her fine flesh as a vampire in a low-cut gown. In *Crash* (2004), Jen toplessly hops atop Don Cheadle and we get a quick view of her naked right teadie.

SKIN-fining Moment:

Crash (0:40) *Jennifer rides Don Cheadle's dong in bed and briefly bares her right-side Espo-teato.*

See Her Naked In:

Crash (2004) Breasts

Cynthia Ettinger

Skin-O-Meter: Brief Nudity

She's blonde, and she's built big and naturally bouncy up top, and she flaunts her chest ornaments in a sheer, low-cut scrap of period-piece lingerie on the HBO freak show *Carnivàle*. You think, "What is the name of this bosomy, billowing broad? Has she come out of nowhere?" The largely lovely leading lady's name is Cynthia Ettinger, and she has trod a long road to *Carnivàle*. Her tracks, and her stretched bra straps, have been everywhere from *Seinfeld* to *ER* to *Touched by an Angel* to *The Practice* to *Felicity* to *Providence* to *Titus* to *Family Law* to *Gilmore Girls*.

SKIN-fining Moment:

Carnivàle "Insomnia" (2003) *Full-bodied sideshow stripper Cynthia gets hot-and-heavy (and how!) with a carny, who pulls down her slip and rubs his lucky mitts all over her mouth-watering Big Top.*

TeleVisions:

Carnivàle Breasts

Alice Evans

Born: August 2, 1971
Bristol, England, UK
Skin-O-Meter: Great Nudity

British actress and former model Alice Evans began filling her acting dossier in France by appearing on the short-lived television series *Elisa Top Modele* in 1996. Finding the Continent more accommodating to her skinematic career than dowdy olde England, Alice appeared in several French films throughout the '90s, including *Mauvaise Passe* (1999), a movie about a male escort in which Alice's character forks over the francs to frolic about with an older Frenchman. Though the plot is clearly a far-fetched fantasy, Alice does flaunt her firm little fried eggs in the bedroom scene. *Sacre Bleu!* Alice also flashes her naked nubbins in the shower in *Monsieur Naphtali* (1999). Unfortunately, she's kept her clothes on in front of the camera since. After landing a near-breakthrough role in the Disney dud *102 Dalmations* (2000), Alice returned to British and French productions with little success, including the flop British television series *The Best of Both Worlds*, which lasted only three episodes.

SKIN-fining Moment:

Mauvaise passe (0:57) *Great bouncing bobbles as Alice settles into a menage-a-trois with a guy and a slinky black-maned minx.*

See Her Naked In:

Mauvaise passe (1999) Breasts
Monsieur Naphtali (1999) Breasts

Linda Evans

Born: November 18, 1942
Hartford, Connecticut
Skin-O-Meter: Brief Nudity

A classy and classic blonde, Linda Evans attended Hollywood High School with fellow starlet-to-be Stefanie Powers and was an early find by connoisseur of blondes John Derek. Given the wattage of Linda's sly smile, the pleasure pillow formed by her pouting bottom lip, the charm of her dimpled chin, the delicate fluting of her long, searching nose, its nostrils flaring with hinted passion, and those eyes so widely trusting and knowing, along with her uncanny ability to squeeze her bosom into a deep crevice of cleavage, the girl was destined for stardom. Unfortunate for skin sightseers, Evans's arena of fame was the traditional small screen, her exposure primarily upon networks that frown upon revealing more than the hint of what lies beneath. The closest ethereal Evans has come to unclothed is in *Mitchell* (1975). With her bare back to the camera, she allows a slight curve of breast to show in shaded profile, and then the kiss off.

SKIN-fining Moment:

Mitchell (0:25) *Linda stands up to get dressed and gives us an okay peek at her upper ass-crackage. It's a little dark. The scene, not her crack.*

See Her Naked In:

Mitchell (1975) RB, Buns

Kim Evenson

Born: November 3, 1962
Bremerhaven, Germany
Skin-O-Meter: Great Nudity

The first thing that must be said about blonde love bundle Kim Evenson is that she carries an amazing, naturally grown rack. Taken individually and judged purely by weight and circumference, Kim's breasts may rate as simply superb. Put the buoyant wonders in combination with one another, factor in the exquisite slope of their heft, and the effect is nothing short of phenomenal. And then expand your view to include that sweet, simmering and immaculately fresh face. Is it any wonder that *Playboy* made her a featured Playmate in their September 1984 issue? Is it any coincidence that *Porky's Revenge* (1985) remains one of the most popular film entertainments of all time? Is there any secret to the impetus behind *Kidnapped* (1986) and *Kandyland* (1987)?

SKIN-fining Moment:

The Big Bet (1:20) *Lit by a single police cruiser light, flickers of Kim's kettle drums, kiester, and kitty are illuminated. Pull over and spread 'em.*

See Her Naked In:

Kandyland (1987) Breasts, Thong
Kidnapped (1986) Breasts, Thong
The Big Bet (1985) FFN, Buns
Porky's Revenge (1985) Breasts
Numerous *Playboy* Videos

Nancy Everhard

Born: November 30, 1959
Wadsworth, Ohio
Skin-O-Meter: Brief Nudity

High, round cheekbones and oversized eyes that can intensify everything from alarm to arousal with the flick of an eyelid are the currency of TV stardom, and wiry blonde bit of intensity Nancy Everhard is a rich lady in the cathode realm. Everhard's been hitting jackpots since her 1982 debut in the aptly titled made-for-TV flick *Born Beautiful* (1982). Nancy's money magnetism has gone on to ring the register on forward-pushing shows such as *Houston Knights*, *The Family Man*, *Reasonable Doubts*, and *The Untouchables*. Behind her, she leaves a trail of men feeling spent.

SKIN-fining Moment:

This Gun for Hire (1:03) *Nancy loses her panties, providing us with some seat, followed by teat as she eases into a bathtub.*

See Her Naked In:

This Gun for Hire (1991) Breasts, Buns

Angie Everhart

Born: September 7, 1969
Akron, Ohio
Skin-O-Meter: Great Nudity

Angie Everhart was told by Eileen Ford, head bitch of the Ford Modeling Agency, that "redheads don't sell," but that didn't stop this five-foot-ten-inch hottie from becoming the first fire-top on the cover of *Glamour* magazine. A model since she was sixteen, Angie debuted on film in *The Last Action Hero* (1993). She went on to more promising fare with *Jade* (1995), opposite lovely Linda Fiorentino, which was her skin debut. Angie exposed her perfect body right down to a pair of shaved lips. Trouble is she's dead, laid out on a morgue slab, if that's your kick. She went goth for *Bordello of Blood* (1996) but strangely kept her clothes on even in character as a vampire/pimp/whore. But *Another 9½ Weeks* (1997), *Sexual Predator* (2001), and *Bare Witness* (2001) gave audiences Angie at her best . . . nude! Sometime around 2000, imperially arousing Angie mounted the lap-throne of none other than King of All Media Howard Stern and further elevated his royally rapturous reputation by proclaiming the radio genius's way with a meat-scepter nothing short of "the best sex I ever had!" Angie keeps Mr. Skin ever-hard.

SKIN-fining Moment:

Jade (0:59:) *Dead heat: Angie lies on the coroner's table, showing some supermodel supersnatch and a nice pair of still-warm whoppers.*

See Her Naked In:

Bare Witness (2001) Breasts, Buns
Sexual Predator (2001) Breasts, Buns
The Substitute 4: Failure Is Not an Option (2000) Breasts
Another 9½ Weeks (1997) Breasts, Buns
Jade (1995) FFN, Buns

f

Marianne Faithfull

Born: December 19, 1946
Hampsted, London, England,
UK
Skin-O-Meter: Great Nudity

Best known as the puffy-lipped, puppy-eyed English blonde girl who left convent school to become a 1960s pop star with songs like "As Tears Go By," multi-faceted icon Marianne Faithfull has always been as famous for her headline sensuality as for her endearing talent. Her romantic peaks and valleys were front-page news while she was little more than a teen, a memory that detracts from the legacy of her *chesty* peaks and valleys (which were similarly committed to film while she was little more than a teen). The slip of nip in *I'll Never Forget What's 'is Name* (1967) is a mere prelude to the wealth of fully offered breast and total bum treat of *Girl on a Motorcycle* (1968). Take *Girl* for a spin, and be a fan of Faithfull forever.

SKIN-fining Moment:

Girl on a Motorcycle (0:06)
Marianne emerges from bed and walks across a room, showing her rack and Faith-furr.

See Her Naked In:

Girl on a Motorcycle (1968) FFN, Buns
I'll Never Forget What's 'is Name (1967) LB

Lola Falana

Born: September 11, 1942
Philadelphia, Pennsylvania
Skin-O-Meter: Great Nudity

Lola Falana may be nicknamed the First Lady of Las Vegas, but at Skin Central she's the Frisky Lady of Lust Vagina. A great act-chest, Lola's set of luscious pipes used to wow audiences in Sin City with their song . . . and bounce. After a few cinematic appearances in the late '60s, Lola found herself in the world of variety TV shows, appearing on *The New Bill Cosby Show, Ben Vereen . . . Comin' at Ya,* and later on Bill Cosby's reprisal *Cos* in 1976. She has also made her fair share of blaxploitation movies, such as *The Liberation of L.B. Jones* (1970), *Lady Cocoa* (1973), and *The Klansman* (1974), most of which feature her pint-sized chocolate milk jugs. Drink up!

SKIN-fining Moment:

Lady Cocoa (1:28) *Nice look at Lola's cocoa puffs while making out with some dude on a boat.*

See Her Naked In:

The Klansman (1974) Breasts
Lady Cocoa (1973) Breasts, Buns
The Liberation of L.B. Jones (1970) Breasts

Anna Falchi

Born: April 22, 1972
Tampere, Finland
Skin-O-Meter: Great Nudity

Finnish-born, flesh-melon-fortified Anna Falchi cried "Arriverderci Helsinki" as a teen, setting off to Rome to make her mark in the sun-kissed cinema of Italy, debuting in *On the Dark Continent* (1993) and raising the eyebrows of producers, modeling agents, tabloid reporters, and the ever-eager paparazzi, who know a knee-weakening sexpot import when they see one. A string of uninspired Euro productions followed, but the only memorable fire she ignited for skin seekers was in Italian horror-meister Michele Soavi's zombie-saturated *Dellamorte Dellamore* (1993), issued on these shores as *Cemetery Man.* Juggling a handful of roles—all of them playing on the fantasies of her mortician costar Rupert Everett—she frequently bursts free of her blouse to reveal a pair of the most curvaceous and cushiony canoles that lire can buy. One such sequence finds her raucously riding a receptive Rupert atop the grave of her recently deceased husband—who ultimately rises from his grave to sink his teeth into his scrumptious former wife. Espresso costs extra.

SKIN-fining Moment:

Dellamorte Dellamore (0:19)
Anna unveils her bombastic bazooms in a cemetery with Rupert Everett. Those knockers will wake the dead!

See Her Naked In:

Bodyguards (2000) LB
Giovani e Belli (1996) Buns
Dellamorte Dellamore (1993) Breasts

Edie Falco

Born: July 5, 1963
Northport, Long Island, New York
Skin-O-Meter: Brief Nudity

An extraordinarily focused performer given to portrayals of intense characters striving for dignity under duress, East Coast indie actress Edie Falco has earned every dime and all the respect she is finally receiving as the mother of Tony's two kids on the HBO franchise-making series *The Sopranos*. Falco's high-strung, hard-shell rawness makes for a real-people quality that is always believable. She is very often subversively sexy, her erotic appeal sneaking in on a subtle level where emotion and character are more affecting than glamor and tease. There's a reason Tony is still bonded to her, and it has much to do with her aura of honest passion in a world of false flash. Edie transmitted the same sub-rosa sexuality as a prison guard on *Oz* as well, although it would be a bad idea to get locked up there with the sole intention of meeting her.

SKIN-fining Moment:

The Sopranos "Sentimental Education" (2004). Mrs. Soprano rises from the bed next to her loverman. We see her bada-bra then get a sweet sampling of Carmella's tasty Italian buns.

See Her Naked In:

Trouble on the Corner (1997) Breasts

TeleVisions:

The Sopranos Buns

Deborah Falconer

Born: August 13, 1965
Sacramento, California
Skin-O-Meter: Great Nudity

Deborah Falconer was married to Robert Downey Jr. Besides an ex-heroin habit in common, the two share an offspring, son Indio. Now divorced, though on good terms with Downey, Deborah is putting her money where her chest is, that is as a singer/songwriter. She recently released a debut album on her own independent label. She has led a semi-successful acting career, debuting in *The Wrong Guys* (1988), playing "John Densmore's girlfriend" in *The Doors* (1991) and a bit part in Robert Altman's *Short Cuts* (1993), which was also her final screen appearance. Before Deborah checked out and sobered up, she managed to flash her itty-bitty titties in the German-made *Mr. Bluesman* (1993). This Falconer is sure to melt your snowman.

SKIN-fining Moment:

Mr. Bluesman (1:11) *Tits on the toilet! Topless Deb squats on the pot and drops a deuce while making goo-goo eyes at her boyfriend as he brushes his teeth.*

See Her Naked In:

Mr. Bluesman (1993) Breasts, Buns

Kate Fallon

Nova Scotia, Canada
Skin-O-Meter: Brief Nudity

Born in the rugged Maritime Provinces of Canada before moving to Montreal, Kate Fallon worked a succession of bartender gigs where her good looks and tight outfits insured a decent income. But it wasn't until she relocated to New York that her sexy star rose, as did the pants of jaded city slickers. Continuing to pour drinks and break hearts with her cheeky hot pants and boob-bobbing low-cut tops, Kate made many friends. She ended up working a stint as associate editor on Al Goldstein's infamous *Screw* magazine and was cast in the low-budget horror yarn *Rock 'n' Roll Frankenstein* (1999), in which she played a Gutted Groupie. Before she got sliced and diced—and poked by a horny Frankie in her wound—Kate treated audiences to a surprisingly hot shot of her dressed like a man and then removed her top for a pleasing peek at her pink-nipped pair. What a drag!

SKIN-fining Moment:

Rock 'n' Roll Frankenstein (0:54) *Kate's cutie-pie casabas get plenty of attention before she's suddenly (and disgustingly) gutted like a fish. Nifty nerples!*

See Her Naked In:

Rock 'n' Roll Frankenstein (1999) Breasts

Debrah Farentino

Born: September 30, 1959
Lucas Valley, California
Skin-O-Meter: Great Nudity

Dark hair, dark eyes, a face that promises a dark erotic surprise, dark and mysterious Debrah Farentino is a twenty-year veteran of the cathode tube. The big mystery is: Why doesn't everybody know her name and the full curve of her grandly rounded behind and the flush blush of chest when it's exposed to the leering light of day? There is no explaining bad luck. Farentino certainly comes equipped with the requisite resplendence, and she's been a hard worker in everything from the daytime soap *Capitol* in 1982 to her end-of-the-century stint on *Get Real*. Don't try to figure out what's gone wrong, just slide in a copy of *Malice* (1993).

Ponder the parted cheeks of Debrah's standing ass shot, magical and mystical even from a distance. Dream about what should have gone right.

SKIN-fining Moment:

Malice (0:26) *She goes De-Brah-less and shows a brief right breast as she lies on top of Alec Baldwin, then gives a glimpse of distant derriere and dugs.*

See Her Naked In:

Malice (1993) Breasts, Buns
Capone (1989) Breasts

Anna Faris

Born: November 29, 1976
Baltimore, Maryland
Skin-O-Meter: Never Nude

Anna Faris shot to fame in the horror spoof hits *Scary Movie* (2000) and *Scary Movie 2* (2001). She literally shoots across the room when her boyfriend comes like a fire hose. Is that Anna's fanny? Could be a body double, but Mr. Skin can dream. Anna has been working as an actress in her native Seattle since age nine and debuted in the low-budget slasher flick *Lover's Lane* in 1999. She's gone on to star in *The Hot Chick* (2002), in which for some reason Rob Schneider plays the title role, and in the disturbing horror shocker *May* (2001) she plays a lesbian vet. A natural blonde—she dyed her locks black to appear more like a Neve Campbell knockoff in *Scary Movie*—maybe one day she'll show her true colors in the buff. All's Faris in love and war.

SKIN-fining Moment:

Scary Movie (1:07) *Anna alleviates her boyfriend's backed-up bozack, setting off a geyser of spooge that sends her sailing towards the ceiling. Then a body double's buns slide in during the money shot.*

See Her Naked In:

Scary Movie (2000) Body Double—Buns

Sharon Farrell

Born: December 24, 1940
Sioux City, Iowa
Skin-O-Meter: Brief Nudity

Sharon Farrell may have started her career with a supporting role in *Kiss Her Goodbye* (1959), but this busty blonde was no kiss-off. It took a few years, but in 1962 she finally found a modicum of fame with a role on the short-run TV series *Saints and Sinners*. After a string of semi-successful cinematic appearances in the '60s, Sharon returned to the boob tube in the '70s for a seemingly endless stretch of made-for-TV movies and a gig on the long-running hit TV series *Hawaii Five-O*. Success reached this comely lass when she was cast in the hit film *The Stunt Man* (1980) opposite the most suggestively named actor outside of Dick Van Dyke, Peter O'Toole. That started a good run for Sharon and for those who wanted to see her shapely form more closely, as they got a good look at one of her massive mammaries in *Out of the Blue* (1980) opposite Dennis Hopper. The plot is as perverse as its leading man, so if the incestuous storylines harsh your boner, then one would be better off checking out *Lonely Hearts* (1982), which features an equally brief look at her mommy mounds. Unfortunately, Sharon returned yet again to the boob-less tube in the '90s with a stint on the hit soap opera *The Young and the Restless*, and her skinitudity has waned ever since. We want Sharon Farrell sharin' her fair all again really soon!

SKIN-fining Moment:

Lonely Hearts (0:52) *Sharon shares her topless schnobs with us as she luxuriates in the sack with Roberts.*

See Her Naked In:

Lonely Hearts (1982) Breasts
Out of the Blue (1980) LB

Lisa Farringer

Skin-O-Meter: Brief Nudity

Lisa Farringer got her big start as one of the groovy love dolls on *Rowan & Martin's Laugh-In*, dancing and performing alongside future skin favorite Goldie Hawn. As beautiful as Goldie, and far bustier, Lisa's career never really took off in quite the same stellar fashion. Choosing to go the blaxploitation route sent her down a road rarely visited by the Academy Awards. She also showed up in the Pam Grier vehicle *Coffy* (1973), which exposes her sole nude scene. She's lounging naked on a couch with another hooker, who's dolled up in a black-lace bra-and-pantie set, when she has to get up to give a john a blowjob. They don't make movies like that anymore.

SKIN-fining Moment:

Coffy (0:34) *Lisa shows the better part of her breasts off while laying on a couch, then proceeds to provide a much nicer peek of her pair, as well as her posterior, when she gets up . . .*

See Her Naked In:

Coffy (1973) Breasts, Buns

Mia Farrow

Born: February 9, 1945
Los Angeles, California
Skin-O-Meter: Great Nudity

Mia Farrow came from the loincloth-covered womb of Tarzan's Jane, Maureen O'Sullivan, and men have been going ape for her ever since. She bedded the ultimate swinger Frank Sinatra but lost him to Satan when he delivered divorce papers to the devil woman on the set of Roman Polanski's *Rosemary's Baby* (1968). Maybe Frank didn't like how frank Mia was with showing off her slender body and perky nips. She got to the bottom of the problem showing off her small but superb can in *John and Mary* (1969). As the flower girl bloomed into a woman and mother, she became less likely to open up and show her flesh petals.

SKIN-fining Moment:

A Wedding (1:10) *Mia poses topless for a painting wearing a bridal veil. Nice li'l wedding cakes.*

See Her Naked In:

Hurricane (1979) LB
A Wedding (1978) Breasts
John and Mary (1969) LB, Buns
Rosemary's Baby (1968) Body Double—Buns / Her—Breasts

Tisa Farrow

Born: July 22, 1951
Los Angeles, California
Skin-O-Meter: Brief Nudity

There are no guarantees for big-screen immortality. Consider the case of Tisa Farrow. She is a beautiful woman—fair, blue-eyed, and bountiful of God-given bust. Her father was movie director John Farrow. Mom Maureen O'Sullivan had been a flashy, hot-bodied movie star swinging through the trees in a skimpy animal-hide one-piece with Tarzan. And still Tisa, unlike her phenomenally famous sister Mia Farrow will pass from this life having been relatively obscure. A film actress by vocation, Tisa plied her trade in a string of European-made exploito pictures and a few lesser-known American titles. About all that is remembered from her movie career are the topless shots in *Some Call It*

Loving (1973) and a profile of boob in shadow with extended nipple in *L'Ultimo Cacciatore* (1980). Wait a second, maybe there is one guarantee for big-screen immortality after all.

SKIN-fining Moment:

Some Call it Loving (1:19) *Tisa's ta-ta's pop out as she's laying in bed and Zalman King pulls down the sheet. A tad dark . . .*

See Her Naked In:

L'Ultimo cacciatore (1980) Breasts
Some Call it Loving (1972) Breasts

Lisa Faulkner

Born: 1973
London, England, UK
Skin-O-Meter: Brief Nudity

That blonde hair cascading down either side of her innocently sultry face, like falling locks of entwined sunshine. That smile, shy only to the point of inviting the first move. Those eyes that don't look away or blink but simply draw you inward and deeper with a steady, beckoning regard. Break the gaze and scan her body. Christ, she's let her blouse fall open. It's impossible not to stare at that tit. It's full, rounded, swelling, heavy as with the milk of nirvana. Gawk for a while, then look back up. London-born, British-bred Lisa Faulkner is pleased at your attention. She does not play games. The promise extended in the purse of her lips is no tease. She is a consuming object of affection in *The Lover* (1992), and she is not there by accident.

SKIN-fining Moment:

The Lover (0:26) *Lisa's love-seat is visible as she strolls bare-assed through an infirmary.*

See Her Naked In:

The Lover (1992) RB, Buns

Sophie Favier

Born: October 5, 1963
Lyon, France
Skin-O-Meter: Great Nudity

If Vanna White were French and loved to show off her naked body (that's redundant) she'd be Sophie Favier. The TV game-show hostess with the moistest from the land of cork-popping beauties is little known Stateside outside of a bit part in *Cheech & Chong's The Corsican Brothers* (1984), in which she was appropriately cast as Lovely #2. Don't let her relative obscurity mislead; Sophie is a talent who exposes all onscreen. She washes down her dangerous curves in *Venus* (1983) and gets hot and manhandled in a randy love scene in *Frank and I* (1984). Lucky Frank, getting his paws on Sophie's massive meat melons. For this game-show hottie, let the games begin!

SKIN-fining Moment:

Venus (0:24) *Sophie shows it all off in the shower. Boppers, burger, and buttshish.*

See Her Naked In:

Frank and I (1984) FFN, Buns
Venus (1983) Breasts, Bush, Buns

Farrah Fawcett

Born: February 2, 1947
Corpus Christi, Texas
Skin-O-Meter: Great Nudity

Tawny blonde dreamboat Farrah Fawcett has been outrageous for almost as long as she has been famous. It's a toss-up as to whether her most erotically charged newsstand appearances have been in the tabloids or *Playboy*, the pages of which fair Farrah graced at fifty. As a young object of fixation, she started popping eyes with her popping nipples, which seemed about to burst out of whatever slinky top she was wearing during her reign on the original *Charlie's Angels* TV series. Fawcett parlayed the appeal of her thick, stand-up knobs into one of the best-selling pinup posters in the history of infatuated maledom. What was all the fuss about? Put on protective glasses and eyeball *Extremities* (1986). A daring and lucky fella licks Farrah's nips, and a rubbery cylinder of erectile tissue stands up to be saluted. A guy could clean his ears out with those things among other places.

SKIN-fining Moment:

Saturn 3 (0:17) *Farrah fools around with Kirk Douglas and we see her niptastic right funbag. That is one major Fawcett!*

See Her Naked In:

Dr. T and the Women (2000) FFN
Farrah Fawcett: All of Me (1997) FFN, Buns
Extremities (1986) RB
Saturn 3 (1980) RB
Myra Breckinridge (1970) Nip-Slip LB

TeleVisions:

Charlie's Angels Nip-Slip RB

Denise Faye

New York, New York
Skin-O-Meter: Brief Nudity

How do a father who's a doctor and a mom who's a psychiatric social worker combine for a daughter with the body of a top-rank stripper? This is only one of the questions that will not come to mind when viewing slinky, stacked, and salacious Denise Faye stealing the entire show in *American Pie 2* (2001). Although she had appeared as a background beauty in such acclaimed features as *Mighty Aphrodite* (1995) and *Donnie Brasco* (1997), Faye's slice of teasing lesbo life took center stage in *Pie 2*. Who's having more fun as rusty-blonde Denise locks lips and tweaks nips with tousled bed-head blonde

Lisa Arturo? Whoever has his finger on the PAUSE button, that's who.

SKIN-fining Moment:

American Pie 2 (0:54) *Bare boobage as Denise and Lisa Arturo give a nice little lesbo show to the Pie boys.*

See Her Naked In:

American Pie 2 (2001) Breasts, Thong

Angela Featherstone

Born: April 3, 1965
Hamilton, Ontario, Canada
Skin-O-Meter: Brief Nudity

Her hair fluctuates from blonde to red to brown, but Angela Featherstone's face is an alluring constant. The clean, fine lines of brow and sculpted cheeks set off the power of Angela's mesmerizing gaze. Her eyes are so blue and deep that they'd be scary except for the reassuring full and soft pads of her lips. If you were falling toward a profound infatuation, Angela Featherstone would be a great place to land. Even as the harrowing girlfriend to Adam Sandler's *Wedding Singer* (1998), Featherstone gave keen eyes two things to wonder about. Uncover Angela's angelic pair in *Dark Angel: The Ascent* (1994). The heavenly dish wanders naked through a clothed crowd, giving one and all a glimpse of paradise.

SKIN-fining Moment:

Dark Angel: The Ascent (0:08) *Angela emerges up into a city street completely starkers. Sweet public T&A.*

See Her Naked In:

Soul Survivors (2001) Breasts
Dark Angel: The Ascent (1994) Breasts, Buns

María Félix

Born: April 8, 1914
Alamos, Sonora, Mexico
Died: April 6, 2002
Skin-O-Meter: Brief Nudity

Reigning as a queen of the silver screens of Mexico and Europe for three decades, Sonora, Mexico-born, black-haired seductress María Félix added flash and fire to the films of world-shaping directors such as Luis Buñuel and Jean Renoir. María's signature character was the strong-headed, independent, sexually supercharged leading lady who by film's end would submit to the macho manhandling of a sensitive but studly dude whose sex drive revved at the same speed as her own. María keeps her cooler-than-ice sunglasses on throughout her daring baring in *Amor y Sexo* (1964), perhaps to keep from being blinded by the eternal luminosity of her anti-gravity orbs.

SKIN-fining Moment:

Amor y Sexo (0:56) *Black-and-white boobage as Maria unbuttons her shirt and turns to flash us. Gracias!*

See Her Naked In:

Amor y Sexo (1964) Breasts

Edwige Fenech

Born: December 24, 1948
Bône, Algeria
Skin-O-Meter: Hall of Fame

Edwige Fenech ranks among the moist prolific act-chests from the classic era of Italian sensual cinema. The statuesque brunette was born in the aptly named town of Bône in Algeria to a French father and a Tunisian mother. She would later move to Europe, where she became a sex star in mostly Italian features. She has made a career out of appearing in such wonderful films as *Sexy Susan Sins Again* (1968), *Swinging Young Seductresses* (1969), *Sex Is a Pleasure* (1969), *Naughty Nun* (1972), *Ubalda, All Naked and Warm* (1973), *La Soldatessa Alle Grandi Manovre* (1978), and the redundant *The Inconsolable Widow Thanks All Those Who Consoled Her* (1974)—

LA SOLDATESSA ALLA VISITA MILITARE:
EDWIGE FENECH DEMONSTRATES HER FLU-
ENCY IN THE UNIVERSAL LANGUAGE. ASIDE
FROM EDWIGE'S FLAWLESS FORM, I LIKE
THAT SHE'D ALLOW THAT PARTICULAR GROUP
OF MOOKS IN THE POSTER TO GET THAT
CLOSE A GANDER AT HER GOODS.

among many, many others. Most of
those movies, as well as such
groundbreaking skin classics as *The
Blonde and the Black Pussycat* (1969),
feature Edwige in at least some state
of undress. Her best films? Where to
begin? She made many classic Italian
Giallo thrillers, as well as many sexy
comedies. Edwige did more movies
with loads of gratuitous nudity than
without, however the majority of
them were rather tame and only a
few featured Edwige giving up the
full monty. Have a look at *Grazie
Nonna* (1975), a.k.a. *Lover Boy*, and
her all-time classic *Cattivi pensieri*
(1976), a.k.a. *Who Mislaid My Wife?*,
for the full Edwige form.

SKIN-fining Moment:

*Cattivi Pensieri (0:23) Full-frontal
glittering goodness followed by super
slo-mo bouncing breast-meat.*

See Her Naked In:

Tais-toi Quand tu Parles! (1981) Breasts,
Buns

Asso (1981) RB
Cornetti Alla Crema (1981) Breasts
Io e Caterina (1980) Buns
Zucchero, Miele e Peperoncino (1980)
Breasts
Il Ficcanaso (1980) Breasts, Buns
Il Ladrone (1979) Breasts, Bush
L'Insegnante va in Collegio (1978) Breasts
L'Insegnante Viene a Casa (1978) Breasts
La Soldatessa Alle Grandi Manovre (1978)
Breasts
La Soldatessa Alla Visita Militare (1977)
Breasts, Bush, Buns
La Vergine, il Toro e il Capricorno (1977)
Breasts
Taxi Girl (1977) Breasts
La Pretora (1976) FFN, Buns
Cattivi pensieri (1976) FFN, Buns
Sex with a Smile (1976) FFN, Buns
La Dottoressa del distretto militare (1976)
Breasts, Bush, Buns
La Moglie Vergine (1975) FFN, Buns
The Sexy Schoolteacher (1975)
Breasts
Grazie Nonna (1975) FFN, Buns
La Poliziotta fa Carriera (1975) Breasts
Escape From Death Row (1975) FFN, Buns
Anna, quel Particolare Piacere (1974)
Breasts
*La Vedova Inconsolabile Ringrazia Quanti la
Consolarono* (1974) Breasts, Bush,
Buns
La Signora Gioca Bene a Scopa? (1974)
Breasts, Buns
Innocenza e Turbamento (1974) Part TK
Ubalda, All Naked and Warm (1973) Breasts,
Thong
*Giovannona Coscialunga, Disonorata con
Onore* (1973) Breasts
Eye of the Black Cat (1972) Breasts
*La Bella Antonia, Prima Monica e Poi
Dimonia* (1972) FFN, Buns
All the Colors of the Dark (1972) Breasts,
Buns
Case of the Bloody Iris (1972) Breasts
5 Bambole per la Luna d'Agosto (1970) FFN,
Thong
Der Mann mit dem Goldenen Pinsel (1969)
Breasts, Buns
Top Sensation (1969) Breasts, Buns
Frau Wirtin Hat Auch eine Nichte (1969)
Breasts, Bush, Buns
The Blonde and the Black Pussycat (1969)
Breasts, Buns

TWO BOOB JUNCTION: SHERILYN FENN IN
TWO MOON JUNCTION.

Sherilyn Fenn

**Born: February 1, 1965
Detroit, Michigan
Skin-O-Meter: Hall of Fame**

Former Playboy Club bunny
Sherilyn Fenn made her first big-
screen impact with a memorable
part in the gender-bender teen flick
Just One of the Guys (1985). After a
few more years of charmingly
goofball youth movies, Sherilyn
showed everything she's got in
Zalman King's erotic carnie classic
Two Moon Junction (1988). Next,
Sherilyn read for each female
character on director David Lynch's
wacko ABC series *Twin Peaks* and
won the part of tarty schoolgirl
Audrey, who, in one of the most
sizzling moments in TV history,
unforgettably ties a cherry stem in a
knot using only her talented tongue.
In 1990, the year *Peaks* debuted,
Sherilyn appeared undressed in the
B-movie *Beauty and the Beast*
knockoff *Meridian* in addition to
spreading herself nude across the
pages of the December issue of
Playboy. Venturing past even *Twin
Peaks* weirdness, Sherilyn snatched
up the armless, legless, often-nude
lead in *Boxing Helena* (1993) after

Kim Basinger backed out. Since then, Sherilyn has kept covered and revealed only emotional nakedness on the Showtime series *Rude Awakening*. Mr. Skin likes physical nakedness better.

SKIN-fining Moment:

Two Moon Junction (1:25) *Sherilyn sheds her threads for some magnificent full-frontal action. Guess what: she's not really blonde!*

See Her Naked In:

Slave of Dreams (1995) LB, Buns
Boxing Helena (1993) Breasts
Backstreet Dreams (1990) RB
Meridian (1990) Breasts
True Blood (1989) Nip Slip RB
Crime Zone (1988) Breasts
Two Moon Junction (1988) FFN, Buns
The Wraith (1986) Breasts

TeleVisions:

Rude Awakening Thong

Sandra Ferguson

Born: March 23, 1967
Pittsburgh, Pennsylvania
Skin-O-Meter: Great Nudity

Soap-opera stars are like American Kennel Club purebreds in that they are among the most finely bred bitches in the entertainment universe and their names are often Biblically long. Take preciously blonde dramatist Sandra Ferguson, who starred as Amanda Cory Fowler Harrison Sinclair during her twelve-year run as a leading femme fatale on *Another World*. Sandra could not have been any more archly innocent and fresh-faced schemey if she'd been the end product of a genetics program to develop the ultimate midwestern vixen. And then she went and misbehaved like any mutt from the neighborhood, pulling out her dugs, nipples and all, for a naked-chest make-out session in *Illegal in Blue* (1995).

SKIN-fining Moment:

Illegal in Blue (0:08) *Fergie shows her funbags while parallel parking.*

See Her Naked In:

Illegal in Blue (1995) Breasts

TeleVisions:

Hotline (Part) TK

Sabrina Ferilli

Born: June 28, 1964
Rome, Italy
Skin-O-Meter: Great Nudity

Sabrina Ferilli is known in her native Italy as a communist, but her career as an actress gets high *Marx* for her skin exposure. She started her career with a bit part in the made-for-Italian-TV movie *Portami la Luna* (1986). Since then, she has gone on to become one of Italy's most beloved female celebrities, largely due to her stellar acting career as well as her stint as the spokesperson for *Spaghetti* brand products. It doesn't hurt that Sabrina has spent quite a bit of time in the nude in her many movies—no, it feels real good. She made her first (and arguably best) skinful performance in the film *Die Falle* (1995), which featured several lingering looks at her massive mammaries as well as some nice muff shots. She has since gone on to appear in some state of undress in *Diario di un Vizio* (1993), *Anche i Commercialisti Hanno un'Anima* (1994), *Ferie d'Agosto* (1996), and *Le Giraffe* (2000). This Sabrina is certainly bewitching.

SKIN-fining Moment:

Die Falle (0:22) *Brief buns and partial tittage followed by full frontal nudity: all visible when Sabrina strips to go skinny-dipping in the sea. That's my kind of fish!*

See Her Naked In:

La Giraffe (2000) Thong
Il Signor Quindicipalle (1998) Thong
Ferie d'Agosto (1996) RB, Thong
Vite Strozzate (1996) Breasts
Die Falle (1995) FFN, Buns
La Bella Vita (1994) Breasts, Thong
Anche i Commercialisti Hanno un'Anima (1994) Breasts
Diario di un Vizio (1993) Buns
Americano Rosso (1991) FFN, Buns

Vanessa Ferlito

Skin-O-Meter: Great Nudity

Lovely Latina Vanessa Ferlito is one of those darkly seductive firecrackers who heats up everything she's been in and adds sparks to her sexy scenes. She hasn't been in much, but so far Mr. Skin likes what he sees. Vanessa began her career in 1999 with a bang on the hit series *The Sopranos*, not that she was whacked or anything. She's since gone on to guest on such high profile boob-tube programs as *Third Watch* and *Law & Order*. Vanessa made her film debut in the unconventional *On Line* (2002), the first movie ever shot almost exclusively via webcam on the Internet. It's about the sexual underworld in New York City, which is promising, though Vanessa manages to keep her clothes on throughout. She lost that inhibition in the John Leguizamo-directed HBO production *Undefeated* (2003). She goes topless by the pool, and Leguizamo allows himself some nice feels of her bitty breasts and meaty ass. It's a good start to a promising career, which will hopefully be showcasing Vanessa's Ferlito-burger soon.

SKIN-fining Moment:

Undefeated (0:38) *Nice view of her tan-lined titlets as she sunbathes topless, followed by action peeks as John Leguizamo pushes her into the pool.*

See Her Naked In:

Undefeated (2003) Breasts, Buns
On Line (2002) Breasts

Cristina Ferrare

Born: February 8, 1950
Cleveland, Ohio
Skin-O-Meter: Brief Nudity

Cristina Ferrare first showed up in filmdom with a supporting role in *The Impossible Years* (1968). After a failed marriage to noted failed auto manufacturer and failed cocaine-smuggling entrepreneur John DeLorean, however, her acting career faltered and she took to hosting talk shows. Local shows in Los Angeles led to nationwide shows such as *Incredible Sunday* and the decidedly feminine oriented *Men Are From Mars, Women Are From Venus*. That isn't to say that the very lovely Cristina never made it as a headlining actress. Her most notable (and skinful) part was as the bisexual, vampiric title character in *Mary Mary, Bloody Mary* (1975). It's a scarce low-budget picture, but if you can lay your meat beaters on a copy, do so, because it features Cristina's only skinitudity. On several occasions she flashes her perky palookas, most often just before killing some hapless guy and right after giving him the best final moments a fellow could ever hope for: he comes, he goes!

SKIN-fining Moment:

Mary Mary, Bloody Mary (0:42) See Helena Rojo pull down Cristina's shirt! See Cristina's awesome cans on full display for a good half minute! See Helena make the lesbian mack moves! So much to see!

See Her Naked In:

Mary Mary, Bloody Mary (1975) Breasts, Buns

Jami Ferrell

Born: June 20, 1974
Muncie, Indiana
Skin-O-Meter: Great Nudity

Let's say a farm-fresh blonde with hair like corn silk and a face and rack that both glow with the intensity of the sun of sex spins into your orbit. This improbably plentiful bundle of pulchritude hails from Muncie, Indiana, and her resumé is replete with credits such as *Playboy's Gen-X Girls* (1998), *Playboy Roommates* (2001), and *Playboy's Barefoot Beauties* (2002). Would it be hard to guess that this midwestern erotic whirlwind—let's call her Jami Ferrell—has a *Playboy* centerfold in her past, say as recently as January 1997? Would it be a leap of faith to predict that her topless jumping jacks and tits-out sunbathing would steal the show in a major feature film, one very much like *Boat Trip* (2002)?

SKIN-fining Moment:

Boat Trip (0:00) Wow! This lounging bikini team includes Shauna Sand, Jami, Teri Harrison, Natalia Sokolova, Deanna Brooks. Jami, Natalia, and Deanna bust out their nude guns.

See Her Naked In:

Boat Trip (2002) Breasts
Fast Lane to Malibu (2000) Breasts
Numerous *Playboy* Videos

Irena Ferris

Skin-O-Meter: Great Nudity

Irena Ferris began her career as one of the many pieces of eye candy and secret balloon smugglers on the hit series *The Love Boat* before taking on a role in the made-for-TV movie *Once Upon a Spy* (1980). Bit parts in more cinematic fare such as *Paternity* (1981) and *Looker* (1981) followed until she landed her breakthrough performance as Blue Eyes in the made-for-TV flick

Cocaine and Blue Eyes (1983). Thankfully, someone took notice, and Irena landed the lead in *Covergirl* (1984), in which she spent the first hour or so flashing her breasts at the drop of a hat—well, more like the drop of a blouse and bra, which is better.

SKIN-fining Moment:

Covergirl (0:19) Nice view of her Ferris Wheels taking off her robe and getting into tub.

See Her Naked In:

Covergirl (1984) Breasts

Chelsea Field

Born: May 27, 1957
Glendale, California
Skin-O-Meter: Great Nudity

A wide-eyed brunette with nice and natural boobies that ace the bounce test, dancer/actress Chelsea Field has enjoyed a long and varied stay in the public eye. She first grooved and shimmied into sight as a *Solid Gold* dancer in 1983 and sprang from that platform to the role of barely covered Teela in *Masters of the Universe* (1987). Chelsea has gone through a phase of playing the motherly wife in mainstream movies such as *The Last Boy Scout* (1991) and *Andre* (1994), and she's done her share of acclaimed TV work in notable series that include *The Bronx Zoo*, *Nightingales*, and *Angel Falls*. Most important, Chelsea has shown up to be counted in sexploitation fare that includes *Dust Devil* (1992) and *Extreme Justice* (1993). Look for the first rise of her full moon when she pops up out of bed in *Harley Davidson and the Marlboro Man* (1991).

SKIN-fining Moment:

A Passion to Kill (0:55) Chelsea gets topless and shows her chugalugs getting it on with Scott Bakula in a garage.

See Her Naked In:

A Passion to Kill (1994) Breasts, Buns
Extreme Justice (1993) LB
Dust Devil (1992) LB
Harley Davidson and the Marlboro Man
   (1991) LB, Buns

Sally Field

Born: November 6, 1946
Pasadena, California
Skin-O-Meter: Brief Nudity

Mr. Skin likes Sally Field . . . really likes her! The little innocent five-foot-two-and-a-half-inch cutie first stole our hearts as the bikini-clad lead on *Gidget*. This irrepressible teen imp went from the beach to the convent as the celibate title character on the hit series *The Flying Nun*. She got out of the habit with a crazy performance in the made-for-TV movie *Sybil* (1976). Sally took home Oscars for *Norma Rae* (1979) and *Places in the Heart* (1984), but it's her work with one-time beau Burt Reynolds that wins a nice booby prize. Films such as *Smokey and the Bandit* (1977), *Hooper* (1978), and *The End* (1978), which exposed some nice cleavage, revealed Sally's sexy side. But when it comes to flesh, Sally's nude scene in *Stay Hungry* (1976) remains her pièce-of-ass de résistance. Talk about a Field of dreams.

SKIN-fining Moment:

Stay Hungry (0:29) *Sally briefly shows her backfield while standing nude and gawking at pictures over the fireplace. Then we see slight side-mammage and a little more cheek as she gets back into bed with Jeff Bridges.*

See Her Naked In:

Stay Hungry (1976) LB, Buns

Jeanna Fine

Born: September 29, 1964
New York, New York
Skin-O-Meter: Great Nudity

Born Jennifer Payson (and once she had a son she doubled up on her work to pay for him), Jeanna Fine changed her name, blew up her flatties to fatties, and rose to the cream of the crop of the adult industry. Her introduction to the world of wank was as a talent coordinator at *Hustler* magazine before beginning an on-and-off porno career (in every sense of the phrase). It began with a meaty role in *Sexaholic* (1985). She has quit the jiz biz three times since then but always seems to come back for more. Jeanna started as a platinum-blonde punkette and morphed into a raven-maned sex machine. Her highlights include: *Hothouse Rose* (1991), *Edward Penishands* (1991), and *New Wave Hookers 5* (1997). If the hairy-palm pictures aren't your bag of nuts, due perhaps to the presence of too many bags of nuts, then check out one of Jeanna's more genteel works. *Halloween Night* (1990) and *Boondock Saints* (1999) both feature her naked, rock-hard body—you'll be rock hard, too. She also appeared in the Matt Stone/Trey Parker comedy *Orgazmo* (1997), but the send up of blue movies is woefully lacking in the skin! Nothing Fine about that.

SKIN-fining Moment:

Eve's Beach Fantasy (0:40) *Fakeroonie torso-orbs getting groped by a hot tub dude as April Adams secretly watches.*

See Her Naked In:

The Boondock Saints (1999) LB
Eve's Beach Fantasy (1995) Breasts
Numerous Adult Movies

Linda Fiorentino

Born: March 9, 1960
Philadelphia, Pennsylvania
Skin-O-Meter: Great Nudity

MR. SKIN'S TOP TEN

Naked Femmes Fatales
. . . Fatal skin-tractions

10. Jaime Pressly
   —*Poison Ivy 3: The New Seduction* 1997

9. Lysette Anthony
   —*Save Me* 1993

8. Rebecca De Mornay
   —*The Hand that Rocks the Cradle* 1992

7. Kathleen Turner
   —*Body Heat* 1981

6. Virginia Madsen
   —*The Hot Spot* 1990

5. Jennifer Jason Leigh
   —*Single White Female* 1992

4. Sharon Stone
   —*Basic Instinct* 1992

3. Mädchen Amick
   —*Dream Lover* 1994

2. Glenn Close
   —*Fatal Attraction* 1987

1. **Linda Fiorentino**
   —*The Last Seduction* 1994

Husky voiced, poker loving, and undeniably alluring in a "she might be able to kick my ass" kind of way, lovely Linda Fiorentino's first role was of the standard love-interest type in the teen romance *Vision Quest* (1985). That led to her skinsational first nude scene as a downtown artist in Martin Scorsese's Soho nightmare *After Hours* (1985) and then an equally revealing arthouse turn in Alan Rudolph's *The Moderns* (1988). Years of relatively low-key projects came next, few of which offered Linda an opportunity to let loose her raw, Philadelphia-bred sexuality. That changed—really changed—with Linda's inimitable turn as a cold-as-nails femme fatale in the neo-noir *The Last Seduction*

SHE DUNNE HIM NUDE: LINDA FIORENTINO
AND GRIFFIN DUNNE IN *AFTER HOURS*.

(1994), highlighted by Linda's head-on encounter with addled dupe Peter Berg against a chain-link fence, followed a year later with a heaping helping of sizzling screen sex sans wardrobe in the sordid thriller *Jade* (1995).

SKIN-fining Moment:

Jade (0:24) *Naked, insanely hot Linda steams up on a chair while talking on the phone. We get a great rear view of her ultra-sweet seat-meat.*

See Her Naked In:

Jade (1995) Breasts, Buns
The Last Seduction (1994) Breasts, Buns
Chain of Desire (1993) LB
Beyond the Law (1992) Breasts, Thong
Strangers (1991) LB
The Moderns (1988) Breasts, Buns
Gotcha (1985) Breasts
After Hours (1985) Breasts

Kate Fischer

Born: November 30, 1973
Adelaide, Australia
Skin-O-Meter: Great Nudity

When you catch Kate Fischer in her movie debut, you known instantly not to throw this one back. That movie, *Sirens* (1994), is a skin classic, and not just because Kate shares screen time with the luscious pair Elle MacPherson and Portia de Rossi. Her character's name is Pru, but Kate is no prude, as she proves in the many gratuitous full-frontal scenes she shares with her carnal costars. Whetting the appetite with such a meaty first course is hard to top. The Aussie arouser then took flight in little-seen local ditties such as *Dust Off the Wings* (1997) and *Pigeon* (1998), but American audiences know her breast for her work as a correspondent on *E! News*, where she joins fellow eye candy such as Jules Asner and Brooke Burke. Yes, Kate keeps good company. While not as bone stroking as her debut, Kate's nipples do their best to escape her wet T-shirt in a scene from *Blood Surf* (2000), which makes Mr. Skin moan, "Kiss me, Kate!"

SKIN-fining Moment:

Sirens (0:25) *Kate flashes her ass and a bit of full-frontal from a distance while wading, then continues to bare her breasts for a very long time when Mr. Camera decides to get a bit closer.*

See Her Naked In:

Sirens (1994) FFN, Buns

Frances Fisher

Born: May 11, 1952
Milford-on-the-sea, England, UK
Skin-O-Meter: Brief Nudity

The daughter of an international oil-refinery construction supervisor, fiery-tressed Frances Fisher was born in Britain but raised around the world, as her daddy's job kept her family on the move. A lengthy New York stage career ultimately led to her first substantial bite at stardom in the mid '70s when she appeared regularly on the boob-tube sudsers *The Edge of Night* and *The Guiding Light*. A series of low-key film projects followed, but it wasn't until 1992 that Frances made her first memorable mark when she portrayed headstrong madam Strawberry Alice in Clint Eastwood's award-winning western *Unforgiven* (1992). Her long-term relationship with Clint, which yielded daughter Francesca Eastwood in 1993, didn't hurt the ole Q rating either! Interestingly, it wasn't as *Unforgiven*'s bordello boss that Frances allowed her flesh flaps to get out for a spell and enjoy some topless Fishering, nor was it the cinematic smash *Titanic* (1997). Her skin scene was primarily saved for the erotic art-house entry *Female Perversions* (1997), which found Frances ridding herself of a bothersome blue blouse and taking a topless turn. Hmmmm . . . is it just a coincidence that the skintastic sequence transpired AFTER she and Eastwood parted ways?

SKIN-fining Moment:

Frame Up (0:52) *Frances lies back topless in bed with Wings Hauser and shows off her Fishers.*

See Her Naked In:

Passion and Prejudice (2001) LB, Buns
Female Perversions (1997) Breasts, Bush, Thong
Frame Up (1991) Breasts

Tara Fitzgerald

Born: September 17, 1968
Sussex, England, UK
Skin-O-Meter: Great Nudity

Starting with her movie debut in *Hear My Song* (1991), Tara Fitzgerald has just said no to her costume designer, preferring to film in her birthday suit. Not only did she expose a lungful of her fist-sized frisky sweater kittens, but she even flashed some pussy, cats! Breast of all, it was only the beginning of what has turned out to be a long and skinful career. This English strumpet blows Mr. Skin's horn in such randy fare as *A Man of No Importance* (1995), *The Student Prince* (1997), *Frenchman's Creek* (1998), and *Conquest* (1998). In the latter, she finally puts on some clothing, but the hem can't quite cover her splendid ass. Her second film remains her mammary opus, the skintacular *Sirens* (1994), in which she strips as naked as costars Kate Fisher, Elle MacPherson, and Portia de Rossi and even does a girl-girl duet. From her full-frontal TV flashes in the mini-series *The Camomile Lawn* (1992) to later-day skinage in *Rancid Aluminum* (2000) and *Dark Blue World* (2001), Tara's ta-tas are terrific!

SKIN-fining Moment:

Sirens (1:00) *Tara's tits bounce around while she fantasizes about running into a group of eager fellers, followed by a friendly shot of the fuzz when she imagines herself naked in church.*

See Her Naked In:

I Capture the Castle (2003) Breasts
Dark Blue World (2001) Breasts
Rancid Aluminium (2000) Breasts, Buns
In the Name of Love (1999) Breasts, Buns
Conquest (1998) Breasts, Buns
Frenchman's Creek (1998) Breasts, Buns
The Student Prince (1997) Buns
A Man of No Importance (1995) Breasts
The Vacillations of Poppy Carew (1995) Breasts
Sirens (1994) FFN
Hear My Song (1991) FFN, Buns

TeleVisions:

The Camomile Lawn FFN

Gabrielle Fitzpatrick

Australia
Skin-O-Meter: Brief Nudity

Having kids is not the end of the world. Sure, a doting dad is required to take the tykes out to kid-friendly movies, something along the lines of *Mighty Morphin Power Rangers: The Movie* (1995). But while sitting in the darkened theater, surrounded by squalling brats and their popcorn-gobbling moms, Dad spies a creamy-skinned redhead with flashing eyes and gleaming teeth and a flexing, sex-infused body that all but bursts from her seamless, Lycra Power Ranger costume. A thorough scrutiny of the end credits turns up the name Gabrielle Fitzpatrick. A few moments of Internet research reveal Gabrielle to be a former model from Australia. Her film and TV credits include a little-seen budget thriller called *Downward Angel* (2000). Papa has a hunch that a blip of Power Ranger nip might slip in *Downward Angel*, and Papa knows best.

SKIN-fining Moment:

Downward Angel (1:11) *Gabrielle soaps up in the shower and her naked left chest Angel points visibly outward.*

See Her Naked In:

Downward Angel (2000) Breasts

Fionnula Flanagan

Born: December 10, 1941
Dublin, Ireland
Skin-O-Meter: Hall of Fame

More Irish than a handful of wee leprechauns sipping Guinness in a field of shamrocks, veteran actress Fionnula Flanagan has found her greatest onscreen success portraying several of James Joyce's lovers in *James Joyce's Women* (1985). Not only did Fionnula write, adapt, and produce the original award-winning play, she also penned and produced the screenplay. Fionnula gives the most skintastic performance of her career in the film, lying naked in bed, her fabulous frontage reaching to the sky and her fur on full display, reciting a monologue while masturbating! For more (unfortunately brief) blinks of her boobs, check out *Crossover* (1980) and *Nightmare in Badham County*

(1976). Fionnula has aged gracefully since her skinematic heyday but continues to land big Hollywood roles in films including *The Others* (2001) and *Divine Secrets of the Ya-Ya Sisterhood* (2002).

SKIN-fining Moment:

James Joyce's Women (1:06) *She shows off tons of fabulous full-frontal flesh during this exceptionally long scene in which she lies on a bed and fingers through the divine secrets of her Ya-Ya.*

See Her Naked In:

James Joyce's Women (1983) FFN
Crossover (1980) Breasts
Nightmare in Badham County (1976) Breasts

Maureen Flannigan

Born: December 30, 1973
Inglewood, California
Skin-O-Meter: Brief Nudity

The regal good looks of blonde descendent of Erin Maureen Flannigan might be described as icy, except that the flush of passion that rises hotter than a blush to her high, sculpted cheekbones melts away any notions of cold. A reigning starlet of the network pantheon, Maureen's corruscating Celtic perfection has flashed forth from recurring segments of *Out of this World*, *Push*, and *7th Heaven*. When a wonderful young woman reaches such heights of lucrative and clothed exposure, the hopes of a skinful future are on a dimmer. But there is always the glimmer of the past, in particular *Teenage Bonnie and Klepto Clyde* (1993). There's a young Flannigan, barely out of her teens, if that, alone in a car with a greasy-haired mook. Suddenly, Maureen's top is tossed over her head, and there *they* are! Popped out into full view, flying around as the sassy lass leaps into the car's backseat. Miracles do happen, and cameras are there to catch them.

SKIN-fining Moment:

Teenage Bonnie and Klepto Clyde (0:44) *She shows her set while screwing Scott Wolf on a stack of cash. Think about that the next time you pull a bill out of your wallet.*

See Her Naked In:

Teenage Bonnie and Klepto Clyde (1993) Breasts

Heidi Fleiss

Born: December 30, 1965
Los Feliz, California
Skin-O-Meter: Brief Nudity

Heidi Fleiss will always be the Hollywood Madam, the fox who ran the cathouse for the big-screen sharks. But after her arrest in 1993 and imprisonment for tax evasion and money laundering a few years later, Heidi went straight . . . to video. She sidestepped to filmdom with *The Doom Generation* (1995) in a cameo as a liquor-store clerk, but for more skin-friendly entertainment we have to go to the videotape. With Victoria Sellers, daughter of celebrated actor Peter Sellers, and stellar-breasted Britt Ekland, Heidi starred in *Sex Tips with Heidi Fleiss and Victoria Sellers* (2001). The ladies of the night reveal how to make your woman a happy hooker but reveal very little of their own charms. For a glimpse of Heidi's hooters, check out her documentary *Heidi Fleiss: The Hollywood Madam* (1995). She's since penned a tell-all tome called *Pandering* in which she reproduces her invitation to President Bill Clinton's inauguration—big surprise—and a letter from Princess Diana that reads: "Thanks, Heidi, what a babe. He rocked my world." Heidi 'ho.

SKIN-fining Moment:

Heidi Fleiss: Hollywood Madam (0:40) *Brief tits, bush, and ass running away from the camera. I'd buy 'em.*

See Her Naked In:

Heidi Fleiss: Hollywood Madam (1995) Breasts, Bush, Buns

Holly Floria

Born: 1966
California
Skin-O-Meter: Brief Nudity

The secret to pixie-faced blonde Holly Floria's improbable success as a secret agent terrorist catcher on the syndicated television docudrama *Acapulco H.E.A.T.* was her ability to squeeze her succulent mounds and sweetly rounded hips into a skimpy swimsuit and then keep her head straight while all around her evil men were losing their concentration in frothy spurts of mental meltdown. Holly had perfected her technique of stringing out male attention using nothing more than her tanned, toned body and a two-piece bathing suit in the rigorous training regimen used by all the natives on *Bikini Island* (1991). Admit it: If Holly Floria was on your tail, you'd be happy for her to bust your ass.

SKIN-fining Moment:

Presumed Guilty (1:02) *Holly gets it on with her guy in bed, presenting us with left hoot, hot buns, and a fast, fuzzy view of her hairy Floria.*

See Her Naked In:

Bikini Island (1991) Buns
Presumed Guilty (1991) LB, Buns

Darlanne Fluegel

Born: 1956
Wilkes-Barre, Pennsylvania
Skin-O-Meter: Great Nudity

Blonde, pouty Darlanne Fluegel wowed with her film debut as one of Faye Dunaway's stable of hot models in *The Eyes of Laura Mars* (1978). It also introduced Darlanne's petite pair in some trashy backstage scenes. She became a cult favorite thanks to her affinity for violent cop and sci-fi dramas—and a growing habit of taking off her top. She was murdered in *Once Upon a Time in America* (1984) but was put to better use in the noir *To Live and Die in L.A.* (1985), which brought her tits flashing for an encore. She continued the tawdry trend in *Freeway* (1988), *Project Alien* (1989), and *Breaking Point* (1993). Then Darlanne moved to the boob tube and ironically kept her little girls concealed on series such as *Crime Story*, *Wiseguy*, and *Hunter*. In recent years, Darlanne has been teaching acting at the University of Central Florida Film School, where she's sure to pass on her topless technique.

SKIN-fining Moment:

To Live and Die in L.A. (0:44) *Nice titlets and taut tail as Darlanne cavorts with her dude in their bedroom.*

See Her Naked In:

Breaking Point (1993) Breasts, Thong
Pet Sematary II (1992) Body Double—Breasts
Project Alien (1989) Buns
Freeway (1988) Breasts
To Live and Die in L.A. (1985) Breasts, Buns
Eyes of Laura Mars (1978) Breasts

Alison Folland

Born: August 10, 1978
Boston, Massachusetts
Skin-O-Meter: Great Nudity

With no prior experience or even an interest in acting, Alison Folland landed her first cinematic role as a result of a mass casting call for *To Die For* (1995). Needless to say, she got the part and has since enjoyed a fairly rapid ascent up the Hollywood food chain. Following a bit part in *Before and After* (1996), Alison landed the lead in the acclaimed arthouse staple *All Over Me* (1997). (No, it's not a porno flick as the title might suggest, nor does it mark the cinematic debut of Monica Lewinsky.) She soon found herself in character roles again, albeit in movies such as *Good Will Hunting* (1997), *Boys Don't Cry* (1999), and *Finding Forrester* (2000). Things could most certainly be worse. Fortunately, Alison, although on the rise in entertainment circles, took some time out to finally flash her fantastic flappers in *Things Behind the Sun* (2001). It's a seriously depressing movie, so beware, but there are ample glimpses of her gargantuan gazongas while she lay

in bed with (the incredibly fortunate) Gabriel Mann. The tryst is very realistic. Alison, was Mann's aim true?

SKIN-fining Moment:

Things Behind the Sun (0:20) *Topless in bed with her boy. The scene is a little dark, but she has wicked-hot whoppers!*

See Her Naked In:

Things Behind the Sun (2001) Breasts

Bridget Fonda

Born: January 27, 1964
Los Angeles, California
Skin-O-Meter: Hall of Fame

It ain't easy being a rebel when your old man is Peter Fonda. But Bridget Fonda has tried to blaze her own trail in the same industry where dad, aunt Jane Fonda, and granddad Henry Fonda became stars. Bridget appeared in both *You Can't Hurry Love* and *Shag* in 1988. She went on to star in such films as Cameron Crowe's *Singles* (reportedly, Crowe wrote Fonda's role specifically for her), *Single White Female* (1992), *Bodies, Rest & Motion* (1993), *Point of No Return* (1993), and *It Could Happen to You* (1994). Bridget also threw her light body into the role of Eleanor Lightbody in *The Road to Wellville* (1994), where her topless bathtub scene leads many a viewer to rub-a-

SINGLE WHITE FEMALE, DOUBLE WHITE FEMALE PARTS: BRIDGET FONDA THROWS (AND STRIPS) DOWN WITH JENNIFER JASON LEIGH.

dub-dub his nub. And her topless debut in *Aria* (1987) has been a skintastic classic for a decade and a half. Bridget played a bong-sucking, ill-fated beach bunny in *Jackie Brown* (1997) and brought her skinful can to *A Simple Plan* (1998) as Bill Paxton's pregnant, crazed wife.

SKIN-fining Moment:

Jackie Brown (1:15) *Nice bun-shot as Bridget walks away after Robert DeNiro has pounded her pooper in the kitchen.*

See Her Naked In:

Kiss of the Dragon (2001) Nip-Slip LB
Break Up (1998) Breasts
Jackie Brown (1997) Buns
Touch (1997) Buns
The Road to Wellville (1994) Breasts
Camilla (1994) FFN, Buns
Single White Female (1992) Breasts, Buns
Leather Jackets (1991) Breasts
The Godfather: Part III (1990) Buns
Scandal (1989) Breasts, Buns
Aria (1987) Breasts, Buns

Jane Fonda

Born: December 21, 1937
New York, New York
Skin-O-Meter: Great Nudity

Being the daughter of Henry Fonda may have helped Jane Fonda land a few acting roles over the years, but her skintastic sexiness and bodacious booberage ensured that she'd stick around even if her name got changed to Hanoi. After starring on Broadway in *Tall Story*, Jane made her film debut by re-creating the role on the big screen in 1960. Next, Jane became one of the first major American actresses to appear nude in a foreign film in *La Ronde* (1964), directed by her lover (and later her first husband) Roger Vadim. Roger next cast a kinky, space-age-costumed Jane in her most boobastic role yet, *Barbarella* (1968), in which Jane popped up on every man's erection radar. In the late '60s Jane got caught up in the anti-Vietnam War movement, but came back to Earth as a prostitute in the clever *Klute* (1971). Jane won an Oscar for that role and scored another for *Coming Home* (1978). She worked with her father on film for the only time in *On Golden Pond* (1981), and caused a workout sensation with her exercise video series throughout the rest of the '80s.

SKIN-fining Moment:

Barbarella (0:03) *Jane's totally naked as she gets out of her space suit in zero gravity, but the damn credits get in the way of her most important parts!*

See Her Naked In:

Old Gringo (1989) LB
The Morning After (1986) Breasts
Coming Home (1978) Body Double—Buns /
    Her—Breasts
Klute (1971) RB
Barbarella (1968) Breasts, Buns
The Game Is Over (1966) Breasts
La Ronde (1964) RB
Les Félins (1964) LB

Michelle Forbes

Born: February 17, 1967
Austin, Texas
Skin-O-Meter: Brief Nudity

Made-in-Texas Michelle Forbes followed a career path similar to many sly and sexy actresses who leave their hometowns behind in search of success on the stage and screen. Arriving in New York in the late '80s, Michelle quickly picked up a part on the leading daytime soap opera *The Guiding Light*, which soon led her piercing gaze and sleek figure to a handful of substantial roles in some notable films, including *The Playboys* (1992), *Love Bites* (1994), and the cult favorite *Swimming with Sharks* (1994). It was in the killer thriller *Kalifornia* (1993) that audience orbs focused on Forbes as she traipsed about sporting a Louise

Brooks bob and some beckoning black undergarments that slipped away for one brief moment to reveal a glimpse of her equally black bush and a set of perky nipples. A series of sadly skinless films and TV shows has since followed, led by roles on *Homicide: Life on the Street* and *Star Trek: The Next Generation*, on which she played the undeniably sexy alien Ensign Ro Laren.

SKIN-fining Moment:

Kalifornia (0:34) *As bedmate David Duchovny descends toward Michelle's mound, we see her furry Forbes' foundation briefly in deliciously fuzzy profile.*

See Her Naked In:

Kalifornia (1993) Bush

Anitra Ford

Skin-O-Meter: Great Nudity

Years before Vanna White was spinning around her letters on *Wheel of Fortune*, Anitra Ford was strutting her stunning stems around a sound stage as one of the original models on the immortal game show *The Price is Right*. Her all-too-clothed TV appearances may have been the impetus to exploit herself the way curvy up-and-coming actresses did in the '70s— by appearing in a string of exploitation films! The result was a full-frontal flash in the women's-prison flick *The Big Bird Cage* (1972), a baring of her buns in *Invasion of the Bee Girls* (1973), and a substantial role in a red negligee opposite Burt Reynolds in *The Longest Yard* (1974). Following her skin trysts, it was back to the tube, where Anitra looked a-nice in a series of guest spots on the most popular cop shows of the era, including *Banacek*, *S.W.A.T.*, *Mannix*, and *Starsky and Hutch*.

SKIN-fining Moment:

Invasion of the Bee Girls (0:47) *Anitra strips to show buns and boobs for a guy by a fire. Nice stingers!*

See Her Naked In:

The Longest Yard (1974) LB
Invasion of the Bee Girls (1973) Breasts, Buns
Stacey (1973) Breasts
The Big Bird Cage (1972) LB, Bush, Buns

Maria Ford

Born: 1966
Pikes Peak, Colorado
Skin-O-Meter: Great Nudity

Some of the hardest-working stars in showbiz are those blondes with the *Playboy*-quality ex-cheerleader faces on top of *Playboy*-quality ex-cheerleader bodies, as typified by prolific and alluring Maria Ford. Maria has made her mark, and frequently so, appearing without a stitch of clothing in films with titles such as *Stripteaser* (1995) and *Strip for Action* (1996). It's pointless to try to tally how many movies Maria has made, because she'll have a new one on the shelves before you're done counting. The Ford oeuvre can be divided into two distinct periods: pre- and post-breast enhancement. The tits are moderate and wholly sexy up until the mid 1990s, as seen in *The Glass Cage* (1996). In the late 1990s, a lift of extra protrusion was built into the shelf, as enjoyed in *The Key to Sex* (1998). Maria's mounds are arguably superior in both the natural and the add-on versions.

SKIN-fining Moment:

Naked Obsession (0:20) *Maria peels to a G-string and pops her pongos into to the face of strip-club customer William Katt.*

See Her Naked In:

Night Calls: The Movie, Part 2 (1999) FFN, Buns
Perfect Fit (1999) Breasts, Thong
I Like to Play Games Too (1998) FFN, Buns
The Key to Sex (1998) FFN, Buns
Stripteaser 2 (1997) Breasts, Thong
Future Fear (1997) Breasts
Strip for Action (1996) Breasts, Thong
Showgirl Murders (1996) Breasts, Thong
Mind Games (1996) Breasts, Buns
Machine Gun Blues (1996) Breasts, Buns
The Glass Cage (1996) FFN, Buns
Burial of the Rats (1995) Breasts
Stripteaser (1995) Breasts, Thong
The Wasp Woman (1995) FFN, Thong
Angel of Destruction (1994) Breasts, Thong
Saturday Night Special (1994) Breasts, Buns
The Unnamable II: The Statement of Randolph Carter (1993) Breasts, Buns
Final Judgement (1992) Breasts, Thong
Ring of Fire (1991) Breasts
The Haunting of Morella (1990) Breasts

Naked Obsession (1990) FFN, Buns
The Rain Killer (1990) FFN, Buns
Slumber Party Massacre III (1990) Breasts, Thong
Deathstalker IV: Match of the Titans (1990) Breasts, Buns
Stripped to Kill II (1989) Breasts, Thong
Dance of the Damned (1988) Breasts, Thong
Le Déclic (1985) FFN, Thong

TeleVisions:

Arli$$ Breasts
Erotic Confessions FFN, Buns
Hotline Breasts
Passion Cove FFN

Amanda Foreman

Born: July 15, 1966
Los Angeles, California
Skin-O-Meter: Brief Nudity

Amanda Foreman is the daughter of late, great film producer John Foreman and actress Linda Lawson. She got her start in the acting business with a small role in the made-for-TV movie *The Preppie Murder* (1989). In spite of giving off sparks onscreen with her sexual electricity, Amanda subsequently appeared in curiously miniscule roles in films such as *Live Wire* (1992), *Forever Young* (1992), and *Sliver* (1993). Finally, in 1998 Amanda landed the career-boosting part she needed as one of the edgier college students on the hit series *Felicity*. Needless to say, her professional life is doing just fine, but a few years back Amanda really busted out. She popped up on the skin-o-scope with quite an audible blip—actually there were two blips: one for each hooter she bared in the made-for-HBO movie *Breast Men* (1997). It's a very nice look at Amanda's pillbox-sized fun-baggage, among a host of other busty babes' boobage. Speaking of lungs, Amanda uses her little two pair as a singer in the L.A. rock band Teen Machine. Mr. Skin

would sure love Amanda to hug and kiss.

SKIN-fining Moment:

Breast Men (0:02) *Amanda bares her barely-a-handfuls to coat them with "Breast Enhancement Cream."*

See Her Naked In:

Breast Men (1997) Breasts

Deborah Foreman

Born: October 12, 1962
Montebello, California
Skin-O-Meter: Brief Nudity

Deborah Foreman launched her acting career in 1982 with a few guest spots on the hit cop drama *T.J. Hooker* before landing a part in the made-for-TV movie *In the Custody of Strangers* (1982). In no time, she managed to make her first-ever appearance on the silver screen in *I'm Dancing as Fast as I Can* (1982). But that was just lighting the fuse of the rocket ride of her career. Deborah was consistently in top form, playing everything from comedic parts to dramatic roles in such productions as *Valley Girl* (1983), *Real Genius* (1985), and on the short-lived TV series *Hot Pursuit*. Then Deborah found her rocket marooned on Planet B in such movies as *Lobster Man from Mars* (1989), *Sundown: The Vampire in Retreat* (1991), and *Lunatics: A Love Story* (1991). That last title ended her love story with the big screen and, besides a guest spot on the TV show *The Marshall*, Deborah has been lost in space. Someone has to rescue the out-of-this-world beauty. You see, the closest Deborah's ever come to flashing any flesh onscreen was in *3:15* (1986). It featured a nice, if brief, look at her bulbous butt as she bounded out of a room clad in no more than a smile. Mr. Skin hasn't smiled as broadly since Deborah's disappearance.

SKIN-fining Moment:

3:15 The Moment of Truth (0:26) *Brief treat of Foreman's fannie when she's running out of bed.*

See Her Naked In:

3:15 The Moment of Truth (1986) Buns

Farrah Forke

**Born: January 12, 1967
Corpus Christie, Texas
Skin-O-Meter: Brief Nudity**

Network TV is a preserve of rare and erotic birds. One of the sexiest that ever flew into the prime-time aviary is bubble-breasted blonde Farrah Forke. With a face that would be perfect for a high-fashion mannequin were it not so animated with intelligence, joy, and wit, fair Farrah has been a natural for cathode stardom. To top off Farrah's Forke appeal, her package is topped off with a heavy emphasis on breast bundles. Longtime fans of the long-running series *Wings* can't remember if they fixated on Farrah more for the way she wrapped her lips around a withering riposte, for the sly sex appeal of her sidelong glances, or for the overwhelming power of her pneumatic sweater classics. The fans who followed Farrah's career to her boob-out, lesberific appearance in *Kate's Addiction* (1999) know exactly what they are obsessing over.

SKIN-fining Moment:

Kate's Addiction (0:37) *After a night of clit-to-clit canoodling with Kari Wuhrer, Farrah wakes up next to her lez love and rises, naked left breast first.*

See Her Naked In:

Kate's Addiction (1999) LB

Claire Forlani

**Born: July 1, 1972
Twickenham, Middlesex, England, UK
Skin-O-Meter: Great Nudity**

Although Claire Forlani was born in England, the better part of her career has been spent playing Americans. And it makes a body patriotic. Claire made her acting debut in the Slovenian production *Gypsy Eyes* (1992), which also happened to feature her first and finest hootage shots. Shortly thereafter she made her first appearance Stateside in the mini-series *J.F.K.: Reckless Youth* (1993), followed by a bit part in *Police Academy: Mission to Moscow* (1994). Thankfully, Claire landed a lead in *Mallrats* (1995), and things took off for this dark-haired beauty with the blockbuster *The Rock* (1996). A star turn in *Meet Joe Black* (1998) led to rumors that she was dating costar Brad Pitt, who had just broken it off with Gwyneth Paltrow. She denies the romance but admits to a brief fling with John Cusack. Her last big role was in *AntiTrust* (2001), a faux Bill Gates thriller that never caught on. Since then Claire has been remanded to such parts as "Sorority Sister" in the comedy *Going Greek* (2001). Hopefully her career isn't going south.

SKIN-fining Moment:

Gypsy Eyes (1:04) *Claire shows several shots of her lovely rack, heavenly heinie, and even a bit of hard-to-see muffshish while making love with Jim Metzler.*

See Her Naked In:

Into My Heart (1998) Breasts
Gypsy Eyes (1992) Breasts, Bush, Buns

Laurie Fortier

**Born: February 25, 1977
Pasadena, California
Skin-O-Meter: Brief Nudity**

Laurie Fortier has spent the better part of her career on campy TV series such as *Running the Halls*, *Push*, and *Rocky Times*. When she gets a gig outside of her series work, it's usually in a guest spot on boob-tube programs such as *Boy Meets World* or *Cupid*. Nevertheless, Laurie has entered the world of cinema on rare occasions, debuting in *To Gillian on Her 37th Birthday* (1996), which is as close to skin as she has yet to come. Laurie strolls about in a tiny G-string bikini, and there are ample shots of her ample ass. That cheeky performance is not much, but it sure cracks Mr. Skin up.

SKIN-fining Moment:

To Gillian on her 37th Birthday (0:16) *In her teenage bedroom, Laurie teaches pal Claire Danes a thing (and two!) about strutting around in a teeny thong bikini. Cheeky!*

See Her Naked In:

To Gillian on Her 37th Birthday (1996) Thong

Brigitte Fossey

**Born: June 15, 1946
Tourcoing, Nord, France
Skin-O-Meter: Great Nudity**

She's a respected icon of foreign cinema, but Brigitte Fossey also crossed over to the raincoat crowd. The former child actress became an international star with the release of the popular *Going Places* (1974)—popular, of course, due to Brigitte's memorable scene as a young new mom who lets actor Patrick Dewaere enjoy a sip of mother's milk the old-fashioned way. Things only got wilder in *Calmos* (1976), in which Brigitte served up some furburgerage in a sexy topless breakfast scene. Then moviegoers thanked God for Brigitte's revealing recline to the missionary position in *Un mauvais fils* (1980). There was less nudity as Brigitte became an elder stateswomen of French cinema, but she made an impressive final nude bow with a full-frontal display in *Enigma* (1983)—and, yes, we know she's being interrogated by a Nazi in the scene, but we have it on good authority that there was a nice Craft Services table right outside of camera range.

SKIN-fining Moment:

Going Places (0:31) *While on a train, Brigitte lets Patrick Dewaere and another guy fondle and suck on her breasts. Tasty!*

See Her Naked In:

Enigma (1983) Breasts, Bush, Buns
Un mauvais fils (1980) Breasts
Calmos (1976) FFN, Buns
Going Places (1974) Breasts

Jodie Foster

**Born: November 19, 1962
Los Angeles, California
Skin-O-Meter: Great Nudity**

Jodie Foster wishes she knew what it was like *not* to be famous. She began her career at age two as The Coppertone Baby whose bathing-suit bottom is pulled down in the teeth of a ribald dog. From that skinful debut, Jodie went on to TV and kiddie movies such as *Bugsy Malone* (1976) and *Freaky Friday* (1977). But it was her role as a streetwalker at age thirteen in *Taxi Driver* (1976) that hooked Mr. Skin. And *Foxes* (1980), her teenager-in-lust classic with ex-*Runaway* Cherie Currie, was a howl. It was a decade until Jodie matured enough for true skinage as a rape victim in *The Accused* (1988), which did for pool tables what *Jaws* (1975) did for the ocean. For a more appealing look at Jodie's apple-sized jugs, and a glimpse of her peach fuzz, check out *Backtrack* (1991). While *The Silence of the Lambs* (1991) made Jodie a superstar, she refused to keep her clothes on for fame's sake and delivered a nasty performance in *Nell* (1994), flashing that pint-sized pair again and taking a nighttime nude dip. Foster may be

Australian for beer, but it's American for babe!

SKIN-fining Moment:

Backtrack (0:45) *Breasts behind textured glass, followed by pillows in plain sight when Jodie opens the door and leans out.*

See Her Naked In:

Nell (1994) FFN, Buns
Backtrack (1991) Breasts, Buns
The Accused (1988) Breasts

Lisa Foster

**Born: 1964
London, England, UK
Skin-O-Meter: Great Nudity**

Lisa Foster spends most of her time now as a digital artist, or something in that vein, but back in the day, this British tart was as hot as an actress could be. She started out her career with a role in the comedy *Spring Fever* (1982), but it wouldn't be until she took on the title role in *Fanny Hill* (1983) that she would finally gain some recognition—and shed some clothing. Lisa was quite nude more or less throughout the film, including a nice little lesbianic tryst with costar Maria Harper, which certainly helped her get recognized here at Skin Central. After *The Blade Master* (1984) and *The Jitters* (1989), Lisa's career was coming to an end, but not before she showed her end again. She exposed some flesh on the cable series *The Hitchhiker*, which is a sure way to get a ride. Foster—it's English for hot nudes!

SKIN-fining Moment:

Fanny Hill (0:09) *Lisa appears gloriously (and gratuitously) nude, preparing for, taking, and getting out of the bath while attended by Frenchy handmaidens.*

See Her Naked In:

Fanny Hill (1983) FFN, Buns

TeleVisions:

The Hitchhiker Breasts

Meg Foster

**Born: May 10, 1948
Reading, Pennsylvania
Skin-O-Meter: Great Nudity**

Always recognized for her other-worldly, pale-blue eyes—which have been used to their utmost in such other-worldly outings as *Ticket to Heaven* (1981), *Masters of the Universe* (1987), and *They Live* (1988)—marvelous Meg Foster is a formally trained actress whose per-formances are often the best parts of any given project she appears in. And, again, it's the eyes that have it. It was audiences' eyes, however, that glazed over when Meg slipped out of her brassiere and let loose her Fosters in *Adam at 6 A.M.* (1970). Meg only had a bit part, but it ignited a skinificant other side of her career, which includes a collection of nip slips in the films *Thumb Tripping* (1972), *Welcome to Arrow Beach* (1974), *A Different Story* (1978), and *The Osterman Weekend* (1983).

SKIN-fining Moment:

Welcome to Arrow Beach (0:40) *Meg gets out of bed and her breasts get into the frame.*

See Her Naked In:

The Osterman Weekend (1983) RB
A Different Story (1978) Breasts
Welcome to Arrow Beach (1974) Buns
Thumb Tripping (1972) Breasts
Adam at 6 A.M. (1970) LB

Sara Foster

**Born: 1981
Skin-O-Meter: Brief Nudity**

Perhaps her struggle to the Hollywood pinnacle was less strenuous than the tough road trudged by naïve outsiders, but don't hate incredibly enticing, young, beautiful, rich, and privileged blonde Sara Foster just because her dad is super-successful composer and producer David Foster. It's not Daddy's dimples and delectable derriere that won Sara her position as hostess of *ET on MTV*, and it's not Papa's svelte, flawlessly smooth, exquisitely proportioned expanse of skin that squeezes into and slips out of a teeny dark bikini in *The Big Bounce* (2004). The only reason to hold anything against Sara Foster is that she's not holding her sweet somethings against you right now.

SKIN-fining Moment:

The Big Bounce (0:06) *Sara's big bouncers look bombastically beauteous in her bikini, plus we see brief bunnage as she sunbathes.*

See Her Naked In:

The Big Bounce (2004) FFN, Buns

Kerry Fox

Born: July 30, 1966
Wellington, New Zealand
Skin-O-Meter: Hall of Fame

Lusty New Zealander Kerry Fox started her career as a police officer on the hit series *Night of the Red Hunter* before moving to Britain and appearing in her first skinful performance, *An Angel at My Table* (1991). It's directed by Jane Campion, no

KERRY FOX (RIGHT) SHOWS SKINTAMACY WITH A FRENCE STICKLER IN *INTIMACY.*

stranger to nudity, and at one point Kerry is naked reading a book while her lover tries to get her attention by fondling her meaty breasts. Since then Kerry hasn't shied away from exposing her curvaceous body, baring her perky hooters in such films as *Shallow Grave* (1994), *The Last Tattoo* (1994), and *A Village Affair* (1994). As provocative as those performances are, it came as quite the surprise when she took on the leading part in *Intimacy* (2000), largely because she actually blew costar Mark Rylance onscreen! Kerry is one randy Fox!

SKIN-fining Moment:

Intimacy (0:04) *Kerry Fox just can't go another second without boinking Mark Rylance, so she strips down to bumpers and beard, then climbs aboard his Oscar Meyer-mobile.*

See Her Naked In:

Intimacy (2000) FFN, Buns
The Last Tattoo (1994) Breasts
Shallow Grave (1994) Breasts
A Village Affair (1994) Breasts
Friends (1993) Bush
An Angel at My Table (1991) FFN, Buns

Samantha Fox

Born: April 15, 1966
London, England, UK
Skin-O-Meter: Great Nudity

If a woman wants to make it as a singer in the ultra-competitive modern music biz, it's essential that she's been blessed with a great set of lungs, and the wondrous chest endowments of 1980s songbird Samantha Fox are prodigious enough that even a deaf man can see that the British-born warbling lassie is fully equipped for superstardom. A model before launching her pop-star career, Samantha's ambitions predictably extended beyond cooing lyrical come-ons and prancing and pouting through promotional videos. The

buoyant and highly elastic lady hopped, skipped, and jiggled into the acting field in such sexy fare as *Rock Dancer* (1994) and *The Match* (1999). Sam commemorated the best year of her life by sharing twelve months' worth of breast and the rest in *Samantha Fox: Calendar Girl* (1997). Proving herself to be quite the 21st-century Fox, Samantha also came out of the closet in 2004 as a lesbian. After a lifetime of getting to look at her own gloriously ultra-female form, going girl-girl crazy seemed to be a natural development.

SKIN-fining Moment:

Samantha Fox: Calendar Girl (0:38) *Heaping helpings of heinie as Samantha has her ass photographed from about 19 different angles.*

See Her Naked In:

Samantha Fox: Calendar Girl (1997) Breasts, Buns

Samantha Fox

Born: December 3, 1951
New York, New York
Skin-O-Meter: Great Nudity

Sex-screen trailblazer Samantha Fox deserves a monument as much as any other American pioneer. Samantha's memorial should be constructed somewhere on the mainland of New York City. That's where the great multitude of her films were made. The Fox shrine should contain interactive exhibits. The greatly interactive nature of its subject is displayed in the roundtable fellatio she doled out to a group of lucky gropers in *Bad Penny* (1978). The displays should incorporate all organic materials, in honor of Samantha's unaffected trollop-next-door sauciness, her pinch of pudge, her habitually smeared lipstick, her hints of cheese at breasts and buns. Finally, any tribute to Samantha must celebrate her aspirations as a real actress, embodied in her portrayal of a junkie sinking into oblivion in *Her Name Was Lisa* (1979). In the mid 1980s Samantha transformed into a B-movie boob flasher and cult-horror screamer in video fodder such as *A Night to Dismember* (1983).

SKIN-fining Moment:

Warrior Queen (0:31) *Sammy dances nude during a medieval orgy with a live snake slithering between her tempting torso-apples, hissing his way toward her hairy Garden of Eden.*

See Her Naked In:

Slammer Girls (1987) Breasts
Warrior Queen (1987) FFN, Buns
Sex Appeal (1986) Breasts, Thong
Streetwalkin' (1985) Breasts
Violated (1984) Breasts
A Night to Dismember (1983) LB
Simply Irresistible (1983) RB
It's Called Murder, Baby (1982) Breasts
Numerous Adult Movies

Vivica A. Fox

Born: July 30, 1964
Indianapolis, Indiana
Skin-O-Meter: Brief Nudity

Since going to war on the libidos and heart rates of soldier boys everywhere as scrumptious Toffee Candette on TV's *China Beach* in 1988, Vivica A. Fox has proven herself to be A. Fox who knows how to prompt her share of wolf whistles. Rising through the soapy ranks of such sudsers as *Days of Our Lives* and *The Young and the Restless* in the early '90s, Lady V made her first skinificant appearance as a family-friendly stripper in the summer smash *Independence Day* (1996). She's since hopped, skipped, jumped, and jiggled in a number of diverse projects targeted at an urban market, including *Set It Off* (1996), *Soul Food* (1997), and *Juwanna Mann* (2002). It was the

popular *Booty Call* (1997), however, that called for more than just a bunch of close-ups of Vivica's garbed booty, as her brief booby-baring bedroom romp with costar Jamie Foxx reveals.

SKIN-fining Moment:

Booty Call (0:30) *As Vivica rides Jamie Foxx surrounded by packing bubbles, her own right-side chocolate chest-bauble pops into view. Nice!*

See Her Naked In:

Booty Call (1997) RB
Independence Day (1996) Thong
Born on the Fourth of July (1989) RB

Jaimee Foxworth

Born: December 17, 1979
Belleville, Illinois
Skin-O-Meter: Great Nudity

Jaimee Foxworth was born on an Air Force base, and when she spreads her wings and takes off, viewers are on cloud nine. Gwyn Foxx, her mother, is a singer and actress, so the apple didn't fall too far from the tree. And while her early fame on the ABC sitcom *Family Matters* is totally wholesome, she eventually bit into that apple and exposed audiences to her original take on sin. Jaimee began her career as a model and acting in TV commercials, but it was her more mature work that gets stiff attention here at Skin Central. When she became of legal age, Jaimee immediately moved her booty into the hardcore penetration world of pornography with *Booty Talk 20: Super Fine Sistas!* (2000), *Adventures of Peeping Tom No. 28* (2001), and *Hot Girlz* (2001). What a difference a dildo makes! *More Black Dirty Debutantes 32* (2002) was Jaimee's last foray into fornication on film, and she retired the stage name Crave. She now works with her mama as an assistant in her talent agency. But

Mr. Skin still thinks Jaimee is fox worthy.

SKIN-fining Moment:

Booty Talk 20: Super Fine Sistas! *Jaimee Fox bangs for all she's worth, showing us her Urkels and every point of entry on her tight brown body as she puts them to meat-packing use, hardcore-style.*

See Her Naked In:

More Black Dirty Debutantes 32 (2002) FFN, Buns
Booty Talk 20: Super Fine Sistas! (2000) FFN, Buns

Joanna Frank

New York, New York
Skin-O-Meter: Brief Nudity

Joanna Frank, who was born with the good fortune to be the sister of noted producer Steven Bochco, started her film career with a supporting role in *America, America* (1963). Unfortunately, the movie's gimmick of gathering attention by repeating its title didn't work. For Joanna that meant spending the latter part of the '60s and the early part of the '70s in guest spots on such series as *The Outer Limits* and *Ben Casey*. She also tried her hand at the drive-in craze with *The Savage Seven* (1968). Then Joanna disappeared. Thankfully, she made her way back into entertainment in the early '80s with a bit part in *Double Exposure* (1982), although without exposing her double exposures. Her big break wouldn't come until her brother gave her a part (as the wife of her real-life husband Alan Rachins) on his hit series *L.A. Law*. 1994 saw the end of the show's run, and Joanna retreated to family affairs. Although the public generally remembers Joanna's turn as "Mrs. Kerwin" in the hit *Say Anything . . .* (1989), Mr. Skin prefers to recall her boobular performance in *Always* (1984). It's worth a look if for no other reason than to see Joanna's marshmallows floating in the hot chocolate-spiked bathtub water. Yum!

SKIN-fining Moment:

Always (0:57) *Joanna frolics topless in the bath and covers her naked right knocker with chocolate powder. Nice Cocoa Pebbles!*

See Her Naked In:

Always (1985) RB

Kristi Frank

Lake Tahoe, Nevada
Skin-O-Meter: Great Nudity

Sometimes to get ahead in business, a girl can do worse than have a great body. The advantage of a fantastic physical container is of utmost importance if a young woman's ambitions veer in the direction of softcore erotic drama, such as that purveyed on the Showtime late-night series *Red Shoe Diaries* during its seven years of premium-cable dominance. The saucy grin and twinkling sensual electricity sparkling from eye to eye are indications of up-and-comer Kristi Frank's confidence in her bodily presence. The "Swimming Naked" episode of *Red Shoe Diaries* proves unequivocally that this confidence is well placed. In the years since her *Red Shoe* plunge, Kristi shifted her sites from erotic fiction to the heated competition of reality TV, appearing as a contestant applying for a high-six-figure position with Donald Trump on *The Apprentice*. If those six figures were awarded on the basis of who brings the best figure to the table, Kristi would have the job in the bag. Alas (and *what* an ass!), Kristi got axed about halfway through the hit reality show's run.

SKIN-fining Moment:

Red Shoe Diaries "Swimming Naked" (1999) *Full-frontal Frankness plus fired-up Kristi-caboose as our ambitious eyeful skinny-dips in all her natural glory.*

TeleVisions:

Compromising Situations Buns
Red Shoe Diaries FFN, Buns

Diane Franklin

Born: February 11, 1963
Plainview, New York
Skin-O-Meter: Great Nudity

A petite powerhouse of neon-hot sex appeal who perfectly matched the look and feel of the go-go '80s, Diane Franklin specialized in horny high-school comedies and modeled her marvelous mug in commercials for Coke, Trident, and Jell-O. Diane's exotic look—all ink-black curls and milk-white skin—made her a natural to play a foxy French exchange student in *Better Off Dead* (1985), as well as the most righteous Princess Joanna in *Bill and Ted's Excellent Adventure* (1989). The bushy-headed beauty's most hair-raising performances, however, focused on her fluffy fro down below. As an inhuman heartbreaker in the immortal teen-sex tragedy *The Last American Virgin* (1982) and the Mother of All Humanity in the off-the-wall Adam and Eve revamp *Second Time Lucky* (1984), Diane proved that her crotch carpet matched her up-top coif, ringlet for ringlet. Naturally, Di put her delicious mini-milkers to potent use in both movies. Her perfect, pink-nosed pair also made a hauntingly hot appearance in *Amityville II: The Possession* (1982). In that incestilicious spooker, Diane continued her oddball-character streak as one hot brotherfucker. At Skin Central, we insist that the time is ripe for Diane's clothes-free comeback, because, Franklin, we give a damn!

SKIN-fining Moment:

The Last American Virgin (1:15) *Diane bares her budding breastage and the top-most curls of her lap-fro while undressing in a doctor's office.*

See Her Naked In:

Second Time Lucky (1984) FFN, Buns
The Summer Girl (1983)
The Last American Virgin (1982) FFN
Amityville II: The Possession (1982) RB

Pamela Franklin

Born: February 4, 1950
Yokohama, Japan
Skin-O-Meter: Great Nudity

Pamela Franklin's charismatic debut as the possessed little girl in *The Innocents* (1961) was the perfect beginning for a hauntingly hot career of devilish pursuits and skinful delights. In *The Night of the Following Day* (1969), Pamela premiered her glowing chest horns to a fiendish young Marlon Brando. As a naughty schoolgirl in desperate need of some discipline in *The Prime of Miss Jean Brody* (1969), Pammie's pointy pair and derrière are anything but scary. Her budding beasties still make the grade, and her red-hot tail earns this nubile nineteen-year-old eXXtra credit. Pam's spellbinding boobage and burning bush are guaranteed to spark an all-consuming fire down below in *The Witching* (1972), as will her sweltering performance sans clothing in *The Legend of Hell House* (1973). Pamela's penchant for provoking screams and wet dreams made her one of the most scorching horror hotties of the early '70s.

SKIN-fining Moment:

The Prime of Miss Jean Brodie (1:23) *Pamela's perky breasts protrude while she's posing nude, followed by a first-rate ass shot as she gets up to put her clothes on.*

See Her Naked In:

The Legend of Hell House (1973) RB
The Witching (1972) Breasts
The Night of the Following Day (1969) Breasts
The Prime of Miss Jean Brodie (1969)
   Breasts, Buns

Laura Fraser

Born: July 24, 1976
Glasgow, Scotland, UK
Skin-O-Meter: Great Nudity

Lovely lass Laura Fraser started her professional acting career while enrolled at the Royal Scottish Academy of Music and Drama with a role in *Small Faces* (1996). Soon after dropping out of the university, Laura landed a leading part in the British TV mini-series adaptation of Neil Gaiman's book *NeverWhere* (1996) and put herself on the fast track to stardom. After landing a few supporting roles, such as Bedroom Beauty in *The Man in the Iron Mask* (1998) and Mariette, the Servant, in *Cousin Bette* (1998), Laura began getting more commanding work in movies such as *Titus* (1999) and *Vanilla Sky* (2001). Laura started to show promise with *Virtual Sexuality* (1999), but be forewarned, there is nothing remotely sexy about this misleading title. For that sort of thing, one needs to seek out her roles in both *Left Luggage* (1998) and *Divorcing Jack* (1998). In the former film, Laura graces us with a full-frontal performance during a skinny-dipping scene with Heather Weeks that leaves us weak in the knees. She exposed her simply marvelous milky-white mammaries in *Jack*, as well, but sadly, she was covered with blood due to a massive chest wound during the scene in question. Unless you are into some pretty serious S&M, the effect is somewhat diminished.

SKIN-fining Moment:

Left Luggage (0:58) *Skinny-dipping fun with Heather Weeks. Laura goes fully frontal nude as the two of them jump in, then shows some brief underwater ass followed by quick boobage and muffwich as she climbs out.*

See Her Naked In:

Divorcing Jack (1998) Breasts
Left Luggage (1998) FFN

Lynne Frederick

Born: July 25, 1954
Hillingdon, Middlesex, England, UK
Died: April 27, 1994
Skin-O-Meter: Great Nudity

Lynne Frederick is perhaps best known for her short-lived marriage to Peter Sellers, but she was a talented actress in her own right. Her career, however, was spotty at best. Lynne started out with a small part in *No Blade of Grass* (1970) and appeared in such notable pictures as *Nicholas and Alexandra* (1971), *The Amazing Mr. Blunden* (1972), and as Catherine Howard in *Henry VIII and His Six Wives* (1973). But somehow she found herself mired in projects like *Vampire Circus* (1972), *Phase IV* (1974), and *The Prisoner of Zenda* (1979), which was her last feature performance. Yet it was with these lesser works that Lynne's greatest works were exposed. She made her skinful debut in *A Venezia Muore Un'Estate* (1972), showing off just about all of her body, but alas, the muff shots are rather brief. She showed off her luscious hoots again with a topless turn in *Four of the Apocalypse* (1975), but for the best look at Lynne's goodies, check out *Schizo* (1977). She shows it all off again, this time for a much more "extended" period, so to speak. Sadly, alcoholism claimed this beautiful lady in 1994. Mr. Skin won't drink to that.

SKIN-fining Moment:

Schizo (0:29) *We see some top ass-crackage in the shower, followed by several looks at Lynne's twins as a slasher approaches.*

See Her Naked In:

Schizo (1976) Breasts, Bush, Buns
Four of the Apocalypse (1975) Breasts
A Venezia Muore Un' Estate (1972) Breasts, Bush, Buns

Alice Fredlund

Skin-O-Meter: Great Nudity

Alice Fredlund did her part in the '70s to put the necessary *B*s in B-movies. Ever ready to bare *Buxom Boobage, Booming Bottom,* and *Blindingly Bright Bush,* this ravishing redhead boasts a brief but flamingly fleshadelic career. Alice indelibly lit up drive-in smashes such as *The Joys of Jezebel* (1970), *The Great Texas Dynamite Chase* (1977), and *The Capitol Hill Girls* (1977) before vanishing like the outdoor venues that so fittingly showcased her larger-than-life work. Although ferociously sexy Fredlund always electrifies onscreen, she's particularly tasty in *Please Don't Eat My Mother* (1972), in which, just before her carrot-topped deliciousness gets fed to a giant flesh-eating plant, she provides an up-close organic study of her pink-tipped booby bulbs and fiery patch of lap grass. Please don't tell my mother what I was doing when I saw that scene!

SKIN-fining Moment:

Please Don't Eat My Mother (1:07) *Alice exposes every inch of her nude form from multiple angles as she chats up a plant-monster. And I don't mean that wild brush growth in her lap.*

See Her Naked In:

The Great Texas Dynamite Chase (1977) Breasts
The Killing of a Chinese Bookie (1976) Breasts
Please Don't Eat My Mother (1972) FFN
Joys of Jezebel (1970)

Paige French

Skin-O-Meter: Brief Nudity

Blonde-haired honey Paige French hit the big time right off the bat, debuting on the popular daytime soap opera *All My Children* in the late '80s. But it was a few years later that Paige caught the attention of the bullpen here at Skin Central.

In *Meatballs 4* (1992), Paige is a real French tickler. The sequel was also known as *Happy Campers*, and with good reason: Paige makes everyone happy when she's flashing that meaty rack. After that skincess, Paige went on to some TV movies and a stint on *The George Carlin Show* in 1994. She's since disappeared, as so many of the fine ones do in time. Let's hope there's another Paige still to be written on this sexy enchantress.

SKIN-fining Moment:

Meatballs 4 (0:27) *Paige doffs her shirt and shows her Meatballs Two while frolicking lakeside.*

See Her Naked In:

Meatballs 4 (1992) Breasts

Anna Friel

Born: July 12, 1976
Rochdale, Lancashire, England, UK
Skin-O-Meter: Great Nudity

After a lot of hard thinking, Mr. Skin thinks the United States and Great Britain should unite via an exchange program for sexy actresses. The U.S. could export an American beauty to star in a skinematic slice of apple hair-pie, and the UK could send a tartlet for a little onscreen Tea & A. Our first import could be British beaut Anna Friel. This Lancashire lovely caused gasps playing a lesbian on the gritty soap *Brookside* with her coming-out episode making front-page news. Anna was an animal in the Aussie flick *The Tribe* (1998). Spotting a couple naked blokes in bed, she instantly went starkers, rocking her pretty kitty up and down in a three-way frenzy. (Her shaggy silken slit made an excellent petting zoo.) Anna floated around with *Dawson's Creek* star Michelle Williams when the two shared a bath in *Me Without You* (2001). *Rogue Trader* (1999) and *The War Bride*

(2001) are also perfect additions to our Yankee wank bank, but as imports they are harder to come by.

SKIN-fining Moment:

The Tribe (0:39) *Anna gets totally nude and then mounts her man. FFN. Oh, what a Friel-ing!*

See Her Naked In:

Watermelon (2002) Breasts
The War Bride (2001) Breasts, Bush
Me Without You (2001) Breasts
Sunset Strip (2000) LB
Rogue Trader (1999) Breasts
Mad Cows (1999) RB
The Tribe (1998) FFN, Buns

Nikki Fritz

Pittsburgh, Pennsylvania
Skin-O-Meter: Hall-of-Fame

Knockout Nikki Fritz brings not only buxom curves and bodacious beauty to the B-films blessed with her presence, she's also an enormously gifted thespian who has studied with some of today's finest acting teachers. Oh, to help this multitalented hottie hone her craft! The Pittsburgh-born power-house grew up in Florida and presently resides in California, where she shines bedazzlingly and seems to fit right in with the tropical topography. Nikki's comic skills and knockeriffic star presence have lit up modern softcore classics such as *Beach Babes From Beyond* (1993), *The Exotic Time Machine* (1997), and two separate entries in the *Bare Wench* series. She was also erotically unforgettable in the mainstream Hollywood hit *Go* (1999). This Fritz is one sexy pussycat.

SKIN-fining Moment:

Showgirl Murders (0:47) *Nikki performs a kinkadelic strip club routine with Maria Ford. She peels off her tights*

to reveal bombers and buns, then Maria drips wax on her tits.*

See Her Naked In:

The Bare Wench Project 2: Scared Topless (2001) Breasts
Fast Lane to Malibu (2000) Breasts, Buns
Sex, Secrets & Betrayals (2000) FFN, Buns
Sinful Obsession (1999) FFN, Thong
Crime and Passion (1999) FFN, Buns
The Bare Wench Project (1999) Breasts, Bush
Secret Pleasures (1999) FFN, Thong
Go (1999) Breasts, Thong
Veronica 2030 (1999) FFN, Buns
Virtual Encounters 2 (1998) FFN, Buns
Black & White (1998) Breasts
Hotel Exotica (1998) FFN, Buns
Hidden Beauties (1998) FFN, Buns
Night Shade (1997) Breasts
The Exotic Time Machine (1997) FFN, Buns
Fugitive Rage (1996) Breasts, Buns
Strip for Action (1996) Breasts
Showgirl Murders (1996) Breasts, Thong
Bikini Drive-In (1995) FFN, Buns
Where Evil Lies (1995) FFN, Buns
Stripteaser (1995) Breasts, Thong
Attack of the 60 Foot Centerfold (1995) Breasts
Terminal Virus (1995) Breasts
A Low Down Dirty Shame (1994) Thong
Bad Blood (1994) Breasts, Thong
Dinosaur Island (1994) Breasts, Thong
Indecent Behavior II (1994) Breasts, Bush, Thong
Beach Babes from Beyond (1993) FFN, Buns
The New Kids (1985) Buns
Spring Break (1983) Breasts

TeleVisions:

Bedtime Stories FFN
Beverly Hills Bordello FFN, Buns
Intimate Sessions Breasts, Buns
Nightcap FFN, Buns
The Pleasure Zone Breasts, Bush, Buns

Sadie Frost

Born: March 27, 1968
London, England, UK
Skin-O-Meter: Great Nudity

One of the hottest strumpets to come out of the UK, Sadie Frost is nothing like her name. The daughter of a convicted anarchist father and hippie/healer mother, sassy Sadie is a chameleon, at her best when adapting to a bare environment. Frost debuted her hot toddies in *Dark Obsession* (1989), but she really caught the Yanks by their wankers in *Bram Stoker's Dracula* (1992) as the fanged, fiery-haired Lucy, the doomed mistress of Dracula. She dyed her dark locks a ravishing red and thrashed around naked with the dark beast in bed. The extended viewing of her creamy-white crumpets was absolutely *fangtastic*. In *Fly Paper* (1997), Sadie was an all-natural brunette but stuck with her skinful strategy of giving her milky mams a bit of screen time. Sadie continued to act her breast in *Rancid Aluminum* (2000); her bare British boobies stood stiffly at attention. Sadie, Sadie the once-married lady filed for divorce from pretty-boy hubby Jude Law in August of 2003. Sadly, Sadie never again showed the world what Jude once had all to himself.

SKIN-fining Moment:

Dracula (0:59) Sophie has vampire convulsions in bed, which send her left breast quaking into view.

See Her Naked In:

Rancid Aluminium (2000) Breasts
Flypaper (1997) Breasts
Crimetime (1996) Breasts
Magic Hunter (1994) Breasts, Bush, Buns
Dracula (1992) Breasts
Dark Obsession (1989) Breasts

Soleil Moon Frye

Born: August 6, 1976
Glendora, California
Skin-O-Meter: Never Nude

Virgil Frye, star of *Take This Job and Shove It* (1981), took something else and shoved it, creating the lovely Soleil Moon Frye. Her name is French for sun, and this busty babe really shined in the early '80s on the hit sitcom *Punky Brewster*. Sadly, her precocious grin and wacky escapades vanished without a trace when the show was cancelled in 1988. Audiences got to watch the bosomy beauty really grow up and out of those training bras into the industrial-strength variety on such series as *Cadets, Where's Rodney?*, and *Grown Ups*. Although Soleil has been acting pretty steadily since her glory days on *Punky*, she is usually stuck in supporting parts in such films as *Twisted Love* (1995), *Mind Games* (1996), and *Motel Blue* (1999). *Mind Games* is the closest Soleil has come to showing off her watermelons, which are overflowing in a lacy over-the-shoulder-boulder-holder. Soleil also teased us with some semi-hooterage in *Pumpkinhead II: Blood Wings* (1994) and as part of the sexy threesome on *Sabrina, the Teenage Witch*, but the viewing public has yet to see what she's still hiding! Let those moons out in the Soleil!

SKIN-fining Moment:

Mind Games Mind Games? It's more like finger games as Soleil uses her own hand to make herself fry before her roommate bursts in on her. Sexy as hell, even if we don't see her Moon or Punky Boobsters.

Mira Furlan

Born: September 7, 1955
Zagreb, Croatia
Skin-O-Meter: Great Nudity

Remember when The Doors sang "The West is the Best"? Well, they were wrong. The East is where Yugoslavian beauty Mira Furlan is from. The problem is that for the early part of her career she only made films on the other side of the former Iron Curtain. She didn't become well known in America until she immigrated here in 1991 and started getting work on such notable programs as *Babylon 5* and *Sheena* and as a voice artist on the hit animated series *Spider-Man*. Of course, she hasn't quite broken into American cinema just yet due to her budding TV career, but she was a huge star in her native country, where she racked up over thirty credits on TV and in the movies in just ten years. Thankfully, she took the time to take on some roles in Yugoslavia, including a topless turn in *Kiklop* (1982) and some savory, full-frontal, unshaven, bushy muffshish in *Lepota Poroka* (1986). Both are muff-sees. Mira, Mira on the wall, you're the prettiest of them all!

SKIN-fining Moment:

Lepota Poroka (1:19) Mira is nude hiding in the grass. We see her full frontal but she is mostly covering herself. Thankfully that big old Eastern European bush is hard to hide.

See Her Naked In:

Spadijer-Jedan Zivot (1986) Breasts
Lepota Poroka (1986) Breasts, Bush
When Father Was Away on Business (1985) Breasts
Kiklop (1982) Breasts

g

Monique Gabrielle

Born: July 30, 1963
Kansas City, Missouri
Skin-O-Meter: Great Nudity

Voluptuous video vixen Monique Gabrielle, a veteran of nearly a dozen skindelicious treats, first raised the eyebrows of audiences (among other things) as *Penthouse* magazine's December 1982 Pet of the Month. Brief but undeniably bombastic nude appearances soon materialized in a string of *Penthouse*-produced videos and similarly willowy walk-ons in such sexy comedies as *Screen Test* (1985), *Emmanuelle 5* (1987), *Miracle Beach* (1991), and, most memorably, as the stripper of every teenage boy's fantasy in the Tom Hanks laff-a-rama *Bachelor Party* (1984). Munificent Monique apparently put it all to rest in the mid '90s; her final appearance was as The Blonde in the family-friendly TV flick *Problem Child 3: Junior in Love* (1995), in which she was indeed provocative—but sadly skin free. A decade on, she remains the bachelor-party accoutrement by which all others are measured.

SKIN-fining Moment:

Bachelor Party (1:11) Monique makes with the full-frontal flesh flash as she strips down for Tom Hanks. Hump, Forrest! Hump!

See Her Naked In:

Fear of a Black Hat (1993) Thong
Angel Eyes (1993) FFN, Buns
Scream Queen Hot Tub Party (1991) Breasts, Buns
Miracle Beach (1991) FFN
Evil Toons (1991) Breasts
Silk 2 (1989) FFN
Amazon Women on the Moon (1987) FFN
Deathstalker II (1987) Breasts, Buns
Emmanuelle 5 (1987) FFN, Buns
Weekend Warriors (1986) Breasts
Bad Girls IV (1986) Breasts, Bush, Buns
Screen Test (1985) FFN
The Big Bet (1985) FFN
Young Lady Chatterley II (1985) Breasts
Hot Moves (1984) FFN
The Rosebud Beach Hotel (1984) Breasts
Love Scenes (1984) FFN
Bachelor Party (1984) FFN
Black Venus (1983) FFN, Buns
Chained Heat (1983) FFN, Buns
Flashdance (1983) Breasts, Thong
Up 'n' Coming (1983) FFN, Buns
Night Shift (1982) Breasts
Numerous Adult Movies

TeleVisions:

Dream On Breasts

Charlotte Gainsbourg

Born: July 22, 1971
London, England, UK
Skin-O-Meter: Hall of Fame

A free spirit, ever ready to take on scandal and take off her clothes, Charlotte Gainsbourg is the spawn

CHARLOTTE GAINSBOURG IN *THE CEMENT GARDEN*. SHE PUTS CEMENT IN MY PANTS.

of the decadent singing duo Serge Gainsbourg and Jane Birkin (best known for their shagadelic single "Je t'Aime [Moi Non Plus]"). With a little help from big daddy, Charlotte shocked the ultra-liberal French at fifteen, appearing in *Charlotte For Ever* (1986), a scandalous semi-autobiographic film that climaxed with father and daughter in bed together. Serge and Charlotte's duet, "Lemon Incest," followed shortly thereafter, furthering their familial infamy. As her papa once said, "Ugliness has more going for it than beauty. It endures." While the Gainsbourg family's collaborations might still be provoking cries of "Mon Dieu," the accumulation of

Charlotte's acting efforts have leaned toward the lovely. Her first go at skinematic beauty was in *Amoureuse* (1993), in which Charlotte debuted her small suckables and gave a long look at her pale Gallic glutes. Since then she has shown her lithe, teeny-titted body in flocks of French flicks such as *The Cement Garden* (1994), *Love, etc.* (1996), and *The Intruder* (1999).

SKIN-fining Moment:

The Little Thief (0:41) Charlotte shows off her youthful, super-tasty boo-boos as she takes off her shirt for some Frenchie.

See Her Naked In:

My Wife Is an Actress (2001) RB, Buns
Passionnément (2000) LB, Buns
The Intruder (1999) Breasts, Buns
Love, etc . . . (1996) Breasts
The Cement Garden (1994) Breasts
Amoureuse (1992) Breasts, Buns
Il Sole Anche di Notte (1990) Breasts, Bush
The Little Thief (1989) Breasts
Charlotte for Ever (1986) Breasts

Anna Galiena

Born: December 22, 1954
Rome, Italy
Skin-O-Meter: Great Nudity

If a skinthusiast's only awareness of top-heavy Italian treasure Anna Galiena is of her minor roles as a buxom ethnic presence in support of American actors such as Robin Williams in *Being Human* (1994) or Jon Bon Jovi in *The Leading Man* (1996), then that skinthusiast is in for a lewd awakening. Seek out two foreign movies that were filmed a dozen years apart: *Jours Tranquilles a Clichy* (1990) and *Senso 45* (2002). The first flick's title translates to *Quiet Days in Clichy*, the second is alternately known as *Black Angel*. Both are foreign features, and both feature great quantities of full-frontal nude lolling and balling such

as are seldom seen outside the private lair of consenting adults. And Anna Galiena's time-defying, ultra-plush figure is of a bountiful perfection as is seldom seen outside the fevered imagination of a skinthusiast in the throes of ecstasy.

SKIN-fining Moment:

Senso '45 (0:39) Loads of full-frontal fun as Anna strips down bareass naked and frolics into the ocean with her equally nude Nazi lover.

See Her Naked In:

Senso '45 (2002) FFN, Buns
Cuestión de Suerte (1996) LB
Jamón, Jamón (1992) Breasts
La Viuda del Capitán Estrada (1991) Breasts
Jours Tranquilles a Clichy (1990) FFN

Denise Galik-Furey

Cleveland, Ohio
Skin-O-Meter: Brief Nudity

The bumbling, bitter, meddling alcoholic mother is a staple of the highest American dramas, appearing with heartrending regularity in the modern-day tragedies of Tennessee Williams and Eugene O'Neil and also casting her caustic spell in network soap operas such as *General Hospital* and *Port Charles*. Endearing blonde Denise Galik-Furey has brought depth and dignity to the role of Rhonda "Cookie" Wexler, a conniving, resentful maternal mess whose selfishly motivated intervening might come across as irredeemable wet-brain malice if presented by a lesser actress. As it is, no matter how often or far away Denise's Rhonda Wexler is exiled from *Port Charles*, there's always a chance she might be allowed to come home again.

SKIN-fining Moment:

Deadly Games (1:13) Two shots of Denise's bare left breast as she bounces atop man-bone in bed.

See Her Naked In:

Deadly Games (1982) LB

TeleVisions:

The Hitchhiker Breasts

Carla Gallo

Born: June 24, 1975
Brooklyn, New York
Skin-O-Meter: Brief Nudity

Carla Gallo was raised in New York, the town so nice they had to name it twice. And Carla is so nice Skin Central is tempted to name her Carla Carla. She attended The LaGuardia School of Performing Arts before pursuing a degree in Theatre Arts at Cornell University. But this smarty-pants is best when she's not wearing any pants. She got to show off her little breasts on an episode of HBO's *Carnivàle* but has otherwise been skingy in her short career. Give her time. She debuted as the girlfriend in the Oedipal masturbation comedy *Spanking the Monkey* (1994), which offered a glimpse of her small wonders in a bra make-out scene. She since has appeared as a guest star on *ER* and *Law & Order*, but it was the critic's darling, short-lived college drama *Undeclared* that gave her career its biggest boost—outside of that topless dance number on *Carnivàle*, of course. Next up, *Sexual Life* (2004), which in title alone has potential. It's time for Carla to let her Gallos out to play again!

SKIN-fining Moment:

Carnivàle "Milfay" (2003) Carla shakes her sweetly petite up-top money-makers while demonstrating "European Muscle Dancing" to carny-goers under a tent along with non-topless Cynthia Ettinger.

TeleVisions:

Carnivàle Breasts

Teresa Ganzel

Born: March 23, 1957
Toledo, Ohio
Skin-O-Meter: Great Nudity

Bursting with bosomness and a sly, kittenish sense of humor, blonde Teresa Ganzel became famous on *The Tonight Show Starring Johnny Carson* as one of the busty "Tea Time Movie Ladies." (Now that's a capital T, and that rhymes with B, and that stands for BOOBS!) Yes, Ganzel had bazoongas and giggles to spare and generously shared them in tit-popping costumes during comedy sketches with Carson and in appearances on *The Love Boat*, *Match Game*, and *Newhart*. On *Three's Company* and *Three's a Crowd*, Teresa had a recurring role as the infamous "Greedy Gretchen," the much-talked-about man-eater of Jack Tripper's dreams. This fluffy-topped funny lady yucked it up with the gut-busting Jim Carrey in the short-lived comedy *The Duck Factory* in the mid '80s. Teresa released her (all natural) gargantuan jigglies from the confines of her clothing in her film debut in *National Lampoon Goes to the Movies* (1981), and her titanic ta-tas gave an encore performance in *C.O.D.* (1981). While doing a little disco dancing, her slurpilicious milk bomb slipped out, with scores of randy men hustling to get the best view.

SKIN-fining Moment:

National Lampoon Goes to the Movies (0:20) If you like your funbags large & jiggly, you'll love this one: a youthful and wonderfully bouncy Teresa Ganzel writhes in bed next to Boon from Animal House.

See Her Naked In:

C.O.D. (1981) RB
National Lampoon Goes to the Movies (1981) Breasts

Terri Garber

Born: December 28, 1960
Miami, Florida
Skin-O-Meter: Brief Nudity

Terri Garber has a career awash in soap operas. With roles on such timeless hits as *Texas*, *Dynasty*, *Santa Barbara*, and *General Hospital*, Terri may only be surpassed by Susan Lucci as the Queen of Soaps. She also made a name with her portrayal of Ashton Main Huntoon in the *North and South* trilogy. Terri does delve into feature films from time to time, having appeared in *Key Exchange* (1985), *Beyond My Reach* (1990), and *Slappy and the Stinkers* (1998), but it was her role in *Toy Soldiers* (1984) that first piqued Mr. Skin's curiosity. In it, she plays Amy, one of a group of kids kidnapped by some rebel types in a nondescript Central American country. In one scene, Terri is forced to take off her top, much to the delight of her captors, as well as the viewing audience. Her last appearance onscreen was credited as Sultry Older Woman in *Thank You, Good Night* (2001). It sounds like she was beginning to carve out a needed career playing mature mamas. Come back, old lady, and make our little man happy.

SKIN-fining Moment:

Toy Soldiers (0:18) A horny platoon of hostile pervs forces Terri to peel off her tank top, turning her exposed right ta-ta into a toy for soldiers.

See Her Naked In:

Toy Soldiers (1984) RB

Nina Garbiras

Born:
New York, New York
Skin-O-Meter: Brief Nudity

A lesser wholly alluring brunette candy face might be satisfied with an ongoing and consistent career as a highly visible television vixen, but not uncommonly attractive Nina Garbiras. Never one to be satisfied with merely being professionally pretty, Nina has always sought to bring dramatic depth to her small-screen roles, playing big in series such as *The $treet*, *Boomtown*, and *Leap Years*. Of course, anyone blessed with such pleasant visuals and highly apparent talent cannot be confined in a box. Nina has consistently made the effort to step to the big screen in independent productions such as *Mixing Nia* (1998), and *You Can Count on Me* (2000). Look for Nina's breakout pair in a rowdy bed rumble in *Bruiser (2000)*.

SKIN-fining Moment:

Bruiser (0:38) Nina mounts her man atop a conference table and her topless Garbiras buck raucously. Then her bang buddy's wife interrupts them and we get a long shot of Nina's na-nas during the post-hump havoc.

See Her Naked In:

Bruiser (2000) Breasts

Ashley Gardner

Skin-O-Meter: Brief Nudity

Women who commit adultery can be hot; in fact, it would be safe to say that hotness is a prerequisite for screwing around. So it should come as no surprise that the voice behind one of America's best-known cheating hearts, Nancy Gribble, the unfaithful marital servant of Dale on the long-running animated series *King of the Hill*, belongs to a set of lungs that have been seen to generate a fair degree of heat on their own. Fetching blonde Ashley Gardner is the human behind the two dimensional Gribble. Although Ashley has been a flesh-and-blood presence on dozens of TV shows, including *The Drew Carey Show* and

The Larry Sanders Show, her best show by far was a slip of nip while having a restaurant conversation with Kevin Bacon in the feature film *He Said, She Said* (1991).

SKIN-fining Moment:

He Said, She Said (1:05) As Ashley jabbers with Kevin Bacon at dinner, her right nip jostles out of her dress and quickly jiggles in plain view.

See Her Naked In:

He Said, She Said (1991) Nip-Slip RB

> "I like to get crazy. I like to be one hundred percent open, and I feel most comfortable doing that in my bedroom."
>
> —JENNIFER GAREIS

Jennifer Gareis

Born: August 1, 1970
Lancaster, Pennsylvania
Skin-O-Meter: Great Nudity

Jennifer Gareis made her film debut in *Weekend at Bernie's II* (1989) in a nondescript, bikini-clad, uncredited role, which she followed up with another no-namer in *The Mirror Has Two Faces* (1996). But this blonde, green-eyed beauty wasn't about to go unrecognized for long. Her career got a giant boost soon after when she landed the role of Grace Turner on the hit daytime soap *The Young and the Restless,* which catapulted her into the limelight. Jennifer went on to appear in *Private Parts* (1997), *Miss Congeniality* (2000), *The Sixth Day* (2000) (as the virtual girlfriend), and *Boat Trip* (2002). But her best role, according to the sexperts here at Skin Central, would be in the little-seen *Luckytown Blues* (2000). In it, she does a wonderful little striptease

for aging hard-ass James Caan's character. Regardless of how old the tough guy is, his ass isn't the only thing that's hard.

SKIN-fining Moment:

Luckytown Blues (0:59) Jen makes James Caan an offer he can't refuse, removing her dress to reveal her robo-rack and skimpy black G-string.

See Her Naked In:

What Boys Like (2001) Breasts
Luckytown Blues (2000) Breasts, Thong

Jennifer Garner

Born: April 17, 1972
Houston, Texas
Skin-O-Meter: Never Nude

The secret of success for brunette television sensation Jennifer Garner—aside from being packaged in a lean and powerful feline body with just the right touch of padding—is her face. Garner's good looks are of the blatantly stunning variety. Jennifer's starring role as Sydney Bristow on the TV action-thriller series *Alias* demands that the seriously hot thespian screw up her mug to show a whole range of emotions, from elated to angry. The Garner features meld so perfectly, and their effect is so exquisitely hypnotic to the observer, that Jennifer's physiognomy retains cover-girl prettiness no matter what freaky urge it is depicting. Of course, it helps that one of Sydney Bristow's best *Alias* disguises is a skimpy, form-fitting bikini that reveals every contour and crease of that catlike body.

SKIN-fining Moment:

Alias "Phase One" (2003) Jen struts her stuff first in two different lingerie get-ups—one black, one red—before strangling some dude who was enjoying the show. You'll be strangling something else as you enjoy the show . . .

Teri Garr

Born: December 11, 1949
Lakewood, Ohio
Skin-O-Meter: Brief Nudity

Teri up your expectations of sexy. Teri Garr tripped the light fantastic as a go-go dancer in about nine Elvis Presley flicks but didn't get her first speaking role until the movie *Head* (1968). No, it's not what you think—*Head* is the mind-blowing psychedelic meltdown starring the prefab four—you know, The Monkees. Her killer gams kicked their way into American living rooms in the '70s thanks to regular appearances on *The Sonny and Cher Comedy Hour* and guest spots on *McCloud.* Teri's talent is unmistakable, from *The Conversation* (1974), *Oh, God!* (1977), and *Close Encounters of the Third Kind* (1977) to her Oscar-nominated performance in *Tootsie* (1982). But for a more revealing taste of Teri there's *One from the Heart* (1982), which finally exposed something near and dear to our heart—her pint-sized, big-nipped hooters. To glimpse Teri's puffy ci-Garrs was worth the wait.

TERI GARR GIVES FREDERICK FORREST TWO FOR THE HARD IN *ONE FROM THE HEART.*

SKIN-fining Moment:

One from the Heart (0:09) *Teri's ta-tas take center stage as she toplessly steps out of the shower.*

See Her Naked In:

One from the Heart (1982) Breasts

Lisa Gastoni

Born: July 28, 1935
Alassio, Savona, Liguria, Italy
Skin-O-Meter: Great Nudity

Lisa Gastoni, who is native to Italy, started her acting career in the UK. In 1959 she landed on the boob tube and appeared in the British series *Skyport* and *The Four Just Men*. Thankfully, when her tenure was over in Britain, she headed back to her native Italy, where the nights are warmer and women are likely to roam about in the nude . . . at least onscreen. Her skin debut came in *Amore Amaro* (1974), which translates to *Bitter Love*, but there was nothing bitter about Lisa's long, well-lit, full-frontal scene, which showcased her lovely, pert breasts and enormous, fluffy bush. *Submission* (1976) also featured her in complete nudissitude, but from more of a distance. Lisa's final film was *L'Immoralita* (1978), and she has been gone from the public eye ever since. Come back, Lisa, you've not run out of Gastoni.

SKIN-fining Moment:

Submission (0:57) *Lisa's forced to strip on a public street: first just one tit, then bare-ass . . . and then full-frontal! Of course she catches a few appreciative glances.*

See Her Naked In:

Submission (1976) FFN, Buns
Amore Amaro (1974) FFN
Labbra di Lurido Blu (1975) Breasts, Buns

Jennifer Gatti

Born: October 4, 1969
Manhattan, New York
Skin-O-Meter: Great Nudity

The wonders of Manhattan will never cease for as long as brunette miracles the caliber of Jennifer Gatti continue to be born there. Her dark locks tumble to either side of a strikingly sensual face; swollen of lip and eyelid, it seems to be lit from within by a flame feeding on equal parts lust and satiation. In the entertainment world, New York is the land of daytime serial dramas, and local legend Jennifer has been fixation-bait since the age of fourteen as a fixture on such soaps as *Search for Tomorrow*, *The Guiding Light*, and *The Young and the Restless*. But Jennifer is a New Yorker in heart and soul. The sexual entanglements of the small-screen realm could leave her only half satisfied, which is why her twins are twice as happy busting out all across the big screen in *Double Exposure* (1993).

SKIN-fining Moment:

Double Exposure (1:24) *Fast right-side fondle puppy while she's supplying some lesboid love to Dedee Pfeiffer.*

See Her Naked In:

Double Exposure (1993) Breasts, Bush, Buns

Erica Gavin

Born: 1949
Hollywood, California
Skin-O-Meter: Great Nudity

Hollywood has big stars, Russ Meyer has bigger ones—and few were as jugantic as Erica Gavin. She debuted in Meyer's classic big-breasted bonanza *Vixen!* (1968)—there should be two exclamation marks, one for each boob. Erica shows off her bombastic bongos

and beats skins with both men and women for a rip-roaring good time. The X-rated, although not hardcore, feature branded Erica, and she followed up her flesh-cess with similar sex stories—*Initiation* (1968), *Erika's Hot Summer* (1972), and another Meyer breastacular, *Beyond the Valley of the Dolls* (1970). Her final skinage was in a more mainstream mam-pleaser, the women-in-prison epic *Caged Heat* (1974), in which Erica got her big girls wet in not one but two shower scenes. When Erica comes clean, everybody just comes.

SKIN-fining Moment:

Vixen! (0:05) *Superb servings of Erica's mountain-sized milk-jugs when her fella frees them from her bikini.*

See Her Naked In:

Caged Heat (1974) Breasts, Buns
Erika's Hot Summer (1970) FFN, Buns
Beyond the Valley of the Dolls (1970) Breasts
Vixen! (1968) Breasts

Anne Gaybis

Skin-O-Meter: Great Nudity

A redhead needn't be genetically predisposed to the crimson mane in order to be real. After all, if skin-screen temptress Anne Gaybis has gone through the trouble to rinse a fiery tone into her hair, then obviously she has an intemperate streak. Gaybis's heat radiates out even from under the black wig that covers her head but leaves the gravity-teasing fullness of her plump breasts undisturbed in *The Best Little Whorehouse in Texas* (1982). Later, Anne would cook as a topless dancer in *Twin Peaks: Fire Walk with Me* (1992) and as a flickering presence in *Showgirls* (1995) and *Bachelor Party* (1984). For the most sizzling slice of Gaybis, go back to *Wham Bam Thank*

You Spaceman (1975) for lingering and loving leering at the thick, dark, tufted evidence that the hair up top is an unnatural red.

SKIN-fining Moment:

Fairy Tales (0:21) Ann plays a naked Snow White—complete with pink nips and brown bush—as the Seven Dwarfs sing and dance in joy.

See Her Naked In:

Twin Peaks: Fire Walk With Me (1992) Breasts
Hollywood Zap (1986) Breasts
Scarred (1984) Breasts
The Lost Empire (1983) Breasts
The Best Little Whorehouse in Texas (1982) Breasts
Fairy Tales (1979) FFN, Buns
Wham Bam Thank You Spaceman (1975) FFN, Buns

Rebecca Gayheart

Born: April 12, 1972
Hazard, Kentucky
Skin-O-Meter: Brief Nudity

You may have creamed to her as "The Noxzema Girl," but Rebecca Gayheart has since made a clean jump from modeling to acting. The curly-maned, huge-eyed hottie's first role was on the NBC soap opera *Loving*, and it led to a hot run on the Fox jiggle-fest *Beverly Hills, 90210*. After her screamingly sexy sorority-girl part in *Scream 2* (1997), Rebecca rolled on with roles in *Urban Legend* (1998) and the *Heathers* (1989) take-off *Jawbreaker* (1999). Sweet!

SKIN-fining Moment:

Vanishing Son (1:08) Rebecca brandishes black bra-and-panties . . . not for long though. Some nipple and a bit of booty, but overall it's too dark.

See Her Naked In:

Vanishing Son (1994) RB, Thong

Judy Geeson

Born: September 8, 1948
Arundel, Sussex, England, UK
Skin-O-Meter: Great Nudity

British-born Judy Geeson started her career with a wee bit part in *Wings of Mystery* (1963) before landing her breakthrough role in the classic *To Sir, with Love* (1967). But after a few more decent roles, in such films as *Prudence and the Pill* (1968) and *Hammerhead* (1968), Judy soon found herself floundering. By the mid '70s, she was well into B-movie scream-queen horror territory, with films such as *Doomwatch* (1972) and *Night Is the Time for Killing* (1975). Finally, fortune smiled upon this ever-so-cute, large-lipped lass, and she landed a high-profile recurring role on the hit TV series *Mad About You*. Having appeared in countless horror and low-budget pictures, one would think that Judy would have a long list of nude credits. In fact, there are only three films in which she let both of her lovely little Geeson's out for an airing. In *Here We Go Round the Mulberry Bush* (1968), we can enjoy her stripping down to only her smile as she turns and runs, bouncing her boobs and buns all the way to the swimming hole. While she is frolicking in the water with lucky Barry Sullivan we also discover that her little beaver's out for a swim. That's the "bush" in the title. Afterwards, back on shore and still nicely naked, she lies down with Sullivan so he can take a dip in her sugar pool. In *Two Into Three Won't Go* (1969), Rod Steiger gets an eyeful as Judy stands at his bedroom door, completely starkers. She darts off, sending her assets bobbling. Later in the flick, her topless form appears at an upstairs window as she waves Steiger "Yoo-Hoo" as he drives

away. *Inseminoid* (1981) offers a futuristic view of Judy's jugs as she's raped by an alien vampire.

SKIN-fining Moment:

Inseminoid (0:31) Judy flashes her flappers, some fanny-osity, and a hint of hoochie as she lies on a table waiting for the alien to fertilize her. Ew.

See Her Naked In:

Inseminoid (1981) FFN
Three Into Two Won't Go (1969) Breasts, Buns
Here We Go Round the Mulberry Bush (1968) Breasts, Buns

Sarah Michelle Gellar

Born: April 14, 1977
New York, New York
Skin-O-Meter: Never Nude

Golden girl Sarah Michelle Gellar emerged from the daytime-TV dungeon of soap-opera acting to worldwide superstardom, knocking dead bloodsuckers and fans alike on the TV phenomenon *Buffy the Vampire Slayer* from 1997 to 2003. Among mere mortals in the movies, she's slinky and sexy as a slasher-dodging beauty queen in *I Know What You Did Last Summer* (1997), and the French-kissing lesson she bestows upon breathtaking Selma Blair in *Cruel Intentions* (1999) ranks among cinema's hottest ever lesbo lip smacks. She makes a lot of noise during an outdoor sex scene in *Harvard Man* (2001), but, unfortunately, Buffy doesn't show muffy.

SKIN-fining Moment:

Cruel Intentions (0:24) In sunny Central Park, Sarah coaches Selma Blair on the specifics of sucking face, providing us with one of cinema's most scintillating (albeit) skinless girl-girl make-out sessions.

Laura Gemser

Born: October 5, 1950
Java, Indonesia
Skin-O-Meter: Hall of Fame

Honey-dipped cup of juicy Java
goodness Laura Gemser is best
remembered as being the Eurasian
reincarnation of the Emmanuelle
character made popular by fellow
flesh-flick star Sylvia Kristel.
Gemser made many erotic cinema
odysseys as Black Emmanuelle
throughout the '70s and '80s in
official and unofficial sequels such
as *Emmanuelle 2* (1975), *Emanuelle in
Bangkok* (1976), and *Emmanuelle
Goes Japanese* (1976). Laura retired
to Italy in the '90s with her (then-
lucky, now-deceased) husband
Gabriele Tinti, with whom she
acted in *Violence in a Women's Prison*
(1982). You may know the film
under the title *Emmanuelle in Hell*,
which is just one of its *seven*
alternate titles! Mr. Skin misses
you, Laura! How about one more
movie? Maybe *Emmanuelle the
Ultimate M.I.L.F.*

SKIN-fining Moment:

*Emanuelle and the Last Cannibals
(1:27) Laura shows her total package
once more as she saves a pal from being
eaten by cannibals. Someone ought to
tell these kids that female flesh is much
better to lick than chew.*

See Her Naked In:

Joe D'Amato Totally Uncut (1999) FFN, Buns
Riflessi di Luce (1988) RB
Top Model (1988) RB
Metamorphosis (1987) Breasts
Il Piacere (1985)
Porno Amore Esotico (1985) FFN, Buns
L'Alcova (1984) FFN
Endgame (1983) Breasts
Les Déchaînement pervers de Manuela
  (1983)
Love Is Forever (1983)
Emanuelle Fuga dall'Inferno (1983) FFN,
  Buns
Caligola: La Storia mai Raccontata (1982)
  FFN
Caged Women (1982)
La Belva Dalle Calda Pelle (1982) Breasts
Famous T&A (1982) Breasts
The Best of Sex and Violence (1981) LB
Die Todesgöttin des Liebescamps (1981) FFN
Brigade Criminelle (1980)
L'Ossessione Che Uccide (1980) FFN
Paura (1980) FFN
Le Notti Erotiche dei Morti Viventi (1979)
  FFN, Buns
The Bushido Blade (1979) RB
Malizia Erotica (1979) FFN, Buns
Porno Holocaust (1979) FFN, Buns
Mavri Emmanouella (1979) FFN, Buns
La Via della Prostituzione (1978) FFN, Buns
Suor Emanuelle (1978)
L'Infermiera di Campagna (1978)
La Mujer de la Tierra Caliente (1978)
Emanuelle e le Pornonotti (1978) FFN
Voglia di Donna (1978)
Velluto Nero (1977)
Emanuelle-Perché Violenza Alle Donne?
  (1977) Breasts
Emanuelle and the Last Cannibals (1977)
  FFN, Buns
Voto di Castità (1976)
Eva Nera (1976) FFN, Buns
Emanuelle in America (1976) FFN, Buns
Emanuelle Nera Orient Reportage (1976)
  FFN, Buns
La Spiaggia del Desiderio (1976) FFN
Emmanuelle Nera (1975) FFN, Buns
Emmanuelle 2 (1975) Breasts, Bush, Buns
Amore Libero (1974)

Carrie Genzel

Born: September 18, 1971
Vancouver, British Columbia, Canada
Skin-O-Meter: Great Nudity

Never has a coveted soap-opera
siren been more forthcoming with a
steamy screen past than brunette
blunderbuss of boobs and behind
Carrie Genzel. Carrie's twin
cannons cannot be overlooked.
Even when they are fully sheathed
in slinky daytime-drama tops, the
explosive stacks make Carrie's
face—high cheeks, a sensual mouth,
and direct, engaging eyes set in the
frame of an auburn mane—into the
second great thing that is noticed
about her. During all of Genzel's
dramatizing on *All My Children* and
Days of Our Lives, idle and idolatrous
minds fantasized visions of Carrie
with her casabas swinging free, and
there was no reason to strain the
imagination. Carrie's generous
helpings are available in easy-serve
portions in the prison-chick flick
Caged Hearts (1995). The nudity is
extensive, intensive, complete, and
accompanied by half a dozen more
mammary-flaunting foxes. In *Caged*,
love lobes fly free.

SKIN-fining Moment:

*Caged Hearts (0:15) Carrie and her
newfound prison-pals appear in all their
naked glory while some prick of a guard
processes their papers.*

See Her Naked In:

The Killer Inside (1996) Breasts
Caged Hearts (1995) Breasts, Bush, Buns
Virtual Seduction (1995) Breasts, Buns

Melissa George

Born: August 6, 1976
Perth, Australia
Skin-O-Meter: Great Nudity

Melissa George boasts as fine a pair
of chest bubbles as has ever popped
out of Australia, putting her high in
the running for Finest Rack
Worldwide, by George. She forged
into acting—after a faltered
"professional roller skating"
career—starring on the hit
Australian series *Home and Away*.
After a few years on that show and
in other Australian productions,
including *Fable* (1997) and the
failed Heath Ledger series *Roar*,
Melissa made the big time in *Dark
City* (1998). Breast of all, she
showed off her twin towers. It was
the only nudity that Melissa has
offered in her career, but it included
a brief glimpse of her furry koala.
Melissa was sweet in *Sugar & Spice*
(2001) and stole Mr. Skin's heart on

the TV series *Thieves*. Here's to seeing more of her champion melons in the future.

SKIN-fining Moment:

Dark City (0:15) By George, she's naked! Melissa shares her natural knockers and nappy nay-nay with us while she gets dressed.

See Her Naked In:

Dark City (1998) Breasts, Bush, Buns

Susan George

Born: July 26, 1950
London, England, UK
Skin-O-Meter: Hall of Fame

Gorgeous Susan George began acting at age four, and she's still going strong. *The Strange Affair* (1968) contains the first appearance of Susan's skin, which may explain why famously macho director Sam Peckinpah got so hot to cast her as the sexually ravaged wife of milquetoast-gone-vigilante Dustin Hoffman in *Straw Dogs* (1971). That film, and its unblinking rape scene, continue to be automatically associated with Susan, even though she doffed her top in the slave-trade exploitation classic *Mandingo* (1975), the *Jaws* (1975) rip-off *Tintorera* (1977), and the gory spooker *The House Where Evil Dwells* (1982). Sweet Sue continues to perform in England, where she lives with her husband, actor Simon MacCorkindale. Mr. Skin wishes she'd uncork her bubblies at least one more time. Cheers!

SKIN-fining Moment:

Straw Dogs (1:00) Susan's stellar sacks get plenty of screen time as she's held down and defiled by a drooling ex-boyfriend.

See Her Naked In:

House Where Evil Dwells (1982) Breasts
Tintorera (1977) Breasts
Mandingo (1975) Breasts

Out of Season (1975) Buns
Straw Dogs (1971) Breasts
The Strange Affair (1968) Breasts, Buns

Ashlyn Gere

Born: September 14, 1959
Cherry Point, North Carolina
Skin-O-Meter: Great Nudity

The term "porn star" is thrown around a lot, but pick it up and dust it off because it belongs pinned to the mammoth mams of Ashlyn Gere, a true captain of carnal cinema. Her X-rated debut was in the hardcore free-for-all *Dreamaniac* (1986), and she's gone on to star in scores of others, so many that she claims to only recall seventy percent of the titles. In other words, Ashlyn's forgotten more sex acts than most of us have had! She became a scream queen and showed off her body for mainstream moviegoers in *Fatal Instinct* (1995) and *Victim of Desire* (1996)—just don't be confused by her non-porno alias, Kim McKamy. The 36-22-33 bombshell is also one of the only adult-film stars to land a regular role on a network TV series—*Space: Above and Beyond* (1995)—while still banging the triple X. Now that's above and beyond the call of duty.

SKIN-fining Moment:

Victim of Desire (0:09) Ashlyn shows off tons of T&A when she sheds her threads for a shower . . . What a body!

See Her Naked In:

Victim of Desire (1996) Breasts, Buns
In the Flesh (1995) Breasts
Fatal Instinct (1991) Breasts
Numerous Adult Movies

Jenna Gering

Born: July 6, 1974
Florida
Skin-O-Meter: Brief Nudity

Love is difficult for a hard-working policeman to come by. The typical detective spends most days poking his nose into the nastiest recesses of human nature, and when he comes up for air, he wants something sweet to the scent, but not cloying or coy. That's why piquant and pulchritudinous blonde Jenna Gering was recruited to provide a taste of saccharin-free sugar for the station-house Romeos of *NYPD Blue* after hard-edged honey-pot Kim Delaney left them flatfooted and brokenhearted. Playing a stripper with a soft spot for boys in blue, Jenna enlivened the final three episodes of *NYPD*'s 2001 season with light-footed, clothing-light pole work that ensured the force would be with her.

SKIN-fining Moment:

NYPD Blue "Under Covers" (2001) Jenna gyrates on a strip-club stage, taking it all off down to a thong and showing most of her left love-pillow. Nobody cops a feel, though.

TeleVisions:

NYPD Blue LB, Thong

> "The first time I watched the film, I said 'Oh my God! I don't have any clothes on!' It's like my evil shadow stepped out and wreaked havoc all over the screen!"
>
> —GINA GERSHON, ON *SHOWGIRLS*

Gina Gershon

Born: June 10, 1962
Los Angeles, California
Skin-O-Meter: Hall of Fame

Considering that you can't spell *vagina* without *g-i-n-a*, it seems only natural that Gina Gershon has played pelvis-pounding labia lovers to legendarily lustful perfection. Ever ready to appear in the buff and dabble with a muff, this founding member of the NYC theater group *Naked Angels* is an all-time fave with skinthusiasts and ladies who munch alike. Gina's high place in the Skintheon of the Greats was forever cemented by her bombastic embodiment of Las Vegas's bisexual stripping starlet extraordinaire Crystal Connors in the one-of-a-kind, over-the-top, down-and-dirty *Showgirls* (1995). This dark-eyed hardbody's incandescent incarnation of rampaging female ferociousness rendered her an instant icon. Gina then furthered her clit-to-clit cred with the twisty, twisted thriller *Bound* (1996), wherein she let loose (*and* tight) as the Sapphic repairwoman of jugadocious Jennifer Tilly's wettest dreams. The girls get their kicks with multiple licks (of every sort), and the classic scene where Jen pets Gina's cooch and diddles her dingle really hits the nail on the head. Oh, Gina, you've got us positively Gershon!

SKIN-fining Moment:

Bound (0:19) Gina bares her bodacious breast and almost a bit of bush while Jennifer Tilly diddles her clitty in a classic lesbo lust-a-thon.

See Her Naked In:

Black & White (1998) RB
This World, Then the Fireworks (1997) RB
Bound (1996) LB
Showgirls (1995) Breasts, Thong
Love Matters (1993) Breasts
Cocktail (1988) RB
Sweet Revenge (1987) Breasts

Jami Gertz

Born: October 28, 1965
Chicago, Illinois
Skin-O-Meter: Brief Nudity

Subtly sultry Jami Gertz may have broken into the big time as a stuffy

prep queen named Muffy on the cult '80s nerd-com *Square Pegs*, but she's somehow always managed to keep her lap fluff under wraps. In fact, despite appearing in such archetypal teen sex comedies as *Sixteen Candles* (1984) and *Mischief* (1985), along with R-rated fare such as *The Lost Boys* (1987) and *Renegades* (1989), the closest Gertz had come to showing her pertness was a microscopic, think-about-blinking-and-you'll-miss-it nip slip in the wasted-youth drama *Less Than Zero* (1987). Fifteen years later (and at least fifteen times sexier), Jami popped that same fleeting teat tip back into view in *Lip Service* (2001), where her deliciously dark, Hershey-Kiss-like milk spout spilled out from under her bed sheets. Shortly after unveiling her coco puff anew, Jami landed back where she began, on the CBS Monday night lineup on the hit comedy *Still Standing*. Coincidence? Mr. Skin thinks not, so all you skingy starlets out there should take note—and take it off!

SKIN-fining Moment:

Less Than Zero (0:41) The briefest of brief nipple slips occurs when Jami sits up in bed with Andrew McCarthy. More please!

See Her Naked In:

Lip Service (2001) RB
Silence Like Glass (1989) Body Double—LB
Less Than Zero (1987) Nip-Slip LB

Nicole Gian

Skin-O-Meter: Great Nudity

All hail this true late-night-cable icon. Nicole Gian was the original "Madame Veronica" during the 1996 season of Showtime's *Beverly Hills Bordello* series before Gabriella Hall and Monique Parent eventually stepped into the role. It was more than anyone expected from the dark

beauty, who made her debut in the Paul Newman/Robby Benson drama *Harry and Son* (1984). Nicole waited over a decade to return in the fitting role of "Dream Girl" in the film *Wish Me Luck* (1995)—and even then she was hiding under the name "Joli Piccolini." She then took her own name while taking off her clothes in films such as *Tainted Love* (1995), *Striking Resemblance* (1997), and *Intimate Deception* (1996). The young gal even took a break from getting us restless with a legit 1997 stint on the daytime soap *The Young and the Restless*.

SKIN-fining Moment:

Intimate Deception (0:17) Nicole wiggles out of her lingerie and under her loverman between the sheets, bare boobles in view.

See Her Naked In:

Hijacking Hollywood (1997) RB
Striking Resemblance (1997) Breasts, Buns
Intimate Deception (1996) Breasts, Buns
Tainted Love (1995) Breasts

TeleVisions:

Beverly Hills Bordello Breasts, Buns

Cynthia Gibb

Born: December 14, 1963
Bennington, Vermont
Skin-O-Meter: Brief Nudity

Bright-eyed, fresh-faced blondes never go out of style, particularly when they are endowed with the million-dollar smile and priceless-gem gaze of Cynthia Gibb. An undisputed star of big and small screen, Cynthia parlayed a modeling career into a shot at acting on the highly dramatized daytime series *Search for Tomorrow*. When producers were searching for a hot new beauty to play opposite Rob Lowe (then a mega box-office attraction) in the hockey flick *Youngblood* (1986), they looked no further than Cynthia Gibb, and neither will any red-blooded viewers of the film. A long, luscious stretch of thigh muscle leads up to the elastic of Cynthia's high-cut white panties as her booty bounty is presented in contour prior to jumping into bed. Once between the sheets with Lowe, Cynthia just can't keep her bulky bosoms under the covers. She has the kind that will never go out of style.

SKIN-fining Moment:

Youngblood (0:49) Hockey groupie Cynthia bares her boobs and butt in bed after ice stud Rob Lowe shoots and scores. I wonder if he went for a hat trick . . .

See Her Naked In:

Youngblood (1986) Breasts, Buns

Courtney Gibbs

Born: August 20, 1966
Dallas, Texas
Skin-O-Meter: Brief Nudity

This former Miss USA didn't make the expected acting debut as another pretty face. Instead, Courtney Gibbs showed up as "Luigi's Girlfriend" on a 1989 episode of *The Super Mario Bros. Super Show!* Yeah, a lot of budding heterosexuals wanted to plumb something that day. Then it was on to a thankless role as a gorgeous salesgirl in the underrated *Joe Versus the Volcano* (1990), followed by the usual soap-opera stint—in this case as a sexpot district attorney on *All My Children*. But this beauty queen went out with a bang in her final screen role to date, stripping down for a bubbilicious bath scene in *The Naked Truth* (1992).

SKIN-fining Moment:

The Naked Truth (0:34) Courtney soaks in a sexy bath, then stands up. Quick nips, slight seat, but most of her Gibb-lets are covered in bubbles.

See Her Naked In:

The Naked Truth (1992) RB, Buns

Rebecca Gibney

Born: December 14, 1964
Levin, New Zealand
Skin-O-Meter: Brief Nudity

She didn't get a proper American debut until the TNT network's remake of *Salem's Lot* (2003). Lucky Australians, however, have gaped at Rebecca Gibney in over twenty *Halifax f.p.* TV movies, in which she plays an Armani-clad forensic psychologist. The New Zealand-born beauty originally made the transition from modeling in *Among the Cinders* (1985), where she fueled the dry drama with some asstastic acting. She's since gone on to become one of Australia's favorite TV personalities. Rebecca's also taken on duties as a daytime-talk-show hostess, although her recent American exposure will also expose more of what she's got Down Under.

SKIN-fining Moment:

Among the Cinders (1:08) Rebecca goes skinny-dipping with buns and breasts in decent (but rather distant) view.

See Her Naked In:

Among the Cinders (1983) FFN, Buns

Susan Gibney

Manhattan Beach, California
Skin-O-Meter: Brief Nudity

Susan Gibney is a California girl, born in Manhattan Beach, who made her name on New York City's competitive Broadway stages. Her headlights shined brighter than those neon lights, but even the Crossroads of the World couldn't expose this gifted temptress to enough popeyes, so she took her hills to the Hollywood Hills. The curvy blonde shook her boob thing on the boob tube, such as NBC's *Happy Family*, playing the older woman with a taste for young meat, and a recurring role on *Crossing Jordan* as well as *Star Trek: The Next Generation* and *Star Trek: Deep Space Nine*. Though she got to show off her out-of-this-world body of work wearing skintight unitards in those outer space dramas, it wasn't until she landed on Showtime's *Bedtime* that the costumes finally came off and her true talents were revealed. She played a lesbian, but even better she appeared topless in a bathtub, which is a sight sexy enough to turn any viewer on to girls.

SKIN-fining Moment:

Bedtime "Episode 10" (1996) Chest-baubles as Sue luxuriates among the bubbles in a bath with Felicity Huffman. They both make me huff, man.

TeleVisions:

Bedtime Breasts

Ariadna Gil

Born: January 23, 1969
Barcelona, Spain
Skin-O-Meter: Great Nudity

Ariadna Gil first strutted her fine stuff as a model for various Spanish fashion magazines. She debuted in *Lola* (1985), but it took several years before she turned heads in *Belle Époque* (1992). And, oh, did the heads (big and small) ever turn! With a well-lit, breast-bouncing sex scene, Ariadna upstaged the film's star, Penélope Cruz, who regrettably remained completely clothed throughout. Since then, Ariadna has become a regular blip on the skin-o-scope with one revealing turn after another. She's thus far managed to escape the American public's eye. (It must be the left eye because it certainly isn't right.) Ariadna rules the European skinematic community, largely due to her breastacular turns in such films as *Malena es un Nombre de Tango* (1996), *Lágrimas Negras* (1998), *Obra Maestra* (2000), and *Desafinado* (2001), which found limited release here in the States under the title *Off Key*. But the skin pick has to be *Segunda Piel* (1999), with its steamy sex scene that finally shed some light on Ariadna's shaving practices—or, more accurately put, lack thereof. Let's just hope it's not her final full-frontal flick.

SKIN-fining Moment:

Desafinado (0:47) Nice shot of Ariadna's hooters in the hallway chit-chatting with Joe Mantegna, followed by an incredible eyeful of her ass as she walks away.

See Her Naked In:

El Lado Oscuro del Corazón 2 (2001) RB
Desafinado (2001) Breasts, Buns
Second Skin (2000) FFN, Buns
Masterpiece (2000) Breasts
Nueces para el Amor (2000) Breasts, Buns
Lágrimas Negras (1998) FFN
Malena es un Nombre de Tango (1996) Breasts
Libertarias (1996) FFN
Los Peores Años de Nuestra Vida (1994) Breasts
Belle Époque (1992) Breasts
Mal de Amores (1992) Breasts
Amo tu Cama Rica (1991) Breasts

Melissa Gilbert

Born: May 8, 1964
Los Angeles, California
Skin-O-Meter: Brief Nudity

From her debut on the hit TV series *Little House on the Prairie*, Melissa Gilbert has been a hot one to watch, going from half pint to double gallons right before our eyes. Mel appeared more rounded and sexier in *The Miracle Worker*

(1979) and *The Dairy of Anne Frank* (1980). She moved to film with *Ice House* (1989), *Funny* (1989), and *Famous* (2000). But it's her big-screen debut, *Sylvester* (1985), that's most worth noting and also marks her skin debut via a brief peek at her boobies when a creep tears off her top in a truck. Hopefully, Melissa will open the door and let her not-so-little houses out again soon.

SKIN-fining Moment:

Sylvester (0:23) Melissa gets manhandled by a would-be rapist who tears her shirt and quickly reveals each of her Little Houses!

See Her Naked In:

Hollywood Wives: The New Generation (2003) Nip Slip LB
Sylvester (1985) Breasts

Pamela Gilbert

Skin-O-Meter: Great Nudity

A tall, smoky brunette with a streamlined contour—aside from those conical breasts dangerously protruding like 1950s taillights—ornamental film star Pamela Gilbert displayed a natural genius for hogging up audience attention while doing little more than walking naked into a pool, paddling across, and walking out again toward the camera. Pamela crammed as much of herself as possible into her pitifully brief two-year work history. *Evil Spawn* (1987) alone is bursting with the dusky goodness of the stark-naked Pamela strut. Those breasts, that artfully cracked ass, the trim triangle of muff thatch. We hardly knew ye, but we shall cherish thee forever!

SKIN-fining Moment:

Lust for Freedom (1:08) Nice peek at Pamela's perky pair and a bit of pussy-

puff as she sits on a bed all hopped-up on goofballs.

See Her Naked In:

Demonwarp (1988) Breasts
Evil Spawn (1987) FFN, Buns
Cyclone (1987) Breasts, Buns
Lust for Freedom (1987) Breasts

Thea Gill

Vancouver, British Columbia, Canada
Skin-O-Meter: Great Nudity

Thea Gill debuted in the nearly pornographic comedy *Bubbles Galore* (1996) in the provocative role of Orgasmic Angel. Yet she managed to remain fully clothed throughout the production. Nothing climatic about that! She earned her orgasmic angel wings, though, in *Papertrail* (1997). The Canadian rip-off of *Seven* (1995) is moist notable for Thea's graphic nude sex scene. American audiences know her best for her lesbian character on Showtime's *Queer as Folk*. To remind you that gay doesn't only mean naked men, Thea fills the screen with ample skin getting down on her love interest Michelle Clunie. Thea's body of work fits the Gill.

SKIN-fining Moment:

Trail of a Serial Killer (0:53) Thea bares her bodacious breasts during this sultry sex scene with Shawn Doyle.

See Her Naked In:

Sightings: Heartland Ghost (2002) Breasts
Trail of a Serial Killer (1997) Breasts

TeleVisions:

Queer as Folk Breasts
Bliss Breasts

Marie Gillain

Born: June 18, 1975
Liege, Belgium
Skin-O-Meter: Great Nudity

Marie Gillain was cast in the Gerard Depardieu flick *My Father the Hero* (1991), and she broke into the acting world with a bang—though she didn't bang Depardieu. Like every other European actress, Marie has been naked in several films—three cheers for French cinema! Her first skin scenes were in *The Bait* (1995). Although they were brief and not all that revealing, it's still a master-bait performance. The real gold mine for some bare Marie, however, would have to be *Harem Suare'* (1999), in which she is basically full frontal for the vast majority of the flick. What was it about? It has furburger! Muff! Cutie cooze! That's what it was about . . . well, that and about a million dead sperm cells. Marie, let them eat cheesecake!

SKIN-fining Moment:

Harem Suare' (0:13) Marie bathes stupendously starkers while beings serviced by a smokin' hot black female servant. FFN. Girl-on-girl grabbing. Great.

See Her Naked In:

Harem Suare' (1999) FFN, Buns
Le Bossu (1997) LB, Buns
The Elective Affinities (1996) Breasts, Buns
L'Appât (1995) Breasts
Marie (1994) Breasts

Eleonora Giorgi

Born: October 21, 1953
Rome, Italy
Skin-O-Meter: Great Nudity

In one of the most thankless debuts in the history of skinema, Eleonora Giorgi got us waving our swords as an uncredited naked beauty in the opening of *Three Musketeers in the West* (1972). It wasn't long, however, before male filmgoers knew Eleonora by name. This icy Italian blonde heated up plenty of films early in her career, including a

shocking full-frontal strip for some sisters in *Diary of a Cloistered Nun* (1973). Eleonora started a virtual g-orgy in theaters with her beach scene in *Born Winner* (1976), while *Disposta a tutto* (1978) featured her naked bod in plenty of amazing settings. She even scored some scream-queen exposure as a doomed beauty in Dario Argento's *Inferno* (1980).

SKIN-fining Moment:

Storia di una Monaca di Clausura (0:15) Eleonora gets stripped down to her naked essence as two creepy-ass nuns get their jollies all the way.

See Her Naked In:

Beyond Obsession (1982) Breasts
Nudo di Donna (1981) Breasts, Buns
Dimenticare Venezia (1979) Breasts, Bush
Disposta a Tutto (1978) FFN, Buns
Suggestionata (1978) FFN
Una Spirale di Nebbia (1977) FFN
L'Ultima Volta (1976) FFN
Liberi Armati Pericolosi (1976) Breasts
The Sex Machine (1975) FFN, Buns
Alla mia Cara Mamma nel Giorno del suo Compleanno (1974) FFN, Buns
Appassionata (1974) FFN, Buns
Il Bacio (1974) Breasts
Storia di una Monaca di Clausura (1973) FFN, Buns

Aria Giovanni

Born: November 3, 1977
San Diego, California
Skin-O-Meter: Great Nudity

Despite her name and exotic dark looks, Aria Giovanni is a sunny California girl from San Diego. She also has one of the most amazing bods to ever emerge from the humble world of internet amateur nudes. She soon graduated to become the September 2000 *Penthouse* Pet, which soon led to the fabulous world of softcore filmmaking—although she's built a hard corps in lesbianic lovefests

such as *Aria and Friends* (2003). Aria also goes where the girls are in *13 Erotic Ghosts* (2002), while her exuberant nature keeps her busy appearing as herself in everything from *Centerfold Babylon* (2003) to the E! Network's *Wild On . . .*, where she aired herself out for a 2003 episode going *Wild on Hollywood Nights.*

SKIN-fining Moment:

Aria (0:49) Operatic eyeful Aria sprawls on the floor in full-frontal resplendence, parting her legs so we can see her G(iovanni) spot.

See Her Naked In:

Aria and Friends (2003) FFN, Buns
13 Erotic Ghosts (2002) FFN, Buns
Survivors Exposed (2001) Breasts
Aria (2001) FFN, Buns
Numerous Adult Movies

Annabeth Gish

Born: March 13, 1971
Albuquerque, New Mexico
Skin-O-Meter: Brief Nudity

Dark-haired, dark-eyed beauty Annabeth Gish was a professional model by age eleven and starred in her first film, *Desert Bloom* (1986), at fifteen. She bloomed into stardom in *Desert* as a troubled preteen plagued by everyday occurrences like family squabbles and nuclear testing. Annabeth's career took off with a starring role in the cult favorite *Mystic Pizza* (1988), with a soon-to-be-globally worshipped Julia Roberts. A bitchin' dish herself, Gish scored as one of four beautiful vacationing teens in *Shag* (1988), opposite screen dreams Phoebe Cates, Bridget Fonda, and Paige Hannah. In 1993 Annabeth briefly interrupted her film career to earn a BA in English. Within a year, she was back on that acting horse in the film *Wyatt Earp* (1994) and the made-for-TV movie *Scarlett* (1994).

She also played an FBI agent on the final season of *The X Files* opposite Robert Patrick, who had a great idea for the show's finale that never came to pass: "It'd be great if we all had some sex," he said. "Group sex!"

SKIN-fining Moment:

The Last Supper (0:47) *Annabeth gets busy with herself in bed, keeping her tight T-shirt on but sending her fingers south for a blistering bout of alone-time lovin'. As non-nude masturbation scenes go, Ms. Gish makes this one a delicious dish.*

See Her Naked In:

Knots (2004) Buns

Robin Givens

Born: November 27, 1964
New York, New York
Skin-O-Meter: Great Nudity

Robin Givens, the 34-22-33 ebony beauty, began her career on the hugely popular *The Cosby Show* in 1985. Bill Cosby liked what he saw and helped steer Robin's flight to fame by helping to cast her on the hit series *Head of the Class*. But she became even more famous for marrying heavyweight champion boxer and ear-eater Mike Tyson. The two went to neutral corners after making newspapers dizzy reporting on their scandalous exploits. Now a free woman, Robin flew the conservative coop and ruffled feathers showing skin in *A Rage in Harlem* (1991) and even giving co-star Eddie Murphy some chocolate milk-sacks to fondle in *Boomerang* (1992). But for the moist skinful view of Robin's nest, check out *Playboy*, which published nude pictures of the act-chest in 1995. Fly, Robin, fly . . . and keep Givens us a boner.

SKIN-fining Moment:

A Rage in Harlem (0:32) *Robin lies in bed with Forrest Whitaker and shows off her chocolate bun-buns.*

See Her Naked In:

Foreign Student (1994) LB, Buns
Boomerang (1992) LB
A Rage in Harlem (1991) Buns

Lola Glaudini

Born: November 24, 1972
New York, New York
Skin-O-Meter: Never Nude

Luscious Lola Glaudini is the daughter of writer Robert Glaudini, who wrote an early episode of *NYPD Blue* and cast his hot offspring in it, which launched this beauty into the wonderful, wanton world of entertainment. Eventually, Lola landed the recurring role of Dolores Mayo on the provocative drama, but things would get far more "blue" as her career took off. She landed some high-profile spots on the boob tube, including a regular spot on *The Sopranos* as an FBI agent trying to infiltrate the mob, but it was the big screen that offered Lola her moist exposure. In *Consequence* (2003), Lola finally—if only briefly—showed off her hidden charms in a lesbian shower scene that is sadly almost skinless despite being a *lesbian shower scene*! On the Joe Pantoliano TV series *The Handler*, Lola proved she's too hot to handle!

SKIN-fining Moment:

Consequence (0:32) *It appears as though Lola shows brief right breast when she is grabbed by Armand Assante, but after extensive analysis at the Mr. Skin laboratories, it has been determined that she is wearing nipple-obscuring modesty tape.*

Judith Godrèche

Born: March 23, 1972
Paris, France
Skin-O-Meter: Great Nudity

Judith Godrèche is one of the plethora of French actresses that could steal your breath with a mere glance in your direction. Her face is beautiful, but you can only tell if you can make it past her heaving, often-glistening bosom. (French women don't sweat . . . they "glisten.") This particular young maiden started off at the tender age of thirteen with a bit part in *L'Eté prochain* (1985). After a few more background roles, Judith landed her first leading part at seventeen in *La Fille de 15 ans* (1989), which ironically translates to *The 15 Year Old Girl*. It features her first topless scene, and it's enough to give you two black eyes from rubbing your face in disbelief of her devastatingly delicious bosom. Though an arthouse sensation with the release of *Ridicule* (1996), she had been showing off her full-frontal nudity as early as *The Disenchanted* (1991). After her obligatory turn opposite Gerard Depardieu in *Bimboland* (1998), Judith finally landed on our shores for a role in the Leonardo DiCaprio flick *The Man in the Iron Mask* (1998). Thankfully, she stayed put long enough to take a role in another domestic production, *Entropy* (1999), in which she schooled her American audience on the benefits of on-screen nudity. Going back to school was never this sexy!

SKIN-fining Moment:

The Disenchanted (1:07) *Full-frontal luminosity as she lights up the living room. Quick scene.*

See Her Naked In:

L'Auberge espagnole (2002) Thong
Entropy (1999) Breasts
The Disenchanted (1991) FFN
Paris s'éveille (1991) Breasts
La Fille de 15 ans (1989) Breasts

Siena Goines

Washington, D.C.
Skin-O-Meter: Brief Nudity

This brown-haired, brown-eyed brown beauty works pretty steadily, but Siena Goines is still overdue for some stardom—and we're not just saying that because she held her own against Cameron Diaz and Christina Applegate in *The Sweetest Thing* (2002). We're saying that because Siena had us holding our own in two 1997 episodes of the cable anthology series *Women: Stories of Passion*. And you'll want to hold on to both your cock and any copies of her amazing sex scenes. Despite the filthy-minded content of *The Sweetest Thing*, Siena Goines is currently a very vocal born-again Christian.

SKIN-fining Moment:

Women: Stories of Passion "Grip Till It Jurts" (1997) Siena shares her sex fantasy with us, along with her socks and seat as she straddles her dream man.

TeleVisions:

Women: Stories of Passion Breasts, Buns

Joanna Going

Born: July 22, 1963
Wasington, D.C.
Skin-O-Meter: Great Nudity

Joanna Going, like many sexy ladies before her, started jumping from bed to bed on daytime TV. From *Search for Tomorrow* to *Another World* and even the gothic take on the genre, the remake of *Dark Shadows*, Joanna used her body to get ahead. She was then featured in the quickly canceled *Going to Extremes*, and it was going, going, gone for Going on the small screen. She made the switch to film, where her slender brunette body with its plum-sized breasts could go further. After well-received roles in *Wyatt Earp* (1994) and *Inventing the Abbotts* (1997), she showed her real assets in *Keys to Tusla* (1997), where she played a stripper. Yes, she strips down to her birthday suit, complete with a snatch of the furry bow between her legs. And in *Lola*

(2001), Joanna takes a sauna—topless—natch. Looks like Joanna is Going to make it after all.

SKIN-fining Moment:

Keys to Tulsa (0:37) Joanna Going makes Eric Stoltz go "boing!" as she reveals her A-cups and thonged ass while stripping.

See Her Naked In:

Lola (2001) Breasts
Commandments (1997) RB
Keys to Tulsa (1996) FFN, Buns
How to Make an American Quilt (1995) Breasts, Buns
Wyatt Earp (1994) Breasts

Meta Golding

Skin-O-Meter: Brief Nudity

Lovely Meta Golding debuted on the hit daytime soap opera *Loving*—and Mr. Skin loves it! From TV she made the leap to the big screen in *Conversations* (1995), which gave her more than mere lip service. She has gone on to appear on episodes of such infamous shows as *V.I.P., C.S.I.,* and *The District*. Meta appeared as Beautiful Girl, the role she was born to play, in the blockbuster *Kiss the Girls* (1997). But her moist notable role was in the dark comedy *The Way We Are* (1997). The producers obviously had big plans for this movie when they landed Hilary Swank. But they couldn't seem to get the star power that they really needed, so they hired the stars' cheaper relatives, such as Jake Busey, Joe Estevez, Bill Cusack, Natasha Gregson Wagner, and Chad Lowe. But the flick is far from a missed opportunity, especially for the brief glimpses of Meta's body. Talk about Meta physics!

SKIN-fining Moment:

The Way We Are (0:18) Break out the hot wax! Topless Meta's right Golding gleams in view as she gets it on in a convertable that's exiting a carwash.

See Her Naked In:

The Way We Are (1997) RB, Buns

Clio Goldsmith

Born: June 16, 1957
Paris, France
Skin-O-Meter: Great Nudity

This heiress comes from one of the wealthiest and most powerful families in Europe—and yet, Clio Goldsmith thought nothing of performing in some of the wildest sexploitation films of the '70s. Well, she's French. This kinky (haired) dark beauty spiced up plenty of fine imports with her daring roles. Highlights include Clio on her knees for a strict domme in the very sweet *Honey* (1981) and teaming up with Virna Lisi for some lesbianic leanings in *La Cadeau* (1980). Sadly, Clio wrapped up her career of unwrapping after a messy divorce in 1985. That didn't keep her out of the spotlight, though.

SKIN-fining Moment:

Le Cadeau (0:39) Clio fiddles with the hair on her head in the bathroom as her bare boom-booms are reflected mesmerizingly in the mirror.

See Her Naked In:

L'Etincelle (1984) RB
Le Cadeau (1981) Breasts, Buns
Honey (1981) FFN, Buns
La Cicala (1980) FFN, Buns
Plein sud (1980) Breasts, Bush

Valeria Golino

Born: October 22, 1966
Naples, Italy
Skin-O-Meter: Hall of Fame

There is no more pleasant surprise than when the unattainable object of desire turns out to be within reach after all. The sultry passion of skintillating, Italian-born temptress Valeria Golino melted the greatest number of hearts when she played Tom Cruise's impossibly sweet and hot girlfriend in *Rain Man* (1988). Her ass in Levi's was enough to cause misty-eye syndrome. As she sparingly flashed nipple for Tom, it was easy to conclude that the fleeting peek was the last we would see of bold brunette Valeria's classic Italian lovelies. It feels so good to be wrong! Two years later, not only were the breasts given the lingering treatment in *The King's Whore* (1990), but the curvaceous bounty of the Golino booty was framed in a tremendous open-crack shot that revealed the musky mystery of the third option! That's an eye winking out at you. A brown one.

SKIN-fining Moment:

The King's Whore (1:03) Valeria shows brief burgerage as we get an amazing open-legged caboose close-up when Timothy Dalton kicks the crap out of her. She's then thrown into the hallway for yet more bunnage and a little breast peep.

See Her Naked In:

Respiro (2002) Breasts
Spanish Judges (1999) Breasts, Bush, Buns
An Occasional Hell (1996) Breasts
Immortal Beloved (1994) RB
Year of the Gun (1991) Breasts, Buns
The King's Whore (1990) Breasts, Buns, Bush
Rain Man (1988) Breasts
Gli Occhiali d'oro (1987) LB
Dernier été a Tanger (1987) Breasts, Bush
Storia d'amore (1986) Breasts, Bush
Piccoli fuochi (1985) FFN, Buns

Melanie Good

Born: February 9, 1969
Rochester, New York
Skin-O-Meter: Great Nudity

Melanie Good turned a sexy nude-modeling career into an even hotter acting career. Good for her, better for us, seeing as she has been prone to showing some serious skin in just about everything she has been

in. Her cinematic debut, a frisky flick called *Die Watching* (1993), featured her first nude scenes on film and some massive breast shots, including one of the young lady being tied to a chair—if you go for bound pleasures. After some other nude-worthy roles in films such as *Psycho Cop Returns* (1993), *Desire* (1993), *Squanderers* (1996), and *One Good Turn* (1995), Melanie landed her moist famous part in the comedy *Private Parts* (1997). Howard Stern, in his exceptional wisdom, placed himself, Fred Norris, and Melanie in an uncomfortable, albeit sexy, ménage of a bubble-bath scene. When Melanie's Good she's great, but when she's wet she's better.

SKIN-fining Moment:

Private Parts (0:30) Sexy shot of Mel's bubble-coated breasts as she seduces the nerd-era Howard Stern.

See Her Naked In:

Private Parts (1997) Breasts, Thong
One Good Turn (1996) Breasts
Desire (1993) RB
Psycho Cop Returns (1993) Breasts, Buns
Die Watching (1993) Breasts

TeleVisions:

Love Street Breasts, Bush, Buns

Karen Lynn Gorney

Born: January 28, 1945
Beverly Hills, California
Skin-O-Meter: Great Nudity

Karen Lynn Gorney was born in Beverly Hills; her dad, Jay Gorney, is the famous songwriter who penned "Brother, Can You Spare a Dime?" But Karen was no loose change and took after her mom, an actress and dancer. After enrolling in the High School of Performing Arts in New York and earning her BFA in Acting at Carnegie-Mellon in Pittsburgh, it was time to make those melons professional, and she

got a gig on the popular soap *All My Children* in 1970. Then, along came *Saturday Night Fever* (1977), which changed everything. As the fine young thing on John Travolta's boogie arm, she became the primordial disco queen and showed off some killer gams. But it was an earlier screen performance that exposed all of her dangerous curves. In *The Magic Garden of Stanley Sweetheart* (1970), Karen took on the sexual revolution with all her weapons bared, from her cute little perky breasts to a patch of flower-child bush. Karen has three names, all right, one for each body part that she gleefully displays. That's a magic number.

SKIN-fining Moment:

The Magic Garden of Stanley Sweetheart (0:59) Fantastic full frontal from Karen when she joins in on some coital fun with Don Johnson and Holly Racimo. Three is the Magic Number!

See Her Naked In:

The Magic Garden of Stanley Sweetheart (1970) FFN, Buns

Heather Gottlieb

Skin-O-Meter: Great Nudity

She's the cute and gawky girl next door—that is if the girl next door is a ticking time bomb of sexuality. Heather Gottlieb began her career innocently enough, first on the kiddie series *Way Cool* and then as a recurring character on the 1996 TV version of *Clueless*. She then proved she was all grown up in *Childhood's End* (1997) while making our trousers grow as a shy young girl who flowers under (and on top of) lesbian lover Denise Edwards. *Edge City* (1998) was another daring turn as a slutty young girl who gets oral on the subject of oral sex. Her sexy role in the romantic comedy *Loving Jezebel* (1999) also got us plenty jezzed. Heather's kept a low profile since the end of the '90s, but we gotta see more of this Gottlieb.

SKIN-fining Moment:

Childhood's End Heather shows her womanhood front grappling girl-girl style with her newfound lesbian lover. Boobs and bush abound.

See Her Naked In:

Childhood's End (1997) FFN, Buns

Elizabeth Gracen

**Born: April 3, 1960
Booneville, Arkansas
Skin-O-Meter: Great Nudity**

With process servers hot on her tail during the Clinton sex scandal, former Miss America Elizabeth Gracen went to the press to admit that she'd enjoyed some gubernatorial groping from Bill Clinton during her days as Miss Arkansas. This put the brakes on Elizabeth's career, which had included a stellar parking-lot sex scene in *Lower Level* (1992)—which, coincidentally, raised dicks to a higher level. Elizabeth even exhibited her breasts spilling from her underwear in the TV movie *Sidney Sheldon's The Sands of Time* (1992). But to really appreciate what prompted Willie's willie, check out her sexy butch look in *Final Mission* (1993). We guarantee that you'll get plenty of emissions from her fabulous topless scene. Gracen couldn't get arrested after her Clinton confessional, despite a great *Playboy* layout, but she did get an IRS audit and the chance to declare personal bankruptcy. Gracen was finally allowed a minor comeback, though, in *Interceptor Force 2* (2002).

SKIN-fining Moment:

Discretion Assured (0:39) Breasts and buns while getting porked by Michael York.

See Her Naked In:

Final Mission (1993) Breasts
Discretion Assured (1993) Breasts, Buns
Lower Level (1991) Breasts, Bush

Aimee Graham

**Born: September 20, 1975
Milwaukee, Wisconsin
Skin-O-Meter: Great Nudity**

That face, the five-foot-nine-inch frame . . . the lovely lacto orbs—no, it's not Heather Graham, but her similarly fine younger sis, Aimee Graham. The hot blonde started her career with a bang in an episode of *Silk Stalkings* (1991). She quickly moved on to the skin-friendly confines of independent features, although she did have bit parts in *From Dust Till Dawn* (1996) and *Jackie Brown* (1997). Aimee's nude career peak was the made-for-cable movie *Reform School Girl* (1994). Talk about a school of hard knockers, Aimee goes topless and gets on to one of her girlie schoolmates for a lesbian tryst. For a more serious side to Aimee's body of work, check out the underrated sicko cult classic *Dance with the Devil* (1997), in which she gets naked in some explicitly rough sex scenes. Those are some fine Graham crackers!

SKIN-fining Moment:

Dance with the Devil (0:47) Amiee flashes her itty-bitties and a touch of ass several times when Javier Bardem rips her clothes off and has his way with her.

See Her Naked In:

Dance with the Devil (1997) Breasts
Reform School Girl (1994) Breasts

TeleVisions:

Fallen Angels Breasts

Heather Graham

**Born: January 29, 1970
Milwaukee, Wisconsin
Skin-O-Meter: Great Nudity**

OH, THOSE GOLDEN GRAHAMS! HEATHER GRAHAM GETS ME HARD(LY) IN *KILLING ME SOFTLY.*

Heather Graham gained a small group of faithful followers after her roles in the indie film *Drugstore Cowboy* (1989) and the cult-classic TV series *Twin Peaks*. Today, her street value has skyrocketed, thanks to her willingness to offer a hit of hooter or toke of tush to appease the drooling masses. Now a gram of Heather's onscreen flesh is the jones of every skin junky, and a nation of horny men are hooked. In *Boogie Nights* (1997), Heather's flash factor was at an all-time high. As the fresh-faced porn star Rollergirl, she sent co-star Mark Wahlberg into a tailspin while doing the horizontal hustle completely naked except for her skates. The exposure led to major parts like the super hit *Austin Powers: The Spy Who Shagged Me* (1999) and the mysterious thriller *From Hell* (2001). With all her popularity, Graham hasn't forgotten how much we all love to see her crackers. In *Killing Me Softly* (2002), she showed her massive mams at great length in super-delicious sex scenes. Oh, those Golden Grahams!

SKIN-fining Moment:

Boogie Nights (0:25) Heather flashes an incredible full-frontal shot when she sheds her threads to boogie with Mark Wahlberg at the behest of Burt Reynolds.

See Her Naked In:

Killing Me Softly (2002) FFN, Buns
Boogie Nights (1997) FFN, Buns

Julie Graham

Born: July 24, 1967
Glasgow, Scotland
Skin-O-Meter: Great Nudity

A wee Scot lassie with bonnie tits and assie, Julie Graham is a graduate of that classical school of British actresses who have learned to drop their knickers when the cameras roll. Unfortunately, this eager student of epidermal drama has never practiced her lessons in Hollywood, but she has extensively showed off her mastery of muff mummery in UK productions that will amply reward skinventurers who track them down. Two particular favorites are *Preaching to the Perverted* (1997) and *With or Without You* (1999). Look for a full screen of Julie's seat meat in *Perverted*, in which her mobility is severely constrained and the nether cheeks are rendered enticingly vulnerable. Graham enjoys a full range of unclothed motion in *Without*, displaying bush, boobs, and tush and indulging in a naked girl-on-girl tussle and a simulated hetero coupling. Cheerio!

SKIN-fining Moment:

With or Without You (0:58) Nice bare boobalas sitting up in bed next to her loverman, then side-seat as she leans over to lap his loin.

See Her Naked In:

Dirty Tricks (2000) Breasts
With or Without You (1999) FFN
Preaching to the Perverted (1997) FFN, Buns
The Near Room (1996) Breasts, Buns
The Big Man (1990) Breasts
The Fruit Machine (1988) FFN, Buns

Lauren Graham

Born: March 16, 1967
Honolulu, Hawaii
Skin-O-Meter: Never Nude

The trouble with TV is that it doesn't provide enough opportunity for sizzling sweethearts like Lauren Graham to get down to skin-ness. The five-foot-nine-inch brunette booty girl has struggled on the small screen, from debuting as a regular on *Caroline in the City* to recurring roles on *3rd Rock from the Sun*, *Law & Order*, and *NewsRadio*, but nothing stuck—except her clothing! Her move to movies offered potential nakedness, especially when she starred in something called *Confessions of a Sexist Pig* (1998), which is also known as *The Taste of Love* yet had no tasteless nudity. Lauren hit it big as a single mom on the hit series *The Gilmore Girls*, but a family-friendly show isn't likely to expose Lauren's lovelies. In fact, she's yet to grace her fans with bare flesh. Lauren comes close in *Sweet November* (2001), where she strips down to black bra and panties and then off they go as she flops about in a sheet-knotting sex scene. Sadly, the blanket covers her breast assets. Just as I was worrying that maybe she was related to preacher Billy Graham, Lauren brought fresh holiday spice to the 2003 raunch comedy *Bad Santa*, stiffening Billy Bob Thornton's candy cane by shaking her ho-ho-ho's in super-sexy, skin-tight undies. You can count on Lauren to always stuff your stocking.

SKIN-fining Moment:

Sweet November (2:14) As Keanu Reeves runs his mouth, Lauren glows white-hot in skin-tight black bra-and-panties. Dude! Pay attention!

Tiffany Granath

Born: May 28, 1972
Los Angeles, California
Skin-O-Meter: Brief Nudity

If the great minds of science are so smart, why don't they straighten out their priorities? Anyone with a modicum of skintelligence who has seen the wonderful rack of Tiffany Granath in such Bunny, Inc. videos as *WildWebGirls.Com* and *Playboy's Cheerleaders* knows that the eggheads would contribute more to mankind by shelving that search for a cancer cure and instead develop a way to enable the human eye to see radio waves. Buxom redhead Granath allowed sitcom phenom David Schwimmer to grope her goods in the HBO movie *Breast Men* (1997), and she occasionally appears with co-hostess Julie Ashton on the Playboy Channel's *Nightcalls*, but if new friends want to deepen their Granath relationship, they are referred to the *radio* version of *Nightcalls*, beamed nightly over XM Satellite Radio. Unfair! Radio is for ugly people (except for you, Howard!).

SKIN-fining Moment:

Breast Men (0:40) David Schwimmer, who was actually paid to be in this movie, shows Tiffany how to massage her tits.

See Her Naked In:

Breast Men (1997) Breasts
Baby Face Nelson (1995) Breasts, Buns

TeleVisions:

Women: Stories of Passion Breasts

Serena Grandi

Born: March 23, 1958
Bologna, Italy
Skin-O-Meter: Great Nudity

Tits don't come much grander than Serena Grandi's massive mammaries, which earned her the right to be compared to past Italian exports like Sophia Loren and Gina Lollabrigida. By the '80s, though, all-American goddesses were showing just as much skin as those liberated Europeans. That's why you might have missed epics such as *La Compagna di viaggio* (1980), in which Serena showed that her ass is just as magnificent as her Italian alps. And if you like women to sport the "natural" look, then *Miranda* (1985) will have you abusing your cock so hard that it should be read its Miranda Rights. Serena will also leave you pretty serene in the wake of *L'Iniziazione* (1987), in which she initiated a young guy to within an inch of his life. There's plenty more, too, but don't miss her reckless reclining in *Le Foto di Gioia* (1987). And yet the closest Serena ever came to American exposure was playing Carol Alt's mother in the TV film *Vendetta: Secrets of a Mafia Bride* (1991).

SKIN-fining Moment:

La Signora della notte (0:08) Full-figured, full-frontal, and totally sexy butt-nekkidness from Serena as she strips down while soaking wet.

See Her Naked In:

Delirium (1987) Breasts, Buns
L'Iniziazione (1987) Breasts, Bush, Buns
Teresa (1987) Thong
La Signora della notte (1985) FFN, Buns
Desiderando Giulia (1985) Breasts, Bush
Miranda (1985) FFN, Buns
La Compagna di viaggio (1980) Breasts

Anais Granofsky

Born: 1973
Toronto, Ontario, Canada
Skin-O-Meter: Great Nudity

Anais Granofsky is best remembered as one of those hot young school kids from the popular Canadian TV series *Degrassi Junior High*. This Great White North black beauty was born to an African American mother and a Russian-Jewish father, and, oh, they taste great together! Anais may be most familiar to American audiences for her stint as Christine Hughes on the TV series *Soul Food*, but it's her writing/directorial debut that made viewers want to eat her up. In the low-budget indie *On Their Knees* (2001) she starred with Ingrid Veninger as sisters of a biracial couple reunited to bury their dead mother. Well, they say write about what you know. Anais must know a bit about streaking, too, because she and Ingrid end up running about the chilly Maritime fields completely naked, with only their fiery bushes to keep them warm. It's enough to bring any man to his knees.

SKIN-fining Moment:

On Their Knees (0:45) Anais and Ingrid Veninger put the great in the great outdoors while romping through a field in this full-frontal extravaganza.

See Her Naked In:

On Their Knees (2001) FFN, Buns

Crystal Celeste Grant

Born: September 20, 1980
Houston, Texas
Skin-O-Meter: Great Nudity

Young, black, and talented Crystal Celeste Grant debuted in *Lawnmower Man 2: Beyond Cyberspace* (1996). But this ebony hottie was not content to be mere gore for horror movies. She bounced around on TV series such as *Sister, Sister*; *Smart Guy*; *The Jersey*; and *Pacific Blue*. But she didn't really get "blue" until teaming up with chronicler of teenage lust Larry Clark. He cast her in one of Skin Central's all-time favorite skintaculars, *Teenage Caveman* (2001). The sci-fi post-apocalyptic sexploitation winner focuses (closely and unclothed) on a group of teenagers who survive doomsday. What do they do? Each other . . . gloriously. The movie makes it Crystal clear that she's a star.

SKIN-fining Moment:

Teenage Caveman (0:27) She frees up her flotation devices for a topless dip in a pool.

See Her Naked In:

Teenage Caveman (2001) Breasts

Faye Grant

Born: July 16, 1957
St. Claire Shores, Michigan
Skin-O-Meter: Brief Nudity

"Believe it or not, I'm walking on air!" sang audiences when they first caught a glimpse of blonde beauty Faye Grant in her debut, the short-lived TV series *The Greatest American Hero*. But she's most famous for fighting alien invaders in the mini-series *V* (1983), the follow-up *V: The Final Battle* (1984), and the series *V*. Too bad none of those reptilian rascals had a ray gun that would zap Faye's clothing off and change the show's title to *X*. For skinage check out her big-screen breast-formances. At first, li'l five-foot-three-inch Faye was timid, not disrobing in *Crossing Delancy* (1988), and maybe it was just too cold in *January Man* (1989). Then came her bedding down with *American Gigolo* Richard Gere in *Internal Affairs* (1990). Faye rode Richard's Gere while one of her hefty jugs overflowed from her top. May Faye Grant us more skin in the future.

SKIN-fining Moment:

Internal Affairs (0:50) Faye straddles Richard Gere in bed, granting us her right breast.

See Her Naked In:

Traces of Red (1992) Thong
Internal Affairs (1990) RB

Lee Grant

Born: October 31, 1927
New York, New York
Skin-O-Meter: Great Nudity

Small roles in the '50s, like a sexy shoplifter in *Detective Story* (1951), didn't prepare men for her hot Oscar-winning performance as one of Warren Beatty's carnal cuts in *Shampoo* (1975). That infamous film also marked her skin debut, albeit with a dark flash of her flesh chesticles. She followed that up with the greatest story about masturbation ever written, *Portney's Complaint* (1976), though she didn't give audiences cause to slap their own meat. That would come in *When Ya Comin' Back, Red Ryder?* (1979). Lee was fifty-two years old and more delicious than ever as she removed her top for a lingering look at her floppy finest. Nowadays Lee keeps busy on the other side of the camera, directing features like *A Matter of Sex* (1984), *What Sex am I?* (1985), and *Down and Out in America* (1986). Doesn't sound like Lee's that down, though it'd be nice to see those mature mams onscreen again.

SKIN-fining Moment:

Shampoo (0:03) Lee bares right side breast-meaty in bed with Warren Beatty.

See Her Naked In:

When Ya Comin' Back, Red Ryder? (1979) Breasts
Shampoo (1975) Breasts

Marcha Grant

Born: May 21, 1937
New York, New York
Skin-O-Meter: Brief Nudity

Marcha Grant has two claims to fame. The first is that at age forty-three she played the lead role of Élodie in *Secrets of the Satin Blues* (1981), a.k.a. *Naughty Blue Knickers,* an erotic drama which follows the sexual awakening of a woman after she discovers a beautiful pair of blue panties. It was co-written by French director Claude Chabrol. Her second claim to fame is that she happens to be the great-great-granddaughter of the one and only General and President Ulysses S. Grant. Now there's a little something you never learned in history class.

SKIN-fining Moment:

Secrets of the Satin Blues (0:02) Marcha goes full frontal before trying on some blue Ulysses S. granny panties.

See Her Naked In:

Secrets of the Satin Blues (1981) FFN, Buns

Leslie Graves

Born: September 29, 1959
Silver City, New Mexico
Died: August 23, 1995
Skin-O-Meter: Brief Nudity

At only four-feet-eleven-inches tall, Leslie Graves still looked like a rising star in the early '80s. Director James Cameron was savvy enough to cast the dark beauty in his first feature, *Piranha II: The Spawning* (1981). She went on to a much smaller role in *Death Wish II* (1982), but Leslie was still unforgettable as an oblivious mega-meloned missy in a lotus position. Then she seemed set to finally break through with a prominent role on the CBS daytime soap *Capitol.* Instead, Leslie disappeared after a nude 1984 photo shoot for *OUI* magazine. She wasn't heard from again until news of her AIDS-related death in 1995.

SKIN-fining Moment:

Death Wish II (1:08) Leslie meditates in the lotus position sans shirt, showing off her life-affirming Death Wish Two.

See Her Naked In:

Death Wish II (1982) Breasts

Teresa Graves

Born: January 10, 1949
Houston, Texas
Died: October 10, 2002
Skin-O-Meter: Brief Nudity

Teresa Graves got her start in 1969 as a regular performer on the hit variety show *Rowan & Martin's Laugh-In.* That sexy success led to such gigs as the series *Turn-On* and *The Funny Side,* as well as an appearance on the made-for-TV special *Ed Sullivan's Armed Forces Tour.* However, after her cop-drama series *Get Christie Love* was cancelled in 1975, Teresa's career officially came to an end. Thankfully, she didn't fade away before making a mocha-mounded skintastic appearance in *That Man Bolt* (1973). Her topless turn in the flick is hot enough to put you in an early Graves.

SKIN-fining Moment:

That Man Bolt (0:40) Teresa takes on Fred "The Hammer" Williamson in the sack, but their nailing gets interrupted by a cock-blocker who blasts a hole in her chest with a gun. Quick nippage as she departs this mortal coil.

See Her Naked In:

That Man Bolt (1973) Breasts

Eva Green

Born: July 5, 1980
Paris, France
Skin-O-Meter: Great Nudity

Mountain-breasted, with a posterior as curvaceous as the coif covering her cooch is lush and full (which is to say delectably so), Eva Green erotically erupted into the reels of world skinema via director Bernardo Bertolucci's NC-17 art-house sensation *The Dreamers* (2003). Playing a ravishing revolutionary in 1968 Paris, Eva exposed every inch of her flawless form in the name of art, politics, and, moist intriguingly, incest, as she shares a bath and another man with Louis Garrell, who co-stars as her twin brother in the film. In real life, Eva honors the skin-exposing tradition established by her mother, awesomely abundant actress Marlène Jobert, who lit up screens a generation ago with naked turns in *Ten Days Wonder* (1972), *La Guerre de polices* (1979), and *L'amour nu* (1981).

SKIN-fining Moment:

The Dreamers (0:48) Boobs and panties as she does a striptease.

See Her Naked In:

The Dreamers (2003) FFN, Buns

Ellen Greene

Born: February 22, 1950
Brooklyn, New York
Skin-O-Meter: Brief Nudity

A tall, blonde goofball with a chest of blessed breast flesh, Ellen Greene is equally adept at arousing laughter and lust. Best remembered as a cleavage-flaunting, ditzy straw top who is seemingly a knockout by accident in Rick Moranis's musical comedy *Little Shop of Horrors* (1986), game-girl Ellen sang and danced her way into the hearts of rack-watchers everywhere. Greene is used to being the slightly offbeat beauty; she played the supporting tart in such flicks as *Talk Radio* (1988) and *One Fine Day* (1996). She is best as a comic siren in laugh fests along the lines of *Naked Gun 33⅓: The Final Insult* (1994) and John Candy's *Wagon's East* (1994). What's so funny about a big, heaving bosom? Ellen started her film career on a different foot, however, the foot that she couldn't see because it was hidden beneath the outcropping of her naked shelf. Try to see past the rack in *Next Stop, Greenwich Village* (1976) and then fast forward a few

decades for her nudie reappearance in *Sex and a Girl* (2001).

SKIN-fining Moment:

Next Stop, Greenwich Village (0:15) Ellen slips out of her bra one whopper at a time—first the right, then the left—on a couch with lucky Lenny Baker.

See Her Naked In:

Sex and a Girl (2001) RB, Buns
Next Stop, Greenwich Village (1976) Breasts

Kim Morgan Greene

Born: 1960
North Carolina
Skin-O-Meter: Great Nudity

Kim Morgan Greene is one of the legion of luscious soap opera hussies, appearing mostly on daytime dramas but seldom seen in cinematic fare. She started her career as Nicole Love #1 on the hit series *Another World* but quickly moved on to the primetime hit *The Colbys*. Soon after her stint on that series ended, Kim made yet another jump, this time to *Days of Our Lives*, but she barely made it there for one season. After a brief turn on the sexy *Silk Stalkings*, Kim turned to movies to make her bread and butter and found out that she was going to have to get a little naked to make it. Thus, her first two outings on the big screen feature Kim's only flesh flashes to date. In *The Soft Kill* (1994) and *Scorned* (1994), Kim revealed what fans of her soap-opera days had been waiting for since the early '80s. Although she appeared topless in *Scorned*, *The Soft Kill* deals her only full-frontal hand, and, although its dark, the full house folds the competition. It'll raise your suit.

SKIN-fining Moment:

Scorned (1:10) A lengthy look at Kim's potent pair as she and Shannon Tweed play "Hide the Finger" in bed.

See Her Naked In:

Scorned (1994) Breasts, Buns
The Soft Kill (1994) FFN, Buns

Judy Greer

Born: July 20, 1975
Detroit, Michigan
Skin-O-Meter: Great Nudity

Judy Greer is one of those Hollywood second bananas who make you want to peel your flesh banana. The comedienne made her debut in the low-budget horror video *Stricken* (1998), which also featured her first skin. The blonde beauty stripped down to black panties for a bed romp, and then everything came off for a shower scene, which is only partially marred by the transparent curtain. She went on to *Jawbreaker* (1999), *Three Kings* (1999), *The Wedding Planner* (2001) (opposite buttastic Jennifer Lopez), and *What Women Want* (2000). What men want is more flesh from this tempting female, and they got it with *What Planet Are You From?* (2000). Judy showed off her plump breasts again in *Adaptation* (2002). That's a reworking we can all get behind!

SKIN-fining Moment:

What Planet Are You From? (0:22) A beauteous shot of Judy's boobies and a flash of snatch, marred only by the addition of a shirtless Garry Shandling.

See Her Naked In:

Adaptation (2002) Breasts
What Planet Are You From? (2000) Breasts, Bush
Stricken (1998) Breasts, Buns

Kim Greist

Born: May 12, 1958
Stamford, Connecticut
Skin-O-Meter: Brief Nudity

Women are not all the same. Some women give their all in pursuit of their dreams, and others sparingly parcel out the rare glimpse here and there along the road to where they want to go. Accomplished actress Kim Greist is of the latter variety. Despite possessing all the womanly attributes accorded to a female who can make a very good living on her looks alone, Kim has opted mostly to shield her vital parts from view. Even as far back as her B-flick exploitation initiation in *C.H.U.D.* (1984), she retained a sweatshirt and panties in the role of a flustered chick, the one who commonly runs around menaced and topless. Having ascended to a recurring role on network goldmine *Chicago Hope*, Kim is probably happy to have done things her way. The only glimpse of Greist goods is a rear, fully nude shot of primarily back in *Brazil* (1985). A lot more people would be happy if she had done things our way.

SKIN-fining Moment:

Brazil (1:24) Kim bares her partial right Brazil-nut and upper-butt peninsula as she romps between the sheets with Jonathyn Pryce.

See Her Naked In:

Brazil (1985) Buns

Jennifer Grey

Born: March 26, 1960
New York, New York
Skin-O-Meter: Brief Nudity

The whirling-bosom choreography of *Dirty Dancing* (1987) could make a man sweat just to watch it, but the moment that really raises the need for a cold shower comes when fleet-footed Jennifer Grey takes a clothed dip in an icy pond with bad boy Patrick Swayze. The girl's nipples, perhaps responding to Grey's training with method maestro Sanford Miesner, pop up through her soaked wife-beater tee and protrude beyond the range of

her prominent pre-scalpel proboscis. Seldom before or since has a PG splash scene caused so many to spill so much. Sadly, subsequent glimpses of Jennifer would be few and fleeting. *Lover's Knot* (1995) shows the flick of what appears to be accidental nip but then captures a full backside view of Jen running up a short flight of stairs that will have cheek cherishers hitting PAUSE, REWIND, PLAY for all the skin-long day.

SKIN-fining Moment:

Lover's Knot (0:43) Brief-but(t)-beautiful bunnage as Jen streaks around the house with her man in hot pursuit. All that dirty dancing paid off!

See Her Naked In:

Lover's Knot (1995) Breasts, Buns

Pam Grier

Born: May 26, 1949
Winston-Salem, North Carolina
Skin-O-Meter: Hall of Fame

MR. SKIN'S TOP TEN

Bush-baring Black Babes
. . . Afro-disiacs

10. Traci Bingham
9. Marilyn Joi
8. Debra Wilson
7. Tanya Boyd
6. Thandie Newton
5. Nicole Ari Parker
4. Josephine Jacqueline Jones
3. Beverly Johnson
2. Vanity
1. **Pam Grier**

The cousin of football legend (and two-headed thing) Rosie Grier, moviedom's all-time A-list queen Pam Grier appropriately debuted in Russ Meyer's masterwork *Beyond the Valley of the Dolls* (1970), where her jumbolicious chocolate milk-bombs fit right in. She next appeared in a series of classic women-in-prison films that were shot in the Philippines, earning a contract with legendary drive-in studio American International Pictures. Pam starred in an array of the most amazing, intense, and outrageous films of the '70s, specializing in the blaxploitation genre, where she became the screen's first female action star, as well as the only action star who gets Mr. Skin really excited by almost never failing to get naked. Among her milestones are *Coffy* (1973), *Foxy Brown* (1974), *Sheba, Baby* (1975), and *Friday Foster* (1975). After blaxploitation petered out, Pam was a regular on TV's *Miami Vice* in the '80s and then returned to urban rump-stomping opposite Steven Seagal in *Above the Law* (1988) and in the blaxploitation throw-back *Original Gangstas* (1993). Superfan Quentin Tarantino wanted to cast Pam in his film *Pulp Fiction* (1994) but instead reworked *Jackie Brown* (1997) into both a tribute and comeback vehicle for this foxiest of all mamas.

SKIN-fining Moment:

Coffy (0:38) Pam sheds her swingin' threads in the bedroom, revealing that high-rise ass and unbelievably monstrous set of mammaries . . . I can dig it!

See Her Naked In:

On the Edge (1985) FFN
Drum (1976) Breasts
Sheba, Baby (1975) LB
Bucktown (1975) Breasts
Friday Foster (1975) Breasts
Foxy Brown (1974) Breasts
The Arena (1973) FFN
Coffy (1973) Breasts, Buns

The Big Bird Cage (1972) Breasts
Black Mama, White Mama (1972) Breasts
Hit Man (1972) Breasts
Women in Cages (1971) Breasts
Big Doll House (1971) Breasts

Simone Griffeth

Born: April 14, 1955
Savannah, Georgia
Skin-O-Meter: Great Nudity

Glowering and gorgeous Georgia blonde Simone Griffeth couldn't have been much more than seventeen years old when she made a full-frontal splash as a free-spirited skinny dipper in *Sixteen* (1972). The slightly surly, wholly angelic nipster-hipster stood still and titty proud as a curious boy's finger zeroed in on her tense nipple, with the camera zeroing in right behind the digit. Griffeth's signature role was as the hottest competitor and gland prize of *Death Race 2000* (1975). The tale of thrills and spills and racetrack romance featured a string of fast-moving cars trying to cling to the track's dangerous curves, but those hairpin turns don't compare to the lethal lines of Simone as she wriggles belly down and wholly exposed, her buttocks out, flexing and twisting.

SKIN-fining Moment:

Death Race 2000 (0:56) Simone undresses and lies in wait for David Carradine, torso sprouts and boo-tay out.

See Her Naked In:

The Patriot (1986) Breasts
Hot Target (1985) FFN, Buns
Death Race 2000 (1975) Breasts, Buns
Sixteen (1972) FFN, Buns

Renee Griffin

Born: May 30, 1968
Long Beach, California
Skin-O-Meter: Great Nudity

Consistency is the better part of ecstasy when applied to pout-lipped blonde baby cakes Renee Griffin. The Long Beach, California, native has demonstrated a consistent penchant for revealing her big, real, buoyant bouncers every time a director calls "Action!" Ecstatic rack fanatics worldwide breathe a little heavier whenever Renee's orbs of excellence circle into view. Not only does the heavenly endowed Renee strip and show 'em, she is usually game for a slippery simulated-sex grind. Sniff out copies of *Showdown in Little Tokyo* (1991), *Number One Fan* (1995), or *Criminal Affairs* (1997), and be prepared to pant.

SKIN-fining Moment:

Showdown in Little Tokyo (0:16) A tattooed Yakuza guy slices off Renee's shirt and bra, freeing her right funbag, which he gropes from behind before somebody hands him a sword.

See Her Naked In:

Criminal Affairs (1997) Breasts
Ladykiller (1996) Breasts, Buns
Number One Fan (1995) Breasts, Buns
The Stoned Age (1994) Breasts
Death Match (1994) Breasts, Buns
Cyborg 2 (1993) Breasts
Showdown in Little Tokyo (1991) Breasts

Melanie Griffith

Born: August 9, 1957
New York, New York
Skin-O-Meter: Hall of Fame

MELANIE GRIFFITH WILL DOUBLE THE LENGTH OF ONE PART OF YOUR BODY IN *BODY DOUBLE*.

For many film fans, Hollywood blonde Melanie Griffith is a prime example of better sexuality through surgery. The nip-and-tuck princess's lips and breasts may in fact be categorized as medical marvels, but they were not always that way. Connoisseurs of fresh-tit, unspoiled exhibitionists can thank Melanie for leaving behind a record of her cheeky youth. Such post-adolescent documents as *Night Moves* (1975) and *Joyride* (1977) preserve the willowy goodness of a gangly kid who just likes to wet down her mouth-sized mams and take her beaver for a swim. Even as late as *Body Double* (1984), *Something Wild* (1986), and *Working Girl* (1988), the booblettes Melanie so generously shares appear to be the ones God blessed her with. Take a look back, and you'll forget that she has also played Lolita's mom.

SKIN-fining Moment:

Something Wild (0:15) Melanie's lip-smackin' milk-balloons bobble as she straddles a handcuffed Jeff Daniels.

See Her Naked In:

Along for the Ride (2000) Body Double—FFN, Buns
Nobody's Fool (1994) Breasts
Shining Through (1992) Breasts
The Bonfire of the Vanities (1990) Nip-slip— Breasts
Working Girl (1988) Breasts
Stormy Monday (1988) Breasts
Something Wild (1986) Breasts, Buns
Fear City (1984) Breasts, Thong
Body Double (1984) Breasts, Buns
Ha-Gan (1977) FFN, Buns
Joyride (1977) Breasts, Buns
Night Moves (1975) FFN, Buns
Smile (1975) Breasts

Tracy Griffith

**Born: October 19, 1965
New York, New York
Skin-O-Meter: Great Nudity**

Maybe she's just a half gene away from superstardom, but to the naked eye, there's no reason that redheaded flame thrower Tracy Griffith shouldn't be at the top of more cast lists. She and half-sister Melanie share a father and a high-watt smile that is all lascivious and delicious. A natural redhead with the pale-pink nipples to prove it, Tracy proudly opened her shirt and displayed her strawberry-tipped small wonders to a younger girl in *The Good Mother* (1988). In *The Finest Hour* (1991), the titillating Ms. T makes the most of the time by wading in a boldly revealing, wet, white T-shirt, which she peels off with sideways-seen flirt of erect nipple. Here's to half fame!

SKIN-fining Moment:

The Good Mother (0:06) Tracy opens her shirt and shows her pink-nosed pups to a curious young girl.

See Her Naked In:

Skeeter (1994) Breasts
The Finest Hour (1991) RB
The Good Mother (1988) Breasts

Rachel Griffiths

**Born: February 20, 1968
Melbourne, Victoria, Australia
Skin-O-Meter: Great Nudity**

Saucy Aussie Rachel Griffiths has gotten unabashedly unclothed (up top and down under!) in arthouse flicks such as *Jude* (1998), *Among Giants* (1998), *Me Myself I* (1999), and *Blow Dry* (2001). But rowdy Rachel's no stranger to skinteresting behavior. She reportedly ran topless through Melbourne's Crown Casino on its opening night as an act of protest. When asked by the local media why she did it, she replied, "If I didn't flash my tits, you wouldn't have put me in the paper!" I agree, Rachel, there's no such thing as bad publicity or nudity. She's now an award-winning ensemble player on the HBO smash *Six Feet Under*, embalming viewers with her sultry sensuality.

SKIN-fining Moment:

Among Giants (0:55) Full-frontal fabulousness and great glutes, too! Watch rackadocious Rachel's jumbo-jackage bobble around as she cavorts underneath a boardwalk with some nude dude.

See Her Naked In:

Blow Dry (2001) Breasts
Me Myself I (1999) Buns
Among Giants (1998) FFN, Buns
My Son the Fanatic (1998) RB
Jude (1996) Breasts
Children of the Revolution (1996) Breasts

Eva Grimaldi

**Born: September 7, 1961
Verona, Veneto, Italy
Skin-O-Meter: Great Nudity**

It's hard for an Italian actress to scandalize nowadays, but Eva Grimaldi stirred up plenty of passion with her role in *La Monaca del peccato* (1986), a.k.a. *The Convent of Sinners*. At least nobody can say Eva is unbelievable as a hot young thing pursued by both priests and nuns. Grimaldi soon found herself working with Federico Fellini in *Intervista* (1987) before heading back to the gutter to star with Fred Williamson in *Cobra nero* (1987), a.k.a. *The Black Cobra*, a remake of Sylvester Stallone's *Cobra* (1986). Eva, incidentally, filled in for Brigitte Nielsen's role. Grimaldi went on to get us gleeful with plenty of nude scenes, including a rough romp with Klaus Kinski in *Paganini* (1989). She shares her talent with the occasional lucky American, too, including Andrew McCarthy as an expatriate with an excellent full-frontal view of Eva in *Jours tranquilles a Clichy* (1990).

SKIN-fining Moment:

La Monaca del peccato (0:03) Breasts and bush while a gaggle of holy-gals do her up in nun-gear.

See Her Naked In:

Mutande pazze (1992) Buns
Cattive Ragazze (1992) Breasts, Buns
L'angelo con la pistola (1992) Breasts, Bush, Buns
Abbronzatissimi (1991) Buns
Per sempre (1991) FFN, Buns
Jours tranquilles a Clichy (1990) FFN, Buns
Paganini (1989) Breasts, Buns
Mia moglie è una bestia (1988) Breasts, Bush, Buns
Quella villa in fondo al parco (1988) FFN, Buns
Intimo (1988) Breasts, Bush, Buns
La Monaca del peccato (1986) FFN, Buns
D'Annunzio (1985) FFN

Amparo Grisales

Manizales, Colombia
Skin-O-Meter: Great Nudity

Amparo Grisales was born in Manizales, Colombia, but was raised in Bogota, more known for its illegal exports than actress sexports. But Amparo was already acting by the age of five, and by thirteen she was filming several soap operas. That led to more work, especially on TV with mini-series coming out of Venezuela, Brazil, Mexico, South Africa, and France. But Amparo knew she was big-time material and moved her Spanish-fly body to Los Angeles, where she's worked in the theater, soap operas, and mini-series, and was even a TV anchor. But if you're looking to drop your anchor, it's best to stick to her work south of the border. She first showed off her maracas in *La Virgen y el fotógrafo* (1982). Once she lost her clothes, she kept them off for a roll in the hey-hey-hey with *De mujer a mujer* (1986) and *Bésame mucho* (1994).

SKIN-fining Moment:

Bésame mucho (0:55) Amparo's tied up in bed, talking to her pervy loverman, displaying terrifically taut and tan ta-ta's.

See Her Naked In:

Bésame mucho (1994) Breasts, Buns
De mujer a mujer (1986) Breasts
La Virgen y el fotógrafo (1982) Bush, Buns

Molly Gross

Georgia
Skin-O-Meter: Brief Nudity

The decidedly ungross Molly Gross was born in Georgia and moved to Seattle, Washington, just in time to be discovered by director Kristine Paterson. Kristine was searching for compelling unknowns to cast in a film about an all-girl rock band, and Molly fit the bill. The resultant *Slaves to the Underground* (1997) has enough nudity to fill a crass exploitation flick, much of it of cuddly Molly and her bubbly boobies. The rusty blonde—replete with full cheeks, pale pink complexion, and shoulder-length shag hair—can't make up her mind if she prefers sharing her smooth, nubile body with another chick of similar appeal or opening up to the possibilities of sharing her nude self with a guy. Her unclothed indecision makes us all winners, but perhaps this highly revelatory role was a case of too-much-shown-too-soon for Molly. She hasn't been seen since.

SKIN-fining Moment:

Slaves to the Underground (0:28) Grrrrl-loving booblets and bunnage during a Sapphic sex snoggle with Marisa Ryan.

See Her Naked In:

Slaves to the Underground (1997) Breasts, Bush, Buns

Florence Guerin

Born: June 12, 1965
Paris, France
Skin-O-Meter: Great Nudity

Florence Guerin started her career with a bit part in the skintastic *Caligula and Messalina* (1982). Time for a pop quiz: Florence did which of the following: A) Shortly thereafter joined a nunnery, B) Settled down to raise her family, or C) Proceeded to get naked at the drop of a hat in just about every movie that she was ever in. If you guessed C, then you get the cake . . . cheesecake, that is. Florence, whose career has become rather spotty in recent years, spent the better part of the '80s in complete nudity, showing just about every inch of her body off from just about every camera angle possible. For some of her better skin shots, look for *Venus* (1983) or *Black Venus* (1983), which are two separate and distinct films that just so happened to be released in the same year. But that's just the beginning. There's also *Le Declic* (1985), *Le Couteau sous la gorge* (1986), and *Profumo* (1987), all of which feature stellar shots of our heroine in all her full-frontal glory. She's a real Florence Nakedgale.

SKIN-fining Moment:

Venus (0:18) Florence flashes full-frontal flesh on the beach. Fantastic!

See Her Naked In:

Rivelazioni Scandalose (1993) Breasts
Cattive Ragazze (1992) Breasts
Alcune signore per bene (1990) Breasts
Scuola di ladri—parte seconda (1987) Breasts
L'Attrazione (1987) Breasts, Bush, Buns
Profumo (1987) FFN, Buns
La Bonne (1986) Breasts, Bush, Buns
Le Couteau sous la gorge (1986) FFN, Buns
D'Annunzio (1985) FFN, Buns
Le Déclic (1985) FFN, Buns
La Joven y la tentación (1984) FFN, Buns
Black Venus (1983) FFN, Buns
Venus (1983) FFN
Le Bourreau des coeurs (1983) Breasts

Blanca Guerra

Born: January 10, 1953
Mexico City, Mexico
Skin-O-Meter: Hall of Fame

She started in Mexican soap operas, but Blanca Guerra's big breasts were obviously meant for the big screen—as proven with her first nude scene in *Pedro Páramo* (1978). It's a nice start, but Blanca truly became an international beauty when she exposed her magnificent bush in *Chile picante* (1983) and *¿Cómo ves?* (1985). Blanca even made it into American video stores with the comedy *Separate Vacations* (1986), in which the lean and luscious bandito stole our sperm while reclining in bed for David Naughton. And don't miss the incredible scene in *El Imperio de la fortuna* (1986) where a lucky hombre gets to ravage Blanca amongst barrels of booze. Now she's back on Mexican TV as a respected icon, but Blanca's beauty still busts through borders—as seen by her cameo in *Clear and Present Danger* (1994).

SKIN-fining Moment:

Pedro Páramo (0:55) Blanca bares a boatload of booby and a long-distance flash of fur burger as she takes off an enormous dress.

See Her Naked In:

Salon Mexico (1996) Breasts
Separate Vacations (1986) Breasts
El Imperio de la fortuna (1986) Breasts
¿Cómo ves? (1985) FFN
Motel (1983) Breasts, Buns
Aquel famoso Remington (1982) Breasts
Cada quien su madre (1982) FFN
Falcon's Gold (1982) Breasts, Buns
Campanas rojas (1982) Breasts
Chile picante (1981) FFN, Buns
Solo Contra La Mafia (1981) Breasts
Perro Callejero 2 (1981) Breasts, Bush, Buns
El sexólogo (1980) Breasts
Dos De Abajo (1980) Breasts, Buns
Mojado Power (1979) FFN, Buns
Estas ruinas que ves (1978) FFN, Buns
Pedro Páramo (1978) Breasts, Bush

Evelyn Guerrero

Born: February 24, 1949
East Los Angeles, California
Skin-O-Meter: Great Nudity

Hot Latina Evelyn Guerrero is breast remembered as making the comic duo Cheech & Chong stop laughing long enough to start spanking their meat-reefers. She appeared in three of their films—*Cheech & Chong's Next Movie* (1980),

Nice Dreams (1981), and *Things Are Tough All Over* (1982)—as Donna. But Evelyn is no joke. She also appeared in *And the Earth Did Not Swallow Him* (1995), a critically acclaimed film adaptation of Tomas Rivera's semi-autobiographical 1971 novella. She first graced the cinema with her spicy presence in *Wild Wheels* (1969). But, more importantly, her first nudie scene was as an S&M Dancer in *Fairy Tales* (1979), which also featured titillating talent such as Linnea Quigley as Sleeping Beauty. It's a muff-see. Evelyn also flashed some less fleshy treats in *Cheech & Chong's Next Movie*. She made more mainstream TV turns on the series *I Married Dora* and *Dallas*. But by *Coyote Moon* (1999), Evelyn seemed finished. The new millennium is less mamnificent without her.

SKIN-fining Moment:

Fairy Tales (0:56) Evelyn struts and shimmies in skintacular full-frontal fashion along with two other kinked-up nude dancers. She's one Mother I'd like to Goose!

See Her Naked In:

Nice Dreams (1981) LB
Fairy Tales (1979) FFN

Monica Guerritore

Born: January 5, 1958
Rome, Italy
Skin-O-Meter: Great Nudity

It doesn't hurt for a gorgeous Italian actress to have a gimmick. Monica Guerritore, for example, adds a touching element to her skinema history by . . . well, touching herself. Monica's masturbation skills are memorably displayed in the thriller *Evil Senses* (1986) and the drama *Fotografando Patrizia* (1985), a.k.a. *The Dark Side of Love*. Your own senses will be feeling pretty good, although the dark side of self love is that guys

might strain their scrotum while following Monica's example. Don't worry, though, Monica isn't flying solo in skintastic epics such as *Scandalous Gilda* (1985), *The Venetian Woman* (1986), and *Strana la vita* (1987).

SKIN-fining Moment:

Love Under the Elms (0:52) Monica shows her incredible rack, complete with a side-helping of ass, when she plays "Show Me Yours and I'll Show You Mine" with Mark Lester outdoors.

See Her Naked In:

Femmina (1998) Breasts, Bush, Buns
Strana la vita (1987) Breasts, Buns
Evil Senses (1986) Breasts, Buns
The Venetian Woman (1986) Breasts
Scandalous Gilda (1985) Breasts, Buns
Fotografando Patrizia (1985) FFN, Buns
La Vela Incartata (1982) Breasts, Buns
Love Under the Elms (1974) Breasts, Bush, Buns

Carla Gugino

Born: August 29, 1971
Sarasota, Florida
Skin-O-Meter: Great Nudity

Director Wayne Wang chose not to give Carla Gugino the lead as a prostitute in his kinky *Center of the World* (2001) because he "was worried that she would eat the movie up with sexuality." Of course he cast the voluptuous beauty as another hooker and, yes, there's skinage. Carla started modeling at fifteen but was deemed too small at five-feet-five-inches. What she lacks in height she more than makes up for in width—around her bountiful bosom. She moved to TV, landing a supporting role on the hit nighttime soap opera *Falcon Crest* (1981). Carla played the typical teenage roles and got a taste of stardom opposite Pauly Shore in *Son in Law* (1993). That led to appearances on the TV drama *Chicago Hope* and the sitcom

Spin City, as well as roles in *Snake Eyes* (1998) and *The Singing Detective* (2002), in which she played another prostitute. But her breast performance has to be in *Jaded* (1996). Her harrowing depiction of an attack victim is redeemed by the ample nudity. You've got to look on the bright side.

SKIN-fining Moment:

Jaded (0:26) Gugino shows some nice butt cleavage as she lays in bed, then a very nice breast shot as she chills out in the shower.

See Her Naked In:

Sin City (2005) Breasts
Judas Kiss (1998) RB
Jaded (1996) Breasts, Buns

Gloria Guida

**Born: November 19, 1955
Merano, Italy
Skin-O-Meter: Hall of Fame**

Italian beauty Gloria Guida, a tall, full-figured, blue-eyed babe, wasn't afraid to show off her fine assets for the camera. Most of her roles required some nudity, and Gloria was always willing to undress for success. She often got quite explicit in her explosively sexploitative performances such as *Blue Jeans* (1975), *La Noviza* (1975), *Scandalo in Famiglia* (1976), and *Peccati di Gioventu* (1975), in which Gloria dished out both erotic sex and full-frontal displays—ever the tawdry trooper. She did gain international recognition for her numerous hot romps in various sex comedies and went on to make thirty films. She worked with a few big players such as John Huston, Rene Cardona Jr., and Ursula Andress. Sadly, Gloria retired from film in 1989, but what a body of work she's left behind (and up front . . . and on top . . . and down under . . . and . . . hair, there, and everywhere)!

LA NOVIZIA: GLORIA GUIDA IS SECOND TO NUN! MY FAVORITE PART OF THIS POSTER IS THE WORD "GIERIG." I UNDERSTAND THE FIRST TWO SENTENCES ABOUT SISTER GLORIA BEING SEXY AND WILD, SO WHATEVER 'GEIRIG" MEANS, IT MUST BE SO HOT THAT I DON'T EVEN WANT A TRANSLATION!

SKIN-fining Moment:

Quella età maliziosa (0:20) Bra-clad Gloria pops out her breasts and some far-off bush as she stands by an open window and does a funkedelic '70s striptease! Get down, mama!

See Her Naked In:

Fico d'India (1980) Breasts, Buns
Indagine su un delitto perfetto (1979) Buns
La Liceale seduce i professori (1979) FFN, Buns
Avere vent'anni (1978) FFN, Buns
La Liceale nella classe dei ripetenti (1978) Breasts, Buns
Travolto dagli affetti familiari (1978) Breasts, Buns
Maschio latino cercasi (1977) FFN, Buns
Scandalo in famiglia (1976) FFN, Buns
L'Affittacamere (1976) FFN, Buns
La Ragazza alla pari (1976) Breasts
Il Medico e la studentessa (1976) Breasts
Quella età maliziosa (1975) Breasts, Buns
La Novizia (1975) FFN, Buns

Il Gatto mammone (1975) FFN, Buns
Blue Jeans (1975) LB, Buns
La Liceale (1975) FFN, Buns
Peccati di gioventu (1975) FFN, Buns
La Ragazzina (1974) FFN
La Minorenne (1974) FFN, Buns

Sophie Guillemin

**Born: December 1, 1977
Paris, France
Skin-O-Meter: Great Nudity**

Sophie Guillemin is all woman— and how. Forget about waif, that fad has been forever eaten up and dismissed in the zaftig fleshy form of this French curvaceous knockout. Sophie is kind of like a French Kate Winslet, and she's just as willing to show it all off onscreen. Sophie did just that in her first-ever feature-film outing, *L'Ennui* (1988). The plot of the film revolves around her character's voracious sexual wants, so it comes as no surprise that she spends most of the film with nothing on but a half-cocked smile—and her lucky co-star is fully cocked. It's hot, and all the furry full-frontal shots are enough to get any red-blooded fellow through a cold, lonely night. Unfortunately, Sophie's been a bit on the skingy side since then, "merely" flashing some of that tremendous ass in *Harry, un ami qui vous veut du bien* (2000). Hopefully, she won't leave the skin behind, but even if Sophie does, she's left a whole lot of love for audiences to wallow in.

SKIN-fining Moment:

L'Ennui (0:28) Sophie takes off her top to reveal some sumptuous chestage, then humps her guy, showing a little ass as she grinds.

See Her Naked In:

Du côté des filles (2001) Breasts
Harry, un ami qui vous veut du bien (2000) Buns
L'Ennui (1998) FFN, Buns

Sienna Guillory

Born: May 31, 1975
Fulham, London, England, UK
Skin-O-Meter: Great Nudity

Sienna Guillory, a native of England, has pretty much stuck to that foggy isle for most of her acting career. She appears in many a BBC production, as well as the prototypical stuffy British film time and time again. She did have a part in *Rules of Engagement* (1999), but it wasn't the one about war and stuff. In fact, it was a short that dealt with a hung-over lush trying to find a computer disk, or something—not necessarily the most skinful platform for this fair lady. Furthermore, even though she has appeared in movies with such provocative titles as *Kiss Kiss (Bang Bang)* (2000), Sienna has yet to truly show onscreen. The closest she has come to fleshing out her performances, so to speak, was in a made-for-TV movie called *Take a Girl Like You* (2001). She played a suburban schoolteacher who gets mixed up with swingers in London and holds on to her virginity to reel in the rogue she loves. Sophie does lose her top but stays pretty much with her back to the camera, which is near blinding due to the glare of the stage lights reflecting off of her pasty white skin. *The Principles of Lust* (2003) gets her in some group grope. Sounds like Sienna is loosening her stiff upper lip and may flash her pink lower ones soon!

SKIN-fining Moment:

Helen of Troy (2003) Regal rump walking into the chamber of men nude, then walking around a bit and standing on a pedestal for all to see. Awesome ass for the ancients!

See Her Naked In:

The Principles of Lust (2003) Breasts, Bush
Take a Girl Like You (2000) LB

TeleVisions:

Helen of Troy Buns

Anna Gunn

Born: August 11, 1968
Skin-O-Meter: Brief Nudity

Square jaw; large mouth; sensitive, fine-line nose; eyes full of wonder, suspense, love or lust, whatever is called for; a curvy athletic body; and medium-caliber, power-packed pistols up top; the good news about Anna Gunn is that she may just now be hitting her skin stride. The highly effective blonde has been in demand as a TV vixen of drama and comedy since an early 1990s one-shot role on *Quantum Leap*. Gunn's small-screen profile peaked with a two-year stint on *The Practice*. Her big-screen profile blew up right along schedule, with her playing foil to some of Hollywood's biggest names in *Junior* (1994), *Without Evidence* (1995), and *Enemy of the State* (1998). And, finally, Anna began establishing a skin profile, proudly thrusting out the splendid contours of her organic pacifiers in *Nobody's Baby* (2001).

SKIN-fining Moment:

Nobody's Baby (0:42) Decent look at Anna's Gunns stretching on a boat deck.

See Her Naked In:

Nobody's Baby (2001) Breasts

Janet Gunn

Born: November 2, 1961
Fort Worth, Texas
Skin-O-Meter: Great Nudity

When you're beautiful, blonde, and busty your career path is genetically laid out before you. And so Janet Gunn followed her good looks to a career as a flight attendant, then showed her durability as a stunt double and her bounce-ability as a Dallas Cowboys Cheerleader. It was only a matter of time before she graced the screen with her alluring presence. She made it big as the gams on the hot cable series *Silk Stalkings*. Janet has also appeared in a fair share of films, including *Night of the Running Man* (1994), which marks her skin debut with a dimly lit bedroom tryst. She came close to showing off a little more in *Marquis de Sade* (1996) but stopped short at a see-through teddy. That's really sadistic. Still, have Gunn, will get horny.

SKIN-fining Moment:

Night of the Running Man (1:09) Janet's two top Gunns are out blazing during some grinding love in bed with Andrew McCarthy.

See Her Naked In:

Night of the Running Man (1994) Breasts

Annabelle Gurwitch

Born: November 4, 1961
Skin-O-Meter: Brief Nudity

Daddy Day Care (2003) featured an impressive all-MILF cast, with Annabelle Gurwitch looking very familiar to guys in the midst of unbuckling their pants. That's because Annabelle is better known as a TV personality than as an actress—specifically, for six years she hosted TBS's *Dinner & a Movie*. But this flame-haired vixen has also been a busy actress since the '80s, and she seriously rings our bells when slipping into a new skin as a sexy alien in the Showtime movie *Not Like Us* (1995). She also shows up in a segment of *Red Shoe Diaries 3: Another Woman's Lipstick*, although she's a lot more naked in a 1994 episode of HBO's comedy *Dream On*. And you can still dream of Annabelle as she hosts the dream-analysis show *The Dream Team with Annabelle and Michael*.

SKIN-fining Moment:

Not Like Us (1:07) A nice lengthy look at Annabelle's bazooms as she receives an odd "tune-up" from a crazy doctor.

See Her Naked In:

Not Like Us (1995) Breasts

TeleVisions:

Dream On LB

Jasmine Guy

Born: March 10, 1964
Boston, Massachusetts
Skin-O-Meter: Great Nudity

Bill Cosby seems to be a pushover for lithe beauties with smoky eyes like Jasmine Guy, and we can all get behind that, Cos. He gave spicy Jasmine her big break on *A Different World* and audiences ate her up. The talented five-foot-two-inch hottie is also a recorded singer, dancer, and sizzling sex symbol. Born of a black dad and white mama, Jasmine is the breast of both worlds. Just take a look at her lovely lungs in *Kla$h* (1995). Her making-love nipple slippage is the stuff of (wet) dreams. If you want to catch a glimpse of Jasmine's finery nowadays you'll have to see her onstage. She's been on Broadway in slinky attire for *Chicago* and has toured with *Grease*. That sounds yummy!

SKIN-fining Moment:

Kla$h (0:28) Sometimes a naked Guy isn't a bad thing—when it's Jasmine Guy, and she's showing her boobs as she shags Giancarlo Esposito.

See Her Naked In:

Kla$h (1995) Breasts, Thong

Maggie Gyllenhaal

Born: November 16, 1977
Los Angeles, California
Skin-O-Meter: Great Nudity

MAGGIE GYLLENHAAL TAKES DICK-TATION FROM JAMES SPADER IN *SECRETARY*.

Maggie Gyllenhaal seemed to come out of nowhere when she rocked Hollywood via the arthouse route in the S&M romantic comedy *Secretary* (2002). But in fact, Mags is part of a Hollywood dynasty, including director dad Stephen Gyllenhaal—she debuted in his *Waterland* (1992)—screenwriter mom Naomi Foner, and younger brother actor Jake Gyllenhaal (the dork from *Donnie Darko* [2001]). Maggie had also already appeared in several movies prior to *Secretary*, such as John Waters's *Cecil B. DeMented* (2000), *Pornographer: A Love Story* (2001), *Donnie Darko*, and *Riding in Cars with Boys* (2001). But after her skintastic performance in *Secretary* everything else falls away—just like Maggie's clothing! From a titty tub scene, frequent masturbation, and a peek at her bruised buns to a fully nude wash down that leaves nothing to the imagination, this is sinema at its breast! Maggie has gone on to appear in *Adaptation* (2002), *Confessions of a Dangerous Mind* (2002), before she upped the ecdysiastical ante in the 2004 HBO drama *Strip Search*. Playing an American prisoner in Red China, Maggie is forced to submit to the titular ordeal and we, the viewers, are forced to witness every naked inch of her long, lithe, supple form being groped, poked, pinched, lifted and spread apart by a commie creep who seems

especially suspicious that she may be hiding something in her Mao-Mao's. As a commentary on personal freedom, *Strip Search* aims to provide food for thought; as an all-points display of Maggie Gyllenhaal in the nude, it's a downright feast for the sort of thoughts that, in some places, can get you locked up!

SKIN-fining Moment:

Secretary (1:41) Maggie generously gives us titties in the bathtub and a grand look at the bush as she reclines with Jimmy Spader.

See Her Naked In:

Strip Search (2004) FFN, Buns
Secretary (2002) FFN

Emily Haack

Born: September 11, 1975
St. Louis, Missouri
Skin-O-Meter: Great Nudity

Modern straight-to-video horror pics provide one of the most reliable alternatives to standard big-studio fare, and Emily Haack, the reigning scream queen of the newest wave in terror skinema, is an earthy, fleshy, fierce, and feisty alternative to sugar-coated confections from the LaLa Land dream factories. There is nothing manufactured about Emily's swaying big-girl chest bombs, nor about her gut-quaking reactions to the twisting plot torments in such razor-edged shock triumphs as *Scrapbook* (2000) and *I Spit on Your Corpse, I Piss on Your Grave* (2001). The primary special effect seems to be to take Emily's clothes away, strip off her makeup, update the pleasures of the Marquis de Sade, and keep the cameras rolling. Obviously, these masterpieces of muff and mayhem should be viewed in their unrated versions whenever possible.

SKIN-fining Moment:

Scrapbook (0:16) Emily shows every inch of her naked form—including boobs, butt, and hairy-gyno—during an intense attack scene.

See Her Naked In:

I Spit On Your Corpse, I Piss On Your Grave (2001) FFN
Scrapbook (2000) FFN, Buns

Eva Habermann

Born: January 16, 1976
Hamburg, Germany
Skin-O-Meter: Great Nudity

Eva Habermann is yet another example of the truth in the German myth of the Master Race. Now, not racially, of course, but in terms of Eva, they certainly win the masturbation race. This tall, stunningly hot buxom blonde is breast known for her role as Zev on the hit sci-fi series *Lexx* and the mini-series *Lexx: The Dark Zone*. But if audiences pine for a peek at Eva's dark zones, then they're to follow her to her homeland and partake in her particularly perverted career there. Yes, she showed off her topless wonders a couple of times on the series, but there's an avalanche of arousing material to be found if one scours her reels in Germany. Her nude debut was in *Weissblaue Wintergeschichten* (1996), and it remains one of her breast. While she's yet to deliver on her furry bits, she continues to flash her finery in *Rosa Roth—Wintersaat* (1998) and *Der Pfundskerl—Tote Buchen keinen Urlaub* (2000). Any of those worthy titles are a mouthful, so it's recommended that you take a photo of erotic Eva to the video store and just shove it at the clerk. Don't worry, he'll understand.

SKIN-fining Moment:

Lexx "Super Nova" (1997) Eva offers up her cosmic coconuts and her ass-teroid while enjoying a stellar shower.

See Her Naked In:

Rotlicht—In der Höhle des Löwen (2000) RB
Der Pfundskerl—Tote buchen keinen Urlaub (2000) Breasts
Angel Express (1999) Breasts
Rosa Roth—Wintersaat (1998) LB, Buns
Weissblaue Wintergeschichten (1996) Breasts

TeleVisions:

Klinik unter Palmen Breasts
Lexx Breasts, Buns

Joan Hackett

Born: May 1, 1942
New York, New York
Died: October 8, 1983
Skin-O-Meter: Brief Nudity

Sadly, Joan Hackett's otherworldly beauty is now in another world, the Great Beyond. After a long battle with ovarian cancer, she died on October 8, 1983. We're not here to mourn the dead but to get off on them. And Joan, while a living, working actress, was a strikingly hot one to watch. She usually played strong, resilient women, such as roles in *The Group* (1966), *Will Penny* (1968), and *Dead of Night* (1977). Not prone to nudity in film, Joan teased us in Paul Simon's *One Trick Pony* (1980). Her luscious, free breasts, meaty ass, and even a very brief glimpse of pubes make us realize how much we miss Joan. It's hard to Hackett without her.

SKIN-fining Moment:

One Trick Pony (1:22) Tits and ass as she emerges from bed while chatting with Paul Simon. You even get a quick side view of her garfunkel.

See Her Naked In:

One Trick Pony (1980) Breasts, Bush, Buns

Dayle Haddon

Born: May 26, 1949
Montreal, Quebec, Canada
Skin-O-Meter: Great Nudity

Elfin Canadian beauty Dayle Haddon used her dark good looks to forge a successful modeling career. She made the cover of *Sports Illustrated* before trying her hand at Hollywood. Disney cast her in *The World's Greatest Athlete* (1973) and had her on the fast track as its leading ingénue. Only she had other ideas, which she exposed in a fleshy spread in *Playboy* magazine. Say good-bye to Disney, hello to Mr. Skin. She has appeared in some big productions such as *North Dallas Forty* (1979) and *Cyborg* (1989), plus a few Woody Allen films. But here at Skin Central she's moist known as the title character in *Spermula* (1976), in which she gave us a nice long look at her lithe young figure. Dayle has not been bashful with her body, from her debut in *Paperback Writer* (1973) to later skintaculars such as *Sex with a Smile* (1976) and an episode of *The Hitchhiker* called "Ghostwriter." She even contributes to CBS's morning program as a "beauty and wellness" editor. Dayle delivers . . . and it's good.

SKIN-fining Moment:

La Supplente (1:10) Full-frontal nakedness in full effect as Dayle strips down and gets sexy . . . all in slow motion!

See Her Naked In:

Le Dernier Amant Romantique (1978) Breasts
Maschio latino cercasi (1977)
Madame Claude (1977) Breasts, Buns
The Cheaters (1976) Breasts
Spermula (1976) FFN, Buns
Sex with a Smile (1976) Breasts, Buns
La Supplente (1975) FFN, Buns
La Cugina (1974) Breasts, Buns
Paperback Hero (1973) Buns

TeleVisions:

The Hitchhiker Breasts, Buns

Julie Hagerty

Born: June 15, 1955
Cincinnati, Ohio
Skin-O-Meter: Brief Nudity

Quirky, funny, and intelligently dopey, Julie Hagerty has brought much mirth to the filmgoing public over the past few decades. Taking off to stardom as a wack-a-holic stewardess in that high-flying marathon of knee slappers and pants wetters, *Airplane!* (1980), Julie has carved out an admirable career spinning countless kooky comic turns. Her portrayal of Albert Brooks's gambling-fool wife in *Lost in America* (1985) was among her proudest roles, aside perhaps from playing Tom Green's mom in *Freddy Got Fingered* (2001). Julie's sole role of skinterest was in *Beyond Therapy* (1987), in which she can be seen taking a shower in attire proper to the activity, although only from the waist up. Cheers to a lady who traded in laughs rather than lust—but who didn't have to!

SKIN-fining Moment:

Beyond Therapy (0:47) In the shower Ms. Hagerty turns toward the camera and we all get a load of her sagerties.

See Her Naked In:

Beyond Therapy (1987) Breasts

Jessica Hahn

Born: July 7, 1959
Massapequa, Long Island, New York
Skin-O-Meter: Great Nudity

In 1987 Jessica Hahn was exposed as the secretary who took more than dictation from TV preacher Jim Baker, husband of the macabrely made-up Tammy Faye Baker. The affair ended the Bakers' ministry but launched Jessica on a career as a super-tramp. She appeared with her massive hooters rolling out of lingerie on an episode of *Married . . . with Children* and continued to work those assets on Howard Stern's radio program, *Howard Stern's Butt Bongo Fiesta* (1992), and *Bikini Summer 2* (1992), as well as various *Playboy* video stroke-a-thons. It's enough to make you go back to church.

SKIN-fining Moment:

Playboy Celebrity Centerfold: Jessica Hahn (0:17) Holy hooters (and hairpie and heinie)! Jessica poses in bed, tempting all comers with her heavenly nude form.

See Her Naked In:

Playboy Celebrity Centerfold: Jessica Hahn (1993) FFN, Buns
Bikini Summer II (1992) Thong

Stacy Haiduk

Born: April 24, 1968
Grand Rapids, Michigan
Skin-O-Meter: Great Nudity

Stacy Haiduk started innocuously enough in a film called *Magic Sticks* (1987), in which she played the Laundromat Lady—but there was nothing to get our stick feeling the magic. But then she landed the coveted role of Lana Lang on the hit series *Superboy*, and her career took flight. She's starred in all manner of TV and film—though her scenes got cut from *Nurse Betty* (2000). Those roles that didn't make it to the cutting-room floor are nude-worthy for exposing her soft and bulging bazookas. For example, in *Luther the Geek* (1990), her natural wonders are squeaky clean in a hot shower scene that still makes us feel dirty. She also flashed the powerful pair in *The Beneficiary* (1996). Her last name is pronounced "Hi-Duke," and we'd like to say hello to her dukes anytime.

SKIN-fining Moment:

Luther the Geek (0:26) Stacy shows her big, bare ka-bobblers as she soaps up a guy in the shower.

See Her Naked In:

The Beneficiary (1997) Breasts
Luther the Geek (1990) Breasts

Leisha Hailey

**Born: July 11, 1971
Okinawa, Japan
Skin-O-Meter: Brief Nudity**

We were all in for a treat when li'l Leisha Hailey made her debut on *Boy Meets World* in 1996. Much like the Yoplait yogurt she advertises on TV, Leisha has since developed into quite a tasty treat. Playing the breast bisexual babe ever on the Sapphically successful cable series *The L Word*, Leisha has come into her element (quite literally). *Lovely, luscious, lip-smackingly fantastic,* and largely in some stage of undress, Leisha is one hell of an actress on one *L* of a show.

SKIN-fining Moment:

The L Word "L'Ennui" (2004) Leisha takes a break from the show's standard same-sex shenaigans to shag a man in the sack. Nice topless view of Hailey's Comets.

TeleVisions:

The L Word Breasts

Haji

**Quebec, Canada
Skin-O-Meter: Brief Nudity**

Behind every breastsploitation hero are breast-hoisting heroines. No jug-genre giantess did more than bra buster Haji to prop up the reputation of Chairman of the Boobs Russ Meyer. Dark and exotic in looks and voice, Haji appeared in more Meyer mammary classics than any other floating rack in the master's stable. Haji's first collaboration with spherically fixated Meyer was in *Motorpsycho* (1965). She established a pattern of creating much of her own dialogue and bleeding psychedelic tendencies of her offscreen life into her characters. Her best-remembered role is that of the bad, bad brunette girlfriend to badder, baddest brunette Tura Satana in the ultimate chesty-chicks-kicking-man-butt flick *Faster, Pussycat! Kill! Kill!* (1966). An exotic dancer before overfilling the silver screen as though it were a piece of skimpy lingerie, Haji often recruited fresh boob flesh for her maestro. In the '90s she retired to Malibu, California, where she starts every day at six A.M. with a round of naked body surfing.

SKIN-fining Moment:

Good Morning . . . and Goodbye! (0:10) Haji shows her breasts and buns as she runs naked through the woods. The tits are a little distant (good thing they're so humungous), but there's a nice butt shot to keep the lads happy.

See Her Naked In:

Good Morning . . . and Goodbye! (1967) Breasts, Buns

Gabriella Hall

**California
Skin-O-Meter: Great Nudity**

While softcore sweeties are often harshly made-up tramps, Gabriella Hall comes across like the nice girl you'd bring home to mother. You'd be lucky if you could, because this fetching brunette may seem poised and prissy on the outside, but she's actually a sex kitten between the sheets. Her scandalous roles in such campy flicks as *Sexual Roulette* (1996) and *Deadly Addiction* (1998), her delicious debut, still steam hot. Maybe that's because she's always naked and none too shy about showing off the nicest pair of tits money can buy, which are topped off with silver-dollar nips. Her curves are in all the right places, and Gabriella's smile is just beguiling enough to let you know that she could bang you until the skin falls off your joystick. What a way to deck the Hall.

SKIN-fining Moment:

Sexual Roulette (0:26) She's naked in the tub, taking it every which way from her lover! FFN, glutes.

See Her Naked In:

The Erotic Misadventures of the Invisible Man (2003) FFN, Buns
Rod Steele 0014: You Only Live Until You Die (2002) Breasts
The Seductress (2000) Breasts, Buns
The Ultimate Attraction (2000) Breasts
Virgins of Sherwood Forest (2000) Breasts, Thong
Alien Erotica 2 (2000) Breasts, Buns
Summer Temptations 2 (2000) Breasts, Buns
The Exotic Time Machine II: Forbidden Encounters (2000) Breasts
Lawful Entry (2000) Breasts
Alien Files (1999) Breasts, Buns
Indiscreet (1998) RB
Shadow Dancer (1998) Breasts
Sweetheart Murders (1998) FFN, Buns
Hot Lust (1997) Breasts
Masseuse 2 (1997) Breasts, Buns
Double Your Pleasure (1997) Breasts, Thong
Scandalous (1997) Breasts, Buns
Desires of Innocence (1997) Breasts
Lolita 2000 (1997) FFN, Buns
Different Strokes (1997) Breasts, Bush, Buns

Beverly Hills Bordello (1997) FFN
The Exotic Time Machine (1997) Breasts, Buns
Guarded Secrets (1997) Breasts
Jane Street (1996) FFN, Buns
Love Me Twice (1996) Breasts, Bush, Buns
Sexual Roulette (1996) FFN, Buns
Centerfold (1996) FFN, Buns
Full Body Massage (1995) FFN, Buns

TeleVisions:

Beverly Hills Bordello Breasts, Bush, Buns
Butterscotch FFN
The Click FFN, Buns
Erotic Confessions Breasts
Intimate Sessions FFN-Buns
Lady Chatterley's Stories FFN
Pleasure Zone FFN, Buns
Women: Stories of Passion Breasts

Jerry Hall

Born: July 2, 1956
Mesquite, Texas
Skin-O-Meter: Brief Nudity

Jerry Hall is from Texas and was one of the first supermodels of the '70s. They don't come much hotter than this tall, blonde, and busty stunner. Yet, she's breast remembered for her lesser half. She snagged the bad boy of rock 'n' roll, Mick Jagger, and stopped the Rolling Stone when she married him. Well, he didn't really stop rolling, and so Jerry divorced him in 1999. Jagger must have been high to let his perfect piece go. But now the smolderingly hot mannequin is available, though she's always been there on the pages of fashion mags for the carnally curious. She's made a name for herself on TV, usually playing herself on episodes of (blow) *Jobs for the Boys*, *Just Shoot Me* (if I can't have Jerry), and *TFI Friday*. She's also blessed the big screen with her presence in *Urban Cowboy* (1980) and gave her sole skin onscreen opposite an equally naked Margot Kidder in *Willie and Phil* (1980). She's made a name for herself with

star turns in *Batman* (1989) and *Freejack* (1992). But if you want to jack off you'll have to see her in person, as she's recently taken over the naked role immortalized by Kathleen Turner as "Mrs. Robinson" in the stage production of *The Graduate*. "Are you trying to seduce me, Mrs. Robinson?" The answer is yes!

SKIN-fining Moment:

Willie and Phil (0:05) Jerry gets dressed, showing her jugs to Ray Sharkey and us.

See Her Naked In:

Willie and Phil (1980) Breasts

Landon Hall

California
Skin-O-Meter: Great Nudity

Landon Hall is a goddess of erotic cinema, and she doesn't seem to make any bones about it—although she certainly produces many . . . boners that is. After her debut as an uncredited brothel girl in *Puppet Master III: Toulon's Revenge* (1991), Landon moved on to bigger and bustier things. She appeared in such classics of the genre as *The Bikini Carwash Company* (1992), *Ladykiller* (1996), *Other Men's Wives* (1996), *Masseuse 2* (1997) . . . and the list just goes on and on. For some of her hottest scenes, be sure to see either *Masseuse 2* or *Masseuse 3* (1998)—they just kept getting better. For some of Mr. Skin's favorite shots, however, be sure to check out *Different Strokes* (1997), in which she's sandwiched in a threesome with hot (not yet) dead chick Dana Plato. There is a really great scene where Landon and Dana are in the shower together, soaping each other up whilst engaging in witty banter. It is a muff-see and another Landon calling.

SKIN-fining Moment:

Different Strokes (0:21) Wet watermelons as she's being soaped up by Dana Plato in the shower.

See Her Naked In:

Sweetheart Murders (1998) FFN, Thong
Masseuse 3 (1998) FFN, Buns
Hotel Exotica (1998) FFN, Buns
The Escort 2 (1998) FFN, Buns
Illusions of Sin (1997) Breasts
Masseuse 2 (1997) Breasts
Different Strokes (1997) FFN, Buns
Maximum Revenge (1997) Breasts, Buns
Stolen Hearts (1997) Breasts
Other Men's Wives (1996) FFN, Buns
Lady Killer (1996) Thong
Cyberella: Forbidden Passions (1996) Breasts
Over the Wire (1995) FFN, Buns
The Dwelling (1991) Breasts
Puppet Master III: Toulon's Revenge (1991) Breasts

TeleVisions:

Beverly Hills Bordello FFN
Erotic Confessions FFN, Buns
Hotline Breasts, Buns
Intimate Sessions Breasts, Bush, Buns

Linda Hamilton

Born: September 26, 1956
Salisbury, Maryland
Skin-O-Meter: Great Nudity

Only two things were able to upstage the super subhuman performance of Arnold Schwarzenegger as a killer robot in *The Terminator* (1984), and both those things were gently swinging from Linda Hamilton's blessed chest. Be honest. What was more impressive, the FX wizardry or lovely Linda's unfettered frolicking as the girl on top in what was probably conceived of as a gratuitous fake sex scene? In *Terminator II* (1991), Linda kept her small but active danglers sheathed in cotton tees. The sequel is generally considered to be a letdown from the original. The conclusion to be drawn is obvious. Also obvious is Linda's nipple appeal in *Separate Lives* (1985). Jim Belushi can't keep his mouth off them.

SKIN-fining Moment:

The Terminator (1:22) Several views of her heroic hooters as she rides Michael Biehn's robot-hating man-rod. Move your hands, Mike, we can't see!

See Her Naked In:

Separate Lives (1995) RB
Black Moon Rising (1986) LB
King Kong Lives! (1986) RB
The Terminator (1984) Breasts

Lisa Gay Hamilton

Born: March 25, 1964
New York, New York
Skin-O-Meter: Brief Nudity

Lisa Gay Hamilton is a true chameleon, with the only constant being that she's incredibly sexy as either a New Jersey housewife in *Palookaville* (1995) or as a tough-talking Army captain in *The Sum of All Fears* (2002). She was especially cute as dykey criminal Lola Jansco in *The Truth About Charlie* (2002), boldly announcing her crush on cute Frenchwoman Thandie Newton. We even have to confess to being turned on by her breast feeding in *Beloved* (1998). And don't forget how she makes squalor seem sensual as Samuel L. Jackson's best girl in *Jackie Brown* (1997). The only role Lisa Gay can't seem to play is that of a box-office star, but it won't be long before Hollywood has to acknowledge her talent, beauty, and sexy bod.

SKIN-fining Moment:

Beloved (0:18) Close-up boobage as a lil' milker sucks on Lisa's hoot.

See Her Naked In:

Beloved (1998) Breasts

Lois Hamilton

Born: 1952
Philadelphia, Pennsylvania
Died: December 23, 1999
Skin-O-Meter: Brief Nudity

Lois Hamilton was no typical Hollywood bimbo. She was an exceptional bimbo who flew a 1936 German WWII bi-plane when she wasn't sculpting, painting, or writing feminist doctrines like *Move Over Tarzan*. Not bad for an Italian baroness who made her name as a popular Ford model in the late '70s. Despite an uncredited start in two Neil Simon films, *Last of the Red Hot Lovers* (1972) and *The Sunshine Boys* (1975), the lovely Lois also went on to a pretty good acting career. She stood out amongst the star-studded cast in *The Cannonball Run* (1981) as Roger Moore's pseudo-Bond girl. Plenty of goofballs went goofy for Lois's bod in *Stripes* (1981), and Lois was also a major temptation as Miss Winter in the TV movie *Invitation to Hell* (1984). But Lois will be best remembered for the comedy *Summer Rental* (1985)—in fact, she makes the whole film memorable as an insecure blonde who keeps dropping her top to get feedback on her boob job. Sadly, we can only remember Lois now, since the big-brained blonde had big personal troubles and committed suicide in 1999 at the age of fifty-seven.

SKIN-fining Moment:

Summer Rental (0:41) Lois tears off her bikini top and asks John Candy to give his opinion on her chest-confections. A classic freeze-frame moment. Sweet!

See Her Naked In:

Summer Rental (1985) Breasts

Suzanna Hamilton

Born: 1960
London, England, UK
Skin-O-Meter: Great Nudity

Suzanna Hamilton is a sweet English lass who is best known Stateside for her role in the classic tale of totalitarian dystopia *1984* (1984). Though she's been acting in her native land since she was a wee child of fourteen, Skin Central stood up and took notice after her quite revealing scenes in the George Orwell story of a bleak future made brighter by the sight of Suzanna's unshaven pubes. They're truly a garden of delight that any man would love to get lost in. It wasn't her first flesh, however. That was opposite Sting in *Brimstone and Treacle* (1982). She showed bush in that too. Are we noticing a trend? Because it's sure one we'd like to get our hands on.

SKIN-fining Moment:

1984 (0:38) Forget Big Brother, check out Big Burger! Suzanna strips for John Hurt and you may hurt yourself when you see her fantastically fur-cious full-frontalage, followed by supple seat-meat.

See Her Naked In:

Die Stimme (1988) Breasts
1984 (1984) FFN, Buns
Brimstone and Treacle (1982) Breasts, Bush

Wendy Hamilton

Born: December 20, 1967
Detroit, Michigan
Skin-O-Meter: Great Nudity

Wendy Hamilton's statuesque five-foot-ten-inch frame was featured in the December 1991 issue of *Playboy* magazine. She's since followed in the footsteps of her predecessors Jenny McCarthy and Pamela Anderson by acting in straight-to-video sextaculars that feature, among other things, her incredible mammoth mammaries! Being a former Playmate, Wendy has been nude in just about every film she has been in. Guess she's typecast as hot and naked, which is a good thing. A highlight is *Ski School II* (1995), which featured her skinfully unclad in the snow. In it, you get a good look at her big, paid-for tits and her round, voluptuous ass. It also starred a then unknown Bill Dwyer of *Battlebots*. For some full-frontal action, as well as some simulated sex, have a look at *The Dallas Connection* (1995). That's a connection we'd like to make.

SKIN-fining Moment:

Ski School II (0:23) Sexy snowbound boobies and bunnage as the sultry Ms. Hamilton paints a guy's portrait in the nude.

See Her Naked In:

The Dallas Connection (1995) FFN, Buns
Midnight Temptations (1995) Breasts, Thong

Ski School II (1995) Breasts, Buns
Scoring (1995) Breasts, Bush, Buns
Numerous Playboy Videos

Jennifer Hammon

Born: March 7, 1976
Winter Park, Florida
Skin-O-Meter: Great Nudity

After a very slow 1996—mainly marked by playing a receptionist on an episode of *The Young and the Restless*—Jennifer Hammon suddenly landed a TV movie plus a role on both *General Hospital* and its companion show *Port Charles*. Oh, and she also made one of the most erotic softcore films of all time. *Allyson Is Watching* (1997) is a stunning, low-budget sexfest, with Jennifer starring as a young acting student who gets involved with several men, one woman, and a murder. Get the unrated version, and you'll see Jennifer and co-star Caroline Ambrose in a rightfully legendary lesbian love scene. Jennifer's solo masturbation scene will also get you Hammoning, especially when the camera reveals her really sheer panties. Jennifer preferred to concentrate on her mainstream career from that point on, guaranteeing herself some sci-fi fans with back-to-back appearances in 2001 on *Star Trek: Voyager* and *The X-Files*.

SKIN-fining Moment:

Allyson Is Watching (0:14) Jenny hears the neighbors next door having some sex and decides to "join the fun." All three B's!

See Her Naked In:

Allyson Is Watching (1997) FFN, Buns

Daryl Hannah

Born: December 3, 1960
Chicago, Illinois
Skin-O-Meter: Hall of Fame

GLEESOME THREESOME: DARYL HANNAH (CENTER) BETWIXT MÉNAGE PALS PETER GALLAGHER AND VALERIE QUENNESSEN IN *SUMMER LOVERS*.

Daryl Hannah once made sweet music with softie rocker Jackson Browne, but her lustrous lungs were destined for greater exposure. That came as an arousing android in *Blade Runner* (1982), but what made laps stand up and take notice was *Summer Lovers* (1982), which marked her skin debut. Life's a beach—if Daryl is sunbathing nude on it. Mixing box office with buff orifices was the mega-hit *Splash* (1984), where, as a mermaid, Daryl managed to flash her watermelons, and we got to sea butt as well. What a piece of tail! Her body of work continued unclothed in *Reckless* (1984) and *At Play in the Fields of the Lord* (1991). The latter showed Daryl exactly as the Lord made her—and settled any questions about her being a true blonde. Even at forty, Daryl is hot enough to grease the pole. Playing a stripper, she worked the pole topless in all her G-strung glory for *Dancing at the Blue Iguana* (2000), proving she's still too hot to Hannah.

SKIN-fining Moment:

Splash (0:27) Great view of Daryl's rock-hard butt cheeks as she makes her first appearance on Liberty Island.

See Her Naked In:

The Job (2003) RB
Dancing at the Blue Iguana (2000) Breasts, Thong

At Play in the Fields of the Lord (1991) FFN, Buns
Roxanne (1987) Buns
Reckless (1984) Breasts
Splash (1984) Breasts, Buns
Summer Lovers (1982) Breasts, Buns

Marcia Gay Harden

Born: August 14, 1959
La Jolla, California
Skin-O-Meter: Great Nudity

Nobody was more surprised than Marcia Gay Harden when she won the Academy Award for Best Actress for *Pollock* (2000). Mr. Skin applauded Marcia's much-deserved recognition, but we at Skin Central have long been absolutely *Gay* for this unique beauty's skinematic achievements. To get a solid Harden in your pants, catch the cable flick *Fever* (1991), in which a jilted lover slices off Marcia's pesky bra and her milky mamacitas bounce bewitchingly into view. Also dig this dark-haired delicacy's bare miles of flawlessly pale flesh in *Crush* (1992), as well as her aforementioned sexy turn as the wife of "splatter" painter Jackson Pollock in the acclaimed film that bears his name. Mr. Skin may not know art, but he knows what makes him go splatter. And, on that front, Marcia is a total masterpiece.

SKIN-fining Moment:

Fever (1:31) One of Marcia's captors un-hooks her bra and out come her kabobs. You'll get a hard-en.

See Her Naked In:

Crush (1992) LB
Fever (1991) Breasts

Kate Hardie

Born: 1969
UK
Skin-O-Meter: Great Nudity

Kate Hardie, daughter of veteran British comedian Bill Oddie, first gained attention in the Denzel Washington/Kevin Kline biopic *Cry Freedom* (1987). She has stuck mostly to her native British Isles, though, and isn't well known in the U.S. Her most notable role Stateside was in *Croupier* (1998), which was an arthouse hit. Kate gave us a good look at her body in *Safe* (1993). The full-frontal scene shows us her gravity-fondled breasts and gargantuan bush. Kate gives her fans a Hardie everytime.

SKIN-fining Moment:

Safe Kate will make you Hardie as she descends a staircase full-frontally nude. Then you can have safe sex.

See Her Naked In:

Heart (1999) Breasts
Croupier (1998) Breasts
Open Fire (1994) Breasts
Safe (1993) FFN, Buns

Tonya Harding

Born: November 12, 1970
Portland, Oregon
Skin-O-Meter: Great Nudity

As everyone knows, Tonya Harding put the "hammer" in Lillehammer at the 1994 Winter Olympics. Narrowly escaping as a co-conspirator in the assault of Nancy Kerrigan, she has moved on to other physical pursuits. Although her official debut in the forgettable *Breakaway* (1996) went unnoticed, her hardcore home video *Tonya and Jeff's Wedding Night* (1994) snagged the flies of every man with a VCR. Tonya's tiny titties scored a perfect ten, and her triple axel around her (now ex) hubby's member was worthy of the gold. Harding still is (and has) a hard ass. She showcased her foxy figure while pummeling Paula Jones on Fox's *Celebrity Boxing* and says she is ready to step into the ring for real. "It is my goal to be a future, undisputed bantamweight champion," she said. While waiting for her next big break, this knockout is currently working as a motivational speaker.

SKIN-fining Moment:

Tonya and Jeff's Wedding Night (0:20) Tonya takes hubby Jeff Gilhooly's hard-ing hardcore-style. FFN, buns, a handful of sperm.

See Her Naked In:

Tonya and Jeff's Wedding Night (1994) Breasts, Bush, Buns

Mariska Hargitay

Born: January 23, 1964
Los Angeles, California
Skin-O-Meter: Never Nude

The stunning result of the union between sex kitten Jayne Mansfield and muscle man Mickey Hargitay, Mariska Hargitay is no stranger to Hollywood and beauty. Although Mariska did not inherit her mother's ample boobage, she does have another fantastic ass-set, a booming backside. Unfortunately, she's kept it under wraps onscreen, using a body double in a shower scene in *Welcome to 18* (1986). Unlike her mother, Mariska tries to steer clear of B-movies, focusing more on becoming a dramatic actress. She paid her TV dues on *Ellen*, *ER*, and *Seinfeld*, where she auditioned for the role of Elaine for the sitcom within the sitcom. (Mariska delivered the line, "It's like a bald convention out there.") Then, like her father, she muscled her way into serious drama as the ass-sertive, leather-clad, sexy detective on *Law & Order: Special Victims Unit*, receiving critical acclaim and the attention of every masochistic man home on a Friday night. Mariska is welcome to handcuff herself to Mr. Skin any day of the week.

SKIN-fining Moment:

Welcome to 18 (0:26) Mariska showers and the camera slides up past somebody's sexy sitter, but since we don't see her face, this may well be a stunt-butt.

See Her Naked In:

Welcome to 18 (1986) Body Double—Buns

Jean Harlow

Born: March 3, 1911
Kansas City, Missouri
Died: June 7, 1937
Skin-O-Meter: Brief Nudity

She spent the Roaring Twenties in bit parts, but Jean Harlow entered the 1930s giving filmgoers plenty to roar about—thanks to a series of racy roles that made her a true legend of skinema. *Hell's Angels* (1930) was her first featured part and remains the only film to offer color footage of Harlow's finest parts. The platinum blonde put color in moviegoers' pants, though, as she churned out classics while showing off her amazing bod. *Red-Headed Woman* (1932) even includes a bracing peek of booby as Jean tosses on a pajama top. Other Harlow hits include *The Public Enemy* (1931) and *Libeled Lady* (1936), all part of an amazing filmography built before her death from uremic poisoning at the age of twenty-six. Her final film, *Saratoga* (1937), was a massive posthumous hit—as was Marilyn Monroe, who frequently cited Harlow as her role model.

SKIN-fining Moment:

Red-headed Woman (0:17) Jean changes shirts and the camera catches a split-second of her stiff-nipped right Harlow. Sexy in its own right, but superbly sack-draining for 1932.

See Her Naked In:

Red-Headed Woman (1932) RB

Claire Harman

UK
Skin-O-Meter: Great Nudity

This buxom British babe got her big break with a guest appearance on an episode of the hit British TV series *Peak Practice*. Then deciding to show off her peaks, she turned her sights toward more skinematic endeavors, landing a bit part in the feature *Sorted* (2000). More small roles followed in films such as *Late Night Shopping* (2001) and the blockbuster *About a Boy* (2002), in which she played the Sketchers shopgirl. But it's her small but memorable role as Young Sally in the critically lauded Michael Caine picture *Last Orders* (2001) that raises our flesh flag. Apparently, young Sally liked doing the horizontal hokey-pokey in automobiles, which is pretty much the crux of what her time on screen was spent doing. This, obviously, led to the baring of her wonderful watermelons. Let's hope those sweet mouthfuls come into season again soon.

SKIN-fining Moment:

Last Orders (0:35) Fantastic long look at Claire's heaving bossoms as she engages in some rumpy-pumpy in a hippie bus. What a fox!

See Her Naked In:

Last Orders (2001) Breasts

Angie Harmon

Born: August 10, 1972
Dallas, Texas
Skin-O-Meter: Brief Nudity

Angie Harmon won *Seventeen's* National Cover Girl Contest at age fifteen, and she's only gotten sexier from there. Beach hunk David Hasselhoff asked, "Coffee, tea, or

MR. SKIN'S TOP TEN
Naked TV Lawyers . . . Law and ardor
10. **Lara Flynn Boyle** —(Helen Gamble) *The Practice*
9. **Deirdre Lovejoy** —(ASA Rhonda Pearlman) *The Wire*
8. **Sharon Lawrence** —(ADA Sylvia Costas) *NYPD Blue*
7. **Blair Brown** —(Molly Dodd) *The Days and Nights of Molly Dodd*
6. **Kathleen Quinlan** —(Lynn Holt) *Family Law*
5. **Susan Dey** —(Grace Van Owen) *L.A. Law*
4. **Portia de Rossi** —(Nelle Porter) *Ally McBeal*
3. **Carey Lowell** —(ADA Jamie Ross) *Law & Order*
2. **Catherine Bell** —(Sarah MacKenzie) *JAG*
1. **Angie Harmon** —(Abbie Carmichael) *Law & Order*

me?" upon seeing the busty brunette on an airplane, and Angie followed Hasselhoff to a short-lived stint on *Baywatch Nights*. Eventually she got cast on the popular TV series *Law & Order*, but her career faltered a smidge in between the beach and the courthouse, and you know what that means: nude scene! Check out her interim effort, *Lawn Dogs* (1997), for a nice glimpse of her tanned hooters. Just remember, New York Giant Jason Sehorn is with her every night, so don't go getting your hopes up.

SKIN-fining Moment:

Lawn Dogs (0:21) Angie's right rocket can be seen in all its proud glory as she boffs Sam Rockwell in his trailer home with little Mischa Barton looking on.

See Her Naked In:

Lawn Dogs (1997) RB

Deborah Harmon

Born: May 8, 1951
Chicago, Illinois
Skin-O-Meter: Brief Nudity

Deborah Harmon launched her career in the spooky made-for-TV movie *The Ghost of Flight 401* (1978). Her special brand of blonde eye candy was just what was needed to sweeten up *The Ted Knight Show* that same year. She finally landed her own series, *What's Up, America?*, and the answer to that question was America's crotches while watching the curvaceous cutie. Deborah promptly lost the show when the prudes in suits at the network saw her topless turn in the comedy *Used Cars* (1980). But you can't keep a hot slut down, and Deborah made bit appearances on the TV series *M*A*S*H* as various sexy nurses for the doctors to play, well, doctor with. She continued on the silver screen, adding pants-popping cameos to *Bachelor Party* (1984) and *Back to the Future* (1985). But after *Mr. Payback: An Interactive Movie* (1995), Deborah's activity in filmdom came to a sudden halt. Men's Harmons have not been the same since.

SKIN-fining Moment:

Used cars (1:04) As Kurt Russell leaps out of bed, Deb's right nipple slipples into view behind him. Nice headlight.

See Her Naked In:

Used Cars (1980) RB

Joy Harmon

Born: May 1, 1940
Flushing, New York
Skin-O-Meter: Never Nude

Joy Harmon might not be the most recognizable name in show biz, but she may have the most recognizable rack! How the hell did Luke keep his hands cool when this 41-22-36 inch frame came out of her shack and started soaping up her jalopy with her own natural sponges? A regular on *You Bet Your Life* after Groucho Marx took a liking to her (bet he took something else to her as well), Joy made literally hundreds of TV cameos in the '60s and '70s and caused thousands of men to take longer showers. She was a building-sized go-go dancer in *Village of the Giants* (1965). But for her hottest scene, check out *Cool Hand Luke* (1967) for yourself . . . and then make sure your water bill is all paid up.

SKIN-fining Moment:

Cool Hand Luke (0:24) To the torture and delight of a prison chain gang, Joy soaps up her roadster and soaks down her flimsy little dress in the sexiest car-wash scene in the history of cinema. Just try to keep cool with your hand, Luke.

Corinna Harney

Born: February 20, 1972
Las Vegas, Nevada
Skin-O-Meter: Brief Nudity

The year 1991 was good for both Corinna Harney and her horny fans, as the Miss August went on to become the *Playboy* Playmate of the Year. Naturally this made Corinna a cornerstone of *Playboy* videos, like her own edition of *Playboy Video Centerfold* (1992) and *Wet & Wild: The Locker Room* (1994). Her subsequent acting career went on to include a vampish turn in *Vampirella* (1996), in which Harney got guys horny with a rack worth sinking your teeth into. The Las Vegas native (changing her billing to Corinna Harney Jones) then made good use of her hometown. She

starred in and produced the Vegas-set *The Road Home* (2003) and appeared in the Vegas-shot comedy *Rat Race* (2001) as a cockalicious cocktail waitress. That's also her as the gorgeous gal at the blackjack table in *National Lampoon's Vegas Vacation* (1997). And guys went wild when Corinna showed up as a Vegas girl gone wild on a 2002 episode of CBS's *CSI: Crime Scene Investigation*.

SKIN-fining Moment:

Vampirella (0:45) Nice shots of her perky pellets as she changes.

See Her Naked In:

Vampirella (1996) Breasts
Numerous *Playboy* Videos

Christine Harnos

Skin-O-Meter: Brief Nudity

Christine Harnos is a dark-haired beauty with ripe melons good for squeezing. Not that she's let many mam-handle her, at least onscreen. The only time she exposed her fruit loops was in *Rebel Highway: Cool and the Crazy* (1994). It's a journey back to simpler times, the '50s to be exact, when girls where horny and the bad boys greased their hair for an easy supply of hand-job lubricant. Christine played one of those open-legged sweethearts and in a tryst exposed her meaty tits for the camera. Christine appeared in the cult hit *Dazed and Confused* (1993) but is more well known for her stint on the popular TV drama *ER*. If someone needs to operate on Christine, it's to remove her from those stubborn clothes she insists on wearing.

SKIN-fining Moment:

Rebel Highway: Cool and the Crazy (0:43) Christine rides the Rebel Highway, indeed. Whilst boning her boy toy in bed, she gives some A+ left lungpop views. But beware the guy-butt!

See Her Naked In:

Rebel Highway: Cool and the Crazy (1994)
Breasts

Jessica Harper

Born: October 10, 1949
Chicago, Illinois
Skin-O-Meter: Great Nudity

Jessica Harper got on the silver
screen thanks to her lungs. No,
those petite pretties offer no
cleavage—at best, they're like rosy
pacifiers—but they belt out quite a
rockin' tune as the singer Phoenix
in *Phantom of the Paradise* (1974).
The perky brunette went on to star
in the Woody Allen comedies *Love
and Death* (1975) and *Stardust
Memories* (1980). But she is best
remembered for her cultist turns
starring in *Suspiria* (1977) and
filling Susan Sarandon's giant bra as
Janet in *Shock Treatment* (1981), the
unsung semi-sequel to *The Rocky
Horror Picture Show* (1975). To get a
rocky picture show of Jessica's flesh
pebbles, check out *Inserts* (1976), in
which her itty-bitty titties are
exposed in bed with Richard
Dreyfuss. Now that rocks!

SKIN-fining Moment:

*Inserts (1:15) Jessica lies in bed topless
for a long, long time and her delicate
demure jujubees get so suckably stiff
you'll swear her A-cups are in 3-D*

See Her Naked In:

Pennies from Heaven (1981) Breasts
Inserts (1975) Breasts

> "I wanted to say to Naomi [Watts]
> the next morning, 'It was good for
> me; was it good for you?' All I can
> say is I'm glad I had a boyfriend at
> the time!"
>
> —LAURA HARRING, ON HER
> *MULHOLLAND DR.* LESBIAN SCENE

Laura Harring

Born: March 3, 1964
Los Mochis Sinaloa, Mexico
Skin-O-Meter: Great Nudity

Laura Harring is the typical Latin
babe with dark flowing hair, tanned
skin, almond eyes, and firm melon-
shaped maracas. This is one
Mexican dish that won't be on the
value menu at Taco Bell! The El
Paso, Texas, resident went from the
Lone Star State to small films in
which she was more than happy to
show us her big Ts. In *The Forbidden
Dance* (1990), she does some dirty
dancing to her native beats, and in
*Silent Night, Deadly Night 3: Better
Watch Out!* (1989), she scrubs up in
a nice bubble bath. Her prime skin,
however, can be found in the David
Lynch wack-off fantasy *Mulholland
Dr.* (2001), which features a full-
frontal Laura engaging in
lesbotronic hijinks with co-star
Naomi Watts. Talk about hard of
Harring!

SKIN-fining Moment:

*Mulholland Dr. (2:01) Big breasted
Laura lies back on the couch waiting for
a topless Naomi Watts to lez out on her.
Woohoo!*

See Her Naked In:

Mulholland Dr. (2001) Breasts
*Silent Night, Deadly Night 3: Better Watch
    Out!* (1989) Breasts

Cristi Harris

Born: December 3, 1977
East Point, Georgia
Skin-O-Meter: Great Nudity

When Mr. Skin first caught a
glimpse of big-breasted blonde
Cristi Harris on the TV show
Growing Pains, I was having some
growing pains of my own. When
she matured into her barely legal
mams and first revealed her massive
talents in *Night of the Demon 2*

(1994), pants across America were
possessed by this young hottie.
Though born in the South and
proudly proclaiming herself a
Georgia Peach, Cristi moved to New
York City when she was fifteen and
hit the naked city's hard pavement
in search of modeling assignments.
They never came, however, until
she moved to Los Angeles, where
she was immediately cast in a
Doritos commercial with then-
unknown Tobey Maguire. The
future *Spider-Man* must have spewed
web when he saw his co-star. Cristi
never hit the big time like Maguire,
but here at Skin Central we applaud
her teen-oriented films—with one
hand clapping and the other
slapping! Check out her les-a-thon
in *Night of the Scarecrow* (1995).
She's really built in *Lurid Tales: The
Castle Queen* (1995), and *Kiss of
Death* (1997) may be the breast look
at Cristi yet. Our Harris pole is
going up!

SKIN-fining Moment:

*Kiss of Death (0:50) As the long grass
blows, it won't be long before Daniel
McVicar does likewise, judging by the
heavy grinding he's doing with Cristi
"Cupcakes" Harris. She shows a great
set of jugs as she takes it all in the great
outdoors. Yummo!*

See Her Naked In:

Kiss of Death (1997) Breasts
Night of the Scarecrow (1995) Breasts
Lurid Tales: The Castle Queen (1995)
    Breasts
Night of the Demons 2 (1994) Breasts

Gail Harris

Born: December 16, 1964
Batley, Yorkshire, England, UK
Skin-O-Meter: Hall of Fame

Gail Harris was born in England—
and now you know why Ben is so
big. This beautiful, sexy blonde
has made more than Big Ben

chime with her hot straight-to-video work. The names say it all: *Takin' it Off* (1985), *Nudity Required* (1988), and the *Masseuse* series of rub-'em-ups. Mr. Skin wonders if Gail can get comfy before a camera without getting undressed? Maybe she can only remember her lines and get into character sans clothing. For some highlights of Gail's girls, as well as her lithe young bod, check out the classic *Sorority House Massacre II* (1990) and *Cellblock Sisters: Banished Behind Bars* (1996). For a spell Gail was married to the lucky prick—literally, that prick was lucky—who parachuted into Michael Jackson's wedding. And here's another nip of trivia: This mother of two girls was the co-creator of *Barely Legal* magazine.

SKIN-fining Moment:

Party Favors (1:01) Gail strips out of a cheerleader costume and shakes her breasts and buns for horny dudes. Awesome bouncing pom-pom action.

See Her Naked In:

Treasure Hunt! (2003) Thong
Masseuse 3 (1998) FFN, Buns
Masseuse 2 (1997) FFN, Buns
Cellblock Sisters: Banished Behind Bars (1996) Breasts, Buns
Masseuse (1996) Breasts, Buns
Galaxy Girls (1995) Breasts
Virtual Desire (1995) FFN, Buns
Forbidden Games (1995) FFN, Buns
Sins of Desire (1992) Breasts
Starlets Exposed! Volume II (1991) Breasts, Bush, Buns
The Haunting of Morella (1990) Breasts, Buns
Hard To Die (1990) Breasts
Sorority House Massacre II (1990) Breasts
Nudity Required (1989) Breasts
Trashy Ladies Wrestling (1987) Breasts, Thong
Takin' It All Off (1987) FFN, Buns
Party Favors (1987) FFN, Buns
Death Feud (1987) Breasts

The Stripper of the Year (1986) FFN, Buns
In Search of the Perfect 10 (1986) Breasts, Bush, Buns
Starlet Screen Test (1986) FFN, Buns
The Girls of Malibu (1986) Breasts, Bush, Buns
Electric Blue (TV Magazine) (1983) Breasts

TeleVisions:

Dream On Breasts, Buns

Jo Ann Harris

Los Angeles, California
Skin-O-Meter: Great Nudity

Jo Ann Harris debuted in the wacky tobaccey exploitation flick *Maryjane* (1968). But when the smoke cleared there was the beautiful '60s swinger topless in her second film *The Gay Deceivers* (1967). Her young, firm, and bulbous boobies were out for all to see, but they didn't get a rise for her co-star, who was trying to avoid the draft by pretending to be homosexual. Why didn't he just tell the authorities she was a trannie? Jo Ann followed that role with *The Beguiled* (1971), in which lucky Yankee Clint Eastwood seduced a boarding school full of southern belles, including young Jo. For another look at her luscious form, check out *The Sporting Club* (1971). Very sporting of her, indeed. She showed the girls again in *Rape Squad* (1974) and then put those sexy cows to pasture.

SKIN-fining Moment:

Rape Squad (0:06) Nice look at her sweet rolls when a meanie makes her take off her top.

See Her Naked In:

Rape Squad (1974) Breasts
The Beguiled (1971) Breasts, Buns
The Sporting Club (1971) RB
The Gay Deceivers (1969) Breasts

Lara Harris

Born: August 22, 1967
Chicago, Illinois
Skin-O-Meter: Great Nudity

Lara Harris has eyes that exude the sultriness of a thousand Arabian nights, and her career started with a story almost as fanciful. She took on the role of the tempting mannequin that comes to lustful life in, you guessed it, *Mannequin* (1987). Her next appearance was as a wife to a real-life mannequin, Charlie Sheen, in *No Man's Land* (1987). She went on to bit parts in big movies such as *The Fisher King* (1991) and *Singles* (1992), but it was her more revealing turn in *The Dogfighters* (1996) that was moist praiseworthy. Lara's heart-shaped ass as well as her magnificently upturned breasts are on display in a scene sure to smack you right in your sex zone. And her movie *Circuit Breaker* (1996) will have you running to your fuse box.

SKIN-fining Moment:

Circuit Breaker (0:05) Ah-whoo! T&A during a dream where she has sex with a werewolf. She really brings out the animal in this dude!

See Her Naked In:

Circuit Breaker (1996) Breasts, Buns
The Dogfighters (1996) Breasts, Buns

Laura Harris

Born: November 20, 1976
Vancouver, British Columbia, Canada
Skin-O-Meter: Great Nudity

Laura Harris is this generation's It Girl. Well, her debut was an uncredited appearance in *Stephan King's It* (1990). But audiences didn't catch on to her charms until *The Faculty* (1998), which featured a completely nude Laura strutting about in the boy's locker room.

Talk about a fantasy made flesh. They should call Laura the Tit Girl! This was not Laura's first skin splash, oh no. She can be found skinny dipping in the sci-fi thriller *Habitat* (1997) and taking another nude swim in the barely seen (though Laura is seen bare) *Best Wishes Mason Chadwick* (1995). Laura makes Mr. Skin's Harris pole rise.

SKIN-fining Moment:

Habitat (1:09) She takes a dip in a strange lookin' pond thing . . . naked! You see breasts but no pubic Harris.

See Her Naked In:

The Faculty (1998) Breasts, Buns
Habitat (1997) Breasts
Best Wishes Mason Chadwick (1995) Breasts, Bush, Buns

Moira Harris

Pontiac, Illinois
Skin-O-Meter: Brief Nudity

Moira Harris was apparently born into a fairly well-known family in Pontiac, Illinois, but we are not sure when. While her age is a secret, it is well known that she has been married to acclaimed actor Gary Sinise, who is also from Illinois, since 1981. Gary is a lucky man because he gets to ride a Pontiac. A number of years after tying the knot, Moira must have got some sort of an itch to get noticed. She took the lead role in an Irish/American production called *The Fantasist* (1986), a freaky low-budget slasher flick. In this film you can see the beautiful Moira in all of her Gary-loving glory. And we can see what attracted Sinise in the first place, Moira's USDA Grade-A meaty buns. He can't leave that behind.

SKIN-fining Moment:

The Fantasist (1:25) Moira's mammaries appear quite quickly as she lays down on the sofa to pose for Christopher Cazenove, who proceeds to play the drum solo from In-A-Gadda-Da-Vida on her naked ass . . .

See Her Naked In:

The Fantasist (1986) Breasts, Buns

Jenilee Harrison

Born: June 12, 1959
Northridge, California
Skin-O-Meter: Great Nudity

Jenilee Harrison first caught men's attention shaking her pom-poms as a cheerleader for the L.A. Rams in the late '70s. Not surprisingly, that led to her role as a cheerleader on an episode of *CHiPs*. But what catapulted her to stardom was her jiggle gig as Suzanne Somers's replacement on *Three's Company*. But then she was replaced by another busty blonde—so is the churn of Hollywood honeys. Jenilee went on to spend a few seasons on *Dallas*. Now Jenilee flashes smile after smile of enormous teeth while hawking various infomercial products. But for a look at Jenilee's best items, check out her short-lived movie career. Her bulbous mounds of love pillows are no curse but a prime target in *Prime Target* (1991) and *Curse III: Blood Sacrifice* (1991). The chance to see her beautiful, round teats spilling over the sides of her chest is a breast buy.

SKIN-fining Moment:

Curse III: Blood Sacrifice (0:56) Cousin Cindy soaks in the bath and we get a brief topless view of Mr. Furleys (but, sadly, no Mr. Curleys).

See Her Naked In:

Fists of Iron (1995) Breasts
Prime Target (1991) Breasts
Curse III: Blood Sacrifice (1990) Breasts

Schae Harrison

Born: April 27, 1963
Anaheim Hills, California
Skin-O-Meter: Great Nudity

She started as an NFL cheerleader for the Seattle Seahawks, but Schae Harrison soon stepped up to her own aerobics workout show on cable television. Her acting career fell into place almost as quickly. You barely see her in the big-screen movie *Twice in a Lifetime* (1985), but Schae quickly moved from a nothing role on *General Hospital* to a 1989 debut on *The Bold and the Beautiful*. She's been with the soap ever since—but that didn't keep Schae from getting down and dirty in the cable thriller *Interlocked* (1998). She gets a cocklock on co-star Jeff Trachta in plenty of sexy scenes, making for an unusually bold and beautiful role for a popular soap star.

SKIN-fining Moment:

Interlocked (0:28) In a business meeting fantasy, Schae hops up on a conference table and shakes her chestcakes free of her dress.

See Her Naked In:

Interlocked (1998) Breasts

Kathryn Harrold

Born: August 2, 1950
Tazewell, Virginia
Skin-O-Meter: Brief Nudity

Kathryn Harrold started her career in the theater before landing a gig on the soap opera *The Doctors*. Her jump to feature films landed her in *Nightwing* (1979), which sadly never took flight at the box office. Still she pressed on, landing such notable gigs as *The Hunter* (1980) and *Bogie* (1980), in which she tackled the role of Lauren Bacall. She shined as the hot icon from movie days past. In the mid '80s Kathryn jumped back on the TV ship for one of the title parts on the short-lived series *MacGruder and Loud*. A string of made-for-TV flicks and not-quite-long-run series followed. Then Kathryn hit the big time, playing Garry Shandling's ex-wife on the hit HBO comedy *The Larry Sanders Show*. She left after one season, though, for the hospital soap *Chicago Hope*. The boob tube is great, but there just aren't enough boobs on it. Kathryn got to show off her shapely body as Albert Brooks's long-suffering girlfriend in *Modern Romance* (1981). In it, she flashed her only flesh to date, including a nice, if a bit distant, full-frontal shot climbing into bed. It's never too late for a follow-up flash!

SKIN-fining Moment:

Modern Romance (0:46) Lightning-quick left hoot and glutes getting under the covers with Albert Brooks.

See Her Naked In:

Modern Romance (1981) LB, Buns

Lisa Harrow

Born: August 25, 1943
Auckland, New Zealand
Skin-O-Meter: Great Nudity

Lisa Harrow isn't the actress on the tip of everyone's tongue, but you sure would like to taste the buxom brunette beauty. She has had quite the nondescript, prolific career, with over thirty mini-series, movies, and TV appearances under her thin and shapely belt since the early '70s. Lovely Lisa has acted with some serious Hollywood heavyweights, such as Anthony Hopkins and Sam Neill. She has most recently taken on the stage lead in *W;t*, about a woman dying of cancer, which ends with a full-frontal scene so as not to be too depressing. It wasn't Lisa's first flesh. She has been completely nude twice in cinema, once at the

beginning of her career and once very recently. There has been some skinage in between, such as *Omen III: The Final Conflict* (1981) and *The Last Days of Chez Nous* (1992), but it's the covers that make this book good reading. For the younger, more svelte Lisa, check out *The Tempter* (1975). In this particular Italian production, the young Lisa gave us a nice brief look at her full-frontal goodies—tempting, indeed. For the older Lisa, check out *Sunday* (1997), in which, thirty-two years after her first flash, she gave us the same full-frontal look, albeit a longer gawk. Compare, contrast, and take notes; you will be quizzed.

SKIN-fining Moment:

The Tempter (0:48) Lisa flashes her tits when she sits up as Glenda Jackson looks for her . . . We found her, Glenda!

See Her Naked In:

Sunday (1997) FFN
The Last Days of Chez Nous (1992) Breasts
The Final Conflict (1981) LB, Buns
The Tempter (1975) FFN, Buns

Deborah Harry

Born: July 1, 1945
Miami, Florida
Skin-O-Meter: Brief Nudity

Deborah Harry made punk rock sexy in the '70s with her band Blondie. That success soon led to movie offers. You celeb-skin fans won't be disappointed by Debbie's lone skin scene in the David Cronenberg mind-bender *Videodrome* (1983). The "tide was high" and so were her nipples during her sex scene with James Woods, who probably got a woody on the set. During this famous scene, Blondie has sex with the pock-faced star while at the same time getting her ears pierced. Now that's penetration!

SKIN-fining Moment:

Videodrome (0:16) The Tide won't be the only thing that's High when you see "Rapture"-ous Debbie get pierced by James Woods.

See Her Naked In:

Videodrome (1983) Breasts

Christina Hart

Skin-O-Meter: Great Nudity

She debuted in the nudie epic *The Stewardesses* (1969), but Christina Hart kept her clothes on in both classic schlock like *The Mad Bomber* (1972) and great films like *Charley Varrick* (1973). But then Christina finally decided to christen the screen with an amazing Hart attack in *The Games Girls Play* (1974). As a politician's sex-crazed daughter who's out to seduce the entire United Nations, Christina literally twirls around in a stunning full-frontal display—and in slow motion, too! That was followed by *Johnny Firecloud* (1975), where Christina further proved that there's nothing sexier than an all-natural, all-American bod. That's why Christina was so effective when cast as Manson Family femme Patricia Krenwinkel in the TV film *Helter Skelter* (1976). She should've been a star, but Christina lost Hart and gave up films after a minor role in the Brian Dennehy comedy *The Check Is in the Mail* (1986).

SKIN-fining Moment:

Games Girls Play (0:02) Christina gets totally naked, leaps into bed, then proceeds to twirl about in all her naked glory.

See Her Naked In:

Mean Dog Blues (1978) Breasts
Johnny Firecloud (1975) Breasts
Games Girls Play (1974) FFN, Buns

Roxanne Hart

Born: July 27, 1952
Trenton, New Jersey
Skin-O-Meter: Great Nudity

Roxanne Hart is best known as the head nurse (does that mean she gives patients head?) from TV's *Chicago Hope*. That is until she stormed into creator David E. Kelly's office and demanded her character have more of a voice on the show. After that, poor Roxanne played an out-of-work actress when she was axed from the drama the very next season. Roxanne's breasts seem just as feisty as she is. She had a brief, and very dark, breast flash in *Highlander* (1986). In the made-for-cable movie *The Last Innocent Man* (1987), she let's us finally see clearly what got the *Highlander* so hot and bothered. Her five-minute topless bedroom scene keeps that innocent man lasting all night, long and hard. Mr. Skin is currently building a time machine to go back to 1987 and work as a production assistant during that day's shoot!

SKIN-fining Moment:

The Last Innocent Man (1:10)
Roxanne shows a great pair of rib pillows after making love with Ed Harris, but when Ed gets a little angry and rips off her blanket, we get something even better . . . muffshish!

See Her Naked In:

The Last Innocent Man (1987) FFN
Highlander (1986) Breasts

Veronica Hart

Born: October 27, 1956
Las Vegas, Nevada
Skin-O-Meter: Hall of Fame

Veronica Hart was a model before she decided to use her body for something more fulfilling—that is filling, as in filling her body with guy's parts as a porno star! The busty beauty made her debut with a role in *Women in Love* (1979). Through the 1980s she racked up over one hundred credits, though she was most often seen in the shadow of porno icon Seka in such flicks as *Princess Seka* (1980) and *Tara* (1981)—but what a shadow that is! Veronica was usually the one picked out for her talents (and "abilities"), winning several Best Actress awards from various adult-film associations. But by the late '80s, she retired from the jiz-biz, and while she doesn't shed her threads on the adult-film circuit anymore, Veronica does appear in various states of undress in more mainstream offerings such as *Cleo/Leo* (1989). She even flashed her massive mammaries on an episode of the hit cable series *Six Feet Under* as (what else) an aging porn star. The part suited her just fine, and the encore appearance of those heaving hooters undoubtedly pleased her legions of fans. You gotta have Hart.

SKIN-fining Moment:

Sex Appeal (0:58) You'll get a Hart-on watching Veronica dance topless for a nice long (and round and bouncy) time for a fella in his bedroom.

See Her Naked In:

The Naked Feminist (2004)
Beauty School (1993) Breasts
Bedroom Eyes II (1990) Breasts
Cleo/Leo (1989) FFN
Sexpot (1988) Breasts
Student Affairs (1987) Breasts
Deranged (1987) Breasts, Buns
Sex Appeal (1986) Breasts
Wimps (1986) Breasts, Buns
Young Nurses in Love (1986) Breasts
Model Behavior (1984) Breasts
It's Called Murder, Baby (1982) LB, Buns
Numerous Adult Movies

TeleVisions:

Six Feet Under Breasts

Nina Hartley

Born: March 11, 1959
Berkley, California
Skin-O-Meter: Great Nudity

Nina Hartley came up with her stage name while stripping in San Francisco. The soon-to-be porno hall-of-famer liked Nina because the Japanese tourists who were shoving dollars in her G-string had no problems pronouncing it. Hartley was in homage to Mariette Hartley of the Polaroid commercials co-starring James Garner. Now she is arguably more famous than either. Nina has appeared in so many X-rated features that you could watch one a day for an entire year without hitting a sloppy second. Known for her deliciously plump derriere, Nina has starred in such rump-pleasing titles as *Anal Annie and the Backdoor Wives* (1984). But she's also appeared in mainstream fare, most notably *Boogie Nights* (1997), as the philandering wife of super-wimp William H. Macy. She managed to show off the least amount of skin of any of the primary cast members, just half a nip and the upper part of her legendary buns. She now defends pornography on such mainstream channels as MTV. Keep up the good fight, girl!

SKIN-fining Moment:

Boogie Nights (0:10) Just a touch of tit and a bit of butt while Nina rides some guy who is most definitely not her hubby.

See Her Naked In:

The Naked Feminist (2004)
Boogie Nights (1997) RB, Buns
Numerous Adult Movies

Cathryn Hartt

Dallas, Texas
Skin-O-Meter: Great Nudity

Cathryn Hartt made her name as the sister of a hottie with more name recognition, TV's sexy blonde bombshell Morgan Fairchild. But Cathryn is a pretty fair child herself. Cathryn was introduced to acting as a child when her sister was too shy to give a book report. Morgan became the first student in what would become *Hartt and Soul*, Cathryn's Texas-based acting school. The big-busted brunette made her professional debut in a remake of *The Creature from the Black Lagoon* (1976). She only played a waitress, but the Creature's gills went ga-ga for what this sensual lady served up. Cathryn continued to sweeten up productions with her eye candy on TV spots and in such films as *Futureworld* (1976) and *The Seduction* (1982), but it wasn't until her appearance in the steamy comedy *Pink Motels* (1983) that she finally let audiences check in . . . her skin. The movie stars wisecracking Phyllis Diller and Slim Pickens as proprietors of a no-tell motel with a clientele of carnal guests. There's the high-school virgin seeking to lose her cherry, a pair of adulterous attorneys trying to get out of their briefs, and a preppie prepping his nerd buddy in the ways of the one-night stand. Cathryn finally fulfills the promise of her pendulous pretties and exposes the whole she-bang. Sadly, it was her sole nudity on screen, and nowadays Cathryn has retired to teaching. If you want to see her ass, you'll have to sign up for her class.

SKIN-fining Moment:

Pink Motel (1:18) Cathryn drops the sheet she's wearing in a motel room and treats her two male companions to an eyeful of pink torso-bumpers.

See Her Naked In:

Pink Motel (1983) Breasts

Imogen Hassall

Born: August 25, 1942
Woking, Surrey, England
Died: November 16, 1980
Skin-O-Meter: Brief Nudity

Imogen Hassall was more famous for her formidable rack, which she displayed in various states of undress at premieres and other public affairs, than her work in film. The English tart with the dark hair and the cleavage that went on forever did make a career for herself on the big screen—where else could such huge hooters be properly displayed? Too bad she was a bit skingy when it came to exposing her tit-tastic talents. In the mid '60s she started appearing in provocatively entitled features such as *Bedtime* (1967) and also on swinging British TV programs such as *The Saint*, *The Avengers*, and *The Persuaders*. While her boobs did their best to escape from the confines of the boob tube, it wasn't until she appeared in the film *El Condor* (1970) that she finally treated audiences to what they'd been waiting to salivate over. Though only a brief skin scene, Imogen didn't disappoint; let's just say it's a muff-see. Imogen went on to jiggle a bit in the Hammer film *When Dinosaurs Ruled the Earth* (1970) and jiggle a bit more in the farce *Carry On Loving* (1970). Her last nudie shot was a glimpse of her famous chest in *Bloodsuckers* (1972). Her jugs remained outstanding, but her career faltered. By *No 1: Licensed to Love and Kill* (1979), a.k.a. *The Man from S.E.X.* and *Undercover Lover*, it was all over. The next year Imogen committed suicide by overdosing on sleeping pills. What a Hassall.

SKIN-fining Moment:

El Condor (0:56) After a gunman bursts in, Imogen confronts him in fabulously full-frontal fashion, then crouches and shows her A-ass-al as she lifts a sheet to reveal a guy beneath her bed. She's got one of those stupendous '70s bods. Oh, I can dig it.

See Her Naked In:

Bloodsuckers (1972) RB
El Condor (1970) FFN, buns

Teri Hatcher

Born: December 8, 1964
Sunnyvale, California
Skin-O-Meter: Great Nudity

"They're real," declared Teri Hatcher to a frustrated Jerry Seinfeld before stomping out his apartment door, "and they're spectacular!" That famous TV moment catapulted the voluptuous brunette's career up, up, and away, as her now "larger profile" convinced network execs to cast her as Lois Lane on the now-defunct ABC hit *Lois & Clark: The New Adventures of Superman*. But before Superman had his eyes on her super mams, Mr. Skin was already watching Teri's tomatoes ripen on the vine in *The Cool Surface* (1994), her first and breast exposure. She went the full monty in *Heaven's Prisoners* (1996), though a pesky balcony railing makes it difficult to see Teri's hairy patch. She's since gone on to one of filmdom's hottest catfights with Charlize Theron in *2 Days in the Valley* (1996) and disrobed for 007, which had him grow a few digits, in *Tomorrow Never Dies* (1997). Teri was born from smart stock—her father's a nuclear physicist and her mom's a computer programmer—but she's left the brains to them and has used her body to succeed from an early age. While at Fremont High School in California, Teri was captain of the Featherettes, a cheerleading dance team, and was voted Most Likely to Become a Solid Gold Dancer by her graduating class in 1982. Instead she became a member of the 1984 Gold Rush, a professional cheerleading squad for the San Francisco 49ers. The 34B-23-34 full-figured temptress had better places to shake her pom-poms and made her show-business debut as a dancing mermaid on *The Love Boat*. The rest is history—that is, the history of a legion of dead semen.

SKIN-fining Moment:

Heaven's Prisoners (0:41) Teri catches Alec Baldwin's eye (and a cold if she's not careful) by stepping out on a balcony in broad daylight completely nude, exposing her tush, bush and Lois Lanes. The only thing preventing this from being a perfect nude scene is a damn railing that obscures a clear shot of her whole naked package. Nonetheless, you still get to see Teri's Hatcher.

See Her Naked In:

Heaven's Prisoners (1996) FFN, Buns
The Cool Surface (1994) Breasts

Amy Hathaway

Skin-O-Meter: Brief Nudity

Blonde, buxom, and leggy Amy Hathaway burst onto the scene with a small role in *14 Going on 30* (1988) and followed that up with the sleazy Charles Bronson ass kicker *Kinjite: Forbidden Subjects* (1989). She managed to keep her pants on for those as well as her next ventures, spots on the TV series *My Two Dads* and *Arresting Behavior*. It wasn't until the Roger Corman-produced schlocker *Last Exit to Earth* (1996) that arousing Amy finally let audiences bang on her cans. She goes back in time to have sex with prehistoric men and returns to the future to repopulate the earth. Amy also plays a good

vamp, as she proved in the skinless but sexy *Joy Ride* (1996). Her father has her in on a scam where she lures unsuspecting marks with her spectacular mams. There's one itsy-bitsy, teeny-weeny bikini scene that won't leave a dry seat in the house. Amy's seat meat runneth over her bathing bottoms in such a pinch-able fashion its hypnotic. Amy and her rump are still working the small screen with appearances on *Felicity* and *Buffy the Vampire Slayer*. On the big screen she's been seen in *The Cure for Boredom* (2000), a.k.a. *Sex & Bullets*, which sadly doesn't live up to its provocative name. But Amy is too frisky a kitten not to end up flashing her pussy soon and letting viewers walk their dogs.

SKIN-fining Moment:

Last Exit to Earth (1:18) Amy's topless orbs wobble in a time machine, but her nips are covered by same contraption. Damn technology!

See Her Naked In:

Last Exit to Earth (1996) Breasts

Anne Hathaway

Born: November 12, 1982
Brooklyn, New York
Skin-O-Meter: Great Nudity

The wide-set lush lips and seemingly innocent brown eyes of Brooklyn-born breathy brunette Anne Hathaway are keeping a secret. At least she thinks she's keeping a secret. Even when Anne's mouth breaks into a widespread smile of pearly white delight, the gorgeous girl behind that flash of invitational tease seems to think that her true deep nature remains hidden. What does harrowingly heavenly Hathaway take us for, blind morons? Are we intended to not notice that hers is a torso worth tossing away one's entire

life's possessions and pursuits on the merest chance of holding and manhandling it for just the briefest flicker of time? Anne gave hints of the Hathaway honey as Meghan Green in the farcical Fox family drama *Get Real*. The cat's out of the bag, along with the fur that warms that pussy, in *Havoc* (2004). Two terms of endearment in *Havoc*'s favor: Bijou Phillips as a co-star and menage-a-trois as a plot point.

SKIN-fining Moment:

Havoc The once-upon-a-time Ella Enchanted puts her princess diary away and uses her own finger like a magic wand to cast a spell on her Havoc hole. Full-frontal self-satisfying fantasticness!

See Her Naked In:

Havoc (2004) FFN, Buns

Aysha Hauer

Skin-O-Meter: Great Nudity

Her father's kicked a lot of ass on screen, but we'd gladly risk the wrath of Rutger for a chance with Aysha Hauer. She's also picked up her dad's knack for shameless roles, starting with sexy turns in *Witchcraft V: Dance with the Devil* (1993) and *At Ground Zero* (1994). Aysha then really put her weird blonde beauty to work in *Welcome Says the Angel* (1996), in which she's supremely sexy as a rock-chick heroin addict with a penchant for chains. It's a star-making role that, unfortunately, didn't get seen by the guys who could make Aysha a star. She's kept a low profile since making *Kick of Death* (1997), but her Gothy goodies are sorely missed.

SKIN-fining Moment:

Welcome Says the Angel (0:54) A flash of fur and a bit of butt when her man-friend rips her pants off then sets into some serious balling.

See Her Naked In:

Welcome Says the Angel (1996) Breasts, Bush, Buns

Darla Haun

Born: November 10, 1964
Los Angeles, California
Skin-O-Meter: Brief Nudity

Some of the skills listed on Darla Haun's resumé include New York, Southern, French, and British accents and burping on cue. With that kind of control of her throat, there's no limit to what she can do. This brunette with the nice boobs can do a lot. She started her career on the boob tube with appearances on *Silk Stalkings*, which led to bouncing spots on *Baywatch* and, finally fulfilling the sexy trilogy, *Son of the Beach*. But Darla didn't ignore the more revealing world of theatrical releases. She revealed her comedic side as Plain White Rapper in *Class of Nuke 'Em High Part II: Subhumanoid Meltdown* (1991), and in *Dracula: Dead and Loving It* (1995) she's billed only as Brunette Vampire. But Darla's dumplings were made for bigger things, and she made things bigger with her role in *Married People, Single Sex* (1993). The story of how several couples spice up their sex lives includes a wife seeking love outside her home, a man who gets more than he expected when he starts making kinky phone calls, and Darla's sole skin scene, in which she flashes her hefty funbags. She continues to work as an infomercial spokesperson and on series such as *Sunset Beach*. May the sun never set on this beautiful beach.

SKIN-fining Moment:

Married People, Single Sex (0:04)
Darla doffs her clothes and exposes her Hauny hooters, Hauny heinie, and even some Hauny hairpie before she slips into a robe.

See Her Naked In:

Married People, Single Sex (1993) FFN, Buns

Annette Haven

Born: December 1, 1954
Skin-O-Meter: Great Nudity

With willow-spry limbs, an ass of sculpted alabaster flesh, a perfect economy of tits, and a face that could have sold anything, Annette Haven single-handedly put the *class* into Classic Porn. From the early 1970s to her mourned retirement from the blue screen in 1989, the incomparably cool and passionate Haven graced more than one hundred hardcore productions. Although the unrivaled goddess of XXX did make one mainstream appearance, offering her milky warm breasts in *10* (1979), the best way to nourish one's soul on the bread of heaven that is Haven is to venture across the adult aisle of the DVD realm. A transcendant experience is waiting, particularly in *"V" The Hot One* (1978), *High School Memories* (1980), *Skintight* (1981), and *Peaches and Cream* (1982). It's hard to go wrong with Annette Haven.

SKIN-fining Moment:

10 (0:50) Dudley Moore spies on a swinger bash through a telescope and gets a glorious eyeful of bare-bosomed Annette patrolling the kink-packed premises in a devastatingly luscious leather dominatrix outfit. Crack that whip!

See Her Naked In:

10 (1979) Breasts
Numerous Adult Movies

Keeley Hawes

Born: 1977
London, England
Skin-O-Meter: Great Nudity

It takes a sex symbol to play a sex symbol, and Keeley Hawes broke out big when she played young Diana Dors in the UK TV bio *The Blonde Bombshell* (1998). Other things broke out big in Keeley's next film, *The Last September* (1999)—which, as it turns out, provides the perfect month for guys to pick some magnificent melons. Hawes's heapin' helpin' of hooters was then matched with some furburgerage in the sexy film *Complicity* (2000). All that was missing was a little lesbianism, so guys were properly Keeleyhauled by her fine Sapphic soothing in the BBC-TV movie *Tipping the Velvet* (2002). Keeley's finally become a hot property with recent A&E cable airings of her critically acclaimed spy show *Spooks*, repackaged here in the States under the title *MI-5*. The series also made the UK gossip columns when Keeley left her husband for co-star Matthew MacFadyen.

SKIN-fining Moment:

Complicity (0:21) Keeley gets really naked, revealing all three B's as she frolics in bed, gets some coffee, and returns to the sheets.

See Her Naked In:

Tipping the Velvet (2002) Breasts
Complicity (2000) Breasts, Bush, Buns
The Last September (1999) Breasts

Goldie Hawn

Born: November 21, 1945
Washington, D.C.
Skin-O-Meter: Hall of Fame

Goldie Hawn socked it to us as the jiggling, giggling, body-painted teen ding-a-ling on *Rowan & Martin's Laugh-in*. This golden go-go girl transitioned to film by starting at the bottom. She bared bountiful backside in *There's a Girl in My Soup* (1970) and emphasized her ass-sets via petite panties in *Shampoo*

(1975). Heading for the top, the Goldster showed a slip of pink nip in the shower in *Best Friends* (1982) and full boobage in the bath in *Wildcats* (1986). Still nifty at fifty, she flashed her fabulously firm fanny in *Town & Country* (2001). Wondering if Gold's dubloons are still perky? Check out her soapy nipple slipple in *The Banger Sisters* (2002).

MMM-MMM-GOLDIE! GOLDIE HAWN'S PINK PANTIES CO-STAR WITH PETER SELLERS IN *THERE'S A GIRL IN MY SOUP.*

SKIN-fining Moment:

Bird on a Wire (0:31) With Mel Gibson beneath her, Goldie's skirt blows up on a ladder and gives us a glorious view of her legendary golden gluteus. You'll be so Hawney.

See Her Naked In:

The Banger Sisters (2002) RB
Town & Country (2001) Buns
CrissCross (1992) Thong
Bird on a Wire (1990) RB, Buns
Overboard (1987) Thong
Wildcats (1986) Breasts
Best Friends (1982) Breasts
Dollars (1972) Buns
There's a Girl in My Soup (1970) RB, Bush, Buns

Linda Hayden

**Born: January 19, 1953
Stanmore, Middlesex, England, UK
Skin-O-Meter: Great Nudity**

In the '70s Linda Hayden ranked right up there with the most popular of Britain's sex symbols. It's easy to see why. At the tender age of fifteen, she made her skinful silver-screen debut in *Baby Love* (1968). And yes, she got naked in the movie, showing off her English Tea & A in a few rather disturbing scenes. (She doesn't look like a mid-teenager, but she is!) A few years later, Linda again flashed her plump rib pillows, and bush in *Blood on Satan's Claw* (1970). Surprisingly, she had only reached the tip of the iceberg at that point, so to speak. Then Linda bared her bushy beaver again to the world via the sex farce *Confessions of a Window Cleaner* (1974). Still, it wasn't her sexiest role. She just gets more randy with age. Next she appeared opposite Udo Kier in the thriller *Exposé* (1975), which offered up quite a bit of gratuitous nudity from both Linda and then-newcomer and future sex kitten Fiona Richmond.

Fiona was certainly hot in the picture, but compared to Linda's masturbatory sequence, she was as frozen as an Eskimo. That Linda ain't Hayden!

SKIN-fining Moment:

Baby Love (0:33) Linda's sweet seat is on full display as she stands naked in front of her mirror.

See Her Naked In:

The Boys from Brazil (1978) Breasts
Love Trap (1977) RB
Confessions from a Holiday Camp (1977) FFN, Buns
Exposé (1975) Breasts
Confessions of a Window Cleaner (1974) FFN
Blood on Satan's Claw (1970) FFN
Baby Love (1968) Breasts, Buns

Salma Hayek

**Born: September 2, 1966
Coatzacoalcos, Veracruz, Mexico
Skin-O-Meter: Great Nudity**

It's hot in Mexico, which explains the South-of-the-Border sexpot Salma Hayek. Her pint-sized, hour-glass figure first made its appearance on the short-lived TV sitcom *The Sinbad Show*. But, oh, her sin is good. Even when stopping short of nudity, like the steamy stripteases in *From Dusk Till Dawn* (1995) and *Dogma* (1999), Salma is naughty. But this spicy dish serves up her hot tamale and chesty chimichangas in many sizzling platters. A tantalizing appetizer being two heaping scoops of juicy boobies ordered up by Antonio Banderas in *Desperado* (1995). The second course: a taste of tit in *Breaking Up* (1997), a side of milk sacks from *The Velocity of Gary* (1998), and a full moon flashed for *The Wild Wild West* (1999). Hope you've saved room for dessert, because there's pie on the menu. The biopic about Mexican artist Frida Kahlo, *Frida* (2002), exposed the more feminine side of Salma with an Ashley Judd lip-lock and crotch-grabbing lesbian lay with Karine Plantadit-Bageot. That stretches Mr. Skin's canvas.

SKIN-fining Moment:

Frida (1:38) Awesome chest-burritos and a small sample of las buttcheekas in grabby lesbo scene with Karine Plantadit-Bageot in bed.

See Her Naked In:

Frida (2002) Breasts, Buns
Wild Wild West (1999) Buns
The Velocity of Gary (1998) RB
Breaking Up (1997) RB
Desperado (1995) Breasts

Lauren Hays

Born: May 21, 1968
Fairfax, Virginia
Skin-O-Meter: Great Nudity

Auburn-haired Lauren Hays is a straight-to-video B-movie vixen. She is scintillatingly hot in that role and will probably never retire from the world of boobs and bad dialogue. When you've got the triple-B moves of this big-breasted thespian, why mess around with anything else? Of course, for the hairy-palm set that enjoys a one-handed ride through the televised world of wank, Lauren's happy career choice provides ample opportunities for gratuitous nudity—which is, of course, the best kind. Lauren is no stranger to that. Like her sometimes co-star Kim Yates, she is quick to shed her clothing for her fans. Thanks! She has always had a killer body (which has killed millions of sperm cells). Her plump, full gazongas and fire-red snatch will have you begging to be burnt. Just about any movie that Lauren's in is worth watching for the inevitable nakedness. For a good, close look at that flaming bush mentioned previously, check

out *Web of Seduction* (1999). You'll get sticky. For a younger, blonder Lauren, go for *Rebecca's Secret* (1998). It all depends on what flavor you prefer, strawberry or vanilla. At Skin Central we like to warm up our tongues on those cold winter nights with Lauren's hot scoops!

SKIN-fining Moment:

Crime and Passion (0:01) It's an all-points nudity lesbo thrown-down with Nikki Fritz. Boobs, buns, bush for both.

See Her Naked In:

Heavenly Hooters (2003) FFN
Perfectly Legal (2002) FFN, Buns
Temptations (1999) Breasts, Bush, Buns
Crime and Passion (1999) FFN, Buns
Stripper Wives (1999) FFN, Buns
Web of Seduction (1999) FFN, Buns
Sex Files: Virtual Sex (1998) FFN
Life of a Gigolo (1998) FFN, Buns
Club Wild Side (1998) FFN, Buns
Dangerous Invitation (1998) FFN, Buns
Rebecca's Secret (1997) Breasts, Buns
Raven (1997) Breasts
Surf, Sand, and Sex (1994) Thong
The Great Bikini Off-Road Adventure (1994) Breasts, Thong
Teasers (1993) Breasts, Buns
Buck Naked Line Dancing (1993) Breasts, Buns
Meatballs 4 (1992) Breasts

TeleVisions:

Beverly Hills Bordello FFN, Buns
Erotic Confessions Breasts, Bush, Buns
Hot Springs Hotel Breasts
Lady Chatterley's Stories FFN, Buns

Susan Hayward

Born: June 30, 1917
Brooklyn, New York
Died: March 14, 1975
Skin-O-Meter: Brief Nudity

A redheaded hottie with a 36½-26-35½ figure, Susan Hayward left Brooklyn, New York, for the fast life of Hollywood. She was one of many

---

MR. SKIN'S TOP TEN

**Favorite Nip Slips
. . . Peek-a-boobs!!!**

10. **Kim Novak**
    —*The Amorous Adventures of Moll Flanders*—1965 (1:36) (right)

9. **Cameron Diaz**
    —*Vanilla Sky*—2001 (1:28) (left)

8. **Julia Louis-Dreyfus**
    —*Seinfeld:* "The Busboy"—1991 (left)

7. **Elvira**
    —*Elvira, Mistress of the Dark*—1988 (0:18) (right)

6. **Jennifer Love Hewitt**
    —*The Tuxedo*—2002 (1:01) (right)

5. **Fay Wray**
    —*King Kong*—1933 (1:12) (right)

4. **Tatum O'Neal**
    —*Little Darlings*—1980 (0:35) (left)

3. **Marilyn Monroe**
    —*The Misfits*—1961 (0:34) (right)

2. **Lucy Lawless**
    —Detroit Red Wings Game: National Anthem—1997 (left)

1. **Susan Hayward**
    —*With a Song in My Heart*—1952 (0:48) (left)

---

starlets in 1939 who auditioned for the part of Scarlett O'Hara in *Gone with the Wind*. Obviously, she didn't get it, but, frankly, my dear, she didn't give a damn. The fire-haired, tenacious act-chest paid her dues in several major-studio releases before hitting the big time with a role in *Beau Geste* (1939). And after that she just hit her stride, eventually garnering five Academy Award nominations for Best Actress and finally winning one for her portrayal of Barbara Graham in *I Want to Live!* (1958). But at Skin Central we want to see her as a live girl dancer. Considering the times, the closest to a peek at her peaks came in the accidental skin of *With a Song in My Heart* (1952). About forty-eight minutes into the musical her left breast clearly pops out of her dress during a song-and-dance number that'll have you doing the Charleston in your pants. Susan was a two-pack-a-day smoker who loved to drink. She was diagnosed with brain cancer in March 1972 and died on March 14, 1975.

SKIN-fining Moment:

With a Song in My Heart (0:48) An early Hollywood nip-slip and still one of the all-time greats. When Susan throws up her left arm during a song-and-dance number, out pops her left-side suckable.

See Her Naked In:

With a Song in My Heart (1952) Nip Slip LB

Rita Hayworth

Born: October 17, 1918
Brooklyn, New York
Died: May 14, 1987
Skin-O-Meter: Never Nude

The ravishing red-haired goddess of every American G.I.'s dreams was actually a Spanish mamacita incognito. Decades before the Latin Explosion brought Hispanic hotties like J-Lo and her bootay grande into fashion, Margarita Carmen Cansino was struggling to find her place in Hollywood. Rita's Poppy and Mommy, both dancers, encouraged their voluptuous dark-haired daughter to follow along in their family's dance steps. Once she hit Hollywood, Rita landed the lead in *The Strawberry Blonde* (1941) and dyed her raven locks red, and thus in Rita Hayworth an American movie queen was born. For a follow-up, she flashed her gorgeous gams and tapped her talented tootsies with Fred Astaire in *You'll Never Get Rich* (1941), emerging as an established star. That same year she posed for *Life* magazine in that

familiar sultry see-through negligee that made her a national pinup favorite. In *Gilda* (1956), Rita's most bumpalicious performance, she donned transparent cock-teasing costumes and performed a partial striptease with such sass and seduction that she earned herself the nickname "The Love Goddess." At the height of her fame, this fiery femme left Hollywood to marry millionaire playboy Prince Aly Khan. Sadly, the union lasted only a few years, but due to unfavorable publicity, a changing climate in Hollywood, and the early onset of Alzheimer's disease, lovely Rita's career never recovered.

SKIN-fining Moment:

Gilda (1:04) Blistering bralessness in black-and-white! Rita's raw rack shows clearly through her sheer top as she turns to talk to her maid.

Lena Headey

Born: 1976
Yorkshire, England
Skin-O-Meter: Great Nudity

She went topless for her torrid debut in *Waterland* (1992), but that was only the start of Lena Headey's numerous nude scenes. This gorgeous Brit then took the title of *Loved Up* (1995) very seriously in a seriously sexy scene. The 1995 mini-series *Band of Gold* further cemented Lena's shameless rep with her role as a dominatrix, while she only made us more Headey clowning around with another gal in *Mrs. Dalloway* (1997). And don't miss one of the great lingerie scenes of all time from a 1997 episode of the cable anthology series *The Hunger*. Her first bid for American stardom was in the college drama *Gossip* (2000), but guys were more dazzled by her brazen nudity throughout *Aberdeen* (2000)—not to mention how her ass and titties

enjoy their freedom in *The Parole Officer* (2001).

SKIN-fining Moment:

Aberdeen (0:04) Lots of looks at Lena's lucky charms as she showers and chats on the phone.

See Her Naked In:

The Parole Officer (2001) Breasts, Buns
Aberdeen (2000) Breasts
Mrs. Dalloway (1997) FFN, Buns
Loved Up (1995) Breasts
Waterland (1992) Breasts

Patricia Healy

UK
Skin-O-Meter: Great Nudity

Patricia Healy has the figure of an hourglass and the looks of a classical Roman bust. So you know what time it is? Time to pillage her sacks like the barbarians we are at Skin Central. The big-breasted beauty made her debut simply as Girl in *The White Bus* (1967). Besides the odd boob-tube appearance, Patricia was not seen or heard from again until making some saucy TV guest spots on *Silk Stalkings* and *NYPD Blue*. But mostly she has been relegated to minor roles in otherwise huge films, such as *The Bodyguard* (1992) and *Heat* (1995), in which she played a hot date to enliven some otherwise unremarkable actor's arm. More recently she has been living in soap-opera heaven as Tammy Hansen on *General Hospital*. She also had a minor role as Adele in the cult film *China Moon* (1994), which offered a silhouetted peek at Patricia's plentiful peaks. For some real skin action, check out *Sweet Poison* (1991), which flashed a nice frontal look at her funbags, as well as a nice detailing of her curvy body. *Ultraviolet* (1992) may be her breast nudity yet, but there's always hope that Patricia will please her fans with more of what we like to call the moist.

SKIN-fining Moment:

Ultraviolet (0:50) Patricia emerges from a pond in wet bra and panties, which she loses when posing for Esai Morales.

See Her Naked In:

China Moon (1994) Breasts
Ultraviolet (1992) Breasts
Sweet Poison (1991) Breasts

Marla Heasley

Born: September 9, 1959
Hollywood, California
Skin-O-Meter: Brief Nudity

Pretty brunette Marla Heasley is breast known as a replacement on the 1984 season of everybody's favorite show about soldiers of fortune who are wanted by the U.S. government, *The A-Team*. She added some much-needed femininity to the he-man cast, which included gold-chain adorned Mr. T. We pity the fool who'd ignore the talents of a sexy minx like Marla. Even though her character was named Tawnia after the daughter of show creator Stephen J. Cannell, sadly, her tenure on the show was short lived, and Marla's career never really bounced back. She remained in the public eye with some guest spots on '80s staples such as *The Love Boat* and *T.J. Hooker*. But to catch Marla's pubic eye, you have to dredge up *Born to Race* (1988). It'll get your motor going. But after the film *Amore!* (1993), our love waned like when the moon hits your eye like a big pizza pie.

SKIN-fining Moment:

Born to Race (0:52) Marla bares her bottom while making out with Joseph Bottoms. That's what I call appropriate behavior!

See Her Naked In:

Born to Race (1988) Buns

Joey Heatherton

Born: September 14, 1944
Long Island, New York
Skin-O-Meter: Brief Nudity

Barry Williams of *Brady Bunch* fame described Joey Heatherton as the "white-hot, vaguely slutty-looking sex goddess" of the '60s. In fact, this crop-topped blonde bopper was one of the sassiest, swingingest chicks around. Little Joey did it all. She released teenage dream singles like "When You Call Me Baby" and made TV appearances on everything from *Route 66* to *I Spy*. It was Joey's work on variety shows such as *The Jackie Gleason Show* and *Dean Martin Presents* that truly showcased her dynamic, sex-kitten energy. She sang, danced, wiggled, and jiggled in teeny frocks, catching the eyes and flies of every red-blooded male with a television set. Her USO tour with Bob Hope caused temporary crippling in many a soldier's wrist. Joey's little figure filled the big screen in *Blue Beard* (1972). She debuted perfectly pointy peaches, proving her tits were as perky as her personality. Expectations were dashed when she appeared in *The Happy Hooker Goes to Washington* (1977) without flashing even an ounce of flesh. Offscreen Joey was everybody's pal. She reportedly slept with a wide variety of men, from Perry Como to the entire Rat Pack. Eventually she married Lance Rentzel, wide receiver for the Dallas Cowboys, but that ended when he was arrested for reportedly exposing himself to a ten-year-old girl. Oh, Joey, will you never win?

SKIN-fining Moment:

Bluebeard (1:52) Fantastic funbaggage as Joey throws open her robes and exposes her globes to Richard Burton.

See Her Naked In:

Bluebeard (1972) Breasts

MR. SKIN'S TOP TEN

Favorite Lesbo Scenes
. . . Bi-namic duos

10. Michelle Williams and Chloë Sevigny
   —*If These Walls Could Talk 2*—2000 (0:57)

9. Laura Harring and Naomi Watts
   —*Mulholland Dr.*—2001 (2:01)

8. Mariel Hemingway and Patrice Donnelly
   —*Personal Best*—1982 (0:18)

7. Angelina Jolie and Elizabeth Mitchell
   —*Gia*—1998 (0:25)

6. Susan Sarandon and Catherine Deneuve
   —*The Hunger*—1983 (1:01)

5. Sarita Choudhury and Indira Varma
   —*Kama Sutra: A Tale of Love*—1996 (1:33)

4. Helen Shaver and Patricia Charbonneau
   —*Desert Hearts*—1985 (1:10)

3. Gina Gershon and Jennifer Tilly
   —*Bound*—1996 (0:19)

2. Marta Kristen and Kathy Kersh
   —*Gemini Affair*—1974 (0:57)

1. **Anne Heche and Joan Chen**
   —*Wild Side*—**1995 (0:40)**

Anne Heche

Born: May 25, 1969
Aurora, Ohio
Skin-O-Meter: Hall of Fame

Call Me Crazy, Anne Heche's 2001 autobiographical account of growing up with a sexually abusive father, rocketed to the top of the *New York Times* bestseller list immediately upon its release. That came as no surprise. Since her much-publicized lesbianic coupling

ANNE HECHE NOT PLAYING THE TITLE CHARACTER IN *PSYCHO*. NOT IN THE MOVIE ANYWAY.

with comedienne Ellen DeGeneres, Anne has consistently been of great pubic—er, public—interest. If she is crazy, Mr. Skin thinks she's crazy like a fox! At nineteen Anne played twins on *Another World*, doubling everyone's pleasure and fun with her blonde-sweet-blonde, bright-eyed good looks. Next, dreamboat Annie appeared in small parts that thankfully showcased all of her naked body parts, in films such as *Girls in Prison* (1994) and the lesbo action-packed *Wild Side* (1995). Her newfound love of labia soon propelled her career upward. She spent a passionate three-and-a-half years of licking and screaming with Ellen DeGeneres and capitalized on her Sapphic success in *Donnie Brasco* (1997), *Volcano* (1997), *Wag The Dog* (1997), and *Psycho* (1998). When her gal-pal union turned sour, she suffered a psychotic breakdown. Tripped out on Ecstasy, this baffled blondie blanked out and found herself in Fresno, calling herself Celestia, while waiting for the mother ship to take her away. In an interview with Barbara Walters, Anne confessed that she created this alter ego to help her cope with life. Regardless of whether she calls herself Anne, Celestia, or Moonzaber God of the Argonauts, whatever planet you're from it's impossible to describe this sexilicious being as anything but heavenly.

SKIN-fining Moment:

Wild Side (0:40) Anne flashes her powerful pontoons and pert posterior whilst paddling Joan Chen's pink canoe in this magically lez-tastic scene.

See Her Naked In:

Psycho (1998) RB, Buns
Return to Paradise (1998) Breasts
The Juror (1996) Breasts
If These Walls Could Talk (1996) Breasts
Wild Side (1995) Breasts, Buns
Pie in the Sky (1995) RB
Girls in Prison (1994) Breasts

Jessica Hecht

Born: June 28, 1965
Princeton, New Jersey
Skin-O-Meter: Great Nudity

Jessica Hecht is best known to all you couch potatoes out there as the carpet-munching siren who stole away Ross's wife on TV's *Friends*. She is most definitely a TV personality, having appeared on *The Single Guy*, *The Heidi Chronicles*, and *What About Joan?* Jessica has appeared in bit movie parts, but her bits are the main part of her sole leading role in *Anarchy TV* (1997). The film featured three of Frank Zappa's kids, Ahmet, Dweezil, and Moon Unit, but is most notable for showing off all of Jessica's amazing assets, from her luscious boobs to her hairy bush. In it, she runs a public (or is it pubic?) access station that the evil Alan Thicke is trying to silence, so they broadcast in the buff. All nudes is good nudes.

SKIN-fining Moment:

Anarchy TV (1:01) Jessica shows some fabulously fluffy full frontal as she gets up from behind her news desk and does some naked aerobics. Exercise has never been this much fun!

See Her Naked In:

Anarchy TV (1997) FFN, Buns

> "I used to have a very large waist and I was shaped like a lemon: no chest, no hips. From the beginning to the end of middle school, when I got to the locker room for gym, everyone made fun of me. For two years, I prayed every night for my breasts to appear. My physical transformation happened when I was seventeen in 1995. When I finished filming *Under Siege 2*, I had become more womanly, more sure of myself."
>
> —KATHERINE HEIGL

Katherine Heigl

Born: November 24, 1978
Washington, D.C.
Skin-O-Meter: Brief Nudity

To quote former boyfriend (and frequent *Tiger Beat* cover fodder) Joey Lawrence, "Whoa!" Katherine Heigl is one hot little momma who is humongous in two very important places. Kat first caught the eyes of skinthusiasts in *My Father the Hero* (1994), spending the majority of the movie in a skimpy white swimsuit. Three years later this tan teen filled up and out and showed the results of her growth spurt (particularly her bare royal rump) in *Prince Valiant* (1997). Kitty made *100 Girls* (2000) a million times hotter when she lost her shirt in a foosball game and tickled tongues with Kewpie-doll co-star Larisa Oleynik. Katherine's mountainously copious cleavage in too-tight, teat-popping tops in *Valentine* (2001) gave everyone at Skin Central a giant *heart-on*. Katherine brought her out-of-this-world beauty to millions of flesh fans on the now-defunct teen TV series *Roswell*. A weekly look at Katherine's extraterrestrials was worth the virtual trip back to high school.

SKIN-fining Moment:

My Father the Hero (0:18) Young Katherine relaxes poolside in a teeny bikini to the dismay of Gerard Depardieu. Then she reveals it's a bun-baring thong and he damn near explodes. You will too.

See Her Naked In:

Prince Valiant (1997) Buns
My Father the Hero (1994) Thong

Amelia Heinle

Born: March 17, 1973
Phoenix, Arizona
Skin-O-Meter: Brief Nudity

Amelia Heinle just had an hour off from her job checking coats at a New York City fashion show when she frantically raced across town for an audition for the soap opera *Loving*. She mistakenly got left off at the studio for *One Life to Live*. When the buxom brunette finally reached the set of *Loving*, she thought her big break had broken into pieces. But they loved her and she got the part, launching this hottie into the daytime world of rape, adultery, and sexy outfits. After testing the cinematic waters in features such as *Liar's Poker* (1999) and *The Limey* (1999), Amelia returned to the boob tube, where she comfortably cut a sexy figure on another soap, *All My Children*. But her Hollywood venture wasn't a total wash thanks to shaking her tail in the erotic thriller *Black Cat Run* (1998), in which she showed her breasts in a very dark sex scene. It's her sole skin to date, but with a body like Amelia's, time is on skin's side.

SKIN-fining Moment:

Liar's Poker (0:17) I'm BUMmed that Heinle doesn't show her heinie (thong only kids). However, who can complain when there are several brief consolation boob shots?

See Her Naked In:

Liar's Poker (1999) Breasts, Thong
Black Cat Run (1998) RB

Jayne Heitmeyer

Born: October 30, 1970
Montreal, Quebec, Canada
Skin-O-Meter: Brief Nudity

Jayne Heitmeyer is a huge-hootered, horseback-riding, guitar-playing Canuck with hot red hair. She started her career in the nondescript Canadian comedy *Coyote* (1992). Since then, she has become sort of a sci-fi icon, choosing roles in several genre films and TV series, such as *Sci-fighters* (1996), which offered the first peek at her mountainous peaks, and *Earth: Final Conflict*. She also did some time on the gritty police drama *Sirens* and played a call girl in *Gleason: The Jackie Gleason Story* (2002), in which her great ones got to mingle with the Great One. She also appeared opposite Stephen Baldwin in *X Change* (2000). Jayne has been selective about her roles, though, and hasn't really gotten around to showing us much of her ass-ets. Her character flashes some poorly lit funbaggage in *Suspicious Minds* (1997), but what nips you can see belong to a Body Double. One of Jayne's first jobs was a steamy bathroom pitch for Cadbury's Crispy Crunch in an advertising campaign that ran in her native land from 1992 through 1996. Her sweets made men reach for their candy bars.

SKIN-fining Moment:

Sci-fighters (1:23) Billy Drago drags Jayne onto the floor and the top half of her right Heitmeyer bobbles on screen.

See Her Naked In:

Suspicious Minds (1997) Body Double. Breasts
Sci-fighters (1996) LB

TeleVisions:

The Hunger Body Double—RB, Thong

Marg Helgenberger

Born: November 16, 1958
North Bend, Nebraska
Skin-O-Meter: Great Nudity

Marg (pronounced *Mar-guh*) Helgenberger got red hot reviews as the stripper-turned-crime-scene-investigator on the CBS smash *CSI*. Probe into this stunning strawberry blonde's past and you'll find that she's been sizzling and showing skin onscreen for quite some time. Her big break came via the 1988 ABC series *China Beach*, where she scored an Emmy for Best Supporting Actress. (Who wouldn't fantasize about being stranded on a desert island with her character, the fiery prostitute K.C.?) Marg was in the breast company, with Traci Lords and Joanna Cassidy, on the ABC fright fest *The Tommyknockers* (1993). That threesome set a record for the most pairs of perfect knocks ever seen together in a TV mini-series. You'll be moved to breed after watching Marg's performances in *Species* (1995) and *Species 2* (1998). She appeared in all her rosy-nipped glory alongside man-eater Natasha Henstridge. Helgenberger's most skinful appearance, in *Frame by Frame* (1995), will really float your boat. Marg is completely nude in the bathtub, and if you look closely you'll get a quick peak of her reddish muffage before she covers it up with her fingers. There is a skindalous rumor going around that Marg will have a flashback on *CSI*, highlighting choice moments from her pole-dancing past. Should this happen, Mr. Skin promises to give the episode a thorough skinvestigation.

SKIN-fining Moment:

Frame by Frame (0:37) Great, multi-angle looks at Marg's delicious pink-tipped mammables as she lies in a bath with her hand on her Helgenbergerage.

See Her Naked In:

Frame by Frame (1996) Breasts, Bush
Species (1995) RB
Death Dreams (1991) Nip Slip RB

Charlotte J. Helmkamp

Born: January 27, 1961
Omaha, Nebraska
Skin-O-Meter: Great Nudity

Charlotte J. Helmkamp has a great set of lungs. The brunette was a competitive swimmer as a teenager, making the Junior Olympic team as a two-time AAU state champion in Iowa. Surprisingly, with such a chest full of talent, Charlotte didn't break out onto the acting scene until several years later, when she took the skinful lead part in the straight-to-video release *Posed for Murder* (1989). She proved that her water-tested boobs were the real deal, as she played the part of a nude model. Thus the clever title and the even more appealing (and Charlotte does some nice peeling) nudity. She's seen in various states of undress throughout the film, so be sure to check it out. Charlotte also briefly bared her bosom in *Frankenhooker* (1990) as one of the prostitutes who James Lorinz hires to complete his girlfriend's body. We're guessing he took her tits.

SKIN-fining Moment:

Posed for Murder (0:22) Charlotte poses for a pervy photog, changing from green lingerie, to a captains hat, to just a thong with her nude nabobs looking swell throughout.

See Her Naked In:

Frankenhooker (1990) Breasts
Posed for Murder (1989) Breasts, Thong
Numerous *Playboy* Videos

Margaux Hemingway

Born: February 19, 1955
Portland, Oregon.
Died: July 2, 1996
Skin-O-Meter: Brief Nudity

Margaux Hemingway had the appearance of a picture-perfect life. The gorgeous granddaughter of Ernest Hemingway, she was one of the most successful models of the 1970s. With her statuesque, six-foot frame and classic facial features, she appeared in high-profile magazines (including the cover of *Time*) and was the spokesperson for Faberge, promoting a fragrance appropriately titled Babe. In 1976 Margaux starred in her first film, *Lipstick*, with her younger sister Mariel Hemingway. Although Marg showed the precious family jewels, the movie wasn't well received. She appeared in other forgettable roles over the years, in films such as *Killer Fish* (1979) and *They Call Me Bruce?* (1982). She flashed flesh in *Inner Sanctum* (1991) and in *Playboy* off and on but could never duplicate the success of modeling. Margaux grew bitter as her career tanked, while sister Mariel gained popularity, appearing in high-profile films like Woody Allen's *Manhattan* (1979). Like her Grand Papa, Margaux suffered from severe bouts of depression, along with epilepsy and eating disorders, and turned to drugs and alcohol for comfort. Her publicized carousing and intoxication landed her a term in the Betty Ford Clinic in 1988, with short-term success. After attempts to parlay her new sobriety into a career, this literary legacy was reduced to autographing X-rated trading cards and taking calls as a psychic-network operator. Perhaps predicting her own bleak future, Margaux took her life on July 22, 1996, by an overdose of barbiturates, cementing her legacy in the suicidal family tradition of her grandfather, his sister, and his father before him.

SKIN-fining Moment:

Lipstick (0:11) Super-quick nippage when Margaux reaches out of the shower to answer the phone.

See Her Naked In:

Double Obsession (1993) RB
Inner Sanctum (1991) Breasts, Buns
Lipstick (1976) Breasts, Bush, Buns

Mariel Hemingway

Born: November 22, 1961
Mill Valley, California
Skin-O-Meter: Hall of Fame

Best known as the granddaughter of Ernest Hemingway, six-foot-tall sexpot Mariel Hemingway made her own name as the May in Woody Allen's May–December relationship in *Manhattan* (1979). Mariel's sweet, tender appeal makes men of all ages want to run through the streets to stop her from leaving us. In addition to male relationships, Mariel has quite an impressive biography. She became a legend among lesbos when she starred as a track athlete in *Personal Best* (1982). Her training in the film included jumping into the sheets with her butch female track pal, Patricia Donnely, and indulging in some (off-camera) sixty-nine during the '76 Olympics. Mariel's mams were expanded from a pert thirty-two to a plump thirty-six inches for her role as former *Playboy* bunny Dorothy Stratten in *Star 80* (1983). A mature Mariel again went girl crazy in *The Sex Monster* (1999). After a three-way with her husband, Hemingway happily humped, bumped, grinded, and licked every pretty girl that crossed her path.

SKIN-fining Moment:

Star 80 (0:24) Celebrated silicone-sackage as Mariel participates in an impromptu photo shoot.

See Her Naked In:

Fourplay (2001) LB
The Celluloid Closet (1996) Breasts, Bush
The Mean Season (1985) Breasts
Creator (1985) Breasts
Star 80 (1983) Breasts
Personal Best (1982) FFN

TeleVisions:

Tales from the Crypt LB

Florence Henderson

**Born: February 14, 1934
Dale, Indiana
Skin-O-Meter: Never Nude**

Florence Henderson is the mom everyone wanted to have—so they could peek in on the pixie blonde beauty as she bathed . . . and maybe get an intimate lesson on the birds and the bees. As Carol Brady on the hit sitcom *The Brady Bunch*, Florence, with her flip 'do and mod minis, was a wholesome heartthrob for primetime. But that role, which also made her a camp icon, was only a launching pad for a career still going strong today. Florence exposed her sense of humor as Shakes's one-night stand in *Shakes the Clown* (1992), played the Amish wife opposite Weird Al Yankovic in his "Amish Paradise" video, and appeared in a cameo in *The Naked Gun 33⅓: The Final Insult* (1994). Unfortunately, she has never appeared nude on film or otherwise. (Some claim that she even has sex with her clothes on.) At any rate, the best look at Big Flo is in *Brady Home Movies* (2000), in which there is a scene where she is bent over in a bathing suit with her legs spread wide. If it hadn't been grainy 8mm film, we may have been able to make out some camel toe. As it is, that's all the footage we've got to hump.

SKIN-fining Moment:

Brady Home Movies (0:21) Swimsuit-clad Mrs. Brady cavorts in the Hawaiian surf, splashing about and bending over with her butt toward the camera. It'll put a Bunch in your pants.

Lori Jo Hendrix

**Born: September 17, 1970
California
Skin-O-Meter: Great Nudity**

"Hey, Joe." This is one "Foxy Lady," eh? It sure would be great to make your way through some "Cross Town Traffic" to get to her "Red House" for a "Little Wing" by the "Fire" on a "Long Hot Summer Night." All right, so Lori Jo Hendrix is no relation to guitar legend Jimi Hendrix, but she still makes some beautiful music for the eyes. Lori Jo is one hot mama who specializes in showing off her incredibly bang-a-licious body, sans clothes of course, in all its top-heavy heaviness. Her paramount pair has to be seen to be believed in such cinematic classics as *A Sensuous Summer* (1991), *Sunset Strip* (1992), *Prison Heat* (1993), and *Babewatch Dream Dolls* (2002), among a host of others. She even had an uncredited role in the blockbuster *XXX* (2002), which was a Vin Diesel vehicle, not hardcore pornography. Let's hope we'll always have Lori Jo's sexadelic tunes in our head.

SKIN-fining Moment:

Prison Heat (0:49) Awesome full frontal when she gets totally nude for the Warden in the shower stall.

See Her Naked In:

Heavenly Hooters (2003) FFN, Buns
Stolen Hearts (1997) Breasts, Thong
Solitaire (1996) Breasts, Bush
Prison Heat (1993) FFN, Buns
Starlet Screen Test III (1992) Breasts
Sunset Strip (1992) Breasts, Thong
A Sensuous Summer (1991) Breasts, Buns

Gloria Hendry

**Born: March 3, 1949
Jacksonville, Florida
Skin-O-Meter: Brief Nudity**

This former *Playboy* Bunny began her career in respected Hollywood films like *For Love of Ivy* (1968), but Gloria Hendry soon moved on to some of the best roles written for women in blaxploitation. Gloria's gazongas helped turn *Black Caesar* (1972) into a genre-spawning classic, and the film's success led to her becoming a brazenly bikinied Bond girl in *Live and Let Die* (1973). Gloria then discovered that the only decent roles for black women were still offered in grindhouse hits such as *Slaughter's Big Rip-Off* (1973) and *Hell Up in Harlem* (1973). Sexy epics like *Savage Sisters* (1974) helped establish Gloria as both a fine actress and a foxy mama. She only managed a few TV roles between 1978 and *Doin' Time on Planet Earth* in 1988, but now Gloria's a respected character actress who, sadly, has put public nudity behind her.

SKIN-fining Moment:

Black Caesar (0:43) Fred "The Hammer" Williamson rips open Gloria's nightgown and her whammer-jammers shake about as she struggles against him.

See Her Naked In:

Black Caesar (1973) FFN, Buns
Slaughter's Big Rip-Off (1973) Breasts

Marilu Henner

**Born: April 6, 1952
Chicago, Illinois
Skin-O-Meter: Great Nudity**

Mammadocious Marilu Henner's future loomed bright when she debuted her honking headlights on the hit series *Taxi*. This ravishing redhead's pointedly braless and bouncy appearance as the only female among a heard of randy cabbies sent engines racing on and offscreen (she dated co-stars Judd Hirsch and Tony Danza during the show's run) and helped fuel *Taxi* through five seasons. During Henner's heyday, her mondo mams revved up Hollywood's horniest A-list actors. She had sessions in the bullpen with *Urban Cowboy* John Travolta and was rumored to have let Burt Reynolds take a crack at her burning bush. At the very least, bad boy Burt got to see Marilu's beautific breasts (and you can too) in all their puffy peach glory during their love scene in *The Man Who Loved Women* (1983). Before *Taxi*, this top-heavy temptress stopped traffic as a stripper in *Between the Lines* (1977), wearing only tiny star-shaped orange pasties to cover her sweet melons. Over the years Marilu has had small parts (sadly, not featuring her whoppingly large chest parts) in feature films such as *Cannonball Run II* (1984), *Johnny Dangerously* (1984), and *L.A. Story* (1991). She also appeared with Reynolds yet again on the series *Evening Shade*. Today she chooses to focus on promoting self-help books that illustrate how she's been able to keep her remarkable beauty through diet and exercise.

SKIN-fining Moment:

The Man Who Loved Women (0:18) Marilu shows her matching headlights when lying in bed with Burt Reynolds, then shows them again, complete with upper butt-crack and a glimpse of boosh as she gets out of bed!

See Her Naked In:

The Man Who Loved Women (1983) Breasts, Bush, Buns
Between the Lines (1977) Breasts

Pamela Hensley

Born: October 3, 1950
Los Angeles, California
Skin-O-Meter: Brief Nudity

There was no shortage of contract girls making the rounds of '70s television, but Pamela Hensley stood out amongst the field. She got a lot of hype in 1975 when she was cast to marry James Brolin's character on the hit ABC show *Marcus Welby, M.D.* She also looked set to break out as James Caan's love interest in *Rollerball* (1975). Instead the trained actress went on to a long career of shining in bad sitcoms and TV movies—oh, and there are still lots of aging sci-fi fans with very, very fond memories of her as Princess Ardala on the 1979 series *Buck Rogers in the 25th Century*. But she certainly made a memorable big-screen debut in *There Was a Crooked Man* (1970), in which Pamela—along with veteran actress Jeanne Cooper—helped break the Hollywood skin barrier by showing her tits in a big-studio Western (starring Henry Fonda, no less). Thank you, Pamela Hensley!

SKIN-fining Moment:

There Was a Crooked Man (0:12) Brief breast canoodling on a pool table with some side-shooter.

See Her Naked In:

There Was a Crooked Man (1970) LB

Taraji P. Henson

Washington, D.C.
Skin-O-Meter: Brief Nudity

Black is beautiful, but Taraji P. Henson is so hot Mr. Skin needs to come up with a better word to describe her booty-liciousness. Something like boobiful or blacktacular. Any way you say it, the Washington, D.C., native is one hot property. She graduated from Howard University and began her professional career with a part on the WB comedy *Smart Guy*. But it was her star turn (and skin turn) opposite Tyrese Gibson and Snoop Dogg in the John Singleton feature film *Baby Boy* (2001) that really made pants stand up and take notice. Her ebony boobs nearly got the black banged off of them in a real hard 'ho down. Taraji continues to show off her finery on TV, co-starring in a CBS *Murder She Wrote* movie called *The Last Free Man* (2001), and she got devilish in *Satan's School for Girls* (2000) with Shannon Doherty and ex-*Charlie's Angels* star Kate Jackson. She's also appeared on *ER*, *Felicity*, and *Sister, Sister*. But let's hope she leaves the boob tube for the boob-friendly big screen again soon.

SKIN-fining Moment:

Baby Boy (0:41) Bouncing boobs abound as Taraji gets her hole handily drilled by tough-guy Tyrese.

See Her Naked In:

Baby Boy (2001) Breasts

Natasha Henstridge

Born: August 15, 1974
Springdale, Newfoundland, Canada
Skin-O-Meter: Hall of Fame

Out-of-this-world Natasha Henstridge left a Canadian trailer park to pursue a career in modeling. She then went from mannequin to man-eater, skyrocketing to skinternational fame in *Species* (1995) and *Species II* (1998). Watch out boy, because Natasha wants to nosh ya in the *Species* series, as a sex-crazed extraterrestrial who eats

NATASHA HENSTRIDGE: SEE THESE IN *SPECIES!*

her mates just after they give her the ultimate pleasure. Luckily she shows her ample extraterrestrials and celestial body throughout both flicks. On a 1997 episode of *The Outer Limits* called *Bits of Love*, 'Tasha plays a computer program designed to ride men's hard drives. Her massive Canadian Mounties will poison your mind in *Bela Dona* (1998). To see handfuls of Natasha's knockable ass, check out *Second Skin* (2000), in which she shows off her bodacious bottom in great length getting out of a bath.

SKIN-fining Moment:

Species (1:22) Natasha lets her hooters out one last time for a ride on the Alfred Molina Express. It's all very sexy until she starts sprouting alien thorns out of her spine! Ew!

See Her Naked In:

Riders (2002) Body Double—Breasts, Buns
Power and Beauty (2002) RB
Second Skin (2000) Buns
Caracara (2000) Breasts
Species II (1998) Breasts, Buns
Bela Donna (1998) Breasts, Bush
Maximum Risk (1996) Breasts, Thong
Species (1995) Breasts, Bush

TeleVisions:

Outer Limits Breasts

Barbara Hershey

Born: February 5, 1948
Hollywood, California
Skin-O-Meter: Hall of Fame

She went through high school as a pom-pom girl, but Barbara Hershey graduated to become cinema's favorite naked hippie. Her wholesome early roles quickly gave way to naked displays in *Last Summer* (1969), *The Baby Maker* (1970), and *Boxcar Bertha* (1972). And don't miss Barbara's definitive display of free love in *Dealing: Or the Berkeley-to-Boston Forty-Brick*

Lost-Bag Blues* (1972). Improbably, Barbara then emerged as a serious actress in the '80s, thanks to her great performance in the intellectual ghost story *The Entity* (1983). [Her ghostly sex scenes would later be parodied by Tori Spelling in *Scary Movie 2* (2001).] Critical acclaim can't keep Barbara's clothes on, though, and she showed off a very sexy maturity in *The Last Temptation of Christ* (1988) and *Drowning on Dry Land* (1999).

SKIN-fining Moment:

Boxcar Bertha (0:52) Babs boinks her boyfriend on the floor. She's completely nude and we see her boobs, buns, and a brief view of Bertha's box.

See Her Naked In:

Drowning on Dry Land (1999) Breasts, Bush
The Last Temptation of Christ (1988) Breasts, Buns
The Entity (1981) Body Double—FFN, Buns
The Stunt Man (1980) LB, Buns
Dealing: Or the Berkeley-to-Boston Forty-Brick Lost-Bag Blues (1972) Breasts
Boxcar Bertha (1972) Breasts, Bush, Buns
The Pursuit of Happiness (1971) Breasts, Buns
Last Summer (1969) Breasts

Sandra Hess

Born: March 27, 1968
Zürich, Switzerland
Skin-O-Meter: Great Nudity

Since it's a Pauly Shore film, everybody probably felt it made perfect sense to cast a Swiss model as a cavegirl in *Encino Man* (1992). Sandra Hess still made her role seem believable—or, at the very least, made the film worth seeing in theaters. Sandra then established herself as a true rising star in *Endangered* (1994), in which she endangerd our zippers once the Swiss Miss got our marshmallows toasting. She kept her clothes on

for *Mortal Kombat: Annihilation* (1997), but her sexy outfit still got us working our joysticks. And don't miss her amazing turn as a femme fatale in the underrated TV movie *Nick Fury: Agent of S.H.I.E.L.D.* (1998). Her icy reserve also came to play in her role as Lieutenant Alexandra "Ice" Jensen on the syndicated series *Pensacola: Wings of Gold*. Sadly, Sandra has recently been keeping a lower profile, concentrating on journalism with her "Hollywood Report" column for a Swiss magazine.

SKIN-fining Moment:

Endangered (0:25) Sandra shows her firm floaters as she splashes about in a lake, followed by some stunning butt as she climbs out, then another rack-flash as she puts on a shirt.

See Her Naked In:

Endangered (1994) Breasts, Buns

Jennifer Hetrick

Born: 1958
Westerville, Ohio
Skin-O-Meter: Brief Nudity

Juicy Jennifer Hetrick is breast known for playing the lovely lunged lawyer wife to the snarly "Arnie Becker" on *L.A. Law*. No mentally competent crotch chaser would ever object to Jenny's jutting jugs in tight, tit-popping power suits throughout her stint as the most alluring of attorneys. An eyeful throughout the '80s and '90s, Jen was most sinful on the short-lived torpedo-teasing TV series *Bodies of Evidence* and in flesh flicks such as the tit-tilating teaser *Squeeze Play* (1980). If lusting after Hetrick's heavy hoots is a crime, Mr. Skin is guilty as sin.

SKIN-fining Moment:

Squeeze Play (0:02) See Jennifer's naked hooters get honked during an opening-credits sex scene. Ah-ooooh-gah!

See Her Naked In:

Squeeze Play (1980) Breasts

Lori Heuring

Born: April 6, 1976
Panama
Skin-O-Meter: Brief Nudity

It's hard to get as much hype as Lori Heuring and still be a relatively unknown actress—but at least this lithesome blonde beauty still has a rabid fan base among men who drooled over her as Miss December in *Maxim*'s 2001 calendar. Lori's biggest role to date was as the heroine of the teen thriller *The In Crowd* (2000), which flopped at the box office but provided a firm look at Lori's bra-clad bod. Then it was back to under-seen epics such as *True Blue* (2001), in which Lori's sexy outfits turn our cocks true purple. And don't miss her role as a beautiful-when-she's-angry Hollywood gal in *Mulholland Dr.* (2001). Her roles are getting smaller, but Lori's still got plenty of years to live up to her blonde ambition.

SKIN-fining Moment:

True Blue (0:59) Lori sashays into a fat guy's bedroom in her black bra and panties, and we get a lightning-quick view of nip when she slips into the sack.

See Her Naked In:

True Blue (2001) LB

Jennifer Love Hewitt

Born: February 21, 1979
Waco, Texas
Skin-O-Meter: Brief Nudity

Jennifer Love Hewitt, affectionately called Jennifer Love Huge-Tits, came by her anatomically accurate nickname as she soared to stardom on Fox's *Party of Five* in the '90s. While still electrifying as a boob-tube tease—check out the often rerun *VH1's 100 Greatest Love Songs* from 2002—Jen has also ignited the big screen with her enormous talents. She provided the screams and launched a million cream dreams in *I Know What You Did Last Summer* (1997), and Mr. Skin knows what you did when you were alone with a copy of that flick on video. She also flashed pantie in *The Suburbans* (1999) and nearly burst through her barely-there wardrobe in *Heartbreakers* (2001). Alas, in the Jackie Chan flick *The Tuxedo* (2002), Jen finally supplied the nip slip that we've all lustfully longed for. Yes, it's underwater and it's barely visible, but Mr. Skin is eternally grateful, Jugs—uh, Jen.

SKIN-fining Moment:

The Tuxedo (1:01) Jennifer Love lets one of those sweet little nips slip during an underwater struggle. Bad news for the editors . . . Great news for us!

See Her Naked In:

The Tuxedo (2002) Nip Slip RB

Virginia Hey

Born: June 19, 1962
Sydney, Australia
Skin-O-Meter: Brief Nudity

Virginia Hey is most well known for her role as Pa'u Zotoh Zhaan on the TV series *Farscape*. She quit the show after three seasons, tiring of shaving her head and wearing full-body makeup that put a strain on her kidneys. Being from Down Under, her first big break came in *Mad Max 2: The Road Warrior* (1981) with Mel Gibson, in which she played the warrior bitch who gave Mel such a hard time. She has also appeared in *Castaway* (1987) and the ill-fated TV series *Dolphin Cove*.

Her most revealing role to date was in *The Living Daylights* (1987), when the camera very unintentionally caught a side view of her left breast as she spun away from a gun-wielding maniac. You can also get a damned good look at her butt on an episode or two of *Farscape*, though it's smothered in odd-colored makeup, if that's your thing. But for Virginia that ain't Hey.

SKIN-fining Moment:

The Living Daylights (1:10) Timothy Dalton uses Virginia to bamboozle a bad guy and we see the side of her left Hey-Hey.

See Her Naked In:

Bullet Down Under (1994) Breasts
Pathos—segreta inquietudine (1988) Breasts, Bush, Buns
The Living Daylights (1987) LB

Anne Heywood

Born: December 11, 1932
Handsworth, England
Skin-O-Meter: Great Nudity

Anne Heywood is the redheaded, big-breasted beauty who gave the English stiff upper lips (among other things) when she was crowned Miss Great Britain in 1949. She took her award-winning body to the big screen with a bit part in *Lady Godiva Rides Again* (1951). And ride she did, with a career spanning nearly forty years with over thirty films under her belt—and who wouldn't want to join them there. She mostly played the good girl in a variety of British, Italian, and German cinema productions, but she has a fairly low profile in America. Anne hasn't been nude all that often in film. She did star as one of the lesbian lovers in *The Fox* (1967) but showed little skin. It was finally her turn in *The Shaming* (1979), in which viewers got to gaze at her plump British breasts and glaze their pants in the process. But it was during a rape scene, which kills the erotic charge. Far better was her exposure in *Ring of Darkness* (1979), in which she played some kind of topless superhero who hangs out with naked ladies. Heywood, it's never too late to show off your mature mams and make our wood hard again.

SKIN-fining Moment:

The Fox (10:00) Anne oils her naked self up in front of a mirror. Multiple breast and bun views ensue in this pioneering nude number.

See Her Naked In:

Ring of Darkness (1979) Breasts
The Shaming (1979) Breasts
La Monaca di Monza (1969) Breasts
The Fox (1968) Breasts, Buns

Catherine Hickland

Born: February 11, 1956
Fort Lauderdale, Florida
Skin-O-Meter: Brief Nudity

Catherine Hickland is married to Michael E. Knight of *All My Children* fame and was once married to David Hasselhoff, who played Michael Knight on talking-car TV hit *Knight Rider* and may be better known for leading a bunch of bathing beauties on *Baywatch*. But Catherine deserves some recognition for her alluring body of work. She's a TV sensation of a sexier sort, with a career on the small screen in daytime soaps. She has been on *Loving, The City, Capitol, The Bold and the Beautiful,* and most recently *One Life to Live*. It was her part—or more specifically her two parts—in *Sweet Justice* (1992), however, that made Mr. Skin's joystick stand up and take notice. Catherine's boobtastic chest lounges in a pool, topless, with her tits floating just under the surface of the water. Sweet Justice, indeed.

SKIN-fining Moment:

Sweet Justice (0:52) Sweet T&A as Cathy enters the hot tub and joins in on the chatty nudefest.

See Her Naked In:

Sweet Justice (1992) Breasts, Buns
Millions (1991) Body Double—Buns

Catherine Hicks

Born: August 6, 1951
Scottsdale, Arizona
Skin-O-Meter: Great Nudity

Catherine Hicks started out giving Ryan hope on the daytime soap *Ryan's Hope* prior to landing the role of Bill Murray's fiancée in *The Razor's Edge* (1984), which offered this blonde honey's first skin. Horror geeks remember her fondly for being the lucky mom who bought Chucky for her son in the original *Child's Play* (1988), and she is most recognizable as the upstanding MILF on *7th Heaven*. But back to her skin appearances—they are brief but worth a wank in *Fever Pitch* (1985) and *Laguna Heat* (1987). You can also see her in a variety of ill-fitting bras in *Eight Days a Week* (1997). No one can call Catherine some country Hicks.

SKIN-fining Moment:

Laguna Heat (1:05) Brief boobage as she gets banged by Harry Hamlin in bed. Dark. Damn.

See Her Naked In:

Laguna Heat (1987) Breasts, Buns
Fever Pitch (1985) LB
The Razor's Edge (1984) LB

Ahmo Hight

Born: TK
Newport Beach, California
Skin-O-Meter: Great Nudity

Ahmo Hight looks vaguely like Sarah Jessica Parker. But unlike the *Sex and the City* star, Ahmo likes to get naked and has appeared in such sexual fare as *Hotel Exotica* (1998), *Club Wildside 2* (1998), *Secret Pleasures* (1999), and *Insatiable Wives* (1999). The latter is a softcore homage to *It's a Wonderful Life* (1946), although it's doubtful the networks will be airing it at Christmastime. She is delightfully nude in all of these films, as well as in *Anna Nicole Smith Exposed: Her Fantasy Revealed* (1998), in which she plays Anna's maid and gets a titty licking from the big-ass queen herself. It's good to be the queen.

SKIN-fining Moment:

Anna Nicole Smith Exposed: Her Fantasy Revealed (0:25) Ahmo shows her juggos and sucks good nipples in a tub with nude-and-lesbo-lovin'-it Anna Nichole Smith. Hugely awesome.

See Her Naked In:

Restless Souls (2001) Breasts, Bush, Buns
Animal Attraction (2000) Breasts
Animal Attraction II (1999) Breasts, Thong
Secret Pleasures (1999) Breasts, Buns
Club Wildside 2 (1998) FFN, Buns
Hotel Exotica (1998) Breasts, Bush, Buns
Anna Nicole Smith Exposed: Her Fantasy Revealed (1998) Breasts, Buns

Mariana Hill

Born: February 9, 1941
Santa Barbara, California
Skin-O-Meter: Great Nudity

Mariana Hill moved around a lot as a kid, which helped her to play so many exotic beauties with foreign accents and led to her being cast as so many darkly attractive out-of-towners. Her delicious Mediterranean looks didn't hurt either. She landed her first major role in *El Condor* (1970), in which we get a lovely full-frontal view of her physiological assets. Mariana is probably most recognizable for her role in *The Godfather* saga as Fredo's sexy wife Deanna Corleone. For another look at Mariana's sweet tits, check out *Medium Cool* (1969). In it, we see her breasts from the side as she thrashes about in bed. Unfortunately, through all the mayhem she manages to cover up her bush. Let's hope she's not too over the Hill for an encore.

SKIN-fining Moment:

Medium Cool (0:36) Sometimes climbing a Hill can be fun—just ask Robert Forster, who gets to hump Mariana Hill after chasing her all over the apartment, butt naked. Nothing's hidden, bush fans!

See Her Naked In:

Schizoid (1980) LB
Thumb Tripping (1972) Breasts
El Condor (1970) FFN, Buns
Medium Cool (1969) FFN, Buns

Raelee Hill

Born: October 24, 1972
Brisbane, Australia
Skin-O-Meter: Brief Nudity

Raelee Hill is best known as one of the sexy out-of-this-world creatures that inhabit the sci-fi TV hit *Farscape*. But she almost didn't get on the series as Sikozu. Originally the redheaded hottie auditioned for the very different role of Utu-Noranti Pralatong. When that went to Melissa Jaffer, the show's producers decided to create a role especially for raunchy Raelee because she'd impressed them so much. This Australian actress has had a swift rise to fame in her own country, with a number of recurring parts on Oz's top programs, including playing Serendipity Gottlieb on *Neighbours* and Constable Tayler Johnson on *Water Rats*. But her breast role to date has to be *Hotel de Love* (1996), in which Raelee exposed her freckled Hills. That's a hotel everybody needs to check out!

SKIN-fining Moment:

Hotel de Love (0:08) Red-maned Raelee strips her top off to expose her tiny-nipped na-nas and leaps on her lad.

See Her Naked In:

Hotel de Love (1996) Breasts

Teresa Hill

Born: May 9, 1969
Burley, Idaho
Skin-O-Meter: Brief Nudity

Teresa Hill was using her svelte brunette body to land a variety of TV commercials when she was hired as Linda Holden (and wouldn't we all love to hold her), one of the mannequins on the failed Aaron Spelling drama *Models Inc*. After that lust opportunity, Teresa moved on to straight-to-video fare. And she landed some big-budget productions, such as the Pauly Shore vehicle *Bio-Dome* (1996) and critic's-darling pictures such as *Twin Falls Idaho* (1999)—appropriate for the twin-titted wonder from Idaho. The boob tube's siren call had her landing on *Melrose Place* for a season. She has also appeared in two *Puppet Master* movies, and her puppets make viewers want to masturbate. But it's her role in the Roger Corman-produced *In the Heat of Passion II: Unfaithful* (1994) that featured her sexiest and most revealing scenes to date. Most recently she appeared in *The New Women* (2001), a black-and-white post-apocalyptic thriller featuring über-lesbian Jenny Shimizu. It's only a matter of time before Teresa exposes her heavenly Hills again.

SKIN-fining Moment:

In the Heat of Passion II: Unfaithful (0:20) Teresa rolls over in bed with Barry Bostwick and we get a lightning-quick glimpse of her left Hill.

See Her Naked In:

In the Heat of Passion II: Unfaithful (1994) Breasts, Buns

Paris Hilton

Born: February 17, 1981
New York City, New York
Skin-O-Meter: Great Nudity

Superhumanly statuesque and blonder-than-blonde, Paris Hilton is named after the City of Lights, but her favorite color is pink, which she's been flashing with her younger sister Nicky Hilton since they got out of diapers. Heiress to the Hilton hotel fortune, Paris is the ultimate party girl, famous for her topless table dancing at New York and Los Angeles hotspots. For her twenty-first birthday, she threw five parties for herself in New York, Las Vegas, London, Hollywood, and Tokyo, going legal with a bang. But the 34-25-35 beauty—who's both waifish and Amazonian at the same time—had already done some big banging on a sex tape leaked to the Internet and then marketed to the masses as *1 Night in Paris*. In the debaucherous documentary, the then nineteen-year-old sexy socialite is displayed every which way *and* loose with her ex-boyfriend, thirty-year-old Rick Solomon, Shannen Doherty's estranged husband. Oh, what a tawdry web they weave! But Paris has been skingy outside of magazine spreads. She's made some guest appearances on the boob tube and has a certified hit with the reality show *The Simple Life*, along with celebrity offspring pal Nicole Richie. Both rich bitches look fine in little more than low-hung hip huggers and tube tops, but Paris has yet to make her hotly anticipated skin debut onscreen. She had cameos in the John Holmes biopic *Wonderland*

(2003) and *The Cat in the Hat* (2003), but she's yet to show her pussy in a Hollywood production. Nonetheless, judging from the hardcore skinthusiasm on display throughout *1 Night in Paris*, we can all still hope that wild-child Hilton's doors will remain open to the possibility of more poon-shows.

SKIN-fining Moment:

1 Night in Paris (1:10) Paris puts her money where her mouth is—and that's a lot of assets. It's too much for her narrow lips to hold, so her boyfriend breaks the bank and spews loose change all over Paris's eyeful towers.

See Her Naked In:

1 Night in Paris (2004) FFN, Buns

Robyn Hilton

Born: 1940
Los Angeles, CA
Skin-O-Meter: Great Nudity

Robyn Hilton is such a video vixen that she starred in the movie *Video Vixen* (1975). The film is a sexy comedy like *The Kentucky Fried Movie* (1977) before there was such a thing and with a lot more skin. The busty lady of humor may be moist mamorable as Mel Brooks's bra-busting, redheaded gal pal Miss Stein in *Blazing Saddles* (1974). Oddly enough, in spite of all her screwball comedy roles in otherwise skinful movies, Robyn's been something of an anomaly. Somehow she remained fully clothed in such pictures as *The Single Girls* (1973), *The Last Porno Flick* (1974), and *Malibu Express* (1985). Her ample cleavage in the Maid Marian outfit from the latter feature more than made up for the lack of out-and-out nudity. Robyn is a bird of many feathers, but she really takes off when we see what's behind the plumage.

SKIN-fining Moment:

Mean Mother (0:53) An extreme close-up of Robyn's rack is seen when Dobie Gray takes her bikini top off at gunpoint by the side of the road. Right on, brother!

See Her Naked In:

Malibu Express (1985) RB
Video Vixens (1975) Breasts
Mean Mother (1973) Breasts

Iben Hjejle

Born: March 22, 1971
Copenhagen, Denmark
Skin-O-Meter: Great Nudity

Iben Hjejle has a last name that cannot be pronounced without an extra vocal cord. But they manage to sing its praises in her native Denmark, where she's a big name. Sadly, she hasn't really made a big splash in the United States . . . yet. She has been acting since 1996 and plays the hooker-cum-housewife in the third official Dogma film *Mifune* (1999). But it was her role in *High Fidelity* (2000) that piqued interest here at Skin Central. In it, she plays John Cusack's "number-one breakup, Laura." There is a great scene that features Iben and Tim Robbins doing the nasty dance, showing us a little of Iben's skin, but not enough—is there ever enough? Hunt out the short foreign film *Nøgen* (1991), where Iben sheds her clothing in a dimly lit scene. If you look closely, you see that she really isn't all blonde, but she is all woman!

SKIN-fining Moment:

High Fidelity (0:34) During John Cusack's fantasy, Iben bares partial party-bobbins while being defiled by Tim Robbins.

See Her Naked In:

High Fidelity (2000) Buns
Nøgen (1991) FFN

Kate Hodge

Born: January 2, 1966
Berkeley, California
Skin-O-Meter: Brief Nudity

From a one shot on the TV drama *thirtysomething* to a slew of sexy appearances on the syndicated hit *Silk Stalkings*, Kate Hodge and her pendulous pair have given new meaning to the term boob tube. The sexy brunette launched into the horror genre on the big screen and became a reluctant scream queen after making her debut in *Leatherface: Texas Chainsaw Massacre III* (1990). She claims to hate scary movies but next found herself starring on the frightening TV series *She-Wolf of London*. With *Rapid Fire* (1992), she attempted to leave the blood and guts behind and expose her more sensual side. It was her first skin onscreen, and it's a walloping scene. The sight of her meaty chest is enough to bring out the monster in a viewer's pants. Continuing the carnal trend, Kate let her big girls out to play in *Desire* (1993) and forever abandoned her beastly career. Sadly, when not being scared stiff, she went a bit limp with short runs on failed sitcoms such as *The George Wendt Show*—which Wendt pretty quick indeed—*The Louie Show*, and *Working*. If Kate wants to repair the Hodge-podge of her career, Mr. Skin suggests she return to the gory origins of her professional life. There's always room for another bosomy beauty in the terror tales.

SKIN-fining Moment:

Desire (1:02) Kate heats up with her man in the sack, going from bra to bare-bazoomed quite nicely.

See Her Naked In:

Desire (1993) LB
Rapid Fire (1992) RB

Susanna Hoffs

Born: January 17, 1959
Newport Beach, California
Skin-O-Meter: Never Nude

Susanna Hoffs, who is a founding member of the newly resurrected girl group The Bangles, got her big acting break in mommy Tamar Simon Hoffs's movie *Stony Island* (1978). No surprise then that she should have the lead role in Tamar's college-girl picture *The Allnighter* (1987). Since she is married to producer/director Jay Roach, it is also no surprise that he cast her in his blockbuster *Austin Powers: International Man of Mystery* (1997) and its sequels as Ming Tea, who plays in Austin's band. It pays to be beautiful and know people in high places. Susanna has woefully never been nude on film or otherwise. She did have some sexy scenes in *The Allnighter*, though. In one, she is seen in her skivvies, fixing her hair, and in another wearing a very flattering swimsuit. But Susanna Hoffs to get nude soon, or Mr. Skin will explode!

SKIN-fining Moment:

The Allnighter (0:40) Susanna primps in front of a mirror while wearing just a bippy top and tight li'l panties. I'd Bangle her!

Sarah Holcomb

Born: 1960
Skin-O-Meter: Brief Nudity

Sarah Holcomb first ignited Mr. Skin's fire with her turn as Maggie O'Hooligan in the comedy classic *Caddyshack* (1980). She also had the lead female role in the Robbie Benson picture *Walk Proud* (1979), about gang life in Chicago. Sarah's career faltered after her role in *Happy Birthday, Gemini* (1980) with Madeline Kahn, and, sadly, this energetic cutie hasn't been seen

since. For those of you who would like to see a little more of Sarah, check out *Animal House* (1978), the fraternity-life classic from the nice people at *National Lampoon*. It was both her screen and skin debut. In it, she played the daughter of the mayor and ended up inexplicably making out with Tom Hulce, who removed her bra only to find it stuffed with tissue. Before she passed out, though, there was a quick glimpse of her jugs. We'll always have *Animal House*, Sarah.

SKIN-fining Moment:

Animal House (0:58) "Fuck her! Fuck her brains out! Suck her tits! Squeeze her buns!" So commands the horny li'l devil on Tom Hulce's shoulder as he surveys Sarah when she's passed out topless in his frathouse bunk, piles of bra-stuffing Kleenex spilled freely on the sheets. One look at Sarah's palatably pubescent nibble-pillows and you'll wonder how he could possibly resist.

See Her Naked In:

Animal House (1978) Breasts

Alexandra Holden

Born: 1977
Northfield, Minnesota
Skin-O-Meter: Brief Nudity

Alexandra Holden is the sweetie who appeared frequently on *Ally McBeal* and *Friends*. She debuted on the TV series *Mr. Rhodes* before moving on to movies such as *In & Out* (1997). She later shook her pom-poms in *Sugar and Spice* (2001) and *Drop Dead Gorgeous* (1999), in which she appeared teste-tinglingly sexy. Since then she's sunken to the depths of B-movie hell, where she will hopefully get naked a lot. *Wishcraft* (2002) marks the beginning of her descent into B-movie obscurity. Sadly, her only skinful turn thus far was on an

episode of the hit HBO series *Six Feet Under*, and, although she was full-frontal in the part, she was also "dead," complete with disgusting autopsy scars running across her beautiful chest. Oh well, beggars can't be choosers, huh? Alexandra will never be penalized for Holden.

SKIN-fining Moment:

*Six Feet Under "In the Game" (2002) The good news: You get to see Ross's coed girlfriend from **Friends** lying on a table full-frontally naked. The bad news: You also get to see all of her autopsy scars.*

TeleVisions:

Six Feet Under Breasts

Marjean Holden

Vail, Colorado
Skin-O-Meter: Great Nudity

Six-foot tall stunningly fit and fine Marjean Holden grew up in Vail, Colorado, so it's no surprise to learn that she's an avid skier. But it's those slopes in her shirt that make for the coolest ride. Marjean is renowned for her figure, one that she keeps strong and shapely with intense workouts of weight training, boxing, and kung fu. She is currently working towards her black belt in wun hop kuen do kung fu, but Mr. Skin prefers her without her belt on. Not long after her debut in *Bill & Ted's Excellent Adventure* (1987), she exposed what an extreme exercise routine can do for a lady. In *Glitch!* (1988) she stripped down to an itsy-bitsy, teeny-weeny bikini, but it was her role as a bump-and-grinder in *Stipped to Kill II* (1989) where Marjean really showed off her perfect form. Her jugs were to die for. She joined Finn Carter, Catherine Hickland, Kathleen Kinmont, and a body double for Michelle McCormick in the hot tub for *Sweet Justice* (1992).

And she is ball-drainingly nice in *Ballistic* (1995). Since then, she's been skingy, but Mr. Skin won't complain after watching her four-armed carnage in *Mortal Kombat 2* (1997) and her bestial performance on the TV series *BeastMaster*. Still, we're Holden on for some more flesh fixes.

SKIN-fining Moment:

Stripped to Kill II (0:17) There's a stage in a strip club. And there are Marjean's breasts gyrating upon it.

See Her Naked In:

Ballistic (1995) Breasts, Buns
Sweet Justice (1992) LB, Buns
Stripped to Kill II (1989) Breasts

Kristina Holland

Born: February 25, 1944
Fayetteville, North Carolina
Skin-O-Meter: Brief Nudity

Kristina Holland was already making the sitcom rounds on such classic TV fare as *Love, American Style* when she landed her breakout role on *The Courtship of Eddie's Father*. Lucky guy, that Bill Bixby, to work so closely with the wide-eyed, buxom brunette beauty. While still on the popular show, though, Kristina put her breast foot forward in the movie *The Strawberry Statement* (1970), and what a sweet statement it was. With its cinematic snapshot of the student college uprisings, it's jam packed with radical politics and even more extreme sex and violence, from blowjobs to Kristina's first and, sadly, only skin scene onscreen. After *Courtship* ended, Kristina worked mostly as a voiceover artist on such TV series as *Wait Till Your Father Gets Home* and *Butch Cassidy and the Sundance Kids*. By the late '70s, Kristina was all but through with the business of show, though she did resurface

doing a voice on *Byzantine: The Betrayal* (1997). Don't be a stranger, Kristina; Mr. Skin would sure like to see how this hippie's hips look now.

SKIN-fining Moment:

The Strawberry Statement (0:12) Kristina trots about topless and naked-tailed, covering her tuft with a towel. Too bad we can't see this Holland's two-lips!

See Her Naked In:

The Strawberry Statement (1970) Breasts, Buns

Xaviera Hollander

Born: June 15, 1942
Surabaya, Indonesia
Skin-O-Meter: Great Nudity

It's said that the brain is the sexiest organ. At Skin Central we'd like to add the voice to that. No, it's not an organ, but when used by Xaviera Hollander it sure perks up our organs! Her sensual tones can get a listener to stand at attention in their pants within moments of her first breathy pant. She landed a coveted Q&A column in *Penthouse* magazine when it was launched, and her "Call Me Madam" has run there for well over twenty years. But she is breast known for her more physical work as a prostitute and madam. In her working prime, Xaviera had a very sellable 38C-27-36½ figure and also a good memory. She exposed her life as a 'ho for hire in the classic novel *The Happy Hooker*. Soon Hollywood came running with *The Happy Hooker* (1975), *The Happy Hooker Goes to Washington* (1977), and *The Happy Hooker Goes Hollywood* (1980). Classics all, but Xaviera was not impressed. She has said you could take your grandmother to these tame adaptations of her carnal career. Xaviera put her

naked body where her mouth was when she starred completely naked in the skintacular *My Pleasure Is My Business* (1975). She played herself, so naturally it's not much of a stretch, but audiences are encouraged to stretch their meat while watching the alluring seductress. You'll be happy you hooked her.

SKIN-fining Moment:

My Pleasure Is My Business (0:14) The Happy Hooker shows her hoots and hairpie as the naked figure in a daydream.

See Her Naked In:

My Pleasure Is My Business (1975) FFN, Buns

Raye Hollitt

Born: April 17, 1964
Wilkes Barre, Pennsylvania
Skin-O-Meter: Brief Nudity

Never has the question "wanna wrestle?" been more appealing than when considering being wedged between Raye Hollitt's creamy, strong thighs. This buxom blonde beauty is most well known for her role as "Zap" on the '80s hit *American Gladiators*, but you might also remember her fabulous frame striking nude body-builder poses for the late John Ritter as Lonnie Jones in Blake Edwards's *Skin Deep* (1989) . . . talk about mudflaps, her buttocks are sublime! For more skintastic peeks at Raye, check out her roles in *Hot Shots! Part Deux* (1993) and *The Last Hour* (1989) with Shannon Tweed. Oh, and last but not least see her jiggle-TV debut as Tina on an episode of *Baywatch*.

SKIN-fining Moment:

Skin Deep (0:27) Raye strips off her bikini for John Ritter and we see her rock-hard ass and some sweet partial titty.

See Her Naked In:

Skin Deep (1989) RB, Buns

Laurel Holloman

Born: May 23, 1971
Chapel Hill, North Carolina
Skin-O-Meter: Great Nudity

Laurel Holloman launched herself into the upper-most echelon of girl-girl greats with the 2004 debut of the Showtime series *The L Word*, on which she plays the pantie-soaking partner of *Flashdance* dazzler Jennifer Beals. These two lovelies made it clear (not-so) straight off that *The L Word* would be a major leap forward in the annals of lezboriffic entertainment, as the opening episode featured Laurel baring bush during a sumptuous skinny-dip scene, followed by graphic Sapphic sex scenes that go on and on and on and only get hotter along the way. But even before all *L* broke loose, Laurel had achieved cinematic lesbian luminary status for her work in *The Incredibly True Adventure of Two Girls in Love* (1995), which included a quick shot of her tits and plenty of chick-on-chick chow-down action. She can also fake some really hot heterosexual sex, as seen by her brazen, bra-clad turn in *Boogie Nights* (1997). Laurel was equally memorable as an enema-loving gal in *Tumbleweeds* (1999), although guys had to wait until *Last Ball* (2001) to see Laurel really unleash her lusciousness. She'll never leave you hollow, man.

SKIN-fining Moment:

The Incredibly True Adventure of Two Girls in Love (1:11) Left tit when Nicole Ari Parker removes her shirt then brief partial nude shots when she moves her hands on her body.

See Her Naked In:

Last Ball (2001)
The First to Go (1997) LB

The Incredibly True Adventure of Two Girls in Love (1995) Breasts

TeleVisions:

The L Word Breasts

Lauren Holly

Born: October 28, 1963
Bristol, Pennsylvania
Skin-O-Meter: Brief Nudity

Any skinatic worthy of the diagnosis yearns to deck his balls with explicit images of a clothing-optional Lauren Holly, but only the most imaginative will be able to do so. Those of us whose devotion to bare facts is less than delusional are forced to make spew with Lauren's moments of skimpy, flimsy, and itty-bitty attire. The Pennsylvania blonde upgraded from working with humorist Andrew "Dice" Clay in *The Adventures of Ford Fairlaine* (1990) to marrying ha-ha man Jim Carrey following the filming of *Dumb and Dumber* (1994), but she's left precious little for chuckleheads-at-large to gawk at. Some experts claim to view quick nipple in *Dragon: The Bruce Lee Story* (1993), and a disputed buttock view graces *Dumber*. Otherwise, Lauren's holly is decked in nightie, lingerie, or bikini.

SKIN-fining Moment:

Dumb and Dumber (0:21) As Lauren hugs Jim Carrey, he lifts up her skirt and—look world!—no panties! Nothing dumb about ogling that dumpling!

See Her Naked In:

Dumb and Dumber (1994) Buns

Jennifer Holmes

Seekonk, Massachusetts
Skin-O-Meter: Great Nudity

Jennifer Holmes started her career with a skin-wonderful role in *The Demon* (1979). The big-breasted beauty immediately caught the carnal attention of the wankensteins at Skin Central with her two topless scenes. With boobs as behemoth as her powerful pair, one glance would have been enough for a lifetime. But two, especially the latter one where she's running around for a very long time with very little on, are what lusty legends are made of. Sadly, it was her only venture into onscreen nudity. Jennifer went on to appear on TV shows such as *Hart to Hart*, *Hawaiian Heat*, and *The Love Boat*, but it was her early-'80s run on *Newhart* that gave her widespread exposure—though not the kind of exposure Mr. Skin likes. After an episode of *Baywatch* in 1993, Jennifer disappeared from the business of show. What a waste; she has so much more to show.

SKIN-fining Moment:

The Demon (1:28) Wearing only panties, Jennifer flees a baddie first by attempting to crawl onto a roof and then, after crashing back down on her bed, running from room to room of a house, bare-rack-first. It's a nice long look at her Holmes, sweet Holmes!

See Her Naked In:

The Demon (1979) Breasts

Katie Holmes

Born: December 18, 1978
Toledo, Ohio
Skin-O-Meter: Great Nudity

Home is where the heart is, but Katie Holmes is where the hard-on is! Katie gave Tobey Maguire an icicle in his pocket in *The Ice Storm* (1997), her film debut. She then turned down the lead on the WB scare-com *Buffy the Vampire Slayer* for the TV hit *Dawson's Creek*. By *Teaching Mrs. Tingle* (1999), Katie was testing the carnal waters with a provocative peek at her brassiered breasts. And *Abandoned* (2000) had Katie abandoning her clothing down to sheer bra and panties. The promise of those teasing glimpses was answered when she finally let her Holmes girls out to play in *The Gift* (2000). Katie is a doomed debutante in a tempting tank top who manages to get topless before she dies. That's the gift that keeps on giving.

SKIN-fining Moment:

The Gift (1:36) Katie pulls her shirt open and bares her large, gravity-mocking mammaries and some skimpy little spankies for Greg Kinnear . . . Sweet Holmes Alabama!

See Her Naked In:

The Gift (2000) Breasts, Thong

Sandrine Holt

**Born: November 19, 1971
England, UK
Skin-O-Meter: Great Nudity**

Beauties don't come much more exotic than five-foot-eleven-inch Sandrine Holt. This glamorous gal first became a star in Canada with *Black Robe* (1991), earning a Canadian Film Academy Award nomination for her role as an Iroquois Indian. The honor was certainly deserved, since Sandrine's character (her boobage was body doubled) spent most of the film topless in a bid for authenticity. Sandrine then went native again while we went bonkers for her boobies in *Rapa Nui* (1994). But she decided to spend the coming years clothed and even graced American television with the John Woo TV movie *Once a Thief* (1996)—and the short-lived series that followed. Sandrine also provided plenty of cheap thrills as a luscious lesbian in *1999* (1998). And it's good to see her making an international bid for stardom, with roles in *Starship Troopers 2: Hero of the Federation* (2004) and *Resident Evil: Apocalypse* (2004).

SKIN-fining Moment:

Rapa Nui (0:12) Sandrine beautifies the outdoors by lying bare-bosomed in the grass with Jason Scott Lee.

See Her Naked In:

Pocahontas, The Legend (1995) Breasts
Rapa Nui (1994) Breasts
Black Robe (1991) Body Double—Breasts

TeleVisions:

Outer Limits Breasts

Leslie Hope

**Born: May 6, 1965
Halifax, Nova Scotia, Canada
Skin-O-Meter: Great Nudity**

Leslie Hope may be from the Great White North, but there's nothing frigid about this shapely igloo. She got her start acting in the U.S. with a two-season stint on the primetime soap *Knots Landing*. She moved on from TV to play the title character in *The Education of Allison Tate* (1986) as well as a meaty role in Oliver Stone's *Talk Radio* (1988). After appearing in the Emilio Estevez/Charlie Sheen sleeper *Men at Work* (1990), she began a career slide, which meant more skin for everyone to enjoy. For some men at wank film works check out a very nude Leslie in *Paris, France* (1993)—ooh-la-la. Leslie played a writer who has a severe case of block until she meets a man in Paris who screws it right out of her. It inspires her—and Mr. Skin, too. *Schemes* (1994) and *Rowing Through* (1996) keep the flesh coming. Hope to see more of you, Leslie.

SKIN-fining Moment:

Paris, France (1:24) In a film packed with full frontals, my favorite is this one, when Leslie's robe opens and out comes her carpet.

See Her Naked In:

Rowing Through (1996) Breasts, Bush, Buns
Schemes (1994) RB
Paris, France (1993) FFN, Buns
Sweet Killing (1993) RB

Kaitlin Hopkins

**Born: February 1, 1964
New York, New York
Skin-O-Meter: Brief Nudity**

It's been a strange career for Kaitlin Hopkins, daughter of Shirley Knight and a talented actress in her own right. She seems to specialize in victims, beginning with her early '90s stint as sexually exploited Dr. Kelsey Harrison on the soaper *Another World*. You'll also find that her nudity in *Little Boy Blue* (1997) occurs during a brutal rape scene. But we're happy to announce that lovely Kaitlin sometimes comes out on top. She's sexually aggressive in a small role in the under-seen *Ted* (1998) and pretty predatory as a horny schoolteacher who compliments Paul Hogan on his ass in *Crocodile Dundee in Los Angeles* (2001). And early in her career, Kaitlin kicked some male ass as an evil succubus who had a satanically sexy coupling in the horror film *Spirits* (1992).

SKIN-fining Moment:

Spirits (0:45) Kaitlin bares the cannage for some "spiritual" sex with her guy, although when things get heated up she turns into a snarling succubus!

See Her Naked In:

Little Boy Blue (1998) RB
Spirits (1990) Breasts

Leslie Horan

**Midway Island, Hawaii
Skin-O-Meter: Brief Nudity**

Plenty of hot young actresses are kept under the sheets once they land a role in soap operas. Leslie Horan's career, though, has included plenty of failed auditions for various soaps. And when this talented beauty finally landed on *General Hospital*, it was only for about a year. But we're not complaining, because Leslie's got too much star power to be hidden away on daytime television. And until she becomes a superstar, Leslie's career can include a few major skindiscretions, such as when she's Horan around with some hot simulated sex in the thriller *Widow's Kiss* (1996).

SKIN-fining Moment:

Widow's Kiss (0:40) While making out with Mackenzie Astin, Leslie loses her bra and we gain a nice look at her breasts.

See Her Naked In:

Widow's Kiss (1994) Breasts

Sacha Horler

Australia
Skin-O-Meter: Great Nudity

Sacha Horler is one sexy piece of heavy thunder from Down Under. A rising star in her native Australia, pretty-faced, poshly padded Sacha has a reputation for taking on bold dramatic roles and delivering skilled performances. And best of all, she's not afraid to do it starkers! She won Best Supporting Actress from the Australian Film Institute for her role as a young, divorced mom dealing with her expanding weight and her own mother's terminal illness in *Soft Fruit* (1999). The already curvaceous cutie purposely put on pounds for the part and was thankfully not ashamed to flash the big and beautiful fruits of her labor. Sacha's titanic tits and boomingly broad bum are showcased best in a scene where

she decides to hop on the scale naked, hoping to weigh a little less. The results are quite phat. Sacha deserves accolades for her role in *Praise* (1998). Her portrayal of Cynthia, a barmaid suffering from chronic eczema, will leave you with an itch dying to be scratched. While giving a Meryl Streep–caliber performance as a character actress, Sasha has voracious casual sex throughout, behaving like the gorgeous goddess she was meant to be.

SKIN-fining Moment:

Soft Fruit (0:33) Sacha gets ready to weigh herself accurately, so she strips completely nude before getting on the scale. Full-bodied FFN.

See Her Naked In:

Soft Fruit (1999) FFN
Praise (1998) Breasts, Bush, Buns

Jane Horrocks

Born: January 18, 1964
Rossendale, Lancashire, England, UK
Skin-O-Meter: Brief Nudity

Jane Horrocks is British and quite prolific, having acted in over forty productions, all in her native land. She debuted in *The Road* (1987) before landing her most eye-catching role as the tiny-titted Bubbles on the hit TV comedy *Absolutely Fabulous*. She had small parts (in film and in her bra) in some Stateside cinema, such as a bit role in *Memphis Belle* (1990) and a voice-only role as Babs the chicken in *Chicken Run* (2000). Outside of Bubbles, Jane is most famous as the lead in *Little Voice* (1998), which was based on a play written especially for her and that booming sound that comes out of those wee lungs. Jane has appeared nude, as most pale, English actresses do, as a matter of

principle. Her precious, teacup-sized breasts can be seen in two made-for-TV British movies, *Alive and Kicking* (1991), in which she plays a strung-out hooker, and *Bad Girl* (1992), which has a very dimly lit scene in which her breasts can be seen very briefly. And in *Life Is Sweet* (1991), those little girls are rubbed flat and hard. Life truly is sweet, at least for the actor who got paid to feel Jane up.

SKIN-fining Moment:

Life Is Sweet (0:50) Jane serves up her (literally) chocolate-covered chest-cherries in bed with David Thewlis.

See Her Naked In:

Bad Girl (TV) (1992) Breasts
Alive and Kicking (TV) (1991) Breasts
Life Is Sweet (1991) Breasts
The Dressmaker (1988) Breasts

Vivian Hsu

Born: March 19, 1975
Taichung, Taiwan
Skin-O-Meter: Brief Nudity

In Hong Kong the name Vivian Hsu makes men sweat. In fact, a lot of other bodily secretions make their way out when the dark-haired hottie is mentioned, let alone when the pixie is seen in the flesh. And she likes to show off what she's got. Vivian is one of the most well known "Photo Girls," the Asian equivalent of being in *Playboy* or being a Page 3 girl in Great Britain. The Taiwanese-born act-chest with a body like a pu-pu platter of delectable parts—pert breasts, silky muff, and meaty ass—is mostly a commodity in her native land and not that well known in America. But her works are well worth finding and wanking to wherever you call home. She is no bashful geisha girl; just take a look at *Chi Luo Tian Shi* (1995), which was only her second film. It translates to *Angel Hearts* and puts the similarly titled U.S. production to shame. Vivian spends much of the movie scrubbing her perfect body clean, showing off her three Bs, and letting audiences get dirty in the process. But the film is filthy with skin, so be sure to hunt it out and watch it alone. For a further look at Vivian's voluptuous body of work, take a gander at her debut *Mo Gui Tian Shi* (1995), a.k.a. *Devil Angel*. The sex scene is a bit dark, but this angel is still heavenly.

SKIN-fining Moment:

Chi Luo Tian Shi (1:38) Breasts, then buns, then all kinds of stuff on the bed. Fur flies.

See Her Naked In:

Devil Angel (1995) Breasts
Chi Luo Tian Shi (1994) FFN, Buns

Season Hubley

Born: March 14, 1951
New York, New York
Skin-O-Meter: Great Nudity

MR. SKIN'S TOP TEN

A Cup All-Stars
. . . Flat is where it's at

10. Ally Sheedy

9. Helen Slater

8. Donna Wilkes

7. Juliette Lewis

6. Koo Stark

5. Jane Birkin

4. Neve Campbell

3. Selma Blair

2. Taryn Reif

1. **Season Hubley**

Season Hubley is a casualty of the fair-weathered climate of Hollywood in the 1970s. An ultra-popular character actress in the '70s, everyone recognized her fair, fresh face. This itty-bitty-tittied blonde appeared on super shows such as *The Partridge Family*, *Kung Fu*, *Starsky and Hutch*, and *Kojak* and was known by the housewife set as the delicious Nurse Candy on the daytime drama *Love of Life*. In 1979 Season starred as Priscilla Presley in the top-rated TV biopic *Elvis* (1979) and found her king in co-star Kurt Russell. The two were married shortly thereafter. Having had a career playing wholesome characters, Season scandalously transitioned to the big screen as a teenage hooker in *Hardcore* (1979). The most scintillating scene in the flick has little Miss Hubley in a peep booth, pressing her teeny tee-tees and naked bod against the glass. As working girl Niki, Season had the hard-edged attitude that made her the perfect hot bitch but unfortunately made her unsuitable for the work she'd done previously. In 1981 she played opposite hubby Kurt in the cult classic *Escape from New York*. Her marriage fell apart, and her winged, funky appearance looked outdated. She divorced Russell and resorted to playing victims in TV movies throughout the '80s and '90s. Forging a comeback in 1994, she co-starred on the failed TV series *Blue Skies*. Unfortunately, Hubley's season in the sun seems to have passed. But there's nothing like a sexy, nudity-packed role to fire up a comeback!

SKIN-fining Moment:

Hardcore (1:06) Season shows all three of her seasons: '70s lap-fro, and two of the most bitable itsy-bitsies ever filmed.

See Her Naked In:

Total Exposure (1991) Body Double—Buns
Vice Squad (1982) LB, Buns
Hardcore (1979) FFN

Kate Hudson

Born: April 19, 1979
Los Angeles, California
Skin-O-Meter: Brief Nudity

Nobody can doubt the pedigree of Kate Hudson, coming from the holy union of mom Goldie Hawn and a genuine Hudson Brother (although Kate considers Kurt Russell to be her real father figure). There's also no doubting that Kate got her mom's sex appeal, as seen by the perfect breasts she sports as '70s rock groupie Penny Lane in *Almost Famous* (2000). That role got her an Oscar nomination and a standing ovation from our crotches. From there, this rising star has established herself as a sexy comic presence in films such as *How to Lose a Guy in 10 Days* (2003) and *Dr. T and the Women* (2000)—in which the film's big climax (and ours) involved her character's lesbian relationship with Liv Tyler. She was also pretty impressive as a rich girl in the college drama *Gossip* (2000). Too bad about her marriage to former Black Crowes frontman Chris Robinson, though.

SKIN-fining Moment:

Almost Famous (1:10) Quick shot of Katie's cannage as she dances in a hotel room with a couple of band members.

See Her Naked In:

About Adam (2000) RB
Almost Famous (2000) LB

Felicity Huffman

Born: December 9, 1962
Woody Creek, Colorado
Skin-O-Meter: Great Nudity

Felicity Huffman, for too long, was best known for playing Dana on the ABC dramedy *Sports Night* (best summed up by stoned teenagers on *Family Guy* thusly: "I finally get Aaron Sorkin's *Sports Night*: it's a comedy that's too good to be funny!"). And despite appearing on numerous episodes of *Frasier* and *Law & Order* along with films such as *Hackers* (1994) and *The Spanish Prisoner* (1997), Felicity has since been usually identified as the wife of actor William H. Macy, whom she married after they rekindled an old romance while they were both making *Magnolia* (1999). And even though her 1996 topless bubble-bath scene on the Showtime program *Bedtime* went largely unnoticed, Felicity forever redefined herself on the same network's *Out of Order* series with a smashing shower sequence on the first season's final episode. From here on in, she will be forever hailed as The Chick with the Un-Freakin'-Believably Long, Thick, Mouth-Wateringly Massive Nipples on that Eric Stoltz Showtime Show.

SKIN-fining Moment:

Out of Order "Put Me in Order" *(2003) Mighty meaty-nippled mams during sex on an office desk with Eric Stoltz.*

TeleVisions:

Bedtime Breasts, Buns
Out of Order Breasts

Kristina Hughes

Leominster, Massachusetts
Skin-O-Meter: Brief Nudity

Kristina Hughes is a member of the group Artists Without Frontiers. She should start one called Artists Without Clothes, because she's moist famous for her breastacular topless and blindfolded appearance in the hilarious movie *Old School* (2003). Though she was only billed as Naked Woman, she offers a skinful addition to the *KY*-covered Lisa Donatz and Corinne Kingsbury. What else do you need to know

about the brunette beauty? Well, Kristina has worked as a photo double for Andie McDowell in her L'Oreal ad campaign and Sandra Bullock on the set of *Miss Congeniality* (2000). The busty babe also landed a recurring role on the TV series *Living in Captivity*, playing a character simply called Dairy Queen. With jugs like Kristina, it's the role she was born to play.

SKIN-fining Moment:

Old School (0:04) Bare casaba'd Kristina and tighty-whitey clad Nicholas Hosking wander out of a bathroom blindfolded while Juliette Lewis waits in bed to make it a menage-a-trois.

See Her Naked In:

Old School (2003) Breasts

Wendy Hughes

Born: July 29, 1952
Melbourne, Victoria, Australia
Skin-O-Meter: Great Nudity

She's one of Australia's most respected and versatile actresses, but Wendy Hughes has somehow never caught on in America—and that's a national disgrace, considering the big-screen debut of Wendy's big'uns in the Aussie import *Jock Peterson* (1974). Wendy showed her whoppers at home, work, and play in that film, and tossed in some full-frontal nudity. There wasn't much more than a slip of the nip in *Lonely Hearts* (1983), but *Flash Fire* (1981) had Hughes getting us sputtering with some underwater nudity. There are also fleeting glances of her finery in *Warm Nights on a Slow Moving Train* (1987). But then Wendy got tired of making films like *Wild Orchid II: Two Shades of Blue* (1992) and concentrated on her career as the Katharine Hepburn of Down Under.

SKIN-fining Moment:

Jock Petersen (0:13) Trouser arouser Wendy strips naked, showing boobs and boosh, then Jack Thompson throws another shrimp in.

See Her Naked In:

The Heist (1989) RB
An Indecent Obsession (1985) LB
My First Wife (1984) Breasts
Lonely Hearts (1982) Breasts
Flash Fire (1981) Breasts
Jock Petersen (1974) FFN, Buns

Dianne Hull

Born: November 24, 1949
Skin-O-Meter: Great Nudity

Dianne Hull's career is split in two. She's a veteran of mainstream TV, with a stint on the Ed Asner cop drama *The Police Story*, as well as one-shot appearances on *Cannon*, *All in the Family*, *Highway to Heaven*, and *Amazing Stories*. Then there's the sexier slice of Dianne to be found in the low-budget glory films of the '70s and '80s. You can spy the svelte sweetie in *The Arrangement* (1969), her debut, *Girls on the Road* (1972), and *Hot Summer Week* (1973). Her most recent film was *The New Adventures of Pippi Longstocking* (1988), which, needless to say, lacks nudity in any semblance. Not that Dianne passed through the heady days of exploitation without flashing some skin. Her naked debut was in *The Magic Garden of Stanley Sweetheart* (1970), in which Dianne romped around a dark living room without a stitch. If you look closely you can see her untrimmed magic garden. The only other nude scene came in a Robert "Freddy Krueger" Englund movie called *The Fifth Floor* (1980) about a young disco dancer wrongly incarcerated in a mental institution. Curvy Dianne exposed her full-frontal glory again. Talk about decking the Hulls.

SKIN-fining Moment:

The Fifth Floor (0:31) Mental patient Diane loses her hospital gown and bares gazongas and glutes while washing up in the shower facilities.

See Her Naked In:

The Fifth Floor (1980) FFN, Buns
The Magic Garden of Stanley Sweetheart (1970) FFN, Buns

Chloe Hunter

Skin-O-Meter: Great Nudity

Chloe Hunter was a national sex symbol before anyone saw her face. That's her perfect navel, stomach, and hand adorning the promotional poster for *American Beauty* (1999)—

MR. SKIN'S TOP TEN

Tied-up Naked Babes . . . Bound to please

10. Claudia Jennings
    —*Deathsport*—1978 (0:31)

9. Nastassja Kinski
   —*Cat People*—1982 (1:47)

8. Lynda Wiesmeier
   —*Wheels of Fire*—1984 (0:34)

7. Judith M. Brown
   —*Big Doll House*—1971 (0:16)

6. Sheryl Lee
   —*Vampires*—1986 (0:39)

5. Anne Parillaud
   —*Innocent Blood*—1992 (1:27)

4. Corinne Clevy
   —*The Story of O*—1975 (1:23)

3. Ursula Andress
   —*Slave of the Cannibal God*—1979 (1:17)

2. Cheri Caffaro
   —*Ginger* 1971—(1:32)

1. **Chloe Hunter**
   —*Spun* 2002—(0:43)

although most people still assume those body parts belong to Mena Suvari. Chloe was already a popular model, but being adored in movie lobbies did nothing for her own acting career. Instead, the former homecoming princess made her skinteriffic mark in the amazing cult film *Spun* (2002). As a screwed-up methadone freak, lucky Jason Schwartzman gets to have some porn-worthy simulated sex with his gorgeous girlfriend—but that's secondary to how Chloe spends most of the film naked and spread-eagle tied to his bed, once he forgets about her in the pursuit of some drugs. Whether you're into bondage or boning, Chloe becomes an instant love object. And that doesn't even get into Debbie Harry as the lesbian next door. . . .

SKIN-fining Moment:

Spun (0:41) Great flopping whoppers as Chloe's tied to the bed, thrashing about while Jason Schwartzman leaves her a phone message, followed by a sweet overhead spread-eagleage.

See Her Naked In:

Spun (2002) FFN, Buns

Heather Hunter

Born: October 1, 1969
New York, New York
Skin-O-Meter: Great Nudity

Heather Hunter was just another frisky teenager dancing at New York City's infamous Latin Quarter when she was discovered by veteran porn star Hyapatia Lee. She suggested the sexually uninhibited wild girl make videos, and to celebrate her eighteenth birthday Heather filmed her first explicit venture, *Heather Hunter on Fire* (1988). That launched a thousand erections and eventually landed Heather at the top of the adult

market as a Vivid Video girl. Not content to suck splooge for a living, Heather jumped to Hollywood for a few mainstream movies, such as the Female in Sex Montage for Spike Lee's *He's Got Game* (1998) and an even smaller role in *Snipes* (2001). Heather fared better in B-movies, specifically *Frankenhooker* (1990), in which she showed off her towering ta-tas. Of course if you want skin, visit the dark recesses of your local rental store's porn section. Heather has recently given up the flesh trade for a singing career. She certainly has the lungs for it. They say the heart is a lonely Hunter, but with Heather it's a heart-on.

SKIN-fining Moment:

Frankenhooker (0:41) Surrounded by other topless prosties, Heather hops out of bed and launches into a breast-and-butt-baring sex dance that'll hook your Franken.

See Her Naked In:

He Got Game (1998) Breasts
Frankenhooker (1990) Breasts
Numerous Adult Movies

Holly Hunter

Born: March 20, 1958
Conyers, Georgia
Skin-O-Meter: Hall of Fame

High-booty bimbos and silicone love-dolls will always have their place in the pantheon of skin, but occasionally it's refreshing to have an intense burst of intelligence mixed in with the flash of animal appeal, and that's where Holly Hunter reigns. The hottest little spitfire ever to roar out of Conyers, Georgia, Holly Hunter won an Oscar for her wrenching portrayal of an erotically frustrated mute in *The Piano* (1993). More important, she opened the eyes of any date-night hostages who might have been dozing off by bending forward and offering her hearty derriere for a long lick from the camera, treating sensitive Sams in theaters across America to backdoor fur and the hint of drapes. Play it again, Holly.

SKIN-fining Moment:

The Piano (1:03) Volcanically hot view of Holly's ass—including a furry rear-angle—before she leans back for a lengthy tittie exposition.

See Her Naked In:

Thirteen (2003) FFN
Harlan County War (2000) Breasts
Things You Can Tell Just by Looking at Her (2000) Breasts
Jesus' Son (1999) RB
Living Out Loud (1998) Breasts, Bush, Buns
Crash (1996) LB
The Piano (1993) Breasts, Buns

Kaki Hunter

Born: 1955
Topanga Canyon, California
Skin-O-Meter: Great Nudity

Porky's (1981). It is an undeniable classic. Kaki Hunter is one of the reasons why. Although she had a rather prolific career before the *Porky's* trilogy, she couldn't seem to get any work after it was through, maybe because she will forever be known as the girl who banged Pee Wee. No amount of acting could take our attention away from that memorable shower scene, where Kaki and her other

MR. SKIN'S TOP TEN
Group Shower Scenes
. . . Steamed clams and misty mams

10. Wendy O. Williams, et al.
   —*Reform School Girls*—1986 (0:26)

9. Anita Strindberg, et al.
   —*Women in Cell Block 7*—1972 (0:28)

8. Anne Heche, Ione Skye, et al.
   —*Girls in Prison*—1994 (1:02)

7. Samantha Janus, et al.
   —*Breeders*—1998 (0:21)

6. Lynda Wiemeier, et al.
   —*Private School*—1983 (0:42)

5. Linda Blair, et al.
   —*Chained Heat*—1983 (0:31)

4. Dina Meyer, et al.
   —*Starship Troopers*—1997 (0:29)

3. Cheryl "Rainbeaux" Smith, et al.
   —*Revenge of the Cheerleaders*—1976 (0:28)

2. Uschi Digand, et al.
   —*Prison Girls*—1972 (0:02)

1. Kaki Hunter, et al.
   —*Porky's*—1981 (1:02)

"high school" friends were showering after gym class, showing off their pseudo-'50s unshaven pies. Kaki will simply be Wendy Williams forever. The original *Porky's* film is the time Kaki got kinky. It is a rather wonderful scene, which climaxes with a young man's Johnson getting pulled through a hole in a wall and features a bevy of beautiful, young, naked women. Not a bad way to be rendered immortal.

SKIN-fining Moment:

Porky's (1:02) Kaki and a ton of her gal-pals spend some quality time in the

shower, and all of them show off a ton of titty, ass, and more massive muffcakes than a feller can shake a stick at.

See Her Naked In:

Porky's (1981) Breasts, Bush, Buns

Neith Hunter

Skin-O-Meter: Great Nudity

Neith Hunter has made herself quite the sexy career on both the boob tube and the big screen, where she's been more than generous in sharing her full-figured brunette body with drooling viewers. She appeared on *Miami Vice, Red Shoe Diaries*, and *Silk Stalkings*. Her work in film has been a bit more varied, from her debut in the comedy *Born in East L.A.* (1987) to the arty *Less Than Zero* (1987) and more genre work as a scream queen in *Near Dark* (1987), *Fright Night Part II* (1989), and *Silent Night, Deadly Night 4: Initiation* (1990), which gave audiences her first skin onscreen. Talk about a hot initiation! She took a short break to return to the small screen after being cast as one of the daytime cuties on the soap *One Life to Live*. But the siren call of nudity brought her back to the silver screen again in the *Playboy*-produced short sex-stories collection *Inside Out* (1992) and then her breast (and butt and bush) showing in *Gentleman's Bet* (1995). It's hard to beat her performance, but it's sure easy to beat off to it! By the end of the millennium, Neith was all skinned out. She hasn't been seen since. Let's hope someone will Hunter down soon.

SKIN-fining Moment:

Gentleman's Bet (0:08) Several spectacular up-close-and-personal shots of Neith's soapy boobs, bush, and butt in the shower.

See Her Naked In:

Gentleman's Bet (1995) FFN, Buns
Inside Out (1992) Breasts, Thong
Silent Night, Deadly Night 4: Initiation (1990) Breasts

TeleVisions:

Red Shoe Diaries FFN, Buns

Rachel Hunter

Born: September 9, 1969
Auckland, New Zealand
Skin-O-Meter: Brief Nudity

Rachel Hunter comes from New Zealand, where they have a talent for producing incredibly hot women. She took her sexy figure and let men around the world ogle it as a fashion model, mostly photographed with little on but a skimpy bathing suit. Check out the *Sports Illustrated Swimsuit Edition* for an eye-pleasing sample. The five-foot-eleven-inch giantess is big in every respect, especially around the chest, where her 36-24-35 figure is hypnotic. Rachel followed her bouncing boobs into acting, debuting in *Winding Roads* (1998). In *Two Shades of Blue* (2000), she lifted the shades on her two mammoth mams, which made the film a classic at Skin Central. Rachel has since appeared as a judge on ABC's venture into reality TV *Are You Hot? The Search for America's Sexiest People*. We can't think of a better person for the job.

SKIN-fining Moment:

Two Shades of Blue (1:22) Breasts and a hint of bunnage on the balcony with Eric Roberts. The ass shot may be body-doubled since you don't see her face.

See Her Naked In:

Two Shades of Blue (2000) Breasts, Buns

Helen Hunt

Born: June 15, 1963
Los Angeles, California
Skin-O-Meter: Great Nudity

Helen Hunt started her career early; at the age of nine she was on *The Mary Tyler Moore Show* playing the daughter of Murray, the bald news writer. Helen has grown up . . . and how! She looks like a nice girl, but beneath that casual exterior is a buxom body made for sin. After a bit part in *Peggy Sue Got Married* (1986), Helen went on to star in the Matthew Broderick monkey movie *Project X* (1987), after which the two briefly dated. Skin Central took notice of this busty beauty when she landed the hot role in *The Waterdance* (1992). It was Helen's sexiest, not to mention nudest, movie to date. She and paralyzed boyfriend Eric Stoltz (whom she also dated) got it on, and Helen took everything off. Mr. Skin couldn't keep his eyes off the blonde honey. America followed once she landed on the hit TV sitcom *Mad About You*, co-starring funnyman Paul Reiser. The success of that show led Helen to an Oscar-winning performance as Carol in *As Good As It Gets* (1997), which also showed off her heavy, creamy sacks. Her career is definitely cresting, with movies such as *Dr. T and the Women* (2000) and *What Women Want* (2000). Hopefully success hasn't spoiled her, and Helen is on the Hunt for more skinful scripts.

SKIN-fining Moment:

The Waterdance (0:51) Helen bares her magnificent mammaries while trying to ride Stoltz's rod, then proceeds to flash some ass when she comes back from the bathroom to clean up "the mess . . ."

See Her Naked In:

Dr. T and the Women (2000) Breasts, Buns
As Good as it Gets (1997) RB, Buns
The Waterdance (1992) Breasts, Buns

Isabelle Huppert

Born: March 16, 1955
Paris, France
Skin-O-Meter: Hall of Fame

There's something about the French . . . oh, yes, they love to get naked, and ooh-la-la Isabelle Huppert has the body for it. Acting since a child and garnering notice on the stage, Isabelle stepped onto the big screen in *La Prussien* (1971), and celluloid instantly became sexuloid. Soon she was *Going Places* (1974) and showing off her *Rosebud* (1975) in a series of scandalous French features, such as the aforementioned titles. American audiences finally got a taste of her sweet pastry in the monumental money-loser *Heaven's Gate* (1980). Isabelle's portrayal of the proprietor of a Wild West brothel was anything but a flop, however. She exposed every inch of her perfect body right down to the hairy beret between her legs. Now she mostly sheds for the croissant munchers at home, but we can still catch her fine foreign ass at the arthouse, which is something to croak about.

SKIN-fining Moment:

Heaven's Gate (1:18) Isabelle bathes bare breasted in a river, then supplies a shot of full-frontal Huppert's gate.

MR. SKIN'S TOP TEN

Prolific A-List Peelers
. . . Breast in show

Theresa Russell—14 Nude Movies

Rosanna Arquette—14

Sharon Stone—14

Sally Kirkland—15

Sophie Marceau—16

Charlotte Rampling—18

Jennifer Jason Leigh—18

Jane Birkin—19

Nastassja Kinski—19

Isabelle Huppert—19

See Her Naked In:

La Pianiste (2001) RB
The School of Flesh (1998) Breasts, Buns
The Bedroom Window (1987) Breasts, Buns
Cactus (1986) Breasts, Buns
Sincerely Charlotte (1986) Breasts
Storia di Piera (1983) Breasts, Bush, Buns
Entre Nous (1983) Breasts
My Best Friend's Girl (1983) LB, Buns
La Truite (1982) FFN, Buns
Lady of the Camelias (1981) FFN
Eaux profondes (1981) Breasts, Bush, Buns
Clean Slate (1981) Breasts, Bush, Buns
Heaven's Gate (1980) FFN, Buns
Loulou (1980) Breasts, Bush, Buns
Violette (1978) Breasts, Bush, Buns
The Lacemaker (1977) FFN, Buns
Dupont-Lajoie (1975) Breasts, Bush
Rosebud (1975) RB, Buns
Going Places (1974) LB

Michelle Hurd

Born: December 21, 1966
New York, New York
Skin-O-Meter: Brief Nudity

Soap operas, situation comedies, and cop shows are the three great proving grounds for female actresses who are striving to develop an urban-edged, sassy, sexy, and no-nonsense intense onscreen persona. Wavy-haired, cocoa-colored biracial beauty Michelle Hurd is a graduate of all three network training acadamies, having matriculated as Dana Kramer on *Another World,* Simone on *Malcom & Eddie,* and Detective Monique Jefferies on *Law & Order: Special Victims Unit.* All these many years of preperation have honed Hurd's instincts and essence, resulting in an exultant casting as Athena Barnes, a striving singer/actress, on the innovative Showtime series *Leap Years.* Catch the *Leap Years* pilot and be in time for a showing of Michelle's mam's and haunches.

SKIN-fining Moment:

Leap Years "Pilot" (2001) *You Hurd it here: Michelle shows her left lung-balloon and lip-smacking panty-packing.*

TeleVisions:

Leap Years LB, Buns

Elizabeth Hurley

Born: June 10, 1965
Hampshire, England
Skin-O-Meter: Hall of Fame

Elizabeth Hurley made eyeballs pop when she arrived on the arm of then-beau Hugh Grant in a nipple-dangling dollop of fabric called a Versace dress for the premiere of *Four Weddings and a Funeral* (1994). Her barely wrapped gifts of two knock-'em-down knockers put her forever at the top of the gossip pages. In time, her relationship with Grant was history, and the rest is her story. Elizabeth's D-cups runneth over in such filmic fleshtaculars as the topless bathing scene in *The Weight of Water* (2000) and her just-covered naughty bits teasing in *Austin Powers: International Man of Mystery* (1997). Her bountiful boobage is uncovered in earlier fare such as *Aria* (1987) and *Shameless* (1995), in which Elizabeth can't seem to keep her shirt on. With her top-heavy arsenal of talent, audiences are Hurley-burley for this girlie.

SKIN-fining Moment:

Aria (0:46) Elizabeth's boobs and buns come out to play as a gent helps her out of her dress before they sing nakedly.

See Her Naked In:

Double Whammy (2001) RB
The Weight of Water (2000) Breasts
Shameless (1995) Breasts
Nightscare (1993) RB, Thong
Kill Cruise (1990) RB
Aria (1987) Breasts, Buns
Rowing With the Wind (1987) Breasts

TeleVisions:

Sharpe's Enemy Breasts

Olivia Hussey

Born: April 17, 1951
Buenos Aires, Argentina
Skin-O-Meter: Great Nudity

Olivia Hussey is most famous for playing Juliet, the gal Romeo goes ga-ga for in Shakespeare's sexiest play. It's also quite a breastacular film. In *Romeo and Juliet* (1968), the Argentina-born actress reveals a nice, brief flash of her young but well-developed juggies. Since then she's kept the corset closed and her career has suffered for it. You just can't keep those big girls under wraps and expect audiences to flock to your openings. Finally waking up to her real talent, Olivia got booby once more as Norman Bates's topless mommy in the cable-TV film *Psycho IV: The Beginning* (1990). See, it pays to be a Hussey.

SKIN-fining Moment:

Romeo and Juliet (1:37) Olivia toplessly rolls off of her Romeo and we get a quick view of her upper balconies.

See Her Naked In:

Bloody Proof (2000) Breasts
Psycho IV: The Beginning (1990) Breasts
Escape 2000 (1981) Breasts
Romeo and Juliet (1968) Breasts

Anjelica Huston

Born: July 9, 1951
Santa Monica, California
Skin-O-Meter: Brief Nudity

Who says nepotism is a bad thing? Not Anjelica Huston. The dark-haired, statuesque, striking beauty got her start in the film industry thanks to her iconic director father, John Huston. He cast her in two of his films, one for each of her plum-shaped jugs, *A Walk with Love* (1969) and *Sinful Davey* (1969). Sinful Anjelica soon moved from beneath the impressive shadow of her famous pop and revealed her chops acting with Anthony Hopkins in *Hamlet* (1969) and later with Jack Nicholson in *The Postman Always Rings Twice* (1981). Although she wasn't Nicholson's love interest in that movie, she shared his bed in real life for a long and heated affair. Back onscreen, Anjelica took advantage of her unique looks and was perfectly cast as the goth wet-dream date Morticia in the *Addams Family* series. For a look at Anjelica's assets, check out her Oscar-winning role as a hit woman in daddy's film *Prizzi's Honor* (1985). She only offered a brief side view of her left tit. That's it, sorry, word of honor.

SKIN-fining Moment:

The Postman Always Rings Twice (1:30) Huston, we have a brief left breast as Anjelica reclines alongside Jack Nicholson in a trailer.

See Her Naked In:

The Perez Family (1995) Breasts
The Postman Always Rings Twice (1981) LB

Tracy Hutson

Skin-O-Meter: Great Nudity

Tracy Hutson sure knows how to get a guy's attention—especially when that guy is named Mr. Skin! This beauty took a while to get her career established, starting with a mere guest role as another beachside beauty on the cable show *Pacific Blue*. But then Hutson stepped in to play porn queen Marilyn Chambers in the cable-TV film *Rated X* (2000). Like most Hollywood porn bios—in this case, covering the career of porn's tragic Mitchell Brothers—there's not a lot

of actual sex onscreen. As Marilyn, though, Tracy gave and showed her all. By the time Tracy showed up as a sexy member of a religious cult in *Endsville* (2000), we had no problem handing over our life savings to her cause.

SKIN-fining Moment:

Rated X (0:38) Racy Tracy gets stripped down and has her funbags fondled by a passel of pretty gals.

See Her Naked In:

Rated X (2000) Breasts

Lauren Hutton

**Born: November 17, 1943
Charleston, South Carolina
Skin-O-Meter: Great Nudity**

Aside from a rather successful modeling career, Lauren Hutton took the world of film by storm in movies such as *Gator* (1976), with Burt Reynolds, and *Once Bitten* (1985), which launched the career of Jim Carrey. Being a former model, and arguably the first supermodel, Lauren is comfortable with her body. That means she strips down quickly to show off her up-turned pretties and uplift every movie she's in. She began exploring filmdom with not one but two nude debuts! Her first full-frontal scene came with *Little Fauss and Big Halsy* (1970), but the shot is distant and kind of hard to see. Then there's *Pieces of Dreams* (1970), which just sports a quick flash of her pert bosom. In her next nude scene, which was in *Permettete? Rocco Papaleo* (1971), Lauren was wild in the bush, talking naked on the phone and giving the phone-sex industry a boost. She has gone on to show her breasts numerous times, exploiting her deliciously tiny nips in *Welcome to L.A.* (1977), *American Gigolo* (1980), *Hecate* (1981), and *Lassiter* (1984), the

latter in which she screws some schmoe to death—literally. What a way to go!

SKIN-fining Moment:

American Gigolo (0:37) A sensual highlighting of Lauren's body parts that focuses on her praise-worthy pair.

See Her Naked In:

Lassiter (1984) Breasts
Hécate (1981) Breasts, Buns
American Gigolo (1980) Breasts
Welcome to L.A. (1977) LB
Permette? Rocco Papaleo (1971) FFN
Little Fauss and Big Halsy (1970) FFN, Buns
Pieces of Dreams (1970) RB

Kimberly Hyde

Skin-O-Meter: Great Nudity

Kimberly Hyde may have fallen off the skin-o-meter after a fleshtastic role in *Video Vixens* (1975), but before that she left a great body of wank. While a fixture in the early '70s randy wave of sexploitation films, kinky Kimberly got her big break in the Oscar-winning Peter Bogdanovich movie *The Last Picture Show* (1971). The black-and-white film burst into pink, at least in the lurid mind of Mr. Skin, when Kimberly offered a titillating full-frontal (and dorsal) shot during the infamous skinny-dipping scene. It's muff-tastic! After that revealing part, she had no problem picking up sexy roles in such films as *The Young Nurses* (1973), *Candy Stripe Nurses* (1974)—are we seeing a trend, here?—and *Foxy Brown* (1974). No, Ms. Brown was not a nurse . . . what a career challenge that must have been! Out of those flicks, she only managed to flash some skin in *Candy Stripe Nurses*, which featured yet another lush look at her lovely hooterage. One out of three isn't shabby, but we miss seeing her Hyde.

SKIN-fining Moment:

The Last Picture Show (0:37)
Kimberly flashes some fantastic full-
frontal flesh when she climbs out of the
pool to greet Randy Quaid and Cybill
Shepherd. Yowza!

See Her Naked In:

Candy Stripe Nurses (1974) Breasts
The Young Nurses (1973) Breasts
The Last Picture Show (1971) FFN, Buns

Joyce Hyser

Born: December 20, 1956
New York, New York
Skin-O-Meter: Brief Nudity

Joyce Hyser made it to the big
screen, if not quite the big time, in
the comedy *The Hollywood Knights*
(1980). She was one of its countless
giggling girls. Joyce parlayed that
credit into a part as an extra in
Valley Girl (1983) and then played a

JOYCE HYSER (RIGHT) CONCEALS HER TWO
GIRLS FROM SHERILYN FENN IN *JUST ONE OF
THE GUYS*.

groupie in *This Is Spiñal Tap* (1984).
The idiot box gave her equally brief
exposure—though sadly, not *in* her
briefs—on *Freddy's Nightmares*, based
on the *Nightmare on Elm Street*
scaries. Her experience incognito

made her the perfect choice for the
lead in *Just One of the Guys* (1985),
in which she played a gal incognito.
Her drag-king act fooled everyone,
complete with a tube sock stuffed in
her pants to pass as a tube steak.
The high-school boy she had the
hots for was confused by his
conflicting emotions. It took a flash
of her medicine-ball-sized bouncers
at the prom to convince her beau
that he wasn't gay. It's one of the
all-time great nude scenes, sure to
knock your socks off.

SKIN-fining Moment:

Just One of the Guys (1:28) Joyce
pulls her prom tux open to show Clayton
Rohner that she is, indeed, female. After
much inspection and testing, the
scientists here at Skin Central have
proven this prognosis to be, indeed,
affirmative.

See Her Naked In:

Just One of the Guys (1985) Breasts

i

Isabelle Illiers

France
Skin-O-Meter: Great Nudity

We're impressed to see Chloë Sevigny giving Vincent Gallo a blowjob in *The Brown Bunny* (2003), but let's not forget Isabelle Illiers and Klaus Kinski in *Les Fruits de la Passion* (1981), a.k.a. *The Story of O, Continued*. Isabelle spends an amazing amount of time naked in her notorious debut, but her lips eventually get covered by Kinski's Eurocock. That's right, there's actual penetration in this penetrating tale of sexual slavery. Of course, nobody was paying attention to foreign sexploitation films in 1981. Even the presence of a semi-respected actor like Kinski didn't count for much. Illiers kept acting, though, keeping her clothes on while becoming a respected comedienne in Italian productions.

SKIN-fining Moment:

Les Fruits de la Passion (0:06) Isabelle hairily bares it all while having her hair combed and tits powdered. Oh, to be a tit-powderer . . .

See Her Naked In:

Les Fruits de la Passion (1981) FFN, Buns
L'Immorale (1980) Breasts

Iman

Born: July 25, 1955
Mogadishu, Somalia
Skin-O-Meter: Brief Nudity

Heaven must be missing an angel, and Africa must be missing a princess. A slinky tower of ebony perfection, Somalian supermodel Iman often appears in the society pages as Mrs. David Bowie. She just as often appears in the dreams of smitten skinsters as a dark-skinned sexual seraphim, the closest we will get in this life to cavorting with the girls of paradise. Quick flashes of the best-possible afterlife love mate can be gleaned from *Out of Africa* (1985) and *Heart of Darkness* (1994). For the most complete view of celestial and sensual Iman, meditate upon her otherworldly orbs rounding out a red corset-and-pantie combination in *Exit to Eden* (1994). Dying would be easy if you could be sure Iman was on the other side.

SKIN-fining Moment:

Exit to Eden (1:21) Iman steams up a crowded shower as two male sex slaves scrub her nude supermodel magnificence, providing us with a fuzzy peek at her left breast.

See Her Naked In:

Exit to Eden 1994) LB, Thong

Deirdre Imershein

Skin-O-Meter: Great Nudity

Deirdre Imershein beamed into show biz in 1990 with a guest spot on *Star Trek: The Next Generation.*

From there, this intergalactically appealing brunette scored a year-long stint on the CBS nighttime soap *Dallas*, followed by a few episodic guest spots on series such as *Cheers* and *Silk Stalkings*. And then that was it for Deirdre's network-TV streak. And that's good news. Fans of the big D (okay, the medium-sized-but-udderly-lovely D) who tuned in to cable in the early '90s could regularly turn on to her soft, natural charms, as Deirdre was a regular on the erotic series *Eden*. You'll also want to loosen your belt for Deirdre's part in *Blackbelt* (1992), in which she displayed her high-impact martial tarts.

SKIN-fining Moment:

Blackbelt (1:07) Deidre sets off her all-natural dairy-bombs.

See Her Naked In:

Blackbelt (1992) Breasts

TeleVisions:

Dream On Breasts
Women: Stories of Passion Breasts, Buns

Sonia Infante

Born: February 17, 1944
Morelia, Mexico
Skin-O-Meter: Great Nudity

Mexican mamacita Sonia Infante was already onscreen and beginning her illustrious career as a teen when she appeared in *Dormitorio para senoritas* (1960). That hit kicked off a slew of films that translate to provocative titles such as *Kill Yourself, My Love* (1961) and *Sex Monster* (1962). The latter is known more commonly as *Rock 'n' Roll Wrestling Women vs. the Aztec Ape*, and it was very nearly Sonia's first skinful moment. Even though she often looked as though she had two pigs writhing about under her sweater, Sonia somehow managed to keep her threads on until she appeared in *La Casa Que Arde de Noche* (1985). She most certainly popped 'em out for that one, though, so be sure to check it out. Those are some massive mammarias, mama!

SKIN-fining Moment:

Los Placeres Ocultos Sonia revels in an erotic trance atop a table as her hairy loverman coats her completely bare body with wine. Intoxicating ta-tas, trim, and tail.

See Her Naked In:

Mujer De Fuego (1988) Breasts, Bush
Los Placeres Ocultos (1988) FFN, Buns
La Casa Que Arde de Noche (1985) Breasts

Randi Ingerman

Born: November 13, 1967
Philadelphia
Skin-O-Meter: Great Nudity

Bellissima Randi Ingerman kicked off her career in the appropriately named Italian production *Too Beautiful to Die* (1988). Immediately afterward she packed up her two plastic chest bags and hopped the pond to Hollywood, where she ignited provocatively titled productions such as *Let's Talk About Sex* (1998) and *Screwloose* (1999) and shared her natural grace and unnatural torso torpedoes with us in a pair of films with decidedly threatening

monikers: *Treacherous* (1994) and *Deadly Rivals* (1993). All these colorful titles are fitting for a beauty named Randi, of course, because after one look at her, "randy" is all you'll feel.

SKIN-fining Moment:

Deadly Rivals (0:18) Bare breasts in bed with her male boner-owner.

See Her Naked In:

Treacherous (1994) Breasts, Buns
Deadly Rivals (1993) Breasts

Eva Ionesco

Born: 1965
Paris, France
Skin-O-Meter: Great Nudity

MR. SKIN'S TOP TEN

TV Stars I Wish Got Naked

. . . Network no-shows

10. **Dawn Wells**
 —(Mary Ann) *Gilligan's Island*
9. **Audrey Meadows**
 —(Alice) *The Honeymooners*
8. **Kim Fields**
 —(Tootie) *The Facts of Life*
7. **Karen Valentine**
 —(Alice) *Room 222*
6. **Katherine Helmond**
 —(Jessica Tate) *Soap*
5. **Connie Hines**
 —(Carol Post) *Mr. Ed*
4. **Kathy Garver**
 —(Cissy) *Family Affair*
3. **Pat Priest**
 —(Marilyn) *The Munsters*
2. **Jan Smithers**
 —(Bailey Quarters) *WKRP in Cincinnati*
1. **Donna Douglas**
 —(Elly May) *Beverley Hillbillies*

Waif-like brunette beauty Eva Ionesco has been famous since she was a child. In fact, she's famous for being a child who's mother, renowned photographer Irina Ionesco, captured her in images that are semi-pornographic and totally scandalous, if marginally legal. Are they child pornography or an artist's unique expression? Whatever, they're too hot to handle. While still a pre-teen, Eva took her notoriety to the big screen in her native France with *Spielen wir Liebe* (1977), which even caused controversy in that progressive land of lust. The movie loosely translates to *Puppy Love*, and while there's no bestiality, Eva and co-star Lara Wendel play adolescents behaving very badly, which can be good for what ails you in certain countries with lenient obscenity laws. Eva continued to push the envelope of good taste with *L'Amoureuse* (1987) and *Monsieur* (1990), which you can watch without guilt or fear of prosecution. This ingenude continues to work to this day, and guys continue to whack off to her ever-maturing mini-mams.

SKIN-fining Moment:

Monsieur (0:53) Eva flashes some black-and-white full-frontal flesh in bed.

See Her Naked In:

Monsieur (1990) FFN
Spielen wir Liebe (1977) FFN, Buns

Jill Ireland

Born: April 24, 1936
London, England, UK
Died: May 18, 1990
Skin-O-Meter: Brief Nudity

When Charles Bronson met Jill Ireland, he reportedly announced to her husband David McCallum, "I'm going to marry your wife." Bronson was serious, too, and the gorgeous blonde soon became a partner to

Bronson in both marriage and movies. (Not surprisingly, she was also a regular co-star of McCallum's during his days on *The Man from U.N.C.L.E.*) Ireland had an icy beauty that played nicely off her craggy husband, and their films together include classics such as *The Mechanic* (1972), *The Valachi Papers* (1972), and *Hard Times* (1975)—plus underrated trash like *From Noon Till Three* (1976) and *Love and Bullets* (1976). Jill jiggled her assets in all of the above, although she showed the most of herself in *Violent City* (1970). Sadly, Jill died of cancer in 1990.

SKIN-fining Moment:

Violent City (1:21) Very brief glimpses of partial right nippage as she lies in bed with Bronson.

See Her Naked In:

Violent City (1970) Body Double—LB, Buns / Her—RB

Kathy Ireland

Born: March 8, 1963
Santa Barbra, California
Skin-O-Meter: Brief Nudity

It was no news flash when Kathy Ireland, the five-foot-eleven-inch statuesque beauty from the *Sports Illustrated Swimsuit Edition* covers, quit the modeling world to pursue a career in acting. But it sure made the pants here at Skin Central tighten in anticipation of watching the arousing sexpot flash on film. She has done well with the career shift, with some comic turns that showcase her high, squeaky voice in *Mom and Dad Save the World* (1993), *Loaded Weapon 1* (1993), *Amore!* (1995), and *Backfire* (1995). The key to cute Kathy's success is her willingness to play goofy people in goofy roles. Kathy has unfortunately never gotten naked in a movie or anywhere else. She has

the dreaded Sandra Bullock no-nudity clause in her contract and even wears pasties when she models "topless." Don't expect to see Kathy's bouncing buoys any time soon. Boob-hoo.

SKIN-fining Moment:

Sports Illustrated 25th Anniversary Swimsuit Video (0:44) Kathy gets sprayed with water and we see the map of Ireland stiffen up under her blue bikini top.

TeleVisions:

Tales from the Crypt Thong

Amy Irving

Born: September 10, 1953
Palo Alto, California
Skin-O-Meter: Great Nudity

Amy Irving is no dummy. She knows how a struggling starlet makes money in Hollywood: marry Steven Spielberg, sign a lucrative pre-nup, have a kid, wait a few years, divorce, and roll around naked in all that filthy cashola. She hedged her bet and it paid off, as she never became superstar material; she used what material God gave her to lure the big bucks. But even such intimate access to the golden-boy director only produced this nugget, arguably her biggest role, the voice of the singing Jessica Rabbit—Kathleen Turner gave the drawn-bad cartoon her smoky sexiness—in the animated hit *Who Framed Roger Rabbit?* (1988). She did play Barbra Streisand's "husband" in *Yentl* (1983), but that's too kinky even for Mr. Skin. Amy keeps busy with character work in titles such as *Deconstructing Harry* (1997) and *Traffic* (2000), but she keeps men busy with her skinful body of work. A little flesh peeked in

Carrie (1976) and its remake *Rage: Carrie 2* (1999). But they were only panty shots, though that still makes us pant. However, *Carried Away* (1996) delivered Amy in the all-together. Her full-frontal shot would be perfect if not for the fact that she shared it with a nude and limp Dennis Hopper. Oh, well, at least we can all see that precious body that Spielberg paid $100 million to screw for four years.

SKIN-fining Moment:

Carried Away (1:11) The Good News: Amy strips out of her bra and panties and shows every nipplicious, hairy-muffed, ass-cracklin' inch of her nude body. The Bad News: Dennis Hopper's there and he's completely nude too.

See Her Naked In:

Carried Away (1996) FFN, Buns
Kleptomania (1995) FFN

Katharine Isabelle

Born: March 10, 1982
Vancouver, British Columbia, Canada
Skin-O-Meter: Never Nude

They could've called it *I Was a Sexy Teenage Werewolf,* but *Ginger Snaps* (2000) helped put the emphasis on Katherine Isabelle and her wild turn as young wolfen Ginger. It was a star-making indie role for Katharine, who was rapidly becoming just another aging child actor. In fact, her big post-*Ginger* role was as "Laughing Girl" in the film version of *Josie and the Pussycats* (2001). *Ginger Snaps,* however, was enough of an indie hit to warrant making both *Ginger Snaps 2* (2003) and *Ginger Snaps: The Prequel* (2003) so we could keep seeing more of Katherine as a sexy wolfgirl in underwear and tight tops. Meanwhile, we creamed over her turn as a big-screen scream queen in *Freddy Vs. Jason* (2003), in which she made for appealing psycho-bait in an inventive shower scene. There's a lot of controversy as to whether or not this overhead topless shot comes courtesy of a body double, but even if they're not Isabelle's, those are some rockin' front door-a-bells.

SKIN-fining Moment:

Freddy vs. Jason (0:12) BODY DOUBLE: Katherine Isabelle's double shows off her front door-a-bells in the shower, overhead shot.

See Her Naked In:

Ginger Snaps Back (2004) Body Double—Buns
Freddy Vs. Jason (2003) Body Double—Breasts

Analía Ivars

Spain
Skin-O-Meter: Great Nudity

You have to be a shameless actress to work with a shameless director like ultraviolent Jesus Franco—which helps to explain why Analía Ivars works so often with the guy. This Eurobabe works with other directors, too, but Franco really gets our franks going with Analía's work in *Tender Flesh* (1998). That one's a real bandwidth burner here at Mr. Skin, with an amazing amount of shots featuring Analía's tender furburgerage. And you'll wish you had eight limbs to work your trouser snake when you see Analía in *Mari-Cookie and the Killer Tarantula* (2001), a.k.a. *Eight Legs to Love You*. Franco puts his camera way down to get some shots that go beyond sexploitation and straight into the gynological.

SKIN-fining Moment:

Tender Flesh (0:31) Long muff shot as Analía climbs onto a counter and puts a "wee" bit of herself into her cooking.

See Her Naked In:

Mari-Cookie and the Killer Tarantula (1998) FFN, Buns
Tender Flesh (1997) FFN, Buns

j

Glenda Jackson

Born: May 9, 1936
Birkenhead, Cheshire, England, UK
Skin-O-Meter: Great Nudity

Glenda Jackson is a real English beauty. In fact, she's even a classy Member of Parliament and the only MP to have won an Oscar—for *Women in Love* (1969) and *A Touch of Class* (1973). And Glenda once had a touch of ass. In fact, *Women in Love* not only garnered her a golden statue but offered up the first view of her pale frame and pancake-sized sweet nipples—not to mention her hairy hippy pits. She briefly did a full-frontal flash in *Sunday, Bloody Sunday* (1971) but hit the right note in *The Music Lovers* (1970), with a Full Monty dance that warms the cockles of our hearts. That Glenda is one action Jackson!

SKIN-fining Moment:

Women in Love (1:24) Breasts when she takes off her gown for Oliver Reed and they settle in for some sexin'.

See Her Naked In:

The Romantic Englishwoman (1975) FFN, Buns
The Music Lovers (1971) FFN
Sunday Bloody Sunday (1971) Breasts, Bush
Women in Love (1969) Breasts
Negatives (1968) Breasts

Janet Jackson

Born: May 16, 1966
Gary, Indiana
Skin-O-Meter: Brief Nudity

Janet Jackson is the hottest member of her famous family, though Michael Jackson does appear to be melting. She is as top-heavy as her wacko sister LaToya but far less scary to lust after. Being born into the Jackson dynasty meant a rocket-ship ride to fame, starting as a youngster on the ghetto sitcom *Good Times*, which led to more TV exposure on *Diff'rent Strokes* and *Fame*. As she developed, Janet put her money where her talent was . . . that is, her luscious lungs. The '80s were Janet's decade; we just got to watch, which was pretty hot. With her "What Have You Done for Me Lately?" attitude and a series of hit records and deliciously sexy videos, Janet was at the top of the musical heap. Janet then returned to acting with a cameo in *Malcolm X* (1992), followed by starring roles in *Poetic Justice* (1993) and *The Nutty Professor II: The Klumps* (2000). Sadly, she's yet to release those chocolate milk sacks onscreen, which surely would shoot to the top of the pants pops. The eagle-eyed out there will catch a brief glimpse of her mams bouncing around like pudding in the made-for-TV concert *All for You from Hawaii* (2002). Then, during a skinstant classic halftime performance at Superbowl XXXVIII in February 2004, Janet almost went *all* the way. At the climax (appropriately enough) of Janet's song-and-dance routine, world's luckiest nancyboy Justin Timberlake tore open the right side of the delectable diva's outfit and her football-sized funbag busted on out with only a miniscule piece of nipple jewelry obscuring part of her ultra-suckable, cocoa-hued areola. I don't know if Michael Jackson ever physically disciplined his chimpanzee Bubbles, but that historic unveiling of half his sister's hooterage had me spanking *my* monkey before the third quarter.

SKIN-fining Moment:

Super Bowl 2004 One nip that shook the world: at the climax (appropriately) of Janet's song-and-dance routine, Justin Timberlake tears open the right side of the delectable diva's outfit and her football-sized funbag busts on out with only a miniscule piece of nipple jewelry obscuring part of her ultra-suckable, cocoa-hued areola.

See Her Naked In:

Super Bowl 2004 (halftime ceremonies) (2004) RB
Janet—Live in Hawaii (2002) Breasts

TeleVisions:

The Tonight Show Buns

LaToya Jackson

Born: May 29, 1956
Gary, Indiana
Skin-O-Meter: Brief Nudity

LaToya Jackson began trading on her famous family name when, coincidentally (or not), The Jackson 5 was waning in popularity and had lost their Motown contract. In 1976 she accompanied her more famous siblings in the Las Vegas variety show *The Jacksons*, which became a one-season TV flop later the same year. Since then her career has been a nepotistic patchwork of one-off guest appearances as herself on such shows as *Mad TV*, *The Howard Stern Show*, and *The Fall Guy*, not to mention her 1992 entry into the Dionne Warwick-pioneered arena of telephone tarot, LaToya Jackson's Psychic Friends Network. Perhaps her most well-known "body" of work is what she's done for *Playboy*. Her 1987 pictorial spread was the best-selling issue in the history of the magazine, and her collection of *Playboy* videos have also been top sellers. Supposedly her manager/husband Jack Gordon prodded her to show off her below-the-nose plastic to the world; they divorced in 1997 after his unsuccessful attempt to get her into hardcore porn.

SKIN-fining Moment:

Playboy Celebrity Centerfold: Lotaya Jackson (0:01) Latoya gets topless and we get to leer at her luscious Jacksons during the intro to her Playboy *video.*

See Her Naked In:

Playboy *Celebrity Centerfold: LaToya Jackson* (1994) Breasts, Buns

Victoria Jackson

**Born: August 2, 1959
Miami, Florida
Skin-O-Meter: Brief Nudity**

Victoria Jackson is the ditzy blonde with the high, squeaky voice who is arguably the moist doable doll in comedy. She made her debut on *The Tonight Show* standing on her head and reciting poetry. After that, her career began to take shape, though nothing can be as shapely as her buxom form. Her body, which is delightfully top-heavy, va-va

voomed to a starring role on *Saturday Night Live* from 1986 to 1992. But the breast part of that late-night institution didn't reveal her true talents until she was featured in *Casual Sex?* (1988). In the movie, Victoria is seen sunbathing nude on the beach with Lea Thompson. The observant will be rewarded by a brief glimpse of Victoria's secret garden as she leans naked from bed in one scene. There's Victoria's dewy patch, if not her Jackson hole.

SKIN-fining Moment:

Casual Sex? (0:27) Victoria and Lea Thompson sunbathe bare-seated outdoors. Nice look at Victoria's Crackson.

See Her Naked In:

Casual Sex? (1988) Buns

Irène Jacob

**Born: July 15, 1966
Paris, France
Skin-O-Meter: Great Nudity**

Irène Jacob started her career in her native France with a role in Louis Malle's holocaust drama *Au Revoir les Enfants* (1987) and began a successful career in the land of stiff baguettes. But in the early '90s, she decided to share her deliciousness with the rest of the world and took on English-language roles with a part in the Steve Buscemi-helmed *Claude* (1993). Since then, Irène has appeared in such notable British and American productions as *U.S. Marshals* (1998), *The Big Brass Ring* (1999), and *My Life So Far* (1999). So far we like what we see. Speaking of her overwhelming beauty, Irène, being French, isn't all that shy in front of the camera and has given up the proverbial goods on a number of occasions. Check out her bustier-busting performances in *The Double Life of*

DOUBLE VISION: IRÈNE JACOB IN THE DOUBLE LIFE OF VERONIQUE.

Veronique (1991), *Othello* (1995), *Incognito* (1997), *The Big Brass Ring*, and *Spy Games* (1999), which happens to feature some of her hotter full-frontal shots. Irène makes Jacob's ladder stiff as a board.

SKIN-fining Moment:

Double Life of Veronique (0:28) Quick flash of her Fur-ronique canoodling with a dude, followed by a double-shot of what Irene's got up-top.

See Her Naked In:

Nés de la mère du monde (2002) Breasts
Mille millièmes (2002) Buns
Lettre d'une inconnue (2001) Breasts
Fourplay (2001) RB
L'Affaire Marcorelle (2000) Breasts
The Big Brass Ring (1999) Breasts, Buns
Spy Games (1999) Breasts, Buns
Incognito (1998) Breasts
Cuisine américaine (1998) LB
Othello (1995) Breasts
Victory (1995) Breasts, Buns
Double Life of Veronique (1991) Breasts, Bush
Les mannequins d'osier (1988) Breasts

Sakina Jaffrey

Skin-O-Meter: Great Nudity

As the daughter of two of India's most noted actors, it could've been expected that Sakina Jaffrey would've just ended up smiling blandly in musical production numbers. Instead, Sakina started her career in New York City in a series of cool indie productions. And when she finally ended up working with her mother—noted actress Madhur Jaffrey—in *Cotton Mary* (1999), the film included the debut of Sakina's perfect breasts. Sakina kept on challenging expectations—and working with her mom—in *Chutney Popcorn* (2000), a fun tale of lovely lesbians. She also added to the international glamour in Jonathan Demme's *Charade* (1963) remake *The Truth About Charlie* (2002). Sadly, though, *American Made* (2003) doesn't show her getting made by an American.

SKIN-fining Moment:

Cotton Mary (1:45) Sakina serves up her Cotton Mary puffs as she dances topless around her kitchen.

See Her Naked In:

Cotton Mary (1999) Breasts

Bianca Jagger

Born: May 2, 1945
Managua, Nicaragua
Skin-O-Meter: Brief Nudity

Bianca Jagger is a Nicaraguan native. She was one of myriad sexual conquests of satyr rock star Mick Jagger, only this Ruby Tuesday stayed the week, even longer, as she wed the notorious hedonist. Bianca tried to parlay her marriage to His Satanic Majesty into an acting career and had some success, such as *The Rutles* (1978), *Couleur Chair* (1979) with Dennis Hopper, and *The Cannonball Run* (1981), as Jamie Farr's girlfriend. No longer married to the Midnight Rambler, sadly, Bianca's career stalled with the sequel *C.H.U.D. II: Bud the Chud* (1989). Bianca's most revealing role to date came in the early Jeff Bridges vehicle *The American Success Company* (1980). In it, we see Bianca in a see-through top, which gives us an ample look at her

MR. SKIN'S TOP TEN

Porn Stars in Mainstream Movies
. . . XXX girls gone mild

10. **Juli Ashton**
    —*Orgazmo* (1997)

9. **Jill Kelly**
   —*He Got Game* (1998)

8. **Alisha Klass**
   —*Cruel Intentions* (1999)

7. **Jeanna Fine**
   —*The Boondock Saints* (1999)

6. **Marilyn Chambers**
   —*Rabid* (1977)

5. **Nina Hartley**
   —*Boogie Nights* (1997)

4. **Annette Haven**
   —*10* (1979)

3. **Kobe Tai**
   —*Very Bad Things* (1998)

2. **Traci Lords**
   —*Not of This Earth* (1988)

1. **Jenna Jameson**
   —*Private Parts* (1997)

bountiful bosom. And you can take that to the (sperm) Bianca.

SKIN-fining Moment:

The American Success Company (0:35) Bianca's Jaggers jostle sexily under a see-through black top as she reclines in the sack.

See Her Naked In:

Blast 'Em (1992) LB
The American Success Company (1979) Breasts

Jenna Jameson

Born: April 9, 1975
Las Vegas, Nevada
Skin-O-Meter: Great Nudity

Jenna Jameson came from the union of a police officer and a showgirl,

and it should be illegal to be as sexy as this blonde bombshell. By the time this vamp was twenty she had moved from the bump-and-grind pole to the pages of skin mags. The demand for a more intimate view of Jenna's talents took her to Los Angeles, where she quickly ruled the randy roost of porno. From softcore to girl-on-girl to a Wicked feature girl, Jenna's come-hither good looks and just come-inducing curves made her a genuine star. She debuted in *Up and Cummers 11* (1994) and continued her carnal appeal in *The Wicked One* (1995), *Jenna Loves Rocco* (1996), and *Virtual Sex with Jenna Jameson* (1999). But you don't have to venture into the dark and mysterious adult section of your video store to appreciate Jenna's body of work. She has been all over the more risqué shows on the E! network and gained mainstream cred as The First Nude Woman on the Radio in the Howard Stern mega-hit *Private Parts* (1997). For another film view of Jenna's privates check out *Dirt Merchant* (1999). It was so good I soiled myself!

SKIN-fining Moment:

Private Parts (1:29) Boobs, butt, and that porn-star poontang as Jenna strips naked and prepares to massage Howard Stern on air.

See Her Naked In:

Getting Naked (2003) Thong
Dirt Merchant (1999) Breasts, Buns
Private Parts (1997) FFN, Buns
Numerous Adult Movies

TeleVisions:

E! Wild On . . . RB, Buns

Samantha Janus

Born: November 2, 1972
UK
Skin-O-Meter: Great Nudity

Samantha Janus's vivacious visage and firm fanny have been quite the rage in her native England since the early '90s. Her BBC credits include the shows *Pie in the Sky* and *Game On!* and the made-for-TV movie *The Grimleys* (in which she played the aptly named Geraldine Titley). Lucky for skinophiles, this sterling stunner has a penchant for stripping down on the big screen in or near showers, as is the case in *Up 'n' Under* (1998) and *Breeders* (1998). She's wearing nothing but suds in both films but only shows a smite of boobage in *Up 'n' Under*. A more satisfying eyeful of Samantha's UK udderage can be seen on the TV dramedy *Demob*, where her nipples tend to stand at attention, poking through whatever little clothing she has on whenever the camera is rolling.

SKIN-fining Moment:

Breeders (0:21) Knobs in the shower and then a pan down to her awesome tush next to the equally amazing-assed Katy Lawrence.

See Her Naked In:

Up 'n' Under (1998) Breasts, Buns
Breeders (1998) Breasts, Buns

TeleVisions:

Demob Breasts

Sam Jenkins

Born: October 18, 1966
Pittsburgh, Pennsylvania
Skin-O-Meter: Brief Nudity

Former model and current sexpot Sam Jenkins jilted hordes of horny girls when she led *Hercules* hunk Kevin Sorbo to the alter. A gorgeous goddess in her own right, Sam is supernaturally sexy in films such as *Bonfire of the Vanities* (1990), *Twenty Bucks* (1993), and *Ed and His Dead Mother* (1993). The latter two flicks feature this feisty fox in scenes exposing her super-powerful bare pair. If that's not enough to slay your dragon diddler, Sam can be

seen shaking her Aphrodites in syndication on series such as *Chicago Hope* and *Hercules: The Legendary Journeys*. Famous in her foxiness, any journey with this juicy jewel is more than enough to give a clash to the fighting titans in your pants.

SKIN-fining Moment:

Ed and his Dead Mother (0:16) Ned Beatty telescopically spies on Sam's naked tail in her bedroom. That ought to make him squeal like a pig.

See Her Naked In:

Ed and His Dead Mother (1993) RB, Buns

Lucinda Jenney

Born: April 23, 1954
Long Island City, New York
Skin-O-Meter: Brief Nudity

Lucinda Jenney is one of Hollywood's more successful character actors, and when you look as hot as she does it's no surprise why. Since her debut in the made-for-TV movie *Out of the Darkness* (1985), Lucinda has appeared in over forty productions and doesn't appear to have even hit her stride yet. She may not be a superstar in the strictest sense of the term, but with supporting appearances in blockbusters such as *Peggy Sue Got Married* (1986), *Rain Man* (1988), *Thelma & Louise* (1991), *Leaving Las Vegas* (1995), *Thirteen Days* (2000), *Crazy/Beautiful* (2001), and *S.W.A.T.* (2003), it would be hard for her to complain . . . OK, so we'll complain a bit. Lucinda's batting average in the skin game isn't all that spectacular. She's only managed to appear nude on film once, in *Sugar Town* (1999), and even then she was pregnant (or at least made to appear so) in the scene in question. Still, it's worth a look if for no other reason than to catch a glimpse of her hella hooters, even if they're resting on a baby gut.

That's all we have until Lucinda loosens up.

SKIN-fining Moment:

Sugar Town (1:21) Pregophile alert! Hugely knocked-up Lucinda bombs the screen with both her bombsatically milk-bloated knockers and bare belly as she goes into labor.

See Her Naked In:

Sugar Town (1999) Breasts

Claudia Jennings

Born: December 20, 1949
Minnesota
Died: October 3, 1979
Skin-O-Meter: Great Nudity

Claudia Jennings was a queen of the drive-in movie exploitation circuit that made film going so pleasurable in the '70s. She starred in such faves as *Unholy Rollers* (1972), *'Gator Bait* (1976), and *The Great Texas Dynamite Chase* (1977), and had been taking off her clothes since her nudie debut in *The Stepmother* (1971), which offered a full-frontal view of why Dad remarried. It wasn't just bush with this babe,

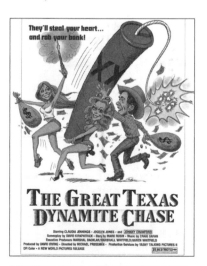

THE GREAT TEXAS DYNAMITE CHASE: TNT AND TN'A! DESPITE THIS CUTE AND CLEVER POSTER, STARS CLAUDIA JENNINGS AND JOCELYN JONES ARE NO CARTOONS!

who could get as rude and kinky as the breast of them, as she proved completely nude and tied to a gurney in *Deathsport* (1978). Sadly, this was almost her last appearance onscreen. Her life was cut short at the age of twenty-nine when she fell asleep behind the wheel of her Volkswagen convertible on her way to Malibu. Around that time, Aaron Spelling wanted her to possibly replace Kate Jackson on *Charlie's Angels*, but her explicit career scared network executives off. She'll always be our angel.

SKIN-fining Moment:

Unholy Rollers (0:32) Some nice shots of Claudia's cans when some of her girlfriends help her out of her clothes at a pool hall.

See Her Naked In:

Famous T&A (1982) Breasts
The Best of Sex and Violence (1981) Breasts
Impulsion (1978) FFN
Deathsport (1978) FFN, Buns
The Great Texas Dynamite Chase (1977) FFN, Buns
The Man Who Fell to Earth (1976) FFN
'Gator Bait (1976) Breasts
Truck Stop Women (1974) Breasts
Bloody Friday (1972) Breasts
Group Marriage (1972) Breasts
Unholy Rollers (1972) Breasts, Buns
Jud (1971) Breasts
The Stepmother (1971) FFN

Rita Jenrette

Born: November 25, 1949
San Antonio, Texas
Skin-O-Meter: Great Nudity

Rita Jenrette is the ex-wife of John Jenrette, the Congressman from South Carolina who went to federal prison for his role in the 1980 Abscam scandal. Her tell-all book *My Capitol Secrets*, about her life as the Congressman's wife, featured a memorable story of her and hubby John having sex on the Capitol steps as other members of Congress walked by, including Tip O'Neil. Talk about a capital offense. You celeb-skin-aholics won't want to miss Rita's imposing rack in her career move to B-horror scream queen in the gore flick *Zombie Island Massacre* (1984). Lovely Rita is why Washington, D.C., is steamy hot.

SKIN-fining Moment:

Zombie Island Massacre (0:01) Great view of her soapy rack while in shower, then again when grinding with her man, still wet and bubbly!

See Her Naked In:

Zombie Island Massacre (1984) Breasts

Jane Jensen

Born: 1968
Indianapolis, Indiana
Skin-O-Meter: Great Nudity

Singer/songwriter/guitarist Jane Jensen is music to our eyes. She is known in the recording world for her debut album "Comic Book Whore," which sums up our interests succinctly. Music is not the only way to sooth Jane's savage breast. She is also a comic artist who did the cartoons in the CD booklet and has appeared in films, the most famous of which is *Tromeo and Juliet* (1996), a B-grade take on the Shakespearean classic in which she spends most of the time bound, blindfolded, and naked. As Juliet, sweet Jane is gloriously sexy and even has a scene where Romeo eats popcorn out of her swollen belly. Wherefor art trou?

SKIN-fining Moment:

Tromeo and Juliet (0:42) Jane's jugs offer a nice distraction when her stomach explodes in a shower of popcorn.

See Her Naked In:

Tromeo and Juliet (1996) Breasts

Maren Jensen

Born: September 23, 1957
Arcadia, California
Skin-O-Meter: Brief Nudity

Sci-fi babes were all the rage in the late '70s, but no one gave Wonder Woman a run for her money more so than the similarly raven-tressed, blue-eyed Maren Jensen. Prior to landing her career-defining role on *Battlestar Galactica* in 1978, Maren spent several years as a top fashion model. That's no surprise; just look at her! What is surprising is that her career never took off as spectacularly as the spaceship she manned onscreen. After *BG* ended, she appeared in a number of guest spots on such series as *The Love Boat* and *Fantasy Island*, where the pretty balloon smugglers are always front-and-center, but she faded away after her performance in *Beyond the Reef* (1981). Fortunately, Maren bared her out-of-this-world chest flesh in Wes Craven's thriller *Deadly Blessing* (1981) before disappearing altogether. Her space-tacular skinbags are on display for a few delectably brief seconds, mostly whilst in or near a bathtub. A very young pantie-clad Sharon Stone also appears in the flick but, alas, remains clothed throughout. Still, it's worth checking out.

SKIN-fining Moment:

Deadly Blessing (0:56) A bare-breasted Maren splashes in the tub and swats at a scary snake.

See Her Naked In:

Deadly Blessing (1981) Breasts, Buns

Jenteal

Born: June 26, 1976
Oklahoma
Skin-O-Meter: Great Nudity

With her fluffy blonde mane, piercing green peepers, and peaches-

and-cream complexion, at first glance Reanne Lynn Rossi looks like your typical, sweet, country cutie from Heartland USA. Masquerading under the moniker Jenteal, this sultry slice of American pie is not the innocent, gentle creature her name suggests. At the tender age of eighteen, Jenteal jumped straight into hardcore, ferociously taking on a three-way fling in *Fresh Meat #1* (1994) and enjoying Sapphic suck-cess with Felicia and Misty Rain in *Fantasy Chamber* (1994). Joining the ranks of porn pioneer Ginger Lynn, in 1994 Jenteal became a *Vivid Video* girl with an exclusive contract for their *Stardust* series. As tasty temptress "Honey Potts," this up-and-comer became so hugely Popu-lar that the series was tamed down for the Playboy Channel. For those with a preference for bolder, more boobilicious bodies of work, check out *Sex Academy 4: The Art of Anal* (1994), *Gangland Bangers* (1995), or *Where the Boys Aren't 9* (1997). Considered one of the naturally prettiest porn princesses around, Jen is also one of the nastiest, most rip-roaring, anything-goes performers in the adult entertainment industry today. Rent any of Jenteal's juice-inducing flicks for a little pup tent in the pants proof.

SKIN-fining Moment:

Made (0:34) In a deleted scene included on the DVD, Janteal shows buns and breasts during an enthusiastic lap dance. Wow!

See Her Naked In:

Made (2001) Breasts, Thong
Animal Instincts III (1995)
Numerous Adult Movies

Joyce Jillson

Born: December 26, 1947
Cranston, Rhode Island
Skin-O-Meter: Brief Nudity

Joyce Jillson began her ascent to stardom just like Ronald Reagan. Before newspapers printed banner headlines like "The Astrologer Who Runs the White House"—she was infamous for doing the President's horoscope—Joyce was hitting the boards on Broadway. She debuted on the little screen in a bit part on the hit series *The Man from U.N.C.L.E.*, but it was her recurring role on *Peyton Place* that made this busty blonde a household name. What made her a skin name, and gave her a panting place in skinstory, was her film work. First and foremost there was *Superchick* (1973); she lived up to the title's promise as her super tits were forever flopping out and bouncing about. Considering the audacious start, her career fizzled out within a few years. She had a cameo as herself in *The Happy Hooker Goes to Washington* (1977) and played a carhop in *Slumber Party '57* (1977), but after that . . . nothing. Maybe with her powers of perception she saw the end coming. At least we got to see her end briefly too.

SKIN-fining Moment:

Superchick (0:04) SuperJoyce shows a bit of superboob while taking her dinner in the bathtub.

See Her Naked In:

Superchick (1973) Breasts, Buns

Gladys Jimenez

Puerto Rico
Skin-O-Meter: Great Nudity

Gladys Jimenez is the queen of daytime soaps, both here and in her native Mexico. This spicy dish began cooking back home on the daytime hit *Te Dejaré De Amar*. Here in the States she acted on *The Young and the Restless* before defecting to *The Bold and the Beautiful*. We're waiting for her to land a role on *The Sexy and the Naked*. Not surprisingly, she's typecast as the exotic, Latin American hot-assed bitch here, whereas in Mexico, everyone is a Latin hot-assed bitch. At least that is what television has taught us. Gladys has done several sexy turns on television shows ranging from *Walker, Texas Ranger* to *Silk Stalkings*, but nothing compares to her role in *Blowback* (1999), which not only featured a nice sex scene but also Senorita Jimenez tied to a cross nude. If you don't want Gladys to die for your sins then seek out *Secrets of a Chambermaid* (1998) for some nice glimpses of her chi-chis. Olé!

SKIN-fining Moment:

Blowback (1:21) She's bare-boobied in a white loin cloth while tied up in a basement.

See Her Naked In:

Blowback (1999) Breasts
Secrets of a Chambermaid (1998) Breasts

Marlène Jobert

Born: November 4, 1943
Algiers, Algeria
Skin-O-Meter: Great Nudity

Carrot-topped cutie Marlène Jobert is the equivalent of Katherine Hepburn in France, with the difference being that this spectacular actress is hip to the nude scene. First featured in films by acclaimed directors, such as Louis Malle's *Le Voleur* (1967) and Jean-Luc Godard's *Masculin, féminin* (1966) (alongside equally boobtastic Brigitte Bardot), Marlène's mojo was most mackin' to the collective croissant lovers in *Le Secret* (1974). It's not exactly hush-hush that this Algerian-born eyeful is free about flashing her firm, freckled flesh in flicks such as *La Guerre des Polices* (1979) and *L'amour Nu* (1981). With enough fiery-red amour to make your member sore, Marlène is skintastic in all her endeavors, but perhaps none moreso than the one she graced us with in 1980: daughter Eva Green, who took up the mantle of Naked Skinternational Sinema Siren with naked brilliance in director Bernardo Betrolucci's NC-17 sensation *The Dreamers* (2003).

SKIN-fining Moment:

Ten Days' Wonder (1:28) Ah, the glory of nature! Jobert and her au natural, perky tush lie in a field with Tony Perkins.

See Her Naked In:

L'Amour Nu (1981) Breasts
La Guerre des Polices (1979) FFN
Pas si méchant que ça (1974) Breasts
Ten Days' Wonder (1972) LB, Buns

Scarlett Johansson

Born: November 22, 1984
New York, New York
Skin-O-Meter: Never Nude

Raspy-voiced, honey-blonde, young, and sexy Scarlett Johansson is an up-and-comer worth watching for a number of reasons . . . well, two big ones, and you know what they are. Though the credits in *The Horse Whisperer* (1998) claim to be "introducing" Scarlett, this red-hot mama had already gotten her teats wet in several small parts, including such movies as *North* (1994) and *Home Alone 3* (1997). But it was her provocative turn as a precocious teenager in *Ghost World* (2000) that made critics sharpen their pencils with praise and put audiences' hands on their tools too. Since then, Scarlett has been on a quick rise in the business and in our pants. She has starred in high-profile films such as *Eight Legged Freaks* (2002) and *Girl with a Pearl Earring* (2003) and made us want to spew a pearl necklace over her

milky white shoulders. In *Lost in Translation* (2003), opposite Bill Murray, Scarlett opens the flick with a close-up of her round eighteen-year-old ass in a tight pair of transparent panties. That's lust in any language.

SKIN-fining Moment:

Lost in Translation (0:00) The film opens as most films should: with Scarlett's super-shapely, panty-clad ass filling the screen.

Azizi Johari

Born: August 24, 1948
New York, New York
Skin-O-Meter: Great Nudity

African American eyeful Azizi Johari is a lusty, dusky dish. One of the first chocolate bunnies to ever grace the cover of *Playboy*, Azizi was dizzyingly delicious in the '70s and early '80s, modeling her magnificent mug and mile-long legs for fashion mags and nudie rags alike. Slaying pant snakes with her super-fly figure, Johari jazzed up movies such as *The Killing of a Chinese Bookie* (1976) and *Dreamer* (1979). While Azizi showed her ample Afro accoutrements in *The Killing*, she is most dreamy in *Body and Soul* (1981). Typecast in the part of "Pussy Willow," this leggy lass is au natural, sporting a spanking ass that would make J. Lo weep. For those with a Johari jones, any of this spectacular blacktress's foxy films add double the dark and lovely wank to your yank bank.

SKIN-fining Moment:

Body and Soul (0:31) Ms. Azizi gets in bed topless with Leon Isaac Kennedy and her naked Joharis get lots of exposure.

See Her Naked In:

Body and Soul (1981) Breasts
The Killing of a Chinese Bookie (1976) Breasts

Tylyn John

Born: July 31, 1966
Encino, California
Skin-O-Meter: Brief Nudity

She's simply billed as the "Redhead," but Tylyn John's sole screen role is a true high point in the history of *Playboy* Playmates. Of course you can find Miss March 1992 featured in plenty of *Playboy* videos, and we particularly like how she still stands out in *Red Hot Redheads* (2001). But to really appreciate Tylyn's talent and titties, get your dick rising to the actioner *Rising Sun* (1993). Tylyn gets sake licked off of her incredibly fine bod while she cavorts with another luscious lady, and then she shows off her incredible ass when jumping on cop Wesley Snipes for a surprise piggyback ride. It's still hard to believe she didn't make Playmate of the Year. Sadly, Tylyn's been troubled by health problems in recent years and has announced her retirement from modeling.

SKIN-fining Moment:

Rising Sun (0:54) Bountiful boobage and butt as she hops atop of Wesley Snipes and starts flailing.

See Her Naked In:

Rising Sun (1993) Breasts, Buns
Numerous *Playboy* Videos

Tracy Camilla Johns

Born: 1963
Queens, New York
Skin-O-Meter: Great Nudity

Tracy Camilla Johns is a native of Queens, New York, and got her big break from the famous Brooklyn director Spike Lee. He cast her in his cinematic debut *She's Gotta Have It* (1986), in which she played a woman who had three simultaneous sexual relationships. The movie brought her limited success, though, spawning only a cameo on *Family Ties* and bit parts in *Mo' Better Blues* (1990), *New Jack City* (1991), and the short-lived television series *Snoops*. Since 1991 this actress has dropped off the radar, and it seems like things are going to stay that way. But her ripe, round gazongas will always be with us thanks to Lee. Check out *She's Gotta Have It* for a heaping helping of two big scoops of chocolate ice cream. You might want to add your own topping.

SKIN-fining Moment:

She's Gotta Have It (0:06) Big bountiful breastages as Tracy has sex by candlelight.

See Her Naked In:

New Jack City (1991) Breasts, Buns
She's Gotta Have It (1987) Breasts, Buns

Adrienne-Joi Johnson

New Jersey
Skin-O-Meter: Brief Nudity

Whether billed as A.J. or Adrienne-Joi Johnson, this stunning young actress has turned in fine performances while looking great in films such as *Sister Act* (1992), *The Inkwell* (1994), and *Hood Rat* (2001) as well as the 1996 NBC mini-series *The Beast*. Of course, some people saw that coming after Adrienne-Joi stood out when making her debut with a bit part in Spike Lee's *School Daze* (1988). But her big contribution to black skinema was in John Singleton's *Baby Boy* (2001), in which she shone as Tyrese's very young mom—and turned a sex scene with Ving Rhames into a hooterific event, augmenting a look at her Almond Joi's with an ample view of her amazing ass.

SKIN-fining Moment:

Baby Boy (1:41) An ultra-brief helping of Adrienne-Joi's ass and sweater-apples as she does the nasty with big Ving Rhames.

See Her Naked In:

Baby Boy (2001) Breasts, Buns

Amy Jo Johnson

Born: October 6, 1970
Cape Cod, Massachusetts
Skin-O-Meter: Brief Nudity

Limber Amy Jo Johnson, or AJ, was a teen gymnast. Besides the pretzel-twisting body fun, she was able to use her talent to jump into the physical role she's best know for, the Pink Ranger on the hit kiddie show *Mighty Morphin' Power Rangers*. No, the Pink part of her name doesn't stand for what you dirty birds out there may think, but AJ still looked red hot in that form-fitting superhero custom. AJ then moved up to slightly more adult fare in the made-for-VH1 movie *Sweetwater* (1999). This drama about a band that opened Woodstock and then disappeared into obscurity was another missed opportunity to see AJ's sweetmeats. She remained on the clothes-friendly confines of TV, in a role on *Felicity*, and appeared on the clothing-optional big screen in *Liars' Club* (2001) and *The Pursuit of Happiness* (2001). Happiness indeed, as we finally got to see AJ's pink-nosed Power Rangers.

SKIN-fining Moment:

Pursuit of Happiness (0:45) Long-range view of grown-up Pink Power Ranger Amy Jo's pink-nosed puppies as she rides a guy in bed.

See Her Naked In:

Pursuit of Happiness (2001) Breasts
Without Limits (1998) Body Double—Buns

Anne-Marie Johnson

Born: July 18, 1960
Los Angeles, California
Skin-O-Meter: Brief Nudity

Though Anne-Marie Johnson had a privileged upbringing in Los Angeles, she has spent much of her career in the television "ghetto" too often reserved for black actors on shows such as the UPN sitcom *Girlfriends* and the syndicated *What's Happening Now*. Aware of her plight but still wanting the dough, she's also spent much of her career trying to break minority stereotypes. She played Althea Tibbs, wife of Virgil Tibbs, on *In the Heat of the Night* from 1988 to 1993 and appeared in Robert Townsend's sleeper hit *Hollywood Shuffle* (1987). Lest you think Anne-Marie is all seriousness, she's worked with Keenen Ivory Wayans more than once, appearing in *I'm Gonna Git You Sucka* (1988) and on the series *In Living Color*. In 1990 she even appeared briefly in the buff as a genetically engineered athlete in the sci-fi flick *Robot Jox*.

SKIN-fining Moment:

Robot Jox (0:35) Anne-Marie steps into the shower and her nude seat gets the sensual soap-up it deserves.

See Her Naked In:

Robot Jox (1990) Buns

Beverly Johnson

Born: October 13, 1952
Buffalo, New York
Skin-O-Meter: Brief Nudity

She was the first black supermodel, but Beverly Johnson has had less luck in Hollywood. That's a shame, too, since Beverly combines comic skill with a killer bod in films such as *Loaded Weapon 1* (1993) and *The Meteor Man* (1993). But we take her sole starring role very seriously, since Beverly stripped down to do some skinny-dipping in her very early film *Ashanti, Land of No Mercy* (1979). Check out that fine bod and you can see why Beverly took the coming decade off to rule the world's runways. Her breasts made an acting comeback in the '90s, too, and you can see her 1996 cable anthology appearance in *Red Shoe Diaries 15: Forbidden Zone*. Otherwise, Beverly's kept us working our Johnsons while she keeps working her body in films such as *54* (1998) and *How to Be a Player* (1997).

SKIN-fining Moment:

Ashanti, Land of No Mercy (0:07) *Bev peels for a skinny dip and we get a nice shot of her ass-shanti. Mercy!*

See Her Naked In:

Ashanti, Land of No Mercy (1979) Breasts, Bush, Buns

TeleVisions:

Red Shoe Diaries LB

MR. SKIN'S TOP TEN

Nude at 18
. . . Grown up at last; shows skin real fast

10. Nastassja Kinski
    —*Stay as You Are* (1978)

9. Emmanuelle Beart
   —*Premiers Desirs* (1983)

8. Virginie Ledoyen
   —*L'Eau Froide* (1994)

7. Bonnie Bedelia
   —*Lovers and Other Strangers* (1970)

6. Asia Argento
   —*Trauma* (1993)

5. Jane March
   —*The Lover* (1992)

4. Brigitte Bardot
   —*Manina, la fille sans voile* (1952)

3. Uma Thurman
   —*Dangerous Liasons* (1988)

2. Drew Barrymore
   —*Doppelganger: The Evil Within* (1993)

1. **Michelle Johnson**
   —*Blame It on Rio* (1984)

Lynn-Holly Johnson

Born: December 13, 1958
Chicago, Illinois
Skin-O-Meter: Brief Nudity

Lynn-Holly Johnson started her career as a professional figure skater. Thus, it's no surprise that she was cast in the lead in *Ice Castles* (1978). Lynn-Holly also played a skater in the Roger Moore–Bond flick *For Your Eyes Only* (1981), but, thankfully, she broke the ice and skated past her career of just playing figure skaters. She went on to appear in the knockout hybrid *Alien Predator* (1986), *The Sisterhood* (1988), and *Hyper Space* (1989) before giving up her acting career altogether in the late '90s to concentrate on family type stuff. Sadly, although she was often quite sexy in those tight figure skater's leotards, Lynn-Holly never showed off any skin onscreen. Well, if you can find *Angel River* (1986) you may catch a fleeting glimpse. It's Lynn-Holly's gift to Johnsons everywhere.

SKIN-fining Moment:

Angel River Lynn-Holly shows the figure she put into her figure skating career. It's a wonder she didn't melt the ice.

See Her Naked In:

Angel River (1986)

Michelle Johnson

Born: September 8, 1965
Anchorage, Alaska
Skin-O-Meter: Hall of Fame

Michelle Johnson managed to make bawdy Brazil even sexier, debuting in *Blame It on Rio* (1984), not even wearing the butt floss of a thong to hide her curvaceous perfection. The naturally busty beauty from Alaska made co-star Demi Moore or less irrelevant, even though Demi exposed her pre-boob-job bitties. How could they compete with Michelle's mammoth mams? And

then Michelle made johnsons stiff with her fully frontal flash. Michelle played the vamp on such series as *The Love Boat* and *Dallas* but saved her va-va-va voom for the big screen. She began her career with a big bang hard to duplicate, and while she's yet to again scale such heights of skindom, Michelle can't keep her hooters in her shirt. The big guns fire in *Genuine Risk* (1990) and *Body Shot* (1993), but they've been silent for a while now. Hopefully the powder is dry and ready to ignite soon.

SKIN-fining Moment:

Blame It on Rio (20:00) *Michelle's magnificent mammaries are out and in full effect while she and the equally topless Demi Moore enjoy some titular time on the beach.*

See Her Naked In:

Body Shot (1993) RB, Buns
Genuine Risk (1990) LB
Beaks: The Movie (1987) Body Double— Breasts
Blame It on Rio (1984) FFN, Buns

TeleVisions:

Tales from the Crypt Breasts

Penny Johnson

Born: March 14, 1961
Baltimore, Maryland
Skin-O-Meter: Brief Nudity

Ever since Penny Johnson's acting debut as the title character in the made-for-TV movie *The Files on Jill Hatch* (1983), she's made quite a name for herself on the boob tube. Unfortunately, while roles on such hit series as *The Paper Chase, General Hospital, The Larry Sanders Show*, and *24* have made Penny a dime or two, they haven't led to much in the way of skinage. Penny has enjoyed her fair share of skinematic successes. She's appeared in supporting parts in a number of wildly popular pictures such as *Swing Shift* (1984), *What's Love Got to Do with It* (1993), and *Absolute Power* (1997), but for some reason leading roles in the cinema have thus far eluded her. Nevertheless, Penny managed to show off her worth in *The Hills Have Eyes Part II* (1985), Wes Craven's follow-up to his original classic thriller. In it, Penny pulled out her poppers, if only for a brief instant, in what will most likely be, at this age and stage of her career, her only skinful turn. We have eyes for her hills! A Penny for your thoughts, a buck for your wet dreams!

SKIN-fining Moment:

The Hills Have Eyes Part II (0:49) *On a school bus, Penny peels off her top and presents her pretty perkers.*

See Her Naked In:

The Hills Have Eyes Part II (1985) Breasts

Sandy Johnson

Born: July 7, 1954
San Antonio, Texas
Skin-O-Meter: Great Nudity

Playboy's Miss June 1974 went on to one of the most bizarre filmographies in Playmate history. Sandy Johnson debuted as John Cassavetes's wife in the big-budget Super Bowl sniper flick *Two Minute Warning* (1976) and followed up with plenty of nudity in *Jokes My Folks Never Told Me* (1978), a live-action version of dirty jokes made for the video and cable market. Oh, and then it was time to star in one of the most profitable films of all time. Sandy was immortalized as a sexually active teen in *Halloween* (1978), although her character, naturally, came to a bloody end. Fortunately, there isn't enough blood in the human body to cover up Sandy's megamelons. Sandy went on to give us a hydraulic lift with some pneumatic nudity in *Gas Pump Girls* (1978) and stripped for another iconic turn in the classic

cheerleader comedy *H.O.T.S.* (1979). And things still got weirder: Sandy (now billed as "Sandi") made it into the cast of *The Best Little Whorehouse in Texas* (1982) and then waited thirteen years to pop up in the Mel Brooks comedy *Dracula: Dead and Loving It* (1995).

SKIN-fining Moment:

Gas Pump Girls (0:05) *Bomp and circumstance! Bare, bouncing beautiful breasts, when her graduation gown gets torn off during ceremony.*

See Her Naked In:

Terror in the Aisles (1984) Breasts
Gas Pump Girls (1979) Breasts
H.O.T.S. (1979) Breasts
Halloween (1978) Breasts
Jokes My Folks Never Told Me (1977) Breasts

Sunny Johnson

Born: September 21, 1953
San Bernardino County, California
Died: June 19, 1984
Skin-O-Meter: Brief Nudity

Sunny Johnson lived a brief life and had an even briefer career, but fortunately she left behind one skintastic appearance in *only* her briefs, that being her appearance as a nude dancer in the trashy smash *Flashdance* (1983). Sunny died in 1984 of a ruptured aneurysm while *Flashdance* was still in theaters, making her premature passing even more tragic. But she experienced more fame and success than many Hollywood dreamers do by the age of thirty, and for that we can still appreciate her mildly skintastic appearances in such fare as *The Night the Lights Went Out in Georgia* (1981), *Dr. Heckyl and Mr. Hype* (1980), and as Otter's co-ed in *Animal House* (1978).

SKIN-fining Moment:

Flashdance (1:15) *Sunny's seen sunnier times as she's carried out of a*

bar in a state of collapse, but we see her sunny-side-ups just fine and dandy!

See Her Naked In:

Flashdance (1983) Breasts, Thong

Victoria Lynn Johnson

Skin-O-Meter: Great Nudity

Any guy would be perfectly happy to jump in the shower with Angie Dickinson. Angie, however, didn't want to show off her impressive aging bod in a shower scene for *Dressed to Kill* (1980). Enter Victoria Lynn Johnson, a gorgeous model who stepped in to provide the film with some daring frontal nudity. Fans of Johnson haven't been shortchanged, though, since Victoria Lynn shows off her amazing face (and all her other parts) in *The Girls of Penthouse* (1984). And even though she only made one film, Victoria Lynn's nudity is memorable enough to rate two skin credits. You'll find her breast parts from *Dressed to Kill* featured in the slasher-film comp *Terror in the Aisles* (1984).

SKIN-fining Moment:

Dressed to Kill (0:02) *As Angie Dickinson's body double, Vicki fills in with her own frontal nudity during the soapilicious shower scene.*

See Her Naked In:

Terror in the Aisles (1984) Breasts
Dressed to Kill (1980) Breasts, Bush

Nahanni Johnstone

Toronto, Ontario, Canada
Skin-O-Meter: Brief Nudity

So far Nahanni Johnstone is probably best known to skinophiles as Mindy in the straight-to-video horror *Big Chill* (1983) parody *Infested* (2002). Nahanni has a great scene where she goes swimming topless then walks onshore with her perfect C (or are those D?) cups a-bouncing before she puts on a T-shirt. Before Nahanni and her twins landed this breakout role, her film roles included *Love in the Time of Money* (2002) and *The Doghouse* (2000). Her more respectable, but less skinorific, work has been on television, in series such as *Third Watch* (as Nicole in 2000) and *Liberty Street* (as Cynthia in the 1995-96 season).

SKIN-fining Moment:

Infested (0:22) Ms. Johnstone shows her Nahannis to great effect as she emerges, topless, from the ocean.

See Her Naked In:

Infested (2002) Breasts

Marilyn Joi

Skin-O-Meter: Great Nudity

The classic blaxploitation films were usually guaranteed to contain violence, vice, and lusciously thick lap fros. True to form, Marilyn Joi's jubilant Nubian nakedness is prominent in countless drive-in fare of the '70s, from *The Student Teachers* (1973) to *Naughty Stewardesses* (1975) to *Cheerleaders' Wild Weekend* (1979). Whether playing "Topless Dancer" or numerous unbilled roles, she has been there (often as Tracy King) to appease viewers' taste for dusky delights, as anyone who caught Marilyn's Joiful—albeit non-nude—swan song performance as "Hooker" in *Satan's Princess* (1990) can attest.

SKIN-fining Moment:

Cheerleaders' Wild Weekend (0:39) Marilyn pops out her chest melons for all in the crowded cabin to ogle.

See Her Naked In:

C.O.D. (1981) Breasts
Cheerleaders' Wild Weekend (1979) Breasts

The Kentucky Fried Movie (1977) Breasts
The Happy Hooker Goes to Washington (1977) Breasts
Nurse Sherri (1977) Breasts, Buns
Ilsa, Harem Keeper of the Oil Sheiks (1976) Breasts, Thong
Tender Loving Care (1974) Breasts
Naughty Stewardesses (1974) Breasts
The Student Teachers (1973) Breasts
Mean Mother (1973) Breasts, Buns
Hammer (1972) Breasts

Angelina Jolie

Born: June 4, 1975
Los Angeles, California
Skin-O-Meter: Hall of Fame

Angelina Jolie may occasionally come off crazier than a bag of cats, but few pussies can make a man's crotch purr like this ultra-C, superhumanly sensuous, luscious-lipped, goth-glam-a-go-go free spirit. Angelina first appeared onscreen opposite her pop Jon Voight in 1982's *Lookin' to Get Out*, but it took a decade before she busted out her big guns in *Cyborg II* (1993). Once unleashed, that powerful pink-tipped twosome proved unstoppable, bouncing from a punky flash in *Hackers* (1994) to the leztastic onslaught of *Gia* (1998)—and beyond! Angie scored a Best Supporting Actress Academy Award for *Girl, Interrupted* (1999) and singled out her date by announcing from the podium, "I am so in love with my brother right now!" Somehow, Angie's subsequent marriage to actor/director/anorexic Billy Bob Thornton (her second, his fifth) got even weirder than that, with the lovebirds flitting about with vials of each other's blood around their necks until their 2002 divorce. O, brother, where art thou!

SKIN-fining Moment:

Gia (0:27) A star is born—in her birthday suit! Angelina embodies the

---

MR. SKIN'S TOP TEN

Naked Daughters of Famous Fathers
. . . Father knows breast

10. Ronald Reagan's daughter Patti Davis

9. Joel Grey's daughter Jennifer Grey

8. William Shatner's daughter Melanie Shatner

7. John Phillips's daughter Bijou Phillips

6. Vic Morrow's daughter Jennifer Jason Leigh

5. Tony Curtis's daughter Jamie Leigh Curtis

4. Peter Fonda's daughter Bridget Fonda

3. Steven Tyler's daughter Liv Tyler

2. Clint Eastwood's daughter Alison Eastwood

1. **Jon Voight's daughter Angelina Jolie**

---

reckless spirit of anything goes '70s supermodel Gia Carangi by strutting around a hallway stark naked, baring her bodacious bosom and supremely squeezable backside to a crowd of astonished onlookers when an elevator opens and grants them a perfect view of her naked voluptuousness.

See Her Naked In:

Taking Lives (2004) Breasts, Bush
Original Sin (2001) Breasts
Pushing Tin (1999) Breasts
Hell's Kitchen (1998) Nip Slip RB
Gia (1998) Breasts, Buns
Mojave Moon (1996) Breasts
Foxfire (1996) Breasts
Hackers (1995) LB
Cyborg 2 (1993) Breasts

Grace Jones

Born: May 19, 1948
Spanishtown, Jamaica
Skin-O-Meter: Great Nudity

Arnold Schwarzenegger complained that Grace Jones was "too tough" during the filming of *Conan the Destroyer* (1984). That's what we like about this androgynous man killer. Arnold must have enjoyed her sexy ways, too, as she attended his 1986 wedding to Maria Shriver on Cape Cod with the only partner that could out-weird her, Andy Warhol. Grace studied theater at Syracuse University before becoming a successful model in Paris—her modeling agency thought her looks too "strong" for New York. Her peculiar and statuesque style made her a hot attraction in New York City's underground and nightlife scenes, and her sexually charged stage shows and songs like "I Need a Man" earned her the title "The Queen of Gay Discos." Yes, gays love her. But men of all sexual perversions find something they can call their own in Grace. She played one of the more bizarre Bond villains in *A View to a Kill* (1985). But for a more revealing shot of Grace check her out in *Vamp* (1986) for an even more bizarre body-painted striptease. She plays another freak in the Eddie Murphy comedy *Boomerang* (1992) and shows off her black booty. Black is beautiful.

SKIN-fining Moment:

Deadly Vengeance (0:14) Pre-freakshow Grace is completely nude on a mattress with her man. FFN and fine fanny.

See Her Naked In:

Boomerang (1992) LB, Buns
Vamp (1986) Breasts
Deadly Vengeance (1981) FFN, Buns
Let's Make a Dirty Movie (1975) Breasts, Buns

Jocelyn Jones

New York
Skin-O-Meter: Brief Nudity

Acting teachers often advise nervous students to picture their audience nude. With Jocelyn Jones, one wonders how many students at the Beverly Hills Playhouse have seen their instructor bare it all on the big screen. Though she devotes far more time to teaching than acting these days, Jocelyn had a promising screen career in the '70s with parts in fare such as *The Other Side of the Mountain* (1975) and *The Enforcer* (1976). Fortunately, she didn't depart without appearing with the late Claudia Jennings in *The Great Texas Dynamite Chase* (1977), where her screen presence was quite boobiquitous.

SKIN-fining Moment:

The Great Texas Dynamite Chase (1:03) Jocelyn enjoys a naked picnic with her boyfriend. Great view of her natural guns.

See Her Naked In:

The Great Texas Dynamite Chase (1977) Breasts

Josephine Jacqueline Jones

Born: 1960
Freeport, Bahamas
Skin-O-Meter: Great Nudity

Crowned Miss Bahamas in 1979, Josephine Jacqueline Jones made her acting debut in the Spanish/American film *Black Venus* (1983), and what a skinorific debut it was! Josephine appeared totally nude throughout this nineteenth-century period piece, which was based on a story by Balzac. Mr. Skin's "ball sac" was throbbing throughout the film, which was also packed with lesbo scenes! The film's follow-up, *Christina* (1984), offered more of the same, but this time with the always naked and incredibly gorgeous Jewel Shepherd. Josephine's last film appearance was in *La Ronde de L'amour* (1989), but overall she left plenty of her posterior—and her front—"behind" for posterity.

SKIN-fining Moment:

Black Venus (0:11) Rack, rump, and rug as she poses for a tuxedo-clad weenie who sketches her.

See Her Naked In:

La Ronde de L'amour (1989) FFN
Warrior Queen (1987) Breasts
Christina (1984) Breasts
Black Venus (1983) FFN, Buns

Marilyn Jones

Born: June 6, 1953
Grosse Pointe, Michigan
Skin-O-Meter: Great Nudity

For someone who started her career in 1969 playing a bordello girl in *Support Your Local Sheriff!* and who once again played a prostitute in the film *The Men's Club* (1986), Marilyn Jones showed precious little skin during her acting career, probably because the vast majority of her work was for television. Eighties television junkies undoubtedly saw Marilyn in at least *something*—she had guest spots on all the biggest shows of the decade, including *Moonlighting*, *Matlock*, and *Remington Steele*, not to mention her recurring roles on *Secrets of Midland Heights* and *King's Crossing*. She's been out of show business since a 1994 appearance on an episode of *Murder She Wrote*. But, thank goodness, she played a *full service* escort in *The Men's Club*, in which she flashed her tits at Harvey Keitel during a hotel bedroom scene.

SKIN-fining Moment:

The Men's Club (1:21) Check out Marilyn's marbles as she talks to Harvey Keitel all topless and such.

See Her Naked In:

The Men's Club (1986) Breasts

Shawnee Free Jones

Skin-O-Meter: Brief Nudity

Shawnee Free Jones would be a notable beauty even if she never made a film, since her father—Franklin Jones, a.k.a. Avatar Adi Da Samraj—is a noted religious leader. Some cult critics even suggest that Shawnee got her start modeling in a lingerie catalogue published by her dad's empire. But at least Shawnee's screen career seems divine, with an amazing nude debut in *L.A. Confidential* (1997). Shawnee freed an amazing set of gorgeous vintage titties in the popular period piece, and you'll boo the good guys when cop Kevin Spacey busts up the hot sex scene. Shawnee then came back in *Something About Sex* (1998), still looking like a classic blonde beauty while riding a guy in a truly wild sex scene. Sadly, her biggest screen role since *L.A. Confidential* has been as Lizzie Borden in the under-seen comedy *Monkeybone* (2001). Shawnee remains a busy young actress, though, and she turned producer to get herself a starring role in *Mr. BBQ* (2002).

SKIN-fining Moment:

L.A. Confidential (0:12) Shawnee frees her cleavage in a hotel room as the press sneaks a photo through the window.

See Her Naked In:

Denial (1998) Breasts, Buns
L.A. Confidential (1997) Breasts

Shirley Jones

**Born: March 31, 1934
Charleroi, Pennsylvania
Skin-O-Meter: Never Nude**

Though remembered today mainly for her role as the mother on *The Partridge Family*, Shirley Jones already had decades of experience on stage and screen before her most prominent role. Named after Shirley Temple, she started out on Broadway, graduating to movie versions of the same musicals. The girl who couldn't say no in *Oklahoma!* (1955) didn't apply this philosophy to nudity, starring mainly in innocuous pictures such as *Carousel* (1960) and *The Music Man* (1962). With attitudes in movies changing in the '60s, she moved to television and currently performs revues of her older work.

SKIN-fining Moment:

The Happy Ending (1:01) Mrs. Partridge peels her shirt off to reveal a bra but doesn't let her pair free.

Sue Jones-Davies

**UK
Skin-O-Meter: Great Nudity**

Monty Python's Life of Brian (1979) wouldn't have been nearly as funny without all the authentic period touches—which, thankfully, include the untrimmed bush of Sue Jones-Davies as Brian's revolutionary love interest. Her toned titties and massive muff are so sexy that we forgot to laugh. Despite her comic highlight, Sue is best known today as a Welsh folk performer, although she occasionally shows up in films such as *The Theory of Flight* (1998). She remains a respected figure of British comedy, too, while UK rock fans still grab their crotches to her sexy turn as Rox on the 1977 TV series *Rock Follies of '77*.

SKIN-fining Moment:

Life of Brian (1:04) Sue shows some seriously shaggy shrubbery when she defends Brian from his mum. There's a delectable chest-duo and a delightful derriere in there, too!

See Her Naked In:

Life of Brian (1979) FFN, Buns

Milla Jovovich

**Born: December 17, 1975
Kiev, Ukraine
Skin-O-Meter: Great Nudity**

More than chicken comes from Kiev, Ukraine. Milla Jovovich is the type of bird that you really want to pluck. The blue-green-eyed waif beauty with the itty bitties and a tall, *svelte* body made for modeling has been doing just that since she was only nine years old. Milla worked on sexy Calvin Klein campaigns, and at twelve years old she made history as the youngest girl ever to appear on an American fashion-magazine cover. Not long after that she was reprising the role that made Brooke Shields famously hot in *Return to the Blue Lagoon* (1991). It also marked the first sighting of her small top. But it was not to be the last. She flashed her fine fanny in *Chaplin* (1992) and made it clear why Charlie Chaplin walked the odd way

---

MR. SKIN'S TOP TEN

Naked Eastern Bloc Babes
. . . Russian undressing

10. Oksana Babiy
9. Ivana Bozilovic
8. Natalia Sokolova
7. Barbora Kodetova
6. Daniela Pestova
5. Jenya Lano
4. Victoria Zdrok
3. Margaret Markov
2. Paulina Porizkova
1. **Milla Jovovich**

MILLA JOVOVICH GETS SOME SAND IN HER GLAND IN *RETURN TO THE BLUE LAGOON*.

> "We were outside in the rain, it was freezing cold, and it was not working. Ashley saw the pain I was in, and without consulting her agents or anything, said, 'Stuff it, I'll do it!'"
>
> —DIRECTOR STEPHAN ELLIOTT ON ASHLEY JUDD'S NUDE SCENE IN *EYE OF THE BEHOLDER*.

he did. Though she wasn't naked in the stoner comedy *Dazed and Confused* (1993), the role cemented her hip credentials. Already a model, act-chest, and even a singer, the sky was the limit for mini-mammed Milla. She took to outer space and again showed off her fit form opposite a lucky Bruce Willis in the sci-fi flick *The Fifth Element* (1997). In *He Got Game* (1998), Milla got tits, and she even unintentionally flashed some gash in the horror-action thriller *Resident Evil* (2002). She kept the fur flying in a lovely out-of-the-shower nude scene in *No Good Deed* (2002). Yes, no good deed goes un-whacked.

SKIN-fining Moment:

The Fifth Element (0:27) Brief right glass-cutter nipple as Milla sleeps in the regeneration chamber.

See Her Naked In:

Resident Evil: Apocalypse (2004) Breasts
No Good Deed (2002) FFN, Buns
Resident Evil (2002) RB, Bush
He Got Game (1998) Breasts, Thong
The Fifth Element (1997) Breasts
Chaplin (1992) LB, Buns
Return to the Blue Lagoon (1991) Breasts

Ashley Judd

Born: April 19, 1968
Granada Hills, California
Skin-O-Meter: Hall of Fame

If you like country-western music, listen to The Judds—but if you prefer thrills a little south of the border, then your destination is Ashley Judd. She's howlingly hotter than her yodel-happy relatives and no bashful southern belle when it comes to showing off. Ash affirmed that Marilyn Monroe was not a natural blonde with her pube-bearing performance as Norma Jean in HBO's *Norma Jean and Marilyn* (1996). That same year, she kept her panties on but forgot to holster her milk guns in *Normal Life* (1996). Those perky pretties are a handful right down to their thumbs-up nipples, which gave audiences a poke in the pants in *Eye of the Beholder* (1999) and made them see double in *Double Jeopardy* (1999).

SKIN-fining Moment:

Norma Jean and Marilyn (0:04) Full frontal in a church-set dream sequence, with extensive ganders at Ashley's Judds. "Oh dear God." indeed!

See Her Naked In:

Double Jeopardy (1999) Breasts, Buns
Eye of the Beholder (1999) Breasts, Buns
Normal Life (1996) Breasts
Norma Jean and Marilyn (1996) FFN, Buns

Janet Julian

Born: July 10, 1959
Evanston, Illinois
Skin-O-Meter: Brief Nudity

Janet Julian dropped out of UCLA after a year to model in New York. Before too long she was starring in commercials and got her big break in 1978 by replacing Pamela Sue Martin as Nancy Drew on *The Hardy Boys/Nancy Drew Mysteries*. She seems to have dropped off the showbiz radar after a 1995 appearance on the kids' television series *Fudge*, but as luck would have it, Janet left behind a few skinorific performances before her showbiz retirement. She was the heroine of the Canadian horror flick *Humongous* (1982), in which there was a nice shot of her very unhumongous ass as she outran a big, mean monster, whom she eventually set on fire. She got briefly naked in *King of New York* (1990) and also had a small role in *Fear City* (1984), a tale of Manhattan strippers who are stalked and murdered by a psycho. She was also pretty hot but non-nude in *Choke Canyon* (1986), which unfortunately does not refer to her gullet!

SKIN-fining Moment:

Humongous (0:20) As Janet pilots a boat, her boyfriend peels down her bikini bottoms and we get some sexy cheek-peeks.

See Her Naked In:

King of New York (1990) LB
Humongous (1982) Buns

Katherine Justice

Born: 1942
Ohio
Skin-O-Meter: Great Nudity

Katherine Justice is the kind of cowgirl cowboys love to ride. She first got in the saddle on the western series *The Big Valley* and followed that up with appearances on other bawdy bronco dramas such as *Gunsmoke* and *The Virginian*. Knowing a good thing when she saw it, Katherine followed her tumbleweed onto the big screen with a performance in *The Way West* (1967) opposite Kirk Douglas. Sadly, by the '70s the genre disappeared, although Katherine did not. But her career was never the same. She did manage to test the sexploitation waters in her sole skinful moment onscreen. In *The Stepmother* (1971), Katherine was completely naked in a few scenes, including a shower montage that stopped just short of muff-tacular. Next, she found employment on the boob tube, with stints on *Falcon Crest* and *Dangerous Women* before leaving the business of show and the possibility of ever showing herself in the nude again. The world's a less hot place when there's no Justice in it.

SKIN-fining Moment:

The Stepmother (0:34) Frequent peeks at Kathy's cannage as she rolls around in bed with her hubby.

See Her Naked In:

The Stepmother (1971) Breasts, Buns

Jane Kaczmarek

Born: December 21, 1955
Milwaukee, Wisconsin
Skin-O-Meter: Brief Nudity

Jane Kaczmarek is the mom on the Fox sitcom hit *Malcolm in the Middle*, and she can even be spied in the buff—albeit with her most important parts just off camera—on some of its more risqué episodes. Now earning the big bucks, it took a while for this unconventional beauty to make it in the superficial world of Hollywood. She worked her way up through the trenches of TV programming such as *St. Elsewhere*, *Hill Street Blues*, and *Remington Steele* before testing her mettle on the big screen, debuting opposite Gene Hackman in the film *Uncommon Valor* (1983). She has made the silver screen sexier thanks to appearances in *Falling in Love* (1984), *Vice Versa* (1988), and *D.O.A.* (1988), but the boob tube has been this brunette's bread and butter. She is the recurring voice of Judge Constance Harm on *The Simpsons* but should be more widely available in movies such as *Widely Available* (1999). It's Jane's only nudity onscreen, and it's boobtacular, as she lets her love sacks free in a bedroom tryst that's sure to have you biting the pillow. Mr. Skin waits with masturbated breath for another look at her jugs.

SKIN-fining Moment:

Widely Available (0:29) Jane gets down to copulating with her man and we see a flash of right breast first, followed by a bit of the left. No telling if Malcolm's in the middle.

See Her Naked In:

Wildly Available (1996) Breasts

Elizabeth Kaitan

Born: 1960
Hungary
Skin-O-Meter: Great Nudity

Elizabeth Kaitan is a Hungarian honey who makes Americans hungry for her big, natural, milky jugs. She came to the United States to become a movie star, and though she's no Hollywood hotshot, her skinful career has made her the money shot here at Skin Central. No one takes you seriously when you take your clothes off in every movie. Who cares; Elizabeth takes her clothes off in every movie she's in! That's batting a thousand in the making-our-bats-hard department. From her first nude appearance onscreen in *Violated* (1984) to her last lustful flash in *Virtual Encounters* (1996), Elizabeth has been the queen of quim. Her blonde hair, big boobs, round ass, and well-trimmed trim—and her willingness to expose them all the time—have made her the act-chest to beat off to. She hasn't been seen much, though,

since *Veronica 2030* (1999), and this sexploitation and scream queen is sorely missed. Speaking of sore, it's been a few years now, Elizabeth, and Mr. Skin's joint has finally recovered from the frantic whacking at your expense. What we're trying to say here at Skin Central is we're ready for another round with your mounds!

SKIN-fining Moment:

Slave Girls from Beyond Infinity (0:38) Grand gander at Liz's large, natural fun-pillows as she cozies up to a fella.

See Her Naked In:

Virtual Encounters (1996) Breasts, Bush, Buns
Vice Academy Part 5 (1996) Breasts
Petticoat Planet (1995) Breasts
Beretta's Island (1994) Breasts
Vice Academy 4 (1994) Breasts
South Beach Academy (1994) Breasts
Desperate Crimes (1993) RB
Vice Academy Part 3 (1991) Breasts
Night Club (1990) FFN
Roller Blade Warriors: Taken by Force (1989) Breasts
Nightwish (1989) Breasts
Friday the 13th Part VII: The New Blood (1988) Breasts
Necromancer (1988) Breasts
Slave Girls from Beyond Infinity (1987) Breasts
Assault of the Killer Bimbos (1987) Breasts
Silent Night, Deadly Night: Part 2 (1986) RB
Savage Dawn (1984) RB
Violated (1984) Breasts, Bush, Buns

TeleVisions:

Love Street Breasts, Buns

Toni Kalem

Born: 1956
Newark, New Jersey
Skin-O-Meter: Brief Nudity

Toni Kalem may be most recognizable for her recurring role on HBO's bad-guy series *The Sopranos*, but she started her acting career on a whim, appearing in an episode of the good-guy series *Starsky and Hutch*. She stuck to TV for a while, appearing on *Another World* for a few seasons, before making her big screen debut in *The Wanderers* (1979). After that came the campy after-school special *The Boy Who Drank Too Much* (1980), starring '80s überkind Scott Baio. Toni still hadn't achieved serious success at this point, having only been seen in the background of big-time flicks such as *Private Benjamin* (1980) and *Paternity* (1981). She finally had a role with some meat in *Running Out* (1983), but few saw it, and it looked like her career was running out of steam. It was during the lull of the early '80s that a window of opportunity opened up, which Toni skinfully exploited in *Silent Rage* (1982). In a bedroom tryst, she rolled around topless, showing off a most bountiful bosom. Most recently, she has appeared in *15 Minutes* (2001) as "Woman at Planet Hollywood." Hopefully, this pretty brunette's fifteen minutes of fame aren't up yet.

SKIN-fining Moment:

Silent Rage (0:46) Brief right boobage twice while Toni makes out in bed with Chuck Norris. Is she the luckiest woman alive or what?

See Her Naked In:

Silent Rage (1982) Breasts

Alexandra Kamp

Born: December 29, 1966
Baden-Baden, Germany
Skin-O-Meter: Great Nudity

It's not only cars, coffee makers, and handguns that the Germans construct with an eye for pleasing, streamlined form and unparalleled functionality. Take one look at former model Alexandra Kamp. Flashing a reddish tinge to her brunette mane, Alexandra has taken her long, sensual, and manifestly strong frame and risen from the catwalk to the bigger-than-life cinema screen. The results are eye boggling. Displaying an amazingly hot actress's points of keenest interest is not verboten on German television. It's a wonder cathode screens across the Vaterland did not melt down with the appearance of Alexandra Kamp's hot spots in *Ein Luge Zuviel* (1997) and *Der Kopp* (1999). For easier rental access to Alexandra's tasty ta-tas, tiptoe into the domestic goof flick *2001: A Space Travesty* (2000).

SKIN-fining Moment:

Eine Lüge Zuviel (0:04) Ass and blurry tits joining Bernd Herzsprung in the shower. Then more tits having sex, which is followed by her lying in bed— dead, naked, and hot!!!

See Her Naked In:

Antonia—Zwischen Liebe und Macht (2001) Breasts
2001: A Space Travesty (2000) Breasts, Thong
Der Kopp (1999) RB
Morgen Gehört der Himmel Dir (1999) Breasts
Ich Liebe eine Hure (1998) Breasts, Thong
Eine Lüge zuviel (1997) Breasts, Buns

Melina Kanakaredes

Born: April 23, 1967
Akron, Ohio
Skin-O-Meter: Brief Nudity

Melina Kanakaredes lit loins afire on *The Guiding Light* then vanished from the boob tube until reappearing as 'cuff-'em-and-rough-'em cop Jimmy Smits's gal pal on *NYPD Blue*, where she exposed some NYPD bunnage. Should this acting gig go south, the Magna cum Laude, synchronized swimming, Miss Ohio 1986 first-runner-up has skills to fall back on. While you're more likely to spy skin at a drunken sorority toga party, Melina's bra-baring scenes have dudes tuning in to the medical mush drama *Providence*, stat.

SKIN-fining Moment:

NYPD Blue "Vishy-Vashy-Vinny" (1995) Brief left NYPD boob as Jimmy Smits takes off her sweater.

TeleVisions:

NYPD Blue Buns

Carol Kane

Born: June 18, 1952
Cleveland, Ohio
Skin-O-Meter: Brief Nudity

Goggle-eyed, waif-like beauty Carol Kane looks like a Botticelli painting come to lustful life. She may be best remembered as Andy Kaufman's kooky wife Simka Gravas on the TV series *Taxi*, but she's been acting since her debut in the movie *Is This Trip Really Necessary?* (1970). Is it ever! Carol has played a goofy girlfriend in *Carnal Knowledge* (1971), a hostage in *Dog Day Afternoon* (1975), Woody Allen's first wife in *Annie Hall* (1977), and a freaked-out babysitter in *When a Stranger Calls* (1979). More recently, she's kept up the monkeyshines opposite Billy Crystal in *The Princess Bride* (1987), Bill Murray in *Scrooged* (1988), and a family of freaks in *Addams Family Values* (1993). But we have to go back to *The Last Detail* (1973) for Carol's best skinage. She plays a hooker who gives AWOL Randy Quaid a sexy send off before he's locked up in the stockade. Carol is completely nude, sitting on a bed smoking, with a hint of her honey-colored bush and her hot-dog tits peeking through her curly blonde locks. Talk about raising Kane!

SKIN-fining Moment:

The Last Detail (1:23) Carol Kane shows her great white pointers and a little babushka as she sits in bed after having banged Randy Quaid.

See Her Naked In:

The Mafu Cage (1978) LB
The Last Detail (1973) Breasts, Bush

Valérie Kaprisky

**Born: August 19, 1962
Neuilly-Sur-Seine, Paris, France
Skin-O-Meter: Hall of Fame**

Valerie Kaprisky debuted in the French flick *Men Prefer Fat Girls* (1981). If that's the case, then they must hate the shapely but sleek booty that this Gallic dollop of gorgeousness loves to expose in film after film, such as in the seaside treat *Year of the Jellyfish* (1984), which boasts lots of topless bathing-beauty views of Valerie's voluptuous va-va-vooms. After establishing a skinful career in her native country, Val tried to break into Hollywood. Her big-budget remake of *Breathless* (1983) with Richard Gere may have flopped at the box office, but it made quite an impression in Mr. Skin's pants. Her nudity left me gasping. But for her skintacular breast-of performance, we have to go back to cheese-eating country and watch *La Femme Publique* (1984), which serves up more furburger than McDonald's serves Big Macs! There's also a hot sex scene that sure doesn't look "simulated." Why bother play

VALÉRIE KAPRISKY AND RICHARD GERE IN *BREATHLESS*. THAT'S NOT HOW YOU MUFF-DIVE, DICK.

acting? No fear of screwing up your lines when you're screwing!

SKIN-fining Moment:

Breathless (0:47) Richard Gere takes off her towel. See those French funbags, fanny, and some fuzz. Nice.

See Her Naked In:

Mouvements du Désir (1994) Breasts
Milena (1991) Breasts
Year of the Jellyfish (1984) FFN, Buns
La Femme Publique (1983) FFN, Buns
Breathless (1983) Breasts, Bush, Buns
Aphrodite (1982) FFN
Superbiester (1981) Breasts

Mitzi Kapture

**Born: May 2, 1964
Yorba Linda, California
Skin-O-Meter: Great Nudity**

Mitzi Kapture seemed like a true trash icon early in her career, sporting a poodle perm while revealing a hot bod in the low-budget movie *Private Road: No Trespassing* (1987). The five-foot-three-inch dynamo also came through with a sterling shower scene in *Lethal Pursuit* (1988) before taking on the hallowed role of former teen hooker Angel in *Angel III: The Final Chapter* (1988). But Mitzi threw us a curve in 1991 by becoming a TV star on the long-running USA detective series *Silk Stalkings*. We got one more look at Mitzi's titzis with *The Vagrant*

(1992), but Kapture had decided to go after a mainstream audience. It'll take a big budget before we can capture Mitzi in the nude again, although she did grace us with a single season of *Baywatch* in 1998.

SKIN-fining Moment:

Private Road (1:29) B.J. and the Bare: Mitzi gets topless while getting some Greg Evigan lovin'.

See Her Naked In:

Lethal Pursuit (1989) Breasts
Private Road (1987) Breasts

Olga Karlatos

**Born: April 20, 1947
Athens, Greece
Skin-O-Meter: Great Nudity**

Olga Karlatos came straight out of Athens, Greece, with a dark beauty that sums up the best of the breed. It's no surprise that she was an international film star throughout the '70s. Things got weird, though, when Olga joined Mia Farrow's sister Tisa in the gory Italian horror hit *Zombie* (1979). It was a weird career choice redeemed by a hot shower scene where Olga finally unveiled some gazongas worth chomping—which, sadly, is exactly what happened to them. The film was a surprisingly smart career move for Olga, though, as she went on to make her American debut in the sexy TV film *Scruples* (1981). Her featured role in the acclaimed *Once Upon a Time in America* (1984) also featured more of her stunning titties, although you can see a lot more of her megamelons in the shower scene from *Murderock—Uccide a Passo di Danza* (1984). Then it was back to the States to play Prince's abused mother in *Purple Rain* (1984). The role made her officially hot enough to sex up a 1986 episode of *Miami Vice*—and that was the last we saw of our favorite Greek pastry.

SKIN-fining Moment:

Zombie (0:39) Olga shows off everything, including some full-frontal action, while taking a shower in front of a cleverly-placed mirror. Kudos to the set designer!

See Her Naked In:

Once Upon a Time in America (1984) RB
Murderock—Uccide a Passo di Danza (1984) Breasts
Zombie (1979) FFN, Buns
Mogliamante (1977) Breasts

Claudia Karvan

Born: May 19, 1972
Sydney, New South Wales, Australia
Skin-O-Meter: Great Nudity

Claudia Karvan may be known to some Americans for her guest spots on the hit series *Farscape*, but the bulk of her career has been firmly rooted in her native Australia. And this gal from Down Under has shown down under! But before that she started her career with a starring role in the Aussie kiddie flick *Molly* (1983) at the tender age of eleven. Since then she has been more or less continually acting, save for a few years in the late '80s when she took some time off for schooling. Claudia has since matured into quite the lovely lady and schooled audiences on the art of seduction by sharing her wonderful beauty via some rather steamy skin scenes, most notably in the short *Touch Me* (1993). In less than a half-hour, Claudia managed to spend about ten minutes completely naked, including some hot full-frontal shots. She has since showed off some hootage in the full-length films *The Heartbreak Kid* (1993), *Flynn* (1996), and *Risk* (2000). But as *Touch Me* proved, sometimes less is more.

SKIN-fining Moment:

Touch Me (0:49) Buns getting an oily massage from another babe. Drippingly hot!

See Her Naked In:

Risk (2000) Breasts, Bush
Flynn (1996) Breasts
Touch Me (1993) FFN, Buns
The Heartbreak Kid (1993) Breasts

Ursula Karven

Born: September 17, 1964
Ulm, Germany
Skin-O-Meter: Great Nudity

In Germany, they say, everyone follows orders. It's understandable when those commands are barked from the sensual mouths of sexy fräuleins such as Ursula Karven. A perfect product of the masturbation race, this leggy blonde was already exposing her assets when still an über-vixen in her native Deutschland. In such T&A-rousing productions as her movie debut *Ein Irres Feeling* (1984), as well as *Tödliches Leben* (1995) and *Liebe Ist Stärker als der Tod* (1999), Ursula made the Fourth Reich rise again . . . in your pants. Thankfully, Ursula decided to dress American wieners with her tasty Kraut. She's at her moist skinful in *Holiday Affair* (2001), and all of her appearances should be as steamy as *Con Express* (2002). Ursula, Mr. Skin is on the fast track for you, baby.

SKIN-fining Moment:

Holiday Affair (0:21) Blindfolded Ursula bares taut, hard-nipped tittage and a hint of bush while getting banged on the floor.

See Her Naked In:

Con Express (2002) Breasts
Holiday Affair (2001) FFN, Buns
Liebe Ist Stärker als der Tod (1999) LB
Rosamunde Pilcher—Dornen im Tal der Blumen (1998) LB
Ich Schenk dir Meinen Mann (1998) Breasts
Tatort—Bei Auftritt Mord (1996) Thong
Tödliches Leben (1995) RB, Buns
Wie Treu Ist Nik? (1986) FFN
Ein Irres Feeling (1984) FFN

Kimberley Kates

Born: August 11, 1971
Louisiana
Skin-O-Meter: Great Nudity

The face of lean, strawberry-blonde Kimberly Kates projects a quality of joyful wantonness that promises purely innocent and entirely prurient sexuality. Kimberly's lasciviously smirking lips and openly yearning eyes are eagerly seeking a vigorous round of fun in the sheets, but all traces of neediness or desperation are excluded from her poised puckering. Gaze at delectable Kates's erotically glowing head shot. She just might be the perfect woman, which explains her casting as the princess vision in *Bill & Ted's Excellent Adventure* (1989). Such a vision of feminine splendor naturally resulted in a captive shower stall performance in *Chained Heat 2* (1993). Kimberly has developed a minor specialty as a topless mattress pal who is choked in the comfort of bed; see her tits quiver as a male paw gets a grip on her throat in *First Degree* (1998) and *Highway* (2001).

SKIN-fining Moment:

Chained Heat 2 (0:30) Full monty when steaming up the shower with Lucie Benes.

See Her Naked In:

Highway (2001) Breasts, Thong
First Degree (1998) Breasts
Armstrong (1998) FFN
Shadow of Doubt (1998) Breasts
Chained Heat 2 (1993) FFN

Rosanne Katon

Born: February 5, 1954
New York, New York
Skin-O-Meter: Great Nudity

Rosanne Katon surprisingly took it all off for a nude spread as Playmate of the Month in the September 1978 issue of *Playboy* magazine *after* she made a name for herself in the movies. In fact, she had been appearing in films since her jug-revealing turn in the skintastic classic *The Swinging Cheerleaders* (1974), as well as on the short-lived TV series *Grady*. By the time she took it off for that frisky Bunny, Rosanne had already pulled out her shirt puppies for meaty roles in *Chesty Anderson, USN* (1976) and *Coach* (1978). The exposure as a stapled, fold-out harlot helped take her career to a new realm, that is the skinless but mainstream hits *Zapped!* (1982) and *Bachelor Party* (1984). That didn't stop her from continuing the tit trend in *Body and Soul* (1981) and *Lunch Wagon* (1982), where she was definitely on the menu. By the early '90s Rosanne's career in the business of show was over—but what a run.

SKIN-fining Moment:

The Swinging Cheerleaders (0:25) Rosy busts out her dusky ding-dongs after she takes off her blouse in the teacher's office.

See Her Naked In:

Body and Soul (1981) LB
Lunch Wagon (1980) Breasts
Coach (1978) Breasts
Chesty Anderson, USN (1976) Breasts
The Swinging Cheerleaders (1974) Breasts

Caren Kaye

Born: March 12, 1951
New York, New York
Skin-O-Meter: Great Nudity

Wherever grown men gather to whine away the remains of the day in the supportive company of one another, be they in lock-down wards, drunk tanks, or Promise Keeper cells, a recurring figure of blame is dear old Dad. The old man is taken to task for being mostly unavailable and harsh when he was around. Pop just never knew how to show his love; it wasn't his fault, but he didn't do us any good with his neglect and abuse. Why couldn't he have caught a screening of *My Tutor* (1983) and its titular heroine as played by brazenly nurturing blonde Caren Kaye? Caren's onscreen appearances formed a long and illustrious span both before and after she played the part of a seductive pedagogue hired by a rich man to deepen the knowledge of his callow son. Candy-lipped Kaye's skin-rich *My Tutor* lessons in love created a serious and lasting epidemic of father envy in those of us who were brought up by lesser men.

SKIN-fining Moment:

My Tutor (0:25) Caren drops her robe and skinny dips in a swimming pool. Those cans are O-Kaye!

See Her Naked In:

My Tutor (1983) Breasts, Buns

Lainie Kazan

Born: May 15, 1940
New York, New York
Skin-O-Meter: Brief Nudity

With her juicy lips like fat sweet dates; her direct, no-bullshit, libido-fed gaze; and a rack commensurate with the size of her big-as-all-heck heart, eternally ethnic Lainie Kazan might be mistaken for just any earthy goddess of sensual delights, until she opens her mouth and belts out a ballad. The torchy singer began her public career as understudy to the wildly popular Barbra Streisand in the 1964 stage production of *Funny Girl*. That trial by fire prepared Kazan for the kitschy kidding and sweet-octave golden throat work necessary for success on *The Dean Martin Summer Show*, and her dramatic and vocal talents have never been far from a screen or cabaret stage near you ever since.

SKIN-fining Moment:

Lust in the Dust (1:03) Lainie shows some veiny seat meat strolling away from the shower, although we don't see her face, so it could be a stunt butt.

See Her Naked In:

Gigli (2003) Thong
Lust in the Dust (1985) Buns

Camille Keaton

Born: 1950
Atlanta, Georgia
Skin-O-Meter: Hall of Fame

Camille Keaton comes from the same stock as funnyman Buster Keaton, but there's nothing comic about the silent movie superstar's great-niece. Slender scream queen Camille premiered in the Italian B-movie *What Have They Done to Solange?* (1972). Later that year she made her skin debut in *Decameron No. 2—Le Alter Novelle di Boccaccio* (1972), with a nice gander at her tiny tits and tailage. But Camille is most notorious as the avenging victim of violence in the feminist exploitation classic *I Spit on Your Grave* (1978). After a brutal attack—featuring her full-frontal glory, if you can stomach the rough stuff—Camille took revenge on her attackers: one gets his meat and potatoes sliced off, another is erotically asphyxiated. Vengeance is mine, saith the (naked) lady! Camille went on to appear in *Raw Force* (1982) and *The Concrete Jungle*

(1982), showing off a bit more skinage, before disappearing from the sexy screen by the mid '90s. Too bad; cinema needs a return of Camille's hot reprisal.

SKIN-fining Moment:

I Spit on Your Grave (1:23) Camille *flashes full-frontal, followed by an excellent shot of her perfect posterior as she prepares for some bathtime fun with Eron Tabor.*

See Her Naked In:

The Concrete Jungle (1982) Breasts, Bush
Raw Force (1981) Breasts
I Spit on Your Grave (1978) FFN, Buns
Decameron No. 2—Le Altre Novelle di Boccaccio (1972) RB, Buns

Diane Keaton

Born: January 5, 1946
Los Angeles, California
Skin-O-Meter: Great Nudity

With her awkward stage presence and plain WASPy looks, it was not a given that Diane Keaton would rocket to stardom. Then came her relationship with Woody Allen. He cast her in a slew of his early, funny movies, climaxing with her Academy Award-winning lead in *Annie Hall* (1977). Not only did guys fall in love with her quirky charms, but gals around the world copped her thrift-store-chic style. Diane bounced from the impish Allen to the Hollywood cocksmith Warren Beatty and from comedy to more serious fare. She appeared as Kay Smith in *The Godfather* series and got an Oscar nomination for her part in Beatty's *Reds* (1981). But this left-handed loony bird made audiences see blue playing an uptight teacher who gets involved in the meet market of '70s New York City. In *Looking for Mr. Goodbar* (1977), Diane melted like chocolate in the groping hands of the groovy singles scene and made her skin debut. Over a quarter

century later, fifty-seven-year-old Diane dared to go bare opposite Jack Nicholson in the romantic comedy *Something's Gotta Give* (2003). When Jack burst in on Diane in the full-frontal buff, something gave all right—in my pants!

SKIN-fining Moment:

Something's Gotta Give (0:31) When Jack Nicholson accidentally walks in on Diane, we get a fast blast of her 57-year-old funbaggage, plus a flash of fur, to boot. Not bad for her age. Not bad at all!

See Her Naked In:

Something's Gotta Give (2003) FFN
Reds (1981) Buns
Looking for Mr. Goodbar (1977) Breasts, Buns

Hayley Keenan

Born: 1980
Skin-O-Meter: Great Nudity

Hayley Keenan wasted no time in shedding clothing and getting a start on her skin career. In what may be the most underrated example of debauchery-laden, gratuitous-nudity-filled celluloid ever, otherwise known as *Teenage Caveman* (2001), she showed off her Hayley's comets. Those milky-white breasts were revealed along with every other female's in the cast! She even got some pretty hot bathtub action with co-star Tiffany Limos. Now that's a debut we can get behind! A role like that would probably mean the end of a lesser babe's career, but with another tit shot (albeit after slitting her wrists in a blood-red bath) in *The Rules of Attraction* (2002) opposite hunkenstein James Van Der Beek and Jessica Biel, skin's the limit for this chick.

SKIN-fining Moment:

Teenage Caveman (0:23) Hayley loses her outfit to hop in hot tub, hoisting out her hooters. Keen (an)!

See Her Naked In:

The Rules of Attraction (2002) Breasts
Teenage Caveman (2001) Breasts

Diane Keen

Born: July 29, 1946
London, England, UK
Skin-O-Meter: Great Nudity

Delicate-boned, dark-haired Diane Keen is a darling of the British TV scene. Famous for lending her lusciousness to series such as *Crossroads, The Cuckoo Waltz,* and the more recent *Brookside,* Diane is a lasting daytime delight. While always the perfect lady in her more popular portrayals, we prefer Diane when she's devilish. The English eyeful was most delicious when serving up her crumpets in flesh flicks such as *The Sex Thief* (1973) and *Sweeney!* (1977). No weenie worth his weight in salt could resist being Keen on ever-delicious Diane in all her skindeavors.

SKIN-fining Moment:

The Sex Thief (1:20) Long scene when she dominates a handcuffed dude. Boobs, buns, and bush.

See Her Naked In:

Sweeney! (1977) RB
The Sex Thief (1973) FFN, Buns

Catherine Keener

Born: March 26, 1960
Miami, Florida
Skin-O-Meter: Brief Nudity

Catherine Keener is the queen of indie movies. The cool guy's sex symbol, this lithe brunette beauty debuted in the Brat Pack flick *About Last Night . . .* (1986) but quickly cemented her reputation with a role opposite Brad Pitt in *Johnny Suede* (1991). She's since made a name for herself as the bitch in *Being John Malkovich* (1999) and flirted with the mainstream in *Death to Smoochy* (2002) and *S1m0ne* (2002). But we love her in small box-office sleepers that show off her small box-office teats. In *Living in Oblivion* (1995) and *The Real Blonde* (1997), Catherine exposed her nipple-swollen twins, if only briefly. Catherine would be even Keener if she let us take a longer peek at her perky set.

SKIN-fining Moment:

Living in Oblivion (0:28) Hairy-pitted Catherine bares her petite peaches while laying in bed.

See Her Naked In:

The Real Blonde (1997) RB
Living in Oblivion (1995) Breasts

Claire Keim

Born: July 8, 1975
Périgord, France
Skin-O-Meter: Great Nudity

We first said "Cripes!" to Claire Keim when this French work of art unveiled her pastries (and some prime furburgerage) in *J'irai au Paradis Car l'enfer est Ici* (1997)—although we were just as happy to see Claire being pretty in blue during her topless scene in *Barracuda* (1997). And now she's become an international star with the arthouse hit *The Girl* (2000), a stunning saga of lesbian loving where Claire defines femininity in the title role. In fact, she defines it by playing a nightclub singer who drives a lovely butch gal crazy with her schizo ways. Claire, fortunately, proves she can be just as inspired with men during her wild sex scenes in the TV movie *Il Giovane Casanova* (2002). Previously, her biggest American exposure had been playing a waitress in a 1994 episode of the syndicated series *Highlander,* but Claire's working on her English and planning to move

into American productions—starting with a role in the low-budget *Ripper: Letter from Hell* (2001).

SKIN-fining Moment:

The Girl (0:20) As her lovergirl saunters up a stairway, Claire provides the ultimate motivation by tossing off her clothes and standing gloriously full-frontal before making a beeline for the bedroom. Mammoth mammos, abundant bush.

See Her Naked In:

Féroce (2002) Breasts, Buns
Il Giovani Casanova (2002) Breasts, Bush, Buns
Les Sens des Affaires (2000) Breasts, Buns
The Girl (1999) FFN, Buns
Le Roi danse (2000) Breasts
Le Juge est une Femme: Dans Avec la Mort (1993) Breasts
Barracuda (1997) Breasts
J'irai au Paradis Car l'enfer est Ici (1997) FFN

Marthe Keller

Born: January 28, 1945
Basel, Switzerland
Skin-O-Meter: Great Nudity

Before there were Ben Affleck and Jennifer Lopez in *Gigli* (2003), there were offscreen lovers Al Pacino and Marthe Keller in *Bobby Deerfield* (1977). This notorious bomb was panned as one of the most inept love stories ever told—and audiences even stayed away from the sight of Marthe's shapely muffins. Sadly, *Deerfield* marked the end of Marthe's busy American career. Already an international star, this Swiss Miss made her American debut wearing out Dustin Hoffman in *Marathon Man* (1976), in which her casual nudity captured the essence of the liberated European woman—except that she shaved her armpits. She's an equally stunning femme fatale in *Black Sunday* (1977), playing a terrorist who

escapes after her shower scene dazzles Israeli agents. Then came *Deerfield*, which meant her incredibly glamorous nude scene in *Fedora* (1978) barely got into theaters. *The Formula* (1980) was another bomb, and Marthe concentrated on her respected screen career in Europe. Americans barely got to see her luscious nakedness in *Femmes de Personne* (1984).

SKIN-fining Moment:

Marathon Man (0:42) After she does Dustin Hoffman on the floor, we see Marthe's marathon mams.

See Her Naked In:

Femmes de personne (1984) Breasts
Fedora (1978) Breasts
Bobby Deerfield (1977) Breasts
Marathon Man (1976) Breasts

Sally Kellerman

Born: June 2, 1937
Long Beach, California
Skin-O-Meter: Great Nudity

Sally Kellerman may have begun her career playing A Girl in *Reform School Girl* (1957), but the husky-voiced, sexy blonde finally got her big break playing Hot Lips O'Houlihan in Robert Altman's classic *M*A*S*H* (1970). She thought she was too fat to strip for the movie's two skin scenes, but thankfully Altman proved a persuasive director. He got her to flash her little wonders for a drooling Robert Duvall and reveal all her goodies in one of filmdom's most famous shower scenes. Sally went on to show skin in other Altman productions such as *Brewster McCloud* (1970) but also shared her ample charms with other directors. She gave up the hootage for more pleasing peeks in *Serial* (1980) and *Fatal Attraction* (1980)—no, not that one. And as this ageless beauty matured she only became more comfortable with nudity. Returning in Altman's *Ready to Wear* (1994), Sally proved she didn't have to wear anything in a hot flash of her roasting chestnuts. The breast is yet to come!

SKIN-fining Moment:

M*A*S*H (1:11) The 4077 pranksters pull the tent down on Sally while she's showering. Side-buns and right-breast. A classic, even if we don't see her Hot Lips.

See Her Naked In:

Ready to Wear (1994) Breasts
Fatal Attraction (1980) Breasts
Serial (1980) Breasts
M*A*S*H (1970) Breasts
Brewster McCloud (1970) Breasts

Sheila Kelley

Born: October 9, 1964
Pittsburgh, Pennsylvania
Skin-O-Meter: Great Nudity

Sheila Kelley gets no respect. She started as a faceless performer in various background roles and as a mid-run replacement on *L.A. Law*. She even had an uncredited role as Mike Myers's ex-girlfriend in *So I Married an Axe Murderer* (1993)— she was merely a photograph in his hand as he recited a poem at some beatnik club. But we'll give Sheila props for her ample show of skin. Her skinful debut was in *Some Girls* (1988), which featured her totally nude, but from a distance. Then there was *Singles* (1993), but again her naked glory was obscured by bad camera angles. But a love of stripping, which took her to many bikini bars to practice her splits and twists on the greased pole, led to *Dancing at the Blue Iguana* (2000), and not only were all bets off, but so were all her clothes! Sheila put her impressive rackshish on full

display during her dance routine at the titular club. She even did some serious spreading, although her G-string somehow remained firmly in place, keeping her naughty bits away from our leering gaze. It's a step in the right erection . . . er, direction, though!

SKIN-fining Moment:

Dancing at the Blue Iguana (0:44) Great toplessness and thongitude during her nudie-club dance routine.

See Her Naked In:

Dancing at the Blue Iguana (2000) Breasts, Thong
Some Girls (1988) Breasts, Buns

Deborah Kellner

Born: January 20, 1977
Corpus Christi, Texas
Skin-O-Meter: Brief Nudity

Blonde beauty Deborah Kellner was born in Texas and got her first acting gig on the TV series *Texas Justice*. But if there's any justice in the world of wank, she'll be pulling out her tumbleweeds on the big screen. And lo and behold, Lady Justice isn't blind, because Deborah did make it to movieland and flashed a cute cupful in the comedy *A Night at the Roxbury* (1998). Those two new wild and crazy guys who play the club-hopping swarms aren't as dumb as they look. They cast Deborah in their film-length *Saturday Night Live* sketch as Topless Woman. There was truth in advertising for that part, and viewers' parts were quite happy indeed for the sexy exposure. Deborah moved on to some bit roles in *Mighty Joe Young* (1998), *Blast from the Past* (1999), and *Beautiful* (2000), in which she played a beauty queen, though there were no shots of her dairy queens. Deborah hit the big time in the hit *Catch Me If You Can* (2002), opposite Tom Hanks and Leonardo

DiCaprio. If Mr. Skin catches her, let's hope she has her cans out again.

SKIN-fining Moment:

A Night at the Roxbury (0:36) Deb emerges from a swimming pool, teasing us with swimsuited seat meat and some left breast that's obscured by nipple tape.

See Her Naked In:

A Night at the Roxbury (1998) LB, Thong

Jill Kelly

Born: February 1, 1971
Pomona, California
Skin-O-Meter: Great Nudity

It only took six years for Jill Kelly to make over four hundred adult films—so most of us should already be familiar with Jill's amazing gazongas. And, like many porn megastars, Jill's also shared her amazing talent in the occasional mainstream production. Her most prominent role was in Spike Lee's *He Got Game* (1998), where she was part of a gleesome threesome that's the ultimate basketball recruitment tool. She also joined other adult stars in cameos for the porn comedy *Orgazmo* (1997) and was pretty amazing as Agent Glory in *Toad Warrior* (1996) and *Max Hell Comes to Frogtown* (2002). After redefining the role of porn star by starting her own production company, Jill recently announced her retirement from performing. Of course, retirements from porn usually last as long as most marriages in Hollywood.

SKIN-fining Moment:

He Got Game (1:35) Jill's jugalos mingle nicely in a ménage-à-trois with also-topless Chasey Lain and Ray Allen.

See Her Naked In:

He Got Game (1998) Breasts
Virtual Encounters (1996) Breasts, Bush, Buns
Numerous Adult Movies

Lisa Robin Kelly

Born: 1975
Southington, Connecticut
Skin-O-Meter: Brief Nudity

Charming belle Lisa Robin Kelly knows how to ring a guy's ding-dong. She loves getting physical, like rock climbing or playing volleyball, and the challenge of the first mixed with the bikinis of the second primed her for a TV career. Before hitting the big time as the feather-back coifed Laurie on *That '70s Show*, she floundered on the small screen for a number of years in the mid '90s. Mr. Skin found the straight-to-video B-movie sequel *Amityville Dollhouse: Evil Never Dies* (1997) from that for-hunger time that really got us salivating over here at Skin Central. In the horror schlock, Lisa let her Robins out of their cage and straddled a lucky guy while wearing only black panties. With the success of *That '70s Show*, we hope Lisa will follow the great '70s tradition of gratuitous nudity.

SKIN-fining Moment:

Amityville: Dollhouse (0:42) In the shed out back, Lisa Robin shows what she's got up front when getting it on with her guy. Nice topless Dollhouses.

See Her Naked In:

Amityville: Dollhouse (1996) Breasts

Moira Kelly

Born: March 6, 1968
Queens, New York
Skin-O-Meter: Great Nudity

Moira Kelly began her career not with a bang but a whimper in bit parts, like the made-for-TV movie *Love, Lies and Murder* (1991) and the theatrically released pedo-nightmare *The Boy Who Cried Bitch* (1991). The banging began when she landed the role of Laura Palmer's best friend Donna in *Twin Peaks: Fire Walk with Me* (1992),

exposing her dark-haired, meaty-melon body for the first time in a graphic sex scene that had Moira's mams a-bouncing. The movie made her a star, and her trajectory has since been split between wholesome fare such as *Mr. Saturday Night* (1992) and *The Lion King* (1994) and more skintastic ventures. For the latter, lap up Moira's topless goodies in *Chaplin* (1992), *Daybreak* (1993), *Little Odessa* (1994), and *The Tie That Binds* (1995). She's since found even more success on TV's hit presidential drama *The West Wing*. Wonder if the Prez gets to play in her Oval Office?

SKIN-fining Moment:

Daybreak (0:43) Moira makes out with Cuba Gooding Jr. with her mammaries exposed for all to enjoy.

See Her Naked In:

The Tie That Binds (1995) Breasts
Little Odessa (1994) Breasts
Daybreak (1993) Breasts
Chaplin (1992) Breasts
Twin Peaks: Fire Walk With Me (1992) Breasts

Sharon Kelly

Skin-O-Meter: Hall of Fame

Flame-maned, milky-skinned, naturally ultra-busty Sharon Kelly radiated intoxicating carnal enthusiasm and Irish-American beauty in over a dozen flesh-packed drive-in blowouts that began with *Teenage Bride* in 1970 and ended with the notorious *Ilsa, Harem Keeper of the Oil Sheiks* six years later. Among her highlights along the way were the hicksploitation ho-down *Sassy Sue* (1972), the *Dragnet*-goes-softcore basher *A Scream in the Streets* (1973), the one-and-only *Ilsa, She-Wolf of the SS* (1974), the Hollywood send-up *Alice Goodbody* (1974), and Russ Meyer's legendary *Supervixens* (1975), in which she

played SuperCherry. Color-splashed Sharon even turned up as Painted Lady in the mainstream smash *Shampoo* (1975). After almost a decade away from movie cameras, Sharon brought her crimson coif, cream-dream physique, and magnificent milkers (which are topped with two of the thickest, sweetest nips you ever drooled over) to the hardcore screen. Acting (and doing *everything* else) under the name Colleen Brennan, she became arguably the last true XXX superstar of the theatrical porn era—and remains the perpetual picture of volcanic redhead perfection.

SKIN-fining Moment:

Shampoo (1:18) Sharon cruises nude around a party with her big ol' painted hooters just a-swingin' in the breeze.

See Her Naked In:

Slammer Girls (1987) Breasts
Ilsa, Harem Keeper of the Oil Sheiks (1976) FFN, Buns
Supervixens (1975) LB
Shampoo (1975) Breasts
The Boob Tube (1975) Breasts, Buns
Hustle (1975) Breasts, Buns
Ilsa, She Wolf of the S.S. (1974) FFN, Buns
Alice Goodbody (1974) FFN, Buns
Carnal Madness (1974) LB
The Beauties and the Beast (1973) Breasts, Buns
A Scream in the Streets (1973) FFN, Buns
Sassy Sue (1972) FFN
Teenage Bride (1970) FFN, Buns
The Dirty Mind of Young Sally (1970) FFN, Buns
Numerous Adult Movies

Patsy Kensit

Born: March 4, 1968
Hounslow London, England
Skin-O-Meter: Hall of Fame

Patsy Kensit started her career at the tender age of six as the movie daughter of Bruce Dern and Mia Farrow in *The Great Gatsby* (1974).

Years later, she grew up as waif-like and hot as Mia, so much so that she played her in the made-for-TV movie *Love and Betrayal: The Mia Farrow Story* (1995). But it was as wacko Mel Gibson's doomed lover in the shoot-'em-up classic *Lethal Weapon 2* (1989) that she finally bared her bitty breasts onscreen. Once you go skin, you don't go back, and Patsy continued flashing her svelte body in such movies as *Timebomb* (1990), *Twenty-One* (1991), *Beltenebros* (1991), *Blame It on the Bellboy* (1992), *Full Eclipse* (1993), *Bitter Harvest* (1993), and *Kleptomania* (1995). But she really stole the show with a full-frontal getting-it-on with her brother in the incestuous *Angels and Insects* (1996). When it comes to sex, this girl is no Patsy.

SKIN-fining Moment:

Angels and Insects (1:01) Patsy makes with the mams and muff as she reclines very sexily in bed.

See Her Naked In:

Shelter Island (2003) FFN, Buns
The One and Only (2002) Breasts
Angels & Insects (1996) FFN
Kleptomania (1995) Breasts
Bitter Harvest (1993) Breasts
Full Eclipse (1993) LB
Beltenebros (1991) Breasts
Twenty-One (1991) Breasts
Timebomb (1990) LB
Lethal Weapon 2 (1989) Breasts

Joanna Kerns

Born: February 12, 1953
San Francisco, California
Skin-O-Meter: Brief Nudity

Joanna Kerns made it OK to lust after Mom. As taboo as that urge may be, her portrayal of the hard-wanking matriarch of the Seaver clan on the hit TV series *Growing Pains* gave Mr. Skin growing pains in his pants. She started her career

back in the late '70s in such films as *Ape* (1976) and *Coma* (1978). Sadly, since hitting the big time she has pretty much, aside from a bit part in a film here and there, spent the better part of her career on the small screen and thus hasn't revealed a whole lot in the way of skinage. She did manage to get naked in *The Watchman* (1992), though all we were treated to was a brief shot of her hellacious heinie and a load of body-double nudity. But mama's got back, and it's all the flesh we have to fantasize with for stingy Joanna.

SKIN-fining Moment:

The Nightman (0:45) Joanna briefly bares her lovely butt as she gets out of bed to put on a robe. Talk about "growing pains"!

See Her Naked In:

The Nightman (1992) Buns

Deborah Kerr

Born: September 30, 1921
Hellensburgh, Scotland
Skin-O-Meter: Brief Nudity

Deborah Kerr puts the Great in Britain, working across the pond to big success on stage and screen. She debuted over here with *Major Barbara* (1941) and made a major impact on the industry. She holds the dubious distinction of being the Susan Lucci of the Oscars, nominated six times without winning, until the Academy finally broke down in 1996 and gave her a lifetime achievement statuette. She was on her way to winning the booby prize for her scandalously wet beachside make-out session with Burt Lancaster in *From Here to Eternity* (1953). It was another pairing with Lancaster in *The Gypsy Moths* (1969) that delivered the sole skin in Deborah's delicious career.

She and Lancaster sucked face on a couch, where Deborah lost her top, and her ample treasure chest spilled its golden goodies. Lancaster got a handful.

SKIN-fining Moment:

The Gypsy Moths (0:52) In a moment of non-clarity, Deborah didn't dare to bare her derriere but to let a body-double provide the exposure. However, she was more than happy to let her hooter come out for Mr. Camera.

See Her Naked In:

The Arrangement (1969) LB, Buns
The Gypsy Moths (1969) Body Double—Buns / Her—LB

Jillian Kesner

Born: November 17, 1950
Portsmouth, Virginia
Skin-O-Meter: Great Nudity

Jillian Kesner is a buffed babe who landed in Holly-wad in 1975, taking on a one-episode role on the television series *S.W.A.T.* playing Miss California . . . beautifully. Next, Jillian landed a gig in the women-in-prison flick *The Student Body* (1976), which happened to feature the earliest-known look at her incredible tits popping out while she's making out in the back of a car. Believe it or not, the flapper flash therein paled in comparison to some of her later work, including *Moon in Scorpio* (1987) and *Roots of Evil* (1992), both of which featured lingering looks at her luscious love bubbles. Jillian's finest flesh-flashing performance, undoubtedly, was her leading turn in *Firecracker* (1981). Not only did she whup some ninja ass in the flick, she did so while topless: Action + Titties = Sure-Fire Hit.

SKIN-fining Moment:

Firecracker (0:46) Just one hell of a good topless karate fight scene. Jillian's breasts are registered with the FBI as lethal weapons.

See Her Naked In:

Roots of Evil (1992) Breasts
Beverly Hills Vamp (1988) Breasts
Moon in Scorpio (1987) Breasts
Firecracker (1981) Breasts, Buns
The Student Body (1976) LB

Arsinée Khanjian

Born: 1958
Beirut, Lebanon
Skin-O-Meter: Great Nudity

With her billowing mane of jet-black ringlets defying containment, it is obvious at a glance that Canadian-raised, Beirut, Lebanon-born actress Arsinée Khanjian is not a woman who will ever grow accustomed to making compromises. Married to iconoclastic Canadian director Atom Egoyan, who like his bride emigrated as a child to the Great White North from the Middle East, Arsinée's full-figured supporting role was a crucial component in her husband's breakthrough project, the intriguing and erotic *Exotica* (1994). To see the divinely dark-skinned Khanjian without her baby fat and sans every stitch of clothing, wearing only the bushy fur God gave her, focus on the French ensemble production *Irma Vep* (1996).

SKIN-fining Moment:

Irma Vep (0:53) Arsinée *hides nothing as she talks on phone in full-frontal glory. This chick has some junk in the trunk—look at them floppers frolic!*

See Her Naked In:

Irma Vep (1996) FFN

Janet Kidder

Toronto, Ontario, Canada
Skin-O-Meter: Brief Nudity

Janet Kidder is tough and gorgeous and she looks like she means business. In other words, she'd easily match her aunt Margot as a perfect big-screen Lois Lane. Instead, the Canadian actress has been busy in TV series and the usual shot-in-Canada syndicated series. The only highlight has been a 1997 episode of *Nikita*, in which Janet joined with her aunt to play the same character in different time periods. Janet finally landed a splashy American role as a horny bisexual honeymooner in *Bride of Chucky* (1998). And she became a true skinterfold in the sci-fi flick *X Change* (2000), in which Janet mounted a guy for a wild ride that sent her taut tits swinging. Her role as a kinky twin in *Darkness Falling* (2002) should've made her a star, but at least the werewolf film *Ginger Snaps 2* (2003) got her back on the horror-sequel scene.

SKIN-fining Moment:

X Change (1:13) Kidder's *sweaty kibbles strain over her mate as she plays the dominant role during some rough-and-tumble bonking.*

See Her Naked In:

Dark Side (2002) Breasts, Buns
X Change (2000) Breasts, Buns
Men with Guns (1997) RB, Buns

Margot Kidder

Born: October 17, 1948
Yellowknife, NW Territory, Canada
Skin-O-Meter: Hall of Fame

Margot Kidder spent the first two-and-a-half years of her life living in a caboose, as her father was a mining engineer in Canada. Maybe that's why she has such an exquisite ass, but it does nothing to explain Margot's meaty mams. She got off the train and into show business, catching the bug onstage in college and ending up a Hollywood star. She made a few films in the U.S., such as *Gaily Gaily* (1969), but found life in the City of Angels too sleazy and retreated home until James Garner lured her back Stateside for his TV series *Nichols*. Margot may have found the film industry a bit seamy, though that didn't stop her from going topless in the British film *Quackser Fortune Has a Cousin in the Bronx* (1970). Once she flashed her Canadian bacon it was sizzling, and there was no turning the fatback. Kinky director Brian De Palma gave her a chilling role in *Sisters* (1972), in which she flashed her igloos again. Though best known as Superman's main squeeze Lois Lane in the mainstream hit *Superman* series, Margot continued to show off her super mams in *92 in the Shade* (1975), *The Amityville Horror* (1979), *Willie and Phil* (1980), and *Little Treasures* (1985). For a big treasure, watch Margot play a murderess in *The Reincarnation of Peter Proud* (1975). After killing her husband, she got full frontal and masturbated in the tub, fantasizing about the dead guy raping her. What a nut—really, read on . . .

SKIN-fining Moment:

Quackser Fortune Has a Cousin in the Bronx (1:03) Margot's *mams are on full display as she bares them for a horny Gene Wilder.*

See Her Naked In:

Little Treasure (1985) Breasts
Willie and Phil (1980) Breasts
The Amityville Horror (1979) Breasts
92 in the Shade (1975)
The Reincarnation of Peter Proud (1975) Breasts, Bush
Sisters (1973) Breasts
Quackser Fortune Has a Cousin in the Bronx (1970) Breasts, Buns

TeleVisions:

The Hitchhiker LB

Nicole Kidman

Born: June 20, 1967
Honolulu, Hawaii
Skin-O-Meter: Hall of Fame

God bless the Land Down Under, and we're not talking about Australia. Nicole Kidman's dewy under bits first saw the delight of day in her homeland, as she showed her superhumanly ideal seat in the 1986 *Oz*-production *Windrider* (1986). Nic expanded to tightening American jeans, baring sweet pink-nipped teats along with that tush in *Dead Calm* (1989), then following with a full-frontal exposure of her red-hot crotch curls in *Billy Bathgate* (1991). In real life, Tom Cruise married this towering skinferno and co-starred with her in director Stanley Kubrick's kink opus *Eyes Wide Shut* (1999). Since her 2001 divorce from Mr. *Top Gun*, Nic's been linked with a number of leading men, let one nip accidentally slip into view in *Moulin Rouge!* (2001), and

starred as a victim of multiple rapes in the controversial *Dogville* (2003). Talk about cruising for a coozing!

SKIN-fining Moment:

Billy Bathgate (0:44) Triple your pleasure as you see Nicole's three B's as she stands totally starkers in front of a three-way mirror. Oh, yes, she's a natural redhead!

See Her Naked In:

Cold Mountain (2003) Breasts, Buns
The Human Stain (2003) Breasts
Birthday Girl (2001) Buns
Moulin Rouge! (2001) Nip Slip RB
Eyes Wide Shut (1999) Breasts, Buns
Portrait of a Lady (1996) Breasts, Buns
Malice (1993) LB, Buns
Billy Bathgate (1991) FFN, Buns
Dead Calm (1989) Breasts, Buns
Bangkok Hilton (1989) RB
Windrider (1986) Breasts, Buns

Susan Lynn Kiger

Born: November 16, 1953
Pasadena, California
Skin-O-Meter: Brief Nudity

The feather-haired 1970s blonde, with her body toned whip thin by endless nights of disco dancing, her eyes big and brimming over with intimations of the one-night-stand, her breasts billowing out unexpectedly, improbably and entirely welcome, this icon of a free-loving decade will never go out of style and in fact spawned an almost instant nostalgia upon her initial appearance. Consider for an instant the languid gaze of guilt-free, bare-faced lust with which feathery blonde Susan Lynn Kiger greets the world. She wore it during her month-long reign as *Playboy* Playmate in January 1977. She kept an expression of sexual dimension in place throughout her sin-free but skinful appearances in *Seven* (1979) and *H.O.T.S.* (1979). And she had

not flinched even unto the new decade, as proven by the sexualized smirk of *The Happy Hooker Goes Hollywood* (1980).

SKIN-fining Moment:

The Happy Hooker Goes Hollywood (0:44) Nice long boob scene when she is playing pool. Susan is the one in the red garter. She gives new meaning to "rack 'em."

See Her Naked In:

The Happy Hooker Goes Hollywood (1980) Breasts
Seven (1979) Breasts
H.O.T.S. (1979) Breasts
Deadly Love (1974) FFN
Numerous Adult Movies

Rya Kihlstedt

Born: July 23, 1970
Lancaster, Pennsylvania
Skin-O-Meter: Great Nudity

Rya Kihlstedt is a mouthful of a name, which is even harder to say because usually her tongue is wrapped around her female co-star. Yes, this busty brunette loves the ladies and has shown her lust graphically in some of her nude onscreen adventures. She debuted with a man, though, Rutger Hauer in *Arctic Blue* (1993) and then got noticed in the TV mini-series *Heaven & Hell: North & South, Book III* (1994). But the role she was born to play was as in the woman-as-a-sexual-predator flick *Jaded* (1996), where she showed off every inch of her supple body during one of the rape scenes. In a weird pit stop, Rya appeared in *Home Alone 3* (1997) and *Deep Impact* (1998) before returning to more girl-friendly territory. That was in the moist made-for-cable drama *Mermaid Chronicles Part 1: She Creature* (2002). She's a mermaid, so you get lots of wet shots of her large scales, plus another lesbian lick off. What a piece of tail!

SKIN-fining Moment:

Jaded (0:26) *"When my baby smiles at me I go to Rya . . ." The statuesque blonde shows her back bacon when running into the water, then her ample breastage. Later, she shows her breasts again as she attacks Valeria Golino.*

See Her Naked In:

Mermaid Chronicles Part 1: She Creature (2001) Breasts
Jaded (1996) FFN, Buns

Jewel Kilcher

Born: May 23, 1974
Payson, Utah
Skin-O-Meter: Never Nude

Boulder-bosomed Alaskan eyeful Jewel Kilcher is known more as a singer-songwriter than as a film star. But she's been starring in Mr. Skin's dreams for years. She released her hugely successful debut album, *Pieces of You*, in 1995. Songs like "You Were Meant for Me" got this hottie noticed for her looks in videos almost as much as the music. This double-D cupped diva made her feature-film debut in the Civil War-era saga *Ride with the Devil* (1999), in which she'll make your south rise again with a breast-feeding scene. Small parts followed in films such as *Almost Famous* (2001), but Jewel has made it clear that music is the most important thing to her. And that's fine with Mr. Skin, as she's revamped her image to compete with today's MTV pop tarts. Jugadocious Jewel's got the weaponry up top to blow away all comers.

SKIN-fining Moment:

Ride with the Devil (1:48) *Mountain-jugged Jewel unleashes her left lung-monster and jams it in the hungry maw of an infant who obviously has the best agent in showbiz.*

James King

Born: April 23, 1979
Omaha, Nebraska
Skin-O-Meter: Brief Nudity

Born Jaime King, the blonde-haired, blue-eyed striking beauty went by her nickname James when she became a teen model. This Nebraska-born, corn-fed lass is so hot she smoked her competition on the catwalk regardless of her mannish name. By the time she was twenty she was sashaying on the silver screen. Soon she would change her name back to the feminine, give up a heroin habit that killed her boyfriend, and devote herself to getting high on sex. Well, she sure gets guys horny. Bit parts in *Pearl Harbor* (2001), *Blow* (2001), and *Slackers* (2002) led to her biggest role yet, kicking ass with Chow Yun-Fat in *Bulletproof Monk* (2003). Fortunately, Jaime managed to land a nice skinful role before she hit the big time. In the would-be *Meatballs* ribald-summer-camp epic *Happy Campers* (2001), a straight-to-video steamer, Jaime showed off her incredible, unequaled breasticles a number of times— once with nipples pierced and eyes painted over her funbags! We can't think of two better reasons to see a movie than that!

"There are about a hundred people sitting there watching you and you're having sex with this guy and he's wearing a thong. . . . You're licking his face and he's licking yours, and its so gross and so nasty, but it's funny too . . . you think 'This is my life. I'm getting paid to have sex with a guy in a thong.'"

—JAMES KING, ON HER *HAPPY CAMPERS* SEX SCENE

MR. SKIN'S TOP TEN
Naked Girls with Guys Names
. . . Not that there's anything wrong with that

10. Toni Collette
9. Bif Naked
8. Bobbie Brown
7. Franka Potente
6. Andie MacDowell
5. Robbi Chong
4. Joey Heatherton
3. Danni Ashe
2. Charlie Spradling
1. **James King**

SKIN-fining Moment:

Happy Campers (0:36) *Spritely supermodel James prances lakeside in a sopping wet, see-through top, then splashes in the water and points her bare nipples up above the surface. King me! King me!*

See Her Naked In:

Happy Campers (2000) Breasts

Alex Kingston

Born: March 11, 1963
London, England
Skin-O-Meter: Hall of Fame

Alex Kingston isn't a doctor, but she plays one on TV—and who wouldn't want to play doctor with this big-hipped, busty redhead? The star of the TV series *ER* can send any hot-blooded man to the emergency room with a severe case of horny. Alex got her first break in her native England on the series *Grange Hill* and followed that up with cinematic success at home and abroad. What a broad, too. Despite her fame she's comfortable with baring all—and how! Her skin-ventures began with *The Fortunes and Misfortunes of Moll Flanders* (1996), a made-for-British-TV movie that gave audiences many prolonged nude looks at Alex's curvaceous bod in the midst of some wildcat lovemaking. But that's just an appetizer; the main course is served up in *Croupier* (1998) and *Essex Boys* (2000). Hope you like meat, because furburger is definitely on the menu. Long live the Kingston!

SKIN-fining Moment:

Essex Boys (0:24) Not one to beat around the bush, Alex opens up her robe for a fantastic full-frontal flesh-flash.

See Her Naked In:

Warrior Queen (2003) Breasts
Essex Boys (2000) FFN
Croupier (1998) FFN
The Fortunes and Misfortunes of Moll Flanders (1996) Breasts, Buns

Kathleen Kinmont

Born: February 3, 1965
Los Angeles, California
Skin-O-Meter: Great Nudity

How has Kathleen Kinmont got naked? Let us count the ways: *Fraternity Vacation* (1985), *Rush Week* (1989), *Bride of Re-Animator* (1990), *The Art of Dying* (1991), *Sweet Justice* (1992), *CIA Code Name: Alexa* (1992), *Final Round* (1993), and *Dead of Night* (1996). It's how she climbed *The Corporate Ladder* (1997), which, by the way, is another flick wherein Kathleen showed off her blonde good looks and super-saline-enhanced big boobs. Kathleen started her career with a bit part in the sex romp *Hardbodies* (1984), and when she met up with Lothario Lorenzo Lamas in the late '80s, whom she married in 1989 (and divorced in 1993), the two were

inseparable onscreen. She even appeared on his doomed TV series *Renegade*. So where does a skin connoisseur begin? At the beginning, with *Fraternity Vacation*, in which she and Barbara Crampton strip down for a very young and happy Tim Robbins. For a peek into her private life (and private parts) with ex-hubby Lamas, watch *Night of the Warrior* (1991), *CIA Code Name: Alexa*, and *Final Round*—the sex scenes appear too realistic for these bad actors to pull off without a bit of penetrating skills.

SKIN-fining Moment:

Fraternity Vacation (0:16) Kathleen strips totally nude alongside Barbara Crampton. Natural knockers and unshaven snizz.

See Her Naked In:

The Corporate Ladder (1997) Breasts, Buns
Dead of Night (1996) Breasts, Buns
Final Round (1993) Breasts
CIA-Code Name: Alexa (1992) Breasts, Buns
Sweet Justice (1992) Breasts
The Art of Dying (1991) Breasts
Night of the Warrior (1991) RB
Bride of Re-Animator (1990) Breasts
Rush Week (1989) Breasts, Thong
Fraternity Vacation (1985) Breasts, Bush, Buns

Nastassja Kinski

Born: January 24, 1959
Berlin, Germany
Skin-O-Meter: Hall of Fame

Nastassja Kinski was born nasty, grown from the seedy seed of infamous Germanic bad boy Klaus Kinski—who hints in his autobiography that he may have slept with his adorable daughter! Her body was toned through a childhood reared in dance, and while her Teutonic tits may be mere sweet gumdrops, her ass is a legendary globe of gloriously gigantic proportion. She first shook

that ass in the West German production *Falsche Bewegung* (1975), but Nastassja's li'l boobs, tush, and bush made their nude debut in *To the Devil a Daughter* (1976). She's one hell of a girl! Arguably, yummy Nastassja is more famous for her naked union with a big, fat snake in a poster that adorned horny men's walls around the world. Quincy Jones certainly enjoyed the sight; he had a baby with Nastassja out of wedlock. But over the years Nastassja has provided her body in a great body of work. She's bumped bottoms with another skinful chick in a steamy shower scene from *Boarding School* (1978) and gave another full-frontal view in the skintacular *Cat People* (1982), with the hooterific Annette O'Toole. And so many others . . . she's acted in her birthday suit in no fewer than twenty films, including *Exposed* (1983), which sums up her career succinctly. And the goodies keep coming, most recently in *Red Letters* (2000) and *Say Nothing* (2001). You can't spell Kinski without "kink."

SKIN-fining Moment:

Stay As You Are (1:25) Nastassja presents all three B's while parading through the kitchen in her beautiful birthday suit.

See Her Naked In:

Say Nothing (2001) Body Double-FFN, Buns
Red Letters (2000) RB
Susan's Plan (1998) Breasts
One Night Stand (1997) RB
L'Alba (1990) Breasts
Maladie d'amour (1987) RB
Harem (1985) Breasts
The Hotel New Hampshire (1984) Breasts
Unfaithfully Yours (1984) Breasts, Buns
Maria's Lovers (1984) RB
Exposed (1983) Breasts
Spring Symphony (1983) Nip Slip LB
Cat People (1982) FFN, Buns
One from the Heart (1982) Nip Slip LB
Tess (1979) LB
Stay As You Are (1978) FFN, Buns

Boarding School (1978) FFN
Tatort—Reifezeugnis (1977) Breasts
To the Devil a Daughter (1976) FFN
Falsche Bewegung (1974) Breasts

TeleVisions:

Dangerous Liaisons RB

Sally Kirkland

**Born: October 31, 1944
New York, New York
Skin-O-Meter: Hall of Fame**

As Sally Kirkland's career matured, so did her mams—straight into almost monstrously bloated

---

MR. SKIN'S TOP TEN

Nude Scenes with an Animal

. . . The booty and the beast

10. Lucy Liu
    —*Flypaper* (1997)—Rattlesnake

9. Barbara Alyn Woods
   —*Striptease* (1996)—Python

8. Claudia Udy
   —*Joy* (1983)—Turtle

7. Edwige Fenech
   —*Top Sensation* (1969)—Goat

6. Tanya Roberts
   —*Beastmaster* (1982)—Ferret

5. Julia Ormond
   —*The Baby of Mâcon* (1993)—Ox

4. Ana Belén
   —*The Creature* (1977)—Dog

3. Laura Gemser
   —*Emanuelle and the Last Cannibals* (1977)—Monkey

2. Bo Derek
   —*Tarzan, the Ape Man* (1981)—Orangutan

1. **Sally Kirkland**
   —*Futz!* (1969)—Pig

---

balloons of fun. By the time she was nominated for an Oscar in *Anna* (1987), those girls deserved their own Golden Globes. She may never have risen to that heady state of superstardom, but she's raised enough pants to keep an army of tailors in business fixing all those popped zippers. Her career of bouncing back and forth from one series to another balanced out with a hefty helping of skinful cinematic work. Sally first flashed skinage in *Futz!* (1969), which featured the bizarre nakedness of Sally riding a hog Lady Godiva–style. In *Coming Apart* (1969), she exposed her full-frontal, unshaven furburger and all-beef patties. Sally then went on to shed her threads in such films as *Big Bad Mama* (1974), *Double Exposure* (1982), *Double Threat* (1993)—she has something for doubles . . . and so do we—*In the Heat of Passion* (1992), and *Amnesia* (1997). And there's more, but oddly less of Sally. Let's explain: she claims that she used money from her role in *ED TV* (1999) to have her breast implants surgically removed. So we have to wonder if the old broad is starting to lose her mind.

SKIN-fining Moment:

Big Bad Mama (0:13) A nice shot of Sally's perky pair and even a bit of derriere as Susan Sennett walks into a bedroom.

See Her Naked In:

Amnesia (1997) Breasts
Guns & Lipstick (1995) LB
Cheatin' Hearts (1993) Breasts, Bush, Buns
Eye of the Stranger (1993) Breasts
In the Heat of Passion (1992) Breasts
Double Threat (1992) Breasts
Forever (1992) Breasts
Cold Feet (1989) RB
High Stakes (1989) Breasts, Thong
Anna (1987) Breasts
Double Exposure (1982) Breasts

Big Bad Mama (1974) Breasts, Buns
Coming Apart (1969) FFN, Buns
Futz! (1969) FFN

TeleVisions:

The Hunger Breasts
Picture Windows Breasts
Women: Stories of Passion Breasts

Mia Kirshner

**Born: January 25, 1976
Toronto, Ontario, Canada
Skin-O-Meter: Great Nudity**

Coming like a red-hot comet from the frozen wasteland of the Great White North, Mia Kirshner melted hearts and filled gonads with her darkly seductive good looks. It was 1990 when she made goth boys smear their lipstick because their hands were so shaky watching the boob sucker on the TV show *Dracula: The Series*. But it was her arty Canadian motion pictures that delivered on the promise of Mia's terrific titty talents. In *Love and Human Remains* (1993), Mr. Skin loved the human remains of Mia's snapped-open lacy black bra. In the following year's *Exotica* (1994), Mia strutted about in a schoolgirl uniform that must have earned her an F for buttoning and an A for skin. Besides the bushel of bosom, she bent over for an up-skirt shot of her peachy butt. Mia lost her appetite for exposure in *Anna Karenina* (1997), *The Grass Harp* (1995), and *Not Another Teen Movie* (2001) but rediscovered her true calling in *Century Hotel* (2002), with its ample lobby and penthouse views. What a house party! In early 2004 Mia followed up on her relatively tame girl-on-girl grapple with Dominique Swain in *New Best Friend* (2002) by lesboliciously exploding all over the Sapphic Showtime series *The L Word*. In the opening episode, Mia bared her puffy nerps and provided more than a mouthful for her munch-happy bedmate Karina Lombard, thereby bringing to mind a whole bevy of "L words"—lick, luscious, lovelies, lap, lapping, licking luscious lovelies lapping laps. . . .

SKIN-fining Moment:

The L Word "Lawfully" (2004)
Topless Mia gets out of bed and wanders around a hotel room wearing only panties and black stockings. Awesome views, awesome long running time, awesome body on this awesome, awesome babe.
A SKINstant classic!

See Her Naked In:

Century Hotel (2001) Breasts, Buns
Exotica (1994) Breasts, Buns
Love & Human Remains (1993) RB

TeleVisions:

The L Word Breasts

Tawny Kitaen

Born: August 5, 1961
San Diego, California
Skin-O-Meter: Great Nudity

Tawny Kitaen is perhaps moist fondly remembered as the wife of *Whitesnake* singer David Coverdale and for being his primary video vixen, climbing all over car hoods and exposing cleavage and G-string-lashed ass. The marriage lasted from 1989 to 1991, and Tawny managed a few non-musical gigs on soaps such as *Capitol* and *Santa Barbara,* as well as hosting the series *America's Funniest People.* When the hot redhead made her silver-screen debut as the title figure in the kink-o-rama comic-strip-inspired adventure *The Perils of Gwendoline in the Land of the Yik Yak* (1984), she was obviously cast for her willingness to be naked onscreen. This talent propelled her into an acting career of sorts, with yet more skinful turns: *Witchboard*

MR. SKIN'S TOP TEN

Sword and Sandal Sirens
. . . Now you see 'em in the coliseum

10. **Darian Caine**
    —*Gladiator Eroticvs* (2001)

9. **Dawn Dunlap**
   —*Barbarian Queen* (1985)

8. **Maria Socas**
   —*The Warrior and the Sorceress* (1984)

7. **Margaret Markov**
   —*The Arena* (1973)

6. **Rosanna Schiaffino**
   —*Minotaur, the Wild Beast of Crete* (1961)

5. **Sandahl Bergman**
   —*Conan the Barbarian* (1982)

4. **Lana Clarkson**
   —*Barbarian Queen II: The Empress Strikes Back* (1989)

3. **Barbi Benton**
   —*Deathstalker* (1984)

2. **Kathleen Beller**
   —*The Sword and the Sorcerer* (1982)

1. **Tawny Kitaen**
   —*The Perils of Gwendoline in the Land of Yik Yak* (1984)

(1985), which featured Tawny's thighbrow as she crashed through a shower door, *Crystal Heart* (1985), *White Hot* (1989), which also featured some ultra-brief furburger served on tight buns, and *Playback* (1995). Of course, she began her career starring opposite Tom Hanks in the hilarious *Bachelor Party* (1984) but only stripped down to a sexy nightgown and a blonde wig. Thankfully, she got that clothing foolishness out of her system early.

SKIN-fining Moment:

Crystal Heart (0:53) Skingoria! In a dream, frontally nude Tawny tosses herself through a glass door. Boobs, bush, and blood result.

See Her Naked In:

Playback (1996) Breasts, Thong
White Hot (1989) Bush
Witchboard (1985) FFN
Crystal Heart (1985) FFN, Buns
The Perils of Gwendoline in the Land of the Yik Yak (1984) Breasts, Buns

Alisha Klass

Born: January 3, 1972
Bellflower, California
Skin-O-Meter: Great Nudity

Few things are stronger than dirt, and few starlet harlots have a more powerful dirty appeal than filthy angel Alisha Klass. Sphincter-centric Alisha thrived during a long and thrillingly sordid career in the XXX milieu with much of her oeuvre coming under the tutelage of poop-chute auteur Seymour Butts. As well as appearing in precisely as many fudge-pack productions as she could shake her tail at, sassy ass Klass also spread and splayed in uncountable skin mags, and evidence of her sexploits for hire is splashed throughout the Internet. Uncommonly pretty for a hardcore thespian, Alisha has tried to make the leap into mainstream and hard-R entertainment. Whatever she does, she always ends up falling back on her ass, lucky for us.

SKIN-fining Moment:

The Center of the World (0:07) Showing off every inch of her sticky sweets on stage at a strip club, Alisha inserts a lollypop into her labia as part of her routine. Klassy!

See Her Naked In:

The Center of the World (2000) Breasts, Bush

Cruel Intentions (1999) Breasts
Numerous Adult Movies

TeleVisions:

Hoop Life FFN
Thrills FFN, Buns

Hanne Klintoe

Skin-O-Meter: Great Nudity

Mike Figgis film fur flasher Hanne Klintoe has only appeared on the silver screen one time, in the coming-of-age drama *The Loss of Sexual Innocence* (1999). It's a skin, er, *sin* that this girl hasn't worked nude more often. In her performance as an erotic Eve, Hanne seems like she was born to swipe the apple from Satan's paws. Cavorting nude with an equally amorous Adam in several metaphorical Garden of Eden sequences, Hanne humps happily. It's a below-the-waist waste that this girl hasn't done more nude work.

SKIN-fining Moment:

The Loss of Sexual Innocence (0:20) Hanne shares her handfuls, as well as her thatch patch, as she gets out of the water and walks to shore.

See Her Naked In:

The Loss of Sexual Innocence (1999) FFN, Buns

Heidi Klum

Born: June 1, 1973
Bergische Gladbach, Germany
Skin-O-Meter: Brief Nudity

If you haven't heard of the five-foot-ten-inch catwalk queen Heidi Klum, you may still be trapped under large graffitied hunks of the Berlin Wall. The winged wonder woman is one of Victoria's Secret's lacy lingerie-laden angels, but it was seeing her bikini-baring bod on the cover of the 1998 *Sports Illustrated Swimsuit Edition* that

first had guys around the world offering to risk sand-in-crack to be a sunblock supplier. Since then, the über-model has graced the covers of bitch bibles like *Cosmopolitan* and *Glamour* and been Michael J. Fox's truly unattainable bed buddy on *Spin City*. Her acting repertoire consists mostly of playing herself on shows such as *Sex and the City* and catwalk-cast cinema such as *Zoolander* (2001), but she did show what's beneath the bikini in *Blow Dry* (2001) and *MTV Uncensored: The Sports Illustrated Swimsuit Issue 2001*. In the latter, Heidi hung the world's luckiest spider monkey off of her high-fashion hooters. You'll be spanking your own pants primate in appreciation.

SKIN-fining Moment:

MTV Uncensored—**Sports Illustrated Swimsuit Issue 2001** *Heidi holds a monkey on the beach with her bare right supermodel mammary in view. I've got a banana, but it's not for her pet!*

See Her Naked In:

MTV Uncensored—Sports Illustrated Swimsuit Issue *2001* (2001) RB
Blow Dry (2001)

Keira Knightley

Born: March 26, 1985
Teddington, London, England, UK
Skin-O-Meter: Brief Nudity

Keira Knightley played the decoy Queen to Natalie Portman's Queen Amidala in *Star Wars: Episode I—The Phantom Menace* (1999), and lots of sci-fi fans were fooled enough to mistakenly butter their popcorn to Keira's gorgeous form. Fortunately, Keira had us creaming over her own fantastic presence, beginning with *The Hole* (2001). No, she didn't play the title role, but Keira had a fantastic scene where she displayed

her breasts as a consolation prize to two guys after Thora Birch broke up their planned gleesome threesome. Keira then broke out big in *Bend it Like Beckham* (2002), a family film where her sexy soccer outfit had us bending our boners. And now, of course, Keira's a rightful star after spilling out of her tight period clothes in *Pirates of the Caribbean: The Curse of the Black Pearl* (2003) and *King Arthur* (2004).

SKIN-fining Moment:

The Hole (0:53) The sexiest tomboy beanpole on the planet proves she's one tastily terrific gal by flashing her ta-ta's in a window.

See Her Naked In:

The Hole (2001) Breasts

TeleVisions:

Doctor Zhivago Breasts

Shirley Knight

Born: July 5, 1936
Goessel, Kansas
Skin-O-Meter: Brief Nudity

Like Shelley Winters before her, Shirley Knight was a sexy '50s starlet who gained weight to become a serious character actress. Shirley was never interested in stardom, anyway. She began as a contract actress in 1958, making the rounds of New York-based television shows like *Playhouse 90*. Despite two Best Supporting Actress Oscar nominations, Shirley was still mainly known as a stage actress when Francis Ford Coppola cast her as a runaway housewife running around in the nude in *The Rain People* (1969). Knight then concentrated on a London stage career, and her film roles stayed pretty chaste—that is until *Indictment: The McMartin Trial* (1995), in which the big gal went to jail and stripped down for a scene worthy of any women's prison movie. It was a daring scene for an older woman and a typically stellar moment from this always-impressive actress.

SKIN-fining Moment:

The Rain People (0:15) Shirley strolls around a motel room with her Knightly Knockers in view before sliding into bed.

See Her Naked In:

Indictment: The McMartin Trial (1995) Buns
The Rain People (1969) Breasts, Buns

Sascha Knopf

Born: February 10, 1975
Long Island, New York
Skin-O-Meter: Great Nudity

It says something good about a gal when she is selected by the nation's two most perceptive and sexually aware filmmakers to portray the epitome of erotically charged femininity. Such a pulse-quickening distinction was bestowed upon brunette wonder bust Sascha Knopf when the Farrelly Brothers selected her to play the carnal creature Gorgeous Tonya in their deeply considered meditation upon appearances and what lies beneath them, *Shallow Hal* (2001). While Sascha's sashaying was eminently sexual in *Shallow*, most viewers couldn't help but notice the actress remained fully clothed. No such constraints apply to *BlackMale* (2000) and *What's the Worst that Could Happen?* (2001).

SKIN-fining Moment:

BlackMale (0:12) Nice tush and (too) brief boobage as the amazing Sascha enjoys a bath.

See Her Naked In:

What's the Worst That Could Happen? (2001) Breasts
BlackMale (2000) Breasts, Buns

Barbora Kodetova

Born: 1970
Czech Republic
Skin-O-Meter: Brief Nudity

The fall of the Iron Curtain was a boon for the creative arts. For the first time since before World War II, creative collaboration was freely possible between the auteurs of the Eastern Bloc and the capitalist producers of Western Europe. The ultimate flower of these collaborations was the baring of classically comely brunette Barbora Kodetova's free-floating breasts in the Italian-shot, Czech-acted televised mini-series *Dune*. A reinterpretation of director David Lynch's stab at the Frank Herbert sci-fi novels, the later version is memorable for Barbora—those otherworldly aquamarine-colored eyes, the stressed twists of her shoulder-length, coal-black hair, the chubby-inducing bulges of pleasingly plump chest bumps.

SKIN-fining Moment:

Dune (mini-series) (2000) Babs changes shirts, spins around, and out come her Chest-Dunes.

TeleVisions:

Dune Breasts

Claudia Koll

Born: May 17, 1965
Rome, Italy
Skin-O-Meter: Great Nudity

Claudia Koll got her big break in the kinky arms of Tinto Brass, who cast her in the exceptionally erotic *Cosi Fan tutte* (1992). The film is one of Signor Brass's better efforts, if for no other reason than he convinced Claudia to bare her meat drapes in several different scenes. That's right, fellas—we're not talking about plain-old furburger, here, but drapes of sweet, juicy pink meat. Claudia has since gone on to a semi-

decent career in Italian film and television and has even bared her breastages in such productions as *Rivière Rouge* (1995) and the series *Linda e il Brigadiere*. Alas, they pale in comparison to her earlier effort. Hopefully, the breast is yet to come.

SKIN-fining Moment:

All Ladies Do It (0:07) Amazing! Stupendous! Close-up gyno, back-bush and even winking browneye as Claudia bends forward and submits to her loverman's probing fingers.

See Her Naked In:

Rivière Rouge (1995) Breasts
All Ladies Do It (1992) FFN, Buns

TeleVisions:

Linda e il Brigadiere Breasts

Alla Korot

Born: November 1, 1970
Odessa, (Ukraine)
Skin-O-Meter: Great Nudity

This Ukrainian will get U-kranking your shaft in plenty of productions, including her chaste TV stints on *All My Children* and the crime drama *The District*. But to really marvel at Alla Korot, check out her boobtastic debut in *Night of the Cyclone* (1990). Your hands will go spinning into your pants once you see her stirring shower scene. We're also praising Alla for her turn on a 1998 episode of the cable anthology show *Red Shoe Diaries*, where she bared plenty of boobage in some simulated sex scenes. We're hoping for more big things from the big things of Alla—who was brought to America at the age of six and grew up to win the California Miss T.E.E.N. pageant. What a country!

SKIN-fining Moment:

Kight of the Cyclone (0:21) Ms. Korot steps out of the shower and we see Alla her tits.

See Her Naked In:

Night of the Cyclone (1990) Breasts, Thong

TeleVisions:

Red Shoe Diaries Breasts, Buns

Sylva Koscina

Born: August 22, 1933
Zagreb, Croatia
Died: December 26, 1994
Skin-O-Meter: Great Nudity

Sylva Koscina started her long and storied career with a small part in *Are We Men or Corporals?* (1955). She then went on to appear in over 120 films until her final role in *Kim Novak Is on the Phone* (1994) shortly before her death. Now that's tenacity! Between those films Sylva appeared in such films as *Casanova & Co.* (1977), *Hornet's Nest* (1970), *Kampf um Rom I* (1968), and *Homo Eroticus* (1971), which isn't nearly as pants stiffening as the title might have one think. Her truly eroticus (read: skinful) appearances started popping in *Kampf um Rom I*, which featured some nice looks at her hippie-era hoots. She went on to show off just about every inch of her hot-assed body in such films as *Nel Buio del Terrore* (1971), *So Sweet, So Dead* (1972), *Sette Scialli di seta Gialla* (1972), *Sex on the Run* (1979), and *The House of Exorcism* (1974), with George the Chauffeur (as portrayed by the very lucky Gabriele Tinti) putting a squeeze on Sylva's chubby tit during a sex scene. Sylva was definitely hot, but thanks to her lasting legacy of onscreen nudity, she will never have to be missed.

SKIN-fining Moment:

Sex on the Run (0:29) Sylvia takes off her top and shows boobs to Tony Curtis. He likes it hot, you know.

See Her Naked In:

Sex on the Run (1979) Breasts
The House of Exorcism (1975) Breasts
Lisa and the Devil (1973) Breasts
Il Tuo Piacere è il Mio (1973) Breasts
To Kill in Silence (1972) Breasts
Beati i Ricchi (1972) RB
So Sweet, So Dead (1972) Breasts
Sette scialli di seta Gialla (1972) Breasts, Buns
Homo Eroticus (1971) Breasts
Nel Buio del Terrore (1971) Breasts
Marquis de Sade: Justine (1969) RB
Kampf um Rom I (1968) Breasts

Harley Jane Kozak

Born: January 28, 1957
Wilkes-Barre, Pennsylvania
Skin-O-Meter: Brief Nudity

Va va voom! Motorcycle momma Harley Jane Kozak gets her nickname from the classic American ride. She began her career with a two-season stint on TV's *Texas*. Tons of television work followed, including roles on such soul-searching soaps as *Santa Barbara* and *The Guiding Light*. Roles in a handful of other quickly canceled TV projects led Kozak to the silver screen, where she appeared in cute and kosher Billy Crystal's *When Harry Met Sally* (1989), *The Jerk* and Steve Martin's *Parenthood* (1989), and Jeff Daniels's (was he *Dumb* or *Dumber*?) *Arachnophobia* (1990). Her only two skin-revealing roles were a quick flash of tit flesh in *Side Out* (1990) and a particularly prurient performance on *Dream On*. We're dreaming we see more of Harley Jane in the near future.

SKIN-fining Moment:

Side Out (0:54) Brief left nippage as Harley is pinned in bed by Pete Horton.

See Her Naked In:

Side Out (1990) LB

TeleVisions:

Dream on LB

Heidi Kozak

Born: 1956
Wilkes-Barre, Pennsylvania
Skin-O-Meter: Brief Nudity

Heidi Kozak got her big break in the business called show with a bit part as a receptionist in the made-for-TV movie *Child's Cry* (1985). Heidi made her first appearance on the silver screen in the fleshtacular B-movie *Slumber Party Massacre II* (1987). Sadly, she managed to be the only woman in the flick who didn't take (all) her clothes off—there are quite a few times that she was clad in little more than her skivvies, though. She wasn't such a tease in *Friday the 13th Part VII: The New Blood* (1988). Like most of the comely young ladies who find themselves on the shore of the infamous Crystal Lake, Heidi found herself in need of a late-night skinny-dipping session, which of course led to some fairly tasty nudity, including some brief full-frontal underwater shots. Then, as is part and parcel to the formula, she got killed by Jason. Man, this guy's got some intimacy problems!

SKIN-fining Moment:

Friday the 13th Part VII: The New Blood (36:00) Nice butt shot stripping off her jean shorts to go for a skinny dip.

See Her Naked In:

Friday the 13th Part VII: The New Blood (1988) Breasts, Bush, Buns

Linda Kozlowski

Born: January 7, 1958
Fairfield, Connecticut
Skin-O-Meter: Great Nudity

It's funny how sometimes the most serious intentions lead to comic endings. When she was a student at New York's Juilliard School for the Performing Arts, the young Linda Kozlowski never could have imagined that the zenith of her artistic pursuits would be as straight man to a slapstick Aussie ham. Though she started highbrow in a made-for-TV *Death of a Salesman* (1985), Linda quickly took the low road to high dollars, hitting the jackpot as leggy, cheek-flashing reporter Sue Carlton in *Crocodile Dundee* (1986). *Dundee* is worth seeing again for a thong effect achieved by Linda's leotard creeping up her butt crack when she squats and pulls down her pants. Her full moons reappeared in *Zorn* (1994), a Swedish TV treat, and her small, serviceable breasts were serviced in *Backstreet Justice* (1994).

SKIN-fining Moment:

Crocodile Dundee (0:31) Linda bends down to get some water from a stream, revealing that her swimsuit has a rumptastic thong. What an Outback!

See Her Naked In:

Backstreet Justice (1994) Breasts
Zorn (1994) Breasts, Buns
Crocodile Dundee (1986) Thong

Stepfanie Kramer

Born: August 6, 1956
Los Angeles, California,.
Skin-O-Meter: Never Nude

The plucky daughter of a violinist pop and model/country-radio spinmeister mom, Stepfanie Kramer piqued our interest, amongst other things, as Dee Dee McCall, the detective we'd love to be searched by, on *Hunter*. It's her role as dirty cop Jack Scalia's snap-happy photojournalist, however, that got her under our skin. The gal with the gun proved she ain't concealing any weapons in the made-for-Cinemax flesh flick *Beyond Suspicion* (1994), in which Stepfanie's skivvy scenes steal the show.

SKIN-fining Moment:

Beyond Suspicion (0:36) BODY DOUBLE: Somebody's sacks step in for Stepfanie's during a sex scene with Jack Scalia.

See Her Naked In:

Beyond Suspicion (1994) Body Double— Breasts

Tina Krause

Born: July 29, 1970
Queens, New York
Skin-O-Meter: Great Nudity

Barely into her thirties, Tina Krause has become a huge fan favorite by . . . well, going barely into her thirties. She's made over forty-four films since her debut in *Rana, Queen of the Amazon* (1994). She's also made just about that many nude scenes. Her continuing bare-boob bonanzas are a big pay off for genre fans, including skintillating appearances in *Vampire Seduction* (1998) and *An Erotic Vampire in Paris* (2002). But to really appreciate Tina's fearless brand of flashing, check out how she turns the blue screen into the boob screen as she flaunts her floating airbags in *Titanic 2000* (1999).

SKIN-fining Moment:

An Erotic Vampire in Paris (1:10) Bloodsucker Tina switches to other, more tastier body fluids in a full-on lesbian scene with Misty Mundae!

See Her Naked In:

Vampire Vixens (2003) Breasts
Girl Seduction (2003) FFN, Buns
Body Shop (2002) Breasts, Buns
An Erotic Vampire in Paris (2002) Breasts, Bush, Buns
Witchouse 3: Demon Fire (2001) Breasts
Titanic 2000 (1999) FFN, Buns
Poetic Seduction: Dead Students Society (1998) FFN, Buns
Vampire's Seduction (1998) Breasts, Bush, Buns

Alice Krige

Born: June 28, 1954
Upington, South Africa
Skin-O-Meter: Great Nudity

Alice Krige went to college dreaming of being a head shrinker. But after only one acting class she decided to become an act-chest, and heads everywhere began to grow in appreciation of this small-breasted brunette beauty. Smart move, too, as the first movie role she landed was in the Best Picture Oscar winner *Chariots of Fire* (1981). But she really burned up the screen with her next part, a booby-prize-winning performance in *Ghost Story* (1981). An aged Fred Astaire must have felt like a young hoofer again when Alice flashed her petite pair with the cherry-sized nipples on top. What a dish! She also got sudsy with a bathtub scene sure to clean up in your pants. Alice's career was moving forward in films such as *Barfly* (1987), *Sleepwalkers* (1992), and the hit British mini-series *Scarlet & Black* (1993), which exposed her bitty-titties. But she became the sex symbol for the pocket-calculator set with her role as the evil Borg Queen in *Star Trek: First Contact* (1996) and the sci-fi TV series *Children of Dune*. But the hairy-palm set find different tasty goodies in Alice's restaurant. On the nudity menu are *Sharpe's Honour* (1994) and *Habitat* (1996), which was sadly her last lustful exposure. But for the best of her breast, check her out as Bathsheba in the Richard Gere Biblical epic *King David* (1985). Somehow, Alice got muffish in a PG-13-rated movie. Don't beat around the bush; get this film and beat off to Alice's bush!

SKIN-fining Moment:

Ghost Story (0:50) T&A standing on a balcony.

See Her Naked In:

Habitat (1997) Breasts
Devils Advocate (1995) Breasts
Sharpe's Honour (1994) LB
Scarlet & Black (1993) Breasts
King David (1985) FFN
Ghost Story (1981) Breasts, Buns

Sylvia Kristel

Born: September 28, 1952
Utrecht, Netherlands
Skin-O-Meter: Hall of Fame

Willowy, naturally slim, with swaying, pleasingly plump and firm breasts and wispy brunette hair, Dutch-born naked beauty Sylvia Kristel exuded cool sensuality as the classic beauty in scores of European skin-heavy romance films. Sylvia's gender-blending sexual aggression in the four *Emmanuelle* films, starting with *Emmanuelle* (1974) and culminating in *Emmanuelle IV* (1984), earned the languorous lovely a worldwide following of skin addicts who haunted the arthouses seeking yet another eyeful of their sleek-hipped siren in all of her full-bushed glory. A subtle and sinuous lovemaker, Sylvia's simulated sex scenes are myriad. Fake sex from Sylvia Kristel is usually far more arousing than real sex from anyone else.

SKIN-fining Moment:

Emmanuelle (0:15) Sylvia shows it all off laying out beside the pool with an equally-hot topless babe. Then she dives in, providing yet more fantastic full-frontal flashes underwater.

See Her Naked In:

Beauty School (1993) Breasts
Hot Blood (1991) Buns
The Arrogant (1987) Breasts
The Big Bet (1985) Breasts
Mata Hari (1985) Breasts
Red Heat (1985) Breasts
Emmanuelle IV (1984) Breasts
Lady Chatterley's Lover (1981) FFN, Buns
Private Lessons (1981) Breasts-Hers/Body Double—Buns
Tigers in Lipstick (1979) Breasts
The Fifth Musketeer (1979) Breasts
Mysteries (1978) RB, Bush
Good-bye, Emmanuelle (1977) FFN
Une Femme Fidèle (1976) FFN
La Marge (1976) FFN, Buns
Alice (1976) FFN
Le Jeu Avec le Feu (1975) Breasts
Emmanuelle 2 (1975) FFN, Buns
Julia (1974) Breasts, Buns
Emmanuelle (1974) FFN, Buns
Because of the Cats (1973) Breasts, Buns
Frank en Eva (1973) FFN

Marta Kristen

Born: February 26, 1945
Oslo, Norway
Skin-O-Meter: Great Nudity

TV-aholics like Mr. Skin will never forget the outer-space-family-Robinson hit series *Lost in Space*. The show aired on network television from 1965 to 1968, but most guys became fans once it played endlessly in afternoon reruns. Let's face it—we didn't watch this sci-fi show for the special effects or to hear the psychotic ramblings of Dr. Smith. We watched to see big, busty blonde Marta Kristen cavorting through the universe as lost spacegirl Judy Robinson. We sure wanted to get lost in her space—the space between her legs! This Finnish/German beauty never made it as a movie star, but she did have a memorable lesbo scene in the obscure film *The Gemini Affair* (1974). Are we seeing double—or in the case of all those boobies, quadruple?

SKIN-fining Moment:

Gemini Affair (0:57) Danger, Will Robinson! Your sister's going lesbo! Marta shows her galactic gazongas and awesome asteroid while make it with full-frontally naked Kathy Kersh.

See Her Naked In:

Gemini Affair (1974) Breasts, Bush, Buns
Once (1974) Breasts

Diane Kruger

Born: July 15, 1976
Hildesheim, Germany
Skin-O-Meter: Brief Nudity

Busty blonde Diane Kruger is on quite a roll. It started with *The Target* (2002), in which her big tush was in the carmera's bullseye rocking and rolling on top of some lucky fellow. The torrid trend continued with *Mon idole* (2002), where she rolls out of bed with her jugs joining her buns for two times the fun. But American audiences know Germany's Teutonic tit from her starring role as Helen, the piece of ass that launched a thousand ships (and erections), in *Troy* (2004). Diane's making sure her Stateside appeal continues with the Chicago-based thriller *Wicker Park* (2004) and the aptly titled *National Treasure* (2004). Before film called, Diane was a ballerina with the

---

MR. SKIN'S TOP TEN

TV Sci-Fi Babes Who Got Naked
. . . Close en-cunt-hairs

10. Claudia Christian
    —*Babylon 5*

9. Virginia Hey
    —*Farscape*

8. Faye Grant
    —*V*

7. Chase Masterson
    —*Star Trek: Deep Space Nine*

6. Marina Sirtis
    —*Star Trek: The Next Generation*

5. Gillian Anderson
    —*The X Files*

4. Pamela Hensley
    —*Buck Rogers in the 25th Century*

3. Jolene Blalock
    —*Enterprise*

2. Maren Jensen
    —*Battlestar Galactica*

1. **Marta Kristen**
    —***Lost in Space***

Royal Ballet in London and then a fashion model. But the 33-23-34 beauty looks right at home naked on the big screen. If dishy Di were related to Freddy Krueger from the *Nightmare on Elm Street* movies, they'd have to re-title the series *Wet Dream on Elm Street!*

SKIN-fining Moment:

The Target (0:09) As Christopher Lambert busts in on her fun in bed with a dude, we see Diane's derriere and left boob as she rolls over, followed by more cheekage as she ducks behind a screen to get dressed.

See Her Naked In:

Troy (2004) Buns
Mon idole (2002) Breasts, Buns
The Target (2002) LB, Buns

Michelle Krusiec

Fallon, Nevada
Skin-O-Meter: Great Nudity

All things considered, Michelle Krusiec was quite sexy in her debut, the made-for-TV movie *Sexual Considerations* (1991). Her things could have been more exposed, though. But that's a small criticism for the introduction of such a sweet Asian talent to the perverted pool of skintertainment. Michelle slowly got her sea legs as the token ethnic, a biological advantage she got from her mother, a Chinese dragon-lady who's fire hot herself. Michelle's temperament for both the tawdry and the comic is reflected in her roles in *Sweet Home Alabama* (2002), *Daddy Day Care* (2003), and *Dumb and Dumberer: When Harry Met Lloyd* (2003). And on the series *One World*, she made the boob tube that much boobier, even if her steamy dumplings are strictly appetizer size. Michelle put those tasty bits on the menu for everyone to sample when she appeared as

"Sushiko, Japanese Masseuse" on an episode of the defunct HBO series *The Mind of the Married Man*. What's on the mind of the married man? Michelle's mams, especially when she offered the show's lead a topless rubdown that stir-fried his brain to thoughts of immoral desire. Does an egg roll come with that? Oh, yes, your egg roll will come!

SKIN-fining Moment:

The Mind of the Married Man "The God of Marriage" (2001) Spa-girl Michelle toplessly massages Mike Binder, who turns down her offer for a "happy ending." Maybe this show should have been called "The Mind of the Married Man who Likes Men."

TeleVisions:

The Mind of the Married Man Breasts

Youki Kudoh

Born: January 17, 1971
Tokyo, Japan
Skin-O-Meter: Brief Nudity

A former kiddie pop sensation, Japanese beauty Youki Kudoh soon made the leap to acting, landing a role in the black comedy *The Crazy Family* (1984). She received good reviews, quickly parlaying her success into roles in such films as *Picture Bride* (1994), *Labyrinth of Flower Garden* (1988), and *Typhoon Club* (1985). Stateside, she's had sultry roles as Russell Crowe's lusty lover in *Heaven's Burning* (1997) and opposite Ethan Hawke in *Snow Falling on Cedars* (1999). Her sexiest role came in the Jim Jarmusch-directed cult fave *Mystery Train* (1989)—she offered a tantalizing peek at her breasts during a hot love scene with her rockabilly boyfriend. It's short but sweet and whets our appetite for the Japanese delicacies she has yet to unveil.

SKIN-fining Moment:

Mystery Train (0:30) Youki loses her black bra and exposes her won-tons during some hotel room hijinks with her boyfriend.

See Her Naked In:

Mystery Train (1989) Breasts

Hitomi Kuroki

Born: October 5, 1960
Fukuoka, Japan
Skin-O-Meter: Great Nudity

In her native Japan, slender but sinfully proportioned Hitomi Kuroki can't walk down the street without legions of company men gasping and clutching their tightly knotted ties to relieve the flashes of distress caused by remembering nude visions of Hitomi. No eager beaver for the limelight of fame, Hitomi waited until the relatively advanced age of twenty-six before making her big-screen debut in *Keshin* (1986), a movie that indelibly impressed her exquisitely contoured form and satiny smooth surface upon the deep conscious of her homeland. Her emoting skills have been in constant demand since that first brave baring, resulting in a steady stream of work that has left Hitomi little time to conquer the mass mind of foreign shores.

SKIN-fining Moment:

Keshin (0:23) Hitomi peels stark naked in a Japanese bedroom, then lays back while a guy samples her sushi. Great view of her titlets, along with some upper butt crack.

See Her Naked In:

Paradise Lost (1997) Breasts
Anego (1988) LB
Keshin (1986) Breasts, Buns

Cheryl Ladd

Born: July 12, 1951
Huron, South Dakota
Skin-O-Meter: Never Nude

The 1970s were a banner decade for the blonde bombshell, and Cheryl Ladd is among the era's hottest broads. Ironically enough, her career began offscreen, as she provided the singing voice for Melody on the hit animated series *Josie & the Pussycats*. After a couple of stints on other less-well-received shows, Cheryl hit the jackpot when she replaced pert-nipped Farrah Fawcett on the hit jiggle show *Charlie's Angels*. Superstardom soon followed, and Cheryl became a permanent fixture on the pop-culture landscape. Whether she followed Fawcett's footsteps into fanny-flashing is a subject of much speculation. These days, she sticks mainly to Hallmark-type fare like *A Dog of Flanders* (1999), but if Demi Moore can bounce back from mommyhood and wow 'em in a bikini, so can this ageless Angel.

SKIN-fining Moment:

Charlie's Angels "Love Boat" (1979) *Cheryl is a blast of pure angelic bliss as she preps for a scuba plunge in one of the teeniest white bikinis seen on TV up to this time.*

Jordan Ladd

Born: January 14, 1975
Hollywood, California
Skin-O-Meter: Great Nudity

Although affiliated with an Angel—juicy Jordon Ladd's mom is the cherubic Cheryl Ladd, the first faux-Farrah—this divine young diva's number of skintillating performances remains a bit shy of heavenly. Jordon has not blessed us in the biblical sense in any of her projects to date, which unfortunately has been a string of rather average TV movies. But fear not, Jordan is rapturous in *The Specials* (2000), where she is celestially sexy in her divine skintimates. Say a prayer we'll be seeing much more of Jordon's godly bod in the near future.

SKIN-fining Moment:

Club Dread (0:55) *Jordan shows off some seriously cute Mary Lou Retton during a marathon makeout/workout session.*

See Her Naked In:

Club Dread (2004) Breasts

Brigitte Lahaie

Born: October 12, 1955
Tourcoing, Nord, France
Skin-O-Meter: Hall of Fame

In a field full of Eurobabes, Brigitte Lahaie is a true icon of foreign sexploitiation. Highlights include her gorgeous melons—and ravishing rubyfruit—in *Grapes of Death* (1978). Brigitte's also totally uninhibited during her simulated sex scenes in *Fascination* (1979) and *The Night of the Hunted* (1980), while her bisexual bonding in *Joy: Chapter II* (1985) makes for a true bandwidth buster. Brigitte even went legit in the artsy biopic *Henry & June* (1990), playing a glamorous whore who ravages another woman in front of an appreciative Maria de Medeiros. She's still active, too, although—as seen by *La Fiancée de Dracula* (2002)—her projects aren't nearly as impressive as her mature bod.

SKIN-fining Moment:

Joy: Chapter II (0:54) *Blow your stack over naked Brigitte lezzying it up on a train with Isabelle Solar. All aboard the FFN-and-buns express!*

See Her Naked In:

Henry & June (1990) Breasts, Buns
Le Couteau sous la gorge (1986) Breasts, Bush
Joy: Chapter II (1985) FFN, Buns
Friendly Favors (1980) FFN
Come Play With Me 2 (1980)
The Night of the Hunted (1980) FFN
Gefangene Frauen (1979) FFN, Buns
Fascination (1979) FFN, Buns
Et la tendresse? . . . Bordel! (1979) FFN

The Grapes of Death (1978) FFN
Numerous Adult Movies

Me Me Lai

Born: 1952
Burma
Skin-O-Meter: Great Nudity

Burmese by birth and British by accent, snooty-sounding but exotically and copiously erotic Me Me Lai played her ethnic heritage to her best advantage while also catering to the most pressing interests of her core audience members. Specializing as the wholly naked native girl who runs through the greenery in anthropological action/adventure sextravaganzas such as *Jungle Holocaust* (1977) and *Eaten Alive* (1980), Me Me made sure that her muff muff was no stranger to clearly illuminated exposure. Catch the coal-black tuft of crotch fluff as Lai lies back on a thick bed of deep tropical grass. Nor did Me Me shy away from serving as the centerpiece to an aboriginal sex ceremony. *Jungle* and *Eaten* make a great double-header of uncivilized carnality.

SKIN-fining Moment:

Au Pair Girls (0:49) Ms. Lai flashes full-frontal flesh following the removal of every last stitch of clothing from her lithe, young frame. My my, Me Me!

See Her Naked In:

The Element of Crime (1984) FFN, Buns
Eaten Alive (1980) Breasts, Bush
Jungle Holocaust (1977) FFN
Au Pair Girls (1972) FFN

Leah Lail

Born: December 27, 1970
Lexington, Kentucky
Skin-O-Meter: Brief Nudity

Blonde, booby, and beautiful, Leah Lail busted out onto the acting scene with more boob-tube appearances than you can shake your stick at (though it's recommended that you try). There was *The Amazing Live Sea-Monkeys*, *The Jackie Thomas Show*, *Seinfeld*, and even a big-screen debut in *Body Waves* (1992)—and, oh, does her body make waves! HBO liked her so much she was cast in a recurring role on its hit series *The Larry Sanders Show*. Smaller parts followed onscreen, such as *D2: The Mighty Ducks* (1994), but her mighty ducks were destined for bigger things. And men's things started stiffening up in 1998 when Leah found herself on the popular Pamela Anderson series *V.I.P.* She went on to make Adam Sandler a horny little devil in *Little Nicky* (2000), but what gets Mr. Skin horny is her brief topless exposure in *Denial* (1998).

SKIN-fining Moment:

Denial (1:07) A distant, brief shot of Leah's boobs when Chas Shaughnessy tries, in vain, to remove her bra, prompting her to take over in the lingerie-removal department. . . .

See Her Naked In:

Denial (1998) Breasts

Chasey Lain

Born: December 7, 1971
Newport, North Carolina
Skin-O-Meter: Great Nudity

A reigning princess during what some experts refer to as the Third Golden Age of Porn (late '80s to early '90s video), Chasey Lain is as notable for the simultaneously expressive and impassive sensuality of her gigantic, unblinking blue eyes as she is for her mammoth, solid-as-two-rocks, soft-as-two-pillows mammaries. Pretty enough to have carved out a career in hard-R nudie exploito material, Chasey's lack of the requisite self-esteem or ambition will forever be counted among the blessings of all who worship at the altar of full-penetration entertainment. Lain's few B-movie boob shots include a two-on-one bed scene in Spike Lee's *He Got Game* (1998) and a flanking maneuver with the overshadowing Ron Jeremy in the decidedly nonorgasmic *Orgazmo* (1997). Live a little, for Chasey's sake, and seek out the XXX.

SKIN-fining Moment:

He Got Game (1:35) Topless in a threeway with Jill Kelly and Ray Allen. She got jugs.

See Her Naked In:

He Got Game (1998) Breasts
Denial (1998) Breasts
Orgazmo (1997) LB
Demon Knight (1995) Breasts
Numerous Adult Movies

Hedy Lamarr

Born: November 9, 1913
Vienna, Austria
Died: January 19, 2000
Skin-O-Meter: Great Nudity

The skin archives cast way back to bring skinthusiasts the forward-thinking breasts and avant-garde backside of Austrian bad girl archetype Hedy Lamarr. How many other flesh icons of the twenty-first century were born in 1913? Hedy was a mere—though stunning—nineteen when all of her was revealed in the Czech film *Ecstasy* (1932). An unusually aptly titled movie, the black-and-white import's lasting import results from ten minutes of Hedy naked as a stripper, frolicking in field and pond. At one point a horse reared its head behind Lamarr's creamy shoulder as her obviously real tits (it was 1932, for God's sake) perked up in the foreground sunshine. *Ecstasy* lifted the spirits of

Depression-era audiences and heralded a New Deal in skinema.

SKIN-fining Moment:

Ecstasy (0:29) She goes chasing after some spooked horses, and wouldn't you know it, she's topless!

See Her Naked In:

Ecstasy (1932) Breasts

Shauna Sand Lamas

Born: September 2, 1971
San Diego, California
Skin-O-Meter: Great Nudity

Shauna Sand Lamas made two very important choices to further her acting career: appear nude in *Playboy* and marry a famous actor. She first started dating Lorenzo Lamas before she appeared as the Bunny's Playmate of the Month for May 1996. Soon after, they were married, and Shauna was off to the races. She first cut her teats with small parts on Lamas's hit series *Renegade*. Not surprisingly, her first big-screen appearance was also opposite her notoriously womanizing husband, in *Black Dawn* (1997). Next, Shauna took a bit part in the Carmen Electra shocker *The Chosen One: Legend of the Raven* (1998). She must have missed her Latino lothario, because she went right back to acting with him, this time in *Back to Even* (1998), in a semi-leading role. Later that year, she and Lorenzo again teamed up, this time for the failed series *Air America*. While Shauna has appeared in some sexy get-ups throughout her film career, she has never been nude in a mainstream movie, so your best bet is to head on down to the local video store and unearth some of her *Playboy* productions. Check out the unintentionally ironically titled *Naturals* (1998), which features nary a natural body in it.

SKIN-fining Moment:

The Chosen One: Legend of the Raven (0:56) Shauna sprawls on the floor in skimpy lingerie, no doubt meditating on how it is to be the luckiest woman alive, married as she was to Lorenzo Lamas.

See Her Naked In:

Numerous *Playboy* Videos

Karen Lamm

Born: 1952
Baton Rouge, Louisiana
Died: June 29, 2001
Skin-O-Meter: Brief Nudity

Karen Lamm is just a girl, but what a girl. This blonde, buxom beauty first made heads turn as a "Girl Clerk" in *Harry O: Such Dust As Dreams Are Made On* (1973) and then as a "Girl on a Motorcycle" in *Thunderbolt and Lightfoot* (1974). In 1975 she played "Patty" on the hit TV series *Starsky and Hutch*, but if you want to see her patty-cakes then check out her next movie, *Trackdown* (1976). Karen got kidnapped, violated, and sold to a pimp to walk the streets as a hooker. Yes, Karen's Lamms were exposed, but it was sadly her only skinful moment onscreen. Karen continued to show up on the boob tube, such as a guest spot on *The Dukes of Hazzard*, and made some more films, but by *The Unseen* (1981) so was she. Life was a beach for Karen; so much so that she married The Beach Boys' late drummer Dennis Wilson . . . twice. He was probably seeing double—yeah, the doubles that Karen kept under her shirt. Sadly, Karen died of heart failure in 2001 and took Mr. Skin's heart-on with her.

SKIN-fining Moment:

Trackdown Ms. Lamm bares her baa-baas as she rises up off the floor topless.

See Her Naked In:

Trackdown (1976) Breasts

Audrey Landers

Born: July 18, 1959
Philadelphia, Pennsylvania
Skin-O-Meter: Never Nude

The '80s gave us a lot of the Landers sisters, mostly on the small screen, where they were often fashioned in as little clothing as possible—and even less dialogue. It's hard to imagine though, or it's hard when you imagine, just how famous older sister Audrey Landers became playing the perennial bubbly blonde for our perpetually perky peckers. Audrey first made her mark as naughty nymph Afton Cooper on *Dallas* and appeared on scores of top-ten TV shows, quickly rising to star status as the "ditz with tits" casting agents called on for window dressing. And box-office receipts were surely boosted when Audrey lent her tail-ents and squeezed into tights and legwarmers for *A Chorus Line* (1985), showing off some fancy footwork and her slinky, taut bod for the big screen. Her only other flashes with flesh were for the flicks *Ghost Writer* (1989), where her skinny-dipping scene gave us just a splash of ass (she covered all the good stuff with her hands), and *California Casanova* (1991), where she shared some brief, soft-focus leg during a love scene, delivering a little on years of TV tease and cheesecaking—and bringing some relief to our collective teen blue balls.

SKIN-fining Moment:

California Casanova (1:20) Audrey takes her clothes off and applies herself most emphatically to a horny dude, but we see only side-nudity and some sexy undie shots as they go at it.

Judy Landers

Born: October 7, 1961
Philadelphia, Pennsylvania
Skin-O-Meter: Never Nude

Before the Hilton sisters, Mother Nature blessed us with the Landers sisters, and if you were a teen in the 1980s, the only crack you were on was the roughly twelve inches of cleavage shared between Judy Landers and her sister Audrey. They helped keep the boob in "boob tube" for over a decade, with appearances on nearly every hit network-television show requiring a dyed-in-the-scalp blonde with the breast-busting bikini to match. Judy emerged from the sexy shadows of older sister Audrey and dove derriere first onto the airwaves, starting with coy, seductive roles on *Vega$* and *Love Boat* and as the appropriately named "Stacks" on *BJ and the Bear*. Her lifelong dedication to gymnastics paid off when she appeared on a few *Circus of the Stars* specials, and her revealing rags kept all big tent poles greased and standing. Moving her moneymakers into movies, Judy landed her lobbers onscreen several times, starting with a bra-and-pantie parade in *Yum-Yum Girls* (1976) as well as skin-lectable roles in *Stewardess School* (1987) and *Club Fed* (1990). But for her most monumental mound mustering, turn all knobs to *Dr. Alien* (1988) and *Ghost Writer* (1989), in which her nudie Neilsen ratings shot through the roof and landed safely in libidos across the nation.

SKIN-fining Moment:

The Yum-Yum Girls (0:19) Audrey cavorts with a pack of female performers in a backstage dressing room, nicely undressing to her bra and panties, both of which are beautifully packed.

Ali Landry

Born: July 21, 1973
Breaux Bridge, Louisiana
Skin-O-Meter: Brief Nudity

They may be fattening and turn your fingers orange, but when Ali Landry hawked Doritos in a commercial that aired during the Super Bowl, millions of mesmerized men put down their pretzels and took to crunching corn chips. When the strutting seductress set off the sprinkler system in that famous ad, it did little to extinguish the fires she set in the laps of lads everywhere. She pointedly parlayed her snack-food sweepstakes into a role on *The Bold and the Beautiful*, where Ali admirers could drop in daily to check out their desired doll. In *Repli-Kate* (2002) Ali undulates in undies and parades in panties much to the delight of Dorito-deranged dudes everywhere.

SKIN-fining Moment:

Repli-Kate (1:14) In a deleted scene on the DVD, Ali lays back beneath her guy and each of her chest-Doritos pops scrumptiously into view.

See Her Naked In:

Repli-Kate (2002) Body Double—Buns/Her—Breasts
Outta Time (2002) LB

Diane Lane

Born: January 22, 1965
New York, New York
Skin-O-Meter: Hall of Fame

It's always nice to see a promising child actor make a smooth transition into adult roles—especially when it's Diane Lane stripping down to show just how grown up she's become. 1987 was a very hot year for guys who'd adored the young star of *Rumble Fish* (1983) and *Streets of Fire* (1984), as Diane showed plenty of adult assets in

both *The Big Town* (1987) and *Lady Beware* (1987). Diane remained a critics' favorite but couldn't count on a comeback until she got indecent in the acclaimed indie *A Walk on the Moon* (1999). This led to her Oscar nod for *Unfaithful* (2002)—a performance which also made a few crotches fervently nod during her adulterous antics.

SKIN-fining Moment:

Unfaithful (0:43) Diane's beautifully buoyant, stiff-nipped dirigibles makes waves in a bathtub with Richard Gere. Aren't you glad I didn't call them "chest-gerbils"?

See Her Naked In:

Unfaithful (2002) Breasts, Buns
A Walk on the Moon (1999) Breasts
Knight Moves (1992) LB
Chaplin (1992) Breasts
Descending Angel (1990) Breasts
Vital Signs (1989) RB
Priceless Beauty (1989) Breasts
Lady Beware (1987) Breasts
The Big Town A (1987) Breasts, Thong
Ladies and Gentleman, The Fabulous Stains (1981) RB, Buns

Sirpa Lane

Born: 1955
Helsinki, Finland
Skin-O-Meter: Great Nudity

Some women of flawless blonde beauty, with their strawberries-and-cream complexions; plump, puffy chest pillows; limber, plush limbs; and ripe, plum-like pudenda just bring out the basest behavior in the male animal. Such was the entirely irresistible effect of fire-eyed Finnish femme Sirpa Lane. Discovered by renowned French man-about-mons Roger Vadim, the Bardot-lite Sirpa rocketed to the leading role in Vadim's assault on smug sexual sensibilities *La Jeune Fille Assassinee* (1974), an exploration of the depths of love and passion that centered upon the rough lust of eroticized asphyxiation. Huffing Sirpa hardly had time to regain her breath when she was being stalked naked and gonadally exposed through a dark forest by a monstrous organ of violent desire in *The Beast* (1975). Bruised but unbowed, Sirpa would survive this forced and animalistic encounter to rise again and inspire men to the greatly satisfying depths of depravity in a career that would stretch into the 1980s.

SKIN-fining Moment:

The Beast (1:04) *First off, we got boobs, butt, and bush galore. But just*

wait till you see Sirpa get eaten by Jacko the Eternally Ejaculating Monster. Wacky!

See Her Naked In:

The Beast (1975) FFN, Buns
Charlotte (1974) FFN, Buns

Jessica Lange

**Born: April 20, 1949
Cloquet, Minnesota
Skin-O-Meter: Great Nudity**

Jessica Lange is one of an exalted breed—an acclaimed dramatist who has spilled her boobs from the dawn of her career and continues to do so during every stage of her artistic maturation. Lange's lungs first popped up as a twenty-something skingénue in *King Kong* (1976) ; her skimpy costume and quivering chest make it easy to see why that big ape is so riled up. Practically one-quarter of a century and two Academy Awards later, the Roman orgy flick *Titus* (2000) was nearly retitled *Tit-us* in honor of the plenitude of breastitude fifty-plus Jessica blessed us with. Between those two eye-popping milestones are the scorching sex scenes with Jack Nicholson in *The Postman Always Rings Twice* (1981), the disturbingly intense nut-ward lust of *Frances* (1985), and an outdoor pee scene in *Rob Roy* (1995). Why do we have the feeling that Jessica is not done yet?

SKIN-fining Moment:

The Postman Always Rings Twice (0:18) *The pubic woman, here, shows once. Jack Nicholson grabs Jessica's underbrush and some fluff peeks out from her panties.*

See Her Naked In:

Titus (2000) Breasts
Blue Sky (1994) Breasts
Everybody's All-American (1988) FFN, Buns
Frances (1982) Breasts, Bush, Buns

The Postman Always Rings Twice (1981)
  Breasts, Bush
King Kong (1976) LB

Heather Langenkamp

**Born: July 17, 1964
Tulsa, Oklahoma
Skin-O-Meter: Great Nudity**

Heather Langenkamp debuted in *The Outsiders* (1983) and followed that up with *Rumble Fish* (1983), not that you'd know it. Her scenes were deleted. Thus, she is known for her true debut in the classic horror hit *A Nightmare on Elm Street* (1984), in which she, alongside a young Johnny Depp and friends, battled the ghoulish Freddy Krueger, who hunts them all down in their dreams. She went on to appear in several more Wes Craven pictures, including *A Nightmare on Elm Street 3: Dream Warriors* (1987), *New Nightmare* (1994), and *Shocker* (1989), though in the latter she just played a corpse. A scream queen icon, Heather did manage to escape the ghetto of gore for a role on the short-lived series *Just the Ten of Us*, as well as the part of Nancy Kerrigan in the made-for-TV movie *Tonya & Nancy: The Inside Story* (1994). While her skintight outfits and ice-skating moves may have titillated us in that one, her only skin scene of real note was in *Nickel Mountain* (1985), in which she flopped around in bed with some lucky guy, showing off her flesh mountains. Oh, for a romp in the Heather.

SKIN-fining Moment:

Nickel Mountain (0.31) *See the Langenkabobs that Freddy Kreuger craved: Heather's topless in pink panties as she wrestles around with her lover, turning Nickel Mountain into a great trip to her silver Dollar Mountains.*

See Her Naked In:

Nickel Mountain (1985) Breasts
A Nightmare on Elm Street (1985) RB

k.d. lang

Born: November 2, 1961
Consort, Alberta, Canada
Skin-O-Meter: Great Nudity

There is no more exotic breed of naked woman than the lesbian. How often can the common guy expect to run across a woman who loves women but has shed her clothing for a man's casual viewing? In light of her fully nude contributions to satisfying bi-curious straight males worldwide, country torch singer k.d. lang deserves a twenty-one-skin salute. Although best known for throaty, high-flying vocals on albums such as *All You Can Eat*, this Canadian iconoclast took a detour into acting in *Salmonberries* (1991). The arty German production succeeded on a number of fronts, the most successful front being the fully nude one of k.d. lang. The songstress stood stripped from her little-boy haircut down to her big-girl bare feet, with her manly/womanly curves and beaver clear for inspection in between. She kind of makes you see the good side to being gay, if you were a woman.

SKIN-fining Moment:

Salmonberries (0:16) Naked k.d. emerges from behind some bookshelves baring both her salmon and her berries.

See Her Naked In:

Salmonberries (1991) FFN

Katherine Kelly Lang

Born: July 25, 1961
Hollywood, California
Skin-O-Meter: Great Nudity

Daytime soap operas are hotbeds of erotic potentialities. Almost all the plotlines are fueled by sexual intrigue, and a disproportionate number of females filling out those plotlines have the pixie-perfect faces of freshly fallen angels and paradisiacally packed bodies that would tempt Satan to reform. The primary drawback of the afternoon melodramas is that the cunning vixens generally never appear anywhere nude while holding down their recurring roles, which puts a damper on the activity of viewers' imaginations. One shining exception is booberific blonde Katherine Kelly Lang. During her thirteen-year reign as vaginally manipulative Brooke Logan on the blockbuster *The Bold and the Beautiful*, Katherine Kelly repeatedly doffed her duds to take on film work that left hardly an inch of her skin to speculation. Nothing, for instance, is subliminal about Lang's seductive skin in the bathtub boning marathon of *Subliminal Seduction* (1996). Purely overt is the flash of fur and the openly hungry nuzzling of her male co-star on K.K.'s brazenly bared knockers.

SKIN-fining Moment:

Subliminal Seduction (0:15) Katherine bares those bodacious boobs and a bit of bathtime boosh in this rather sexy tub-schtupp scene.

See Her Naked In:

Subliminal Seduction (1996) Breasts, Bush
Till the End of the Night (1994) Breasts

Kim Lankford

Born: June 14, 1962
Montebello, California
Skin-O-Meter: Great Nudity

Breezes blow and waves crash. Whether rising or setting, the sun casts a rosy-pink tinge so that every flesh-colored thing takes on the tinge of lanky California redhead Kim Lankford's conical, palm-sized, nipple-topped chest cakes. Some years are better than others for West Coast beauties, and 1978 brought the season when Kim Lankford's earthy, tangy vintage bloomed into its full-bodied palate. Not only did Kim's all-day-sucker eyes, apple cheeks, and silly-sally smile bring a face of effervescent fun to the NBC comedy *The Waverly Wonders*, the lean, lovely teen also waved her wonder twins and dashed buns out into the nighttime surf of *Malibu Beach* (1978). Why can't they all be California girls?

SKIN-fining Moment:

Malibu Beach (0:33) Kim's keister shines as she runs into the water to join skinny-dippers, then we see tits as she gets out. By the looks of things, the water's cold.

See Her Naked In:

Malibu Beach (1978) Breasts, Buns

TeleVisions:

The Hitchhiker Breasts

Jenya Lano

Moscow, Russia
Skin-O-Meter: Brief Nudity

Back before the fall of communism, the only glimpse the free-world fan of females ever got of Russian women was during the Olympics. Those buff, swaggering, square-jawed, mustachioed lady athletes of the USSR gave no clue to the feminine delights being kept under glasnost back home, a prime example of which is big-busted, blonde pussy-face Jenya Lano. Perhaps sharp-eyed American lovers of liberty and natural hydraulics noticed Jenya's implausible risers squeezing together for attention in the midst of all the blood and mayhem in *Blade* (1998). If not, track down the documentary-style spoof *Fashionably L.A.* (1999). Be prepared to pledge allegiance to Jenya's giants.

SKIN-fining Moment:

The Shield "The Spread" (2002)
Jenya shows us her upper ass-crack and almost all of her huge right boob from behind while she's bouncing on some dusky wang, causing her boyfriend to freak.

See Her Naked In:

Stealing Candy (2002) Breasts
Fashionably L.A. (1999) Breasts
Blood Money (1999) Breasts

TeleVisions:

The Shield RB, Buns

Ruby Larocca

New Jersey
Skin-O-Meter: Great Nudity

This dish of devilish delights, performing under the name Ruby Larocca, is guaranteed to rock your socks off. As one of Seduction Cinema's most skinterestingly Sapphic creatures, she specializes in sinematic girl-on-girl action with gorgeous gal-pal muff munchers Misty Mundae and Darian Caine. Frequently involved in twobees and threebees, Ruby's appearances have twice and thrice the usual freebee tingle. This bewitchingly bare jewel will take your tool and put it to work as the blonde filling between a Caine-Mundae sandwich in *Mummy Raider* (2001). Equally leztastic in *Witchbabe: Erotic Witch Project 3* (2001), Larocca brings her ripe peaches and fuzzy rubyfruit to the table in the ménage-a-munch with Paige Richards and, again, the ever-misty Mundae. In real life, Ruby and Misty are breast buddies, which explains their juicy twosome couplings in many of Larocca's flicks. These best of fiends will warm your heart and hard-ons with

their sisterly soul-smooching and lovely lass-licking in *Master's Plaything* (2002), *The Erotic Mirror* (2002), and *Lustful Addiction* (2003). No newbee to the skin scene, Ruby will be rocking cock-a-doodle-doos for a long time to come.

SKIN-fining Moment:

Mummy Raider (0:32) Ruby is the blonde filling in the Darian Caine-Misty Mundae sandwich in this full-frontal lesbianic sextravaganza!

See Her Naked In:

Lustful Addiction (2003) Breasts, Bush
Dr. Jekyll & Mistress Hyde (2003) FFN, Buns
Flesh for the Beast (2003) FFN, Buns
SpiderBabe (2003) Breasts, Bush
Girl Seduction (2003) FFN, Buns
Master's Plaything (2002) Breasts, Bush
Lord of the G-Strings: The Femaleship of the String (2002) Breasts, Buns
Satan's School for Lust (2002) FFN
The Erotic Mirror (2002) FFN
Gladiator Eroticvs (2001) Breasts, Bush, Buns
Blood for the Muse (2001) Breasts, Thong
Seduction of Cyber Jane (2001)
Mummy Raider (2001) FFN, Buns
Witchbabe: Erotic Witch Project 3 (2001) Breasts, Buns
Erotic Survivor (2001) FFN, Buns

> "I hate pretty-looking boys. I'd rather have a guy with a potbelly than one who's in the gym all the time and watches what he eats."
>
> —ALI LARTER

Ali Larter

Born: February 28, 1976
Cherry Hill, New Jersey
Skin-O-Meter: Brief Nudity

Ah! There's something about a Jersey girl—and, no, it's not toxic residue in her DNA (just kidding, Garden Staters!)—we're talking about a smoldering and sultry Springsteen-country sexuality that

can stop traffic. Born in charming Cherry Hill, Ali Larter possesses such carnal qualities. Ali looked absolutely astounding in *Jay and Silent Bob Strike Back* (2001) as a leather-clad cat thief. But it was her role as Darcy Sears, Dawson's deliriously delightful darling in *Varsity Blues* (1999), that showcased this stunning sweetie's sexy stuff. In the football-themed teen hit, Ali forever altered popular conceptions of swimwear and desert toppings alike by electrifying the screen in a whipped-cream bikini that did more for cherries than Smuckers ever has. In 2004, Ms. Larter came clean and showed off her back-Ali during a doggystyle sex scene in the flick *3-Way*. You can make your own whipped cream while watching that one.

SKIN-fining Moment:

Varsity Blues (0:52) Ali frothily rewrites the history of human swimwear by debuting the "whipped-cream bikini" to James Van Der Beek. Perfect placement of maraschino cherries, as well.

See Her Naked In:

3-Way (2004) Buns

Dagmar Lassander

Born: June 16, 1943
Prague, Czechoslovakia
Skin-O-Meter: Great Nudity

Dagmar Lassander got her start in *Sperrbezirk* (1966). By the early '70s she hit her stride, appearing nude in European sexploitation pictures such as *Femina Ridens* (1969), *La Lupa mannara* (1976), which is also known as *Naked Werewolf Woman*, *Atti Impuri all'italiana* (1976), and *S.A.S. a San Salvador* (1982). Each one of those tongue-twisting treasures featured her magnificent muff and heavenly hootage on full display. Sadly, she gave up her skinful ways by the '80s. She managed to parlay her past into a semi-lucrative acting career with roles in such films as *La Famiglia* (1987), *L'Ingranaggio* (1987), and *Passi d'amore* (1989), which means *Steps of Love*—well worth climbing. Unfortunately, she hasn't done a whole lot since then, and it's beginning to look like she isn't planning on it any time soon— Dagmar it!

SKIN-fining Moment:

Werewolf Woman (0:17) Dagmar displays her breasts and muff whilst doing a little self-exploration.

See Her Naked In:

S.A.S. Malko—Im Auftrag des Pentagon (1982) FFN, Buns
Werewolf Woman (1976) FFN, Buns
Atti Impuri all'italiana (1976) Breasts, Buns
Dandelions (1974) FFN, Buns
L'Iguana della Lingua di Fuoco (1971) Breasts
Femina Ridens (1969) Breasts

Sanaa Lathan

Born: October 19, 1971
New York, New York
Skin-O-Meter: Brief Nudity

Sanaa Lathan is the product of a bicoastal union between entertainment professionals: her father, a television producer, her mother, a Broadway actress. No doubt, then, that she would go into the business called show. She made her big-screen debut in *Drive* (1996). It was only a bit part, but she followed it up with guest spots on *Moesha*, *In the House*, and *Family Matters*, all in the span of a few months. In 1997 Sanaa appeared on the sitcom *Built to Last*, which was unfortunately built to be canceled. After a stint on the short-lived Al Franken sitcom *LateLine*, Sanaa took a brief turn in the Wesley Snipes vampire action picture *Blade* (1998).

That in turn led to bigger and better roles in movies such as *Life* (1999) and *The Best Man* (1999). Sanaa first unleashed her massive round breasts to the world in *Love & Basketball* (2000) opposite Omar Epps. He apparently liked what he saw, seeing as they ended up hot and heavily engaged. It is also noteworthy to add that Sanaa again released her heaving bosom, this time for Snipes when she teamed up with him for *Disappearing Acts* (2000). Looks like the only disappearing act was her bra from her boobs.

SKIN-fining Moment:

Love & Basketball (0:46) Sanaa's bared right basketball is a slam dunk, even if it is a lightning-quick peep.

See Her Naked In:

Love & Basketball (2000) RB
Disappearing Acts (2000) RB

Carole Laure

Born: August 5, 1951
Montreal, Quebec, Canada
Skin-O-Meter: Hall of Fame

Carole Laure was a teacher in Montreal, where she was raised, when she realized it's better to teach by dirty example. She talked the talk and walked the walk with her first notable appearance in the film *Mon Enfance à Montréal* (1971) and has since appeared in more Canadian, American, and French television and cinema than you can shake a meat stick at. Thankfully, the exotic Carole has also been kind enough to show off her sizzling Canadian bacon. Some of her more liberating roles include *Sweet Movie* (1974), the aptly titled *Get Out Your Handkerchiefs* (1978), *Un Assassin qui Passe* (1981), *La Mort d'un Bucheron* (1984), and *Sweet Country* (1986). That's two sweets, but all of the aforementioned tidbits deliver some

view of her beautiful tits and several full-frontal scenes. Oh, Canada!

SKIN-fining Moment:

Sweet Movie (1:30) Carol twists about nude while being covered in chocolate. T&A.

See Her Naked In:

Rats and Rabbits (2000) Breasts
Elles ne Pensent qu'à ça . . . (1994) Breasts
La Nuit avec Hortense (1988) Breasts
Sweet Country (1986) FFN, Buns
Heartbreakers (1984) Breasts
The Surrogate (1984) Breasts
Un Assassin qui Passe (1981) Breasts, Buns
Au Revoir à Lundi (1979) FFN
La Jument Vapeur (1978) RB
Get Out Your Handkerchiefs (1978) FFN
L'Ange et la Femme (1977) Breasts
Blazing Magnum (1976) Breasts
La Tête de Normande St-Onge (1975) Breasts
Sweet Movie (1974) Breasts
La Mort d'un Bûcheron (1973) FFN, Buns
Fleur bleue (1971) FFN

Ashley Laurence

Born: May 28, 1971
California
Skin-O-Meter: Great Nudity

Typecasting can be a good thing if a lady wants to make a living, and checks have been rolling in for striking Brit brunette Ashley Laurence ever since she helped scare the pants off legions of fixated adolescents as the imperiled, plucky, and totally bed-worthy Kristy Cotton in *Hellraiser* (1987). Ashley's stressed, screaming sensualist so resonated among the *Hellraiser* hellions that she became inseparable from the success of the series and resumed her demon-battling role in the second, third, fifth, and sixth installments of the ever-popular series. In *Hellraiser: Hellseeker* (2002), Ashley stripped to boudoir wear. Lovely Laurence is at least three times as explicit while pretending to ride rod in *Triplecross* (1995), which bears the unofficial alternate title *Triple-Bs*, as in buns, boobs, and beav.

SKIN-fining Moment:

Triplecross (0:42) During a lengthy lovemaking bout, Ashley airs out her love-bombs, backdoor, and even a bit of bushala.

See Her Naked In:

A Murder of Crows (1999) Breasts, Thong
Triplecross (1995) Breasts, Buns, Bush

Avril Lavigne

Born: September 27, 1984
Napanee, Ontario, Canada
Skin-O-Meter: Brief Nudity

Avril Lavigne is the no-nonsense MTV star who looks sexy even in cut off Dickies and a wife-beater. She was born in Napanee, Ontario, Canada—oh, Canada! At sixteen she moved to Manhattan and began work on her debut album, dropping out of high school after eleventh grade when she scored a record deal. When Avril was almost eighteen, she released "Complicated," the first single from her debut album *Let Go*. The album went straight to the top of the pops. Even Mr. Skin popped off to it. A petite skater girl from a small town, Avril has redefined sexy for the teeny-bopper set. She's got Grammy nominations and MTV awards, but the one thing she's missing is the skin exposure that we here at Skin Central covet. Her videos may not offer much more than a tough-girl pose, but we caught a live performance on Canada's Much Music where her low riders were riding so low that she mooned the audience! Looks like Avril's got a sex kitten purring beneath that tomboy.

SKIN-fining Moment:

Much Music Awards (2002) Avril cracks a smile and beautifully complicates the performance of her smash hit by bending over so her upper butt crack can get some quality exposure.

TeleVisions:

Much Music Awards Buns

Lucy Lawless

Born: March 29, 1968
Mount Albert, Auckland, New Zealand
Skin-O-Meter: Brief Nudity

Lucy Lawless is a born beauty. She won the Mrs. New Zealand pageant in her homeland, which landed her a part on the hit comedy series *Funny Business*. There was nothing funny about this brunette's appeal. She rode the vehicle of her good looks to other indigenous productions like *Within the Law* (1990), *A Bitter Song* (1990), and *The End of the Golden Weather* (1991) before landing a role on the hit series *For the Love of Mike*. For those who love Lucy, she took her career to the next lusty level, moving to the U.S. and finding work on *The Ray Bradbury Theatre*, *The X-Files*, and, most important, on *Hercules: The Legendary Journeys*. She was first cast as Lyla but later tried out for the ass-kicking Xena, was cast, and dyed her hair to distinguish herself from the prior role. Xena was such a tempting warrior that her character was spun off, and the rest is history. Despite her name, Lucy's film and TV career has been very law abiding, at least in terms of breaking the skin barrier. She's strutting about scantily clad, but sadly always clad. For an unintentional peek at Lucy's lovelies, check out the lungful beauty belting out the National Anthem at a Redwings game in Detroit on May 6th, 1997. She also belted out one of her meaty boobs as it rolled out from her descending

LUCY, FLAWLESS: GLAMAZONIAN MS. LAW-LESS IN HER FAMOUS *XENA: WARRIOR PRINCESS* GET-UP.

top while she reached for that elusive high note. Now that *Xena* is off the air, maybe Lucy will get (intentionally) loose.

SKIN-fining Moment:

Redwings Game: National Anthem (1997) As Lucy sings "The Star-Spangled Banner," her pink nippled left bomber bursts out of her Uncle Sam costume and into the air like rockets' red glare.

See Her Naked In:

Redwings Game: National Anthem (1997) Nip Slip LB

TeleVisions:

Xena: Warrior Princess FFN, Buns

Gail Lawrence

New York City, NY
Skin-O-Meter: Great Nudity

Fresh-faced, vulnerable, naïve, and idealistic are not terms generally befitting the women of sin cinema, unless that woman is strawberry-blonde nymph Gail Lawrence. Under the porn name Abigail Clayton, Gail revealed her charming, youthful essence in a series of XXX triumphs that, unfortunately, were confined to the short span of years between 1976 and 1980, a time of unlikely innocence in the sex business. Even the jaded moguls of hardcore recognized Lawrence's core innocence, casting her in the title role of *Seven into Snowy* (1977), a penetrating retelling of the Snow White fairy tale. Fans of arty French filmmaking can treat themselves to an excruciatingly full strolling ass shot in *Ciao Maschio* (1977), which translates to *Bye Bye Monkey*. Considering Gail's many nude scenes, a more appropriate title might be *Spank Spank Monkey*.

SKIN-fining Moment:

Bye Bye Monkey (0:11) The good news is that Gail goes full-frontal on the bed. The bad news is: so does Gérard Depardieu.

See Her Naked In:

Maniac (1980) Breasts, Bush
Bye Bye Monkey (1977) FFN, Buns
Numerous Adult Movies

Sharon Lawrence

Born: June 29, 1961
Charlotte, North Carolina
Skin-O-Meter: Brief Nudity

A bursting ball of entertainment energy, Sharon Lawrence has appeared on stage, television, and screen with a vixenish vengeance since the early 1990s, and she shows no sign of turning in her SAG card or for sagging anywhere at all. The saucy sprite is best known for her seven-year stint as Dennis Franz's spirited squeeze on *NYPD Blue* and may hold the skin-stinction of being the only actress to shed more thread while working on television than in the movies. On *NYPD Blue* Sharon had no reservations about giving her

corporate suit the boot and remaining silent and sexy for the cameras—broadcasting her bulletproof buns more than once, including a controversial shower scene with screen hubby Franz where she bailed out her buns for a little interrogation titillation. And since her rear-ended role as a primetime, pant-suited pretty has expired, Sharon has moved on to series comedy, television movies, and the occasional direct-to-video action-fest, flashing her bikini for the sitcom *Fired Up* and showing off her skimmies for the mini-series *Degree of Guilt* (1995). Sharon always takes on a variety of screen personae and never looks behind her—a place where most of our eyes have been locked for a long time.

SKIN-fining Moment:

NYPD Blue "The Final Adjustment" (1994) Sharon steps into the shower and stuns the world with her athletic ass. Then Dennis Franz joins her. His ass is not so athletic.

TeleVisions:

NYPD Blue Buns

Isild Le Besco

Born: November 22, 1982
France
Skin-O-Meter: Great Nudity

Young French actress Isild Le Besco, unlike her older actress sister Maïwenn Le Besco (who played an alien in *The Fifth Element* [1997]), has figured out how to keep the audiences "coming" back for more—boobies and bush! Though she's barely legal drinking age in the U.S., Isild has already shown more skin than the vast majority of American actresses her age. This is probably due to the fact that she is French. In 2003 television audiences in her homeland got a

double eyeful of her fabulous au natural front in the made-for-boob-tube flick *La Maison du Canal* (that's French for "Home of the long dark tunnel of love" or something like that). The year 2000 was also quite skinorific for Isild. She got finger fiddled by the Marquis de Sade in *Sade* (2000) and played the sluttier half of a quasi-lesbian fifteen-year-old couple in *Girls Can't Swim* (2000). Who cares if she can swim; the most important thing is that she goes into the water topless! That translates to beaucoups des tits pour nous!

SKIN-fining Moment:

Sade (1:18) Breasts and bush as two fellas toy with Isild's butt-naked body.

See Her Naked In:

The Cost of Living (2003) Breasts
La Maison du canal (2003) Breasts, Buns
Sade (2000) FFN
Girls Can't Swim (2000) Breasts, Buns

Dorothy Le May

Skin-O-Meter: Great Nudity

They don't make porn starlets like they used to, and in the case of redhead street angel Dorothy Le May it's too bad they don't. Skin scouts who have never ventured into hardcore territory may nonetheless carry a cerebral imprint of Le May's lighter-than-air bosom as it floated onscreen in Blake Edwards's *10* (1979). The more reckless epidermal explorers can only scoff at their timid brethren and exhort the mousy muff hunters to go all the way, especially for Dorothy Le May. The rewards include soft, copper-colored tufts atop and below, lissome limbs like milk in a flesh mold of the Sabine women, a mouth never completely shut, a tongue never far behind her not-quite-touching teeth, a sexual hunger never far from erupting and consuming all who are its witness. Start with *Taboo* (1980) and press deeper from there.

SKIN-fining Moment:

10 (0:50) Dudley Moore squires Dorothy around a swinger's bash and we see her Les Mams and Les Mudflaps.

See Her Naked In:

Simply Irresistible (1983) FFN, Buns
Taboo (1980) FFN
10 (1979) Breasts, Buns
Numerous Adult Movies

Cloris Leachman

Born: April 30, 1926
Des Moines, Iowa
Skin-O-Meter: Brief Nudity

Cloris Leachman first stepped out as a runner-up in the 1946 Miss America pageant and curled her captivating looks and fledgling acting aspirations into a half-century of steady work and acclaim. Her first skip with stardom came when she was tapped as the bleak blonde femme fatale in *Kiss Me Deadly* (1955), and she's paved a golden path in entertainment ever since, with a focus on the funny. Whoever said humor isn't the key to sex appeal has never seen Cloris in her prime, where during her stint on TV's *Mary Tyler Moore*, she brought life to the archetypal blonde bimbo. But on the big screen, Cloris was a bit racier in character choices, playing a lady of ill repute in *Butch Cassidy & The Sundance Kid* (1969), then quickly giving a glimpse of her door knockers and warm welcome mat in *The People Next Door* (1970)—at age forty-four. Her turn as Melba in *Crazy Mama* (1975) gave us a brief peek at her firm bum cakes—plus a hilarious scene involving her in little more than a low top and high stockings. This award winner proves that

both wits and tits make the ideal Hollywood success story.

SKIN-fining Moment:

The People Next Door (0:59) Cloris rises from the sack and shows back-crack plus a little side right breast as she tosses on a robe.

See Her Naked In:

Crazy Mama (1975) LB, Buns
The People Next Door (1970) RB, Buns

Kelly LeBrock

Born: March 24, 1960
New York, New York
Skin-O-Meter: Brief Nudity

> **MR. SKIN'S TOP TEN**
>
> **Best PG Nude Scenes**
> . . . Not parental guidance, Pleasantly Gratuitous
>
> 10. **Stella Stevens**
>   —*Monster in the Closet* (1986) (0:17)
> 9. **Beverly D'Angelo**
>   —*Hair* (1979) (0:59)
> 8. **Daryl Hannah**
>   —*Splash* (1984) (0:28)
> 7. **Tanya Roberts**
>   —*Sheena* (1984) (0:54)
> 6. **Gilda Texter**
>   —*Vanishing Point* (1971) (1:19)
> 5. **Sheree North**
>   —*Lawman* (1971) (1:19)
> 4. **Elizabeth McGovern**
>   —*Ragtime* (1981) (0:53)
> 3. **Barbara Williams**
>   —*Oh, What a Night* (1992) (0:59)
> 2. **Julie Warner**
>   —*Doc Hollywood* (1991) (0:15)
> 1. **Kelly LeBrock**
>   —*The Woman in Red* (1984) (1:14)

No matter what dirty tricks time or fortune may have in store, Kelly LeBrock will always know that for one stirring moment hers was the embodiment of Hollywood's highest concept of the ultimate hot chick. *Weird Science* (1985) presented the skinteresting proposition that two computer-geek adolescents had the power to create and interact with the most amazingly rad-bodied, dream-faced woman of their deepest yearning dreams. The computer fired up, and out popped Kelly. Sadly, *Weird Science* was aimed at a kid crowd, and nothing much of Kelly really popped out, which certainly disappointed the advanced-placement kids. Satisfaction could be found a year earlier in the Gene Wilder vehicle *The Woman in Red*, which capped off with deliciously naked LeBrock popping out of bed and popping eyes with her hot bod and bush. LeBrock rocked.

SKIN-fining Moment:

The Woman in Red (1:14) Kelly flashes her tits while getting her groove on with Gene Wilder, then shows more-than-a mouthful of muff when her husband comes home early. This is rated PG-13!

See Her Naked In:

The Woman in Red (1984) Breasts, Bush, Buns

Shakara Ledard

Nassau, Bahamas
Skin-O-Meter: Brief Nudity

Much of the allure exerted by the exotic atolls and sandy beaches of the Caribbean comes from fervid imaginings of the lovely native creatures gamboling bikini-clad and topless through the frothy, warm surf. No visualization of island femininity is more likely to pop a dreamer's thermometer than

Bahamian beauty Shakara Ledard. Even if she weren't posing to sell Dove moisturizing bars or cocking her drum-tight buns in a national Levi's campaign, one look at Shakara's supernaturally gleaming ebony countenance and matching mouth-watering body would be enough to know that here glows a model of the genus super. Aside from providing full-color sensationalism to the Victoria's Secret bible of lingerie, Shakara's dusky peaks and curves are prominent in that definitive resource for athletic apparel, the *Sports Illustrated Swimsuit Edition*. Spurts more than sports came to mind when Shakara's chocolate nipples popped up unfettered and nibble ready in *MTV Uncensored—Sports Illustrated Swimsuit Issue 2001* (2001).

SKIN-fining Moment:

MTV Uncensored—**Sports Illustrated Swimsuit Issue 2001** *Shakara shakes her way free of a bikini top amidst some dunes and then covers her own dusky hills with a sheer orange scarf, but we get a refreshing blast of stiff nipple along the way.*

See Her Naked In:

MTV Uncensored—Sports Illustrated Swimsuit Issue *2001* (2001) RB

Brandy Ledford

Born: September 12, 1969
Redondo Beach, California
Skin-O-Meter: Great Nudity

Brandy Ledford got her start as Jisel in the May 1990 issue of *Penthouse* magazine, even though she seems to have dropped this particular credit off her resumé. Though she may not like to admit it now, this shoot propelled her all-American good looks and bountiful bosom into a promising film and television career. Her first "big" break was a

bit part as the Fiber-Op Girl in *Demolition Man* (1993), soon followed by her first nude appearance opposite Shannon Tweed in *Indecent Behavior* (1993). She soon abandoned the "erotic thriller" genre but took a very skinerrific role in *Zebra Lounge* (2001), once again leaving very little to the skinophile's imagination. She also has appeared in such films as *National Lampoon's Last Resort* (1994), *My 5 Wives* (2000), and *Rat Race* (2001). Much of her work has been on television, with appearances on *Baywatch*, several episodes of *Silk Stalkings*, and the hit sci-fi series *The Invisible Man*, which has garnered her largest fan base to date.

SKIN-fining Moment:

Indecent Behavior (0:59) Brandy ditches her outfit for Jan-Michael Vincent, treating us all to her boom-booms and butt-butt.

See Her Naked In:

Separate Ways (2001) Breasts
Zebra Lounge (2001) Breasts
Irresistible Impulse (1996) Breasts
Killing for Love (1995) FFN, Buns
Demolition Man (1993) Breasts
Indecent Behavior (1993) Breasts, Buns

Virginie Ledoyen

Born: November 15, 1976
Aubervilliers, France
Skin-O-Meter: Hall of Fame

If it weren't for France, we would have no French kissing, no French Lick, and no Virginie Ledoyen. Ledoyen is a tart and delicate pastry treat whose very celluloid presence makes men of all nations forget our differences, uniting us in the realization that we share a common sweet tooth. The first taste of Virginie for most American sugar lovers came when the eye-candy confection shed the strings of her

bikini and bared the sides of her cupcake breasts for Leonardo DiCaprio in *The Beach* (2000). Frenchmen have been glazing over at the sight of Ledoyen's savory puffs since the scrumptious mademoiselle pulled her nightgown over her head and proudly displayed her sugar-spun bush in *Le Voleur d'enfants* (1991). There have been many mouth-watering snacks in the meantime; *Fin Août, Debut Septembre* (1998) in particular is worth seeking out.

SKIN-fining Moment:

Heroines (1:33) Virginie gets out of bed nude, puts on a CD and performs a naked dance of seduction. Titlets and tail.

See Her Naked In:

De l'amour (2001) Breasts, Bush, Buns
The Beach (2000) Breasts
En Plein Coeur (1998) Breasts
Jeanne et le Garçon Formidable (1998) Breasts, Bush
Fin Août, Debut Septembre (1998) Breasts, Bush
Héröines (1997) FFN, Buns
Les Sensuels (1995)
L'Eau Froide (1994) Breasts
La Règle de l'homme (1994) FFN, Buns
Les Marmottes (1993) Breasts
Le Voleur d'enfants (1991) FFN

Joie Lee

Born: 1963
Brooklyn, New York
Skin-O-Meter: Brief Nudity

Joie Lee, the lusciously ebony skinny bitty booby, owes her career to her brother. No, not "brother" like the proud and strong African American community, but her biological brother, the wildly successful impish director Spike Lee. He has cast her in almost everything he has ever done. Joie debuted in *She's Gotta Have It* (1986) before appearing in *School*

Daze (1988), *Do the Right Thing* (1989), *Mo' Better Blues* (1990), *Crooklyn* (1994), *Get on the Bus* (1996), and most recently *Summer of Sam* (1999). Her only nude scene to date was in *Mo' Better Blues* (1990), in which you can glimpse her right breast for about a tenth of a second. I guess Spike didn't want to be caught looking at his sister's goodies. But for us it's a Joie.

SKIN-fining Moment:

Mo' Better Blues (1:06) Joie shows right jugalina in bed with Denzel Washington. Directed by brother Spike!

See Her Naked In:

Mo' Better Blues (1990) RB

Loletta Lee

Born: January 8, 1966
Kwangchow, China
Skin-O-Meter: Great Nudity

Chinese charmer Loletta Lee gives Mr. Skin plenty to cheer about, and from the looks of her, she'd be plenty of fun to chew on. Actually, she gets chewed on in quite a few of her titles (as Ms. Lee isn't too chaste), most notably in *Bu kou niu de nu hai* (1994), a.k.a. *Girls Unbuttoned,* and *Yu po tuan er zhi yu nu xia jing* (1996), a.k.a. *Sex and Zen II.* Seeing Loletta in all her full-frontal glory, most of the time whilst in the midst of an acrobatic sex session, is worth the effort of tracking these down, as you will probably be very "relieved" several times throughout each one! (In the case of *Sex and Zen II,* that acrobatic sex is with Asian lovely Qi Shu.) Most of her titles are in Cantonese and very difficult to find in America—no huge surprise, with silly titles like *Porky's Meatballs* (1986), *Terror in a Woman's Prison* (1988), *United Family Joyful* (1989), *The Musical Vampire* (1990), *Chicken à la Queen* (1990), *Pom Pom & Hot Hot*

(1992), and *The Pink Bomb* (1993). Loletta has made it over here for a few bit parts, most notably in the flopmeister *Street Gun* (1996), but for skin, check out the aforementioned flicks or her softcore romp *Crazy Love* (1993), in which she stars alongside the aptly named Tom Poon.

SKIN-fining Moment:

Yu po tuan er zhi yu nu xia jing (1:18) The beautiful Loletta is getting slammed hard for a long time by the beautful Qi Shu. Luscious lesbianism, all-points nudity for both beauties.

See Her Naked In:

Sex and Zen 2 (1996) Breasts, Buns
Yu po tuan er zhi yu nu xia jing (1996) Breasts
Bu kou niu de nu hai (1994) FFN, Buns
Crazy Love (1993) Breasts, Bush, Buns

Robbie Lee

Born: September 1, 1954
Hollywood, California
Skin-O-Meter: Great Nudity

Sometimes the brightest stars have the shortest flash, and such was the blink of light known as Robbie Lee. A strawberry blonde in the Linda Blair mold, only fresher and without the satanic undertow, Robbie Lee achieved full nudity in her first movie role of note, as part of a bank-robbing pussy posse in the tits-and-tommyguns classic *Big Bad Mama* (1974). Budding nymphette Robbie looks so innocent, skinverts will almost feel guilty fixating on her cheeky assets as she strips and prepares for bedtime action with another girl and a stepdaddy. Robbie was promoted to a girl-gang leader in *Switchblade Sisters* (1975). Despite baring her snarly adolescent soul and soft, girlie chest buds, her flaring arc soon fell back to earth, never to be seen again.

SKIN-fining Moment:

Big Bad Mama (0:51) Robbie and Susan Sennett shed their threads and head to bed with Tom Skerritt, baring their buns in the process.

See Her Naked In:

Switchblade Sisters (1975) Breasts
Big Bad Mama (1974) Breasts, Buns

Sheryl Lee

Born: April 22, 1967
Augsburg, Bavaria, Germany
Skin-O-Meter: Hall of Fame

Sheryl Lee is what we call a Mr. Skin shoo-in. Find a show she's in, and she's likely to be showin'. The German-born, American-raised strudel-puss set the tone for her career in *Twin Peaks: Fire Walk with Me* (1992) by dancing topless, lounging in a bar booth topless, and engaging in topless feigned sexual intercourse. Of course, nobody does simulated lovin' like Sheryl Lee. Sheryl hit a full-frontal, bush-accessorized stride and indulged another bout of topless putative coupling in *Backbeat* (1994), added a dash of handcuffs to the formula in *The World, Then the Fireworks* (1997), and graduated to being the creamy filling between two stripped studs in *Kiss the Sky* (1998). Germany's loss is humanity's gain.

SKIN-fining Moment:

Twin Peaks: Fire Walk With Me (1:21) Sheryl sits bare-boobied in a booth at a nightclub chatting up some chick. Only in Twin Peaks . . . get it?!?!

See Her Naked In:

Angel's Dance (1999) FFN
Kiss the Sky (1998) Breasts, Buns
Vampires (1998) Buns
This World, Then the Fireworks (1997) Breasts
Bliss (1997) Breasts
The Blood Oranges (1997) Breasts
Mother Night (1996) Breasts
Homage (1996) Breasts

Notes From Underground (1995) Breasts
Backbeat (1994) FFN, Buns
Twin Peaks: Fire Walk With Me (1992) Breasts

TeleVisions:

Kingpin Breasts
Red Shoe Diaries Breasts

Sook-Yin Lee

Vancouver, British Columbia, Canada
Skin-O-Meter: Brief Nudity

Canadian-born, exhibitionistic Asian lovely Sook-Yin Lee first captured the frosty hearts of snowbound popular-culture fans as lead singer of the influential pop-punk band Bob's Your Uncle. In 1995 Sook-Yin's sweet lips and dulcet tones won her a spot as a veejay on MuchMusic, the north-of-the-border equivalent of MTV. Just like down here in the wicked United States, music-channel personalities of the female gender are subject to fixation in the male viewer's imagination. Hetero-curious males may fully appreciate Sook-Yin's status as an important performance artist but can't help wondering and asking aloud, "What would Sook-Yin Lee look like naked?"

SKIN-fining Moment:

The Art of Woo (0:56) Sook-Yin briefly bares her egg rolls in bed, then flashes ass as she gets up.

See Her Naked In:

The Art of Woo (2001) Breasts, Buns

Sung Hi Lee

Born: April 1, 1970
Seoul, Korea
Skin-O-Meter: Great Nudity

Why should kids have all the fun? We adults are perfectly content to allow the tykes their enjoyment of sleekly sensational Asian love kitten Sung Hi Lee as she leaps and bounds through sound stage and back lot as Kiri on the pre-adolescent action fest *Mortal Kombat: Conquest*. Just don't let the rug brats ask us to share our prized portions of former Hawaiian Tropic representative Sung Hi's high-flung chest beauties as they are presented in *Playboy's The Girls of Hawaiian Tropic*. Let the youngsters grow up a few years before they see how Sung Hi's tender flesh plays with yellow body paint in *Error in Judgment* (1998).

SKIN-fining Moment:

A Night on the Water (0:22) Sung Hi shows off her impressive Asian Apples and one helluva sweet can as she does a sexy strip for her latest conquest.

See Her Naked In:

The Girl Next Door (2004) Breasts, Thong
Error in Judgment (1998) Breasts, Buns
A Night on the Water (1998) Breasts, Buns
Butterfly (1997) Breasts, Buns

Erica Leerhsen

Born: February 14, 1977
Ossining, New York
Skin-O-Meter: Great Nudity

Red is among the most striking of hair hues, especially when the copper top is bobbing above the supple, nipple-activated form of cream-and-sugar delight Erica Leershen. The pale perfection of Erica's heavenly complexion is worth an extended first look, but it's her tidbit tits that inspire a neck-jerking double take when their nips pop prominently beneath a flimsy T-shirt on a third-season *Sopranos* stint as a pouting sprite wielding a tennis racket. The leering lens caught Leershen in full-frontal, crimson-thatched glory and with a fetching twist of totally naked behind in *Blair Witch 2: Book of Shadows* (2000), a performance so provocative that even old Leatherface saw red, and Erica also landed a lead as an imperiled teen in the classy remake *Texas Chainsaw Massacre* (2003).

SKIN-fining Moment:

Blair Witch 2: Book of Shadows (0:44) On a videotape, willowy witch Erica casts a bare-hootered hex as she frolics topless in the forest.

See Her Naked In:

Blair Witch 2: Book of Shadows (2000) FFN, Buns

Phoebe Legere

Skin-O-Meter: Brief Nudity

Phoebe Legere claims to have descended from passengers on the Mayflower. That's another thing we can thank the Pilgrims for, bringing the genes that generations later developed into this blonde bombshell. A denizen of New York's Lower East Side and its music/performance art crucible, Phoebe has a four-octave range, so pity her neighbors in those thin-walled tenements when she's having a screaming orgasm. A Vassar graduate with a master's degree in music composition from NYU, Phoebe got into the music biz at age fifteen and claims some A&R scum raped her when she brought him her tape. But she persisted and was described as the hetero '90s version of Bette Midler during her tenure at the gay bathhouses of New York. She's been on film in the documentary *Mondo New York* (1987) and even wrote and starred as a female wrestler with supernatural powers in a parable about corruption in the entertainment business called *Marquis de Slime* (1996). But she is best known as Toxie's main squeeze in *The Toxic*

Avenger, Part II (1989) and *The Toxic Avenger Part III: The Last Temptation of Toxie* (1989), in which she briefly flashed her little softies. That's something to sing about!

SKIN-fining Moment:

The Toxic Avenger, Part II (0:33) *Phoebe flashes her flappers while making out with The Toxic Avenger.*

See Her Naked In:

The Toxic Avenger Part III: The Last Temptation of Toxie (1989) RB, Thong
The Toxic Avenger, Part II (1989) RB
Mondo New York (1987) Bush, Buns

Kristin Lehman

Toronto, Ontario, Canada
Skin-O-Meter: Great Nudity

Unconventional blonde beauty Kristin Lehman is well known to fans of such TV series as *Poltergeist: The Legacy* (on which she had a co-starring role from 1998 to 1999) and *Judging Amy* (where she played Dr. Lily Reddicker in the 2002–03 season). Lucky for skinophiles, Kristin appeared in all her bare-breasted glory in the Canadian horror flick *Bleeders* (1997), and her rounded ass cheeks were on alluring display in a pulling-down-the-panties scene in Bruce McCulloch's *Dog Park* (1998). No topless shots here, but at least the former *Kids in the Hall* performer filmed Kristin in a lengthy diatribe wearing only a white T-shirt over her bulging breasts.

SKIN-fining Moment:

Bleeders (1:10) *Kristin's bouncin' bazongas appear as she strips off her top and gets down to some seriously frantic fragglin'.*

See Her Naked In:

Dog Park (1998) Buns
Bleeders (1997) Breasts

Hudson Leick

Born: May 9, 1969
Cincinnati, Ohio
Skin-O-Meter: Great Nudity

For centuries, the spin on women was that they were the gentler sex, given to minimizing conflict, bringing forgiveness and diplomacy where strife and resentment might reign, but that was before *Xena: Warrior Princess* burst upon the Zeitgeist and wiped all that sweet-and-sassy propaganda away. Blonde and bodacious Hudson Leick can look like a bowl of sugared cream poured into the body of a waking wet dream, and she played that look to perfection as Shelly Hanson on *Melrose Place*, but it was when she put on cleavage-enhancing armor and picked up a sword in 1995 as Callisto, the Queen of Battle, on *Xena: Warrior Princess* that Hudson transformed into a dangerous and delightful archetype for a new, nasty femininity.

SKIN-fining Moment:

Denial (0:43) *Hudson's spectacular set bounces about during this long, sweaty, heaving-and-humping sex scene with Ryan Alosio.*

See Her Naked In:

Denial (1998) Breasts
The Last Hand (1997) Breasts

Barbara Leigh

Born: November 16, 1946
Raingold, Georgia
Skin-O-Meter: Great Nudity

Probably no one outside of Studio 54 had more fun or "dated" more celebrities in the '70s than the skintacular bronzed brunette goddess Barbara Leigh. Barbara began modeling at age nineteen after she was discovered in a Beverly Hills nightclub. Strangely,

she had moved to L.A. to work as a nurse, a role she reprised in *The Student Nurses* (1970), *sans* scrubs. Helloooo nurse! She first hit the small screen in a Coca-Cola commercial and appeared in about fifty commercials altogether. Movie work soon followed, including the role of Jean, Rock Hudson's wife, in *Pretty Maids All in a Row* (1971) and the female lead opposite Steve McQueen in *Junior Bonner* (1972). In 1975 Barbara was signed on to play the bare-bosomed bloodsucker *Vampirella* for Hammer Films, but the movie was never made. Heartbroken, Barbara retired from acting, but she still has legions of fans around the world. She currently works for *Playboy* magazine.

SKIN-fining Moment:

The Student Nurses (0:41) *Barb bares boobs and several hints of bush as she lays in the sand with what appears to be a relative of Fabio.*

See Her Naked In:

Famous T&A (1982) Breasts
Mistress of the Apes (1979) Breasts
Terminal Island (1973) Breasts
The Student Nurses (1970) Breasts, Bush

Janet Leigh

Born: July 6, 1927
Merced, California
Skin-O-Meter: Brief Nudity

Picked from obscurity in 1947 and thrust into the Hollywood spotlight, Janet Leigh was typecast as the virginal ingénue for the early part of her career. She quickly took to her instant stardom, co-starring and hobnobbing with the sexiest leading men of the day. Janet's girl-next-door charm, vulnerability, and quiet sensuality made her an instant hit, but her superstar status came only after she married drag-inclined Tony

MR. SKIN'S TOP TEN

Solo Shower Scenes
. . . One hand washes
the udder

10. Stella Stevens
   —*Slaughter* (1972) (1:14)

9. Angelina Jolie
   —*Mojave Moon* (1996) (0:51)

8. Simone Griffeth
   —*Hot Target* (1985) (0:09)

7. Dyanna Thorne
   —*Ilsa, the Tigress of Siberia* (1977)
   (1:08)

6. Lana Wood
   —*Demon Rage* (1981) (0:20)

5. Stephanie Beacham
   —*Superbitch* (1973) (0:28)

4. Sherilyn Fenn
   —*Two Moon Junction* (1988) (0:07)

3. Beverly D'Angelo
   —*Vacation* (1993) (0:19)

2. Jill Schoelen
   —*The Stepfather* (1987) (1:14)

1. **Janet Leigh**
   —***Psycho* (1960) (0:45)**

Curtis in 1951, which led to a string of hits in almost every genre. Despite these successes, it was her scant but sinful forty-five minutes of screen time in Alfred Hitchcock's *Psycho* (1960) that would burn her name, and naked frame, into cinema history. We first peeped on Janet peeling down to her bra and slip early in the movie, making way for that famous shower scene, where throughout she revealed just enough soaking skin to give us a perfect picture of her, ahem, Hollywood hootenannies. Leigh also went off with her get-up in Orson Welles's film noir classic *Touch of Evil* (1958), where we see just a touch of Janet's planets during a strip-to-the-slip scene,

allowing us to conjure up plenty of our own evil thoughts.

SKIN-fining Moment:

Psycho (0:45) Very brief and blurry nipple shot in Hitchcock's ultra-famous, frantically edited shower scene.

See Her Naked In:

Psycho (1960) RB

Jennifer Jason Leigh

**Born: February 5, 1962
Hollywood, California
Skin-O-Meter: Hall of Fame**

Nobody's ever mistaken Jennifer Jason Leigh for a bimbo. Both critics and fans had to respect those mammaries so memorably seen in *Fast Times at Ridgemont High* (1982). Jennifer's acting skills then kept abreast with her . . . er, breasts as she showed real talent in films such as *Miami Blues* (1990) and *Single White Female* (1992). And it doesn't take a big budget to get those big'uns flashing, as seen in artsy productions such as *The King Is Alive* (2000). She hasn't lived up to the early predictions of stardom, but Jennifer remains a skinsation to fans of both taut performances and her taut little bod.

SKIN-fining Moment:

Flesh and Blood (1:06) JJL bares B-B-B! Naked as a lima bean, she jumps into a steaming bath and has an underwater shag with Rutger Hauer.

See Her Naked In:

The Machinist (2004) Breasts
Skipped Parts (2000) RB
The King Is Alive (2000) Breasts
Thanks of a Grateful Nation (1998) Breasts
Georgia (1995) Breasts, Buns
Mrs. Parker and the Vicious Circle (1994)
   Breasts
Single White Female (1992) FFN
Rush (1991) Buns

Crooked Hearts (1991) Breasts
Backdraft (1991) LB
Miami Blues (1990) Breasts
Last Exit to Brooklyn (1989) Breasts
Heart of Midnight (1988) RB
Sister Sister (1987) Breasts
Flesh and Blood (1985) FFN, Buns
Girls of the White Orchid (1983) Breasts
Fast Times at Ridgemont High (1982) Breasts
Eyes of a Stranger (1981) Breasts

Roberta Leighton

**Born: March 23, 1953
Minneapolis, Minnesota
Skin-O-Meter: Brief Nudity**

Roberta Leighton is primarily a creature of late '70s and early '80s television soaps, but skinophiles need look no further than their local video store to catch the only real (but still saliva-inducing) skin she ever committed to celluloid. Roberta's first professional acting gig was on a 1976 episode of *Barnaby Jones*, which led to the biggest role of her career, Cassandra "Casey" Reed on *The Young and the Restless*, a role she played off and on for twenty years. After appearing in the cinematic bomb *Barracuda* (1978), Roberta atoned for her sins by baring her itty bitties for the entire first fifteen minutes of *Stripes* (1981). In this seminal comedy, Roberta ran around in only her underwear while her boyfriend, played by Bill Murray, begged her not to leave him for good. (Spoiler: She leaves.) After *Stripes*, Roberta returned to the boob tube for one season of *General Hospital* before returning to *The Young and the Restless* in 1984. She spent two seasons on *Days of Our Lives* and hasn't been seen since 1998.

SKIN-fining Moment:

Stripes (0:08) Roberta exits the bathroom in panties only, and we get a quick view of her itty-bitties as she jiggles into a shirt.

See Her Naked In:

Stripes (1981) Breasts

Kasi Lemmons

Born: February 24, 1961
St. Louis, Missouri
Skin-O-Meter: Brief Nudity

Did light-skinned soul sister Kasi Lemmons feel she had something to prove? Success-driven at an early age, creamy Kasi landed a part directly out of high school in the made-for-TV drama *11th Victim* (1979). With only a pause to shake her blonde dreadlocks and twitch her high, taut, globicular tail feathers, sweet (not sour) Lemmons burst from the big screen with a stunning turn in director Spike Lee's African-American sorority sendup *School Daze* (1988). Kasi's acting credentials received a universal stamp of approval with her portrayal of Special Agent Ardelia Mapp in the monster hit *Silence of the Lambs* (1991), but she'd already proven herself, in *Vampire's Kiss* (1989), to be a hot mouthful of milky chocolate under the nipple-teasing lips of bloodsucker Nicolas Cage.

SKIN-fining Moment:

Vampire's Kiss (0:05) Kasi loses her black bra and gives bloodsucker Nicolas Cage two more fun things to put his mouth on.

See Her Naked In:

Vampire's Kiss (1989) Breasts

Ute Lemper

Born: July 4, 1963
Münster, Westfalen, Germany
Skin-O-Meter: Great Nudity

Ute Lemper is a Teutonic tootsie, a singer/actress/model from Germany whose sleek blonde good looks would make her a star even if lungs were only good for squeezing. She started her career as a model, but her big break came in 1983 when she played a pussy in the stage hit *Cats*. Her film debut was in a West German piece, *Drei Gegen Drei* (1985). By 1989 she became renowned for her singing ability, having released a concert video, as well as performing on numerous soundtracks and CDs. In the early 1990s Ute moved to the United States, making her most notable screen appearance in the fashion send-up *Ready to Wear* (1994), in which she appeared very pregnant and very naked alongside a slew of other nude-worthy models. She has since moved back to Germany but has returned Stateside to vamp as the sexy Velma in *Chicago* on Broadway. You've got to love the singer, not the song.

SKIN-fining Moment:

Ready to Wear (2:02) Ute displays milk-bloated bombers and thick thatch as she struts naked down a runway—massively pregnant.

See Her Naked In:

Ready to Wear (1994) Bush, Buns

Heidi Lenhart

Born: August 22, 1973
Los Angeles, California
Skin-O-Meter: Great Nudity

Heidi Lenhart owes her good looks to her mother, Cheryl Saban, who once graced the pages of *Playboy* magazine as a Playmate of the Month. But her acting career can be traced directly to her stepfather, Haim Saban, who heads up the Saban Entertainment Group and surely has a goodly number of connections in the entertainment industry. Heidi started her acting career in the made-for-TV movies *The Girl Who Came Between Them* (1990) and *A Quiet Little Neighborhood, a Perfect Little Murder* (1990) before taking on a role on the *Saved by the Bell*-esque series *California Dreams*. Mr. Skin's dreams came true when she moved from TV to cinema, especially in the nudie spectacular *Red Meat* (1997), in which she appeared completely nude for a good deal of the time that she was onscreen. That's a meal you can really sink your teeth into.

SKIN-fining Moment:

Red Meat (0:58) Heidi offers some very perky T&A as she entices a man into her bed.

See Her Naked In:

Red Meat (1997) Breasts, Buns

Rula Lenska

Born: September 30, 1947
St. Neots, Cambridgeshire, England, UK
Skin-O-Meter: Brief Nudity

With a full, strawberries-and-cream face and calculating green eyes, redheaded Rula Lenska has enjoyed a long and varied career as a supporting actress on British telly and also in the films those people make. Capable of high drama, low drama, and farce, pinkly pale Rula has flashed her dramatist flair in such disparate examples of Limey fare as the Peter Sellers goof *Undercovers Hero* (1973) and the wacky action of *Royal Flash* (1975), not to mention the departure into farcical histrionics as The Narrator in *Spice Girls' Girl Talk* (1997).

SKIN-fining Moment:

Oh, Alfie! (0:12) Here the hell is Rula Lenska: showing her kabobblers after toplessly rolling off Alan Price.

See Her Naked In:

Oh, Alfie! (1975) Breasts
Undercovers Hero (1973) Breasts

Kay Lenz

Born: March 4, 1953
Los Angeles, California
Skin-O-Meter: Great Nudity

Sultry-eyed brunette Kay Lenz is our kind of actress—a successful looker with a way-busy career who isn't above showing some skin here and there. She's appeared on a veritable shitload of TV shows, including *The Andy Griffith Show*, *Simon & Simon*, *Hill Street Blues*, *Murder She Wrote*, *Moonlighting*, and *Once and Again*. She earned critical acclaim for her starring roles in the films *Lisa Bright and Dark* (1973) and the Clint Eastwood-directed drama *Breezy* (1973) but has spent most of her career as a supporting player. Whatever the size of her role, we're grateful that she's stayed skinful throughout. She's bared skin in several films, including *Breezy* and *The Passage* (1979). Her most revealing onscreen moments can be seen—and savored—in the James Woods prison drama *Fast Walking* (1981).

SKIN-fining Moment:

Fast Walking (1:27) Kay's nay-nays get a splashtastic hosing down by James Woods outside.

See Her Naked In:

Stripped to Kill (1987) Breasts, Thong
Fast Walking (1981) Breasts
The Passage (1979) Breasts
Moving Violation (1976) Breasts
Breezy (1973) Breasts, Buns

Melissa Leo

Born: September 14, 1960
New York, New York
Skin-O-Meter: Great Nudity

Like many a hot young thing before her, Melissa Leo started her career on the set of the daytime soap opera *All My Children*. She was the sexy one . . . with red hair. Shortly after she landed that part, she garnered a role in the film *Streetwalkin'* (1984), which featured her first topless shots. Although the scenes are rather brief, it's a hot look at her soft, small wonders. After a turn in the made-for-TV movie *Silent Witness* (1985), Melissa took another skinful role in *Always* (1985) opposite actor/director Henry Jaglom. Again, you only get to see her handfuls for a brief instant, this time as she slides into a pool for a little commando swimming. Since then she has gone on to a supporting role on *Homicide: Life on the Street*, which landed her some choice parts, most notably in *The Ballad of Little Jo* (1993), the mini-series *Scarlett* (1994), and *Under the Bridge* (1997). Let's hope her nudity isn't under the bridge and Melissa lets her Leos roar again.

SKIN-fining Moment:

Streetwalkin' (0:15) Ms. Leo doffs her top in a strip club and gives a customer something to see-o.

See Her Naked In:

Silent Witness (1985) Breasts
Always (1985) Breasts
Streetwalkin' (1984) Breasts

April Lerman

Born: February 6, 1969
Chicago, Illinois
Skin-O-Meter: Brief Nudity

April Lerman's biggest role was as boy-crazed Lila on the 1984 debut season of CBS's sitcom *Charles in Charge*—and we could've watched her mature if she hadn't been replaced when the canceled series renewed itself as a syndicated show. Instead, it was a quiet April until she suddenly returned in full bloom for *Sorority House Party* (1992). The little girl proved she'd grown up and out as she went topless-turvy in bed with a long-haired rock guy. Sadly, April promptly disappeared again, leaving Nicole Eggert no competition as Charles's sexiest grown-up charge.

SKIN-fining Moment:

Sorority House Party (0:50) April enjoys some topless lovin' from her boyfriend in bed and we see her jiggling sorority houses.

See Her Naked In:

Sorority House Party (1993) Breasts

Anna Levine

Born: September 18, 1957
Skin-O-Meter: Hall of Fame

Character actress/sex-scene specialist Anna Levine's movie career has been like her bra—holding two big, separate spheres in one. Anna is respected by the acting cognoscenti for her nuanced depictions of auxiliary characters in such important pictures as *Heaven's Gate* (1980), *Wall Street* (1987), and *Unforgiven* (1992). Simultaneously, large-mammed Levine earned the admiration of discerning skinthusiasts with her uninhibited and enthusiastic portrayals of broads who like to swing their jugs in the open air. Though her rack appears in countless low-budget boob operas, Anna stretches the skinvelope with a lesbo-riffic gynecologist's fantasy that includes a wink of shaved clam in *Fiona* (1998). In *Bridget* (2002), the adventurous, veteran nudist is marched blindfolded and attire deprived into a city street after enduring a grueling ordeal of nude pushups while surrounded by a ring of menacing men. It's easy to feel the mystique of being one of them, thanks to Anna's raw emoting.

SKIN-fining Moment:

Fiona (0:21) A great flash of Anna's hooters while she shoots dope in the bathtub next to a guy. What a robo-rack!

See Her Naked In:

Bridget (2002) Breasts, Bush, Buns
Fast Food Fast Women (2000) FFN, Buns
Six Ways to Sunday (1999) Breasts
Fiona (1998) FFN, Buns
Sue (1997) FFN
Drunks (1997) Breasts
Jaded (1996) Breasts, Buns
I Shot Andy Warhol (1996) Breasts
Angela (1995) Breasts
Handgun (1994) LB
Blood Run (1994) Breasts, Buns
White Hot (1989) Breasts

> "I need someone who's going to strip me down and say, 'Do it!' I've never done nude scenes, and I can't wait. I can't wait to be abused in a film. Maybe it's a secret fantasy burning inside of me."
>
> —CHARLOTTE LEWIS, PRIOR TO HER SKIN DEBUT.

Charlotte Lewis

Born: August 7, 1967
Kensington London, England
Skin-O-Meter: Great Nudity

She has been referred to as the "R-rated Marcia Brady," but Charlotte Lewis is much more than that. She started acting in her native England, where she landed a role on the long-running series *Grange Hill*. But Hollywood beckoned. First she seemed to go bust in the box-office sinker *Pirates* (1986), but then she was cast opposite Eddie Murphy in *The Golden Child* (1986) and things turned, well, golden for the temptress. Charlotte has not only posed for *Playboy*, she also gets naked a lot onscreen to pay the bills. She's been on *The Red Shoe Diaries* and the made-for-cable

scorcher *Sketch Artist* (1992), in which she played a high-priced hooker who made love upside down while watching a fashion video. For *Men of War* (1994) she shared a wilderness bath with Dolph Lundgren. But her sexiest scene was a lesbianic tryst with Alyssa Milano in *Embrace of the Vampire* (1994). Oh, to get caught in Charlotte's web.

SKIN-fining Moment:

Storyville (0:17) Charlotte takes out of her martial arts outfit and eases into a hot tub. Buns and bombers.

See Her Naked In:

The Glass Cage (1996) Breasts
Men of War (1994) Breasts
Excessive Force (1993) Breasts
Storyville (1992) Breasts, Buns
Sketch Artist (1992) Breasts, Thong
Bare Essentials (1991) Thong
Dial Help (1988) RB

TeleVisions:

Red Shoe Diaries Breasts

Fiona Lewis

Born: September 28, 1946
Westcliffe-on-Sea, Essex, England, UK
Skin-O-Meter: Great Nudity

Fiona Lewis debuted in *Tell Me Whom to Kill* (1965) and sealed her fate as a scream queen. She went on to appear in *Dr. Phibes Rides Again* (1972), *Dracula* (1973) (where she played the luckless Lucy), and *The Fury* (1978). It was with The Who's lead throat Roger Daltrey in *Lisztomania* (1975) that Fiona first showed her hooters. Though mostly topless, there was a fleeting glimpse at her lower frontal goodies, proving that Fiona was game for skin. She followed that film with another bawdy turn, this time in the blaxploitation picture about life on the

plantation, *Drum* (1976). This film featured her, as well as every other female in the cast, topless at least once.

SKIN-fining Moment:

Lisztomania (0:00) Topless Fiona gives Roger Daltrey a double-shot of her mouthfuls in bed.

See Her Naked In:

Tintorera (1977) FFN, Buns
Drum (1976) Breasts
Lisztomania (1975) Breasts
Blue Blood (1973) Breasts, Bush
Villain (1971) Breasts

Jazsmin Lewis

Cleveland, Ohio
Skin-O-Meter: Great Nudity

Multi-talented, racially diverse Ohio native Jazsmin Lewis first took her rocking rack and slamming seat cushions to the stage as a backup vocalist and bass player for funky-beat headliners such as George Clinton and Zapp. Lucky for fans of visual stimulation, Jazsmin left music behind and took her cushiony, beckoning lips; moody, mystic eyes; and showstopping rear into the skinematic realm with a soulful supporting role in the keeping-it-real cop drama *Broken Bars* (1995). Jazsmin rocked her rhythm on television shows such as *Martin*, *Saved by the Bell: The New Class*, and *Hang Time* and cemented her position as a bouncy love bunny to place on nudity watch.

SKIN-fining Moment:

How to Be a Player (0:21) Jazsmin jiggles down the stairs topless in zebra panties at Pierre Edwards's home.

See Her Naked In:

How to Get the Man's Foot Outta Your Ass (2003) Breasts
How to Be a Player (1997) Breasts

Juliette Lewis

Born: June 21, 1973
Los Angeles, California
Skin-O-Meter: Great Nudity

Audiences got their first taste of Juliette Lewis in the blockbuster movie *Christmas Vacation* (1989) as the third and perhaps sexiest Audrey Griswold. She got serious opposite Robert De Niro in the remake of *Cape Fear* (1991), and you know what happens when an actress gets serious . . . they soon get nude. Juliette showed her first onscreen titty in *Kalifornia* (1993), although it was just a brief flash. *Natural Born Killers* (1994) offered

some more scant nudity. For the breast of Juliette, watch *Strange Days* (1996). Several scenes in this sci-fi head-scratcher showed her bitty boobies in lengthy, well-lit shots. Since then, Juliette's been free with her chest in *Some Girls* (1998), *Men* (1998), and *Picture Claire* (2001). Better (and wetter) still, Juliette took a plunge into toplessness in *Blueberry* (2004), providing us with a wide-open, underwater, spread-eagle crotch shot. It's one of the all-time great servings of celebrity furburgerage, complete with a peek at Juliette's pink-berry. Sweet *and* ripe!

SKIN-fining Moment:

Blueberry (1:50) Juliette serves up sumptuous submerged burger as she's underwater and opens her legs wide, filling the screen with her sweet Blueberry pie!

See Her Naked In:

Blueberry (2004) FFN, Buns
Picture Claire (2001) Breasts
Some Girl (1998) Breasts
Men (1998) Breasts
Strange Days (1995) Breasts
Natural Born Killers (1994) Nip Slip LB
Kalifornia (1993) LB

Marilyn Lightstone

Born: 1941
Montreal, Quebec, Canada
Skin-O-Meter: Brief Nudity

What do Sonja from *Heathcliff & the Cadillac Cats* and Crasher from *Challenge of the GoBots* and both Alice Mitchell and Martha Wilson of *Dennis the Menace in Cruise Control* have in common? Simply that, just like several of the highlighted voices of *Inspector Gadget*, *Kissyfur*, and *The Super Mario Bros. Super Show!*, they emanate from the golden throat of acclaimed Montreal-born veteran of screen and sound studio Marilyn Lightstone. Redheaded and

matronly Marilyn has also put a face along with the voice in such feature films as *Spasms* (1983), *The Wild Pony* (1983), and *The Surrogate* (1984).

SKIN-fining Moment:

In Praise of Older Women (0:45) In a scene full of hip-grinding and fumbling clothing removal, all we see are a couple of quick right breast shots while Marilyn ravages Tom Berenger on the floor.

See Her Naked In:

In Praise of Older Women (1978) RB

Marie Liljedahl

Born: February 15, 1950
Stockholm, Sweden
Skin-O-Meter: Great Nudity

Marie Liljedahl is quite possibly one of the most important figures in the history of erotic cinema. Sadly, she isn't a household name anywhere outside of Skin Central. Maybe she would have had better luck if she changed her name to something easier to pronounce, like Marie Lusty. She started her career with a big bang that puts the one that began the universe to shame. *The*

MARIE LILJEDAHL STICKS TO HER STORY IN *ENGENIE . . . THE STORY OF HER JOURNEY INTO PERVERSION.*

Seduction of Inga (1967) may seem tame by today's crude standards, but it ranks as one of the hottest X-rated movies ever thanks to Marie's lead role. Sure, the movie is pretty convoluted, but Marie got pretty naked several times, even showing a little thighbrow in one particular scene. She went on to appear in seven more softcore skin flicks, like the smartly asked question *Do You Want to Remain a Virgin Forever?* (1969), the intriguing *Eugenie . . . The Story of Her Journey Into Perversion* (1969), and the delightfully lesbianic *Ann and Eve* (1970). Then in 1971 Marie gave up the life. She's since appeared in interviews on special edition DVDs of her classic films, but we wait drooling for her triumphant return to sinema.

SKIN-fining Moment:

Inga (1:15) A great view of Marie's superb sweater treats as her man does a little carpet munching off-camera.

See Her Naked In:

Eugenie . . . the Story of Her Journey Into Perversion (1970) FFN, Buns
Ann and Eve (1970) Breasts
Inga (1967) Breasts, Buns

Tiffany Limos

Born: January 31, 1980
Mesquite, Texas
Skin-O-Meter: Great Nudity

Tiffany Limos was born in Texas, where they like them big. She may not be huge, but she knows what she likes. Tiffany was watching porno by age five, after she found tapes her father left in the VCR. That made going to a strict Catholic school a little confusing, she said, even though later her knowledge of porn stars endeared her to her friends. At fifteen she moved to New York to model for the Ford

Agency. Tiffany's film career started off innocently enough with an uncredited turn as Miss Texas in the hit flick *Bully* (2001) but has thankfully moved on to more skin-centric work. Tiffany appeared in *Teenage Caveman* (2001), which was pretty much all about teenagers having sex. Tiffany did her part to exemplify this within the film, showing off damn near every inch of her supple body in several scenes, including a sex scene that feels awfully real, as well as some pretty hot lesbianic stunts with Hayley Keenan. In the even more explicit *Ken Park* (2002), she played Peaches and got it on with two guys. Yes, big things are in store for this randy vixen.

SKIN-fining Moment:

Ken Park (1:23) Tiffany plays hardcore and exposes every inch of her dusky, flawless form while taking on a pair of mooks, at least one of whom gets his knob slobbered right on camera!

See Her Naked In:

Ken Park (2002) Breasts, Bush
Teenage Caveman (2001) Breasts, Buns

Christina Lindberg

Born: December 6, 1950
Göteborg, Sweden
Skin-O-Meter: Great Nudity

Sometimes selfishness is a virtue, especially when a stunning young lady has been blessed with tits to spare but still keeps those extra heaping wonders to herself. Such a virtuously over-stacked lass was Sweden's Christina Lindberg in her prime. A mesmerizing nymph who gamboled in clothing-optional art flicks and horror thrillers from the late '60s to the mid '70s, Christina had a hypnotic, otherworldly, distracted quality to her beauty. Typified in sexual-awakening fare such as *Maid in Sweden* (1969) and

Anita (1973), Christina always seemed to be listening within herself for the soft trembling of an oncoming orgasm.

SKIN-fining Moment:

Was Schulmädchen Verschweigen (0:35) Breasts and brief side nude trying to tempt a guy. Then she makes him kiss her lucky lindbergs.

See Her Naked In:

Sängkamrater (1975) FFN, Buns
Around the World with Fanny Hill (1974) Breasts, Bush
Was Schulmädchen Verschweigen (1974) Breasts, Bush
Thriller: A Cruel Picture (1974) FFN, Buns
Furyou Anegoden Inoshika Ochou (1973) Breasts
Anita—Ur en Tonårsflickas Dagbok (1973) FFN, Buns
Every Afternoon (1972) FFN, Buns
Schulmädchen—Report 4: Was Eltern oft Verzweifeln Läßt (1972) FFN
Exponerad (1971) Breasts
Smoke (1971) Breasts
Rötmånad (1970) FFN, Buns
Maid in Sweden (1969) Breasts, Buns

Janine Lindemulder

Born: November 14, 1968
La Mirada, California
Skin-O-Meter: Hall of Fame

Janine Lindemulder is one of the few celebrities known by only one name. But before she was a Vivid porn star, Janine worked in "legitimate" cinema, debuting in the Italian film *Moving Target* (1988) opposite the head-turning Linda Blair. Janine, of course, got naked throughout the course of the film, so she was pretty much a shoo-in for a role in the T&A flick *Spring Break USA* (1989). That film exposed Janine's assets, along with the other bouncing beauties in the movie. She went on to appear in the little-seen *Caged Fury* (1989) but soon realized that being a B-movie bimbo didn't pay nearly as well as simply going all the way for the camera. So she became an adult-film star. Over sixty credits later, she still refuses to have sex with anyone but women onscreen. Check out *Where the Boys Aren't 12* (2000) and wish you were there.

SKIN-fining Moment:

Janine & Vince Neil: Hardcore & Uncensored (0:28) Janine moshes atop Vince's Motley Tool. Full frontal, full penetration. Rock on!

See Her Naked In:

Janine & Vince Neil: Hardcore & Uncensored (1998) FFN, Buns
Denial (1998) Breasts
The Price of Desire (1996) FFN, Buns
Spring Break USA (1989) Breasts
Moving Target (1988) Breasts, Buns
Numerous Adult Movies

Christa Linder

**Born: December 3, 1943
Berchtesgaden, Bavaria, Germany
Skin-O-Meter: Great Nudity**

Claudia Schiffer is not without precedent as a vision of superior Germanic genetics in the realm of engineering über-blondes. The otherworldly blue-eyed dream of feminine excellence that Bavarian-born actress Christa Linder shared with a grateful and gleeful world in dozens of European and Mexican films from the mid 1960s through 1980 not only equals her sweet-pouting supermodel countrywoman in puissant insouciance, but far surpasses the modern mannequin in skin-flaunting generosity of spirit. Whether baring her cotton-tail buns in the Mexican-made *La Noche de los Mil Gatos* (1972) or flexing her tanned and trim gluteus to maximus effect in the Swedish-lensed *Bel Ami* (1976), Christa

Linder flashed an ass that even the sublime Ms. Schiffer should kiss, which would put her lips directly upon the portal to paradise.

SKIN-fining Moment:

Mi Amorcito de Suecia (0:49) When Julio Alemán climbs in the shower to try to free Christa, the Austrian cutie doesn't seem to care that her fabulous frontage is on full display.

See Her Naked In:

El Sexólogo (1980) Breasts
La Hora del Jaguar (1978) Breasts
Víbora Caliente (1976) Breasts
Bel Ami (1976) FFN, Buns
La Governante (1975) Breasts
Tutti Figli di Mamma Santissima (1973)
Racconti di Viterbury—Le Più Allegre Storie del '300, I (1973) Breasts, Buns
Fra' Tazio da Velletri (1973) Breasts, Buns
Mi Amorcito de Suecia (1972) Breasts, Buns
Confessioni Segrete di un Convento di Clausura (1972) FFN, Buns
La Noche de los Mil Gatos (1972) Breasts, Buns
El Imponente (1972) Breasts, Buns
Decameron '300 (1972) FFN, Buns
El Ardiente Deseo (1970) Breasts
Die Liebesquelle (1965) Buns

Traci Lind

**Born: April 1, 1966
Louisville, Kentucky
Skin-O-Meter: Great Nudity**

Southern girls have nothing to lose except their clothes, which is luckily what blonde beauty Traci Lind has done in more than one of her movies. Born in Kentucky, Traci got her start in modeling at age thirteen when Elite head man John Casablancas discovered her at a shopping mall. In 1984 she landed a season-long stint on the long-running soap opera *Ryan's Hope*. Most of her work since has been in film, starting with the forgettable *My Little Girl* (1986) and continuing the mediocre trend

with such masterworks as *Moving* (1988), *Fright Night II* (1989), and *Spellcaster* (1992). She briefly appeared nude in *Survival Quest* (1989), in which she's seen topless in a wilderness bath, but the view is from quite a distance, so it really isn't all that great. Her most eye-popping and entertaining role to date was in *The Road to Wellville* (1994), in which she gave Matthew Broderick's character, and everyone else, a hard-on when she shed her turn-of-the-century scrubs to display her titties and perfectly round ass.

SKIN-fining Moment:

The Road to Wellville (0:27) One sweet keister and a side-peek at her left A-cup as Traci stands naked in an elevator.

See Her Naked In:

The Road to Wellville (1994) LB, Buns
Survival Quest (1989) Breasts

Rosemarie Lindt

**Germany
Skin-O-Meter: Great Nudity**

Hair lank and long and reddish brunette; the idealized heart-shaped cherub face that might have seemed placid except for being flushed with erotic radiance; breasts that sloped at a high natural angle and held firm, pointing up; shapely, contoured rear loaves; a tangled muff of thick love matting—sexploitation starlet Rosemarie Lindt had been blessed with all the aspects of physical attraction. Like a true beauty, lovely Lindt generously shared all her gifts throughout the 1970s in what seemed like a never-ending series of X-rated European art films. Look for highbrow titles such as *The Sweet Sins of Sexy Susan* (1967), *Sexy Susan Sins Again* (1969), *Salon Kitty* (1976), and

Porno-Erotic Western (1979) for Rosemarie's bottom line. She holds nothing back.

SKIN-fining Moment:

Salon Kitty (0:53) Rack, rump, and rug as Rosemarie runs around the room with some fat old horny Nazi bastard.

See Her Naked In:

Salon Kitty (1976) FFN, Buns
Who Saw Her Die? (1972) Breasts, Bush, Buns

Laura Linney

Born: February 5, 1964
New York, New York
Skin-O-Meter: Great Nudity

Laura Linney's shapely form first appeared onscreen in *Lorenzo's Oil* (1992), and it really greased our pole. After a few made-for-TV flicks, the stage-trained Laura returned to the silver screen for another sweet-girl-in-the-background part in *Dave* (1993). Not long after that, Laura appeared in the cable mini-series about the queer life, *Tales of the City* (1993), which featured her, as well as a few members of the supporting cast, in little more than a smile. She went on to grace the big screen again in *Absolute Power* (1997) as the daughter of master thief Clint Eastwood and opposite Jim Carrey in *The Truman Show* (1998). Not shy about baring all for her art, Laura's most impressive skin was in the little-seen flick *Maze* (2000), in which she spent a great deal of her time onscreen posing nude for artist Rob Morrow. The Indians call it maze, we call it a grand full-frontal sextacular.

SKIN-fining Moment:

Maze (0:30) Laura bares every last inch of her stunning frame when posing nude for Rob Morrow, including several peeks at her pubies.

See Her Naked In:

Kinsey (2004) LB

P.S. (2004) Nip Slip—RB
Love Actually (2003) Breasts
The Life of David Gale (2003) Breasts, Bush, Buns
Maze (2000) FFN, Buns

TeleVisions:

Further Tales of the City FFN

Lio

Born: June 17, 1962
Mangualde, Portugal
Skin-O-Meter: Great Nudity

A native of Portugal whose artistic endeavors have emanated primarily from France, bushy-browed brunette Lio has been equated to a European version of Madonna, except without the world domination and the children's book. Like America's Material Girl, Lio is known by but a single name, and she balances two simultaneous careers, one as a musical sensation, the other as a movie star. Although the pouting, passion-kissed face of Lio has yet to become anywhere near as famous as Madge's, the scrumptious Latina lovely has garnered a string of positive acting reviews, beginning with her screen debut, *Les Années 80* (1983). Lio has also left a legacy of titty and assy on film, which might be a lesson to her Stateside counterpart.

SKIN-fining Moment:

Jalousie (0:21) As she peels to pose for a painting, Lio provides plenty to see-o. Fun-balloons, fur bush, and fanny.

See Her Naked In:

Jalousie (1991) FFN, Buns
Sale Comme un Ange (1990) Breasts

LisaRaye

Born: September 23, 1967
Chicago, Illinois
Skin-O-Meter: Brief Nudity

LisaRaye is black, beautiful, and built like a babe—it's no wonder *Black Men* magazine voted her the Sexiest Woman of 2001. Her career began with a part in the little-seen movie *Reasons* (1996), and she trudged forth, scoring roles in films such as *Date from Hell* (2001) and *The Wood* (1999) and on TV series such as *The Parent 'Hood* and *In the House*. Her most memorable contribution to skinema came in the Ice Cube-helmed film *Player's Club* (1998). Lisa bumped and grinded her way across the silver screen, appearing nude several times throughout the film. She's played it tame since, but perhaps director Spike Lee will get his mitts on her and cast her in a sequel to *Girl 6* (1996).

SKIN-fining Moment:

The Players Club (0:24) Lisa flashes her fine flappers on stage as she does her striptease "thang."

See Her Naked In:

The Players Club (1998) Breasts, Buns

Sacheen Littlefeather

Born: 1947
Salinas, California
Skin-O-Meter: Brief Nudity

Sacheen Littlefeather was born Maria Cruz but took advantage of her Native American heritage when her career took off shortly after her appearance in *Il Consigliere* (1973). At the Academy Awards ceremony that year, Sacheen made headlines by standing in for Marlon Brando and refusing his Best Actor statuette on his behalf, saying that her leg hurt or that she had a Wounded Knee . . . or something like that. She got cheers and jeers from the audience, but, unfortunate for Sacheen, this pretty much landed her in the stereotype of "squaw-in-trouble" for the remainder of her career, which, not surprisingly, didn't last all that long. She claims the FBI blacklisted her. Thankfully, before that happened Sacheen flashed some skinitude in *Johnny Firecloud* (1975). In that film she played a squaw in danger of being raped by a bunch of oppressive white fellas, who just so happened to remove her blouse for a nice look at her big bow and arrow. That sure made us play with our Littlefeather!

SKIN-fining Moment:

Johnny Firecloud (0:56) Littlefeather has her phony funbags exposed as a bunch of rednecks ravage her in a school classroom. Long scene with plenty of goofy symbolism.

See Her Naked In:

Johnny Firecloud (1975) Breasts

Lucy Liu

Born: December 2, 1968
Queens, New York
Skin-O-Meter: Great Nudity

The Fox dramady *Ally McBeal* got a new lease on life when Asian love doll Lucy Liu arrived on the scene, playing sexual and predatory legal eagle Ling Woo. Lucy's erotic prowess stood out on a show that was front loaded with sensual high achievers. Slinky and searing Lucy captured the mass imagination and transformed her sex appeal into star power, landing high-profile, but no nipple, roles in the two *Charlie's Angels* (2000 and 2003) mega-productions. But along with a future, the sublime Ms. Liu had a past. Look back and see Lucy's rear cheeks quiver as she walks butt naked in *Flypaper* (1997). Oh, and there in the near distance are her itty-bitty titties flexing on a

stripper pole in *City of Industry* (1997).

SKIN-fining Moment:

Flypaper (1:24) Delicious T&A as Lucy eases into an empty pool with her guy. They get it on until a snake bites them.

See Her Naked In:

Payback (1999) Thong
Flypaper (1997) Breasts, Buns
City of Industry (1997) Breasts

Kari Lizer

Born: 1962
Los Angeles, California
Skin-O-Meter: Brief Nudity

Los Angeles native Kari Lizer didn't have far to go for her Hollywood break. Sugar-faced and impish, with a topping of fluffy blonde hair, Kari was cute enough for the close-up frame of the TV camera, and her full-breasted, athletically proportioned, bouncing body perfectly suited the head-to-toe needs of big-screen cinematography. Her credible and attractive performances in low-brow feature-film diversions such as *Smokey Bites the Dust* (1981) and *Gotcha!* (1985) resulted in Kari being drafted to the small screen, where her most enduring gig was as Cassie Phillips on *Matlock*. Learning on the job, Kari moved into the writer's role, injecting her wit and pathos in scripts for acclaimed series such as *Boston Common* and *Will & Grace*. The luscious looks of Kari Lizer might have been lost forever, except that while shaking her pom-poms and her ta-tas as a hyperactive cheerleader in *Private School* (1983), her left melon escaped and flew forever free for all eternity.

SKIN-fining Moment:

Private School (0:30) A split-second moment of sexiness as Kari's left

lungnut decides to burst on out of her cheerleader uniform.

See Her Naked In:

Private School (1983) LB

Arroyn Lloyd

Mallorca, Spain
Skin-O-Meter: Great Nudity

If one country has an excess of desirable products, especially a country like Spain which seems to be overflowing with cinnamon-skinned packages of softly curved seduction, then it is only fair that the surplus goodness be exported to Hollywood, California. Beautiful and brilliant Arroyn Lloyd is Mallorca, Spain's loss, but the world's gain. The blonde-tressed mop top popped into the pop-culture eye as a regular gust of fresh-faced air on the NBC teen comedy *One World*, which led to guest spots on top-notch shows such as *Home Improvement*, *Seven Days*, and *The Practice*. Look for Arroyn playing racier than on TV with skinful suggestiveness in *Shadow Hours* (2000) and *Mic and the Claw* (2000).

SKIN-fining Moment:

Red Shoe Diaries "Caged Bird" (1999) Arroyn sings like a lesbian nightingale while toplessly shagging her Sapphic cellmate.

See Her Naked In:

Mic and the Claw (2000) RB, Buns

TeleVisions:

Red Shoe Diaries Breasts

Emily Lloyd

Born: September 29, 1970
London, England
Skin-O-Meter: Great Nudity

After her splashy debut as a slutty teen in the English hit *Wish You*

Were Here (1987), Emily Lloyd was touted as one of the most talented—and hottest—young actresses around. Then she came to America and promptly earned a reputation as a complete wreck of an actress. After being fired from at least three different movies, Lloyd returned to concentrate on European roles that had us willing to forgive any craziness. She was sensationally sexy in *When Saturday Comes* (1996) but really returned to her wild blonde roots in *Woundings* (1998), in which she fearlessly flaunted her English eggies while having sex with a soldier boy. At this rate, it won't be long before Hollywood comes begging for a second chance.

SKIN-fining Moment:

Wish You Were Here (0:41) Emily cavorts in her backyard and silences a shouting neighbor by shooting her lovely teenage moon in his direction.

See Her Naked In:

The Honeytrap (2002) Breasts, Buns
Woundings (1998) Breasts
Wish You Were Here (1987) Buns

Sabrina Lloyd

Born: November 20, 1970
Fairfax, Virginia
Skin-O-Meter: Brief Nudity

There wasn't much sliding beneath the tight tops that Sabrina Lloyd sported on the Fox sci-fi show *Sliders*. We were already more than fans, though, having spotted Sabrina in the HBO young-lesbian drama *More Than Friends: The Coming Out of Heidi Leiter* (1994). Sabrina slid out of *Sliders* after three seasons for a role on the acclaimed-but-canceled *Sports Night*, which was followed by the quickly cancelled *Madigan Men*. Sabrina's busy in the indie-film scene, though, including showing off her

acting assets and her amazing ass in the low-budget romance flick *Dopamine* (2003).

SKIN-fining Moment:

Dopamine (0:15) Sabrina Lloyd takes a post-sex pee-break and we see her naked ass along the way.

See Her Naked In:

Dopamine (2003) Buns

Amy Locane

Born: December 19, 1971
Trenton, New Jersey
Skin-O-Meter: Great Nudity

With a button-cute face that brims over with corn-fed impertinence, Amy Locane has built up a cottage industry in playing adventurous teens who are diving boobs-first from the cusp of sexual awakening, epitomized by her topless dry hump in *Going All the Way* (1997). Blonde and sweet to see, but with an undercurrent of impending depravity, Amy began her high-school hottie career opposite leading man Johnny Depp in the John Waters directed *Cry-Baby* (1990). Next, all smirky and sexy, she leapt to a recurring part on that bastion of campy sexual antics, *Melrose Place*. The big screen gave Amy the freedom to flaunt her free-floating breast flesh, a freedom she must have been yearning for. The lovely Locane has all the concupiscent allure of jailbait, with none of those pesky drawbacks. Her pair wafts and her butt bubbles bounce as she rides a horse naked in *Carried Away* (1996), preparatory for a tumble in a stack of hay with a much older man.

SKIN-fining Moment:

Carried Away (0:35) Stark naked on a black stallion, her breasts and buns bounce as she rides circles around Dennis Hopper in the stable.

See Her Naked In:

End of Summer (1997) Breasts
Going All the Way (1997) Breasts
Carried Away (1996) FFN, Buns
Criminal Hearts (1995) Body Double—Breasts
Airheads (1994) Thong

Sondra Locke

Born: May 28, 1947
Shelbyville, Tennessee
Skin-O-Meter: Great Nudity

Although she may go down in cinematic history as a former long-time love of actor/director Clint Eastwood, adventurously boobular and asstastic Sondra Locke has left a legacy of skin fit to immortalize her on her own merits. A strawberry blonde with achingly large, expressive green eyes and the puffy, creamy matched set of boobies and buns that often emerge in women blessed with a submerged redhead gene, it's easy to see how Sondra snagged *Dirty Harry*. Eastwood was so taken with Locke's loveliness that she appeared in a host of his star vehicles, including *Sudden Impact* (1983). Her most revelatory teaming with the tough-guy squinter came in *The Outlaw Josey Wales* (1976), where only the sudden intervention of cruel fate prevented every stitch of clothing from being torn from Sondra. Still visible were fine views of straining nipples and wriggling bum.

SKIN-fining Moment:

Death Games (0:18) Sondra soaks in a bath with Colleen Camp, then stands up and shows off her Clint-Eastwood-pleasin' caboose when the girls invite Seymour Cassell to join them for a splashtastic threeway.

See Her Naked In:

The Gauntlet (1977) Breasts, Buns
Death Game (1977) Breasts, Buns

The Outlaw Josey Wales (1976) LB,
Buns
Suzanne (1974) Breasts

Anne Lockhart

Born: September 6, 1953
New York, New York
Skin-O-Meter: Great Nudity

Anne Lockhart is lucky. She got an
inside track to her successful career
thanks to Mommy, *Lassie*'s June
Lockhart. Her first role came in *Jory*
(1972) opposite Robby Benson, but
she soon turned to the boob tube as
her main source of income,
appearing on various episodes of
basically every TV series from 1972
on. She does, however, boast a
rather formidable film career,
although with a lot of questionable
material such as *Slashed Dreams*
(1974). Of course, this leads to
onscreen nudity, as was the case
with *Joyride* (1977) opposite the
likes of Melanie Griffith and Robert
Carradine. Talk about a joyride,
Anne went topless in a few scenes,
but good luck trying to find the
video, as it is long out of print and
very few rental places carry it. Cross
your fingers that it's reissued on
DVD soon. Since then, she has kept
her top on and gone on to appear on
the series *Battlestar Galactica* as well
as lending her voice to *The Little
Mermaid* (1989) and *Total Recall*
(1990). If Anne would only let us
recall her totally hot body again,
she'd have a lock on our heart-on.

SKIN-fining Moment:

Joyride (1:01) June Lockhart's little
girl is topless in the jacuzzi with her
three pals. Mom should be proud!

See Her Naked In:

Young Warriors (1983) Body Double—
Breasts, Buns
Joyride (1977) Breasts

Heather Locklear

Born: September 25, 1961
Westwood, California
Skin-O-Meter: Never Nude

You've followed her sylph-like
blonde progress from *T.J. Hooker* to
Dynasty to *Melrose Place* to *Spin City*,
and you've slavered in the shadow
of her image. The epitome of the
brazen television vixen, Heather
Locklear managed to play a pitch-
perfect bitch for several years
running and still come across as
someone intrinsically wholesome
whom most men in America would
love to spend a few years of quality
time with. Stylish, poised,
impeccable, and maintaining her
physical prime for more than two
decades, Heather Locklear is some
kind of miracle.

SKIN-fining Moment:

Spin City "She's Got Habit" (2001)
Spin Clitty! Heather Sucks Sapphic face
with co-star Charlie Sheen's real-life
wife, Denise Richards.

Katie Lohmann

Born: January 29, 1980
Scottsdale, Arizona
Skin-O-Meter: Great Nudity

When you surgically enhance your
bosom, have long luscious blonde
hair, and like to show skin, it's no
surprise that your first acting jobs
are playing a "dancer" and then a
"centerfold." Katie Lohman burst
onto the scene in pleasing performances in *Hot Club California*
(1999) and the randy comedy
Tomcats (2001). Since then, she has
landed roles in such notable fare
as *Artificial Intelligence: AI* (2001),
playing an uncredited "pleasure
mecha." The vast majority of her
work has been in less popular and
more ribald fare like *Sex Court: The
Movie* (2002), *Mummy's Kiss*

(2002), *The Model Solution* (2002),
and *DarkWolf* (2003). Moist
revealing is the straight-to-video
Shannon Tweed release *Dead Sexy*
(2001), which featured Katie in all
her full-frontal glory. In fact, if you
hit the pause button at just the
right time, you can catch a glimpse
of meat drapes amidst the hanging
gardens.

SKIN-fining Moment:

DarkWolf (0:00) Bare bazombas as
she lap dances at strip club during the
opening credits.

See Her Naked In:

National Lampoon's Dorm Daze (2003)
Breasts, Thong
DarkWolf (2003) Breasts
Autofocus (2002) FFN
Sex Court: The Movie (2002) Breasts,
Bush
The Model Solution (2002) Breasts
Mummy's Kiss (2002) Breasts
Dead Sexy (2001) FFN
Talk Sex (2001) Breasts
Hot Club California (1999) FFN
Numerous *Playboy* Videos

Kristanna Loken

Born: October 8, 1979
Ghent, New York
Skin-O-Meter: Brief Nudity

Years of modeling and a score of
mostly forgettable TV appearances
taught Kristanna Loken the
importance of staying in shape—but
she was in for the workout of her
life with her breakout role in the
Arnold Schwarzenegger vehicle
Terminator 3: Rise of the Machines.
The blonde, B-cupped beauty spent
countless hours getting sweaty in
the gym, gearing up for her
motherboard-mangling nude scene
in *T3*. The Norwegian-bred babe
managed to pack fifteen pounds of
toned, tanned muscle onto her
droolworthy five-foot-eleven-inch

frame and showed every inch in a "birthing" scene that will have you saying, "Hasta la vista," to your pants. End result? A groin-grabbingly hot cyborg babe-a-tron who has skinophiles everywhere moaning, "Domo Arigato, Mr.Roboto!"

SKIN-fining Moment:

Terminator 3: Rise of the Machines (0:06) Brief nippage (her hair's in the damn way) and awesome ass as Kristanna climbs out of a store window and walks down the street naked. Lethally hot.

See Her Naked In:

Terminator 3: Rise of the Machines (2003) Buns
Academy Boyz (2001) Breasts

Gina Lollobrigida

Born: July 4, 1927
Subiaco, Italy
Skin-O-Meter: Brief Nudity

Sad is the man who looks at what is and says, "If only," especially if he is grieving an overview of Italian glamour queen Gina Lollobrigida. While it is true that hourglass-perfect Gina never reached the heights of American fame achieved by European rivals Sophia Loren and Brigitte Bardot, in her homeland Lollobrigida was second to none. A second runner-up in the 1947 Miss Italy contest, former art student Gina followed a short modeling stint with a long-running career in cinema. Her Stateside debut came in *Beat the Devil* (1954), followed by a pair of films that increased her profile and the skimpiness of her costumes: *Trapeze* (1956) and *Solomon and Sheba* (1959). Throughout the 1960s Lollobrigida made movies at the rate of two a year, but her heart was in Italy. In the 1980s she ran for Parliament and

won a seat. For winning looks at Gina's lingerie-clad seat, don't miss *Les Belles de Nuit* (1952).

SKIN-fining Moment:

Les Belles de Nuit (0:39) Brief black-and-white booty as she gets into pool. Turn around so we can see your 'gina, Gina!

See Her Naked In:

Les Belles de Nuit (1952) Buns

Karina Lombard

Born: January 21, 1969
Tahiti
Skin-O-Meter: Great Nudity

Tahitian-born and toasted to a lightly browned perfection, svelte and velvety Karina Lombard's exquisite and exotic beauty caught the eye of fashion lens man Bruce Weber during a trip to New York. Weber's provocative photos of this raven-haired vision of sensuality entitled Karina to a career as a skinternational supermodel. Perhaps because her maternal grandparents are Lakota Indians from South Dakota, Lombard decided to base herself in the United States and study acting at the Strasberg Institute. After a bit part in Oliver Stone's *The Doors* (1991), Karina stepped up and stripped down to play the lead in the erotically charged *Wide Sargasso Sea* (1993). Lissome Lombard received a lifetime appreciation award from the IBTC (Itty Bitty Titty Committee) for that performance alone and, more recently, took high, hard honors from the esteemed GGGGGGG Group (Guys Going Ga-Ga for Girl-Girl Grappling) in appreciation of her Sapphoriffic achievements between the sheets—and between the thighs of Mia Kirshner—on the blisteringly hot Showtime lesborama series *The L Word*.

SKIN-fining Moment:

Wide Sargasso Sea (0:36) Some swashbuckling dude removes Karina's clothing and lays her down on their fancy bed. We see her nice itty-bitties and lush muff.

See Her Naked In:

Footsteps (1998) RB
Last Man Standing (1996) Breasts
Legends of the Fall (1994) Breasts
Wide Sargasso Sea (1993) FFN, Buns

TeleVisions:

The L Word Breasts

Nia Long

Born: October 30, 1970
Brooklyn, New York
Skin-O-Meter: Brief Nudity

We've watched Nia Long grow from a sweet girl with nice nubs (which she had when making *The B.R.A.T. Patrol* [1986]) to a full-blooded woman with enormous Nubian knockers (which she flashed during *In Too Deep* [1999]). She shared the all-too-brief scene with L.L. Cool J, but we like to think she showed 'em just for us. Brooklyn-born Nia has had all sorts of acting gigs over the course of her career, doing the soap opera *The Guiding Light*, flicks such as *Boyz N the Hood* (1991) and *Stigmata* (1999), and the television show *The Fresh Prince of Bel Air*. She can currently be seen in *How to Get the Man's Foot Outta Your Ass* (2003). Sadly, we've yet to see Nia's panty hamster. C'mon baby, help a brutha out.

SKIN-fining Moment:

Boyz N the Hood (1:17) Nia starts out in her undies, cuddling with Cuba Gooding Jr. As he makes his way up her body, her left cocoa-puff nip pops into view.

See Her Naked In:

In Too Deep (1999) Breasts
Boyz N the Hood (1991) LB

Shelley Long

Born: August 23, 1949
Fort Wayne, Indiana
Skin-O-Meter: Brief Nudity

Shelley Long was made for TV, but she began her career in the improv group Second City before trying out the movies. She debuted in the little-seen *The Key* (1977) but quickly moved to guest spots on various TV series, such as *The Love Boat*, *Family*, and *M*A*S*H*, where she was more likely to be seen. And what a sight this svelte blonde comic is! Back in the movies, she strutted her stuff in a prehistoric fur bikini in *Caveman* (1981) and played a happy hooker opposite Henry "The Fonz" Winkler in *Night Shift* (1982), which featured a few scenes where she was clad only in a nightie or her undies. Shelley returned to TV land and finally hit the big time with a starring role on the ensemble sitcom *Cheers* as the quirky barmaid Diane Chambers. And everybody wanted to get Diane in Chambers for a flesh meeting. Her success led back to films like *Irreconcilable Differences* (1984) and *The Money Pit* (1986). Then Shelley's career hit the skids. Poor choices such as *Troop Beverly Hills* (1989), *Don't Tell Her It's Me* (1990), and *Frozen Assets* (1992) put her in the "Where Are They Now?" file. But when she took the torch from Florence Henderson, appearing as Carol Brady in the nostalgia-fad-exploiting *Brady Bunch* movies of the mid-to-late '90s, things turned around for this hottie. She ended up in the skintacular *Dr. T and the Women* (2000) but didn't show off her body of wank. Not satisfied with mere teasing, Mr. Skin uncovered Shelley's full-moon flash in *Hello Again!* (1987) from the downside of her career. Hope she hits bottom again if it looks this sweet.

SKIN-fining Moment:

Hello Again! (1:01) A not-so-Long bit of Shelley's bum is bared when her hospital gown blows open. Cheers!

See Her Naked In:

Hello Again! (1987) Buns

Jennifer Lopez

Born: July 24, 1970
The Bronx, New York
Skin-O-Meter: Brief Nudity

Is there anyone on earth who is outside the realm of Jennifer Lopez's magnificent nates? At the very start of this multi-faceted Latina gem's rise to prominence, so much was made of Jennifer's posterior mounds that the girl's many other attributes were often lost in its shadow. What about those tits for instance? Firm, high riders with nipples that are forever protruding from one slinky top or another, the soft side meat continually on display in revealing award-show wear. And don't discount the mesmerizing Lopez face with its blend of languor and fervent passion. The face's delicious lips are a call to salivation. The slashing cheeks and flashing eyes are bedroom beacons. And by the time you finish marveling at the physical perfection of Jennifer Lopez, she has established herself as the world's most revered dancer/singer/actress, advancing from *In Living Color* Fly Girl to a self-contained industry with profits and synergy to rival many Fortune 500 companies. All based on that roaring butt. J. Lo, as the lofty Ms. Lopez has come to be universally known, ensures that skin desires are inflamed by squirming into the most revealing scraps of fabric when posing on red carpets and talk-show couches. A few roles

J-SHOW: JENNIFER LOPEZ IN U TURN

from Jennifer's back story feature her pop-up nips in all their glory. Exult in J. Lo's erectile tissue in *Money Train* (1995) and *U Turn* (1997).

SKIN-fining Moment:

Money Train (0:55) Some nice, but ultra-quick, shots of J. Lo's nips while she rides Wesley Snipes's Money Train. All aboard!

See Her Naked In:

U Turn (1997) LB
Money Train (1995) Breasts

Traci Lords

Born: May 7, 1968
Steubenville, Ohio
Skin-O-Meter: Great Nudity

With an explosive body too volcanically erotic to keep covered, a screen-scorching carnal radiance too incandescent to be toned down, and an all-encompassing sexual appetite too omnivorous to be anything but the real deal, ruling superstarlet of mid '80s porn Traci Lords, did, in fact, prove to be too good to last. In fact, Traci proved to be underage at the dizzying height of her triple-X eminence. And, well, that's too bad. Soaring past even the most popular of her adult-film contemporaries, Traci became the number-one box-office draw in the last days of theatrical hardcore via classics such as *Talk Dirty to Me III* (1984). Alas, these happy, slappy days had to come to an end. In the spring of 1986, Traci set up her own company and released *Traci, I Love You*, a runaway smash that would prove to be the last—and only legal—appearance of La Lords in a full-penetration sex endeavor. While preparing to promote the video, the messy truth wiggled out that, after three years in the porn biz, Traci had only recently turned eighteen, thus rendering her eighty or so previous productions very much against the law in the U.S. Millions of dollars were lost. Threats were made against the outed adolescent. But Traci took a shot at fame away from the blue screen and achieved a career trajectory never thought possible for an ex-pornie. After a period away from the (s) limelight, Traci reemerged in the Roger Corman remake *Not of This Earth* (1988), showcasing her famously upturned boobs and magnificently puffy nipples in an R-rated milieu that kicked off a major career as a direct-to-video B-movie heroine. She also tore things up memorably in John Waters's *Cry-Baby* (1990) and on TV as a sadistic cult leader who spiced up *Melrose Place*. Her no-holes-barred 2003 autobiography *Traci Lords: Underneath It All* earned good reviews and strong sales, providing its author with yet another medium to boast about conquering. Now if she'd only break new ground in the arena of gloriously maturing beauties who choose to do stunningly explicit nude scenes (again).

SKIN-fining Moment:

Not of This Earth (0:25) Tracy's incredible tits and awesome ass appear as she towels off and talks to lucky Lenny Tuliano.

See Her Naked In:

Extramarital (1997) Breasts
Not of This Earth (1988) Breasts, Buns
Numerous Adult Movies

Alicia Lorén

Skin-O-Meter: Great Nudity

After the Fox network rejected the too-sexy-for-prime-time series *Manchester Prep*, the pilot was gussied up with nudity and sent out to video as *Cruel Intentions 2* (2000). This was ultimately a triumph for fans of sexy sisters, as Alicia Lorén teamed with twin sis Annie Sorell for a skintillating shower scene. We're not talking about mere matching titties, either. Alicia and Annie showed off a sisterly intimacy that rates as a classic in three categories: lesbians, showers, and sisters. Of course, it's slightly easier to tell Alicia from Annie now that she's being billed under the "Lorén" surname—strangely enough, just in time to co-star with Annie in the twisted short film *Mad Twin* (2003).

SKIN-fining Moment:

Cruel Intentions 2 (0:36) This twin (on the right) drops her robe and drives some dude wild with her own set of twins in this long, steamy shower scene.

See Her Naked In:

Cruel Intentions 2 (2000) Breasts

Sophia Loren

Born: September 20, 1934
Pozzuoli, Campania, Italy
Skin-O-Meter: Brief Nudity

Remembered primarily for her roles in saucy Italian sex comedies such as *Boccaccio '70* (1962) and *Marriage Italian-Style* (1964), volcanically voluptuous Sophia Loren is indisputably hot, hot, hot—a sex symbol for the ages. However, this skinema siren also has the acting chops to back up the low-cut gowns and come-hither looks, giving her a depth and range beyond many of her peers. The raven-haired cannoli received the first Oscar for a performance given entirely in another language as the lead in the intense Italian war drama *Two Women* (1961). Hollywood called, and she held her own alongside leading men John Wayne, Cary Grant, Frank Sinatra, and Alan Ladd while continuing to turn out quality work in international productions such as *El Cid* (1961) and *Arabesque* (1966). Sadly, she's also held onto most of her clothing through the years— notable exceptions being her brief topless scene in *Era Lui...Si! Si!* (1952) and a mouthwatering appearance in a soaking-wet, sheer dress in *Boy on a Dolphin* (1957). Proving that age ain't nothin' but a number (in this case, about 38DD), the lascivious legend stripped down to her black, lacy skivvies in *Ready to Wear* (1994) at a very sexy sixty-something. Now that's amore!

SKIN-fining Moment:

Boy on a Dolphin (0:05) Super-sultry Sophia climbs out of the water and into a boat with her sopping dress clinging mo(i)st delectably to her ultra-succulent Italian Alps.

See Her Naked In:

Era Lui . . . Si ! Si ! (1951) Breasts

Lisa Loring

Born: February 16, 1958
Kwajalein, Marshall Islands
Skin-O-Meter: Brief Nudity

Everybody has to grow up someday, even child stars from the golden age of TV. But the loss of a cute sprite from childhood reveries isn't so bad if, like Lisa Loring, that former prepubescent celebrity moves into adulthood and gifts her long-time fans with footage of her matured cans. Every twisted little kid in 1960s America developed an enduring crush on Lisa when she set down the Christina Ricci template in her character Wednesday Thursday Addams from the classic TV series *The Addams Family*. Twenty-one years after the show was canceled in 1967, Lisa rewarded the patience of her dedicated admirers with an ass shot that showed slot and a floating view of her frontal lobes in *Iced* (1988).

SKIN-fining Moment:

Iced (1:09) No-longer-little Wednesday shows off her all-grown-up pumpkins, ass, and gash while getting some guy's thing in a bath tub. Kooky and ooky!

See Her Naked In:

Iced (1988) FFN, Buns

Lori Loughlin

Born: July 28, 1964
Queens, New York, USA
Skin-O-Meter: Never Nude

Cute and cuddly, sweet and sassy, wholesome and virginal are not generally attributes equated with the object of a sensual obsession, but all these terms apply to sandy blonde Lori Loughlin. Although she made her biggest dent in the mass consciousness during a seven-year run as the frustratingly straight-laced "Becky Katsopolis" on *Full House*, Lori began her rise to fixation bait in a series of 1980s teenybopper flicks that included *The New Kids* (1985), *Secret Admirer* (1985), *Back to the Beach* (1987), and *The Night Before* (1988).

SKIN-fining Moment:

Suckers (0:51) Brief butt and breasts during a sex scene, but Lori's face is out of the frame. I call BODY DOUBLE!

See Her Naked In:

Suckers (1998) Body Double—Breasts, Buns
The New Kids (1985) Body Double—Buns

Julia Louis-Dreyfus

Born: January 13, 1961
New York, New York
Skin-O-Meter: Brief Nudity

The lesson of Julia Louis-Dreyfus is: Don't be fooled by a frumpy pre-sentation. During the raven-haired, cheeky stunner's eight-year run on the massive comedy hit *Seinfeld*, Julia's cleavage displays were so few that she might have counted them on the nips of her own two tits—although she unwittingly unveiled half that equation when her Hershey-Kiss-like left-side milk spigot slipped into view when she bent down on the 1991 episode "The Busboy." During early stints on laugh-arousing institution *Saturday Night Live* and as a regular on *Day by Day*, unsuspectingly juggy Julia managed to charm and beguile but never as a knockout bosom flaunter. Then came Louis-Dreyfus's surprise appearance at the Emmy show, squeezed lusciously into a dress slit almost to the navel, with boobs dripping out like the thinking man's J. Lo. Now her mammaries are never far from mind.

SKIN-fining Moment:

Seinfeld "The Busboy" (1991) Julia bends down in a nightgown and her left-side yadda-yadda-yadda pops into view.

See Her Naked In:

Troll (1986) Thong

TeleVisions:

Seinfeld Nip Slip LB

Tina Louise

Born: February 11, 1934
New York, New York
Skin-O-Meter: Brief Nudity

Any male kid (and many females) of the '60s or of the later rerun generations who didn't grip himself in a squeeze of ecstasy every time Ginger popped up on *Gilligan's Island*, raise your hand; the hand that did not hold that popping ecstasy. Those three liars and numb nuts with their hands up are the same trio of dopes who could conceive of wanting to be rescued from that island paradise. When Tina Louise made her critically acclaimed feature debut in the serious drama *God's Little Acre* (1958), she could not have known that her fame would be confined to Gilligan's little acreage. Though the steamy redheaded temptress has worked steadily in TV and a few films since her island days, it's only as Ginger that she continues to inhabit and inspire the fantasy life of skinema fans everywhere. A flash of side breast in *Mean Dog Blues* (1978) is almost enough to dislodge Tina's iconic image embedded during the aficionado's formative years, but not quite.

SKIN-fining Moment:

Mean Dog Blues (1:16) Ginger lays on a massage table, and as she gets up we get an ultra-quick side breast shot.

See Her Naked In:

Mean Dog Blues (1978) RB

Courtney Love

Born: July 9, 1964
San Francisco, California
Skin-O-Meter: Great Nudity

"I am not a woman, I'm a force of nature," Courtney Love quipped wittily in response to her infamous antics. With a list of public offenses that reads like a resumé for a bouncer at the Bada Bing, it's interesting that such a ball buster would pick a moniker like Love for a last name. A multitude of harassments, arrests for disorderly conduct and assault and battery, these are not the acts of Gandhi. How could this seemingly ultra-violent vixen associate herself with anything as warm and fuzzy as love? Was this the force that catapulted Courtney toward making grunge-god hubby Kurt Cobain and herself the wickeder, more drug-addled '90s version of doomed idols Sid and Nancy or the vibe that led this mammary flashing, mosh pit mangling, punk princess to become the front fox for Hole? Maybe not. Courtney's choice of a name is actually one of her most revealing qualities, and it's right there, as blatant as her frequent flashes of nudity. Deep down, all this hardcore hottie wants from the world is to be loved and adored. Her flesh-and-blood beauty was more than lovely in *The People vs. Larry Flynt* (1996). In playing Lord Larry's ultimate *Penthouse* Pet, Althea, Love portrayed a shocking certain realness that's intoxicating. Not only did she flaunt every inch of her plastic fantastic frame (from blow lips to bush), she displayed a rare moment of vulnerability that was as bone inducing as any beaver shot. Make this gorgeous goddess of gall's dream come true by worshiping her in all her naked glory as soon as possible. For a rocking, riotous good time, a little Love may be all you need.

SKIN-fining Moment:

The People vs. Larry Flynt (1:49) The good news: we see Courtney's breasts and beaver under water. The better news: she's dead.

See Her Naked In:

Taff (2003) RB
Beat (2000) RB
The People vs. Larry Flynt (1996) FFN, Buns

Deirdre Lovejoy

Skin-O-Meter: Brief Nudity

Redheaded, with a malleable, meaty face that can look plush with passion, bulging with irritation, settled in contemplation, or swollen with yearning, actress Deirdre Lovejoy brings a gravity to her roles that accounts for her several stolid appearances as lawyers or reporters in such broadcast-television fare as *Kingpin*, *Law & Order*, *Strong Medicine*, *Spin City*, and *Third Watch*. Deirdre expanded her type in film work but has always remained solid in small parts in *Number One* (1998), *Random Hearts* (1999), and *The Talented Mr. Ripley* (1999). Deirdre managed to make the role of Assistant State Attorney Rhonda Pearlman both heavy and lighter than air by fishing out her fleshy floater in a topless tryst with a dick-motivated detective on HBO's cops-and-dopers drama *The Wire*.

SKIN-fining Moment:

The Wire "The Buys" (2002) Bare-chested Deirdre does her boyfriend in bed and her bare right lovejoy lingers in front of the camera.

TeleVisions:

The Wire RB

Linda Lovelace

Born: January 10, 1949
The Bronx, New York
Died: April 22, 2002
Skin-O-Meter: Great Nudity

Although her renown is limited among smut consumers of today, Linda Lovelace was at one time—and in the long run will probably ultimately be—the most famous porn star in the world. Linda, due to her anatomically stunning performance in the beyond hugely successful porno chic movie *Deep Throat* (1972), became the first woman in the adult business whose name could appear in the Johnny Carson monologue and be recognized by a vast majority of the folks at home. A daughter of the Bronx, Linda had a brittle edge to her willowy beauty, her face as often as not set in a sullen pout. A 1969 lead role in a canine-appreciation film went largely unnoticed, but Lovelace rose like the sun of sin in *Deep Throat*. Starring as a sexually dissatisfied housewife who discovers that her clitoris has been embedded in the lower ranges of her esophagus, Linda's circus-like ability to swallow immense flesh swords and keep them down without gagging won her a vast celebrity but no credibility and not much more cash. Sadly, such was the recipe for bitterness and recriminations.

SKIN-fining Moment:

Deep Throat Linda opens wide and inch by inch, introduces dirty doctor Harry Reems to (at least) the top of her tonsils, deftly demonstrating the movie's titular technique. A star is blowin'!

See Her Naked In:

Deep Throat (1972) Breasts, Bush, Buns
Numerous Adult Movies

Jacqueline Lovell

Born: December 9, 1974
Beverly Hills, California,
Skin-O-Meter: Great Nudity

Jacqueline Lovell started her career under the name Sara St. James and appeared on the fringe of erotica, often in adult films but not really engaging in any "encounters." Her first major film was *Animal Instincts III* (1996), in which she played the part of a Cleaning Lady. There are few cleaning ladies who have racks like Jacqueline's or such a propensity for sex. The film marked one of her finer lesbian scenes, opposite veteran Tara Hayes. Needless to say, Jackie never really broke into mainstream cinema and continued to act in nudity-filled roles through to the end of her career in 2000, when she gave up the movie business in order to raise her children. Then out of the blue movies came *Rod Steele 0014: You Only Live Until You Die* (2002), in which she played Pussy L'Amour. Guess baby formula is expensive. Still, you've got to Lovell it.

SKIN-fining Moment:

Femalien (0:22) Jackie takes off her blouse and gets verrrry comfortable with her naked self on a lounge chair.

See Her Naked In:

Legally Exposed (2003) FFN, Buns
Sex, Lies, and Politics (2003) FFN, Buns
Rod Steele 0014: You Only Live Until You Die (2002) Breasts, Thong
The Ultimate Attraction (2000) FFN, Buns
Women of the Night (2000) FFN
The Killer Eye (1999) Breasts
The Key to Sex (1998) FFN, Buns
Black Sea 213 (1998) FFN, Buns
Lolita 2000 (1997) FFN, Buns
I'm Watching You (1997) FFN, Buns
Hideous! (1997) Breasts
The Exotic House of Wax (1996) Breasts
Virtual Encounters (1996) FFN
Who Killed Buddy Blue? (1996) FFN, Buns
Femalien (1996) Breasts, Bush
Damien's Seed (1996) FFN, Buns
Head of the Family (1996) FFN, Buns
Hard Time (1996) Breasts, Bush, Buns
Nude Bowling Party (1995) FFN, Buns
Animal Instincts III (1995) Breasts, Buns
All Nude Glamour (1995) FFN, Buns

TeleVisions:

The Click Breasts, Buns
Red Shoe Diaries FFN, Buns

Carey Lowell

Born: February 11, 1961
New York, New York
Skin-O-Meter: Brief Nudity

Carey Lowell had big dreams of becoming an actress. And more hotties like her should get their luscious butts onscreen. She debuted as background scenery in *Dangerously Close* (1986) and as a model in *Club Paradise* (1986). But she sure made sweet eye candy. Carey made a brief skin debut in the classic talking-penis comedy *Me and Him* (1988). She looked like she would make it when cast as Pam Bouvier, the newest Bond Girl, in *License to Kill* (1989), her sexiest role to date with cleavage aplenty. But that promise was cut short after appearing in *The*

Guardian (1990). Thankfully, that film offered Carey's true talents to the world, uncovering her breasts for a nice little bedroom scene. That same year, Carey landed a recurring role on the hit series *Law & Order*, which raised her image. Gerbil connoisseur Richard Gere noticed, and after she left the series and he left model Cindy Crawford, the two shacked up. She may have left movies behind, but we'll never forget her behind.

SKIN-fining Moment:

The Guardian (0:37) Carey canoodles with her husband in bed and we get two nice ganders at her mammary glanders.

See Her Naked In:

Road to Ruin (1991) Buns
The Guardian (1990) RB
Me and Him (1988) RB

Lynn Lowry

Born: October 15, 1947
Cahokia, Illinois
Skin-O-Meter: Great Nudity

Lynn Lowry is one of the first and best in the sexy category we like to call Scream Queens. What is a scream queen? Well, it amounts to a lack of clothing and the propensity to be cast by low-budget horror-film directors in everything that they do. Lynn debuted in the no-budget schlocker *The Battle of Love's Return* (1970), which was directed by and starred Troma Films honcho Lloyd Kaufman. But Lynn made her nude debut in *I Drink Your Blood* (1971), stripping down for a sexy Satanic ritual. She scored a better-than-average role in *Sugar Cookies* (1973), which featured Lynn's sugar cookies and all of her full-frontal glory for the first time ever. After a brief turn on the equally brief series *How to Survive a Marriage*, Lynn returned to horror flicks. She got the lead in *Shivers* (1975), in which she portrayed a nurse who fell prey to a parasite that had been secretly introduced to her by some mad-scientist type and made her turn into a sex-crazed maniac. She then, through her sexual exploits, infected the majority of the people living in her Canadian apartment community. She ended up cat food in *Cat People* (1982) and has been missing in action since the mid-'90s. Even scream queens have to rest.

SKIN-fining Moment:

Sugar Cookies (0:03) Lynn shows it all off—including a hint of the muff—before sexily sticking a gun into her mouth.

See Her Naked In:

Cat People (1982) Breasts
Shivers (1975) Breasts
Sugar Cookies (1973) FFN, Buns
Score (1972) FFN
I Drink Your Blood (1970) LB, Buns

Susan Lucci

Born: December 23, 1946
Scarsdale, New York
Skin-O-Meter: Never Nude

It took Susan Lucci nineteen nominations before she won her Daytime Emmy award, but the long-running soap star has gotten plenty of standing ovations from our trousers. Her character Erica Kane has been making *All My Children* America's sexiest soap for over three decades. In fact, Erica is only one of two characters left from the original *All My Children* pilot episode. Susan's also translated her sexy presence to plenty of TV movies, bringing

daytime heat to primetime in epics such as *The Woman Who Sinned* (1991) and *Seduced and Betrayed* (1995)—although we were really feeling Lucci in her role as a sexy demonic gatekeeper in Wes Craven's TV-movie epic *Initiation to Hell* (1984).

SKIN-fining Moment:

Seduced and Betrayed (0:44) BODY DOUBLE! Very, very brief booty as she dives into a swimming pool, tempting a wide-eyed younger guy.

See Her Naked In:

Seduced and Betrayed (1995) Body Double—Buns

Joanna Lumley

Born: May 1, 1946
Srinagar, Kashmir, India
Skin-O-Meter: Great Nudity

Joanna Lumley is best known for her role on the hit Brit-com *Absolutely Fabulous*, where she excelled as an excessive, boozy, druggie love kitten. But she has had a very long and fruitful career spanning more than three decades and shows no sign of letting up. Joanna began her career quietly enough in an uncredited role in the little-seen *Some Girls Do* (1965), and she was definitely one of the girls who did! She quickly moved up the proverbial ladder with a bit part in the Bond flick *On Her Majesty's Secret Service* (1969). Less than a year later, Joanna was commanding starring roles, and she took the lead part of Fanny Hill in the sex romp *Games That Lovers Play* (1970). Not surprisingly, the film was replete with nudity, including that of our heroine Joanna. Her familiar blonde locks were noticeably gone in lieu of her natural brunette coif, but it was hard to notice when her pert, young tits were dead center on the

screen. After the film was made, Joanna shot to superstardom through various television and film roles, so her clothes remained (sadly) on for the remainder of her career. But we have our mammaries.

SKIN-fining Moment:

Games That Lovers Play (0:14) Nice breast shot followed by a good bit of butt as she climbs out of a red bed.

See Her Naked In:

Games That Lovers Play (1970) FFN, Buns

Deanna Lund

Born: May 30, 1937
Oak Park, Illinois
Skin-O-Meter: Brief Nudity

It's a long and winding road from the rodeo rings of Florida to the bed of television host Larry King, but luscious-lipped lovely Deanna Lund made the trip, and she looked good on every twist and turn. As a ten-year-old riding and roping in the kiddie rodeo circuit of Florida, perky Deanna could not have guessed that her pretty face and preternatural perseverance would lead her to cult-TV immortality. A struggling actress in the 1960s, filling such parts as Android in *Dr. Goldfoot and the Bikini Machine* (1966) or a lesbian stripper in Frank Sinatra's *Tony Rome* (1967), Deanna was on the verge of splitting from show biz when she landed the part of Valerie Ames Scott on the eternal sci-fi classic *Land of the Giants*. After a season of being menaced by mice the size of Buicks and dodging pencils as big around as one-hundred-year-old sequoias, Lund was ready for a lasting career popping up in shows such as *Batman*, *The Waltons*, and *The Incredible Hulk*. In the 1990s she would win the affections of Larry

King and look back and marvel at how one pretty little girl could have come so far.

SKIN-fining Moment:

Roots of Evil (1:33) From "Land of the Giants" to Glands that Are Giant; Deanna doffs her top and bares her luscious lunds in bed with Brinke Stevens.

See Her Naked In:

Roots of Evil (1992) Breasts

Jamie Luner

Born: May 12, 1971
Los Angeles, California
Skin-O-Meter: Great Nudity

Jamie Luner holds the dubious distinction of being the only person to play three different roles on the hit sitcom *Growing Pains*. She played Sheena Berkowitz, Kara Daye, and Cindy Lubbock, which was, of course, the character that she continued to play on the not-quite-as-famous sitcom *Just the Ten of Us*. That attention got her cast in several made-for-TV movies, as well as the steamy hit series *Savannah*, *Melrose Place*, and *Profiler*. Perhaps the most notable aspect of Jamie's career is that she has never shied away from onscreen nudity, which gives us a high-five in our pants. Her first nude scene came in the erotic thriller *Tryst* (1994), which placed her as the object of the titular adulterous affair. There are some nice topless moments, although her outing in *Sacrifice* (2000) shines as her most skintabulous role to date. The film placed her as an ex-prostitute who hooked up with Michael Madsen to help him find the killer of his daughter. Of course, during their search, they needed to stop and have sex. Thus began the nude scene, which featured a nice side shot of her melons and a tush flash as she rode Mr. Madsen like a stallion. Whoa, Nellie! That's some

thoroughbred action.

SKIN-fining Moment:

Tryst (1:13) Breasts in the hotel room changing as her dude watches, then more topless and panty shots getting her slip ripped off by him.

See Her Naked In:

Sacrifice (2000) Breasts, Buns
Tryst (1994) Breasts

Cherie Lunghi

Born: April 4, 1953
London, England, UK
Skin-O-Meter: Great Nudity

In her native Britain, fair and lovely Cherie Lunghi has never been far from the leering public eye since her acclaimed 1978 debut in the BBC mini-series *Kean*. Brunette, with skin as pale as linen, and a flawless oval face lustrous and implacable like a piece of bone china, Cherie could be the model for a painting of a fairy princess. No wonder then that she was cast as legendary lady Guinevere in *Excalibur* (1981), the story of King Arthur, his Knights of the Round Table, and the magic sword that saved a kingdom. And what made the sword magic? Perhaps it was the vicinity of Cherie Lunghi's creamy butt crack and mesmerizing lung flesh that nips out while noodling with her knight in shining amour.

SKIN-fining Moment:

King David (0:28) See Cherie's chest-cherries as she lays topless for a good long time in bed next to Richard Gere. It's a great clip, even if she doesn't show her lap-gerbil.

See Her Naked In:

King David (1985) Breasts
Excalibur (1981) Breasts, Buns

TeleVisions:

Strangers Breasts, Bush, Buns

Patti LuPone

Born: April 21, 1949
Northport, Long Island,
New York
Skin-O-Meter: Brief Nudity

Patti LuPone may be best known as the solid-as-a-rock mom on the ABC family series *Life Goes On*, but onstage she's an icon. In 1979 she was strutting her ample stuff in the finest theaters the world has to offer. Patti soon made the jump to the big screen with her film debut in *Witness* (1986). Although she has been around for years, it was *Summer of Sam* (1999) that really scored points with Mr. Skin. In that flick Patti played the hard-boiled New York Italian mother of one of the film's central characters. She has recently remarried when her twenty-something wayward son moves back home. Frisky as a couple of co-eds, Patti and her new hubby cannot keep their hands off each other. In one scene Patti takes her top off so her man can fondle her massive motherly flapjacks . . . just then her son walks through the door and wrecks all the fun. You fans of *Life Goes On* won't want to miss this scene. It is the only time you'll get to see what's under her apron.

SKIN-fining Moment:

Summer of Sam (0:33) Nice shots of Lupone's lung-pillows as she's fooling around with her hubby on the couch, plus a little extra jiggle when son Adrien Brody shows up and causes some embarassment.

See Her Naked In:

Summer of Sam (1999) Breasts

Kelly Lynch

Born: January 31, 1959
Golden Valley, Minnesota
Skin-O-Meter: Great Nudity

Kelly Lynch was discovered on an elevator—talk about going up! This leggy beauty first kicked into the biz as a model for the Elite Agency in the early '80s. She quite rightly made her first onscreen performance in a documentary about modeling, *Portfolio* (1983). After bit supporting parts in *Bright Lights, Big City* (1988) and *Cocktail* (1988), Kelly made the leap to stardom with a part in the Gus Van Sant downer *Drugstore Cowboy* (1989). It also featured one of her first nude scenes, although it was only a side shot. The role was enough to garner a part in *Road House* (1989), and this time when Kelly got nekkid she showed all of tit—if only for a brief instant. Thankfully, when her career didn't rocket to the stars like everyone thought it would, Kelly took a part in the little-seen *Warm Summer Rain* (1989), which was awash in some of her finest nude scenes to date. There was a wonderful little full-frontal romp as well as some great ass shots and sex scenes. Since then, her skin scenes have become fewer and farther between, as well as more brief, like in *Homegrown* (1998). Still, it is always nice to see Kelly's incredible rack and tight-assed body. If we have to die, Lynch us!

SKIN-fining Moment:

Warm Summer Rain (1:11) We've got bush! Nice shot when she runs out of the burning house.

See Her Naked In:

The Slaughter Rule (2002) Buns
Cold Around the Heart (1998) Breasts, Buns
Homegrown (1998) Breasts, Buns
Persons Unknown (1996) Breasts
Desperate Hours (1990) Breasts
Road House (1989) Breasts, Buns
Warm Summer Rain (1989) FFN, Buns
Cocktail (1988) Thong

TeleVisions:

The Hitchhiker LB

Carol Lynley

Born: February 13, 1942
New York, New York
Skin-O-Meter: Brief Nudity

Just a kid when she made the transition from posing for Coca-Cola ads to flashing her bobby-socked ankles as Sally Graves in 1957's *Junior Miss* TV series, strawberry blonde and perfectly pretty Carol Lynley parlayed her all-American beauty and ease of line delivery into a film career that cranked out two movies per year in the 1960s and lasted into the 1990s. Versatile enough to play a nun twice on TV, Carol had ten pages of the March 1965 *Playboy* devoted to her habit-forming figure. While lovely Lynley's most memorable role was as a go-go-booted, hot-pants-wearing band singer in *The Poseidon Adventure* (1972), to glimpse the most of Carol's cans, put your buck on *Bad Georgia Road* (1977) or *Blackout* (1988).

SKIN-fining Moment:

Blackout (1:01) Carol leans back bare bazoomed and a lucky hand grabs her loose left Lynley.

See Her Naked In:

Blackout (1988) Breasts
Bad Georgia Road (1977) RB

Amber Lynn

Born: September 3, 1963
Newport Beach, California
Skin-O-Meter: Great Nudity

Satiny blonde XXX goddess Amber Lynn was not always a buff and burnished superstar of the skin screen. When the slim and wholly sexualized fireballer made her *Casino of Lust* (1983) debut, she was cute, unsophisticated, and voracious. But video was just taking over from film as the

medium of choice for adult-film marketeers. Amber entered hardcore skinema when the industry was on the cusp of a major upheaval. Her personal reinvention coincided with a revolution in the way people viewed sexually explicit material, and she was not alone. A whole new pantheon of superstars spontaneously erupted along with the home-viewing bonanza triggered by the advent of the VCR. Along with Amber, Ginger Lynn, Christy Canyon, and Traci Lords became bedroom names in almost every American household that had a TV and a tape deck. Amber's star arc outsoared and outlasted them all. Her strutting high-caliber glamour became a template for dozens of Vivid Video franchise girls. The continuation of Amber Lynn's style and attitude can be clearly seen in the femme-machismo stage personas of mainstream mega-stars such as Britney Spears.

SKIN-fining Moment:

52 Pick-up (0:23) Boobage opening her shirt while being videotaped at a party.

See Her Naked In:

52 Pick-Up (1986) Breasts
Evils of the Night (1985) FFN, Buns
Numerous Adult Movies

Meredith Scott Lynn

Skin-O-Meter: Brief Nudity

Her kiddie career dates back to the final season of *The Facts of Life*, but Meredith Scott Lynn isn't some fading starlet. After plenty of stints on failed series, an older, wiser, and sexier Meredith concentrated on a big-screen career. Too bad that her first showcase was gyrating over the credits of *A Night at the Roxbury* (1998). The film—based on that annoying *Saturday Night Live* sketch about two overgrown club kids—couldn't compete with Meredith's mam-shaking opening. Then our trousers got quaking during her turn in the plastic-vagina farce *Standing on Fishes* (1999), as Meredith finally unveiled her charming bod. She's since gone on to the multiplexes with *Legally Blonde* (2001) and *Hollywood Homicide* (2003), but Meredith still needs some smart producer to tap her star power.

SKIN-fining Moment:

Standing on Fishes (0:10) Meredith gets plonked, and her right nipple gives a few slipples from behind her arms.

See Her Naked In:

Standing on Fishes (1999) RB

Theresa Lynn

Born: July 1, 1964
Louisville, Kentucky
Skin-O-Meter: Great Nudity

Howard Stern fans will remember Theresa Lynn's planetary-sized *Private Parts* from the 1997 movie of the same name. In one of the film's hottest scenes, Theresa, playing one of Stern's horny listeners (a character appropriately named "Orgasm Woman"), turns on her radio, hikes up her skirt, rips open her blouse, and straddles a stereo speaker. As Stern makes vibrating noises over the airwaves, Theresa caresses her gloriously gigantic jugs to full climax. Theresa's large-scale lemons can also be seen in *New York Cop* (1996) and *Marilyn Chambers' Bedtime Stories* (1993). Suffice it to say, we've come across plenty of Lynns over the years (such as porn star Ginger, country singer Loretta, former Boston Red Sox outfielder Fred), and Theresa's definitely our favorite.

SKIN-fining Moment:

Private Parts (1:54) Theresa's huge ta-tas are unleashed as she enjoys an aural orgasm from Howard.

See Her Naked In:

Psycho Sisters (1998) Breasts
Private Parts (1997) Breasts
New York Cop (1996) Breasts, Buns
Vampire Vixens from Venus (1995) Breasts
Marilyn Chambers' Bedtime Stories (1993) Breasts, Thong

TeleVisions:

The Sopranos Breasts, Thong

Melanie Lynskey

Born: May 16, 1977
New Plymouth, New Zealand
Skin-O-Meter: Brief Nudity

We've wanted to go down under New Zealand native Melanie Lynskey ever since her topless tub scene opposite Kate Winslet in *Heavenly Creatures* (1994). The busty beauty beat out six hundred hopefuls for the part of Pauline Parker, a murderous teen lesbian with killer cantaloupes. She showed a lighter—but thankfully dirtier—side in *Detroit Rock City* (1999), in which she played Beth Bumsteen, a KISS fan who rocked 'n' rolled all night by humping co-star Sam Huntington in a church confessional. The voluptuous Melanie can also be seen shaking her (sadly, covered) pom-poms in *But I'm a Cheerleader* (1999) and her booty in *Coyote Ugly* (2000). Hopefully, it won't be long before Melanie once again shares her monster milk duds with the masses.

SKIN-fining Moment:

Heavenly Creatures (1:20) Relaxing in an incredibly lucky bathtub with naked Kate Winslet, Melanie's mammaries bubble up above the surface.

See Her Naked In:

Heavenly Creatures (1994) Breasts

Natasha Lyonne

Born: April 4, 1979
New York, New York
Skin-O-Meter: Never Nude

As a child actress, young Natasha Lyonne (born Natasha Braunstein of New York City) got her feet wet portraying Meryl Streep's niece in *Heartburn* (1986) and adorable little Opal on TV's *Pee Wee's Playhouse*. It was a decade and a high-school diploma later that Woody Allen—no stranger to younger women—took notice and cast her in his musical fantasy *Everyone Says I Love You* (1996). Like her other fans, the Woodman must have grooved on the magenta mane and game-for-anything attitude that Natasha had only hinted at in her younger years. From that point on, Natasha found herself getting feisty, frisky, and nearly naked in such memorable indie-styled offerings as *Modern Vampires* (1998), the first two *American Pie* entries (1999, 2001), and *Slums of Beverly Hills* (1998), the storyline of which revolved around the neuroses that Natasha endured when her adorable teenage breasts began to bloom. Said breasts filled the screen for a few moments

> "I'm a 32A. You could have fit eight sets of me into Vivian's bra. I'd sit on my bed listening to Carole King's *Tapestry* with these prosthetic breasts, crying my eyes out. Alan [Arkin] and I ended up playing ball with them when I didn't have to wear them. We even gave them names—after all, they did kind of get to star in the movie."
>
> —NATASHA LYONNE, ON WEARING GIANT FAKE BREASTS IN *SLUMS OF BEVERLY HILLS*

during the film, but they appear to be those of a body double. Audiences have yet to see Natasha's genuine article (she came close again when she played a hooker in 2002's *Night at the Golden Eagle*), though their taste for Sapphic sequences was sated a bit in *But I'm a Cheerleader* (1999), which found Natasha engaging in a lustful, lippy onscreen kiss with co-star Clea Duvall.

SKIN-fining Moment:

Slums of Beverly Hills (1:13) BODY DOUBLE! You get a good up-close look at SOMEBODY's ripe breasts after Natasha's doctor draws an incision line.

See Her Naked In:

Slums of Beverly Hills (1998) Body Double—Breasts

Elena Lyons

New Orleans, Louisiana
Skin-O-Meter: Brief Nudity

She's got the soft butch looks of Gina Gershon, and Elena Lyons is just as capable of stunning girl-girl teases. It's worth digging up the *Tootsie*-influenced rock comedy *Face the Music* (2000) to see Elena's scenes with a guy in drag. She also made our Crotch Stretch Indefinitely when she appeared on a 2000 episode of *CSI: Crime Scene Investigation* with Amy Carlson as her lethal lesbian lady friend. Elena's brooding beauty was also used to good effect in the thriller *Devil's Prey* (2001). Still, it took the sunny ambience of the slasher comedy *Club Dread* (2004) to finally get Elena naked in a scene that raised a machete in our pants.

SKIN-fining Moment:

Club Dread (0:04) Captain Caaaaaaaavvvvvveboobs! Elena and Tanja Reichert shimmy around in a cave, letting their jubs fly free. Elena's the brunette fox.

See Her Naked In:

Club Dread (2004) Breasts

Wendy Lyon

Canada
Skin-O-Meter: Great Nudity

Tight tokus, mouth-watering melons, and a golden, Enchanted Forest-like snatch—that's our official scouting report on the wickedly hot Wendy Lyon. This Canadian cupcake showed every glorious inch of her bodacious bod in *Hello Mary Lou: Prom Night II* (1987), an unrelated sequel to the 1980 Jamie Lee Curtis horror hit. Wendy played Vicki Carpenter, an innocent high schooler possessed by the spirit of angry dead trollop Mary Lou Maloney. Under the maniacal mind control of Mary Lou, an oft-naked Vicki dabbled in murder (bad) and lesbianism (good). Wendy's poon-tastic performance as Vicki came two years after her debut as Prissy Andrews in the made-for-TV movie *Anne of Green Gables* (1985). Talk about stretching as an actor—she went from playing Prissy to showing her prissy. Bravo!

SKIN-fining Moment:

Hello Mary Lou: Prom Night II (1:05) She strips off her towel and walks full-frontal into the shower with Beverley Hendry. Then more nakedness stalking her. Nice!

See Her Naked In:

Hello Mary Lou: Prom Night II (1987) FFN, Buns

Jennifer MacDonald

Skin-O-Meter: Great Nudity

A familiar and welcome presence in a nice assortment of direct-to-video films and TV shows in the mid '90s, Jennifer MacDonald actually kick-started her career with a role in . . . a live-action video game! 1994's *Wing Commander III: Heart of the Tiger* found the lithe and limber Jen appearing as Lt. Robin "Flint" Peters, alongside fellow performers Ginger Allen and Mark Hamill. The interactivity immediately catapulted Jennifer up the entertainment ladder, while simultaneously stripping her of all unnecessary garmets. She appeared wonderfully without her top in such straight-to-tapers as *Object of Obsession* (1994), *T-Force* (1994), and *Dead Weekend* (1995), as well as in an installment of Zalman King's *Red Shoe Diaries* (1994). Her most engaging erotic entry was the cleverly titled *Headless Body in Topless Bar* (1996), which found Jennifer's frequently "Topless" stripper Candy doing the ole grind for a drunk and his decapitated buddy. Jennifer's latest skin was in the slasher flick *Campfire Tales* (1997), which found the able actress's assets looking a bit more, er, inflated and gravity defying than they did in previous years. The person to ask would have to be co-star Ron Livingston, who came to grips with what Jennifer had to offer.

SKIN-fining Moment:

Object of Obsession (0:16) Jen shows all her full-frontal goods when she doffs her dress on a videotape.

See Her Naked In:

Campfire Tales (1997) LB
Dead Weekend (1995) Breasts
Headless Body in Topless Bar (1995) Breasts, Buns
T-Force (1994) Breasts
Object of Obsession (1994) FFN

TeleVisions:

Dream On Breasts
Red Shoe Diaries Breasts, Buns

Kelly MacDonald

Born: February 23, 1976
Glasgow, Scotland
Skin-O-Meter: Great Nudity

A brassy, sassy Scottish lassie, Glasgow's Kelly MacDonald aroused everyone with her very first film role in the tantalizing, trend-setting *Trainspotting* (1996). As heroin addict Ewan McGregor's love interest, Kelly kicked audiences in the head with her skintastic enthusiasm during a wild-and-flailing, post-nightclubbing sex scene set to Blondie's '80s dancehall standard "Atomic." It's to McGregor's—and the audience's—shock when it's discovered the next morning that Kelly's character is a lustful, Lolita-esque schoolgirl. Her career firmly established, Kelly then appeared immediately, if not skin-worthily, in such projects as *Cousin Bette* (1998), *Splendor* (1999), and *The Loss of Sexual Innocence* (1999). Kelly's dual MacDonalds most recently saw the flicker of the silver screen in the British production *Some Voices* (2000) in a scene where she shared a bath with co-star Daniel Craig, who must regret that he wasn't on the receiving end of any of the action McGregor so enjoyed opposite Kelly four years earlier.

SKIN-fining Moment:

Trainspotting (0:25) Kelly drops her dress to reveal her casabas, gets high on Ewan MacGregor's meat-syringe then flashes some full-frontal fuzz as she gets dressed afterward.

See Her Naked In:

Some Voices (2000) Breasts
Trainspotting (1996) Breasts, Bush

Andie MacDowell

Born: April 21, 1958
Gaffney, South Carolina
Skin-O-Meter: Brief Nudity

Always appealing Andie MacDowell, a South Carolina-sired siren, took the modeling route to silver-screen stardom, looking pretty in advertisements for L'Oreal cosmetics and Calvin Klein jeans before snagging her first film role as Jane in *Greystoke: The Legend of Tarzan, Lord of the Apes* (1984). With nearly thirty films under her slender belt, including such sexy stocking stuffers as *Sex, Lies, and Videotape* (1989) and *The Object of Beauty* (1991), Andie remains one of the few major actresses to more-or-less remain safely tucked away within the warm confines of her blouse, the only exception being the 1993 straight-to-tape titillator *Ruby Cairo* (renamed *Deception* for its Stateside video release), which found MacDowell engaged in a brief and dimly lit topless bedroom romp with co-star Liam Neeson. Praise the lord for the ever-present paparazzi, who occasionally manage to snap the kind of sensational, unsolicited shot of Andie that everyone wants to see.

SKIN-fining Moment:

Deception (1:26) Brief flashes of T&A as Andie has some sex on the couch with Viggo Mortensen.

See Her Naked In:

Deception (1993) LB, Buns
Object of Beauty (1991) Body Double—Buns

Ali MacGraw

Born: April 1, 1938
Pound Ridge, New York
Skin-O-Meter: Great Nudity

After seeing Ali MacGraw play a smoldering bitch in heat, how could any danger-loving thrill seeker be satisfied with a secure and predictable nice girl? Even in her sweetest role, that of fey Jenny opposite Ryan O'Neal in *Love Story* (1970), Ali was foul mouthed and prone to disturbing emotional outbursts. But imagine the make-up sex! MacGraw rode her buns to success, saying, "Hello, butt shot!" in *Goodbye, Columbus* (1969) not once but twice. *The Getaway* (1972) presented a profile in nipples, and Ali left the set with her marriage to super-producer Robert Evans in tatters and new beau and co-star Steve McQueen on her wing. The simpering and scintillating brunette

suffered a career lacuna while caring for an ailing McQueen and has since appeared most notably on the *Dynasty* series and in a yoga video.

SKIN-fining Moment:

Goodbye, Columbus (0:51) Goodbye, Columbus; hello casabas! Our willowy heroine peels down for as skinny-dip and we get a load of her petite-but-potent-nipped Ali McGraws.

See Her Naked In:

Blast 'Em (1992) RB
Just Tell Me What You Want (1980) Breasts
The Getaway (1972) Breasts
Goodbye, Columbus (1969) Breasts, Buns

Simmone Mackinnon

Born: March 19, 1973
Mount Isa, Queenland, Australia
Skin-O-Meter: Brief Nudity

Castoff debtors, lunatics, and convicts from the British Empire are generally credited with settling the continent nation of Australia, and if English skinthusiasts had known long, inhumanly sexy water siren Simmone Mackinnon were to descend from these motley rejects, they might have lobbied to hold some back. The coolly simmering and salty Simmone spent a few years hissing and clawing her way to the top of a Down Under production of *Cats* and became an international object of fixation after getting her fur wet as Allie Reese on *Baywatch Hawaii*. Before viewers had a chance to dry themselves off, sumptuous Simmone was back in the water as a *Deep Shock* (2003) scientist investigating squiggly eels emerging from a fissure deep under the sea. Squiggly eels have a knack for emerging wherever Simmone Mackinnon ventures.

SKIN-fining Moment:

The Lost World "Nectar" (1999) Glowing globes as Simmone rises from an underground body of water with the

top half of her own body completely unclothed.

TeleVisions:

The Lost World Breasts

Shirley MacLaine

Born: April 24, 1934
Richmond, Virginia
Skin-O-Meter: Brief Nudity

If there is such a phenomenon as reincarnation, it would be a good thing if more women came back as a young Shirley MacLaine. Shirley's youthful vitality and top-shelf jiggle power were obvious to the producers of her first big Broadway show, *The Pajama Game*, who plucked the game pajama babe out of the chorus line and shoved her into a lead, a limelight she has never relinquished. Celluloid evidence of the undoubtedly scrumptious nips, nubs, and nates of Shirley is sadly scant, confined to a few seconds of *Desperate Characters* (1971), but her warm, giving sensuality is much in evidence. Savor plenty of silky-soft skin in *Irma la Douce* (1967) as vintage MacLaine plays a tight-bodied Parisian woman of loose morals, heart of gold, and overflowing brassiere.

SKIN-fining Moment:

Desperate Characters (1:22) Kenneth Mars takes off Shirley's shirt and her cosmic casabas orbit into view.

See Her Naked In:

Terms of Endearment (1983) Nip Slip RB
Desperate Characters (1971) Breasts
Woman Times Seven (1967) Buns

Elle MacPherson

Born: March 29, 1963
Sydney, New South Wales, Australia
Skin-O-Meter: Great Nudity

Elle MacPherson, all six boobalicious feet of her, was once rejected by a

ELLE MACPHERSON GETS WET BETWEEN PORTIA DE ROSSI AND KATE FISCHER IN *SIRENS*.

modeling agency for being too tall and busty. That didn't stop the lofty lovely from being on the cover of the *Sports Illustrated Swimsuit Edition* three times, not that she was modeling much more than skin. She debuted on the big screen in Woody Allen's comedy *Alice* (1990) with only one line, but who cares what she says. Elle's talents are more visual, as she proved as a nude artist's model in the skintacular classic *Sirens* (1994). Her alarmingly hot 36-24-35 palette colors a full-frontal canvas and is sure to ruffle the bristles on anyone's paintbrush. She's an Elle of a girl!

SKIN-fining Moment:

Sirens (0:25) Elle bares two huge reasons for her nickname "The Body" as she enjoys a clothes-free swim session with her gal-pals.

See Her Naked In:

Sirens (1994) FFN, Buns

TeleVisions:

A Girl Thing Breasts

Elizabeth MacRae

Born: 1936
Fayetteville, North Carolina
Skin-O-Meter: Brief Nudity

An attractive, familiar-faced character actress, Elizabeth MacRae, of Fayetteville, North Carolina, is probably best known to audiences for her role as lovely Lou-Ann Poovie on the '60s TV comedy *Gomer Pyle, U.S.M.C.* and supporting turns on the popular soap operas *General Hospital* and *Days of Our Lives*. Lovely Liz's only nude appearance to date was of the full-frontal nature, albeit a bit brief. She portrayed a deceptively sensitive and sexy party girl named Meredith who manipulated surveillance expert Gene Hackman into bed in Francis Ford Coppola's acclaimed film *The Conversation* (1974). The nudity is seen in long shot from quite a distance, but it definitely kept audience's surveillance systems on alert. She was last seen in a small role in *Eddie and the Cruisers II: Eddie Lives* (1989).

SKIN-fining Moment:

The Conversation (1:14) Liz strips while drunken Gene Hackman is sprawled on a bed. Spiffy sacks and seat-cushions.

See Her Naked In:

The Conversation (1974) FFN, Buns

Amy Madigan

Born: September 11, 1950
Chicago, Illinois
Skin-O-Meter: Great Nudity

Amy Madigan is married to man-enough-to-be-bald Ed Harris. She's one of those actor's actors who has been active in theater and cinema for years. That means she's no star, which may have to do with her un-Barbie-like looks. But Mr. Skin still thinks she's a doll. She may not look like Pamela Lee, but who would throw her out of bed for eating crackers? Unless you wanted to do her on the floor—kinky. She made her debut in the made-for-TV teenage-angst drama *Crazy Times* (1981) before heading to the big screen in the lead role of *Love Child* (1982), which garnered her much critical acclaim but left her without many openings in Tinseltown. She finally got Hollywood to notice in *Field of Dreams* (1989) as Kevin Costner's stalwart wife. Then came the meatier role as John Candy's girlfriend in *Uncle Buck* (1989). She courted controversy as Sarah Weddington in the TV movie *Roe vs. Wade* (1989). But we prefer Amy nekkid onscreen. She showed some great skin with soon-to-be hubby Harris in *Alamo Bay* (1985). The brief flash of her itty-bitty titties paled in comparison to her full-frontal, semi-lesbianic turn in *Female Perversions* (1996). In that film she joined Tilda Swinton, who happened to be fully clothed, in a bathtub. It sure beats her voiceover in Ken Burns's *Jazz*.

SKIN-fining Moment:

Love Child (0:53) Buns, boobs and Beau Bridges! He and Amy enjoy some conjugal relations at a women's prison.

See Her Naked In:

Female Perversions (1997) FFN, Buns
The Prince of Pennsylvania (1988) LB, Buns
Nowhere to Hide (1987) RB
Alamo Bay (1985) Breasts
Love Child (1982) Breasts, Buns

Madonna

**Born: August 16, 1958
Bay City, Michigan
Skin-O-Meter: Great Nudity**

Named after the biblical icon, Madonna could stir even the messiah's loincloth to sin. She first discovered her arousing talents shaking her pom-poms as a cheerleader in high school and then escaped to New York and fame and fortune. While her musical career—with hits such as "Like a Virgin," "Justify My Love," and "Erotica"—propelled her to the top of the charts in videos that mimicked the moves of peepshow

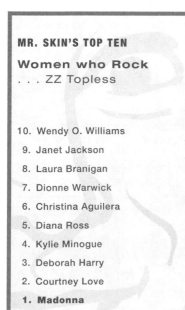

MR. SKIN'S TOP TEN

Women who Rock
. . . ZZ Topless

10. Wendy O. Williams
9. Janet Jackson
8. Laura Branigan
7. Dionne Warwick
6. Christina Aguilera
5. Diana Ross
4. Kylie Minogue
3. Deborah Harry
2. Courtney Love
1. **Madonna**

MADONNA SERVES WILLEM DAFOE A FACE FULL OF MATERIAL CURLS IN *BODY OF EVIDENCE*

girls, Madonna's bump and grind on the big screen offered a more skinful side of the boy toy. *Desperately Seeking Susan* (1985) and *Vision Quest* (1985) popped her cinematic cherry, but it was the low-budget *A Certain Sacrifice* (1985) where Madonna first flashed her golden records. In the documentary *Truth or Dare* (1991), Madonna dared to show more skin and continued the tasty trend with *Dangerous Game* (1993) and *Swept Away* (2002). But her moist pleasing role onscreen was *Body of Evidence* (1993), in which Madonna masturbated and got into some mufftacular kinky sex. Talk about blonde ambition!

SKIN-fining Moment:

Body of Evidence (1:08) Madonna airs out her up-top Material Girls while she reclines in an open robe and pets her pussy. Papa don't bleach.

See Her Naked In:

Swept Away (2002) Breasts, Buns
The Next Best Thing (2000) Thong

Dangerous Game (1993) Breasts, Buns
Body of Evidence (1993) FFN, Buns
Madonna: Truth or Dare (1991) Breasts
A Certain Sacrifice (1985) Breasts

Virginia Madsen

**Born: September 11, 1963
Chicago, Illinois
Skin-O-Meter: Hall of Fame**

Her brother Michael is one of Hollywood's scariest tough guys, but we'd risk any wrath to lick on this *Candyman* star's goodies. Virginia Madsen (and her right breast) made her debut in *Class* (1983), before growing up and out

MR. SKIN'S TOP TEN

Top 10 Right Breast *Only* Scenes
. . . In support of women's rights

10. Helen Slater
—*Happy Together* (1988) (0:17)
9. Erinn Bartlett
—*100 Women* (2002)
8. Rita Coolidge
—*Pat Garrett and Billy the Kid* (1973) (1:48)
7. Vivica A. Fox
—*Booty Call* (1997) (0:29)
6. Heather Thomas
—*Red Blooded American Girl* (1990) (1:19)
5. Candice Bergen
—*A Night Full of Rain* (1978) (1:04)
4. Shannon Whirry
—*Me, Myself & Irene* (2000)
3. Fran Drescher
—*Cadillac Man* (1990) (0:07)
2. Julia Roberts
—*Pretty Woman* (1990) (1:35)
1. **Virginia Madsen**
—*Class* (1983) (0:20)

in films such as *Creator* (1985) and *The Hot Spot* (1990). She only got more becoming while bedding down with Mathilda May in *Becoming Collette* (1992). Virginia even ranked as a minor scream queen after roles in genre classics such as *Dune* (1984) and *Candyman* (1992). Sadly, Madsen's most prominent roles are now restricted to chaste made-for-TV productions. Maybe she shouldn't have turned down that lead role in *Basic Instinct* (1992).

SKIN-fining Moment:

Class (0:21) When Andrew McCarthy rips open Virginia's blouse, her racktastic right-side bazoombo bursts out into view.

See Her Naked In:

Blue Tiger (1994) LB
Becoming Collette (1992) Breasts
Candyman (1992) Breasts
The Hot Spot (1990) Breasts, Bush, Buns
Gotham (1988) FFN
Long Gone (1987) Buns
Slam Dance (1987) Breasts
Fire with Fire (1986) Breasts, Buns
Creator (1985) Breasts, Buns
Class (1983) RB

TeleVisions:

The Hitchhiker Breasts

Mía Maestro

Buenos Aires, Argentina
Skin-O-Meter: Brief Nudity

Born in Argentina, Mía Maestro went to Berlin to become a cabaret singer and then made a splashy big-screen debut in the *Oscar*-nominated foreign film *Tango* (1998). She made it to American arthouses in *Timecode* (2000), which was the first of what would be several roles opposite Salma Hayek. She was a sexy refugee in *HBO's For Love or Country: The Arturo Sandoval Story* (2000) and provided some local beauty in the Mexico-set

Picking Up the Pieces (2000). But Mía really got American audiences mewling with *Frida* (2002). She doesn't join Salma in any of this bio's bisexual exploits (she's playing family, perv), but Mía still shows off her ample ass in an amazing sex scene. Mía's since been concentrating on Spanish language productions, but she obviously speaks our language.

SKIN-fining Moment:

Frida (1:15) Fast-but-tasty tail meat as she grinds atop Alfred Molina on the floor, only to get busted by jealous Salma Hayek.

See Her Naked In:

Frida (2002) Buns

Ann Magnuson

Born: January 4, 1956
Charleston, West Virginia
Skin-O-Meter: Great Nudity

Ann Magnuson came from the crucible of the New York mid '80s post-punk performance scene. She played ex-porn stars in one-woman shows and led a heavy band called Bongwater. She was the perfect choice for the punkette whom David Bowie fondled and then bit in the chic vampire thriller *The Hunger* (1983). It was both her film and skin debut and gave America a peek at the sweet melons that downtown denizens had been drooling over for years. She next appeared with another street urchin named Madonna, playing Cigarette Girl in *Desperately Seeking Susan* (1985)—no nudity in that or the several forgettable TV movies that followed. If Ann was going to sell out, she might as well show a bit! But Ann stayed very clothed during supporting roles in *Making Mr. Right* (1987) opposite John Malkovich, *Tequila Sunrise* (1988) with Mel Gibson, and *A Night in the Life of Jimmy Reardon* (1988) co-starring

River Phoenix. She returned to television in 1989 for a role on the hit series *Anything but Love* but could still be seen onscreen, most impressively as horny multi-limbed Calli in the Chris Elliott comedy *Cabin Boy* (1994). Ann has not forgotten her free and sleazy roots, though. In *The Caveman's Valentine* (2001) opposite Samuel L. Jackson, Ann showed us how nicely a woman can close in on perfection through the process of aging by baring her breasts for a little jungle lovin'.

SKIN-fining Moment:

The Hunger (0:05) Ann flashes her perky poppers for a brief instant when David Bowie gets himself a squeeze.

See Her Naked In:

The Caveman's Valentine (2001) Breasts
The Hunger (1983) Breasts

Lorna Maitland

Born: November 19, 1943
Glendale, California
Skin-O-Meter: Great Nudity

A killer California blonde who reportedly sports a 42D chest, Lorna Maitland was discovered by that legendary filmmaker whose body of work boasts the most cantilevered, casaba-cavorting of casts, Russ Meyer. In 1964 he created a vehicle for said devastating discovery, the eponymously titled *Lorna*, which found his lusty leading lady carousing about topless for the better part of ninety minutes, eagerly engaging in all manner of erotic encounters while her husband works at the local salt mines. Lovers of big, bouncing, bodacious breasts made the film an underground smash, which was undoubtedly the impetus for Lorna's subsequent appearances in two more works by the master, *Mudhoney* (1965) and the succulently structured stripper documentary *Mondo Topless* (1966). Lorna gave it all she's got (and she's got it!!!) in a pair of other non-Meyer projects, *Hot Thrills and Warm Chills* (1967) and *Hip, Hot & 21* (1967), before tucking in her wayward wonders and disappearing from the screen altogether.

SKIN-fining Moment:

Lorna (0:34) Lorna luxuriates on the bank of a river, losing her clothes and leading the camera on in for a luscious close-up of her enormous upper endowments.

See Her Naked In:

Hip, Hot & 21 (1967)
Hot Thrills and Warm Chills (1967)
Mondo Topless (1966) Breasts, Buns
Mudhoney (1965) Breasts, Buns
Lorna (1964) Breasts, Buns

Paula Malcomson

Belfast, Northern Ireland
Skin-O-Meter: Great Nudity

Need wood? Check into *Deadwood*, HBO's Old-West-set drama that runs rampant with foul language, fouler behavior, and fine, fine ladies of a certain profession that are sure to put steel in any cowpoke's six-shooter. Chief among the mining camp's most treasured chests is that of Paula Malcomson, who plays the ever-appropriately monikered Trixie, jewel in the crown of a bawdy establishment named The Gem. The Irish-born beauty brings a blast of the Emerald Isle to *Deadwood*'s dusty trails, illuminating the path of randy pioneers with the two bright bulbs upon her chest.

SKIN-fining Moment:

Deadwood "Deep Water" (2004)
Your wood will most certainly not be dead after you catch a glimpse of Paula's full-frontlage and dainty duff as she gets out of bed!

TeleVisions:

Deadwood FFN, Buns

Wendie Malick

Born: December 13, 1950
Buffalo, New York
Skin-O-Meter: Brief Nudity

Just Shoot Me had lots of guys just watching to see Wendie Malick parading in sexy outfits. Fortunately, Wendie's pre-sitcom days included showing a little panty in *A Little Sex* (1982), thanks to a bathrobe that conveniently flew open. Sadly, she's since kept guys hoping for more. Wendie was even one of the few actresses to keep her clothes on in HBO's series *Dream On*. She also failed to cash in on her skin during a four-year stint on *Baywatch*. Malick didn't give us males something to lick our chops over until *Divorce: A Contemporary Western* (1998), where the lithe beauty jumped from her bath and revealed her gorgeous ass and timeless titties.

SKIN-fining Moment:

Divorce: A Contemporary Western (1:25) Wendy steps out of the tub and we get a fast gander at her globes and glutes.

See Her Naked In:

Divorce: A Contemporary Western (1998) Breasts, Buns

Kym Malin

Born: July 31, 1962
Dallas, Texas
Skin-O-Meter: Great Nudity

Like many a bodaciously built blonde *Playboy* Playmate of the '80s (think Kimberly MacArthur, Shannon Tweed, and Lynda Wiesmeier, for starters), titillating Texan Kym Malin, *Playboy*'s May 1982 Playmate of the Month, tore

off her top as window dressing for such silly sex comedies of the day as *Joysticks* (1983) and *Weird Science* (1985). She submitted a couple of similarly topless turns in *Die Hard* (1988) and *Roadhouse* (1989) before appearing at her most pulchritudinous as a Vegas nightclub entertainer/secret agent in *Picasso Trigger* (1989) and *Guns* (1990), two straight-to-tape sagas by boobs-and-bullets auteur Andy Sidaris. A couple more Sidaris straight-to-tapers followed—*Enemy Gold* (1993) and *The Dallas Connection* (1994), but Kym with a "Y" hasn't been seen onscreen since.

SKIN-fining Moment:

Joysticks (0:18) Kim loses a strip video game and we win when she bares her bo-bo's and beds the guy who beat her.

See Her Naked In:

Guns (1990) FFN, Thong
Picasso Trigger (1989) Breasts
Weird Science (1985) Breasts
Joysticks (1983) Breasts
Numerous *Playboy* Videos

Camryn Manheim

Born: March 8, 1961
Caldwell, NJ
Skin-O-Meter: Brief Nudity

Camryn Manheim is best known as defense attorney Ellenor Frutt on the David E. Kelley courtroom drama *The Practice*, the role that landed her an Emmy award in 1998 and a Golden Globe in 1999. Born Debra Frances Manheim in Caldwell, New Jersey, this size twenty-two dedicated her Emmy to "all the fat girls" out there. Manheim's ample assets have filled screens both large and small since the early '80s, and New York theater critics praised her plentiful stage presence in the 1996 one-woman show *Wake Up, I'm Fat!* Manheim gave big girls everywhere a boost by baring it all in her solitary skinematic stint in *The Road to Wellville* (1994). If you like big butts and you cannot lie, don't miss it. Manheim shows more seat meat in this movie than even Sir-Mix-A-Lot could imagine!

SKIN-fining Moment:

The Road to Wellville (1:13) Full-figured Cammy bravely bares her whole-lotta-side-skin and upper ass-crackage while face down on a massage table.

See Her Naked In:

The Road to Wellville (1994) Buns

Karin Mani

Skin-O-Meter:Great Nudity

Little is known about exploitation kitten Karin Mani. She showed up on the TV mini-series *From Here to Eternity* (1979) before hitting the big screen with a bit part in the comedy *Utilities* (1981). Karin only performed in two more pictures during her short but hot career, but what pictures they were. In *Alley Cat* (1982), Karin was a hottie who single-handedly cleaned up crime in the dirty city. She trained for her black belt in karate and practiced her cunt-fu on the scumbags who come out at night. Karin was locked up as a vigilante, which meant that the bloody violence was punctuated with leeringly long shower scenes. She followed up that classic with a part in the second of the teenage hooker cult hit series *Avenging Angel* (1985), which found her in the shower again showing off her furry angel wings. Since that film Karin has been woefully absent from skintertainment. Let's hope this alley cat comes back to wag her tail again.

SKIN-fining Moment:

Alley Cat (0:01) Karin peels off her nightgown and pops out her nice udders, which we see in a mirror, as the opening credits roll.

See Her Naked In:

Avenging Angel (1985) FFN, Buns
Alley Cat (1982) FFN, Buns

Taryn Manning

Born: November 6, 1978
Tucson, Arizona
Skin-O-Meter: Brief Nudity

In her short-but-skyrocketing career, Taryn Manning has surrounded herself with some of the biggest stars of song and screen and, better still, joined the celebrity skin set early and sexily. Born November 6, 1978, in Tucson, Arizona, Manning is a "triple threat"—she sings, dances, and acts. She made her small-screen debut on an early-1999 episode of *The Practice* and spent the late '90s in various bit parts, including Groupie in the made-for-TV movie *Come On, Get Happy: The Partridge Family Story* (1999) and the short-lived series *Get Real*. These spots landed her large-screen supporting roles as a troubled teen in *Crazy/Beautiful* (2001), *Crossroads* (2002), *8 Mile* (as Eminem's ex), and *White Oleander* (2002) (with Michelle Pfeiffer). Finally, in the Civil War epic *Cold Mountain* (2003), Taryn briefly aired out her not-so-mountainous-but-udderly-mouth-watering right ta-ta in a must-freeze-frame moment. Here's hoping all this fresh exposure will soon "boob-st" Taryn into her own leading role.

SKIN-fining Moment:

Cold Mountain (1:12) Taryn and a plus-size prostie statisfy Phillip Seymour Hoffman until some spoil sport interrupts their ruckus. Lightning quick flash of nip, but it's definitely Taryn's mamming.

See Her Naked In:

Cold Mountain (2003) Breasts

Jayne Mansfield

Born: April 19, 1933
Bryn Mawr, Pennsylvania
Died: June 29, 1967
Skin-O-Meter: Great Nudity

America split the atom, but far more powerful in its arsenal was bombshell Jayne Mansfield, whose flesh missiles could pop off an entire city of men with one flash. Her 40-23-37 jugantor figure made her more than a Marilyn Monroe knockoff, but a knockout of boobalicious dimensions. Girlie mags first introduced the curvaceous cutie, but the pages of pinup pulps couldn't hold Jayne's bountiful beauty, and soon stage and screen beckoned. Broadway's *Will Success Spoil Rock Hunter?* exposed Jayne's ample body of work to the public and led to a frisky film version in 1957. But Jayne could never rise above her image as a sloppy-second sex symbol like Mamie Van Doren and Diana Dors. That's a good thing. It meant revealing performances in movies such as *Promises, Promises* (1963), in which juggy Jayne let it all hang out. Lost to us too soon in a June 29, 1967, tragic car accident, this anything-but-plain Jayne had all the goods to be oh so bad.

SKIN-fining Moment:

Promises! Promises! (0:04) The bubble-bath that forever shook up cinema! Bombshell Jayne bares her titanics in the tub, setting off the modern era of celebrity skin.

See Her Naked In:

The Wild, Wild World of Jayne Mansfield (1968) Breasts
Promises! Promises! (1963) Breasts, Buns

Jeane Manson

Born: October 1, 1945
Ohio
Skin-O-Meter: Great Nudity

You never know what's going to become of a skinsational gal like Jeane Manson. She started out making the usual rounds of low-budget films, including a memorable nude stroll that led to some beach-blanket boning in *The Young Nurses* (1973). Then she appeared as *Playboy*'s Miss August 1974—which usually launches an American career. Instead, Jeane went off to France and became one of the county's most beloved entertainers. She sold over twenty million records between 1976 and 1996, even though nobody in America was paying attention. She's also a respected stage actress in her adopted homeland. Jeane still graced American audiences with a token appearance in the Charles Bronson film *10 to Midnight* (1983) looking like a perfect '80s hairhopping blonde. Those Manson melons were also as ripe as ever. Jeane's still a regular presence on Parisian television, as well, so her amazing career (and potential for nudity) is still far from over.

SKIN-fining Moment:

10 To Midnight (1:25) Jeane sheds her boulder-holder in preparation for some Paid-For-Lovin' with Gene Davis.

See Her Naked In:

10 To Midnight (1983) Breasts
The Young Nurses (1973) FFN, Buns
Hot Thrills and Warm Chills (1967)

Shirley Manson

Born: August 26, 1966
Edinburgh, Scotland, UK
Skin-O-Meter: Brief Nudity

One look in the mirror and those guys in the band Garbage knew they needed a hot femme vocalist. They made a fine choice in Shirley Manson, who'd previously been wasted in lesser UK acts such as Goodbye Mr. McKenzie and

Angelfish. The stunning Scottish songstress contributes more than just a great bod and stunning red hair. She's also the band's lyricist and guitarist and kept Garbage at the top of the charts even after becoming a blonde in 2001. She displayed one hell of an A-side of her C-size while sporting a low-cut top on the *VH-1 Fashion Awards* too. Shirley's also any man's treasure in the Garbage music videos, posing as a dominatrix for "Queer" and a Jane Fonda-style sex kitten for "Stupid Girl."

SKIN-fining Moment:

VH1 Fashion Awards (1996) As Shirley fronts her rock combo Garbage, her not-trashy-at-all-right-titlet repeatedly peeps into view through her unbuttoned blouse. Now that's the type of fashion that deserves an award.

TeleVisions:

The VH1 Fashion Awards RB

Mary Mara

Syracuse, New York
Skin-O-Meter: Brief Nudity

You may not have heard of Mary Mara, but chances are you've seen her in one of her countless supporting TV or movie roles in the past fourteen years. One of the hardest-working actresses of screen and stage, Mary made her debut in the made-for-TV movie *The Preppie Murder* (1989) and has appeared in such films as *Blue Steel* (1990), *The Hard Way* (1991), *True Colors* (1991), *A Civil Action* (1998), and *K-PAX* (2001). Her familiar face also has repeatedly graced the small screen on hit series such as *ER* and *Nash Bridges*. A graduate of the Yale School of Drama, Mary honed her acting chops on the stage, appearing opposite Michelle Pfeiffer and Mary Elizabeth Mastrantonio in the New York Shakespeare Festival production of *Twelfth Night*, among

other heavyweight theater productions.

SKIN-fining Moment:

Stranger Inside (0:02) Mary scrambles to keep her most scrumptious bits covered during a prison strip search, but those boobies have just got to be free.

See Her Naked In:

Stranger Inside (2001) Breasts

> "It is something actresses need to go through, and I think they look forward to being naked in a movie. I don't know why, but it is something you need to exhaust from yourself."
>
> —SOPHIE MARCEAU

Sophie Marceau

Born: November 17, 1966
Paris, France
Skin-O-Meter: Hall of Fame

Sophie Marceau doesn't waste time. She appeared in her first film at age thirteen, and only a few years later the French tickler shocked even jaded Parisian audiences as a happy hooker in *L'Amour Braque* (1985). Muff's the word on her full-frontal explicit performance. Best known to Americans as the Princess who wanted to get Mel Gibson's kilt off in *Braveheart* (1995), Sophie has saved her moist skinful roles for her horny homeland. In *Beyond the Clouds* (1995), Sophie showed that she's beyond underwear, needing only her dark patch of pubes to keep warm . . . and to keep audiences hot.

SKIN-fining Moment:

Beyond the Clouds (0:49) Sophie flashes the total package as she gets up out of bed and walks to the window and back.

See Her Naked In:

Belphégor—Le fantôme du Louvre (2001) Buns
La Fidélité (2000) Breasts, Bush, Buns
The World Is Not Enough (1999) RB
Firelight (1997) Breasts
Marquise (1997) Breasts
Beyond the Clouds (1995) FFN, Buns
La Fille de d'Artagnan (1994) Breasts
Fanfan (1993) Breasts
Pour Sacha (1991) FFN, Buns
Pacific Palisades (1990) FFN
Mes Nuits Sont Plus Belles que vos Jours (1989) Breasts
The Student (1988) FFN, Buns
Descent into Hell (1986) FFN, Buns
L'Amour Braque (1985) FFN, Buns
Police (1985) Breasts
Joyeuses Pâques (1984) Breasts

Jane March

Born: March 20, 1973
Edgware, London, England
Skin-O-Meter: Hall of Fame

Jane March follows the beat of a different drum. At fourteen the five-foot-two-inch, eighty-eight-pound English strumpet left her blue-collar life behind for a modeling career. By seventeen she was starring in *The Lover* (1991) and doing things with an older Chinese man that makes Mr. Skin's egg roll. Jane's realistic sex scenes exposed her young, juicy furburger, whetting the appetite for more skinage. And she didn't disappoint in her follow-up, the erotic thriller *Color of Night* (1994), with *Die Hard*'s Bruce Willis just getting hard as Jane strutted wearing only her birthday suit throughout most of the movie. Bruce found his sexy co-star delicious as he licked up sweet Jane in a swimming-pool scene. Since then Jane's nudity hasn't been on the menu, except in a few foreign productions such as *Agent Provocateur* (1996). Let's hope Jane marches right back into the skin of things soon.

SKIN-fining Moment:

Color of Night (1:00) Jane and Bruce Willis boink in both a pool and bed, as she shows off every last inch of her completely naked, absolutely magnificent body.

See Her Naked In:

Agent Provocateur (1996) Breasts
Color of Night (1994) FFN, Buns
The Lover (1992) FFN, Buns

Constance Marie

Born: September 9, 1969
Hollywood, California
Skin-O-Meter: Brief Nudity

Being typecast is nothing to scoff at, particularly if that type is the salsa-hot and sweetly saucy barrio-bred beauty who shines as a beacon of feminine pulchritude no matter what environment she finds herself cast in. Glowing brown beauty Constance Marie fits the stereotype to a T, and that T, as seen in *The Last Marshall* (1999), is apt to be of the skimpy wife-beater variety, with Marie's moneymakers flouncing around inside bra free. For a pick-me-up shot of Constance Marie, keep the eye tuned to the cathode tube. This perky and stimulating Hollywood native has brought spice and sass to *Santa Barbara*, *Union Square*, *Early Edition*, and *The George Lopez Show*.

SKIN-fining Moment:

My Family (1:05) Very brief right breast while making love outside. Sort of an orange tint. Who likes these colors getting in the way like that?

See Her Naked In:

My Family (1995) RB

Heidi Mark

Born: February 18, 1971
Columbus, Ohio
Skin-O-Meter: Great Nudity

Heidi Mark is most famous for being the former wife of riotous rocker Vince Neil of Motley Crue. (Although the two excelled at burping contests—"I can burp louder than Vince," Heidi says—they parted company citing "irreconcilable differences" in 2001.) Heidi left her true mark on the American public by pairing with *Playboy*, appearing as both a Playmate in July of 1995 and star of yank wank wares like *Playboy Video Playmate Calendar 1997* (1997) and *Playboy: Girls of the Internet* (1998). Like every bronzed blondie born to wear a bikini, Mark made the double-D grade running on a beach in *Baywatch: Forbidden Paradise*. Her foxy frame was fetchingly featured in big-screen fare such as *Swim Suit: The Movie* (1997) (ahhh . . . typecasting) and as a sextra in *Rock Star* (2001). Although this heart-stopping hottie has yet to appear totally nude, she did bare her mondo mams on *The Red Shoe Diaries: Luscious Lola*. Oh-la-la-Lola! With the days of Crue coddling in her past, it's just a matter of time before we see a bit more of Heidi's hyde. Mark our words: In all her awesome assemblage of hooterage, young Heidi has yet to hit her stride.

SKIN-fining Moment:

Red Shoe Diaries "Mercy" (1995) Heidi's guy makes his mark and we see her buns, breasts, and bush as they copulate in the kitchen.

See Her Naked In:

Weapons of Mass Distraction (1997) Breasts
Numerous Playboy Videos

TeleVisions:

Red Shoe Diaries Breasts, Bush, Buns

Margaret Markov

Born: 1951
Yugoslavia
Skin-O-Meter: Great Nudity

Margaret Markov showed a genius for appearing in 1970s sexploitation classics as an enslaved woman attempting to escape her confining circumstances while also escaping the confines of her clothes. Although she initially played slightly off character in the biker pic *Run, Angel, Run* (1969) and in the Rock Hudson farce *Pretty Maids All in a Row* (1971), Margaret found her footing in *The Hot Box* (1972). As a nurse leading a revolt of women imprisoned in a steamy jungle, Margaret let her melons do much of the emoting for her, as did most of her cast mates. Mammerific Markov hit her enslaved stride in *Black Mama, White Mama* (1972), spending almost the entire movie tits out and chained to African American boobular icon Pam Grier, also tits out. The two temptresses tussled topless until they learned to get along, bringing a smile to the faces of all witnesses.

SKIN-fining Moment:

***The Hot Box* (0:45)** *Margaret joins a jumble of bare-bosomed bathing beauties in a stream and we enjoy a lengthy visit with her milky Markovs.*

See Her Naked In:

The Arena (1973) Breasts, Buns
The Hot Box (1972) Breasts
Black Mama, White Mama (1972) Breasts

Shae Marks

Born: June 1, 1972
New Orleans, Louisiana
Skin-O-Meter: Great Nudity

Shae Marks entered a bikini contest at age sixteen . . . and lost! Well, she came in second. Her girlfriend, who's now a dancer in Hotlanta, came in first. But Shae still shimmied her sexy form into an acting career, starting with the aptly titled *Scoring* (1995). They say write what you know, but there should be an appendix: act what

you know. Shae went on to play a centerfold who is slain by a man posing as a woman in the kinky thriller *Cover Me* (1995). She didn't really find her niche, however, until she joined up with the skinful cast of the *L.E.T.H.A.L. Ladies* series of films with a part as Tiger in *Day of the Warrior* (1996). She went on to reprise the role in *L.E.T.H.A.L. Ladies: Return to Savage Beach* (1998), and, naturally, both films featured her impossibly gigantic melons on full naked display. Since then, she has gone on to appear in such "mainstream" flicks as *Love Stinks* (1999) and on the TV series *Black Scorpion* (2001), so let's hope she hasn't left her skinful ways behind—or forgotten her skinful behind! We sure can't forget it or anything else she's shared and bared. Because hot Marks this spot!

SKIN-fining Moment:

***L.E.T.H.A.L. Ladies: Return to Savage Beach* (0:47)** *Shae's cartoonishly huge (and hot) chest balloons are bursting out all over while she grinds with a guy, and we also learn, from a look at her lap, that she doesn't completely sha(v)e.*

See Her Naked In:

L.E.T.H.A.L. Ladies: Return to Savage Beach (1998) FFN, Buns
Day of the Warrior (1996) Breasts
Scoring (1995) Breasts
Cover Me (1995) Breasts, Buns
Numerous *Playboy* Videos

Kelli Maroney

Born: December 30, 1964
Minneapolis, Minnesota
Skin-O-Meter: Great Nudity

Blonde hair, big boobs, and show-biz aspirations can lift a pretty girl to celebrity blockbuster paradise. They can also steer her to a comfortable show-biz limbo from which she can give succor and

inspiration to legions of diversion-starved lads who are satisfied with the small pleasures of simple entertainments such as provided by *Slayground* (1987) and *Chopping Mall* (1987), both of which greatly benefit from the buxom blondness of pretty household no-name Kelli Maroney. Although her career kicked off with two seasons on the high-profile *Ryan's Hope* and a quick ensemble turn in the vaunted springboard to superstardom *Fast Times at Ridgemont High* (1982), it's Kelli's work in the horror-hacker genre that qualified her for a seat in the revealing steam of *Scream Queen Hot Tub Party* (1991).

SKIN-fining Moment:

***Scream Queen Hot Tub Party* (0:30)** *Body beautiful Kelli ditches her pom-pom-girl duds, lotions up her nude boobs and buns, then gets to working on her muscle mass.*

See Her Naked In:

Face Down (1997) FFN, Buns
Scream Queen Hot Tub Party (1991) Breasts, Buns

Laure Marsac

Born: February 18, 1970
Paris, France
Skin-O-Meter: Great Nudity

Vampires, especially the stylish sub-breed of those defiling bloodsuckers who group together onscreen in movies Oscar-nominated for art direction, are very choosy about the virginally sweet child-women they ceremoniously disrobe, slay, and slurp upon. The ideal sacrifice must be fair of skin, fine-boned of face, with a blondeness reminiscent of a stilled breeze, a wiry wisp of which blondeness must cover the juncture at the top of her thighs. When she stands, a drugged satiation must cause her eyes to droop as if in satisfied lust, and her breasts must be plump and buoyant, as if filled and bobbing with life's most important fluid. In short, the perfect victim and party favor is embodied by French actress Laure Marsac, as full-frontally revealed in *Interview with the Vampire* (1994).

SKIN-fining Moment:

Interview with the Vampire (1:16) *The bloodsuckers strip Laure naked on stage, unleashing her love-lumps and landing strip.*

See Her Naked In:

Interview with the Vampire (1994) FFN, Buns
L'Homme Voilè (1987) FFN, Buns

TeleVisions:

Strangers Breasts, Buns

Paula Marshall

Born: June 12, 1964
Rockville, Maryland
Skin-O-Meter: Brief Nudity

The world is not always fair, and repeated rolls of the dice do not guarantee fame and fortune in this crap shoot called life, but at least well-traveled actress Paula Marshall was born with a high draw from the gene-pool lottery. From her lustrous, thick black hair, to her captivating, dark-eyed gaze, to the tongue-teasing twist of her full, flexing lips, to the tooth-flashing gusto of her lusty laugh, to her plush, soft hips and rounded, high-riding tits, Paula Marshall is a winner top to toe. Her home-run looks have been pitched on series such as *Wild Oats, Chicago Sons, Cupid, Snoops, The Weber Show*, and *Hidden Hills*. Still, the jackpot of super celebrity eludes lucky lady Paula.

SKIN-fining Moment:

The New Age (1:06) *Paula rolls over and sits up after a massage, providing fast but relaxing glimpses at her full-frontal fineness.*

See Her Naked In:

The New Age (1994) Breasts, Bush
Hellraiser III: Hell on Earth (1992) LB

Ruth Marshall

Toronto, Ontario, Canada
Skin-O-Meter: Brief Nudity

While *Will & Grace* has made the gay man/straight gal friendship mainstream, Ruth Marshall did it a decade ago with *Dharma & Greg's* Thomas Gibson. In *Love & Human Remains* (1993), Ruth's skintroduction to big-screen breast baring, her plus-sized, plush pillows overpowered the dark film's other kinky characters and sexploration themes. From her debut in the promisingly titled yet disappointing flick *The Myth of the Male Orgasm* (1993), Ruth's career fizzled after starring opposite *Achy Breaky Heart* mullet man Billy Ray Cyrus on the TV series *Doc*. Unearthing Marshall's mammaries may have saved the doomed *Doc*, but with a country crooner covering coronaries in the concrete jungle, there's only so much one baby Ruth can do.

SKIN-fining Moment:

Love & Human Remains (0:45) *Big, bare juggalos laying back in bed while Joanne Vannicola kisses her way south, then another shot as they canoodle and Ruth rises out of bed. Udderlicious!*

See Her Naked In:

Love & Human Remains (1993) Breasts

Cristina Marsillach

Born: September 30, 1963
Madrid, Spain
Skin-O-Meter: Brief Nudity

While her milk wagons aren't as massive as her sister Blanca's, creamy Cristina Marsillach is no slouch. Ask Italian and Spanish filmgoers about Cristina's fantastic

flesh cushions and they'll tell you about films like *Opera* (1987), in which she plays a theater singer who's stalked by a psychopath (finally—a reason to go to the opera). American audiences will recognize Cristina's wonderful woofers from *Every Time We Say Goodbye* (1986), in which she starred opposite a young Tom Hanks. It might be one of Hanks's more obscure films, but Cristina makes it a movie to remember.

SKIN-fining Moment:

Opera (0:23) *Cristina's cans are uncovered as a serial killer prepares to butcher the sleeping gal.*

See Her Naked In:

Opera (1987) Breasts
Every Time We Say Goodbye (1986) Breast
La Gabbia (1986) FFN
1919, crónica del alba (1983) Breasts

Pamela Sue Martin

Born: January 5, 1954
Westport, Connecticut
Skin-O-Meter: Great Nudity

A tease is always forgiven if she eventually puts out, and there are no hard feelings against Pamela Sue Martin. Pamela Sue's specialty was the bad girl. In a pinch she could do the good girl in distress. Whatever the role, with her delicate, pretty features Martin played the soiled angel angle to perfection. She came to light in *To Find a Man* (1971) as a teenage girl who is pregnant and doesn't want to be, and she continued along the stressed damsel route as a teen girl on a sinking ship in *The Poseidon Adventure* (1972). The tease played on during her 1977 stint as Nancy Drew on TV. Finally, the full-frontal payoff came in *The Lady in Red* (1979), where, as bank robber John Dillinger's last girlfriend, Martin played stick-'em-up after dropping her top. In the early 1980s, Pamela's bad streak matured as Fallon Carrington Colby on the primetime soap *Dynasty*, although her bad behavior never again included anything of great skinterest.

SKIN-fining Moment:

The Lady in Red (0:25) Nancy Drew stands nude in prison with dozens of other naked gals, before being asked to bend over for "further inspection."

See Her Naked In:

The Lady in Red (1979) Breasts

Maria Marx

Skin-O-Meter: Great Nudity

In filling the crucial supporting roles of tortured inmates while casting actresses for a classic concentration-camp flick, budding filmmakers should keep key points in mind. The ideal candidate for a featured prisoner must of course have no objection to being stripped of every last stitch of clothing at the merest provocation. She should be tall so that when she is marched nude past a gauntlet of clothed guards her bare skin is not lost in their sea of khaki. Hair color? Preferably brunette to offset the hue of the blonde villainess. The face must be capable of holding an expression that—though suffused with dread and resignation—retains and highlights the endearing symmetry of vulnerable beauty under duress. In short, commit to memory a clip of statuesque and doomed Maria Marx enduring her naked torments in the all-time abomination *Ilsa, She Wolf of the S.S.* (1974), and pick the prospect who most closely resembles it.

SKIN-fining Moment:

Ilsa, She Wolf of the S.S. (0:54) Maria's strapped naked to a table by horrible Nazi bitches with electrodes on her big, awesome breasts and something absolutely evil attached to her bush.

See Her Naked In:

Ilsa, She Wolf of the S.S. (1974) FFN, Buns

Marsha Mason

Born: April 3, 1942
St. Louis, Missouri
Skin-O-Meter: Great Nudity

Seeing as she is originally from Missouri, there is every reason to hope that Marsha Mason will appear in a show-me state. This former vampire girl from the gothic soap opera *Dark Shadows* did indeed live up to the Missouri motto and stepped, if only briefly, into the light of the bare-top. From 1973 to 1982, Marsha was married to Midas-touch script man Neil Simon and garnered four Oscar nominations while playing the lead in hubby's creations. No need to clutter this space with their names. The pictures to see are *Blume in Love* (1973) and *Cinderella Liberty* (1973), both of which are graced with in-bed views of the Mason chest.

SKIN-fining Moment:

Cinderella Liberty (0:38) Marsha sits up topless in bed next to James Caan and we get a tasty treat of her Mason mints.

See Her Naked In:

The Image (1990) LB
Cinderella Liberty (1973) Breasts
Blume in Love (1973) Breasts

Athena Massey

Born: November 10, 1971
Orange, California
Skin-O-Meter: Great Nudity

Athena Massey must be put at the very top of any cable TV fan's list of ladies to watch. There is something extra hot about a gorgeous, incredibly well-built actress who isn't afraid to get nude in lower-budget films. She's so damn hot it burns. But in Athena's case, you may wish to put her on the watch list twice—once for the left and once for the right. That rack is definitely two to watch. But this lady is no booby. She speaks multiple languages—all of them dirty. Athena took over a starring role in the highly popular sex trilogy *Poison Ivy 3: The New Seduction* (1997). The previous flicks exposed both Drew Barrymore and Alyssa Milano, so you can bet Athena can't be that far behind—plus, she's got Jaime Pressly to help boost interest. Speaking of behinds, Athena has a tush that any prospector would love to swing his flesh-pick into, not to mention two of the greatest breasts medical science has to offer. In addition to her movie roles she can also be seen as Lieutenant Eva in the hit video game *Command & Conquer*. Athena's star is definitely on the rise, and now that I mention it, so are many pants here at Skin Central!

SKIN-fining Moment:

Undercover (0:56) Athena bursts into a room with buns and boobs a-blazin' clad in a nice black latex S&M cop getup.

See Her Naked In:

Body Parts (1999) Breasts
Poison Ivy 3: The New Seduction (1997) Breasts
Star Portal (1997) FFN, Buns
Termination Man (1997) Breasts, Bush, Buns
The Unspeakable (1996) Breasts, Bush
Virtual Combat (1996) Breasts
Undercover (1995) Breasts, Bush, Buns

TeleVisions:

Red Shoe Diaries FFN, Buns

Chase Masterson

Born: February 26, 1963
Colorado Springs, Colorado
Skin-O-Meter: Great Nudity

A li'l plastic surgery on that freaked out nose of hers and it's all good. Oh, what's that you say? It's only a prosthetic? She's playing an alien? Then Chase Masterson is one out-of-this-world babe! Chase is best known for her role in *Star Trek: Deep Space 69*—oh sorry, that was a typo. It should read: *Star Trek: Deep Space 9*. And who wouldn't want to trek deep into the space between Chase's legs? She is also the first cousin of smokin' Olivia and Maryam D'Abo. Chase does have some movie credits but probably nothing you would remember, like *A Moment of Passion* (1993). Oh, you might want to check that out for a not-so-chaste view of Chase. The celeb-skin-aholics out there will be completely "lust in space" over Chase's mam-terson's in the low-budget sci-fi movie *Digital Man* (1995). Chase makes the threat of alien invasion seem a lot less scary, messed up nose and all.

SKIN-fining Moment:

Digital Man (0:28) Side-nudity while in bed as Don Swayze downs a cool one. And nobody's cooler than Don Swayze.

See Her Naked In:

Digital Man (1995) Breasts, Bush
Married People, Single Sex (1993) Breasts, Buns
In a Moment of Passion (1993) LB

Fay Masterson

Born: March 31, 1974
UK
Skin-O-Meter: Brief Nudity

Fiery-haired Fay Masterson is surprisingly anonymous for someone so skinsational. Appearing alongside leading lads like Mel Gibson in *The Man Without a Face* (1993) and Tom Cruise in *Eyes Wide Shut* (1999), Fay's sexual spark, ravishing red mane, and miles of milky-white skin make for some serious competition with her chicas. In her brief bit of brilliance in *Eyes Wide Shut*, Fay fueled a future rivalry with strawberry sweetheart Nicole Kidman. You can be sure that darling Nikki kept her peepers wide open during this sexy starlet's small but tent-inducing stint. Me-ow-wow-wow! Even the charismatic, crotch-revealing cowgirl Sharon Stone needed a short lasso to keep Russell Crowe and Leo DeCaprio from going off half-cocked in *The Quick and The Dead* (1995). Fay's performance as a gun-slinging goddess of the gulch gave new meaning to the phrase ride 'em cowboy! Most important, Masterson has no qualms about baring boobage. In *Sorted* (2000), Fay guided her lover's lucky hands up and down the slope of her shapely, pink-nipped knockers. Mr. Skin trusts that Fay will sort out all the rivalry and sexual tension and become master of the leading-lady circuit soon.

SKIN-fining Moment:

Sorted (1:04) Riding man-rod recklessly in bed, Fay's nay-nays sway away.

See Her Naked In:

Sorted (2000) Breasts

TeleVisions:

Strangers Body Double—Breasts

Mary Elizabeth Mastrantonio

Born: November 17, 1958
Lombard, Illinois
Skin-O-Meter: Great Nudity

Mary Elizabeth Mastrantonio has the distinction of having the longest name ever nominated for an Oscar, for her supporting role in *The Color of Money* (1986). The dark, exotic, Mediterranean fox made her film debut as Gina, the doomed sister of Tony Montana in the classic film (and gangsta-rap sample) *Scarface* (1983). Says director Brian De Palma, "I was looking for someone who could play a virginal younger sister and transform herself into a wild Latin sexpot." He got that and more from Mary Elizabeth's hot performance. And with a smoking bod like that, it was only a matter of time before she flashed her goods. In fact, *Scarface* offered a brief tease. She continued the flesh trend in the aforementioned *The Color of Money* as well as *The Abyss* (1989), *Robin Hood: Prince of Thieves* (1991), and *White Sands* (1992). But for Mary Elizabeth's breast view, take a gander at those gallon-sized jugs in *January Man* (1989). Director Pat O'Connor liked what he saw so much he married her. Lucky bastard.

SKIN-fining Moment:

The January Man (0:42) Mary Elizabeth's rackstronio will inspire much masturbationio as she's splayed out topless in bed next to Kevin Kline.

See Her Naked In:

White Sands (1992) LB
Robin Hood: Prince of Thieves (1991) Buns
The Abyss (1989) Breasts
The January Man (1989) Breasts
The Color of Money (1986) Breasts
Scarface (1983) LB

Chiara Mastroianni

Born: May 28, 1972
Paris, France
Skin-O-Meter: Great Nudity

The pressure on Chiara Mastroianni began while she was an embryo floating in the gulf of warm fluids within her mama's belly. All the world held the highest of expectations for the spawn of dream-quality French beauty Catherine Denueve and Italy's leading Latin lover Marcello Mastroianni, and Chiara has grown up to be just as precious and pretty as anybody could have predicted her to be. Plus, she has inherited her mother's willingness to bare the divine circumstance that is her physical form to the camera's unblinking, everlasting eye. Look at perfectly bred loveliness for the ages in *N'oublie pas que tu vas mourir* (1995) and *Cameleone* (1996).

SKIN-fining Moment:

N'oublie pas que tu vas mourir (1:34) Fabulous mam-uloses as she leans back for a beef injection in bed.

See Her Naked In:

Carnage (2002) LB, Bush, Buns
Caméléone (1996) Breasts
N'oublie pas que tu vas mourir (1995) Breasts

Samantha Mathis

Born: May 12, 1970
Brooklyn, New York
Skin-O-Meter: Great Nudity

Samantha Mathis broke into acting crotch first via a commercial for Always Slender Pads, a feminine hygiene product for teens. Moving the focus a bit north, this petite firecracker sizzled in her long and lingering topless scene in *Pump Up the Volume* (1990). It certainly pumped Mr. Skin up, only to have the next decade be a letdown of one skinless role after another. Fortunately, Samantha garnered new attention with the release of *Attraction* (2000). The attraction was simple: a flash of gash, handfuls of Mathis's melons in a performance-art scene, and a wickedly cracked ass. Missed that? She showed her terrific tush again on TV's *Mists of Avalon* in a scene that makes my lap misty.

SKIN-fining Moment:

Pump Up the Volume (1:13) One of the great gratuitous teen-flick tit-reveals. Sam shows her mams while getting cozy outside with Christian Slater.

See Her Naked In:

Attraction (2000) Breasts, Buns, Bush
Pump Up the Volume (1990) Breasts

TeleVisions:

The Mists of Avalon Buns

MARLEE MATLIN: *SEE NO EVIL,* **BUT DO SEE HER BOOBIES!**

Marlee Matlin

Born: August 24, 1965
Morton Grove, Illinois
Skin-O-Meter: Great Nudity

When Marlee Matlin won her Oscar for *Children of a Lesser God* (1986) she did it without ever uttering a word onscreen. She also became only the fourth actress to win an Oscar in her first film role. But Marlee couldn't hear the applause. That's because she's completely deaf and has been since an illness made her so at eighteen months. That's all fine and dandy, but have you seen her body? That thing deserves an award of its own. The fact that Marlee is deaf seems to overshadow everything she does, and people forget that she is a fantastic-looking piece of ass with two world-class jugs. She showed off her round tush in a skinny-dipping scene from her booby prize-winning performance, but the breast was yet to come. Marlee's melons were ripe and juicy in *In Her Defense* (1986), *Hear No Evil* (1993) and *Two Shades of Blue* (2000). And no, they're not silent movies.

SKIN-fining Moment:

Children of a Lesser God (0:47) Marlee hugs William Hurt in the water and we see her submerged left suck-pillow.

See Her Naked In:

Two Shades of Blue (2000) Breasts
In Her Defense (1998) Breasts

Hear No Evil (1993) Breasts
Children of a Lesser God (1986) Buns

Robin Mattson

Born: June 1, 1956
Los Angeles, California
Skin-O-Meter: Great Nudity

A powerhouse of boobilicious blonde ambition, Robin Mattson is known in soap-opera circles for her uncanny ability to play scheming, fair-haired fireballs with such perfection. This devious diva has appeared in most every daytime drama imaginable, beginning with *The Guiding Light* to her most recent stint on *All My Children*, spanning a sex-filled, successful career over three decades. Much like her conniving characters, Robin herself has a skinteresting past. In the early years, Mattson's mams were on full display at your local drive-in theater in *Candy Stripe Nurses* (1974). As a tasty Florence Nightingale in training, randy Robin gave some lucky bird a little chirp in the gymnastics room, taking his temp with her tats and baring both backside and bush in preparation for a skinjection. Sweet, fast-fast-fast relief! You'll also howl over glimpses of Mattson's round robins in *Wolf Lake* (1978) when she flashed her rack to a pack of horny lumberjacks. Timberrrr! From days performing dirty deeds on the soaps to wild nights flashing funbags for us mopes, Robin is one dirty little birdie who shouldn't be missed.

SKIN-fining Moment:

Bonnie's Kids (0:07) Robin washes up her naked Mamm-sons in a bathroom.

See Her Naked In:

Take Two (1988) Breasts
Wolf Lake (1978) FFN
Candy Stripe Nurses (1974) Breasts, Bush, Buns
Bonnie's Kids (1973) Breasts

Mathilda May

Born: February 8, 1965
Paris, France
Skin-O-Meter: Hall of Fame

Mathilda May is to die for in *Lifeforce* (1985)—literally! As the tempting and clothing-deprived Space Girl, she spent the entire movie nude, but one kiss from her outer-space lips sucked you dry—what a way to go, though! Mathilda had no dialogue in the film, but her fleshy planets, Milky Way-smooth ass, and black hole speak volumes. Daughter of a prima ballerina for the Sweden Malmo Ballet Company, Mathilda was born fit for bearing skin. As a dancer herself since age eight, the only fat on her jiggles in her mammoth mams. For a closer look at that treasure chest behold the aptly named *The Tit and the Moon* (1994). Mathilda delivered on the carnal promise of her provocative movie titles like *Naked Tango* (1990)—Mathilda May, Mr. Skin have this dance?

SKIN-fining Moment:

Lifeforce (0:21) Mathilda wakes up on the lab table totally naked, and proceeds to show off every last bit of her bangtabulous body, including a hint of pubitude, before planting a killer kiss on the spaceman.

See Her Naked In:

The Tit and the Moon (1994) Breasts
Toutes Peines Confondues (1992) FFN
Becoming Colette (1992) Breasts, Buns
La Conquete de la Peur (1991) LB, Buns
Naked Tango (1990) Breasts, Bush, Buns
Trois Places Pour le 26 (1988) Breasts, Buns
La Passerelle (1988) FFN, Buns
La Vie Dissolue de Gérard Floque (1987) Breasts
Letters to an Unknown Lover (1985) Breasts, Buns
Lifeforce (1985) FFN, Buns

Melanie Mayron

Born: October 20, 1952
Philadelphia, Pennsylvania
Skin-O-Meter: Brief Nudity

Some people have a knack for being at the forefront in the march for social advancement, and tousle-head Melanie Mayron, as the neurotic struggling photographer Melissa Steadman on the boomer-angst ensemble television event *thirtysomething*, headed the line for molding and defining the expectations and acceptances of her generation. And of course she would be. Mayron started out ahead of the curve in the early 1970s as a cast member in a road show of the groundbreaking musical *Godspell*. She remained ahead of the curve by putting her own curves on view, first as Ginger the hitchhiker in *Harry and Tonto* (1974), and later as a single, struggling photographer in *Girlfriends* (1978). In both flicks, Melanie is a picture-perfect point of focus.

SKIN-fining Moment:

Harry and Tonto (0:57) Long shot of Melanie's Ralphy buoys toweling off in a room with Art Carney.

See Her Naked In:

Girlfriends (1978) LB, Bush, Buns
Harry and Tonto (1974) Breasts

Debi Mazar

Born: August 15, 1964
Queens, New York
Skin-O-Meter: Brief Nudity

Debi Mazar could kick Fran Drescher's ass—and that's a catfight we'd love to watch. The Queens native with the hard-as-nails New Yawk voice has been called a Fran clone from the very first time she appeared on film. There are some similarities between the two, but where Fran is a likable TV character, Debi is a big-screen

DEBI MAZAR SHOWS HER CUTE SACKS TO JOHN CUSACK IN *MONEY FOR NOTHING.*

bad ass. She looks like one of those pinups from a '40s mechanics calendar or a tough-talking mob girl in films of the same era. Debi is not what you might call traditionally beautiful, but her offbeat looks and "screw you" attitude bring the whole package home into one fabulous babe. She got her big break playing a coke whore in *Goodfellas* (1990), but we prefer her role in *Money for Nothing* (1993), where she wore nothing while rubbing down her li'l fun pair with dollar bills. She made a TV splash in the cast of *L.A. Law* and hit the gossip rags by being romantically linked to men as diverse as Quentin Tarantino and perverse as Pee Wee Herman. Maybe she'll hook up with Fran in real life and turn our fantasy life into a white-hot turn-on.

SKIN-fining Moment:

Money for Nothing (0:40) Debi's rolling in money! Literally! And she's showing her dainty nubbins! Literally!

See Her Naked In:

Money for Nothing (1993) Breasts

Rachel McAdams

Born: October 7, 1976
London, Ontario, Canada
Skin-O-Meter: Brief Nudity

Blonder than blonde, built to thrill, and possessed of simmering, sexual undercurrents that threaten (or promise) to explode at any moment to hysterical heights of excess, Rachel McAdams could not have seemed more at home in well-known teen-flick hits, fittingly titled *The Hot Chick* (2002) and *Mean Girls* (2004). Fans of Rachel's natural knockout looks and perpetually volatile allure are advised to look beyond the *Hot* and the *Mean*, however, and dredge up a heretofore forgotten relic of Rachel's pre-Hollywood past. The 2002 Canadian obscurity *My Name Is Tanino* provides an incendiary introduction to Rachel in the raw, and as her star rises in the realm of mainstream entertainment, it may well be the world's last opportunity to ogle Ms. McAdams's apples for quite a spell. Find it and bewitch yourself.

SKIN-fining Moment:

My Name Is Tanino (0:03) Rachel's no Mean Girl—she nicely gives up some boob shots when she's splashing around in the ocean.

See Her Naked In:

The Notebook (2004) Breasts
My Name Is Tanino (2002) Breasts

Kimberly McArthur

Born: September 16, 1962
Fort Worth, Texas
Skin-O-Meter: Great Nudity

Mr. Skin would like to offer Kimberly McArthur a complimentary back massage, not just for the love of her aching shoulders, which must be killing her from carrying around such heavy hooterage, but also as a ceremonial tribute to her skinsational career in the '80s. Like the multitudes of perky-peeked pinups before her, this former *Playboy* Playmate of January 1982 parlayed her jamambo juggedness into a suc*sex*ful stint in film. Kimberly's kazoongas are a medical marvel in

Young Doctors in Love (1982). Her pointedly perfect presence in a Santa Claus hat, behemoth breasts bouncing bare, nips popping in the icy breeze, will fill you with tingly tidings of great joy. Ho! Ho! Ho! Thanks for the Christmas mammaries, Kimmy. Rodney Dangerfield was an easy mark for the charms between Kim's arms in *Easy Money* (1983). Surprising Kim sunbathing in all her naked glory, randy Rodney got no respect at all. McArthur's double-D digits and bushy beaver, however, are highly regarded, adding up to some major cha-ching for the ding-a-ling. After years of airing out her massive mams in the '80s, Kim sadly disappeared from the public's watchful fly. Anyone who knows the whereabouts of this big busted beauty, please let her know that Mr. Skin will gladly help her take a load off.

SKIN-fining Moment:

Easy Money (0:47) Kimberly sunbathes topless in a backyard, causing Rodney Dangerfield to wonder if her udderly humungous glory-pillows are worth losing $10 million. You will, too.

See Her Naked In:

Malibu Express (1985) Breasts
Easy Money (1983) Breasts
Young Doctors in Love (1982) Breasts
Numerous *Playboy* Videos

Harlee McBride

Born: 1954
California
Skin-O-Meter: Great Nudity

Harlee McBride is the star of the softcore classic *Young Lady Chatterly* (1977) and its salacious sequel *Young Lady Chatterly II* (1985). If you are interested in seeing this sweet, innocent-looking lady in the buff, then you'll need look no further than these late-night cable perennials. Harlee has the face of an

angel with the body of a sinner. Her breasts are perfectly kissable, and her ass just begs to be cupped by masculine hands (or, as happens in her films occasionally, some lustful lady fingers). In real life, Harlee is married to funnyman and *Law & Order: Special Victims Unit* star Richard Belzer. So there's a lesson in the success of scrawny, pock-marked Belz in scoring an international sex symbol: brush up on your jokes, folks!

SKIN-fining Moment:

Young Lady Chatterley II (0:20) Marvel at Ms. McBride's melons as her masseuse becomes her masturbatory manipulator! Man, oh man!

See Her Naked In:

Young Lady Chatterley II (1985) FFN
Young Lady Chatterley (1977) FFN, Buns

Jenny McCarthy

Born: November 1, 1972
Chicago, Illinois
Skin-O-Meter: Great Nudity

Imagine your perfect pal. He loves sports that make you bleed, can burp the alphabet without apology, matches you pint for pint at the pub, and makes you laugh so hard you shoot beer out of your nose. Now give that buddy booming boobies and the sun-kissed charm of any girl who ever stepped foot on *Baywatch* and you have Jenny McCarthy. This blonde beach bunny actually grew up in an Irish Catholic family on Chicago's south side. Rough and ready to rumble (yet ridiculously ravishing), Jenny decided to drop out of college and do something with her life. She took some snapshots of her fine frame and walked right into *Playboy*'s corporate office. *Playboy* made her Playmate for October 1993 and she was soon a smoking skinsation with a host spot on

MTV's *Singled Out*. Jenny was so scorchingly hot in the mid '90s, a poll revealed that one in five men in the U.S. had masturbated to her at least once. As her poke appeal rose, she landed *The Jenny McCarthy Show* and the short-lived sitcom *Jenny*. This vulgar vixen finally let her freak flag fly onscreen, combining her Playmate pleasantness with the humor of a truck driver. Since then, this burping bombshell has thrived on blonde ambition, starring in such teen scream fests as *Scream 3* (2000) and *Scary Movie 3* (2003) and making yank banking guest appearances on *Less Than Perfect*, *The Drew Carey Show*, and *Charmed*. While this lovely lass may not have charmed the world with her special gifts, Jenny has flashed, flaunted, and farted her way into our hearts.

SKIN-fining Moment:

Playboy: The Best of Jenny McCarthy (0:10) Bomp and circumstance: Jenny's graduation gown magically comes undone and out come her FFN playmates and close-trimmed centerfold.

See Her Naked In:

Playboy's Wet & Wild: The Locker Room (1994) FFN
Playboy The Best of Jenny McCarthy (1996) FFN, Buns
Numerous *Playboy* Videos

Tane McClure

Born: June 8, 1959
Pacific Palasades, California
Skin-O-Meter: Great Nudity

If a woman's breasts are bigger than average, lighter than air, and visible often enough, she will find that she has very little need to speak. All she needs to do is take in a sharp huff of breath, bust the buttons on her blouse, point her stacks at what she wants, and all the hetero-blooded males in the vicinity will be cutting one another's throats to be the first to bring it to her. Superstardom, in a

trashy, sexploitative vein, seems to be what the loudly and clearly expressive body of Tane McClure wanted, and a list of more than three dozen movies highlighting her high-riding Himalayas is what she got. Plus, aside from revelatory rounds in *Lap Dancing* (1995), *Stripshow* (1996), and *Bare Deception* (2000), she was tapped to be Reese Witherspoon's mom in *Legally Blonde* (2001).

SKIN-fining Moment:

Surf, Sand, and Sex (0:34) Red-light rack and rug as Tane makes out with a man in a restaurant.

See Her Naked In:

Bare Deception (2000) FFN, Buns
Shadow Hours (2000) Breasts, Bush, Buns
Go (1999) Breasts, Thong
Hot Lust (1997) Breast, Buns
Illicit Dreams 2 (1997) FFN, Buns
Lovers, Liars, and Thieves (1997) Breasts
Night Shade (1997) Breasts, Buns
Scorned 2 (1997) Breasts
Stripshow (1996) Breasts, Buns
Who Killed Buddy Blue? (1996) Breasts
Sexual Roulette (1996) Breasts, Buns
Target of Seduction (1995) Breasts, Buns
Caged Hearts (1995) Breasts, Bush, Buns
Bikini Drive-In (1995) Breasts
Lap Dancing (1995) Breasts, Thong
Surf, Sand, and Sex (1994) Breasts, Bush
Inside Out II (1992) Breasts
Hot Under the Collar (1991) Breasts
Death Spa (1988) Breasts, Bush
Death House (1987) Breasts
Crawlspace (1986) Breasts

TeleVisions:

Nightcap FFN, Buns
Pleasure Zone Breasts, Buns
Sherman Oaks Breasts, Buns

Lorissa McComas

Born: November 26, 1970
Columbus, Ohio
Skin-O-Meter: Great Nudity

Lorissa McComas has done skinsationally well for herself. With a head for business and a body for

skin, this thirty-four double D-light built a successful strip-o-gram service right out of college. A dusky dish served hot and fresh in thirty minutes or less? How skinventive! One of Lorissa's best qualities is her willingness to work hard for her money, and she's worked so hard for it honey, appearing in hundreds of magazines and calendars since her first *Playboy* modeling job in 1991. The skinergizer bunny of the B-movie, Lo has flashed her cafe au lait flesh in over thirty-seven movies in the past ten years. While each of her efforts is a guaranteed deposit in your yank bank for future reference, Mr. Skin recommends *Love Games* (1998), where Lorissa makes showing her fuzzy fro down below into a lusty, libidinous sport. Game on, McComas!

SKIN-fining Moment:

Can It Be Love (0:55) A guy peeps on Lorissa through a two-way mirror as she changes. He spies her bazooms and butt. So do we.

See Her Naked In:

Slaughter Studios (2002) Breasts
Raptor (2001) Breasts
Hard as Nails (2001) Breasts, Thong
Undercurrent (1999) Breasts, Thong
The Bare Wench Project (1999) Breasts
Voyeur (1999)
Testing the Limits (1998) FFN, Buns
Love Games (1998) FFN, Buns
Live Nude Shakespeare (1997) FFN, Buns
When Passions Collide (1997) FFN, Buns
Erotic Heat (1996) FFN, Buns
Arranged Marriage (1996) FFN, Buns
Body Language (1996) Breasts, Buns
Hindsight (1996) Breasts
Lap Dancing (1995) FFN, Buns
Virtual Desire (1995) Bush, Thong
Stormswept (1995) FFN, Buns
Piranha (1995) FFN, Buns
Wish Me Luck (1995) Breasts, Buns
Droid Gunner (1995) Breasts
Babes, Bikes and Beyond (1994) Breasts, Buns
Can It Be Love (1992) Breasts, Thong, FFN, Buns

TeleVisions:

Arli$$ Breasts, Buns
Sherman Oaks Breasts

Catherine McCormack

Born: January 1, 1972
Alton, Hampshire, England
Skin-O-Meter: Great Nudity

The British are a practical people, and the national trait of doing what is necessary and sensible extends to their actors of the female persuasion. When a vaunted thespian of the caliber of strikingly regal redhead Catherine McCormack is called upon to perform a realistic and hopefully rousing love scene, she intuitively knows to cast aside all pretense of shielding her modesty with an artfully placed towel, sheet, or shirttail. Not only are the snowy mounds of Catherine McCormack heaving tokens to authenticity in passionately portrayed embraces during erotic encounters in *Loaded* (1994) and *The Tailor of Panama* (2001), but the nipples are always convincingly hard. It must have something to do with that bit about the Brit stiff upper lip.

SKIN-fining Moment:

Braveheart (0:38) Catherine gets topless and shows her brave-tarts by a lake with Mel Gibson.

See Her Naked In:

The Tailor of Panama (2001) Breasts
Shadow of the Vampire (2000) Breasts
Dangerous Beauty (1998) Breasts, Buns
Braveheart (1995) Breasts
Loaded (1994) Breasts

Mary McCormack

Born: February 8, 1969
Plainfield, New Jersey
Skin-O-Meter: Brief Nudity

Mary McCormack is best known as Queen to the King of All Media's heart and hard-ons in Howard Stern's *Private Parts* (1997). Although Mary quite contrary stopped short of showing her own growing garden of secret delights, her brief flesh flash in a black lacy bra was enough to put a nice little shock in our jocks. Always an angel-faced vision of the girl next door, Mary's easy-going, earth-girl appeal caused a profound bang down below in *Deep Impact* (1998) and made Russell Crowe's cock *a-doodle-doo* in *Mystery, Alaska* (1999). Although McCormack's performance with Kevin Spacey in *K-Pax* (2001) was out of this world, she was most heavenly in *World Traveler* (2002). In her one and only skinematic glimpse of greatness, Mary's globalicious glutes were seen in a dark yet bone-brightening scene. Recently, Mary gave David Spade's ding-a-ling a luminary leap as his surrogate screen mom in *Dickie Roberts: Former Child Star* (2003). What brilliant, skincestuous fun for all. Mary is one little lamb who will be followed wherever she goes.

SKIN-fining Moment:

World Traveler (0:30) Mary flashes some of that high-rise ass when Billy Crudup peeks in on her.

See Her Naked In:

World Traveler (2001) Buns

Maureen McCormick

Born: August 5, 1956
Los Angeles, California
Skin-O-Meter: Brief Nudity

Maureen McCormick may have been in the business called show since age six when she won the Baby Miss San Fernando Valley contest, but she'll be forever known as the hottest chick on the '60s sitcom phenomenon *The Brady Bunch*. As wholesome as this archetypal California girl is, that's how naughty

MR. SKIN'S TOP TEN

TV Babes I Can't Believe Got Naked
. . . Emission possible

10. **Vanna White**
    —(Host) *Wheel of Fortune*

9. **Sally Field**
   —(Sister Bertrille) *The Flying Nun*

8. **Juliet Mills**
   —(Nanny) *Nanny and the Professor*

7. **Cloris Leachman**
   —(Phyllis) *The Mary Tyler Moore Show*

6. **Melody Patterson**
   —(Wrangler Jane) *F Troop*

5. **Pamela Sue Martin**
   —(Nancy Drew) *Nancy Drew Mysteries*

4. **Amy Jo Johnson**
   —(Kimberly Hart) *Mighty Morphin Power Rangers*

3. **Tina Louise**
   —(Ginger) *Gilligan's Island*

2. **Justine Bateman**
   —(Mallory Keaton) *Family Ties*

1. **Maureen McCormick**
   —(Marcia) *The Brady Bunch*

Mr. Skin's thoughts about her are. Maureen couldn't overcome the squeaky-clean image of Marcia Brady, although she tried. In the rarely seen *Texas Lightning* (1981), Maureen got roughed up and out of her top by a couple of randy rednecks. The brief nipple shot must be milked for all it's worth, as Maureen is hardly seen outside of a G-rated *Brady* reunion. The blonde beauty is using her lungs for more melodic works lately, like *When You Get a Little Lonely*, a country CD inspired by her days singing with the Brady Kids, and as the voice of the Pillsbury Dough Boy. Mr. Skin wishes Maureen would come into his kitchen for some poppin' fresh dough!

SKIN-fining Moment:

Texas Lightning (1:04) Marcia Brady still has hair of gold—and a nip of pink—in this fast flash of her Brady bump.

See Her Naked In:

Texas Lightning (1980) RB

Daisy McCrackin

Skin-O-Meter: Brief Nudity

Flame-maned, naturally dazzling Daisy McCrackin has been adding bulk to hollow weenies since her appearance in the fright fest *A Crack in the Floor* (2000). Those suffering from lactose intolerance will need to steer clear of Ms. D's dairy drippers in *Halloween: Resurrection* (2002), as the beautiful bulk of her milky-white mams is boobilicious enough to scare the pants off you. For a frightful, delightful time, any dollop of Daisy will do.

SKIN-fining Moment:

Halloween: Resurrection (0:51) A meager hint of hooter making out with Luke Kirby.

See Her Naked In:

Halloween: Resurrection (2002) Breasts

Julie McCullough

Born: January 30, 1965
Honolulu, Hawaii
Skin-O-Meter: Brief Nudity

Former child star Julie McCullough has suffered a lot of growing pains in her skinsational career. A blonde bombshell with a gorgeous face and knockout body, Julie appropriately began as a bikini model in Honolulu. Her memorable mountains caught the fly of a visiting *Playboy* photographer, who lured her into his stable of boobilicious bunnies, making her Playmate of the Month in February

1986. While modeling shortly after, Julie captured the attention of Hollywood producers, who found her aura of girlish innocence and wholesome all-American good looks perfect for the part of Kirk Cameron's love interest on the family-friendly sitcom *Growing Pains*. When *Playboy* decided to rerun Julie's jugilicious photo spread to capitalize on the curvy cutie's popularity, she was let go. Cameron's overbearing, born-again-Christian mother found the photos to be "against God." Since God created this angelic vision, Mr. Skin finds it heresy not to worship her in all of her naked loveliness. To bow down at McCullough's alter, check out Julie's juiciness in *Playboy Video Playmate Calendar 1988* (1987) and *Playboy Prime Time Playmates* (2002). Growing up isn't easy, Julie, but we certainly appreciate the rod-stiffening results.

SKIN-fining Moment:

Big Bad Mama II (0:12) Julie jumps topless into a pond, followed by the also bare-bazoomba'd Danielle Brisebois.

See Her Naked In:

Big Bad Mama II (1987) Breasts
Numerous *Playboy* Videos

Mary Beth McDonough

Born: May 4, 1961
Van Nuys, California
Skin-O-Meter: Brief Nudity

Growing up a wholesome-looking mid-American beauty, Mary Beth McDonough was perfect to play one of the sympathetic siblings of America's favorite family of the '30s in *Homecoming: A Christmas Story* (1971). The show was so full of homegrown warm and fuzzy appeal that it spawned the long-running TV series *The Waltons*. Mary Beth's portrayal of "Erin," the angst-filled yet angelic middle child, was an

integral part of the show's success and resulted in the spinoff TV specials *A Wedding on Walton's Mountain* (1982) and *Mother's Day on Walton's Mountain* (1982), which compose the majority of Mary's cinematic resumé. In an effort to escape from a mountain of a pristine pigeonhole, Mary made her skinful debut in *One of Those Nights* (1998). Getting in touch with her inner repressed wild child, Mary had a little ex sex with a former hubby, who freed McDonough's mammy mounties from the confines of her top. You'll have to calm your own *John Boy* down after watching her eye-popping perky peaks. Mary Beth continued the Walton legacy in *A Walton Easter* (1997), proving that she's every bit the cutie pattootie she's always been.

SKIN-fining Moment:

One of Those Nights Mary Beth squats on a fellow's crotch, then yanks down her top and invites us all to adore her Walton's Mountains.

See Her Naked In:

One of Those Nights (1998) Breasts

> "I wanted to do nudity; it's about a certain physical liberation for myself as an actor."
>
> —FRANCES MCDORMAND

Frances McDormand

Born: June 23, 1957
Chicago, Illinois
Skin-O-Meter: Brief Nudity

Frances McDormand is a feisty firecracker of a film star with a penchant for low-key, real-life dramatics that bring an organic authenticity to whatever character she assays. Whether it be the mother of a rock-journalist prodigy in *Almost Famous* (2000) or a massively pregnant rural sheriff in *Fargo* (1996) or her debut as a kittenish and adulterous wife in *Blood Simple* (1984), McDormand's seemingly easy, natural delivery belies the fact that she is a well-studied Yale graduate. Also belied in many of McDormand's depictions is a taut sexuality, fully revealed in the flash of beav in Robert Altman's *Short Cuts* (1993) and as the tittie-twisting record producer who flashes her pop tops in *Laurel Canyon* (2002).

SKIN-fining Moment:

Short Cuts (0:45) A fleeting bit of full-frontal fun as Frannie passes through a doorway nakedly.

See Her Naked In:

Laurel Canyon (2002) Breasts
Short Cuts (1993) LB, Bush

Karen McDougal

Born: March 23, 1971
Gary, Indiana
Skin-O-Meter: Great Nudity

Imagine the mixed disappointment of all the daddies whose kids were in the last pre-school class taught by former children's pedagogue Karen McDougal. Busty and beautiful in the way of a corn-fed, small-town pageant winner, Karen's days in the classroom were doomed when she was selected to reveal her multi-faceted charms in the centerfold slot of the December 1997 issue of *Playboy*. While the fathers of the sons who had been lucky enough to gaze upon Karen's super shelf all through nap time gazed in turn, with equal parts longing and loss, at the copious curves of their kids' former teacher as shown in the Bunny book, Karen was being elevated to Playmate of the Year for 1998. Once she'd appeared as "Roger Corwin's girl at party" in *Charlie's Angels* (2000), all hopes for her return to

the playground were dashed. And the rest of us should rejoice.

SKIN-fining Moment:

The Arena (0:36) Karen's amazingly round balloons make plenty of appearances during some steamy softcore sex.

See Her Naked In:

The Arena (2001) Breasts, Buns
Numerous *Playboy* Videos

Natascha McElhone

Born: March 23, 1971
Hampstead London, England
Skin-O-Meter: Great Nudity

She's English, which accounts for the steely reserve. She's a former model, which explains the perfect posture and self-possession. She has a singular inspirational beauty of a face, which makes for affecting, prolonged, full-screen close-ups. And she comes packaged in a smoking, lithe, long, and lean athletic body, but that still doesn't explain the miracle of Natascha McElhone's forever-lasting (don't forget to PAUSE, REWIND, PLAY) stint standing fully naked in full light as a high-breasted, sweet-hipped, thick-bushed artist's model in *Surviving Picasso* (1996). Most skin readers will have been impressed by Natascha as the stunning young Irish terrorist who made out with old Robert DeNiro in *Ronin* (1998). Those skinvestigators

NATASCHA MCELHONE IN *SURVIVING PICASSO*.
APPARENTLY SHE'S UNFAMILIAR WITH
HANNIBAL LECTOR'S IDEA OF SUCKING FACE.

are advised to bypass the shadowy profile nudity of *Solaris* (2002) and make a beeline back to *Picasso*.

SKIN-fining Moment:

Surviving Picasso (0:21) Natty removes her dress and stands bare-assed naked for a clearly intrigued Anthony Hopkins.

See Her Naked In:

Solaris (2002) RB, Buns
Surviving Picasso (1996) FFN

Graem McGavin

Skin-O-Meter: Great Nudity

Flirty filmstress Graem McGavin presents a picture-perfect physiognomy of the 1980s play date, sporting a fluffy, feathered, and frosted coif; a quirky face with high, blushing apple cheeks; and big, beckoning eyes. Also evocative of that era is Graem's rack, which, true to the times, she shows off in such percolating period pieces as *My Tutor* (1983) and *Angel* (1984). *My Tutor*, wherein Graem gives some shag-head mook a pop quiz in backseat carnality, offers the best views of her plump, pre-silicone pleasure cushions, vintage early 1980s.

SKIN-fining Moment:

My Tutor (0:21) She gets topless in a backseat with Matt Lattanzis. Great Maems, Graem!

See Her Naked In:

Angel (1984) Breasts
My Tutor (1983) Breasts

Vonetta McGee

Born: January 14, 1948
San Francisco, California
Skin-O-Meter: Great Nudity

The 1970s were a boon time for African American thespians, who were suddenly presented with a plethora of roles in dozens of melanin-heavy films populated by and aimed at urban black folks. Many of the cinema's most important performers of color got their first shot at celluloid glory in these blaxploitation pics, but creamy licorice twist Vonetta McGee was not among them. Though she would provide a mellow ebony glow to such triumphs of the genre as *Blacula* (1972), *Hammer* (1972), and *Shaft in Africa* (1973), Vonetta first showed her sass and ass, plus a bitty of titty, in the spaghetti western *Il Grande Silenzo* (1968).

SKIN-fining Moment:

Shaft in Africa (0:44) Bare backside as she reclines naked with Richard Roundtree in a hut. Careful! Vonetta's heat might ingnite the straw walls!

See Her Naked In:

Shaft in Africa (1973) Buns
Hammer (1972) RB, Buns
Il Grande Silenzo (1968) Breasts, Buns

Kelly McGillis

Born: July 9, 1957
Newport Beach, California
Skin-O-Meter: Hall of Fame

It takes a special actress to make an Amish woman come off as sexy, and Kelly McGillis did just that by taking off her top and employing her special rack in *Witness* (1985). Despite the acclaim won by the Newport Beach, California–spawn for that nuanced performance and two more in *Top Gun* (1986) and *The Accused* (1988), McGillis faltered along her career path and stumbled into a series of projects that highlighted her nipples as much as they did her emoting. From the beachfront nudity of *Grand Isle* (1991) to the breasts bared through ripped bodice in *Painted Angels* (1998) to the perfectly lit, perfect absence of clothing during the lesbianic tryst of *Monkey's Mask*

TITNESS: KELLY MCGILLIS'S AMISH UDDERS WILL HAVE YOU CHURNING *BUTTER IN WITNESS*

(2001), McGillis's loss in professional stature has been a gain for skin sleuths everywhere.

SKIN-fining Moment:

Witness (1:18) Harrison Ford stumbles in as Kelly's using a wash-basin to polish her Amish apples. You'll churn your own butter!

See Her Naked In:

The Monkey's Mask (2000) Breasts, Buns
Painted Angels (1998) Breasts
Grand Isle (1991) FFN, Buns
Cat Chaser (1989) FFN, Buns
The House on Carroll Street (1988) Breasts
Made in Heaven (1987) LB
Witness (1985) Breasts

Elizabeth McGovern

Born: July 18, 1961
Evanston, Illinois
Skin-O-Meter: Great Nudity

With a mug like a cherub and a body to tempt gay Satan himself, Elizabeth McGovern began her career as the ultimate actress seductress. Although her character stayed fully clothed in *Ordinary People* (1980), daring darling Elizabeth looked quite extraordinary in Milos Forman's *Ragtime* (1981) as the naked embodiment of baby-faced fleshly pleasure. Look for a bounty of high-held chest bags in *Ragtime*, and then look closely at *Once Upon a Time in*

America (1984), and McGovern's furry honeypot will slip into view.

SKIN-fining Moment:

Ragtime (0:53) Elizabeth drops her dress and we get a glimpse of her lap-floss before an ultra-long treat of her teats.

See Her Naked In:

Women & Men: Stories of Seduction (1990) Breasts
Johnny Handsome (1989) RB
Once Upon a Time in America (1984) Breasts, Buns, bush
Racing with the Moon (1984) Breasts
Ragtime (1981) FFN, Buns

Rose McGowan

Born: September 5, 1973
Florence, Italy
Skin-O-Meter: Great Nudity

This Italian import with the Irish name has been making teens (of all ages) horny as hell ever since her bare double-Ds debuted in *The Doom Generation* (1995). Rose's terrifically too-tight turtleneck provided her with a landmark pokie-nipped performance in *Scream* (1995), which she followed by freeing her mega milkers again in *Going All the Way* (1997) and *Lewis and Clark and George* (1998). Rose's rack was kept covered in the poisonous comedy *Jawbreaker* (1999), in which her then real-life boyfriend, shock rocker Marilyn Manson, appeared as a greaseball who made it with McGowan from behind. Much more enjoyable was when Rose accompanied Manson to the 1998 MTV Awards. She "wore" a dress that seemed to be nothing more than a few strands of black spaghetti spread far apart and clinging to Rose's curves only by her Satanic freak boy's mental power. Damn him!

SKIN-fining Moment:

The Doom Generation (0:14) Stunning eyeful of Rose's massive chest-

blossoms in the tub, followed by more mammage as she messes with her man.

See Her Naked In:

Lewis and Clark and George (1998) Breasts
Going All the Way (1997) Breasts
The Doom Generation (1995) Breasts, Buns

Peggy McIntaggart

Born: September 6, 1961
Midland, Ontario, Canada
Skin-O-Meter: Great Nudity

Buxom and statuesque blondes who broadcast their life-affirmative personalities through glittering brown eyes and dazzling broad smiles of sensual invitation are a comfort and a motivation to the lone male dreaming of a better future to come. Comfort and motivation are both ratcheted up a couple of excruciating notches when, as in the case of *Playboy* Playmate for January 1990 Peggy McIntaggart, that inspiring blonde deigns to doff her duds and display her buds. In flesh-flashing moments during fun flicks as varied as *Into the Night* (1985) and *Lady Avenger* (1989), the comely, chesty comforts of Peggy are a reminder that a better future is now here.

SKIN-fining Moment:

Into the Night (0:43) Ms. McIntaggart steps out of a store dressing room with her top down and naked Pegs exposed. Jeff Goldblum enjoys a Brundlefly-ful.

See Her Naked In:

Far Out Man (1990) Breasts, Thong
Lady Avenger (1989) Breasts
Beverly Hills Cop II (1987) Breasts
Into the Night (1985) Breasts
Numerous *Playboy* Videos

Lonette McKee

Born: July 22, 1954
Detroit, Michigan,.
Skin-O-Meter: Brief Nudity

Lonette McKee is not your average soap star. In addition to her role as Sarah Ruth Bennett on *As the World Turns*, this money cocoa honey is also a consummate film and theatre virtuoso. A particular favorite at Mr. Skin is Lonette's bare-boob debut, which involved rolling around in bed nekkid with Wesley Snipes, in Spike Lee's tale of interracial dalliance *Jungle Fever* (1991). This dark-haired doll showed up in another Lee movie, as the revolutionary rabble-rouser's mom in *Malcom X* (1992) (dude, your mom is hot). McKee is much more than just skintillating though; she showed off her funny bone (hey now, keep yours in your pants Mr.) in the Richard Pryor vehicles *Which Way is Up?* (1977) and *Brewster's Millions* (1985). The lovely Lonette is also known as quite the song bird, making good use of her perky pipes as a Billie Holiday-type character in *Round Midnight* (1986). As well as belting it out in the Harlem heyday flick *The Cotton Club* (1984) and in her entree into cinema stardom *Sparkle* (1976), she is also a Tony and Drama Desk award nominated stage actress.

SKIN-fining Moment:

Dangerous Passion (0:39) Lonette gets comfy in a car with Carl Weathers and out comes her right breast.

See Her Naked In:

Jungle Fever (1991) LB
Dangerous Passion (1990) RB
Which Way Is Up? (1977) LB

Jacqueline McKenzie

Born: October 24, 1967
Sydney, New South Wales, Australia
Skin-O-Meter: Great Nudity

Who isn't a fan of all things Down Under? Not just *that* down under, you silly skinsters; we're talking about nubile Australian native Jacqueline McKenzie playing anguished indie-film appetizers in both *Romper Stomper* (1993) and *Angel Baby* (1995). Speaking of Down Under, Fosters may be Australian for beer, but flesh fans are hoping that McKenzie is Australian for *bare*—all Mr. Skin can say is, stay tuned skin supporters. Flaxen-haired femme fatale Jacqueline took her dramatic-arts background to the edge as an alluring angst-ridden Aussie opposite John Lynch in the provocative lunatics-in-love story *Angel Baby*. In addition to smoldering onscreen, Jackie received wide acclaim and several awards for this portrayal. The brooding beauty also acquired oodles of accolades for her role as an abused runaway and epileptic in the controversial *Romper Stomper*. Her co-star Russell Crowe shot to stardom as well for his role as an inexorable bully and brute, not to mention neo-Nazi gang leader, in this cautionary tale of hate mongering with a love-triangle twist. You can also check out Jackie Mac in *The Divine Secrets of the Ya-Ya Sisterhood* (2002) (if you're into chick flicks) and *Deep Blue Sea* (1999) (if you're into good-old-fashioned, cheesy Peter Benchley rip-offs . . . mmm, sharky).

SKIN-fining Moment:

Romper Stomper (0:19) Fascist funbags and partial buns as Jackie has frenzied sex with skinhead Russell Crowe.

See Her Naked In:

The Human Touch (2004) FFN, Buns
Angel Baby (1995) FFN, Buns
Romper Stomper (1993) Breasts, Buns

Lindsey McKeon

Born: March 11, 1982
Summit, New Jersey
Skin-O-Meter: Brief Nudity

There's nothing like a naïve, brown-eyed, blonde nymph whose full lips are parted in an intake of vulnerability to arouse the instincts to cuddle and protect. Even when luscious young angel-faced Lindsey McKeon is playing a conniving kitten vixen attempting to pussywhip her smitten boyfriend into committing a cold-blooded murder on her behalf, as is her character's wont in *Class Warfare* (2001), still the impulse is to warm up a glass of milk, tuck her into a soft quilt in front of a smoldering fireplace, and cuddle until dawn, shooing the demons away and cradling her head in your strong, protective arms. And then she pops out of her bikini in *Shredder* (2002), and a whole new set of urges arise.

SKIN-fining Moment:

Shredder (0:53) Lindsey loses her leopard print bra while sucking face with her fella. Lots of side-breast and a shreddingly quick hint of right nip.

See Her Naked In:

Shredder (2002) RB

Zoe McLellan

Born: November 6, 1974
La Jolla, California
Skin-O-Meter: Brief Nudity

Captain's log: subject: Zoe McLellan, not merely the angelic ingénue from the penultimate panoply of hobgoblinry *Dungeons & Dragons* (2000), but also a considerable heavenly body in one of our favorite chapters of space travel's supreme ongoing sagas. Dear Lieutenant Ohura: I'm sorry, but after years of pursuing your haughty space-suited posterior, I'm jumping star ship for ampler astral pastures, i.e. *Star Trek Voyager's* finest guest nova. This busty, brown-eyed beauty is the extreme egghead's wet dream, though Zoe is not just for the geek elite. It doesn't

matter if you're into D&D, science fiction, or just a fan of the TV-lite-style variants of hard-boiled noir/detective fare, Zoe has covered all the bases (yes, Mr. Skin knows you want to round hers). For example, in addition to several *Star Trek Voyager* episodes, consider Zoe's scientifically proven appeal for her guest spots on the TV series *Sliders*, plus appearances on *The Invisible Man*, *Silk Stalkings*, *Diagnosis Murder*, and recurring roles on *JAG*. For those who would rather not think of Zoe as *the* revenge of the nerds, check out the Z-woman in supporting roles in *Inventing the Abbotts* (1997), *Stranger in My House* (1999), and opposite Harvey Keitel in *Imaginary Crimes* (1994).

SKIN-fining Moment:

Stranger in My House Zoe hops up out of the bath and her sudsy lovelies swing breastastically into view.

See Her Naked In:

Stranger in My House (1999) Breasts

Barbara McNair

Born: March 4, 1934
Racine, Wisconsin
Skin-O-Meter: Brief Nudity

Singin', dancin', wise-crackin' Barbara McNair was a whirlwind wunderkind of stage, screen, recording studio, and nightclub revue, with classy, brassy good looks and talent to spare. Musically inclined from an early age, Barbara studied voice at the American Conservatory of Music in Chicago and graduated almost directly to heady highs of performing at the Persian Room in New York's Plaza Hotel and in L.A.'s Coconut Grove. With her sleek moves and svelte looks, McNair's natural segue was into the arenas of movie and TV, giving depth and color to such small-

screen fare as *The Redd Foxx Show* and *Mission Impossible*. Barbara's big-screen credits include *Stilleto* (1969), *Venus in Furs* (1969), and *They Call Me Mr. Tibbs* (1970). Perhaps her greatest triumph, a monumental achievement for a black woman of her day, was to be host of her own musical variety series, *The Barbara McNair Show*.

SKIN-fining Moment:

If He Hollers, Let Him Go! (0:39) Babs bares boobs and buns while easing into the sack with her loverman. She should have turned on the lights!

See Her Naked In:

If He Hollers, Let Him Go! (1968) Breasts, Buns

Kate McNeil

Born: 1959
Philadelphia, Pennsylvania
Skin-O-Meter: Brief Nudity

The blush of an Irish rose spreads upon the cheeks of fair-haired lady lovely Kate McNeil, a fetching crimson flush that has been her go-to stalwart since her big-screen debut in *Beach House* (1979) and had still not deserted the comely lassie in *Escape Clause* (1996). In the years between that pair of glowing career highlights, Kate's budding blush has reflected red and impassioned, rising as regular as the morning sun across TV horizons that include *As the World Turns*, *WIOU*, and *Bodies of Evidence*. The first evidence of Kate's pink-nippled body was uncovered in *Monkey Shines* (1988), and shine is what those monkeys do.

SKIN-fining Moment:

Escape Clause (0:20) Kate canoodles with Andrew McCarthy, loses her white bra, and locates her pink nipples for us to see.

See Her Naked In:

Escape Clause (1996) Breasts
Monkey Shines (1988) RB

Kristy McNichol

Born: September 11, 1962
Los Angeles, California
Skin-O-Meter: Great Nudity

It's always fulfilling to watch little darlings bud into full-grown tittie terrors, especially when the progression from tiny top to popping tart is accompanied by rampant rumors of incipient lesbianism, as was the case with child actress turned adult temptress Kristy McNichol. Kristy became a prospect to watch in *Little Darlings* (1980). She played a fifteen-year-old chicklet with a chip on her shoulder who's engaged in a contest with Tatum O'Neal to see which virgin can split her cherry first. Neither sprite won, but viewers who kept track of McNichol were rewarded doubly by the bubbly two boobs of Kristy in *Two Moon Junction* (1988) and a flying glimpse of nip behind a fleeting sheet in *Dream Lover* (1986).

SKIN-fining Moment:

Two Moon Junction (0:42) Kristy bares her "little darlings" in an open shirt while she talks with Sherilyn Fenn, then she takes it off for an unobscured view.

See Her Naked In:

Two Moon Junction (1988) Breasts
Dream Lover (1986) RB
Just the Way You Are (1984) LB

Jenny McShane

Minnesota
Skin-O-Meter: Great Nudity

Juicy-jugged Jenny McShane first romped about in tit-popping tops alongside Latin lover Lorenzo Lamas in *The Rage* (1997). Anyone who's seen this beautifully boobied blonde in small but hugely tit-tilating parts in *Wayne's World 2* (1993), *Never Say Die* (1995), and *Cyborg Cop III* (1995) can attest to the raging hormones that follow her

every move. You'll want to take a bite of this delicious dish watching her skinful turns in *Shark Attack* (1999), *Stag* (1997), and *Monsoon* (2001). Monsooner or later, the downpour of testosterone inspired by this tasty tempest is going to catch Hollywood by storm.

SKIN-fining Moment:

Stag (0:14) Jen's the entertainment at a bachelor party, so out come her pups and thong-clad posterior.

See Her Naked In:

Shark Attack 3: Megalodon (2002) Breasts
Monsoon (1999) Breasts, Buns
Stag (1997) Breasts, Thong

Janet McTeer

Born: May 8, 1961
Newcastle, England
Skin-O-Meter: Brief Nudity

Englishwoman Janet McTeer is another fish in the seemingly endless stream of talented actresses from across the pond who have found recent critical success in Hollywood. She made her feature debut with a very small role in the Michael Caine/Sigourney Weaver flick *Half Moon Street* (1986). For the past fifteen years she has mostly been seen on the stages of London's West End and in her 1997 Tony award-winning role on Broadway in *A Doll's House*. Throughout this doll's career she has been applauded for her chameleon-like ability to become almost any role she is offered. Her lanky six-foot frame, flowing locks, and penetrating blue eyes have drawn comparisons to Meryl Streep, whom Janet herself calls her inspiration. She earned a Best Actress nomination for her role in *Tumbleweeds* (1999), in which she went on a cross-country trip with her daughter. The Oscar nominee has appeared nude twice, each deserving a booby prize. She

showed her crumpets in the BBC presentation *Portrait of a Marriage* (1992) and also in *Dead Romantic* (1992). Dammit, Janet, you're one live wire!

SKIN-fining Moment:

Portrait of a Marriage (2:28) Left McTeat and McTail as Ms. McTeer gets out of bed. Then some more when she's putting on a robe.

See Her Naked In:

Dead Romantic (1992) Breasts, Buns
Portrait of a Marriage (1990) Breasts, Buns

Heather Medway

Skin-O-Meter: Brief Nudity

It's hard to compete with a Dodge Viper for va-voom factor, but the high headlights, soft shocks, and curve-hugging chassis of souped-up brunette sports model Heather Medway leave the car in a cloud of burning rubber. As Detective Cameron Westlake, hot-wired Heather was one of two people allowed to drive the crime-solving armored vehicle on the network cop drama *Viper*. She's the only one of those two who also convincingly portrayed a highly paid fashion icon on *Models Inc.* Perhaps Heather's authenticity as a runway mannequin derived from her days as a New York model; or the reality of her artful depiction might have sprung from her stint on *Star Search* as a spokesmodel. Either way, that Dodge Viper had one lucky car seat.

SKIN-fining Moment:

The Fear (0:30) After some shadowy snuggling with her man in the sack, Heather gets startled by a mannequin-looking thing outside their bedroom and her right bobbler pops into view. It's super-fast, but this is why nature gave us the power to freeze-frame.

See Her Naked In:

The Fear (1995) RB

Mariangela Melato

Born: September 18, 1941
Milan, Italy
Skin-O-Meter: Great Nudity

Nobody's saying that Madonna isn't sexy, but she had a big bikini top to fill in her recent remake of *Swept Away* (2002). Specifically, she had to match Mariangela Melato's perfect presence in the original *Swept Away* (1974)—including a beach sex scene that's a legend in European cinema. Of course, Mariangela went on to even greater glories, with guys buffing their boners to her sizzling topless woman-on-top antic in *Attenti al Buffone* (1976). Her films became a little less classic in the '80s, but Mariangela never quit being an icon of Italian sexuality—as seen by her orgasmic emoting in *Notte d'estate con Profilo Greco, Occhi a Mandorla e Odore di Basilico* (1987).

SKIN-fining Moment:

Swept Away (1:10) Bare tits as a rather enthusiastic Giancarlo Giannini rips off Mary's top and ravages her on the beach.

See Her Naked In:

Summer Night (1987) Breasts, Buns
Dimenticare Venezia (1979) Breasts
Attenti al Buffone (1976) Breasts
Nada (1974) Breasts
Swept Away (1974) Breasts

Wendel Meldrum

Born: April 15, 1958
Rome, Italy
Skin-O-Meter: Great Nudity

Born in Italy, a country that's shaped like a boot or a twisted hard-on, depending on your perspective, lovely Wendel Meldrum left her homeland for fame and fortune in the U.S. Unlike most aspiring actresses, she actually achieved that goal, landing a two-year stint on *Knots Landing* playing P.K. Kelly. Unfortunately, Wendel's silver-screen debut wasn't as successful. She appeared opposite another soap star, Patrick Duffy, in *Vamping* (1984). The experience must have left a bad taste in her mouth, because Wendel stayed off the marquee for some time and strutted her talents in such made-for-TV fare as *Breakfast with Les and Bess* (1985), *Stark* (1985), and *Dallas: The Early Years* (1986). She also showed up on *The Pursuit of Happiness*, *The Wonder Years*, and as the "low-talker" on *Seinfeld*. Thankfully, Wendel returned to the warm glow of the projector's lights with a small role as Pretty Girl with Dog in the bow-wow comedy *K-9* (1989). It was less than notable, albeit well-described. Never one to give up that easily, the intrepid Wendel took another try at the big time and hit with a supporting role as one of the folks who got to hang out with Rip Torn's Walt Whitman in *Beautiful Dreamers* (1990). Not only did the film feature her most substantial role to date, it also presented her heavy breasts joined by a hairy bush in a skinny-dipping scene that would make even the queer poet get up to bat for the other team. It's her only skinage caught on film, but whoa Wendel, it's enough to keep a guy busy for at least five minutes or so.

SKIN-fining Moment:

Beautiful Dreamers (1:07) Wendel slowly unwraps her big, pale globes and thick-a-licious bush as she hops into the river with her hubby.

See Her Naked In:

Beautiful Dreamers (1990) FFN

Marisa Mell

Born: February 25, 1939
Vienna, Austria
Died: May 16, 1992
Skin-O-Meter: Great Nudity

With the influx of fetchingly foreign femmes from Latin and Asian locales into the global entertainment pool, it's easy to overlook the contributions of European womanhood to the cause of exotic sensual mesmerization, unless of course you take even one quick glance at the full-lipped, razor-cheeked, tiger-eyed face of Viennese brunette Marisa Mell. Even before she takes off her clothes, this exquisite example of Austrian Alps and valleys exudes a palpable hypnotic allure. Then she strips in such continental treats as *Una sull'altra* (1969), *Marta* (1971), and *L'Osceno Desiderio* (1977) to reveal a body of perfect comic-book proportions. But no comic book ever flashed the fur of *La Belva col Mitra* (1977).

SKIN-fining Moment:

La Belva col Mitra (0:38) A flash of full-frontal fun and a lot more of Marisa's Mell-ons during this bedroom romp.

See Her Naked In:

Corpi Nudi (1983) FFN
Sex on the Run (1979) LB
La Belva col Mitra (1977) FFN
L'Osceno Desiderio (1977) Breasts, Bush
Nel Buio del Terrore (1971) Breasts
Marta (1971) Breasts
Perversion Story (1969) Breasts

Tamara Mello

Born: February 22, 1970
Orange County, California
Skin-O-Meter: Great Nudity

Television is a great place to watch chicks, especially since saucy angel-cake starlets of Tamara Mello's caliber are paid to strut their prime, fine tails in the service of primetime coming-of-age tales. California native Tamara's exotic brunette sizzle put extra pizzle into the WB's *Popular*, a high-school jiggle festival in which Tamara played the class activist, with an ass that could convince Yogi the Bear to get active on a honey fast. The unfortunate limitations of television voyeurism are summed up as lack of snatch, a drawback Mello addresses, and undresses, in the feature film *Scorpion Spring* (1995). Look for Tamara lifting her skirt in the bus station, instantly transforming the location to a bush station. Tam also showed her mams (and some sweet side bunnage) in the flick *Infidelity* (1997), a.k.a. *Hard Fall*. Here's hoping that many more such treats will be forthcoming in this scrumptious crumpet's future.

SKIN-fining Moment:

Scorpion Spring (0:15) Tamara lifts her dress and serves up a sumptuous slice of her hot-hot hairpie.

See Her Naked In:

Infidelity/Hard Fall (1997) Breasts, Buns
Scorpion Spring (1995) Bush

Eva Mendes

**Born: March 5, 1978
Houston, Texas
Skin-O-Meter: Brief Nudity**

This is the tale of a sadly underutilized instrument of beauty finally being recognized and appreciated. After a slew of straight-to-video missteps (*Children of the Corn V: Fields of Terror* [1998]) and worse (*A Night at the Roxbury* [1998]), Miami Latin hottie Eva Mendes writhed and quaked into mass ass consciousness as the busty, underdressed girlfriend of Denzel Washington in *Training Day* (2001). Her quivering mounds of soft brown goodness must have caught the eye of more than the paying audience. Eva won the lead female part in *2 Fast 2 Furious* (2003), and there's no looking back, unless it's to admire her 2 Hard 2 High back shelf.

SKIN-fining Moment:

Training Day (1:37) See every inch of Eva when Ethan Hawke busts into her

bedroom. She hops up next to Denzel Washington and all three B's fly into view. Fast and a bit too fuzzy.

See Her Naked In:

Training Day (2001) FFN, Buns

Mary Mendum

Skin-O-Meter: Great Nudity

Decadence just isn't what it used to be. Nowadays, if an onscreen lesbian is willing to be filmed while undergoing erotic humiliation training that includes peeing on demand and aiming the flow upon the hand that commands her, you can bet she's a real-life, manly, truck-driving dyke on some late-night-cable documentary show. In the 1970s, such scenarios were presented with dignity, grace, and a high degree of feminine beauty that included every external inch of milky, doe-eyed blonde Mary Mendum. The proof of better times behind us is amply found in *The Image* (1975). Mendum's bush, buns, boobs? All copiously displayed in ultra-explicit, jaw-dropping frailty. Plus, a stream of pee is shown arcing from atop her pussy.

SKIN-fining Moment:

The Image (1:01) Marilyn Roberts commands the completely naked Mary to bend over for a nice from-the-rear gyno shot, then nearly drowns her, after which Mary pees on Marilyn's hand. This chick has some bladder capacity!

See Her Naked In:

The Image (1975) FFN, Buns

Xuxa Meneghel

**Born: March 27, 1963
Santa Rosa, RS, Brazil
Skin-O-Meter: Brief Nudity**

Like many South American sex symbols, Xuxa Meneghel—best

> With *Training Day*, it was presented to me as a topless scene. And when I sat down with [director] Antoine Fuqua and talked to him about why she was topless in this scene, he said, no one's going to go for full nudity. And I said, well, I will. So it was basically my idea."
>
> —EVA MENDES

known as the singular Xuxa (pronounced shoo-shah)—made a splash on a popular soap opera. Her role on the Brazilian hit *Elas por Elas* was soon matched by stellar recording success. Xuxa's subsequent sexy film career took a bizarre turn, however, when she began hosting a popular children's television show. Her outfits still remained incredibly sexy, most probably due to both her core audiences sharing a breast fixation. *Amor estranho Amor* (1982) is strictly for grownups, though, thanks to a sizzling strip scene that reveals more than just baxuxas.

SKIN-fining Moment:

Amor estranno Amor (0:23) Xuxa bares her bubas while wearing a furry white bikini bottom and getting fitted for a crazy white teddy-bear costume. A horny li'l bugger spies on the semi-surreal proceedings.

See Her Naked In:

Amor estranho Amor (1982) Breasts, Buns

Alex Meneses

Chicago, Illinois
Skin-O-Meter: Great Nudity

Alex Meneses is one hot Hispanic hoochie-coochie, and it shows in the roles that she has been offered. They almost always involve characters of Latin roots and sexy ways. She's actually a mix of Mexican and Ukrainian, which is a rather combustible combo. Her big debut was in the made-for-cable sci-fi comedy *Amanda and the Alien* (1995), in which she got rather naked. Most of the shots are just boobs, but there is a fleeting shot of her spicy ass if you care for a brief taste. She then went on to appear in *Kissing Miranda* (1995), in which she played the title role, who is (surprise!) Hispanic and (surprise again!) naked. After that, Alex

portrayed the small-time hood Cleopatra in the crime drama *The Immortals* (1995). Then, Alex was fortunate enough to land another saucy Spanish role on the hit series *Dr. Quinn, Medicine Woman*, where she stayed put for two seasons. Alex hasn't given up her love of skin. In *Auto Focus* (2002), she played an exotic dancer who showed *Hogan's Heroes* actor Bob Crane the path to depravity with a nipple slip along the way. Also check out the series *Hot Line* for her role in the episode titled "Payback," in which she shed her inhibitions, as well as her clothes, for a few lust-worthy scenes. Payback is a bitch!

SKIN-fining Moment:

Amanda and the Alien (0:24) Nice look at Allie's gorgeous bongos and buxom behind as she's getting into the shower.

See Her Naked In:

Auto Focus (2002) LB
Amanda and the Alien (1995) Breasts, Buns
Kissing Miranda (1994) LB

TeleVisions:

Hotline Breasts, Bush, Buns

Idina Menzel

Born: May 30, 1971
Long Island, New York
Skin-O-Meter: Brief Nudity

If all the world is a stage, then singing, dancing star of stage and screen Idina Menzel can't help but win rave reviews when she struts down to the corner deli to pick up lox and bagels. Menzel took the world by storm as a wailing, squealing, gyrating, breast- and bun-flexing, Tony-nominated dervish in the long-running Broadway smash musical *Rent*. The built, quasi-ethnic brunette spun off from the *Rent* tempest and landed a

role in *Just a Kiss* (2002). Idina's boobs flailed like battling storm fronts as she grinded like an off-white tornado upon the pelvis of a dude. Prepare to be drenched by a sudden downpour.

SKIN-fining Moment:

Just a Kiss (0:04) Idina shows off her rack several times while she viciously rides a scared-looking Ron Eldard in this rather psychedelic sex scene.

See Her Naked In:

Just a Kiss (2002) Breasts

Heather Menzies

Born: December 3, 1949
Toronto, Ontario, Canada
Skin-O-Meter: Brief Nudity

A sandy-haired Canadian with the tawny complexion of a Malibu beach girl and the svelte athleticism of a supermodel flexing her lithe leanness for a *Nike* ad, '70s siren Heather Menzies was perfect as the running buddy of Gregory Harrison on *Logan's Run*, a network continuation of the successful sci-fi flick of the same name, in which citizens of the future are compelled by law to die before they got old. The only way to survive the cutoff date (age thirty) was to hit the road and hightail it for "Sanctuary." Heather, with her chirpy grin, feathered shag, and taut, trim, toned tush, made fleeing look fun. The show ran for only a year, but Heather's cult following grew stronger and wider with every decade that has passed.

SKIN-fining Moment:

SSSSSSS (0:44) Heather's hills are alive, but we can't quite see them during a distant shot as she charges into the water for some skinny-dip time with Dirk Benedict.

See Her Naked In:

SSSSSSS (1973) Buns

Michèle Mercier

Born: January 1, 1939
Nice, France
Skin-O-Meter: Great Nudity

She began her film career in 1957, but Michèle Mercier didn't become an international favorite until *Shoot the Piano Player* (1960)—a classic François Truffaut film that would be memorable even without Michèle being resplendent in her raw roundness. Her topless scene was pretty daring for the time, but Michèle was just getting warmed up, as seen when her hot body wowed French audiences in Technicolor in *Angélique, Marquise des Anges* (1964). This was the first of several films based on the popular book series about a noblewoman in the court of Louis XIV. Michèle's melons really worked the period costumes, too—and she still managed to get exceptionally naked by 1964 standards. (Keep in mind that the *Angélique* books were generally considered fun for the whole family.) Michèle remains associated with the Angélique character, but we also find her unforgettable in *Lady Hamilton—Zwischen Schmach und Liebe* (1968), in which she reclined to show off an amazing naked bod. Michèle now only makes the occasional film appearance, but she's seen aging to great effect in *La Rumbera* (1998).

SKIN-fining Moment:

Shoot the Piano Player (0:21)
Beautifully bouncing bosoms as a topless Michele relaxes in bed with her man.

See Her Naked In:

Lady Hamilton—Zwischen Schmach und Liebe (1968) Breasts, Buns
Shoot the Piano Player (1960) Breasts

Michèle Mercure

Canada
Skin-O-Meter: Great Nudity

All the gorgeous hippies weren't in the United States, you know. Michèle Mercure is a perfect example of the Canadian flower children who helped forge the sexual revolution up North. Michèle's particularly stunning in *Loving and Laughing* (1971), where she's all sunny innocence as a naked gal frolicking on the beach—and also happy to share her shower stall with a girlfriend. It's a much different Michèle than we see in *East End Hustle* (1976), where she had a hardened look that made her topless tough-girl pose seem even sexier. Hey, it was a long way from the '60s by then. Michèle worked steadily, though, until a turn as a lovely secretary in *Au Pays de Zom* (1983). Then she went the way of the Summer of Love.

SKIN-fining Moment:

Loving and Laughing (1:18) Some mercurial full-frontal exhibitionism as Michèle runs out of the water to her towel with a naked friend, then a decent butt-shot as they writhe on the ground. Nice tan lines!

See Her Naked In:

East End Hustle (1976) Breasts, Bush
Loving and Laughing (1971) FFN, Buns

Roxane Mesquida

Born: October 1, 1981
Marseille, France
Skin-O-Meter: Great Nudity

Roxane Mesquida hails from the baguette-raising, beret-twirling land of France, a country that likes its women hot and undressed onscreen as much as possible. She started her career innocently enough in *Marie Baie des Anges* (1997) and quickly lost that innocence in *The School of Flesh* (1998). Although she remained clothed throughout, the film undoubtedly convinced her to take on a more daring part. That came

with the role as the elder sister at the center of a summertime love affair in Catherine Breillat's controversial *À ma Soeur!* (2001), or *Fat Girl*. But that's fat as in PHAT: Pretty Hot And Tempting. Although the film lacked the "punch," so to speak, of her more controversial picture *Romance* (1999), it still managed to put all of Roxane's goody-goods on full display and featured some fairly explicit sex. No, there wasn't any penetration shown, but the mood was right. In any respect, the part led to another Breillat film for the sultry young actress, *Sex Is Comedy* (2002). While it didn't make us want to slap our funny bone, we did slap another bone.

SKIN-fining Moment:

À ma Soeur! (0:56) Roxanne turns on her red light and shows us all of it in this sultry sex scene.

See Her Naked In:

Sex Is Comedy (2002) FFN
Very Opposite Sexes (2002) Breasts
Les Paradis de Laura (2002) FFN, Buns
À ma Soeur! (2001) FFN
The School of Flesh (1998) Breasts

Debra Messing

Born: August 15, 1968
Brooklyn, New York
Skin-O-Meter: Brief Nudity

Male homosexuality is one of the most baffling conditions known to heterosexual man. How, for instance, can a testicle-bearing human stand in the vicinity of auburn-tressed, waifish pixie face Debra Messing, less than an arm's length away from her compact and impactful torso, and even dare to pretend not to pop a boner? Such is the incomprehensible premise of *Will & Grace*, the NBC staple of a guy and a gal who can sleep under the same roof without the guy making any attempt to slip into bed with the gal. But improbability never rests in the roles of Messing. Doll-like and delightful, Debra donned an air of New Testament debauchery and exposed her entire naked form in profile as infamous harlot Mary Magdalene, whose life was saved—although her hole went unserved—by the Prince of Peace in *Jesus* (1999). Again, who can believe such a premise? Honestly, could Christ have died a virgin with a temptress such as the memorable Messing willing and open for His taking?

SKIN-fining Moment:

Jesus (0:06) Quick side shot of Debra's rump when she squats to put on a robe. Sadly it's all seen through a curtain, so there's not much to see.

See Her Naked In:

Jesus (1999) Buns

LoriDawn Messuri

Portland, Oregon
Skin-O-Meter: Great Nudity

Redhead LoriDawn Messuri may not have been able to decide on a first name, but she has no hesitation about shedding her threads onscreen. Her big-screen debut was in *Malibu Nights* (1997), in which she had the female lead, although it sadly didn't garner enough attention (or skin time) for this very comely young lass. She also appeared in *Madam Savant* (1997), but it was *I'm Watching You* (1997) that finally made audiences take notice. It marked her first nude scenes, and what nude scenes they were. Not only did she have a delightfully luscious lesbian tryst, she also went full frontal to reveal her fluffy blonde bush in a steamy masturbatory sequence—possibly one of the best ever in a mainstream movie. She then went on to appear in *Word of Mouth* (1999), *The Seventh Sense* (1999)—

"I see naked boobies"—and *Insatiable Wives* (2000), with a title more scandalous than the film itself. She starred in the big-snake horror flick *Python* (2000), where LoriDawn got to play dirty with one of her co-star's snakes. Can't wait to see what LoriDawn slithers into next.

SKIN-fining Moment:

Word of Mouth (0:14) LoriDawn proves she's a natural redhead while her man mouths her from head to hooters to hairpie to heinie.

See Her Naked In:

Fatal Blade (2000) Breasts
Python (2000) Breasts
Word of Mouth (1999) FFN, Buns
The Big Hustle (1999) FFN, Buns
Intimate Nights (1998) Breasts, Buns
I'm Watching You (1997) FFN, Buns

TeleVisions:

Passion Cove FFN, Buns

Bess Meyer

Evanston, Illinois
Skin-O-Meter: Brief Nudity

The 1980s ended on a high note for grinning imp Bess Meyer, a stalwart of silver and small screen who could be depended on for a knowing smirk, a cocked hip, and a wisecrack. Take two of Bess's feature credits and feel free to jump to conclusions: *In the Mood* (1987) leads to *She's Out of Control* (1989), and who would not want to take that leap along with the pert and perky punkette? Bess toned down her gritty, witty game to go doper slow as Female Stoner in the Winona Ryder breakthrough *Heathers* (1989). Few *Heathers* viewers stopped to realize that Meyer's own breakout had come with a slip of unfettered skin in *One More Saturday Night* (1986). This story of dating woes in a small

Minnesota town relied on a bit of Bess to dispel the chill.

SKIN-fining Moment:

One More Saturday Night (1:02) Bess lays topless in bed next to Tom Davis. It's a trade-up from Al Franken. For both of them.

See Her Naked In:

H.P. Lovecraft's Necronomicon, Book of the Dead (1994) Body Double—Breasts
One More Saturday Night (1986) LB

Dina Meyer

Born: December 22, 1968
Queens, New York
Skin-O-Meter: Great Nudity

Dina Meyer, a ravishing auburn-haired beauty, first gained attention playing the role of a professor's wife who fell in love with Jason Priestley on Fox's *Beverly Hills, 90210*. From there, she moved into films and was most memorable in *Starship Troopers* (1997) as a simultaneously sexy and tough military officer who happened to shower topless with the troops. What a way to keep morale (and other things) up. Dina was born in Queens, New York, and began acting as a child in local commercials. Her first big break came when actor/director Forest Whitaker cast her in his HBO film *Strapped* (1993), and she continued to wow in *Star Trek: Nemesis* (2002). Dina is a workout freak who takes very good care of her body. Any doubts? Check out her naked buns in *Poodle Springs* (1998), the sight of which could make even a blind man testify that she is one hot piece of ass. This Meyer sure pleases our wiener.

SKIN-fining Moment:

Starship Troopers (1:21) Meyer makes with the mammaries as she prepares to take a ride on the Casper Van Dien Machine.

See Her Naked In:

Eye See You (2002) Buns
Poodle Springs (1998) Buns
Starship Troopers (1997) Breasts

Michelle Meyrink

Born: September 1, 1962
Vancouver, BC, Canada
Skin-O-Meter: Brief Nudity

Michelle Meyrink is best known for '80s-era comedies, including *Revenge of the Nerds* (1984), *Joy of Sex* (1984), and *Real Genius* (1985). It doesn't take a real genius to tell that sexy Michelle is no nerd. Although her career came to an end long ago, following her role in *Permanent Record* (1988), Mr. Skin enjoys dusting off her earliest performance opposite Nicolas Cage and Deborah Foreman in the hilarious fish-out-of-water comedy *Valley Girl* (1983). Naturally, one of my favorite scenes is the "Gratuitous Underwear Dancing" sequence, in which all of the females in the cast join up for some pantie-clad partying. But even that pales in comparison to Michelle's shower scene. She's completely nude, albeit behind a translucent screen, so despite the distortion there's plenty of nipple and muff to be seen—Holy Belly Beard, Batman!

SKIN-fining Moment:

Valley Girl (0:59) Milk-bombs, muffshish and bum-cakes, teasingly seen through a frosted-glass shower door.

See Her Naked In:

Valley Girl (1983) FFN

Julie Michaels

California
Skin-O-Meter: Great Nudity

Danger is Julie Michaels's middle name. This athletically alluring angel of death-defying feats has literally saved the asses of lookers like Pamela Anderson and Jaime Pressly, working it as an action stunt double in flicks such as *Barb Wire* (1996) and *Poor White Trash* (2000). "Surviving is the key," Julie says of her risky endeavors, "not only in acting, but in life." Behind the scenes, Julie's muscular meat seat has miraculously survived. In front of the camera, this California cutie is equally D-lightful. With her innocent face, fluffy blonde hair, and curvy cupfuls, Jules is easily as fetching as the foxes she fights for. Her skinful debut in *Road House* (1989) brought her brick-house figure into focus as she flaunted her taut and tan tittles in a little dirty dancing with Patrick Swayze. Sawdust and lust! Ohh-wee. Combining her talent for showing ass and kicking it, Julie bared boobage, and bush battling FBI agents in *Point Break* (1991). Freakin' *Boobiliciously Intense*, man! With all of Ms. Michaels's spectacular acts, as both featured player and bad-guy slayer, it's hard to tell which of her talents are more skincredible.

SKIN-fining Moment:

Road House (1:19) Julie bares her happy ho-ho's while doing a little dance on stage.

See Her Naked In:

Jason Goes to Hell: The Final Friday (1993) Breasts, Buns
Witchboard 2 (1993) Breasts
Doctor Mordrid (1992) Breasts, Buns
Point Break (1991) FFN
Road House (1989) Breasts

Nicki Micheaux

Detroit, Michigan
Skin-O-Meter: Brief Nudity

Nicki Micheaux was an army brat and she grew up to be Major Hottie. But it wasn't until she marched onto the small screen that civilians got to admire her—and viewers love a girl *not* in uniform. She first made men salute (in their pants) when she got drafted onto the boob tube—and that's cable, where boobs actually can appear on the tube. Yet her exposure on HBO's *Six Feet Under* and even a sexy turn as the seductress Lila on Showtime's *Soul Food* didn't expose her black beauties. Just when it looked like her skin was AWOL, Nicki got cast on the F/X series *The Shield*. In one episode she lost her fatigues and streaked through the precinct house, which had all the officers reaching for their love guns. Things are looking up for one armed soldiers in TV land, as Nicki is set to play Velvet on the series *The Ranch*, an "erotic comedy" about the goings-on inside a Nevada brothel. Hopefully, the fur will fly in that cathouse.

SKIN-fining Moment:

The Shield "Streaks and Tips" (2004) Nicki's left-breast and bare BOO-ya bounce beautifully as she streaks through a police station while the cops cheer. You'll join them—one-handed!

See Her Naked In:

The Ranch (2004) Breasts, Thong

TeleVisions:

The Shield LB, Buns

Ann Michelle

Born: August 11, 1952
Chigwell, Essex, England
Skin-O-Meter: Great Nudity

British-born Ann Michelle was a staple of UK horror and thriller flicks in the '70s. The buxom 36-26-36 beauty debuted in the thriller *Psychomania* (1971), a trying tale of a motorcycle gang called "The Living Dead," where to join the club you had to kill yourself. She next appeared in *Virgin Witch* (1972), which may be about women who refused to wear clothes, since that just about sums up the entire movie. Watch it for some great shots of Ann, who appears in all her full-frontal glory, as well as her sister Vicki Michelle, who appears in the shadow of her sister's rampant clothing-optional turn. Although Ann appeared in the skin classic *Young Lady Chatterley* (1977), she remained clothed throughout. If you want some more of this brazen British tart, check out *House of Whipcord* (1974) and *Mistress Pamela* (1974), both of which feature Ann in some manner of undress. After an equally fleshy turn in *The Haunted* (1979), Ann disappeared for a while, popping up once more in an episode of *Casualty* in 1986, only to disappear again forever. Ann's absence is a casualty we'll never recover from.

SKIN-fining Moment:

Virgin Witch (0:27) Ann poses full-frontal-tastically for a pervy photog outdoors, then shows us her seat when they commence to getting it on.

See Her Naked In:

The Haunted (1979) Breasts
French Quarter (1978) Breasts
House of Whipcord (1974) Breasts
Mistress Pamela (1974) Breasts
Virgin Witch (1971) FFN, Buns

Shelley Michelle

Born: April 3, 1966
Hollywood, California
Skin-O-Meter: Great Nudity

Backup singers often have larger plans for wider world domination, and the global aspirations of former Kid Creole supporting broad Shelley Michelle have in no small part been buoyed by her air-light, blonde mounds of uplifting roundness. The bodaciously stacked siren sings not a note in a body of film work that includes *Bikini Summer* (1991), *The Naked Truth* (1992), *Married People, Single Sex* (1993), *Midnight Blue* (1996), and *Rising Sun* (1993), in which she plays a naked sushi tray, but she projects a high, sweet tone that will be music to a skinthusiast's eyes.

SKIN-fining Moment:

Overexposed (0:54) Shelly wears a wig—and nothing else—as she gets into bed with a dude.

See Her Naked In:

.com for Murder (2001) Breasts
Midnight Blue (1996) LB, Buns
Lover's Concerto (1995) FFN
Tornado Run (1995) RB, Thong
Married People, Single Sex (1993) Breasts, Thong
Hexed (1993) Breasts, Buns
Rising Sun (1993) Breasts, Thong
Nails (1992) Breasts, Buns
The Naked Truth (1992) FFN, Buns
Bikini Summer (1991) Breasts, Buns
Overexposed (1990) LB, Bush, Buns

Vicki Michelle

Born: December 14, 1950
Chigwell Essex England, UK
Skin-O-Meter: Great Nudity

Vicki Michelle pretty much lived in the shadow of her sister Ann Michelle throughout her career, although she shined in her own way as an actress. Her debut was in a film that her sister undoubtedly got her picked up for, that is the deliciously tempting *Virgin Witch* (1971). She appeared completely naked, with a nice long look at her furry British bush, although the majority of the film's nudity came from her saucy sister. She followed up *Witch* with a turn in *Alfie Darling* (1975). Vicki took some more bit parts in the late '70s before landing a role on the TV series *'Allo 'Allo*. Vicki, unlike her sister, has stayed relatively active in her career as of late, appearing most recently in *The Colour of Funny* (1999). Color Vicki . . . hot!

SKIN-fining Moment:

Virgin Witch (31:00) Vicki lets us in on her bathtub time, boobs and buns included.

See Her Naked In:

Virgin Witch (1971) FFN, Buns

Mako Midori

Born: March 26, 1944
Taiwan
Skin-O-Meter: Great Nudity

Mako Midori is not to be confused with veteran Japanese actor Mako or veteran porno actress Midori. The Taiwanese actress got her start in Japanese film with a part in *Nihiki no Mesuinu* (1964). Her career in cinema remained prolific until the late '70s, although she is sporadically active to this day. Unfortunately, outside of Japanese arthouse cinema fans, Mako is fairly unknown here in America. Mr. Skin took notice of this exotic beauty, though, when she appeared in *Blind Beast* (1969). The movie is a bizarre S&M trip through the senses with Mako as a model kidnapped by a blind artist who takes her to his lair, which is more or less a giant ware-house filled with huge sculptures of naked women. (I don't know about art, but this I like!) To cut to the chase, Mako and the blind man spend most of the movie banging away in this raw space, which offers up plenty of nice looks at Mako's magnificent melons, although she stops just short of full-frontal exposure. It's pretty hot until the end, where she goes blind, he cuts off her arms and legs and then stabs himself. Talk about ruining the mood.

SKIN-fining Moment:

Blind Beast (0:00) Mako's mammos appear in a variety of bondage photos that open the movie.

See Her Naked In:

Blind Beast (1969) Breasts

Izabella Miko

Born: January 21, 1981
Lodz, Poland
Skin-O-Meter: Brief Nudity

With a slightly crazed smile, slightly dazed eyes, wholly hot body, and totally fresh face, Polish pixie Izabella Miko couldn't look anything other than multi orgasmic if she tried. Every picture the pale, blonde waif appears in should be titled *Woman on the Verge . . . of a Climax*. A back injury sustained soon after coming to the U.S. to study ballet made Izabella available to audition for a part in the under-revealing *Coyote Ugly* (2000). The fair immigrant lass won the part of Cammie, but the role was limited to a bit of camel-toe tease. In Miko's follow-up flick, *The Forsaken* (2001), her shirt was largely forsaken, which is good for the sake of admiring her snowy chest peaks, small, pink-tipped, soft, and lovely. No wonder she exists in a state of constant excitation.

SKIN-fining Moment:

The Forsaken (0:01) Skingoria! Izabella is blonde and hot and bloody all over as she scrubs off some pesky plasma in the shower. Great pale nips.

See Her Naked In:

The Forsaken (2001) Breasts

Alyssa Milano

Born: December 19, 1972
Brooklyn, New York
Skin-O-Meter: Hall of Fame

Alyssa Milano played Tony Danza's daughter on the TV series *Who's the Boss?*, teaching viewers the joys of watching a young girl develop, buy a bra to handle her blossoming charms, and then lose her virginity. When the show was canceled, Alyssa lost the bra, and her massive talent spilled over onto the big screen. In *Embrace of the Vampire* (1994), she embraced more than gothic occultism, but lesbianism and threesomes, too. For *Poison Ivy 2: Lily* (1995), Alyssa's bouncingly firm dynamic duo showed why two are better than one. Returning to the small screen didn't mean buttoning up her expressiveness. She went topless for *The Outer Limits* and sent audiences out of their minds. Bewitching with Shannen Doherty, Rose McGowan, and Holly Marie Combs on TV's *Charmed*, Alyssa definitely puts a spell on you.

SKIN-fining Moment:

Embrace of the Vampire (0:50) Alyssa shows "Hoots the Boss" as she poses topless for Charlotte Lewis's Polaroid just prior to their lesboid lip-lock.

See Her Naked In:

Below Utopia (1997) LB
Hugo Pool (1997) Breasts
Fear (1996) Thong
Poison Ivy 2: Lily (1995) Breasts, Buns
Deadly Sins (1995) RB
Embrace of the Vampire (1994) Breasts, Buns

TeleVisions:

Outer Limits Breasts

Aubrey Miles

Philippines
Skin-O-Meter: Great Nudity

Life is grittier and sex is steamier in the Philippines, facts borne out by the steamy, gritty sexual performances of Aubrey Miles, who, despite her Anglicized name, is a native-born Manila celebrity who has dominated the island nation's entertainment industry as a singer, actress, and TV host. It's impossible to imagine an American woman in a similar position, especially one blessed with the dreamy, pure Miles vision of fragility and innocence, relishing the roles that Aubrey so sexily animated in *Prosti* (2002) and *Xerex* (2003). In *Prosti*, Aubrey's brothel-dwelling character is first prodded and poked by a madame inspecting her fleshly goods and then leaves a string of customers and packed houses of rabid viewers drained and satisfied, finishing the film naked in the midst of multiple mirrors, which reflect her rack unto eternity.

MR. SKIN'S TOP TEN

Childhood TV Stars Who Got Naked
. . . Growing up in pubic

10. **Kristy McNichol**
    —(Buddy) *Family*

9. **Patty Duke**
    —(Patty/Cathy Lane) *The Patty Duke Show*

8. **Dana Plato**
    —(Kimberly Drummond) *Diff'rent Strokes*

7. **Mary Beth McDonough**
    —(Erin) *The Waltons*

6. **Melissa Gilbert**
    —(Laura Ingalls) *Little House on the Prairie*

5. **Lisa Loring**
    —(Wednesday) *The Addams Family*

4. **Maureen McCormick**
    —(Marcia) *The Brady Bunch*

3. **Danielle Brisebois**
    —(Stephanie) *All in the Family*

2. **Lisa Bonet**
    —(Denise Huxtable) *The Cosby Show*

1. **Alyssa Milano**
    —(Samantha) *Who's the Boss?*

SKIN-fining Moment:

Prosti (0:07) Aubrey's udders bounce in full view as she gets probed and examined by a whorehouse madam.

See Her Naked In:

Xerex (2003) Breasts
Prosti (2002) Breasts

Sarah Miles

Born: December 31, 1941
Ingatestone, Essex, England
Skin-O-Meter: Great Nudity

When a talented actress's artistic imperative intersects with her impulse to shed her clothing, the God of skintertainment smiles, such as He often has during the inspired nude performances of seriously stripping thespian Sarah Miles. Born at the outset of World War II, the amazing lady Miles matured into a look of distressed sensuality and almost painful erotic longing, a demeanor that suited her long-limbed, thin-hipped form and medium-sized chest risers. After establishing her credentials on the London stage, Sarah migrated to Hollywood productions in the very early 1960s, almost always attached to projects of advanced artistic merit, which meant that she could be expected to become unattached to her clothing. Her erectile nips and alfresco toplessness in *The Man Who Loved Cat Dancing* (1973) and *The Sailor Who Fell from Grace with the Sea* (1976) were considered daring for their time, but Sarah's greatest dare was yet to come. In *Steaming* (1985), well into her forties, Sarah exposed tons of bush, her ass crack, tits that were holding up remarkably well, and an arch of bare foot both high and mighty.

SKIN-fining Moment:

The Sailor Who Fell from Grace with the Sea (0:45) Bare-boobied Sarah's lap is as shaggy as Kris Kristofferson's kisser. You can compare as they get it on here.

See Her Naked In:

Steaming (1985) FFN, Buns
The Sailor Who Fell from Grace with the Sea (1976) FFN, Buns
The Man Who Loved Cat Dancing (1973) Breasts
Lady Caroline Lamb (1972) RB
Ryan's Daughter (1970) RB

Sylvia Miles

Born: September 9, 1932
New York, New York
Skin-O-Meter: Great Nudity

Fearless blonde actress Sylvia Miles's long and flashy career is synonymous with New York City. Her signature roles as hard-boiled carnal women have been in gritty carnal New Yawk stories such as *Murder, Inc.* (1960), *Midnight Cowboy* (1969), and Andy Warhol's *Heat* (1972). Miles can play a chippie with a chip on her shoulder better than any other Oscar-nominated broad around. And like a city where possibilities never sleep, when Sylvia drops her chip, her bra and panties might fall right along with it. Her totally nude zipless boff with Jon Voight in *Cowboy* made everyone come in a New York minute; it was the shortest performance ever nominated for an Academy Award.

SKIN-fining Moment:

Midnight Cowboy (0:20) A quick glimpse of Sylvia's salamanders, as well as a little bootay, as she rolls about in bed with Jon Voight.

See Her Naked In:

The Funhouse (1981) LB
The Sentinel (1977) Breasts, Buns
Heat (1972) Breasts
Midnight Cowboy (1969) Breasts, Buns

Penelope Milford

Born: 1948
St. Louis, Missouri
Skin-O-Meter: Great Nudity

Penelope Milford started acting in the B-movie mystery *Man on a Swing* (1974) opposite Joel Grey. But her next role was more nude-worthy. She portrayed one of the racy conquests of Rudolph Valentino in the taboo-busting *Valentino* (1977). Things really started percolating for the perky actress when she appeared in both *Endless Love* (1981) and the comedy *Take This Job and Shove It* (1981)—oh, to take Penelope and shove her with endless love.

SKIN-fining Moment:

Valentino (1:25) Penelops bares all three B's while banging Rudolph Nureyev in bed. It's a crazy, stylized, long scene. Don't let the face-paint scare you.

See Her Naked In:

Blood Link (1982) Breasts
Valentino (1977) FFN, Buns

Mirta Miller

Born: August 16, 1948
Buenos Aires, Argentina
Skin-O-Meter: Great Nudity

Luscious, sleek Mirta Miller may not have been born with an evil streak, but she surely knew how to play a depraved villainess, and she could also suffer the torments of the saints as a victim of nefarious evildoers both living and dead. Born in Buenos Aires, Argentina, the prodigious brunette was barely into her teens when she was cast as Carmencita in the film adaptation of brooding Frenchman Jean Paul Sartre's play *No Exit* (1963).

Alternately titled *Sinners Go to Hell*, the dire entertainment presaged the diabolical turn Mirta's career would be celebrated for today. Typical of the countless European horror flicks she sexed up is *Vengeance of the Zombies* (1972), in which, scantily clad and heaving of bosom, Mirta fell into the clutches of living-dead creeps who needed her voluptuous, narcotized body as the centerpiece for a vile pagan ritual. Watch at your own risk—risk of entrancement.

SKIN-fining Moment:

Gatti Rossi in un Labirinto di Vetro (0:21) Nice tan-lined ta-ta's as she smokes in bed and chats up a black chick.

See Her Naked In:

Yo Hice a Roque III (1980) Breasts
Suave, Cariño, muy Suave (1978) Breasts
Niñas . . . al Salón (1977) Breasts
La Oscura Historia de la Prima Montse (1977) Breasts, Buns
Alcalde por Elección (1976) Breasts, Buns
Gatti Rossi in un Labirinto di Vetro (1975) Breasts
Dr. Jekyll y el Hombre Lobo (1972) Breasts

Penelope Ann Miller

Born: January 13, 1964
Los Angeles, California
Skin-O-Meter: Great Nudity

There was a time in the early '90s when it appeared that Penelope Ann Miller was on the verge of superstardom. This L.A. native was the main female in a string of box-office hits, and her giggly intelligence was something that audiences seemed to be taking a liking to. In films such as *Kindergarten Cop* (1990) and *Other People's Money* (1991) she proved that smart and normal could be very sexy. She also played off her seductive, sexual side in a couple of gangster flicks: *The Freshman* (1990), where she embodied the tempting, underage daughter of godfather Marlon Brando, and *Carlito's Way* (1993), where she showed the world her marvelous mams go-go dancing in a tempting topless scene. The roles for this lanky redhead seem to have dried up in recent years, although she scored a surprise hit with the horror film *The Relic* (1997). Let's hope she keeps it up—and us while she's at it.

SKIN-fining Moment:

Carlito's Way (1:00) Penelope peels on a strip club stage, providing us with a primo look at her Penelo-c's.

See Her Naked In:

Carlito's Way (1993) Breasts

TeleVisions:

The Hitchhiker Breasts

Mary Millington

Born: November 30, 1945
Kenton, Middlesex, England, UK
Died: August 19, 1979
Skin-O-Meter: Great Nudity

What is it with fun-time party girls leaving this world too young? Take, for example, Great Britain's empire treasure Mary Millington. It seems so unfair that a statuesque, stacked, and simmering lady of Millington's stature would be unable to help herself. How is it possible that the bearer of those bountiful boobs and bobbing buns (first seen serving the needs of humanity in 8mm Brit loops with titles like *Miss Bohrloch* and *Erotic Inferno*) could not take cheer from the anatomy that granted cheer to so many others? Think of the multitudinous sorrows released at the viewing of happy, generous Millington in such sex farces as *I'm Not Feeling Myself Tonight* (1976) and *Keep It Up Downstairs* (1976). Mary's habitually dignified and inviting expression exhibited the regal self-possessed aplomb such as is expected in the royal box at Ascot. Hopefully she is reigning, with a harp and wings (and not much else to hide her heavenly form) in a better place.

SKIN-fining Moment:

Keep It Up Downstairs (0:58) *Millington monkeys around in a tree-house with an old geezer, showing off her perksters and ripe rear all the while.*

See Her Naked In:

The Playbirds (1978) FFN, Buns
Come Play with Me (1977) FFN, Buns
Keep It Up Downstairs (1976) Breasts
Numerous Adult Movies

Donna Mills

Born: December 11, 1942
Chicago, Illinois
Skin-O-Meter: Brief Nudity

Though she is blonde, blue-eyed, svelte, and possesses tightly compact chest nuggets, Donna Mills's body of work presents a cautionary tale of squandered possibilities. A 1960s pioneer of the dramatic TV series, Mills caught the spotlight with featured parts in *The Secret Storm* and *Love Is a Many Splendored Thing*. Though widely seen, these shows featured very few of the parts of Donna that were widely desired to be seen. The ambitious actress posed for a revealing *Playboy* spread, which indicated a willingness to play naked. Starring as Clint Eastwood's girlfriend in *Play Misty for Me* (1971), Donna took a topless dip in a pond, a scene idyllic and erotic, though shot from a great distance. There is no further filmed record of Donna's treasures; her producers and directors must be taken to task for this wasted resource.

SKIN-fining Moment:

Play Misty for Me (1:10) Ms. Mills shows a side view of her right hill while hugging Clint Eastwood under a waterfall. Bet that made his day.

See Her Naked In:

Play Misty for Me (1971) RB, Buns

Hayley Mills

Born: April 18, 1946
London, England, UK
Skin-O-Meter: Great Nudity

A little girl who grew up fast and must have caused her parents (the stiff-upper-lip Brit actor John Mills and playwright Mary Hayley Bell) no end of grief and heart attacks, impertinent imp Hayley Mills starred in six Walt Disney films over a five-year span, most memorably playing twins in *The Parent Trap* (1961). After turning eighteen and outgrowing her Disney contract, Hayley ran off with her luscious thick lips and wide-eyed insouciance and married Roy Boulting, her director on *The Family Way* (1966). Hayley was all of twenty; Boulting was a young-thinking fifty-two. Such an impetuous move should indicate a taste for skin daring, but Mills's bare dramatics are confined to a few moments of boobs and buttocks in *Deadly Strangers* (1974). Hayley's is a life of truth more titillating than the fictions in which she played.

SKIN-fining Moment:

The Family Way (0:49) Hayley stands in a tub wearing a towel that manages to expose her delectable post-Disney derriere three times.

See Her Naked In:

Deadly Strangers (1974) Breasts, Buns
The Family Way (1966) Buns

Juliet Mills

Born: November 21, 1941
London, England, UK
Skin-O-Meter: Great Nudity

Her godmother was Vivien Leigh, her godfather was Noel Coward, and she comes from one of England's most respected acting families—and yet Juliet Mills is best known for the goofy '70s sitcom *Nanny and the Professor* and the Italian horror hit *Beyond the Door* (1974). What went right? Juliet never set out to compete with teen-queen sister Hayley and forged her own happy path to stardom. Thankfully, this included *Avanti!* (1972), in which the former child actress showed off her maturity, along with her bountiful nannies and gorgeous ass. This Brit beauty (all five-feet-two-inches of her) has only gotten sexier in the ensuing decades. Juliet's still popular, too, currently bewitching soap fans as sexy sorceress Tabitha on the daytime series *Passions*.

SKIN-fining Moment:

Avanti! (1:24) Join Jack Lemmon as he enjoys Mills's milky moos on the beach while she waves to a bunch of clearly titillated sailors.

See Her Naked In:

Avanti! (1973) Breasts, Buns

Sofia Milos

Zurich, Switzerland
Skin-O-Meter: Never Nude

Versatility is money in the bank for an actress, and copper-complected Sofia Milos, with her thick mane of brunette ringlets, earth-goddess full figure, and striking, strong facial features, has a rich range of ethnicities at her disposal. Though born in the snowy-white heights of Zurich, Switzerland, softly zaftig Sofia descends from Greek and Italian parentage, which has allowed her to play Italian on HBO's monster hit *The Sopranos*, Hispanic on the TV cop drama *CSI: Miami*, eastern European on the goofy sitcom *Caroline in the City*, and just plain adorable on *The Secret Lives of Men*. Whatever her presumed race, religion, or origin,

Sofia always comes from the land of full and sexy chest pillows.

SKIN-fining Moment:

The Ladies' Man (0:11) As Ladies' Man Tim Meadows makes it with Miss Milos, we see her pastie-plastered ladies' mams.

Yvette Mimieux

Born: January 8, 1942
Hollywood, California
Skin-O-Meter: Brief Nudity

The magic of Yvette Mimieux's name evokes the exotic allure of far-off places, a rich, sensual resonance of old-world charm and wiles. Is she from the glittering lights of Paris? The mysterious alleyways of Marseilles? Hardly. She was a hometown Hollywood girl, discovered when a motion-picture press agent's helicopter made an emergency landing out in the scrubs where Yvette was horseback riding. The petite French/Spanish hybrid shot to fame and the national libido portraying the innocent, free-loving future girl Weena, who always looked one shimmy from falling out of her toga in *The Time Machine* (1960). Although Mimieux could always be counted on for an erotically charged screen presence, her only true exposure occured during an altercation with a horny guard in Roger Corman's overcooked, overlooked classic *Jackson County Jail* (1976), which, contrary to expectations, failed to provide the requisite shower scene.

SKIN-fining Moment:

Jackson County Jail (0:39) A guard attacks Yvette in her Jackson County jail cell, tearing her top and exposing her moo-moos.

See Her Naked In:

Jackson County Jail (1976) Breasts

MR. SKIN'S TOP TEN

Babes on the Toilet
. . . Poop tarts

10. Sandra Oh
    —*Prey* (1995) (0:12)

9. Elizabeth Berridge
   —*When the Party's Over* (1992) (0:03)

8. Barbara De Rossi
   —*La Cicala* (1980) (1:29)

7. Deborah Caprioglio
   —*Paprika* (1989) (0:11)

6. Paz Vega
   —*Sex and Lucia* (2001) (0:22)

5. Nadia Fares
   —*Elles n'oublient jamais* (1994) (0:17)

4. Portia de Rossi
   —*Women in Film* (2001) (0:27)

3. Deborah Falconer
   —*Mr. Bluesman* (1993) (1:11)

2. Charlotte Alexandra
   —*A Real Young Girl* (1976) (0:20)

1. Rachel Miner
   —*Bully* (2002) (0:18)

Rachel Miner

Born: July 19, 1980
Skin-O-Meter: Great Nudity

Rachel Miner is certainly no slouch when it comes to acting ability, playing the tot version of Mia Farrow's character in the Woody Allen feature *Alice* (1990) at age ten and followed it up with a five-season stint on the long-running hit soap opera *The Guiding Light*. From 1998 to 2000 Rachel was married to fellow child thespian Macauley Culkin, which may have helped her career, since she later took a skinful shot at the big screen in *Bully* (2001). In the controversial tale of teen murder, Rachel and Bijou Phillips seem to be competing to

see who can show off her naked glory the most. Bijou gave it a valiant effort, but Rachel's many full-frontal scenes, not the least of which takes place on a toilet, gave her the big win, one-free-hand down.

SKIN-fining Moment:

Bully (0:18) Nice side shot of Rachel's itty-bitties while she takes a leak followed by a fur-burger flash when she stands up. No shit!

See Her Naked In:

Bully (2001) FFN, Buns

TeleVisions:

NY-Lon Breasts, Buns

Liza Minnelli

Born: March 12, 1946
Los Angeles, California
Skin-O-Meter: Brief Nudity

Brunette firecracker Liza Minnelli has not always been the befuddled butt of a joke about gay marriage. With a crackerjack showbiz lineage that includes wizard of awes Judy Garland for a mother and revered Hollywood director Vincente Minnelli for a pa, tripping and traipsing Liza had no sooner toddled past the diaper pail than she was being groomed for stardom of stage and screen. The childhood years of dance training produced a trim and cuddly bundle of sensual energy. The typical Minnelli hard-boiled ingénue—as evidenced in *The Sterile Cuckoo* (1969) and *Tell Me That You Love Me, Junie Moon* (1970)—was a wisecracking cutie given to flamboyant and effervescent flaunting of her physical attributes. Liza's flaunting mostly stopped just short of nudity, such as the revealing anti-androgyny of her costuming in *Cabaret* (1972), but a moony peek of chair cheeks graced *Junie Moon*.

See Her Naked In:

Tell Me That You Love Me, Junie Moon (1970) Buns

Kylie Minogue

Born: May 28, 1968
Melbourne, Victoria, Australia
Skin-O-Meter: Brief Nudity

Though recognized worldwide as a pop-singing sensation who knows how to put a pair of metallic hot pants to best use, Australian wonder waif Kylie Minogue started her assault on show biz as a child actress. At the tender age of seven, Minogue had a pivotal role on *Neighbours*, one of the top TV soaps Down Under. The sweetly warbling nymph's on-camera experience certainly gave her an advantage when posing for promotional film clips, as any sharp-eyed viewer of MTV will recognize. For a fuller glimpse of the simmering Sheila's assets, track down *The Delinquents* (1989), a Romeo and Juliet fable set in 1950s Australia made interesting by fleeting perky peeks of Kylie.

SKIN-fining Moment:

The Delinquents Kylie quickly blasts the screen with a peek at her topless poptarts. It's fast, but I just can't get her out of my head, out of my head, out of my head . . .

See Her Naked In:

The Delinquents (1989) Breasts

Kristin Minter

Born: 1971
Miami, Florida
Skin-O-Meter: Great Nudity

A tan-complected Florida fox who flew to Europe for a modeling career after high school, Kristin Minter came back to America and landed an up-front, sassy spot as gum-popping Randy on the TV mega-hit *ER*. People wanted to see more of Kristin's teasing and seldom sexually appropriate receptionist Randy, and people got what they wanted when Minter quit the show to advance in a career as an often topless and occasionally bottomless specialist. Starting as far back as *Flashfire* (1993), Kristin has been unable to keep her perfectly circular rib ornaments under wraps; more recently she has failed to shield her booty and bush from prying eyes. Although the burger is mostly shadowed in *Tick Tock* (2000), its owner indulges in plenty of udder and utter nudity, including a wholly stripped, outdoor sprint.

SKIN-fining Moment:

Tick Tock (0:37) Bare breasts as she bludgeons a dude to death. Then we see her ass as she takes off, followed by brief full-frontal while she runs out of house, then more all-points-nudity as she crosses a lawn and hoses the blood off outside.

See Her Naked In:

Diamond Men (2001) Breasts, Thong
Tick Tock (2000) FFN, Buns
Savage (1995) Breasts, Buns
Flashfire (1993) Breasts, Thong

Miou-Miou

Born: February 22, 1950
Paris, France
Skin-O-Meter: Great Nudity

A face built upon delicate bone structure that is at once fragile and vulnerable to loves and lusts but never weak, expressive brown eyes like pools of physical and psychic emotions, lips quivering with the adrenaline of life, Miou-Miou is the quintessential French actress of the *nouvelle vague* film movement of the 1950s and 1960s, with one exception. Miou-Miou's groundbreaking, adventurous cinema career didn't get off the ground until the 1970s, which means that along with raw feeling and gritty, real sensuality, her performances were infused with generous helpings of meaningful nudity. Bask in the revelatory wonders of *Going Places* (1974), an unflinching exploration of the hippie generation's aftermath. In her role as a moll who services a gang of thugs, Miou-Miou doesn't flinch from baring her breasts, her buttocks, her bush, and her soul.

SKIN-fining Moment:

Going Places (0:46) This scene is sure to erect your Eiffel Tower! We get a long, lusty look at Miou-Miou's fluffy muffy, tiny teats, and ripe rump.

See Her Naked In:

Elles (1997) Breasts
La Lectrice (1989) Breasts, Bush
Dog Day (1984) Breasts
Josepha (1982) Breasts
La Derobade (1979) FFN
Jonah—Who Will be 25 in the Year 2000 (1976) Breasts
Marcia trionfale (1976) Breasts
La Grande trouille (1975) Breasts
Going Places (1974) FFN, Buns
Destroy Yourselves (1968) Breasts

Irene Miracle

Born: January 24, 1954
Stillwater, Oklahoma
Skin-O-Meter: Great Nudity

Irene Miracle is her real name, and that's the most normal thing about this talented actress's bizarre career. Born in Oklahoma, the globe-trotting beauty found herself providing sex appeal in the Italian thrillers *L' Ultimo Treno della Notte* (1975) and *La Portiera Nuda* (1976)—the latter of which included a miraculous lingering shower scene. Irene then made a quantum leap in quality in *Midnight Express* (1978), the hit film that also made Irene a Golden Globe winner for Best Motion Picture Acting Debut. Of course, *Midnight Express* was really the American debut of Irene's own golden globes, shown under glass in a fine fantasy sequence. Irene followed that with a lovely turn as a doomed lady in the horror import *Inferno* (1980) and then kept a low profile with TV appearances. Her career has since been a bizarre mix of low-budget schlock and fascinating indie films such as *The Last of Philip Banter* (1986). At least her more bizarre choices give us the occasional cheap thrill, such as a gratuitous bathtub scene that gets us watching in *Watchers II* (1990). Still, it's heartbreaking to see her lovely throat slit by a damn puppet in *Puppet Master* (1989).

SKIN-fining Moment:

Midnight Express (1:40) Irene puts her chest-miracles on the glass so Brad Davis can have a self-conjugal visit in prison. "Oh, Billy! . . ."

See Her Naked In:

Watchers II (1990) Breasts
In the Shadow of Kilimanjaro (1986) Breasts
Midnight Express (1978) Breasts
La Portiera nuda (1976) Breasts, Buns

Soledad Miranda

Born: July 9, 1943
Seville, Spain
Died: August 17, 1970
Skin-O-Meter: Great Nudity

Haunting beauty, an untimely death, and a legacy of sexy-spooky horror films have combined to create a massive cult following for the stunningly gorgeous and unfairly doomed Soledad Miranda. Born in Seville, Spain, in 1943 and tragically taken by a road accident in 1970, Soledad is the undisputed,

eternal Queen of European Vampire Flicks. Expert critics of the genre describe her in language such as "pale, mysterious, enigmatic, provocative, unknowable." She looked like a lucky cross between Ali McGraw and Salma Hayek, only more refined, and willing to provide prolonged access to her thatch, breasts, and ass crack. Any movie in which she appeared provides a valuable watching experience. Of particular skinterest are *Vampyros Lesbos* (1970) and *Eugénie DeSade* (1970). After her death, Soledad's spirit is said to have visited the dreams and possessed the actresses working with Jesus Franco, the Spanish director who discovered her and created her greatest works.

SKIN-fining Moment:

Eugénie De Sade (0:13) Sexy Señorita Soledad, pantiless, flops facedown on a bed and wiggles her bare booty tantalizingly.

See Her Naked In:

The Devil Came from Akasava (1971) Breasts, Bush, Buns
She Killed in Ecstasy (1970) FFN, Buns
Eugénie (1970) FFN, Buns
Vampyros lesbos (1970) FFN, Buns
Eugénie De Sade (1970) FFN, Buns
Nightmares Come at Night (1970) LB, Buns

> "I thought he'd pay me a compliment, but he didn't say a thing. He could at least have said I had nice boobs. But if you produce real bosoms, men get terrified."
>
> —HELEN MIRREN, ON TOM WILKINSON WATCHING HER FILM A NUDE SCENE IN *PRIME SUSPECT*

Helen Mirren

Born: July 26, 1945
Chiswick London, England, UK
Skin-O-Meter: Hall of Fame

Helen Mirren is the great dame of British stage and screen . . . plus, she's one royal babe. Yes, Helen is in the twilight of her years, but if all mature matrons looked this good, Mr. Skin would be cruising the old-age home for talent. She was once called "Shakespeare's Slut" because early in her career Helen happily accepted controversial roles that required her to bare her "tea and crumpets" to the world. In *Age of Consent* (1969) and *Savage Messiah* (1972) she displayed her royal jewels in all their full-frontal majesty. And she has not only exposed for the arthouse crowd, she showed all in *Caligula* (1979) and even flashed her giant jugs, albeit through a sheer top, in *Excalibur* (1981). Regardless of her age, Helen has one of the finest sets of natural funbags on the big screen, and with her reputation as a wild child, we can bet that we will see them again soon. In *Calendar Girls* (2003), a true story based on a bunch of crusty broads who stripped for skin photos to adorn a calendar, Helen proved you're never too old to get a rise.

SKIN-fining Moment:

Savage Messiah (1:14) A lithe, lovely and youthful Ms. Mirren parades through a mansion with her bountiful breasts and beautiful bush bared for a wonderfully long time.

See Her Naked In:

Calendar Girls (2003) Breasts
The Roman Spring of Mrs. Stone (2003) FFN
The Passion of Ayn Rand (1999) LB, Buns
Royal Deceit (1994) Breasts, Bush, Buns
Cause Célèbre (TV) (1991) Breasts, Buns
The Cook, the Thief, His Wife & Her Lover (1989) FFN, Buns
Pascali's Island (1988) LB
Cal (1984) RB, Bush, Buns
Hussy (1980) FFN, Buns
Caligula (1979) FFN
Savage Messiah (1972) FFN, Buns
Age of Consent (1969) Breasts, Bush, Buns

Elizabeth Mitchell

Born: March 27, 1970
Dallas, Texas
Skin-O-Meter: Great Nudity

There's nothing like a sexy, critically acclaimed movie to lift a pretty actress up from obscurity. You probably don't know Elizabeth Mitchell by name, but bet you'll remember her as Angelina Jolie's lesbian lover in HBO's model biopic *Gia* (1998). The sex scenes between the dark and brooding Angelina and the pale and sweet Elizabeth are by far some of the most erotic ever seen on celluloid. Elizabeth is a fantastic looking woman: Her tall, leggy frame and perfectly formed scoops of vanilla are topped off by one of the most angelic faces in Hollywood. She has mostly appeared on the boob tube, most recently with Rob Lowe on the series *The Lyon's Den*, and she's been onscreen in such features as *Nurse Betty* (2000) and *The Santa Clause 2* (2002). All Mr. Skin wants for Christmas is Elizabeth's two front boobs!

SKIN-fining Moment:

Gia (0:25) Elizabeth sheds her threads and inhibitions for some lesbolicious photographic fun with Angelina Jolie.

See Her Naked In:

Gia (1998) Breasts, Buns

Ella Mitchell

Skin-O-Meter: Brief Nudity

Ella Mitchell is a sex symbol for those who like their booty super-sized. Baby's got back—and front and side—and it's just dripping off her luscious mountain of a body like an avalanche of love. It's enough to make your volcano erupt, if you go that way. Ella first appeared in *Lord Shango* (1975) in a bit part as a singer—as if this mammoth mama could ever just be a bit player. After twenty-five years in relative obscurity, she reappeared as the impetus behind Martin Lawrence's transformation in *Big Momma's House* (2000). And lord, how she is one big momma. When she sits her naked buns on the toilet, your pipes will spew.

SKIN-fining Moment:

Big Momma's House (0:11) Brace yourselves for one massive ass-shot as Ella drops her threads before showering.

See Her Naked In:

Big Momma's House (2000) Buns

Radha Mitchell

Born: January 1, 1973
Melbourne, Australia
Skin-O-Meter: Brief Nudity

The *Alien* (1979) rip-off *Pitch Black* (2000) made Vin Diesel a star, but it might as well have left Radha Mitchell stranded on that damn desolate planet. This gorgeous Aussie blonde deserves a lot better, and not just because she looked so damn hot in that skimpy T-shirt while being stalked by monsters. Mitchell is also a fine actress, and we'd admire her work in the indie hit *High Art* (1998) even if it didn't include a sizzling lesbian love scene with Ally Sheedy. But it does, so that's another reason to ravage our rods over Radha. She's also brought her sexy presence to plenty of other projects—including *Phone Booth* (2002) and the indie thriller *Visitors* (2003)—so it won't be long before she finally lands on Planet Stardom.

SKIN-fining Moment:

High Art (1:10) Radha feeds her bare right nipple to hungry girl-lover Ally Sheedy.

See Her Naked In:

High Art (1998) RB

Rhona Mitra

Born: August 9, 1976
Paddington, London, England
Skin-O-Meter: Great Nudity

Before there was a blockbuster movie and its smash-hit sequel, there was a video game called *Tomb Raider*, one of the first to capitalize upon a sexy, curvy superheroine, namely Lara Croft. When the animated Lara blew up to be an international sales sensation, the obvious move for the interactive *Tomb Raider 2* was to replace the cartoon chick with a real, live, flesh-and-blood superheroine, or at least an actress who boasts the face and body of one, and that's where British brunette Rhona Mitra came in. Rhona is the stunning action figurine with the stunning figure in the original live-action game, and she donned the erotically charged Croft costume at trade shows and fan events. When was the last time Angelina Jolie was seen mingling with a mob of game boys?

SKIN-fining Moment:

Hollow Man (0:58) Rhona reflects over her rackage in front of a vanity mirror.

See Her Naked In:

The Life of David Gale (2003) Buns
Hollow Man (2000) Breasts
The Man Who Made Husbands Jealous (1997) Breasts

Shanna Moakler

Born: March 28, 1975
Providence, Rhode Island
Skin-O-Meter: Great Nudity

If a girl is pretty enough, she can do whatever she wants, and maybe it's her outrageous, beach-friendly, blonde good looks that empower model turned actress turned model Shanna Moakler to do things backwards from what most unfairly fair vixens would do. After gaining the Miss USA crown in 1995, the Providence, Rhode Island–stunner turned to the worlds of movies and TV for further veneration, making worship-worthy appearances in *Poison Ivy 3: The New Seduction* (1997), *The Wedding Singer* (1998), *Love Sucks* (1998), and *Love Stinks* (1999). She moved in as the live-in girlfriend of Golden Boy boxer Oscar de la Hoya and subsequently sued him for palimony. Only after amassing all these career highlights did Shanna strip and pose for the centerfold of the December 2001 issue of *Playboy*. With a rear bumper like Shanna's, it might make sense for her to move backwards, but it's all about what's up front in the 2004 indie comedy, *Seeing Other People*. At the 24-minute mark, Shanna busts out her meaty melons while sitting on a bed with funnyman Jay Mohr. And he *ain't* laughing!

SKIN-fining Moment:

Seeing Other People (0:24) Shanna sits on a bed and we see her chest-people.

See Her Naked In:

Seeing Other People (2004) Breasts
Poison Ivy 3: The New Seduction (1997) Thong
Numerous *Playboy* Videos

Katherine Moennig

Born: December 29, 1976
Philadelphia, Pennsylvania
Skin-O-Meter: Brief Nudity

When Daddy's a violin maker and Mama's a Broadway dancer, darling daughter is less likely to grow up to be an accountant than to blossom into an edgy, sexy actress who brings a sense of erotic propulsion to a gay female character on a groundbreaking Showtime series delving into the lesbian subculture, and that's the story of sharp-featured brunette Katherine Moennig. Having made her stage debut at the age of ten in a kiddie production of *Winnie the Pooh*, cool-hot Kate took her first takes in front of the network camera as Jake in *Young Americans*, and she tossed her boyish duds aside to flash her initial beaver, boob, and bun exposure as a skinny-dipping sprite on same-sex cable sensation *The L Word*.

SKIN-fining Moment:

The L Word "Pilot" (2004) Dark-haired (and darker-bushed) Katherine dives full-frontally nude into a backyard pool, then treats us to some underwater ass just before she dives all over a topless blonde, Wet! Wet! Wet!

TeleVisions:

The L Word FFN, Buns

Gretchen Mol

Born: November 8, 1972
Deep River, Connecticut
Skin-O-Meter: Great Nudity

Fetchin' Gretchen Mol worked as a hat-check girl at a restaurant where she was discovered by her agent-to-be, who got the five-foot-six-inch busty blonde a Coke commercial. It's the real thing! Gretchen uncorked on the big screen, where her naturally big and beautiful boobs were featured in *The Last Time I Committed Suicide* (1996), *Just Looking* (2000), and *Attraction* (2000). While she bubbles just below superstardom, usually playing the girlfriend eye candy in films like *Donnie Brasco* (1997) and *Rounders* (1998), Gretchen always makes Mr. Skin pop off. She's at her skinful best in *Forever Mine* (1999), where she teased in a low-cut bathing suit then delivered with three hot sex scenes. Perhaps this unabashed explosion of old-school eroticism is what led producers, in 2004, to cast Gretchen in a biopic dedicated to iconic vintage pinup queen Bettie Page. A beauty for all ages, Gretchen makes every man want to Mol her.

SKIN-fining Moment:

Forever Mine (0:17) Gretchen gives up her gargantuan globes during some hot-and-heavy sex with Joseph Fiennes, then offers up an encore flash when she lounges in bed.

See Her Naked In:

Attraction (2000) LB
Just Looking (2000) RB
Forever Mine (1999) Breasts
The Last Time I Committed Suicide (1996) Breasts

Ángela Molina

Born: October 5, 1955
Madrid, Spain
Skin-O-Meter: Hall of Fame

Spanish actress Ángela Molina is not very well known in the United States, but she has been steaming up the screen in her native land since the mid 1970s, having appeared in more than eighty films to date. She gained widespread attention for her role in the critically acclaimed joint French/Spanish effort *That Obscure Object of Desire* (1977). As is the case with most fawned-over foreign films, there's plenty of artistic nudity in this flick to satisfy even the most pretentious and discriminating tastes, including that of our heroine. In the flick *Gli Occhi, la Bocca* (1982), Ángela also showed everything below *Those Eyes, That Mouth*—her full-frontal scenes revealed an incredibly furry muff that is not to be missed! Ángela didn't make a blip on Hollywood's radar screen until appearing in the *Rocky*-esque boxing drama *Streets of Gold* (1986). Still a major star in Spain, she hasn't appeared in an American film since starring opposite Gérard Depardieu in Ridley Scott's *1492: Conquest of Paradise* (1992).

SKIN-fining Moment:

That Obscure Object of Desire (1:21) FFN as Angela struts about a strip club stage for a most appreciative audience of Japanese businessmen.

See Her Naked In:

Edipo Alcalde (1996) Breasts
Le Voleur d'enfants (1991) Breasts
The Things of Love (1989) Breasts
La Sposa era Bellissima (1986) Breasts, Buns
Lola (1985) RB
Demonios en el Jardin (1982)
The Eyes, the Mouth (1982) FFN
Marginado—Kaltgestellt (1980) FFN
Le Buone Notizie (1979) Breasts
La Sabina (1979) Breasts
That Obscure Object of Desire (1977) FFN, Buns
Nunca es Tarde (1977) Breasts
Camada Negra (1977) LB
La Ciutat Cremada (1976) Breasts
Las Largas Vacaciones del 36 (1976) LB
No Quiero Perder la Honra (1975) Breasts

Kelly Monaco

Born: May 23, 1976
Philadelphia, Pennsylvania
Skin-O-Meter: Great Nudity

Not ashamed of her body, which includes some of the meatiest chest Betties ever whipped out for a how-de-do, Kelly Monaco did what most former nude models do: She tried out her acting skills on the hit series *Baywatch*. After that golden opportunity went south, Kelly appeared as one of the sexy cheerleaders in the Trey Parker/Matt Stone comedy *BASEketball* (1998) before showing off her voluptuous bod again as a Baywatch Woman Guard in the little-seen *Welcome to Hollywood* (2000). For a boobalicious peek at Kelly's treasures, check out the Jessica Alba flick *Idle Hands* (1999); it's the first time (other than her multitude of *Playboy* videos) that she showed her massive mammaric melons to the camera. She then went on to appear in the made-for-TV movie *Late Last Night* (1999), which again flashed the flesh, and *Mumford* (1999). Kelly most

recently landed a role on the *General Hospital* spinoff *Port Charles*. If you really want to see her in all of her naked glory, may we suggest buying a few of her better *Playboy* videos, namely *Naturals* (1998), which ironically doesn't boast one natural beauty.

SKIN-fining Moment:

Idle Hands (1:07) Young Kelly's smashing pair of pleasure-pumpkins massaged by not one, not two, but three non-idle hands in the front seat of a car.

See Her Naked In:

Late Last Night (1999) Breasts
Idle Hands (1999) Breasts
Numerous *Playboy* Videos

MR. SKIN'S TOP TEN

Best Nude Scenes in a Car

. . . Auto-erotica

10. **Natasha Gregson Wagner**
    —*Lost Highway* (1998) (1:07)
9. **Linnea Quigley**
    —*The Return of the Living Dead* (1985) (0:39)
8. **Teri Polo**
    —*Quick* (1993) (1:06)
7. **Sandy Johnson**
    —*Gas Pump Girls* (1979) (0:30)
6. **Lisa Baur**
    —*Animal House* (1978) (1:16)
5. **Rosanna Arquette**
    —*Crash* (1996) (1:15)
4. **Kelly Preston**
    —*Secret Admirer* (1985) (0:53)
3. **Graem McGavin**
    —*My Tutor* (1983) (0:22)
2. **Kate Vernon**
    —*Dangerous Touch* (1993) (0:29)
1. **Kelly Monaco**
    —*Idle Hands* (1999) (1:07)

Constance Money

Skin-O-Meter: Great Nudity

Slender, dark-blonde, distinguished by small but prominent tits and ass, topped off by a face as pure as the sex of a first romance, Constance Money rocketed into the porn pantheon with her virgin leading role in *The Opening of Misty Beethoven* (1976). She will never be dislodged from her top XXX all-time ranking, on the merits of that one performance alone. Money was full frontally included among the posse of prime blue-screen pussy wielders in Blake Edwards's *10* (1979). Anyone on the fence about delving into the Golden Age of theatrically released hardcore should come on over and track down *Beethoven*. Also investigate two other features directed by Money's mentor, Radley Metzger: *Barbara Broadcast* (1977) and *Maraschino Cherry* (1978).

SKIN-fining Moment:

The opening of Misty Beethoven (1:17) The entire flick leads to the moment when Constance is deemed worthy to accept the dong of her sexual mentor, Jaime Gillis. Hoots, heinie, wide-open hair pie, plus hardcore blowjob and buffing action. Talk about a money shot!

See Her Naked In:

10 (1979) FFN
The Opening of Misty Beethoven (1976) Breasts, Bush, Buns
Numerous Adult Movies

Marilyn Monroe

Born: June 1, 1926
Los Angeles, California
Died: August 5, 1962
Skin-O-Meter: Great Nudity

M&M isn't the only sweet thing with a sleek candy shell that tastes delicious. There's M&M, as in Marilyn Monroe, the go-to girl for bombshell beauty. Born Norma Jean

---

MR. SKIN'S TOP TEN

Naked '50s Legends
. . . Bullet bra busters

10. Arlene Dahl
9. Debrorah Kerr
8. Tempest Storm
7. Eleanor Parker
6. Carroll Baker
5. Blaze Starr
4. Bettie Page
3. Mamie Van Doren
2. Jayne Mansfield
1. **Marilyn Monroe**

Baker, Marilyn reinvented herself as a bleached blonde and stopped time with her hourglass figure. She made men want to handle their tools posing for various automotive catalogues, but her career really got into gear on the big screen. After bit parts, Marilyn made the sidewalk sizzle in *The Asphalt Jungle* (1950) and proved that *Gentlemen Prefer Blondes* (1953). She showed *How to Marry a Millionaire* (1953)—all you need are million-dollar knockers. And not only did *Some Like It Hot* (1959), but everyone loved Marilyn when she was hot—and she was never less than steamy. But Marilyn's exposure onscreen remained teasingly short of skin until she starred in the unfinished film *Something's Got to Give* (1962). Although middle-aged, Marilyn was hardly finished as a sex symbol. Her naked pool swim made no ands, ifs, and lots of butt shots about it, with a good measure of her massive mams on display. It's great to finally see why U.S. presidents, baseball legends, and even literary nerds went ga-ga for Marilyn's ta-tas.

SKIN-fining Moment:

The Seven Year Itch (1:14) Marilyn steps over a New York City subway gate in a flowing white dress. Her skirt blows up, her hands scramble to cover her crotch and one of the most iconically sexual images in all of cinema is immortalized. Even if we don't get to see her hair-ilyn.

See Her Naked In:

Something's Got to Give (1962) Breasts, Buns
The Misfits (1961) Nip Slip RB

Sasha Montenegro

Yugoslavia
Skin-O-Meter: Hall of Fame

Yugoslavia-born Sasha Montenegro was very young when her parents moved to Argentina, and she has made Latin America her home ever since. Before becoming famous as the wife of former Mexican president Jose Lopez Portillo, she was one of the biggest nude stars of '70s Mexican cinema and appeared in more than seventy films, television series, and miniseries. She made her debut in *Un Sueno de Amor* (1972) and helped usher in a permissive new era of skinema in the formerly prudish Mexican film industry. Some of Sasha's most skintastic moments, however, appear in her '80s body of work, most notably in *Las Tentadoras* (1980) and *El Hijo de Pedro Navaja* (1986), both of which featured several full-frontal shots of her fantastic body and fluffy black muff. Though she appeared to retire from acting in 1991, she turned up on the 2002 TV series *Las Vias del amor*, so there's hope yet she may treat fans to another flash of flesh.

SKIN-fining Moment:

Blanca Nieves y sus 7 Amantes (0:37) Following a full-frontal dip in the deep blue sea, snowy Sasha is chased by six naked dwarfs. Hi-ho!

See Her Naked In:

La Taquera Picante (1988) FFN
Solitario Indomable (1988) FFN, Buns
Solicíto Marido para Engañar (1987) Breasts
El Hijo de Pedro Navaja (1985) Breasts
Pedro Navaja (1984) FFN, Buns
Extraño Matrimonio (1984)
Entre Ficheras anda el Diablo—La Pulquería 3 (1983) FFN
La Golfa del Barrio (1983)
Blanca Nieves y sus 7 Amantes (1981) FFN, Buns
La Pulquería 2 (1981) FFN, Buns
Las Tentadoras (1980) FFN
Noches de Cabaret (1978) FFN, Buns
Muñecas de Medianoche (1978) FFN, Buns
Bellas de Noche 2 (1977) Breasts
Bellas de Noche (1975) RB
Un Amor Extraño (1974) Breasts, Buns

Belinda Montgomery

Born: July 23, 1950
Winnipeg, Manitoba, Canada
Skin-O-Meter: Brief Nudity

With chubby cheeks, lips pursed as if they'd just been pulled off the nipple, and a layer of plush flesh padding that placed her budding bod halfway between prematurely voluptuous and sleek within a coating of baby fat, Canadian blonde Belinda Montgomery made her initial mark in the cathode realm in a string of 1960s roles as a basically good kid who has undergone some corrupting duress. Belinda would weather her troubled teens okay in the end, growing up to be the motivated mother of the world's youngest medical student and most adolescent doc, *Doogie Howser, M.D.* Montgomery's shot at domestic bliss came only after several years as the on-and-off estranged wife of Don Johnson on *Miami Vice*.

SKIN-fining Moment:

The Todd Killings (0:43) While grappling with a bad-intentioned guy, Belinda's bare bedazzlers flop out of her nightgown top.

See Her Naked In:

The Todd Killings (1970) Breasts

Elizabeth Montgomery

Born: April 15, 1933
Hollywood, California
Died: May 18, 1995
Skin-O-Meter: Brief Nudity

The debate over which supernatural babe was hotter, Sam from *Bewitched* or Jeannie from *I Dream of Jeannie*, will be argued until the end of time. But if a choice must be made between these two enchantresses, Mr. Skin would have to side with Elizabeth Montgomery simply because she's shown some of her breast parts onscreen, while her bottled competitor remained covered up. Elizabeth, the daughter of movie star Robert Montgomery, began acting on Daddy's early '50s TV show *Robert Montgomery Presents*. The good reviews she received and the fact that she was born into Hollywood royalty opened many doors for this strikingly beautiful actress. The role of Samantha Stevens, the suburban housewife and practicing witch, was created as a vehicle for Elizabeth, and it made her a household name. But she became a Skin Central name for her more mature roles after the nose twitching ended. For instance, she portrayed an axe murderer chopping up mama and papa in *Legend of Lizzy Borden* (1975), in which she stripped naked to do the dirty deed and revealed her pink nipple and soft bosom. Then there was another glimpse of nipple when Elizabeth stared topless into a mirror in *Between the Darkness and the Dawn* (1985). Those performances really put a spell on you.

SKIN-fining Moment:

Legend of Lizzie Borden (1:27)
Ultra-fleeting glimpse of Elizabeth's nipple peeking out of her dress while she gives her father forty whacks . . .

See Her Naked In:

Between the Darkness and the Dawn (1985) LB
Legend of Lizzie Borden (1975) LB Euroversion only

Julia Montgomery

Born: July 2, 1960
Kansas City, Missouri
Skin-O-Meter: Great Nudity

Julia Montgomery was still in high school when she landed her role on the soap opera *One Life to Live*, but this gorgeous actress earned her screen immortality thanks to awesome teen comedies. *Senior Trip* (1981) and *Up the Creek* (1984) were a good warm-up, but Julie didn't really heat up until her role as a sorority sister in *Revenge of the Nerds* (1984), in which her boobies were broadcast via hidden video cameras. Damn, those nerds know a lot about technology. Julia reprised her role in *Revenge of the Nerds III: The Next Generation* (1992) and *Revenge of the Nerds IV: Nerds in Love* (1994) but hasn't made another appearance since her role as a young sex maniac's mom in *Milk Money* (1994). But for non-nerdish delights, check out her quick slip of the nip in the low-budget indie *South of Reno* (1988).

SKIN-fining Moment:

Revenge of the Nerds (0:49)
Cheerleader Julia takes off her robe for a shower and—hooray!—out bounce her naked pom-poms.

See Her Naked In:

South of Reno (1988) Breasts
Revenge of the Nerds (1984) Breasts

Sheri Moon

Skin-O-Meter: Brief Nudity

Sheri Moon never had any aspirations of being an actress. She was interested in doing cartoon voice overs, she says, but then a ten-year relationship that led to marriage with rock icon Rob Zombie ended all that. Thankfully, Zombie knows talent when he sees it and cast the curvaceous blonde as Baby in *House of 1,000 Corpses* (2003), where she definitely got her hands dirty. Sheri isn't named Moon for nothing—she flashed that round, hard, meaty delight in chaps and a G-string and also when her pair of low riders gave the camera a cracking good view of her butt cleavage. Look closely and Sheri even flashes her jugs. She is set to appear in the Tobe Hooper remake of the cult classic *The Toolbox Murders* (2004). Maybe Sheri will

---

MR. SKIN'S TOP TEN

**Naked TV Moms
. . . Mommie Rearest**

10. Edie Falco
—*The Sopranos*

9. Bess Armstrong
—*My So-Called Life*

8. Jane Kaczmarek
—*Malcolm in the Middle*

7. Susan Clark
—*Webster*

6. Deborah Harmon
—*Just the Ten of Us*

5. Annette O'Toole
—*Smallville*

4. Barbara Alyn Woods
—*Honey, I Shrunk the Kids: The TV Show*

3. Joanna Kerns
—*Growing Pains*

2. Meredith Baxter
—*Family Ties*

1. **Elizabeth Montgomery**
—*Bewitched*

add her box to the cinematic mix she's exposed onscreen. It'd sure make Mr. Skin's tool happy.

SKIN-fining Moment:

House of 1,000 Corpses (0:24)
Frighteningly sexy seat-meat as Ms. Moon (indeed!) treats us to a rear-view of her way-low-cut pants in a liquor store.

See Her Naked In:

House of 1,000 Corpses (2003) RB, Buns

Barbara Ann Moore

Born: August 21, 1968
Spokane, Washington
Skin-O-Meter: Great Nudity

Any blonde who has a million-dollar smile and at least twenty grand worth of rack has a steadily rising career path in front of her. All she needs to do is keep an eye on the ground beneath her protruding shelf and put one foot in front of the other. The gratifying grin and mesmerizing mounds of Barbara Ann Moore perfectly augment her satin-soft, straw-colored mane and perfectly captivated the attention of *Playboy*'s talent scouts when brought to their attention. A December 1992 reign as Playmate of the Month served as a stepping stone for Barbara Ann, who strode head up and tits out onto the breast-revealing sets of *Wild Malibu Weekend* (1994), *Temptress* (1994), and *Cyber Bandits* (1995), all of which led to her crowning achievement: the role of a dancing fembot in *Austin Powers: International Man of Mystery* (1997).

SKIN-fining Moment:

Temptress (0:18) You'll pop your cork when you see Barbara's breasts as she poses in a large champagne glass.

See Her Naked In:

Cyber Bandits (1995) Breasts, Thong
Temptress (1994) Breasts
Wild Malibu Weekend! (1994) RB
Numerous *Playboy* Videos

Candy Moore

Born: August 26, 1947
Maplewood, New Jersey
Skin-O-Meter: Brief Nudity

Working with a legendary self-taught genius can be tough on a mere kid in her teens, but indomitable blonde child actress Candy Moore not only survived her three years as Chris, daughter to copper-top comedienne extraordinaire Lucille Ball, but the spunky sprite went on to thrive in TV and big-screen roles for almost twenty years. After outgrowing the domesticity of *The Lucille Ball Show*, Candy moved in with that other paragon of '60s family fare, *The Donna Reed Show*. Candy would later be on her own in episodes of *Leave It to Beaver* and *Rawhide*. Although the sweetly named New Jersey native would never strip down to raw hide or beaver, she did drop the veil of modesty in the classic drive-in skin vehicle *Lunch Wagon* (1980). Good for a snack or a meal.

SKIN-fining Moment:

Lunch Wagon (0:53) First she sweetly cozies next to a guy while wearing a robe, then she undoes the top and we see Moore Candy.

See Her Naked In:

Lunch Wagon (1980) Breasts

Demi Moore

Born: November 11, 1962
Roswell, New Mexico
Skin-O-Meter: Hall of Fame

A true legend of movie nakedness, Demi Moore has earned her place in Mr. Skin's Hall of Masturbation. *Indecent Proposal* (1993), *The Scarlet Letter* (1995), and (of course) *Striptease* (1996) showed unpreskindented amounts of nudity from a major star. Demi also spent her prime movie-star years famously stripping twice for the

GEE, STRING! DEMI MOORE THONGS UP THE STAGE IN *STRIPTEASE*.

cover of *Vanity Fair*. But even if she had used stardom as an excuse to keep her clothes on, we'd still be raving about Demi displaying her epidermis in films such as *Blame It on Rio* (1984) and *About Last Night . . .* (1986). She kept her clothes on for her comeback in *Charlie's Angels: Full Throttle* (2003), but her lascivious licking of Cameron Diaz proves that Demi's as shameless as ever.

SKIN-fining Moment:

Striptease (1:15) Demi's busts out her robo-dirigibles and thonged buttcheeks while she gyrates on a table for an understandably grateful Burt Reynolds.

See Her Naked In:

G.I. Jane (1997) Buns
Striptease (1996) Breasts, Thong
The Scarlet Letter (1995) Breasts, Buns
Indecent Proposal (1993) Breasts, Buns
The Seventh Sign (1988) FFN
About Last Night . . . (1986) Breasts, Buns
Blame It on Rio (1984) RB
No Small Affair (1984) LB

Jessica Moore

Born: August 8, 1967
Urbino, Pesaro, Italy
Skin-O-Meter: Great Nudity

More is unarguably more when it comes to tallying the erotic impact of nude sexual hijinks from Italian-born beauty Jessica Moore. Jessica has not only shown more God-given breasts, more plush, firm buns, and more tastefully trimmed bush than most of her contemporaries on her home continent and Stateside, but she does more with her abundant stuff while she has it out. Bountifully bosomed Moore's first lead in a feature came as a budding writer immersing herself in the sex-for-pay demimonde while researching a book on nude modeling and prostitution in *Undici Giorni, Undici Notti* (1986). Jessica is a girl who strips naked and then gets down to business. Even as the titular poser in her full-skinned follow-up *Top Model* (1988), she refuses to stand still when there is a stud to mount and romp in cowgirl superior.

SKIN-fining Moment:

Top Model (0:03) She strips to the bone in a warehouse filled with mannequins. Boobs, bush, and buns in the house! Moore! Moore! Moore!

See Her Naked In:

Non Aver Paura della Zia Marta (1989) FFN, Buns
Riflessi di Luce (1988) RB
Top Model (1988) FFN, Buns
Undici Giorni, Undici Notti (1986) FFN, Buns
La Monaca del Peccato (1986) FFN, Buns

Julianne Moore

Born: December 3, 1961
Fayetteville, North Carolina
Skin-O-Meter: Hall of Fame

Naturally radiant redhead Julianne Moore leapt from live theater and soap-opera roles to a burgeoning big-screen career that exploded with an intensity as glowing as her scarlet muff with her bottomless breakthrough in *Short Cuts* (1993). J-Mo (as Mr. Skin likes to call her) first bared her delicious rose-tipped buds in *Body of Evidence* (1993) and followed with freckly fleshtastic turns in *Boogie Nights* (1997), *The*

> "I called her up and said 'Julianne, I've got a part I want you for, I'm sending you a script, but there's just one thing—the part calls for you to be naked from the waist down for about five minutes. There was a pause, and she said 'I can do that. And Bob, I've got a bonus for you. I'm a natural redhead.'"
>
> —*SHORT CUTS* DIRECTOR ROBERT ALTMAN ON JULIANNE MOORE

Big Lebowski (1998), and *The End of the Affair* (1999). Here's hoping that Julianne, one of the classiest, ass-iest figures in all of contemporary film, continues to roll out her own red carpet.

SKIN-fining Moment:

Short Cuts (2:17) Fire on the hole! Bottomless Julianne argues with Matthew Modine and proves what a natural redhead she is for two glorious minutes.

See Her Naked In:

The End of the Affair (1999) Breasts
The Big Lebowski (1998) FFN, Buns
Boogie Nights (1997) Breasts
Short Cuts (1993) Bush, Buns
Body of Evidence (1993) Breasts, Buns

Kenya Moore

Born: January 24, 1974
Detroit, Michigan
Skin-O-Meter: Brief Nudity

You've seen the fantastic blacktress Kenya Moore on almost every African American sitcom on TV, which works out perfectly because you won't be able to get enough of this café au lait cutie in action. This Miss USA of 1993 perked up the pee pees of every red-blooded male on *The Fresh Prince of Bel-Air, Living Single, The Parent Hood, The Parkers*, and her own short-lived sitcom *In the House*. Kenya's curves translate well on the big screen, especially

when playing the willing fill-in for a skinperienced married couple's ménage in *Trois* (2000). Although the lighting is poor, there's no denying that Kenya has a booming, blacktacular bod. Vive la nudity! When it comes to seeing this delicious, dusky dish, sometimes *Moore* is more.

SKIN-fining Moment:

Trois (0:33) Gary Dourdown sucks on some chick's nipple. In the movie, the milk-spout belongs to Kenya's character, but since we don't see her face in the shot, we're forced to call BODY DOUBLE!

See Her Naked In:

Trois (2000) Buns

Mandy Moore

Born: April 10, 1984
Nashua, New Hampshire
Skin-O-Meter: Brief Nudity

A blonde hottie of the recently jailbait variety, scintillating songstress Mandy Moore owes her success to a great set of lungs. Make that two great sets of lungs, one inside and one popping out from the surface of her nubile chest. Think of Mandy as a classy Christina Aguilera; she's not shy about flaunting her steamy post-adolescent vixen appeal, but she seems sweetly nonvirginal, as opposed to Aguilera's wild child. Mandy's approach may prove to be longer lasting. She's been increasingly successful in crossing over to an acting career, especially in bra-flouting titles such as *All I Want* (2002). For a peek at what may yet come from Mandy, track down *Rove Live* (2000), a concert performance tape. Mandy's nipple puckers hard and sweet under a sheer top as her face contracts in a soulful rounding of lips as if squeezing out a deeply felt O. Her hand grasps a microphone and points it with blatant phallic imagery toward that rounded mouth. You may need ice water as you groove to the beat of Mandy's dented shirt, but there'll be no cooling down from the actual debut of Mandy's right-side mammary spout in the drama *How to Deal* (2003). Bending toward a window, Mandy's tank top flops open and provides a lickety-quick nip slip that's at once satisfying but will also have you crying "Moore! Moore! Moore!"

SKIN-fining Moment:

How to Deal (0:33) Super-quick, semi-dark nip-slip as Mandy walks to a window in a wide-open-sleeved shirt that shows off her right Mammary Moore. It's brief but awesome.

See Her Naked In:

Chasing Liberty (2004) Body double—buns
How to Deal (2003) Nip Slip RB

Mary Tyler Moore

Born: December 29, 1936
Brooklyn, New York
Skin-O-Meter: Never Nude

As Laura Petrie on *The Dick Van Dyke Show* and Mary Richards on *The Mary Tyler Moore Show*, Mary Tyler Moore assured office-bound women across America in the '60s and '70s that it was OK to wear the pants in the family if need be. Of course, she could just as easily have convinced women to wear no pants if she had continued her first TV role as Happy Hotpoint, the Hotpoint Appliance Elf, whom she played on a commercial during *The Ozzie and Harriet Show* in 1955. Famous more for her spunk than her sexiness, Mary has always been a looker, though she's never shed her skivvies onscreen. She was once offered $1 million to appear nude in *Playboy* but turned it down! Mary began her career as a dancer but hung up her tap shoes in favor of

acting because she "wanted to be a star," and she remained a very major one until 1980. She will always be remembered more for her TV work than her less-than-stellar film resumé, which includes such odd role choices as *What's So Bad About Feeling Good?* (1968), *Don't Just Stand There* (1968), and the Elvis Presley dud *Change of Habit* (1969), in which she played a nun. Though she still acts and was nominated for a Best Actress Oscar for her turn in *Ordinary People* (1980), she is best known today for her vegetarianism and animal rights and Diabetes activism. Feeling a bit frisky in 1996, Mary showed off her bra-clad torso in the Ben Stiller vehicle *Flirting with Disaster* (1996), looking stunning even at her (very) advanced age.

SKIN-fining Moment:

Flirting With Disaster (0:10) MTM raises her shirt to show off the gravity-defying buoyancy of her t's, which reside in a bra, cup-size B.

Melissa Anne Moore

St. Charles, Illinois
Skin-O-Meter: Great Nudity

Blonde, built, and sparkling-fresh of face, as an actress Melissa Anne Moore has been both a prodigy and a late, fully matured, and enticingly ripe bloomer. The eye-catching form of Melissa Anne first attracted the public gaze in an action thriller from pre-video days, *Assault* (1971). Apparently the limelight was slightly too bright for the stacked and twinkling ingénue, as she does not appear to have graced the screen again until *Killzone* (1985). After the release of that video-shelf stalwart, it was impossible to keep Melissa Anne out of camera range and equally tough to keep her shirt on while she was there, screaming and fleeing, alternately predator and prey in dozens of

cheapo horror flicks with a combined wardrobe budget of just over seventy-eight bucks.

SKIN-fining Moment:

Hard To Die (0:21) Melissa Anne offers up her maw-maws during a long, loveley topless shower scene.

See Her Naked In:

Compelling Evidence (1995) Breasts
Stormswept (1995) Breasts
Bikini Drive-In (1995) Breasts
Angelfist (1993) Breasts, Bush, Buns
Da Vinci's War (1993) Breasts, Buns
One Man Army (1993) Breasts
Consenting Adults (1992) Buns
The Other Woman (1992) Breasts
Scream Queen Hot Tub Party (1991) Breasts
Hard To Die (1990) Breasts
Sorority House Massacre II (1990) Breasts, Buns
Vampire Cop (1990) Breasts
The Invisible Maniac (1990) Breasts, Buns
Repossessed (1990) Breasts
Scream Dream (1989) Breasts
Evil Spawn (1987) Breasts

Jeanne Moreau

Born: January 23, 1928
Paris, France
Skin-O-Meter: Great Nudity

Jeanne Moreau has over one hundred credits to her name, debuting in *Dernier Amour* (1948) before going on to play in what would amount to a number of B-movies. That all changed when she was picked up by legendary auteur Louis Malle for his film *Ascenseur pour l'echafaud* (1958). Many credit Malle with bringing fame to the comely starlet, but the fact is that she had been acting onstage and in film for twenty years prior, as he was quick to point out. Jeanne did appear in mostly European cinema but jumped over to the States for some time, appearing in such flicks as *The Victors* (1963), *The Yellow Rolls-Royce* (1964), and *The Train* (1965)—guess they weren't so creative about movie titles back then. Jeanne may be best remembered as the lead in François Truffaut's French threesome *Jules et Jim* (1961). Never exactly shy about showing off her beauty, she flashed brief delights in *Les Amants* (1958). *La Notte* (1960) is an erotic masterpiece that made her an international star, and she's also a hoot(er) in *The Bride Wore Black* (1967). But it was her role in *The Immortal Story* (1968) that first grabbed Skin Central by its collective balls. It offered a tantalizing glance at Jeanne's goodies, although she had them discreetly covered with her hands. It wouldn't be until *Je t'aime* (1974) that we would finally see what she was trying so desperately to hide. It was worth the wait.

SKIN-fining Moment:

Je T'aime Bare-juggled Jeanne brushes her hair while a bug-eyed perv peeps in her bedroom window.

See Her Naked In:

Je t'aime (1974) Breasts
The Bride Wore Black (1968) Breasts
The Immortal Story (1968) RB
Mademoiselle (1966) RB
La Notte (1960) Breasts
Les Amants (1958) LB

Marguerite Moreau

Born: April 25, 1977
Riverside, California
Skin-O-Meter: Great Nudity

We're all animal men on the island of Marguerite Moreau, who's certainly grown up since debuting in *The Mighty Ducks* (1992). She worked steadily through the '90s while maturing into a proper beauty—and, incidentally, earning a bachelors degree in political science from Vassar College. This brainy beauty also became a sex symbol in the comedy *Wet Hot American Summer* (2001) as a fabulously fickle

camp counselor. She then vamped it up in *Queen of the Damned* (2002) and sported scorching lingerie while taking over Drew Barrymore's role in the made-for-cable sequel *Firestarter 2: Rekindled* (2002). Things finally got easier for our eyestrain when Marguerite went skinematic in *Easy* (2003). She also created a whole new death cult as Manson disciple Patricia Krenwinkel in the remake of the classic TV film *Helter Skelter* (2004).

SKIN-fining Moment:

Easy (1:12) Marguerite-aville is clearly clothing optional, as Ms. Moreau opts to offer us eyefuls of her boobs and a quick blast of buns.

See Her Naked In:

Easy (2003) Breasts, Buns

Rita Moreno

Born: December 11, 1931
Humacao, Puerto Rico
Skin-O-Meter: Brief Nudity

Talent, versatility, perseverance, and a hot rack and backside have been the mainstays of Puerto Rican wonder woman Rita Moreno's forty-plus years holding the fickle light of fame. As Anita, she was the only Latina in all of *West Side Story* (1961). In the early 1970s hers was a signature character on the long-running PBS kids show *The Electric Company*. As a sultry ingénue she labored beneath Marlon Brando as the acting heavy's longtime romantic liaison. And she recently kept an entire prison of caged testosterone at bay as Sister Peter Marie on the HBO melodrama *Oz*. Her nip slips are few and far between. Chi-chi spottings in *Marlowe* (1969) and *The Night of the Following Day* (1969) weren't followed up until Rita's bubble buns broke the surface as she swam butt naked in *The Four Seasons* (1981) at the tender age of fifty.

SKIN-fining Moment:

Marlowe (1:32) Rita bares her pasty-covered tweeters while dancing at a strip club before some prick shoots her.

See Her Naked In:

The Four Seasons (1981) Buns
Marlowe (1969) Breasts, Thong
The Night of the Following Day (1969) LB

Chesty Morgan

Born: 1928
Poland
Skin-O-Meter: Great Nudity

No Polish joke, Lillian Wilczkowsky came to America from her native Poland, and her American dream was every man's hottest fantasy fulfilled. You might recognize her better by her stage name, which was first Zsa Zsa but later became the immortal Chesty Morgan. Chesty doesn't begin to describe the heavy, soft, udderly natural, and inhumanly large breast bombs that explode from this goddess's chest. Some think of Chesty as a camp classic, but Mr. Skin is very serious when discussing the Baroness of Boobdom. She made her mark in film (and a stain on her fans' pants) in a series of sexy sexploitation movies in the early '70s. In the aptly titled *Deadly Weapons* (1973), Chesty smothered men to death with her huge hooters. What a way to go! Then Chesty returned with *Double Agent 73* (1974), in which her breasts were used for all manner of odd activities, including becoming a spy camera to photograph secret documents. Her last movie appearance was in *The Third Hand* (1981), and we can guess what that was used for. In recent years, Chesty has become more of a cult figure and is the star of numerous Web sites erected (no pun intended) in her honor. Chesty, you are the besty!

SKIN-fining Moment:

Double Agent 73 (0:15) *Fire away at Chesty's 73-inch (!!!) cannons when she strangles a nurse with them and then photographs the evidence with her "tit-cam."*

See Her Naked In:

Casanova (1976) Breasts
Double Agent 73 (1974) Breasts
Deadly Weapons (1973) Breasts

Cindy Morgan

**Born: September 29, 1954
Chicago, Illinois
Skin-O-Meter: Great Nudity**

"You have such small tits," Chevy Chase says as he rubs mineral oil over Cindy Morgan's sleek and sexy back in a scene from *Caddyshack* (1980). He's massaging her shoulder blades—what a card! He turns her over and we see Cindy's glorious bosom and rosy nips. We see a lot more when Michael O'Keefe beds down the hot blonde later in the movie. After that comedy classic, sadly, we didn't get to see a lot of Cindy's scrumptious body. She went on to star in Disney's cult sci-fi curiosity *Tron* (1982), but primitive CGI covered her best assets. Cindy took her sweet looks to TV and a short stint on the primetime soap *Falcon Crest*, but TV skin isn't up to our high standards here at Skin Central. Cindy continues to work sporadically, most recently as a voice in *Tron 2.0* (2003), an animated take on the original, which means we don't even get to see a dressed Cindy. Cindy, come back, take off your shirt, and let's see that perky pair again . . . please!

SKIN-fining Moment:

Caddyshack (0:58) *"Lacey Underall" shows whats under her bra as she messes with Michael O'Keefe in Ted Knight's bed.*

See Her Naked In:

Caddyshack (1980) Breasts

Debbi Morgan

**Born: September 20, 1953
Dunn, North Carolina
Skin-O-Meter: Great Nudity**

Debbi Morgan started her career in film but soon found her niche in soap operas. She first appeared on *All My Children* in 1982 and stayed on for a tumultuous eight years until she left the hit series in 1990. After a stint on the sleeper *Generations*, Debbi moved on to *Loving* for a few years before finally landing in the big time on *General Hospital* in 1997. After one year in residence, she moved on to *GH's* spinoff *Port Charles*, where she spent another few years. After awhile it was time to strut her luscious dark meat back on film, where she appeared in the hits *She's All That* (1999), *The Hurricane* (1999), and *Love and Basketball* (2000). But the call of the boob tube was too strong for this busty beauty to resist, and she returned with roles on *Soul Food* and *Boston Public*. Although she's never shown her pubic, the surprise hit *Mandingo* (1975) exposed her breast talent. But it was Debbi's debut in *Cry Uncle!* (1971) that garnered our accolades here at Skin Central. In it, she marks her best nudie performance with a boob-, butt-, and bush-baring turn opposite some lucky white dude. Check it out for some steamy jungle lovin'.

SKIN-fining Moment:

Cry Uncle! (0:42) *Nice view of Debbi's Mocha mounds and buns taking off her clothes and lying in bed.*

See Her Naked In:

Mandingo (1975) Breasts
Cry Uncle! (1971) Breasts, Buns

Jaye P. Morgan

**Born: December 3, 1931
Mancos, Colorado
Skin-O-Meter: Brief Nudity**

Multi-talented, multimedia star Jaye P. Morgan was a household name as a pop vocalist years before a television sat unblinking in every living room. Despite the fact that Jaye P. contributed to the dignified dawning of the cathode age, it is thanks to vulgar exploitation that she is fondly recalled by adoring masses today. The warbling wonder had her first top-ten hit way back in 1951 with "Life Is Just a Bowl of Cherries." As the 1950s matured, Morgan acted like an adult on *Eddie Fisher's Coke Time*, *The Perry Como Show*, *Toast of the Town*, and her very own *Jaye P. Morgan Show*, all of which are mere footnotes in broadcast history. Mention *The Gong Show*, a 1970s bastion of crass mockery disguised as a talent contest for day-pass mental patients, however, and the eternally vibrant image of *Gong* panelist Jaye P. Morgan springs to life. Morgan's *Gong* legacy will endure long after the final episode of *Masterpiece Theater* has dissolved in the heaping landfill of discarded popular culture.

SKIN-fining Moment:

The Gong Show Movie *Celebrity panelist Jaye P. chucks her top and bangs out her pink-nippled double gongs.*

See Her Naked In:

The Gong Show Movie (1980) Breasts

Shelley Taylor Morgan

Skin-O-Meter: Great Nudity

She's best known for her soapy stints on *Days of Our Lives* and *General Hospital*, but Shelley Taylor Morgan also made some very impressive contributions to the skintorium. One of her first roles was as Bar-Bro in *The Sword and the Sorcerer* (1982), in which her bra bowed out and made room for some wild topless shots of her fine wenchy bod. Shelley then appeared in *Malibu Express* (1985), where we held our own while she held her own against skin icon Sybil Danning. Shelley displayed plenty of her ample ass and bodacious breasts, but that was before taking a break from acting after 1989.

SKIN-fining Moment:

Malibu Express (0:28) Shelley lets her taut twosome and prominent posterior out to play during a roll in the sack.

See Her Naked In:

Malibu Express (1985) Breasts, Buns
The Sword and the Sorcerer (1982) Breasts

Morganna

Born: July 4, 1947
Louisville, Kentucky
Skin-O-Meter: Great Nudity

She didn't get a farewell speech, but December 12, 1999, marked a sad day in baseball as Morganna the Kissing Bandit retired from her career on the field. Fully known as "Morganna Cottrell," the buxom blonde became a legend for dashing out during games to kiss athletes, a pastime that began when she took a bet to kiss Pete Rose during a 1971 Cincinnati Reds game. Morganna came from a skinematic background, though, and you can field her home-run hooters in the classic bawdy sex comedies *Indian Raid, Indian Made* (1969) and *Riverboat Mama* (1969). The former *Playboy* model and exotic dancer went out as a beloved figure, too, with gullible journalists happy to cite her age as forty-seven and willing to repeat her boast of a natural sixty-inch bust. True fans will note that Morganna began her burlesque career as a perfect 36-24-36.

SKIN-fining Moment:

Indian Raid, Indian Made (1:25) Morganna does a long, seductive snake dance and her tremendous tom-toms will rouse the snake in your pants.

See Her Naked In:

Indian Raid, Indian Made (1969) FFN, Buns

Louisa Moritz

Born: 1946
Havana, Cuba
Skin-O-Meter: Great Nudity

The sight of busty, Cuban-born Louisa Moritz is enough to raise the Cuban cigar in your pants. Even better, she'll smoke it! No brainless beauty, Louisa charted high on an IQ test and was offered a scholarship to the Barbizon School of Modeling, but sadly her mother would not allow her to attend. When the revolution came, Louisa left for the U.S. and decided her revolution would be televised. She began modeling on runways and in teen magazines such as *Seventeen*. Her movie debut was in *The Man From O.R.G.Y.* (1970). She played a young hooker who inherited a fortune from one of her late clients, and the representatives of the deceased spent half of the movie looking for the girl with a tattoo on her derriere to give her the inheritance. She moved to TV with mamorable performances on *Love, American Style*, but her breast shows remain onscreen, such as the cult hit *Deathrace 2000* (1975), *Six-Pack Annie* (1975), and *The Happy Hooker Goes to Washington* (1977). They all showed off her large, natural funbags. She even showed up as one of the girlfriends smuggled into the nut house for a drunken good time by Jack Nicholson in *One Flew Over the Cuckoo's Nest* (1975). But she remains forever the hot Latina from *The Last American Virgin* (1982)

who got more than pizza delivered from a pack of horny boys. Nowadays Louisa is studying to be a lawyer. Hope she doesn't pass the bar, because it'd be a blast to sit and drink with her.

SKIN-fining Moment:

The Last American Virgin (0:42) Huge, honkin' Mexi-mams as she gets stripped and services two out of three American no-longer-Virgins.

See Her Naked In:

Hot Chili (1985) Breasts
The Last American Virgin (1982) Breasts, Buns
Lunch Wagon (1980) Breasts
The Happy Hooker Goes to Washington (1977) RB, Buns
Six-Pack Annie (1975) Breasts, Thong
Death Race 2000 (1975) Breasts, Buns

Sara Mornell

Skin-O-Meter: Brief Nudity

Bubbly and delicious brunette Sara Mornell was almost too busy to take her trouser-snake-rousing shower in the comic horror knock-off *Python* (2000). The hard-working, talented, sexually intriguing, all-American thespian has been sharpening her emoting skills at the network TV grindstone since appearing in the 1995 pilot for the long-running series *JAG*. The demanding creators of *Judging Amy*, *Becker*, *ER*, *Dharma & Greg*, and *Six Feet Under* have been monopolizing Mornell's talents. Luckily, she was able to break away and treat her broad, moistened back and left breast to a public *Python* shower.

SKIN-fining Moment:

Python (1:07) Quick glimpses of Sara's left boob in the shower before some idiot flushes the toilet and ruins the show.

See Her Naked In:

Python (2000) LB

Anita Morris

Born: March 14, 1943
Durham, North Carolina
Died: March 1, 1994
Skin-O-Meter: Great Nudity

Anita Morris first appeared in movies back in 1972, but it wasn't until she lost the lead of Xaviera Hollander to Lynn Redgrave in the pants-popping feature *The Happy Hooker* (1975) that people took notice. Thankfully, the part Anita did get offered ample room to show off both her orchestra and balcony. It proved to be her only skin offering, but what a whopper—and we had it our way. She went on to appear on the series *The Berrengers* in the mid '80s before finding real success on the big screen with the classic comedy *Ruthless People* (1986). She also appeared in the really strange, albeit nudity-filled, *Aria* (1987), but, alas, she remained clothed throughout. Next, Anita cuddled up to George Burns in the comedy *18 Again!* (1988), which made the aging comic feel not only 18 years old but 18 inches hard! By the early '90s Anita was working her sweet stuff on the hit mini-series *Trade Winds*. Her last role was in *Radioland Murders* (1994). She died of cancer that same year. Voyeuristic lust just hasn't been the same since she's been gone. We Anita Morris!

SKIN-fining Moment:

The Happy Hooker (0:59) Anita lays naked on a table while a hungry horndog turns her into a human ice-cream sundae.

See Her Naked In:

The Happy Hooker (1975) Breasts

Mari Morrow

Miami, Florida
Skin-O-Meter: Brief Nudity

Mari Morrow got her big break on an episode of *Family Matters* back in 1992. Since then, she's appeared on an episode of basically every black-com to hit the airwaves, from *The Fresh Prince of Bel-Air* and *The Sinbad Show* to *The Jamie Foxx Show*. Makes one kind of wonder why there was never *The Mari Morrow Show*. In spite of her many boob-tube appearances, Mari's found enough time to appear episodically, as it were, on the silver screen. Most of her cinematic appearances have been in such fare as *Children of the Corn III* (1995), *Undercover Heat* (1995), and *House Party 4: Down to the Last Minute* (2001). She's also scored parts in more mainstream movies, such as *Virtuosity* (1995) and *Dead Man on Campus* (1998). The beautiful, buxom young lass also had a playful turn in *How to Be a Player* (1997), in which she appeared in her first-ever skin scenes. Mari flashed her enormous rack in the flick, which is more than enough for any player to play with. Screw the boob tube, sister, work it on the big screen. It's the only screen large enough to do her massive mams justice. Good Morrow to you!

SKIN-fining Moment:

How to Be a Player (1:26) Lingering looks at Mari's dairies while she boinks Bill Bellamy.

See Her Naked In:

How to Be a Player (1997) Breasts

Emily Mortimer

Born: December 1, 1971
London, England,
Skin-O-Meter: Great Nudity

Oxford-educated English strumpet Emily Mortimer first made a splash Stateside with a meaty role (pun very much intended) in the Val Kilmer flick *The Ghost and the Darkness* (1996). After a few forgettable turns in British productions, she returned to Kilmer's side in *The Saint* (1997). Her career has mostly been centered on European films such as *The Last of the High Kings* (1996) and *Elizabeth* (1998). She has gained some notoriety in the United States for the films *Notting Hill* (1999), *Scream 3* (2000), and *The Kid* (2000), opposite Big Daddy Bruce Willis. Emily's first naughty role was in *Coming Home* (1998), in which she appeared in some state of undress in numerous scenes. Check it out for great looks at her bulbous breasts floating in a bubble bath, as well as some steamy love scenes. She continued to give up the flesh in pictures such as *Formula 51* (2001), *The Sleeping Dictionary* (2002), and *Young Adam* (2003). But her piece de resistance has to be *Lovely & Amazing* (2001), in which she is both. It may be an art-house chick flick, but fellas, go ahead and let your better halves talk you into this one. Emily puts herself on full-frontal display for her lover in the movie in what might be the most bizarre skin scene ever recorded. While she poses, the lucky guy that she's standing in front of goes on a lengthy tirade about everything that is wrong with her body (not that we noticed anything), including her fluffy muff, which is plainly visible in a few brief shots. He says she should trim it. We say she should braid it and get back into bed.

SKIN-fining Moment:

Lovely & Amazing (1:19) Emily asks Dermot Mulroney to evaluate her naked form, offering up her booming bazookas and fluffy below-beard. She gets an A-plus from Mr. Skin!

See Her Naked In:

Young Adam (2003) FFN, Body Double—Buns
The Sleeping Dictionary (2002) Breasts
Lovely & Amazing (2001) FFN, Buns
Formula 51 (2001) Breasts
Coming Home (1998) Breasts

Samantha Morton

Born: May 13, 1977
Nottingham, England, UK
Skin-O-Meter: Great Nudity

Samantha Morton has been sweet and she's been lowdown, but either way she brings to the screen a simple, unmistakable beauty. An actor since age thirteen, the Nottingham, England, native's portrayal of mute laundress Hattie in Woody Allen's *Sweet and Lowdown* (1999) snapped co-star Sean Penn's guitar strings and also earned her an Oscar nomination. But it was her role as Iris in the Brit production *Under the Skin* (1997) that got under the skin. Samantha showed plenty of skin when sweet Iris dressed up as her dead mother and embarked on a series of sordid one-night stands. Samantha hit the big time in *Minority Report* (2002), where she played a wet and bald clairvoyant. She claims not to do nudity but has gotten her juicy flesh out in *This Is the Sea* (1998), *Jesus' Son* (1999), *Morvern Callar* (2002), and *In America* (2002). So take that with a grain of Morton salt.

SKIN-fining Moment:

Under the Skin (0:56) Some quick but nice glances at her big, wobbly, upturned boobs while she washes up in a crappy bathroom.

See Her Naked In:

Enduring Love (2004) Buns
Code 46 (2003) Body Double—Bush
In America (2002) Breasts
Morvern Callar (2002) Breasts, Bush, Thong
Jesus' Son (1999) LB, Bush, Buns
Under the Skin (1997) FFN, Buns

TeleVisions:

Band of Gold Breasts

Carrie-Anne Moss

Born: August 21, 1967
Vancouver, British Columbia, Canada
Skin-O-Meter: Brief Nudity

Carrie-Anne Moss kicks ass, and her ass looks great in the latex she sports for her most notable role in *The Matrix* (1998) and its sequels. The Canadian-born actress was named after the Hollies' 1967 song "Carrie Anne," and she's as lovely as that English group's famous harmonies. Carrie-Anne mixes a model's ultra-chic image and long, thin body with a tough-guy persona that Clint Eastwood would be proud of. Her stand-out performance as the super-sexy, leather-clad, cyber-ninja Trinity made a nation of horny men rediscover the beauty of leather pants. But delve back a bit in her career and Carrie-Anne is even hotter without the fetish gear. In *The Soft Kill* (1994), she got down and dirty for a topless bedroom tryst, and *Red Planet* (2000) found her completely naked and wet from a shower—but she managed to cover up the good bits. In *The Matrix: Reloaded* (2003), she finally consummated her love for Keanu Reeves at what appeared to be an orgy. Again she's nude but tastefully obscured by a well-placed arm. Don't complain too loudly; Carrie-Anne is one tough broad! If ever an actress could break the male stronghold on action flicks, it's this girl. No Moss gathers on this rollicking beauty.

SKIN-fining Moment:

The Soft Kill (1:10) Carrie-Ann gets worked up with Michael Harris, providing us a peek at her pre-Matrix Trini-titties.

See Her Naked In:

Red Planet (2000) LB
The Soft Kill (1994) Breast

Kate Moss

Born: November 16, 1974
Addiscomb, Croydon, Surrey,
England, UK
Skin-O-Meter: Brief Nudity

Kate Moss may have figured as the Twiggy of the '90s, but unlike that '60s icon, Kate was happy to take her clothes off at the drop of a camera flashbulb. She first got into modeling when a guy who said his sister owned a modeling agency chatted up the fourteen-year-old Kate on an airplane. He said that she should be a model, and the world agreed. Über-waif Kate became an instant sensation via Calvin Klein's controversial "Heroin Chic" print ads and crossed all borders as the first covergirl to adorn Russian *Vogue*. Kate has pranced in her birthday suit through any number of racy fashion spreads—with a massive furry bush appearing like an anchor, the only thing keeping the rail-thin hottie from floating off on a breeze like a leaf. But she has sadly not blessed the moving pictures with much of her assets. She did offer a quick tit slip in the British TV movie *Inferno* (1992), in which she shared the screen with fellow pinups Tyra Banks, Helena Christensen, and Eva Herzigova. But other than an appearance in the comedy *Blackadder Back & Forth* (1999), Kate has few acting credentials and less nude screen time. A rolling stone gathers no Moss, and neither, it appears, does the silver screen. Let's hope that changes soon. This slinky siren is too hot and is burning for some skinamatic exposure.

SKIN-fining Moment:

Inferno (0:06) It's a supermodel nip-slip as Kate cavorts in a tub with two little boys. Courtesy of Michael Jackson productions.

See Her Naked In:

Inferno (1992) Nip Slip RB

Paige Moss

Bowie, Maryland
Skin-O-Meter: Brief Nudity

It's said that a rolling stone gathers no moss. But turn the page on that axiom and discover Paige Moss, who would be a hoot to roll no matter how stoned one may be. The brunette cutie is breast known to fans of Showtime's *The Ranch*, which is not about cattle but udderly worth rounding up. Paige plays one of the legal hookers on the brothel soap. She's a Bettie Page-looking school-girl turn-on that's sure to have audiences hitting the (stroke) books. She started her career on the only slightly less raunchy *Beverly Hills, 90210* and had a recurring role on *Buffy the Vampire Slayer* as Veruca. But Paige's bark is much better than her bite, and by bark Mr. Skin means the soft, white flesh that this young girl is only now beginning to expose. It's been worth the wait.

SKIN-fining Moment:

The Ranch (0:18) Ms. Moss has some boss li'l bo-bos, as she so kindly shows us when she gets doggie-plowed on a bed by a dorky-looking dude.

See Her Naked In:

The Ranch (2004) Breasts

Melissa Mounds

Born: October 9, 1959
Skin-O-Meter: Great Nudity

The most striking feature about blonde-tressed porn star, exotic dancer, and part-time feature-film actress Melissa Mounds is a double helping of heaping hooters. Mounds's mams are bigger than large. Think of the normal superhuman vixen and the overblown balloons that you are wont to fantasize rising from the flesh above her rib cage. Then expand by two, and chances are you're in the ballpark of Melissa's stadium-rocking rack. Stalkers of

porno theaters and strip clubs that book national figures with supernatural figures will be familiar with mammoth Melissa, but clean livers also have an option to embrace the pleasing excess of Mounds. Undergo the heavy-glanded humor of *Flesh Gordon Meets the Cosmic Cheerleaders* (1989). Just be sure your imagination doesn't get a hernia from carrying Melissa's loads around with you for the next week or so.

SKIN-fining Moment:

Flesh Gordon Meets the Cosmic Cheerleaders (0:54) She serves up her cosmic-casabas on a golden platter. Sterling!

See Her Naked In:

Flesh Gordon Meets the Cosmic Cheerleaders (1989) Breasts
Numerous Adult Movies

Bridget Moynahan

Born: September 21, 1972
Binghamton, New York
Skin-O-Meter: Never Nude

A towering pinnacle of feminine perfection, ice-eyed brunette Bridget Moynahan is so obviously a former model that she might as well carry her face as though it were her ticket to fame and fortune. Wait a minute. That face is a ticket to fame and fortune, especially when coupled with an athletic, graceful body boasting a full accoutrement of bumps and valleys. Bridget is far and away the most attractive and articulate female ever to appear on the HBO gal fest *Sex and the City*, and as such, she rightfully claimed the show's prize male, Mr. Big, only to cast him off when he later turned out to be unworthy of her.

SKIN-fining Moment:

The Recruit (1:11) Bridget peels to a black bra as she preps for the pole of Colin Farrell. After the lovin, she throws

on his shirt and buttons up. No nips, but still sexy even though, you know, the whole Colin Farrell thing.

Cookie Mueller

Born: August 1, 1949
Baltimore, Maryland
Died: November 10, 1989
Skin-O-Meter: Brief Nudity

Her filmography is almost entirely based on being one of the bizarre "Dreamgirls" in the repertory company of cult director John Waters. Still, there's nothing gross or shocking about the bizarre beauty of Cookie Mueller. Not even a vulgar visionary such as Waters could make this Cookie less than appetizing. Her wild hair and heavy mascara added slutty sex appeal to epics including *Female Trouble* (1974) and *Polyester* (1981). Don't feel bad about her kinky coupling that proves fatal to a fowl in *Pink Flamingos* (1972), either; Waters assures us that the chicken was promptly plucked and eaten afterwards. Mueller's offscreen life was equally daring, as she traveled the world and kept journals of her strange adventures, right up to her death from AIDS-related illness in 1989.

SKIN-fining Moment:

Pink Flamingos (0:28) In a moment of tenderness and exquisite taste, Cookie strips to full frontal nudity while Danny Mills (really) cuts a chicken's throat. Cookie and Danny then (really) get it on while the bird cockadoodle-doos between their bucking bodies. Really.

See Her Naked In:

Pink Flamingos (1972) FFN

Becky Mullen

Skin-O-Meter: Great Nudity

Did you hear the one about the Farmer's Daughter? After

captivating young men as a brawler on *GLOW: Gorgeous Ladies of Wrestling*, Becky Mullen—then known as "Sally, the Farmer's Daughter"—fulfilled fans' fantasies by going on to skinematic greatness. Her bazongas made their bow in *Affairs of the Heart* (1992), and Mullen kept us mulling her melons with hot sex scenes in *Forbidden Games* (1995) and *Sinful Intrigue* (1995). She's kept a low profile since the mid '90s, but we know that, somewhere, Mullen still casts a giant shadow.

SKIN-fining Moment:

Affairs of the Heart (0:52) Becky takes off her bikini top and busts out her Mullens before diving into a pool.

See Her Naked In:

Forbidden Games (1995) Breasts
Sinful Intrigue (1995) Breasts, Buns
Affairs of the Heart (1992) Breasts
Hard Hunted (1992) Breasts, Thong

TeleVisions:

Rude Awakening Breasts, Buns

Lillian Müller

Born: August 19, 1952
Grimstad, Norway
Skin-O-Meter: Great Nudity

Norway is a distant, isolated land, set in a cold, northern clime of darkness all winter long, the ancestral home of fierce, marauding Norsemen and frankly Satanic hard-rock music. The flip side of that dismal image is sunny, scrumptious vision of comfort and awe Lillian Müller. The truly blonde and naturally built snow bunny from Grimstad hopped to America's shores and shook her cotton tail right onto the centerfold of *Playboy*'s August issue in the hot summer of 1975. The following year, this warm, gregarious,

eternally bright Norsewoman spread happiness and cheer throughout her adopted land as Playmate of the Year, and immortality was not far behind.

SKIN-fining Moment:

Sex on the Run (0:16) Lillian strips down for bare-boob-and-butt lesbianics with Olivia Pascal and another blonde.

See Her Naked In:

Sex on the Run (1979) Breasts, Buns

Chelsea Mundae

Born: January 16, 1974
Skin-O-Meter: Great Nudity

The sexual revolution will be televised and it's being broadcast from New Jersey, home of the erotic empire of Seduction Cinema. One of its rising (pants) stars is the delectable Daisy DeWright, better known to the hairy-palm set as Chelsea Mundae and real-life older sister of Seduction supernova Misty Mundae. Chelsea first made her mark as Daisy in *The Vampire's Seduction* (1998), where she did the near impossible, turning a steamy lesbian ménage-a-trois into something even sexier. From the big bang of her debut things just got better with *Satan's School for Lust* (2002) and her signature role opposite her sibling Misty in the sapphic spectacular *Sin Sisters* (2003).

SKIN-fining Moment:

Sin Sisters (0:12) Brief bush as Chelsea struts around poolside in a bikini top, followed by breasts and full-

> "As sweet and innocent as I may appear to be, I'm just as much a sexual deviant as many of my fans."
>
> —MISTY MUNDAE

bodied FFN as sister Misty Mundae kisses her on the nose before pushing big sis into the water.

See Her Naked In:

Sin Sisters (2003) FFN
Satan's School for Lust (2002) Breasts, Bush

Misty Mundae

Born: October 16, 1979
Illinois
Skin-O-Meter: Hall of Fame

The beginning of the week isn't so hard to take when it's a Misty Mundae. The lithe star of Seduction Cinema's freaky funhouse factory in New Jersey puts out carnal sinema at its breast. Not that mouth-watering Misty is exactly busty, but she's no booby prize. Her petite treats up top go deliciously well with her bottom galore and an eager beaver's taste for the Pine Barrens of her Sapphic co-stars' nether regions. It all started with *Vampire Seduction* (1998), which sucks . . . in all the right places! Misty's face has that goth-next-door charming quality, and she shows her truly dark and desirable colors in movies like *Lust in the Mummy's Tomb* (2001), *Erotic Survivor* (2001), *Playmate of the Apes* (2002), and *Dr. Jekyll & Mistress Hyde* (2003). With Seduction Cinema's girl-on-girl sexy spoofs in the randy realm, Misty sits nude upon the throne as its libidinous queen.

SKIN-fining Moment:

Lord of the G-Strings: The Femaleship of the String (1:00) Misty, A.J Khan, Darian Caine, and Barbara Joyce enjoy some fabulous full-frontal Lesbianic four-way fun by the fire.

See Her Naked In:

Sexy American Idle (2003) Breasts, Thong
That 70's Girl (2003) FFN, Buns
Screaming Dead (2003) FFN
Dr. Jekyll & Mistress Hyde (2003) FFN, Buns

Vampire Vixens (2003) FFN, Buns
Sin Sisters (2003) FFN, Buns
Lustful Addiction (2003) FFN, Buns
Girl Seduction (2003) FFN, Buns
SpiderBabe (2003) FFN, Buns
The Erotic Mirror (2002) FFN, Buns
Roxanna (2002) Breasts, Bush
An Erotic Vampire in Paris (2002) FFN, Buns
Lord of the G-Strings: The Femaleship of the String (2002) FFN, Buns
Satan's School for Lust (2002) FFN, Buns
Play-Mate of the Apes (2002) FFN, Buns
Master's Plaything (2002) FFN, Buns
Lust in the Mummy's Tomb (2001) FFN, Buns
Erotic Survivor (2001) FFN, Buns
Mummy Raider (2001) FFN, Buns
Witchbabe: Erotic Witch Project 3 (2001) FFN, Buns
Seduction of Cyber Jane (2001) FFN, Buns
Gladiator Eroticvs (2001) FFN, Buns
The Vibrating Maid (2000) FFN, Buns
Vampire's Seduction (1998) FFN, Buns
Poetic Seduction: Dead Students Society (1998) Breasts

Amparo Muñoz

Born: June 22, 1954
Vélez Málaga, Málaga, Andalucía, Spain
Skin-O-Meter: Hall of Fame

Before she was even twenty-one years old, brunette sight sensation Amparo Muñoz had already reigned for a year as Miss Spain and had proudly claimed the crown of Miss Universe for 1974. Her future was mapped out for her: A staid succession of corporate shill spots and, if she behaved, her waning years in the limelight as a respected, respectable broadcast journalist. "Fuck all that," Amparo must have said, in her delightfully saucy and spicy accent, because the world's best woman cast that boring, straight-laced future to the dust and embarked upon a film career that has revealed a surprising depth of emotive talent and stupendous quantities of bush, buns, and titties! Check out the royal beauty's thick bush as she engages in fur-flying fisticuffs with an equally naked big-boobed brawler in *Sexo Contra Sexo* (1980).

SKIN-fining Moment:

Sexo Contra Sexo (0:58) Amparo and another naked babe stage a Skintastic cat-fight at a funeral. FFN, buns and a dead body!

See Her Naked In:

Si las Mujeres Mandaran (1982) Breasts
La Mujer del Ministro (1981) FFN, Buns
Sexo Contra Sexo (1980) FFN, Buns
El Sexólogo (1980) Breasts
Mírame con Ojos Pornográficos (1980) FFN, Buns
Mama Turns 100 (1979) FFN
L'Anello Matrimoniale (1978) Breasts
Del Amor y de la Muerte (1977) FFN, Buns
La Otra Alcoba (1976) Breasts
Tocata y Fuga de Lolita (1974) Breasts

Caroline Munro

Born: January 16, 1950
Windsor, Berkshire, England, UK
Skin-O-Meter: Brief Nudity

Brunette ravisher Caroline Munro is a child of the 1950s, reared in a conservative tradition but unable to contain the burgeoning sexuality of her stacked and packed, tan and taut frame. The quintessential prim and proper English convent schoolgirl was also the consummate erotic tease. While only seventeen, in swinging 1967, Caroline was already working for *Vogue* magazine in the midst of the love revolution that was then engulfing London. She provided skimpy-clothed window dressing for the James Bond spoof *Casino Royale* (1967). By the time ten years had passed, Munro's smoldering look and her line delivery had matured to the point where she co-starred opposite Roger Moore in the real James Bond blockbuster *The Spy Who Loved Me* (1977). In the intervening decade, sinfully shapely Caroline reigned, a crotch-melting combination of carnal and chaste, as the cleavage-accentuating main mammary attraction in a string of horror classics including *The Abominable Dr. Phibes* (1971), *Dr. Phibes Rises Again* (1972), and *Dracula A.D. 1972* (1972). Despite a moral conflict that prevented Caroline from agreeing to venture beyond near nudity, the line was inadvertently crossed as her breast escaped a low-cut tunic while the star boarded a boat in *The Golden Voyage of Sinbad* (1974). More-deliberate exposure came in *Captain Kronos—Vampire Hunter* (1974) and as spacey heroine "Stella Star" in *Starcrash* (1979).

SKIN-fining Moment:

The Golden Voyage of Sinbad (0:51) Caroline gets lugged by Sinbad from ship to shore and her right nipple gets justled from her top into view. Not bad for a G-rated flick.

See Her Naked In:

The Golden Voyage of Sinbad (1974) Nip Slip RB

Odessa Munroe

Skin-O-Meter: Great Nudity

Odessa Munroe initially took flight on an episode of *Dark Angel* and quickly scored an unforgettable role as one of the topless table-tennis-playing hookers in the hit comedy *Saving Silverman* (2001). The film lacked any trace of Amanda Peet's perfect peaks, so it was truly saved by the presence of Odessa and Tracy Trueman battling it out—and bouncing about—over a lengthy game of Ping-Pong. Tracy definitely has the bigger rack, but Odessa, as number two in the boob department, tries harder. And we got harder for it. But, then, Odessa's ogle orbs got harder, too. Check her out as Victim #1 in the instant-classic horror smackdown *Freddy vs. Jason* (2003). In the opening moments, Odessa doffed her top for a skinny dip and showed off her almost achingly obvious new breast implants. Then Jason massacred her with his machete. Hey, big guy, Mr. Skin isn't crazy about silicone sackage either, but that's taking disapproval too far.

SKIN-fining Moment:

Saving Silverman (0:25) Odessa serves up her boingers to play some tittilicious topless Ping-Pong.

See Her Naked In:

Final Destination 2 (2003) Breasts
Freddy vs. Jason (2003) Breasts, Bush, Buns
Saving Silverman (2001) Breasts

Janet Munro

Born: September 28, 1934
Blackpool, England, UK
Died: December 6, 1972
Skin-O-Meter: Brief Nudity

Janet Munro is the daughter of Scottish comedian Alex Munro, but there's nothing funny about this almond-eyed cutie. Spunky Janet was a staple of British TV, so much so that she was deemed Miss TV 1958, but international fame came when she caught the eye of family-friendly tycoon Walt Disney. She signed with the Mouse for an unprecedented five-movie contract, where the spirited, brunette-banged ingénue made such classics as *Darby O'Gill and the Little People* (1959), *Third Man on the Mountain* (1959), and *The Swiss Family Robinson* (1960). To shuck the wholesome-sweetheart label, Janet moved on to spicier parts, including a critically lauded role in *Bitter Moon* (1963). But it was *The Day the Earth Caught Fire* (1961) that forever changed this good girl to a skin girl. The movie is about the cover-up of a global disaster, but for Janet it's all about uncovering her globe-sized honkers. Sadly, alcoholism, two

failed marriages, and the strain of raising two children took her from the big screen, and in 1972 she died of a heart ailment. Her last screen time was as a boozing pop star in *Sebastian* (1968). Dammit, Janet, why'd you have to leave us?

SKIN-fining Moment:

The Day the Earth Caught Fire (0:45) Squeaky-clean Janet towels herself off, allowing a brief glance at her black-and-white high-beams. Nifty nippage for 1961!

See Her Naked In:

The Day the Earth Caught Fire (1961) Breasts

Brittany Murphy

Born: November 10, 1977
Atlanta, Georgia
Skin-O-Meter: Never Nude

Hot-bodied blonde heartthrob Brittany Murphy has blown up and is on the verge of becoming a giant movie star. To her credit are a long list of acclaimed roles in everything from *Clueless* (1995) to *Girl, Interrupted* (1999). Look at the parts that make up Murphy's whole. A face where a lascivious leer is as equally at home as a sweet smile of seduction. A tight, bulging, highly mobile pair of butt orbs that are continually showcased in clinging, sheer fabrics. Chest ornaments of a thrilling elasticity, the buoyant profiles of which are consistently presented in vibrating ensembles that just skirt full exposure. A daring, brash sexual side as shown in the torrid make-out with Eminem in the kinetic *8 Mile* (2002) and the bikini-clad splits-and-all pole dancing of *Spun* (2002).

SKIN-fining Moment:

Don't Say a Word Mental patient Brittany flails about her padded cell sans bra and flashing panties, occasionally touching herself. You can touch yourself

too. *I'll never tell.*

See Her Naked In:

Spun (2002) Thong

Ornella Muti

Born: March 9, 1955
Rome, Italy
Skin-O-Meter: Hall of Fame

Ornella Muti first garnered attention as the princess in *Flash Gordon* (1980). She plays Ming's saucy, sex-crazed daughter and delivers her lines in such a filthy, suggestive tone that she'd make men come just reading the phone book. The full, 35C-24-35-figured love doll was already a sexsation in her native Europe, having starred in many fleshtaculars such as *La Moglie più Bella* (1970), her skin debut, *Paolo il Caldo* (1973), and *Il Mio Primo Uomo* (1975). But her breast foreign exposure was in *La Ragazza di Trieste* (1983)—suffice it to say, it's a muff-see. Even in middle-age Ornella is, like most decent Italian actresses, still showing off her whack-tabulous body. If you don't care for movies with subtitles, rent *Tales of Ordinary Madness* (1983) or *Widows* (1998) for some great shots of her Neopolitan naughty bits. That she's hot is a Muti point.

SKIN-fining Moment:

Appassionata (1:29) Muti gets out of bed and struts to the door with her dumplings, derrierre and Delta of Venus in view.

See Her Naked In:

Somewhere in the City (1998) Breasts
Widows (1998) RB
I Inconnu de Strasbourg (1998) Breasts
Tatiana, la Muñeca Rusa (1995) Breasts, Buns
El Amante Bilingüe (1993) FFN, Buns
La Domenica Specialmente (1991) LB, Bush, Buns

Il Viaggio di Capitan Fracassa (1991) Breasts
Codice Privato (1988) LB, Buns
Cronaca di una Morte Annunciata (1987) Breasts
Swann in Love (1984) Breasts
La Ragazza di Trieste (1983) FFN, Buns
Tales of Ordinary Madness (1983) Buns
Famous T&A (1982) Breasts, Buns
Il Bisbetico Domato (1980) Breasts
Primo Amore (1978) Bush
La Dernière Femme (1976) FFN, Buns
Il Mio Primo Uomo (1975) Breasts, Buns
Romanzo Popolare (1974) Breasts, Bush
Appassionata (1974) FFN, Buns
Una Chica y un Señor (1974) Breasts
Paolo il Caldo (1973) Breasts, Buns
Un Posto Ideale per Uccidere (1971) RB
Summer Affair (1971) Breasts, Buns
La Moglie più Bella (1970) FFN

Cynthia Myers

Born: September 12, 1950
Toledo, Ohio
Skin-O-Meter: Brief Nudity

Cynthia Myers meet Russ Meyer . . . men around the world prepare to pop off. The bigger-is-better busty beauty had only an uncredited appearance in *They Shoot Horses, Don't They?* (1969) when she was cast as the bass player of the all-huge-boobed all-girl band the Carrie Nations in the Roger Ebert/Russ Meyer breastacular *Beyond the Valley of the Dolls* (1970). Nudity was, of course, a prerequisite for working with Meyer, and Cynthia didn't disappoint. She appeared for an instant in completely nude repose, although the lighting was atrocious, and all you see is a silhouette of her gargantuan, real breasts. She followed that up with a turn in the Sam Elliott vehicle *Molly and Lawless John* (1972), only to disappear from sight after that. Then, thanks to technology, she returned with her own Web site to wow the wicked world online with her mammary memorabilia. She's got a big heart and an even bigger bosom that she still shares with her adoring fans.

SKIN-fining Moment:

Beyond the Valley of the Dolls (1:25) *It's her happenings, and she busts them out! Sizzling Cynth gets lesbionic with Erica Gavin, showing off some zaftig left zoobie and groin-grabbingly good glutes in the process!*

See Her Naked In:

Molly and Lawless John (1972) Breasts
Beyond the Valley of the Dolls (1970) Breasts, Buns

n

Kathy Najimy

Born: February 6, 1957
San Diego, California
Skin-O-Meter: Brief Nudity

Kathy Najimy is probably most well known for her chest—it's huge and packs a powerful punch—that is as a singer. Yes, those luscious lungs helped her land the role of the nun with incredible singing ability in the *Sister Act* (1992 and 1993) franchise. She has also voiced numerous animated productions, including the TV series *Hercules*, *Stuart Little*, and as Peggy Hill on *King of the Hill*. After her big break in *Soapdish* (1991), Kathy went on to appear in a number of box-office successes, although never in a leading role. Some of her credits include *The Fisher King* (1991), *Hope Floats* (1998), and *The Wedding Planner* (2001). She has also played on a number of TV series, including *Veronica's Closet* and *Chicago Hope*. Kathy was kind enough to bust out of her enormous bra for an unforgettable turn in the otherwise forgettable *Nevada* (1997). She doffed her duds in the film for a dip with the star attraction, Amy Brenneman. Although her gargantuan tits stayed submerged during the scene, if you look close, you can make out some nippage. That's a big tease.

SKIN-fining Moment:

Nevada (0:52) Kathy relaxes in a hot tub and we see her right-side Peggy Hill under the bubbles.

See Her Naked In:

Nevada (1997) RB

Bif Naked

Born: June 15, 1971
New Delhi, India
Skin-O-Meter: Brief Nudity

Bif Naked? More like Buff Naked. This heavily inked, out-and-proud bisexual scorcher is a taut and tempting rock chick run wild! Of course, Bif is best known for her hard metal-punk assault. But this glam goddess is no one-trick pony, though we'd love to ride her. Bif may not be boffo box office, but she has cut herself a sexy figure on the big screen. She made some TV cameos on *Buffy the Vampire Slayer* and *Once a Thief*. Her first big-screen appearance was as a Russian Soldier in *Archangel* (1990) and then a Liquor Store Manager in *The Boys Club* (1997), which showed her range, if not her skin. That is until *Lunch with Charles* (2001). It wasn't a box lunch, but Bif got buck Naked showing off her tom-tom tits and bass-drum derrierre for Mr. Camera. It marked the first—and hopefully not last—time Bif rocked out the flesh tunes.

SKIN-fining Moment:

Lunch with Charles (0:31) Bif's naked! She skinnydips in a river with friends showing her taut ta-ta's and high-rise hind-cakes in the process. Nice tats!

See Her Naked In:

Lunch with Charles (2001) Breasts, Buns

Francesca "Kitten" Natividad

Born: February 13, 1948
Wattichiquaqua, Mexico
Skin-O-Meter: Hall of Fame

Holy mam-oley! Francesca "Kitten" Natividad has had one boobiliciously bare career. Voted Miss Nude Universe in 1970 and 1971, Francesca landed a topless non-speaking role in *The New Centurions* (1972). While dancing in a strip club, this mammoth-mammed, Mexican mamacita was discovered by legendary boobster movie director Russ Meyer, who brought her into his bevy of buxom beauties and gave her the purrfect nickname, Kitten. Kitten showed off her super shakers in Meyer's all nude Greek Chorus in *Up!* (1976) and *Beneath the Valley of the Ultra-Vixens* (1979). After catting around with Russ for a few years and getting implants in her already humungo hooters, Kitten sank her claws into hardcore, co-starring with the jumbo johnsoned John Holmes in *John Holmes and the All-Star Sex Queens* (1980). Often described as "a nymphomaniac Charo on speed," this skinergizer bunny has revealed her righteous rack in nearly every performance! Mr. Skin recommends tamer tinglers like *Takin' It Off* (1985) and *Night Patrol* (1984), just enough Kitten to send up your tree. Meow-wow-wow! Sadly, Francesca suffered from breast cancer and underwent a double mastectomy in October of 1999. With her wild Latina beauty and personal charm still intact, Kitten will always be muy caliente.

SKIN-fining Moment:

My Tutor (0:10) Kitten bombs Matt Lattanzi with her legendarily larger-than-life milk-monsters.

See Her Naked In:

United Trash (1996) Breasts
The Girl I Want (1993)
Inside Out II (1992) Breasts
Another 48 Hrs. (1990) Breasts
Takin' It All Off (1987) FFN, Buns
Bad Girls IV (1986) Breasts
The Stripper of the Year (1986) FFN
Takin' It Off (1985) FFN, Buns
The Tomb (1985) Breasts, Thong
Bodacious Ta Ta's (1984) FFN, Buns
Night Patrol (1984) Breasts
The Wild Life (1984) Breasts
An Evening with Kitten (1983) Breasts, Thong
My Tutor (1983) Breasts
Titillation (1982) Breasts
The Gong Show Movie (1980) Thong
The Lady in Red (1979) Breasts
Beneath the Valley of the Ultra-Vixens (1979) FFN, Buns
Up! (1976) FFN, Buns
Numerous Adult Movies

Elise Neal

Born: March 16, 1970
Memphis, Tennessee
Skin-O-Meter: Brief Nudity

Serious dance training is an excellent preparation for a young lady about to sally forth into the big, bad world. The hours of stretching and all that frenetic leaping and bounding teach a budding woman to be resilient, to move with grace through the rough patches, to set her sights high and keep her chin up, and also to remain whippet thin with a pair of buttocks high and solid like God's own throw pillows. Downhome brown-sugar sweetie Elise Neal from Memphis, Tennessee, was a disciplined, whip-sharp dancer before she ever did her first music-video shimmy or melted the cool of basketball Hall of Famer George "Iceman" Gervin in a campaign for *Nike* shoes. The propulsive explosiveness from those long-gone dancing days lifted Elise to two seasons on *Seaquest DSV*, four years starring on *The Hughleys*, and sassy, classy movie credits such as *Scream 2* (1997) and *Playas Ball* (2003). In a boob tube breakthrough, Brave Elise bared her chest along with her soul as a breast-cancer patient on the edgy medical drama *Chicago Hope*. She and the producers intended to show women nationwide that they can have a sweet-looking rack despite suffering from cancer and undergoing skin grafts. Elise's beauties overflow with hope to spare. Ms. Neal is a trip fantastic.

SKIN-fining Moment:

Chicago Hope "Cutting Edges" (1994) In a boob tube breakthrough, brave Elise bares her chocolate chestberries in a hospital bed to a posse of medicos.

TeleVisions:

Chicago Hope Breasts

Holly Near

Born: June 6, 1949
Ukiah, California
Skin-O-Meter: Great Nudity

Holly Near began her career onstage, in the first nudie musical on Broadway, *Hair*. In the early '70s she made the transition to TV on such swinging hits as *All in the Family*, *The Mod Squad*, and *The Partridge Family*. She was featured in *Slaughterhouse Five* (1972) but was put to better use in the hippie love-in *The Magic Garden of Stanley Sweetheart* (1970), in which she exposed her burning bush—along with every other inch of her womanly body. By the mid '70s she was focusing full time on her political activism through her music and independent record label. An accomplished songwriter and folk singer, her composition "We Are a Gentle, Angry People" appears in "Singing the Living Tradition," the official hymnal of the Unitarian Universalist Association. She returned to the screen, both small and large, briefly in the late '80s for a guest spot on *L.A. Law* and in *Dogfight* (1991) and *Heartwood* (1998), but she's left our hard wood a little softer since her absence. Holly, we prefer you Near.

SKIN-fining Moment:

The Magic Garden of Stanley Sweetheart (0:36) Holly comes on to Don Johnson with a full-bodied full-frontal. Get warm to her fluffy fire-snatch.

See Her Naked In:

The Magic Garden of Stanley Sweetheart (1970) FFN

Kate Nelligan

Born: March 16, 1950
London Ontario, Canada
Skin-O-Meter: Brief Nudity

Cool Kate Nelligan was born in the Great White North and began her career North of the border before hightailing it for England. That brought her to the U.S. to pursue an acting career both onstage and in movies and television. She got the sexy role of Lucy in *Dracula* (1979), but her career didn't take off until she got on the Al Pacino/Michelle Pfeiffer vehicle *Frankie and Johnny* (1991). Playing a mattress-hopping wiseacre waitress, Kate exposed her comic side, which allowed her to break out of the icy-cold mold that she was seemingly trapped in. Next, she landed a role in Barbra Streisand's *The Prince of Tides* (1991), which garnered her an Oscar nod. *Frankie and Johnny* director Garry Marshall said of Kate: "Anyone who can play Nick Nolte's mother for Streisand and a slut for me has quite a range." Of course, all that wouldn't matter if she hadn't shown a little skin in her long and storied career, and lo and behold, she certainly did in the lady-falls-for-Nazi-spy drama *Eye of the Needle* (1981) opposite Donald Sutherland. There were a few breast shots, as well as a brief glimpse of her heinie as she rose from bed. It'll make your Third Reich rise again!

SKIN-fining Moment:

Eye of the Needle (0:52) Kate towels up in the bathroom and Donald Sutherland gets a gander at her left globe.

See Her Naked In:

Eye of the Needle (1981) Breasts, Buns

Nena

Born: March 24, 1960
Hagen, Germany
Skin-O-Meter: Brief Nudity

Anyone who has memories of the middle 1980s, no matter how vague, can recall the plaintive opening vocal rise of the 1984 new-wave hit from Germany, "99 Luftballons." Mixed in with the sensory recollection of that saccharine but soul-wrenching guttural cry and subsequent bouncy pop melody is a less vague remembrance of a female singer cavorting and emoting with starry-eyed face lifted beseechingly and mildly scoldingly to the camera, in a pose of heartfelt but pretty angst that would become a template for generations of warbling, socially aware songstresses to come. The band and the singer were both named Nena, and the reason she is remembered and they are forgotten is that video exalts the hot-chick star.

SKIN-fining Moment:

Gib Gass—Ich will Spass! (1:12) As Nena changes clothes, we get to see some close cheek peekage courtesy of her undersized underpants, plus a chart-bursting blast of her right luftballoon.

See Her Naked In:

Der Unsichtbare (1987) Breasts
Gib Gas—Ich will Spass! (1982) Nip Slip RB, Buns

Francesca Neri

Born: February 10, 1964
Trento, Italy
Skin-O-Meter: Hall of Fame

Sex, nudity, and horror are a family affair for Italian beauty Francesca Neri. Like her mesmerizing Mediterranean momma Rosalba Neri (of *Marquis de Sade: Justine* [1969] fame), Francesca has flashed flesh in a number of screamingly sexy skindeavors. Mostly known in the States as the mouthwatering dish in *Hannibal* (2001), when it comes to showing skin, Francesca is a tasty meal best served on native soil. In *Outrage* (1993), Neri did the nasty with Antonio Banderas, offering a skintimate bite of her yummy cannoli and furburger below. What tasty teats and eats! Francesca dabbled in a horny cornucopia of skinful sex acts in *The Ages of Lulu* (1990). As a young married woman obsessed with S&M and homosexual sex, Francesca lived for butt-pirate porn and the old slap and tickle. Offering something for everyone, she friskily shaved her furry mound, indulged in backdoor bouts of the old in-and-out, and had a ménage with her husband and a female impersonator and a bit of blindfolded fun with her own brother. Holy skincestuous fun, Batman! Any of Francesca's flicks are guaranteed to bring you *Neri* to an explosion of the skinses.

SKIN-fining Moment

Outrage (0:43) Full-frontal rack and furburger as Francesca scrubs up in the shower.

See Her Naked In:

Live Flesh (1998) Breasts
Outrage (1993) FFN, Buns
Las Edades de Lulú (1990) Breasts, Bush

Rosalba Neri

Born: June 19, 1939
Milan, Italy
Skin-O-Meter: Hall of Fame

Some people grow into greatness, and such was the path to glory of Italian cult siren Rosalba Neri. Brunette, but with a streak of reddish highlights, Rosalba's radiant countenance began lighting up foreign silver screens when the girl was a mere fifteen, but it wasn't until the matured woman had cracked the age of thirty that the sloe-eyed seductress with the sensual mouth and the blood-red nipples dared to bare and dramatize in *Marquis de Sade: Justine* (1969). The stage was set for Rosalba's reign as queen of the damned, the deranged, and the disrobed. See her sleek glowing form in situations of danger and delight in *99 Mujeres* (1969), *Sexy Susana Knows How* (1970), *La Figlia di Frankenstein* (1971), and *Alla Ricerca del Piacere* (1972).

SKIN-fining Moment:

Alla Ricerca del Piacere (0:13)
Rosalba drugs Barbara Bouchet so she can take advantage of her! Slo-mo, all-points naked lesbianism ensues.

See Her Naked In:

Racconti di Viterbury—Le Più Allegre Storie del '300, I (1973) RB, Buns
Il Plenilunio delle Vergini (1973) Breasts
Primo Tango a Roma—Storia d'amore e d'alchimia (1973) RB, Buns
Confessioni Segrete di un Convento di Clausura (1972) Breasts, Buns
L'Amante del Demonio (1972) Breasts
Alla Ricerca del Piacere (1972) Breasts, Buns
Slaughter Hotel (1971) FFN, Buns
La Figlia di Frankenstein (1971) Breasts, Buns
Sexy Susana Knows How (1970) Breasts
Top Sensation (1969) Breasts, Buns
Marquis de Sade: Justine (1969) Breasts
99 Mujeres (1969) Breasts

Bebe Neuwirth

Born: December 31, 1958
Princeton, New Jersey
Skin-O-Meter: Brief Nudity

Bebe Neuwirth may not be a household name, but she's probably graced the screen of every TV in the civilized world at some point between 1986 and 1993 as psychiatrist Dr. Lilith Sternin-Crane on the long-running series *Cheers* (for which she won an Emmy). But don't be put off by Bebe's steely facade and barbed tongue on that show—there's more than meets the eye beneath those stern gray power suits. Like, for instance, her tight ass, perky tits, and taut, toned body, which looks more like age twenty-five than forty-five. Bebe began her career as a dancer and still appears in such racy Broadway musicals as *Chicago* and *Cabaret*. She got her start as part of the *Chorus Line* dance troupe and has won two Tony awards for her stage work. The stage might be the best place to catch her in a skimpy outfit, as she has never appeared nude onscreen. She appeared in an organ-throbbing black thong in *The Associate* (1996), however, and played a hooker who instructs a co-star in the art of fellatio in Woody Allen's *Celebrity* (1998). Also check out *Summer of Sam* (1999) for a super-steamy sex scene with co-star John Leguizamo. Though clad only in a bra (and showing no bush), she's still a million times hotter than many actresses half her age, most of whom possess less than half her acting ability.

SKIN-fining Moment:

The Associate (0:59) Black-lingerie-clad Bebe struts toward Whoopi-Goldberg-in-White-Face, lands on her lap, then grinds her groin lapdance-style, with her sweet, thonged Keister pointed straight at the camera. Nice Ass-ociate!

See Her Naked In:

The Associate (1996) Thong

Amber Newman

Born: 1978
Tipp City, Ohio
Skin-O-Meter: Great Nudity

Blend a husky, Kathleen Turner-esque voice with Brooke Shields's smoldering eyes, and you get Amber Newman. This comely young lady hails from the Buckeye State and has made a career out of playing strippers, lap dancers, and hookers. Just check out such skin classics as *Lap Dancing* (1995), Jesus Franco's *Tender Flesh* (1997), *Sin in the City* (2001), and *Sex Secrets and Lies* (2003). Amber is kind to skinaholics everywhere and appears in some stage of undress in absolutely everything that she has done, often taking part in some rather explicit sex scenes. One of the breast is her carnal performance in *Sex Files: Sexually Bewitched* (2000), which featured a hot masturbatory sequence. Also check out *Sex Files: Sexual Matrix* (1999), where she is just plain hot. In short, if you happen to notice Amber on a video box cover, check it out for some excellent, well-lit and completely gratuitous nudity, which is, of course, Mr. Skin's favorite kind!

SKIN-fining Moment:

Tender Flesh (0:03) *Amber throws every bit of herself in a long, lusty, full-frontal dance number.*

See Her Naked In:

Sex Secrets And Lies (2003) Breasts, Buns
Sexual Magic (2001) FFN, Buns
Virtual Girl 2: Virtual Vegas (2001) Breasts, Thong
Sin in the City (2001) Breasts, Bush
Lawful Entry (2000) FFN, Thong
Sex Files: Sexually Bewitched (2000) FFN, Buns
Erotic Possessions (2000) Breasts
Alien Erotica 2 (2000) FFN
Body of Love (2000) Breasts, Bush, Buns
Virgins of Sherwood Forest (2000) Breasts, Thong
Night Calls: The Movie, Part 2 (1999) FFN, Buns
Sex Files: Creating the Perfect Man (1999) FFN, Buns
Dungeon of Desire (1999) FFN, Buns
Sexual Matrix (1999) Breasts, Bush
Scandal: On the Other Side (1999) FFN, Buns
Pleasurecraft (1999) FFN, Buns

Timegate: Tales of the Saddle Tramps (1999) Breasts, Buns
The Perfect Man (1999) FFN, Buns
Ancient Desires (1999) Breasts, Buns
Mari-Cookie and the Killer Tarantula (1998) FFN, Buns
Tender Flesh (1997) FFN, Buns
Lap Dancing (1995) Breasts
Vamps: Deadly Dreamgirls (1995) FFN, Thong

TeleVisions:

Erotic Confessions FFN
Passion Cove FFN, Buns

Julie Newmar

Born: August 16, 1933
Los Angeles, California
Skin-O-Meter: Great Nudity

The bodacious 37-26-37 Julie Newmar is forever etched in the collective male libido as the original Catwoman from the camp classic TV series *Batman*. But Julie's no one-trick pony (even though that one trick is terrific). She even showed up as herself in the Patrick Swayze/Wesley Snipes drag-queen

---

MR. SKIN'S TOP TEN

Actresses Who've *Only* Shown Buns

. . . No ifs, ands—only butts

10. Shelley Long
 9. Deborah Foreman
 8. Lori Petty
 7. Dana Barron
 6. Marla Heasley
 5. Sabrina Lloyd
 4. Anne-Marie Johnson
 3. Joanna Kerns
 2. Victoria Jackson
 1. **Julie Newmar**

---

flick *To Wong Foo, Thanks for Everything, Julie Newmar* (1995). Julie has been working the tail end of her career as an aging sex kitten in *Deep Space* (1987), *Ghosts Can't Do It* (1990), and *Oblivion* (1994). But for a glimpse of Julie's assets in primetime, check out *Mackenna's Gold* (1969), where she played the Native American "Hesh-Ke" and was seen from afar bathing in a spring. At least the aging but purr-fect stunner is still willing to let her pussy out.

SKIN-fining Moment:

Mackenna's Gold (1:09) Julie romps in a muddy pond, providing not-so-easy-to-see views of her T&A, punctuated by bare butt when she hops ashore.

See Her Naked In:

Mackenna's Gold (1969) Buns

Thandie Newton

Born: November 6, 1972
Zambia
Skin-O-Meter: Great Nudity

Thandie Newton, whose full name Thandiwe means Beloved in some African language, actually gained critical acclaim for portraying Beloved in the Oprah Winfrey-financed *Beloved* (1998). She is the daughter of a Zambian princess and a well-to-do British father, so it seems like she had all the breaks, which she more or less did. When her family fled Africa during a time of uprising, Thandie decided to try her hand at acting. She was cast in the sleeper flick *Flirting* (1992), which starred Nicole Kidman and just so happened to feature Thandie's first nude scene. She went on to act in the 2Pac vehicle *Gridlock'd* (1997), which also happened to feature her in the buff. She continued the carnal trend in *The Leading Man* (1996) opposite Jon Bon Jovi and *In Your Dreams* (1997). Just when it seemed she

would break out of her pretty-naked-girl roles, Thandie again opted to shed her duds for *Besieged* (1998) and *Beloved*, the latter of which featured her only full-frontal shot to date. She went blockbuster with *Mission: Impossible II* (2000) but failed to gain box-office clout with the disappointing *The Truth About Charlie* (2002), so there's hope for a return to form for this skinful star. Her body is sweet as Thandie.

SKIN-fining Moment:

Beloved (2:28) Oprah leads the gigantically pregnant—and entirely naked—Thandie on a walk. Amazing ass, shag coochie, milky mo-mo's and sexy mega-belly.

See Her Naked In:

Beloved (1998) FFN, Buns
Besieged (1998) Breasts
In Your Dreams (1997) Breasts
Gridlock'd (1997) Breasts
The Leading Man (1996) Breasts, Bush
Flirting (1992) Breasts

Kelly Nichols

Born: June 8, 1959
West Covina, California
Skin-O-Meter: Great Nudity

Wavy redhead Kelly Nichols became a hall-of-infamy-quality porn starlet, but she didn't start out that way. With her sunshine-bright cheerleader face and lithe, streamlined bod, Kelly made a quick stop on the *Penthouse* Pet stepping stone and tried to rocket herself from that platform into Hollywood stardom. Kelly's delightful dimples appeared in the blockbuster *King Kong* (1976) ; unfortunately, her scene was there and gone within the flickering of an eyelid. A long and lingering look at Nichols front and back and up and down provided the highlights of the slasher flick *The Toolbox Murders* (1978). After being pursued in the nude throughout *Toolbox*, Kelly went to work with her own box and ratcheted up a string of successes with triple-X tools throughout the early 1980s.

SKIN-fining Moment:

The Toolbox Murders (0:22) Psycho killer Cameron Mitchell interrupts Kelly's bath, causing her to streak nude through her apartment before settling on a bed and scorching the screen with her buoyant boppers and one of the most full-bodied muffs in movie history.

See Her Naked In:

Model Behavior (1984) Breasts
Deathmask (1984) Breasts
The Toolbox Murders (1978) FFN, Buns
Numerous Adult Movies

Julia Nickson-Soul

Born: 1958
Singapore
Skin-O-Meter: Brief Nudity

When opportunity knocks, Singapore-born skin slinger Julia Nickson-Soul answers the door ready to hop to as the desired Asian du jour. Since she appeared on a 1983 episode of *Magnum, P.I.*, versatile Julia has portrayed any manner of almond-eyed nationals in features as diverse as *Rambo: First Blood Part II* (1985) and *Harry's Hong Kong* (1987) and even performed her flower-blossom best on the spaced-out TV series *Babylon 5*, on which viewers couldn't even be sure she was from this planet. Luckily, Julia has been generous with her jewels. Her views to a thrill in *Man Against the Mob: The Chinatown Murders* (1989) and *White Tiger* (1995) make totally superfluous the question of her country of origin.

SKIN-fining Moment:

White Tiger (1:04) Julia toplessly shows off her pink-nosed tigers as she gets animal-like with Gary Daniels.

See Her Naked In:

White Tiger (1995) Breasts
Amityville: A New Generation (1993) LB
K2 (1991) Buns
Man Against the Mob: The Chinatown Murders (1989) Breasts

Nico

Born: October 16, 1938
Cologne, Germany
Died: July 18, 1988
Skin-O-Meter: Great Nudity

She had a voice of doom and a Teutonic blonde perfection that dared to take on the ravages of time and destiny. To her generation and to all those rebellious hearts that followed, she became the ultimate underground icon. She is Nico. Although she is best known for having sung on the first record by New York City art-noise band and Andy Warhol protégés The Velvet Underground, Nico was actually taking a step down when she signed on as a rock 'n' roll siren. Big eyes, big lips, big cheekbones, a sculpted nose, and an expression of placid certitude, Nico had reigned as a top European model, mothered a love child with a top European actor, and appeared as herself in a top Federico Fellini film, *La Dolce Vita* (1960).

SKIN-fining Moment:

Strip-tease (0:43) In groovy black-and-white, Nico unveils her swingin' knockos at a strip club. Nice, even if we don't get to see her Velvet Underground.

See Her Naked In:

Strip-tease (1963) Breasts

Daria Nicolodi

Born: June 19, 1950
Florence, Italy
Skin-O-Meter: Brief Nudity

Longtime companion to Dario Argento and mother to the arousing Asia Argento, Daria Nicolodi is often referred to as the Deep Red Diva from what is perhaps her most famous role as Gianni in her hubby's film *Deep Red* (1975). Although Dario and Daria allegedly never officially tied the knot, with their names being the same—one the feminine, the other masculine—they make a perfect union, as illustrated by their frisky and sexually ambitious offspring. Daria is still quite active in films and has most recently starred in her daughter's directorial debut, which is appropriately enough called *Scarlet Diva* (2000). Although Asia might be following in the big footsteps of her family's business, she has already surpassed her mother in terms of onscreen nudity.

SKIN-fining Moment:

Schock (0:30) Two great looks at her cute glutes in the shower.

See Her Naked In:

Schock (1977) LB, Buns
La Proprietà non è più un furto (1973) FFN, Buns

Brigitte Nielsen

Born: July 15, 1963
Helsingor, Denmark
Skin-O-Meter: Great Nudity

Brigitte Nielsen's stardom soared through the zipper when she latched onto Sylvester Stallone's Italian Stallion and rode that beast from *Rocky IV* (1985) to *Cobra* (1986). After dropping out of school to pursue a career as a model, she landed a role in *Red Sonja* (1985) for a barbaric good time. Metal breastplates and mini animal skirts must have attracted the pint-sized, pumped-up affection of Stallone, who ended up marrying the statuesque beauty and sharing her well-toned body in the spotlight. Brigitte maintained her exposure in B-movies like *Mission of Justice* (1992) and *Chained Heat II* (1993). Be sure to catch what snared Sly in such skintaculars as her rump-a-thon in *Bye Bye Baby* (1988) and a wet topless pool scene in *Domino* (1989), plus a finger-licking-hot masturbation scene sure not to leave a dry seat in the house.

SKIN-fining Moment:

Domino (1:04) Brigitte canoodles with her self in a super-sexy white lingerie get-up, feeling up her own massive, naked right-side fake-a-bago.

See Her Naked In:

Bye Bye Baby (1989) RB, Buns
Domino (1989) Breasts, Buns

Connie Nielsen

Born: July 3, 1965
Elling, Jutland, Denmark
Skin-O-Meter: Great Nudity

Connie Nielsen is one Great Dane (no, not a dog, she's Danish born and bred), who got her cinematic start in Italy before heading to the U.S. for the big-budget bonanzas that made her famous. That fame first fanned the flames of male libidos in the Keanu Reeves thriller *The Devil's Advocate* (1997), playing the K-dude's Satan-spawned sister who was hell-bent on incest. She appeared very nude in the movie's climactic final scene, with a long, decently lit full-frontal shot. That arousing introduction led to a role in the blockbuster *Gladiator* (2000), as the wise-beyond-her-years sister of Commodus. That must have been a pleasant change for her, because in *Gladiator*, it's her brother, not her, who is bent on incest, which seems to be a running theme for her. Connie's star continued to rise in *One Hour Photo* (2002) and *The Hunted* (2003). But that doesn't mean

she's neglected flashing her fine flesh. She wasn't so innocent in her topless scene for *Innocents* (2000). And in the foreign art-house thriller *Demonlover* (2002), about corporate spying and pornographic anime, Connie went back to her devilish ways by showing off her sinful skin. Connie can be our demon lover anytime.

SKIN-fining Moment:

The Devil's Advocate (2:10) Connie strips completely naked and attempts some incest with her bro Keanu Reeves by tempting him with her fake dubloons, dainty derriere, and sugary Danish.

See Her Naked In:

Demonlover (2002) Breasts
Dark Summer (1999) Breasts, Buns
The Devil's Advocate (1997) FFN, Buns
Voyage (1993) LB, Buns

Lisa Niemi

Born: May 27, 1957
Houston, Texas
Skin-O-Meter: Great Nudity

Texans know how to steal a show when they really want to, and lanky, limber, loaded of breast Lisa Niemi must have truly desired to purloin the thunder from *Slam Dance* (1987). The tall blonde native of Houston had a background in dance and theater, steeped in childhood training and young-adult experience hoofing across Broadway floorboards in shows such as *Hellzapoppin* with Jerry Lewis. Button flies were poppin' from Dallas to Juarez when the rhythmic dramatist paraded like a stark, raving nudist across the *Slam Dance* set, erasing from memory every other aspect of that otherwise entirely memorable film.

SKIN-fining Moment:

Slam Dance (54:00) Complete and total nakedness as Lisa argues with Tom Hulce before a kid wanders in. Lucky

kid—he sees her perfect boobs and pubes. We do, too.

See Her Naked In:

Slam Dance (1987) FFN, Buns

Barbara Niven

Born: February 26, 1953
Portland, Oregon
Skin-O-Meter: Great Nudity

Barbara Niven is perhaps most famous for her roles on *The Bold and the Beautiful* and *Pensacola: Wings of Gold* or perhaps for her interpretation of Marilyn Monroe in the HBO movie *The Rat Pack* (1998) or as Goldie's Stepmother in the lesbianic fantasy that was *Foxfire* (1996). But nothing has broken this buxom talent into the big time . . . yet. She was kind enough, though, to bust out her massive hooters a few times, most notably in *Depraved* (1996). She appeared fully nude from behind during a sex scene, but the crème de la crème was her topless rendezvous with a bubble bath. Get a load of those floaters!

SKIN-fining Moment:

Illegal Entry: Formula for Fear (1:02) Babs gets topless and feeds her nipplilicious Nivens to her man's mouth.

See Her Naked In:

Depraved (1996) Breasts, Buns
Illegal Entry: Formula for Fear (1993) Breasts

Cynthia Nixon

Born: April 9, 1966
New York, New York
Skin-O-Meter: Great Nudity

Cynthia Nixon may seem like a tomboy, but beneath her spunky good looks lurks the lust of an Amazonian sex goddess as wild as her dyed-red hair. The New York native first made her name onstage and has won numerous acting awards for her strut in front of the footlights. While her movie work may be more on the sidelines, the intrepid viewer can find himself pleasantly rewarded for digging deep into her oeuvre. She debuted in the naughty teen comedy *Little Darlings* (1980) as Sunshine Walker, a pre-teen flower child who is involved in the summer-camp-wide contest to see who can lose their virginity first. She went on to appear in such notable films as *Amadeus* (1984) and *Addams Family Values* (1993), though her roles were almost non-existent. The only starring parts she could land, it seems, were in obscurities like *I Am the Cheese* (1983) and *Baby's Day Out* (1994). Of course, you no doubt recognize Cynthia as one of the lovely ladies on the hit HBO series *Sex and the City*. Like her co-stars, the carnal Kim Cattrall and the knockout Kristin Davis, Cynthia has shown off her meaty melons throughout the scandalous series. She also appeared quite topless in *Advice From a Caterpillar* (1999), which again found her in a very small role, although she was naked for the better part of her time onscreen. She should listen to that caterpillar more often.

SKIN-fining Moment:

Sex and the City "The Domino Effect" (2003) Ms. Nixon pulls no tricks and shows her topless knick-knacks in the sack while paddywhacking Blair Underwood.

See Her Naked In:

Advice From a Caterpillar (1999) Breasts
O.C. and Stiggs (1987) Buns

TeleVisions:

Sex and the City Breasts

Stephanie Niznik

Bangor, Maine
Skin-O-Meter: Great Nudity

From Bangor, Maine, to the college campuses of North Carolina to the hills of Hollywood to the mean streets of Salt Lake City, Utah, such are the landmarks on the far-flung path taken by sparkling pale blonde Stephanie Niznik in her pursuit of dramatic stardom. Fine-featured, cerebral, light as a gossamer pastry, Stephanie came to life in Bangor and earned a Masters in Fine Arts from North Carolina's Duke University and promptly put the diploma to use in stage productions of *Crimes of the Heart* and *Dial M for Murder*. Matinees led to sound stages with guest spots on *Dr. Quinn, Medicine Woman*; *JAG*; and a plethora of others, which eventually won the upwardly mobile career girl the coveted next-door-neighbor role on the surprise-hit series *Everwood*, filmed in Salt Lake City. At home in Hollywood, formerly nasty Niznik must reflect that all the males in Utah will be ever wood if they ever happen upon her full-frontal exposure in *Exit to Eden* (1994).

SKIN-fining Moment:

Exit to Eden (0:37) Stephanie gives Dana Delany a hand putting on her robe and you can compare their awesome orbs and fuzzy-wuzzles.

See Her Naked In:

Spiders II: Breeding Ground (2001) Breasts
Exit to Eden (1994) FFN

Margaret Nolan

Born: August 1, 1943
Hampstead, London, England, UK
Skin-O-Meter: Brief Nudity

Margaret Nolan is breast known for her purrfectly arousing role as the sex kitten "Dink" in *Goldfinger* (1964). With her bushy blonde mane and out of this world mea-surements, there is nothing dinky about this alluring English muffin. The PR department of *Goldfinger* proudly published Madge's mea-surements at 41-23-37, raising the gazonga gold standard to an all-time, bone-inducing high. Also a mammarific model in the '60s, Nolan was a natural at playing the naked nymph, hawking her humongous hooters between the pages of *Playboy*. This pinup warmed peter pullers in abundance during her curve-clutching career in flicks like *Bikini Paradise* (1967) and *No Sex Please: We're British* (1973) but was sadly skingy about revealing her pointed peaks onscreen. After a short-lived role on the TV series *Crossroads* in the '80s, Nolan is now nowhere to be found. Are you there, Margaret? It's us, your fans. We miss your pecker-perking presence.

SKIN-fining Moment:

Carry On Girls During a crazy bikini catfight, Margaret's sizable casaba's slip free of her swimsuit top. Carry On Girls, indeed!

See Her Naked In:

Carry On Girls (1973) Nip Slip RB

> "If you eat right and you exercise and you get breast implants, you can look like us."
>
> —GENA LEE NOLIN

Sheree North

Born: January 17, 1933
Los Angeles, California
Skin-O-Meter: Brief Nudity

Sheree North was once the heir apparent to the bosomy mantel of Marilyn Monroe, until 20th Century-Fox decided to focus on Jayne Mansfield instead. Oh, well, Sheree didn't mind. Her talents shaking her fine rack gave her a string of successes dancing through roles on the silver screen and TV throughout the '50s. She disappeared for a while after that, coming back with a part in *Destination Inner Space* (1966)—and to taste Sheree's inner space, whoo-whee! After that, she began to take on more "worldly" roles, appearing as a topless dancer in *The Gypsy Moths* (1969) and again showing some of her top-heavy skin in *Lawman* (1971) opposite very-happy-to-grope-her Burt Lancaster. Ah, Sheree amore!

SKIN-fining Moment:

Lawman (1:19) Sheree shows the North and South points of skinterest on her naked chest in bed with Burt Lancaster.

See Her Naked In:

Lawman (1971) Breasts
The Gypsy Moths (1969) LB

Judy Norton-Taylor

Born: January 29, 1958
Santa Monica, California
Skin-O-Meter: Brief Nudity

If you're a young woman who's spent her career as part of America's most wholesome family, where do you go to prove that you're all grown up? In the case of Judy Norton-Taylor—beloved to America as little Mary Ellen from *The Waltons*—the answer was obviously *Playboy*. Judy's sizzling photo layout was a big seller for the magazine, and guys could also enjoy scenes from the photo shoot in *Playboy Video Magazine, Vol. 10* (1986). Now she's a sexy older actress showing up in small TV roles as simply "Judy Norton"—but that's probably a welcome change of pace for this sexy farm girl, who, after seven *Waltons* TV movies, probably doesn't want to answer to "Mary Ellen" ever again.

SKIN-fining Moment:

Playboy Video Magazine, Volume 10 (0:45) Judy shows her Walton

mountains and fully-bloomed underbrush in still photos from her Playboy *spread.*

See Her Naked In:

Playboy Video Magazine, Volume 10 (1986) FFN

Désirée Nosbusch

Born: January 14, 1965
Esch/Alzette, Luxembourg
Skin-O-Meter: Hall of Fame

There is no higher honor for a German actress than to record a song with "Der Kommisar" himself. Désirée Nosbusch proudly sang with Falco on the song "Kann Es Liebe Sein"—but we, of course, are more likely to go insane for her kanns. Désirée first got us desirous with some full-frontal flaunting during her debut in *Nach Mitternacht* (1981). *Der Fan* (1982) got guys harDer with plenty of Nosbusch bush, and she closed out the '80s with skinema appearances in films such as *Die Klette* (1986) and *Good Morning, Babylon* (1987). Désirée also ditched her clothes for a 1985 episode of the HBO series *The Hitchhiker*. She's been staying clothed in recent years, but the outspoken radio host and Euroactress has stayed busy with plenty of scandals—including a sordid case where her sixty-year-old lover was murdered by his son. We'd be upset if our father was getting to dick a dame like Désirée too.

SKIN-fining Moment:

Der Fan (1:16) Désirée Noscbusch shows busch—and boobs and buns—as she figures out that the fella on the floor is dead, then proceeds to cut him up for storage in the freezer.

See Her Naked In:

A.D.A.M. (1988) Breasts
Good Morning, Babylon (1987) Breasts
Die Klette (1986) Breasts

Questo e quello (1983) Breasts, Buns
Der Fan (1982) FFN, Buns
Nach Mitternacht (1981) FFN, Buns

TeleVisions:

The Hitchhiker Breasts

Kim Novak

Born: February 13, 1933
Chicago, Illinois
Skin-O-Meter: Brief Nudity

Buxom blonde glamour gal Kim Novak got her start as Miss Deepfreeze, modeling Frigidaires on television in the early '50s. With her curvaceous chestage and hypnotizing hips, Kim went from Ice Queen to Teen Dream, warming hearts and pants on and off screen. This sultry sex kitten pawed her way through most of the Rat Pack, including Frank Sinatra, Peter Lawford, and Sammy Davis Jr., the latter love fest resulting in purrrfect 1950s scandal. No matter whom she dated or what she wore, Kim's cunning curves made her the talk of the walk of fame. Her D-lightful attributes and charming personality were bewitchingly beautiful in *Bell Book and Candle* (1958) and the farcical sex-fueled romp *Kiss Me Stupid* (1964). Kim was at her most dazzling and dizzying in *Vertigo* (1958) with Jimmy Stewart. Double-diddle inspiring, she played two mysterious (mammoth-mammed) characters, both dressed in sexy skin-hugging suits. Kim's look in the film left such a mark on director Paul Verhoeven's shorts, he made ice-pick princess Sharon Stone wear exact replicas for her sexpot role in *Basic Instinct* (1992). Although Kim's career slowed after the '60s, she continued to dress to impress, flaunting her still-firm finger pillows in a plunging, black, groan-ganking gown at the 1979 Oscars. This super-sized superstar will always be Breast Actress here at Skin Central.

SKIN-fining Moment:

The Amorous Adventures of Moll Flanders (1:36) Kim robs a store, then runs off and hides around the corner, but only the tip of her teat gets busted. Nip-slip alert!.

See Her Naked In:

The Amorous Adventures of Moll Flanders (1965) Nip Slip RB

Mia Nygren

Sweden
Skin-O-Meter: Great Nudity

Sylvia Kristel wasn't getting any younger, so the Emmanuelle producers gave her a complete makeover in *Emmanuelle 4* (1984). Her character went through extensive cosmetic surgery, and the wrappings were removed to reveal the much younger Mia Nygren. This stunning starlet then made sure that all of her new parts were working. Mia quickly indulged in plenty of sex and nudity with partners of both genders. It was an impressive debut, but the wild gal's only other skinema contribution was *Plaza Real* (1988)—and then it was see ya, Mia. Maybe she just went back to looking like Sylvia Kristel.

SKIN-fining Moment:

Emmanuelle IV (0:15) Mia explores every inch of her nude body while strutting around her house. FFN, buns.

See Her Naked In:

Plaza Real (1988) Breasts
Emmanuelle IV (1984) FFN, Buns

Lena Nyman

Born: May 23, 1944
Stockholm, Sweden
Skin-O-Meter: Great Nudity

Sweden-born sweetie Lena Nyman has been making movies in her native land since the mid '50s and continues filming to this day. But she'd be just another cold Swedish fish if it weren't for a pair of arthouse sex films that she starred in back in the swinging '60s. Alternately called "one of the most important pictures I have ever seen in my life" by Norman Mailer or "vile and disgusting" by Rex Reed, *I Am Curious (Yellow)*—(1967) hit American shores like an invading army of perversion when it opened in 1969. It became the highest grossing foreign film release of its day. The explicit feature broke down the last vestiges of the Hollywood production code and paved the way for the mainstreaming of actual hardcore porn like *Deep Throat* (1972) and *Caligula* (1979). Lena really blew viewers' horns (among other things). She is far from the normal Hollywood sex kitten, a shapely and attractive beauty but not without flaws. She didn't have any problem with nudity, though, and there's plenty of it. She followed that up with *I Am Curious (Blue)*—(1968)— the colors are from the Swedish flag. The rest of her career hasn't been as skinful, but that double-header of carnality gives her a special place of distinction in the Skin Central Hall of Fame. Color us hot.

SKIN-fining Moment:

I Am Curious (Yellow) (1:32) In this super-long scene, we start with some serious banging and end with a screaming match, where the only thing you don't see of Lena is the underside of her feet.

See Her Naked In:

I Am Curious (Blue) (1968) FFN, Buns
I Am Curious (Yellow) (1967) FFN, Buns

O

Shauna O'Brien

Born: October 17, 1970
Pasco, Washington
Skin-O-Meter: Great Nudity

When you look as scrumptious as Shauna O'Brien, guys just want to eat you up. And she's a dish that's best served hot. Of course, Shauna is sizzling as one of the queens of the sexy end of the B-movie spectrum. She's carved a niche for herself as the California dreamer in *Beverly Hills Workout* (1993), *Wild Malibu Weekend!* (1994), and *Beverly Hills Bordello* (1997), in which her character's motivation is to take off her clothes as quickly as possible. She actually had a bit part in *Another 48 Hrs.* (1990), but her "mainstream" career just doesn't seem to want to take off—at least, not as easily as her clothing does. That is all fine and good for Shauna, who is more willing to entertain through titillation than through actual acting ability. And with her figure, that's a lot of tit. Not only that, she makes it a habit to perform the most realistic sex scenes this side of Paris. For some Shauna highlights, check out *The Escort* (1997) and its sequel, as well as *Friend of the Family* (1995) and its sequel. She's so good and busty, it's always worth coming back for more mams.

SKIN-fining Moment:

Friend of the Family (0:44) Lezbo-a-go-go! Shauna shows full-frontal ferociousness while going girl-girl-crazy with Griffin Drew in a tub.

See Her Naked In:

Baberellas (2003) Breasts, Thong
Survivors Exposed (2001) Breasts
15 minutes of Fame (2001) FFN, Buns
Platinum Blonde (2001) FFN, Buns
Summer Temptations 2 (2000) FFN, Buns
The Seductress (2000) FFN
Erotic Possessions (2000) FFN, Buns
Scandal: The Big Turn On (2000) FFN, Buns
Sex Files: Creating the Perfect Man (1999) Breasts, Buns
Voyeur (1999) FFN, Buns
The Escort 2 (1998) Breasts
Striking Resemblance (1997) FFN, Buns
The Escort (1997) Breasts, Buns
Beverly Hills Bordello (1997) FFN, Buns
Body Armor (1996) Breasts
Friend of the Family 2 (1996) FFN, Buns
A Passion for Murder (1996) Breasts, Buns
Friend of the Family (1995) FFN, Buns
Over the Wire (1995) FFN, Buns
Seduce Me: Pamela Principle 2 (1994) Breasts, Buns
Wild Malibu Weekend! (1994) Breasts, Thong
Beverly Hills Workout (1993) FFN, Buns

TeleVisions:

Beverly Hills Bordello FFN, Buns

Taaffe O'Connell

Skin-O-Meter: Great Nudity

Intense-looking blonde Taaffe O'Connell has been prompting Taaffe pulls since 1975, when she made her debut on an episode of *Starsky and Hutch*. She spent the '70s putting plenty of bounce in jiggle television and managed an appearance as a ring girl in *Rocky II* (1979). Then her big'uns hit the big screen in *Galaxy of Terror* (1981), although Taaffe's titties were seen to better effect in films such as *Caged Fury* (1984) and *Hot Chili* (1985). Taaffe only works sporadically nowadays, but her memorable double Connells still get us saying "O"—as proven when her *Galaxy of Terror* footage was recycled for the remake of *Not of this Earth* (1988).

SKIN-fining Moment:

Galaxy of Terror (0:42) When a slimy alien bug wants a taste of Taafe, he thoughtfully exposes her breasts before infiltrating her interspecies-style.

See Her Naked In:

Not of This Earth (1988) Breasts, Buns
Hot Chili (1985) Breasts
Caged Fury (1984) Breasts
Galaxy of Terror (1981) Breasts, Buns

Frances O'Connor

Born: June 12, 1967
Oxford, Oxfordshire, England
Skin-O-Meter: Great Nudity

Frances O'Connor has gotten us blundering for our zippers in films like *Kiss or Kill* (1997) and *Bedazzled* (2000). This lithe brunette has also become a regular presence in classy British productions, which—not too surprisingly—resulted in some classical nudity from *Madame Bovary*

(2000). The British lassie has started to assault the local multiplexes, too, making a big splash as the mom with an electronic boy in *Artificial Intelligence: A.I.* (2001)—although we'd prefer seeing her with an electronic toy. Anyway, Frances is now officially a rising star in Hollywood, with roles in *Timeline* (2003) and *Iron-Jawed Angels* (2004). Her nude scene in *Book of Love* (2004) keeps our trousers rising too.

SKIN-fining Moment:

Madame Bovary Frances goes for some natural nookie with a guy against a tree. Quick caboose, bolstered by side right boobage.

See Her Naked In:

Book of Love (2004) Bush
Madame Bovary (2000) Breasts

Glynnis O'Connor

Born: November 19, 1956
New York, New York
Skin-O-Meter: Great Nudity

You might recognize Glynnis O'Connor as the earthy beauty of Robbie Benson's dreams in *Ode to Billy Joe* (1976). Although Glynnis played the perfect wholesome hottie in the flick, she was more fleshtastic in her second feature

CALIFORNIA DREAMING: IT'S MORE LIKE CALIFORNIA CREAMING TO THE MAM-AS AND THE FLOPPAS IN THIS SUN-SOAKED LOBBY CARD THAT APTLY AMPLIFIES THE MOVIE'S FEEL-GOOD FLOW—ALONG WITH GLYNNIS O'CONNORS' GLOBES.

with Benson, *Those Lips, Those Eyes* (1980). Those Tits! This bonnie lass whipped out her stellar shamrocks, causing the heartthrob (and fans of skinema) to pulsate in a place further down below. Glynnis has shown her lucky charms in other flicks, such as *Melanie* (1982) and *California Dreaming* (1979), each being a Gallic globed vision of perky perfection. Glyn has gone on to appear in estrogen-inducing films featured on Lifetime and in guest appearances on *Law & Order*. Although we at Skin Central hope Glynnis continues to have the luck of the Irish, we find her hiatus from nudity to be a real crime.

SKIN-fining Moment:

California Dreaming (0:11) Glynnie's twins glimmer when she pulls off her nightie and walks to the bathroom.

See Her Naked In:

Melanie (1982) Breasts
Those Lips, Those Eyes (1980) Breasts, Buns
California Dreaming (1978) Breasts

Reneé O'Connor

Born: February 15, 1971
Katy, Texas
Skin-O-Meter: Brief Nudity

Reneé O'Connor got her big break with a gig on an episode of *Tales from the Crypt* in 1990, but, alas, her scenes were deleted before the show was aired. She had previously done some work on *The Mickey Mouse Club*, *NYPD Blue*, and in the Roy Scheider thriller *Night Game* (1989), but these were brief, blink-and-you'll-miss-it fleeting encounters with fame. The sexy blonde Texan finally landed some work of note, first in the made-for-TV movie *Changes* (1991), then in the feature film *Stone Cold* (1991), which has nothing to do with wrestling. Most people recognize her for her part on the hit syndicated series *Xena: Warrior*

Princess, on which she played Gabrielle, Xena's trusty sidekick. As the show matured, so did the relationship between the two characters, who ended up bathing together and sharing a kiss as writers skirted around the issue of whether the two were in fact lovers *and* fighters. *Xena* is also your best bet for catching the sexy lass nude, as she's been filmed in some compromising positions, all of which somehow manage to cover up the dirty bits. Since *Xena* has been canceled, Reneé has been avoiding the camera with her main squeeze in New Zealand, but hopefully this Kiwi lover will peel soon.

SKIN-fining Moment:

Xena: Warrior Princess "The Haunting of Amphipolis" (2000) Shrieking like some kind of monkey-woman, she pounces on Xena and, as they roll around, we see a flash of Reneé's nice monkey rump.

TeleVisions:

Xena: Warrior Princess Buns

Jennifer O'Dell

Born: November 27, 1974
Hawaii
Skin-O-Meter: Brief Nudity

Jennifer O'Dell is an O'Doll! Jennifer has risen to stardom by getting a rise out of her pop-eyed male audience in a multitude of guest appearances on shows such as *Renegade*, *Silk Stalkings*, *Pacific Blue*, and *Beverly Hills, 90210*. She's been onscreen, too, of course, most notably in *Sometimes They Come Back . . . For More* (1998) and *Point Doom* (1999). For the more skinful side of Jennifer, she did manage a few nip slips and pubic glances on her television series *The Lost World* and showed some brief hootage in *Point Doom*. But *Sometimes* featured her best flesh to date, including one of her topless body on an examination table, complete with enormous, natural jugs sagging down into her pits. Unfortunately, the scene also involved Jennifer being tortured and killed, but hey, let's not be so picky.

SKIN-fining Moment:

Sometimes They Come Back . . . For More (1:16) Jen's splayed out on a table with her bare O'Del's drenched in blood. Skingortastic.

See Her Naked In:

Point Doom (1999) Breasts
Sometimes They Come Back . . . For More (1998) Breasts

TeleVisions:

Nip/Tuck RB, Buns

Devon Odessa

Born: January 18, 1974
Parkersburg, West Virginia
Skin-O-Meter: Brief Nudity

People are still mourning the cancellation of the 1994 TV series *My So-Called Life*, and it's not just overgrown, misunderstood teens. Plenty of well-adjusted men miss their weekly chance to ogle divine Devon Odessa. This perky blonde provided plenty of so-called boners while trying to pass as a high-school student. She certainly got straight Aaah's from us. Her subsequent career has been a weird mix, including the hit Christian thriller *The Omega Code* (1999). Fortunately, Devon also sinned and skinned in the college drama *The Sterling Chase* (1999), playing a luscious lipstick lesbian losing her lover to societal pressure. Damn that societal pressure!

SKIN-fining Moment:

The Sterling Chase Devon looks devine with her dairy spouts in plain view as she slips inside a shirt.

See Her Naked In:

The Sterling Chase (1999) Breasts

Rosie O'Donnell

Born: March 21, 1962
Commack, Long Island, New York
Skin-O-Meter: Never Nude

Some like 'em hot, some like 'em big. If you can't decide, then Rosie O'Donnell is your kind of woman. She started her career by losing to Rick Ducommun on *Star Search*, but you can't keep a large woman down, and she used her runner-up money to move out to L.A. and pursue her acting career. She vaulted into the limelight by appearing as a veejay on the fledgling VH1 network before she tried her hand at some serious acting and stand-up. For *A League of Their Own* (1992), she got to play ball with her pussy-eating pal Madonna. In the smash hit *Sleepless in Seattle* (1993), just being on the same set as the luscious Meg Ryan must have made this behemoth dyke's panties cream up. To get her fans' rocks off, she appeared in *The Flintstones* (1994) as Betty Rubble. But for all you tubby chasers, the cream is found in the fetish comedy *Exit to Eden* (1994). Rosie finally exposed her sexual side in a leather-and-latex outfit that left audiences craving a bite. She has since gone on to a successful daytime talk show and is now in semi-retirement. If she returns to the spotlight, then everything will be coming up Rosie.

SKIN-fining Moment:

Exit to Eden (1:13) Whole-lotta-Rosie makes like a pork sausage in a hard-stretched black leather dominatrix get-up. And if that suit smells half as bad as it looks . . .

Bulle Ogier

Born: August 9, 1939
Boulogne-Billancourt, France
Skin-O-Meter: Brief Nudity

Just when the hype was dying down from the '60s, Bulle Ogier came along to remind Americans that French films were still packed full of ooh-la-la. Plenty of guys packed the arthouses to check out Bulle's valley in *La Vallée* (1972). And those long legs made the trip to her valley very pleasurable, while Bulle's modest French pastries also made for a real treat. She then became a true international star with the worldwide success of *The Discreet Charm of the Bourgeoisie* (1972). *Maîtresse* (1976) further established Bulle as a truly shameless starlet, dolled up in fetish outfits as a seriously sick dominatrix. But Bulle can also be sexy in normal settings, as seen when she went topless in *Tricheurs* (1984). She's gone on to become one of France's busiest actresses (and a respected screenwriter), although the nude scenes have fallen by the wayside. Bulle is still sexy in clothed roles, though, as seen in *Irma Vep* (1996), in which her bitchy character casually announced the lesbian yearnings of one of her party guests.

SKIN-fining Moment:

La Vallée (0:15) Side view of ass and brief look at her right tit being tweaked during sex.

See Her Naked In:

Tricheurs (1983) Breasts
La Vallée (1972) RB
Piège (1968) Breasts

Lani O'Grady

Born: October 2, 1954
Walnut Creek, California
Died: September 25, 2001
Skin-O-Meter: Great Nudity

Lani O'Grady is best remembered as Mary, the braniac med student daughter on the classic '70s dramedy *Eight is Enough*. In real life, Lani hailed from a famous family herself, being the sister of Don O'Grady of *My Three Sons* fame. Lani's career didn't get off to the smoothest start, though. She was featured in a few downer television productions, such as *The Headmaster* and *Cage Without a Key* before her feature-film debut in *Massacre at Central High* (1976). The only thing massacred in that was Lani's clothing. She let loose her bountiful, bouncing breasts for a nice, long topless scene that would prove to be her only. Aside from her various *Eight is Enough* reunions, she more or less quit acting after *The Kid with the Broken Halo* (1982) to pursue work as a talent scout. Takes one to know one.

SKIN-fining Moment:

Massacre at Central High (1:10) Lovely Lani walks out of a tent to fetch Cheryl Smith for a little ménage-à-trois action with Robert Carradine. Remember kids, it's good manners to share!

See Her Naked In:

Massacre at Central High (1976) Breasts

Sandra Oh

Born: 1971
Nepean, Ontario, Canada
Skin-O-Meter: Great Nudity

Korean Canadian Sandra Oh first exposed her Asian charms with the lead performance in the made-for-TV movie *The Diary of Evelyn Lau* (1993). And she's only gotten better since. Sandra skyrocketed to stardom with a recurring role on the hit cable series *Arli$$*. Since then it has been nothing but top-shelf movies for her top-notch body. She's been in *Bean* (1997), *The Red Violin* (1998), *Waking the Dead* (2000), and *The Princess Diaries* (2001), not to mention the sexually ambiguous mini-series *Further Tales of the City* (2001). Thankfully, some

incredibly intelligent individual decided to cast Sandra in the stripper flick *Dancing at the Blue Iguana* (2000), leading to her first notable skin scenes, including a nice topless routine in the vicinity of a brass pole. If anyone ever told you that dreams don't come true, here's proof that they lied . . . Oh yeah!

SKIN-fining Moment:

Dancing at the Blue Iguana (0:10) Her dance sequence starts with some excellent thongness and is soon followed by a nice look at her little nubbins.

See Her Naked In:

Dancing at the Blue Iguana (2000) Breasts, Thong
Guinevere (1999) RB

Kelsey Oldershaw

Skin-O-Meter: Great Nudity

We grabbed our crotch STAT when Kelsey Oldershaw appeared as "Nurse Tess" on the 2003 season of *ER*—although we almost had to turn the channel to get the *CSI* crew to clean up the crime scene in our pants. Kelsey was overdue for a high-profile turn after finally getting some attention via her role in the spooky romance short *Cinema/Vérité* (2001). The feature *The Affair* (2003) also showcased Kelsey as a cheating wife with a preference for lowlifes. We were already counting on Kelsey, though, having been turned on to this hot young talent when she donned a bikini as a perfect girlfriend on a 2003 episode of the WB sitcom *Run of the House*.

SKIN-fining Moment:

The Affair (0:23) With buns this bangin', she's GOTTA show 'em off. She lies in bed with her dude, tuchus up.

See Her Naked In:

The Affair (2003) Breasts, Buns

Lena Olin

Born: March 22, 1956
Stockholm, Sweden
Skin-O-Meter: Great Nudity

With her dark brown hair and olive complexion, Lena Olin looks more like a native of the Mediterranean Sea than the North Sea. Truth is, this Swedish splendor got her start from Ingmar Bergman, the director who championed fellow Scandinavian sirens like Liv Ullman and Pernilla August. One of Lena's earliest roles was a short film called *Glasmastarna* (1981), or *The Glaziers*, in which she climbed in and out of a bubble bath, exposing both front and back sides for the delight of Swedish skinsters. It's sure to heat up the frozen tundra. Her breakthrough role came with *The Unbearable Lightness of Being* (1988), in which she let Juliette Binoche snap photos of her disrobed rump. After receiving a Best Supporting Actress Oscar nomination for her role as a young temptress in *Enemies: A Love Story* (1989), another nude revue, she appeared in several less critically acclaimed American features. She may be the most famous parent on TV, playing Jennifer Garner's double-crossing, KGB-card-carrying, long-thought-dead-in-a-car-crash mom on the hit series *Alias*. But for the best and most bizarre view of Lena, visit *Romeo Is Bleeding* (1994), in which she played a kinky Russian assassin whose favorite pastime is wrapping her thighs around Gary Oldman's head. That's quite a face off.

SKIN-fining Moment:

The Unbearable Lightness of Being (1:29) Ms. Olin provides plenty to ogle as she seductively poses for Juliette Binoche's camera. Nice breasts, nicer buns.

See Her Naked In:

The Ninth Gate (1999) Body Double—LB, Buns

Romeo is Bleeding (1994) Breasts, Thong
Enemies: A Love Story (1989) Breasts
The Unbearable Lightness of Being (1988)
    Breasts, Buns

Kate O'Mara

Born: August 8, 1939
Leicester, Leicestershire, England,
UK
Skin-O-Meter: Great Nudity

Is there such a thing as a GILF? Grandmotherly Kate O'Mara defined the term when she appeared on the UK prison drama *Bad Girls* as a high-class hooker. Even in a wheelchair, Kate was still handicapable of making our zipper break out of our pants. Not bad for a British beauty whose career goes back to TV appearances in 1957. Kate's a legend of stage and screen in England, but her biggest splash in America was a 1986 stint on *Dynasty* as Joan Collins's striking sister. The oft-married O'Mara is also famously plainspoken, and she famously got O'Muffish with an amazing sex scene in the drama *Whose Child Am I?* (1974). Though she's still stunning, check out more of her younger bustline in Hammer Horror classics like *The Horror of Frankenstein* (1970) and *The Vampire Lovers* (1970).

SKIN-fining Moment:

Whose Child Am I? (0:32) After getting a big O from her boyfriend, Kate shows her O'Mammaries and O'Muffala in bed and again in the shower.

See Her Naked In:

Whose Child Am I? (1974) FFN, Buns

Tatum O'Neal

Born: November 5, 1963
Los Angeles, California
Skin-O-Meter: Great Nudity

If ever arose a case of divided erotic loyalties, it popped up during viewing of *Little Darlings* (1980). The conflicted alliance came in trying to pick a preferred winner when budding tots Tatum O'Neal and Kristy McNichol squared off as feuding brats competing to see which of the post-pubescent pretties could pop her cherry first. The scales tipped in Tatum's favor and stayed that way when her dark left nipple popped from her bikini top and into plain sight during a spell of pool-time frolic. Although the rusty-blonde progeny of Irish ham Ryan O'Neal had previously won an Oscar for her toddler role in *Paper Moon* (1973), the future ex-Mrs. John McEnroe's peak was yet to come. Peek at the twin delights and definite but slight ridge of muff displayed for the delectation of Richard Burton and all others who are wise enough to watch *Circle of Two* (1980).

SKIN-fining Moment:

Circle of Two (0:57) Long scene of Tatum's taters as she stands behind a chair talking to Richard Burton. Those are some funky funbags!!!

See Her Naked In:

The Home Front (2002) RB
Circle of Two (1980) Breasts
Little Darlings (1980) Nip Slip, LB

Jennifer O'Neill

Born: February 20, 1948
Rio de Janeiro, Brazil
Skin-O-Meter: Brief Nudity

A former Ford model most famous as the face of Cover Girl cosmetics, Jennifer O'Neill always has a picture-perfect presence. How appropriate that this haughty hottie hails from the banana-exporting country Brazil, since Jen has been inspiring banana-sized boners since her first sultry appearance in *Summer of '42* (1971). This Brazilian bombshell rounded up a tornado of lust in the dust in *Rio Lobo* (1970), leaving the Duke helpless to say anything except "Well, howdy partner" to the mighty tingle in his dingle. Skinematically speaking, Jennifer was selective about showing her tan and taut frame. A brief brown nip slip in *Committed* (1988) and a viewing of her hot-crossed bunnage in *Glass Houses* (1972) make this well-cut, rare gem's bare juiciness even more arousing. Today, Jennifer can be seen in bewitching bitch roles in such films as *Full Exposure: The Sex Tapes Scandal* (1989) and *The Cover Girl Murders* (1993) on the Lifetime network. Jen's own lifetime achievement as tasty eye candy will always be sweetly remembered.

SKIN-fining Moment:

The Masters (0:34) Jen joins Franco Nero by a window, supplying us with a quick view of her naked sitter and side right boob.

See Her Naked In:

Gente di rispetto (1975) Buns
Glass Houses (1972) Buns

Yoko Ono

Born: February 18, 1933
Tokyo, Japan
Skin-O-Meter: Brief Nudity

Who cares if she broke up the Beatles? This pioneering performance artist has a hot little bod that's prompted plenty of penises to break up zippers. Yoko Ono was free with her body back in the '60s, building her reputation with displays like "Cut Piece," in which an eager audience disrobed Yoko a snip at a time. She was also eager to strip once John Lennon brought her to the national stage—as we're all reminded by her nude scenes in the documentary *Imagine: John Lennon* (1988). Don't forget her tawdry early role in the sleazy *Satan's Bed* (1965), either, in addition to her Bed-In that helped hippies host a revolution between the sheets.

SKIN-fining Moment:

Imagine: John Lennon (0:57) Yoko appears full-frontally naked on an album cover alongside John. There's enough hair between them that it takes a moment to tell who's who. Look for her Japanese submarines.

See Her Naked In:

Imagine: John Lennon (1988) FFN

Amanda Ooms

Born: September 5, 1964
Kalmar, Kalmar län, Sweden
Skin-O-Meter: Hall of Fame

Sometimes venturing far afield can be a most worthwhile endeavor. Especially if the wayfaring explorer happens upon the richly exotic foreign delights of Amanda Ooms. Born and bared in Sweden, Ooms's sensual pout and splendid pair have graced the skinema of her homeland since the mid 1980s. She has displayed and splayed in everything from *The Mozart Brothers* (1986) to *Så vit som en snö* (2001). Having gone so far as to gobble gonads in *Hotel St. Pauli* (1988), it's nothing short of remarkable that Ooms has also made her mark as a serious lead actress in internationally acclaimed dramas. She is the beautiful pianist cured of blindness in *Mesmer* (1994). Anyone with Amanda's eye appeal deserves to be able to see herself.

SKIN-fining Moment:

Så Vit Som en Snö (1:24) Meaty buttage, bouncing bare B-cups and lofty lap-fluff as Amanda climbs a hill and is startled by a parade of male nakedness on horseback.

See Her Naked In:

Så Vit Som en Snö (2001) FFN, Buns
Recycled (1999) Breasts, Buns
Getting Hurt (1998) Breasts
Jagd Nach CM 24 (1997) Breasts
Chainsmoker (1997) Breasts, Buns
Wilderness (1996) Breasts, Buns
De Tussentijd (1993) Breasts
Ginevra (1992) Breasts
Buster's Bedroom (1990) Breasts
Kvinnorna På Taket (1989) FFN
Hotel St. Pauli (1988) FFN, Buns

Julia Ormond

Born: January 4, 1965
Epsom, Surrey, England, UK
Skin-O-Meter: Great Nudity

It once appeared that the Brit beauty Julia Ormond was set to be the next big babe. She starred opposite Richard Gere in *First Knight* (1995) and Harrison Ford in Sydney Pollack's sexy *Sabrina* (1995) remake. The silky brunette held her own next to her Hollywood heavyweight hunks—and turned many a head with her curvy figure and 36C bust. Unfortunately, the public wasn't prepared for such a hot Sabrina, and since then Julia has only appeared in mundane movies with negligible nudity like *The Prime Gig* (2000). To see the moist of Julia's fantastic frame, dig up Peter Greenaway's art-kink masterpiece *The Baby of Mâcon* (1993). Julia plays a seventeenth-century bad girl whose shining moment is a sloppy seduction of Ralph Fiennes in a barn. After an angry steer gores Fiennes before they can consummate their love, Julia alleviates her sexual frustrations by killing it—without bothering to put her clothes on. I guess that's a little hamburger to go with the buns.

SKIN-fining Moment:

The Baby of Mâcon (1:03) Julia gets naked with Ralph Fiennes in a barn. Then some magic kid points his finger, there's blood everywhere and Julia gets

full-frontal as she slaughters a cow. Some villagers show up; Julia stays naked. Completely ridiculous, entirely sexy.

See Her Naked In:

The Prime Gig (2000) LB
Smilla's Sense of Snow (1997) Buns
Legends of the Fall (1994) RB
The Baby of Mâcon (1993) FFN, Buns
Nostradamus (1993) LB

TeleVisions:

Traffic Buns

Phina Oruche

UK
Skin-O-Meter: Brief Nudity

How did Phina Oruche end up playing a security guard on a 2003 episode of the syndicated series *She Spies*? After all, she's one of the sexiest and funniest femmes currently being neglected by Hollywood. Despite stealing scenes and tightening groins in films such as *How Stella Got Her Groove Back* (1998) and *High Freakquency* (1998), Phina's only star turn has been in the skintastic flick *The Forsaken* (2001). She's also fairly fangtastic, putting a bat in our pants as an evil, sexy sucker. Phina's character didn't survive that film, but her own career is way overdue for a major resurrection.

SKIN-fining Moment:

The Forsaken (0:50) Topless Phina gets ferocious in a backseat as she sinks her fangs into a fella, her naked right cocoa-puff swinging every which way. Phine-a!

See Her Naked In:

The Forsaken (2001) RB

Debbie Osborne

Skin-O-Meter: Great Nudity

"He conquered the hills, piece by piece!" reads the tagline to Bethel G.

Buckalew's sexploitation film *Tobacco Roody* (1970). It marked hot Debbie Osborne's first appearance in the warm, mosquito-attracting glow of the drive-in theater. Not surprisingly, Debbie appeared in several states of undress in that particular feature. Ol' Buckalew must have enjoyed what he saw because he cast her in his sexy *Country Cuzzins* (1970) and *Midnight Plowboy* (1971). Both films again featured the comely young kitten in all her light-auburn-haired full-frontal glory . . . all nicely trimmed, combed, and parted in the middle, ready for company to come and play as they most often did in steamy simulated sex scenes. As if Buckalew hadn't served up enough chances for little Debbie to strut her sweet stuff onscreen, equally notable smut servers Robert Anderson and Corey Allen gave her some skin time in *Cindy and Donna* (1970) and *The Erotic Adventures of Pinocchio* (1971), respectively. Unfortunately, that just about rounded out Debbie's career, which has been on "vacation" since 1972. Come back, Debbie, so we can come!

SKIN-fining Moment:

Tobacco Roody (0:55) In the back of a van with a dirty old man, Debbie displays her deliriously delicious little bare body and parts her legs wide, proving her natural redhead status, as well as rendering it so her gynecologist no longer has anything on the rest of us.

See Her Naked In:

Midnight Plowboy (1971) FFN
Tobacco Roody (1970) FFN, Buns
Country Cuzzins (1970) FFN, Buns

Maureen O'Sullivan

Born: May 17, 1911
Boyle, County Roscommon, Ireland
Died: June 23, 1998
Skin-O-Meter: Never Nude

As a true Hollywood legend, Maureen O'Sullivan appeared in classics such as *Pride and Prejudice* (1940), *The Big Clock* (1948), and even *Bonzo Goes to College* (1952). She even managed an impressive comeback with *Hannah and Her Sisters* (1986) and *Peggy Sue Got Married* (1986) before her death in 1998. But this Irish lassie lassoed herself some skinematic greatness with her role as the proverbial "Jane" in the popular *Tarzan* series. Maureen was sexy in *Tarzan the Ape Man* (1932), but *Tarzan and His Mate* (1934) featured amazing early nudity, including a backlit disrobing scene and some flashilly FFN skinny dipping. Alas, when it comes to the flesh, Maureen's Jane is a Cheetah! The boobs and beav belong to Olympic swimming gold medalist and naked body double Josephine McKim. Still, Maureen always provides plenty to thump your, uh, chest over.

SKIN-fining Moment:

Tarzan and His Mate (0:41) Tarzan throws his mate Maureen into a river, and, on the way down, her dress gets torn by a branch revealing ultra-astonishing full-frontal jungle arms and lap-brush courtesy of body double Josephine McKim.

See Her Naked In:

Tarzan and His Mate (1934) Body Double— FFN, Buns

Carré Otis

Born: September 28, 1968
San Francisco, California
Skin-O-Meter: Great Nudity

Carré Otis's career has certainly seen its ups and downs . . . and ins and outs! After several years reigning high on the fashion-model circuit, Carré took a shot at acting with her soon-to-be ex-husband Mickey Rourke in *Wild Orchid*

(1990), which raised more than a few eyebrows for their said-to-be less-than-simulated sex sequence. Unfortunately, her career quickly came tumbling down, both in the modeling realm and in Hollywood, when her battle with bulimia reached epic proportions and she nearly died from a heroin overdose. By 1996, though, Carré had pulled herself back together and, better still, has continued to take her clothes off. She's since returned to modeling (with a much more robust figure) and even landed an acting gig opposite Rourke, of all people, in *Exit in Red* (1996). She's also added to her skinful features with a hooter flash in *Under Heavy Fire* (2001), so it looks as if Carré's career is back on the breast track that we could have hoped for!

SKIN-fining Moment:

Wild Orchid (1:44) Carré gets the meat from Mickey Rourke in a scene rumored to be the real deal. Her tits, trim and tail are certainly real!

See Her Naked In:

Under Heavy Fire (2001) Breasts
Wild Orchid (1990) FFN

Annette O'Toole

Born: April 1, 1954
Houston, Texas
Skin-O-Meter: Great Nudity

When Annette O'Toole passes away, her tombstone will read: "Here lie some of the most beautiful, natural breasts ever photographed, and the lucky guy from *Spiñal Tap* got more than any one man can handle by marrying her." Or something like that. Mr. Skin is just jealous of Michael McKean. Annette has been acting since she was in her teens, starting off in an episode of *My Three Sons*. She has appeared on countless TV shows, from *Gunsmoke* and *The Virginian* to *Hawaii Five-O* and *Nash Bridges*. Annette had a brief part as Nick Nolte's pissed but understanding girlfriend in *48 Hrs.* (1982) before co-starring in *Superman III* (1983). Then she finally revealed her awesome twosome in the pussy thriller *Cat People* (1982), which offered a couple of glances at her mammalian magnificence. But the real booby prize was her turn opposite Martin Short in the sleeper *Cross My Heart* (1987)—let's just say she's not wearing any cross-your-heart bra. The last half of the film takes place in a bedroom with the obviously retarded Short having a difficult time consummating his relationship with arousing Annette. Why does he come up Short? With Annette as the temptress, there's not an O'Toole out there that would have any difficulty getting it on.

SKIN-fining Moment:

Cat People (1:31) *Annette's massive, milky-white mammaries come out when she takes her clothes off in the locker room.*

See Her Naked In:

Cross My Heart (1987) Breasts, Buns
Cat People (1982) Breasts

Tamayo Otsuki

Born: May 29, 1959
Skin-O-Meter: Great Nudity

On the 1991 TV series *Davis Rules* sexbomb Tamayo Otsuki played a schoolteacher, which was a step up from her debut in *Mortuary Academy* (1988) where she was billed Madonna-style as simply "Tamayo." Her best-known role remains the Korean shop owner who's gunned down in the comedy *Don't Be a Menace to South Central While Drinking Your Juice in the Hood* (1996). Tamayo is also a brazenly sexy gal, however, and she stripped for Japanese *Playboy* in a comic photo layout celebrating pubic hair. *Anarchy TV* (1997) even featured her as a hooker who joined the cast in a wild full-frontal dance routine. Sadly, Tamayo's kept a low screen profile since then, but you might still get lucky and find her performing her stand-up comedy.

SKIN-fining Moment:

Anarchy TV (1:01) *Tamayo shows it all off as she leads the naked crew in some Birthday Suit Aerobics!*

See Her Naked In:

Anarchy TV (1997) FFN, Buns

Miranda Otto

Born: December 16, 1967
Brisbane, Queensland, Australia
Skin-O-Meter: Great Nudity

Miranda Otto is best known to American audiences for her parts in *The Thin Red Line* (1998), *What Lies Beneath* (2000), and the last two installments of *The Lord of the Rings*. But those supporting roles belie her star power Down Under, back in her native Australia, that is. She wasted no time jumping to the top of the proverbial heap, taking on the title role in her debut film, *Emma's War* (1986). Before her fateful venture to Hollywood, Miranda commanded starring roles in such notable Australian pictures as *Initiation* (1987), *The 13th Floor* (1988), and *The Girl Who Came Late* (1991)— well, at least she came. Hopefully, that star power will prevail here in America. Mr. Skin would like to see her stick around . . . or her around a stick. Miranda's not so shy about shedding her threads onscreen, either. She first flashed her flappers in *The Nostradamus Kid* (1993) and thankfully continued the trend in such films as *Love Serenade* (1996), *True Love and Chaos* (1997), and *In the Winter Dark* (1998). She even briefly flashed some titty during a sex scene with Tim Robbins in *Human Nature* (2001), but it paled in comparison to her earlier exposure. Keep it up, Miranda, you're Otto control!

SKIN-fining Moment:

Julie Walking Home (1:26) *Don't miss this glimpse of Otto's Hotto Tottos!*

See Her Naked In:

Julie Walking Home (2001) Breasts
Kin (2000) Breasts, Bush
True Love and Chaos (1997) LB
Love Serenade (1996) Breasts
The Nostradamus Kid (1993) RB, Buns
Emma's War (1986) Breasts, Buns

Danielle Ouimet

Born: June 16, 1947
Montreal, Quebec, Canada
Skin-O-Meter: Great Nudity

You didn't have to be from England to be a sexy victim of a lesbian vampire. Danielle Ouimet started out in Canada, where she did amazing early work as a sexbomb in *Valérie* (1969). She was in her true prime as the title character, showing off her fine Canadian peaks in a steamy bath scene. She also cavorted nude with girlfriends and a lucky man in the sexfest *L'Initiation* (1970). Danielle didn't become truly immortal, though, until she was cast in the cult classic *Daughters of Darkness* (1971) as a young newlywed seduced by Delphine Seyrig. It's an amazing feminist film with plenty of hot scenes to please the guys. Danielle didn't try hard to follow that sex act, though, and it was over a decade before she returned in the 1985 TV series *L'Or du temps*—and then another seventeen-year wait before she showed up as a sexy grandma in *L'Odyssée d'Alice Tremblay* (2002).

SKIN-fining Moment:

Here and Now (0:53) Both Danielle and Celine Lomez show their upper decks with some other girls in the sauna. Long Ouimet scene.

See Her Naked In:

Daughters of Darkness (1971) Breasts
Here and Now (1970) Breasts
Valérie (1969) Breasts

Camilla Overbye Roos

Copenhagen, Denmark
Skin-O-Meter: Great Nudity

Though Camilla Overbye Roos started her career in Danish films such as *Drengen der forsvandt* (1984) and *Forbryelsens element* (1984), she wasted no time making her way to Hollywood. Small roles on TV shows such as David Lynch's *Hotel Room* and some low-profile film appearances led to a bit part in the waterlogged blockbuster *Titanic* (1997). Roles in *The Beat Nicks* (2000), *Thicker Than Thieves* (1999), and *The Guilty* (2000) followed, and things continue to look bright for the big-busted up-and-comer.

SKIN-fining Moment:

Vicious Circles (0:26) Camilla and Carolyn Lowery both bare their sweaty fun-sacks in the steamroom. Bang-up boobulars, babes!

See Her Naked In:

The Contract (1999) Breasts, Buns
On the Border (1998) Breasts, Buns
Vicious Circles (1997) Breasts

Susie Owens

Born: May 28, 1956
Arkansas City, Kansas
Skin-O-Meter: Brief Nudity

Late-bloomer Susie Owens got our boxers blooming when she became *Playboy*'s Miss March 1988 at the age of thirty-one. She also took her time about finally making a skinematic appearance—after, that is, the usual brilliant show in productions such as *Playboy Video Playmate Calendar 1989* (1988). Susie finally made her acting debut in *They Bite* (1996) and has confined her nude appearances to the Bunny Ranch ever since—not that we mind visiting there to enjoy her massive talents.

SKIN-fining Moment:

They Bite (1:06) We see her breasts and her tush while straddling a guy in bed. Then her vagina turns into an alien beast! Huh?

See Her Naked In:

They Bite (1996) Breasts, Buns
Numerous *Playboy* Videos

Catherine Oxenberg

Born: September 22, 1961
New York, New York
Skin-O-Meter: Great Nudity

Catherine Oxenberg made her big debut as her hotness Princess Diana in *The Royal Romance of Charles and Diana* (1982). Then, from 1984 to 1986, she out-bitched the bitchiest, landing a coveted role on the iconic TV soap *Dynasty*. She continued working in made-for-TV crap until landing a part opposite Amanda Donohoe in madman Ken Russell's wacky whack-off horror favorite *The Lair of the White Worm* (1988). Catherine later reprised her role as the doomed Princess Di in *Charles and Diana: Unhappily Ever After* (1992). Her career slowed a bit following her run on *Acapulco H.E.A.T.*, so she turned to some serious nudie fare to pay the bills, a move always applauded by Mr. Skin. Check out the women in prison flick *Time Served* (1999) for a great deal of nudity from carnal Catherine. In that movie, she is arrested and forced to undergo a strip search. Her firm, round tits do make a worthwhile appearance, but her delightful backside steals the show.

SKIN-fining Moment:

Time Served (0:19) Great, typical women-in-prison scene of Catherine having to strip before entering the pokie that's made extraordinary by her bare-breasted heat.

See Her Naked In:

Frozen in Fear (2000) Breasts, Thong
Time Served (1999) Breasts, Buns

Hilit Pace

Skin-O-Meter: Great Nudity

As a quirky normal gal with strange sex appeal, Hilit Pace doesn't get nearly enough roles—but when she works, she's unforgettable. Her presence livened up the daytime soaper *All My Children* between 1999 and 2001, and she enjoyed a sexy turn in the film *Chasing the Dragon* (2000). Hilit then raised our zippers to the hilt as a dancer who enchanted a traitorous FBI agent in *Master Spy: The Robert Hanssen Story* (2002). This real-life tale originally aired on CBS, and Hilit was a reliable made-for-TV stripper. The DVD version, though, allowed Hilit to unhinge in full NC-17 mode. She brazenly displayed her boobies and a thong-wrapped ass and shined in an aborted oral-sex scene. Somebody needs to pick up the Pace on this gal's career!

SKIN-fining Moment:

Master Spy: The Robert Hanssen Story (0:55) Gazongas and a G-string as she peels in a strip club.

See Her Naked In:

Master Spy: The Robert Hanssen Story (2002) Breasts, Thong

TeleVisions:

Master Spy: The Robert Hanssen Story Breasts, Thong

Judy Pace

Born: June 15, 1946
Los Angeles, California
Skin-O-Meter: Great Nudity

Judy Pace was one of the most gorgeous young actresses of '60s cinema, but this black beauty didn't let herself get stuck in any kind of genre. After debuting in a schlock-horror classic as one of *13 Frightened Girls* (1963), Judy appeared in upscale classic films such as *The Fortune Cookie* (1966) and *The Thomas Crown Affair* (1968). Her sexy presence was put to good use on the TV series *Peyton Place*, and she was unforgettable in *Three in the Attic* (1968), where she was part of a trio of cuties who locked up their cheating boyfriend so they could drain him of his manhood. She was also in the sexy semi-sequel *Up in the Cellar* (1970). And when Judy finally decided to do blaxploitation, she chose the classic *Cotton Comes to Harlem* (1970) to show some classic nudity. She retired in 1973 and left a gap in sexy cinema that hadn't been seen since Greta Garbo went off to be alone.

SKIN-fining Moment:

Cotton Comes to Harlem (0:31) Judy keeps the nudie Pace and flashes all 3 B's getting into a lush lavender bed, then later showing a little more shadowy T&A running away, the tease.

See Her Naked In:

Cotton Comes to Harlem (1970) FFN, Buns

Joanna Pacula

Born: January 2, 1957
Tomaszow, Lubelski, Poland
Skin-O-Meter: Hall of Fame

After appearing in a few unpronounceable Polish movies, Joanna Pacula landed the lead female role in the hit mystery *Gorky Park* (1983) opposite William Hurt. And it also marked the pretty Pole's first onscreen nudity. The brunette beauty has gone on to appear in *The Kiss* (1988), *Tombstone* (1993), *My Giant* (1998), and *The Hit* (2001). While her bedroom romp with Hurt in *Gorky Park* didn't hurt the eye, it was her turn in *Husbands and Lovers* (1992) that grabbed attention like a girl giving her first hand-job. In the film, Joanna explored taboo sexual matters, such as sadomasochism and bondage with her lover, while her husband made love to other women. She appeared completely nude in much of the film, including some sweet shots of her scrumptious bush and buns. She has also appeared nude in *Every Breath* (1992), *The Art of Murder* (1999), and others, but *Husbands and Lovers* remains her greatest skin role to date. And that's no Polish joke.

SKIN-fining Moment:

Gorky Park (1:21) Joanna is in bed and gets completely naked right before William gives her the big "Hurt."

See Her Naked In:

The Art of Murder (1999) Body Double—FFN, Buns
Business for Pleasure (1997) Buns
Last Gasp (1995) RB
Private Lessons II (1993) Buns
Husbands and Lovers (1992) FFN, Buns
Every Breath (1992) Breasts, Buns
Black Ice (1992) LB, Buns
The Kiss (1988) Breasts
Not Quite Paradise (1986) LB
Gorky Park (1983) Breasts

Joanna Page

UK
Skin-O-Meter: Brief Nudity

Drool, Britannia! English eyeful Joanna Page is fast proving to rank high among the 21st century's most reliably—and robustly—naked skinternational starlets. Her full-bodied, bare-boobied turns in the decidedly British-flavored hits, *From Hell* (2001) and *Love, Actually* (2003) bode well for not only for lovers of UK T&A, but for all those who find the bare breasts of buxom blondes unbeatable in terms of entertainment. And that means you. Joanna is a real Page-turner . . . on.

SKIN-fining Moment:

From Hell (0:08) Sexy backal-nudity (no crackle, though) as Joanna rides man-rod, punctuated by an appearance of her pink-nosed pups.

See Her Naked In:

Love, Actually (2003) Breasts
From Hell (2001) Breasts

Holly Palance

Born: August 5, 1950
Los Angeles, California
Skin-O-Meter: Brief Nudity

Holly Palance is proof that hot chicks come from cool cucumbers. Her father is the hard-ass character actor Jack Palance. She started her career opposite another granite-faced actor, this one being the comic John Cleese, in *Golf Etiquette* (1973). She subsequently spent her youth in one bit part after another in such films as *The Omen* (1976), *Dickens of London* (1976), and *The Strange Case of the End of Civilization as We Know It* (1977). She finally landed a good supporting role in *The Comeback* (1978) and went on to appear in such semi-notable productions as *Under Fire* (1983), *The Thorn Birds* (1983), and *The Best of Times* (1986). Her career abruptly ended after her turn in *Cast the First Stone* (1989). It's a drag that Holly never got that superstar role that she must have yearned for, but, thankfully, her career didn't come to its screeching halt before she had a chance to bare her beautiful bosom for the camera in *Tuxedo Warrior* (1982). The movie is no classic, but it's definitely worth the look just to see Daddy Jack's little girl all grown up, if you catch our drift.

SKIN-fining Moment:

Tuxedo Warrior (0:32) Holly's not wearing a tuxedo while getting some from her guy. That's why we can see her hoots.

See Her Naked In:

Tuxedo Warrior (1982) Breasts

Aleksa Palladino

New York
Skin-O-Meter: Brief Nudity

Aleksa Palladino first made a name for herself as the latter half of *Manny & Lo* (1996), playing the pregnant runaway sister of Scarlett Johansson. The indie caught the attention of Hollywood, who soon scooped up the beautiful, brunette, and talented young actress. Since then Aleksa has appeared in such fare as *Number One Fan* (1997), *A Cool, Dry Place* (1998), and Woody Allen's *Celebrity* (1998). Things are looking up for this boobtastic babe—that is viewers' things. Although Aleksa starred in many an arthouse favorite, her career didn't really hit the mainstream until an appearance in *Storytelling* (2001) opposite Selma Blair. Aleksa definitely appeared in Blair's skinful shadow in the film but managed to turn a few heads with her first ever nudity. She provided the icing on Selma's (cheese) cake by flashing full-frontal muff and hooterage in photographs that some lucky person took and another equally lucky guy perused. It may not be "live," so to speak, but it's sure to enliven that monster in your pants. You just have to wonder who got to keep those pictures for their personal album after the production was complete.

SKIN-fining Moment:

Storytelling (0:16) Aleksa flashes a bit of all her B's in a series of bondage photos that Selma Blair finds rather distasteful.

See Her Naked In:

Storytelling (2001) FFN

Anita Pallenberg

Born: January 25, 1944
Rome, Italy
Skin-O-Meter: Great Nudity

Italian eyeful Anita Pallenberg is breast known for riding on the coattails and cocks of the Rolling Stones. Anita was a '60s skinsation who went from flaunting her lofty frame in fashion mags like *Harper's Bazaar* to boinking bizarre, beat-obsessed beaus. This randy rock lover hopped atop Brian Jones's jock, moved on to Keith Richards, who sired her two children, before finally having a fast and furious fling with Mick Jagger. Now that's amore. Skinspired by Anita's magnificent mug, endless legs, and insatiable lust, The Rolling Stones penned "Angie" and "You Got Silver" in homage to her hornage. While bopping the band, Anita still found time to eke out a skinsational career shaking her moneymaker in the psychedelic '60s classic *Barbarella* (1968) and baring boobage in *Candy* (1968). What deliciously sweet cannoli teats! Today Pallenberg's rocker-romping lifestyle is as dead as the '60s. Clean, sober, and still fantastically fit, she spends her skinergy designing sexerific clothing in London. Any of this tall temptress's offerings will leave you crying, "*Anita* more!"

SKIN-fining Moment:

Performance (0:47) Anita shows T&A in a hot tub with Mick Jagger and Michelle Bretton. Nice Rolling Stones!

See Her Naked In:

Performance (1970) Breasts, Buns
Candy (1968) LB

Gretchen Palmer

Born: December 16, 1961
Chichopee, Massachusetts
Skin-O-Meter: Great Nudity

Gretchen Palmer first made the film rounds with bit parts in such features as *Fast Forward* (1985), *The Malibu Bikini Shop* (1985), and *Crossroads* (1986). No one seemed to notice, so she made the guest appearance rounds on such series as *Matlock* and *21 Jump Street*. Again, no one seemed to care, so she took the role of Hooker in *Red Heat* (1988) and, by baring her breasts and buns, gave her career the boost that it needed—and audiences got a boost in the pants for good measure. Gretchen would still be stuck in bit parts in movies like *Wishmaster* (1997), *Starquest II*

(1997), and *Moonbase* (1998) before she would finally find fame in the erotic thriller *Trois* (2000). The movie was rated NC-17, but it surprisingly contained very little in the way of nudity, although Gretchen managed to show off some of that scrumptious ass and the side of a tit here and there. It may not be all that skinful, but it sure is hot. With a body like Gretchen's got, who wouldn't want to Palmer?

SKIN-fining Moment:

Tales from the Crypt "Ear Today, Gone Tomorrow" (1996) Top-notch, torrid T&A as Gretch aggressively gyrates atop the lap of Tommy Lee Jones.

See Her Naked In:

Trois (2000) Buns
Red Heat (1988) Breasts, Buns

TeleVisions:

Bedtime Breasts, Buns
Perversions Breasts, Thong
Tales from the Crypt Breasts, Buns

Rebecca R. Palmer

UK
Skin-O-Meter: Great Nudity

Rebecca R. Palmer burst onto the scene with a bit part in the made-for-British-TV movie *Alice Through the Looking Glass* (1998). Then she landed another bit part in *Elephant Juice* (1999), but it was her completely naked shot in *Quills* (2000) that first brought Rebecca to Mr. Skin's carnal attention. However, even that paled in comparison to her role in *Intimacy* (2001). In that particular feature, Rebecca and Kerry Fox both engaged in some explicit sex, although Rebecca's scenes were a smidgen tamer than Kerry's. Nevertheless, it's a nude-worthy addition to her body of wank.

SKIN-fining Moment:

Intimacy (1:19) Boobies and beav as Rebecca R. Palmer has chatty relations with Mark Rylance.

See Her Naked In:

Quills (2000) RB
Intimacy (2000) FFN

Gwyneth Paltrow

Born: September 28, 1972
Los Angeles, California
Skin-O-Meter: Great Nudity

Class and ass are an intoxicating concoction, and they mix in equal parts in svelte blonde knockout Gwyneth Paltrow. While small in boobage, there is nothing paltry about Paltrow's package. The 33½-25-35, five-foot-nine-inch statuesque stunner first freed her cute cupfuls in *Flesh and Bone* (1993). Her flesh gave Mr. Skin a bone. She continued the torrid trend with *Mrs. Parker and the Vicious Circle* (1994) and *Moonlight and Valentino* (1995) and made the Bard grab his quill in *Shakespeare in Love* (1998). An equal-opportunity flasher, Gwyneth dropped drawer for a touch of tush in *Hush* (1998) and showed more literary titties in *Sylvia* (2003). She donned a "fat suit" as a corpulent cutup in the comedy *Shallow Hal* (2001), but there's no hiding Gwyenth's sexy body of work.

SKIN-fining Moment:

Shakespeare In Love (0:46) Oscar-winner Gwyneth shows off her Golden Globes while banging Bard Joseph Fiennes.

See Her Naked In:

Sylvia (2003) Breasts, Buns
Shallow Hal (2001) Thong
Shakespeare In Love (1998) Breasts
Hush (1998) Body Double—LB, Buns
Mrs. Parker and the Vicious Circle (1994)
  Breasts
Flesh and Bone (1993) LB

Irene Papas

Born: September 3, 1929
Chilimodion, Corynth, Greece
Skin-O-Meter: Brief Nudity

Few actresses have appeared in as many international classics as Irene Papas—including *The Guns of Navarone* (1961), *Zorba the Greek* (1964), *Anne of the Thousand Days* (1969), and *Z* (1969). Fortunately, this dark Greek also turned us into geeks with a skinternational turn in the classic *The Trojan Women* (1972). Her display of T&A is truly award worthy, and the former dancer has maintained a bod that makes us all want to become Greek diners. We're still panting for Papas in recent films such as *Jacob: A TNT Bible Story* (1994) and *Captain Corelli's Mandolin* (2001).

SKIN-fining Moment:

The Trojan Women (1:11) Irene bends down topless to wash herself in a water basin and we get a glance at Papas's mamas.

See Her Naked In:

The Trojan Women (1972) Breasts

Vanessa Paradis

Born: December 22, 1972
St-Maur-des-Fossés, Val-de-Marne, France
Skin-O-Meter: Great Nudity

Say what you will about Johnny Depp, but we'd also stay in Paris if our bedmate was Vanessa Paradis. She started out as a model, but Vanessa became a film star when her debut role in *Noce blanche* (1989) won her the French equivalent of the Oscar. It also gave us guys massive erections, as Vanessa displayed her luscious tits and heart-stopping, heart-shaped ass. Then she returned before the camera in *Élisa* (1995) to provide more Paradis in a full-frontal nude scene. She's worked steadily in films since then, although she's

settled for staying sexy with her clothes on. As mentioned, she lives with and has two children by Johnny Depp now, so maybe she's lost interest in advertising.

SKIN-fining Moment:

Noce Blanche (0:09) Brief full frontal as Vanessa gets out of bed in front of her professor, followed by a wondrous shot of her plump little butt. Tres bien!

See Her Naked In:

Élisa (1995) FFN, Buns
Noce blanche (1989) Breasts, Buns

Jessica Paré

Born: 1982
Montreal, Quebec, Canada
Skin-O-Meter: Great Nudity

Jessica Paré looks like Liv Tyler—if Liv had gargantuan jugs and liked to show them off at every opportunity. Yes, Jessica puts the sexy but shy Liv to shame. She has only been acting since 1999 and has already climbed the ladder into the realm of A-list actresses. The Canadian, in all her glory, has also put those very same mammoth mammaries on proud display many a time, first in the French-language film *En Vacances* (1999). Then, in the goalie-turned-supermodel drama *Stardom* (2000), Jessica showed off her dogs again, this time in somewhat better lighting—and, boy, does it make a man howl. However, the pièce de résistance for getting out her piece happened to be the picture *Lost and Delirious* (2001), which placed her and Piper Perabo in a lesbianic tryst which included some naked sack romping as well as extracurricular topless nudity from both actresses. Jessica is sure to take the cinematic world by storm, and there is no doubt here that she will do it naked.

SKIN-fining Moment:

Lost and Delirious (0:29) Jessica presses her jugtastic pair of Pares

LUST AND DAIRYLICIOUS: JESSICA PARÉ WITH PIPER PERABO IN HER LAP (AND TRAINING-BRA-ERA MISCHA BARTON IN THE BACK-GROUND) IN *LOST AND DELIRIOUS*.

against Piper Perabo during a lickilicious lesbo love scene.

See Her Naked In:

Lost and Delirious (2001) Breasts
Stardom (2000) FFN, Buns
En vacances (1999) Breasts

Monique Parent

Born: November 4, 1965
San Luis, California
Skin-O-Meter: Great Nudity

As Peter Cushing was to Hammer Horror, Monique Parent is to skinsational skinema—specifically, a fine acting presence who's believable as both a classy businesswoman and a nude maid. This riveting redhead first caught Mr. Skin's eye with some Sapphic shenanigans in *Secret Games* (1991). She was just getting warmed up while getting us overheated, though. Monique's got a throbbing softcore portfolio, including bondage with Kate Vernon in *Dangerous Touch* (1993), shacking up with Tane McClure in *Stripshow* (1995), and (reportedly real) mutual masturbation with Jennifer Burton in *Play Time* (1994). The unpredictable Monique has also recently taken to billing herself as "Scarlet Johansing"—which is a puzzling development, since you'd more likely expect that from some porn star following in the footsteps of Dru Berrymore.

SKIN-fining Moment:

Dangerous Touch (0:51) Ms. Parent whelps out her baby-feeders and birth-canal before joining Kate Vernon in bed.

See Her Naked In:

Wicked Temptations (2002) FFN
Close Enough to Touch (2001) Breasts
The Seduction of Maxine (2001) FFN
The Pornographer (1999) Breasts, Thong
Temptations (1999) FFN, Buns
Club Wildside 2 (1998) FFN, Buns
The Key to Sex (1998) FFN, Thong
Sweetheart Murders (1998) Breasts
Seaside Seduction (1998) Breasts
Club Wild Side (1998) Breasts
Lebensborn (1997) FFN, Buns
Lovers, Liars and Thieves (1997) Breasts, Bush, Buns
Tender Flesh (1997) FFN
Beverly Hills Bordello (1997) Breasts, Bush, Buns
Hot Lust (1997) FFN
Desire: An Erotic Fantasy Play (1996) FFN, Buns
Busted (1996) FFN, Buns
Masseuse (1996) Breasts, Bush
Love Me Twice (1996) Breasts, Buns
Dark Secrets (1996) FFN, Buns
Ladykiller (1996) Breasts
Stripshow (1996) FFN, Buns
Morgana (1995) FFN, Thong
Mirror Mirror III: The Voyeur (1995) FFN, Buns
Midnight Confessions (1995) FFN
Galaxy Girls (1995) Breasts, Buns
Blonde Heaven (1995) FFN, Thong
Scoring (1995) Breasts
Vicious Kiss (1995) Breasts
Married People, Single Sex II: For Better or Worse (1995) Breasts
Play Time (1994) FFN, Buns
Bikini Med School (1994) FFN
Sexual Outlaws (1994) Breasts
Love Street 1: I Dreamed of Angels Crying (1994) FFN, Buns
Dangerous Touch (1994) FFN
Body of Influence (1993) Breasts
Night Eyes 3 (1993) Breasts, Thong
Divorce Law (1993) FFN, Buns
. . . And God Spoke (1993) Breasts
Dragon Fire (1993) Thong
Sins of Desire (1992) FFN, Buns

Buford's Beach Bunnies (1992) Breasts
Secret Games (1991) RB, Bush, Buns
Black Tie Nights FFN, Buns

TeleVisions:

Beverly Hills Bordello Breasts, Bush, Buns
Erotic Confessions FFN, Buns
Hotline Breasts, Bush, Buns
Intimate Sessions Breasts, Buns
Passion Cove Breasts, Bush, Buns

Anne Parillaud

Born: May 16, 1960
Paris, France
Skin-O-Meter: Hall of Fame

Although Anne Parillaud started her career with a bit part in the French flick *Un amour de sable* (1977), Stateside voyeurs didn't get an opportunity to ogle the baguette-hardening honey until she originated the title role of *La Femme Nikita* (1990). Since then Anne has appeared in such notable English-language movies as *Frankie Starlight* (1995), *The Man in the Iron Mask* (1988), and *Dead Girl* (1996). But it was *Innocent Blood* (1992), which featured a very naked Anne parading about in all her full-frontal glory, that gave Americans an idea of what French film lovers had known for decades. Needless to add, this lusty lady is more than forthcoming with her onscreen skinitudity, making full-frontal appearances in such pictures as *Pour la peau d'un flic* (1981), *Le Battant* (1983), and *Juillet en septembre* (1988). In *Patricia* (1980), she explored lesbianism—always the adventurer. Anne even showcased her casabas for her role in *Shattered Image* (1998) and *Gangsters* (2002), showing the world that, like fine French wine, her corks only get better with age.

SKIN-fining Moment:

Innocent Blood (0:05) Anne ambles around her apartment completely nude, showing tasty titlets, great glutes, and a little patch of womb-groom.

See Her Naked In:

Gangsters (2002) Breasts, Buns
Shattered Image (1998) Breasts
À la folie (1994) FFN, Buns
Map of the Human Heart (1992) Breasts
Innocent Blood (1992) FFN, Buns
La Femme Nikita (1991) RB
Juillet en Septembre (1988) Breasts, Buns
Le Battant (1983) FFN
Pour la peau d'un flic (1981) FFN
Girls (1980) Breasts
Patricia (1980) FFN, Buns

Eleanor Parker

Born: June 26, 1922
Cedarville, Ohio
Skin-O-Meter: Brief Nudity

Eleanor Parker is often forgotten as both a former star and a pioneering Queen of Kink. Check out the women's prison drama *Caged* (1950), where her sweet character became a skinhead chain smoker who fascinates predatory warden Agnes Moorehead—and that's one of her more respectable films! In fact, the role led to her first Oscar nomination. Eleanor went on to another Oscar bid as Kirk Douglas's wife in *Detective Story* (1951) and a third as an afflicted opera star in *Interrupted Melody* (1955). She definitely deserved a medal for her topless turn in *An American Dream* (1966), in which she tormented her lover with a lit cigarette. Eleanor also gave Ann-Margret some feminine competition in *The Tiger and the Pussycat* (1967). By the '70s, though, she was reduced to TV projects like the 1972 pilot for *Fantasy Island*. Parker's been retired since 1991, but she'll always be a skinematic icon.

SKIN-fining Moment:

An American Dream Quick left knob when Ellie reaches over to turn the TV dial. Nice set.

See Her Naked In:

An American Dream (1966) LB

Kay Parker

Born: August 28, 1944
Birmingham, England, UK
Skin-O-Meter: Great Nudity

Kay Parker is one classy lady. She gets filmed doing unspeakable acts for the camera, always glowing hot and never looking tarnished. Arguably the queen of the classic era of pornography, Kay brings an almost subtle casualness to all her roles that suggests that she, in fact, enjoys what she is doing and even considers the genre an "Art Form." I don't know about art, but I know what I like . . . oral satisfaction, and

Kay bobs among the most talented slurpers ever involved in the suck industry. At the ripe old age of thirty-three, Kay ventured from her home in England to Hollywood, where she dove into the porno business boobs first with a part in *Seven Into Snowy* (1977). The top-heavy performer humped her way through such productions as *Sex World* (1978), *Body Talk* (1982), and *Tomboy* (1983), working her magic on many a hard-on, as well as many willing female participants. To watch her rump-rolling, giddy-up-little-cowgirl sex scene is to sit in absolute awe—no need for that Viagra prescription. Naturally, Kay's biggest success was as the incestuous mother in the classic *Taboo* (1980). The film appeared at the end of the so-called Sexual Revolution but somehow did more for the movement than anything in the previous two decades when it was supposedly swinging in full force. There wasn't a dry lap in the house when Kay woke up her sleeping son with a little lip lock to the groin. Oh-Kay!

SKIN-fining Moment:

Taboo (0:54) No longer able to abstain from the appeal of her on-screen son, Mama Kay slides into junior's bed and offers him access to the very portal from which he was originally produced. Kay satisfies her offspring with her magnificently matronly milk bags, motherly seat-meat, and wooly mammoth of a muff, as well as kissing him long, deep and sloppily on some place other than his cheek. What a lucky motherfucker!

See Her Naked In:

Taboo (1980) FFN
Numerous Adult Movies

Mary-Louise Parker

Born: August 2, 1964
Fort Jackson, South Carolina
Skin-O-Meter: Great Nudity

Three names can be disconcerting. Part-Swedish hottie Mary-Louise Parker has been confused with other tri-named tramps like Mary Stuart Masterson, Penelope Ann Miller, and Catherine Mary Stewart, but she's a threesome who stands apart from the others. The Southern belle from South Carolina moved to New York City to pursue a career onstage. While we'd prefer it be on the tawdry footlights of Times Square's flesh parlors, Mary-Louise made a name for herself in the more highfalutin theater world. The big screen beckoned and she followed, landing her debut in the AIDS drama *Long Time Companion* (1990) as one of the characters without a dick. Since then she's made people with dicks very happy, especially with her skin debut in *Grand Canyon* (1991), flashing those big-nippled titties in bed. Parker's pretties continued to be *Naked in New York* (1993) and elsewhere in *Let the Devil Wear Black* (1999), *Goodbye Lover* (1999), which added tush to her body of work, and *The Five Senses* (1999). Talk about ending the millennium with a bang . . . and then storming into the twenty-first century like a fox! In the 2004 HBO mini-series *Angels in America*, Mary Louise stunned viewers with a heavenly full frontal. *Angels in Hair-merica*, anyone?

SKIN-fining Moment:

Angels in America (2003) Stunning butt followed by awesomely furry full-frontalage as Mary-Louise talks to a Patrick Wilson. Angels in Hair-merica!

See Her Naked In:

Master Spy: The Robert Hanssen Story (2002) Breasts
Let the Devil Wear Black (1999) Breasts
The Five Senses (1999) Breasts
Goodbye Lover (1999) Buns
Naked in New York (1993) LB
Grand Canyon (1991) Breasts

TeleVisions:

Angels in America FFN, Buns
Master Spy: The Robert Hanssen Story Breasts

Molly Parker

Born: July 17, 1972
Maple Ridge, British Columbia, Canada
Skin-O-Meter: Great Nudity

If you like your sex served up hot with a heaping side of perversion, then Molly Parker is your kind of actress. The Canadian-born thespian is no stranger to explicit and bizarrely sexual roles. Her skin debut was a little shocker called *Kissed* (1996), which had morbid Molly getting it on with a stiffy— literally, the dead—as she played a gal into necrophilia. And in *Suspicious Rivers* (2000) she played a hooker who gets roughed up. But that's nothing compared to her magnum nude opus *The Center of the World* (2001), in which a dot-comer hired her (playing another prostitute, natch) to accompany him for a fling in Las Vegas. She'll do anything for money, which means so many lap dances the male lead ends up with calluses on his pecker. With her almond-shaped face, chalk-white complexion, and willowy figure, she's the ultimate good girl gone bad. Obviously, Molly has no problem flashing her fantastic flesh, like she did in *In the Shadows* (1998) and *The Five Senses* (1999). Good golly, Miss Molly!

SKIN-fining Moment:

The Center of the World (0:24) Molly shows her chest-dollies and buff buns while doing a long striptease for Peter Sarsgaard.

See Her Naked In:

The Center of the World (2000) Breasts, Buns
Suspicious River (2000) Breasts, Bush, Buns

The Five Senses (1999) RB, Buns
In the Shadows (1998) Breasts
Kissed (1996) FFN

Nicole Ari Parker

Born: October 7, 1970
Baltimore, Maryland
Skin-O-Meter: Great Nudity

Nicole Ari Parker is our cup of Joe: she's hot, black, strong, and tasty. Oh, yeah, Nicole is pretty talented too. She's held her own against the big boys in productions like *Remember the Titans* (2000), *Blue Streak* (1999), and *The End of Violence* (1997). It'll only be a matter of time before this talented and beautiful lassie is recognized for her incredible abilities. Until that fateful day, Mr. Skin would like to recognize Nicole for her incredible body, which has been put on full skinful display a number of times. She flashed her flappers in *Boogie Nights* (1997), pulled out her poppers in *Loving Jezebel* (1999), and flipped full frontal in *Mute Love* (1998). Mmm! Muff-tastic! Did anyone else notice that Laurel Holloman was in the first two films listed above? Of course Nicole and Laurel have enjoyed fairly parallel careers, including their big-break flick, the lesbo coming-of-age story *The Incredibly True Adventure of Two Girls in Love* (1995). Seeing as they've worked together several times since then, we're guessing they really enjoyed that ultra-plasmatically hot lez-tronic four-tittied sex-fest at the end of the flick. Mr. Skin did!

SKIN-fining Moment:

Mute Love (0:53) Brief boobage in the tub then some fabulous furry full-frontage while facing a mirror.

See Her Naked In:

Mute Love (1999) FFN
Boogie Nights (1997) Breasts

The Incredibly True Adventure of Two Girls in Love (1995) Breasts

Sarah Jessica Parker

Born: March 25, 1965
Nelsonville, Ohio
Skin-O-Meter: Never Nude

Three words: Sarah Jessica Parker. Three more words: no-nudity clause. From her humble beginnings as TV's first New Wave nerd sex symbol on the short-lived sitcom *Square Pegs* to her reign as queen of the frisky fashionistas on HBO's *Sex and the City*, Sarah Jessica has cut an alluring figure. With her long face, curly blonde locks, and curvaceous busty body, she first came to notice as a vapid party girl in the Steve Martin comedy *L.A. Story* (1991). She looked good in a skimpy black bikini in *Honeymoon in Vegas* (1992) but never stripped on The Strip. That damn clause. The closest we got to a peek at Parker's skin came in *Striking Distance* (1993), in which Sarah Jessica went for a tumble between the sheets. She was wearing underwear. Three final words: why, why, why?

SKIN-fining Moment:

Honeymoon in Vegas (0:32) Sarah hops up out of the hotel pool in a bikini that perfectly showcases her brickhouse build.

Heather-Elizabeth Parkhurst

Born: January 16, 1972
San Francisco, California
Skin-O-Meter: Great Nudity

So whatever happened to The Swedish Bikini Team? Former member Heather-Elizabeth Parkhurst barely got out of the bikini. The former beauty queen— officially Miss Mission Beach and

Miss Cancun—went on to spend lots of time poolside on the sexy Showtime series *Sherman Oaks*. Heather was also willing to ditch the titular clothing for some skintastic sunning in *Bikini Summer III: South Beach Heat* (1997). Don't miss her turn in the horror epic *The Granny* (1995), either, where she formed a trinity of charmers with Shannon Whirry and Stella Stevens. Heather has plenty of proud skinematic moments, including the unique honor of setting her boobies on stun for director William Shatner when he directed a 1997 episode of the HBO sci-fi anthology series *Perversions of Science*. And if you're more of a literary type, you can marvel at Heather in comic book form as the model for the fictional heroine Tommi Gunn.

SKIN-fining Moment:

Bikini Summer 3 (0:22) It's a plastic-fantastic fest as Ms. Parkhurst parties topless with pals in and out of a shower.

See Her Naked In:

Bikini Summer 3 (1997) FFN, Buns
The Granny (1995) Breasts
Conflict of Interest (1993) Breasts
Inside Out II (1992) Breasts, Thong

TeleVisions:

Perversions of Science Breasts, Buns
Sherman Oaks Breasts, Buns

Barbara Parkins

Born: May 22, 1942
Vancouver, British Columbia, Canada
Skin-O-Meter: Great Nudity

Most film fans remember Sharon Tate and Patty Duke as stars of the incredibly sordid *Valley of the Dolls* (1967). Barbara Parkins tends to be forgotten as the movie's third gritty gal, despite her own impressive body of work. Parkins first became a sex symbol in 1964, starring on the scandalous soap *Peyton Place*. After the murder of Sharon Tate, though,

Barbara fled Hollywood and spent her career bringing class and sex appeal to European productions like *Puppet on a Chain* (1972) and *Shout at the Devil* (1976). She also became a '70s scream queen after memorable—and kinky—roles in *The Mephisto Waltz* (1971) and *Asylum* (1972). She even served up her bare boobies in *Breakfast in Paris* (1981). Barbara announced her retirement in 1997, but her long, strange career certainly doesn't rule out a surprise comeback.

SKIN-fining Moment:

Breakfast in Paris (0:41) Right breast, while rolling over in bed followed by both bombers when she sits up.

See Her Naked In:

Breakfast in Paris (1982) Breasts
The Mephisto Waltz (1971) LB

Dian Parkinson

Born: November 30, 1944
Jacksonville, North Carolina
Skin-O-Meter: Great Nudity

Announcer Rod Roddy's cry of "Come on down!" spoke to the zippers of many guys ogling *The Price Is Right* hostess Dian Parkinson. The former beauty queen built a long career out of posing with groceries between 1975 to 1993—until it all fell apart after she filed a sexual harassment suit against host Bob Barker. Actually, some would say that the long-running presenter was reacting poorly to having been fired. In any case, things turned out delightfully for Dian. Her acting background consisted of guest spots on *The Mary Tyler Moore Show* and *Vega$*, but *Playboy* decided that the age was right for a fifty-year-old nude model. This led to taped appearances in *Playboy Celebrity Centerfold: Dian Parkinson* (1993) and *Playboy's Celebrities* (1999), both featuring Dian in all her scandalous glory.

SKIN-fining Moment:

Playboy Celebrity Centerfold: Dian Parkinson (0:05) The Price Was Right, and Dian's body is tight as she peels off a business suit to model her birthday suit. Plinko!

See Her Naked In:

Playboy's Celebrities (1999) FFN, buns
Playboy Celebrity Centerfold: Dian Parkinson (1993) FFN, Buns

Tammy Parks

Born: May 30, 1965
Long Island, New York
Skin-O-Meter: Great Nudity

Tit-popping tease Tammy Parks first pumped penises and stopped hearts in *Night Visions* (1991). Thanks to the nudetastic vision that is Tammy, this film spurned an insatiable yen for skin from the tasty-teated treat. Fiery topped, feisty, and always full of fun, Tammy tempted in flicks such as *Secret Games 3* (1994), *Attack of the 60 Foot Centerfold* (1995), and *Nude Bowling Party* (1995). For a ball-busting good time, catch this striking sexpot in full-frontal flinging flicks such as *Marilyn Chambers' Little Shop of Erotica* (1998) and *Virtual Desire* (1995). After envisioning Ms. Parks in all her perky-peaked, red-rugged refinement, you'll want to park your kiester in front of the TV for more.

SKIN-fining Moment:

Play Time (1:33) Tammy plays black-and-white FFN lesbian football with an anonymous brunette as a warm-up to a menage.

See Her Naked In:

Blood for the Muse (2001) Breasts, Thong
Titanic 2000 (1999) FFN, Buns
Masseuse 3 (1998) Breasts, Bush
Game of Pleasure (1998) Breasts
Marilyn Chambers' Little Shop of Erotica (1998) FFN
Desire (1997) FFN, Thong

Stolen Hearts (1997) Breasts, Thong
The Way We Are (1997) Breasts
Day of the Warrior (1996)
Deadly Currency (1996) Breasts, Buns
Midnight Tease II (1995) Breasts, Thong
Virtual Desire (1995) FFN, Buns
Droid Gunner (1995) Breasts, Buns
Attack of the 60 Foot Centerfold (1995)
   Breasts, Thong
Nude Bowling Party (1995) FFN, Buns
Smooth Operator (1995) Breasts
Illegal in Blue (1995) LB, Thong
Scoring (1995) FFN, Buns
Lover's Concerto (1995) FFN, Buns
The Dinner Party (1994) FFN, Buns
Play Time (1994) FFN, Buns
Secret Games 3 (1994) Breasts, Buns
Bare Exposure (1993) Breasts, Bush, Buns
Numerous Adult Movies

TeleVisions:

Compromising Situations Breasts, Buns
Erotic Confessions Breasts, Buns

Dolly Parton

Born: January 19, 1946
Sevierville, Tennessee
Skin-O-Meter: Never Nude

Dolly Parton is known for three things: great country music and her impossibly enormous mammaric mountains. Born in rural Tennessee, one of twelve children living with both of her parents in a one-room cabin, by the age of twelve Dolly was performing her musical act on Knoxville TV stations, and by thirteen she played the Grand Ole Opry. That's pretty impressive for a little girl from way back in the hills with a pair of gorgeous flesh hills. In 1967 Dolly finally hit the big time with a secure spot on the hit variety series *The Porter Wagoner Show*. When that gig dried up, she started her own variety series, *Dolly*, in 1976. Acting being the next logical step, Dolly won a part in the hit office flick *Nine to Five* (1980). The movie got her an Oscar nod for Best Song, but, sadly, she didn't win it. As if it matters. Dolly's mantle

sports more *Grammys* than you could shake a stick at . . . plus she's got a fine pair of trophies that she carries around with her daily. Since then, she's appeared in such memorable pictures as *The Best Little Whorehouse in Texas* (1982), *Rhinestone* (1984), and *Steel Magnolias* (1989), which made Dolly's dumplings a matinee idol. Unfortunately, in spite of her infamous top-heavy five-foot frame, Dolly has never shown any skinage onscreen outside of some massive cleavage, which is truthfully more than most actresses can offer even with their shirts off. Hello, Dolly!

SKIN-fining Moment:

The Best Little Whorehouse in Texas (0:17) There's nothing little jouncing and a-jiggling in Dolly's black lingerie ensemble as she entices Burt Reynolds with her southern charm (s) and cleavage the size of the state where the movie takes place.

Julia Parton

Born: July 4, 1964
Kentucky
Skin-O-Meter: Great Nudity

There are two ways to look at Julia Parton. Either keep the eyes peeled and the finger on the pause button while auditing such skin tease fare as *Vice Academy 4* (1994) and *The Naked Detective* (1996) (moderately quick reactions will be required to capture the bustuesque brunette with her bazooms rocketing to and fro), or Parton searchers seeking a more relaxed viewing experience can opt to slip into a XXX presentation, something along the lines of *Pleasure Zone* (1982). Prepare for long, languorous looks at long and leggy Julia, plus she'll be licking lingam. Both methods of appreciation guarantee titanic tit thrills.

SKIN-fining Moment:

Heavenly Hooters (0:47) Julia's marvelous mammaries and muffshish are

shown in a rather up-close-and-personal manner as the camera pans down her naked body.

See Her Naked In:

Sex Secrets And Lies (2003) FFN, Buns
Heavenly Hooters (2003) Breasts, Bush
Dangerous Pleasures (2001) Breasts
The Naked Detective (1996) FFN, Buns
Vice Academy 4 (1994) Breasts
New York Nights (1994) FFN, Thong
Marilyn Chambers: Wet & Wild Fantasies (1994) FFN
Good Girls Don't (1993) Breasts, Thong
Vice Academy Part 3 (1991) Breasts
The Rosebud Beach Hotel (1984) Breasts, Buns
Love Skills: A Guide to the Pleasures of Sex (1984) FFN, Buns
Erotic Images (1983) Breasts
Numerous Adult Movies

Christine Pascal

Born: November 29, 1953
Lyon, Rhône, France
Died: August 30, 1996
Skin-O-Meter: Great Nudity

Christine Pascal started her career with a part in the French film *The Clockmaker of St. Paul* (1973). She didn't show her working parts but subsequently went on to appear in over thirty productions, in many of which she did expose her skinful ways. Christine also penned and directed numerous films throughout her thirty-three-year-long career, which tragically ended in 1996 when she committed suicide. Nevertheless, this talented, stunning beauty left her trademark good looks and wit on everything she ever appeared in, setting the bar, as it were, for everyone else in the entertainment industry, most notably with her performance and award-winning directorial effort in *Le Petit Prince a Dit* (1992). But Christine really made heads turn when she lowered the bar in terms of nudity, most notably in *Que la Fête Commence* (1974), which featured several lingering looks at her completely naked body. She went full frontal again for roles in *Des Enfants Gâtés* (1977) and *Train d'Enfer* (1984) but sadly gave up her fleshful ways and not long after her very flesh. What a waste; but at least she left a fine body of work to whack off to in fond remembrance.

SKIN-fining Moment:

Que la fête commence . . . (0:58) Christine gives good full frontal hanging out with equally naked party guests. Pruning shears have never touched this stunner's shrubbery.

See Her Naked In:

Train d'enfer (1984) Breasts
Des enfants gâtés (1977) FFN
Que la fête commence . . . (1974) FFN

Olivia Pascal

Born: May 25, 1957
Munich, Germany
Skin-O-Meter: Hall of Fame

There is something to be said for the more liberal attitudes toward nudity and sex in Europe, and that something is Olivia Pascal. Although her hair has appeared in various tones of brunette, Olivia's eyes are always seductively hooded, her mouth is forever slightly parted and she exudes an eternal schoolgirl insouciance. The fact that she was able to transition into a successful, long-running career in German television in the mid 1980s after reigning the previous decade as the Continent's queen of softcore erotica attests to the open-mindedness of our heavy-breathing brothers across the sea. Olivia's title turn as *Vanessa* (1977), in which she excelled at girl-to-girl nipple fencing and muff cupping and squeezed a bunch of red grapes between her soft thighs so the sweet wine dripped down and mixed with the nectar from her honeypot, attests to the innovative

and licentious liberality of Fatherland filmmakers.

SKIN-fining Moment:

Vanessa (0:17) How's this for sexadelic 70's surrealism: a fully naked Olivia on a maroon velvet waterbed, getting a massage from an Asian man with a moustache, while a topless, buck-toothed girl drinks OJ and watches.

See Her Naked In:

Coconuts (1985) Breasts
Cola, Candy, Chocolate (1979)
Sex on the Run (1979) FFN
Summer Night Fever (1978) Breasts
Popcorn und Himbeereis (1978) FFN, Buns
Insel der tausend Freuden (1978) FFN, Buns
Vanessa (1977) FFN, Buns
Behind Convent Walls (1977) Breasts, Bush
Sylvia im Reich der Wollust (1977) FFN, Buns
The Fruit Is Ripe (1976) FFN, Buns

Elsa Pataky

Born: July 18, 1976
Madrid, Spain
Skin-O-Meter: Brief Nudity

Guys have gone wacky for Elsa Pataky ever since she became a regular presence on Spanish television on late-'90s series such as *Al salir de clase* and *Tio Willy*. This Eurobeauty was also regularly featured in Spanish films before landing a role in *Beyond Re-Animator* (2003). The third entry in this beloved horror series was eagerly awaited, and Elsa animated plenty of trouser snakes as a reporter trapped amongst undead craziness. Sadly, *Beyond Re-Animator* was generally considered to be a disappointment. Pataky was soon stripping in Spanish in *Atraco a las 3 . . . y media* (2003), but it shouldn't take a mad scientist to soon revive her skinternational career.

SKIN-fining Moment:

Beyond Re-Animator (0:36) Quick look at Elsa's left chest orb as she cuddles with a chatty guy in the sack.

See Her Naked In:

Beyond Re-Animator (2003) LB
Atraco a las 3 . . . y media (2003) Breasts

Tatjana Patitz

Born: March 25, 1966
Trelleborg, Sweden
Skin-O-Meter: Great Nudity

Tatjana Patitz caught the eyes (and flies) of the world by walking the runway directly to every man's zipper. With her blonde buxomness and lengthy legs, this German supermodel (who was born in Sweden) is every man's fantasy and gets off on it, availing her ass-sets to fashion magazines and films such as *Ready to Wear* (1994) and *Rising Sun* (1993). In the latter she gave Wesley Snipes's snake a shake by baring her hard-tipped *tatjs*. Mr. Skin can hardly keep his son from rising just thinking about it. In *Restraining Order* (1999), you'll have to hold back from instantly relieving yourself at the site of Patitz's Swedish meatballs. What Hôt and tastë teats! Be it a nip slip on the catwalk or tit pop at the box office, Tatjana's offerings are guaranteed to add an entire library to your wank bank.

SKIN-fining Moment:

Rising Sun (0:06) Some sweet cheek-crackage and some side-glimpses of the heavy hangers as Tatjana watches TV naked.

See Her Naked In:

Restraining Order (1999) LB
Rising Sun (1993) FFN, Buns

Tera Patrick

Born: July 25, 1976
Great Falls, Montana
Skin-O-Meter: Great Nudity

Tasty Thai temptress Tera Patrick is known mainly for showing her pa'nang under her own name as well as other noms de porn, but she's also had legitimate skinematic roles. Okay, so *The Seduction of Maxine* (2000) isn't exactly Bergman, but next to the likes of *Up and Cummers 80* (2000), *Ass Angels* (2000), and *Fluffy Cumsalot, Porn Star* (2003), anything else seems legitimate. Tera has also hosted a skinternet talk show and done USO tours with the equally booberific Salma Hayek. She's fluent in Hungarian as well as a registered nurse with a degree in microbiology, so it's clear the D in her D-cup doesn't stand for dummy!

SKIN-fining Moment:

The Howard Stern Show (2004) *After submitting to Howard's infamous "Tickle Chair," Tera kicks back topless on the couch, her huge moon boobs absolutely mouthwatering even with the pixelation.*

See Her Naked In:

The Seduction of Maxine (2001) Breasts, Buns
Numerous Adult Movies

TeleVisions:

The Howard Stern Show

Melody Patterson

Born: April 16, 1949
Inglewood, California
Skin-O-Meter: Brief Nudity

Melody Patterson made primetime really primetime for lovers of shapely beauties. Her portrayal of rooting-tooting cowgirl Wrangler Jane on the hit series *F Troop* rustled up ratings and hard-ons in the mid '60s. Sadly, after the show ended its run, Melody wasn't able to corral much of a career. She made a brief go at it with guest spots on *The Monkees*, *Adam-12*, *Green Acres*, and *Hawaii Five-O*, where she met her

husband and future ex James MacArthur, a.k.a. Danno. She made a few movies, including an uncredited appearance in *The Harrad Experiment* (1973), but by that point her profession had gone out to pasture. Melody managed to eke out a bit of a skin scene in *The Cycle Savages* (1969), but very little other than her naked back and brief bunnage can be seen. Melody, that's such a sad song.

SKIN-fining Moment:

The Cycle Savages (0:33) Mel poses for a portrait from behind. Upper-buttage and side-nubbin.

See Her Naked In:

The Cycle Savages (1969) Buns

Alexandra Paul

Born: July 29, 1963
New York, New York
Skin-O-Meter: Great Nudity

Long-nippled Alexandra Paul started her career with a role opposite delicious Daryl Hannah in the highly touted made-for-TV movie *Paper Dolls* (1982). But it wasn't until she took it off (at least down to a skintight swimsuit) on the über-hot series *Baywatch* that her star finally rose—as did our less celestial bodies. Since her stint on the bouncing babe booty show ended in 1997, Alexandra has been flaunting her stuff in such fare as *Arthur's Quest* (1999), *Revenge* (1999), and the nighttime soaper *Melrose Place*. However, Mr. Skin has uncovered a few skin-eletons in Alexandra's carnal closet, like when she bared her petite bosom for her role in *American Nightmare* (1983). Although she went on to show boobitudity in such films as *American Flyers* (1985) and *Sunset Grill* (1993), Alexandra's pièce de résistance was *8 Million Ways to Die* (1986), which featured a lingering

look at her totally naked frame, complete with furburger. More like eight million ways to get hard!

SKIN-fining Moment:

8 Million Ways to Die (0:26) Tight-bodied, furry full-frontal as Alexander stands in bathroom as Jeff Bridges enters.

See Her Naked In:

Sunset Grill (1993) Breasts, Buns
Millions (1991) Breasts
8 Million Ways to Die (1986) FFN
American Flyers (1985) Breasts
American Nightmare (1983) Breasts

TeleVisions:

The Hitchhiker Breasts

Meilani Paul

California
Skin-O-Meter: Great Nudity

Whaaazup? Well, our penises after Meilani Paul appeared in yet another hot commercial campaign—specifically, as one of Ray Charles's "Uh-Huh Girls" in the popular Pepsi ads. Meilani managed to parlay her presence into an acting career and even married series star Adrian Paul while making her debut on the *Highlander* TV series. The marriage didn't last, but Meilani was soon proudly displaying her new surname—and surreal titties—in trashy epics such as *Call Girl* (1995) and *The Corporate Ladder* (1997). *Hard Time* (1996) featured a detailed stripping scene that even Ray Charles couldn't miss seeing. Meilani's recently toned down her skinematic antics, but she's still working steadily. Under her new screen name of "Melanie Hall," she even managed to play the multiplexes in Ashton Kutcher's sci-fi hit *The Butterfly Effect* (2004).

SKIN-fining Moment:

The Corporate Ladder (0:41) Plastic fantastics as she peels down her dress and sashays into a pool.

The Corporate Ladder (1997) Breasts, Thong
Hard Time (1996) Breasts, Buns
Call Girl (1995) Breasts, Buns

Julie Payne

Born: September 11, 1940
Terre Haute, Indiana
Skin-O-Meter: Brief Nudity

As the child of actors John Payne and Anne Shirley, Julie Payne is known in Hollywood as a true legacy of Old Hollywood. That still couldn't stop her from getting her start on shows such as *Love, American Style* and *Sanford and Son*. Fortunately, Julie also made it into a few classic counter-culture films, including *The Strawberry Statement* (1970) and *THX 1138* (1971). Julie's always worked steadily and has matured into a true MILF figure—as seen in *American Wedding* (2003) and her role as Larry David's mother-in-law on HBO's *Curb Your Enthusiasm*. Julie also bared a bouncing boob just as she reached the cusp of mature beauty in *Private School* (1983), playing a cheerleading coach whose pop gets topped as part of a very practical joke.

SKIN-fining Moment:

Private School (0:30) Julie's left jewel pops out of her cheerleading outfit when she jumps up. Cheers!

See Her Naked In:

Private School (1983) LB

Amanda Pays

Born: June 6, 1959
London, England, UK
Skin-O-Meter: Brief Nudity

Because of her deep voice as a schoolgirl, Amanda Pays was cast as a man in plays, but as this Brit blossomed she became a model. This led to acting, and she soon starred on *Max Headroom* as Theora

Jones. On *The Flash*, Amanda didn't actually do said action, but we can at least look at her luscious lycra-clad lovelies in *Leviathan* (1989). The one part to date that warrants watching her alone is *Solitaire for 2* (1995). It Pays to show more skin.

SKIN-fining Moment:

Solitaire for 2 (0:55) Amanda delivers some light right nip-slippage during a too-dark sex tussle.

See Her Naked In:

Solitaire for 2 (1995) RB

Dixie Peabody

Skin-O-Meter: Great Nudity

Tall and lean with a rat's nest of a beehive hairdo, Dixie Peabody looks more like an ass-kicking biker chick than most women in biker flicks, who tend to play something closer to flower-painted hippies. In the revenge thriller *Bury Me an Angel* (1971), where Dixie sought the killers of her brother, she not only looked sexy straddling a shotgun but managed to get naked for a full-frontal skinny dip. This is the only biker flick written and directed by a woman and offers a perverse perspective perfectly suited to Dixie's cups. She followed up that drive-in classic with a Roger Corman production called *Night Call Nurses* (1972) about three sexy nurses working in a psychiatric ward. There's a plotline about an abused prisoner and threatening notes, but all that is forgotten as the bevy of beauties get naked, including a fine topless scene by Dixie. Then she disappeared from filmdom. Hopefully, she's not just whistling Dixie.

SKIN-fining Moment:

Night Call Nurses (0:35) Dixie serves up her cups for a group of rather impressed onlookers.

See Her Naked In:

Night Call Nurses (1972) Breasts
Bury Me an Angel (1971) Breasts, Bush, Buns

Pandora Peaks

Born: April 12, 1964
Atlanta, Georgia
Skin-O-Meter: Great Nudity

A veteran of stripper stage, skin-magazine shoot, and porno set, implausible blonde Pandora Peaks and her gigantic jugs have spawned a parallel career in hard-R sexploitation and straight-R mainstream flicks. Although she always plays the type of foxy girl who walks around with a pair of chest balloons inflated to the size of dirigibles, Pandora's appeal is durable, easily translating into the slightly less risqué arena. With a chest sized with the aim of making an impression way out in the cheap seats of vast strippertoriums, Pandora's big-screen impact is sudden and sensational. Gasp at the glory as she knocks Demi Moore out of the picture frame in *Striptease* (1996).

SKIN-fining Moment:

Do or Die (1:09) Some very long peeks at Pandora's very huge Peaks as she gets some man-prong outside.

See Her Naked In:

Pandora Peaks (2001) FFN, Buns
Return of the Ultra Vixens (2000) Breasts, Bush
Visions and Voyeurism (1998) FFN
Striptease (1996) Breasts
Do or Die (1991) Breasts

Jacqueline Pearce

Born: December 20, 1943
Byfleet, England, UK
Skin-O-Meter: Brief Nudity

Jacqueline Pearce is best known as the nearly bald Servalan, Empress of the Federation, on the English cult sci-fi series *Blake's 7*. The character was originally written for a man, not unlike Ripley in *Alien* (1979) and Honor Blackman's Cathy Gale role on *The Avengers*. Lucky for Jacqueline's admirers, the change in sex occurred, and a hard-on fantasy of a queen bitch was born. Jacqueline's fetishistic costumes on the show garnished a special interest from fans. "I did get a letter from a man who asked whether I'd go around one night and chastise him, but would I not go before ten p.m., because his mother didn't go to bed until 9:30. But I went and she slept through it," she laughs, tongue in cheek. The success of the show sent her to L.A. to court film fame. "I went out to establish myself in a film career and I ended up working in a strip club called The Losers, the irony of which escaped me for many years." She began her movie career with *Plague of the Zombies* (1966). She finally shed those sexy outfits for her sexier body in *White Mischief* (1987), in which she was soaking wet, from her naked floppers to her meaty ass. While Jacqueline still works to this day, she's yet to repeat such a Pearce-ing performance.

SKIN-fining Moment:

White Mischief (0:06) Jackie rises from a bathtub and displays her sudsy super-soakers and big, round rump to a gaggle of gawkers.

See Her Naked In:

White Mischief (1988) Breasts, Buns

Patricia Pearcy

Skin-O-Meter: Brief Nudity

Pretty-knobbed Patricia Pearcy began as a daytime diva on *One Life to Live*. With her ravishing red hair and peaches-and-cream complexion, Pat moved on with her own life, taking small parts in bigger productions such as *The Goodbye Girl*

(1977) and *Delusion* (1980). It's no figment of your imagination that this carrot-topped cutie can be one randy red fox. To see sly Patricia in all her freckled fury, check out *Cockfighter* (1974) and *Squirm* (1976). Both flicks will make your rooster restless when Pearcy peels out her perty little pair. For those with a taste for strawberry sweetness, Pat is where it's at.

SKIN-fining Moment:

Cockfighter (0:28) Patrice bares her pert pretties while taking pipe from Warren Oates next to the lake.

See Her Naked In:

Squirm (1976) LB
Cockfighter (1974) Breasts

Barbara Peckinpaugh

Skin-O-Meter: Great Nudity

No true skinema fan can look back at the 1980s without pining for Barbara Peckinpaugh. This icy blonde had a severe look that dripped styling mousse, and her amazing natural bod defied both gravity and cosmetic surgery. Peckinpaugh got us pawin' our peckers in *Shadows Run Black* (1986), but she's equally stunning in skinsational films such as *Basic Training* (1985), *Roller Blade* (1985), and *Bad Girls II* (1984). She even made it to the multiplexes as one of Melanie Griffith's fellow porn stars in Brian De Palma's *Body Double* (1984). Barbara was also happy to play straight softcore scenes, including a turn where she called herself "Chrissy" in the documentary *Best Chest in the West* (1984). She also provided some educational content in *Love Skills: A Guide to the Pleasures of Sex* (1984). Barbara went out like a winner, too, providing a definitive shower scene while soaping up in *Electric Blue 51* (1987).

SKIN-fining Moment:

The Witching (0:02) During an occult ceremony, Babs bares all three B's and gets her nipples pinched as other weirdies dance around her in a circle.

See Her Naked In:

Shadows Run Black (1986) FFN, Buns
Roller Blade (1985) FFN, Buns
Basic Training (1985) Breasts
Bad Girls II (1984) Breasts
Body Double (1984) Breasts
Erotic Images (1983) Breasts
Homework (1982) Breasts
The Witching (1972) FFN, Buns
Numerous Adult Movies

> "Usually I'm splicing the scene into 2-second portions of nipples or saying, 'Artist's buttocks will be shown for 3 seconds in this shot,' but for this scene I was just like, 'Where do you want to put the camera?'"
>
> —AMANDA PEET ON *IGBY GOES DOWN*

Amanda Peet

**Born: January 11, 1972
New York, New York
Skin-O-Meter: Great Nudity**

A leggy, auburn brunette who has one of the most mobile and expressive faces of any gorgeous actress of her generation, Amanda Peet is a delightful big-screen presence. Amanda's oversized, crystalline-clear, blue-green eyes see deep into your secret desires, and her mouth spreads in that wide, wry grin that let's you know she shares those desires. Peet is so confident in her enduring attraction that she can play the psycho-bitch girlfriend of *Saving Silverman* (2001) and still she seems like the ideal lifetime companion. A whiz at exuding simultaneous comic and sensual appeal, Amanda causes climaxes and chuckles while pointing a pistol and protruding her nipples in *The Whole Nine Yards* (2000).

SKIN-fining Moment:

The Whole Nine Yards (1:06) Amanda stands in a doorway with a gun, showcasing her killer B-cups and only a bannister blocks a view of her peet-moss.

See Her Naked In:

Igby Goes Down (2002) Breasts
The Whole Nine Yards (2000) Breasts

Courtney Peldon

Born: April 13, 1981
New York
Skin-O-Meter: Brief Nudity

With so many actresses emerging as alumnae from the MTV sexfest *Undressed*, how could Courtney Peldon stand out? This fearless all-American gal grabbed the most memorable role in the bad-taste comedy *Say It Isn't So* (2001), opening her blouse to reveal some absurd nipple piercings on an absurd pair of prosthetic breasts. What's truly absurd is that, somehow, it was still hot. The moment was also overdue for those Peldon fans who'd been pulling their peckers ever since the young starlet hit legal age. And now those same fans can court Courtney in her recurring role as Becky Emerson on the TV series *Boston Public*, as well as applauding both her pomps and circumstances in the flick *Reality Check* (2002), where she at last graduated to real-deal rack exposure.

SKIN-fining Moment:

Reality Check (0:23) Courtney is really the kind of upstanding young lady any gentleman would like to get to know better. And by "upstanding" I mean "strips down at a wacky party and tosses aside her feather boa to flash her fog lights."

See Her Naked In:

Reality Check (2002) Breasts

Ana Luisa Peluffo

Born: October 9, 1929
Queretaro, Mexico
Skin-O-Meter: Great Nudity

England has Michael Caine, France has Gérard Depardieu, and Mexico has Ana Luisa Peluffo to appear in just about every other film made in the country. In fact, she's made over 160 films since 1954—and that includes some pioneering early nudity. Ana didn't let her age get in the way of showing us some Technicolor titties, either. She was forty-six years old when she showed off her amazing ass and mature muffins in *El Reventón* (1975). She's also stunning in her full-frontal glory in *La Guerra de los sexos* (1978). And don't miss her senior shower scene in *Una Rata en la oscuridad* (1978). Ana's still beautiful today, too, and we won't be complaining if her two hundredth film includes a salute to her booby bicentennial.

SKIN-fining Moment:

Cada quien su madre (0:50) Ana Louisa proves to be quite the life of the party, traipsing around utterly starkers in a room full of aroused onlookers—which will include you! FFN, buns, hilarious bad dancing.

See Her Naked In:

Corrupción (1983) Breasts
Cada quien su madre (1982) FFN, Buns
Una Rata en la oscuridad (1978) FFN, Buns
La Guerra de los sexos (1978) FFN, Buns
Deseos (1977) Breasts
El Reventón (1975) FFN, Buns
Ángeles y querubines (1972)
La Fuerza del deseo (1955) Breasts

Elizabeth Peña

Born: September 23, 1959
Elizabeth, New Jersey
Skin-O-Meter: Great Nudity

As a young Hispanic actress, Elizabeth Peña was struggling through the usual roles in ethnic indie films. Then she managed an impressive turn as a politically minded maid in *Down and Out in Beverly Hills* (1986), followed by the unexpected success of the Richie Valens biopic *La Bamba* (1987). Suddenly, Elizabeth was the hottest Latina actress in film history. That didn't last long, though, as Hollywood's big vision for Elizabeth involved casting her as a maid on the 1987 sitcom *I Married Dora*. That halted her rising star, but nothing could tone down Elizabeth's extreme sex appeal. Peña got us popping with skinematic turns in *Jacob's Ladder* (1990) and *Across the Moon* (1994) and then matured into MILFdom in *The Pass* (1998). She still steals the occasional hit, such as *Rush Hour* (1998), but she relies on the indie world to give her the occasional starring role in films such as *Lone Star* (1996).

SKIN-fining Moment:

Jacob's Ladder (0:17) Elizabeth gets dressed and we get to see the good stuff that goes into her bra.

See Her Naked In:

The Pass (1998) RB
Across the Moon (1994) LB
Dead Funny (1994) LB
Jacob's Ladder (1990) Breasts
La Bamba (1987) RB

Piper Perabo

Born: October 31, 1977
Toms River, New Jersey
Skin-O-Meter: Great Nudity

Versatility is the mark of an excellent actress, and coltish cutie Piper Perabo has the makings of excellence. In *Coyote Ugly* (2000) Perabo flitted about as a skinny blonde with a huge and toothy smile, looking like the gawky tomboy next door who grew up to be a fashion model. The only disappointment in the way she turned out was that she went through the entire movie without showing nips or better. This oversight was overturned when, as a *brunette* (hence the accolade for versatility), perky Piper revealed a hearty helping of boob in *Lost and Delirious* (2001), which might better have been titled *Naked and Bi-Curious*. In this Canadian film celebration of boarding-school girls going south for the simmer, the

naked yearning on Perabo's face is perfectly complemented by the yearn-worthy nakedness of her baby-soft nymphet form. Pipe up, Piper!

SKIN-fining Moment:

Lost and Delirious (0:28) Piper plies her petite ping-pongs on humungo-jugged Jessica Pare as they go at it girl-girl-style.

See Her Naked In:

Lost and Delirious (2001) Breasts
Coyote Ugly (2000) Thong

Tonie Perensky

Skin-O-Meter: Great Nudity

Sure, brown-haired babe Tonie Perensky is no big-name actress, but she's a big-titted actress, and that's worth a lot to Mr. Skin. The sultry starlet kicked off her career with a bit part as a waitress in the TV movie *Another Pair of Aces: Three of a Kind* (1991) and has appeared (however briefly) in a string of B-movies ever since. Along the way, she's treated skin fanatics to two particularly hot bare-bodied scenes. Check her out as "Darla" in the ill-conceived *The Return of the Texas Chainsaw Massacre* (1994) starring pre-fame Renée Zellweger and Matthew McConaughey, and you'll get an eyeful of her gravity-defying gazongas. She upped the ante with a hot topless dance number in *Varsity Blues* (1999), proving this skin star is no flash in the pan.

SKIN-fining Moment:

Varsity Blues (1:01) I'm hot for teacher! Tonie shows tits and tail while strutting for her students at a strip club.

See Her Naked In:

Varsity Blues (1999) Breasts, Thong
The Return of the Texas Chainsaw Massacre (1994) Breasts

Rosie Perez

Born: September 6, 1964
Brooklyn, New York
Skin-O-Meter: Great Nudity

Pugnacious Puerto Rican beauty Rosie Perez has fostered a career that's as reliant on her body as it is on her considerable acting talents. The Brooklyn, New York, native began her career as a dancer on *Soul Train* and later became a choreographer of videos and stage shows for such performers as Bobby Brown and Diana Ross. She made her film debut as Spike Lee's steamy, ice-melting girlfriend in *Do the Right Thing* (1989), then went on to earn an Oscar nomination for *Fearless* (1993). Both *White Men Can't Jump* (1992) and *The 24 Hour Woman* (1999) provided brief glimpses of Perez's kung-fu-carved body, but she earned a black belt in Mr. Skin's book for the wild, hyperkinetic, cult phenomenon *Perdita Durango* (1997), a.k.a. *Dance with the Devil*. The unedited version featured Rosie's rosy breasts and a ton of bun as she portrayed the girlfriend of a superstitious criminal bent on human sacrifice. That's a devilishly sexy dancer Mr. Skin would partner with anytime!

SKIN-fining Moment:

Do the Right Thing (1:22) Hot knockers as Spike Lee rubs ice all over Rosie's naked upper anatomy.

See Her Naked In:

The 24 Hour Woman (1999) RB
Dance with the Devil (1997) Breasts, Buns
White Men Can't Jump (1992) Breasts, Buns
Do the Right Thing (1989) Breasts

Elizabeth Perkins

Born: November 18, 1960
Queens, New York
Skin-O-Meter: Great Nudity

Because she's of Greek descent, we can't leave Elizabeth Perkins behind! The Queens, New York–born, Vermont-raised, and now Los Angeles-based cutie is a pert-breasted wonder. Elizabeth got her chops on the stage and debuted onscreen in *About Last Night . . .* (1986), in which she shared screen time with pre-implanted Demi Moore. But it wasn't until *He Said, She Said* (1991) that we got to she Liz's itty bitties—and we said "Yum!" Elizabeth's fame enlarged when she starred opposite Tom Hanks in *Big* (1988). She also played Wilma in the big-budget bonanza *The Flintstones* (1994) and provided one of the voices in the blockbuster *Finding Nemo* (2003), but we prefer her less animated and more skinful roles. For instance, *Moonlight and Valentino* (1995), in which Liz let one of her rosy nips float by in a steamy bathtub scene. But more titillating is the Hollywood send-up *I'm Losing You* (1988), which offered her petite pair getting manhandled. That's enough to Perkins up the dead!

SKIN-fining Moment:

I'm Losing You (0:54) Stunning flash of fur followed by Ms. Perkins' topless perkables atop Andrew McCarthy.

See Her Naked In:

I'm Losing You (1998) Breasts, Bush
Moonlight and Valentino (1995) RB, Buns
He Said, She Said (1991) Breasts

Millie Perkins

Born: May 12, 1938
Passaic, New Jersey
Skin-O-Meter: Brief Nudity

You won't find many debuts more depressing than Millie Perkins's turn in *The Diary of Anne Frank* (1959). Her touching turn as the title character made her an overnight star—which soon led to Millie indulging herself in some very bizarre roles. Her follow-up to *Frank* had her co-starring with Elvis Presley in *Wild in the Country* (1961), and it wasn't long before Millie abandoned Hollywood in favor of low-budget weirdness, including the legendary existential westerns *Ride in the Whirlwind* (1965) and *The Shooting* (1967). Millie also showed up in the drive-in classic *Wild in the Streets* (1968) and the legendary cult item *Cockfighter* (1974). Nobody was surprised when Millie finally went skinematic with some kinky castrating sex scenes in *The Witch Who Came from the Sea* (1976). Perkins remains a respected actress, but the closest she's come to the mainstream remains TV guest spots and a few seasons on the nighttime soap *Knots Landing*. Otherwise, Perkins prefers to lend a hot older presence to bizarre indies such as *Slamdance* (1987), *Two Moon Junction* (1988), and *Necronomicon* (1994).

SKIN-fining Moment:

The Witch Who Came from the Sea (0:16) Millie bewitches a duo of drug dudes by baring her topless Perkins before she ties up the stoned stooges.

See Her Naked In:

The Witch Who Came from the Sea (1976) Breasts

Denise Perrier

France
Skin-O-Meter: Brief Nudity

Nobody knows what Denise Perrier did for sixteen years after winning the title of Miss World, but eventually she resurfaced in *Le Bourgeois gentil mec* (1969). We last saw this French pastry in *Diamonds Are Forever* (1971), where she was one of the few of Bond's blondes to bare her ooh-la-las to Sean Connery—and the lucky viewers get a peek as well. With only a pause button, Denise's delights are forever too. We don't know where this sparkling beauty is now, but we're happy to drink her water any time!

SKIN-fining Moment:

Diamonds are Forever (0:35) Sean Connery frees Denise of her pesky bikini top and we see Boob, Left Boob. This Perrier sure is bubbly!

See Her Naked In:

Diamonds are Forever (1971) LB

Valerie Perrine

Born: September 3, 1944
Galveston, Texas
Skin-O-Meter: Great Nudity

Based on three films she accessorized to simmering copper-top perfection in the early 1970s, Valerie Perrine is among the most memorable red-hot redheads in cinema history. No red-blooded skin seeker who saw *Steambath* (1972) will soon forget the rosy glow and steamy sheen of Valerie's pearly pink flesh as she shed her towel and invaded the all-male bathhouse sanctum. Fresh from that vision of ginger goodness, pulchritudinous Perrine perked her redhead nipples and cocked her

VALERIE PERRINE IN *SLAUGHTERHOUSE-FIVE*, CLEAVAGE TEN.

curvy redhead hips as a naked sex symbol on a distant planet in *Slaughterhouse-Five* (1972). Who needs Technicolor? As Honey Harlow, stripper burlesque queen in the black-and-white film *Lenny* (1974), Valerie's sultry standing butt shot will have sharp-eyed skinsters tasting red.

SKIN-fining Moment:

Slaughterhouse-Five (1:27) Several looks at Val's chest-pals as she rassles with some guy in a futuristic dome setting.

See Her Naked In:

The Border (1982) Thong
Can't Stop the Music (1980) Breasts
Lenny (1974) Breasts, Thong
Steambath (1972) RB, Buns
Slaughterhouse-Five (1972) Breasts, Buns

Essy Persson

Born: June 15, 1941
Gothenburg, Sweden
Skin-O-Meter: Great Nudity

Essy Persson deserves a special place in every skinophile's heart. She explored virgin territory fearlessly, appearing in highly erotic films in an age when that sort of thing wasn't quite accepted by the general public, not even in erotically charged Europe. In fact, her first film, *Jag—en kvinna* (1965), was banned in Finland when it was first released. Thankfully, the producers brought it to America, where select audiences embraced the frank sexuality and tame-by-today's-standards nude scenes. (There are a few brief glimpses of Essy's hooters . . . no wonder it was banned!) She went on to show off her incredible body again in *Lejonsommar* (1968) as well as *Therese und Isabell* (1968), the latter featuring some pretty steamy lesbian action, which was exceptionally rare back then. It's definitely not as daring as some of today's offerings, but the hairy trails it blazed are historic! If not for the likes of Essy and her revolutionary counterparts, the face of skinema would be forever different. Essy is an essential Persson in the evolution of skin.

SKIN-fining Moment:

Therese and Isabelle (1:44) Essy proves she's a female Persson as she lies topless in the woods alongside her gal pal.

See Her Naked In:

Cry of the Banshee (1970) Breasts
Lejonsommar (1968) LB
Therese und Isabell (1968) Breasts, Buns
Jag—en kvinna (1965) Breasts

Bernadette Peters

Born: February 28, 1948
Queens, New York
Skin-O-Meter: Brief Nudity

Pink, pouty, and protuberantly stacked, Bernadette Peters is one of the gleaming lights of the Great White Way. She got her first gig in the business called show as a five-year-old performer on Horn and Hardart's kiddie-talent radio program and, by age eleven, was appearing on Broadway in *Most Happy Fella*. This pint-sized, red-headed, ultra-curvy cutie has been making fellas moist happy ever since. Bernadette was almost typecast as the squeaky-voiced dumb blonde with her successful run in the stage smash *Dames at Sea*, prompting her to try some TV gigs in the '70s. Ultimately Bernadette's greatest fame came from co-starring opposite funnyman Steve Martin in the one-of-a-kind comedy classic *The Jerk* (1977). As sexy as Bernadette is, she's not been quick to slip out of her girlishly tempting outfits. The sole time she offered up some skin time was a brief bit of breast in *Pink Cadillac* (1986). We'd like to see more of her pink caddies, but in the meantime she continues with the provocative roles, most recently playing a stripper's mom in the Broadway revival of *Gypsy*. Bernadette, you burn us up!

SKIN-fining Moment:

Pink Cadillac (1:24) Bernadette's pink left torso-bumper rolls into view as she smooches Clint Eastwood.

See Her Naked In:

Pink Cadillac (1989) LB

Vicki Peters

Born: September 9, 1950
Minneapolis, Minnesota
Skin-O-Meter: Brief Nudity

While some girls pose for *Playboy* as a stepping stone to a movie career, Vicki Peters seems to have taken the reverse route from Hollywood to Hef. Miss July's genuine jutting jugs justify *Blood Mania* (1970), filmed a full two years before she became a Playmate in 1972. From sprockets to staples, her spotlight then apparently Peters out. If only Vicki continued to pursue acting, she could have become a star like fellow Playmates Claudia Jennings, Dorothy Stratten, or . . . wait, maybe she's better off after all.

SKIN-fining Moment:

Blood Mania (1:05) Vicki makes it more like "Boob Mania" in a topless sex scene.

See Her Naked In:

Blood Mania (1970) Breasts

Joanna Pettet

Born: November 16, 1942
London, England, UK
Skin-O-Meter: Brief Nudity

Serious actress Joanna Pettet got a major break alongside Candace Bergen, Jessica Walter, and Joan Hackett in *The Group* (1966), an adaptation of Mary McCarthy's sordid paperback about old college friends. Then she became a sexbomb as "Mata Bond" in the James Bond spoof *Casino Royale* (1967). This shagalicious role had her vamping it up as the daughter of James Bond and Mata Hari. *Playboy* quickly featured her in a 1968 pictorial, and she made her skinematic move in the brothel comedy *The Best House in London* (1969). Sadly, a string of bad films left her spending the '70s in TV movies, along with episodes of *The Love Boat* and *Fantasy Island*. Joanna had a skintastic decade in the 1980s, though. She retired in 1990, but not before showing those non-petite Pettets in the low-budget flick *Double Exposure* (1982) and the Shakespearean adaptation *Othello, el comando negro* (1982).

SKIN-fining Moment:

Double Exposure (0:55) Joanna shares her juggalos with psycho-boy in bed. Be careful!

See Her Naked In:

Othello, el comando negro (1982) LB
Double Exposure (1982) Breasts
The Best House in London (1969)

Angelique Pettyjohn

Born: March 10, 1943
Las Vegas, Nevada
Died: February 12, 1992
Skin-O-Meter: Great Nudity

Hugely blessed Angelique Pettyjohn and her big, big hooters made her first splash in show biz as a guest-spot specialist (or breast-spot specialist) on such hip go-go shows as *Get Smart*, *Batman*, and *Star Trek*. The divine, massive Pettyjohn also did the starlet shimmy in kooky classics such as *The Love Rebellion* (1965), *Clambake* (1967), and *The Mad Doctor of Blood Island* (1968). Perhaps pulled down by the weight of her dependent hefties, Angelique

followed her funbags into hardcore via *The Curious Female* (1969). Her overblown talents would be witnessed in several other gems of the gonadal genre. Later she would reemerge as a breast-spot specialist in such legitimate fare as *Repo Man* (1985) and *Biohazard* (1984).

SKIN-fining Moment:

G.I. Executioner (0:59) Delightfully long scene with Angie as a naked, gun-wielding, post-coital maniac! Nice T&A action.

See Her Naked In:

Biohazard (1984) Breasts
Body Talk (1982) Breasts
Titillation (1982) Breasts
G.I. Executioner (1973) Breasts, Buns
The Curious Female (1969) Breasts, Buns
Heaven with a Gun (1969) Breasts
The Mad Doctor of Blood Island (1968) LB, Buns
Numerous Adult Movies

Lori Petty

Born: March 23, 1963
Chattanooga, Tennessee
Skin-O-Meter: Brief Nudity

Don't cry for Lori Petty. The sometimes waiflike, sometimes vixenish starlet has been a featured performer on both big screen and TV tube but has never blossomed into a major media sensation. Feisty, tasty, and trim, Petty's rise to skin icon was undermined by roles as the tomboy next door (Willie in *Bates Motel* [1987]) or as a hotter star's gawky sister (to Geena Davis in *A League of Their Own* [1992]). Pretty Petty was given a lead as the titular chick in *Tank Girl* (1995). Unfortunately, the concept of a female action cartoon hero was slightly ahead of its time. Still, Lori carved out a comfortable career as a blonde, a redhead, and a brunette, and she even showed her ass in surf and crime caper *Point Break* (1991).

That brief glimpse of split tail was just enough to show that we should be crying for ourselves and the many sides of Petty that have gone unseen.

SKIN-fining Moment:

Point Break (1:14) Extremely quick flash of Tank Girl's tuchus as she bolts out of Keanu Reeves's bedroom.

See Her Naked In:

Point Break (1991) Buns

Dedee Pfeiffer

Born: January 1, 1964
Midway City, California
Skin-O-Meter: Great Nudity

Dedee Pfeiffer, who is the younger sibling of Hollywood ultra-siren Michelle Pfeiffer, launched her acting career way back in 1985 with an appearance on an episode of the hit series *Simon & Simon*. Shortly thereafter, Pfeiffer the Younger turned her attention to the silver screen, landing a part as a hooker in her sister's heist comedy *Into the Night* (1985), although Dedee regrettably kept herself pretty covered up for the role (Michelle, however, showed all). The nudity tables turned when the lovely young Dedee finally pulled out her savory, all-natural, perky breasts for a shower scene in *The Horror Show* (1989). Unlike her famous elder sis, Dedee has turned out to be a bit less than abashed. She flashed her flappers time and again in such films as *Deadly Past* (1995), *Radical Jack* (2000), and *Double Exposure* (1993), which unfortunately only featured a single exposure for the comely kitten in the form of a single-breast-baring lesbian love scene with Jennifer Gatti. The sensuous makeout session between the two babes more than made up for the lack of a double tit shot. Dedee may not be a double-D, but she gets an A from Mr. Skin.

SKIN-fining Moment:

Double Exposure (1:24) Deedee shows her left beebee while lesbo-lovin' it up in bed with Jennifer Gatti.

See Her Naked In:

Radical Jack (2000) LB, Thong
Deadly Past (1995) Breasts
Double Exposure (1993) LB
The Horror Show (1989) Body Double—Breasts, Buns

> "Now the reason is my children, but back then it was my father. He would have disowned me. My dad would have killed me."
>
> —MICHELLE PFEIFFER, ON NO LONGER APPEARING NUDE

Michelle Pfeiffer

Born: April 29, 1958
Santa Ana, California
Skin-O-Meter: Brief Nudity

Groin-crunchingly beautiful Michelle Pfeiffer wasn't always a star. She began her career with such duds as *National Lampoon*'s short-lived *Delta House* series and in movie flops such as *Charlie Chan and the Curse of the Dragon Queen* (1981) and *Grease 2* (1982). But when you look as impossibly enchanting as Michelle, people take notice. Although Michelle was unforgettably electrifying in her all-latex outfit as Catwoman in *Batman Returns* (1992), her most noteworthy onscreen nudity remains a blisteringly sexy naked stroll past Jeff Goldblum in *Into the Night* (1985). Another skin scene of note came in *A Thousand Acres* (1997), in which she showed off her right boob during an examination. It's a smidgen weird, though, since her left tit is covered with a pretty grotesque prosthetic. Let's hope that in the pfuture, Ms. Pfeiffer won't be as pfinicky with her perfect pflesh.

SKIN-fining Moment:

Into the Night (0:27) Sweet shot of Michelle's superb ass while she stands nude with one leg up on the toilet.

See Her Naked In:

A Thousand Acres (1997) RB
Into the Night (1985) RB, Buns

Bijou Phillips

Born: April 1, 1980
Greenwich, Connecticut
Skin-O-Meter: Great Nudity

Bijou Phillips is the progeny of none other than late Mamas and Papas founding member John Phillips, so it comes as no surprise that she's a rather free spirit. By the age of thirteen she had given up on school in favor of a career as a model. In keeping with her genes, Beej is also a singer and titled her first album *I'd Rather Eat Glass* in reference to a rumor about the prospect of her returning to modeling. In 2000 Bijou took a go at acting with a role in *Black & White*, which was filmed in naked color and marked her first time flashing hootage onscreen, in a bisexual threesome out in the woods, no less. Although Bijou's *Black* girl-on-girl smooch was as steamy as one could imagine, the film paled in comparison, by sheer skinful standards, at least, to her turn in *Bully* (2001). Bijou left absolutely nothing to the imagination in the flick, so don't back down from the title: stand tall and see Bijou's all.

SKIN-fining Moment:

Bully (0:36) Nice, up-close-and-personal flash of Bijou's Camel Toe hanging out of the side of her spankies . . . It's quick, so don't blink, or you'll miss it.

See Her Naked In:

Havoc (2004) FFN, Buns
Bully—Behind the Scenes (2002) Breasts

Bully (2001) Breasts, Bush
Black & White (2000) Breasts

Bobbie Phillips

Born: January 29, 1972
Charleston, South Carolina
Skin-O-Meter: Great Nudity

Star of UPN's *Chameleon* movies Bobbie Phillips lives up the title, blending in for more than a decade in everything from *Married . . . with Children* to *The Sopranos*. It's on the big screen, however, that we see her as God (and her plastic surgeon) made her. Bobbie bared her bold and beautiful boobies in *Showgirls* (1995) and *Red Shoe Diaries: Luscious Lola*, but in *The Hustle* (2001) Phillips phlaunted her phabulous phur in all its phull-phrontal phenomenality. Phew!

SKIN-fining Moment:

Showgirls (0:19) Bobbie sticks out her gorgeous Mama Earth titties and asks if they've somehow gotten any bigger.

See Her Naked In:

The Hustle (1997) FFN
Cheyenne (1996) Breasts
Showgirls (1995) Breasts, Thong

TeleVisions:

Red Shoe Diaries Breasts

Michelle Phillips

Born: June 4, 1944
Long Beach, California
Skin-O-Meter: Great Nudity

It's a small skinthusiast who envies any other man his skin conquests. Therefore we salute and congratulate musician Papa John Phillips for his long-ago dominion over achingly sweet proto waif Michelle Phillips. While the eternally delectable Michelle has matured into an ageless graceful beauty worthy of

MAMA MICHELLE PHILLIPS GETS NUDE WITH RUDOLF NUREYEV IN *VALENTINO*—AND ALL HER LEAVES ARE BROWN!

respectful leers even on her worst days, Michelle in her youthful prime was a vision such as would inspire the painters of the Renaissance to idolatry. As a golden-throated teenager, and John's concubine, Michelle rocketed to superstardom in the 1960s vocal group The Mamas and the Papas. Her lilting, lovely high notes were such that would inspire her collaborators to adultery, and extramarital dalliances are credited with breaking up the band, which cast fair Michelle upon the rocky shore of show bushness. Groove to the soaring harmonies of nipple, bush, and bum in *Valentino* (1977). Naked Michelle is what California dreaming is all about.

SKIN-fining Moment:

Valentino (0:51) Michelle's little chest-mamas and furry crotch-papa make beautiful music in a tent with Rudy Nureyev. And even though Michelle's blonde, all her leaves are brown . . .

See Her Naked In:

Valentino (1977) Breasts, Bush, Buns

Samantha Phillips

Born: February 25, 1966
Los Angeles, California
Skin-O-Meter: Great Nudity

Blonde and boobular Samantha Phillips is an L.A. woman for the new millennium. She's ambitious and she's busy, and she uses her naked body as fame currency. Well-rounded in more than the physical sense, Samantha has been a member of an all-girl rock group, The Lykettes, and the co-host of a radio talk show, *Sheena & Sam*. However, the former *Penthouse* Pet of the Month (June 1993) has reaped the greatest exposure in the realm of sexploitation quickie flicks. Her flurry of furry activity has produced a long list of casual-sex credits. Start with *Scandal: On the Other Side* (1999). Prepare for Samantha highlighted and naked for toss-around sex on white backgrounds—on a bed and in a shower stall. For some snickers with the dropped knickers, opt for *The Bare Wench Project 2: Scared Topless* (2001). Be advised: Samantha is scared bottomless as well.

SKIN-fining Moment:

The Bare Wench Project 2: Scared Topless (0:37) Samantha flashes every last inch of her own incredible body while she takes a turn dancing naked by the campfire.

See Her Naked In:

Treasure Hunt! (2003)
The Bare Wench Project 2: Scared Topless (2001) FFN, Buns
The Escort III (1999) Breasts
Scandal: On the Other Side (1999) FFN
Butter (1998) Breasts
Moonbase (1998) Breasts
Fallen Angel (1997) FFN, Buns
The Dallas Connection (1995) Breasts, Thong
Sexual Malice (1994) Breasts
Angel 4: Undercover (1993) Breasts
Sex Crimes (1992) Breasts, Thong
Phantasm II (1988) Breasts

TeleVisions:

Hot Springs Hotel Breasts, Buns

Rainbow Phoenix

Born: March 31, 1973
Crockett, Texas
Skin-O-Meter: Brief Nudity

If eccentricity were an industry, the family of unconventionally cute Rainbow Phoenix would be the Carnegie-Mellons of odd characterization. A lesser-known sibling of dynastic actors River, Joaquin, Summer, and Liberty Phoenix, Rainbow's moniker might seem like a bit of a hippie-dippy handle, but it's not the young actress's real name, which is Rain Joan of Arc Phoenix. Despite appearing on the TV series *Family Ties* back in 1987 and playing a cello in the REM video for "At My Most Beautiful," Rainbow's career has

MR. SKIN'S TOP TEN

Women of Color
. . . B-hue-tiful babes

10. Ellen Greene

9. Karen Black

8. Jamie Rose

7. Erin Gray

6. Pink

5. Jennifer Grey

4. Kaki Hunter

3. Vanna White

2. Scarlett Johansson

1. **Rainbow Phoenix**

not yet quite reached the pot of gold. She has managed to flash her burnished pubes, however, in *Even Cowgirls Get the Blues* (1994), and time and beauty are still on her side.

SKIN-fining Moment:

Even Cowgirls Get the Blues (0:49) Rainbow drops her duds with the other cowgirls and points just her bare muff at the camera.

See Her Naked In:

Even Cowgirls Get the Blues (1994) Bush

Summer Phoenix

Born: December 10, 1978
Winter Park, Florida
Skin-O-Meter: Great Nudity

She may never be as famous as her movie-star siblings River and Joaquin, but who would you rather see naked—her marquee brothers or neo-hippie ingénue Summer Phoenix? The intense and natural brunette beauty has been knocking audiences dead since she guest starred on *Murder, She Wrote* at the age of six. A child of Christian missionaries, Summer shared her blessed boobs, buns, and bush in *eSTheR KaHN* (2000). The game girl's motto must be, "If you're going to try something new, you might as well try it buck naked." Summer toned back to tits-only for her bare-top role in *The Believer* (2001). There's still plenty of time for Summer to let her clothes fall.

SKIN-fining Moment:

eSTheR KaHN (1:32) Summer strips fabulously nude for a dude and delights with her sizable, suckable, sweet seat and stunningly lush muff.

See Her Naked In:

The Believer (2001) Breasts
eSTheR KaHN (2000) FFN

Paloma Picasso

Born: April 19, 1949
Paris, France
Skin-O-Meter: Great Nudity

She could've just been Pablo's daughter, but Paloma Picasso is a fine piece of art—and ass—herself. The bizarre beauty made her mark as a designer and also became her best creation. She stood out in the '70s with pale skin contrasted by bright-red lipstick and dark hair. (The look would later be popularized by the all-femme band in those Robert Palmer videos.) Those same features landed her a starring role in the artsy horror anthology *Immoral Tales* (1974), where Paloma peeled off her clothes and palled around with women as the bloodthirsty Elisabeth Bathory. Sadly, she was just slumming and soon returned to running her fashion empire.

SKIN-fining Moment:

Immoral Tales (1:09) It's a "babia majora" as Paloma has her clothes ripped off, revealing her fine flopsies, furry funbox, and fantastic fanny in the midst of an orgy.

See Her Naked In:

Immoral Tales (1974) FFN, Buns

Cindy Pickett

Born: April 18, 1947
Norman, Oklahoma
Skin-O-Meter: Great Nudity

Blonde bombshell Cindy Pickett first made heads turn when she landed on *The Guiding Light* in the mid '70s. Not just another pretty face on daytime TV, Cindy tested the cinematic waters with her film debut . . . and they were hot! *Night Games* (1980), directed by Roger Vadim, explored the lustful fantasies of a housewife, which included lots of skinny dipping with another naked gal pal, some lesbianism, and, of course, full nudity. The film's tagline read: "Bardot . . . Deneuve . . . Fonda. Roger Vadim exposed them all to the world. And Now he has discovered a new star, Cindy Pickett—a woman of the '80s—in a new American film that is elegant, erotic, and explicitly free." And how! But after such a promising start, Cindy fell back into the boobless terrain of the tube on the hit series *St. Elsewhere*. She returned to the big screen with some big hits such as *Ferris Bueller's Day Off* (1986) but never fulfilled her early promise. It's enough to make a person paint a Pickett sign and protest.

SKIN-fining Moment:

Night Games (1:14) A fleeting glance at a full-frontal Cindy as she emerges from the tub for some guy dressed up like a gold-plated superhero.

See Her Naked In:

Night Games (1980) Breasts, Bush, Buns

Rebecca Pidgeon

Born: October 10, 1963
Cambridge, Massachusetts
Skin-O-Meter: Brief Nudity

This multi-talented, sexy Scot started the bulk of her acting work while her successful career as jazz/folk singer/songwriter/bandleader was in full swing. Rebecca Pidgeon graced the boards in hubby David Mamet's stage productions, later moving gracefully into most of his movies, where she remains a skinlicious staple. Her soft, strong-willed roles come across with such an intellectual charge, it's hard to determine what's sexier: her postmodern beauty or the non-traditional approach she takes with her characters. Probably a perfect balance of both, as her performances glow with naïve sexuality, yet give off an unattainable vibe. A perfect femme fatale, Pidgeon has played women bordering on that title in movies such as *The Spanish Prisoner* (1997) and *Heist* (2001), both for man-of-the-house Mamet. But it wasn't until after her seventh star turn for him in *State and Main* (2000) that she was required to clear the nest of those breast pidgeons and show what her Broadway beau has enjoyed after performances for years.

SKIN-fining Moment:

State and Main (1:10) Rebecca pops out from behind a red curtain and we peep at her pink nipple.

See Her Naked In:

State and Main (2000) RB

Silvia Pinal

Born: September 12, 1931
Guaymas, Sonora, Mexico
Skin-O-Meter: Great Nudity

Americans may know Silvia Pinal best from the nosebleed channels on their TV dial, where she is a regular on the hotly expressive Spanish-language programs. But south of the border they know this Mexican hot tamale for her south-of-her-border exposure. She began her career as a leading lady in the '40s, but it was under the direction of the famous surrealist Luis Buñuel in the bizarre religious morality tale *Simon of the Dessert* (1965) that she first revealed her tortilla-busting breast burritos. The shot is from above as Silvia pulls her low-slung neckline down behind her high-rising bust line. Viewers' shots were heard below the belt. It wasn't until *Divinas palabras* (1977) that she delivered the hole package, stripping naked in a crowd, causing a bit of shock until some gal pinched Silvia's nipples and everything got crazy. She was

forty-six years old when she made that movie, and she appears to be maturing nicely. There's no doubt audiences' Pinals will be pleased.

SKIN-fining Moment:

Divinas palabras (1:36) Surrounded by a crowd of scary types, Silvia does the only sensible thing and strips all her clothes off. FFN and buns. Wow.

See Her Nake In:

Divinas palabras (1977) FFN, Buns
Simon of the Desert (1965) Breasts

Pink

Born: September 8, 1979
Philadelphia, Pennsylvania
Skin-O-Meter: Brief Nudity

This firecracker is so hot her hair turned fluorescent! Pop tart Pink continues the sexy sounds of Philly Soul, but with a twist—she's far sexier than any of the Stylistics or the Spinners. Pink has not shown her pink, but being a staple on MTV means lots of skinage. Her first solo album had her in heavy rotation with the video "Just Like a Pill," which was not at all hard to swallow, with Pink reenacting the rose-petal scene from *American Beauty* (1999) that made men red hot for Mena Suvari. And "Lady Marmalade" offered a foursome of foxy females (hot tramp Christina Aguilera, chocolate sweetie Maya, nasty Lil' Kim, and massive mama Missy Elliot) in various states of undress. Pink is setting her pretty sights on movies, featured in the role she was born to play: herself. But *Ski to the Max* (2001) is far from skin to the max, nor is *Rollerball* (2002) equal to the skintertainment of Roller Girl in *Boogie Nights* (1997). But (t) back on the small screen, shocking Pink improved upon a tradition established by Dan Ayckroyd's refrigerator repairman by flashing a little brown when the back of her pants slipped crack-

revealingly low during her December 2003 performance on *Saturday Night Live.*

SKIN-fining Moment:

Saturday Night Live (2002) Pink almost shows brown! Bodacious butt-crack as the pop diva performs.

TeleVisions:

Saturday Night Live Buns

Jada Pinkett

Born: September 18, 1971
Baltimore, Maryland
Skin-O-Meter: Brief Nudity

It was a different world for the drooling voyeurs of TV land when that fine and hot ebony princess Jada Pinkett made her first major impact in 1991. That was when she landed a supporting role on the hit series *A Different World*, but it wasn't until Jada appeared in the surprise hit *Menace II Society* (1993) that she would finally reach stardom—and become a menace to flaccid members everywhere. She has since appeared in such notable productions as *A Low Down Dirty Shame* (1994), *Demon Knight* (1995), *The Nutty Professor* (1996), *Scream 2* (1997), *Bamboozled* (2000), and *Ali* (2001), opposite her hubby Will Smith. As her acting career steams ahead, Jada is yet to appear in the buff on celluloid. You may remember some skin scenes in *Jason's Lyric* (1994), but aside from a few shots of her supple ass, all were done by a body double. Don't be jaded, Jada, give up the Pinkett.

SKIN-fining Moment:

Jason's Lyric (1:16) Brief bunnage in a hiked-up dress while Allen Payne schtups Jada in a store.

See Her Naked In:

Jason's Lyric (1994) Body Double—Breasts / Her—Buns

Marie-France Pisier

Born: May 10, 1944
Dalat, Vietnam
Skin-O-Meter: Great Nudity

Marie-France Pisier was born during WWII in Vietnam, where her father was a French colonial governor. By age seventeen this French pastry was living in Paris and appearing in experimental films, her first being *L'amour à vingt ans* (1962). No intellectual lightweight, Marie found time for college in between her '60s films shoots, completing her law and political science degrees at the University of Paris. After appearing in a number of obscure French art films, Marie gained international attention in 1975 for her Cesar award-winning performance in *Cousin, Cousine* (1975). This also meant a wider audience for her Gallic gallivanting. Hollywood finally caught a full-frontal glimpse of Marie's furry French souffle in *The Other Side of Midnight* (1977), but before you could say *Sacre Bleu!* Marie had disappeared from American screens and was back in European films such as *Le Soeurs Brontë* (1979), *French Postcards* (1980) (where she once again bared her baby bon-bons), and *Chanel Solitaire* (1981). Marie wrote the best-selling novel *The Governor's Party* in 1990 and went on to direct the film version of the book. She still directs and appears in French films and TV.

SKIN-fining Moment:

The Other Side of Midnight (1:17)
Super-sexy full-frontal as she preps herself for some fireside lovin' by rubbing ice and oil all over her naked form.

See Her Naked In:

Les Nanas (1985) Breasts
French Postcards (1979) Breasts
The Other Side of Midnight (1977) FFN, Buns
Sérail (1976) FFN

Maria Pitillo

Born: January 8, 1965
Elmira, New York
Skin-O-Meter: Brief Nudity

Blonde starlet Maria Pitillo made her first TV appearance in a Pepto-Bismol commercial and soon landed her first bit part on a 1984 episode of *Miami Vice*. Too bad her skin has also remained more or less fully coated onscreen so far, but she's still working, so there's still hope! In 1986 she made her feature-film debut playing a masseuse alongside Danny DeVito and Joe Piscopo in *Wise Guys* (1986). Soap stardom soon followed when she played southern bad girl Nancy Don Lewis on *Ryan's Hope* from 1987 to 1989. Since then her film career has been more successful than her TV stints, as she has appeared on more than one failed sitcom, including *Partners* and *House Rules*. Her first "big" film role was in the CBS Schoolbreak Special *What If I'm Gay?* (1987), in which she had nothing whatsoever to do with the lead male character's decision to hit for the other team. Her biggest film roles to date were as brunette coffee-shop owner Gloria McKinney, who fell for Greg Kinnear, in *Dear God* (1996) and news reporter Audrey Timmonds in the remake of *Godzilla* (1998).

SKIN-fining Moment:

White Palace (0:27) Ms. Pitillo briefly flashes her titillo's while having sex with James Spader.

See Her Naked In:

White Palace (1990) RB

Ingrid Pitt

Born: November 21, 1937
Poland
Skin-O-Meter: Great Nudity

To this day, a large cadre of skindustrious film fans are devoted to the mannered, period-piece vampire movies put out by Britain's Hammer Studios in the early 1970s. The force behind this continued fascination is the voluptuous presence of cleavage-and-fangs villainess Ingrid Pitt. Ingrid's full-chested charms rose above all the elaborate Victorian costuming and ponderous speechifying that cloaked the genre at that time. Her whiter-than-milk dairy queens heaved heavy and full in a passion for blood. On the bottom line, Pitt graced *The Vampire Lovers* (1970) with one of the most mesmerizing butt shots of all time. The ass-rich actress stood in a bathtub and lifted her legs to step over the rim, giving loads of backside movement and allowing study of the half loaves in all various stages of tension and repose. Ingrid will forever have a seat among the Pantheon of Skin.

SKIN-fining Moment:

The Wicker Man (1:00) Insouciant Ingrid doesn't seem to mind being walked in on while bathing; in fact, she makes no move to cover those buoys.

See Her Naked In:

The Wicker Man (1973) Breasts
Countess Dracula (1970) Breasts
The Vampire Lovers (1970) Breasts, Buns

Mary Kay Place

Born: September 23, 1947
Port Arthur, Texas
Skin-O-Meter: Brief Nudity

During her long and varied career, perky Mary Kay Place has made her mark as a creator and performer in some of the most groundbreaking entertainments of her time. After an uncredited minor part in Barbra Streisand's *What's Up, Doc?* (1972), Mary Kay garnered accolades as a writer for *The Mary Tyler Moore Show*, one of the best-crafted series ever to be on TV. M.K. took her place in front of the cameras portraying a recurring character on *Mary Hartman, Mary Hartman*. From Fernwood, she hitched a ride to high Hollywood, showing a tiny nipple spill in *The Big Chill* (1983). Place's resumé is capped with a pair of pressed boobies in a tight-squeezing shower shared with Martin Short in *Captain Ron* (1992). Derriere beware: The ass shot is a butt double. Too bad we have no Place posterior for posterity.

SKIN-fining Moment:

Captain Ron (0:32) Mary-Kay is the woman, her chest is the naked Place as she showers with Marin Short. Overhead view.

See Her Naked In:

Captain Ron (1992) Breasts

Dana Plato

Born: November 7, 1964
Maywood, California
Died: May 8, 1999
Skin-O-Meter: Great Nudity

MR. SKIN'S TOP TEN

Real Suicide Girls

10. Wendy O. Williams

9. Savannah

8. Romy Schneider

7. Jean Seberg

6. Brenda Benet

5. Lani O'Grady

4. Lois Hamilton

3. Margaux Hemingway

2. Dana Plato

1. **Marilyn Monroe**

Dana Plato had a short, wild ride that even the great philosopher Plato couldn't make sense of. She debuted as a Tennis Fan in the TV series *The Bionic Woman* (1975) after she passed on the possessed-child role that Linda Blair would eventually play in *The Exorcist* (1973). Her mom didn't like the tone of the demonic material, so it wouldn't be until Dana landed the part of Kimerbly Drummond, the white girl with two black brothers, on *Diff'rent Strokes* that things took off. Dana was eventually bumped from the program when she became pregnant. She struggled to find work and, instead, found trouble: drug addiction and a criminal record for forging Valium prescriptions and even robbing a video store. Where else to go but the always inviting arms of softcore exploitation? Delicious Dana offered some *Compelling Evidence* (1995) with a topless titty-sucking scene and went every which way *and* loose with a threesome, skinny dipping, and a lesbo shower rubdown in *Different Strokes: The Story of Jack and Jill . . . and Jill* (1997)—well worth a stroke or two. After appearing on *The Howard Stern Show* in 1999, where Dana swore she was cleaning up her act, the thirty-four-year-old mother of one checked out with an OD ruled a suicide. It may take different strokes, but that was one unkind cut.

SKIN-fining Moment:

Different Strokes (0:21) Dana shows her chest-Drummonds while helping Landon Hall with those "hard-to-reach areas" in the shower. Nice!

See Her Naked In:

Different Strokes (1997) Breasts, Buns
Compelling Evidence (1995) Breasts

Martha Plimpton

Born: November 16, 1970
New York, New York
Skin-O-Meter: Brief Nudity

Martha Plimpton was born for show business. Her father is Keith Carradine and her mother is Shelley Plimpton, so it makes perfect sense that this natural talent was already in movies by age ten, appearing in a small part in *Rollover* (1981). She went on to do a series of Calvin Klein commercials (we'd sure like to get between her and her Calvins!) before making a name for herself in *The Goonies* (1985). On the set of *The Mosquito Coast* (1986) she met River Phoenix and became romantically entangled with the pretty-boy, vegetarian, tree-hugging, dope fiend. She's also dated such Hollywood hunks as Christian Slater and Jon Patrick Walker. But we're unlikely to get our hands on the sweet blonde's petite tits, so for compensation we have her brief skin scenes in *I Shot Andy Warhol* (1996). While she appeared to be a good ride, her bedroom antics were filmed in arty silhouette. Even worse is *Eye of God* (1997), where Martha was topless, but as a gutted-down-the-middle corpse. But that's all she's showing (for now). Martha, my dear, please, one well-lit scene is all Mr. Skin asks.

SKIN-fining Moment:

I Shot Andy Warhol (0:16) Martha gets topless for a sapphic tussle with Lili Taylor as a horny dude watches and whacks.

See Her Naked In:

Eye of God (1997) Breasts
I Shot Andy Warhol (1996) Breasts

Shelley Plimpton

Skin-O-Meter: Great Nudity

Hippies were meant to be naked, and flower child Shelley Plimpton proved that on several skinful occasions during her short-lived stage and screen career. Discovered in her teens by the producers of the stage play *Hair*, she went on to perform in that clothing-optional Broadway hit on and off for several years, taking time—and her clothes—off to appear in two of the love generation's cult cinema classics, where her Haights and Ashbury were on grand display. A former groupie herself who cavorted with the likes of The Rolling Stones, Shelley was cast as Arlo Guthrie's bare band babe in *Alice's Restaurant* (1969), in which she dropped her sun dress in a bid to bed the star. And in *Glen and Randa* (1971) Plimpton went full frontal for a frolic in the post-apocalyptic wasteland for her director/husband. Sadly, after one more skin-friendly role in *Fore Play* (1975), this svelte sexpot put her woodstocks away and bowed out of the acting arena, seemingly to raise a family. But for a brief time she was a patchouli-oil princess, prompting a generation to tune in and turn on with her body in its 100% organic, all-natural form.

SKIN-fining Moment:

Glen and Randa (0:01) Great view of Shelley's forest while in the forest with Glen. Long scene.

See Her Naked In:

Glen and Randa (1971) FFN, Buns
Alice's Restaurant (1969) Breasts

Amanda Plummer

Born: March 23, 1957
New York, New York
Skin-O-Meter: Hall of Fame

So refined and high toned is leggy New York-native Amanda Plummer that she might be easily misperceived as being British. The daughter of critically regarded thespians Christopher Plummer and Tammy Grimes, artfully bred Amanda began her career as a serious stage actress. Although she won two Tony awards for her live dramatics, Amanda eventually gave

in to the allure of film and skin. Don't expect typical titty twisting. The best part of *Butterfly Kiss* (1996) is one long lesbianic tryst, with Plummer's body wrapped in chains throughout. *8½ Women* (1999) is distinguished by the odd fetishistic appeal of Amanda naked in traction in a hospital bed, the freaky fun of fully nude Plummer bathing a giant four-legged pig, and twin bouncing butts as our heroine bounds into the distance riding a big white horse. Hooray for artistic vision.

SKIN-fining Moment:

American Perfekt (0:46) Side-skinnage as Amanda gets it on with Robert Forster, followed by some bonus breastosity when the deed is done.

See Her Naked In:

The Apartment Complex (1999) Breasts
8½ Women (1999) Breasts, Buns
American Perfekt (1997) Breasts
Butterfly Kiss (1996) FFN, Buns
Cattle Annie and Little Britches (1981) Breasts

Rossana Podestà

Born: June 20, 1934
Tripoli, Libya
Skin-O-Meter: Brief Nudity

Director Robert Wise needed an actress to play the title role in his historical epic *Helen of Troy* (1956), and Elizabeth Taylor and Ava Gardner just weren't sexy enough. Instead, he chose Italian beauty Rossana Podestà—and not for her oral skills, either. In fact, Rossana didn't speak English and had to learn her lines phonetically. Nobody cared, though, since Rossana was well established as an international actress. Besides, her blonde Helen erected plenty of Trojan horses in the pants of male moviegoers. Rossana spent the rest of her career in Italy, though, where she later went skinternational in *Le Ore nude* (1964) and got heteros erect in

Homo Eroticus (1971). The Libyan-born beauty didn't retire from the screen until 1985, but she still went out as a legendary MILF in films such as *Segreti segreti* (1985).

SKIN-fining Moment:

Le Ore nude (1:13) Rosie shows her rump while running toward a car after a skinny-dip. It's quick, but pretty cool for 1964.

See Her Naked In:

Le Ore nude (1964) Buns

Haydée Politoff

Born: May 25, 1946
Paris, France
Skin-O-Meter: Great Nudity

Add a little France to your pants without taking a costly, smoke-filled trip. Haydée Politoff has enough foxy French flavor to get your jets racing here Stateside. Since la nudité is as common in Europe as tiny dogs and Bush bashers, the Lady Haydée doesn't disappoint in showing her sun-kissed skin. She featured her firm, freckly flesh in films such as *Bora Bora* (1968) and *Il Delitto del diavola* (1971). With buoyant baguettes and booming buns as poppin' fresh as Haydée, any of her movies will give you your just desserts.

SKIN-fining Moment:

Bora Bora (0:36) Haydée's hooters come out to play at the behest of Corrado Pani.

See Her Naked In:

The Virgin of Bali (1972) Breasts
Il Delitto del diavolo (1971) Breasts, Buns
Bora Bora (1968) Breasts

Cheryl Pollak

Born: August 31, 1967
Rialto, California
Skin-O-Meter: Great Nudity

In the bevy of beauties that once was *Melrose Place*, you might recognize Cheryl Pollak as the sexy little home wrecker who wooed Billy away from Alison. This California girl has been wrecking peckers since her debut in the horror comedy *My Best Friend is a Vampire* (1988). Later she achieved suck-sess grabbing Christian Slater by the tators in the DJ diatribe *Pump up the Volume* (1990). Whose stump wouldn't be pumped by Cheryl's co-ed charms and peaches-and-cream complexion? After a few attempts as a femme fatale on short-lived series such as *Hotel Malibu* and *Live Shot*, Pollak was victorious in her vixenism in *No Strings Attached* (1997). Her skinful stint as a nudist painter made Vincent Spano *Van Gogh off* half cocked. Pretty as a picture and still fit for the hung, Cheryl's only peril is that she's underappreciated by the mainstream.

SKIN-fining Moment:

No Strings Attached (0:40) Cheryl busts out the boob-stuff in bed with Vincent Spano.

See Her Naked In:

No Strings Attached (1997) Breasts

Sarah Polley

Born: January 8, 1979
Toronto, Ontario, Canada
Skin-O-Meter: Brief Nudity

Sarah Polly, chesty young beauty from the Great White North, doesn't care about fame or fortune in Hollywood, which is maybe why the industry is showering her with both. She made her position clear early on after being blacklisted by Disney for refusing to take off a peace symbol at a ceremony during the Gulf War. Sarah was only twelve at the time. She also lost some back teeth in a clash with the police while attending a political

demonstration when she was sixteen. This feisty little independent (who stands only five-foot-two) debuted at the age of six in *One Magic Christmas* (1985), but it was her starring turn in the Terry Gilliam flick *The Adventures of Baron Munchausen* (1988) that got her noticed. More recently Sarah's star rocketed via roles in *The Sweet Hereafter* (1997), *eXistenZ* (1999), and *Go* (1999). Her go-to film in terms of nudity, however, is the drama *Guinevere* (1999), in which she revealed her really huge Big Macs. Mr. Skin especially likes the scene where Sarah, while walking down a hallway, is wearing nothing but a towel. The Canuck can also be seen wearing only a bra (and sadly a skirt) in the aforementioned *Go*, in which she had to strip for some drug dealer who's afraid she's wired (if I were a cop, I'd hide my mike someplace else—if only to get a couple of actresses really naked).

SKIN-fining Moment:

Guinevere (0:58) Sarah sure can fill out a towel, even if this Polly won't show her cracker.

See Her Naked In:

The Law of Enclosures (2000) RB
Guinevere (1999) Breasts

Teri Polo

Born: August 29, 1969
Dover, Delaware
Skin-O-Meter: Great Nudity

Teri Polo began her career on the soap opera *Loving*, and audiences have been loving this little blonde cutie ever since. She moved on to the big screen in movies such as *Born to Ride* (1991) and *Mystery Date* (1991), with smaller parts in ensemble pieces *Passed Away* (1992) and *The House of the Spirits* (1993). But it was the smash-hit comedy *Meet the Parents* (2000) that put Teri on the verge. Since then she's been

playing with big boys like John Travolta in *Domestic Disturbance* (2001) and Andy Garcia in *Unsaid* (2001). But that doesn't mean she's too shy to show skin. Her debut debauchery came in *Quick* (1993), in a slightly violent sex scene that showed off her round and bouncy rumptasticness. She also shared her small-nippled mini-milkers during a front-seat carnal car hump. Here's hoping she never puts the brakes on her love of showing skin.

SKIN-fining Moment:

Quick (1:06) Nice view of Teri's ta-tas as she toplessly mounts a guy for some clumsy car-sex.

See Her Naked In:

Second String (2002) LB
The House of the Spirits (1994) Breasts
Quick (1993) Breasts, Buns

Kitt Pomidoro

Skin-O-Meter: Great Nudity

The competition for newscaster positions at the major networks is ruthless and cutthroat. For most candidates, a position reading events of the day to the camera is a lifelong ambition, pursued with dedication and abandon. Would-be news anchors hone their presentation skills on college campuses, on cow-town stations, in front of every mirrored surface they ever encounter. And then there is brunette bombshell Kit Pomidoro, a network news sensation who was hired as much for her ability to talk while she takes off her clothes as for any affinity for articulating the pressing issues of our time. Information junkies who tune in to the Playboy network's *Weekend Flash* current events wrap-up will have no problem paying attention as Kit and her co-anchors present current events while slipping out of their garments, but anyone who hopes to pass a quiz covering the material he has just seen is hopelessly deluded.

SKIN-fining Moment:

The Exhibitionist Files (1:23) Kitt shows tit and mitts her clit, masturbating full-frontally nude while she knows someone is watching. Someone besides you, that is.

See Her Naked In:

The Exhibitionist Files (2002) FFN, Buns

TeleVisions:

Weekend Flash FFN, Buns

Alice Poon
Skin-O-Meter: Great Nudity

What's in a name? If you're Alice Poon, everything, considering her roles often feature a little skin-sum on the menu. Possessing a super tight body and rich, caramel flesh that would make even Ming beg for mercy, Alice splits her time between bare bits and stunt work, showing she's not afraid to work without a net, or without a wardrobe, for the right project. Her first turn sans silk was for the sexually super-charged auto fetish flick *Crash* (1996), where while on all fours she was on the receiving end of James Spader's tongue and gearshift. Then on the erotic vampire cable series *The Hunger*, Alice showed off her Shanghai sacks for the creatures of the night. After a few well-placed, fully clothed roles, she returned to skindom with her role as the masseuse on the make for Mark Wahlberg in *The Corruptor* (1999), pressing her pointy perks up against his back during a full-service rubdown. And a happy ending may be in the price of admission for Alice as well, as she took a turn, and a lot of spills, in the Hollywood remake of the sci-fi thriller *Rollerball* (2002), playing

an exotic, tough-as-nails contestant.

SKIN-fining Moment:

Crash (0:05) Left dangler as she gets it doggy-style from James Spader.

See Her Naked In:

The Corruptor (1999) Breasts
Crash (1996) Breasts

TeleVisions:

Leap Years Breasts, Buns, Bush
The Hunger Breasts, Thong

Paulina Porizkova

Born: April 9, 1965
Prostejov, Czechoslovakia
Skin-O-Meter: Great Nudity

Paulina Porizkova is best known for her many appearances in *Sports Illustrated*'s annual swimsuit edition, as well as for her plethora of magazine photo shoots and modeling gigs, including one (wonderful) appearance in the pages of *Playboy* magazine in August 1987. Not surprisingly, she has given acting a shot or two. Quite surprisingly, she proved her talents were more than two-dimensional. Paulina first graced the silver screen in the let's-drool-over-young-models docu-drama *Portfolio* (1983), which she followed up with a part in *Covergirl* (1984), both of which featured her in roles as a living mannequin. Naturally, she shined. She rose to a new challenge in *Anna* (1987) and has since enjoyed a semi-successful screen career in such films as *Arizona Dream* (1993), *Female Perversions* (1996), and *The Intern* (2000). Not a stranger to nudity, Paulina first let a nipple slipple in *Her Alibi* (1989). But for her best sex-luloid skin, check out *Thursday* (1998), in which she went completely naked for most of her time onscreen, which she spends forcibly (!) having sex with some

lucky guy whom she has tied-up in a chair. Mr. Skin wishes every day of the week was as tawdry as *Thursday*.

SKIN-fining Moment:

Thursday (0:56) Incredible! Paulina peels to reveal her supermodel mammaries and ass while mounting tied-up Thomas Jane and riding his rod on a kitchen chair. You will be SO jealous of Ric Ocasek.

See Her Naked In:

Knots (2004) RB
Thursday (1998) Breasts, Buns
Her Alibi (1989) Nip Slip RB

Susie Porter

Australia
Skin-O-Meter: Hall of Fame

Susie Porter reigns supreme as one of Australia's hottest sexports, starting her career with *Idiot Box* (1996) and never looking back. Soon she was commanding more notable roles in movies such as *Mr. Reliable* (1996) and the Glenn Close–helmed *Paradise Road* (1997). It seems odd then that once achieving an admirable level of fame she would begin shedding her clothes at every possible turn. Oddly *great!* Starting with a tit-revealing turn in the randy comedy *Welcome to Whoop Whoop* (1996), Susie got more and more daring with every performance, subsequently showing off some more hootage in *Feeling Sexy* (1999), then making her first full-frontal exposure in *Better Than Sex* (2000). For the most Porter bang for your Porter buck, though, one need look no further than the whodunit *Monkey's Mask* (2000), which featured several fully nude dalliances between Susie and glamazon Kelly McGillis. It's so hot in fact that it warmed the cockles of one George Lucas, who subsequently cast cutie Susie in part two of his epic saga, *Star Wars:*

Attack of the Clones (2002). She's certainly out of this world.

SKIN-fining Moment:

The Monkey's Mask: (0:49) Susie lays back for a full-frontal tongue-bath from the also naked Kelly McGillis. Leztastic!

See Her Naked In:

Better than Sex (2000) FFN
The Monkey's Mask (2000) Breasts, Bush, Buns
Feeling Sexy (1999) Breasts, Buns
Welcome to Woop Woop (1996) Breasts, Bush, Buns

Parker Posey

Born: November 8, 1968
Baltimore, Maryland
Skin-O-Meter: Great Nudity

Svelte sweetie Parker Posey was named after the hot model of the '50s, Suzy Parker, and she shares that beauty's classy allure. Parker has also been named the "Queen of Indies" by *Time* magazine and has appeared in some thirty films since 1994, most of them low-budget art-house productions. But the wet dream of the horn-rimmed glasses set started her career in 1991 with a stint on the hit soap opera *As the World Turns*. She quickly moved on to the mini-series *Tales of the City* and all of its sequels, *Sleepless in Seattle* (1993), and *Coneheads* (1993). But it was in less mainstream fare such as *Dazed and Confused* (1993), *Amateur* (1994), and *The Doom Generation* (1995) that she truly bloomed. Yes, she continues to sneak into big-budget pictures like *You've Got Mail* (1998) and *Scream 3* (2000), but we appreciate her low-budget turns, as they seem to turn up Parker's itty bitties more often than not. She first flashed her thimble-sized thingies in *Sleep with Me* (1994). Once free, they refused to remain undercover. Parker treated us to her tiny teats with such breastastic exposure in *Party Girl* (1995), *The Misadventures of Margaret* (1998), *The Anniversary Party* (2001), and *Personal Velocity* (2002). Sadly, she has yet to do a full-frontal scene. It's time she Parker her Poseys and let us take in her furry bouquet.

SKIN-fining Moment:

Sleep with Me (0:57) Now here are some posies that are ripe for the pickin'! Parker pulls off her top and exposes her bite-sized boobies to Eric Stoltz.

See Her Naked In:

Personal Velocity: Three Portraits (2002) RB
The Anniversary Party (2001) Breasts
The Misadventures of Margaret (1998) Breasts
Party Girl (1995) LB
Sleep with Me (1994) Breasts

Markie Post

Born: November 4, 1950
Palo Alto, California
Skin-O-Meter: Never Nude

As Public Defender Christine Sullivan, *Night Court*'s Markie Post skipped the jiggle and simply showcased her stunning breasts in all kinds of professional outfits—and the occasional cunning casual clothing. Before that, though, Markie showed off her booming boobies in plenty of bikinis on the TV show *The Fall Guy*. Her early fans will also never forget Markie as a busting brunette on a 1977 episode of *The Love Boat*, where she turned a skimpy one-piece bathing suit into an over-the-shoulder-boulder-holder. Markie finally got a well-deserved, big-screen showcase as Cameron Diaz's foxy mother in *There's Something About Mary* (1998), but she can't help heating up modest made-for-TV fare. *Visitors of the Night* (1995) had a nude Markie getting probed by aliens, while her skinny-dipping scene in *Tricks of the Trade* (1988) caught the censors sleeping for a slip of a nip. Sadly, a lot of masturbatory fantasies were recently aborted when nobody picked up Markie's pilot for a revival of the old Saturday morning stand-by *Electra Woman and Dyna Girl*.

SKIN-fining Moment:

Tricks of the Trade (0:59) As Cindy Williams tsk-tsks, Markie enjoys a few laps of moonlit skinny-dipping in a pool. No clear nudity, but we almost see some underwater buttage.

Franka Potente

Born: July 22, 1974
Dülmen, Germany
Skin-O-Meter: Great Nudity

Her last name translates to "powerful," and that's a good description of sinewy siren Franka Potente. She may be best known to American audiences for her roles in such films as *Blow* (2001), *Storytelling* (2001), and, of course, the worldwide smash *Run Lola Run* (1998). But the German goody actually began her career years ago with a role in *Nach Funf im Urwald* (1996), which also marked the first time that she flashed some hootage on film. She went on to appear in all her boobular glory in such Teutonic fare as *Easy Day* (1997), *Drei Madels von der Tankstelle* (1997), and *Coming In* (1997) before making the trek across the pond. Thankfully, American audiences have finally been treated to Franka's potentes in *The Bourne Identity* (2001) opposite Matt Damon. Franka, my dear, I give a damn!

SKIN-fining Moment:

Nach Fünf im Urwald (1:13) Franka strips to her panties before diving into a swimming pool. Ich ben ein Boob-liner!

See Her Naked In:

I Love Your Work (2003) Breasts
Blueprint (2003) RB
Bin ich schön? (1998) RB
Easy Day (1997) RB
Die Drei Mädels von der Tankstelle (1997) Breasts
Coming In (1997) Breasts
Nach Fünf im Urwald (1996) Breasts

Annie Potts

Born: October 28, 1952
Franklin, Kentucky
Skin-O-Meter: Brief Nudity

After spending most of her youth doing stage work, Annie Potts, a kickin' chick from Kentucky, finally broke into Hollywood with a string of TV work, leading to her raucous role as the "If the van is a-rockin'" customized cutie who woos and screws Mark Hamill in *Corvette Summer* (1978), which featured a brief but memorable glimpse of her dashboard ornaments and tail end. She's spent the past two decades as a strong and always sexy supporting character actress, lending her pretty and witty style to numerous TV shows, movies, and Lifetime dramas, including a seven year tour of booty on the ensemble sitcom *Designing Women*. Her homegrown good looks and, ahem, southern charms, made her a favorite on that show and ushered in a newfound love for old-fashioned and delicious debutantes. For an eyeful of Annie's own southern bells, they were on ample display in *Who's Harry Crumb* (1989), albeit trapped in a see-through bra, and in *Texasville* (1990), where she paraded around in tight-fitting tank tops, bras, and low-shoulder dresses, serving up a family-sized gander at both her Mason and her Dixon.

SKIN-fining Moment:

Corvette Summer (0:51) Hard-to-see hootage in a van with Mark Hamill.

See Her Naked In:

Corvette Summer (1978) Breasts

> "I just promised lots of sexual favors for the part of Molly and they said, 'OK, we'll put you in the show.' But the only drawback to that is now I have to do it every week."
>
> —SARAH-JANE POTTS ON HOW SHE LANDED ON TV'S *FELICITY*

Sarah-Jane Potts

Born: August 30, 1979
Bradford, West Yorkshire, England, UK
Skin-O-Meter: Great Nudity

Lucious Liverpoolian Sarah-Jane Potts is best known in the U.S. for her tawdry turn as the fresh-faced flatmate on teen melodrama *Felicity* but cut her zipper teeth onscreen in her homeland for years prior to stimulating Statesiders with her bangers and mash. Back home, Sarah-Jane had no reservations undoing her britches to get her thespian career on the fast track— gladly giving Brits the tits as a juvenile delinquent in the downbeat TV movie *Meat* (1994) and playing tasty tarts on several TV shows and mini-series. Since then she's given her rapidly growing fanbase a peek at her very own BBC (Boobs, Buns, and Cootchie) during a sweat bead-inducing bedroom romp in *Wonderland* (1999) and has kept her resumé fresh with several sweet and sexy supporting roles in indie flicks and syndicated television shows. She most recently worked her burning-hot bum off in *Afterschool Special* (2003) and on the WB network's revamped *Tarzan* series. "Me Tarzan, you Sarah-Jane?" No, she didn't play the ape-man's main squeeze, but she no doubt had fans on both sides of the Atlantic banging on their chests during every episode.

SKIN-fining Moment:

Wonderland (0:13) Ultra-sexy boomers, bushala, and bottom as she mixes it up with her hipster boyfriend in bed.

See Her Naked In:

Wonderland (1999) Breasts, Buns

Brittney Powell

Born: March 4, 1972
Würzburg, Germany
Skin-O-Meter: Great Nudity

A naughty knockout, Brittney Powell was a *Playboy* staple in the '90s. Although Britt never made it to bunny, she did more than her fair share of flaunting her firm frame from tats to toes in video flicks such as *Girls of Spring Break* (1991) and *Bikers, Babes and Beyond* (1994). Equally enticing on the series *Eden*, Powell was powerless to stop islanders from snatching at her ample apples on the *Fantasy Island*-skinspired weekly love fest. For those with tamer tastes, Brittney was perfectly professional in movies such as *Airborne* (1993) and *Dragonworld* (1994) and on the soap opera *General Hospital*. Mr. Skin prefers the Britt exposing at least a bit o' tit, as in the mainstream movie *Fled* (1996). For more glimpses of this gorgeous German's sweet T&A, flee to your video store schnell!

SKIN-fining Moment:

Round Trip to Heaven (0:36) As she slips into a swimsuit, we see quick slips of topless Britt's bits.

See Her Naked In:

Fled (1996) Breasts
Babes, Bikes and Beyond (1994) Breasts, Thong
Round Trip to Heaven (1992) Breasts

Romina Power

Born: October 2, 1951
Los Angeles, California
Skin-O-Meter: Great Nudity

As the daughter of Hollywood icon Tyrone Power, Romina Power could have come to America and used her father's famous name. Instead, Romina chose to follow a European career in the tradition of her mother, respected actress Linda Christian. Her career started with the sexy film *Menage all'italiana* (1965). But then Romina really got our Italian breads rising with *Marquis de Sade: Justine* (1969), a shameless kinkfest where the bold young actress hung topless in the breeze while being mercilessly abused—which is still nothing compared to how we're abusing ourselves whenever we watch these scenes. Romina's still a popular actress (and singer) in Italy, but she only got more respectable in later years. Still, she's earned the right to be respected as a pioneer in cinematic sadomasochism.

SKIN-fining Moment:

Marquis de Sade: Justine (0:57)
Ponder Power's pellets as she poses nude for a painting. Positively perfect!

See Her Naked In:

Marquis de Sade: Justine (1969) Breasts, Buns

Stefanie Powers

Born: November 2, 1942
Hollywood, California
Skin-O-Meter: Brief Nudity

Born Stefania Zofia Federkiewicz, Stefanie Powers wisely chose to change her name to something easy to fit your mouth around, just like she is. While best known for her leading role on the hit '80s series *Hart to Hart*, her career started with a bit part in *Tammy Tell Me True* (1961). Although she spent the next few years in various cinematic outings, she pretty much eschewed that particular milieu in favor of countless television gigs and guest appearances. Some of her more interesting endeavors included the failed series *The Girl from U.N.C.L.E.*, the failed series *Doctors*, and the incredibly brief and ultimately failed series *The Feather and Father Gang*. Hmm, notice a trend here? Logically, due to the bulk of her work appearing on network television, Stefanie never really got the chance to show off that bodacious bod quite like some of us hoped. She did manage to free her flappers ever so briefly in *Crescendo* (1972) as well as in *Little Moon and Jud McGraw* (1976). She got nude in *The Invisible Stranger* (1976), but we only saw her from the back—with a bit of a butt flash. It's a tease, but hopefully the Powers that be will get frisky in her old age and expose some of that mature mammaliciousness.

SKIN-fining Moment:

Crescendo (1:11) In bed with James Olson, Stefanie uncovers her hootastic Hart-to-Harts. First James treats them like his personal Olson twins. Then he shoves Stef forward when a gunman enters, and her double-barrels bounce bedazzingly.

See Her Naked In:

The Invisible Strangler (1976) Buns
Bronco Busters (1976) Breasts
Crescendo (1970) Breasts

Taryn Power

Born: September 13, 1953
Los Angeles, California
Skin-O-Meter: Brief Nudity

Taryn Power was conceived by a blow from the infamous flesh sword of super swashbuckler Tyrone Power. She started her career in the Spanish-language Colombian production *María* (1971). Of course, she played the title role in the film, but, unfortunately, 1971 wasn't exactly a banner year for Colombian cinema in the States. Taryn next followed in her daddy's footsteps and took a turn toward the hallowed hills of Holly-wad, although from the distance of a role in the made-for-British-TV movie *The Count of Monte Cristo* (1975) with the likes of Richard Chamberlain and Tony Curtis. It was a step in the right direction, anyway. Finally, Taryn landed her first American skinematic gig as the gentle collegiate love interest of war-torn Dennis Hopper in *Tracks* (1976). It's a triumphant treat, representing the best-ever looks at Taryn's real powers, namely those sitting high on her chest. Sure, they're brief looks at best, and the right hooter makes its appearance a full half-hour before the left one, but voyeurs can't be choosers. Taryn returned to the blimey shores of Bri-tit-ain for a turn in *Sinbad and the Eye of the Tiger* (1977). In spite of its misleading G rating, this fantasy offered prime bunnage and brief breastitudity from both Taryn and none other than Jane Seymour—and you do "see more"—not bad for a kiddie flick. Unfortunately, Taryn pretty much dropped off the map after that, landing roles here and there in flicks such as *Serpiente de mar* (1984) and *Eating* (1990), neither of which served to flash any more flesh than she had flashed before. Her absence is Taryn us apart!

SKIN-fining Moment:

Sinbad and the Eye of the Tiger (1:16) Taryn presents some super-quick bunnage as she goes for a distant skinny-dip with a gal-pal.

See Her Naked In:

Sinbad and the Eye of the Tiger (1977) RB, Buns
Tracks (1976) Breasts

Joan Prather

Born: October 17, 1950
Dallas, Texas
Skin-O-Meter: Great Nudity

Though she is most widely known as dutiful and daughterly Janet Bradford on television's *Eight Is Enough*, the beguiling brunette with the small but serviceable rack and firm, tightly formed butt pack is best remembered for her buns-out performance in a more sinister kind of family drama. The Angie Dickinson star vehicle *Big Bad Mama* (1974) would have been nothing without innocent lasses ripe for Angie's corrupting influence, and sweet-cheeked Joan Prather was prime for debauching. From the moment Joan showed up with her arms spread and tied to the headboard of a brass bed, with sinful Angie menacing her from the other end, it was obvious that Joan would undergo an education of the sensual variety. Sure enough, by the time the film is ready to climax, Prather has learned to drop all pretense of clothing, cling on to the nearest stud, and turn her finely turned chair cheeks to the discerning camera. Two buns are enough.

SKIN-fining Moment:

Big Bad Mama (1:15) Joan briefly bares her boobies and offers up a decent shot of ass shortly before planting a knee in Tom Skerritt's wedding tackle.

See Her Naked In:

Famous T&A (1982) Breasts
The Best of Sex and Violence (1981) Breasts
Smile (1975) Buns
Big Bad Mama (1974) Breasts, Buns
Bloody Friday (1972) Breasts

Victoria Pratt

Born: December 18, 1970
Toronto, Ontario, Canada
Skin-O-Meter: Great Nudity

Victoria Pratt started her adult life as a kinesiologist shortly after graduating summa cum laude (then again, summa don't . . .) from York University. Naturally, this brainy babe used her knowledge of the human body's goings-on to perfect her own. She's earned several martial-arts belts, track championships, and fitness-magazine writing credits. Oh, yeah, she has one hell of a tight body too! In 1998 Victoria made the next logical step and took a two-episode gig on the hit syndicated series *Xena: Warrior Princess*. Shortly thereafter she took her chiseled ass on over to the action series *Once a Thief*, but, sadly, the series tanked shortly after she arrived. Vicky has since spent the better part of her time flashing her athleticism on such series as *Forbidden Island*, *Cleopatra 2525*, and *Mutant X*, but every now and again she pops up in a feature film for us to pop off to. Consider *Whatever It Takes* (1999), featuring the nicknamed trio of Don "The Dragon" Wilson, Fred "The Hammer" Williamson, and Andrew "Dice" Clay. Although Victoria didn't appear in the credits, it's kind of hard to miss her thirty seconds onscreen, considering that she's topless with nothing on but a thong and a smile while seducing The Hammer. I'd make a joke about being "nailed" by The Hammer, but it would just be too obvious.

SKIN-fining Moment:

Whatever It Takes (0:39) Great view of her phony funbags and thonged-ass seducing Fred "The Hammer" Williamson. Hammer, don't hurt 'em!

See Her Naked In:

Whatever It Takes (1999) Breasts, Thong

TeleVisions:

Xena: Warrior Princess Nip Slip RB, Thong

Paula Prentiss

Born: March 4, 1939
San Antonio, Texas
Skin-O-Meter: Great Nudity

Paula Prentiss debuted in the Spring Break classic *Where the Boys Are* (1960). Where are the boys? Anywhere that brunette beauty Paula is! Not surprisingly, she reached the heights of superstardom shortly thereafter, landing parts in such screwball comedies as *The Honeymoon Machine* (1961), *Bachelor in Paradise* (1961), and *The Horizontal Lieutenant* (1962). After a stint on the television series *He & She* and a role in the hooker comedy *What's New, Pussycat?* (1965), Paula moved into what Mr. Skin likes to call the "Gratuitous Nudity" stage of her career. In one short year Paula notably flashed flesh two times. First, she bared her breasts in a bathtub scene with Elliott Gould in *Move* (1970). But let's move on to her turn in the classic war comedy *Catch-22* (1970). In that particular production, Paula can be seen, albeit from a distance, in all her furry full-frontal glory. As quickly as her Gratuitous Nudity stage began, it came to an all-too-premature end. Currently, she spends the better part of her time filming instructional videos about how to conduct business meetings and such with her husband, actor/director Richard Benjamin. May we suggest they turn their entrepreneurial ways towards couples sex videos?

SKIN-fining Moment:

Catch 22 (0:22) Fuzzy (but not in the good way) full-frontal as Paula peels off and tosses her dress to Alan Arkin.

See Her Naked In:

Move (1970) Breasts
Catch 22 (1970) FFN

> "I worked my ass off for this body and I'm going to enjoy it!"
>
> —JAIME PRESSLY

Jaime Pressly

Born: July 30, 1977
Kinston, North Carolina
Skin-O-Meter: Great Nudity

Jaime Pressly was unforgettable in *Poison Ivy: The New Seduction* (1997), combining a tough-girl attitude with unbearably sweet all-American beauty. Her role as Violet really let her loose, too, with lots of nude scenes and domineering antics. *The Journey: Absolution* (1997) offered a tamer role and just as much nudity, but then Hollywood came calling for this hot property. She's kept her clothes on for the transition to rising starlet, but there have still been plenty of highlights: her matter-of-fact, anonymous blowjob at the beginning of the Jerry Springer epic *Ringmaster* (1998), scenes of her as a gun-toting child bride in *Poor White Trash* (2000), and plenty of lesbian teases in *Tomcats* (2001). And don't forget how Jamie got us banging our piñata in the horror/bikini epic *Piñata: Survival Island* (2002).

SKIN-fining Moment:

Poison Ivy 3: The New Seduction (0:30) Hootage and thong-clad heinie as Jaime goes for a topless dip in the pool.

See Her Naked In:

Poison Ivy 3: The New Seduction (1997) Breasts, Buns
The Journey: Absolution (1997) Breasts, Thong

Cyndy Preston

Born: May 18, 1967
Toronto, Ontario, Canada
Skin-O-Meter: Brief Nudity

It's okay to call her another pretty face since Cyndy Preston used to be an international model for top agencies. But she's also a graduate of the Juilliard School of Drama and a respected Canadian actress. We've got a lot of respect for her Great White titties, too, especially as seen in her role as a crazy bikinied (and later topless) groupie in *Whale Music* (1994). Cyndy's also a warm Canadian dream in *Picture Windows* (1995), and she convinced our dick that she was a real stripper in *The Ultimate Weapon* (1997). Her appearance on *The X Files* was also pretty cool, although Mr. Skin prefers his ladies to actually keep their skin *on*. But that's okay, because Cyndy showed some prime boobage as the weird wife in the cable sequel (and subsequent series) *Total Recall 2070* (1999). Americans can now even press their flesh to Preston's role as evil Faith Roscoe on ABC's *General Hospital*.

SKIN-fining Moment:

Total Recall 2070 (0:12) Shirtless Cyndy bares her little byndi's while making out with her man-friend.

See Her Naked In:

Total Recall 2070 (1999) RB
The Ultimate Weapon (1997) Thong
Whale Music (1994) LB, Buns

TeleVisions:

Picture Windows Breasts
Total Recall 2070 RB

BUMPER CAR: KELLY PRESTON BUFFS HER FRONT-END WITH DOUG MCKEON IN *MISCHIEF.*

Kelly Preston

Born: October 13, 1962
Honolulu, Hawaii
Skin-O-Meter: Hall of Fame

At the tender age of twenty Kelly Preston already measured a respectable 34-24-34, and her top-heavy talents only expanded (way, way out!) from there. She took that fine figure on the road as an Elite Agency model, then turned to a role on the now-defunct soap opera *Capitol* before heading off to cinematic efforts like *Christine* (1983), *SpaceCamp* (1986), and *Twins* (1988), which would prove to be her breakthrough role. She has since appeared in *Citizen Ruth* (1996), *Nothing to Lose* (1997), *Jack Frost* (1998), and one of the many Kevin Costner baseball movies, *For Love of the Game* (1999). She married noted Scientologist John Travolta and converted to the controversial faith, which fortunately does not forbid nudity, because she has a legacy of it onscreen. Kelly started her skinful ways when she shed her bountiful boobage in the back of a car in *Secret Admirer* (1985). Next, she turned it up a notch with a full-frontal turn in *Mischief* (1985). Kelly has since appeared in all her boobtacular glory in *52 Pick-Up* (1986), *Spellbinder* (1988), *A Tiger's Tale* (1988), and *Double Cross* (1994). Let's hope Kelly is back to Preston those big girls onscreen soon.

SKIN-fining Moment:

Mischief (0:59) Mrs. Travolta reveals her hugely hot torso-tonnage, a bit of butt, and even a flash of fur-burger when she doffs her duds and gets ready for some lovin'.

See Her Naked In:

Jerry Maguire (1996) RB
Double Cross (1994) LB, Buns
Love Is a Gun (1994) Body Double—Breasts, Buns

A Tiger's Tale (1988) Breasts
Spellbinder (1988) Breasts
Twins (1988) Thong
52 Pick-Up (1986) Breasts, Buns
Mischief (1985) FFN, Buns
Secret Admirer (1985) Breasts, Buns

Brenda Price

Born: December 18, 1972
Middletown, Connecticut
Skin-O-Meter: Great Nudity

Deliciously dark-maned, dusky-hued, drum-tight Brenda Price may not be history's only newswoman to boast a past peppered with provocative nude shots but—stop the presses!—she may well be the sexiest. Better still, Brenda's appropriately proud of her on-camera peel down in the 2002 epic *The Road From Erebus*. It only makes sense that this aspiring actress and media siren would be at once so wicked hot and downright cool, as she's also the voice of current events on Florida's uproarious *Lex and Terry* morning radio show. Amidst the non-stop mayhem of the Sunshine State's premiere FM madmen, Brenda beams smarts, savvy, a razor-sharp sense of humor, and blistering sensuality via her daily newscasts. CNN? NPR? MSNBC? Forget them! Let's have some more T&A from this headline hottie who redefines the concept of "fox news."

SKIN-fining Moment:

The Road From Erebus (0:37) Miss Price's luscious plums bounce beautifully as she hops on her man and goes for a pony ride.

See Her Naked In:

The Road From Erebus (2002) Breasts

Justine Priestley

Born: December 31, 1967
Vancouver, British Columbia, Canada
Skin-O-Meter: Great Nudity

Giving up is just not in the nature of winners, and the fact that she has reinvented herself as a fleshly canvas for the filmic arts is why Justine Priestley, though hardly a household name, is a boner fide winner. After an abbreviated television career that started with the straight-to-cathode movie *The Substitute* (1993) and petered out with sporadic guest spots on Aaron Spelling productions, valiant Vancouver-bred vulva owner Justine tripped the light skintastic. In the year 2000 Justine won the sexploitation trifecta, wagering her highly favored seat meat in three top-rated B-rankers: *Up Against Amanda* (buns while she stood lookin' out the winda'), *Rage Against the Innocents* (augmented by two spank-happy naked nymphs who were rightly fascinated by Justine's compact, muscular, and flexed ass), and *A Crack in the Floor* (look for ass crack in the shower).

SKIN-fining Moment:

Up Against Amanda (0:27) Quickie shot of her posterior while changing in the bathroom.

See Her Naked In:

Up Against Amanda (2000) LB, Buns
A Crack in the Floor (2000) Buns
Rage of the Innocents (2000) Breasts, Buns

Victoria Principal

Born: January 3, 1950
Fukuoka, Japan
Skin-O-Meter: Great Nudity

In the 1970s, while starring on CBS's global mega-smash *Dallas*, Victoria Principal burned about as hot as any sex symbol ever had. Lately, however, she is more likely to be seen hawking her private line of cosmetics in late-night infomercials than scorching up tawdry nighttime soap plots. As Pam Ewing, the wife of idealistic oil heir Bobby Ewing,

MR. SKIN'S TOP TEN

Rarely Seen Nudity
. . . Lust and Found

10. Josie Bissett
    —*Desideri* (1990)

9. Mary Beth McDonough
    —*One of Those Nights* (1998)

8. Barbara Bach
    —*Ecco noi per esempio* (1980)

7. Stephanie Beacham
    —*Super Bitch* (1973)

6. Stockard Channing
    —*Sweet Revenge* (1977)

5. Jennifer O'Neill
    —*Glass Houses* (1972)

4. Melanie Griffith
    —*Ha-Gan* (1977)

3. Barbara Streisand
    —*The Owl and the Pussycat* (1970)

2. Sophia Loren
    —*Era Lui . . . Sì! Sì!* (1951)

1. **Victoria Principal**
   —***The Naked Ape* (1972)**

she displayed the virtues all men want in their women: She was supportive, loving, and had the kind of body that could make any man's drill spout a gusher! In the early '80s she became a spokeswoman for a national chain of fitness centers. The spots featured Victoria adorned in skintight Spandex showing off her mammoth D-cup dumbbells. This led her to produce a string of popular workout tapes and books. She's since been seen briefly skinful in *Love in Another Town* (1997). Very early in her career she appeared nude in the sex farce *Naked Ape* (1972), but it was never released on video. Victoria Principal is naked in a bad flick and we aren't able to rent it? I believe it's time we all write our congressmen!

SKIN-fining Moment:

Love in Another Town (1:05) An ultra-quick view of Victoria's secret (her right one) as she makes love to her man. It's quick, but it's there.

See Her Naked In:

Love in Another Town (1997) RB
The Naked Ape (1972) Breasts

Joan Pringle

New York, New York
Skin-O-Meter: Great Nudity

Joan Pringle has been a familiar face on television ever since she had a regular role on *Ironside*—which, sadly, means this lovely mocha blonde has seldom opened her blouse to give us a regular Irondick. Joan still remains a welcome presence in TV movies, guest spots, and the ocassional feature film. She also graced us with a short stint in blaxploitation, starring in the dead gangsta ghost story *J.D.'s Revenge* (1976). She uncapped her Pringles twice in that one, with the opening love scene being preferable to when she's attacked by her possessed (and horny) boyfriend.

SKIN-fining Moment:

J.D.'s Revenge (0:28) Partial left boobage as Glynn Thurman fondles her, then a nice eyeful of the unobscured orb as she lays back on the bed.

See Her Naked In:

J.D.'s Revenge (1976) Breasts

Emily Procter

Born: October 8, 1968
Raleigh, North Carolina
Skin-O-Meter: Brief Nudity

Emily Procter began her celebrity ascent slowly with a guest spot on an episode of *Friends* and small roles in such blockbusters as *Leaving Las Vegas* (1995) and *Jerry Maguire*

(1996). But it wouldn't be long before the skinematic community took notice of this blossomingly bosomed belle. Now that she's done her time on the hit series *The West Wing*, playing a conservative Republican hottie, this gorgeous young lady should have her pick of the lusty litter. In terms of skin, Emily put her best boob forward, landing a plum role in the made-for-HBO movie *Breast Men* (1997). Playing one of the many recipients of the then-new breast-augmentation technology around which the movie revolved, Emily showed off her plumb plums both before and "after" the operation—even though her real rack is a wholly natural wonder. She went on to show off her perky pillows again in *Body Shots* (1999), but was almost lost in the shadow of Tara "I'll Suck Your Cock For a Thousand Dollars, Mr. Lebowski" Reid's sex scene with Jerry O'Connell. Almost . . . It's kind of hard to miss her hooters all dressed up in kinky S/M gear whilst whipping Ron Livingston. With this Procter, there's no gamble that the breast is yet to come.

SKIN-fining Moment:

Breast Men (0:43) Emily opens her vest and shares her flawless chest with Dr. David Schwimmer.

See Her Naked In:

Body Shots (1999) Breasts
Breast Men (1997) Breasts

Kristin Proctor

Born: April 16, 1978
Los Angeles, California
Skin-O-Meter: Brief Nudity

Crinkle-nosed blonde bit of heaven Kristin Proctor may have the best-educated pair of breasts in all filmdom. At the tender age of nineteen, this twin-torpedoed

prodigy was accepted at the American Repertory Theater/Moscow Art Theatre School and appeared in numerous productions on the Moscow stage. Later, Kristin and her mammaries matriculated at the Harvard University Institute for Advanced Theater Training and at London, England's Royal Academy of Dramatic Arts. With all this learning under her chest, it was a cinch for bra-buster Kristin to peel off her shirt and let the twins ace their exams as Aimee, the girlfriend of an inadvertent drug dealer, on the HBO cops and crackheads series *The Wire*.

SKIN-fining Moment:

The Wire "Hard Cases" (2003) Kristin proves she's not wearing a wire—or bra—as she changes her shirt while sitting on a bed exposing her nicely sizable casabas. A guy tries to cop a feel. You'll understand why!

TeleVisions:

The Wire Breasts

Renee Props

Born: February 15, 1962
Oklahoma
Skin-O-Meter: Brief Nudity

Spunky brunettes are more fun—because they try harder. The extra effort a dark-haired lass puts out is evident and typified in the high-watt smile and dancing dimples of shiny-eyed Renee Props, an accomplished actress whose willingness to be pleasing is a pleasure in and of itself. Long-time dedicated fans of eternal soap *As the World Turns* to this day gather around the electric fire and recount the glad memories brought to mind at the mention of pert and perky Renee during her incarnation as Ellie Snyder Anderson. On a personal account, remember when you went to see *Get Shorty* (1995), and suddenly you got a biggy? That was right after eager-to-be-of-service Props popped up onscreen.

SKIN-fining Moment:

Free Ride (0:13) Props to Renee for showing off her topless treats in the shower.

See Her Naked In:

Free Ride (1986) Breasts

Mowava Pryor

South Hill, Virginia
Skin-O-Meter: Great Nudity

Like a tiny chocolate-coated version of Britney Spears, Mowava Pryor first appeared on the teen scene on the updated version of *The Mickey Mouse Club*, *MMC*. Relating more to co-Mouseketeer Christina Aguilera, Mowava was less goody-two-shoes and more nudie-two-boobs, making lust in the dust with Lorenzo Lamas in *SnakeEater* (1988). Your peter would be hard pressed (or pressed hard) to find a flaw in Pryor's lack of attire onscreen. Mowava gained more sexposure in skinfully sexy supporting roles in TV movies such as *The Cover Girl Murders* (1993) and *Dead by Midnight* (1997). Let's hope we'll be seeing *Mowava* Ms. Pryor in the near future.

SKIN-fining Moment:

SnakeEater (0:07) Mowava's chocolate donuts fill the screen quite nicely, and stay tuned for a nice peek at the tush.

See Her Naked In:

SnakeEater (1988) Breasts, Buns

Dawn Marie Psaltis

Born: November 3, 1970
Woodbridge, New Jersey
Skin-O-Meter: Brief Nudity

One of the bustiest babes to ever step into the ladies lion den of lust that is World Wrestling Entertainment, Dawn Marie Psaltis proves that a little definitely goes a long way toward making your day. Decked in the itsiest of bitsy bikinis, pouncing on piles of gorgeous WWE gal pals like the jugsy Jacqueline Moore, Dawn is most on when it comes to flashing flesh. At her breast (and mostly undressed) on the series *WWE's Velocity* and in *WWE Divas: Desert Heart* (2003), Dawnie's plastic fantastic can't be beat. With such gargantuan gazongas and glorious glutes, Dawn Marie is the sexy *Psalt* of the earth needed to get down and dirty.

SKIN-fining Moment:

The Vampire Carmilla (0:01) Ms. Psaltis pshows her psacks while pswapping psaliva with psome psucker, but psadly, we don't psee the crack of Dawn.

See Her Naked In:

The Vampire Carmilla (1999) Breasts

Linda Purl

Born: September 2, 1955
Greenwich, Connecticut
Skin-O-Meter: Brief Nudity

Linda Purl, who was at one time Mrs. Desi Arnaz Jr., landed her first big break with a role in the sci-fi picture *Time Travelers* (1966). But it would take a few years before audiences finally took note of the stunning young ingénue in *Jory* (1972). Sadly, Linda's cinematic career slowed down a bit shortly thereafter, and she took to boob-tube work. She landed a recurring role on *Happy Days* as Gloria in 1974 and returned as the much more notable Ashley Pfister toward the end of the show's run. Pfister . . . you bet! Although Linda certainly provided some eye-popping candy on the series, the Days would have been much Happier had she been allowed to shed her threads. Thankfully, Linda left one notable skinful skeleton in her career closet. In *Crazy Mama* (1975) she flashed some distant T&A when Bryan Englund and Don Most opened the door to the bathroom while she was drying off after a shower. It's brief, so be ready on that pause button! Since then, Linda has spent the better part of her time on TV, as well as touring with her nightclub act, so her career has been a bit on the skingy side. She may be well into middle age at this point, but Mr. Skin is still pulling for another glimpse of Linda's Purl.

SKIN-fining Moment:

Crazy Mama (0:53) The bathroom door slides open and we see Linda's love-Purls and pert posterior.

See Her Naked In:

The High Country (1981) Buns
Crazy Mama (1975) Breasts, Buns

q

Valérie Quennessen

Born: 1957
Paris, France
Died: March 1989
Skin-O-Meter: Great Nudity

If any sleek-bodied brunette with shockingly sexy, otherworldly green eyes and a dancer's long, strong, limber limbs ever needed one more reason to buckle up her seat belt before hitting the highway, let that deciding bit of inspiration be Valerie Quennessen. Parisian-born and supernaturally stunning, Valerie focused her youthful energy into becoming an actress. She studied the craft at the prestigious and arduous Conservatoire National d'Art Dramatique de Paris from 1976 to 1979. So bright was her star as a student that she worked in a steady stream of local cinema projects during that time, amassing an impressive resumé of French-language films by the time she graduated. Quennessen's powerful allure first entranced American eyes as a bra-straining, snake-handling princess in *Conan the Barbarian* (1982). Her entire body worked wonders in *Summer Lovers* (1982). Tragically, an automobile accident took Valerie before she could show more.

SKIN-fining Moment:

Summer Lovers (0:20) French chest-pastries, lovely bunnage, and a flash of the fur as Val goes nude sunbathing with Petey Gallagher.

See Her Naked In:

Summer Lovers (1982) FFN, Buns

Linnea Quigley

Born: May 27, 1958
Davenport, Iowa
Skin-O-Meter: Great Nudity

No one in Davenport, Iowa, would have ever guessed that homespun hero Linnea Quigley, their little innocent towheaded sweetheart, would grow up to be the queen of the scream queens. Besides a few mainstream roles in Cheech & Chong flicks and *Play it to the Bone* (1999), in which she played an overdosed hooker, Linnea has stuck to the B-movie/horror genre, and with much success. She nearly owns it. Linnea is quite adept at portraying hot chicks who get naked and then quickly die, which is more or less what you have to do to succeed in that field. Perhaps this is the origin of the expression "Dying to succeed." (Sadly, this scenario cuts her onscreen skin time short, but short skin time is better than no skin time . . . so no bitching!) Linnea has wrangled everything from the living dead and imps hidden in bowling trophies to Freddy Krueger, and, although she usually loses the battle, she also loses her clothes, too, which makes it all worthwhile. From her legendary, fully nude striptease as horny punkette Trash in *Return of the Living Dead* (1985) to . . . well, to damn near everything she's been in, Linnea's lovelies are on the loose! She's been in over sixty productions since the late '70s and doesn't show any signs of slowing down in spite of the fact that her hella hooters are well into their forties—that's years, not inches. And they still look great in every possible way, in every possible light, from every possible angle that Linnea's willing to show them in. As well she should be. Breasts like that don't come around every day. She should be proud . . . surely her plastic surgeon is. However she got that bod, Mr. Skin bows down to the queen. We're not worthy!

MR. SKIN'S TOP TEN

Scream Queens
. . . Horror hotties

10. Tina Krause
9. Tiffany Shepis
8. Monique Gabrielle
7. Emily Haack
6. Elvira
5. Julie Strain
4. Michelle Bauer
3. Debbie Rochan
2. Brinke Stevens
1. **Linnea Quigley**

SKIN-fining Moment:

The Return of the Living Dead
(0:19) Pontoons, posterior and patch-
covered poontang as Linnea strips naked
and respectfully dances atop someone's
gravestone.

See Her Naked In:

Sex Files: Pleasureville (1999) Breasts, Bush,
Buns
Death Mask (1998) Breasts, Buns
Mari-Cookie and the Killer Tarantula (1998)
Thong
Jack-O (1995) Breasts, Buns
Pumpkinhead II: Blood Wings (1994) Breasts
Heavy Petting Detective (1993) Breasts
Scream Queen Hot Tub Party (1991) Breasts
Freddy's Dead: The Final Nightmare (1991)
Breasts
Linnea Quigley's Horror Workout (1990)
Breasts, Buns
Murder Weapon (1990) Breasts, Buns
Vice Academy Part 2 (1990) Breasts, Thong
Virgin High (1990) Breasts
Sexbomb (1989) Breasts
Assault of the Party Nerds (1989) Breasts
Witchtrap (1989) FFN, Buns
Deadly Embrace (1989) Breasts, Buns
Vice Academy (1988) Breasts
A Nightmare on Elm Street 4: The Dream
Master (1988) Breasts
Dr. Alien (1988) Breasts
Hollywood Chainsaw Hookers (1988) Breasts
Creepozoids (1987) Breasts
Night of the Demons (1987) Breasts, Bush
Nightmare Sisters (1987) Breasts
Beverly Hills Girls (1986) Breasts, Bush, Buns
Silent Night, Deadly Night: Part 2 (1986)
Breasts
The Return of the Living Dead (1985) FFN,
Buns
Savage Streets (1984) FFN
Silent Night, Deadly Night (1984) Breasts
Get Crazy (1983) LB, Thong
Young Warriors (1983) Breasts, Buns
Still Smokin' (1983) Breasts, Buns
Graduation Day (1981) Breasts
Don't Go Near the Park (1981) LB
Psycho from Texas (1981) Breasts, Bush,
Buns
Stone Cold Dead (1979) RB, Buns
Fairy Tales (1979) Breasts
Auditions (1978) FFN, Buns

MR. SKIN'S TOP TEN

Naked Movie Mental Patients
. . . Loontang

10. **Christina Ricci**
    —*Prozac Nation* 2001

9. **Elisabeth Shue**
   —*Molly* 1985

8. **Edy Williams**
   —*Hellhole* 1985

7. **Béatrice Dalle**
   —*Betty Blue* 1986

6. **Gwyeth Paltrow**
   —*Sylvia* 2003

5. **Samantha Eggar**
   —*The Brood* 1979

4. **Maggie Gyllenhaal**
   —*Secretary* 2002

3. **Jessica Lange**
   —*Frances* 1982

2. **Diane Hull**
   —*The Fifth Floor* 1980

1. **Kathleen Quinlan**
   —*I Never Promised You a Rose*
   Garden 1977

Kathleen Quinlan

Born: November 19, 1954
Pasadena, California
Skin-O-Meter: Great Nudity

Kathleen Quinlan was plucked out
of the classroom by director George
Lucas while he was scouting for
talent at her high school—good
choice, Lucas. This busty brunette
has that girl-next-door quality—if
that girl was a lustful slut! She
debuted in *American Graffiti* (1973),
with a choice, one-line role as Peg.
She was supposed to be the next big
thing, but her career faltered after a
turn as a multiple-personality head
case in *I Never Promised You a Rose
Garden* (1977). One of those

---

personalities must have been a
stripper, because this drama offered
Kathleen's first skin and a hot
bareback ride on a very happy
horse. She followed that with a bevy
of roles in less than stellar made-
for-TV fare and lethargic cinema
like *The Promise* (1979) and *Hanky
Panky* (1982). For some real hanky
panky, check out her performance
as the tripped-out reporter who
weds Jim Morrison in a satanic
ritual in *The Doors* (1991). Kathleen
got starkers with Val Kilmer in an
orgy of satanic delights. After that
she went on to parts in *An American
Story* (1992), *Apollo 13* (1995)—for
which she garnished an Oscar
nomination—*Breakdown* (1997), and
Event Horizon (1997). What her
nude scenes lack in duration, they
more than make up for in sinful
potency. Even a brief view of her
top-heavy frame diving into a pool
and several fanny shots in *The Last
Winter* (1984) will warm the cockles
of your hard-on.

SKIN-fining Moment:

The Doors (1:01) All 3 B's and tons 'o
blow during long scene with Val Kilmer.

See Her Naked In:

Apollo 13 (1995) LB
Trial By Jury (1994) Thong
The Doors (1991) Breasts, Bush, Buns
The Last Winter (1984) Breasts, Buns
Sunday Lovers (1980) FFN, Buns
I Never Promised You a Rose Garden (1977)
Breasts

Maeve Quinlan

Born: November 16, 1969
Chicago, Illinois
Skin-O-Meter: Great Nudity

Maeve Quinlan is known to soap-
opera fans worldwide as bodacious
blonde "Megan Conley" on the popular CBS serial *The Bold and the
Beautiful*. Appearances on shows
such as *JAG* and *General Hospital*

have also kept the curvaceous cutie busy on the boob tube. Her film career has thus far consisted mostly of small roles in low-profile flicks such as *Instinct to Kill* (2001) and *Totally Blonde* (2001), but things took a turn for the tawdry with her role in controversial director Larry Clark's latest, *Ken Park* (2002). Mammacious Maeve was featured fully nude, the recipient of a fairly graphic bout of lap licking. Hope this sparks a trend among other similarly hot TV-bound tarts.

SKIN-fining Moment:

Ken Park (0:16) Maeve shows shaved beav and bare fake-a-bagos as her hipster toyboy gives her hardcore head.

See Her Naked In:

Ken Park (2002) Breasts, Bush, Buns

Patricia Quinn

Born: May 28, 1944
Belfast, Northern Ireland, UK
Skin-O-Meter: Great Nudity

Patricia Quinn has big red lips that you'd like to have wrapped around your big, long . . . you know. Those pleasurable puckers open up the cult classic *The Rocky Horror Picture Show* (1975), singing "Science Fiction, Double Feature" in her role as Magenta. That kinky part may be what made her famous, but Patricia is a very accomplished actress of the stage and screen, although admittedly things seemed to slow down for her at the end of the '90s. She started her career with bit parts in four different films: *Up the Front* (1972)—playing another maid, this time for hot tramp Mata Hari— *Rentadick* (1972), *The Alf Garnett*

Saga (1972), and *Adolf Hitler: My Part in His Downfall* (1972). Talk about a way to start off a career! She then landed meatier roles in the mini-series *Shoulder to Shoulder* (1974) and the *Love School* series before reaching fetishistic perfection in *RHPS*. She has since been in the celebrated mini-series *I, Claudius* (1976), in which she flashed a bit of her pretties, *Beauty and the Beast* (1976), and the follow-up to *RHPS*, *Shock Treatment* (1981). While her *Rocky* togs were quite sexy, to get a better look at this lilting Irish lass, you should check out the hilarious *Monty Python's Meaning of Life* (1983), in which she helped John Cleese teach an all-boys' school class a lesson in the birds and the bees. And there's the "Witching Time" episode of the TV series *Hammer House of Horror*, where she's bewitchingly topless. Thanks for the mammaries, Patricia.

SKIN-fining Moment:

I, Claudius "What Shall We Do About Claudius?" (1976) Patricia's right popper bops into view as she hops into bed. And, hey, her nipple's magenta!

See Her Naked In:

Monty Python's the Meaning of Life (1983) Breasts

TeleVisions:

Hammer House of Horror Breasts
I, Claudius RB

Robin Quivers

Born: August 8, 1952
Baltimore, Maryland
Skin-O-Meter: Never Nude

Robin Quivers makes breast men quiver. Howard Stern's long-reigning Queen of All Media off-sets her partner's stern remarks with a hearty laugh that comes bellowing from her beautifully behemoth brown bosom. While Robin delivers the news, Stern delivers the nudes, but surprisingly he's never been able to get Robin to pop the tops on her superlative super-soakers. Baltimore native Robin has been working alongside Howard every morning for over two decades, and aside from various Stern-related TV series and video outings— *Howard Stern's Butt Bongo Fiesta* (1992) comes to mind—she has only appeared as an "actress" in a few productions. *Private Parts* (1997) marked her most famous foray onto the big screen, and she was playing herself. She also turned up in the made-for-TV *Deadly Web* (1996) and *An Alan Smithee Film: Burn Hollywood Burn* (1997). The closest we've come to delighting in Robin's dusky dairy dirigibles was when she flashed her double-parachute-sized boulder-holder once on the show. It was a fleeting moment, but unforgettably, flabbergastingly great! Fly, Robin, fly off that top again soon, and this time burn the bra!

SKIN-fining Moment:

The Howard Stern Show (2001) The (Dairy) Queen of All Media pulls open her shirt and flashes her 50,000-watt chocolate-milksack-stuffed bra. Whoa! I think Little Mr. Skin must have swallowed some of Robin's "Master Cleanser."

r

Pamela Rabe

**Born: April 30, 1959
Oakville, Ontario, Canada
Skin-O-Meter: Great Nudity**

Amongst the lovely naked maidens of *Sirens* (1994), Pamela Rabe really stood out with her athletic frame and earthy sexuality. Unlike the other hippie-dippy ladies (including Elle MacPherson) on Sam Neill's isle, Pamela stood out as a tough gal who'd be equally at home effortlessly stripping in some L.A. nightclub. Instead of capitalizing on stealing those sex scenes, though, the Canadian native stayed in Australia and kept her ravishing Rabes undercover in local productions—although some smart international productions still take advantage of her imposing talent and beauty.

SKIN-fining Moment:

Sirens (0:52) Pam poses in all her bare-bosomed, hairy-holed glory for painter hubby Sam Neill.

See Her Naked In:

Paradise Road (1997) Breasts
Sirens (1994) FFN

Victoria Racimo

**Born: December 26, 1950
New York, New York
Skin-O-Meter: Great Nudity**

Though Victoria Racimo has shown skin in several of her films, she's spent most of her career playing fully-clothed Native American women with character names like Running Moon, Anne Greyfeather, Napewaste, and Appomosiscut. Perhaps it's the "wise woman" stereotype that kept her luscious hide covered up in furs and feathers all that time? Fortunately, in her turn as the Asian Mai Lee Foon in *G.I. Executioner* (1973) (billed as "The wildest nude shootout in film history!"), she spent most of her time onscreen completely naked. Victoria's exotic good looks have landed her several other choice roles, including the camp nurse in *Ernest Goes to Camp* (1987), Rachel in *Choke Canyon* (1986) (spoiler: nothing goes in her throat), and her most recent screen credit as Katrin in the Native American belief-heavy *White Fang II: Myth of the White Wolf* (1994).

SKIN-fining Moment:

The Magic Garden of Stanley Sweetheart (1:16) Let there be light! Victoria flashes some full-frontal flesh getting crazy with Don Johnson, Karen Lynn Gorney, and a heaping helping of paint.

See Her Naked In:

G.I. Executioner (1973) Breasts, Buns
The Magic Garden of Stanley Sweetheart (1970) FFN

Cristina Raines

**Born: February 28, 1952
Manila, Philippines
Skin-O-Meter: Brief Nudity**

Cristina Raines left Manila behind for the Hollywood dream and began showing up on American TV in the early '70s. Her first small-screen role was in the made-for-TV tearjerker *Sunshine* (1973), where she appeared in flashbacks as breast-cancer casualty Kate Hayden. Her resumé boasts an extensive list of TV bit parts, including appearances on such hits as *Kojak, The Love Boat, Fantasy Island, The Fall Guy,* and *Moonlighting,* not to mention the lead role in the 1980 primetime soap *Flamingo Road.* She also kept busy with film throughout the '70s and '80s. Her most skintastic appearance was in the horror flick *The Sentinel* (1977), in which she played Alison Parker, a fashion model inhabiting a New York brownstone that doubles as a portal to hell. Not only is this film chock full of huge stars like Ava Gardner, Christopher Walken, and Burgess Meredith, there's a fantastic scene where Cristina sits opposite Beverly D'Angelo and watches her masturbate! The scene isn't a *bit* scary, but it is, um, "hair" raising . . .

SKIN-fining Moment:

The Sentinel (0:33) Christina's topless in a wacky black-and-white dream sequence. At the end of the clip, she bows into the lap of Chris Sarandon, who's enjoying his Morticia chair.

See Her Naked In:

The Sentinel (1977) LB

Jeramie Rain

Born: October 8, 1948
West Virginia
Skin-O-Meter: Great Nudity

Stunning beauty Jeramie Rain only made three films—and only one of them has really become a classic—but she couldn't have chosen better titles to showcase her titties. Actually, the trashy comedy *Preacherman* (1971) doesn't have nearly enough Rain, but *Last House on the Left* (1972) is a shower of perversion, made more so by Jeramie displaying her ju-jus while playing a real psycho. *The Abductors* (1972), part of Cheri Caffaro's series of films as slutty secret agent Ginger, was Jeramie's real showcase of skin. She steals the show as a young woman kidnapped by the white slave industry. She's no mere victim, though, and the defiant spitfire puts up plenty of full-frontal fights while sporting a sexy *Klute* 'do.

SKIN-fining Moment:

The Abductors (0:02) A nice triple-titty feature for Jeramie, Honey Well, and Ined Som as they're being gagged and restrained.

See Her Naked In:

The Last House on the Left (1972) Breasts
The Abductors (1972) FFN, Buns

Arcelia Ramírez

Born: October 15, 1967
Mexico City, México D.F, Mexico
Skin-O-Meter: Great Nudity

Hotter than a handful of jalapeños, Mexican actress Arcelia Ramírez has been spicing up Spanish-language cinema since her debut in the short dramatic film *El Centro del laberinto* (1985). Since then she's peppered her performances with more than a few peeks at her perky pups and pretty poon. *Ay yi yi!* In her most skinematic performance to date, *La Mujer de Benjamín* (1991), Arcelia played the lust interest of an old bachelor named Benjamin who plots her abduction when she fails to respond to his love letters. As passions tend to run hotter south of the border, Arcelia has gotten naked in more than one of her films, including the fiery melodramas *En un claroscuro de la luna* (1999) and *Así es la vida* (2000).

SKIN-fining Moment:

La Mujer de Benjamín (1:18)
Beautiful breasts and ass as she gets into a wash tub and scrubs up for an old-timer's entertainment. Hot!

See Her Naked In:

Así es la vida (2000) FFN
En un claroscuro de la luna (1999) Breasts
La Mujer de Benjamín (1991) Breasts

Charlotte Rampling

Born: February 5, 1945
Sturmer, England, UK
Skin-O-Meter: Hall of Fame

Charlotte Rampling made her debut in *The Knack, And How To Get It* (1965), in an uncredited role as eye candy, which she shared with such sweets as Jacqueline Bisset and Marlo Thomas. This marked the beginning of one of cinema's most enigmatic careers. In *Max, My Love* (1986) Charlotte portrayed a woman who is in love with a monkey. Talk about swinging. Then there's the mind-blowing Sean Connery sci-fi film *Zardoz* (1974), in which Charlotte exposed her hand-sized teats for a treat. But that wasn't her first flesh. Her skin debut was in *'Tis a Pity She's a Whore* (1972), although you don't see us complaining. One of her strangest nude scenes highlights the disturbing film *The Night Porter* (1974). She played a Holocaust survivor reunited with the Nazi who tortured and raped her. Charlotte was completely nude and looked oddly alluring as concentration camp chic. As she matures, she only gets hotter. Case in point: *Hammers Over the Anvil* (1991), the Australian epic that featured our Charlotte giving Russell Crowe a lesson in bedroom rodeo riding. And in *The Swimming Pool* (2003) she held her own with nude-comer Ludivine Sagnier. Keep on Rampling, Charlotte!

SKIN-fining Moment:

The Night Porter (1:12) Charlotte spends a good 90 seconds topless as she huskily serenades a room full of appreciative Germans.

See Her Naked In:

Swimming Pool (2003) FFN
Under the Sand (2000) Breasts
Signs & Wonders (2000) Breasts
Hammers Over the Anvil (1991) Breasts, Buns
Angel Heart (1987) RB
Mascara (1987) Breasts
Max, mon amour (1986) Buns
Tristesse et beauté (1985) Breasts
He Died with His Eyes Open (1985) Breasts, Buns
The Purple Taxi (1977) Breasts
Foxtrot (1975)
Farewell My Lovely (1975) Breasts
Yuppi du (1975) Breasts
The Night Porter (1974) Breasts, Bush, Buns
La Chair de l'orchidée (1974) FFN
Zardoz (1974) Breasts
Caravan to Vaccares (1974) FFN, Buns
'Tis a Pity She's a Whore (1972) Breasts

TeleVisions:

Radetzkymarsch Breasts, Buns

Anne Ramsay

Born: September 11, 1960
Skin-O-Meter: Never Nude

Anne Ramsay isn't your typical Southern California girl. She doesn't have bleached blonde hair or even big meaty breasts. But if you like a plain Jane with a small pair who sports some of the thickest nipples west of the Mississippi, then she's your cup of tease. She'd been acting since graduating from UCLA, but it wasn't until landing on the hit series *Mad About You*, playing Helen Hunt's sister, that things started percolating. If only the show explored the taboo of sisterly love (but we're getting ahead of ourselves). Then she landed a role opposite Madonna in *A League of Their Own* (1992), playing a first baseman whom viewers wanted to hit a homerun with. Though she's worked steadily on other TV shows such as *Doctor, Doctor*, as a nutty psychiatrist, and on the big screen in *Planet of the Apes* (2001), Anne never revealed her true assets. Even when she appeared on the Showtime lesbian soap opera *The L Word* (see, told you we'd get back to that), Anne used a body double. In an episode entitled "Limb From Limb," Anne's lips are sealed, but her stand-in's sunken chest is a pirate's dream, especially if that Jolly Roger likes to finger her large, pink, jewel-like nipples. Yo ho 'ho!

SKIN-fining Moment:

The L Word "Limb From Limb" (2004) BODY DOUBLE: Someone's left lung-cushion turns up twice in bed with Mia Kirshner. Sexy. Succulent. But suspicious.

TeleVisions:

The L Word Body Double—LB

Anne Randall

Born: September 23, 1944
Alameda, California
Skin-O-Meter: Brief Nudity

Beautiful blonde and overall ideal woman Anne Randall found her way into acting after appearing as *Playboy*'s Playmate of the Month in May 1967. Unlike so many Playmates before and after her, though, this "girl next door" actually scored some decent roles and showed that she had a shred of acting ability to boot. Shortly after her nude spread in the magazine, Anne landed a cameo on an episode of *The Monkees* and quickly moved on to cinematic roles in films such as *The Split* (1968), *The Model Shop* (1969), and *Hell's Bloody Devils* (1970). Her first title role accompanied her only skin scenes in the flop *Stacey* (1973), a.k.a. *Stacey and Her Gangbusters*. Before dropping out of the acting community just before the 1980s, Anne had a fair amount of small-screen success, including stints on the hit soap opera *Days of Our Lives* and later on the hit (among dirty old Southern men) *Hee Haw*.

SKIN-fining Moment:

Stacey (0:01) Anne roars into the opening moments of the movie by opening her race-car jumpsuit and busting out her naked championship cups.

See Her Naked In:

Stacey (1973) Breasts

Theresa Randle

Born: December 27, 1964
Los Angeles, California
Skin-O-Meter: Brief Nudity

A brief perusal of Theresa Randle's career to date reads almost like a who's who of black cinema. In addition to appearing in three Spike Lee "joints" (*Jungle Fever* [1991], *Malcolm X* [1992], and *Girl 6* [1996]), she's also starred alongside Martin Lawrence and Will Smith in *Bad Boys* (1995) and *Bad Boys II* (2003), Chris Rock in *CB4* (1993), Michael Jordan in *Space Jam* (1996), and Michael Jai White in *Spawn* (1997). Robert Townsend directed her in her most well-known role to date, that of Natalie Cole in the made-for-TV biopic *Livin' for Love: The Natalie Cole Story* (2000). She made her screen debut in the Ally Sheedy flick *Maid to Order* (1987) and landed her first starring role in *Girl 6* in 1996.

SKIN-fining Moment:

Girl 6 (0:06) Theresa gets topless during a phone-sex job interview. You're hired!

See Her Naked In:

Girl 6 (1996) Breasts

Sheeri Rappaport

Born: October 27, 1977
Dallas, Texas
Skin-O-Meter: Great Nudity

Texas-born and raised in Rockland County, New York, Sheeri Rappaport started her career in guest spots on various teeny-bopper shows like *Clarissa Explains It All*, *7th Heaven*, and *Beverly Hills, 90210*. She's matured nicely on TV, as evident by her role as Mary Franco on the nudity-friendly *NYPD Blue*. She debuted with a bang and a bit of a surprise. Instead of her prerequisite ass shot, "You see everything but my butt," she says. But side views of Sheeri's pendulous knockers just didn't cut it for the professionals here at Skin Central, so we dug a wee bit deeper. Thankfully, we came across a little gem called *Little Witches* (1996), which featured a bevy of Catholic school girls, including Sheeri and skin favorite Landon Hall, who get trapped in their school during spring break and thus decide to get naked and practice witchcraft. In that respect, it is a bit like *The Craft* (1996), although this movie featured nudity, while *The Craft* just caused blue balls.

SKIN-fining Moment:

Little Witches (0:17) Breasts and white panties as Sheeri strips out of her Catholic school plaid skirt in the bedroom window for all the construction workers to see. *You go, girl!*

See Her Naked In:

Little Witches (1996) Breasts, Buns

TeleVisions:

NYPD Blue RB

Rie Rasmussen

Born: February 14, 1982
Copenhagen, Denmark
Skin-O-Meter: Brief Nudity

The secret of a successful debut as a model-actress was not lost upon serpentine brunette Rie Rasmussen. A tall and sinuous Dane whose beauty is so extreme she must be classified as exotic, Rie was the insanely sexualized stunner who upstaged über-blonde Rebecca Romijn-Stamos in Brian De Palma's gleefully cheesy and sleazy *Femme Fatale* (2002). Former model-only Rasmussen's recipe for the scintillating transition to hyphenate? Stick to pure, unadulterated eroticism. The Romijn-Rasmussen toilet-stall face-sucking tittie grope has been seared as a classic carnal caper in the memories of skinthusiasts worldwide. The fond memory is partially due to Rebecca, who showed nary a nip, but mostly thanks to the revelatory plunge of Rie into top-down skinema.

SKIN-fining Moment:

Femme Fatale (0:10) Rie makes-out with Rebecca Romijn-Stamos in a bathroom, and her not-so-concealing boob-holder goes "Bye-Bye."

See Her Naked In:

Femme Fatale (2002) Breasts

Heather Rattray

Born: April 26, 1966
Moline, Illinois
Skin-O-Meter: Brief Nudity

Heather Rattray made her acting debut at age eleven in the rated G family flick *Across the Great Divide* (1976), playing an orphan who crossed the Rockies with her brother and a frontier drifter in the year 1876. Other similarly syrupy family fare followed, including *The Sea Gypsies* (1978), *The Further Adventures of the Wilderness Family* (1978), and *Mountain Family Robinson* (1980). Aside from a small 1978 role on the hit soap *The Guiding Light*, Heather didn't turn up onscreen again until 1990, when, obviously bored with working with hicks and animals, she appeared in the horror flick *Basket Case 2* (1990). A complete change of pace from her earlier work, Heather gave a glimpse of her grown-up rack in this film. Heather's last work was a three-year stint on the soap *As the World Turns* from 1990 to 1993.

SKIN-fining Moment:

Basket Case 2 (1:21) Super-quick boobage spills out from Heather's open shirt as she struggles with Kevin Von Hentryck.

See Her Naked In:

Basket Case 2 (1990) RB

Andrea Rau

Born: 1947
Stuttgart, Germany
Skin-O-Meter: Great Nudity

Andrea Rau is the Teutonic equivalent of Dana Plato. She started acting at the age of five with a bit part in *Fight of the Tertia* (1952) and really didn't slow down until she hit the "best-before date" stage of her career. Unlike Dana, though, Andrea seemed to have a bit longer shelf life, not resorting to skin

scenes until she was in her mid-twenties. Her nude debut was in *Sexy Susana Knows How* (1970)—and how!—followed by *Daughters of Darkness* (1971). After that little French gem, Andrea went legit again but only until *Das Netz* (1976), or *The Net*, and with her furry fine full-frontal nudity, she can catch us in her net anytime. She pulled one more full-frontal credit in *Vertreibung aus dem Paradies* (1977), a.k.a. *Expulsion from Paradise*, but shortly thereafter she expelled horny men from the paradise of her naked form and hasn't been seen since. But unlike Dana, she didn't OD and therefore may surprise us with a scandalous second act.

SKIN-fining Moment:

Daughters of Darkness (1:08) There's some bush and left tit in a swanky bathroom as a guy carries her into a shower. She does not want to go and we see some T&A as she struggles, followed by lingering full frontal as she lies dead on the floor.

See Her Naked In:

Die Vertreibung aus dem Paradies (1977) FFN, Buns
Das Netz (1976) Breasts
Beyond Erotica (1974) FFN, Buns
Daughters of Darkness (1971) FFN, Buns
Sexy Susana Knows How (1970) FFN, Buns
Das Stundenhotel von St. Pauli (1970) FFN

Gina Ravera

San Francisco, California
Skin-O-Meter: Brief Nudity

Gina Ravera landed her first acting gig on an episode of *In Living Color* shortly before taking on skinematic efforts such as *Lambada* (1990), a.k.a. *The Original Erotic Dance*, as it's translated from its Italian title. She returned to the boob tube for a gig on *Silk Stalkings* and continued on in the world of the small screen for a few years, appearing (completely clothed, unfortunately) in such made-for-TV fare as *White Male* (1994) and *W.E.I.R.D. World* (1995). Thankfully, she took on a clothing-optional role in the skintastic classic *Showgirls* (1995) as the one decent character in the decadent tale. She played a bubbling G-string seamstress, who was rewarded for her charity and goodwill with a brutal rape at the hands of an evil rock star. She did, however, show, and it's her only nude time onscreen, which creates a moral dilemma for the hairy-palm set. Ah, jerk on, it's only a movie.

SKIN-fining Moment:

Showgirls (1:50) Showgirls is all fun-and-gam(e)s up until Gina meets the Lurch-like, rock star of her dreams and he tears her dress off while his gang of no-goodniks pounces on her, pricks-first. G-stringed booty and lots of discomfort ensue.

See Her Naked In:

Showgirls (1995) Buns

Ola Ray

Born: August 26, 1960
St. Louis, Missouri
Skin-O-Meter: Great Nudity

Ola Ray started a career in skinema as Hooker #1 in *Body and Soul* (1981). Ola then appeared as yet more hookers in both *48 Hrs.* (1982) and *Night Shift* (1982), although she managed to keep herself pretty well covered up throughout both movies. She returned to her skinful ways as one of the doomed college students in the Charles Bronson thriller *10 to Midnight* (1983). Although the better part of Ola's hooter exposure in the flick appeared while she was being murdered (and rather violently, at that), the lingering moments that led up to the homicide, which featured Ola in the shower, are well worth the entry fee. What a rack! Next Ola was tapped to play Michael Jackson's "girl-

friend" in the classic rock video for his hit song "Thriller," which shot her into the spotlight, at least for a little while. After a bit part in *The Man Who Loved Women* (1983), as well as a turn as a *Playboy* Playmate in the hit cop flick *Beverly Hills Cop II* (1987), however, Ola gave up her acting career in favor of more musically minded endeavors. She's got the lungs for it. Hopefully, she'll be in a video of her own before too long. It's our only Ray of hope.

SKIN-fining Moment:

10 To Midnight (1:27) Ola bares her breasts and butt a few times when Gene Davis barges in on her in the shower before a psycho ruins the fun with a murder rampage.

See Her Naked In:

10 To Midnight (1983) Breasts, Buns
Body and Soul (1981) Breasts
Numerous *Playboy* Videos

Dolly Read

Born: September 13, 1944
Bristol, Avon, England, UK
Skin-O-Meter: Brief Nudity

Dolly Read came about her fame the honest way: She appeared in *Playboy* magazine as its May 1966 Playmate then married funnyman Dick Martin of the hit series *Rowan & Martin's Laugh-In*. Of course, at that point Dolly had no need to appear in any films, since she was already famous, but she did, God bless her and that smoking body. She appeared in a few films, but her only starring role was also her last film appearance, the Roger Ebert/Russ Meyer production *Beyond the Valley of the Dolls* (1970). The satire of the popular book *Valley of the Dolls* is a Meyer classic, even if it doesn't offer as much skin as his earlier sexploitation steamers. There's one seriously campy scene after another, including gratuitous nudity and several sex scenes, some

with Dolly in all of her topless glory. Hello, Dolly!

SKIN-fining Moment:

Beyond the Valley of the Dolls (0:32) Hello, Dollies! The dairy queen gets topless and tussles with her own torso-torpedos while primping in the mirror.

See Her Naked In:

Beyond the Valley of the Dolls (1970) Breasts

Jemma Redgrave

Born: October 1, 1965
London, England, UK
Skin-O-Meter: Great Nudity

She's the granddaughter of Sir Michael Redgrave, niece of Vanessa and Lynn Redgrave, and cousin of Natasha Richardson—which makes Liam Neeson her . . . cousin-in-law? Anyway, Jemma Redgrave didn't have to pay too many dues entering the family business. But even a theatrical blueblood can bare her boobies, and Jemma went further than that in *The Buddha of Suburbia* (1993). Her full-frontal flaunting is uniquely European in that a) she's naked on a TV series and b) well, just check out that mighty muff.

SKIN-fining Moment:

The Buddha of Suburbia: (Mini-series) (1994) Full-frontal monster muffish standing nude while ironing. Nice.

See Her Naked In:

The Acid House (1998) Body Double—RB

TeleVisions:

The Buddha of Suburbia FFN

Lynn Redgrave

Born: March 8, 1943
London, England, UK
Skin-O-Meter: Great Nudity

Currently active members of the British acting clan that spawned rowdy redhead Lynn Redgrave include her controversial sister Vanessa and dainty nieces Natasha and Joely Richardson. Their hammy lineage goes back generations and is as venerable an English tradition as salted kippers and soiled knickers. Lovely Lynn's pantie-twisting title turn as *Georgy Girl* (1966) won the strutting strumpet a Best Actress Oscar, and her pitch-perfect portrayal of international madame Xaveria Hollander in *The Happy Hooker* (1975), while showing nary a hooter, is a reward in and of itself. Ever-ready Redgrave waited until her sixty-seventh year to dare to bare top to bottom, reveling in the revealing of tush, tits, and a glimpse of red bush in *Touched* (1999).

SKIN-fining Moment:

Getting it Right (0:46) Lynn busts out her English T's while cozying up to a young fella, then they flop around as she roughhouses with him.

See Her Naked In:

Touched (1999) Breasts, Buns, Bush
Shine (1996) LB
Calling the Shots (1993) LB, Buns
Getting it Right (1989) Breasts
The Happy Hooker (1975) Thong

Vanessa Redgrave

Born: January 30, 1937
London, England, UK
Skin-O-Meter: Great Nudity

Vanessa Redgrave, unlike her hooker-playing sister Lynn Redgrave, didn't wait until she was eligible for her pension to peel for the camera. Of course, she has had quite the acting career, like her sib, and thankfully passed on her incredible features (read: "perky tits") to her hot daughters Joely Richardson and Natasha Richardson. She has made her career out of memorable perfor-mances in *Blowup* (1966) (which was also her skin debut), *Morgan!* (1966)

VANESSA REDGRAVE IN *STEAMING.* YOU WILL BE.

(for which she was nominated for the Best Actress Oscar), *Isadora* (1968), *Mary, Queen of Scots* (1971) (another Oscar nod), and *Julia* (1977) (for which she finally snared the statuette). As mentioned before, Vanessa has offered up some tantalizing glimpses of her hootage, from a brief shot in *Isadora* to some more brief-but-steamy looks in *Steaming* (1985). Most of the time she is nude onscreen, though, Vanessa tends to be pointing the important parts away from Mr. Camera, as she did in *Steaming*, *Orpheus Descending* (1990) and *Un Tranquilo posto di campagna* (1969). No matter, we would be just as happy looking at her high-rise ass as we would her itty bitties.

SKIN-fining Moment:

Isadora (0:47) Vanessa dances around totally nude, annoying her boyfriend with her three B's as he tries to paint. What a homo!

See Her Naked In:

Orpheus Descending (1990) Buns
Steaming (1985) RB, Buns
Agatha (1979) Buns

Yanks (1979) LB, Buns
Out of Season (1975) FFN
Un tranquillo posto di campagna (1969) Buns
Isadora (1968) FFN, Buns
Blowup (1966) RB

> "I actually like it a lot. I get to express my sexuality in a safe environment, and I love the idea of people watching me and getting off on it."
>
> —KIRA REED ON HER STATUS AS A VIDEO SKIN ICON

Kira Reed

Born: October 13, 1971
Santa Clara, California
Skin-O-Meter: Great Nudity

If you have ever seen a single movie on Cinemax involving a softcore sexual situation, chances are Kira Reed was in it. Her mouth-watering double-D cups are all natural, and she's been naked in everything she's ever been in, making her rise head, shoulders, and chest above the rest of the T&A crowd. OK, so she isn't known for appearing in serious pieces of art, but that's not to say that she's a bad actress. Her movies are always high quality and feature intricate plots, most of which involve her in some state of undress or another. Kira got her big break as "Dream Girl" in the relatively mainstream movie *Fortress* (1993) opposite Christopher Lambert. Since then she's appeared in nearly fifty films and has been naked in every damn one of them. Thus, if you see her on a video, pick it up, for you surely will never find a hotter, more naked actress than she. Currently Kira and her twins can be seen on *Playboy* TV's *Sexcetera*, reporting on erotic events around the world.

SKIN-fining Moment:

Cheerleader Ninjas (0:12) Kira plays an inflatable doll come to life, with real tits, real rump, and a real-close-shaved bush! Hot damn!

See Her Naked In:

Legally Exposed (2003) Breasts, Thong
Rod Steele 0014: You Only Live Until You Die (2002) Breasts, Buns
15 Minutes of Fame (2001) Breasts, Bush
Chained Rage: Slave to Love (2001) FFN, Buns
Sexual Intrigue (2000) FFN, Buns
American Virgin (2000) Breasts
Rage of the Innocents (2000) FFN, Buns
Fast Lane to Malibu (2000) Breasts, Buns
Sexual Intrigue (2000) FFN, Buns
The Mistress Club (1999) FFN, Buns
Forbidden Highway (1999) FFN, Buns
Surrender (1999) Breasts
Alien Files (1999) FFN
Secrets of a Chambermaid (1998) FFN, Buns
Cheerleader Ninjas (1998) Breasts, Bush
Madam Savant (1997) FFN, Buns
Fallen Angel (1997) FFN, Buns
The Night That Never Happened (1997) Breasts, Buns
Scandalous (1997) FFN
Losing Control (1997) Breasts, Bush, Buns
Maui Heat (1996) FFN, Buns
The Lady in Blue (1996) Breasts, Buns
Damien's Seed (1996) Breasts
The Price of Desire (1996) FFN, Buns
Numerous Adult Movies

TeleVisions:

Beverly Hills Bordello Breasts, Bush, Buns
Erotic Confessions FFN, Buns
Intimate Sessions Breasts, Buns
Nightcap FFN, Buns
Passion Cove Breasts, Bush, Buns
Red Shoe Diaries Breasts, Bush, Buns
Women: Stories of Passion Breasts

Pamela Reed

Born: April 2, 1949
Tacoma, Washington
Skin-O-Meter: Brief Nudity

Actress Pamela Reed was born in Washington and raised in Maryland; she returned to the Northwest to—believe it or not—work on the Trans-Alaska Pipeline! Slammin' Pam makes Mr. Skin think of some pipe *I'd* like to lay! Pam was almost thirty when she started making the casting rounds in New York and L.A., but before long, Pam was nailing regular roles on weekly TV series such as *The Andros Targets*, *Tanner 88*, and *Grand*. Her movie debut would happen in the role of true-life cowgirl Belle Starr in the western *The Long Riders* (1980). Producers came running for this girl-next-door type, using Pam for smaller roles in films like *Melvin and Howard* (1980), *The Right Stuff* (1983), and *Cadillac Man* (1990). Her most famous film role, though, was as Arnold Schwarzenegger's LAPD partner in *Kindergarten Cop* (1990). She even got to ape Ahhhhnold's German accent while playing his sister. Mr. Skin will spot her while she does her squat thrusts any day.

SKIN-fining Moment:

The Long Riders (0:18) Pam stands in a bathtub and bares her nude panty-hams while reaching out to embrace David Carradine. It's a plenty nice patoot, but could possibly belong to a BODY DOUBLE.

See Her Naked In:

The Long Riders (1980) Buns

Saskia Reeves

Born: 1962
London, England, UK
Skin-O-Meter: Great Nudity

Saskia Reeves has commanded considerable star power in her native Britain for over two decades. An actress of great versatility and shameless skinthusiasm, her film credits include chick flicks such as *Antonia and Jane* (1991), incest flicks such as *Close My Eyes* (1991), and lesbian flicks such as *Butterfly Kiss* (1995), in which she appeared topless in a hot lesbian scene with Amanda Plummer. She bared her first butt shots in the made-for-British-TV movie *Children Crossing* (1990). A few years later she re-teated her bare breasts for *Cruel Train* (1995) and showed off just about everything else in *Traps* (1994), *Close My Eyes*, and *Antonia and Jane*. In 1999 she made her American screen debut as Mrs. Cratchit in the made-for-TV movie *A Christmas Carol* (1999). Perhaps with the foresight that appearing in a sci-fi production is the best way to get tons of buzz from millions of geeks, Saskia also appeared in the American television mini-series version of *Dune* in 2000. This classy dame has one killer all-natural body, so whenever you can catch it in all its naked glory, don't pass up the chance.

SKIN-fining Moment:

Close My Eyes (0:29) Saskia gives new meaning to the term "brotherly love" in this incest scene, where she shows her sweater sisters and a even a thatch flash.

See Her Naked In:

Butterfly Kiss (1996) Breasts
I.D. (1995) RB
In the Border Country (1991) Breasts
Close My Eyes (1991) FFN, Buns
Antonia and Jane (1991) Breasts

Tanja Reichert

West Vancouver, British Columbia, Canada
Skin-O-Meter: Brief Nudity

This sultry blonde subordinate seems to have appeared out of thin air and floated down to Earth on a cleavage cloud from heaven. A West Vancouver, Canada, native, Tanja Reichert's notable appearances include *Poltergeist: The Legacy* and *Scary Movie* (2000), but her big break came in the role of snappy assistant Karen Petrusky on the series *Relic Hunter*. The show regularly displayed quite the bevy of beauties, and we often got a good gander at Tanja's grrreat cleavage in this role. To see her in her full naked glory however, skinfans will want to check her out in the thriller *Sanctimony* (2000) starring Eric Roberts, Michael Paré, and Casper Van Dien. The best scene featured a topless, black-thong-laden Tanja sleeping angelically when the villainous Casper entered and forced himself on her. What started rather violently turned out to be quite passionate, as she became an equal aggressor. Who knew pushing Tanja's head down into a pillow and ripping off her panties could inspire animal lust in her! In any case, the scene is hot enough to breathe new life into any old relic (i.e., skinfans everywhere).

SKIN-fining Moment:

Club Dread (0:04) Captain Caaaaaaaavvvvvveboobs! Tanja and Elena shimmy around underground, letting their jobs fly free. Tanja's the blonde knockout.

See Her Naked In:

Club Dread (2004) Breasts
Sanctimony (2000) Breasts, Buns

TeleVisions:

Poltergeist: The Legacy FFN

> "I can make a scene that's not supposed to be sexy, very sexy. It's a power you're born with. It's not a physical thing. It comes from inside. It's all in the eyes."
>
> —TARA REID

Tara Reid

Born: November 8, 1975
Wyckoff, New Jersey
Skin-O-Meter: Great Nudity

MTV veejay Carson Daly broke Tara Reid's heart, but she busted his hard-on when the couple went kaplooie in 2003. Daly's loss is America's gain,

as tight Tara is on the prowl. The veteran act-chest has been a TV staple since age six, growing up big on the little screen from *Saved by the Bell: The New Class* to the torrid tales on sudsy stories like *Days of Our Lives*. It was the day of everybody's life when Tara made her big-screen debut in the stoner comedy *The Big Lebowski* (1998). "I'll suck your cock for a thousand dollars," she tells Jeff Bridges's character, The Dude, and theaters quickly emptied as ATMs around the country were flooded with horny hopefuls. Tara appeared in the skinless but no less filthy *Cruel Intentions* (1999), the innocent tease of girl-group grope *Josie and the Pussycats* (2001), and the not-so-innocent *American Pie* (1999) and *Van Wilder* (2002). But for a taste of Tara's ta-tas, check out *Body Shots* (1999). Love those shots of her body.

SKIN-fining Moment:

Body Shots (1:07) Tara's ta-ta's flip, flop and fly deliciously as she rides Jerry O'Connel. Ass-tastic crack, too!

See Her Naked In:

Body Shots (1999) Breasts, Buns
Around the Fire (1999) RB

Taryn Reif

Born: February 13, 1976
New York City, New York
Skin-O-Meter: Great Nudity

Oh give me a home where the crocodile roam and the girls flit about naked all day, and seldom are heard a bone-crunching word from the croc as he swallows his prey. As the antihero of *Blood Surf* (2000), a.k.a. *Krocodylus*, eats his way through the surfer population, skin devotees will be more interested in the skin stylings of oft bare-breasted Taryn Reif and "chums." Taryn, a tiny-boobed blonde waif from NYC, began her career as a child actor on several soaps and gained fame as a fabulous babe on

the smash MTV show *Undressed*. You can also get your fill of Taryn in the made-for-TV movie *Rocket's Red Glare* (2000) and starring as Shawna Quinlan on the soap *One Life to Live*.

SKIN-fining Moment:

Blood Surf (0:12) Taryn is stripped to her bare A-cuppage, then bent over by a horny guy on the docks.

See Her Naked In:

Blood Surf (2000) Breasts, Thong

Francesca Rettondini

Verona, Italy
Skin-O-Meter: Brief Nudity

Veronese vixen Francesca Rettondini is one hefty-teated treat. Even her last name sounds like a meaty Mediterranean meal. A tit-topping popular dish in her native land, Francesca fumes with steamy goodness in Italian films such as *Ragazzi della notte* (1995) and *La Cena* (1998) and gives scores of signores weekly wank fare in reruns of the TV series *Angelo il custode* (2001) and *Elisa di Rivombrosa* (2003). Yanks will get the most bank from Fran's sexy stint Stateside in *Ghost Ship* (2000). The site of her bare booming boobage will have seamen and land lubbers alike lubed and ready to storm her peaked port. Mouthwateringly mammeriffic in all her skindeavors, even a dash of Ms. Rettondini will leave your weenie wanting more.

SKIN-fining Moment:

Ghost Ship (1:01) Francesca briefly bares a wobbler for Isiah Washington.

See Her Naked In:

Ghost Ship (2002) Breasts

Gloria Reuben

Born: June 9, 1964
Toronto, Ontario, Canada
Skin-O-Meter: Great Nudity

Canadian Gloria Reuben started acting as a child on the series *Polka Dot Door* in 1971. But this foxy black mama was all grown up by the time she appeared in movies like *Immediate Family* (1985) and *Wild Orchid II: Two Shades of Blue* (1992). *Orchid II* featured Gloria's first real exposure, which is not surprising, given the facts that the director was skineaste Zalman King and the film starred erotic-flick-seal-of-approval Mickey Rourke. King had the stroke-worthy stroke of brilliance to team glorious Gloria with fleshy firecracker Nina Siemaszko. Gloria is best known for her stint on the hit television drama series *ER*, in which we were all tempted to take two of Gloria's tits and call her in the morning! Though she made more than a few shafts rise in *Shaft* (2000), Mr. Skin knows that Gloria is at her barest and best in the made-for-cable thriller *Indiscreet* (1998), where she put the *hot* in hot tub. What's love got to do with it? Not a thing, Gloria—this is *lust*! On her current cable-TV series *1-800-Missing*, Gloria's portrayal of a hot FBI agent has viewers everywhere wanting to phone in and order the Reuben!

SKIN-fining Moment:

Indiscreet (0:22) Gloria shows glutes during a drunken dip. Then Luke Perry carries her out of the water.

See Her Naked In:

Indiscreet (1998) Breasts, Buns
Wild Orchid II (1992) Breasts
Shadow Hunter (1992) Buns

Candice Rialson

Born: December 18, 1952
Santa Monica, California
Skin-O-Meter: Hall of Fame

Bountiful Candice Rialson strutted off topless go-go stages as a teen and into the world of B-movie

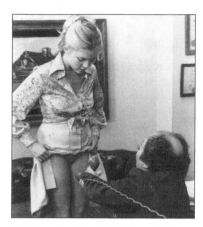

REACH OUT AND MUFF SOMEONE: CANDICE RIALSON LETS HER BOX CHAT IN *CHATTERBOX.*

stardom during the swinging '70s. For ten years she ruled the roost of fine-feathered females showing off her lusciously large chestables in cult items with titles that tell it all. The blonde bombshell was purrfect in *Pets* (1974); a sweet fantasy made flesh in *Candy Stripe Nurses* (1974); a winning advertisement for summer school in *Summer School Teachers* (1974); and, in *Chatterbox* (1977), she had a muff that couldn't be muzzled. Yes, her cooze conversed and even sang. Candice also spiced up some mainstream affairs such as her debut as Girl In Bikini in *The Gay Deceivers* (1969) and bit parts in *The Eiger Sanction* (1975), *Logan's Run* (1976), and the made-for-TV movie *Guilty or Innocent: The Sam Sheppard Murder Case* (1975). With a lot of skintastic performances already heating up her decade of dominance, it was *Hollywood Boulevard* (1976) that showed off Candice's jiggling juggies to best effect. By the '80s this wet dreamboat had run aground and was never to be heard of again. Mr. Skin remains at half-mast.

SKIN-fining Moment:

Chatterbox (0:15) Check out Candice's cans when she's strapped to a bed in front of a large audience while her

pussy is singing. Yes. Her pussy is singing.

See Her Naked In:

Chatterbox (1977) Breasts, Bush, Buns
Hollywood Boulevard (1976) Breasts
Summer School Teachers (1975) Breasts, Buns
Mama's Dirty Girls (1974) Breasts, Buns
Candy Stripe Nurses (1974) Breasts
Pets (1974) Breasts

Marissa Ribisi

Born: December 17, 1974
Los Angeles, California
Skin-O-Meter: Brief Nudity

Dazed and Confused (1993) isn't just a cult classic. It also showcased the coming decade's sexiest young actresses, with Marissa Ribisi stealing scenes as a determined young Texas teen. This intense young beauty has been working regularly ever since, with some of her sexier outfits being in *Reform School Girl* (1994), *The Brady Bunch Movie* (1995), and *True Crime* (1999). She also scripted herself some good roles in *Some Girl* (1998) and *According to Spencer* (2001). But Marissa really got us massaging our rib in *100 Girls* (2000), in which she stood out from the other 99 by doffing her underwear for a torrid topless scene.

SKIN-fining Moment:

100 Girls (1:11) A nice long sequence of pans up and down her undy-clad body, followed by a blast of Marisa's naked Ri-boobies.

See Her Naked In:

100 Girls (2000) Breasts

Christina Ricci

Born: February 12, 1980
Santa Monica, California
Skin-O-Meter: Great Nudity

Goth darn, that Christina Ricci is one hot weirdo! Her debut as

Cher's youngest daughter in *Mermaids* (1990) was followed by the unholy grail of gothic turn-on, Wednesday Addams in *The Addams Family* (1991) and *Addams Family Values* (1993). The just-five-foot darkly arousing imp grew up—and out—before our very pop-eyes. She played an oversexed teenager in *The Ice Storm* (1997), a lovely Lolita in *The Opposite of Sex* (1998), and a barely legal gal pal to legendary nutball Vincent Gallo in *Buffalo 66* (1996). The buxom beauty lost some of her baby fat, but thankfully none of her sweater sacks, and strutted that new willowy form as the new hot bitch on TV's *Ally McBeal*. And then the gods answered Mr. Skin's prayers. Christina's colossal chest was at last revealed in *Prozac Nation* (2001). The release of this story about a Harvard student's bout with depression has been on hold for years, and Mr. Skin waits with bated breast.

SKIN-fining Moment:

Prozac Nation (0:04) Screw antidepressants! The sight of rackodocious, fluff-muffed Miss Ricci full-frontally starkers, sitting on a bed, will snap you out of your funk in a jiff.

See Her Naked In:

Prozac Nation (2001) FFN

Denise Richards

Born: February 17, 1971
Downers Grove, Illinois
Skin-O-Meter: Great Nudity

With flashing eyes of emerald green and lips like plump, candied slabs of love, Denise Richards is pretty enough to have secured a movie career without ever having shown anything. Indeed, her breakthrough role in *Starship Troopers* (1997) was a fully clothed jaunt, although no amount of fabric could conceal the trundling treasures of her heaving

---

MR. SKIN'S TOP TEN

Ménage-à-trois Scenes

. . . Two's company, three's a wow

10. Eva Green, Michael Pitt, and Louis Garrel
    —*The Dreamers* (2003) (0:50)

9. Donna Wilkes, Lindsay Freeman, and an older guy
   —*Fyre* (1978) (1:13)

8. Alice Evans, Daniel Auteuil, and some chick
   —*Mauvaise Passe* (1999) (0:57)

7. Sondra Locke, Colleen Camp, and Seymour Cassel
   —*Death Game* (1977) (0:18)

6. Tiffany Limos and two guys
   —*Ken Park* (2002) (1:23)

5. Andrea Thompson and two dudes
   —*Manhattan Gigolo* (1986) (0:18)

4. Debbi Morgan, Maureen Byrnes, and David Kirk
   —*Cry Uncle* (1971) (0:17)

3. Mary Collinson, Madeleine Collinson and a dude
   —*Some Like it Sexy* (1969) (0:36)

2. Maribel Verdú, Diego Luna, and Gael Garcia Bernal
   —*Y tu mamá también* (2001) (1:34)

1. **Denise Richards, Neve Campbell, and Matt Dillon—** *Wild Things* 1998 (0:57)

---

chest. Those beauties, and the booty that backs them up, were brought to light in *Wild Things* (1998). Playing a devious and oversexed rich chick, Denise started off by doing a bold bikini strut but soon discarded that top for wilder things. The film's highlight was a three-way grope and slurp that featured Matt Dillon and Neve Campbell going hot and bothered

---

for the bare breasts and sucking tongue of pop-top Richards. In a celebratory mood, Matt dribbled champagne through Denise's cleavage and tongued the bubbly off. His is not the only cork that will pop.

SKIN-fining Moment:

Wild Things (0:57) Denise busts out her bodacious bombers for some bubbly-covered three-way lovin' with Matt Dillon and Neve Campbell.

See Her Naked In:

Wild Things (1998) Breasts

Kim Richards

Born: September 19, 1964
Minneola, New York
Skin-O-Meter: Never Nude

Boys who grew up watching *Nanny and the Professor* can remember the strange trouser-stirring sensation that popped up whenever young Kim Richards appeared onscreen. Our ache hardened as she parlayed the part into high-profile Disney films and TV shows, including *Escape to Witch Mountain* (1975) and *Hello, Larry* (1979). Like a precursor to the Olsen twins, millions waited for the little blonde-headed honey to reach the age of eligibility, and thankfully she didn't disappoint. While child stars can sometimes rot with age, Kim grew up real good, as evidenced by her pointy-nippled performance in the teen gang flick *Tuff Turf* (1985). Film historians often refer to this movie as the only one in which Kim flashed her flesh cakes, but they're sadly mistaken. Those feed bags belong to her body double, the fetching Fiona Harris. Truth is, we've never seen Kim's creamy nougats and probably never will, as she's retired. Her absence has fans everywhere asking, "Dear Prudence, won't you come out to play?"

SKIN-fining Moment:

Tuff Turf (1:29) Kim's character gets topless opposite James Spader, but those boobs are a Body Double's and not Little Richards.

See Her Naked In:

Tuff Turf (1984) Body Double—Breasts

Joely Richardson

Born: January 9, 1965
London, England, UK
Skin-O-Meter: Great Nudity

The sister of actress Natasha Richardson and the daughter of actress Vanessa Redgrave and director Tony Richardson, Joely Richardson got a later start than her big sis. But she is no less off-beat than her sib, often winding up in freaky arthouse fare such as Peter Greenaway's *Drowning By Numbers* (1988). In the twisted tale she played one of three murderesses, all named Cissy Colpitts. Joely proved she was no sissy, tackling the notorious Hollywood musical *I'll Do Anything* (1993). Though she's no dog—as is evidenced by her pouty lips and steely eyes—Joely came on board for the successful remake of *101 Dalmatians* (1996). One of her greatest roles, without a doubt, happened in *Sister My Sister* (1994), which cast her as a maid having an incestuous, lesbian love affair with her sister. This maid leaves more than mints on the pillow! In *Hollow Reed* (1996) she played the divorced mother of a young boy who was abused by her live-in boyfriend. Her highest profile role to date may have been in the Mel Gibson Revolutionary War flick *The Patriot* (2000), in which she played the sister of Mel's dead wife. Joely puts enough hustle in that bustle to make anyone a *minute* man!

SKIN-fining Moment:

Lady Chatterley (2:17) Joely strips off, showing everything but the internal workings, then runs around outside in the rain while her bit of nasty chases after her.

See Her Naked In:

Maybe Baby (2000) LB, Buns
I'll Do Anything (1994) Bush
Lady Chatterley (1992) FFN, Buns
Drowning By Numbers (1988) Breasts
Wetherby (1985) Breasts

Miranda Richardson

Born: March 3, 1958
Southport, Lancashire, England, UK
Skin-O-Meter: Great Nudity

Pale beauty Miranda Richardson has played everything from a cold-blooded killer to a ditzy Queen of England. After paying her dues in the British theater, Miranda brought her corseted boobs to the boob tube in Rowan Atkinson's *Black-Adder* comedies. She finally got her big film break in director Mike Newell's *Dance with a Stranger* (1985), playing a woman who winds up getting executed for murder. A simple tongue-lashing would have sufficed! Miranda turned down the role that went to Glenn Close in *Fatal Attraction* (1987) and instead appeared in Steven Spielberg's *Empire of the Sun* (1987) playing a doctor's wife who winds up in a Japanese prison camp. It beats being boiled like a dead rabbit! Miranda had bigger roles in the drama *Damage* (1992) and the penis-Russian-roulette masterpiece *The Crying Game* (1992). Miranda made the most of her small role as a radio-station secretary in Robert Duvall's *The Apostle* (1997), and she made the most of her bodice-busting breasts in Tim Burton's *Sleepy Hollow* (1997). You can read Mr. Skin *those* Miranda rights any day!

SKIN-fining Moment:

Damage (1:40) Miranda takes off her shirt to ask Jeremy Irons if she is good enough for him. One look at her tits and the answer is obvious!

See Her Naked In:

Spider (2002) Body Double—Breasts, Buns
Swann (1996) RB
The Night and the Moment (1994) Nip Slip LB
Century (1993) Breasts
Damage (1992) Breasts
Dance with a Stranger (1985) Breasts

Natasha Richardson

Born: May 11, 1963
London, England, UK
Skin-O-Meter: Great Nudity

The daughter of British actress Vanessa Redgrave and director Tony Richardson—and the sister of fellow hottie Joely Richardson—Natasha Richardson was named after the heroine in Leo Tolstoy's novel *War and Peace*. And who wouldn't want to go to war for this piece? Little four-year-old Natasha's film debut was a family affair, playing her mom's bridesmaid in *Charge of the Light Brigade* (1968), which daddy Tony directed. After training at the Old Vic, performing Shakespeare, Natasha began taking supporting roles in films such as *Every Picture Tells a Story* (1984). Natasha's been carving out her own sexy cinematic path with strong film roles such as *A Month in the Country* (1987) and the Mr. Skin favorites *Patty Hearst* (1988) and *The Handmaid's Tale* (1990). But Natasha still loves the stage, and she won a Tony for her portrayal of Sally Bowles in *Cabaret*. These days Natasha is married to ol' Schindler himself, Irish actor Liam Neeson. "This watch . . . this watch could have been used to note the time of one more of Natasha's nude scenes!"

SKIN-fining Moment:

The Comfort of Strangers (0:45)
Long, loving looks at Natasha's
knockerage as she lays in bed.

See Her Naked In:

Past Midnight (1992) Breasts
The Comfort of Strangers (1990) Breasts
The Handmaid's Tale (1990) Breasts
Patty Hearst (1988) Breasts

Salli Richardson

Born: November 23, 1967
Chicago, Illinois
Skin-O-Meter: Great Nudity

A colorful combination of African,
Cherokee, Italian, and Irish heritage,
Salli Richardson is one saucy slice of
all-American pie. After playing
"Pretty Girl" in the Damon Wayans
wack-fest *Mo' Money* (1992), this
delightful dish hit her stride
showing skin in *Posse* (1993),
leaving lusty men longing to ride
her dusty trails. Since then Sally has
found stunning suck-cess in movies
such as *A Low Down Dirty Shame*
(1994) and *Antwone Fisher* (2002)
and series such as *Rude Awakening*
and *Family Law*. Any of this
tantalizing treat's skindeavors will
leave your crying for mo' of Salli's
malted mams.

SKIN-fining Moment:

Posse (1:11) Salli succumbs to the
charms of Mario Van Peebles and serves
him a naked helping of her topless
coconuts.

See Her Naked In:

Posse (1993) Breasts

Fiona Richmond

Born: 1945
Hilborough, Norfolk, England, UK
Skin-O-Meter: Hall of Fame

Foxy Fiona Richmond began her
career as the "French Stripper" in

the Australian comedy *Barry
MacKenzie Holds His Own* (1974) and
apparently liked disrobing so much
that she continued to do it for
several years after. She made our
bologna pony whinny in the
controversial Aussie flick *Exposé*
(1976)—which was banned in
Britain due its graphic sex and
violence (though not necessarily in
that order)—*Hardcore* (1977)—not
to be confused with the 1979
George C. Scott film of the same
name—and *Let's Get Laid* (1977),
allowing grateful viewers to drink in
her hairy goblet and magnificent
milk wagons. Though we haven't
seen her since *Eat the Rich* (1987),
we often think of Fiona's apples.

SKIN-fining Moment:

Exposé (0:05) Bazoombas and booty
abound when Fiona gets it on with a
creepy, rubber-gloved cretin.

See Her Naked In:

Love Trap (1977) Breasts, Bush
Hardcore (1977) FFN
Exposé (1975) Breasts, Bush, Buns

Deborah Richter

Born: August 31, 1961
Los Angeles, California
Skin-O-Meter: Great Nudity

Comely Deborah Richter really
embodies (ahem) the spirit of the
quintessential 1980s young babe.
This sassy brunette with the never-
ending rack could make a priest
kick a hole in a stained-glass
window. Besides being Jean-Claude
Van Dumb's gal pal in *Cyborg*
(1989), this jugtastic chick
showcased her undressed best in
the super '80s teen steamer *Hot
Moves* (1984). Deborah, who was
crowned Miss California in 1975,
appeared in several TV mini-series
after her debut in the movie *One on
One* (1977) and was once married to
the scruffy dude from *Hill Street
Blues*. She also occasionally

appeared on the show as his
onscreen wife.

SKIN-fining Moment:

Hot Moves (1:09) Debbie shows off
her topless snack-cakes while disrobing
for some fun with a fellow.

See Her Naked In:

Cyborg (1989) LB, Buns
Hot Moves (1984) Breasts

Rena Riffel

Inglewood, California
Skin-O-Meter: Great Nudity

Few actresses have a career as
schizo as Rena Riffell, whose
waffles have heated up many a
mainstream hit and indie smash.
She started out dying way too soon
as a sexy sacrifice in *Satan's Princess*
(1990). Before long, though, Rena
was mooning in the multiplexes as
strippers in *Showgirls* (1995) and
Striptease (1996). Her shape even
stole the show in HBO's breast-
heavy *Breast Men* (1997), providing
both topless thrills and bikinied
bliss. She's also sexed up acclaimed
indie films such as *Goat on Fire and
Smiling Fish* (1999) and *The
Pornographer* (1999). And check out
Candyman 3: Day of the Dead (1999),
in which Rena proved that she can
still make her naughty nudity seem
fresh and spontaneous. Hopefully,
this hottie will return to more high-
profile projects such as David
Lynch's *Mulholland Drive* (2001).

SKIN-fining Moment:

Showgirls (0:24) Rena strips starkers
as Kyle MacLachlan and Gina Gershon
*look on. She even offers up a From-the-
Rear peek at her Vertical Smile!*

See Her Naked In:

White Slave Virgins (2003) FFN
The Pornographer (1999) Breasts
Candyman 3: Day of the Dead (1999)
  Breasts, Thong

Chained Heat III: No Holds Barred (1998) Breasts, Buns
Scandalous Behavior (1998) Breasts, Bush
Breast Men (1997) Breasts
Striptease (1996) Breasts, Thong
Showgirls (1995) Breasts, Bush, Buns
Undercover (1995) Breasts
Satan's Princess (1990) Breasts

Diana Rigg

Born: July 20, 1938
Doncaster, Yorkshire, England, UK
Skin-O-Meter: Brief Nudity

Diana Rigg is such a staple of British pop culture that she was knighted in 1994. Call her Dame Diana, please. It's a fitting title for one of the hottest dames ever to squeeze into a leather jumpsuit. Diana is renowned the world over via her role on the hit '60s series *The Avengers*, where she played Mrs. Emma Peel, and, oh, to see her peel! Diana also made for an indelible Bond Girl in the only George Lazenby installment of the film series, *On Her Majesty's Secret Service* (1969). Not that Diana is simply a shockingly beautiful piece of ass. This talented lass has appeared in everything from Shakespearean theater to horror flicks, and she's both talented and hot as hell. Of course, we are moist grateful that the stunning Diana got out of those tight leather outfits that she made so popular on *The Avengers* just long enough to show a little skin in *The Hospital* (1970) opposite George C. Scott. It isn't much, admittedly. We wish we could Rigg more skin time for this Old Britannia.

SKIN-fining Moment:

The Hospital (0:57) Extremely brief shots of her body when George C. Scott tears off her clothes. Don't blink!

See Her Naked In:

The Hospital (1970) Buns

Molly Ringwald

Born: February 18, 1968
Roseville, California
Skin-O-Meter: Great Nudity

Good golly, but Molly Ringwald would be a guilty pleasure, except that the eternally postpubescent tease is the ripening embodiment of innocent, naïve eroticism. There is no shame in sitting through sentimental teen fodder such as *Sixteen Candles* (1984), *Pretty in Pink* (1986), or *The Breakfast Club* (1985). Especially not *The Breakfast Club*, with its lingering up-skirt shot focusing on Molly's cotton-fresh pantie shield, a view that gives rise to thoughts of wonder, as in: "I wonder if Molly's lower lips are as full and lust swollen as the facial labia that she nibbles on so adorably whenever experiencing a frisson of adolescent sexual tension?" Ringwald's signature characters are usually gawky and endearing, like a curvy gosling in the process of transforming into a sleekly sensual swan. Molly left the Brat Pack nest and spent a few years in Paris, gaining a Continental outlook that resulted in *Malicious* (1995). See Molly all grown up and smoking a cigarette. She also smoked in a topless girl-on-top boff with her remarkably mature chest pillows tossing in the breeze.

SKIN-fining Moment:

Malicious (0:24) Molly hangs her gorgeous, stunning hefty mammaries straight into the camera as she mounts her tied-up fella. Those nipples are beyond Pretty in Pink!

See Her Naked In:

Malicious (1995) Breasts

Jennifer Rivell

Born: June 5, 1973
West Chester, Pennsylvania
Skin-O-Meter: Brief Nudity

Bitchin' babe Jennifer Rivell is linked to bad boy Bam Margera, the most skateboard-friendly alum of MTV's *Jackass*. Though playing herself, Bam's better half, on Bam's spinoff neck-breaking saga *Viva La Bam* on MTV, she made her first appearances in Bam's pre-*Jackass* skate video *CKY2K* (2000). She's not just the hot babe in Bam's life; thanks to his writing and directing debut, *Haggard: The Movie* (2003), Jenn's the hot babe of everyone's dreams.

SKIN-fining Moment:

Haggard The Movie (1:09) Brunette bombshell Jen most decidedly does not live up to this flick's title, as evidenced by her delicious dumplings as she unsheaths them from a black bra before beddy-bye.

See Her Naked In:

Haggard: The Movie (2003) Breasts

Cheryl Rixon

Skin-O-Meter: Brief Nudity

Cheryl Rixon first busted out with an Australian scandal in 1975, after posing nude on a motorcycle with a star of the popular detective series *Homicide*. Her big-screen debut was in the sexless Aussie sex comedy *Plugg* (1975), and then Rixon revved up American dix on the pages of *Penthouse*—ultimately becoming Pet of the Year in 1980. Her American debut soon followed in the cult comedy *Used Cars* (1980), in which Cheryl doffed her top for a guerrilla live broadcast. Ignored at the time, the film is now considered a classic—which is good news for Cheryl, since her only other memorable role turned out to be in *Dark Secrets* (1998), a wild erotic thriller directed by porn veteran John T. Bone.

SKIN-fining Moment:

Used Cars (0:29) Cheryl gyrates atop a car during a commercial when her dress gets torn off and she's topless. Nice lemons!

See Her Naked In:

Used Cars (1980) Breasts

Lois Robbins

Skin-O-Meter: Brief Nudity

Any man who has ever been out of work for a few months at a time and has fallen into the habit of spending the spare hours in front of the TV as the daytime dramas play out their plotlines of adultery, betrayal, and more adultery has been shocked to find his mind veering sharply gutterward as the day progresses. Much of the blame for this bawdy bent of thought can be laid upon full-lipped, jutting-jaw Latina spitfire Lois Robbins. The pleasure-packed curves of voluptuous Lois have signified and justified, posed and pouted, schemed and dreamed as a regular libidinal attraction on what seems like every soap in the world, including *Another Life, Loving, Ryan's Hope, All My Children*, and *One Life to Live*. The irony of it is that with all those suds rising up around Lois's body of work, the tube may never feel clean again.

SKIN-fining Moment:

Kingpin "French Connection" (2003) Look close for several neatnip-slips as bra-clad Lois struggles with a guy and he flips her onto the floor.

TeleVisions:

Kingpin Nip Slip RB

> "When you act with your clothes on, it's a performance. When you act with your clothes off, it's a documentary. I don't do documentaries."
>
> —JULIA ROBERTS

Julia Roberts

Born: October 28, 1967
Smyrna, Georgia
Skin-O-Meter: Brief Nudity

She's *America's Sweetheart*, but guys are still grateful for Julia Roberts's whorish past in *Pretty Woman* (1990)—where, despite all you've heard about Shelley Michelle as her body double, Julia still provided a definitive slip of the nip. The film also offered Julia in plenty of sexy outfits, which have thankfully been a mainstay of this Georgia beauty's subsequent career. She's the highest-paid actress in Hollywood, and we've paid lots of attention to her tight outfits (and tighter underwear) in films such as *The Pelican Brief* (1993) and *My Best Friend's Wedding* (1997). And don't forget those Oscar-worthy, bra-busting tops in *Erin Brockovich* (2000).

SKIN-fining Moment:

Pretty Woman (1:35) Mega-quick peek of Julia's right nerp as she pulls off her nightie.

See Her Naked In:

Pretty Woman (1990) RB

Layla Roberts

Born: October 22, 1974
Kealakekua Kona, Hawaii
Skin-O-Meter: Great Nudity

What's the MrSkinny on this babe? Being a Hawaiian native and all-around hottie, of course Layla Roberts had to cameo on *Baywatch*. Guest spot or not, watching Layla's terrifically tall, tan, bikini-clad bod bounce around will float any guy's buoy. In addition to her guest appearance on the boob-fest that is *Baywatch*, this busty blonde can also be seen briefly as a comely stripper in the astronomically popular asteroidal thriller *Armageddon* (1998). There's even more for the science-fiction devotee in Layla's

repertoire, although the real test of manhood is being able to wait to see Layla bare it all as Grendel's mom in Christopher Lambert's futuristic version of *Beowulf* (1999). Layla is not the only thing in this low-budget bonanza that transforms monstrously—only diehard B-movie fans will have the patience NOT to fast forward to the naked parts.

SKIN-fining Moment:

Beowulf (0:31) In the days of old, when knights were bold, fair maidens wore metal lingerie like Layla does here. And if they had large, natural torso-towers like Layla, it was awesome when they took it off like she does here, too.

See Her Naked In:

Beowulf (1999) Breasts
Numerous *Playboy* Videos

Kathleen Robertson

Born: July 8, 1975
Hamilton, Ontario, Canada
Skin-O-Meter: Brief Nudity

Thrown into a world of rich-kid teen angst, shopping, and well-dressed heavy petting, Kathleen Robertson was a refreshing burst of Joan Jett-style, kick-ass grrrl power before she became one of the assimilated on the hit series *Beverly Hills, 90210*. Remember when Kathleen first appeared as Clare, a spiky-haired rebel with a toughie swagger and a mouth on her as rough as Leather Tuscadero? Ah, those were the days. Well, captivating Kathleen has certainly come a long way since then and was even a pro long before. Starting out as a child actress in Canada, Kathleen starred on the series *My Secret Identity* and *Maniac Mansion*. Following these roles and her stint on *90210*, the mucho talented Ms. K went on to play bit and larger parts in such films as *Dog Park* (1998), *Nowhere* (1997), *Psycho Beach Party* (2000), *Beautiful* (2000), *I Am Sam* (2001), and *Scary Movie 2* (2001).

SKIN-fining Moment:

XX/XY (0:06) Kathleen serves just a taste of her tight tail as a threesome kicks off involving her, Maya Stange, and one lucky dork.

See Her Naked In:

XX/XY (2002) Buns

Kimmy Robertson

**Born: November 27, 1954
Hollywood, California
Skin-O-Meter: Brief Nudity**

When people talk about Kimmy Robertson, they usually mention *Twin Peaks*, but they're not just referring to the quirky David Lynch-created TV series in which she starred. As drool-inducing ditz Lucy Moran, Kimmy's petite but perfectly pert sweater melons kept channel changers gooed, er, glued to their sofas throughout the show's early '90s run. A bouncy blonde with a Betty Boop voice, Kimmy originally wanted to be a ballerina but wound up taking off her ballet shoes to slip into a skimpy bikini for randy teen romp *The Last American Virgin* (1982). Although she scored most of her major points with *Peaks*, you can catch Kimmy's (unfortunately) clothed cans in *Speed 2: Cruise Control* (1997) and *Stuart Little* (1999). She's currently keeping her mouth filled with voiceover work.

SKIN-fining Moment:

Bad Manners (0:37) It's Triple Peeks as Twin Peaks Kimmy shows all three B's on her way into the shower.

See Her Naked In:

Bad Manners (1984) FFN, Buns

IN HER? SPANKED 'EM! TANYA ROBERTS IN *INNER SANCTUM.*

Tanya Roberts

**Born: October 15, 1954
The Bronx, New York
Skin-O-Meter: Hall of Fame**

Model turned off-Broadway actress turned full-time night-emission fodder, Bronx bombshell Tanya Roberts began appearing in film roles that played to her buxom strengths such as *The Yum-Yum Girls* (1976) and *California Dreaming* (1979). In *Tourist Trap* (1979), the camera dispensed with all the preliminaries and just focused on her long and lovely legs. In 1980 Tanya signed on to replace Shelly Hack on TV's jiggleriffic *Charlie's Angels*. After one season of strip-searches and concealing weapons in her bikini, Roberts went back to big-screen horror films and T&A exploitation. Tanya's best known for the sword-and-sandal epics *Beastmaster* (1982) and *Sheena, Queen of the Jungle* (1984), in which she showed Marc Singer that a hot, naked girl can be even more fun than a sackfull of muskrats. Tanya tumbled back into TV as Velda in

Mike Hammer: Murder Me, Murder You (1983), where she had viewers ready to aim and shoot! After skintastic stints in sexy flicks such as *Inner Sanctum* (1991), Tanya scored yet another signature TV role as "Midge Pinciotti" on *That '70s Show*. Perfect casting, as no one else would be hot enough to play ravishing redhead Laura Prepon's mother. But someone should have told the show's writers that you're never too old to breastfeed!

SKIN-fining Moment:

Sheena (0:54) Aweome jungle jugs and beauteus gluteus as Tanya saunters into the lake and teases Ted Wass.

See Her Naked In:

Deep Down (1994) Breasts
Almost Pregnant (1992) Body Double—Buns / Her—Breasts
Sins of Desire (1992) Breasts, Buns
Legal Tender (1991) Breasts, Buns
Inner Sanctum (1991) Breasts, Buns
Night Eyes (1990) Breasts, Bush, Buns
Purgatory (1988) FFN, Buns
Sheena (1984) FFN, Buns
The Beastmaster (1982) Breasts, Buns

Louise Robey

**Born: March 14, 1960
Montreal, Quebec, Canada
Skin-O-Meter: Great Nudity**

Racy redhead Louise Robey rose to popularity through her role as Micki Foster on the small screen on the *Friday the 13th* TV series. This Montreal native and singer-slash-songwriter-slash-actress-slash-model-slash-former lady of Buford Manor—take a deep breath—will take you by the heart when she takes you by the hand (Mr. Skin means that figuratively of course . . . he doesn't want to know what's in your hand right now). You can also review Louise's many (but sadly, clothed) talents by checking her out in *Raw Deal* (1986), *Triple Identity* (1986), and *The Money Pit* (1986). You may also note that acting is only one of Ms. Robey's many gifts, as she has had a hit single, "One Night in Bangkok," and adorned the pages of Paris *Vogue* at the tender age of nineteen. Her marriage to and subsequent divorce from Lord Charles F.T. de VereBeauclerk, Earl of Buford, is, to say the least, fascinating—but we're here for skinography people, not petty gossip!

SKIN-fining Moment:

Play Nice (0:35) Robey rides man-rod in bed, pumping and moaning as her soft sacks sway sensationally.

See Her Naked In:

Play Nice (1992) Breasts

Eva Robins

Born: December 10, 1958
Bologna, Italy
Skin-O-Meter: Brief Nudity

So what if she was born a man? Nobody's perfect, but Eva Robins still gets tantalizingly close—especially as transsexuals go. (For the record, Eva claims to be a hermaphrodite.) The former Roberto Coatti is now a sexy cinematic femme, still best remembered as the psyche-shredding beauty on the beach in Dario Argento's *Tenebre* (1982). After doffing her top for a crowd of pleased young men, Eva fulfilled many a foot fetishist's dream by taking revenge on a tormentor with one of her spiked heels. Eva then co-starred with Lou Ferrigno in *The Adventures of Hercules* (1983)—although nobody probably had the nerve to mention Eva's past to the former Hulk. In a particularly daring move, Eva also went full frontal in the thriller *Mascara* (1987). She's since made a nice transformation into a sexy older gal, as seen in later projects like *Cattive inclinazioni* (2003).

SKIN-fining Moment:

Tenebre (0:22) This Eva tempts a whole passel of Adams with her apples. She pulls down her top on the beach and then it's off to the races. That little minx!

See Her Naked In:

Tenebre (1982) Breasts

> "You know, I really love the Mr. Skin Web site. That '50s style is so nice. You go to some of these celebrity sites and you feel kind of dirty. At Mr. Skin, you feel like you're having a grand old time."
>
> —DEBBIE ROCHON

Debbie Rochon

Born: November 3, 1968
Salt Lake City, Utah
Skin-O-Meter: Great Nudity

After a decade-plus run as one of the most skintillating figures in B-moviedom, dairylicious dish Debbie Rochon has ratcheted up over one hundred film credits and presently reigns as one of the scorchingly Sapph-tastic sirens of Seduction Cinema alongside gorgeous gal pals Misty Mundae and Darian Caine. Ever youthful and with a face so naturally beautiful it almost defies belief, Debbie has most recently delighted in Seduction's skintastic girl-on-girl-crazy spoofs such as *Witchbabe: Erotic Witch Project 3* (2001) and *Play-Mate of the Apes* (2002). Prior to finding her perfect fit with the Seduction studio, Debbie electrified even her most obscure offerings and brought bona fide superstar power to cult classics such as *Tromeo & Juliet* (1996) and *Head Cheerleader Dead Cheerleader* (2000). In *Final Examination* (2003), Debbie offered her D-lightful divots for an in-depth chestal check up on the couch. After a thorough going

over, you'll agree that her ample apples earn an A-plus. A busty, thrusty beauty in all her skindeavors, not-so-little Debbie is guaranteed to scare—and tear—the pants off you every time.

SKIN-fining Moment:

Broadcast Bombshells (0:25) Debbie goes starkers before donning a sultry little S/M getup.

See Her Naked In:

Final Examination (2003) Breasts
American Nightmare (2002) Breasts
Dead & Rotting (2002) Breasts
Bleed (2002) Breasts
Witchbabe: Erotic Witch Project 3 (2001) Breasts
Sandy Hook Lingerie Party Massacre (1999) Breasts
Santa Claws (1996) Breasts
Scream Queens' Naked Christmas (1996) Breasts, Thong
Tromeo and Juliet (1996) RB
Broadcast Bombshells (1995) FFN, Thong
Abducted II: The Reunion (1994) Breasts
The Regenerated Man (1994) Breasts

Lela Rochon

Born: April 17, 1964
Los Angeles, California
Skin-O-Meter: Brief Nudity

Lela Rochon's perky puppies easily upstaged Spuds McKenzie in some Budweiser commercials back in the '80s. From there this African American actress rapidly moved up from the chorus line in Lionel Richie videos. Among other honors, she was one of *People*'s Fifty Most Beautiful People in the World in 1996. The big screen has also taken advantage of Lela's big assets. Her stripping scene always gets gangs bangin' in *Gang Related* (1997), and *Waiting To Exhale* (1995) had us all holding our breath waiting for her to drop that bra. (She didn't.) And the lovely Lela currently has us all arrested as a sexy cop on Lifetime's *The Division*.

SKIN-fining Moment:

Gang Related (0:21) Lela lights up a strip club stage with her butt-floss G-string and smokingly sensuous moves.

See Her Naked In:

Gang Related (1997) Thong

> "I'll take being on *Baywatch* over being prom queen any day!"
>
> —BRANDE RODERICK

Brande Roderick

Born: June 13, 1974
Novato, California
Skin-O-Meter: Great Nudity

Hollywood is full of blonde *Playboy* models who think they can act. But beautiful Brande Roderick was actually right! The hottest honey on the long-running jigglethon *Baywatch Hawaii*, Brande makes her yellow one-piece—not to mention viewers—scream for joy. Since appearing in the pages of *Playboy*, Brande's reportedly been romantically linked to everyone from Fred Durst to Big Hef himself. Having successfully made the leap from *Playboy*-produced fare like *Sex on the Beach* (1997) and *Playboy Playmate Video Calendar* (2001) to big-budget, A-list blockbusters like *Starsky & Hutch* (2004), California girl Brande has accomplished every centerfold's dream.

SKIN-fining Moment:

Sheer Passion (0:13) Brande looks dandy serving up full-frontal candy while initially dancing for and then doing the dirty with a dude. You'll pop a Roderick!

See Her Naked In:

Sheer Passion (1998) FFN, Buns
Club Wildside 2 (1998) FFN, Buns
Life of a Gigolo (1998) Breasts
Numerous *Playboy* Videos

Kate Rodger

Sugarland, Texas
Skin-O-Meter: Great Nudity

If not for one woman's courage and generosity, the world in large part might have forever remained ignorant of the splendor that is the magical rise and amazing stamina of copper-tinged brunette Kate Rodger's jutting, thumb-sized nipples. That brave and giving female is, of course, Kate Rodger herself. A veteran of daytime melodramas, having waxed histrionic on the likes of *General Hospital* and *Days of Our Lives*, daring and baring, randy lassie Rodger has made a life's work of spreading the cheer of her bosom, her buns, and sometimes her bush in such skin-flaunting features as *Last Stand* (2000), *Chained Heat III: No Holds Barred* (1998), and *Poison Ivy 2* (1995).

SKIN-fining Moment:

Hell Mountain (0:56) Kate gets stripped topless, tied up, lowered into a pit by wicked lesbos and whipped. Kinktastic!!!

See Her Naked In:

Last Stand (2000) Breasts
Chained Heat III: No Holds Barred (1998) Breasts, Buns
Hell Mountain (1998) Breasts
Walnut Creek (1996) FFN, Buns
Club V.R. (1996) Breasts
Poison Ivy 2: Lily (1995) Breasts

TeleVisions:

Women: Stories of Passion Breasts, Buns

Michelle Rodriguez

Born: July 12, 1978
Bexar County, Texas
Skin-O-Meter: Never Nude

In *Girlfight* (2000), delicious-but-deadly Michelle Rodriguez proved she could kick ass. But in the bikini blockbuster *Blue Crush* (2002), Michelle showed that she's got a pretty nice ass of her own. Michelle's folks moved the family around a lot, seasoning the Texas-born babe in Puerto Rico, the Dominican Republic, and New Jersey. After extra work in *Summer of Sam* (1999) and *Cradle Will Rock* (1999), Michelle finally got her chance to be a star after answering an open call for a bodacious boxing babe. *Girlfight* punched down the doors to Hollywood for Michelle, and she went on to star in *The Fast and the Furious* (2001), in which she had a hip-grindin' good time with Vin Diesel—no doubt causing Vin to pump a little oil of his own. She starred opposite Colin Farrell in the big-budget blockbuster *S.W.A.T.* (2003), where she showed off the ammo that gives every marksman an itchy trigger finger.

SKIN-fining Moment:

Blue Crush (13:00) Surf's up as Michelle hangs ten and wears a skimpy bikini that accentuates her perfect two. That'll put a long-board in your shorts.

Mimi Rogers

Born: January 27, 1956
Coral Gables, Florida
Skin-O-Meter: Hall of Fame

Mimi Rogers is the biggest talent to come out of Hollywood in decades—just take one look at her two titacular towers. Roger that! The melon-mounted marvel from Coral Gables, Florida was married to Tom Cruise, who is about as big as one of Mimi's monster mams. She may not share the same level of stardom as her former husband, but then his chest never looked as good as Mimi's in *The Rapture* (1991), *Bulletproof Heart* (1994), and *Reflections in the Dark* (1995). A glimpse of Mimi's mamas is more than enough boobage for even the most diehard tit man, but if you want to risk a jug

OD then go for the uncut stuff in *Full Body Massage* (1995). Mimi got oiled up and rubbed down, sending her fleshy mounds every which way *and* loose. It makes Mr. Skin want to do a little self-message.

SKIN-fining Moment:

Full Body Massage (1:11) Ultimate milk-monster Mimi gets her jug-gantic Jolly Rogers worked over by Bryan Brown's luckiest mitts in the history of the world.

See Her Naked In:

The Door in the Floor (2004) FFN, Buns
Reflections in the Dark (1995) Breasts, Buns
Full Body Massage (1995) Breasts, Buns
Bulletproof Heart (1994) Breasts
The Rapture (1991) Breasts

Kristin Rohde

Skin-O-Meter: Brief Nudity

Cruelty doesn't necessarily make a person bad. Some people are mean not out of any inherent malice but because they are insecure, afraid of making themselves vulnerable to being disliked or rejected. Or, in the case of a brutal, antagonistic, and sadistic female prison guard as played by comely Kristin Rohde on the HBO murder and sodomy prison-life extravaganza *Oz*, a broad may play tough titty because it's just not good policy to look like a pussy. And in the course of her *Oz* tenure, the tender impulses that Rohde's Officer Claire Howell so viciously tried to disguise with sneering contempt emerged as surely as love must. Then her life really went to shit.

SKIN-fining Moment:

Oz "Gray Matter" (2000) In the locker room, Kristin proves that under her guard uniform, she's just one of the girls by losing the top and showing off her dairy-dinks.

TeleVisions:

Oz Breasts

Elisabeth Röhm

Born: April 28, 1973
Düsseldorf, Germany
Skin-O-Meter: Brief Nudity

Former soap star Elisabeth Röhm, a German-born beauty with looks reminiscent of a younger Sheryl Lee, got her big break playing salty-tongued detective Kate Lockley on the WB's sultry vamp-camp hit *Angel*. She left the show in 2001 for a plum role on *Law & Order*, a veritable breeding ground for hot young actresses (see also brunette barristers Angie Harmon, Carey Lowell, and Jill Hennessey). Her buttoned-up, feminist-charged role as Assistant D.A. Serena Southerlyn hasn't made her a flesh fanatic's fave, but where there's smoke, there's fire—and Mr. Skin has a feeling it won't be long 'til this smoldering beauty heats up the big screen with her fiery, fleshy self.

SKIN-fining Moment:

Eureka Street Eureka! Elisabeth bounds up in bed rack-first. Raw and order.

See Her Naked In:

Eureka Street (1999) Breasts

Maria Rohm

Born: February 25, 1945
Vienna, Austria
Skin-O-Meter: Great Nudity

As part of notorious director Jesus Franco's repertory crew, Maria Rohm was as daring as she was gorgeous—especially considering that she was committing some groundbreaking nudity in films like *Eugenie . . . the Story of Her Journey Into Perversion* (1970). Any proper film historian will marvel at Maria's Rohmin' hands as they give Marie Liljedahl one of the sexiest baths in film history. Maria went on to be equally shameless as a horny slave girl in *Venus in Furs* (1970). Any of her films come highly recommended, since Maria always knows how to work her awesome blonde beauty—which, sadly, also explains why the aging actress has been working strictly behind the scenes as a producer since 1989.

SKIN-fining Moment:

Marquis de Sade: Justine (1:19) Rosemary Dexter and Maria enjoy a skinny-dip that turns into a splashy catfight and strangulation. Maria shows her boobs and bush.

See Her Naked In:

Eugenie . . . the Story of Her Journey Into Perversion (1970) FFN, Buns
Jesus Franco's Venus in Furs (1969) Breasts, Buns
Girl from Rio (1969) Breasts, Buns

Marquis de Sade: Justine (1969) Breasts, Bush

María Rojo

Born: August 15, 1943
Mexico City, Mexico
Skin-O-Meter: Great Nudity

How can there be any opposition to NAFTA when a worker so skilled and eager as Maria Rojo is just waiting to have her talents imported to the USA? One of Mexico's national treasures, alternately bubbling and simmering Rojo has been a fixture on Latin TV and silver screens since the 1960s. Maria's first English-language role consisted of her plump and perky chi-chis doing the talking through two scenes of Roger Corman's *Candy Stripe Nurses* (1974). Since then Rojo's sexposure has come on both sides of the border, not neglecting the area south of her own border. Bite into the spicy pulp of a totally hairy simulated-sex close-up in *El Apando* (1976). Whack the pinata as the lovemaking Latina tumbles beaver-first from a hammock in *Homework* (1990). Marvel at the immaculately preserved mangoes in *De Noche Vienes* (1997), wherein forty-seven-year-old Maria flashed all, wearing nothing more than a big smile.

SKIN-fining Moment:

El Apando (0:42) See Maria's mammaritas and muffala as she gets a cavity exam from a female guard who really ought to enjoy her job more than she seems to.

See Her Naked In:

De noche vienes, Esmeralda (1997) FFN
Forbidden Homework (1992) Breasts
Homework (1990) Breasts, Buns
Lo que importa es vivir (1987) Breasts
El Apando (1976) FFN
Candy Stripe Nurses (1974) Breasts

Lina Romay

Born: June 25, 1954
Barcelona, Spain
Skin-O-Meter: Hall of Fame

Smoldering brunette Lina Romay is the bella donna of Spanish horror skinema. The long-time live-in love of blood-and-boobies auteur Jesus Franco has shown her dusky hot stuff in at least one hundred foreign-language flicks. Even at age forty-three Romay couldn't stop tossing her clothes away; middle-aged and muy caliente, Lina hung her Barcelona beaver in *Tender Flesh* (1997). Hot at any age, Romay in her prime is a burning vision of knee-weakening lust. Try to stand up to her challenging nineteen-year-old's glare in *Les Avaleuses* (1973). The only refuge from the harrowing need of her eyes was the bold beauty of her knowing nymph's body. Generous in youth, she showed it all, including open-sesame buttock views as she squirmed in a bathtub of blood. Beware of racing pulse.

SKIN-fining Moment:

Les Avaleuses (0:00) Full-frontal nudity wearing a cape and walking towards the camera in the opening credits.

See Her Naked In:

Vampire Junction (2001) FFN, Buns
Mari-Cookie and the Killer Tarantula (1998) FFN, Buns
Tender Flesh (1997) FFN
Ilsa, the Wicked Warden (1980) LB
Elles font tout (1978) FFN, Buns
Jack the Ripper (1976) Breasts, Thong
Die Marquise von Sade (1976) FFN, Buns
Exorcisme (1974) Breasts, Bush
Les Avaleuses (1973) FFN, Buns

Sydne Rome

Born: March 17, 1951
Akron, Ohio
Skin-O-Meter: Hall of Fame

Though Sydne Rome grew up in Ohio and got her start in the UK film *Some Girls Do* (1969), she made her mark in Italian-made films that played up her classic American-girl looks. In Roman Polanski's *What?* (1972), Sydne played an American whose trip to a Mediterranean villa turns into a sexy, bizarre *Alice in Wonderland*-like farce. Lucky for viewers everywhere, someone keeps stealing Sydne's clothes throughout the whole flick. Then-living legend Marcello Mastroianni never seemed to have as much fun in his whole career as when he got to smack Sydne's tight, jeans-clad booty—one of two spankings saucy Sydne received—or when he got to don tiger skins and ravish young Sydne. In *La Race de seigneurs* (1974), Sydne sexed it up with Alain Delon, who also sexed it up with erotic legend Jeanne Moreau. You've got to feel for poor Alain; Mr. Skin challenges you to pick between those two honeys!

SKIN-fining Moment:

What? (0:08) Sydne strips down to go to sleep, treating us to muliple views of her teats, plus a little lap-fur when she slips between the sheets.

See Her Naked In:

Looping—Der lange Traum vom kurzen Glück (1981) Breasts
Wanted: Babysitter (1975) FFN
El Clan de los inmorales (1975) Breasts
Il faut vivre dangereusement (1975) Breasts
La Sculacciata (1974) FFN, Buns
Creezy (1973) Breasts
What? (1972) FFN, Buns

TeleVisions:

Das Erbe der Guldenburgs Breasts

Rebecca Romijn-Stamos

Born: November 6, 1972
Berkeley, California
Skin-O-Meter: Great Nudity

With legs that rise all the way up to paradise, a face that is the portal to nirvana, and a torso that is the fleshly embodiment of God-given ecstasy, honey-blonde superhuman Rebecca Romijn-Stamos is a woman whose impending divorce from John Stamos has been a bigger boon for lagging erections than the invention of Viagra. With Stamos out of the way, the rest of us are free to dream the dreams of true men! Our transcendent visions will include randy Rebecca's groin-charming semi-striptease and bi-gender macking as featured in the deadly hot *Femme Fatale* (2002), and we will awake to a reality wherein the brightest shining star of *Sports Illustrated Swimsuit 99* (1999) walks among us on this planet, a free and available woman.

SKIN-fining Moment:

Femme Fatale (1:36) A ravishing full-frontal splashdown as Rebecca takes a plunge into water. There's some bubbles in the way, but trust us . . . It's all there!

See Her Naked In:

Godsend (2004) Breasts
Femme Fatale (2002) FFN
Rollerball (2001) Breasts

Jamie Rose

Born: November 26, 1959
New York, New York
Skin-O-Meter: Brief Nudity

She's a straight-to-video vixen, a bit-part tart, a TV-tease cutie, but still redhead Jamie Rose has shown enough sophisticated sass to pierce a skin lover's heart. Although she was a queen of sexy-pout emoting on the network series *St. Elsewhere* and *Lady Blue*, blushing Rose's bouncy blossoms were most coveted in her role as Victoria on primetime jiggle-Jello melodrama *Falcon Crest*. The thorny issue with this fine, freckled Rose is that her sexposure is limited to a scattering of three-blink bits in a handful of early-1980s flicks, then it was back to *Ally McBeal* guest spots. Which is why God invented DVD freeze-frame technology.

SKIN-fining Moment:

Heartbreakers (0:08) Jaime shows off her impressive rack while making out with Nick Mancuso shortly before Peter Coyote performs the cock-block of the century . . .

See Her Naked In:

Rebel Love (1985) RB
Tightrope (1984) Buns
Heartbreakers (1984) Breasts
Just Before Dawn (1981) Breasts

Sherrie Rose

Born: February 24, 1966
Hartford, Connecticut
Skin-O-Meter: Great Nudity

Blonde B-movie fixture Sherrie Rose may have missed full-on fame by a country mile, but Mr. Skin isn't about to complain. She's one of the finest purveyors of straight-to-video skinema, and for that we applaud her. Of particular note is her bare-rumped romp in *Me and Will* (1998), but don't miss her blazing-hot love scenes in *Double Threat* (1992) and *Devil in the Flesh* (1998). For more flesh-flashing fun, just stay tuned—there's undoubtedly more to come.

SKIN-fining Moment:

Me and Will (0:45) Scoops, seat, and snizz as Sherrie skinny-dips in a creek with equally bare Melissa Behr.

See Her Naked In:

Devil in the Flesh (1998) Breasts
Me and Will (1998) FFN, Buns
New Crime City (1994) FFN, Buns
Double Threat (1992) Breasts
Inside Out (1992) Breasts
Inside Out II (1992) Breasts
Unlawful Entry (1992) Breasts
Maximum Force (1992) Breasts
A Climate for Killing (1991) Breasts
Summer Job (1989) Breasts

TeleVisions:

Dream On Breasts
Tales from the Crypt FFN

Charlotte Ross

Born: January 21, 1968
Winnetka, Illinois
Skin-O-Meter: Brief Nudity

Being a prime specimen of the sexy-smart style of blonde, seething with a snarling sexuality, Charlotte Ross is perfectly suited for soap-opera stardom. Which explains why the wickedly wonderful Ross played so well on that long-running chronicle of relationship crisis *Days of our Lives*. Charlotte's web of ambition, talent, and primetime pulchritude explain why she was snatched out of daytime psychodrama and high-beamed into a higher boob-tube profile. So driven is Ross in her pursuit of craft that she went ass-out on *NYPD Blue* during the show's 2003 season. Watching and hoping, skinthusiasts are keeping their fingers crossed that Charlotte will one day challenge the big screen's sex-scene boundaries.

SKIN-fining Moment:

NYPD Blue "Rude Awakening" (2003) Great glutes as she drops her robe to take a shower, followed by tits and almost bush when she walks over but gets interrupted by a lucky kid. It's amazing (and commendable) that this was on ABC.

See Her Naked In:

Kidnapped in Paradise 1999) Thong

TeleVisions:

NYPD Blue Buns

Diana Ross

Born: March 26, 1944
Detroit, Michigan
Skin-O-Meter: Brief Nudity

Her voice has triggered untold millions of eargasms. Her big, big eyes spill over with pleading and promise. Her angular, thin body constricts with the wiry musculature of the marathon-humping sexual athlete. She is wrapped in an ebony sheen of black and beautiful soul. Here and there, in paparazzi shots and on variety-show guest spots, she has shared snippets of nipple and a nates sashay. Supreme diva Diana Ross has made a home for herself in the libidinal subconscious of every man over forty in the world. She's a prime fixture at wet-dream central, and she's done so with only one flash of onscreen flesh. See what so many of us have so long imagined in *Mahogany* (1975).

SKIN-fining Moment:

Mahogany (1:25) Diana shows her supremely teeny ta-ta's one at a time. We see lefty through the side of her dress, then righty when she puts on a robe.

See Her Naked In:

Mahogany (1975) Breasts

Isabella Rossellini

Born: June 18, 1952
Rome, Italy
Skin-O-Meter: Great Nudity

Famous for being the pleasing product of actress eyeful Ingrid Bergman and Italian film director Roberto Rossellini and for her magnificent mug and modeling career, skin aficionados know the alluring Isabella Rossellini breast as the tormented, touched-in-the-head torch chanteuse "Dorothy Vallens" in David Lynch's bizarro film *Blue Velvet* (1986). At her best undressed, wearing only a fright wig and a ferocious amount of furburgerage, Rossellini was the complete opposite of frightening. Thanks to the ever-free flesh

---

> **MR. SKIN'S TOP TEN**
>
> **Most Skin-famous Body Doubles**
> . . . Sleight-of-gland
>
> 10. NOT Maureen O'Sullivan's naked bod in *Tarzan and His Mate* (1934)
>
> 9. NOT Britt Ekland's buns in *The Wickerman* (1973) (0:58)
>
> 8. NOT Andie MacDowell's buns in *Object of Beauty* (1991)
>
> 7. NOT Marisa Tomei's breasts in *Slums of Beverly Hills* (1998)
>
> 6. NOT Kim Richards's breasts in *Tuff Turf* (1984) (1:29)
>
> 5. NOT Jennifer Connelly's double-dildoed buns in *Requiem for a Dream* (2000) (1:31)
>
> 4. NOT Teri Copley's naked bod in *Down the Drain* (1990) (0:32)
>
> 3. NOT Angie Dickinson's full-frontal in *Dressed to Kill* (1980) (0:02)
>
> 2. NOT Brooke Shields's naked bod in *The Blue Lagoon* (1980) (0:27)
>
> **1. NOT Isabella Rossellini's buns in *Death Becomes Her* (1992) (1:20) *The body double was a then-unknown Catherine Bell**

---

flashing of her European ancestry, Isabella continued to be a skintastic suck-cess, baring her rosy-nipped bitty B-cups in films such as *Dames Galantes* (1990) and *The Innocent* (1993). Vixenly vicious in her skindeavors yet always gorgeous and glamorous, it's no wonder that directors David Lynch and (former husband) Martin Scorsese found this marvelous Mediterranean mama to be their main monkey-spanking muse.

SKIN-fining Moment:

Blue Velvet (1:40) Shocking (and shockingly hot) full-frontal on Kyle MacLachlan's porch walking like a zombie.

See Her Naked In:

The Innocent (1993) Breasts
Death Becomes Her (1992) Body Double— Buns
Dames Galantes (1990) RB
Blue Velvet (1986) FFN, Buns

Katharine Ross

Born: January 29, 1940
Hollywood, California
Skin-O-Meter: Brief Nudity

A whole generation graduated from girls to women once they saw Katherine Ross as elegant beauty Elaine Robinson in *The Graduate* (1967). The role made her a star, but Katherine's next roles were just window dressing in films like *Butch Cassidy and the Sundance Kid* (1969). Fortunately, this inspired the dark beauty to head overseas for *Le Hasard et la violence* (1974), where Katherine combined a gritty role with nude footage of her in her prime. Then she came back to America to prove that plastics really were the future in *The Stepford Wives* (1975). Katherine was equally sexy as both a scantily clad housewife and as a huge-breasted replacement model. Ross went boss again in *The Betsy* (1978), in which guys started tripping once her infant got to sipping. (She was also featured in the instructive 1987 video *Breastfeeding Your Baby: A Mother's Guide*.) Sadly, the selective Ms. Ross—who's aged magnificently— wasn't interested in stripping onstage as Mrs. Robinson in the recent stage version of her breakthrough film.

SKIN-fining Moment:

The Betsy (1:05) A meager tenth of Katherine's nipple appears for about a tenth of a second while she breast-feeds a baby. Move your head, kid!

See Her Naked In:

The Betsy (1978) LB
Le Hasard et la Violence (1974) RB
They Only Kill Their Masters (1972) RB, Buns

Tracey Ross

Born: February 27, 1959
Brooklyn, New York
Skin-O-Meter: Great Nudity

The soap operas are a demanding proving ground for starlets of note who hope to become actresses of acclaim. Back in the mid-1980s, an ambitious dreamer with creamy brown skin, thick candied lips, eyes that filled with flashes of passion, hunger, cunning, and kindness appeared as out of nowhere as Diana Douglas on the ABC hyper-drama *Ryan's Hope* and established herself as the most-promising African American lady thespian ever to grace that show. Not for nothing had Tracey Ross been named *Star Search*'s first $100,000 Model Spokesperson. The Ross promise was fulfilled to a degree beyond Ryan's wildest hope during Tracey's flesh-flashing frenzy in *Small Time* (1998), an orgy of skin that incorporated Hershey-tipped breasts, a brief burst of bush, and buns wafting through the air as their owner is held aloft for a standup humping.

SKIN-fining Moment:

Small Time (0:37) A few nice shots of Tracey's sweaty stack while she sucks down a bit of Booger Sugar.

See Her Naked In:

Unconditional Love (1999) Breasts
Small Time (1998) Breasts, Bush, Buns
Best Defense (1984) Breasts

Yolonda Ross

Omaha, Nebraska
Skin-O-Meter: Brief Nudity

With only a handful of roles, Yolonda Ross has proven herself to be one of the most versatile young actresses around. And she's proven herself to be several handfuls with her nude scene in *Stranger Inside* (2001), an acclaimed women's prison flick that begins with a traditional strip-and-shower scene. Catfight fans will be happy with where the plot goes from there, even though it's a pretty serious film. Yolonda's yams have pretty much stayed hidden in subsequent parts, but she's set up for a long career of playing unforgettable gals.

SKIN-fining Moment:

Stranger Inside (0:04) You'll be no Stranger to Yolanda's full-frontally naked form after watching her show it all as she preps for a strip search. It's great, even if we don't get to see Inside.

See Her Naked In:

Stranger Inside (2001) FFN

Cynthia Rothrock

Born: March 8, 1957
Delaware
Skin-O-Meter: Brief Nudity

Powerful and with a body benefiting from a lifetime of rigorous physical training, blonde and buxom Cynthia Rothrock belies the forbidding butch image of the female athlete. Since the tender age of thirteen, Rothrock has been mastering the martial arts of the Orient, at one point going five years straight as undefeated Kickboxing/Weapons Lady Champion. Of course, it's hard to make a legitimate living cracking skulls. In 1985 Cynthia turned to chop-suey cinema, traveling to Hong Kong to appear in her first karate caper flick, *Yes, Madam!* (1995). Rothrock's reign of victory has extended for forty-five-plus action movies. In a tribute to her pull as a puncher and a kicker, the furious-fisted star has kept her battling garb intact in all but one of her roles. A long make-out scene highlights *Sworn to Justice* (1996), affording Cynthia a quick profile in boobage.

SKIN-fining Moment:

Sworn to Justice (0:49) It's a brief look at Cynthia's Rothrocks (in poor lighting)—but due to her proclivity for remaining fully-clothed on film, we'll take it!

See Her Naked In:

Sworn to Justice (1996) RB

Myriem Roussel

Born: February 26, 1962
Rabat, Morocco
Skin-O-Meter: Hall of Fame

Jean-Luc Godard has a rep for uncovering many alluring actresses, but we'd like to extend an extra hearty *merci* to the director for unearthing (and disrobing) Moroccan lovely Myriem Roussel. He's featured her in several of his films, which are often packed with nudity and suffused with sexuality. Get a load of Myriem in *Hail Mary* (1985), in which she played the Holy Mother as a gas-station attendant. Myriem dropped trou to reveal the hottest bush in Bethlehem—and then some. Her full-frontal scenes in *Passion* (1982) are also worth a lingering look.

SKIN-fining Moment:

Passion (0:41) Myriem sits atop the stage naked to all the world, brushing her hair all sexy-like.

See Her Naked In:

Die Venusfalle (1988) Bush
La Monaca di Monza (1986) Breasts, Bush
Bleu comme l'enfer (1986) Breasts, Buns
Hail Mary (1985) FFN, Buns
Tristesse et beaute (1985) Breasts, Bush, Buns
Passion (1982) Breasts, Bush, Buns

Victoria Rowell

Born: May 10, 1960
Portland, Maine
Skin-O-Meter: Brief Nudity

You've seen black and beautiful Victoria Rowell everywhere. She's popped up in everything from *The Distinguished Gentleman* (1992) to *Dumb & Dumber* (1994) to *Barb Wire* (1996). She's that hot yet down-to-Earth chick whose milky-soft skin seems to glow from within. Victoria began training as a ballerina at a very early age, eventually dancing with the American Ballet Theater II. And you thought legs like those came out of nowhere? It was a long, hard road to the movies for Victoria, who spent eighteen years in foster care. The big-hearted babe gave back to the community when she founded the Rowell Foster Children's Fine Arts Scholarship Fund, which provides ballet training for foster kids. Rowell made her film debut in the Bill Cosby debacle *Leonard Part 6* (1987), but just a few years later her beautiful eyes and bewitching smile brought her fame as Drusilla on *The Young and the Restless*. Parts in other films began pouring in, but it wasn't until *Dr. Hugo* (1998) (also known as *Eve's Bayou*) that Victoria finally gave the world what it had long been waiting for: a peek at one of her perky peaks. Here's hoping that Victoria doesn't make us wait so long for another journey across her chest Alps.

SKIN-fining Moment:

Dr. Hugo (0:07) A little slipple of her left nipple when a lucky doc performs an examination of her chest.

See Her Naked In:

Dr. Hugo (1998) LB

Misty Rowe

Born: June 1, 1952
San Gabriel, California
Skin-O-Meter: Great Nudity

Skin scouts who grew up during the 1970s feel a twang of nostalgia to this day when the strains of a fiddle and a steel guitar remind them of *Hee Haw*. It wasn't the country music or the rapid-fire one-liners that kept the skin sprouts popping up in front of the TV every week for the *Hee Haw* ritual. We were there for the Hee Haw Honeys. These comely corn-pone chicks twisted their down-home hips into skintight Daisy Dukes and hog-tied their bursting barnyard hooters in cropped and knotted gingham blouses. The most memorable of the Honeys was platinum blonde Misty Rowe. Misty's resemblance to a young and soft Marilyn Monroe won her the title role in a Marilyn bio pic, *Good-bye, Norma Jean* (1975), in which Misty freed her young and soft chesty chickadees from their holsters and carried them just as natural and high and flighty as she might please.

SKIN-fining Moment:

Goodbye, Norma Jean (0:59) Topless Misty shows her Hee-Haws during a photo shoot.

See Her Naked In:

National Lampoon's Class Reunion (1982) Breasts
Goodbye, Norma Jean (1975) Breasts
Hitchhikers (1971) Breasts

Paige Rowland

Born: May 27, 1967
Greenwood, South Carolina
Skin-O-Meter: Brief Nudity

Equally adept at playing blonde or brunette, and heart-haltingly hot in either hue, transplanted Southern belle Paige Rowland has been lauded as a soap-opera performer of the week for her nuanced, anguished, and outright alluring portrayal of Kit Montgomery Fisher on daytime mainstay *All My Children*. Prior to tackling the role of Kit—a spunky but troubled prison graduate trying to carve out a life of love and dignity in the outside world—Paige provided a pivotal turn on the equally revered soap *Days of Our Lives*. With all that drama in her professional life, it's a wonder that rousing Rowland is able to maintain her marriage, her Christian faith, and her production company. Watch for Paige's self-scripted historical romance *Theodosia* coming soon, God willing.

SKIN-fining Moment:

Lady in the Box Paige plays the Lady in the Bath. Her right nip makes brief, bubblicious cameos.

See Her Naked In:

Lady in the Box (2001) RB

Michelle Ruben

Born: September 15, 1970
Phoenix, Arizona
Skin-O-Meter: Brief Nudity

When you have a body like Michelle Ruben, it's only natural that the first film you're cast in is an erotic explosion like *The Story of O: Untold Pleasures* (2001). Michelle's outlandish curves and pouty lips have caused many an O in their day—especially for viewers of *Son of the Beach*, who never got to read the rolling credits in favor of Michelle's recurring distraction as the string biniki-clad Wrap-up Girl. Michelle's mams were on hand for Cuba Gooding Jr.'s mystifying career choice *Boat Trip* (2002). Michelle and the other members of the "Swedish suntanning team" were a few of the redeeming/jiggling virtues of the film and kept viewers swabbing the deck. Michelle crossed over into the mainstream, kind of, with *Confidence* (2003), in an uncredited—but anatomically incredible—role as an exotic dancer.

SKIN-fining Moment:

Boat Trip (0:39) Brief bombers as camera pans across a room packed with prime pretties to Michelle. Then she starts the topless jumping jacks.

See Her Naked In:

Confidence (2003) Breasts
Boat Trip (2002) Breasts

TeleVisions:

Six Feet Under Breasts, Thong
Son of the Beach Thong

Jennifer Rubin

Born: November 11, 1962
Phoenix, Arizona
Skin-O-Meter: Great Nudity

More former fashion models should follow the revealing career curve of lovely Jennifer Rubin. A brunette of the aching-with-longing variety, Rubin's face is accessorized by soft, sex-swollen lips. Her warm, brown eyes reflect pools of molten passion deep enough to drown in. Her body is long, tawny, and toned, as befits the hot lights of the runway. Her breasts? Double handfuls of billowing nirvana topped by a pair of the most active stand-up nipples ever captured by the leering lens. The miracle is how often and to what lengths those breasts have been captured. Expect top-shelf beauty and the leisure in which to savor it from Jennifer's titles. Two particular favorites that showcase her two particular favorites are *Saints and Sinners* (1996) and *A Woman, Her Man and Her Futon* (1992).

SKIN-fining Moment:

Bitter Harvest (0:36) Frequent visits from Jennifer Rubin's rackage as she messes around with a Baldwin and a bathrobe.

See Her Naked In:

Saints and Sinners (1996) Breasts
Deceptions II: Edge of Deception (1995) Breasts
Stranger by Night (1994) Breasts
Red Scorpion 2 (1994) Breasts
Playmaker (1994) Breasts, Bush
Bitter Harvest (1993) Breasts
The Fear Inside (1992) Breasts
A Woman, Her Men and Her Futon (1992) Breasts
Delusion (1991) Breasts
Blueberry Hill (1988) LB

Sara Rue

Born: January 26, 1979
New York, New York
Skin-O-Meter: Great Nudity

Early in her career, full-bodied bombshell Sara Rue played second fiddle to leaner leading ladies like model-perfect co-star Leslie Bibb on the WB's cult teen series *Popular* and boby-boned babe Kate Beckinsale in the blockbuster *Pearl Harbor* (2001). Today, ABC execs are confident that the superhumanly stacked Sara is woman enough to carry a captivating tune all on her own in the comedy *Less Than Perfect.* Fiery, feisty, and fun-fun-funny, Sara's weekly helping of mega-sized sweetness is stealing hearts and steeling hard-ons across America. But Sara is not always full of sugar and spice and everything nice. Those who'd like to see this good girl get down are in for a Rue-d awakening by her titanically tit-ilating turn in the Stevie Nicks-skinspired comedy *Gypsy 83* (2001). Miss this scene and you'll Rue it for the rest of your life! We at Skin Central are pants-poppingly pleased to welcome Sara and her more-than-mammoth mam baring to the biggest of the big time!

SKIN-fining Moment:

Gypsy 83 (1:00) Sumptuously sizable, super-mega-ultra-stacked Sara shows off how she's More Than Perfect by busting out her bone-popping, jaw-droppingly huge, udderly all-natural Hindenburgs for a horny hooter-hunting fellow who gets to enjoy her humungous heaps hands-first.

See Her Naked In:

Gypsy 83 (2001) Breasts

Jennifer Runyon

Born: April 1, 1960
Chicago, Illinois
Skin-O-Meter: Brief Nudity

Jennifer Runyon cut her teeth on TV fare such as *The Fall Guy, Charles in Charge,* and *Quantum Leap,* but she's best known to fans of '80s comedy as the incredibly hot student body whom Bill Murray tests for clairvoyant ability in the beginning of *Ghostbusters* (1984). Jen's most titillatingly taunting moment on film comes in the tits-n-zits comedy *Up the Creek* (1984), in which a bunch of misfits took part in a white-water-rafting race where the only white-water that counted was the gallons that wound up on the girls' wet T-shirts. Jennifer finally delivered the skinage in the shoot-em-up flick *Killing Streets* (1991), in which she finally revealed the rosy-nipped chest bombs we've long suspected her of smuggling. Jennifer seemed to disappear after her appearance in *Carnosaur* (1993), but skineastes everywhere eagerly await this bodacious blonde's return!

SKIN-fining Moment:

Killing Streets (1:01) Quick casabas when she's getting slipped the salami in the sack.

See Her Naked In:

Killing Streets (1991) Breasts
Till Death Do Us Part (1991) Body Double—Breasts, Thong

Betsy Russell

Born: September 6, 1964
San Diego, California
Skin-O-Meter: Great Nudity

She's not a household name, but Betsy Russell is a legendary figure to fans of film nudity. Her topless horse-riding scene in the teen sex comedy *Private School* (1983) got plenty of crotches bouncing. Betsy then took on the role of ass-kicking former prostitute Angel, formerly played by Donna Wilkes, turning in a shamelessly sexy performance in *Avenging Angel* (1985). Betsy's boobies were once again out of her blouse in *Out of Control* (1984), and you'll never see a sexier *Tomboy* (1985) than Betsy in the title role. She even went semi-legit in the tawdry TV movie *Roxanne: The Prize Pulitzer* (1989), but now Betsy only shows up in the very occasional small film.

SKIN-fining Moment:

Private School (0:19) Betsy's bouncing boobs steal the show as she discovers the joys of topless horseback riding!

See Her Naked In:

Delta Heat (1992) RB, Buns
Tomboy (1985) Breasts
Out of Control (1984) Breasts, Buns
Private School (1983) FFN, Buns

Jane Russell

Born: June 21, 1921
Bemidji, Minnesota
Skin-O-Meter: Never Nude

For as long as most moviegoers can remember, Jane Russell's name has been synonymous with the word "bombshell." It's no wonder, as the brunette-tressed beauty gained her fame in no small part due to the twin towers adorning her über-curvaceous frame. Funny thing, though—those fame-making funbags were deemed so scandalous for their time that the release of her debut role in Howard Hughes's burlesque western *The Outlaw* (1943) was delayed not once but twice. The film finally gained widespread release in 1946 and was an immediate smash, natch. Russell's talents went beyond the mere corporeal—she was a gifted comedienne to be sure—but her acting skills were mostly underutilized, barring standout roles in the saucy comedies *Gentlemen Prefer Blondes* (1953), alongside fellow sex goddess Marilyn Monroe, *Gentlemen Marry Brunettes* (1955), and her titular role in *The Revolt of Mamie Stover* (1956). Her career may have simmered down after the early '60s, but to this day, the image of Jane in a low-cut prairie-girl top makes men hanker for a tumble in the hayloft.

SKIN-fining Moment:

The Outlaw (0:46) Vintage volcano of voluptuousness Jane bends down and creams the screen with the cleavage between her Texas-sized two-guns as she checks on Billy the Kid.

Keri Russell

Born: March 23, 1976
Fountain Valley, California
Skin-O-Meter: Brief Nudity

Though her career's been somewhat quiet of late, Mouseketeer turned teen drama queen Keri Russell wasted no time rising to fame in the lead role on the WB's fan favorite *Felicity*. Sadly, skin watchers were out of luck with the curly haired cupcake's straight-laced role as a love-sick, collegiate Bridget Jones type. She wasn't always so skingy, though. Before Keri hit it big on the flesh-restrictive TV airwaves, she took a topless romp in the low-budget teen sex comedy *Eight Days a Week* (1997). Whereas Felicity bored us with hippie skirts and long sleeves, her *Eight Days* character treated viewers to a pulse-pounding peek at her tan bod clad only in white cotton panties. For more racy, pre-WB thrills, check her out in *The Babysitter's Seduction* (1996), a creepy and kinky murder mystery featuring captivating Keri as the sitter in question. Now if only someone could seduce Keri into returning to her early days and nudie ways.

SKIN-fining Moment:

Eight Days a Week (0:01) Keri cavorts in a lawn sprinkler during the opening credits while wearing only the skimpiest white T-shirt. A few squirts in and we get a niptastic see-through view of her little Felicititties.

See Her Naked In:

Eight Days a Week (1997) Breasts

Theresa Russell

Born: March 20, 1957
San Diego, California
Skin-O-Meter: Hall of Fame

A rare combination of talent and tits, Theresa Russell is a skinophile's dream come true. A former teen model, Theresa dropped out of high school to devote herself to her craft. She made her film debut in Elia Kazan's *The Tycoon* (1976) and played opposite Dustin Hoffman in *Straight Time* (1978). Rather than shy away from risky, sexually tinged material, Theresa embraced it with her roles in *Bad Timing: A Sensual Obsession* (1980), *Aria* (1988), *The Razor's Edge* (1984), and *Insignificance* (1985). While it's hard to narrow down her finest skinematic moment—simply because there have been so many— you can't go wrong watching the tight-tushed thesp bare all in *Black Widow* (1987) or in the titular role in *Whore* (1991).

SKIN-fining Moment:

Bad Timing: A Sensual Obsession (0:31) The good news: we see various views of Theresa's full-frontal nudity. The bad news: she's having sex with the also naked Art Garfunkel.

See Her Naked In:

Luckytown Blues (2000) Breasts
Wild Things (1998) Breasts, Buns
Public Enemies (1996) Breasts
Grave Indiscretion (1995) FFN
Hotel Paradise (1995) Breasts, Bush, Buns
Trade Off (1995) Breasts
The Spy Within (1994) Breasts
Whore (1991) Breasts, Buns
Cold Heaven (1990) Breasts
Impulse (1990) LB
Black Widow (1987) FFN, Buns
Eureka (1983) FFN, Buns
Bad Timing: A Sensual Obsession (1980) FFN
Straight Time (1978) Body Double—LB

Carmen Russo

Born: October 3, 1959
Genoa, Italy
Skin-O-Meter: Great Nudity

Curvy Carmen Russo raised Italian stick stallions in the '80s with her hugely skinful stint in cinema.

Frequently naughty and naked, this generously jugged Genoan displayed her al dente tortellinis with scrumptious results in skintastic flicks such as *Patrick Still Lives* (1980), *Les Filles de madame Claude* (1980), and *Mia moglie torna a scuola* (1981). *Grazzi* to this former Miss Teenage Italy of 1972 for coming through with the goods in her short but skintilating career. With more than six nude-tastic flicks to choose from, take a gander at this Italian eyeful's fly-filling films today.

SKIN-fining Moment:

Ring of Darkness (0:03) Carmen carouses topless with some Speedo dude in a spooky outdoor setting.

See Her Naked In:

Amiche mie (1982) Breasts, Thong
Mia moglie torna a scuola (1981) FFN, Buns
Infermiera nella corsia dei militari (1980) Breasts, Bush, Buns
Patrick Still Lives (1980) FFN, Buns
Le Porno killers (1980) FFN, Buns
Les Filles de madame Claude (1980) FFN, Buns
Ring of Darkness (1979) Breasts

Rene Russo

Born: February 17, 1954
Burbank, California
Skin-O-Meter: Great Nudity

In a classic rock-chick-to-riches story, strikingly tall blonde Rene Russo was plucked out of a crowd of hyperventilating nubiles at the age of seventeen at a Rolling Stones concert and placed on the path to modeling superstardom. Although she became one of the defining mannequins of the 1970s, young beauty Rene was too brainy to be satisfied by merely standing around looking perfectly amazing. She wanted to look amazing while talking and emoting at the same time, so she set her sights on a movie career. She kept

those sights set for a long time and didn't hit the main stage until she'd passed forty. Let us all praise perseverance and also the exquisitely preserved sights of Rene Russo. *The Thomas Crown Affair* (1999) is a treat for feasting eyes. Topless and sunbathing, Russo's high-beam nipples outshine the blinding orb in the sky. Don't stare too long, because you want to be able to see Rene's ride-'em-cowgirl love tussle with Pierce Brosnan.

SKIN-fining Moment:

The Thomas Crown Affair (1:01) Rene reveals her rack several times during this long, sweaty, drunken sex sequence with Brosnan. Pierce Brosnan.

See Her Naked In:

The Thomas Crown Affair (1999) Breasts

Kelly Rutherford

Born: November 6, 1968
Elizabethtown, Kentucky
Skin-O-Meter: Brief Nudity

Kelly Rutherford has been an international star since 1989, when her short-lived soaper *Generations* somehow became a massive hit in Turkey. This pale blonde beauty remains a Turkish delight to her fans at home, too, most notoriously for her role as Dixie Cousins on the hipster western TV show *The Adventures of Brisco County Jr.* There's also been a short stint on *Melrose Place* and a sexy spy turn on the recent TV show *Threat Matrix*. Kelly's also taken the occasional break from TV to get sexy on the big screen, most notably in *Scream 3* (2000) and *Angels Don't Sleep Here* (2000), in which Kelly's smallish Rutherfords can finally be glimpsed amongst some hot simulated sex.

SKIN-fining Moment:

Angels Don't Sleep Here (0:51) Kelly's kabobbles make a brief appearance as she and her bedmate canoodle.

See Her Naked In:

Angels Don't Sleep Here (2000) Breasts

Amanda Ryan

UK
Skin-O-Meter: Great Nudity

Amanda Ryan was just another young British starlet until *Metroland* (1997), when she used all of her talent—and every inch of her luscious Brit bod—to be the ultimate lure from monogamy. Her devastating sexuality got another star turn that same year on the cable anthology series *The Hunger*, where plenty of guys got goofy over Amanda's gothy presence. She's since concentrated on working in UK television, but Amanda can still steal the occasional big-screen scene, as seen by her period outfits in *Elizabeth* (1998).

SKIN-fining Moment:

Metroland (1:22) Amanda shows her collection of B's as she perkily waits in bed for some Christian Bale-banging.

See Her Naked In:

Elizabeth (1998) Breasts
Metroland (1997) FFN, Buns

TeleVisions:

The Hunger Breasts, Thong

Blanchard Ryan

Boston, Massachusetts
Skin-O-Meter: Brief Nudity

Mr. Skin knows why sharks hunger for our women. Blanchard Ryan is the newest in a proud line of naked (master) bait that have tempted the man-eaters of the sea. She's this millennium's *Jaws* morsel, only times have changed and nudity in a mainstream movie doesn't have to be silhouetted. Blanchy opens *Open Water* (2004) with a splash of full-frontal nudity that will make you afraid to go to the movies again,

because how can even the most sexciting productions live up to her udderly unexpected flesh-fest? Before this summer thriller sent her to the top of the marquee, Blanchard had been toiling in obscurity, literally playing an "Unknown" in *All My Children* but showing promise in provocatively titled productions such as *Remembering Sex* (1998). One thing's for certain, after seeing Blanchard's ripe, rich, round mangoes and delicious dark patch in *Open Water*, she'll be remembered much more fondly than as a mere seafood-for-seafood.

SKIN-fining Moment:

Open Water (0:10) Blonde beauty Blanchard Ryan lies next to her hubby in bed with both of her bouyant, all-natural Great Whites bobbling atop the sheets in plain sight. Blanch then follows up with a fuzztastic blast of full frontal when she reaches over to turn out the light. That'll raise a dorsal fin—in your pants!

See Her Naked In:

Open Water (2003) FFN

Marisa Ryan

Born: November 20, 1974
New York, New York
Skin-O-Meter: Great Nudity

Television is a fertile breeding ground for little ladies who need to be liberated into leading ladies who are willing to expose their fertile breeding mounds. In the textbook case of button-nose blonde Marisa Ryan, yesteryear's child star has once again become yesterday's exposed rear end. Skinthusiasts who blossomed into their vocation at a young age will remember responding to Marisa's girl-next-door (only prettier) appeal when she played the teenage daughter to *Major Dad*. Papa's little girl grew up to be plush and protuberant in all the right places, a fact she puts to cinematic proof in *Slaves to the*

Undergound (1997). This grunge-rock musical keys on Marisa's lesbie-friendly, clothing-free fondling with randy rocker Molly Gross. *Trash* (1999) has a throwaway up-from-under view of Marisa's heaving breast. Nothing garbage about it.

SKIN-fining Moment:

Slaves to the Underground (0:28) Marissa's rack and rump goes clit-to-clit with dark-haired Molly Gross while footage of their band jamming is intercut with the good stuff.

See Her Naked In:

Trash (1999) LB
With or Without You (1998) Breasts, Buns
Slaves to the Underground (1997) Breasts, Buns

Meg Ryan

Born: November 19, 1961
Fairfield, Connecticut
Skin-O-Meter: Great Nudity

Meg Ryan is the ultimate hot girl next door who isn't averse to taking her top off. For three years she was on *As the World Turns* as one of the legion of oversexed vixens on daytime TV. Meg's world turned to film . . . and the opportunity to show off some of that lily-white skin. In *The Presidio* (1988), her flopping handfuls dangled in a sex scene with Mark Harmon. *When Harry Met Sally* (1989) got audiences in the mood, with her gonad-shaking fake orgasm at Katz's Deli. You want a schmear with that? Meg went on to light Val Kilmer's fire with a topless scene in *The Doors* (1991). To get a boner, witness Meg's display of flesh in *Flesh and Bone* (1993). It worked for co-star and husband Dennis Quaid—and yet he chose to end his marriage to America's Sweethard-on. Now that Russell Crowe's hitched, Meg's single and likes to mingle. Genitalmen, start your engines.

SKIN-fining Moment:

In the Cut (1:06) Meg's pegs and pert forty-something fanny as she gets undressed and slides into bed with Mark Ruffalo. And look close—Sally shows Hairy!

See Her Naked In:

In the Cut (2003) FFN, Buns
Flesh and Bone (1993) RB
The Doors (1991) RB
The Presidio (1988) RB
D.O.A. (1988) RB
Promised Land (1988) LB

Tracy Ryan

Born: March 14, 1972
Kitchener, Ontario, Canada
Skin-O-Meter: Great Nudity

Tremendously tantalizing Tracy Ryan isn't just one of the fastest-rising starlets in the realm of high-octane, minimal-clothing, direct-to-video entertainment, she's one of the most beguilingly beautiful lovelies to light up screens of any type in some time. Over the past few years, this hard-bodied blonde (who's also soft and round in *all* the right places) has established herself as a B-movie queen with A-plus talent and sex appeal to spare in dozens of fun, frisky features that never skimp on scintillating heat and full-body contact. And not only is Tracy an extraordinary performer in outrageously exciting good-time movies such as *Girl for Girl* (2000) and *The Seduction of Maxine* (2001), she's generous with the gifts nature bestowed upon her, regularly disrobing to display her impossibly perfect, shockingly home-grown attributes. Tracy, we love you!

SKIN-fining Moment:

Web of Seduction (1:11) After an FFN-and-fanny-revealing peel-down, Tracy gets all friendly with her own

fingers in a window while a guy ogles across the way.

See Her Naked In:

Forbidden (2002) FFN
The Seduction of Maxine (2001) Breasts
Close Enough to Touch (2001) Breasts, Buns
Tender is the Heart (2001) Breasts
Hollywood Sex Fantasy (2001) FFN, Buns
Instinct to Kill (2001) Breasts, Buns
Girl for Girl (2000) FFN
Fast Lane to Malibu (2000) FFN, Buns
Hot Club California (1999) FFN, Buns
Web of Seduction (1999) FFN, Buns
Numerous Adult Movies

Lisa Ryder

Born: October 26, 1970
Edmonton, Alberta, Canada
Skin-O-Meter: Brief Nudity

Theater geek turned sci-fi seductress Lisa Ryder got her start acting in small-time productions with a theater group she helped form in wintry Toronto. Bit parts on TV shows such as *Kung Fu: The Legend Continues* (1993) and *Earth: Final Conflict* (1997) followed. Her cult following started to blossom when she landed the role of lady cop Tracey Vetter on the short-lived series *Forever Knight*. The lithe, cat-eyed blonde hit her stride playing the kick-ass space bitch Beka Valentine on *Gene Roddenberry's Andromeda* alongside former *Hercules* stud Kevin Sorbo. She's now a way-sexy fixture of the syndicated sci-fi set, a role we hope she expands to less, shall we say, restrictive pastures. For a funny, frisky take on a topless scene, check her out in *Jason X* (2001). Her sexy cyborg character Kay-Em 14 bares boob, detachable nipples and all.

SKIN-fining Moment:

Jason X (0:28) Lisa, playing an android, bares her robo-rack and all is fine and mammary until her nipples slide

off and roll across the floor. Damn tit-nology.

See Her Naked In:

Jason X (2001) Breasts

Winona Ryder

Born: October 29, 1971
Winona, Minnesota
Skin-O-Meter: Brief Nudity

Winona Ryder . . . how true. Mr. Skin would love to ride this five-foot-four-inch 34-22-34 power-house. Winona is a mystery girl: she's actually a blonde who's been dying her hair black since age eleven and also tries to hide her humongous hooters—no such luck on the latter count. Ever since debuting in *Lucus* (1986), audiences have discerned something trying to burst out from her buttoned blouse. From titty holsters in *Great Balls of Fire* (1989), goth goodies in *Edward Scissorhands* (1990), and a see-through chemise in *Dracula* (1992) to a side of booby meat served briefly in *The House of Spirits* (1993) and wet T-shirt wonder in *Girl, Interrupted* (1999), Winona has yet to uncork her giant jugs. Then *Autumn in New York* (2000) proved the season to be sleazing. In a bedroom tryst with *American Gigolo* Richard Gere, her rosy bud slipped out from its silk vase top for a quick glimpse of Winona's blooming boobies. Savor the bouquet.

SKIN-fining Moment:

Autumn in New York (1:23) After years of smuggling those booming balloons under her shirt, the pink-tip of Winnie's right rounder peeks out of her hard-working nightgown.

See Her Naked In:

Autumn in New York (2000) Nip Slip RB

S

Sable

Born: August 8, 1967
Jacksonville, Florida
Skin-O-Meter: Great Nudity

To Rena Mero—better known by her ex-World Wrestling Entertainment moniker Sable—clotheslines aren't for laundry, they're for knocking down opponents. The high-haired, big-boobed blonde has ridden wrestling's resurgence better than any other biceps-busting babe of the ring, so when she filed a $110 million breach-of-contract suit against the WWE because it wanted her to expose her breasts, it looked like she was biting the hand that was feeding her. Her supposed modesty was thankfully short lived. Just take a gander at her great home video extravaganza *Sable Unleashed* (1997). You may not see a softer side of Sable, but you'll certainly see skin. But for the best view of this titanic athlete's toweringly awesome T&A, check out the 2003 thriller *The Final Victim*, in which Sable showered long and lustfully in a well-lit scene that's guaranteed to turn the Hulk Hogan in your pants into a raging Andre the Giant.

SKIN-fining Moment:

The Final Victim Sable goes from WWE to T&A. You'll put yourself in a choke-hold.

See Her Naked In:

The Final Victim (2003) Breasts, Buns

Melissa Sagemiller

Born: June 1, 1974
Washington, DC
Skin-O-Meter: Brief Nudity

Discovered by the Ford Modeling Agency at fifteen, Melissa Sagemiller was born to flaunt her flawless face and fantastic frame. After years of catwalk prowling, this pretty pussy took her first role in the lukewarm flick *Get Over It* (2001). Over her own apparent anonymity, Mel added some much-needed heat to *Soul Survivors* (2001). Seen only from behind, Mel's topless turn was made all the more steamy by the site of teeny-weenie see-through panties. Equally ass-tastic with better shots of breastage, Melissa showed off her fetching figure in *The Love Object* (2003) and *The Clearing* (2004). While scrumptious in the gender-bending comedy *Sorority Boys* (2002), this co-ed cutie used a body double for her steamy shower scenes. Regardless, Mr. Skin pledges his allegiance and undying devotion to Ms. Sagemiller in all her skindeavors.

SKIN-fining Moment:

Soul Survivors (0:00) A fleeting side-shot of Melissa's breastage, but the payoff is in the see-thru panties!

See Her Naked In:

Love Object (2003) Breasts, Buns
Sorority Boys (2002) Body Double—Breasts
Soul Survivors (2001) LB

Ludivine Sagnier

Born: July 3, 1979
La Celle-Saint-Cloud, Yvelines, France
Skin-O-Meter: Great Nudity

It's been a while since Hollywood started howling over a French starlet's hooters. Ludivine Sagnier, however, is a breakout talent who's got executives breaking out the Kleenexes. As the mysterious girl of *Swimming Pool* (2003), she got everyone in a little villa—including repressed author Charlotte Rampling—getting all wet and excited. But that's nothing new for Ludivine, whose ludicrously hot bod is best appreciated in *Water Drops on Burning Rocks* (1999). This sexfest featured her in full-frontal French splendor, plus some truly memorable simulated (and kinda kinky) sex. Her scene at a topless beach in *Bon plan* (2000) also got guys popping their tops. Ludivine finally made her American film debut in *Peter Pan* (2003), and, yes, we're all feeling really bad for lusting after Tinkerbell.

SKIN-fining Moment:

Swimming Pool (0:27) Mammoth, tan milk-bombs as she sits talking to Charlotte Rampling outside.

See Her Naked In:

La Petite Lili (2003) FFN, Buns
Swimming Pool (2003) FFN, Buns
Les Frères Hélias (2002) FFN, Buns
La Banquise (2000) Buns

Bon plan (2000) Breasts
Water Drops On Burning Rocks (1999) FFN, Buns

Eva Marie Saint

Born: July 4, 1924
Newark, New Jersey
Skin-O-Meter: Brief Nudity

An etheral and deceptively still pond of blonde, subtle and dramatic actress Eva Marie Saint seemed to effortlessly radiate a simultaneous depth of beauty and familiarity of feature that enabled her to play the perfectly gorgeous girl up the block, such as in her Oscar-winning film debut opposite Marlon Brando in *On the Waterfront* (1954). Another classic Eva Marie Saint role, such as the one she sprung on Cary Grant in Alfred Hitchcock's definitive thriller *North by Northwest* (1959), is as the chance encounter who, aside from being virtuous, courageous, durable, and a triffle cynical, also just so happens to offhandedly possess world-class cheekbones, eyes to tie the glibbest cad's tougue, and a tidy, gravity-defying figure. Eva Marie is the most heavenly Saint in all of Hollywood's paradise dreams.

SKIN-fining Moment:

Loving (0:57) Saint be praised! Eva Marie pivots while yakking with George Segal in the john and we get a rare glimpse of her right chest-divot.

See Her Naked In:

Loving (1970) RB

Theresa Saldana

Born: August 20, 1954
Brooklyn, New York
Skin-O-Meter: Great Nudity

Brooklyn-born beauty Theresa Saldana got her big break as Robert De Niro's sexpot sis in *Raging Bull* (1980). (What bovine in his right mind wouldn't rant over this Italian eyeful's full-figured charms?) Thankfully, right out of the pen tempting Terri bared her bellissimo body during her premier in *Nunzio* (1978). Then she lent her tit-tastic talents to TV, perfecting her Mediterranean magnetism in *Sophia Loren: Her Own Story* (1980), nearly surpassing the real-life Loren with her stellar sex appeal. Going from starlet to harlot, Theresa played a prostitute in the flesh-filled farce *The Night Before* (1988). Mr. Skin was hooked on looking at this dark-eyed dish decked in tit-popping tops and micro minis throughout. Luscious Lady T can still be seen as a mighty MILF on reruns of the series *The Commish*. Any of Theresa's tasty offerings are guaranteed to be delish!

SKIN-fining Moment:

Nunzio Theresa leans in to seduce David Proval and her open robe exposes her sexy Saldamas.

See Her Naked In:

Nunzio (1978) RB

MR. SKIN'S TOP TEN

Flavorite Naked Actresses
. . . Spice racks

10. Toni Basil
 9. Season Hubley
 8. Kasi Lemmons
 7. Saffron Burrows
 6. Rosemarie Lindt
 5. Ginger Lynn Allen
 4. Kristin Minter
 3. Nathalie Baye
 2. Melissa Sagemiller
 1. Jennifer Salt

Jennifer Salt

Born: September 4, 1944
Los Angeles, California
Skin-O-Meter: Brief Nudity

Jiggly jugged Jennifer Salt got her start in the late '60s thriller *Murder à la Mod* (1969). Since then this sweet slice of pie added a dash of much-needed sugar to flicks such as *Brewster McCloud* (1970), *Sisters* (1973), and *It's My Turn* (1980). Jenny certainly took her own turn at stardom as the innocently alluring "Eunice" on the spoof-errific series *Soap*, proving to be a striking suckcess throughout the show's run. Putting her bout with bubbles behind her, today Jennifer writes for the skintastic series *Nip/Tuck*. Whether sizzling in front of the camera or smoldering behind the scenes, Jen has a certain yen for skinema.

SKIN-fining Moment:

Midnight Cowboy (0:31) It's not much, but it is a lightning fast butt flash as Jennifer runs away.

See Her Naked In:

Midnight Cowboy (1969) Breasts, Buns

Candy Samples

Born: April 12, 1940
Kansas City, Missouri
Skin-O-Meter: Great Nudity

Professional blonde sexhibitionist Candy Samples brought a legendarily large pair of lung ornaments into show-biz with her, and then she made them even bigger, so big that you would be tempted to designate them as "fabled," except that filmic evidence exists of their enormity, and fables are imaginary. Set up a viewing of *Prison Girls* (1972) or *Superchick* (1973) and prepare to be floored by the knockout dimensions of Candy's naturally grown knockers. Then, after you put your jaw back in its socket, brace yourself for the enhanced reality of Samples's supersized mega-mams in *Pandora Peaks* (2001). Whoever said "less is more" had a much shallower understanding of the universe than does Candy Samples.

SKIN-fining Moment:

Up! (0:03) Candy's dandy as she wears a mask and punishes Hitler in a sexadelic dungeon. See her sweet mega-sacks fly!

See Her Naked In:

Pandora Peaks (2001) FFN
Best Chest in the West (1984) Breasts
Up! (1976) FFN, Buns
Superchick (1973) Breasts
Prison Girls (1972) FFN, Buns
Numerous Adult Movies

Laura San Giacomo

Born: November 14, 1962
Hoboken, New Jersey
Skin-O-Meter: Never Nude

Laura San Giacomo carries the weight of her awesome talents with poise and class—and a bit too much reserve, as she's yet to let those fat twins out for air. In the history of Hollywood, with its bra-runneth-over starlets, Laura's cleavage looms legendarily extra large. When she finally opens her shirt, the resulting avalanche of boobage may kill us all—but what a way to go. Men first stared pop-eyed at the bountiful act-chest when she was introduced in *Sex, Lies and Videotape* (1989), which skimped on the first part. She went on to play a wisecracking, but not crack-revealing, friend of Julia Roberts in *Pretty Woman* (1990) and has since settled into the sitcom *Just Shoot Me*. TV has been very good to Laura and to her hard-up fans, too, as evident in the made-for-TV movie *The Stand*. In the apocalyptic drama, queen Laura literally does the Devil. While even the Prince of Hardness can't get Laura to exorcise her clothing, she does writhe and wiggle

almost out of her white lacy bra beneath Satan's staff. When she's bad she's the best.

SKIN-fining Moment:

Under Suspicion (0:49) Laura lays Liam Neeson in a fancy bed and leans up several times so we can almost see all of her luscious, ultra-large lacto-lovelies. Unfortunately, it is just "almost."

Aitana Sánchez-Gijón

Born: November 5, 1968
Rome, Italy
Skin-O-Meter: Great Nudity

What do you get when you combine a little pasta sauce with salsa? You get delicious dish Aitana Sánchez-Gijón. This Spanish-Italian eyeful has more than enough form to satisfy your craving for the caliente. Although Aitana's sex-elicious stints Stateside in *A Walk in the Clouds* (1995) and *Love Walked In* (1997) were nicely spicy, this sweet-teated tamale is a more tempting treat in servings from her native lands. Flesh-filled faves such as *Celos* (1999), *La ley de la frontera* (1995), and *Bajarse al moro* (1988) are enough to plump your sausage, but any of this mucha muchacha's movies will leave you with an aftertaste for additional Aitana.

SKIN-fining Moment:

Bajarse al moro (0:21) Aitana divulges her adorable hootage a few times as she tries on a few outfits.

See Her Naked In:

Celos (1999) Breasts, Buns
Yerma (1999) Breasts
Love Walked In (1998) LB
La ley de la frontera (1995) Breasts
La leyenda de Balthasar El Castrado (1995) FFN, Buns
Havanera 1820 (1992) Breasts
Bajarse al moro (1988) FFN

TeleVisions:

La Regenta FFN, Buns

Victoria Sanchez

Born: January 24, 1976
Canary Islands, Spain
Skin-O-Meter: Great Nudity

Victoria Sanchez found a quick way to stand out amongst the sexy female alumnae of MTV's *Undressed*. She sprouted hair as the star of *Wolf Girl* (2001), a humble made-for-cable film that got critical acclaim worthy of an indie. As a beautiful sideshow freak, Victoria managed to show off both her fine acting skills and some impressive nudity—despite both her talent and her body occasionally being covered in extensive make-up. The former Canadian child star also got our pupils rolling with a sexy turn in *Satan's School for Girls* (2000), while her recent regular role on the kiddie show *Tales from the Neverending Story* left us with some neverending erections. But for real grown-up action, check out Sanchez's sizzling sex scene from the cable series *Bliss*.

SKIN-fining Moment:

Blood Moon (1:12) Boobs waking up then looking in the mirror and noticing her hair is gone.

See Her Naked In:

Blood Moon (2001) Breasts

TeleVisions:

Bliss LB

Dominique Sanda

Born: March 11, 1948
Paris, France
Skin-O-Meter: Hall of Fame

French beauty Dominique Sanda was married and divorced by age eighteen. Yes, this busty blonde knew that she could get far on her looks, farther than being some guy's ball and chain—though any guy who sees her wants to jerk his chain and play with his balls. She first worked as a *Vogue* model before director Robert Bresson gave her a starring role in *Une femme douce* (1969). Following that movie, she continued with naked performances in *First Love* (1970) and *The Conformist* (1970). In the latter, she played a young woman who commits suicide when her husband doesn't bang her. Yet she still managed to make this film her skin debut. And things only got hotter from there on out. Next she played a not-so-nice Jewish girl in *The Garden of the Finzi-Continis* (1971) and made Torahs everywhere unroll like salivating tongues thanks to her great nudity. One of her many crowning achievements was the full-frontal flash in Bernando Bertolucci's epic *1900* (1976). Dominique kept her fleshy resumé thick with good references, from *Beyond Good and Evil* (1977) to *A Room in Town* (1982), which was sadly her last lustful close-up. She appeared in *Playboy* at the height of her sexually explicit career in the '70s and continues to work today. Viewers would *wank* her, if only Dominique would let them see her middle-aged mams.

SKIN-fining Moment:

The Garden of the Finzi-Continis (1:13) Chest-pontoons while a guy peeps at her through window.

See Her Naked In:

A Room in Town (1982) Breasts, Bush
Le Voyage en douce (1980) FFN
Cabo Blanco (1980) Breasts, Buns
Beyond Good and Evil (1977) FFN
The Inheritance (1976) FFN
1900 (1976) FFN
Steppenwolf (1974) LB, Bush
Story of a Love Story (1973) Breasts
The Garden of the Finzi-Continis (1971) Breasts
The Conformist (1970) Breasts
First Love (1970) Breasts
Une femme douce (1969) Buns

Stefania Sandrelli

Born: June 5, 1946
Viareggio, Italy
Skin-O-Meter: Hall of Fame

Stefania Sandrelli was only fifteen when she established herself as an international beauty in the arthouse hit *Divorce, Italian Style* (1961). But by the time of the equally successful import *Il Conformista* (1970), Stefania demonstrated a bountiful nudity that proved she wasn't like the other girls—including Sophia Loren, frequently touted as her great rival for Italian hearts, minds, and hard-ons. Stefania was less interested in working outside of Italy, though. She was, however, a lot more adventurous onscreen, as Stefania proved in *The Key* (1983). This film fell just short of hardcore action, and Stefania seemed very enthused to be smashing barriers and raising erections. There's more full frontal in *Una Donna allo specchio* (1984), while Stefania kept her countrymen jamming with more hot nudity in *Jamón, jamón* (1992). That older bod only proved to be sweeter and curvier in *Caramelle* (1995). Stefania's still busty and busy as ever and even made it back to the American art-houses in *Stealing Beauty* (1996).

SKIN-fining Moment:

The Key (0:03) Every last bit of Stefania's stellar body is put on display in this rather bizarre scene, when the old dude poses her under a desk lamp, allowing for plenty of vaginal close-ups . . .

See Her Naked In:

Caramelle (1995) LB, Buns
Jamón, jamón (1992) Buns
D'Annunzio (1985) Breasts, Bush, Buns
Mamma Ebe (1985) FFN
Il Momento magico (1984) LB
L'Attenzione (1984) Breasts, Bush
Una Donna allo specchio (1984) Breasts, Bush, Buns

The Key (1983) FFN, Buns
La Disubbidienza (1981) Breasts
Desideria: La vita interiore (1980) Buns
Dove vai in vacanza (1978) Breasts, Buns
Les Magiciens (1976)
Delitto d'amore (1974) Breasts, Buns
Black Belly of the Tarantula (1972) Breasts, Buns
The Conformist (1970) RB, Buns
L'Amante di Gramigna (1969) Breasts, Buns

Mia Sara

Born: June 19, 1967
Brooklyn, New York
Skin-O-Meter: Hall of Fame

After her screen-stealing romp as the innocently sexy high-school girlfriend in *Ferris Bueller's Day Off* (1986), vampy Mia Sara's career was expected to take off. Fate had other plans, plans that included an extensive list of skin exposure, and the only thing that fate has allowed Sara to take off is her clothing. Mia is cute and quirky. Her big google eyes are complemented by a teasing, taunting smirk of a mouth. The face has remained in a look of perpetual surprise (as if she has just discovered her joy button) mixed with an expression of glazed anticipation (as if she intends to flip that buzz switch again at the first opportunity). Check out her stages of undress and make that same face yourself.

SKIN-fining Moment:

Black Day, Blue Night (0:50) Great looks at Mia's topless mamma-mias when she gets it on with Gil Bellows.

See Her Naked In:

Undertow (1996) Breasts
The Set Up (1995) Breasts
Black Day, Blue Night (1995) FFN, Buns
Timecop (1994) Breasts
Blindsided (1993) RB
Caroline at Midnight (1993) Breasts
Any Man's Death (1989) RB
Apprentice to Murder (1987) Breasts

TeleVisions:

Strangers RB

Susan Sarandon

Born: October 4, 1946
New York, New York
Skin-O-Meter: Hall of Fame

Although her outspoken political beliefs ensure that she will never be conservative radio host Rush Limbaugh's favorite celebrity, odds are that in a blind touch test, actress Susan Sarandon's full, rich rack would rank in any worthy

groper's all-time Bra of Fame. Susan today is a tit-stacked treat for those who appreciate a well-matured hang of hooters and finely aged piece of seat meat. Sarandon's blushing bum in *Twilight* (1998) proves that age is no obstacle to artful arousal. For the sheer power of naïve, stoned lust, few epidermal debuts match the skintastic nudie gymnastics of budding Susan's flicking tips as a milky-white hippie chick in *Joe* (1970). It's the rare creature whose front-and-center features hold up for almost thirty years of big-screen scrutiny.

SKIN-fining Moment:

Atlantic City (0:50) Sexy Susan washes her ample hootage as a horny ol' Burt Lancaster peeps on in.

See Her Naked In:

Twilight (1998) Body Double—RB, Buns
The Celluloid Closet (1996) Breasts
White Palace (1990) Breasts
Sweet Hearts Dance (1988) Breasts
Bull Durham (1988) RB
The Hunger (1983) Breasts
The Tempest (1982) Breasts
Atlantic City (1981) LB
King of the Gypsies (1978) RB
Pretty Baby (1978) Breasts
The Other Side of Midnight (1977) Breasts
Lovin' Molly (1974) RB
Fleur bleue (1971) Breasts
Joe (1970) Breasts, Bush

Leilani Sarelle

Born: September 28, 1966
California,
Skin-O-Meter: Brief Nudity

Few skinophiles will forget the deep, seemingly endless soul kiss long-legged Leilani Sarelle shared with fellow blonde Sharon Stone in the hit erotic thriller *Basic Instinct* (1992). Too bad she hasn't followed through on that early prurient promise. Sure, she's had a few flesh-baring escapades in flicks such

as *The Harvest* (1992), and *Breach of Trust* (1995), but just as her muff-diving lover must have been thinking, we need *more*.

SKIN-fining Moment:

The Harvest (1:19) Leilani provides a hair-fest during some full-frontal fooling around with Miguel Ferrer.

See Her Naked In:

Breach of Trust (1995) Breasts
The Harvest (1993) FFN

Isabel Sarli

Born: July 9, 1935
Concordia, Entre Rios, Argentina
Skin-O-Meter: Great Nudity

Here's a reminder that today's kids didn't invent sex: Isabel Sarli was Miss Argentina in 1955 when she took up an offer from director Armanda Bo to pose nude in the film *El Trueno entre las hojas* (1956). She was the country's first nude actress, and the controversy was accompanied by national acclaim. Isabel went on to make over twenty-eight films with Bo, the great majority of which featured her incredible bod either swimming or showering or both. Isabel even became a talented actress, as seen by a very sexy doffing in *La Diosa impura* (1963). Her talent also fleshed out her legitimacy when the outlandish *Fuego* (1969)—featuring a hot masturbation scene—finally brought her to American art-houses. She retired when Bo died but still gave her fans one last thrill by showing off her aged perfection in *La Dama regresa* (1996)—which translates to *The Lady Comes Back*, just as her fans come again and again.

SKIN-fining Moment:

La Diosa impura (1:08) Isabel bares her boobs for Mr. Artist so he can paint a picture . . . How thoughtful of her!

MR. SKIN'S TOP TEN

Hottest Hookers Onscreen
. . . The whore the bare-ier

10. **Patricia Arquette**
    —*True Romance* (1993)

9. **Jamie Lee Curtis**
    —*Trading Places* (1983)

8. **Nancy Travis**
    —*Married to the Mob* (1988)

7. **Randi Brooks**
    —*Tightrope* (1984)

6. **Vanity**
    —*52 Pick-Up* (1986)

5. **Barbara Hershey**
    —*The Last Temptation of Christ* (1988)

4. **Xavier Hollander**
    —*My Pleasure is my Business* (1974)

3. **Rebecca De Mornay**
    —*Risky Business* (1983)

2. **Elisabeth Shue**
    —*Leaving Las Vegas* (1995)

1. **Susan Sarandon**
    —*Pretty Baby* (1978)

See Her Naked In:

El Sexo y el amor (1973)
Fiebre (1970)
Éxtasis tropical (1969) Breasts
Fuego (1969) Breasts
La Tentación desnuda (1965) Breasts
La Diosa impura (1963) Breasts

Catya Sassoon

Born: September 3, 1968
New York, New York
Died: January 1, 2002
Skin-O-Meter: Great Nudity

When you are the heiress to a hairstyling empire, it seems there is just about nothing that you can't have. Such was the case with Catya Sassoon, who was the offspring of style magnate Vidal Sassoon and actress Beverly Adams. Catya wasn't the cat's meow, however, until she bought herself some new tits and miscellaneous plastic surgery, all of which was paid for by your hard-earned hair-care dollars. Sadly, Catya's career and life came to an untimely end on New Year's Day, 2002, when she died after a New Year's Eve party. Okay, get that image out of your mind, change channels, and enjoy the fact that bionic Catya shared what she had when she still had it in such B-movie teasers as *Secret Games* (1991), her skin debut featuring a topless sunbathing scene, and *Angelfist* (1993), where she's shagged rotten in a nice "simulated" sex scene with some lucky actor. Ooh, la-la, Sassoon!

SKIN-fining Moment:

Angelfist (0:35) Catya's cooch finally pops up as she makes with the full frontal in the shower.

See Her Naked In:

Bloodfist VI: Ground Zero (1994) Breasts
Angelfist (1993) FFN
Inside Out IV (1992) Breasts, Thong
Dance With Death (1991) Breasts, Buns
Secret Games (1991) Breasts

Inés Sastre

Born: November 21, 1973
Valladolid, Madrid, Spain
Skin-O-Meter: Great Nudity

Except for the sensual welcome of her wide smile and open gaze, Spanish super-beauty Inés Sastre might be a tad intimidating. What do you say about a woman who speaks four languages, earned a degree in French literature from the Sorbonne, interviewed the Dalai Lama as an ambassador for UNICEF, and was Spain's representative to the world during the 1992 Olympics? Normally you would say, "Here is a broad who is overachieving in compensation for her homely looks." But Sastre could make a blind man stare. The gorgeous and brainy Spaniard has been in movies since she was thirteen, was an Elite model at fifteen, and was a phenomenal naked presence in *Beyond the Clouds* (1995). Her nipples were teased to aching erection in a scene that makes that condition painfully contagious.

SKIN-fining Moment:

Beyond the Clouds (0:26) Inés bares her boobs as a guy gropes her globes in bed.

See Her Naked In:

Vidocq (2001) Breasts
Beyond the Clouds (1995) Breasts

Jennifer Saunders

Born: July 6, 1958
Lincolnshire, England, UK
Skin-O-Meter: Brief Nudity

Jennifer Saunders is an English muffin, a funny lady who not only makes one laugh but is a tasty treat as well, especially with melted butter drooling all over her fleshy body. She met Dawn French at school, and the two teamed up to bring an alternative comedy to the mainstream in Britain. *French and Saunders* made the stiff-upper-lip isle stiff a bit further south thanks to the two tarts' quick wit and sexy ways. Jennifer is a full-figured gal with brown hair and boobs that jiggle often thanks to her infectious laugh. Everybody across this green globe of ours was laughing once Jennifer expanded a sketch to launch the hit TV series *Absolutely Fabulous*. On it, she caused a storm of controversy with her pill-loving, liquored-up, drug-addled, couture-wearing, gigolo-boffing waste case of a character Edina Monsoon. Nothing is sacred for this sexy lady. She's squeezed her hourglass body into such tight-fitting outfits that often more of her was slipping out than contained within. But she went all out for her humorous role in *The Supergrass* (1985), her sole skin onscreen. Take a hit, it'll get you high!

SKIN-fining Moment:

The Supergrass (0:44) White bra, black panties, side right breast, sexy pajamas. Not quite nude, but Jen's jiggly juggles are always Absolutely Fabulous.

See Her Naked In:

The Supergrass (1985) RB

Tracie Savage

Born: November 7, 1962
Ann Arbor, Michigan
Skin-O-Meter: Brief Nudity

Blonde, buttoned-down, and businesslike as she delivers her reports of death and disaster on Los Angeles, California's *Channel 4 News*, Tracie Savage looks as though she must have at one time exuded a boyish sort of charm and beauty. And then those honkin' hooters had to grow in and ruin the whole coltish silhouette! As she sits behind the news desk or bustles about with microphone and camera crew in the field, it's hard to imagine Tracie with nipples erect in a long and steamy shower. But consult the hard evidence, which can be ogled in *Friday the 13th Part 3: 3D* (1982). Water spits off Tracie's chest slope. Breast flesh and back splash both seem to come shooting right off the screen. It's as if a paw could reach up from the front seats and work a spot of lather into the Savage cleavage. Now there's a news flash.

SKIN-fining Moment:

Friday the 13th, Part 3: 3D (1:02) And now, the news: future newscaster Tracie soaps up while Jason lurks . . . and that's not a machete in your pants. Originally, Tracie's two C's were in 3D!

See Her Naked In:

Friday the 13th, Part 3: 3D (1982) Breasts

Savannah

Born: October 9, 1970
Laguna Beach, California
Died: July 11, 1994
Skin-O-Meter: Great Nudity

Doomed beauty was never more doomed nor more beautiful than in the sadly spent life of icy porn goddess Savannah. Having become accustomed to the life of celebrity and cash as the teenage companion to rocker Gregg Allman, Savannah used the assets at her disposal to achieve the only prominence that was within her grasp. Those assets consisted of an agonizingly classic blonde, blue-eyed surfer girl head, something like the mug of an angel that has learned to tease and please, attached to the taut, baby-soft, perfectly stacked boobs and butt of a body that might be Satan's own party favor. Poor little Shannon Wilsey (her real name) reached the height of XXX superstardom. From the heights, she saw only a sad and inevitable decline. Rather than take that plunge, Savannah fatally shot herself on July 11, 1994.

SKIN-fining Moment:

Sorority House Massacre II (0:44) Savannah and her enormous breasts get their collective groove on (and off) at a strip club.

See Her Naked In:

Legal Tender (1991) Breasts
The Invisible Maniac (1990) Breasts, Buns
Sorority House Massacre II (1990) Breasts, Thong
Numerous Adult Movies

Teresa Ann Savoy

Born: July 18, 1955
London, England, UK
Skin-O-Meter: Great Nudity

A perfect specimen of the petulant, bratty, spoiled British schoolgirl who might be either an urchin imposter or a real-life princess, Teresa Ann Savoy was too hot for the chilly sexual climes of her native land. Her icy charms were melted in the caressing sun of Italian skinema. Wavy blonde hair falls across Teresa Ann's flawless milky shoulders to crash upon her naturally rising peaks of chest flesh. A rear so high and mighty and prim and proper that one can hardly imagine it containing a quim and pooper. But there is no need to imagine. Cast your eyes upon *Penthouse* publisher Bob Guccione's prescient *Caligula* (1979). Again and again, sweet Savoy poses for the up-skirt shot—only with no skirt and no panties. Her downy soft butt cheeks twist open and reveal the dual orifices winking within. It's as if Heaven is revealed as a great place to get laid in.

SKIN-fining Moment:

Salon Kitty (1:13) Perfect young yaboos and bountiful blonde boosh as Teresa pours some champagne for herself and some lucky German.

See Her Naked In:

Caligula (1979) FFN, Buns
Salon Kitty (1976) FFN, Buns
Private Vices, Public Pleasures (1975) FFN, Buns

Greta Scacchi

Born: February 18, 1960
Milan, Italy
Skin-O-Meter: Hall of Fame

Born in Italy and coming of age in England and Australia, light-haired stunner Greta Scacchi mixes Mediterranean heat with steely British nerve. Simmering and cool, like a hot knife in ice, this simultaneously exotic and refined temptress has been cast again and again in the role of glamorous seductress. While there are worse things to be typecast as, go-getter Greta has flourished in a variety of roles and genres: tony Brit period dramas (*Emma* [1996]), big budget thrillers (*Presumed Innocent* [1990]), and broad comedy (*The Coca-Cola Kid* [1985]). The string that runs through Scacchi's body of work is a willingness to work her body without a stitch of clothing. In *The Coca-Cola Kid* alone she is a triple threat to visual complacency—buns, boobs, and bush!

SKIN-fining Moment:

The Coca-Cola Kid (0:49) You'll have a 7-up when you see the mighty mounds, muff, and seat-meat as mama Greta scrubs up with her daughter in the shower.

See Her Naked In:

Cotton Mary (1999) LB
The Red Violin (1998) LB, Buns
Turtle Beach (1992) RB, Buns
Salt on Our Skin (1992) Breasts, Buns
Fires Within (1991) Breasts, Buns
Shattered (1991) Breasts
Presumed Innocent (1990) Breasts, Buns
La Donna della luna (1988) FFN, Buns
White Mischief (1988) Breasts
A Man in Love (1987) Breasts, Buns
Good Morning, Babylon (1987) Breasts
The Coca-Cola Kid (1985) Breasts, Bush, Buns

The Ebony Tower (1984) FFN, Buns
Heat and Dust (1982) Breasts, Buns

Michele Scarabelli

Born: April 11, 1955
Montreal, Quebec, Canada
Skin-O-Meter: Great Nudity

Brunette beauty Michelle Scarabelli started out as many young starlets do—with bit part after bit part in schlocky B-movies. Thankfully, she stripped down in a few of these appearances. She bared bush and boobs on an episode of *The Hitchhiker* and lost her top once more in *Perfect Timing* (1984). She later cleaned up her act, much to Mr. Skin's chagrin, when she hit it big as a lead actress on the popular sci-fi series *Alien Nation*. Sure, she sported a speckled, egg-shaped cranium on the show, but a hot bod is a hot bod. With any luck, this still-sexy actress will crash land a role in more skinful territory soon.

SKIN-fining Moment:

Perfect Timing (1:11) Michele makes with the hinder and hooters as she spends some cuddle-time in bed with her man.

See Her Naked In:

Perfect Timing (1986) Breasts, Buns

TeleVisions:

The Hitchhiker Breasts, Buns

Rosanna Schiaffino

Born: November 25, 1938
Genoa, Liguria, Italy
Skin-O-Meter: Brief Nudity

This classic work of ass . . . make that art made her debut in *Totò, lascia o raddoppia?* (1956), quickly joining the ranks of other dark donnas who had Americans pining for a slice of Italian. Rosanna Schiaffino never broke through like Sophia Loren, but men were leerin' in swords-and-sandal epics such as *Minotaur, the*

Wild Beast of Crete (1961) and *Romulus and the Sabines* (1961). Rosanna also lengthened some inseams when she wrapped herself up as a harem girl in *The Long Ships* (1963). She appeared in the occasional mainstream American feature, but Rosanna would only bare her Italian Alps in homegrown productions, including *Trastevere* (1971) and *La Trastienda* (1975), which really put the spotlight on Rosanna's rosiest attributes. She retired from the screen in 1977, but her skinematic legacy still gets our noodles al dente.

SKIN-fining Moment:

Trastevere (1:06) Ganja-zonked Rosie shows her left chest-blossom while goofily gabbing with a pair of policemen.

See Her Naked In:

La Trastienda (1975) RB
Trastevere (1971) Buns, LB
Minotaur, the Wild Beast of Crete (1961)

Maria Schneider

Born: March 27, 1952
Paris, France
Skin-O-Meter: Hall of Fame

Maria Schneider broke into acting back in 1969 with an uncredited role in *Les Femmes* but didn't really hit the spotlight here in America until she popped up (and out) opposite Marlon Brando in the X-Rated classic *Last Tango in Paris.* Naturally, she showed off every last inch of her magnificent body several times in the flick, including some rather explicit sex sequences that scandalized audiences and packed art theaters around the world. Since then, though, Maria's career has been spotty at best, although she's managed to manifest her mammaries a time or two in such pictures as *The Passenger* (1975) and *La Derobade* (1979), which also featured another furry flash worthy of the ol' pause button.

SKIN-fining Moment:

Last Tango in Paris (1:31) Maria shows it all while Marlon Brando scrubs all three of her B's in a bathtub.

See Her Naked In:

La Derobade (1979) Breasts, Bush
A Woman Like Eve (1979) LB
Last Tango in Paris (1972) FFN, Buns
Hellé (1971) LB, Bush

Romy Schneider

Born: September 23, 1938
Vienna, Austria
Died: May 29, 1982
Skin-O-Meter: Hall of Fame

Romy Schneider had everything going for her as an actress. Born into Germany's premier acting dynasty, this child of film and theater was talented, connected, driven, and to top it off, beautiful in the way of an unattainable ideal. It was as though she had sparkling cut diamonds for eyes. Romy's regal mien allowed her to specialize in playing royalty onscreen, but she also knew how to please the commoners. Her rabble-rousing nude scenes span a string of European films from the late 1960s through the 1970s, and many are attainable in all of Romy's original splendor. Although this queenly performer kept her pubic crown to herself, the seat of power was visible and felt almost within reach in *La Piscine* (1969).

SKIN-fining Moment:

Innocents with Dirty Hands (0:10) Laying in bed with her loverman, Romy shows us some side-skin, followed by an okay view of her rich, dark nip-nips.

See Her Naked In:

Le Vieux fusil (1975) LB
Innocents with Dirty Hands (1975) Breasts, Buns
L'Important c'est d'aimer (1975) Buns
Love at the Top (1974) Breasts
Le Trio infernal (1974) Breasts

Max et les ferrailleurs (1971) LB
La Califfa (1970) Breasts, Buns
Les Choses de la vie (1970) Buns
La Piscine (1969) Breasts
10:30 P.M. Summer (1966) LB
Boccaccio '70 (1962) LB

Jill Schoelen

Born: 1966
Burbank, California
Skin-O-Meter: Great Nudity

After a long career that started off as background fluff in early 1980s boob-tube filler, slight, lithe brunette Jill Schoelen is poised for skinmortality. Despite a face that is as cute as a young Beaver Cleaver, only without the homoerotic overtones and grafted onto the body of a state cheerleading champion, much of Jill's film work has been largely ignored. Some interest was stirred by the starlet's stirring soul baring in *Thunder Alley* (1985), a story of sex and drugs on the highway to hell. That interest dropped its jaw and became a mouth-breathing devotee during viewing of *The Stepfather* (1987), one of the great shower epics of all time. There is absolutely nothing gratuitous about the fully nude rear views of Schoelen's tight, shapely ass, a butt that will live in perpetuity, right alongside her lovingly soaped natural chest nibs. Watch and wash.

SKIN-fining Moment:

The Stepfather (1:13) In one of skinema's all-time great gratuitous nude scenes, all the action in the movie stops so Jill can strip down, step into the shower, soap up those sweet young funbags and then towel off and get dressed in order to go back to dodging her deadly Daddy.

See Her Naked In:

The Phantom of the Opera (1989) Breasts
Cutting Class (1989) Breasts
The Stepfather (1987) Breasts, Buns
Thunder Alley (1985) LB

Julia Schultz

Born: June 15, 1979
San Diego, California
Skin-O-Meter: Brief Nudity

When Julia Schultz was only eleven years old she was already using her body as a way to get ahead (oh, if only Mr. Skin could get her to give me head!), modeling and strutting her premature stuff in local beauty pageants. At fifteen the Southern Californian's mother moved her to Milan, Italy, to hit the catwalks of high-fashion. After making her name in print and on the runway, the leggy blonde returned Stateside, graduated high school, and did what any self-respecting hottie would do: She waltzed into the *Playboy* offices to try to get noticed. It didn't take much, and not a year after leaving school Julia was Miss February 1998 and things kicked into high gear—at least in men's pants. Naturally, Julia sought fame and fortune as an act-chest. She certainly has the equipment. And who wouldn't want to see her onscreen? On the boob tube, Julia got small parts on shows such as *Pensacola: Wings of Gold* and *Grosse Pointe*. She used her not-so-small parts to land her eye-candy roles in movies such as *Love Stinks* (1999), *Nutty Professor II: The Klumps* (2000), and *Tomcats* (2001). But it was her topless flash from a car in *Forsaken* (2001) that had viewers pulling at their foreskins. Since then Julia has been rather skingy. In *Rush Hour 2* (2001), she's sexy but skinless. But we're not complaining. Her father is former Hells Angel "Dutch" Schultz and is now her manager, so we don't want to get him angry.

SKIN-fining Moment:

The Forsaken (0:06) In the passenger seat of a moving car, Julia flashes her jugaboos at a passing motorist.

See Her Naked In:

The Forsaken (2001) Breasts
Numerous *Playboy* Videos

Wendy Schumacher

Born: 1971
Skin-O-Meter: Great Nudity

Wendy Schumacher first exposed her two meaty chops in the little-seen sci-fi flick *Star Hunter* (1995). If stardom was her game, she left that movie with no awards on her wall—but audiences did get the pleasure of a quick shot of her twin trophies, and they bagged big ones. She starred in the softcore sextravaganza *Animal Instincts III* (1996) and left nothing to the imagination. Her ample boobage is front-and-center, joined by her plump rump and even some shag shots so vivid you can almost count the hairs. Her professional path has thankfully continued on the road to skin in *Scorned 2* (1996), *Fugitive Rage* (1996), and *Black Widow Escort* (1998). By the dawn of the new millennium, Wendy decided she needed a change and switched up her stage name to Alexander Keith, but a flesh bomb by any other name still strips as sweet.

SKIN-fining Moment:

Animal Instincts III (1:04) In her opulent bathroom, Wendy peels to full-frontal fineness while inviting equally naked Jenteal to join her for a boob-sucking, cliddle-diddle bath. This sight inspires two insanely hot maids to make it a side-by-side lesbian foursome as they lock (and lick) loins on the bathroom floor. What kind of maniac wrote this movie?

See Her Naked In:

The Capitol Conspiracy (1999) Breasts, Buns
Scorned 2 (1997) Breasts
Fugitive Rage (1996) Breasts, Buns
Animal Instincts III (1995) FFN, Buns
Star Hunter (1995) LB

Hanna Schygulla

Born: December 25, 1943
Königshütte, Germany
Skin-O-Meter: Great Nudity

Hanna Schygulla is the blonde muse of renegade German helmsmen Rainer Werner Fassbinder. She worked with the eccentric leather-clad bad boy since her debut in *The Bridegroom, The Actress and the Pimp* (1968). Fassbinder didn't direct that one, but he did play the "Pimp." By Fassbinder's *Liebe ist kälter als der Tod* (1969), Hanna was already showing off her sisters—two plump betties, with a round rump, and even a taste of pubic hair to get caught between some lucky fellow's teeth. It was the beginning of a skinful career that has stretched her naughty nudity to *Warszawa* (1992). But Hanna was a national treasure unknown on U.S. shores until Fassbinder kicked the bucket. After that Hanna was hotfooting it to Hollywood for roles. She played opposite Lee Marvin in *The Delta Force* (1986) and starred in the *Desperately Seeking Susan* (1985) knockoff *Forever, Lulu* (1987), where Hanna was looking very Debbie Harry—only with her tits hanging out. You've got to Hanna it to the girl!

SKIN-fining Moment:

Liebe ist kälter als der Tod (0:54) Nice breastage and flash of muff as she strips to lay on bed next to a guy, followed by a lingering shot of her dazzling dumper.

See Her Naked In:

Warszawa (1992) FFN
Forever, Lulu (1987) Breasts
Il Futuro è donna (1984) LB
Storia di Piera (1983) LB, Buns
Die Fälschung (1981) RB
Die Ehe der Maria Braun (1979) Breasts, Bush, Buns
Whity (1971) Breasts
Warnung vor einer heiligen Nutte (1971) Breasts, Buns

Rio das Mortes (1971) Buns
Katzelmacher (1969) RB
Liebe ist kälter als der Tod (1969) Breasts, Bush, Buns

Annabella Sciorra

Born: March 24, 1964
Whethersfield, Connecticut
Skin-O-Meter: Great Nudity

Wiry brunette spitfire Annabella Sciorra has long been a tantalizing blip on the skin-sighting radar. As Tony Soprano's hot-tempered girlfriend for one high-temperature season of *The Sopranos*, Annabella put the *whoa* in HBO. Her specialty is hard-edged loner women who squint out at the male world with a hint of vulnerability and thinly veiled romanticism. Passion imbues her every crooked flash of smile. Her flame-throwing sensuality is a searing highlight of *Prison Stories: Women on the Inside* (1990), *Internal Affairs* (1990), and *Whispers in the Dark* (1992). Careful. Don't get burned.

SKIN-fining Moment:

The Hand that Rocks the Cradle (0:08) Quick right-side rackage as Annabella leans back at the doctor's office.

See Her Naked In:

Whispers in the Dark (1992) Body Double—Buns
The Hand that Rocks the Cradle (1992) RB
Internal Affairs (1990) RB
Prison Stories: Women on the Inside (1990) RB

TeleVisions:

The Sopranos Thong

Yvonne Sciò

Italy
Skin-O-Meter: Great Nudity

The only thing Italian-born international libido sensation

Yvonne Sciò needs to win the hards and minds of the male American public is her face. With eyes of a cool, soothing shade of blue seen in the depths of Lake Como, lips as mouth-watering and plump and inviting to the tongue as a tube of homemade pasta, a complexion white as powdered-sugar snow, Yvonne's is the kind of mug that causes instant fixation. And then her puffy, rising boobs turn out to be every whit as natural and mesmerizing as her frank and inviting gaze. Plus, her splendid rear cheeks pull off the neat trick of being simultaneously plush and trim. There is no point in resisting the allure of Yvonne Sciò. She holds all the sex-appeal cards. Lucky for us, she shows her hand generously in *Redline* (1997) and *Layover* (2001).

SKIN-fining Moment:

Layover (0:20) It's Laywatch! Breasts and thonged buttage during some shadowy sex with David Hasselhoff amidst chain-link fencing. Dig those thick, pink, meaty nips . . . Yvonne's that is.

See Her Naked In:

Layover (2001) Breasts, Thong
Redline (1997) Breasts, Bush, Buns
Sabato italiano (1992) Breasts

Tracy Scoggins

Born: November 13, 1959
Dickinson, Texas
Skin-O-Meter: Great Nudity

Millions thrilled to the snotty sexual jujitsu of tall, tight Texan Tracy Scoggins in the classic television gawk series *Dynasty*, *The Colbys*, and *Babylon 5*. Untold millions more of wide-eyed insomniacs with lust on the mind have watched as if in a hypnotic trance as enterprising Tracy bends, stretches, and flexes through endless infomercials hawking her exercise videos. A relatively small cognoscenti has sniffed out Tracy's nostril-widening flashes of flesh in celluloid sensual delights such as *The Gumshoe Kid* (1990) and *Alien Intruder* (1992). The gravity-defying *Gumshoe* chest balloons will increase heart rates much more effectively than any exercise tape.

SKIN-fining Moment:

The Gumshoe Kid (1:11) Tracy bares her behemoth breasts in the shower with Jay Underwood, complete with a nice touch of Slo-Mo to lengthen the exposure. What a rack!

See Her Naked In:

Dead On (1993) LB
Alien Intruder (1992) LB, Buns
Play Murder for Me (1991) Breasts
Ultimate Desires (1991) Breasts, Buns
The Gumshoe Kid (1990) Breasts, Thong
In Dangerous Company (1988) LB

Nicolette Scorsese

Skin-O-Meter: Great Nudity

She's no relation to Martin, but Nicolette Scorsese gets the kind of showcase roles you'd expect a gal to score through nepotism. We wouldn't mind scoring with Scorsese, either, especially as Chevy Chase's fantasy of a perfect gift in *Christmas Vacation* (1989). We only get a glimpsette of her nipplettes, but Nicolette makes up for that in her coming-from-behind sex scene with Julian Sands in *Boxing Helena* (1993). (Sherilyn Fenn's watching it all too.) And don't miss her dolled up—in clothes, sadly—as a trashy Marilyn Monroe wannabe in the kitschy *Girls in Prison* (1994). Nicolette's kept a low profile since her turn as a "Busty Barmaid" on an episode of *NYPD Blue*, but we're still hoping

to see more of this brunette bombshell.

SKIN-fining Moment:

Boxing Helena (1:24) Nicolette frees her nay-nays from a bra and makes nookie with Julian Sands as Sherilyn Fenn spies on the action.

See Her Naked In:

Boxing Helena (1993) Breasts, Thong

Izabella Scorupco

Born: June 4, 1970
Bialystok, Poland
Skin-O-Meter: Great Nudity

Polish-born beauty Izabella Scorupco was tall and blonde enough to fit in when her family moved to Sweden. In fact, the seventeen-year-old fit in well enough to become a star with her debut in the film *Only We Can Love Like This* (1998). Izabella then used her fluency in four languages to launch an international modeling career before returning to the screen to play a woman masquerading as a man in *Petri tårar* (1995), which featured a scene where she hopped out of a medieval hot tub. She then upstaged Pierce Brosnan's Bond debut as a Russian computer whiz in *GoldenEye* (1995) before returning to skinternational productions such as *Dykaren* (2000), which, despite the title, features Iza in a hot heterosexual sex scene. Izabella's since returned to English-language productions, saving dude-in-distress Christian Bale from dragons in *Reign of Fire* (2002) and getting our heads spinning in *Exorcist: The Beginning* (2004).

SKIN-fining Moment:

Petri tårar (1:04) Lots of hot-tub brewed boobies as Izabella relaxes, and

then a mega-quick peek at the bush as she leaps out of the bubbles.

See Her Naked In:

Dykaren (2000) LB
Petri tårar (1995) Breasts, Bush, Buns
Vampires of Love (Music Video) FFN
Ingen Kan Älska Som VI (1988) LB

Kristin Scott Thomas

Born: May 24, 1960
Redruth, Cornwall, England, UK
Skin-O-Meter: Hall of Fame

Kristin Scott Thomas is so gifted and glamorous that she actually survived starring in Prince's noted debacle *Under the Cherry Moon* (1986). Of course, the aftermath required an exile in France, but that just meant her pleasant pastries soon came popping up in *Force majeure* (1989). This was followed by a wonderful shot of her shapely ass and cute titties being sent out to sea in *Le Bal du gouverneur* (1990). She also provided some lesbian loving in Roman Polanski's erotic thriller *Bitter Moon* (1992). *Four Weddings and a Funeral* (1994) finally made Kristin an international star, and *The English Patient* (1996) provoked international hard-ons when Kristin went full-frontal in a bathing scene with Ralph Fiennes. And don't forget all the random hard-ons prompted by Kristin's sexy scenes in *Random Hearts* (1999).

SKIN-fining Moment:

The English Patient (1:14)
Phenomenal phull-phrontal when Kristin disrobes and gets in and out of a tub with Ralph Fiennes. Tastilicious titlets, mouth-watering mounds of muff.

See Her Naked In:

Amour et confusions (1997) Breasts
The English Patient (1996) FFN
The Pompatus of Love (1996) RB

Bitter Moon (1994) Breasts
Masterpiece Theatre: Body and Soul (1994) FFN
Un été inoubliable (1994) FFN, Buns
Framed (1990) Breasts
Le Bal du gouverneur (1990) Bush, Buns
Force majeure (1989) Breasts

Serena Scott Thomas

Born: September 21, 1961
Nether Compton, Dorset, England, UK
Skin-O-Meter: Great Nudity

Just as Natalie Wood had sister Lana in *Diamonds Are Forever* (1971), Kristin Scott Thomas had Serena Scott Thomas to fill in as a Bond girl in *The World Is Not Enough* (1999). It was a typically sexy and minor role for Serena, whose career hasn't been nearly as highbrow as her sister's. In addition to a great guest shot on *Buffy the Vampire Slayer,* her other big parts have been as a regular on Don Johnson's TV show *Nash Bridges* and playing Princess Diana in the TV movie *Diana: Her True Story* (1993). She's also shown off her other biggest parts, of course, looking supremely sexy in *Relax . . . It's Just Sex* (1998) and *The Brothel* (2003).

SKIN-fining Moment:

Harnessing Peacocks (0:46) You'll have to harness your own peacock when you see Serena standing stark naked in front of a mirror trying on her new hat.

See Her Naked In:

Relax . . . It's Just Sex (1998) LB
Harnessing Peacocks (1993) FFN, Buns

Debralee Scott

Born: April 2, 1953
Elizabeth, New Jersey
Skin-O-Meter: Brief Nudity

A perky pepper pot with a knack for broad comedy, New Jersey's Debralee Scott is fondly remembered as Rosalie "Hotzie" Totzie from the warmly regarded *Welcome Back, Kotter. Kotter* launched the meteoric career of John Travolta, and for a while Debralee wasn't far behind. Earlier she had caught a role in *American Graffiti* (1973), a movie that launched many meteoric careers of its own, and Scott had every reason to believe that Hotzie would soon be rocketing among the stars. Unfortunately, her skyrocket fizzled and she soon fell into the *Police Academy* ring of career limbo. Debralee Scott is listed here due to her role as a frontally nude corpse in *Dirty Harry* (1971). Her performance is a tad stiff, but it's worth a peek.

SKIN-fining Moment:

Dirty Harry (1:10) Hotzie Totzie is full-frontally nude, dirty, and hairy, being pulled from sewer. She is dead too. But she is still Hotzie Totzie naked.

See Her Naked In:

Dirty Harry (1971) FFN

Jean Seberg

Born: November 13, 1938
Marshalltown, Iowa
Died: September 8, 1979
Skin-O-Meter: Brief Nudity

Megalomaniac director Otto Preminger discovered Jean Seberg at the University of Iowa and nearly destroyed her career by casting the young girl as "Joan of Arc" in *St. Joan* (1957). The film was a disaster, but Seberg limped along until Jean-Luc Godard made her an existential sex symbol in *Breathless* (1961). Jean then worked steadily overseas, with films like *A Fine Madness* (1966) capitalizing on her offhand sex appeal. She finally made it back to American productions in *Paint Your Wagon* (1969). The Lee Marvin/Clint Eastwood musical was another big flop, but nobody minded how Seberg's copious cleavage came flopping out when a lusty Lee Marvin grabbed her blouse. *Airport* (1970) was a proper hit, but Seberg—typically—followed mainstream success with daring nude scenes in *Macho Callahan* (1970) and *Kill!* (1971), although the latter is most likely a body double. Then it was back to baring her 'bergs in European productions such as *Camorra* (1972), as she struggled with both personal problems and FBI surveillance prompted by her association with the Black Panthers. The troubled actress was found dead in Paris from a barbiturate overdose in 1979.

SKIN-fining Moment:

Macho Callahan (1:01) David Janssen rips Jean's blouse open and we see berg, but that right-side rack-half may belong to a body double.

See Her Naked In:

Kill! (1972) Body Double—RB—Buns
Questa specie d'amore (1972) Breasts, Buns
Macho Callahan (1970) Body Double—Breasts, Buns

Edie Sedgwick

Born: April 20, 1943
Santa Barbara, California
Died: November 16, 1971
Skin-O-Meter: Great Nudity

The legend of Edie Sedgwick has been blown up to mythic proportions in memoirs and art work from those whose paths, however briefly, intersected with her crazy orbit. A daughter of wealth and privilege, Edie traipsed away from the bosom of her blue-blood family to hang out with the geeks and freaks of Andy Warhol's infamous Factory, a New York City loft that was a magnet to the brightest and most demented lights of the '60s guerrilla-art counterculture. Charmed by Edie's manic pixie motor-mouth energy, Warhol cast her in several of his underground flicks, most notably *The Chelsea Girls* (1967). Although Sedgwick was incapable of unwrapping a candy bar without sexualizing the act, she remained fully clothed in her Warhol flings. Her floppers came flapping out in her last picture, a show called *Ciao! Manhattan* (1972). The picture proved the adage that if an actress is going to loll around, she might as well loll around in her panties with her titties tossing about.

SKIN-fining Moment:

Ciao! Manhattan (0:14) Edie bares her meaties while dancing around clad only in panties.

See Her Naked In:

Ciao! Manhattan (1973) Breasts

Kyra Sedgwick

Born: August 19, 1965
New York, New York
Skin-O-Meter: Brief Nudity

Born and raised in Manhattan, sweet-faced, supple-skinned Kyra Sedgwick made her show biz debut at the age of sixteen with a recurring role on the Gotham-based soap opera *Another World*. Not long after that she made her move into motion pictures, landing substantial roles in the sadly skin-free *War and Love* (1985), *Kansas* (1988), and *Born on the Fourth of July* (1989). Kyra's adorable girl-next-door persona was put aside for a series of sizzling sex scenes with her real-life husband Kevin Bacon in the silly but staggeringly sex-filled comedy *Pyrates* (1991), which found Kyra's cans and "kuru" noticeably on display.

SKIN-fining Moment:

Pyrates (0:19) Kyra gets porked by Kevin Bacon, riding his sausage first in a see-through black nighty, then with her chest-eggs flipping in the open air.

See Her Naked In:

The Woodsman (2004) Breasts
Pyrates (1991) Breasts, Buns

Xenia Seeberg

Born: April 4, 1972
Geldern am Niederrhein, Germany
Skin-O-Meter: Brief Nudity

German jolter Xenia Seeberg got her start as a servant girl in the Euro production *Farinelli the Castrato* (1994)—and, man, that must've been one sad castrato with a girl like Xenia running around. The bouncing blonde then became a skinema favorite with her amazing bound knockers in *Knockin' on Heaven's Door* (1997). Her shameless antics made the former lingerie model a natural to step in to replace the departing Eva Habermann as the nymphomaniac love slave "Xev Bellringer" on the bizarre sci-fi series *Lexx*. Xenia took over the role in 1998 and also took full advantage of how those Europeans don't mind nudity on television. We're especially fond of the episode where the bubbles in a bubble bath fail to work in a concealing manner. It's no surprise that Xenia's stayed a big favorite in Germany, but we're fLexxing our zippers in hopes of a skinternational return.

SKIN-fining Moment:

Lexx "P4X" (2001) Xenia showers aboard her space ship, showing the upper crack of her galactic glutes and her orbitally orgasmic right torso-globe.

TeleVisions:

Lexx RB, Buns

Pamela Segall

Born: 1968
Skin-O-Meter: Brief Nudity

A soulful brunette blend of tomboy gamine and grunge goddess, heartbreaker Pamela Segall has a

versatility of presentation that has allowed her to create a panoply of memorable characters using only her tongue and her mouth. Though she has plenty of proud credits in front of the camera, including featured spots in *Willy/Milly* (1986), *Say Anything . . .* (1989), and *Bed of Roses* (1996), starry-eyed Segall collects her checks primarily for voice work in animated features. Hers are the plaintive tones that sound from the mouth of adolescent Bobby Hill on *King of the Hill*. Imagine the exclamations that might percolate up from Bobby were he to stumble upon a copy of *Eat Your Heart Out* (1997). Pretty Pamela proffered a full boob profile in front of a steamed-over mirror, her nipples popping way out at attention. The voice-over artist leaves us speechless.

SKIN-fining Moment:

Eat Your Heart Out (0:08) Fleeting right-side rackage, giving her guy a gander.

See Her Naked In:

Eat Your Heart Out (1997) RB

Emmanuelle Seigner

Born: June 22, 1966
Paris, France
Skin-O-Meter: Hall of Fame

Pooh to those fancy pants actresses who deem themselves such brave artistes because they cradle a profile of teat or lift a rear cheek for an artfully shadowy mood piece. These posers pale, they are dashed to mediocrity, they pule and whine like mangy alley cats when exposed to the luminous, exultantly naked presentations of French and fabulous delicacy Emmanuelle Seigner. The Parisian pouter was discovered at the age of seventeen by pervy Polish genius Roman Polanski, who no doubt saw something special deep inside her. The diminutive director seems to have dedicated his relationship with Seigner to showing the rest of mankind every secret thing that he saw in her. When Emmanuelle casts aside her clothing in a film, rest assured that the clothing will stay cast aside for a while. Her sweet, swoon-inducing moon rises so much in *Bitter Moon* (1992) that the casual viewer is liable to develop a fixation. *Le Sourir* (1994), replete with extensive studies of Emmanuelle's trimmed vulva hedge, will only feed the fires of fixation. After Seigner's, it's tough to go back to any other backside.

SKIN-fining Moment:

Bitter Moon (0:30) A great look at Emmanuelle's perfect pair as Peter Coyote laps spilled milk off of her goodies.

See Her Naked In:

Corps à corps (2003) FFN
The Ninth Gate (1999) Breasts, Buns
Buddy Boy (1999) Breasts
R.P.M. (1997) Breasts, Buns
La Divine poursuite (1997) Bush
Le Sourire (1994) FFN, Buns
Bitter Moon (1994) Breasts, Buns
Frantic (1988) RB
Cours prive (1986) FFN
Détective (1985) Breasts

Mathilde Seigner

**Born: January 17, 1968
Paris, France
Skin-O-Meter: Great Nudity**

She's been a star in France for some time, but Mathilde Seigner didn't break through in America until the international success of *With a Friend Like Harry . . .* (2000). Mathilde, however, has been a friend to our penises ever since her nude debut in *Le Sourire* (1994). She put on a fascinating full-frontal frolic as part of a trilogy of trouser-trilling trumpets. Mathilde followed that up with some major assitude during her night-swimming scenes in *Vacances bougeoises* (1995) before making us even inSeigner with titillating turns in films such as *Mémoires d'un jeune con* (1996) and *L'homme que j'aime* (1997). Mathilde's also capitalized on her post-*Harry* success with a swell shower scene in *Betty Fisher and Other Stories* (2001) and some trystin' in *Tristan* (2003).

SKIN-fining Moment:

Le Sourire (0:56) Mathilde shakes her coconuts and divulges the bush as she dances all disco-like.

See Her Naked In:

Tristan (2003) Breasts
Betty Fisher and Other Stories (2001) Breasts
Belle Maman (1999) Breasts
L'homme que j'aime (1997) LB
Pêcheur d'Islande (1996) Breasts
Mémoires d'un jeune con (1996) Breasts
Vacances bougeoises (1995) Buns
Le Sourire (1994) FFN

Susan Sennett

**Born: September 25, 1945
Skin-O-Meter: Great Nudity**

It was a short film career, but Susan Sennett spent it as a true drive-in queen. *Tidal Wave* (1973) was a cheap Japanese disaster movie that had new scenes added with American actors—including Lorne Greene giving a speech to the UN. The brutal kidnapping drama *The Candy Snatchers* (1973) starred Susan as the titular treat, spending the entire movie in bondage while dolled up as a schoolgirl. Three turned out to be the fucky number as Susan stripped for Tom Skerritt in *Big Bad Mama* (1974). This final role had Susan flexing her form in every position short of full frontal. A few years later, though, Susan would settle into marital bliss with rock star Graham Nash. The couple made headlines when Nash performed a concert in a high school cafeteria as a special event for people who—like Susan—were born on Leap Day.

SKIN-fining Moment:

Big Bad Mama (0:51) Susan shows caboose and just a bit of the side of her tit when she and her sister climb into bed with Tom Skerritt.

See Her Naked In:

Big Bad Mama (1974) Breasts, Buns

Assumpta Serna

**Born: September 16, 1957
Barcelona, Spain
Skin-O-Meter: Hall of Fame**

You could say that Barcelona-born bombshell Assumpta Serna went from bits to tits. After small roles in Spanish flicks such as *La Orgia* (1977) and *Lulu de Noche* (1985), Assumpta brought her lactating maracas to Hollywood for a recurring role on television soap series *Falcon Crest*. That led to bigger and breaster things, mainly *Wild Orchid* (1990), in which she almost stole the film. That's no small feat, considering the flick showed Carré Otis and her heavenly cooze in several gratuitous nude scenes. But Assumpta stiffened our shorts by showing off her creamy chimichangas in a hot limo scene. She's appeared in dozens of films since, but none more mammarable.

SKIN-fining Moment:

Wild Orchid (0:39) Assumpta offers up a ton of titty shots when her top gets ripped off in a crowd of crazed people.

See Her Naked In:

Nana (2001) Breasts
Nostradamus (1993) RB
Wild Orchid (1990) Breasts
Matador (1986) FFN
Violencia criminal (1986) FFN
Lola (1985) Breasts
La Joven y la tentación (1984) Breasts
Le Cercle des passions (1983) Breasts

Joan Severance

**Born: December 23, 1958
Houston, Texas
Skin-O-Meter: Hall of Fame**

Joan Severance is a credit to model-turned-actresses everywhere. Why waste that statuesque, black-haired, high-assed beauty on getting married and raising kids somewhere back in your native Texas? When Joan's big acting break on the 1980s network sensation *Wiseguy* failed to fire up an A-list career, the extra-stacked Severance promptly took her place at the head of the Bs. Joan began a creative partnership on Showtime's skintillating *Red Shoe Diaries*, where she was muff-baring muse to mentor Zalman King. King is the crown prince of skinsational erotic thrillers, and his expertise is epitomized in *Lake Consequence* (1992). Joan shined in an outdoor sex scene. She shined in an indoor sex scene. She shined wetly in a shower stall lesbo sex scene. What, no underwater sex scene? They had a lake right there, for God's sake. Well, that's what's great about Joan Severance. There is always more to look forward to.

SKIN-fining Moment:

See No Evil, Hear No Evil (1:11) Joan drops her towel and reveals her tanned torso torpedoes while Gene Wilder pretends to have a gun in his pocket.

See Her Naked In:

In Dark Places (1997) Breasts
Profile for Murder (1996) Breasts
Payback (1995) Breasts, Bush
Black Scorpion (1995) Breasts, Buns
Dangerous Indiscretion (1994) Breasts, Buns
Criminal Passion (1994) Breasts, Buns
Illicit Behavior (1992) Breasts, Buns
Lake Consequence (1992) Breasts, Bush
Almost Pregnant (1992) Breasts, Thong
Another Pair of Aces (1991) Breasts
Write to Kill (1990) Breasts
See No Evil, Hear No Evil (1989) Breasts

TeleVisions:

Red Shoe Diaries Breasts, Bush, Buns

Chloë Sevigny

**Born: November 18, 1974
Springfield, Massachusetts
Skin-O-Meter: Great Nudity**

Chloë Sevigny started her professional life as an intern for

BLOW, BUNNY: CHLOË SEVIGNY AND THE MOUTH THAT MADE ART FILMS FUN AGAIN IN *THE BROWN BUNNY.*

Sassy, a magazine that once likened underground publisher and MrSkin.com contributor Selwyn Harris to mucous. Fortunately, she soon made the move to acting with an enchanting, altogether amazing performance in the super-dark flick *Kids* (1995) and has since risen to indie-film superstar status. In 1998 she managed to make us wince and applaud simultaneously when she pulled some tape off her nipples in *Gummo*, but Chloë's skinful ways were still only warming up. In 1999 and 2000 Chloë hit two back-to-back unbelievably boobular Lesbianic Grand Slams, first with Hilary Swank in *Boys Don't Cry* (1999), then with Michelle Williams in the HBO flick *If These Walls Could Talk 2* (2000). Taking that momentum to a new height, Chloë scandalized the 2003 Cannes film festival with her appearance in writer-director-producer-scaryman Vincent Gallo's ego epic *Brown Bunny*. The climax of the movie features Chloë performing hardcore, open-jawed, porno-style oral sex on Gallo. Critics were unanimous in declaring that *Brown Bunny* blows and Mr. Skin thinks so too—and I mean that as the highest (and hardest and deepest and gooeyest) of praise!

SKIN-fining Moment:

The Brown Bunny (1:15) At the climax of this ultimate skinematic ego trip, Chloë opens wide and provides

writer/director/star/scary guy Vincent Gallo with a wet, sloppy, tonsil tickling, Jenna-Jameson-style hardcore oral report, up-close and all real and right there on the screen, forever after rendering him the Blown Bunny.

See Her Naked In:

The Brown Bunny (2003) FFN
If These Walls Could Talk 2 (2000) Breasts
Boys Don't Cry (1999) Breasts
Gummo (1998) RB
Kids (1995) Bush

Carmen Sevilla

Born: October 16, 1930
Sevilla, Andalucía, Spain
Skin-O-Meter: Brief Nudity

It's not just aging Hollywood stars who find themselves on the B-movie circuit. Carmen Sevilla was one of Spain's greatest musical stars during the 1950s and eventually went international with the French production *El Amor de Don Juan* (1956). Carmen then concentrated on dramatic roles throughout the '60s, although the pickings got lean by the '70s. While former MGM starlets like Debbie Reynolds made movies such as *What's the Matter with Helen?* (1971), Carmen was appearing in *The Boldest Job in the West* (1971)—sadly, it's a bank job—and doffing her top with Donald Pleasance in *La Loba y la Paloma* (1974), a.k.a. *House of the Damned*. *Strip-tease a la inglesa* (1975) was another promising title, but Carmen was ready to retire from the screen in 1978, although she returned in 1986 to concentrate on a TV career.

SKIN-fining Moment:

La Loba y la Paloma (0:42) Carmen's cans come out to play when her man rips off her shirt and makes with the lovin'.

See Her Naked In:

Nosotros, los decentes (1976) LB
La Loba y la Paloma (1974) Breasts

No es bueno que el hombre esté solo (1973) LB
La Cera virgen (1972) LB

Cara Seymour

UK
Skin-O-Meter: Great Nudity

We never thought we'd become Cara Seymour fans after her scary cameo as an egg-harvesting gal in *You've Got Mail* (1998)—but that was before her dramatic turn as one of Christian Bale's sexier victims in *American Psycho* (2000). Her sullen prostitute brings a tone of real decadence to a ménage a doom, and we also get to see more of Cara's beautiful breasts and buns. Cara has since brought her erotic moodiness to roles in *Dancer in the Dark* (2000) and as Nicolas Cage's love interest in *Adaptation* (2002).

SKIN-fining Moment:

American Psycho (0:44) We get brief breasts and side-angle nakedness as Cara canoodles in a frantic ménage with Christian Bale and Krista Sutton.

See Her Naked In:

American Psycho (2000) Breasts

Jane Seymour

Born: February 15, 1951
Middlesex, England, UK
Skin-O-Meter: Great Nudity

To be acknowledged by the slightly skewed half-smile of British star of stage and dream Jane Seymour, having met the glittery challenge of her eyes as they look down her long, refined nose, this contact is to risk being mesmerized and enchanted. Seymour's first step in world seduction was as a swinging '60s London model, which was but a short skip to the femme fatale lead opposite James Bond in *Live and Let Die* (1973). Jane's rarefied sensuality and ass-long hair have never faded

from style; she's been a class-act fixture on the small screen for more than twenty years. Her most lasting impression is from *Lassiter* (1984), in which, fully naked, she adorned a bed with her so sophisticated seat cushions raised to be appraised. And there is that smile, slightly skewed, fully verticle.

SKIN-fining Moment:

Lassiter (0:10) Great glute shot as Jane rests bare-assed atop Tom Selleck, followed by side right tittle.

See Her Naked In:

The Tunnel (1987) Breasts, Buns
Lassiter (1984) RB, Buns
Sinbad and the Eye of the Tiger (1977) Nip Slip RB, Buns

Polly Shannon

Born: September 1, 1973
Kingston, Ontario, Canada
Skin-O-Meter: Great Nudity

Her mom writes children's TV shows, but Polly Shannon has had a very grown-up career. She even flashed her lovely smallish breasts during her film debut in *Love & Human Remains* (1993)—but she only showed up long enough to get murdered in the opening scenes. Polly got better, though, and made it hard for us to lose our erections in *Hard to Forget* (1998), in which she really gave (and came) her all in a simulated sex scene. Then she showed up as a kinky college gal majoring in group sex in the daring *Harvard Man* (2001). And, in tribute to her Canadian heritage, Polly wanted our testicles cracking when she walked around in her underwear in the hokey comedy *Men with Brooms* (2002).

SKIN-fining Moment:

Harvard Man (1:21) Distant dairyage in bed while making out with Rebecca Gayheart.

See Her Naked In:

Harvard Man (2001) Breasts
The Girl Next Door (1999) Breasts, Buns
Hard To Forget (1998) Breasts, Buns
Love & Human Remains (1993) Breasts

TeleVisions:

The Hunger Breasts
Outer Limits Breasts, Buns

Cornelia Sharpe

Born: October 3, 1947
Selma, Alabama
Skin-O-Meter: Brief Nudity

Were there so many gorgeous, naked girls in the '70s that Cornelia Sharpe could be overlooked? After debuting as a foxy roller-derby star in *Kansas City Bomber* (1972), Cornelia's cans made their debut in her role as Al Pacino's soapy girlfriend in the classic *Serpico* (1973). The combination of a prestigious hit film and Cornelia's amazing natural tits should've made this Alabama beauty a superstar. Instead she went on to get guys super hard with some simulated sex in *The Reincarnation of Peter Proud* (1975). Sadly, this misunderstood thriller derailed a few careers. Sharpe shed her clothes again for *The Arab Conspiracy* (1976), but she was out of the business after being underused in the underrated snake thriller *Venom* (1982).

SKIN-fining Moment:

Serpico (0:41) Bubbly view of Cornelia's sharpies in a bathtub with Al Pacino.

See Her Naked In:

The Arab Conspiracy (1976) Breasts
The Reincarnation of Peter Proud (1975)
   Breasts, Buns
Serpico (1973) Breasts

Melanie Shatner

Born: August 1, 1964
Los Angeles, California
Skin-O-Meter: Brief Nudity

It's no surprise that Captain Kirk's daughter's first two roles were in a 1966 *Star Trek* episode and *Star Trek V: The Final Frontier* (1989). Melanie Shatner still went on to become a genre figure in her own right, helped by her sexy firm jawline and jugs that jiggle like Jell-O at warp drive. Her dark beauty got our trousers beaming up in direct-to-video fun like *Cthulhu Mansion* (1990), but Melanie's melons really Spocked our interest with her shower-curtain tease in *Bloodstone: Subspecies II* (1993). Then she pushed our phasers to the final frontier by showing her ample ass and galactic gazongas in *Bloodlust: Subspecies III* (1994).

SKIN-fining Moment:

Bloodlust: Subspecies III (0:04) Brief left breast and buns taking off blood-stained dress. Long shot.

See Her Naked In:

Bloodlust: Subspecies III (1993) LB, Buns

Shari Shattuck

Born: November 18, 1960
Atlanta, Georgia
Skin-O-Meter: Great Nudity

Nobody's mixed the mundane and the mainstream like Shari Shattuck. This southern beauty spent the early '80s as a regular presence on TV shows such as *Mike Hammer* and *Knight Rider*. But when it came time for her big-screen nude debut, Shari unleashed her big'uns in the women's prison flick *The Naked Cage* (1985). She's amazing as the gullible blonde who finds herself up against vengeful inmates and a sexually submissive warden. Shari kept appearing on wholesome TV shows such as *Who's the Boss?* and *Life Goes On* before moving into soaps such as *The Young and the Restless*. Meanwhile, Shari kept shucking her clothes in tawdry epics

such as *A Man of Passion* (1989), *The Spring* (1989), and *Immortal Sins* (1992). Her dedication paid off when she was brought in to replace Lisa Pescia as homicidal maniac "Dr. Claire Archer" in *Body Chemistry 3: Point of Seduction* (1994).

SKIN-fining Moment:

Dead On (0:15) Awesome eyefuls of her natural udders and backdoor during a long, lusty lovemaking session.

See Her Naked In:

Point of Seduction: Body Chemistry III (1994)
   Breasts, Buns
Dead On (1993) Breasts
Immortal Sins (1991) Breasts
The Spring (1989) Breasts, Buns
Desert Warrior (1988) Breasts
Tainted (1988) Breasts, Buns
A Man of Passion (1988) Breasts
The Naked Cage (1986) Breasts, Buns

Helen Shaver

Born: February 24, 1951
St. Thomas, Ontario, Canada
Skin-O-Meter: Hall of Fame

The national animal of Canada happens to be the beaver, and comely Canuck cream puff Helen Shaver's nationalistic pride is visible in the way she lets hers roam free when the cameras are rolling. Blonde and ethereal, with a stare as deep and engulfing as all outer space, Helen and her great white milk spouts are high-profile ambassadors from the Great White North. Although she's appeared fully swathed in such fare as *The Amityville Horror* (1979) and *The Color of Money* (1986), the Helen chest can be checked in breast epics spanning from *High-Ballin'* (1978) to *Rowing Through* (1996), even engaging in a breasty-to-chesty girl-on-girl love tussle in *Desert Hearts* (1985). Her fine, furry fold is fuzzy and fun in *In Praise of Older Women* (1978), which might have been titled *In Praise of Canada's National Animal* in consideration of Helen's ankles being gripped and held apart to expose her unleashed beav.

SKIN-fining Moment:

Desert Hearts (1:10) Helen shows her hangers during some super-hot lesbo lovin' with Patricia Charbonneau in bed.

See Her Naked In:

Rowing Through (1996) Breasts
Innocent Victim (1990) LB
The Believers (1987) RB, Buns, Bush
The Men's Club (1986) Breasts
The Park Is Mine (1986) Breasts
Desert Hearts (1985) Breasts
The Osterman Weekend (1983) Breasts, Bush
In Praise of Older Women (1978) FFN, Buns
High-Ballin' (1978) Breasts, Buns

Fiona Shaw

**Born: July 10, 1958
Cork, Ireland
Skin-O-Meter: Great Nudity**

She's best known as Aunt Petunia in the *Harry Potter* films, but Fiona Shaw is actually a respected London stage actress who was a late bloomer to both film and nudity. She was already in her thirties when she made her big-screen debut in *Sacred Hearts* (1985). Then her sharp, mature beauty made its own belated, full-frontal debut in the historical drama *Mountains of the Moon* (1990). Her sexy hair-waxing scene (trust us) got us all wanting to sniff this Petunia. Our erections only got greater when she stripped down again in *For the Greater Good* (1991). Fiona's finery is mainly still reserved for the stage, but this Irish vixen's next booty will be appreciated by many young fans who already have a crush on their favorite aunt.

SKIN-fining Moment:

Mountains of the Moon (0:33) Fiona gets totally nude, with a hint of pubic sproutage, while letting Patrick Bergen wax the hair off her legs. Shaw 'nuff!

See Her Naked In:

For the Greater Good (1991) FFN, Buns
Mountains of the Moon (1990) Breasts, Bush

Vinessa Shaw

**Born: July 19, 1976
California
Skin-O-Meter: Brief Nudity**

As a teen actress Vinessa Shaw was replaced on the 1994 adventure series *McKenna* by Jennifer Love Hewitt. That's okay, though, since Vinessa was jettisoned into the big leagues when Stanley Kubrick cast her as the prostitute "Domino" in *Eyes Wide Shut* (1999). Cameron Diaz beat her out for the starring role in *Gangs of New York* (2002), but Vinessa's stunning as an FBI agent in a nurse uniform in *Corky Romano* (2001). She's also extremely believable as a masturbatory icon in the sex comedy *40 Days and 40 Nights* (2002). Naturally, dirty old man Woody Allen knew how to showcase Vinessa in *Melinda and Melinda* (2004). Still, her most important film is the underseen *L.A. Without a Map* (1998), where a revealing bathing suit allowed Vinessa to join her actress mother Susan Damante-Shaw in the annals of skinema.

SKIN-fining Moment:

L.A. Without a Map (1:14) Vinessa lies in bed, and we get a partial peek at her left lacto-launcher.

See Her Naked In:

L.A. Without a Map (1998) LB

Carol Shaya

**New York, New York
Skin-O-Meter: Great Nudity**

"Freeze, this is a bust!" Carol Shaya became an overnight sensation—and scandal—when the blonde New York City police officer posed nude for *Playboy*. She was promptly fired by the NYPD, who claimed that Carol had broken policy by posing in her official uniform. Carol had her eye on bigger things, though, and we had our eye on her bigger things when she starred as a cop in *Silent Prey* (1997). It wasn't just the criminals coming clean during Carol's fine shower scene. Her titties also got terrorized later in the film, but rest assured that this muscular Miss comes out on top.

SKIN-fining Moment:

Silent Prey (0:23) Ms. Shaya is a showa, delighting us with both her Carol-cannons as she steps into the shower.

See Her Naked In:

Silent Prey (1997) Breasts, Buns

Katt Shea

**Detroit, Michigan
Skin-O-Meter: Great Nudity**

An anomaly among B-movie boob queens, Katt Shea played the naked bimbo airhead in cheapo camp classics with names like *Hollywood Hot Tubs* (1984). Unlike the great multitude of her fellow flashers, Shea did not slip from semi-notoriety into total obscurity. Indeed, the crafty camera tease learned while she earned and graduated to a job behind the lens. Katt has directed such lowbrow high spots as *Stripped to Kill* (1987), *Poison Ivy* (1992), and *Last Exit to Earth* (1997). Still, her roots remain enticingly visible in such pleasing fare as *My Tutor* (1983) and *Barbarian Queen* (1985).

SKIN-fining Moment:

Preppies (0:20) Katt bares her boobs and just a hint of heinie while torturing some dork through the window.

See Her Naked In:

Barbarian Queen (1985) Breasts
Hollywood Hot Tubs (1984) Breasts

My Tutor (1983) Breasts
Preppies (1982) Breasts, Buns

Rhonda Shear

Born: November 12, 1954
New Orleans, Louisiana
Skin-O-Meter: Brief Nudity

There are benefits to not being able to sleep, not the least of them being a working familiarity with the wacky, stacked, goofball appeal of delightfully dippy brunette knockout Rhonda Shear. Much of America's insomniac population owes the shreds of its remaining sanity to the comforting bumbling presence of Rhonda as the reassuringly halfway competent hostess of *USA Up all Night,* an early-morning marathon of cheesy cheap flicks shown in their most condensed and censored form. If *USA Up* had shown pictures in their entirety, the silly but skintillating Shear might have been in the unique position of introducing a film that starred her own friendly boobies and butt, such as *Basic Training* (1985) with its basic girl-on-top pony ride.

SKIN-fining Moment:

Basic Training (0:07) Rhonda's tits make a lovely appearance as she bounces on a boner just before Ann Dusenberry puts a damper on the bedtime fun.

See Her Naked In:

Basic Training (1985) Breasts

Ally Sheedy

Born: June 13, 1962
New York, New York
Skin-O-Meter: Brief Nudity

Though some see her as a case of arrested promise, idiosyncratic Hollywood outsider Ally Sheedy has always stuck to her guns and is not afraid to poke her nipples out like thumbs. Sheedy's high watermark for public recognition was undoubtedly as a proto-Goth freaky-deaky chick in *The Breakfast Club* (1985). This introverted, troubled teen showed no skin, but her quirky intensity was obviously sexual in its nature. Hints of a hot core were seen in *Bad Boys* (1983) and *One Night Stand* (1995), but those hints were fleeting, covered in sheets and shrouded in shadow. The actual view came in *High Art* (1998), a touching romance tinged with drug addiction, lesbianism, and one of Sheedy's swinging udders.

SKIN-fining Moment:

Bad Boys (0:12) Super quick glimpse of Ally's left titty as she leans forward.

See Her Naked In:

High Art (1998) Breasts
Macon County Jail (1997) Body Double—
　　Breasts, Bush
One Night Stand (1995) RB
Blue City (1986) LB
Bad Boys (1983) LB

Tamie Sheffield

Born: July 27, 1969
Mechanicsburg, Pennsylvania
Skin-O-Meter: Great Nudity

Pulse-quickening Pennsylvania native Tamie Sheffield's bio would read like that of many other golden-haired straight-to-tape starlets—if she weren't such a jock! Following her premiere as free-spirited femme fatale Zoey in the video premiere *Wildflower* (1999), which found her eagerly unleashing her top to reveal a perfect pair of enhanced orbs, she took her athletic prowess to a fascinatingly skintriguing extreme: In 2000 she burst into the consciousness of a certain segment of the population when she appeared as the popular wrestler Sandy on UPN's syndicated series *Women of Wrestling*—better known as *W.O.W.* Wow!! It was back to stripping starlet stylings with her turn in *Cheerleader Massacre* (2002), along with numerous appearances on TV and on the glossy pages of calendars and trading cards.

SKIN-fining Moment:

Cheerleader Massacre (0:46) Tamie flashes some titty and just a bit of butt while getting ready for a shower.

See Her Naked In:

Confidence (2003) Thong
Cheerleader Massacre (2002) Breasts, Buns
Wildflower (1999) Breasts, Bush, Buns

Deborah Shelton

Born: November 21, 1952
Norfolk, Virginia
Skin-O-Meter: Hall of Fame

Former Miss USA 1970 Deborah Shelton had gotten wet to great effect in *Blood Tide* (1982), but her film career was stalled until Brian De Palma cast her in *Body Double* (1984). The film was notorious before production even began, with De Palma attempting to cast porn star Annette Haven in the role that ultimately went to Melanie Griffith. As a gorgeous mystery woman, Deborah jumped into sexy scenes that included changing out of her panties in an upscale store. Deborah went on to three seasons of *Dallas* and then really got her body working double time. *Nemesis* (1993) featured some feral full frontal, while *Sins of the Night* (1993) and *Silk Degrees* (1994) offered Shelton shelling out hot love action. *Plughead Rewired: Circuitry Man II* (1994) had Deborah doffing her top under the bright desert sun. She's kept a low profile lately, but Deborah's body still has us double diddling.

SKIN-fining Moment:

Nemesis (0:37) Ms. Shelton's posterior is punctuated as she turns and gives her lover a massive roundhouse, thereby revealing two heaving hooters and a quick, blissful bush.

See Her Naked In:

Circuitry Man II: Plughead Rewired (1994) Breasts
Silk Degrees (1994) Breasts
Sins of the Night (1993) Breasts, Bush, Buns
Nemesis (1993) FFN, Buns
Blind Vision (1990) Breasts

Marley Shelton

Born: April 12, 1974
Los Angeles, California
Skin-O-Meter: Never-Nude

She started out as a child actor named "Marlee," but Marley Shelton dropped the extra "e" as a hot young actress. She hasn't, however, been especially generous about dropping her bra or panties, although in the 1994 TV movie, she does flash some sweet (albeit distant) cheekage before jumping into a lake for a giddy skinny-dip. That taste of tuchus has only whetted the pub(l)ic's appetite for more of Marley. One tantalizing tease occurs in the slasher flick *Valentine* (2001), wherein Marley wraps herself in a towel while audience members wrap their hands around their . . . other kind of members. Marl also made a wholesome love interest for Tobey Maguire in *Pleasantville* (1998) and was equally sexy in the kinky comedy *Bubble Boy* (2001). In addition, the former prom queen got us shaking our pom-poms as a knocked-up cheerleader in *Sugar & Spice* (2001). Marley's just as sexy offscreen, too, as she proved by her bouncing conversation while guesting on *The Late, Late Show with Craig Kilborn*.

SKIN-fining Moment:

Hercules in the Underworld (0:36) Somebody shows what's in her underpants. *It's supposed to be Marley jumping bare-assed in a lake, but it's a body double.*

See Her Naked In:

Hercules in the Underworld (1994) Body Double—Buns

Hilary Shepard

Born: 1961
New York, New York
Skin-O-Meter: Great Nudity

The sci-fi genre has been kind to sultry-eyed Hilary Shepard. While best known for playing spacy villainess "Divatox" in a couple of *Power Rangers* incarnations, she's also made appearances in *Attack of the 50-Foot Woman* (1993), *Last Exit to Earth* (1996), and the TV series *Deep Space Nine*. Pretty tame fare for a gal who got her skinematic start granting peeks in films such as the Rob Morrow vehicle *Private Resort* (1985) and *Weekend Pass* (1984). Given the eye-popping loveliness of Hil's all-natural D-cups, it seems a shame to keep 'em sealed up in a space suit.

SKIN-fining Moment:

Private Resort (0:36) Great looks at Hilary's heaving hootage and booty-licious buns as she strips for Rob Morrow.

See Her Naked In:

Peacemaker (1990) LB, Buns
Private Resort (1985) Breasts, Buns
Weekend Pass (1984) Breasts, Buns

Jewel Shepard

Born: January 3, 1958
Flatbush, Brooklyn, New York
Skin-O-Meter: Great Nudity

Brooklyn gal Jewel Shepard took an amazing path to L.A. stardom. While working as a stripper, her car broke down in front of auto designer George Barris's shop, home of the Batmobile and the Monkeemobile.

Barris got her a job modeling for car shoots, and her acting career soon took off. Her second nude role made her a true gazonga goddess, playing the beauty whose top got popped by telekinetic Scott Baio in the film *Zapped!* (1982). Shepard's since gone on to doff her clothes in plenty of films (and to do some voice work on the *Garfield & Friends* cartoon show). We're particularly fond of her muscular mammaries in *Caged Heat II: Stripped of Freedom* (1993), but her earlier, softer, brunette years are just as sparkling. Jewel's also promoted her nudie career in the documentary *Jewel Naked Around the World* (1995) and *If I'm So Famous, How Come Nobody's Ever Heard of Me?* (1994), a video version of her autobiography. And she returned to acting—after an eight-year absence—as a hooker in the critically acclaimed film *The Cooler* (2003).

SKIN-fining Moment:

The Sex and Violence Family Hour (1:09) Various angles on Jewel's all-points nudity as she dances and chats.

See Her Naked In:

Jewel Naked Around the World (1995) FFN, Buns
Caged Heat II: Stripped of Freedom (1994) FFN
Roots of Evil (1992) RB
Mission: Killfast (1991) Breasts, Buns
Hollywood Hot Tubs 2: Educating Crystal (1989) LB
The Underachievers (1987) Breasts
Party Camp (1986) Breasts
Christina (1984) FFN, Buns
The Sex and Violence Family Hour (1983) FFN, Thong
My Tutor (1983) LB
Zapped (1982) Breasts
Raw Force (1981) Breasts

Cybill Shepherd

Born: February 18, 1950
Memphis, Tennessee
Skin-O-Meter: Great Nudity

Cybill Shepherd kicked off her career as a model after winning the 1966 Miss Teenage Memphis beauty pageant. Fortunately director Peter Bogdanovich serendipitously picked up a copy of *Glamour* that happened to feature young Cybill on the cover and proceeded to cast her in his cult classic *The Last Picture Show* (1971), launching the aspiring actress into a long and fruitful career, as well as an affair with ol' Pete. Naturally Bogdanovich made sure that Cybill shed her threads a number of times in *Picture Show*, which led to several gratuitous ganders at her globes, as well as an incredible ass shot which we're sure helped Cybill out in garnering her Golden Globe nod for Most Promising Newcomer. With a behind like that, though, she should have won!

SKIN-fining Moment:

The Last Picture Show (0:39) A quick shot of Cybill's nibblers while she sheds her threads on the diving board to join her skinny-dipping pals in the pool.

See Her Naked In:

The Last Picture Show (1971) Breasts, Buns

Tiffany Shepis

Born: September 11, 1979
New York
Skin-O-Meter: Great Nudity

Tiny Tiffany Shepis stands five-feet-three-inches and stands out in any number of cheap horror films—usually thanks to a bulging bust line that harnesses the lung power of a true scream queen. She made her debut as a classical beauty in *Tromeo and Juliet* (1996) and went on to plenty of Troma productions. There was never anything sheepish about Shepis, and she really got us shearing our zippers in *Vinyl Dolls* (2002). She scared our penises out of our pants with her amazing towel toss in *Bloody Murder 2: Closing Camp* (2003), and *Delta Delta Die!* (2003) had us holding our own while Tiffany held her own against a cast of veteran scream queens. There's A-list talent packed into that Shepis shape, too, which is why she remains one of the busiest actresses on the B-movie scene.

SKIN-fining Moment:

Bloody Murder 2 (0:23) Tiffany reveals her rack and a hint of hairless crotch in the shower with Tom Mullen.

See Her Naked In:

The Deviants (2004) Breasts, Buns
The Hazing (2004) Breasts, Buns
Delta Delta Die! (2003) Breasts, Thong
Bloody Murder 2 (2003) FFN

Delia Sheppard

Born: 1961
Copenhagen, Denmark
Skin-O-Meter: Great Nudity

Danish-born Delia Sheppard started her acting career at the ripe old age of thirteen in the South African production *The Spots on my Leopard* (1974). She later had the foresight to remove all her inhibitions (as well as her duds) for a spread in *Penthouse*, where she became the Pet of the Month for April 1988. After her spread (and she was thoughtful enough to use her fingers to spread 'em, if you know what we mean), delicious Delia went on to an illustrious career getting small parts in some agreeably goofy low-budget productions. She scored some Hollywood work, as well, such as *The Adventures of Ford Fairlane* (1990) and *Any Given Sunday* (1999), specializing in parts that called for screen-igniting eye candy. With a filmography including titles like *Sexbomb* (1989), *Secret Games* (1992), and *Naked Force* (1992), you can count on this electrifying act-chest to deliver her goods. Check out *Night Rhythms* (1992) for her hottest scene to date, which involves another bleached blonde in a rumbling-tumbling lesbianic romp that leaves you guessing which one is which.

SKIN-fining Moment:

Haunting Fear (1:10) Extensive examination of Delia's full-frontal fineness while she gets it on with her fella.

See Her Naked In:

Sex Files: Pleasureville (1999) FFN, Buns
Dead Boyz Can't Fly (1992) Breasts
Sins of Desire (1992) FFN, Buns
Animal Instincts (1992) Breasts
Night Rhythms (1992) FFN
Roots of Evil (1992) Thong
Secret Games (1991) Breasts
Mirror Images (1991) Breasts, Bush, Buns
Haunting Fear (1991) Breasts
Witchcraft 2: The Temptress (1990) Breasts
Sexbomb (1989) FFN, Buns

Nicolette Sheridan

Born: November 21, 1963
Worthing, Sussex, England, UK
Skin-O-Meter: Great Nudity

Although blonde heart-stopper Nicolette Sheridan made her first imprint upon mass skin consciousness while bikini clad in *The Sure Thing* (1985), she is not to be confused with a vacuous beach bunny. Sleek and streamlined, like a female version of a top-of-the-line Jaguar, this British-born seductress is sophisticated, cunning, ambitious, and more than a little dangerous. Nicolette was most widely known from her stunning turn on the TV hyper-drama *Knots Landing*, on which she was a vixen to be drooled over then reckoned with. Aerodynamic and small up top, Sheridan's sweet back bumper permitted her to get away with anything, especially the hearts of all who prayed they could see more of it. Those prayers were answered, perhaps by Satan, in *Raw Nerve* (1999). Nicolette's arching, high-end ass perched without so much as a thong. Do those cheeks frame the gates to paradise? Or are they split by an on ramp for the highway to hell?

SKIN-fining Moment:

Raw Nerve (0:24) Sweet teats and a perfect posterior as Nicolette enjoys some lusty mirror-sex with Mario Van Peebles.

See Her Naked In:

Raw Nerve (1999) Breasts, Buns

> "What comes between me and my Calvins? Nothing!"
>
> —BROOKE SHIELDS

Robin Sherwood

Skin-O-Meter: Great Nudity

She didn't have much of a career, but Robin Sherwood certainly rates as one of the great lost talents of the '70s and '80s. This shapely brunette mixed her raw sensuality with a wholesome beauty. That's why directors loved to showcase her hot, naked bod amongst scenes of violence, as best displayed in *Death Wish II* (1982). Her mammaries also made for a memorable victim in *The Love Butcher* (1982). That was pretty much the end of Robin's eggs onscreen, though, and she retired from acting. Fortunately, Robin is also sure to prompt wood in her clothed roles in *Loose Shoes* (1977), *Tourist Trap* (1979), *Serial* (1980)—and even with her fun cameo in *Blow Out* (1981).

SKIN-fining Moment:

Death Wish II (0:15) Robin bares her breasts when thugs have their way with her in a warehouse.

See Her Naked In:

Death Wish II (1982) Breasts
The Love Butcher (1975) Breasts, Buns

Brooke Shields

Born: May 31, 1965
New York, New York
Skin-O-Meter: Brief Nudity

Sometimes people feel guilty for no good reason, but if a guy experiences a twinge of shame while contemplating the early work of child model turned grown-up television star Brooke Shields, then he probably really does have something to repent. As a child prostitute putting her cherry up for auction in *Pretty Baby* (1978), thirteen-year-old Brooke threw the Zeitgeist into a conflicted tizzy. On the one hand, the kid was just so damn otherworldly, innocent, willing, and beautiful. On the other hand, she was a kid. To further confuse desire and taboo, Brooke's next big move was to show off her fifteen-year-old nipples during a love scene in *The Blue Lagoon* (1980). But that was long ago, and Brooke has grown up into a woman whose here-and-now beauty wipes out all memory of the past. Thank God, or we'd all be in therapy.

SKIN-fining Moment:

The Blue Lagoon (0:27) Brooke's body double bares her chest-bubble and pseudo-Shields shag while cavorting underwater with the all-too-actually bare-assed Christopher Atkins.

See Her Naked In:

The Blue Lagoon (1980) Body Double—
    Breasts, Bush, Buns
Just You and Me Kid (1979) Buns
Pretty Baby (1978) Breasts, Buns

Jenny Shimizu

Born: June 16, 1967
Los Angeles, California
Skin-O-Meter: Brief Nudity

Models are tall, Aryan creatures of almost supernatural conformity to accepted standards of beauty, right? Not if that model is Asian tattooed alterna-chick Jenny Shimizu. A little bit androgynous and a whole lot photogenic, little Jenny—as the story goes—was a happy lesbian auto mechanic discovered by a Calvin Klein scout when the taco-loving Asian pulled up on her Hog to L.A.'s trendy Club Fuck. Next stop modeling stratosphere, putting a face to creations from many of the most cutting-edge designers in fashion, posing for the lenses of legendary photographers, strutting her cross-gender sex appeal in over-the-line music videos. Jenny has returned to her mechanic ways, but not before leaving a record of her boyish chest and tiny popping nipples in *Foxfire* (1996).

SKIN-fining Moment:

Foxfire (0:42) Nice look at Jenny's A-cups getting a tattoo from Angelina Jolie.

See Her Naked In:

Foxfire (1996) Breasts

Sofia Shinas

Windsor, Ontario, Canada
Skin-O-Meter: Great Nudity

Sadly, Sofia Shinas will be best remembered as Brandon Lee's co-star when he died during the shooting of their death scenes in *The Crow* (1994). She's worked steadily in sexy direct-to-video thrillers since then (including two with C. Thomas Howell), but let's not neglect her early career in cheap shot-in-Canada cable anthology films. The compilation *Red Shoe Diaries 12: Girl on a Bike* (2000) featured her nude "Borders of Salt" segment, but watch out for the body double. Shinas truly shined, though, on the 1995 "Valerie 23" episode of *The Outer Limits*, in which she played a fully functional party doll of the future. And we really hunger for Sofia in the 1997 "Footsteps" episode of Showtime's *The Hunger*, in which her vampish looks and incredible bod were shown off to devastating effect.

SKIN-fining Moment:

The Outer Limits "Valerie 23" (1995) Robo-Sofie supplies William Sadler with a T&A-rifle lesson in her fully functioning anatomy. More humid than human.

TeleVisions:

The Hunger Breasts
Outer Limits Breasts, Bush, Buns
Red Shoe Diaries Breasts

Pamela Susan Shoop

Born: June 7, 1948
Hollywood, California
Skin-O-Meter: Brief Nudity

Ugh, that stooooopid Michael Myers. You know, of *Halloween* fame (not to be confused with international man of mystery *Austin Powers* actor Mike Myers). He just had to go heat things up a little too much in the hot tub for the all-natural naughty nurse played by Pamela Susan Shoop. She can really raise your blood pressure in the second installment of John Carpenter's maniac magnum opus *Halloween II* (1981). Ah well, these horror genre films are always "potboilers" anyway—get it? OK . . . let's move on, shall we? Pam is also a smokingly sexy, seasoned character actress. Hence her luscious bod is not her only fecundity; her career has been long and fruitful too. As a teen she was a regular on the popular '70s soap *Return to Peyton Place* and has pretty much been a drive-by guest on every conceivable made-for-TV kitsch catchall. Highlights include *Mannix, Hawaii Five-O, The Mod Squad, Night Gallery, Wonder Woman, CHiPs, The Incredible Hulk, Battlestar Galactica, Knight Rider, Fame,* and *Kung Fu: The Legend Continues.* Phew, that list is a tongue twister . . . don't even say it.

SKIN-fining Moment:

Halloween II (48:00) Pamie shows her topless pumpkins as she hops in and out of a whirlpool with Leo Rossi.

See Her Naked In:

Halloween II (1981) Breasts

Kathy Shower

Born: March 8, 1953
Brookville, Ohio
Skin-O-Meter: Great Nudity

Poster-perfect blonde Kathy Shower has had the ultimate B-movie boob-queen career. Initially cradling her melons on *Three's Company, CHiPs,* and *Simon & Simon* guest spots, Kathy parlayed her television exposure into a slot as *Playboy*'s Playmate for May 1985. The initial appearance of her sunny bounties in Hefner's guide to the good life resulted in Shower reigning as Playmate of the Year for 1986, and the rest has been the breast of times. Aside from a slew of *Playboy* videos, comely Kathy has bounced through twenty-plus sexploitation flicks. Collect them all, but start with *Erotic Boundaries* (1997). See Shower cross all erotic lines—going solo for phone sex, legs open as she squirms beneath a man, and humping her mound as an equally attractive female specimen feasts on her steamy clam.

SKIN-fining Moment:

The Further Adventures of Tennessee Buck (0:59) Kathy, appearing in all her naked glory, gets a nice, oily rubdown courtesy of a bunch of native babes, baring her bodacious bosom in the process. Wow!

See Her Naked In:

Love Letters: A Romantic Trilogy (2001) Breasts, Bush
Erotic Boundaries (1997) FFN, Buns
Hindsight (1996) Breasts
Irresistible Impulse (1996) Breasts
To the Limit (1995) Breasts
Married People, Single Sex II: For Better or Worse (1995) Breasts
Sexual Malice (1994) Breasts
Improper Conduct (1994) Breasts
L.A. Goddess (1993) FFN
Wild Cactus (1993) Breasts
Bedroom Eyes II (1990) Breasts, Buns
Out on Bail (1989) Breasts
Velvet Dreams (1988) Breasts, Buns
Frankenstein General Hospital (1988) Breasts
The Further Adventures of Tennessee Buck (1988) Breasts
Numerous *Playboy* Videos

TeleVisions:

Hotline Breasts
Women: Stories of Passion Breasts, Buns

Elisabeth Shue

Born: October 6, 1963
Wilmington, Deleware
Skin-O-Meter: Great Nudity

Elisabeth Shue is the archetypal girl-next-door beauty with the drop-dead

IF THE SHUE TITS: ELIZABETH SHUE IN *LEAVING LAS VEGAS.*

body under her puffy sweater. In *Adventures in Babysitting* (1987), she was the babysitter trapped in big, bad Chicago with a bunch of troublemaking kids. In *Cocktail* (1988), Liz played the sweet rich girl being wooed by blue-collar bartender Tom Cruise against her daddy's will. And she exposed first skin: a sideways shot of her topless bundles. Then Liz decided it was time to grow up or forever be typecast as the cheerleader. In *Leaving Las Vegas* (1995), she shattered her previous image by portraying a street-walking whore and allowing her mammoth mams to get handled and sucked before sitting nude in a shower. Elisabeth was nominated for an Oscar for the role, and it has made her one of Hollywood's most sought-after actresses—and we're always seeking a fresh glimpse of her gorgeous form. Dig the slip of the nip in *Blind Justice* (1994), her bawdy bits in *Cousin Bette* (1998), and, good golly Miss *Molly* (1999). Elisabeth shows off her meaty round tush, which is as appetizing as her hefty hooters. If the Shue fits, wear it— and, oh, to strap on Elisabeth!

SKIN-fining Moment:

Leaving Las Vegas (1:20) Fantastic close-ups of Shue's shakers as she pours tequila on her naked chest and has Nicolas Cage lick 'em clean.

See Her Naked In:

Molly (1999) Bush, Buns
Cousin Bette (1998) RB, Buns

The Trigger Effect (1996) LB
Leaving Las Vegas (1995) Breasts
Blind Justice (1994) RB
Radio Inside (1994) LB
Link (1986) Body Double—RB, Buns

Qi Shu

Born: April 16, 1976
Taiwan
Skin-O-Meter: Great Nudity

Asian actress Qi Shu is one karate-kicking hottie. This Taiwanese tiger is breast known in Chinese skinema for her manic movements while boxing heads and baring boobage in action films such as *Sex & Zen II* (1996) and *Street Angels* (1996). Stateside Qi is more famous for her tamer trysts, such as *Gorgeous* (1999) and the French and English flick *The Transporter* (2002). While gorgeous in both films, this tasty dish's *mu goo gi pan* is most delish in imports from her native land.

SKIN-fining Moment:

Yu po tuan er zhi yu nu xia jing (1:18) The beautiful Qi Shu is slamming the beautiful Loletta Lee during a long, energetic bout of lesbiosity.

See Her Naked In:

Iron Sister (1999) Breasts, Buns
Viva! Island Girl (1999) Breasts
Sex and Zen 2 (1996) FFN, Buns
Yu po tuan er zhi yu nu xia jing (1996) Breasts, Bush, Buns
Street Angels (1996) Breasts
Viva Erotica (1996) Breasts

Nina Siemaszko

Born: July 14, 1970
Chicago, Illinois
Skin-O-Meter: Great Nudity

What can be said about Nina Siemaszko, a fresh breeze from the Windy City? Let's talk breasts. Nina's chest boasts a moderately full rack that slopes to form a pleasing, firm contour, bulging to

the sides with a quality of roundness about equal in volume to the curvature of the hang on the boob bottoms. Nipple diameter is appropriate to overall tit size. The beauties swing and sway in a natural way and are inviting to face and paw. The best place to experience the free-floating contentment of Siemaszko's bra contents is in Zalman King's *Wild Orchid 2* (1992), in which Nina was cast as a young girl pushed by circumstances into the fast lane of life as a high-priced call girl.

SKIN-fining Moment:

Wild Orchid II (0:27) Nina shows us her top-knobs and tush while putting on clothes with Wendy Hughes.

See Her Naked In:

More Tales of the City (1998) Breasts
Wild Orchid II (1992) Breasts
Lost Angels (1989) Buns

TeleVisions:

Red Shoe Diaries FFN

Karen Sillas

Born: June 5, 1965
Brooklyn, New York
Skin-O-Meter: Great Nudity

Whether due to her commitment to craft or bad breaks, wonderfully emotive Karen Sillas and her fully expressive fun balloons are known to far less skin fanatics than are prepared to adore her. A dirty blonde with a face that jumps with excitement, much of Karen's acting has been in live theater. When she has placed her proud protruders in front of a movie camera, it's usually been for some indie effort doomed to selective screening. Picky viewers are sure to be pleased by the sweet gropes of *Sour Grapes* (1998) and by Karen's guaranteed-to-please performance as a chick-loving nude figure model in *Risk* (1994).

SKIN-fining Moment:

Risk (0:20) Karen poses for a figure-drawing class. What a figure! What a class! And we see her boobies.

See Her Naked In:

On the Edge (2001)
Sour Grapes (1998) LB
Female Perversions (1997) Breasts
Risk (1994) Breasts, Buns

Alicia Silverstone

Born: October 4, 1976
San Francisco, California
Skin-O-Meter: Brief Nudity

Perfection is a tough act to follow, but impishly beautiful blonde Alicia Silverstone consistently achieves the impossible. In giving a perfect rendition of the spoiled but adorable high-school princess, replete with miniskirts, mini-tops, popping sexpot eyes, and pouting sexpot lips in *Clueless* (1995), Alicia seemed to be on a path to teasing and temptation from which there could be no deviation. But she had achieved a wholly opposite perfection in *The Crush* (1993). Stealing scene after scene as a precocious Lolita with a heart full of malice, simmering Silverstone leaves sweetly concupiscent Cher totally in the *Clueless* dust. The teenage temptress of *Crush* is the most evil little darling ever to squirm about in a falsely modest pink bikini. Nothing nipworthy is actually shown, but the effect is every bit as strong as if those bikini bottoms had dropped to the ground. Almost a decade later, Alicia proved to be as perky as she was in her big-screen prime on her NBC series *Miss Match*, where she also provided her most skinful effort to date—via a stunning look at her chest charms behind a sheer shower curtain while sudsing up with her loverman. Nice work, Miss Mams!

SKIN-fining Moment:

The Crush (0:25) Alicia ably demonstrates the all-powerful allure of the female teen body in a bikini as Cary Elwes just can't pull himself away from gawking at her through a window.

See Her Naked In:

The Crush (1993) Body Double—Buns

TeleVisions:

Miss Match Breasts

Victoria Silvstedt

Born: September 19, 1974
Skelleftehamn, Sweden
Skin-O-Meter: Great Nudity

Skintillating Swedish knockout Victoria Silvestedt, an Amazonian blonde in the great Scandinavian tradition, achieved international skin status as *Playboy*'s Playmate of the Year in 1997. She's been teasing audiences ever since as appropriately overwhelming window dressing in such sexy comedies as *BASEketball* (1998), *Out Cold* (2001), and *Boat Trip* (2002). Remarkably (but not regrettably), the only time she let loose her scrumptious Swedish meatballs in a feature film was in the Australian beach flick *Boardheads* (1998).

SKIN-fining Moment:

Boardheads (0:52) A fun frolic with Vicki's plastic fantastics as she peels down her bikini top for a beach bum.

See Her Naked In:

Boat Trip (2002) Thong
Out Cold (2001) RB
Ivansxtc (2000) LB
Bodyguards (2000) Breasts
Boardheads (1998) Breasts
Numerous *Playboy* Videos

TeleVisions:

E! Wild On . . . Breasts, Thong

Jessica Simpson

Born: July 10, 1980
Abilene, Texas
Skin-O-Meter: Never Nude

After losing out to Christina Aguilera and Britney Spears for a place on *The Mickey Mouse Club*, Jessica Simpson kept auditioning and earned her own place in the '90s as a leading pop songstress. The five-foot-three-inch dynamo was a hit artist by the age of seventeen, which meant we only had to wait one year before pulling our puds to the sexy shots we've pulled from her many MTV appearances—not to mention an amazing outfit she sported for *The Tonight Show*. Sadly, Jessica's held on to her chaste image, while Christina and Britney are slutting it up. She's also become very quotable on her MTV reality series *Newlyweds: Nick & Jessica*, where her oblivious statements are as memorable as her bikini footage. Speaking of bikinis, don't miss Jessica's hooterific bathing suit on *That '70s Show*. It's no wonder that Ashton Kutcher later sought her out to get *Punk'd*.

SKIN-fining Moment:

Newlyweds: Nick & Jessica (2003) See Jessica force her awesomely flawless form into a wetsuit. Watch that bombastically beautiful body bounce and bobble and jiggle and shimmy and . . . you get the picture. It's awesome.

Suzi Simpson

Born: November 16, 1968
Athens, Greece
Skin-O-Meter: Great Nudity

Born in Athens, Greece, but raised in America, former Catholic school girl Suzy Simpson emerged as one of the many Pamela Anderson-esque centerfolds to grace the pages of *Playboy* in the early '90s. The beautifully breasted bella—who provides an engaging argument for the actual existence of Greek goddesses—parlayed that appearance into a boob-and-buns-baring feature role in the Andy Sidaris–directed straight-to-tape *Enemy Gold* (1993). She followed her golden appearance as secret agent "Becky Midnite" in the Sidaris caper with an equally skintastic supporting role in the video premiere *The Last Road* (1997). Suzi's astounding assets haven't been seen in a feature film since, but there's still hope.

SKIN-fining Moment:

Enemy Gold (0:09) Suzi shows those boobzies while tossing on a new outfit in the john.

See Her Naked In:

The Last Road (1997) Breasts
Enemy Gold (1993) Breasts, Buns
Numerous *Playboy* Videos

Molly Sims

Born: May 25, 1973
Murray, Kentucky
Skin-O-Meter: Brief Nudity

Super sexpot Molly Sims simmers and glimmers with gorgeousness. With beauty and brains to boot, this long-legged lovely studied pre-law before prancing her fine frame down the catwalk. First modeling her marvelous mug, mini-mams, and hamhocks for fashion mags, Molly warmed with her form in *Sports Illustrated* and served as hostess with the most-ass on MTV's *House of Style*. Now Molly is set up in Skin City, taunting and teasing on the series *Las Vegas*. Good golly, Miss Molly! We'd sure love a ball.

SKIN-fining Moment:

Las Vegas "Donny, We Hardly Knew Ye" (1994) Molly changes shirts in front of some business suited bozo, supplying us with super hot right side-boob, including a glimpse of nip smack dab in the midst of NBC primetime.

TeleVisions:

Las Vegas RB

Lori Singer

Born: November 6, 1957
Corpus Christi, Texas
Skin-O-Meter: Hall of Fame

Is it possible for God to give one woman too many good things? The excesses of good fortune don't seem to have done any harm to long, lissome blonde beauty Lori Singer, nor to the legions of aficionados who admire her many and varied attributes. As smart as she is sensually appealing, Texas-bred Lori began a modeling sideline in the late 1970s to finance her study of classical cello at the prestigious and arduous Juilliard School for the Performing Arts. She sprang from the catwalk to the squawk box with a featured role as a cellist on the hit series *Fame*, which was but a hop and skip away from being cast opposite Kevin Bacon in *Footloose* (1984), which showered Singer in fame beyond all reckoning. Mensa member Lori refused to allow renown to ruin her. Unspoiled and natural as the day the Good Lord broke the mold after fashioning her, the streaky blonde with the faraway eyes has shared her skintastic gifts in half a dozen instances of epidermal generosity. The bounty is best appreciated in *The Last Ride* (1994).

SKIN-fining Moment:

Sunset Grill (1:14) Lori's nips are nice and stiff as she gets up from some hot and sweaty schtupping.

See Her Naked In:

The Last Ride (1994) Breasts
Short Cuts (1993) Breasts, Bush, Buns
Sunset Grill (1993) Breasts, Buns
Made in U.S.A. (1988) LB
Summer Heat (1987) Breasts
Trouble in Mind (1986) LB

WICKED-HOT MARINA SIRTIS GETS WHIPPED AND STRIPPED BY FAYE DUNAWAY IN *THE WICKED LADY.*

Marina Sirtis

Born: March 29, 1960
East London, England, UK
Skin-O-Meter: Great Nudity

Deep outer space is said to be a cold and lonely place, which accounts for why the crew of the Starship *Enterprise* made sure to never leave behind hot companion Marina Sirtis. In her role as Counselor Deanna Troi on *Star Trek: The Next Generation*, busty, lusty, London-born Marina fueled the rocket-propelled fantasies of a cross-generational selection of sci-fi nerds and outright pervs. But there was life before interplanetary liftoff for Sirtis, some of it shirtless with her chest globes lifting off in orbits all their own. The mammary planets were most fetchingly aligned in *The Wicked Lady* (1983). Worlds were set spinning when Marina flashed bush while dashing from bed and fled with exposed tits heaving. A raucous mob of townsfolk sputtered as though they had been visited by an alien lifeform.

SKIN-fining Moment:

The Wicked Lady (1:20) FFN after Faye Dunaway catches her in the sack with Alan Bates. Wicked!

See Her Naked In:

Paradise Lost (1999) Breasts
Death Wish III (1985) Breasts
Blind Date (1984) Breasts
The Wicked Lady (1983) FFN

Claire Skinner

UK
Skin-O-Meter: Great Nudity

Claire Skinner is one of the few hot-blooded British actresses ever to make a splash Stateside, but her name isn't as recognizable as, say, Catherine Zeta-Jones. Maybe Claire should find herself an aging Hollywood playboy like Michael Douglas to ball. Even without that advantage Claire has led a wonderful career, appearing in just over twenty productions (mostly on the BBC) in just over a decade. Oddly enough, her penchant for onscreen nudity didn't really materialize (or dematerialize) until later, with her big nudie debut in *A Dance to the Music of Time* (1997), in which she went balls-out full frontal with a couple of nice ass shots thrown in for good measure. Her biggest hits on this side of the pond were as the decapitated midwife in *Sleepy Hollow* (1999) and as Magda in *Bridget Jones's Diary* (2001). But for a bigger thrill, check out Claire's little scenes in *Second Sight* (1999), *Mauvaise passe* (1999), and *Perfect Strangers* (1999). Let's hope this English strumpet doesn't remain a stranger long.

SKIN-fining Moment:

Mauvaise passe (0:53) Quick nips and a hint of lap-lint while she's getting worked on by a guy in bed.

See Her Naked In:

Perfect Strangers (2001) Breasts
Second Sight (1999) Breasts
Mauvaise passe (1999) Breasts, Bush

TeleVisions:

A Dance to the Music of Time FFN, Buns

Jennifer Sky

Born: October 13, 1977
Palm Beach, Florida
Skin-O-Meter: Great Nudity

Where do the television networks find all these impossibly hot, sweet, dream chicks who populate the silly dramas and somber comedies aimed at their fourteen to twenty-five demographic? Case in point, Jennifer Sky. At times a platinum blonde, always perky, and playful with big, flashing eyes and an inviting blast of smile, Jennifer has been an aching object of supporting-role desire on *Emerald Cove*, *SeaQuest DSV*, *Out of the Blue*, *Buffy the Vampire Slayer*, *General Hospital*, *Xena: Warrior Princess*, and *Cleopatra 2525*. The TV gods have so many of these perfectly fine filler chicks. Why not toss a few into the breast-infested waters of basic cable and the silver screen? TV is too confining a limit for this Sky.

SKIN-fining Moment:

My Little Eye (0:43) Jennifer in the Sky with Tits Out. As she humps and grinds Bradley Cooper, we see her awesome rackage.

See Her Naked In:

My Little Eye (2002) Breasts

Ione Skye

Born: September 4, 1971
Hertfordshire, England, UK
Skin-O-Meter: Great Nudity

The great thing about hippie parents is that when their daughters go into show business they have no hesitation about flaunting their natural nudity. Ione Skye, whose dad is '60s Sunshine Superman Donovan, plays true to form, and what a form it is. Slightly pigeon toed, with full girlish hips and freshly budded chest ornaments, Ione jumped right into the skin mix with *The Rachel Papers* (1989). She still hadn't put her clothes back on ten years later with *Mascara* (1999). In between, her flower-child juglettes were onscreen tripping in *Gas Food*

Lodging (1992), *Rebel Highway: Girls in Prison* (1994), and *Four Rooms* (1995).

SKIN-fining Moment:

The Rachel Papers (1:05) Overhead views of Ione's sumptuous mammaries first in bed, then in the bath with her lover-dude.

See Her Naked In:

Mascara (1999) Breasts, Bush, Buns
Four Rooms (1995) Breasts
Girls in Prison (1994) RB
Gas Food Lodging (1992) Breasts
The Rachel Papers (1989) Breasts

Helen Slater

Born: December 15, 1963
Massapequa, Long Island, New York
Skin-O-Meter: Great Nudity

"Look! Up in the sky, it's a bird, it's a plane . . . it's a hot chick!" That's Helen Slater, who got to wear the blue and red leotard as *Supergirl* (1984). The film may have been a failure at the box office, but what an introduction to such a sexy lady. The visibility she received from her debut splash scored her some ripe roles in über-'80s hits, most notably *The Secret of My Success* (1987), *Ruthless People*, and *The Legend of Billie Jean* (1985), in which she played the title role of the down-home martyr opposite Christian Slater (no relation). She also appeared in *City Slickers* (1991) and the ill-fated Lloyd Bridges journalism TV drama *Capital News*. Thankfully a downward turn in Helen's career brought about some skin flashitude. Check out *Happy Together* (1988) for her brief debut breast shot. For a more satisfying gander at Helen's Supergirls, see *A House in the Hills* (1993), in which she appeared more or less nude for about half of the movie. That's a house that's built to move.

SKIN-fining Moment:

A House in the Hills (0:15) Helen shows her breasts in the mirror while trying on lingere.

See Her Naked In:

A House in the Hills (1993) Breasts
Betrayal of the Dove (1992) Breasts
Happy Together (1989) RB

Amy Sloan

Born: May 12, 1978
Whitehorse, Yukon, Canada
Skin-O-Meter: Great Nudity

She was a psycho we'd gladly be locked up with in *Gothika* (2003), but Amy Sloan made it to the big time as Howard Hughes's neurotic mom in *The Aviator* (2004). This red-haired Canuck has been a skinematic favorite ever since her role in the sci-fi flick *X Change* (2000). This serious young actress gave her all in a sizzling sex scene that showcased her tiny titties and a stunning ability to orgasm. It's never been more obvious that big things were coming a starlet's way—and we certainly like the way that this starlet is coming.

SKIN-fining Moment:

X Change (0:27) Curly-locked Sloan screams her way through a goofy sex scene with Kyle MacLachlan, cheerfully showing off her squeakers and kazoo.

See Her Naked In:

X Change (2000) Breasts, Buns

Amy Smart

Born: March 26, 1976
Topanga Canyon, California
Skin-O-Meter: Great Nudity

Flawless blonde Amy Smart played against her last name as a naïve co-ed on the TV college drama *Felicity* from 1999 to 2001, but this ferociously sexy California girl has the brains to back up her killer body. After plying her trade as a ballerina, model, and up-and-coming actress in flesh-friendly fare such as *Varsity Blues* (1999), Amy displayed savage comedic instincts in a succession of big-screen comedies such as the cross-country campus caper *Road Trip* (2000), in which she spectacularly went topless, and the frantic farce *Rat Race* (2001), which featured a bizarrely sexy scene in which Amy suggestively siphoned gas from a car. Talk about crude oil!

SKIN-fining Moment:

Road Trip (0:17) Amy sheds her shirt and serves up her adorable Smarties as she gets sexy with a very thankful Breckin Meyer.

See Her Naked In:

Road Trip (2000) Breasts

Allison Smith

Born: December 9, 1969
New York, New York
Skin-O-Meter: Great Nudity

Cute as a button, and far nicer to put on, Allison Smith in her trademark brown bob haircut is a cuddle-friendly actress who is not nearly as famous as she should be. Recognizable from her role as Mallory on TV's *The West Wing*, the part is just not as substantial as this hot piece deserves. She debuted as young Eva Peron in the made-for-TV *Evita Peron* (1981), which was a great role for the budding beauty, but it only led to guest spots on shows like *Hunter* and *Wolf*, neither of which served to bolster her career. After starring as Jane Curtin's daughter on the CBS sitcom *Kate & Allie*, young Allison went off to cinema land to get herself killed by Jason Vorhees in the ninth *Friday the 13th* installment, *Jason Goes to Hell* (1993). Allison landed the challenging role of a young college student who is forced into a sexual encounter in the socially conscious *A Reason to Believe* (1995). But the real reason to believe is Allison's full-frontal turn in the Spanish flick *Los Años Bárbaros* (1998). She showed all coming out of the ocean, which from the hard, rock-like nipples centered on her dripping boobies, appears to be a quite chilly surf.

SKIN-fining Moment:

Los Años Bárbaros (1:22) Allison gets nude on the beach with Hedy Burress and two friends. FFN and buns in the summer sun.

See Her Naked In:

Los Años Bárbaros (1998) FFN, Buns

Amber Smith

Born: March 2, 1972
Tampa, Florida
Skin-O-Meter: Great Nudity

In the world of the high-fashion supermodel, Amber Smith is a breath of fresh heat. The *Sports Illustrated* swimsuit model and catwalk temptress enjoys flaunting her talents—clothed, semi-clothed, and fully naked. Amber, in her post-modeling film career, embraces this ideal with a body made for lingerie, swimsuits, or, best, nothing at all. In Howard Stern's *Private Parts* (1997), Amber played the listener who related the story of her first lesbian experience. In an unforgettably erotic scene, she slowly described, in delectable detail, how she was seduced while away at summer camp by an equally girl-happy counselor. For more revealing looks at Amber, check out *How to be a Player* (1997), *Tell Me No Lies*

(2000), and *Deception* (2000). When it comes to eye candy, Amber is the sweetest.

SKIN-fining Moment:

The Funeral (0:43) Bare bombers in a scene rumored to be real sex. Watch how she wipes herself after Paul Hipp pulls out.

See Her Naked In:

Amber Smith: R.A.W. (2003) FFN, Buns
Crime Scene (2001) Breasts, Bush, Buns
Starstruck (2000) Breasts
Tell Me No Lies (2000) Breasts
L.A. Confidential (1997) LB
How to be a Player (1997) Breasts, Thong
Laws of Deception (1997) Breasts, Thong
Lowball (1997) FFN
The Funeral (1996) Breasts

TeleVisions:

Red Shoe Diaries FFN, Buns

Anna Nicole Smith

Born: November 28, 1967
Mexia, Texas
Skin-O-Meter: Hall of Fame

Things are just bigger in Texas. Take former Playmate of the Year and Guess? Jeans supermodel Anna Nicole Smith, who made it sexy to be a full-figured woman again in the famished times of waifs like Kate Moss. It's especially nice to have that weight divided between her brontosaurus breasts and planetoid posterior. *Playboy* took her from chicken-flinging obscurity to centerfolds and table dances. Anna famously married paralyzed ninety-year-old billionaire J. Howard Marshall, whom she met at a topless club, in 1994. Anna Nicole may have been more than Marshall could handle, as he died a year later, and a court battle between the volcanically voluptuous widow and her (really) old man's family ensued. She ended up walking away with

millions, but that didn't stop the temptress from sharing the wealth—at least in scores of saucy *Playboy* videos! We're particularly fond of the wet lesbian scrub-a-dub from *Anna Nicole Smith Exposed: Her Fantasy Revealed* (1998). She's appeared in more multiplex-friendly features, like her debut in *The Hudsucker Proxy* (1994) and *Naked Gun 33⅓: The Final Insult* (1994). And, of course, there have been the sexploitation thrillers *To the Limit* (1995) and *Skyscraper* (1995). For a more intimate look at the life and times of Anna Nicole, there is the reality TV show from the E! Entertainment network. How much bigger can this gal get?

SKIN-fining Moment:

To the Limit (1:13) Anna Nicole makes the most of herself in the shower. Massive mongo-bombers and frontal-fuzz as she lets her own fingers do the diddling.

See Her Naked In:

Anna Nicole Smith Exposed: Her Fantasy Revealed (1998) FFN, Buns
To the Limit (1995) FFN, Thong
Skyscraper (1995) Breasts, Buns
Numerous *Playboy* Videos

"What Pam Grier was to blaxploitation movies, what Bruce Lee was to kung fu movies, what Burt Reynolds was to good-ol'-boy movies, Rainbeaux Smith was to cheerleader movies. She truly has, without trying whatsoever, a Marilyn Monroe quality. She doesn't look like Monroe at all; she just has that kind of vacantness. She's not so much acting as she is existing. Imagine Marilyn Monroe as kind of a '70s hippie junky, then you kind of have Rainbeaux Smith."

—QUENTIN TARANTINO ON CHERYL "RAINBEAUX" SMITH

Cheryl "Rainbeaux" Smith

Born: June 6, 1955
Los Angeles, California
Died: October 25, 2002
Skin-O-Meter: Hall of Fame

The late Cheryl "Rainbeaux" Smith is the definitive '70s drive-in starlet, an ethereal nymph who brought inimitable star power and A-plus class to numerous B-movie classics. The waify blonde's film career skyrocketed from her lead in the art-short *The Birth of Aphrodite* (1971) and a bit part in the same year's biopic *Evel Knievel*. Cheryl changed her name to Rainbeaux Smith over the course of appearing

---

MR. SKIN'S TOP TEN

Naked Cheerleaders
. . . Rah rah sis BOOB bah

10. **Rosanne Katon**
    —*The Swinging Cheerleaders* (1974)

9. **Marilyn Joi**
    —*Cheerleaders' Wild Weekend* (1979)

8. **Diane Lee Hart**
    —*The Pom Pom Girls* (1976)

7. **Kari Lizer**
    —*Private School* (1983)

6. **Tamie Sheffield**
    —*Cheerleader Massacre* (2002)

5. **Bambi Woods**
    —*Debbie Does Dallas* (1978)

4. **Mary Louise Weller**
    —*Animal House* (1978)

3. **Michelle Drake**
    —*The Hollywood Knights* (1980)

2. **Mena Suvari**
    —*American Beauty* (1999)

1. **Cheryl "Rainbeaux" Smith**
    —*Revenge of the Cheerleaders* (1976)

in more than twenty-five motion pictures, every one of which is noteworthy, before she seemingly disappeared after 1982's *Parasite*. Sadly, the reason for Cheryl's absence was an extended battle with drug addiction that led her to destitution and jail and, ultimately, contributed to her tragic death in 2002. Fortunately, Rainbeaux will shine forever through her skintastic legacy, starting with 1974's *The Swinging Cheerleaders* and continuing on through such mammariffic milestones as *Caged Heat* (1974), *Revenge of the Cheerleaders* (1975), *The Pom Pom Girls* (1976), *Massacre at Central High* (1976), *Drum* (1976), and *Cinderella* (1977), to name just a few. In the 1975 send-up *Video Vixens*, Rainbeaux sensationally displayed her comedic talents (along with her entire body) as the Twinkle Twat Girl, hawking an unabashed feminine hygiene spray. Offscreen Cheryl performed live with Cheech & Chong and often sat in as a drummer for Joan Jett. There was nothing this multitalented knockout couldn't do . . . except find happiness in a world for which she was too beautiful.

SKIN-fining Moment:

Cinderella (0:30) Rainbeaux glows full-frontal perfection as she's bathed by Linda Gildersleeve and Yana Nirvana.

See Her Naked In:

Parasite (1982) Breasts
The Best of Sex and Violence (1981) Breasts
Cinderella (1977) Breasts, Bush, Buns
The Incredible Melting Man (1977) Breasts
Fantasm Comes Again (1977)
Slumber Party '57 (1977) Buns
Drum (1976) Breasts
Revenge of the Cheerleaders (1976) Breasts, Bush, Buns
Massacre at Central High (1976) Breasts, Bush, Buns
The Pom Pom Girls (1976) Breasts

Video Vixens (1975) FFN
Farewell My Lovely (1975) FFN
Caged Heat (1974) FFN, Buns
The Swinging Cheerleaders (1974) Breasts

Jaclyn Smith

Born: October 26, 1947
Houston, Texas
Skin-O-Meter: Never Nude

Jaclyn Smith was the only constant *Angel* during the five-year run of *Charlie's Angels*, and she wasn't in a hurry to ditch TV after the series ended. One of her few big-screen excursions, *Nightkill* (1980), offered a nice gratuitous shower scene, but it's strictly chaste. That's because Jaclyn has always taken pride in her family values. She even took issue when *Angels* producers suggested that her character, Kelly Garrett, may have been a call girl in her early days. Thankfully, Jaclyn wasn't too devout to bare phenomenal cleavage on network television. And she's been just as sexy in her other TV projects and could still steal a scene in her unbilled cameo in *Charlie's Angels: Full Throttle* (2003).

SKIN-fining Moment:

Charlie's Angels "Angels in Chains" (1976) The Angels, undercover behind bars, are forced to uncover for a pervy prison guard. Jaclyn's way of opening her towel so he can take a gander is especially skinspirational.

Julie K. Smith

Born: August 18, 1967
Nuremberg, West Germany
Skin-O-Meter: Great Nudity

Juicy, jug-heavy Julie K. Smith first slipped out of her clothing for small roles in the exploitation flicks *Pretty Smart* (1986) and *Angel III: The Final Chapter* (1988), followed by her reign as *Penthouse*'s February 1993 Pet of the Month, but that was only a harbinger of things to come. Since

then, Julie has followed suit by shedding her suit to reveal her bountiful boobs and remarkably resilient rear in no less than a dozen straight-to-tape spectaculars, including *Midnight Tease 2* (1995), *Sorceress II: The Temptress* (1996), *The Bare Wench Project* (2000), and, most recently, *Bad Bizness* (2002). Undoubtedly, Julie's most highly regarded group of taped titillaters are those she appeared in for babes-and-bullets auteur Andy Sidaris, who put Julie to work as an undercover lethal lady code-named Cobra in his productions *The Dallas Connection* (1994), *Day of the Warrior* (1996), and *Return to Savage Beach* (1998).

SKIN-fining Moment:

Pretty Smart (1:14) Hefty-hoots and hair below as Julie puts a pillow between herself and her boyfriend in bed.

See Her Naked In:

Bad Bizness (2003) Breasts
Baberellas (2003) Breasts, Thong
Wolfhound (2002) Breasts
Cheerleader Massacre (2002) Breasts
Survivors Exposed (2001) Breasts
The Bare Wench Project (1999) Breasts
L.E.T.H.A.L. Ladies: Return to Savage Beach (1998) Breasts, Buns
Day of the Warrior (1996) Breasts
The Dallas Connection (1995) Breasts, Buns
Midnight Tease II (1995) Breasts, Thong
Angel III: The Final Chapter (1988) Breasts
Pretty Smart (1987) Breasts, Bush, Buns
Disorderlies (1987) Breasts, Buns

TeleVisions:

Erotic Confessions Breasts, Bush, Buns

Lauren Lee Smith

Born: June 19, 1980
Vancouver, British Columbia, Canada
Skin-O-Meter: Never Nude

Canadian up-and-comer Lauren Lee Smith got her big break bouncing her B-cups alongside Sylvester

Stallone in *Get Carter* (2000). Soon this former model found herself kicking ass with fellow fox Jessica Alba on *Dark Angel* and bopping her bouncies about on the short-lived MTV boy-band parody *2Gether: The Series*. After parading her peaches-and-cream complexion in TV family fare such as *Christy: The Movie* (2001) and *The Survivors Club* (2003), little Lauren Lee was lured into the luscious world of lesbianism. She became one of the Sapphic co-stars on the Cinemax series *The L Word*, the perfect environment for a lovely lady like Lauren Lee.

Madeline Smith

Born: August 2, 1949
Hartfield, Sussex, England, UK
Skin-O-Meter: Great Nudity

Dark-haired English beauty Madeline Smith debuted in the British comedy *The Mini-Affair* (1967), which unfortunately had nothing to do with hot chicks in miniskirts doing the nasty. She's most recognizable as Miss Caruso, the Italian secret agent whom James Bond unzipped with his magnetic wristwatch at the beginning of *Live and Let Die* (1973). After a role in the serial Santa Claus thriller *Silent Night, Deadly Night* (1984), however, Madeline wasn't naughty or nice, but gone from cinema. Thankfully, she did so after she showed off her sweater meat in a few flicks, most notably *The Vampire Lovers* (1970), in which she cavorted in the nude with Ingrid Pitt, and *Up Pompeii* (1971), in which she took a bubble bath. Thanks to DVD, the sun will never set on her British Empire.

SKIN-fining Moment:

The Vampire Lovers (0:49) Breasts when she gets her dress pulled down by Ingrid Pitt. Sucktackular!

See Her Naked In:

Up Pompeii (1971) Breasts
The Vampire Lovers (1970) Breasts

Maggie Smith

Born: December 28, 1934
Ilford Essex, England, UK
Skin-O-Meter: Brief Nudity

When a thespian in the prime of her advanced career has retained the versatility to play with aplomb both Mother Superior in the *Sister Act* flicks and Professor McGonagall in the *Harry Potter* films, then that far-ranging ham should be awarded some grand prize, like a knighthood for instance, and that's just the distinction that has been bestowed upon Dame Maggie Smith. A rapid-talking terror on the London stage while hardly out of her teens, Smith has brought her refined, gutsy glory to scores of critically acclaimed films in Britain and the States, winning two Oscars over here, the first as a kooky teacher in *The Prime of Miss Jean Brodie* (1969), the second as an Oscar-nominated actress on Oscar night in Neil Simon's *California Suite* (1978). Oscar was treated to a blush of plush Dame flesh in the second winner.

SKIN-fining Moment:

California Suite (1:05) Maggie puts on a nightgown and we see her left mammie.

See Her Naked In:

My House in Umbria (2003) RB
California Suite (1978) LB

Martha Smith

Born: October 16, 1953
Cleveland, Ohio
Skin-O-Meter: Great Nudity

A statuesquely structured babe-alicious blonde, Ohio-born Martha Smith implanted herself into millions of male minds as sexy southern belle Babs Jensen in the immortal comedy *Animal House* (1978). It's hard to believe she didn't bare the Babs boobies in that effort (though she did look damn sexy!) considering she bared it ALL as the July 1973 centerfold in *Playboy*. Following her trip to the Delta House, Martha went on to appear on the soap opera *Days of Our Lives* and then on to primetime prominence on the successful series *Scarecrow and Mrs. King*. But the gorgeous gamine did grace her admirers with some naughty naked niceties in the bizarre thriller *Blood Link* (1982).

SKIN-fining Moment:

Blood Link (0:51) Bare milk-wagons in bed while two dudes somehow fail to pay attention.

See Her Naked In:

Blood Link (1982) Breasts, Buns

Melanie Smith

Born: December 16, 1962
Scranton, Pennsylvania
Skin-O-Meter: Great Nudity

Boldly brunette with eyes of brown; a strong, dimpled chin; a full mouth full of sensual expression; and a tightly packed body that presents that most wonderful of dilemmas—whether to fixate upon the top shelf or bottom cheeks—it is only natural that saucy seductress Melanie Smith's simmering emoting should have been featured on three of the most definitive shows of the late twentieth century. *Seinfeld, Melrose Place*, and *Beverly Hills, 90210* all would have been somewhat poorer if not for the riches contributed by Melanie. And Smith still manages to exude innate sex appeal when her face is obscured by a mask of extraterrestrial grotesquerie, such as worn by Tora Ziyal on the cathode cult classic *Star Trek: Deep Space Nine*.

SKIN-fining Moment:

The Baby Doll Murders (0:09) Mel gets topless and eases her flotation devices into a hot tub with a dude.

See Her Naked In:

The Baby Doll Murders (1992) Breasts

Sukie Smith

London, England, UK
Skin-O-Meter: Brief Nudity

How hot is Sukie Smith? She can make a gay man straight. Well, at least in the movies. Her most skintacular role to date has been as a flawless tart in *The Lawless Heart* (2001), seducing an identity-confused Tom Hollander. Before flaunting her front, this lass from London was on the telly since the late '80s, getting her *Peak Practice* on the soap of the same name. She made her mark as a maid in the Gilbert and Sullivan flick *Topsy Turvy* (1999). But it's her most recent film that is the very model of her modern major genitals.

SKIN-fining Moment:

The Lawless Heart (0:37) Sukie shows her ta-ta's and tookie in a full frontal flash as she opens a door and grabs her clothes from some goof.

See Her Naked In:

The Lawless Heart (2001) FFN

Yeardley Smith

Born: July 3, 1964
Paris, France
Skin-O-Meter: Brief Nudity

Squinty, smiley cutie-pie Yeardley Smith is forever being cast in comedic sidekick TV roles that downplay the kissable softness of her lips, the nuzzle-worthy nature of her cheeks, the trim and compact pop of her nether cheeks, and the savory, billowy, pale milk sacks that linger undetected

beneath her sweater. Chances are that Yeardley's perky surface has caught the eye of casual tube viewers as a quirky supporting character on shows such as *Herman's Head*, *The Tracy Ullman Show*, and *Dharma and Greg*. And undoubtedly you've heard her girlish voice as Lisa Simpson on the cartoon institution *The Simpsons*. The casual eye muses, "Let me undress this appetizing crumpet. What might I find?" If the generous helping of chest fodder on view in *Ginger Ale Afternoon* (1989) is any indication, the casual eye will spy a sadly overlooked treasury of tit.

SKIN-fining Moment:

Ginger Ale Afternoon (0:53) It's Lisa Simpson's love-balloons as Yeardley loses her top in a trailer! Ay Carumba!

See Her Naked In:

Ginger Ale Afternoon (1989) Breasts

Carrie Snodgress

Born: October 27, 1946
Park Ridge, Illinois
Died: April 1, 2004
Skin-O-Meter: Great Nudity

A neurotic's sweetheart, a nerd's valentine, Carrie Snodgress started her acting career on Chicago stages before making her debut in the TV drama *The Whole World is Watching* (1969). She followed that with a cameo as one of the Commune Hippies in *Easy Rider* (1969) and landed her first semi-leading role in the TV movie *Silent Night, Lonely Night* (1969) opposite Lloyd Bridges. But it wasn't until she took the lead in *Diary of a Mad Housewife* (1970), in which she played a chick bent on adultery due to her overbearing husband's behavior, that the world really started

watching. Carrie scored an Academy Award nomination for her honest, comic, and skinful performance. She showed off her big-nippled little boobies and a totally adorable and perfectly squeeze-friendly tush. She quit the business in the '70s for the hippie life before returning to the silver screen in *The Fury* (1978). Since then she's remained active, if not as renowned as in her heyday. Carrie appeared in the Mr. Skin favorite *Wild Things* (1998), and though she didn't get nude or involve herself in any of the film's famed lesbianic lick-a-thons, Neve Cambell and Denise Richards did. Carrie hopefully learned something from her young thespian co-stars. Alas, the song of this ex-wife of rock legend Neil Young ended on a sad note in April 2004, when Carrie died too young, at age fifty-seven.

SKIN-fining Moment:

Diary of a Mad Housewife (0:01) Nice, well-lit look at her enormously nippled na-na's while getting dressed during a conversation with Richard Benjamin.

See Her Naked In:

Rabbit, Run (1970) Buns
Diary of a Mad Housewife (1970) Breasts, Buns

Susan Marie Snyder

Born: July 18, 1964
Dundee, Oregon
Skin-O-Meter: Brief Nudity

The life of the soap-opera actress is a heightened reality of high-strung emotions, overt sexuality without the benefit of accompanying nudity, and betrayal and reversals of fortune always impending like doom, held at bay only by the whims of plot-challenged writers. Starring in the soaps is a high-stress job, and the women who do it would certainly benefit if they could occasionally get everything off their chests, starting with shirt and bra. Goo-goo-eyed blonde vixen Susan Marie Snyder has a history of vamping and camping on television melodramas that spans ten years and includes crucial roles on *As the World Turns* and *Santa Barbara*. How did she do it and not crack under the stress? She must have sent her tits out for air every time the cameras stopped.

SKIN-fining Moment:

Sleepaway Camp II: Unhappy Campers (0:08) Susan yanks up her T-shirt and flashes her yaboos. No wonder they're happy campers!

See Her Naked In:

Sleepaway Camp II: Unhappy Campers (1988) Breasts

Leelee Sobieski

Born: June 10, 1982
New York
Skin-O-Meter: Brief Nudity

L'IDOLE: SEESEE LEELEE. THIS ULTRA-RARE POSTER FOR MS. SOBIESKI'S MOST SKINTAS-TIC MOVIE IS ALMOST AS HARD TO FIND AS THE FLICK ITSELF.

She looks like she's destined to play Helen Hunt's daughter, but Leelee Sobieski has already become a movie star through her own dazzling looks. She was a little too young to be properly ogled in *Eyes Wide Shut* (1999), but her bra-clad appearance perfectly summed up adolescent sex appeal. Nothing wrong with being gleeful about Leelee in *The Glass House* (2001), though, especially since she helped turn the film into the *Citizen Kane* (1941) of bikini scenes. Her skimpy outfits also proved that she's worth a road trip in the thriller *Joy Ride* (2001)—and don't miss her commentary on the DVD, which included a mention of how she's an expert on international porn. But Leelee really made history in the network TV movie *Uprising* (2001), in which she displayed some discreet full-frontal nudity. The film's plot is historically important, too, but you'll understand if we're distracted by Leelee's soft, full curves. Leelee followed up with even more see-see in the 2002 Canadian flick *The Idol* (aka *L'idole*), wherein she shows off her sumptuously full-bodied form in profile. She may be sideways, but Leelee's T&A are awesome— straight-up!

SKIN-fining Moment:

The Idol (0:49) Leelee shows her left breastski and buoyant backside as she combs her hair completely nude.

See Her Naked In:

The Idol (2002) LB, Buns

Maria Socas

Buenos Aires, Argentina
Skin-O-Meter: Great Nudity

B-movie producers find some amazing things when they head out to shoot films in cheap locales. And two of those most amazing things are on the chest of Maria Socas, an Argentinean beauty who worked

steadily after her country became a magnet for low-budget filmmaking. She boldly embraced American standards of nudity in *The Warrior and the Sorceress* (1984), where the striking brunette first bewitched our swords. She also had us raising a stalk with her role as an Amazon Queen in *Deathstalker II* (1987). After *Wizards of the Lost Kingdom* (1985), though, Maria concentrated on local projects and remains a real favorite in her homeland.

SKIN-fining Moment:

The Warrior and the Sorceress (0:15) Maria's wonderfully gratuitous tits light up a dungeon. Hoo-gah!

See Her Naked In:

The Warrior and the Sorceress (1984) Breasts

Sonja Sohn

Skin-O-Meter: Brief Nudity

Although her mix of African American and Korean American heritage; her exotic, laid-back, and coolly sensual good looks; her tight as twin drums buns; and her emerging fame and wealth as a rising star in the glittery showbiz firmament may tend to separate sugary brown Sonja Sohn from the rest of us, there's one thing we all have in common with her character Detective Shakima Greggs on the hit HBO narco-drama *The Wire*. "I dig girls," announces Detective Greggs right out of the gate; and who among us can find a bone of contention in that assertion? To see beyond the lingerie-tight denim and body-hugging T's of Sonja's customary *Wire* wardrobe, trip out on her trembling erectile titties in *Slam* (1998).

SKIN-fining Moment:

Slam (1:14) Saul Williams slips some sausage into Sonja and her pair of stiff-nipped suckables stand at attention.

See Her Naked In:

Slam (1998) Breasts

Natalia Sokolova

Born: October 15, 1976
Moscow, Russia, Soviet Union
Skin-O-Meter: Great Nudity

One look at the firm, orbicular flotation devices rising upon the chest of eye-pleasing, Moscow-born blonde Natalia Sokolova, and it's impossible to remember what basis we ever had to hold a grievance against our new friends the Russians. How could an Evil Empire have produced this playful vision of beneficent and bountiful femininity? Surely, no regime hostile to our capitalist society would send out one of its fairest daughters to blow up as a *Baywatch* babe and infiltrate *Playboy* magazine as its centerfold for April 1999. Sign up for the *Boat Trip* (2002) cruise and see how easily this sexy Soviet emissary and her bottoms-only bikini take to the American sexploitation tradition of the topless sundeck.

SKIN-fining Moment:

Boat Trip (0:00) Prepare yourself for this plethora of bikini-team meat-pontoons. Shauna Sand, Jami Ferrell, Teri Harrison Natalia and Deanna Brooks. Jami, Natalia, and Deanna forget their tops—and we win!

See Her Naked In:

Boat Trip (2002) Breasts
Numerous *Playboy* Videos

P.J. Soles

Born: July 17, 1955
Frankfurt, Germany
Skin-O-Meter: Brief Nudity

Half-informed sexperts believe that perky sweetheart P.J. Soles is a cult star due to her performance as a rabid fan in the Ramones' *Rock 'n' Roll High School* (1979). What must be realized is that Soles was a cult star even before being teamed up with the rebels from Rockaway Beach. P.J. played a secondary screamer in two massively influential scary movies: First overshadowed by Sissy Spacek in *Carrie* (1976) and then in the shade of Jamie Lee Curtis in *Halloween* (1978), where we all enjoyed her topless jack-o(ff)-lanterns!

SKIN-fining Moment:

Halloween (1:03) P.J.'s right T.T. pops up when her boyfriend hops off her in bed.

See Her Naked In:

Terror in the Aisles (1984) Breasts
Halloween (1978) Breasts

Suzanne Somers

Born: October 16, 1946
San Bruno, California
Skin-O-Meter: Great Nudity

It took three women to make *Charlie's Angels* a classic of '70s jiggle television. *Three's Company* only needed Suzanne Somers. (Sorry, Joyce DeWitt.) Suzanne was having a last laugh, too, since she originally lost out on the role of *Angels*'s Jill Monroe to Farrah Fawcett. Suzanne had already established herself as one of L.A.'s sexiest '70s blondes, thanks to a sexy scene on *Starsky and Hutch* and some poolside nudity in the Dirty Harry hit *Magnum Force* (1973)—although she was killed off too soon to get her name in the credits. The success of her sitcom also gave Suzanne a chance to get even sexier in the TV movie *Zuma Beach* (1978) and the big-screen film *Nothing Personal* (1980). From there it was salary disputes and plenty of TV movies. But if you ever see reruns of her '90s family sitcom *Step by Step*, listen for the discreet references to her kinky sex life with TV hubby Patrick Duffy.

SKIN-fining Moment:

Magnum Force (0:27) Super-sacked Suzanne skinny-dips at a pool party and just when you marvel at how she could never drown with those gorgeous double-barrels, a crazed gunman puts an end to everyone's good time.

See Her Naked In:

Magnum Force (1973) Breasts

Elke Sommer

Born: November 5, 1940
Berlin, Germany
Skin-O-Meter: Great Nudity

Defying the conventional wisdom that nobody laughs and comes at the same time is sensual and silly sex-screen pioneer Elke Sommer. Ranked number thirty-one on *Playboy*'s list of the One Hundred Sexiest Stars of the Century, Elke and her bare breasts made a serious impact when they burst upon the public in *Sweet Ecstasy* (1962). Although shot in black-and-white and with her nipples covered by the mashing mitts of a hulking Euro hunk, Elke's tits were a brazen dare to all the swinging '60s starlets. Elke was just as effective at tickling funny bones. Her kooky bombshell foil to Peter Sellers in *A Shot in the Dark* (1964) is a key to why that movie is regarded as the best Pink Panther outing of all. Speaking five languages, Sommer was a bright, breasty star in the cinema of an equal number of nations. Her budding youth is amply documented on several continents. Her ample maturity can be sampled in *The House of Exorcism* (1975). By 1975 Elke's unsinkables were thirty-five years old and filmed in color but were still mashed by some hulking Euro hunk's mitts.

SKIN-fining Moment:

The House of Exorcism (1:11) Nice nude bazooms as she snoozes in bed as a fruity looking guy peels her clothes off.

See Her Naked In:

I Miss You, Hugs and Kisses (1978) LB
The House of Exorcism (1975) Breasts
Die Reise nach Wien (1973) Breasts
Lisa and the Devil (1973) Breasts
The Invincible Six (1968) Breasts
The Wicked Dreams of Paula Schultz (1968)
  Buns
The Victors (1963)
Zarte Haut in schwarzer Seide (1961)
  Breasts

Annie Sorell

Skin-O-Meter: Great Nudity

Along with her twin sister Alicia Lorén, Annie Sorell helped compile the unaired TV series *Manchester Prep* into the R-rated extravaganza known as *Cruel Intentions 2* (2000). The identical twins were sent into Sebastian's shower to seduce him away from his potential girlfriend, and the topless twosome made their point by shamelessly making out with each other. It's truly a milestone in twins tweaking our testicles. And look for the short film *Mad Twins* (2003), in which the duo returned as identical cheerleaders in the midst of an identity crisis.

SKIN-fining Moment:

Cruel Intentions 2 (0:36) Double your pleasure when Annie drops her robe alongside identical sis Alicia. Then hang on for bare-bazooka'd twincest!

See Her Naked In:

Cruel Intentions 2 (2000) Breasts

Louise Sorel

Born: August 6, 1940
New York, New York
Skin-O-Meter: Brief Nudity

She's in her sexy sixties now, but Louise Sorel remains one of the hottest babes on daytime television—and always in demand on shows such as *Days of Our Lives, All My Children,* and *Passions.* This beguiling brunette has been a regular presence on TV since 1963, including a glammy turn as one of William Shatner's space babes on a 1969 episode of *Star Trek.* Louise then swung into the '70s with a skinematic debut in the counterculture comedy *B.S. I Love You* (1971). It was mostly TV movies from there, although Louise kept things tawdry with her turn as a gangster's slutty moll in the blaxploitation-lite epic *Get Christie Love!* (1974). Sorel got us coming again as she sported a nurse's uniform in *Airplane II: The Sequel* (1982), and she was a major MILF as Wendy Schall's mother in *Where the Boys Are '84* (1984). We don't know what to make of her appearing in *Woof! Woof! Uncle Matty's Guide to Dog Training* (1997), though.

SKIN-fining Moment:

B.S. I Love You (0:09) Slight right-side rackshish getting groped in bed. Fast and dark.

See Her Naked In:

B.S. I Love You (1971) RB

Heidi Sorenson

Born: August 5, 1960
Vancouver, British Columbia, Canada
Skin-O-Meter: Great Nudity

Lots of *Playboy* Playmates go on to films, but they're usually just window dressing. Heidi Sorenson—Miss July 1981—actually went on to show some real comedic talent. She was just another sexy Vestal Virgin in Mel Brooks's *History of the World: Part 1* (1981), but Heidi was lots of fun while doffing her top in *Spies Like Us* (1985). She can get a dramatic rise in our trousers in a dramatic role, too, like when she stripped down for a sex scene in *Suspect Device* (1995). You can also see her posing very seriously in *Playboy Video Magazine, Vol. 5* (1983).

SKIN-fining Moment:

Dream On "Martin Tupper in Magnum Force." (1994) Bouncing robo-boobs while riding that Body By Jake dude on a couch, followed by buns when they're interrupted and she jumps up.

See Her Naked In:

Suspect Device (1995) Breasts, Buns
Numerous *Playboy* Videos

TeleVisions:

Dream On Breasts, Buns

Mira Sorvino

Born: September 28, 1967
Tenafly, New Jersey
Skin-O-Meter: Brief Nudity

Grown from the seed of character actor Paul Sorvino, Mira Sorvino came to acting after earning a degree in East Asian studies from Harvard. So maybe she can tell us if it's true what they say about Asian women. She made a splash as the call-girl-with-a-statue-of-gold in her Academy Award–winning performance for Woody Allen in *Mighty Aphrodite* (1995). However provocative the role (and dirty-minded her director), there was not a hint of skin to be found on the reels. Mira has remained as chaste as the girl next door, but she did get cheeky in one scene and topless in another as Marilyn Monroe for the made-for-HBO movie *Norma Jean and Marilyn* (1996). She paired off with Ashley Judd, as the before-she-was-blonde bombshell, who got the best skin scenes. Reportedly Mira had to get drunk before taking off her dress and flashing her mams. Poor Mira, poor Mira . . . pour Mira another drink!

SKIN-fining Moment:

Norma Jean and Marilyn (2:04) Mira yanks down her dress and serves up her Norma Jean and Marilyns.

See Her Naked In:

Norma Jean and Marilyn (1996) Breasts, Buns

Shannyn Sossamon

Born: October 3, 1979
Hawaii
Skin-O-Meter: Brief Nudity

Shannyn Sossamon is a beguiling blend of French, Hawaiian, Dutch, Irish, Filipino, and German heritage, all of which combine to make this dark-eyed delight the best of all worlds. Early-starter Shannyn was living on her own in L.A. at seventeen with ambitions of becoming a professional dancer. While working as a DJ at Gwyneth Paltrow's birthday bash, the svelte sweetie was discovered and cast as Heath Ledger's love interest in the blockbuster *A Knight's Tale* (2001). And it's been only up from there (for both her career and our pants). She next starred as the temptress who made it extremely difficult for Josh Hartnett to keep his vow of chastity in *40 Days and 40 Nights* (2002). Shannyn offered first skin in a sexy nude scene where Hartnett had some great fun fingering her entire body with a feather while she was wearing nothing but black panties and some leaves. Talk about a fashion statement. Check out those perfectly formed and slightly swollen nipples! Now we know why everyone wants to become an actor! Her next role was as a virgin in *The Rules of Attraction* (2002), and, sadly, there was no more skin than a shot of Shannyn in a black bra. She re-teamed with Ledger and director Brian Helgeland for the thriller *The Order* (2003), in which the real thrills came when her left boob slipped briefly into view.

SKIN-fining Moment:

40 Days and 40 Nights (1:07) While Josh Hartnett works her with flower petals, we see part of Shannyn's luscious right chest-bud.

See Her Naked In:

The Order (2003) LB
40 Days and 40 Nights (2002) RB

Renée Soutendijk

Born: May 21, 1957
Amsterdam, Noord-Holland,
Netherlands
Skin-O-Meter: Great Nudity

Renée Soutendijk is a well-respected actress in her native Holland, performing in over forty film and stage productions since her debut in *Pastorale 1943* (1978). In the U.S. this Dutch delight is breast known for her association with flesh flasher extraordinaire Paul Verhoeven (director of *Showgirls* [1995] and *Basic Instinct* [1992]). Infamous for his characterizations of vicious vixens, Verhoeven revved up Renée's randy side in *Spetters* (1980) and *De Vierde Man* (1983). Both flicks offered a taste of her tiny-tipped höötlets and an intimate skintastic swim in her deliciously de-fuzzed dyke. Outside of work with Verhoeven, Soutendijk's sexcapades Stateside were sauciest in *Eve of Destruction* (1991). As a crazy femmebot with a ticking time bomb inside her fantastic frame, her nakedness will leave you on the verge of exploding. Although most of Renée's films were box-office bombs Stateside, this delicious Dane will always be a skinematic success here at Skin Central.

SKIN-fining Moment:

Spetters (0:55) Extended tittie peeks as Renee plays Pull the Pony with Hans van Tongeren's happy hog.

See Her Naked In:

De Flat (1996) Breasts
Eve of Destruction (1991) Breasts
De Vierde man (1983) FFN, Buns
Van de koele meren des doods (1982) FFN, Buns
Spetters (1980) Breasts

TeleVisions:

The Hitchhiker Breasts

Catherine Spaak

Born: April 3, 1945
Boulogne-Billancourt, France
Skin-O-Meter: Great Nudity

Thank God for the universal language of skin. If it weren't for the fascination that crosses all borders, a willowy brunette temptress of the caliber of Catherine Spaak might not enjoy the Stateside acclaim that she does today. Although she did appear in a few American movies, most notably *Hotel* (1967) opposite Rod Taylor and Karl Malden, the French-bred Spaak built the bulk of her career in Continental cinema. Many of these European films received only the most limited release in the U.S., and the bulk of them speak in tongues that are alien to our ears. But there is nothing foreign about the high-riding chair cheeks and chest peaks of *The Libertine* (1969). Catherine's bikini lines and nipples in *Il Gatto a nova code* (1971) seem right at home. And her high-yield striptease from *Bruciati da cocente passione* (1976) would be a welcome next-door addition at Anytown, USA.

SKIN-fining Moment:

Una Ragazza piuttosto complicata (0:55) Cathy goes for a nice long stroll bare-assed in the forest while some clever fella decides to film what he sees.

See Her Naked In:

Bruciati da cocente passione (1976) Breasts
La Via dei babbuini (1974) Breasts
Il Gatto a nove code (1971) Breasts
The Libertine (1969) Breasts, Buns
Una Ragazza piuttosto complicata (1968) Breasts, Buns

Sissy Spacek

Born: December 25, 1949
Quitman, Texas
Skin-O-Meter: Hall of Fame

Sissy Spacek is a quirky bundle of sexiness. Freckle faced and innocent, like the girl next door whom you just know is a freak behind her half-drawn shades, Sissy has managed to translate her weirdness into box-office clout— and get nude a few times along the way! Sissy is known for her edgy and dark roles and debuted as a prostitute in *Prime Cut* (1972). But it is the starring role in the classic horror yarn *Carrie* (1976) that made Sissy a household name. She wowed audiences before the credits even stopped rolling in the infamous mufftastic teenage shower scene. She won an Oscar for *Coal Miner's Daughter* (1980), playing country legend Loretta Lynn and showing off her powerful lungs as a singer. But we prefer seeing her breasts more clearly in flicks such as *Welcome to L.A.* (1977) and *Raggedy Man* (1981). Miss Spacek is no Sissy when it comes to skin.

SKIN-fining Moment:

Carrie (0:02) Sissy shows boobs, and buns, and the naturally red-haired Spacek between her legs in the high school shower room as she freaks out over getting her period.

See Her Naked In:

Raggedy Man (1981) Breasts
Welcome to L.A. (1977) Breasts
Carrie (1976) FFN, Buns
Prime Cut (1972) Breasts, Bush, Buns

Donna Spangler

Born: November 2, 1962
Los Angeles, California,
Skin-O-Meter: Great Nudity

Urban legend has it that the short-lived women's athletics TV series *PWOW: Powerful Women of Wrestling* was canceled because it inspired too many people in the home audience to indulge in powerful strangleholds, and

poultry activists panicked that not a single American chicken would be left unchoked if the show were not halted immediately. A primary cause of all that concern was generously chested, candy-faced, power-buns blonde Donna Spangler. After inspiring so many fantasies of tag-team grappling, Donna squirmed naturally into the arena of sexploitative cinema. See her grip and slip in a hot-oil grudge match with Kym Malon in *Guns* (1990), and then join the two as they play nice in the shower.

SKIN-fining Moment:

Guns (0:30) Great look at Donna's spectacular Spanglers in the shower.

See Her Naked In:

Space Girls in Beverly Hills (2001) Breasts
Dinosaur Valley Girls (1996) Breasts
Hollywood Dreams Take 2 (1995) Breasts
Roots of Evil (1992) Breasts
Guns (1990) Breasts, Thong

TeleVisions:

Compromising Situations Breasts, Buns

"I don't believe in drugs or even smoking."

—BRITNEY SPEARS

Britney Spears

Born: December 2, 1981
Kentwood, Louisiana
Skin-O-Meter: Never Nude

Britney Spears's first love was a rodent. She tried out for *The Mickey Mouse Club,* but the producers said she was too young! The now-buxom brat from rural Louisiana kept on truckin' and ended up in a couple of theatrical productions, which gave her the experience (and time enough to "grow up") to land

that coveted *MMC* role opposite barely legal temptress Christina Aguilera in 1993. But the big time came after her stint on *The Club*, when Britney made beautiful and sexy music history with her debut album. Her provocative hot-to-trot Catholic schoolgirl jail-bait videos and Lolita-like photo spread in *Rolling Stone* magazine kept fans stiff, and one of the most incandescent chapters in pop-stardom history was ignited. Suggestive radio hits and explicit MTV clips made Brit one of the most famous figures in the world, where her lung power and debates over her "real or fake?" torso torpedoes kept her on everyone's lips as she matured from T&A-intensive adolescence to raunchily ripe young womanhood. Britney returned to acting, if only briefly, with a cameo in *Longshot* (2001) as a "flight attendant," which is sort of like a hooker of the friendly skies. She went on to star in *Crossroads* (2002), but besides a few bathing-beauty shots, Britney has teased by not delivering the skin. Hit us Britney—two more times!

SKIN-fining Moment:

Nickelodeon Kids Choice Awards (1999) As she performs "Baby . . . One More Time," 18-year-old Brit's pokey nips turn her white top into a pair of hugely protruding pop peaks and this kiddie award show into the stuff adults-only entertainment usually only wishes it could be as hot as. Hit us Britney, a billion more times!

Carol Speed

Born: March 14, 1945
Bakersfield, California
Skin-O-Meter: Brief Nudity

With the resurgence of interest in the blaxploitation sub-genre, African American ass kicker Carol

Speed's resumé can probably pull more juice now than it could in her heyday. Though never reaching the market penetration of a Pam Grier, stacked soul sister Speed did rack up a strong batch of ghetto-fabulous credits. Her frankly sensual, lazy-eyed stare can be seen looking insolently out from *Black Samson* (1974), *Disco Godfather* (1979), and *The Mack* (1973). A morality tale of pimpin' and consequences, *The Mack* is a message movie with more than one point—two of them being Carol's erect, upward-straining, chocolate-dipped nipples. In *The Big Bird Cage* (1972), a chick prison flick that also features the divine Ms. Grier, Carol kneels in surrender. Desperation and abandon struggle on her face. Her tittie slips from its confining garment and makes a flash for freedom.

SKIN-fining Moment:

The Mack (0:23) Topless Carol shows her Speed Demons in the sack with Max Julien.

See Her Naked In:

The Mack (1973) Breasts
The Big Bird Cage (1972) LB

Dona Speir

Born: February 7, 1964
Norwalk, California
Skin-O-Meter: Great Nudity

If top body Dona Speir were a pro basketball player, she would be what is known as "a franchise player." Such a baller can ensure the profitability of an entire franchise with just his own exceptional talents. Dona is such a baller. Spier's exceptional talents include breasts as big as her head and just as visible. She also has the smooth, muscled legs and firm, ripped glutes of a person who makes her living with her physique. Her face is framed in a mane of brightly cast blondness. She is a franchise package.

Since 1987, as super secret agent Donna Hamilton, Speir has been the go-to gal in director Andy Sidaris's flashy series of spy-chick erotic thrillers. The highly successful, often imitated, never duplicated Sidaris formula can be distilled to bombs and boobs and beaches and Bond gadgetry and hot tubs that double as think tanks. The intangible that pulls it all together? Dona Speir.

SKIN-fining Moment:

Do or Die (1:21) Great flotation devices and fanny as she frolics in a pool with Erik Estrada. Nice CHiPs!

See Her Naked In:

Fit to Kill (1993) Breasts, Thong
Hard Hunted (1992) Breasts
Do or Die (1991) Breasts, Buns
Guns (1990) Breasts, Thong
Click: The Calendar Girl Killer (1990) Breasts, Buns
Picasso Trigger (1989) Breasts, Buns
Savage Beach (1989) FFN, Buns
Hard Ticket to Hawaii (1987) Breasts, Buns
Numerous *Playboy* Videos

Georgina Spelvin

Born: January 3, 1936
Texas
Skin-O-Meter: Great Nudity

Georgina Spelvin was perhaps the best actress ever to appear in a hardcore XXX movie. Such a statement perhaps doesn't sound like much in the way of praise to anyone who has not yet exulted in her performance as Justine Jones, a suicidal spinster in Gerard Damiano's masterpiece *The Devil in Miss Jones* (1973). Georgina deserved an Academy Award nomination for her tortured, frantic portrayal of a voluptuary doing *everything* humanly possible to overcome being damned to an eternity of sexual frustration. The exalted Ms. Spelvin went on to a long XXX career, bumped over to *Police Academy* (1984) cameos and

the like, and even dipped back into the porn bath with *Still Insatiable* (1999). Nothing has ever dimmed the eternal flame ignited by *The Devil in Miss Jones*.

SKIN-fining Moment:

The Devil in Miss Jones (0:48) Miss Jones gets devilish with a snake, and not of the pants-python variety. An actual serpent slithers around Georgina's lap-nest before she invites him into her mouth and gives head to the snake's head.

See Her Naked In:

The Devil in Miss Jones, Part II (1982) Breasts
Honky Tonk Nights (1978) Breasts
I Spit on Your Corpse! (1974) Breasts, Buns
Devil in Miss Jones (1973) FFN, Buns
The Twilight Girls (1957) Breasts
Numerous Adult Movies

Charlie Spradling

Born: October 15, 1968
Fort Worth, Texas
Skin-O-Meter: Great Nudity

Jet-black hair and a high pair of stand-alone boobs have a way of entrancing even the most wayward male. The inky-dark mane and rousing rack of tantalizing Texan Charlie Spradling are augmented by a pair of buttocks you could eat off of and a sly, sexy, bold prettiness of face that the hopeful skinthusiast associates with a woman who's more than willing to deliver on her tease. Who could hope to resist such charms? Not the blood-sucking protagonist of *To Sleep with a Vampire* (1992), who falls under the sway of Charlie's full moon and twin risers as she does a pelvic-perfect twist as a pole-dancing stripper. Young Dracula is so smitten that he forgets to pull the shades as the sun comes up.

SKIN-fining Moment:

Meridian (0:28) Great looks at topless Charlie's angels by the fire and on the sofa.

See Her Naked In:

A Midsummer Night's Rave (2002) Breasts
Johnny Skidmarks (1998) RB
To Sleep with a Vampire (1992) Breasts, Thong
Puppet Master II (1990) Breasts
Wild at Heart (1990) Breasts
Mirror, Mirror (1990) Breasts, Buns
Meridian (1990) Breasts
Twice Dead (1988) Breasts

Pamela Springsteen

Born: September 7, 1960
Freehold, New Jersey
Skin-O-Meter: Brief Nudity

Nobody could blame Pamela Springsteen for trying to tap some of that Bruce juice during the 1980s. She had us tapping some juices ourselves with her film debut as a cheerleader in *Fast Times at Ridgemont High* (1982). She didn't leap to stardom like co-stars Nicolas Cage and Sean Penn, but Pamela got us reckless in the theater with another cheerleading turn in *Reckless* (1984). She also showed up in the classic *Modern Girls* (1986) before finally making her own mark as the transgendered slasher "Angela" in *Sleepaway Camp II: Unhappy Campers* (1988) and *Sleepaway Camp III: Teenage Wasteland* (1988). After shooting those two films back-to-back, She made us all happy campers with some skinny dipping in *Dixie Lanes* (1988). Pamela soon retired from acting, though, and is now established as a successful photographer.

SKIN-fining Moment:

Dixie Lanes (1:00) It's knockers-by-night when topless Pam talks to her dude as they wade in a moonlit pond.

See Her Naked In:

Dixie Lanes (1988) Breasts

Dina Spybey

Born: August 29, 1966
Columbus, Ohio
Skin-O-Meter: Brief Nudity

That high voice may sound like a whiny joke, but we took Dina Spybey very seriously as Monique Jr. in *Striptease* (1996). This unconventional beauty held her own against the likes of Demi Moore—and we've been holding our own while following Dina's other sexy roles. We spied her spilling out of her underwear in *Julian Po* (1997), and she was supremely sexy as a '60s gal in *Isn't She Great* (2000). Dina was even unrelentingly cute while playing an irritating party planner on the HBO series *Six Feet Under*. She's had bad luck with critically acclaimed but quickly canceled TV series like *Greg the Bunny*, but major productions such as *The Haunted Mansion* (2003) suggest that Dina will keep scaring our pants off.

SKIN-fining Moment:

Striptease (0:05) Dina does her share of opening credit hooter-and-heinie action with a little dance on the club stage.

See Her Naked In:

Striptease (1996) Breasts, Thong

Ilona (Cicciolina) Staller

Born: November 26, 1951
Budapest, Hungary
Skin-O-Meter: Hall of Fame

A carpetbagger and a carpet muncher, Ilona "Cicciolina" Staller is the only woman in history to become elected to a legislative body of a country other than her own origin and also to have been paid to dive and chew muff rug on film. The Hungarian-born dark-rooted blonde was elected along with her big boobs and well-earned reputation for tarnished virtue to the Italian Parliament during a low-news period of the 1980s. She'd sucked and smirked her way through tons of Euro-pop fodder, such as *La Supplende* (1975) and *L'Ingenua* (1975). In tracking down evidence of Cicciolina's future parliamentary body of work, one clue: The older the film, the better.

SKIN-fining Moment:

La Supplente (0:33) Ilona shares a dude with another girl and shows full breasts, bush, and buns in this wacky high-speed sex scene.

See Her Naked In:

Replikator (1994) FFN, Buns
Senza buccia (1979) FFN
Inibizione (1976) FFN
La Supplente (1975) FFN, Buns
La Liceale (1975) Breasts, Thong
L'Ingenua (1975) FFN, Buns
Numerous Adult Movies

Maya Stange

Australia
Skin-O-Meter: Great Nudity

After several years as a popular presence in Australia, Maya Stange finally came to America in the acclaimed indie *XX/XY* (2002)—and it only took one look for Americans to start coming to this strange Aussie beauty. She seemed strangely boyish at first, but Maya quickly proved herself to be all woman once she unleashed her Australian coconuts during a wild sex scene. Her countrymen, of course, already had the pleasure of seeing Maya's mammaries in the tropical love film *In a Savage Land* (1999). Maya also made for a sexy rocker in *Garage Days* (2002) and seems set to keep guys groping Down Under for many more years.

SKIN-fining Moment:

XX/XY (0:06) Maya makes it a threesome with redhead Kathleen Robertson and a dude. You can see her tittables several times, but you have to look close.

See Her Naked In:

XX/XY (2002) Breasts
In a Savage Land (1999) FFN

Taylor Stanley

Born: August 12, 1975
Boston, Massachusetts
Skin-O-Meter: Brief Nudity

Taylor Stanley got a lot of attention with a recurring role on the Michael J. Fox sitcom *Spin City*, but Hollywood's yet to take advantage of this young beauty. We've certainly taken advantage of her sexier scenes, though, whether it was her short stint on the soaper *Another World* or her fine casual nudity in *The Waiting Game* (1999). Fetishists may also want to check out Taylor's work in the film *Secret Cutting* (2000)—although we're glad to point out that her work in *Little Pieces* (2000) isn't a sequel.

SKIN-fining Moment:

The Waiting Game (0:54) Taylor serves up some tit with a side of "brief ass" whilst rolling over in bed.

See Her Naked In:

Knight Club (2001) Breasts
The Waiting Game (2000) RB

Claire Stansfield

Born: August 27, 1964
London, England, UK
Skin-O-Meter: Great Nudity

When a girl's topping six feet at the age of sixteen, a modeling career is kind of in the cards—especially if she blossoms into a dame like Claire Stansfield.

Hollywood, however, hasn't known what to do with this amazing Amazon, and she's usually an unforgettable presence in forgettable films. Don't miss her as a buxom bounty hunter in *Red Shoe Diaries 5: Weekend Pass* (1995) or as a tough gal holding her own (while we hold our own) in *Gladiator Cop* (1994). Claire's also firmly on top of Eric Roberts in the scorching *Sensation* (1994). She also made for a sexy beastie on a 1993 episode of *The X Files*. But for true trouble, marvel at Claire's recurring role as the evil witch "Alti" on episodes of *Xena: Warrior Princess*. Claire's foul-mouthed antics at Xena conventions have since made her a fan favorite. Sadly, MTV passed on her pilot for *The Sausage Factory*, which would've starred Claire as a lascivious librarian with a taste for young boys.

SKIN-fining Moment:

Sensation (1:05) Claire's cannage makes a few appearances as she lustily rides Eric Roberts's rod.

See Her Naked In:

The Outpost (1995) Buns
Sensation (1994) Breasts, Thong
Gladiator Cop (1994) Breasts

TeleVisions:

Red Shoe Diaries Breasts, Thong

Koo Stark

Born: April 26, 1956
New York, New York
Skin-O-Meter: Great Nudity

England's royal family has been inundated with scandal in its long and salacious history, but sexalicious Koo Stark provided the first real regal raunch of the modern media age. In the late '70s Koo began dating Prince Andrew, and it was reported that Queen Elizabeth was actually quite taken

with the pretty little British actress—until someone mentioned that Koo made her living appearing Stark naked in softcore porn films! *Emily* (1977) featured the potential Princess in a lesbian shower suck down and a five-minute masturbation scene. It went on to be the highest grossing British film of the year, fueled by peeping peasants wanting to watch their possibly future ruling lady get off. The Queen went royally mad and banned Andrew from continuing the relationship. The press had a field day and essentially ended Koo's acting career. To this day it's alleged that many inside the walls of Buckingham Palace believe that Koo was Andrew's one true love. Mr. Skin wishes the Queen had lightened up a bit, because Princess Koo does have a ring to it.

SKIN-fining Moment:

Emily (0:32) Nice views of Koo's cuddlies as she talks to, then kisses, her older lesbian lover.

See Her Naked In:

Cruel Passion (1977) Breasts, Bush, Buns
Emily (1977) FFN, Buns
Las Adolescentes (1975) Breasts

> "Porn killed stripping. And now with those tape rentals, well, nudity seems like nothing at all. But in my day nudity was so rare—so special. Society thought that to be a stripper was to be a prostitute. But I always felt that I was an artist, entertaining."
>
> —BLAZE STARR

Blaze Starr

Born: 1932
West Virginia
Skin-O-Meter: Great Nudity

The West Virginia redhead who will forever reverberate through history as Blaze Starr is the most scandalous stripper in the history of bug-eyed men. If it weren't for the Bible's market saturation, Blaze and her unveiling dances would be better known than Salome worldwide. Bounteous Blaze actually has achieved a Biblical proportion in the state of Louisiana. As a young strip and strutter, Starr's blazing affair with Louisiana Governor Huey Long was primary among the dirt used to chase the all-powerful governor from office. See the cans that cost the little king his kingdom in *Blaze Starr Goes Nudist* (1960). The always-smiling copper top's creamy-white largesse is bigger than life, busting out of just about every frame.

SKIN-fining Moment:

Blaze Starr Goes Nudist (0:53) *Sometimes a title says it all and here, Blaze almost shows all. Romping amidst nudist camp bliss, we see Ms. Starr's bodacious Blazers and booty-cakes when she confers with a couple of clothes-free laundresses.*

See Her Naked In:

Blaze Starr Goes Nudist (1960) Breasts Buns

Ingrid Steeger

Born: April 1, 1947
Berlin, Germany
Skin-O-Meter: Hall of Fame

There's a lot to say about Berlin-born Ingrid Steeger, but the English translations of her early movie titles best sum it up: *Guess Who's Sleeping with Us Tonight?* (1969), *Me, a Groupie* (1970), *The Sex Adventures of the Three Musketeers* (1971), *Sex at the Olympics* (1972), *Massage Parlour* (1972), *Emanuelle Meets the Wife Swappers* (1973)—and this is only skimming the surface! Her Deutsch mammophones have been everywhere in Germany since her days as a pinup queen and star of

many sex comedies. These days she's considered more respectable. Though none of her commercial work is that successful, she and her revolving door of romances are constantly covered by the German gossip press. Who cares if she hasn't shown new skin in a while when there's so much of it to catch up with?

SKIN-fining Moment:

Calendar Girls (0:50) *Ingrid demonstrates a bevy of porking positions as part of a Sex Ed program. She also demonstrates what a sexy womans breasts, buttocks, and vagina-hair looks like.*

See Her Naked In:

Zwei Kumpel in Tirol (1978) FFN, Buns
Junge Mädchen mögen's heiß, Hausfrauen noch heißer (1973) FFN, Buns
Liebesmarkt (1973) FFN, Buns
Schulmädchen-Report 5: Was Eltern wissen sollten (1973) FFN, Buns
Liebe in drei Dimensionen (1973) FFN, Buns
Hochzeitsnacht-Report (1972) FFN, Buns
Mädchen, die nach München kommen (1972) FFN, Buns
Blutjunge Verführerinnen 2 (1972) FFN, Buns
Schulmädchen-Report 4: Was Eltern oft verzweifeln läßt (1972) FFN, Buns
Massagesalon der jungen Mädchen (1972) FFN, Buns
Nurses Report (1972) FFN, Buns
Blutjunge Verführerinnen 3 (1972) FFN, Buns
Zum zweiten Frühstück: Heiße Liebe (1972) FFN, Buns
Der Lüsterne Türke (1971) FFN, Buns
Die Goldene Banane von Bad Porno (1971) FFN, Buns
Die Stewardessen (1971) FFN
Sonne, Sylt und kesse Krabben (1971) FFN, Buns
Blutjunge Verführerinnen (1971) FFN, Buns
Die Sexabenteuer der drei Musketiere (1971) FFN, Buns
ich, ein Groupie (1970) FFN, Buns
Die Liebestollen Baronessen (1970) FFN, Buns

Josefine—das liebestolle Kätzchen (1969) FFN, Buns

TeleVisions:

Zwei himmlische Töchter Breasts

Mary Steenburgen

Born: February 8, 1953
Newport, Arkansas
Skin-O-Meter: Great Nudity

Tall and thin, just a little more graceful than gawky, with tightly wound dark hair and a face that is fetching at least, seductive at most, accomplished actress Mary Steenburgen is the domesticated man's sexpot. Most commonly seen portraying a mother, a wife, a coworker, or a grown sibling, Mary reminds us that there is sensuality in maturity, that a home life is a great place for a sex life, that settling down needn't be the end of being riled up, as husband Ted Danson surely knows. Steenburgen's suburbanized demeanor is also a reminder not to judge a skinful body by its cover. For a few hotter sides of Mary, look into her fully nude, Oscar-winning prance through a strip bar in *Melvin and Howard* (1980). Think that flash is a fluke? Fast forward twenty years and admire Steenburgen's high-end rear in *Life as a House* (2001), which features a mid-forties long-running butt shot with no cheek double. Just her own double cheeks.

SKIN-fining Moment:

Melvin and Howard (0:31) *Steenburgen shows cheeks and ta-ta's when she strips off her waitress uniform and struts nude in front of an entire bar. She is full-frontal ONLY in the VHS full-screen version.*

See Her Naked In:

Life as a House (2001) RB, Buns
Melvin and Howard (1980) FFN, Buns

Simonetta Stefanelli

Born: November 30, 1954
Rome, Italy
Skin-O-Meter: Great Nudity

She'll always be remembered as Michael Corleone's doomed first wife in *The Godfather* (1972) and not just because Simonetta Stefanelli provided the film's most thrilling nudity. Her unforgettable acting has also made Simonetta a legend of Italian cinema. Her sinister sexiness in *Lucrezia giovane* (1974)—a retelling of the saga of Lucrezia Borgia—is enough to let her poison us anytime. Simonetta also showed off her ta-tas in a magnificent scene from *La Nuora giovane* (1975), and it was a meeting of the tittie titans when Simonetta co-starred with Edy Williams in *Peccati in famiglia* (1975), a.k.a. *Scandal in the Family*. Sadly, Simonetta looks to have firmly retired that firm bod at the start of the '90s.

SKIN-fining Moment:

The Godfather (1:50) As Michael Corleone's Sicilian bride, Simonetta shows her Italian Alps, thereby making Al Pacino two offers he can't refuse.

See Her Naked In:

Peccati in famiglia (1975) FFN, Buns
La Nuora Giovane (1975) FFN, Buns
Lucrezia Giovane (1974) FFN, Buns
La Profanazione (1974) Breasts, Buns
The Godfather (1972) Breasts
Non commettere atti impuri (1971) Breasts, Buns

Leslie Stefanson

Born: May 10, 1971
Fargo, North Dakota
Skin-O-Meter: Brief Nudity

An Ivy League-educated model turned actress with strong Scandinavian roots, Leslie Stefanson made her way up the entertainment ladder from her small-town trappings in Minnesota to amass quite a portfolio of wholesome, corn-fed good girls. With angelic features and a body that could stop a tractor dead in its tracks, Leslie's appearances not only turn heads, they turn out to be well acted. Whether she's the cute girl next door in *Flubber* (1997), a waitress in *As Good as it Gets* (1997), or a Kennedy in the mini-series *The Women of Camelot* (2001), she gets the job done and always looks damn good doing it. Her performance as the sex-crime victim in *The General's Daughter* (1999) has brought her the most notice, and controversy, to date—as she gave a five-star skin salute during a disturbing spread-eagle S/M scene. Hopefully we meet Leslie under more pleasant skin circumstances the next time a role calls for a peek at her Midwest molehills and muffin.

SKIN-fining Moment:

The General's Daughter (0:19) Totally naked, but dead as Travolta approaches her.

See Her Naked In:

The General's Daughter (1999) FFN

Pamela Stephenson

Born: December 4, 1949
Auckland, New Zealand
Skin-O-Meter: Great Nudity

Few remember her 1985-86 stint on *Saturday Night Live*, but don't blame Pamela Stephenson—after all, she wasn't allowed to regularly strip like she did on the BBC's hilarious series *Not the Nine O'Clock News*. Anyway, Pamela's short *SNL* gig was so depressing that she gave up comedy soon afterwards, leaving behind an impressive body of work that featured her impressive body. Big blondes don't come much funnier and stunnier, as Pamela proved by showing off her laugh lines in British comedies such as *Bloodbath at the House of Death* (1985) and *Stand Up, Virgin Soldiers* (1976). Americans also got to ogle Pamela's plumpers in a revealing scene from Mel Brooks's *History of the World: Part I* (1981). She now resides in Los Angeles with her husband—and legendary UK comedian—Billy Connolly, where she enjoys life as Dr. Pamela Connolly, distinguished lecturer on psychology. Now that's a punchline!

SKIN-fining Moment:

Stand up Virgin soldiers Pam shows mams and a flash of her can when she strips before hitting the sheets. My soldier's no virgin, but he is standing up.

See Her Naked In:

Bloodbath at the House of Death (1985) Breasts
History of the World Part I (1981) Breasts
Stand Up Virgin Soldiers (1976) Breasts, Buns

Lesli Kay Sterling

Born: June 13, 1965
Charleston, West Virginia
Skin-O-Meter: Great Nudity

Ah, there's nothing like the secret life of soap stars. Lesli Kay Sterling—best known as "Lesli Kay"—has spent over seven years starring on the popular daytime drama *As the World Turns*. She's also made some amazing skinematic contributions that capitalize on her magnificent mega-melons and sizzling soft-butch sex appeal. Lesli kept her clothes on in the classic *Forbidden Games* (1995) but made a full-frontal plunge on "The Gardener" episode of Cinemax's *Hot Line*. Don't miss her getting plowed from behind during a very stimulating simulated sex scene. Lesli then showed her globes in *Galaxy Girls* (1995) before indulging her Sapphic side as a space sheriff in *Petticoat Planet* (1995). She returned to late-night cable on the

"Table Service" episode of Showtime's *Women of Passion* and took it indoors and outdoors in *Guarded Secrets* (1997)—which should also please fans of thong bikinis. Lesli's pretty daring in daytime too. In 2002 she thrilled bondage fetishists when her character on *As the World Turns* was bound and gagged in the back of a car.

SKIN-fining Moment:

Galaxy Girls (0:11) Lesli soaks up a lot of sun by tanning herself topless and talking to her gal-pals.

See Her Naked In:

Guarded Secrets (1997) Breasts, Buns
Galaxy Girls (1995) Breasts
Petticoat Planet (1995) Breasts

TeleVisions:

Hotline FFN, Buns
Women: Stories of Passion Breasts, Buns

Brinke Stevens

Born: September 20, 1954
San Diego, California
Skin-O-Meter: Great Nudity

Brunette, with breasts the perfect size for palming and a rear asset that is every bit as pert as her clever, pretty face, Brinke Stevens is a faux bimbo. The San Diego, California-born skinstress has flashed and flounced through more than eighty B-grade productions since her debut in *Necromancy* (1972). Her camera-ready rack, bush, and buns show up in such dopey-sounding titles as *Slave Girls from Beyond Infinity* (1987) and *Droid Gunner* (1995). Who could guess that the owner of these so-often soapy knockers also possessed a master's degree in marine biology? In fact, not only did Brinke appear in *Teenage Exorcist* (1993), she wrote the damn thing. What kind of bimbo ever did a thing like that?

SKIN-fining Moment:

Nightmare Sisters (0:43) Brinke bobbles in the tub with Michelle Bauer and Linnea Quigley. Breasts, buns, and bubbles abound.

See Her Naked In:

The Bad Father (2002) Breasts, Bush, Buns
Hybrid (1997) Breasts
Illicit Dreams 2 (1997)
Eyes Are Upon You (1997) FFN, Buns
Droid Gunner (1995) Breasts, Thong
Teenage Exorcist (1993) Buns
Roots of Evil (1992) Breasts
Haunting Fear (1991) FFN
Scream Queen Hot Tub Party (1991) FFN, Buns
Murder Weapon (1990) LB
Bad Girls From Mars (1990) Breasts
Phantom of the Mall: Eric's Revenge (1989) Breasts
The Jigsaw Murders (1989) LB
Sorority Babes in the Slimeball Bowl-O-Rama (1988) FFN, Buns
Nightmare Sisters (1987) Breasts, Buns
Fatal Games (1984) LB, Buns
Body Double (1984) Breasts
Emmanuelle IV (1984) Breasts
Red Hot Rock (1984) Breasts
Private School (1983) Breasts, Buns
More Candid Candid Camera (1983) Bush, Buns
The Man Who Wasn't There (1983) RB, Buns
Sole Survivor (1982) Breasts
The Slumber Party Massacre (1982) Breasts, Buns

Carrie Stevens

Born: May 1, 1969
Buffalo, New York
Skin-O-Meter: Brief Nudity

We sure do like nude women, and Carrie Stevens was gorgeous as *Playboy*'s Miss June 1997. We're also grateful for her nakedness in *Playboy* videos like *Playmates: Bustin' Out* (2000). Carrie, however, has a special talent for looking amazing in skimpy clothing. We'd almost be as happy if she kept on that black negligee in *Jane Street* (1996). And

we gladly whip out our own pistols when pistol-packing Carrie simulates some hot sex in *Cruel Game* (2001)—but check out how amazing she looks in that leopard-skin bikini! Is it any wonder that we're just as enthused about her appearance on *E! Wild On . . . ?*

SKIN-fining Moment:

Jane Street (0:54) Boobs and butt while banging her boytoy. Carrie on, Stellar Stevens.

See Her Naked In:

Cruel Game (2001) Breasts, Buns
Jane Street (1996) Breasts, Buns
Numerous *Playboy* Videos

TeleVisions:

E! Wild On . . . Breasts

Connie Stevens

Born: August 8, 1938
Brooklyn, New York
Skin-O-Meter:Great Nudity

From her origins as platinum-haired jailbait to her peak as a brassy blonde dame, Brooklyn-born Connie Stevens always exuded sex appeal with a capital peel. Plucked from one of the more exciting regions of obscurity as a seventeen-year-old by Jerry Lewis and featured front and center in *Rock-a-Bye Baby* (1958), Stevens's bombshell body and schoolgirl naïveté raised the antennae and the hopes of skin scouts throughout the land. Connie's marriage to teen heartthrob Eddie Fisher resulted in a spate of 1960s beach flicks. Bikinis and the twist screwed the developing blonde deeper into the mass skinful consciousness. Stevens waited until her thirties to reward an expectant nation, unveiling the flesh behind the fame in two more-than-approriately titled adventures, *The Sex Symbol* (1974) and *Scorchy* (1976). Both pictures are recommended for the climactic unveiling of a sexual body a lifetime in the making, especially the former. A recently discovered uncut version of *The Sex Symbol* includes fresh flesh from Connie thought to be lost forever. Now you can lust at it forever.

SKIN-fining Moment:

Scorchy (0:57) *Connie's casabas show up towards the end of this scene, which sees her boyfriend dead and herself molested.*

See Her Naked In:

Scorchy (1976) Breasts
The Sex Symbol (1974) Breasts, Bush, Buns

Stella Stevens

Born: October 1, 1938
Yazoo City, Mississippi
Skin-O-Meter: Great Nudity

Fashion in the swinging '60s demanded breasts, the bigger the better. None were larger than superior sweater buster Stella Stevens. She added the exclamation marks to *Girls! Girls! Girls!* (1962) with Elvis Presley, made Jerry Lewis crazy in *The Nutty Professor* (1963), and had Dean Martin pop off in *The Silencers* (1966). By the Me Decade Stella was finally showing off more of herself. As the prostitute who tamed Jason Robards in *The Ballad of Cable Hogue* (1970), she flashed her bubbliscious butt. Stella's rack is to die for in *Slaughter* (1972), whether getting wet in the shower or letting ex-football player Jim Brown get his paws all over her pigskins. A native of Hot Coffee, Mississippi, Stella liked her men hot and black. Even at forty-eight, Stella's bellas were knockouts. Take a gander at her glandular greatness in *Monster in the Closet* (1986). If those ta-tas were in Mr. Skin's closet, I'd never come out!

SKIN-fining Moment:

Slaughter (1:14) *Stella's stellar set and fantastic fanny come into view as she finishes up in the shower and meets some sleazeball hiding in her room.*

STELLA STEVENS IN SLAUGHTER: JIM BROWN STARS IN THE POSTER, BUT THE MOVIE CONTAINS ONE STELLA PERFORM-ANCE. THIS IS A SLAMMIN' EXAMPLE OF BLAXPOITATION POSTERS AT THEIR BEST—PACKED WITH BAD-ASS BROTHERS, BIG GUNS, AND THE SWEET-STACKED SISTERS WHO MAKE ALL THAT VIOLENCE WORTHWILE.

See Her Naked In:

Last Call (1990) Nip Slip LB
Monster in the Closet (1986) Breasts
Slaughter (1972) Breasts, Buns
The Ballad of Cable Hogue (1970) Breasts, Buns

Cynthia Stevenson

Born: August 2, 1963
Piedmont, California
Skin-O-Meter: Brief Nudity

Cynthia Stevenson knows that every really hot chick role needs a less hot chick best friend. Cynthia may not be smoking, but she's cooking up something with that girl-next-door cute allure. She has cheerleader pep and little-sister looks, and they have served her well professionally. Cynthia's greatest exposure came in Robert Altman's satirical look at Hollywood, *The Player* (1992). She is the ever-loyal assistant/lover of oblivious studio player Tim Robbins. The hot-tub scene sticks out as one of the film's high points thanks to Cynthia's perky nubs making their screen debut. How about an encore?

SKIN-fining Moment:

The Player (0:19) *Cynthia shows her shirtless bobbins in a hot-tub with Tim Robbins.*

See Her Naked In:

Live Nude Girls (1995) LB, Thong
The Player (1992) Breasts

Alana Stewart

Born: 1946
Nacogdoches, Texas
Skin-O-Meter: Brief Nudity

Those reality shows are serious business, as proven when a beauty like Alana Stewart was voted out of the TV series *I'm a Celebrity, Get Me Out of Here!* Of course, some people would say that Alana barely counts as a celebrity, mainly being famous as the ex-wife of Rod Stewart and George Hamilton. Those people haven't seen Alana's important screen work in *Night Call Nurses* (1972), where the tall blonde provides a prescription of simulated sex, with a healthy portion of ample ass and outstanding tits. She made a few more films with a lot less nudity, which explains why Alana is now known best as a socialite and TV personality—even co-hosting a short-lived morning show with ex-hubby George.

SKIN-fining Moment:

Night Call Nurses (0:28) Alana flashes some ass and hooterific goodness while making out with Richard Young.

See Her Naked In:

Night Call Nurses (1972) Breasts, Buns

Alexandra Stewart

Born: June 10, 1939
Montreal, Quebec, Canada
Skin-O-Meter: Great Nudity

Her far-seeing green-eyed gaze tends to give Québecois thespian Alexandra Stewart an air of distance, although her passion is no more removed than just below the surface of her skin. In more than one hundred film credits, in titles ranging from *Tarzan the Magnificent* (1960) to *Exodus* (1960) to *Under the Cherry Moon* (1986), Alexandra's strong, handsome features are often set in a mask of determination. This force of will is intrinsically sexual—how else to account for an array of leading men that includes Peter Lawford, Paul Newman, and Prince? What did they all see in her? A half dozen of Stewart's titles display the answer in pink-skinned glory.

SKIN-fining Moment:

Femmes (0:16) Full-on frontal fun in the sun! Naked Alex gets fondled by the ever-busy Helmut Berger on a beach, most likely getting sand in those hard-to-reach places.

See Her Naked In:

Femmes (1983) FFN, Buns
In Praise of Older Women (1978) Breasts, Bush, Buns
Because of the Cats (1973) Breasts
Ils (1970)
Kemek (1970) Breasts

TeleVisions:

The Hitchhiker Breasts

Catherine Mary Stewart

Born: April 22, 1959
Edmonton, Alberta, Canada
Skin-O-Meter: Brief Nudity

Lean and athletic Catherine Mary Stewart is missing the genetic makeup to be a bimbo. Back home in Canada, Mom is a physiologist, Dad is a renowned marine biologist, and brother Alan is a scientist with his own TV show. At seven Catherine Mary veered away from her family's academic bent to study dance. By nineteen she'd toured the world with various dance troupes and moved to London, England, to further pursue her dramatic career, a gambit that resulted in appearances on *Knight Rider* and *Hotel*, which in turn led to a recurring role on *Days of Our Lives*. The rest is history: Surfer Girl in *The Beach Girls* (1982), Gwen in *Weekend at Bernie's* (1989), and Lia in *Cafe Romeo* (1992).

SKIN-fining Moment:

Psychic (0:45) Catherine Mary lets her right-side chest-gremlin slip after getting it on with Zach Galligan.

See Her Naked In:

Psychic (1992) RB

Mink Stole

Baltimore, Maryland
Skin-O-Meter: Brief Nudity

It takes a special woman, even with the dedicated assistance of a special husband, to challenge a deranged, poop-chewing drag queen; an obese, toothless, egg-gulping retard hag; and a feckless poultry perv to a contest to determine who are "the filthiest people alive," and that special woman, at least as portrayed in the midnight classic *Pink Flamingos* (1972), is Mink Stole. Skinny, strident, and shameless, Stole burst into underground prominence as one of travesty director John

Waters's first super-duper stars, a cadre of gritty prole freaks from Baltimore whose working-class confrontationalism was a refreshing, unpretentious counterbalance to the socialite superstars slumming in the Andy Warhol Factory up north. Although her string of films for the Maryland maniac spans from *Roman Candles* (1966) to *A Dirty Shame* (2004), Mink distinguished herself from most of Waters's other collaborators by carving out a niche career in B-list TV and film fare that includes *Lost Highway* (1997), *Pink as the Day She Was Born* (1997), and *But I'm a Cheerleader* (1999).

SKIN-fining Moment:

Pink Flamingos (0:35) Full-frontal outrage as Mink makes it with Mr. Marble in bed, complete with graphic toe-sucking.

See Her Naked In:

Pink Flamingos (1972) FFN

Sharon Stone

Born: March 10, 1958
Meadville, Pennsylvania
Skin-O-Meter: Hall of Fame

She's complained that she was tricked into doing the scene, but Sharon Stone has still done very well after exposing her pussy in *Basic Instinct* (1992). She kept on flashing in plenty of sexy scenes, including *Intersection* (1993), *The Quick and the Dead* (1994), and *The Specialist* (1994)—not to mention pulling a nice orgasm in *Sliver* (1993). Sharon's been maturing nicely, too, as seen by her amazing aging ass in *The Muse* (1999) and a surprisingly hot sex scene with Ellen DeGeneres in HBO's *If These Walls Could Talk 2* (2000). She's now back on the comeback trail, but let's also not forget all of Sharon's important early work—especially a gratuitous topless scene in *Irreconcilable Differences* (1984) and her amazing aerobics in *Total Recall* (1990).

SKIN-fining Moment:

Basic Instinct (0:27) Panty-free Sharon crosses and uncrosses her legs as Wayne Knight grabs a sweet peek and hair-riffic history is made!

See Her Naked In:

A Different Loyalty (2004) Breasts
If These Walls Could Talk 2 (2000) Breasts, Buns
The Muse (1999) RB, Buns
The Quick and the Dead (1995) Breasts
Intersection (1994) LB
The Specialist (1994) Breasts, Buns
Sliver (1993) Breasts, Buns

Basic Instinct (1992) FFN, Buns
Year of the Gun (1991) LB
Scissors (1991) Breasts
Total Recall (1990) Nip Slip RB
Blood and Sand (1989) Breasts
Action Jackson (1988) Breasts
Cold Steel (1987) Breasts
Irreconcilable Differences (1984) Breasts

Sherri Stoner

**Born: July 16, 1965
Santa Monica, California,
Skin-O-Meter: Brief Nudity**

The high-school path of young, sprightly Sherri Stoner must have seemed fated from the moment her name was first called out in that initial freshman-year homeroom. Here was a girl destined to smoke up every day, drop out, drop a pair of kids with different fathers, and spend the remainder of her days watching daytime TV and cursing the mailman for being late with her check. But Sherri Stoner defied all expectations, rising to the challenge imposed by her moniker and establishing herself while still a minor as a major force on the cathode tube, her whip-thin, pleasingly padded body and wonder-waif grin brightening the flat lands of *Little House on the Prairie*, which led to a feature-film career culminating in *Reform School Girls* (1986). Sherri's frantic, naked struggle while pinned to the institutional bathroom floor beneath a ratty trio of tough-chick attackers hearkened to the victim a lesser girl might have become, were she burdened with the same name as Sherri Stoner.

SKIN-fining Moment:

Reform School Girls (0:05) Ass and brief bush as they shower and get sprayed for bugs. Sherri provides the seat-meat in the center and then on the far left.

See Her Naked In:

Reform School Girls (1986) Breasts, Buns

Guylaine St-Onge

**St-Eustache, Québec, Canada
Skin-O-Meter: Brief Nudity**

It's the fast lane to an erection whenever Guylaine St-Onge shows up onscreen—although guys also have to look for her as "St. Onge," which must be kind of galling for a gal from the Canadian town of St-Eustache. Anyway, this Canuck first struck us with plenty of guest spots on Canadian-shot shows such as *La Femme Nikita* and the Showtime edition of *The Outer Limits*. Guylaine finally got a recurring role as the alluring alien "Juda" on the 2001 season of *Earth: Final Conflict*, which allowed that series to go out with a bang—in our briefs, that is. Guylaine's still causing guy stains at Skin Central, most recently with a wild sex scene in *One Way Out* (2002). She's surrounded by enough candelabra to make you think she's screwing Liberace, but that's all the better to see her incredible, natural breasts. Nice jewelry too.

SKIN-fining Moment:

One Way Out (0:12) Guylaine's heaving hooters are on display as she bangs Jim Belushi.

See Her Naked In:

One Way Out (2002) Breasts, Buns

Tempest Storm

**Born: February 29, 1928
Eastman, Georgia
Skin-O-Meter: Brief Nudity**

Known as the "Fabulous 4D Girl" due to her larger-than-life natural Nerf balls, Tempest Storm wanked weenies as a burlesque stripper after WWII. You too can take a walk down mammary lane and give your boinker a blast from stripping days past watching Tempest's eruption of flesh in *Mundo Depravados* (1967), *Striptease Girl* (1952), and *Paris After*

Midnight (1951). Double your pleasure and fun with twice the amount of tornados for your yank in *Teaserama* (1955), featuring the stealthy Ms. Storm and the boobilicious Bettie Page. Tit-tastic! Most of Tempest's films feature her fleshtastic performances but don't actually zoom in on skin. For a little more of Storm's form, catch double-D director Doris Wishman's titilating *Double Agent 73* (1974). Along with fellow jumbo-jugged striptresses Chesty Morgan and Blaze Starr, Tempest allowed a trio of horny onlookers to pat her mouthwatering melons. Quadruple D-licious! When no other port in the *Storm* will do, D-scriminating sailors and gents continue to look to Tempest for safe harbor in the haven of her hooters.

SKIN-fining Moment:

Double Agent 73 (DVD bonus feature) Tempest kicks up a storm by unleashing her double thunder-guns amidst a gaggle of gawking guys.

See Her Naked In:

Double Agent 73 (1974) LB

Madeleine Stowe

Born: August 18, 1958
Eagle Rock, California
Skin-O-Meter: Hall of Fame

A refined tropical blend of British and Costa Rican parentage, sultry, cocoa-colored brunette screen star Madeline Stowe's career has been a journey into nudity. She started out projecting both virginal and maternal qualities (always fully clothed) in *The Nativity* (1978) at the tender age of twenty. Stowe matured steadily, revealing more of herself on a learning curve that is as full and sensually lulling as the contour of her hips. Start with *Stakeout* (1987) for a lingering, panoramic ass shot that displays Stowe's stowaway from every which way. Move on to

Short Cuts (1993). A far more confident and consummate professional pretends to be a fully, frontally nude figure model. Studying the craft really pays off!

SKIN-fining Moment:

China Moon (0:21) Madeleine strips bare in a canoe with Ed Harris, exhibiting her taut twosome and poof of poonanny.

See Her Naked In:

China Moon (1994) FFN
Blink (1994) Breasts
Short Cuts (1993) LB
Unlawful Entry (1992) Breasts, Buns
The Two Jakes (1990) Buns
Revenge (1990) Breasts, Thong
Tropical Snow (1989) Breasts, Buns
Stakeout (1987) RB, Buns

> "I'm a real life warrior. I'm strong. Women want to be me. Men want to fuck me. I've created this dark, looming vixen character. Who else is there?"
>
> —JULIE STRAIN

Julie Strain

Born: February 18, 1962
Concord, California
Skin-O-Meter: Great Nudity

Julie Strain is about the most multi-talented six-foot-two-inch lady in the skintertainment industry. She acts. (Well enough to serve as Geena Davis's understudy in *Thelma and Louise* [1991].) She directs. (You just have to see *Lingerie Kickboxer* [1998] to believe it.) She models. (Ever heard of *Penthouse*? Julie reigned as Pet of the Year in 1993. How about *Playboy*?) She is, beyond a shadow of a doubt, a modern-day goddess. And did I mention that she's *really* tall? Since Julie first showed up in all her topless wonder at the beginning of 1989's *Picasso*

Trigger, she's gone on to appear in some state of undress or another in over ninety films. Needless to say, finding some flesh-flashing from this filly on film isn't all that hard to do. For some of her finest mam-and-glutes-filled moments, try checking out *all* of her *Penthouse* videos (*Satin & Lace* [1992] is especially worthy), as well as her hit cable series *Judge Julie* and such skinematic productions as *Masseuse 3* (1998) and *The Bare Wench Project* (1999). Really, if you catch Julie on the cover of a video box, just go ahead and pick it up; you really can't go wrong.

SKIN-fining Moment:

Masseuse 3 (0:45) Gravity-mocking, goddess-great gazongas, gluteus and gash ignite the screen as Julie accepts a dong doggie-style, then rides the pink pony. Feel the Strain!

See Her Naked In:

Heavenly Hooters (2003) Breasts, Thong
Baberellas (2003) FFN
Treasure Hunt! (2003) Breasts
Delta Delta Die! (2003) FFN, Buns
Hellcats in High Heels 3 (2002) FFN, Buns

MR. SKIN'S TOP TEN

Naked and at Least Six Feet Tall
. . . Towering skinfernos

6'0" Mary Woronov

6'0" Geena Davis

6'0" Mariel Hemingway

6'0" Elle Macpherson

6'0" Brooke Shields

6'0" Uma Thurman

6'0" Shannon Tweed

6'0" Tracy Tweed

6'1" Brigitte Nielsen

6'2" Julie Strain

Bleed (2002) Breasts
13 Erotic Ghosts (2002) FFN, Buns
Blood Gnome (2002) Breasts
Sex Court: The Movie (2002) Breasts, Bush, Buns
The Bare Wench Project 2: Scared Topless (2001) FFN, Buns
How to Make a Monster (2001) Breasts
.com for Murder (2001) Breasts
Millennium Queen (2000) Breasts, Bush
The Rowdy Girls (1999) Breasts
The Bare Wench Project (1999) FFN, Buns
Masseuse 3 (1998) Breasts, Bush, Buns
L.E.T.H.A.L. Ladies: Return to Savage Beach (1998) Breasts, Buns
Lethal Seduction (1997) Breasts, Thong
The Last Road (1997) FFN, Buns
Bikini Hotel (1997) Breasts, Thong
Red Line (1996) FFN
Victim of Desire (1996) Breasts, Buns
Dark Secrets (1996) Breasts, Buns
Day of the Warrior (1996)
Busted (1996) Breasts, Bush, Buns
Blonde Heaven (1995) Breasts, Thong
The Dallas Connection (1995) Breasts, Thong
Big Sister 2000 (1995) Breasts
Married People, Single Sex II: For Better or Worse (1995) Breasts, Thong
Morgana (1995) Breasts, Thong
Midnight Confessions (1995) Breasts, Buns
Virtual Desire (1995) FFN, Buns
The Mosaic Project (1995) Thong
Buck Naked Golf (1994) Breasts, Buns
Sorceress (1994) Breasts
Play Time (1994) FFN, Buns
Squanderers (1994) Breasts, Buns
Fit to Kill (1993) Breasts, Thong
Buck Naked Line Dancing (1993) Breasts, Buns
Psycho Cop Returns (1993) Breasts, Buns
Enemy Gold (1993) Breasts, Thong
Future Shock (1993) Thong
Witchcraft 4: Virgin Heart (1992) Breasts, Thong
Night Rhythms (1992) LB
Bad Love (1992) Breasts
Carnal Crimes (1991) Breasts
Mirror Images (1991) Breasts, Thong
Out for Justice (1991) RB
Sunset Heat (1991) Breasts
Guns (1990) Breasts
Picasso Trigger (1989) Breasts
Hard Ticket to Hawaii (1987) Breasts

Susan Strasberg

Born: May 22, 1938
New York, New York
Died: January 21, 1999
Skin-O-Meter: Brief Nudity

A fragile, fair-skinned brunette, her face a map of sensitivity and intelligence where all roads lead to a cool core of hipster sensuality, Susan Strasberg was the daughter of Lee Strasberg, perhaps the most inventive and influential acting coach of the cinematic era. As a descendent of an innovator like Lee, and coming into her heyday during the radical 1960s, it was only natural that Susan would flirt with serious experimentation. That means she took her shirt off and emoted while the cameras were running. Under the kaleidoscopic lighting treatment of *The Trip* (1967), Susan's skin slid on hippie-dude skin in a free-love free-for-all. *Psych-Out* (1968) offered a freaky flash of breast flesh. For the breast of Strasberg, consult *Le Sorelle* (1969). A full view of her mounds reclining in all their full glory is capped off by a mad bare-bottom dash.

SKIN-fining Moment:

The Trip (0:17) Susan sheds her shirt and climbs into bed for a make-out session with Peter Fonda, but thanks to the crazy lighting all that can be seen is her right boob and even then, it's only for an instant.

See Her Naked In:

In Praise of Older Women (1978) Breasts
Le Sorelle (1969) Breasts, Buns
Psych-Out (1968) RB
The Trip (1967) LB

Dorothy Stratten

Born: February 28, 1960
Vancouver, British Columbia, Canada
Died: August 14, 1980
Skin-O-Meter: Great Nudity

MR. SKIN'S TOP TEN

Favorite Playmates in Movies

. . . They give me a Huge Hefner

10. **Kimberly McArthur**
　　—February '82

9. **Lynda Wiesmeir**
　　—July '82

8. **Anna Nicole Smith**
　　—May '92

7. **Pamela Anderson**
　　—February '90

6. **Cynthia Meyers**
　　—December '68

5. **Kathy Shower**
　　—May '85

4. **Shannon Tweed**
　　—November '81

3. **Stella Stevens**
　　—January '60

2. **Claudia Jennings**
　　—November '69

1. **Dorothy Stratten**
　　—**August '79**

Greed, jealousy, and possessive vengeance combined to create the insanity that robbed the world of one of *Playboy*'s most beautiful Playmates ever, Dorothy Stratten. An import from the same area of Canada that would later spawn Pamela Anderson, Dorothy had the blessings of a phenomenal, nature-crafted blondness, pure and touching charisma, and a body that would have exuded irresistible sex appeal even had it been inhabited by a bitter crone rather than the bundle of breasts and sunshine that was Dorothy. Take one glance at her fine bottom, full breasts in profile, and shag haircut in *Autumn Born* (1979) and be forever smitten. The young Ms. Stratten had the great good fortune to be *Playboy*'s Playmate of the Year for 1980. She had the greater misfortune to fall into the clutches of psychotic manager/husband Paul Snider and a clique of selfish gropers. The bio-pic *Star 80* (1983) conveys the sordid, predatory depravity of the murderous milieu that destroyed her. But Mariel Hemingway as the doomed sun, though lovely in her own light, could not be expected to duplicate the luminous essence of Dorothy Stratten.

SKIN-fining Moment:

Autumn Born (0:46) A nice long visit with Dorothy's bum and bobblers as she strips down for a bath.

See Her Naked In:

Hugh Hefner: Once Upon a Time (1992) RB
Dorothy Stratten, The Untold Story (1985) FFN, Buns
Autumn Born (1979) Breasts, Buns

Meryl Streep

Born: June 22, 1949
Summit, New Jersey
Skin-O-Meter: Brief Nudity

Universally presented as the standard by whom all other actresses are judged, Mery Streep's name is often invoked by budding serious-chick thespians who self-deprecatingly remark, "I may not be Meryl Streep, but . . ." But, Honey, at least you can take your clothes off and be just as good at it as the great Streep herself. In fact, it's a sad wanna-be leading lady who can't outdo Streep in using her naked instrument to raw effect. Dame Meryl's combined exposure of nips and buttocks in their entirety—a quick flash of chest flesh in *Silkwood* (1983) and some shadowy shared bathtub footage in *Bridges of Madison County* (1995)— are less award worthy than a single afternoon of work from an underappreciated artist such as Edy

Williams or Vanessa del Rio. Still, there is time, and the right role may yet roll along and strip Streep.

SKIN-fining Moment:

Silkwood (0:24) The world's most acclaimed actresses surprises her boss (and us) with one of the world's best-loved nipple-flashes.

See Her Naked In:

Adaptation (2002) Body Double—Breasts
The Bridges of Madison County (1995) Breasts, Buns
Silkwood (1983) LB

Barbra Streisand

Born: April 24, 1942
Brooklyn, New York
Skin-O-Meter: Brief Nudity

Is there a man in the free world who has not been touched by the fame of acclaimed singer/actress/writer/director/producer Barbra Streisand and not been brightened for that contact? Unabashedly, proudly, boldly ethnic, this original Brooklyn diva took to the Broadway stage in 1962 as Miss Marmelstein in *I Can Get It for You Wholesale* and thrust her nose out before her like the prow of a particularly invincible and implausibly erotic battleship. With that sleek, sensual, prominent proboscis complemented by full gourmand lips and eyes as big and wonderstruck as a ten-year-old's on her first trip to Bloomingdale's, Streisand played sassy and wisecracky as comedienne Fanny Brice in *Funny Girl* (1968). A rapidly articulate, streetwise persona was established, and like a destroyer in a sea of rowboats, Barbra Streisand plowed through the froth and flume in such hits as *What's Up, Doc* (1972), *The Way We Were* (1973), *A Star Is Born* (1976), and *The Main Event* (1979). With each project, Barbra took greater behind-the-scenes control until, with *Yentl*

(1983), Queen Showbiz not only functioned as writer, director, producer, and star, she also sang the title tune. On the side, Barbra sold more record albums than any other female in the history of America.

SKIN-fining Moment:

The Owl and the Pussycat (0:45) La Streisand peels for George Segal and we get a split-second serving of Babs's slabs. Mammaries, light the corners of my mind . . .

See Her Naked In:

The Owl and the Pussycat (1970) Breasts

Connie Strickland

Skin-O-Meter: Great Nudity

Boobilicious blonde Connie Strickland made great skinematic strides in her short career in '70s sexploitation. In *Secretary* (1971), Connie comes to question who's the boss by mastering the art of *dick*-tation. Mr. Skin's typing pool doth overfloweth. As the vengeful vixen in *Rape Squad* (1974), this juicy jugged outlaw makes the breast po-litical statement possible by sudsing in a tub with five foxy female vigilantes. Connie jiggles her giant gazongas jubilantly and flittingly flashes her fur patch while dipping in with her Sapphic sisters. Ra-ra-tits-boob-ba! For more of Connie's curvaceous cups and other general boobery, check out *Centerfold Girls* (1974). Each and every sexploitive skindeavor from the lovely Connie is guaranteed to be *cantastic!*

SKIN-fining Moment:

Bummer! (0:32) Tits and ass when she and Diane Lee Hart strip naked and shower in front of some fat guy.

See Her Naked In:

The Centerfold Girls (1974) Breasts
Black Samson (1974) Breasts, Buns
Rape Squad (1974) Breasts, Bush
Bummer! (1972) Breasts, Buns

Anita Strindberg

Sweden
Skin-O-Meter: Great Nudity

If ever there was a two-legged, spry-breasted argument for a Europe without borders, that argument was Anita Strindberg. Sometimes blonde, sometimes brunette, always with tapered pegs and uplifted chest ornaments, Anita was a Swede born and bred but traveled freely across the continent to Italy. The Italian skinema quickly roped the mellow traveler into a string of spaghetti sexploitation pics with titles like *The Eroticist* (1972), *Eye of the Black Cat* (1972), and *The Antichrist* (1974). This sinsationalist fare sometimes focused on violent vengeance, other times opted for harrowing horror, but always tossed in dashes of dazzling flesh, often that of Anita Strindberg. Her reign was the 1970s. Pick any title and prepare to be pleased.

SKIN-fining Moment:

Una Lucertola con la pelle di donna (0:07) Great breast shot when she rips off her top.

See Her Naked In:

L'Ossessione che uccide (1980) Breasts
La Segretaria privata di mio padre (1976) Breasts, Bush, Buns
Milano odia: la polizia non può sparare (1974) Breasts
The Antichrist (1974) Breasts, Buns
Contratto carnale (1974) Breasts, Buns
Eye of the Black Cat (1972) Breasts
Diario segreto da un carcere femminile (1972) LB, Buns
Una Lucertola con la pelle di donna (1971) Breasts
La Coda dello scorpione (1971) Breasts

Sherry Stringfield

Born: June 24, 1967
Colorado Springs, Colorado
Skin-O-Meter: Brief Nudity

People do funny things. Sometimes they work hard all their lives and achieve exactly what they have been striving for, then they walk away. A nation of skin watchers is left to wonder, "Geez, why did Sherry Stringfield show her great ass in a series of great quick shots on *NYPD Blue* way back in 1993 and then basically pull a disappearing act? Why did she remove from us the strong, compassionate sensuality of her face and the hope of seeing her breasts, more of her ass, and maybe even her bush?" There is no answer for such questions. After only one year at *NYPD Blue*, portraying David Caruso's ex-wife, Stringfield opted out of her contract. After two seasons on *ER*, she ditched that gig. In 2001 she negotiated a deal to return to *ER* for three more terms. Women. Don't ever try to figure what makes them tick.

SKIN-fining Moment:

NYPD Blue "True Confessions" (1993) Sherry rises from bed next to David Caruso and ignites ABC primetime with most of her right chest-rocket and a great blast of her booming backside.

TeleVisions:

NYPD Blue RB, Buns

Tara Strohmeier

Skin-O-Meter: Great Nudity

Big-boobied brunette Tara Strohmeier spent the better part of the '70s flaunting her fine frame in skinema. Flesh freaks know top-heavy Tara breast as the naughty nightingale in Roger Corman's *Candy Stripe Nurses* (1974) and the sizzling sexpot in *The Kentucky Fried Movie* (1977), but all this busty babe's skindeavors are equally finger-licking good. Worshipers of womping woolies will get a rise out of Strohmeier's surprisingly large suck-sacks in films such as *The*

Student Teachers (1972), *Hollywood Boulevard* (1976), and *Malibu Beach* (1978). Any look at Tara's titilating double D-lights is guaranteed to be hotter than your most boobtastic day at the beach.

SKIN-fining Moment:

Hollywood Boulevard (0:33) Great glistening gazongas as she sunbathes topless with Candice Rialson.

See Her Naked In:

Van Nuys Blvd. (1979) Breasts
Malibu Beach (1978) Breasts
The Kentucky Fried Movie (1977) Breasts
Hollywood Boulevard (1976) Breasts
Cover Girl Models (1975) Breasts
The Student Teachers (1973) Breasts

Brenda Strong

Brightwood, Oregon
Skin-O-Meter: Brief Nudity

Standing at a statuesque six-feet tall in her bare fishnet pantyhose, glacially pale brunette Brenda Strong is an aptly named vessel of erotic puissance. This gem-eyed beauty's plentiful television appearances are varied and accomplished, but a pertinent aspect of her appeal can be summed up by adding together the titles from two of her early 1990s series: *Scorch* and *Twin Peaks*. The heat of Brenda's high-end shelf added simmer to the skinful *Weekend Warriors* (1986) and popped thermometers as Nurse Gretchen in the Mel Brooks laugh attack *Spaceballs* (1986). Get pleasantly warm as Brenda emerges braless from the sea, makes love behind a veil of mosquito netting, and squeezes her thong-split buns into a tight dress in *Undercurrent* (1998).

SKIN-fining Moment:

Undercurrent (0:54) Like Botticelli's Venus, Brenda emerges topless from the sea. Only this goddess's clam shells are perfectly bare!

See Her Naked In:

Undercurrent (1999) Breasts, Thong
Weekend Warriors (1986) Breasts

Sally Struthers

Born: July 28, 1948
Portland, Oregon
Skin-O-Meter: Brief Nudity

Sally Struthers was a secret pleasure of the groundbreaking early 1970s TV series *All in the Family*. While most viewers claimed to watch the show for its scathing sarcasm and social commentary, an equally devoted contingent was fixated beyond help upon the bulging sweaters, baby-doll voice, denim-clad chair cheeks, and naïve girly face of Archie Bunker's sweet and kindly bombshell daughter, Gloria. Those discerning skincentrics who detected heaving mounds of joy beneath Struthers's fully clad persona were proven correct by a pair of 1970s classic films, both of which highlighted the classic pair of Archie's kid. The tits are bare and breathtaking beneath Jack Nicholson in *Five Easy Pieces* (1970). In *The Getaway* (1972), long before Steve McQueen slugs her across the chops, Sally does a totally sexy boogie in black panties and a tie-top that totally reveals bobbling side boobage. If we could have our druthers, we'd take classic Struthers.

SKIN-fining Moment:

Five Easy Pieces (0:34) You get some nice views of topless Sally's "easy pieces" as Jack Nicholson carries her into the bedroom.

See Her Naked In:

Five Easy Pieces (1970) Breasts

Imogen Stubbs

Born: February 20, 1961
Newcastle-Upon-Tyne, England, UK
Skin-O-Meter: Great Nudity

Green-eyed, fair-skinned blonde Imogen Stubbs is a film actress who has no trouble playing the role of a brainy, sensitive, and intuitive beauty. The British-born daughter of a Naval officer was educated at prestigious and rigorous Oxford University and has honed her stagecraft with the Royal Shakespeare Company and upon the boards of the Strand Theatre and the Haymarket, two venues for drama steeped in traditions of excellence and intelligence. Discerning American cinema connoisseurs will recall Imogen's shaded interplay with equally adept Emma Thompson in the costumed period piece *Sense and Sensibility* (1995). Vulgarians will forever recall blinking during Imogen's shirtless appearance in *Blind Ambition* (2000), a reflexive twitch intended to protect gawking eyeballs from the piercing protrusions of her hyper-erect nips.

SKIN-fining Moment:

Fellow Traveller (0:54) Imogen's guy diddles her stiff-nipped boobles in bed until erectile dysfunction ruins the fun.

See Her Naked In:

Blind Ambition (2000) Breasts
Fellow Traveller (1989) Breasts
Deadline (1988) FFN
A Summer Story (1988) Breasts
The Rainbow (1988) Breasts, Bush, Buns

Trudie Styler

Born: January 6, 1955
Birmingham, England, UK
Skin-O-Meter: Brief Nudity

Being Mrs. Sting takes a special kind of woman. She must be beautiful. She must be adventurous and freewheeling. She must be regal in bearing—and in baring. She must have a broad, hot, British bum and a passion for portraying the arts of love. She must be Trudie Styler. And she must be seen in *On the Q.T.* (1999) to be believed. Pushing forty-

five, mature, and a multiple mother, Trudie throws all modesty and the notion of using a body double to the wind. She sprawls out in full-length full nudity beside and beneath a starkers lad who looks young enough to have sprung from her loins rather than springing into them. May there always be an England!

SKIN-fining Moment:

On the Q.T. (0:39) Some nice shots of Mrs. Sting's chest-things in a choppily edited sex scene involving some dude playing his instrument.

See Her Naked In:

On the Q.T. (1999) Breasts
The Scold's Bridle (1998) Breasts, Buns, Bush
Grave Indiscretion (1995) Buns
Fair Game (1988) Buns

Emma Suárez

Born: June 25, 1964
Madrid, Spain
Skin-O-Meter: Great Nudity

Impish nymph Emma Suárez is one of those miracles of Spanish genetics. Her skin is the tawny rich tan of a born brunette, while her mane of thick, heavy locks falls with the sun-kissed insouciance of a natural blonde. Emma is a pretty and playful sprite, a teasing grin often accompanying her glowers of passion, but a come-on from this star of European screen is no tease. A veteran of acclaimed features since appearing in *Memorias de Leticia Valle* (1979) at age fifteen, sweet and spicy Suárez has shared the full enjoyment of her heavy, high-riding breasts and ripely rounded rear in a wide selection of arty foreign fare. Be one among the masses who benefits from Emma's breastly busses in *Kisses for Everyone* (2000).

SKIN-fining Moment:

Contra el viento (0:55) Great flash of hooter when she opens her top for Bruce McGuire.

See Her Naked In:

Kisses for Everyone (2000) LB, Buns
Pintadas (1996) FFN, Thong
Earth (1996) Buns
Enciende mi pasión (1994) FFN, Buns
The Red Squirrel (1993) Body Double—
    Bush / Her—Breasts, Buns
Contra el viento (1990) Breasts, Buns
Hot Spot (1985) Breasts

Tara Subkoff

Born: 1973
Skin-O-Meter: Great Nudity

All it takes to be a star in Mr. Skin's boorish book is for a budding talent to take off her clothes. By that definition, Tara Subkoff is well on her way to the stratosphere. She hasn't had all that bad of a career thus far, no leads really, but she did debut as a crazy mute in *When the Bough Breaks* (1993) and played part of a girl-girl amore in *All Over Me* (1997). That was followed by bit parts in such notable flicks as *As Good As It Gets* (1997), *The Last Days of Disco* (1998), and *American Pie* (1999). Tara landed a somewhat more impressive turn in *The Cell* (2000), but we prefer her bit parts—especially when those bits are her perky little tits. She finally showed the goods in the made-for-cable flick *Teenage Caveman* (2001), appearing amongst a bevy of first-time skinsters in the sci-fi thriller. It's worth tracking down to see Tara and her teeny-bopper pals in all their naked glory whilst swimming, and in Tara's case, engaging in some pretty convincing sex on a warehouse floor. Now that's some manly work we can all get behind!

SKIN-fining Moment:

Teenage Caveman: (1:13) Breasts and side nudity getting naked in a warehouse with a dude. Then having sex.

See Her Naked In:

Teenage Caveman (2001) Breasts

Catherine Sutherland

Born: October 24, 1974
Sydney, New South Wales, Australia
Skin-O-Meter: Brief Nudity

You know Catherine Sutherland as the sexy blonde superhero wrapped up in a skintight pink leotard, The Pink Ranger on the hit kiddie series *Mighty Morphin' Power Rangers*. Who can't get enough of the shapely beauty kickin' ass in an outfit that leaves little to the imagination? While being a role model for the kids takes up most of this hot young actress's time, she did manage to branch out and portray a recently murdered girl in the J. Lo thriller *The Cell* (2000). Since she has no lines, the director must have decided to make her part a little more memorable, so he painted her up in some white make-up (head-to-toe) and laid her out buck naked for the world to see. That's right: You can see the Pink Ranger stark-raving naked in a role as a corpse. If you look closely, you'll catch a fleeting glimpse of her namesake between those athletic legs.

SKIN-fining Moment:

The Cell (0:13) Nude laying dead on a table. She's a tad bit pale.

See Her Naked In:

The Cell (2000) Breasts, Bush

Krista Sutton

Canada
Skin-O-Meter: Great Nudity

"It was mostly just, um, body language," Krista Sutton said of her controversial skinematic debut as a hot-to-trot hooker in *American Psycho* (2000). It was Sutton's scorchingly sexy three-way scene with Christian Bale and Cara Seymour that earned the film's NC-17 rating, not the ultra-violence. It is true that this cunning Canuck was dangerously dizzying in her short eight-minute scene, busting nuts with her Canadian Mounties in all their pointed glory. When *Psycho* star Bale asked Krista to take off her dress, she was more than ready. "I had to go for it," she says. "I kind of surprised myself . . . the bustier comes off, and you get to see the real goods, no false advertising." As a testament to her terrific two, a rash of serial wankings broke out in North America after the flick's release. Since *American Psycho*, Kris has been flaunting her fine frame in Canadian theater productions, including the mufftastic *Vagina Monologues*. Mr. Skin is more than willing to lend his ears to this pretty pussy's ramblings, anytime, anywhere.

SKIN-fining Moment:

American Psycho (0:44) Quickbits of T&A as Krista makes up one-third of a Balehooker Sandwich.

See Her Naked In:

American Psycho (2000) Breasts, Thong

"I didn't want to be known for nudity, but I'll never say never."

—MENA SUVARI

Mena Suvari

Born: February 9, 1979
Newport, Rhode Island
Skin-O-Meter: Brief Nudity

Anyone who doubts the greatness of the U.S. need only see prototypical American blonde Mena Suvari's American trilogy. First, sit up and snap to attention for smirky, flirty Suvari's teasing tantalization in the camp hetero-teen coming-of-age film *American Pie* (1999). Next, zip through to Mena's flat-on-her-back climax in *American Beauty* (1999). Prepare to fire a one-gun salute as the conflicted post-adolescent girl's billowy breasts float atop her heaving chest like buoys guiding the ships of free-market enterprise. Then, if any doubt as to the manifest destiny of unilateral sexism remains, consult *American Virgin* (2000). Mena's character displays her capitalist Yankee ingenuity by intending to lose her virginity on the Internet while a huge paying audience hooks up via sensory replicating gear to share the experience.

SKIN-fining Moment:

American Beauty (1:47) An open-bloused Ms. Suvari treats Kevin Spacey (and the viewer) to a lengthy look at her love-buds.

See Her Naked In:

American Beauty (1999) Breasts

Dominique Swain

Born: August 12, 1980
Malibu, California
Skin-O-Meter: Brief Nudity

A little bit surly and a whole lot pretty, Malibu blonde Dominique Swain is a little girl who grew up fast. As a fifteen-year-old cheeky tit bit in *Face/Off* (1997) and *Lolita* (1997), Dominique looked like a lot of things—young, fresh, nubile, actualized, sexualized—and none of them were naïve or innocent. Since reaching the age of consent, bad girl Swain has been taking increasingly risqué roles. After a bout of bra-and-pantie clad self-inspection in *Girl* (1998), Dominique went fully bare, but covered up, for a 2001 PETA ad and twitched her butt with her bikini bottom firmly up her cheek crack in *Dead in the Water* (2002). The promise of the teenage temptress came true in *New Best Friend* (2002) when Dominique went titties out while putting the lesbo bed moves on brunette tasty treat Mia Kirschner. Welcome to adulthood.

SKIN-fining Moment:

New Best Friend (0:47) A few quick snippets of Dominique's funbags as she enjoys a co-ed lesbian tryst with the equally sexy Mia Kirshner.

See Her Naked In:

New Best Friend (2002) Breasts

Hilary Swank

Born: July 30, 1974
Lincoln, Nebraska
Skin-O-Meter: Great Nudity

It's the rare leading lady who can impersonate a boy and still come off sexy. Tall, with rangy, lean limbs and torso and a striking face that is equal parts strength and sensuality, Hilary Swank burst into the A-list portraying a woman who passes as a man in *Boys Don't Cry* (1999). *Boys Don't* won Hilary an Oscar and exposed her bush and hips in a graphic depiction of what boys sometimes do. The film's harsh realities were softened with some nuanced lesbian make-out scenes, which hint at Hilary's potential to become a skinternational superstar. Let's hope that the Academy Award doesn't go to her head.

SKIN-fining Moment:

Boys Don't Cry (1:22) Girl does show: some meanies pull down Hilary's tightie-whiteys and get stunned by her Swanky female private parts.

See Her Naked In:

Boys Don't Cry (1999) RB, Bush, Buns

Jackie Swanson

Born: June 25, 1963
Michigan
Skin-O-Meter: Great Nudity

Hip hips hurray to Jackie Swanson for giving us weekly wank fare as the naïve yet nastily nubile poor little rich girl on *Cheers*. This curvy cutie gave the whole bar a bone as Kelly, the wife of dim-witted bar meister Woody (making Mr. Harrelson's nickname on the show all the more apropos). K-E-L-L-Y . . . Why? Because she's fine, fine, fine. Aside from baring her beauty in Bean Town, this blonde bimbolina knocked knockwursts in *Slamdance* (1987) and filled the void of her absence on *Cheers* in the sci-fi westerns *Oblivion* (1994) and *Oblivion 2: The Backlash* (1996). Jackie's juicy, all-American allure in curve-clutching costumes was out of this world! Those with a Jackie jones can still catch this fair-haired fox cruising along the freeway of lust in car commercials. Still fine at forty, Jackie has plenty of miles left on her *Oh*dometer.

SKIN-fining Moment:

Lethal Weapon (0:01) Jackie treats us to her topless Lethal Weapons just before she leaps out of a high rise.

See Her Naked In:

Perfect Victims (1988) Breasts, Bush, Buns
Lethal Weapon (1987) Breasts

Kristy Swanson

Born: December 19, 1969
Mission Viejo, California
Skin-O-Meter: Never Nude

If nobody likes a tease, how come the world is so in love with California blonde Kristy Swanson? Sunshine-fresh Swanson's only nude role to date, a head-to-knees fully nude rear shot in *Getting In* (1994), showcases a pair of tightly clenched, cheese-free butt cheeks. Sadly, the seat meat, though savory, is the property of a body double and has come no closer to Kristy's pepper pot than have the rest of us. Still, Swanson maintains a lingerie-clad hold on mass affection. A pro of screen and tube,

Kristy's list of credits is long and studded with prominent entries. Is there a common thread? The peekaboo hottie dons a bra-and-panties combo or a tasteful bikini almost every time out. Such costuming is a ray of hope. One of these outings, some little bit is bound to slip.

SKIN-fining Moment:

Higher Learning (0:31) The original Buffy doesn't get in the buff, but she'll put a stake in your pants when you see her here in bra-and-panties making out with a college dude who turns creepy.

See Her Naked In:

Getting In (1994) Body Double—Buns

Rochelle Swanson

Skin-O-Meter: Great Nudity

You really have to love a girl who has no illusions about where her talents lie. Rochelle Swanson is just such a girl. The former nude model turned softcore actress has made a career out of giving people exactly what they want . . . our kind of people, the kind who dedicate themselves to serving the demanding dictates of Skin Central. This dark-haired beauty even augmented her bosom to bazooka size just to make sure everybody would be happy when she took her shirt off, which she does a lot. So everybody's happy! When this bombshell shows up in a film, within thirty seconds she's exposed every inch of her knockout body. Where to begin? Why not at the beginning with *Sorceress* (1994), not really her first skin time, but what a time. Rochelle is the meat between the bawdy bread of Julie Strain and Toni Naples in a lesbo sandwich that is just one of the carnal treats on the menu. Rochelle is better than a Swanson Hungry Man Dinner.

SKIN-fining Moment:

Hard Bounty (0:38) Breasts and buns as she bucks a cowboy's flesh-bronco.

See Her Naked In:

On the Border (1998) Breasts, Buns
Mutual Needs (1997) Breasts, Buns
Walnut Creek (1996) Breasts, Buns
Hungry for You (1996) Breasts, Buns
Hard Bounty (1995) Breasts
Night Fire (1994) Breasts, Thong
Illicit Dreams (1994) Breasts
Indecent Behavior II (1994) Breasts, Buns
Secret Games 3 (1994) Breasts, Buns
Sorceress (1994) Breasts, Buns

TeleVisions:

Love Street Breasts, Buns
NYPD Blue Thong
Sherman Oaks Breasts

Stephanie Swift

Born: February 7, 1972
Louisiana
Skin-O-Meter: Great Nudity

For some starry-eyed, post-adolescent cream puffs, the allure of on-camera sexual stardom is an end in itself, but for a more down-to-earth and worldly erotic performer of the caliber of small-breasted brunette waif Stephanie Swift, appearing in roughly two hundred full-penetration erotic entertainments is merely a stepping stone to greater fame. Though her thin, pliant body and its amazingly expandable orifices can be gawked at in a glut of goopy blue-screen classics that includes *Sweet Little Pervert* (1998), *Encino Housewife Hookers* (1998), and *What Makes You Cum?* (1999), Stephanie's talents really shine and soar during her challenging forays upon the legitimate screen. See her naked skin bathed in blood in the crimson thriller *Cabin Fever* (2002). Bask in her full-frontal effrontery in the criminal romance *Perfectly Legal* (2002). Don't be shy about reaping the rewards of Stephanie Swift's higher aspirations.

SKIN-fining Moment:

Cabin Fever (DVD bonus feature) Stephanie and Janelle Perry get topless and bloody as part of the DVD menu. And since this is a menu, I'd like to order more naked Stephanie . . . swift!

See Her Naked In:

Cabin Fever (2002) RB
Perfectly Legal (2002) FFN, Buns
The Ultimate Attraction (2000) FFN
Major Rock (1999) Breasts
The Price of Desire (1996) FFN
Numerous Adult Movies

TeleVisions:

Beverly Hills Bordello Breasts

Tilda Swinton

Born: November 5, 1960
London, England, UK
Skin-O-Meter: Great Nudity

She has the intense, focused presence within her being of an orgasm addict longing for a fix. A shrink wrap of translucent, porcelain-white skin. Fine, fiery-red hair. A flashing emerald gleam in her eyes. And she'll proudly parade her bush in the cause of dramatic verisimilitude. Is there a reason not to acclaim Tilda Swinton the most sensational female pubic figure to come out of Britain since Lady Godiva? Before broaching any argument, inspect the evidence. In *Orlando* (1993), Tilda's exploration of a sexually morphing being will solidify the sexual leanings of those viewers who pride themselves on being among the skingnoscenti. Enter *Female Perversions* (1997), and case closed. Presenting herself as a brunette, Tilda brings her nympho lawyer character to life as though she is redhead hot, full frontally showing all she's got.

SKIN-fining Moment:

Orlando (0:56) Full-frontal fantasticness as Tilda ogles her suddenly changed-to-female form in a mirror. Don't ask. Just leer.

See Her Naked In:

Young Adam (2003) Breasts, Bush
The War Zone (1999) RB
Female Perversions (1997) FFN, Buns
Orlando (1993) FFN

Amanda Swisten

Born: December 20, 1978
New York, New York
Skin-O-Meter: Brief Nudity

One of the greatest traditions in the United States is the bachelor party, an all-night bacchanal of booze, broads, and bad behavior that sends the groom-to-be to the altar sated, glutted, and—if he's not careful—pining over the next twenty years for a stack-topped blonde whom he knew only briefly and imperfectly for one fleeting night, that last night of hopeful freedom. The perfectly rounded and flush breasts of electric blonde Amanda Swisten are examples of miraculous erotic perfection that will haunt a husband until his last dying breath, or until he starts cheating, whichever comes first. He will dream, and he may stray, but he will be hard-pressed to locate a playmate so dirty-sweet of face and exquisitely endowed of body as Amanda Swisten in the role of bachelor-party temptress in *American Wedding* (2003).

SKIN-fining Moment:

American Wedding (0:45) Stripteasin' in a French maid's outfit, Amanda's tittastic torpedoes thrust out as she tickles Finch with her. . . . . . . feather duster.

See Her Naked In:

The Girl Next Door (2004) Breasts, Thong
American Wedding (2003) Breasts

Brenda Sykes

Born: June 25, 1949
Shreveport, Louisiana
Skin-O-Meter: Brief Nudity

Big of Afro and booming of bootay, Brenda Sykes is an African Queen of the '70s exploitation scene. This foxy brown bombshell had her first jam as "Jelly" in *The Liberation of L.B. Jones* (1970). Free to take on more skinsational roles, Brenda was bootilicious in *Getting Straight* (1970) and *The Skin Game* (1971). Ever the chocolate charmer, Brenda landed a leading-lady role as a rich black bitch with a craving for vanilla love in *Honky* (1971). Hershey's Kisses were never so tempting. Brenda bounced bad guys as the tough "Tiffany" in *Cleopatra Jones* (1973), her scantily clad curves a vision of blacktastic beauty! Grabbing Middle America by the crotch, this dark and lovely lassie created twice the bang for your yang, playing perky-topped twins on the *Ozzie and Harriet* spinoff *Ozzie's Girls*. At the end of her career, soul sista Sykes lit a fuse with her loveliness in the racy racial flick *Mandingo* (1975), finally exploding in her heart-pounding skinful debut in *Drum* (1976). As her last picture, beautiful Brenda left the '70s skinematic screen with a bang.

SKIN-fining Moment:

Black Gunn (0:45) Brenda sits up topless in bed and—Pow! Pow! There go her Black Gunns.

See Her Naked In:

Drum (1976) Breasts
Mandingo (1975) Breasts
Black Gunn (1972) RB
Honky (1971) Breasts
Getting Straight (1970) Breasts

t

Kobé Tai

Born: January 15, 1972
Taipei, Taiwan
Skin-O-Meter: Great Nudity

Ever speculate what the most exotic of *Charlie's Angels*, Lucy Liu, might look like in hardcore XXX action? Well look no further than any porn entertainment boasting the taut, tawny torso of Kobe Tai, and speculate no more. Simply drop your jaw in wonder. The mass of mainstream skin seekers caught a stiffening glimpse of Kobe Tai as the acrobatic sex toy who winds up a Las Vegas bachelor party in *Very Bad Things* (1998). Unfortunately, after providing the movie with several swirling moments of all-nude life affirmation, Kobe's character is rendered a stiff. Her corpse is dragged around for the rest of the film, which seems like a poor casting decision. In the skin universe, Kobe Tai survives and tends to the rest of the stiffs until the end credits roll.

SKIN-fining Moment:

Very Bad Things (0:15) Kobe Tai's one on—and takes it off—as a bachelor party stripper. Great fake gazongas.

See Her Naked In:

Very Bad Things (1998) Breasts, Buns
Numerous Adult Movies

Patricia Tallman

Born: September 4, 1957
Saugatuck, Michigan
Skin-O-Meter: Brief Nudity

It might help to be a sci-fi geek if you plan to sit down and enjoy a continuous replay of the classic 1994 through 1998 years of the TV space-travel series *Babylon 5*. Then again, it might also help if you are a male with a pulse and two working eyes, both of which will focus on the redheaded wonder of tall, athletic, and treasure-chested Patricia Tallman, glowing and glowering in her role as telepath Lyta Alexander. One look at Patricia's milky complexion and the profile of her marvelous milkers triggers the desire to see more of her. The irony is that in much of Patricia's best film and broadcast work, her appearance is meant to go undetected. In a career parallel to her front-and-center acting, towering Tallman is one of Hollywood's most in-demand stuntwomen, risking hide and hair in pictures that range from *Monkey Shines* (1988) to *Forest Gump* (1994). To enjoy Patricia without all that dangerous artifice, check her darling dual dugs in *Knightriders* (1981).

SKIN-fining Moment:

Knightriders (0:46) Patricia shows her boobs from the semi-safety of the trees, but unfortunately there's no bush.

See Her Naked In:

Knightriders (1981) Breasts

MR. SKIN'S TOP TEN

Actresses who Should Have Left Their Clothes *On*!
. . . Send this dish back

10. **Aida Turturro**
    —*Illuminata* (1998)

9. **k.d. lang**
    —*Salmonberries* (1991)

8. **Carol Kane**
    —*The Last Detail* (1973)

7. **Tonya Harding**
    —*Tonya and Jeff's Wedding Night* (1994)

6. **Carol Burnett**
    —*Pete 'n' Tillie* (1972)

5. **Rosie O'Donnell**
    —*Exit to Eden* (1994)

4. **Camryn Manheim**
    —*The Road to Wellville* (1994)

3. **Ella Mitchell**
    —*Big Momma's House* (2000)

2. **Kathy Bates**
    —*About Schmidt* (2002)

1. **Jessica Tandy**
    —*Cammilla* 1994 (She was 85!!!)

Jessica Tandy

Born: June 7, 1909
London, England, UK
Died: September 11, 1994
Skin-O-Meter: Brief Nudity

It should come as a slight surprise that *Driving Miss Daisy* (1987) biddy Jessica Tandy was at one time, in a galaxy far, far away, long, long ago, a hot chick with a body worth squinting at. Alas, the young Jessica never took her clothes off when a camera was present. A contrarian and obstinate eccentric, Tandy opted not to show her candy until the age of eighty-five. Catch her from behind in *Camilla* (1994). Her rump jumps joyously upon the shore of a vast body of water, as naked as it was three-quarters of a century, plus a decade, earlier—at the day of her birth. The thrill of skin never dies!

SKIN-fining Moment:

Camilla (0:47) Tons of ass and a hint of breast as 85-year-old Jessica goes for a naked swim with Bridget Fonda. It looks like she's already been in the water for quite a while . . .

See Her Naked In:

Camilla (1994) Buns

Amanda Tapping

**Born: August 28, 1965
Rochford, Essex, England, UK
Skin-O-Meter: Never Nude**

Born in Britain and raised in Canada, Amanda Tapping raises pants across the globe. She first made her mark on TV productions filmed in the Great White North, such as *Forever Knight, Goosebumps, Due South,* and *The X-Files.* While Amanda wasn't ready to go X-rated, she did venture to Hollywood to heat up her career in the mid '90s. *Rent-a-Kid* (1995) wasn't exactly a skin bonanza, but the made-for-TV movies *Net Worth* (1995) and *Remembrance* (1996) helped cement her name in the industry. When she landed a role in the film *Booty Call* (1997), Mr. Skin was ready to pop the flesh champagne and celebrate. Only Amanda continued with her

skingy ways even in that nude-fest. For her role on the sic-fi series *Stargate SG-1,* the "SG" might as well stand for "Sorry, guys," because our chance of seeing Amanda's Tappings is almost nil. But then out of that darkness appeared *The Void* (2001), with Amanda's T&A in delicious close-up. Only there was no shot of her finery with a face attached, meaning that it was probably a body double. But at this point, that's all we have.

SKIN-fining Moment:

The Void (0:26) BODY DOUBLE: Those are not Amanda's breasts and buns you see. Sorry.

See Her Naked In:

The Void (2001) Body Double—Breasts, Buns

Sharon Tate

**Born: January 24, 1943
Dallas, Texas
Died: August 9, 1969
Skin-O-Meter: Brief Nudity**

It is a tragedy of immense proportions that beautiful blonde bombshell Sharon Tate is remembered for anything other than her tremendous, big-hearted, sensual appeal. Tate was one of the most pleasing actresses ever to commit her image to film. Her personality was as big and full as her brassiere. She possessed the intelligence of a natural comedienne and the physique of a swimsuit model. Her face was hospitable, winning, eager that you be pleased, and entirely suitable for the cover of *Vogue* magazine. After a brief stint on *The Beverly Hillbillies,* Sharon enjoyed a few roles on film. Her credits are unconscionably brief, and every film she appeared in has moments to cherish. In *13 Chairs* (1969), those moments are naked. Director and future Tate

husband Roman Polanski initially thought Sharon was not right for the lead part in *Fearless Vampire Killers* (1967). He changed his mind after seeing her in costume. Alas, Sharon will forever be most horribly remembered for falling prey to the "Helter Skelter" antics of the murder-crazed Manson family, who slaughtered her while she was nine months pregnant, along with a house full of party-goers, in the infamous slayings of August 1969. But as her film work endured, it gave life to the early-'80s non-hit by the Jim Carroll Band, "It's Too Late to Fall in Love with Sharon Tate."

SKIN-fining Moment:

Valley of the Dolls (1:22) As a pair of business suited sleazies watch a lurid movie of Sharon peeling down and slipping beneath the sheets, we get some bare-nipple flashes of the tips of her left Tate.

See Her Naked In:

13 Chairs (1969) Breasts
Valley of the Dolls (1967) LB
The Fearless Vampire Killers (1967) RB

Audrey Tautou

**Born: August 9, 1978
Beaumont, France
Skin-O-Meter: Great Nudity**

Elfin gamine Audrey Tautou first came to the notice of American males when they accompanied their girlfriends to the arthouse sensation *Amélie* (2001). The guys wondered, "Who is this equivalent of Audrey Hepburn on a honey croissant? Will she ever be seen with her boobies, which are undoubtedly savory, and her buns, which assuredly are taut and toothsome, exposed to the leer of the lens?" A bit of back-tracking is all that is necessary to clear up these questions. Big-eyed Audrey's shockingly bountiful boobies bounce during a bathtub soak in *Le*

Boiteux (1999), but the real Tautou sugar high hits in *Le Libertin* (2000). The savories up front, the taut and toothsome behind—they are every speck as delectable as our hopes and imaginations could have conspired.

SKIN-fining Moment:

Le Libertin (1:04) Tautou's tasty tater tots practically jump off the screen as she milk-tubs with Vahina Giocante.

See Her Naked In:

Dirty Pretty Things (2002) LB
God Is Great, and I'm Not (2001) Breasts
Le Libertin (2000) Breasts, Buns
Le Boiteux (1999) Breasts

Delores Taylor

Born: September 27, 1939
Winner, South Dakota
Skin-O-Meter: Brief Nudity

Few can compete with Delores Taylor as an icon of earthy hippie sexuality. As a sensitive teacher in *Billy Jack* (1971), Delores was the perfect lover to the angry half-breed, and nobody blamed Billy for kicking ass after some creepy kids assaulted her sunburnt beauty. Also, Delores looked plenty hot when she was seen bathing naked in a stream. The *Billy Jack* movies were a family affair for star/writer/director Tom Laughlin, so it's no surprise that Delores—being Laughlin's real-life wife—also showed up in *The Trial of Billy Jack* (1974) and *Billy Jack Goes to Washington* (1977). (She also got a pseudonymous credit for the screenplays.) Throughout the trilogy, Delores is always a somber beauty who represents the best of true American values.

SKIN-fining Moment:

Billy Jack (1:14) Delores is fully nude bathing in a creek while two thugs peep. We get distant shots and one close-up view of the buns. Not bad for PG.

See Her Naked In:

Billy Jack (1971) Buns

Elizabeth Taylor

Born: February 27, 1932
Hampstead, London, England, UK
Skin-O-Meter: Never Nude

Everybody knows that Elizabeth Taylor is a Hollywood legend. She gets less credit for some legendary sexual antics. She was certainly an outrageous sex symbol in *Cleopatra* (1963), and her offscreen sexploits were equally shocking. But when the '70s came along, La Liz helped define the cinematic sexual revolution. Audiences had already seen Elizabeth win an Oscar in her underwear for *Butterfield 8* (1960). She followed that with a sexy bath alongside Mia Farrow in *Secret Ceremony* (1968). Liz used a body double for *Reflections in a Golden Eye* (1970) and *Ash Wednesday* (1973), but she still revealed an interest in shocking roles. *X, Y and Zee* (1972) featured Liz determined to seduce her husband's mistress. Audiences also still get amazed when the legend gives a blowjob to a lucky motorist in *Driver's Seat* (1975). Of course, Taylor today has gone back to being the dignified movie star in retirement—but fans of trash cinema are ready to fire off their own twenty-one-gun salute to this shameless diva.

SKIN-fining Moment:

Cleopatra (0:30) The Queen of Hollywood, playing the naked Queen of Egypt, gets a royal rub-down, and all ever the most observant horndogs get is some side right asp-cheek. Not really enough to erect a pyramid in your pants today, but this was the height of scandal circa '63.

See Her Naked In:

Ash Wednesday (1973) Body Double—Breasts, Buns
Reflections in a Golden Eye (1967) Body Double—LB, Buns

Lili Taylor

Born: February 20, 1967
Glencoe, Illinois
Skin-O-Meter: Brief Nudity

It's the rare actress who is secure enough in her allure that she can play a frump. Lili Taylor often downplays her looks and even went so far as to star in *Dogfight* (1991) as a woman who is invited to a party by a group of guys who are having a contest to see who can pick up the ugliest girl. Even in that role, Lili's spooky sensuality shone through. With her highly emotive, elfin-nymph face and lank, dark hair, Taylor exudes an intense physical personality that was strong enough to cast her as a love lead in the HBO hit *Six Feet Under*. Plus, she carries a surprisingly full load of lung flesh, ready for viewing in *Household Saints* (1993).

SKIN-fining Moment:

Bright Angel (0:26) Brief breasts while swimming on her back, then a nice dripping wet boob shot when getting out of the water.

See Her Naked In:

I Shot Andy Warhol (1996) Breasts
Household Saints (1993) Breasts
Bright Angel (1991) Breasts

Lisa Taylor

Born: 1951
Oyster Bay, New York
Skin-O-Meter: Brief Nudity

The occasional porn star may cross into the mainstream, but Lisa Taylor remains a true pioneer. She began by starring in British schoolgirl spanking loops that led to a noted obscenity trial in 1974. The ensuing scandal soon made Lisa a very popular bad girl. She left behind the world of shorts—and her own shorts, too—for shocking scenes like her gleesome threesome in *Let's Get Laid* (1977). She's the best thing in the sex farce, too. Lisa soon landed a feature role in the major American film *The Eyes of Laura Mars* (1978), in which she played a glamorous lesbian model who gets killed way too early in the film. Her acting career never really took off, but Lisa remains an icon of both underground sex and mainstream modeling.

SKIN-fining Moment:

Love Trap (0:37) Lisa's little lugnuts occupy the screen as she picks up the phone to chat. Call 1-900-ANT-HILL now!

See Her Naked In:

Eyes of Laura Mars (1978) RB
Love Trap (1977) Breasts, Bush
Numerous Adult Movies

Maui Taylor

Born: June 28, 1983
Brighton, UK
Skin-O-Meter: Great Nudity

One-half exotic Filipino filly, one-half stodgy old Britannia, and completely red hot and finger-licking good is the best way to describe Asian act-chest Maui Taylor. And that's no typo: Maui's wowees are a sight for sore eyes (and the cause of many sore members from too much tugging and loving). The top-heavy honey is only a wee five-feet-two-inches tall but already has a big career. It began on the boob tube when she was twelve, with series such as *TGIS* and *Anna Karenina*. Her conservative father insisted Maui relocate from gloomy England to the tropical paradise of the Philippines to prevent her from being drawn into the wild life. Instead she became a sex star in

films such as *Gamitan* (2002) and *Hibla* (2002). *Sex Drive* (2003) brought her T&A into overdrive and burned rubber. She continues to make a name for herself as Asia's sluttiest slut in productions like *Huling birhen sa lupa* (2003) and *Bugbog sarado* (2003). Dad must be so proud. Maui joined Aubrey Miles and Diana Zubin for the *FHM* 2003 calendar. Save that date!

SKIN-fining Moment:

Sex Drive (0:56) Maui gets stripped, groped, and orally pleasured as her perky pears stand at full attention.

See Her Naked In:

Huling birhen sa lupa (2003) Breasts
Bugbog sarado (2003) Breasts, Buns
Sex Drive (2003) Breasts, Buns
Hibla (2002) Breasts
Gamitan (2002) Breasts

Sandra Taylor

Born: December 26, 1966
Westchester, New York
Skin-O-Meter: Great Nudity

It's ironic that March 1991 *Penthouse* Pet of the Month Sandra Taylor's fame flowered on the radio. Known back then as Sandi Korn, Taylor was a frequent guest on Howard Stern's radio show and was soon cast in a variety of Taylor-made roles. She stripped before a leather-clad crowd in Rosie O'Donnell's S & M comedy *Exit to Eden* (1994), which offered up more skin than the average Hollywood comedy. She stripped as Shannon Tweed's body double in *Possessed by the Night* (1994). Then she peeled again in *Under Siege 2: Dark Territory* (1995). After that, she continued her hot streak, getting naked with Patricia Staples in *Women of the Night* (2000). In recent years, lamentably, she's sacrificed quantity skin time for quality screen time, appearing in respectable films like *L.A. Confidential* (1997),

Runaway Bride (1999), and *The Princess Diaries* (2001). It looks like a Taylor-fade to me.

SKIN-fining Moment:

Possessed By the Night (1:05) Sandy plays body double for Shannon Tweed, substituting in her naked bombers and butt during a solo cliddle-diddle.

See Her Naked In:

Women of the Night (2000) Breasts
Exit to Eden (1994) Breasts
Possessed by the Night (1994) Breasts, Thong
Lady In Waiting (1994) Breasts, Bush, Buns

Vida Taylor

London, England, UK
Skin-O-Meter: Brief Nudity

The world of skinema is filled with mysterious ladies of lusciousness, but none quite like Vida Taylor. She may have only made two films, but they're both genre classics with memorable full-frontal nudity. The drive-in classic *God Told Me To* (1976) has Vida being abducted by aliens for some intergalactic nookie. *Clash of the Titans* (1981) is a big-budget fantasy that features Vida doling out some mother's milk and strolling naked down a beach. We don't know much about this London lady, though, including whether she was much of an actress. She doesn't really have dialogue in either film. That amazing bod, however, does a lot of talking.

SKIN-fining Moment:

Clash of the Titans (0:11) Vida pumps the milk of life into her son on the beach, baring her volcanically inviting Mount Olympuses. The PG-rating here stands for Pretty Great!

See Her Naked In:

Clash of the Titans (1981) RB, Buns
God Told Me To (1976) Breasts, Buns

Leigh Taylor-Young

Born: January 25, 1944
Washington, D.C.
Skin-O-Meter: Great Nudity

Leigh Taylor-Young was a prim and proper lass whose only thought was on honing her craft as an actor. She gained fame after replacing Mia Farrow on the then-fledgling series *Peyton Place* and then became a hippie icon as the groovy chick who fed Peter Sellers pot-laced brownies in *I Love You, Alice B. Toklas!* (1968). Following the free spirit of the era, Leigh let love beads out for a nude debut in *The Big Bounce* (1969). The film also introduced her to her future hubby, Ryan O'Neal, who got her pregnant while he was still married to Joanna Moore. That union didn't last once O'Neal's tryst with Barbra Steisand went public. She had a few more notable appearances in movies like *The Adventurers* (1970), *The Buttercup Chain* (1970), and *The Horsemen* (1971), which featured one of Leigh's very few nipple slipples. Let's hope this flower girl blooms nude anew . . . and soon!

SKIN-fining Moment:

The Big Bounce (0:14) Leigh strips for a full-frontal skinny-dip and also supplies some splashtastic seat views as she paddles around the pool. You'll feel the Big Bounce in your pants.

See Her Naked In:

The Horsemen (1971) LB
The Big Bounce (1969) FFN, Buns

Valeria Bruni Tedeschi

Born: November 16, 1964
Turino, Italy
Skin-O-Meter: Great Nudity

The alternatingly sky-blue and sea-green eyes of auburn-blonde, Italian-born dream-bait Valeria Bruni Tedeschi twinkle with sly delight and happy mischief. The honey-toned happy sacks swinging from Valerie's tender and flushed chest seem to have a hilarious effect on the former fashion model. Whenever she breaks them out, she seems to bust out in a grin and a guffaw. Tedeschi's thick, dark bush of love fuzz also appears to create a fizz of fun and frivolity within her head when she lets it out for air. Down in the dumps? There is a remedy. In *C'est la vie* (1990), *Oublie-moi* (1995), *Les Menteurs* (1996), and *Ah! Si j'étais riche* (2002), Valeria's naked good cheer is infectious.

SKIN-fining Moment:

Oublie-moi (0:48) Valeria strips down, gets fully frontalfied (bush ahoy!), then slips into bed. Oh, this is ever so nice.

See Her Naked In:

5X2 Cinq fois deux (2004) FFN, Buns
Ah! Si j'étais riche (2002) Breasts, Thong
Ceux qui m'aiment prendront le train (1998) Breasts
Les Menteurs (1996) Breasts
Oublie-moi (1995) FFN
C'est la vie (1990) Breasts

April Telek

Born: April 29, 1975
Vancouver, British Columbia, Canada
Skin-O-Meter: Great Nudity

Whoever invented the circuit of international beauty pageants deserves an entire wing named after him in the Hall of Skinfamy. Thanks to such contests of female comeliness, dazzling blondes such as the Great White North's April Telek are plucked from the obscure and drab masses and raised to a prominence—in April's case during her reign as Miss Canada—that positions their goddess-quality physicality to be worshiped by the appreciative masses and also exposes a young and impressionable lady to the ego fulfillment of being a revered public figure while putting out little more effort than smiling, flexing the glutes, and sticking out the chest. Where else, other than on the beauty-pageant stage, will she find such gratification? Probably nowhere, but if she's April Telek, she can search for stardom on the motion-picture screen in such guises as Blonde Singer, Bikini Girl, Sexy Girl, Receptionist, and Flight Attendant, important roles that might go woefully unfilled if not for the stream of beauties directed Hollywood way by the beauty-pageant circuit.

SKIN-fining Moment:

Bounty Hunters II: Hardball (0:25) April shows her breasts in a window. Distant, but hey, it's boobies.

See Her Naked In:

Bounty Hunters 2: Hardball (1997) Breasts

TeleVisions:

Outer Limits Breasts
The Hunger RB

Victoria Tennant

Born: September 30, 1950
London, England, UK
Skin-O-Meter: Brief Nudity

Victoria Tennant is best known as the English strumpet who blew funnyman Steve Martin's horn so well that he married her. Well, we don't know exactly what went on behind closed doors, but the two made an amorous couple when they starred together in Martin's *L.A. Story* (1991). No one-note thespian, Victoria appeared in *Whispers* (1989), in which she exposed some brief breastage, although some of the scenes appeared as if they were a body double. She enjoyed some success in *All of Me* (1984), where she met her future ex-hubby. She also appeared in the hit *The Handmaid's Tale* (1990). Besides

Whispers, Victoria has showed little skin in her lengthy career. We wish she'd speak up. But for now that's all we've got to hail Victoria.

SKIN-fining Moment:

Whispers (0:42) Victoria's left breast momentarily isn't so secret as it slips into view while she beds Chris Sarandon.

See Her Naked In:

Whispers (1989) LB

Jill Terashita

Skin-O-Meter: Great Nudity

Jill Terashita (and her incredible, edible breasts) gambled big and won her way to B-movie semi-stardom back in 1985 with a bit part in *The Big Bet*. (Unfortunately, the twins stayed covered throughout—although that would soon change!) After another quickie part in *Terminal Entry* (1986), Jill finally landed a part of some note in the horror flick set in an abandoned funeral parlor *Night of the Demons* (1987). In addition to the savory skinage provided by the film's star, Linnea Quigley, Jill generously flashed her sweater flesh whilst engaged in some sort of naughtiness in a coffin with one of her male co-stars. The following year Jill went for a re-teat performance in the equally campy *Sleepaway Camp III: Teenage Wasteland* (1989). After that memorable mammary appearance, Jill only managed to land one more skinematic role with a bit part in *Why Me?* (1990). Why you, Jill? Just look at your boobs!

SKIN-fining Moment:

Night of the Demons (0:57) Bare juggled Jill gets a meat-stake driven through her holiest-of-holies as she gets it on with her guy in a coffin. Scary hot!

See Her Naked In:

Sleepaway Camp III: Teenage Wasteland (1988) Breasts
Night of the Demons (1987) Breasts

Sylvie Testud

**Born: January 17, 1971
Lyon, Rhône, France
Skin-O-Meter: Great Nudity**

Sylvie Testud "gives a performance of bone-chilling intensity," *The New York Times* said of this French fury's performance in *Murderous Maids* (2000), the horrific real-life account of two Sapphic siblings who murder their rich employers. Mr. Skin agrees and adds that this Gallic goddess is equally bone inducing in most every flick. Bouncing boobage between German and French cinema, Sylvie is ever ready to give an all-knockers-out, knockout performance in most of her films. Sexy Sylvie bared *le bush* right off the bat in her skinematic debut *Jenseits der Stille* (1996) and followed up by whipping out her cocoa-tipped nips in *Karnaval* (1999). Her tit-tastic talents and greatest showing of earthly bare beauty in the latter snagged the fly of director Jean-Pierre Denis of *Murderous Maids*, who cast her in the role of lead murderess. As a result, she gave the world lusciously lickable love scenes with onscreen sister Julie-Marie Parmentier steamy enough to make Caligula blush.

SKIN-fining Moment:

Jenseits der Stille (1:08) Sylvie flashes brief, distant FFN while nighttime skinny-dipping with Sibylle Canonica.

See Her Naked In:

A Loving Father (2002) LB
Murderous Maids (2000) Breasts, Bush
La Captive (2000) Bush
Karnaval (1999) Breasts
In Heaven (1998) Breasts
Jenseits der Stille (1996) FFN

Tia Texada

**Born: December 14, 1972
Louisiana
Skin-O-Meter: Brief Nudity**

Simmering Latina sensation Tia Texada has traveled all across this great land since her days as a young girl in Louisiana, and she has taken up permanent residence in that section of the mass male consciousness that appreciates dusky cleavage heaving with a sheen of slightly sweaty passion. Seen regularly on TV cop drama *Third Watch* as tough-talking, straight-shooting, hard-ass, and sassy Sergeant Cruz, tempting Tia has sprinkled her spicy seasoning on shows ranging from *Malibu Shores* to *The Mind of the Married Man*. Her sizzle pops most freely in big-screen fare, such as the devilishly insane shelf of chest flesh flashed in *Crazy as Hell* (2002).

SKIN-fining Moment:

Crazy as Hell (1:20) Tia flashes just a touch of titty in bed with Eriq La Salle during this ultra-dark scene . . .

See Her Naked In:

Crazy as Hell (2002) Breasts

Gilda Texter

Skin-O-Meter: Great Nudity

In the beloved B-movie/muscle-car opus *Vanishing Point* (1971) our post-*Easy–Rider* pill-poppin' hero, Kowalski, on a mysterious cross-country journey, meets up with a cavalcade of characters the likes of which Homer's *Odyssey* never saw. Of the various freaks and geeks Kowalksi meets up with, the most eye-popping one in Mr. Skin's estimation would have to be the character of the Nude Rider, played with naked aplomb by the pert and luxuriously locked Gilda Texter. Way too short, but nonetheless very sweet, Gilda's tour de force involves the sun shining on her pixie-like, au natural body and tiny, perky breasts as her ass-length hair tousles furiously behind her. The delicious tease is trying to catch a glimpse of her nether regions, but alas this hirsute pursuit is mostly in vain . . . but you can't blame a guy for trying, right? T&A will have to suffice, but oh what a boon for the drive-in era that must have been.

SKIN-fining Moment:

Vanishing Point (1:17) Gilda's globes and gluteus are in full effect as she chugs along on a motorcycle, then engages Barry Newman in some idle chit-chat.

See Her Naked In:

Runaway, Runaway (1971) FFN, Buns
Vanishing Point (1971) Breasts, Buns
Angels Hard as They Come (1971) Breasts

Charlize Theron

Born: August 7, 1975
Benoni, South Africa
Skin-O-Meter: Hall of Fame

An exquisite pale complexion; a perfect, symmetrical smile; a taunting, plump bottom lip; soul-seeking eyes lidded in languorous abandon; yellow-gold hair as finely spun as angel's breath—former model and current big-screen sultry star Charlize Theron is South African-born of German heritage, but who can be sure she was not dropped directly from heaven? How else to account for the divine inspiration that compels Charlize to continue her habit of shedding her clothing long after she has accumulated enough star power to contractually opt out of showing so much as a nipple? There Theron was, breasts and nips to the bright lights in *2 Days in the Valley* (1996). Here she is still in *Reindeer Games* (2000), flashing ass crack almost to the level of brown eye. And there is

plenty of Theron skin to squint at in between.

SKIN-fining Moment:

2 Days in the Valley (0:37) James Spader rips open her teddy and we see Charlize's teat-treats.

See Her Naked In:

Head in the Clouds (2004) Breasts
Monster (2003) Breasts
The Yards (2000) Breasts
Reindeer Games (2000) Breasts, Buns
Sweet November (2000) Breasts
The Cider House Rules (1999) Breasts, Buns
The Devil's Advocate (1997) FFN
2 Days in the Valley (1996) Breasts

Tiffani-Amber Thiessen

Born: January 23, 1974
Long Beach, California
Skin-O-Meter: Never Nude

If you like big butts and you can't deny it, look no further than TAT. For her sheer buxom bootiliciousness Tiffani-Amber Thiessen (affectionately nicknamed TAT by Mr. Skin) deserves to go to the head of her class. TAT first earned good marks as the scantily clad sweetie of *Saved By the Bell*, pumping new life into the bones of barely eighteen lovers everywhere. Smart enough to know that nice girls finish last, Tiffani traded nice for nasty, putting the ohhh in *Beverly Hills, 90210* as the bewitching bitch "Valerie Malone." Mammoth of mouth, overflowing boobage, and booming bootay, Tiffani was the perfect reminder that even in California bigger is better. Since, Thiessen has graduated to film. In the TV movie *Buried Secrets* (1996), her succulent brown nips are boldly visible under a matting of bubbly goodness. It's no secret what we'd like to bury after seeing her ta-tas. TAT-TASTIC! Always one to stuff a wild bra and

undies, Tiffani steamed up the scene in painted-on lingerie in the hit *The Ladies Man* (2000). Every day is a good day and the forecast is always hot now that Tiffani has joined the cast of *Good Morning Miami. Mucha Muchacha!* Fourteen years after her debut on *Saved*, TAT is still where it's at.

SKIN-fining Moment:

Fastlane "Asslane" (2003) Bra-clad Tiff falls to her knees smack at the crotch of Peter Facinelli and then orally services Facinelli's peter. The sucking's simulated but, still, this is T.A.T. giving a BJ on TV!

Betty Thomas

Born: July 27, 1948
St. Louis, Missouri
Skin-O-Meter: Brief Nudity

Betty Thomas was not always a big-shot director. Back before she ruled at the helm of such laugh-a-licious pictures as *The Brady Bunch Movie* (1995), Howard Stern's *Private Parts* (1997), and the Sandra Bullock drying-juicer flick *28 Days* (2000), boob-carrying Betty was a big-top object of desire. Thomas and her bouncing betties got their start in the laff racket, honing their chops with Chicago's Second City improv troupe. As early as the proto skit-comedy pic *Tunnelvision* (1976), Thomas was securing her reputation as a yuckster who was game to flash titty if a titter were likely to ensue. Betty put her best breasts forward in *Loose Shoes* (1980), wearing a loosely flapping denim vest and nothing else above the waist.

SKIN-fining Moment:

Tunnelvision (0:19) The director of Private Parts *keeps hers covered with just panties and teeny pasties during a game show parody. Awesome jiggliness, though.*

See Her Naked In:

Loose Shoes (1980) RB

Heather Thomas

Born: September 8, 1957
Greenwich, Connecticut
Skin-O-Meter: Brief Nudity

There's no better way for a new TV show to distinguish itself than to feature a bodacious bikini babe in the opening titles. Heather Thomas set the precedent for this scheme in 1981 with *The Fall Guy*, which featured her big smile, big feathered blonde hair, and big . . . well, you get the picture. As stuntwoman Jodi Banks, the Greenwich, Connecticut, native's infamous assets were the cherry on the cheesecake appeal for the show's five-year run. Her career since then has been less high-profile, but sexy all along. On the big screen, she played the object of telekinetic dork Scott Baio's lust in *Zapped!* (1982), only to be replaced by a body double in the blouse-busting climax.

SKIN-fining Moment:

Red Blooded American Girl (1:19) Very brief right breast as Heather enjoys a rather lengthy softcore sex scene.

See Her Naked In:

Red Blooded American Girl (1990) RB

Andrea Thompson

Born: May 22, 1959
Dayton, Ohio
Skin-O-Meter: Hall of Fame

Andrea Thompson was born in Dayton, Ohio, but caught the world-traveling bug at age seven when her family moved to Australia. When she graduated from high school, another bug, the acting one, bit her, and it wasn't too long before she started landing parts in such skinful fare as

---

MR. SKIN'S TOP TEN

Best Nude Scenes in Black and White
. . . Women of no color

10. Debbi Morgan
    —*Cry Uncle!* (1971) (0:17)
9. Jennifer Connelly
    —*Mulholland Falls* (1996) (0:02)
8. Hedy Lamarr
    —*Ecstasy* (1932) (0:29)
7. Sally Kirkland
    —*Coming Apart* (1969) (0:51)
6. Josie Bissett
    —*All-American Murder* (1991) (1:07)
5. Valerie Perrine
    —*Lenny* (1974) (0:14)
4. Angelina Jolie
    —*Gia* (1998) (0:25)
3. Cybill Shepherd
    —*The Last Picture Show* (1971) (0:40)
2. Jayne Mansfield
    —*Promises! Promises!* (1963) (0:59)
1. **Andrea Thompson**
    —*A Gun, a Car, a Blonde* **(1996) (1:08)**

Nightmare Weekend (1986), *Hot Splash* (1987), and *Manhattan Gigolo* (1986), the latter of which featured a rather scandalous look at her completely naked body, including a peek at her poonanny. By 1987, though, Andrea was garnering roles in more recognizable affairs such as *Wall Street* (1987), *Delirious* (1991), and *Babylon 5* (1994), and it seemed as if her skintastic days on the silver screen were long gone. Nevertheless, she managed to pop up one more time in all her naked glory in 1997's *A Gun, a Car, a Blonde*, which featured one of her finest full-frontal flashes, albeit in black and white. Regardless, it's worth a look at that shaved-up

beav, at any cost, especially considering that she's since gone on to land anchor gigs on *Headline News* and Court TV. Now that she's all journalistic, the chances of any more full-on furburger flashes may be long gone . . . but just think of the headlines that would generate!

SKIN-fining Moment:

A Gun, a Car, a Blonde (1:08) This just in . . . Andrea appears outside in all her fabulous full-frontal glory. Film at eleven . . .

See Her Naked In:

A Gun, a Car, a Blonde (1997) FFN, Buns
Hot Splash (1987) Breasts, Buns
Nightmare Weekend (1986) LB
Manhattan Gigolo (1986) FFN, Buns

TeleVisions:

Arli$$ Breasts

Cynthia Thompson

Skin-O-Meter: Great Nudity

Cynthia Thompson's boomingly bare boobage made her a cinch for the Skin Central nomination for Breast Actress in the '80s. In *Tomboy* (1985), this tall and taut all-American girl debuted her delicious breast pillows, separating the men from the boys with a mere flash of flesh. Boobtastic! Cyn's passion for skin continued in *Cave Girl* (1985). Her bouncing blonde tresses, rock-hard bottom, and pointed perky peeks will make your *dino sore* from repeated bones. Thompson's tendency toward naked is best expressed in *Camping del terrore* (1987). Her long, lingering flesh flashes are guaranteed to put a pup tent in your pants. Following a thorough in*chest*igation, it seems that after her achingly alluring tit popping in the '80s, Cynthia went poof! It's no mystery that we are sorely missing in action with her disappearance.

SKIN-fining Moment:

Camping del terrore (0:50) Brief but excellent full-frontal flash from Cynthia.

See Her Naked In:

Rescue Force (1989) Breasts
Camping del terrore (1986) FFN
Cave Girl (1985) Breasts, Buns
Tomboy (1985) Breasts

Emma Thompson

**Born: April 15, 1959
Paddington, London, England, UK
Skin-O-Meter: Great Nudity**

With her high-toned Brit accent and the frosty reserve of her beautiful but deliberately placid face, very serious English actress Emma Thompson might come off as a bit of a cold fish. Do not be deceived by outward rectitude. Chill rivers run deep, hot, and tight—just like the crack of this lordly lady's ass. Look and ye shall find Emma's inner skinitude. For starters, reference regal Thompson's scorching screw scene with Jeff Goldblum in *The Tall Guy* (1990). Look at those leaping lung ornaments! And here is the aforementioned deep, hot, tight ass crack in a close-cropped, split-cheek butt shot. Who could ask for more? Everyone. And a bit more is to be found, particularly in *Carrington* (1995). Prim and proper Emma plays a painter with an itchy punani.

SKIN-fining Moment:

The Tall Guy (0:34) Enjoy eyefuls of Emma's meaty boobage and suprisingly neat seat as she goes at it with Jeff Goldblum.

See Her Naked In:

Imagining Argentina (2003) RB
Wit (2001) Breasts
The Winter Guest (1997) RB
Carrington (1996) RB
The Tall Guy (1990) Breasts, Buns

TeleVisions:

Angels in America (mini-series) Body Double—RB

Lea Thompson

**Born: May 31, 1961
Rochester, Minnesota
Skin-O-Meter: Great Nudity**

Lea Thompson is most commonly known for her role as a high-school sweetheart in *Back to the Future* (1985). She was that saucy brunette with the chirpy, pale sex appeal. Remember her milky-white bosom squeezed into a deep ball of cleavage by her strapless '50s gown? Well, back up a few more years, and lanky Lea seems a lot more grown up playing a high-school sweetheart pressing her full and rounded bare milkers up against Tom Cruise's lucky chest in *All the Right Moves* (1983). Then jump ahead a few more years and catch up with Thompson's sun-baked can as she lay naked belly down on simmering beach sands in *Casual Sex* (1988). Backward and forward, Lea Thompson is a woman with a skinful past.

SKIN-fining Moment:

All the Right Moves (1:04) Lea shows All the Right Boobs—and a hint of pubes—as she doffs her duds in preparation for some pubescent poon-pounding from Tom Cruise.

See Her Naked In:

Casual Sex? (1988) Buns
All the Right Moves (1983) FFN, Buns

Kim Thomson

**Born: 1960
London, England, UK
Skin-O-Meter: Great Nudity**

Since we humans, in our purest sense, are, in the words of the great

theologian Sting, merely "spirits in the material world," it is only natural that we tend to experience the grace of God in a physical manner, especially if we are a tight-bodied, hard-nippled, full-bushed, lithe, and lissome redhead blessed with curiosity and passion, as embodied by British-born slice of paradise Kim Thomson in *Stealing Heaven* (1988). Kim plays a twelfth-century Parisian student of scriptures who is possessed by the Lord in a manner that leaves her quivering and quaking in orgasmic bliss, with her priestly professor hovering in the same state above her. It is a scene never to be repeated now that all these pesky clergy-molestation cases have popped up.

SKIN-fining Moment:

Stealing Heaven (0:47) Kim leans back and displays her lip-smacking strawberry nipples and a tasty dollop of her natural red nether-nettles.

See Her Naked In:

Stealing Heaven (1988) FFN

Callie Thorne

**Born: November 20, 1969
Massachusetts
Skin-O-Meter: Brief Nudity**

An angular brunette with the svelte, sexy body and dark, piercing eyes of a classic femme fatale, Callie Thorne isn't a household name yet, but hopefully she'll soon be a bedroom name. The hot act-chest is just beginning to get noticed, but she debuted way back in a bit part in *Ed's Next Move* (1996), a romantic comedy that somehow avoided the skin exposure associated with romance. It was her role on the critic's darling TV series *Homicide: Life on the Streets* that kept her busy for the latter half of the '90s. Too bad the boob tube rarely shows any boobs. Callie made her way back to the big screen in *Next Stop Wonderland* (1998), not that viewers got to savor her wonder glands. She appeared in other provocative titles such as *Giving It Up* (1999) and *Whipped* (2000), yet surprisingly it was a return to the small screen, albeit on cable, that finally introduced Callie's adoring public to her adorable jugs. As "Elena McNutly" on HBO's *The Wire*, Callie is McNut-drainingly sweet. She gets intimate with her man, and suddenly her mams are jiggling all over the place. That's the kind of Thorne in Mr. Skin's side that pricks so good.

SKIN-fining Moment:

The Wire "The Prologue" (2003) Callie gets schtupped by a stud standing up, and we get a great view of her left breast.

TeleVisions:

The Wire LB
Rescue Me Breasts

Dyanne Thorne

Born: October 14, 1932
Greenwich, Connecticut
Skin-O-Meter: Hall of Fame

One woman's failed dream can launch the erotic reveries of ten million men. Perhaps her gigantic rack of God-given jugs doomed the harshly beautiful Dyanne Thorne to a life of hard-R sexploitation; perhaps these physical attributes destined her for skinmortality. Either way, she initially wanted to be a serious stage actress and pursued a classical education in the dramatic arts. Any skinthusiast with a twist toward the sextreme will swear that not a day of that schooling has gone to waste. Learn the lessons of *Ilsa, She Wolf of the S.S.* (1974). Dyanne, as the evil camp warden Ilsa, is one of the most compelling villainesses in the history of sadistic pleasures. Plus,

she very generously shares her huge, 100% organic chest cushions with her star pupils. Thorne proved to be such an effective teacher of sexual treachery that her Ilsa character was ripped off by pale imitators, and she reprised the role twice, in *Ilsa, Harem Keeper of the Oil Sheiks* (1976) and *Ilsa, the Wicked Warden* (1980).

SKIN-fining Moment:

Ilsa, the Wicked Warden (0:02) Brief bush then her enormous bazooms are seen as she gets into the tub.

See Her Naked In:

Ilsa, the Wicked Warden (1980) FFN, Buns
Ilsa, the Tigress of Siberia (1977) FFN, Buns
Ilsa, Harem Keeper of the Oil Sheiks (1976) Breasts, Buns
Wham Bam Thank You Spaceman (1975) Breasts
Ilsa, She Wolf of the S.S. (1974) Breasts, Buns

Courtney Thorne-Smith

Born: November 8, 1967
San Francisco, California
Skin-O-Meter: Never Nude

How's this for budget breast reduction? When Courtney Thorne-Smith was unhappy about her 36DD cup size, she embarked on a rigorous yoga program that redistributed her body fat and decreased her chest size to a C. Mr. Skin still gives them an A, though. The giant-jowled California blonde has been acting since high school, when she was handpicked to star as Charlie Sheen's girlfriend in *Lucas* (1986). She does good as a better half and is most famous for playing one on the Jim Belushi sitcom *According to Jim*. You have to give that comic slob a point for good taste. Although you can see her buff bod in a bikini in *Revenge of the Nerds II: Nerds in Paradise* (1987), she didn't appear nude until—believe it or not—an episode of the

TV show *Ally McBeal*. It's just a glimpse of her rear end, butt I'll take it.

SKIN-fining Moment:

Ally McBeal (1999) Courtney traipses nude into Gil Bellows's office, giving Gil plenty to bellow about as she bares her glutes and some side-boob that's blocked by one of those attorney-type lamps. There ought to be a law!

Frankie Thorn

Born: August 27, 1964
Minnesota
Skin-O-Meter: Great Nudity

If you are a sucker for carrot tops with tit-tastic boobs to boot, look no further than Frankie Thorn. Frankie is rouge-tastic! Red from head to toe, her carpet matches her drapes, and she gives tours to prove it. You'll be horny over Thorn's form in *Bad Lieutenant* (1992), where, in all her pale perfection, she bared both her pink-tipped nips and burning bush. Just thinking about it makes Mr. Skin salute! Frankie's flesh flash in *Warm Texas Rain* (1998) will bring on a hot and wet sprinkle fest. Her freckled front flaps and fiery patch of thatch put the *ohh* in the Alamo, and boy do we remember. I can't decide which feature I love best about this curvy, crimson-haired harlot. I am *Thorn* between her perky pomegranates and her ruby fruit. Whatever it is, I want more, because *Frankie*, Miss Scarlett, I do give a damn.

SKIN-fining Moment:

Bad Lieutenant (0:26) Nice look at Frankie's full-frontal flesh while she lays on a hospital bed and a few nuns cover her nudeness.

See Her Naked In:

Warm Texas Rain (1998) FFN, Buns
Bad Blood (1994) Breasts
Bad Lieutenant (1992) FFN, Buns

Linda Thorson

Born: June 18, 1947
Toronto, Ontario, Canada
Skin-O-Meter: Brief Nudity

Linda Thorson kicked off her career by replacing Diana Rigg as a vengeful vixen on the hit series *The Avengers* in the late '60s. A mere twenty years old at the time, her nubile wiles and tit-tastic stats (a reported 38-25-36) highlighted weekly in can-clutching leather costumes caught the fly of horny crooner Frank Sinatra, who left his *hard-on in Thorson's Crisco*. Their union was so skintense, later in life Linda made him godfather to her son. Although cock-poppingly curvy, being a graduate of the Royal Academy of Dramatic Arts, Linda opted to boast her brains rather than bare her beauty, receiving critical acclaim for dramatic roles in *Lady Killer* (1973) and *The Greek Tycoon* (1978). Thorson was an amazing mammarific magnet to men, even though she remained mostly clothed throughout her stint in cinema. Now nifty at fifty-something, Linda lovers are still buzzing about this honey's hot bod and box-office offerings in her heyday.

SKIN-fining Moment:

Valentino (0:43) Very brief left nip while she's pinned beneath a dude in bed, stiff, but quick.

See Her Naked In:

Straight Into Darkness (2003) Breasts
Valentino (1977) LB

Ingrid Thulin

Born: January 27, 1926
Sollefteå, Ångermanland, Sweden
Died: January 7, 2004
Skin-O-Meter: Great Nudity

A Swedish blonde with a daunting, icy beauty that only deepened with age, peerless in portraying the angst of a compromised soul struggling with easy evil, brooding erotic legend Ingrid Thulin was already established as an acclaimed world-class actress when she took on her defining title role in the premiere swastikas-and-sex immorality tale *Salon Kitty* (1976), plus she was fifty years old. Indeed, Ingrid was a serious cinema veteran of forty-two when she flashed her first onscreen skin in the scary and unnerving *Hour of the Wolf* (1968). She kept her middle-aged, mouthwatering mounds in play for arthouse perennials *The Damned* (1969) and *Cries and Whispers* (1972), but it was as madame to the Third Reich in *Salon Kitty* that Ingrid seized her lasting skinfamy.

SKIN-fining Moment:

Salon Kitty (0:36) Nice long nip-slip as Ingrid croons a tune in a Nazi nightclub.

See Her Naked In:

After the Rehearsal (1984) Breasts
Salon Kitty (1976) Breasts, Buns
La Cage (1975) LB
Viskningar och rop (1972) FFN, Buns
Short Night of the Glass Dolls (1971) RB
La Caduta degli dei (1969) Breasts
Hour of the Wolf (1968) Breasts

Uma Thurman

Born: April 29, 1970
Boston, Massachusetts
Skin-O-Meter: Great Nudity

Exquisite exoticism and implicit eroticism are the hallmarks of the queen of quirky Uma Thurman. The daughter of Buddhists and the goddaughter of high priest of LSD Timothy Leary, Uma comes into her freaky squealy appealy honestly. Named after a Hindu goddess, the former model was cast as the Goddess of Love in *The Adventures of Baron Munchausen* (1988). She played a goddess of nipple teasing. Her breasts were

---

MR. SKIN'S TOP TEN

Period Pieces of Ass
. . . Powdered wig
poontang

10. **Marina Sirtis**
   —*The Wicked Lady* (1983)

9. **Valeria Golino**
   —*Immortal Beloved* (1994)

8. **Amanda Donohoe**
   —*The Rainbow* (1989)

7. **Kate Winslet**
   —*Quills* (2000)

6. **Maribel Verdù**
   —*Goya en Burdeos* (1999)

5. **Annette Bening**
   —*Valmont* (1989)

4. **Marisa Berenson**
   —*Barry Lyndon* (1975)

3. **Elizabeth Berridge**
   —*Amadeus* (DVD deleted scene) (1984)

2. **Julìa Ormond**
   —*The Baby of Mâcon* (1993)

1. **Uma Thurman**
   —*Dangerous Liaisons* (1988)

---

straight up for worship in *Dangerous Liaisons* (1988), a safe bet to please those who yearn for heavenly rib cushions. Need more? Try *Where the Heart Is* (1990). Hint: That organ lies directly under the left tit.

SKIN-fining Moment:

Dangerous Liaisons (1:00) Uma opens her nightie and out explode her 18-year-old boomas in bed with John Malkovich.

See Her Naked In:

Vatel (2000) RB
Mad Dog and Glory (1993) Breasts
Jennifer Eight (1992) Body Double—Breasts, Buns
Where the Heart Is (1990) Breasts

Dangerous Liaisons (1988) Breasts
The Adventures of Baron Munchausen (1988) RB

Rachel Ticotin

Born: November 1, 1958
Bronx, New York
Skin-O-Meter: Brief Nudity

Upon meeting Rachel Ticotin, comedian Richard Pryor said, "She looks good enough to sop with a biscuit." As such, this Latin lovely has proven sop-worthy to many a man. The producers of *Fort Apache, the Bronx* (1981) cast her as Paul Newman's girlfriend even though she had never before spoken in front of a camera (her sexy topless bathtub scene didn't require much skill in dialogue delivery, anyway). After her debut, Rachel starred in a succession of forgettable films over the years. She had a minor role in *Falling Down* (1993), and you may be able to spot her naked tush in *Don Juan DeMarco* (1995)—if you can see around Marlon Brando's gargantuan gut. She's most recently appeared with fellow sizzling Latina Rachel Welch on the PBS series *American Family*. That's four spicy meatballs!

SKIN-fining Moment:

Fort Apache, the Bronx (1:25)
Fleeting funbaggage in the bath as Paul Newman adds some bubbles.

See Her Naked In:

Don Juan DeMarco (1995) Body Double—Buns
Fort Apache, the Bronx (1981) LB

Maura Tierney

Born: February 3, 1965
Boston, Massachusetts
Skin-O-Meter: Brief Nudity

Maura Tierney's portrayal of Lisa Miller on the long-running NBC sitcom *News Radio* exemplified what the girl in the next cubicle should be: smart, sexy, sassy, and beautifully built. But it's the Boston native's feature-length film debut in *Dead Women in Lingerie* (1991) that revealed what she does *after* work. In the low-budget slasher parody, Maura made love to a protecting policeman, giving skinsters the only available glimpse of her curvaceous body in the buff. Since then, she's abandoned such brassiere-busting roles in favor of supporting parts in big-budget Hollywood flicks. She played Jim Carrey's wife in *Liar Liar* (1997) and earned critical praise as a political consultant having an interracial affair in *Primary Colors* (1998). Plus, she plays doctor on *ER*. Yes, that Maura can really Tierney us on.

SKIN-fining Moment:

Dead Women in Lingerie (1:09)
Quick slip of the left nip when Maura tussles with her fella between the sheets and moves on top to mount him.

See Her Naked In:

Primary Colors (1998) RB
Dead Women in Lingerie (1991) LB

Pamela Tiffin

Born: October 13, 1942
Oklahoma City, Oklahoma
Skin-O-Meter: Great Nudity

You can't keep a girl down on the farm, not when she has the wild, willful, adventurous streak of Oklahoma-born brunette Pamela Tiffin. The panhandle was just not hot enough to hold this stirring dish of flashy teeth, shiny eyes, and a kisser sweet as spiced honey. Even shooting up on a trajectory toward Hollywood stardom in hit flicks such as *Summer and Smoke* (1961) and *State Fair* (1962) wasn't enough to keep sexual and experimental Pamela from jetting off to decadent old Europe, where she dropped her gingham top, squirmed out of her

PAMELA TIFFIN SHOWS HER *DOS AMIGOS* IN *LOS AMIGOS*.

dungarees, and, more often than not, went blonde to loll around naked in sexy foreign fare such as *Il Vichingo venuto dal sud* (1971), *Una Giornata nera per l'ariete* (1971) and *Deaf Smith and Johnny Ears* (1972).

SKIN-fining Moment:

Il Vichingo venuto dal sud (1:35)
Just a peek at Pamela's left popper laying on a movie set with Lando Buzzanca, followed by a side-shot of her ass when the director desides that it's time for another take . . .

See Her Naked In:

La Signora è stata violentata (1973) RB, Body Double—Buns
Deaf Smith & Johnny Ears (1972) Buns
Una Giornata nera per l'ariete (1971) LB, Buns
Il Vichingo venuto dal sud (1971) LB

> "I have never been with a man who has performed any kind of good cunnilingus. Guys always act really bored."
>
> —JENNIFER TILLY

Jennifer Tilly

Born: September 16, 1958
Harbor City, California
Skin-O-Meter: Hall of Fame

Her cartoon voice might alienate the squeamish of ear (while turning on others), but brunette knocker knockout Jennifer Tilly could stay in bed for the rest of her life and her fame would continue to grow, spread by one avid skinthusiast to the next. For as long as the skin obsession exists, those in the know will crow about the volcanic girl-on-girl eruption that is *Bound* (1996). Jennifer's nipple-mashing, tongue-thrashing, libido-trashing lesbo grip and grope with gonad-getter Gina Gershon is enough to seal Tilly's top spot in the rotation. Save another slot in the random-repeat carousel for *Fast Sofa* (2001), a feature unforgettable for the jutting jumbo jugs of Jennifer.

SKIN-fining Moment:

Bound (0:19) Jennifer's right tit and the better part of her spanktastic ass come out to play with an equally-naked Gina Gershon during this lengthy lesbianic interlude.

See Her Naked In:

Hollywood North (2003) LB
Fast Sofa (2001) Breasts
Dancing at the Blue Iguana (2000) Breasts, Thong
Bound (1996) RB, Buns
The Getaway (1994) Breasts, Buns
Made in America (1993) Body Double—Buns
Shadow of the Wolf (1992) Breasts

Meg Tilly

Born: February 14, 1960
Texada, British Columbia, Canada
Skin-O-Meter: Great Nudity

The older and less-exposed sister of screen burner Jennifer, Meg Tilly hit the skindar in a little baby-boomer extended music video called *The Big Chill* (1983). Marvelously malleable Meg (a former dancer) starred as the yoga-addicted nymph who does seven sides of splits while dressed in form-fitting tights that leave only the rosy pinkness of her epidermis to the imagination. The viewing public was poised to see more. More was shown in *The Girl in a Swing* (1989). Meg swings her girl stack in

a make-out scene and a splashing water frolic. How long must we wait until we see more Meg?

SKIN-fining Moment:

The Girl in a Swing (1:14) Meg shows her shirtless Hillys during a trip to the beach.

See Her Naked In:

The Girl in a Swing (1989) Breasts, Buns

Marilù Tolo

Born: January 16, 1944
Rome, Italy
Skin-O-Meter: Great Nudity

Mediterranean mama Marilù Tolo is most famous for flaunting her flesh in English-language movies such as *Bluebeard* (1972) with the randy Richard Burton and *The Greek Tycoon* (1978) alongside the always-virile Anthony Quinn. While skinfully stunning with Burton and Quinn, this regal Roman beauty is most revealing when ravished on native soil. Tastiest in Italian skin fare such as *My Dear Killer* (1971) and *Jus primae noctis* (1972), this delicious dish's bare meat seat and tasty teats are quite the sweet treat. Always al dente, Tolo's top-heavy tortellinis are a *Marilù* skinspiration when you're down in the pumps.

SKIN-fining Moment:

The Greek Tycoon (0:26) Marilù flashes some ass, then several shots of furry full-frontal when she gets out of bed, then proceeds to kick Anthony Quinn's ass.

See Her Naked In:

The Greek Tycoon (1978) Breasts, Bush, Buns
Prigione di donne (1974) Breasts, Buns
Il Trafficone (1974) Breasts
Bluebeard (1972) Breasts
Jus primae noctis (1972) Breasts, Buns
My Dear Killer (1971) Breasts
Confessions of a Police Captain (1971) LB, Buns

Jeana Tomasina

Born: September 18, 1955
Milwaukee, Wisconsin
Skin-O-Meter: Great Nudity

The entertainment career of dark and endearing Jeana Tomasina, her face blessed with a gripping blend of full, sugary lips; striking, high cheeks; and smoldering, taunting eyes, is a testament to purely pleasurable endeavoring. Hot tomato Tomasina's first film role was in the adventure thriller *The Capture of Bigfoot* (1979) as Dancer. Dancing can of course be a dramatic activity but is far more often a joyous expression of bodily delight. And what bodily expression could be more delightful than Jeana's one-month reign as *Playboy*'s featured Playmate in November of 1980? Why, nothing more than the happy hooters and ebullient heinie of Jeana Tomasina, both cracking naked cleavage smiles for fun and froth in *The Beach Girls* (1982).

SKIN-fining Moment:

The Beach Girls (0:51) Jeana drops her bikini top and delivers two swollen mams for a bizarrely disinterested sea captain.

See Her Naked In:

The Beach Girls (1982) Breasts, Buns
Double Exposure (1982) Nip Slip LB
Numerous *Playboy* Videos

Marisa Tomei

Born: December 4, 1964
Brooklyn, New York
Skin-O-Meter: Never Nude

Playing herself, Marisa Tomei was attracted to Jason Alexander on *Seinfeld* and won a Best Supporting Actress Oscar for *My Cousin Vinny* (1992) as the foul-mouthed girlfriend of Joe Pesci (reuniting her with the Brooklyn accent she trained so hard as a young actress to lose). But Marisa's best known to skin aficionados as the stunning brunette who has yet to shed and shine in all her naked glory. Mr. Skin went to the videotape and after close inspection unearthed *Untamed Heart* (1993), with its very quick peek of a nip and a pinch of pube. Hopes were high with *The Slums of Beverly Hills* (1998) when Marisa stopped a car by flashing her perky pair, but they belonged to a body double. Marisa's Tomei-toes are too ripe to remain on the vine.

SKIN-fining Moment:

Slums of Beverly Hills (0:04) BODY DOUBLE! Marisa's character steps into the shower, but somebody else's super soakers fill the frame.

See Her Naked In:

Slums of Beverly Hills (1998) Body Double— Breasts

Tamlyn Tomita

Born: January 27, 1966
Okinawa, Japan
Skin-O-Meter: Brief Nudity

Tamlyn Tomita is one ripe tomato with some seriously tasty skinematic juice. Hotter than wasabi, delicate dish Tamlyn sizzled as the Japanese sexpot who turned Ralph Macchio into a man in *The Karate Kid, Part II* (1986). Tam's tea seduction ceremony was one of the steamiest '80s teen movie scenes to date . . . no kidding about it. A silk-clad vision of Asian allure, simply letting loose her long black tresses from the confines of her barrette, Tamlyn set kettles boiling socking the Karate Kid right in the groan. This eyeful from the Orient shed her teen-queen image and clothes in *Come See the Paradise* (1990) with Dennis Quaid. Her heavenly olive-skinned sexiness will send you to ecstasy again and again. Celebrate your good fortune by watching Ms. T turn up the heat in *The Joy Luck Club* (1993) by serving up her dark-

nipped dumplings. She's guaranteed to be all that and *dim sum*. For a weekly Tomita wankfest, check her out on the TV series *JAG*. With every endeavor, Tamlyn just gets more skinsational.

SKIN-fining Moment:

The Killing Jar (0:29) Snazzy ass followed by supple chest-bubbles as Tamlyn turns over to get some tool from her man in bed.

See Her Naked In:

Killing Jar (1996) Breasts, Buns

Angel Tompkins

Born: December 20, 1943
Albany, California
Skin-O-Meter: Great Nudity

Angel Tompkins started out playing the hot blonde on programs such as *Wild Wild West* and *Dragnet 1967*, soon graduating to roles as the hot blonde in movies such as *Hang Your Hat on the Wind* (1969) and *I Love My . . . Wife* (1970). Angel won a Golden Globe for her role opposite Elliott Gould in the latter and realized the award was for anatomy and not acting. *Prime Cut* (1972) showed some of her Grade-A dairy product, followed by boobs-a-plenty in *The Don Is Dead* (1973), *How to Seduce a Woman* (1974), *The Teacher* (1974), and *The Naked Cage* (1986). Between film gigs in the '70s, she appeared on every TV program that was ever made. She's ostensibly retired now, but this Angel has earned her wings in the annals of skin.

SKIN-fining Moment:

The Teacher (0:09) Topless on a boat airing out her Angels as a binocular guy spies.

See Her Naked In:

Murphy's Law (1986) Breasts, Thong
The Naked Cage (1986) Breasts
Walking Tall Part II (1975) Breasts

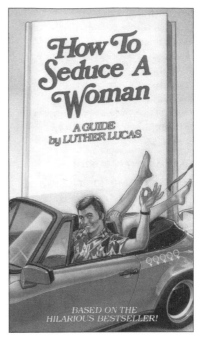

HOW TO SEDUCE A WOMAN: HOW TO NOT SEDUCE A WOMAN: HANG THIS POSTER OVER YOUR BED. I DON'T KNOW WHO THE INCREDIBLY COOL GUY IN THE POSTER IS, BUT THE LEGS BELONG TO ANGEL TOMPKINS, AND THAT ALONE SEDUCED ME INTO SEEING THE MOVIE.

How to Seduce a Woman (1974) Breasts
The Teacher (1974) Breasts, Bush, Buns
The Don Is Dead (1973) LB
Prime Cut (1972) LB
I Love My Wife (1970)

Jill Tompkins

Skin-O-Meter: Great Nudity

Let all good men now praise the blonde brave enough to play a booby, easy-lay bimbo! Stacked and sweet of face, sensual pro Jill Tompkins has the guts to play a male-pleasing stereotype. This flaxen-haired baby doll with the softly zaftig, God-grown breast flesh might have gone the easy route and embraced a bitter feminist rhetoric that insists the male gender is unworthy of having its fantasies catered to. Jill might have hidden her natural graces to the impoverishment of testicle owners as a whole, but she is made of better stuff. Gorge on Jill's better stuff shown in the buff as the courageous cutie pretends to bone in *Sex Files: Pleasureville* (1999). Then begin yodeling the praises of Jill Tompkins, muff-baring iconoclast.

SKIN-fining Moment:

Lawful Entry (0:38) Claudia is "defrocked," showing her fantastic fleshmelons before doing a little "plea bargaining" with the D.A.

See Her Naked In:

Lawful Entry (2000) Breasts, Thong
Sex Files: Pleasureville (1999) FFN, Buns
Virtual Encounters 2 (1998) FFN

Angelica Torn

London, England, UK
Skin-O-Meter: Brief Nudity

She's blonde and those hooters are real, both real as in natural and real, *real* big, and that's just two reasons why Angelica Torn is a big hit with Mr. Skin. The daughter of respected thespians Rip Torn and Geraldine Page, her debut came in the Bruce Willis/Paul Newman movie *Nobody's Fool* (1994), and nobody felt foolish watching her in the mamorable scene in which she played strip poker and lost . . . gloriously. It must be quite a burden carrying around that pendulous pair, but she does it well. Now, if only she'd do Mr. Skin. Angelica has played suicide poet Silvia Plath onstage and admitted in an interview that she was raped at nineteen and suffered abusive boyfriends. But as far as her acting goes, all the hits are in the box office. After her eye-opening career start, Angelica went on to roles in *The Sixth Sense* (1999) and *Domestic Disturbance* (2001), but the only

thing disturbing is trying to top that top-heavy display from her first film. Angelica, it leaves us all Torn up.

SKIN-fining Moment:

Nobody's Fool (1:26) Angelica loses at strip poker next to Bruce Willis. We win when she takes out her two-ton torso-torpedoes.

See Her Naked In:

Nobody's Fool (1994) Breasts

Maria Tornberg

Sweden
Skin-O-Meter: Great Nudity

Maria Tornberg is one Swedish dish best served naked and cold. Blonde and bubbling with nip-popping breastage, Maria modeled her marvelous mug in Sweden before moving to the U.S. to pursue acting. Faster than you can say BOO(b), Tornberg's tempting tats landed her one and only tit-illating role in the cop comedy *Super Troopers* (2001). With bare boobs like stealth bombers, Maria is the most arresting feature in the flick. They bounce and flounce with a mind of their own, causing moans of ecstasy from skin lovers everywhere. The real crime in this flick is that Maria didn't have enough screen time to adequately display the depth of her boobilicious beauty. How do you solve a problem of not enough Maria? Pause repeatedly during the good parts of *Super Troopers* and wait patiently for her next big bone-inducing break.

SKIN-fining Moment:

Super Troopers (0:44) Tornberg's teriffic ta-tas jiggle all about as she gets silly in bed with a cop.

See Her Naked In:

Super Troopers (2001) Breasts

Beth Toussaint

Born: September 25, 1962
Pleasant Hill, California
Skin-O-Meter: Brief Nudity

Classy ladies do not come a dime a dozen. A woman minted of frosted brunette Beth Toussaint's caliber is of rare and precious mettle and worth her weight in golden-tanned thighs. The diamond-clear luster of Beth's million-dollar gaze has enriched such platinum-rated network hits as *Dallas* (on which Beth played among the demigods of divinely inspired prosperity as Tracy Lawton) and *Savannah* (on which the southern belles ring true and pure like they were cast from melted paving stones pried off the streets of paradise). Still, if seeking the best return on your entertainment buck, shell out for a rental of schlock cinema classic *Berserker* (1987), where the price of admission is more than covered by the raw and rude uncovering of Beth's erectile nipples and deep-dish ass crack.

SKIN-fining Moment:

Berserker (0:39) Beth bares her boobage and the side of her buns a few times as she enjoys a moonlit scrogging.

See Her Naked In:

Berserker (1987) Breasts, Bush, Buns

Katharine Towne

Born: July 17, 1978
Hollywood, California
Skin-O-Meter: Brief Nudity

Her father wrote *Chinatown* (1974), but Katharine Towne owes her career more to nipples than nepotism. She first caught our zippers as the bloodsucking "Sunday" on a 1999 episode of *Buffy the Vampire Slayer*. Her battle with Sarah Michelle Gellar was easily the best catfight in the show's history. Then we went to Towne as Katharine went redhead while showing off her incredible T&A from behind in *Go* (1999). That was followed by a sexy turn as a punky lesbian in *But I'm a Cheerleader* (1999). Katharine kept her megamelons covered at the multiplex for *Evolution* (2001) and *Mulholland Drive* (2001), but she let loose with a mind-blowing orgasm in the under-seen *Sol Goode* (2001). Then she got—and provided— meaningful exposure from a thrilling thong in *Sweet Home Alabama* (2002). It's a scene that made us all southern men!

SKIN-fining Moment:

Go (0:46) Katharine literally sets the room on fire as she engages in a three-way with a guy and another chick. Somebody's cigarette ignites paper in the waste basket and, as hot as it gets your own temperature will be sent through the roof by bare upper-deck and back door on this Towne-house.

See Her Naked In:

Sol Goode (2001) LB
Go (1999) Breasts, Buns

Michelle Trachtenberg

Born: October 11, 1985
New York, New York
Skin-O-Meter: Never Nude

Michelle Trachtenberg has known how to get a man's attention since she was but a wee lass barely out of diapers. In her first TV commercial for Wisk detergent she played a daughter who threw a glassful of cranberry juice at her father. That's one way to make guys take notice. The boob tube kept the little princess employed with various guest appearances on *Law & Order* and *Clarissa Explains It All*. Then she landed on the daytime soap *All My Children*, where she played one of the cutest autistic children Mr. Skin

has ever come across. Of course, she might as well have been cast on *The Young and the Skinless*, because she was too immature for any one-handed viewing. All that changed when Michelle landed on the fifth season of *Buffy the Vampire Slayer* playing Sarah Michelle Gellar's sister. Audiences got to watch her grow up on camera as their pants grew tight at the sexy sight. But Mr. Skin got really excited when the now-legal lust muffin was cast in the hot comedy *Eurotrip* (2004). She didn't cross the skin barrier but got awfully tempting in a string bikini and when flashing her bra-covered rack while hitchhiking. What a trip!

SKIN-fining Moment:

Euro Trip (0:42) On a nude beach, Michelle peels to a teeny blue bikini but stops before she joins the naked throng. Still, there's awe-inspiring ogleage of her bottom-boobs, ultra-taut tummy and even a tiny taste of camel toe.

Keegan Connor Tracy

Born: December 3, 1971
Windsor, Ontario, Canada
Skin-O-Meter: Great Nudity

Canadian cutie Keegan Connor Tracy is tiny yet mightily hot. With three names, three perfect areas on her fine-boned frame, and three times the strength and bitchiness of girls thrice her size, she's triple the woman of most starlets in one petite package. This pixie bitch got her start making guest appearances on TV series like *Viper*, *First Wave*, and *The Net*. Her sprightly spitfire sex appeal landed her a regular role on the cable series *Beggars and Choosers*, where this finicky fox beseeched the audience to behold her bare boobage. For such a small sexpot, her ta-tas topple over her small stature like two tasty marshmallows on a stick. What sweet, tasty teats! Tracy tantalized

audiences with her luscious lungs in her first major picture *Duets* (2000). Take one look at this willowy, whirling dervish's devilish demeanor in any of her appearances, and you'll come singing her praises.

SKIN-fining Moment:

Blackwoods (0:21) Keegan bares just a bit of thong-clad butt and a hint of tit here and there during this rather frantic sex sequence.

See Her Naked In:

Blackwoods (2002) LB, Thong

TeleVisions:

Beggars and Choosers Breasts

Deborah Tranelli

Born: July 6, 1955
Skin-O-Meter: Great Nudity

The great state of Texas is so gall dang big that they can make room for more dysfunction junctions in any one Lone Star town than many entire countries are able to accommodate. TV doesn't lie, and according to thirteen consecutive years of CBS network reality, *Dallas* is a Texan burg that puts the indecent inhabitants of both Sodom and Gomorrah to shame. Angelic-looking brunette wisp of wonder and wickedness Deborah Tranelli may not have been the most evil seductress or craftiest conniving charmer in her decade as Phyllis on the long-running, adult soap drama, but she managed to last ten years in a cauldron of bedroom and boardroom betrayal without ever being knocked off.

SKIN-fining Moment:

Naked Vengeance (0:59) Deb treats us to all three B's while taking on a guy in a lake, recreating the time-honored exploitation movie tradition of seduction/castration/killing.

See Her Naked In:

Naked Vengeance (1985) FFN, Buns

Kylie Travis

Born: April 27, 1970
London, England, UK
Skin-O-Meter: Great Nudity

Life imitates art for Australian-raised model/actress Kylie Travis. She's best known for her role as über-hot bitch on wheels Julie Dante on the short-lived (but much-remembered) *Melrose Place* spinoff *Models, Inc.* The Aaron Spelling-produced soap series about a scandal-ravaged modeling agency may have been canned, but its unabashed trashiness and stunner-packed cast (Kylie's comely co-stars included Carrie-Anne Moss and Garcelle Beauvais) made it fun while it lasted. What next for the flaxen-haired looker? Naturally, she co-founded her own modeling agency, Models West, while continuing to appear on television shows such as *Central Park West*, *Ed*, and *Renegade*. Whether she's acting or modeling, where Kylie goes, our roving eyes shall follow.

SKIN-fining Moment:

Eyes of the Beholder (1:08) Kylie will make you smiley when she drops her top and shows her torpid twosome to some tuxedo-clad dude.

See Her Naked In:

Eyes of the Beholder (1992) Breasts

Nancy Travis

Born: September 21, 1961
New York, New York
Skin-O-Meter: Great Nudity

A delightful goof ball who maintains the seductive aplomb of a ingénue while carrying around a massive head of twisted blonde hair, Nancy Travis is the kind of happy-go-plucky hottie who has secured ongoing roles on at least half a dozen network series, most of them intentionally comic. TV, of course, is a fleeting medium, even with reruns, but movies, thanks to video and DVD, play forever. Never will skinsters forget or tire of Nancy's skin-clad rise to fame in *Married to the Mob* (1988). Rising from the cheesy bathtub in a Jersey-hinterland motel room, Nancy flexes her high, satin-smooth couch cushions. She turns her torso this way and that, presenting a full range of backside profiles, and takes a permanent place in the seat of skin affection. Her spin as Andy Garcia's pantie-losing wife in *Internal Affairs* (1990), though less revealing, is even more brain searing.

SKIN-fining Moment:

Married to the Mob (0:16) A long look at Nancy's back bacon as she smokes in bed, followed by more ass and mammage when she hugs Dean Stockwell.

See Her Naked In:

Internal Affairs (1990) LB
Married to the Mob (1988) Breasts, Buns

Stacey Travis

Dallas, Texas
Skin-O-Meter: Brief Nudity

Nostalgia can be a source of deep disappointment if explored carelessly, especially in the realm of beloved television series of yore. In resurrecting a revered cultural touchstone of the past, there are rules to be followed, the most paramount of them being that a central role must be filled by a stunning, summery, blue-eyed blonde whose fresh and sexy smile is capable of lighting up a TV screen with the radiance of wholesome lust. One such blonde is sugar-spun creation Stacey Travis, who did her bit as Cruise Director Suzanne Zimmerman to ensure the success of 1970s retread *The Love Boat: The Next Wave*. That *The Next Wave* is not still pulsating upon the tube today may be the fault of many factors, but Stacey Travis is blameless. What more could she have done, other than go topless?

SKIN-fining Moment:

Dracula Rising (0:43) Stacey gets wet with Christoper Atkins in an aquatic setting. We see her flotation devices up top, plus underwater bush and buns.

See Her Naked In:

Dracula Rising (1993) FFN, Buns
Hardware (1990) Breasts, Buns

Terri Treas

Born: July 19, 1959
Kansas City, Kansas
Skin-O-Meter: Brief Nudity

Terri Treas is best known for her spotty-scalped chrome-dome character Cathy Frankel on the hit series *Alien Nation*. But the out-of-this-world beauty had been acting for almost a decade before that star-raising gig. She first appeared as a fan dancer in *All That Jazz* (1979). For a while, Terri was utilized for her dancing talents only, that is, until she was cast as one of the many young ladies who populated the Chicken Ranch in the double-D Dolly Parton flick *The Best Little Whorehouse in Texas* (1982). You can catch her massive cleavage and animal-print garters in an "Oh, you caught me" sex scene. She then went on to appear in such notable series as *Seven Brides for Seven Brothers* and *Santa Barbara* and such feature films as *The Nest* (1988), *The Terror Within* (1989), and *House IV* (1992). But she has pretty much left the acting career behind to pursue her screenwriting profession. Thankfully, Terri didn't leave the camera behind before she had the chance to show some hootage. In the opening scene of *The Fabulous Baker Boys* (1989), she can be spied in bed with nary a thread on her luscious bod. Now that's fabulous, boys.

SKIN-fining Moment:

The Fabulous Baker Boys (0:01) Quick look at Terri's right breast in bed during opening scene.

See Her Naked In:

The Fabulous Baker Boys (1989) RB

Peggy Trentini

Born: June 22, 1968
Newport Beach, California
Skin-O-Meter: Great Nudity

Royalty is not something to be worked at or achieved. True, a particularly foxy and frolicsome commoner can marry into the exalted ranks, but only her offspring will be accepted as of true regal blood. The crown, you see, is bestowed at birth, and it could not have been long after she'd popped from her mother's chute that the sensual sovereignty of exalted boobular blonde Peggy Trentini became obvious to all who gazed upon her courtly combination of form and functionality. The coronation of Peggy into the constellation of ruling racks occurred in her role as the topless Christmas Elf in *Young Doctors in Love* (1982). Trentini's loyal and devoted subjects have subsequently benefited from her princess-like prurience in numerous gifts of noblesse nudity, including *Virtual Combat* (1996), *Vampirella* (1996), and *Human Desires* (1997).

SKIN-fining Moment:

Human Desires (0:11) Loads of full-frontal lesbianic goodness in the sack with Dawn Ann Billings.

See Her Naked In:

Poison (2000) Breasts, Buns
Carnal Desires (1999) Breasts, Bush, Buns
Masseuse 3 (1998) Breasts, Thong
Masseuse 2 (1997) Breasts
Human Desires (1997) Breasts, Buns
Vampirella (1996) Breasts
Virtual Combat (1996) FFN
Virtual Desire (1995) Breasts, Thong
Demon Knight (1995) Breasts, Thong
Up the Creek (1984) Breasts
Young Doctors in Love (1982) Breasts

TeleVisions:

Beverly Hills Bordello FFN, Buns
Erotic Confessions FFN, Buns
Hotline Breasts, Bush, Buns
Nightcap FFN, Buns

Paula Trickey

Born: March 27, 1966
Amarillo, Texas
Skin-O-Meter: Great Nudity

From beauty queen to sexed-up starlet, Paula Trickey has quite the crafty career. While in high school, this Oklahoma eyeful pranced her titillating, tall frame down the catwalk in pageants, winning the title of Miss Oklahoma. Paula put her runway skills to good use in her first film, *Maniac Cop 2* (1990), strutting and stripping onstage. Her bubbling boobage and rock-hard heinie were most arresting. Trickey went on to lend her major mams to a minor part in *Black Scorpion* (1995) and the cable series *Dream On*. Next, Paula was pleased to spread her sexiness to the masses on TV, starring as curvy cop "Cory McNamara," Sergeant of the Santa Monica Bike Patrol on *Pacific Blue*. The athletically alluring Paula is D-lightful, bouncing about half naked on her bike at the beach, leaving your boys a-twitter in shades of blue. It's not *Trickey* to figure out why this buxom brunette is enjoying so much skinematic suck-sess. She's absolutely boobilicious!

SKIN-fining Moment:

Maniac Cop 2 (0:41) Paula peels out of an orange swimsuit in a go-go cage. Breasts and thonged-up buns.

See Her Naked In:

A Kiss Goodnight (1994) Thong
Maniac Cop 2 (1990) Breasts, Thong

TeleVisions:

Dream On Breasts

Sarah Trigger

Born: 6/
London, England, UK
Skin-O-Meter: Great Nudity

Strawberry blonde and equally adept at portraying a strumpet or a vestal vision, London-born cream dream Sarah Trigger's sinuous and sensuous screen presence creates a dynamic erotic tension that makes viewers feel that they need apply just one twitching finger and they'll fire away. Sarah started off her cinematic career loaded for nudity, rising up from metallic satin sheets in the UK-produced drama *Fellow Traveller* (1989) with her fine, firm, puffy-nipped fellows traveling directly into the ranks of all-time great racks.

SKIN-fining Moment:

Deadfall (0:42) Good looks at Sarah's milksacks during a long, multi-position bedroom boffing.

See Her Naked In:

Deadfall (1993) Breasts
Paradise (1991) Breasts
Fellow Traveller (1989) Breasts

Marie Trintignant

Born: January 21, 1962
Paris, France
Died: August 1, 2003
Skin-O-Meter: Great Nudity

Doe-eyed, wet-lipped, tiny-tipped brunette Marie Trintignant is a uniquely French confection, seemingly conceived and assembled in the salons and ateliers of Paris to achieve the greatest delicacy of erotic impact. Though fine of line and fragile of temperament, Marie exhibits no hint of frailty as she frolics in full, tawny-skinned nudity throughout her all-too-brief span of cinema immortality. Sadly and far too swiftly, Marie was removed from our midst at age forty-one in 2003. Her naked padding and pouting and posing and pleasing will live on in *Nuit d'été un ville* (1990) and *Betty* (1992) for as long as men gather to savor fluffy, fragrant bush.

SKIN-fining Moment:

Nuit d'été enville (0:02) Marie first flashes some boobies, then a bit of butt, and then the entire furry package as she gets out of bed and heads for the chair.

See Her Naked In:

Noyade interdite (1997) Breasts, Bush
Les Marmottes (1993) Breasts, Bush, Buns
Betty (1992) Breasts, Bush, Buns
Nuit d'été en ville (1990) FFN, Buns
Wings of Fame (1990) Bush, Buns
Série noire (1979) FFN, Buns

Idy Tripoldi

Skin-O-Meter: Great Nudity

Appearing in three films during a short stint in the late '70s and early '80s, the nicely enticing Idy Tripoldi's career in skinema was entirely too tiny for such a long-legged vision of lusciousness. Thankfully, this randy redhead flashed the entirety of her top-heavy flesh in all her skindeavors, revealing her fuzzy patch of thatch the first time out in *Auditions* (1978). With her softcore efforts hardening the limpest of biscuits, Idy should have taken Hollywad by storm. Alas, we'll just have to live happily ever after relying on our dirty dreams and reliving this

heavenly hottie's sexcapades in *Fairy Tales* (1979).

SKIN-fining Moment:

Auditions (1:01) Idy proves she's natural all-over from her strawberry-blonde hair to her ravishingly buxom rack when she busts out her naked bod for a shot at the big time.

See Her Naked In:

Famous T&A (1982) FFN
Fairy Tales (1979) FFN, Buns
Auditions (1978) FFN, Buns

Jeanne Tripplehorn

Born: June 10, 1963
Tulsa, Oklahoma
Skin-O-Meter: Great Nudity

What happens to a gorgeous young girl when all her life schoolyard wits have been calling her Triple Horny? If she's something like Tulsa, Oklahoma's Jeanne Tripplehorn, she takes her terrific tapered legs, scintillating sculpted ass, breath-taking breasts, and drop-dead face to Hollywood. Once in the city of glitz, she commits her heavenly goods to celluloid in one of the most sex-drenched blockbusters in box-office history, leaving the busters back home to be forever triple horny. Given a second viewing, *Basic Instinct* (1992) discloses itself to be a Jeanne Tripplehorn vehicle. Her brown-tipped boobs swing and sway all the way out of their busted bra. Her torso is pawed and her neck chomped. She's bent butt-up over the back of a sofa, flesh bare except for stockings and garters, and endures a smart round of spank therapy. And then she shows skin never more. Jeanne has yet to follow up her auspicious skinema debut. Her ass appears to appear in *Waterworld* (1995). Alas, the illusion is created by a bun double. Please, Jeanne, give us more. The busters back in Tulsa have suffered enough.

SKIN-fining Moment:

Basic Instinct (0:35) Jiggling jugs and bouncy buns as Jeanne and Michael Douglas fill the living room with their angry lovemaking.

See Her Naked In:

Waterworld (1995) Body Double—Buns
Basic Instinct (1992) Breasts, Buns

Monica Trombetta

Skin-O-Meter: Great Nudity

It may be unfair to refer to the men and women of our nation's beleaguered police forces as swine, but there is a good case to be made that the creators of network cop shows have a streak of piggish male chauvinism. How else to account for the tendency to fill ancillary female roles with actresses, such as Monica Trombetta, whose sexual allure could be felt from a distance of three city blocks? It seems unfair to the criminals to place dusky brunette Monica and her mocha mounds in the vicinity of the interrogation rooms of *Third Watch*, *Law & Order*, *Homicide*, and *NYPD Blue*. Her scintillating looks unjustly sweat the crooks, and they'll admit to anything if only she will promise to turn up the heat even further.

SKIN-fining Moment:

Raw Nerve (1:17) Check out Monica's mountains while she screws Mario Van Peebles in front of the mirror.

See Her Naked In:

Raw Nerve (1999) Breasts

Tracy Trueman

Skin-O-Meter: Brief Nudity

Tracy Trueman touts one of the best pairs of tits in skinematic history. A bootilicious bouncing brunette with a pouty-lipped, come-hither look, Tracy's perfectly round, pointy-nipped nuggets were at their gold standard breast in *Saving Silverman* (2001). Even in her small (but big at heart) part as a prostitute, her hooters will have your tooter hooked on all things Tracy. In *Life or Something Like It* (2002), Ms. T (and A) stole the show in a bit part as Ed Burns's (s) ex-wife. Now that Hollywood has caught a glimpse of what this hoochie mama can do, you better believe we'll be seeing a lot more of Tracy. It's *Trueman*, so get used to it.

SKIN-fining Moment:

Saving Silverman (0:25) Tracy's titties make up one-half of this sexy topless Ping Pong team!

See Her Naked In:

Saving Silverman (2001) Breasts

Lin Tucci

Skin-O-Meter: Brief Nudity

When it comes to bra sizes, there's double-D, triple-D, triple-E, and then there's Lin Tucci. Lin is every breast man's fantasy, a full-bodied redhead with jamambo jugs and booty to match. In the skin classic *Showgirls* (1995), Lin played the aptly-named Henrietta Bazoom, and her Large Marge-sized hooters completely filled the big screen. In a film that stars Elizabeth Berkley and Gina Gershon and has lesbians, strippers, taboo sex, and more meat than a butcher's shop, Lin is its biggest and breastest star. Sadly, it was the first and last time her beautiful berthas popped up on film. Fortunately, they were large enough to remain permanently etched in our mammaries.

SKIN-fining Moment:

Showgirls (0:21) As the Cheetah Club's Mistress of Ceremonies, round-and-raunchy Lin storms the stage between strip acts and punctuates her dirty jokes by popping the top off her dress four honkin' times.

See Her Naked In:

Showgirls (1995) Breasts

Tamara Tunie

Born: March 14, 1959
McKeesport, Pennsylvania
Skin-O-Meter: Brief Nudity

Tamara Tunie is primarily a creature of the boob tube, having spent the majority of her career in the role of attorney Jessica Griffin McKechnie on the long-running soap *As the World Turns*. When not playing a hardball lawyer, she's playing a hard-boiled police lieutenant's wife on *NYPD Blue* and a thick-skinned medical examiner on *Law & Order: Special Victims Unit*. She also appeared on *24* for the 2001–02 series. This Carnegie-Mellon University graduate got her start in theatre; her second stage job was as a backup singer for Lena Horne in the Tony award-winning Broadway hit *Lena Horne: The Lady and Her Music*. Among her smattering of film roles, Tamara's most skintastic roles to date are her scenes alongside a horny ghost in *Spirit Lost* (1996) and as Al Pacino's naughty neighbor in the *Faust*-y Keanu Reeves vehicle *The Devil's Advocate* (1997). In a rather skintilating scene, her ittie-bittie cocoa puffs stand up like radio control knobs, and those dials have *got* to be standing out at least half an inch!

SKIN-fining Moment:

The Devil's Advocate (0:57) Tamara takes off her top in the dressing room, to explain the benefits of breast augmentation to Charlize. We're all impressed.

See Her Naked In:

The Devil's Advocate (1997) Breasts

Robin Tunney

Born: June 19, 1972
Chicago, Illinois
Skin-O-Meter: Great Nudity

An impish brunette who habitually wears a look of surprise and awe, an expression always on the verge of breaking into tears or into the throes of orgasm, Robin Tunney is the type of girl he-men love to protect. Robin developed her dramatic powers under the wing of such strong leading males as Arnold Schwarzenegger and Pauly Shore. The plucky sparrow has now ventured out to fly on her own, arms raised, shirt off, shooting starward, tits in the astral breeze! Tunney first flexed her muscles during a shirt-shirking hurry in *End of Days* (1999). The bra-free empowerment felt so good that she tossed the garment and sprung loose at every opportunity in *Supernova* (2000).

SKIN-fining Moment:

Supernova (0:11) You'll find more of Tunney's twins here as she disrobes in a futuristic co-ed locker room. Gotta love the future.

See Her Naked In:

Cherish (2002) LB
Investigating Sex (2001) Breasts, Buns
Supernova (2000) Breasts
End of Days (1999) Breasts

TeleVisions:

Dream On RB

Paige Turco

Born: May 17, 1965
Springfield, Massachusetts
Skin-O-Meter: Brief Nudity

Paige Turco kicked off her skintertainment career in 1987 when she landed a recurring gig as Dinah Morgan Mahler #2 on the long-running soap opera *The Guiding Light*. By 1989 she saw the light and took a role as Melanie Courtlandt Rampal on competing daytime drama *All My Children*. Hey, at least she was no longer a stinky number two! The silver screen came next (but you men will have to wait to come . . . be patient) with a turn as the ass-kicking April O'Neil in the hit kiddie flick *Teenage Mutant Ninja Turtles II: The Secret of the Ooze* (1991). Although she reprised the role in *Teenage Mutant Ninja Turtles III* (1993), the franchise went down the proverbial tube, and Paige returned to the boob tube for her bread and butter. Since the early '90s Paige has spent her time divided between such serial gigs as *Party of Five*, *The Agency*, and *American Gothic* and independent skinema such as *Vibrations* (1995), *Dead Funny* (1994), and *Urbania* (2000). *Dark Tides* (1998) features one of Paige's few skin scenes. Although it's a fleeting shot of her enormous hooters, it's more than worth a look. Hopefully, she'll turn the Paige on her bashfulness and get down to the bare facts.

SKIN-fining Moment:

Dark Tides (0:45) Paige is off-the-charts sexy as she changes shirts on a boat, baring a bite of her left floatation device in the process. I'd like to suck on that lifesaver.

See Her Naked In:

Dark Tides (1998) LB

Bree Turner

Born: March 10, 1977
Palo Alto, California
Skin-O-Meter: Never Nude

A five-foot-eight-inch blonde, Bree Turner should change her first name to Head because she's been turning them on since launching her career as a deliciously sexy dancer in such films as *The Big Lebowski* (1998), *My Best Friend's Wedding* (1997), and *She's All That* (1999). Her first

speaking role was as Allison, the pet-shop girl in *Deuce Bigalow: Male Gigolo* (1999). What did she say? Who knows?! All eyes were on her erect twins that she dunked into the water of an aquarium when asked to get some snails. She must like to get her hooters wet, because she followed *Deuce* with another wet T-shirt scene in *Sorority Boys* (2002). Bree also appeared in the cheesy-and-teasy MTV soap opera *Undressed* but kept her clothes on. Maybe MTV will launch a show called *Dressed* and we'll finally see Bree's breasts.

SKIN-fining Moment:

Deuce Bigalow: Male Gigolo (0:02) Pet store clerk Bree double dips her potently pert T-shirt clad pair into a fishtank when scooping out snails, then leans back with her see through wet-spots showing off her sumptuous rack.

Guinevere Turner

Born: May 23, 1968
Boston, Massachusetts
Skin-O-Meter: Great Nudity

Guinevere Turner has made some serious marks as a lesbian. Aside from her turn as Bus Station Attendant in *Dogma* (1999), she's played a labia-licker in just about every movie she's been in, most notably in *Kiss Me Guido* (1997) as Indignant Lesbian and in *Go Fish* (1994), which she co-wrote (and where she showed off her pierced nipples). Although our movie-going society dictates that once one is "out" as a pussy pumper, then you're stuck playing only lesbian-type roles, Guinevere bucked the trend by not only penning the script for *American Psycho* (2000) but also appearing in the film as one of Christian Bale's victims. Sure, she engaged in some bisexual three-way action, but the strength of the script definitely showed her versatility and ability to wear something other than the "Gay

Hat." Thankfully, when Gwen puts on that Gay Hat, it's usually the only thing she's wearing! She flashed her flappers in her first-ever skinematic role, *Go Fish*, and continued the trend in *The Watermelon Woman* (1996) and the aforementioned *American Psycho*. Mr. Skin especially enjoyed her turn in *Preaching to the Perverted* (1997), though. It featured a nice full-frontal flash or two from the gorgeous Gwen. What a Turner on!

SKIN-fining Moment:

The Watermelon Woman (0:41) Lickylesbo sex with Cheryl Dunye brings Lady Guinevere's royal boobs and bunnage, and even a teensy touch of the muff!

See Her Naked In:

American Psycho (2000) Breasts
Preaching to the Perverted (1997) FFN, Buns
The Watermelon Woman (1996) Breasts, Bush
Go Fish (1994) Breasts

Janine Turner

Born: December 6, 1962
Lincoln, Nebraska
Skin-O-Meter: Brief Nudity

Her hair is usually cut short, but not like a boy's, like a former model's, a look that is augmented by a face with features so perfectly symmetrical and pretty and bold that one look is enough to know that it has graced the covers of dozens of magazines. Janine Turner is both a veteran of the fashion runways and the daytime airwaves, starting her acting career as a slinky tormentress on the soaps *General Hospital* and *Another World*. Her peak of popularity came as another slinky tormentress on the freaky CBS drama *Northern Exposure*. For a peek at Janine's slinky tool of torment, try *Monkey Shines* (1988), and watch Turner's bad moon rise and shine.

SKIN-fining Moment:

Dr. T and the Women (0:39) Brief upper butt-crack twice in Dr. Hamster's office.

See Her Naked In:

Dr. T and the Women (2000) Buns
A Secret Affair (1999) RB
Monkey Shines (1988) Buns

Kathleen Turner

Born: June 19, 1954
Springfield, Missouri
Skin-O-Meter: Hall of Fame

In the early 1980s shadowy blonde Kathleen Turner was a one-woman recipe for spontaneous combustion. Take that whiskey voice and the dangerously hot sparks that shot off from her sparkling, sex-ready eyes and cross them with the electrified erotic vibrancy of her bedroom athlete's nates and TNT-tipped titties. All Kathleen had to do was light a match, and *bang!*: Sexplosion. It's no coincidence that this sizzling vixen's first major appearance was in a movie called *Body Heat* (1981). She climbed on top and rocked her buttocks in a high-temperature hump scene, the mercury rising in her nipples so that they protruded an extra inch. That sweat running down the crack of her backside? It's the proof of the theory of hot fusion put into action.

SKIN-fining Moment:

Body Heat (0:24) A happy gander at Kathleen's long-nipped little globes as she leads William Hurt around by his johnson.

See Her Naked In:

The War of the Roses (1989) LB
Julia and Julia (1987) Breasts
Prizzi's Honor (1985) LB
Crimes of Passion (1984) Breasts
A Breed Apart (1984) Breasts
The Man with Two Brains (1983) Buns
Body Heat (1981) Breasts, Buns

Bahni Turpin

Skin-O-Meter: Brief Nudity

She's one of the sexiest and most gifted young African American actresses out there today—so, naturally, Bahni Turpin spends a lot of time playing a female prisoner. It's a waste of her talent, but at least Bahni's boobies are being appreciated by her biggest fans. She's a very sexy inmate in *Brokedown Palace* (1999) and certainly worth stirring up some baby batter as the imprisoned "Baby Bomber" in *Rain without Thunder* (1992). But Turpin really gets us tapping our testicles in *Girls In Prison* (1994), where Bahni shares her topless body with Ione Skye during a swell Sapphic shower scene.

SKIN-fining Moment:

Girls in Prison (0:23) Bahni's left headlight rubs up against Ione's right one during a showtime make-out session.

See Her Naked In:

Girls in Prison (1994) LB

TeleVisions:

Women: Stories of Passion Breasts

Aida Turturro

Born: September 25, 1962
New York, New York
Skin-O-Meter: Brief Nudity

Although she has been a formidable presence in East Coast independent films for many years, it is her portrayal of Janice Soprano, Tony's little sister, on *The Sopranos* that Aida Turturro has finally made her mark. Equal parts flaky and fearsome, Aida's character is lusty and busty and has a penchant for landing in the sack with the show's most psychotic villains, which makes for kinky foreplay that is best not emulated by the home audience. Turturro's massive mammary mounds are no secret, as even an Eskimo's formal wear could not conceal them. What is little known is that the jamambos are not only put on display in her brother John Turturro's film *Illuminata* (1998), but they are gnawed on by a male co-star. Aida's feast of chest flesh could cure famine forever.

SKIN-fining Moment:

Illuminata (1:11) Tony Soprano's sister dropps her top and hoists out her heavingly heavy milk-monsters.

See Her Naked In:

Illuminata (1998) Breasts

Shannon Tweed

Born: March 10, 1957
St. John's, Newfoundland, Canada
Skin-O-Meter: Hall of Fame

Shannon Tweed burst onto the skinematic scene the old-fashioned

---

MR. SKIN'S TOP TEN

Video Vixens
. . . Straight to titty-o

10. Jacqueline Lovell
9. Monique Parents
8. Misty Mundae
7. Lisa Boyle
6. Maria Ford
5. Landon Hall
4. Shannon Whirry
3. Gabriella Hall
2. Athena Massey
1. **Shannon Tweed**

way: with a spread in *Playboy* back in November 1981. (Now *there's* a collector's issue!) Not surprisingly, Tweed landed the coveted Playmate of the Year title, as well as a spot in Hugh Hefner's bed shortly thereafter. Although the fling with Hef didn't last and she's since gone on to a long and tongue-tastic relationship with Kiss bassist Gene Simmons, Shannon's then-budding acting career certainly has panned out prodigiously. In 1982 she landed a part as Diana Hunter on the long-running hit soap opera *Falcon Crest* and has since appeared in several series, including *Days of Our Lives, Fly By Night*, and as the star of HBO's *1st and Ten*. Shannon's also managed to appear in over sixty feature films, beginning with *Of Unknown Origin* in 1983. The better part of her filmography features rather scandalous features, although naturally, for her best skinematic nudity, one need look no further than her pantheon of *Playboy* videos. Regardless, we'd be remiss in not mentioning 1998's straight-to-video classic *Singapore Sling*, in which Shannon engaged in what appears to be some not-so-simulated sex. Don't miss it—because she doesn't!

SKIN-fining Moment:

Hot Dog . . . The Movie (0:42)
Shannon strips to her panties and beds a ski-bum. Those boobs could melt the Matterhorn.

See Her Naked In:

Dead Sexy (2001) Body Double—Breasts
The Rowdy Girls (1999) Breasts
Powerplay (1999) Breasts
Dead by Dawn (1998) Breasts, Buns
Scandalous Behavior (1998) FFN, Buns
Naked Lies (1998) Breasts
Shadow Warriors II: Hunt for the Death Merchant (1998) Breasts
Forbidden Sins (1998) Breasts
Human Desires (1997) Breasts, Buns

Stormy Nights (1996) Breasts
Victim of Desire (1996) Breasts
Electra (1996) Breasts
Indecent Behavior 3 (1995) Breasts
The Dark Dancer (1995) Breasts, Buns
Scorned (1994) Breasts, Buns
Hard Vice (1994) Breasts
Indecent Behavior II (1994) Breasts, Buns
Night Fire (1994) Breasts
Possessed By the Night (1994) Breasts, Bush, Thong
Illicit Dreams (1994) Breasts, Buns
Model By Day (1994) Breasts
Cold Sweat (1993) Breasts, Bush, Buns
Night Eyes 3 (1993) FFN, Buns
Indecent Behavior (1993) Breasts, Buns
Sexual Response (1992) Breasts, Bush, Buns
Night Eyes 2 (1992) Breasts, Buns
The Last Hour (1991) Breasts, Buns
The Firing Line (1991) RB, Buns
Last Call (1990) Breasts
In the Cold of the Night (1989) RB
Lethal Woman (1989) Breasts
Hot Dog . . . The Movie (1984) FFN, Buns
The Surrogate (1984) Breasts
Of Unknown Origin (1983) RB
Numerous *Playboy* Videos

TeleVisions:

The Hitchhiker Breasts

Tracy Tweed

Born: May 10, 1965
St. John's, Newfoundland, Canada
Skin-O-Meter: Great Nudity

Imagine the exquisite torment of growing up a preteen male next door to the family Tweed of British Columbia. It's not enough that this northern gene pool has produced the all-time poster girl for ultra-blonde extra-stacked Canadian womanhood (pre-Pamela Anderson division) in Shannon, but they went and produced a little sister, Tracy, who is just as hot. And the younger ones are always wilder, that's a well-known fact. The neighborhood must have been one unending game of "Let's spy on the Tweeds." Ogle

the peaks the B.C. kids were straining to peek in *Sunset Heat* (1991) and *Night Rhythms* (1992). With the miracle of video, there is no need to risk trespassing charges, or worse.

SKIN-fining Moment:

Sunset Heat (0:19) Topless Tracy *treats us to her Tweed-ers while she gets poled by Michael Pare.*

See Her Naked In:

Night Eyes 3 (1993) Breasts, Thong
Night Rhythms (1992) Breasts, Bush, Buns
Sunset Heat (1991) Breasts, Buns

Twiggy

Born: September 19, 1949
Neasden, England, UK
Skin-O-Meter: Brief Nudity

Posterity's images of swinging '60s London have largely been subsumed by the goofy metropolitan mugging of Mike Meyers and his Austin Powers persona, but in the real-time real world of that fabulous and frivolous decade, no face or figure gave the Beatles a better run for their money as pop ambassadors of English chic as did the big-eyed, pencil-thighed über-waif Twiggy. Whether photographed cocking her hip in a Saville Row mini-dress upon the cover of *Vogue* or snapped while cavorting along Carnaby Street in the company of British Invasion royalty or even while in a pose of curtsying to meet the Queen, Twiggy couldn't help but seem to be thinner and richer than everyone else in the picture.

SKIN-fining Moment:

John Carpenter's Body Bags (1:20)
A pair of peeks at Twiggy's lap-wiggy when Mark Hammil gets busy with her in bed.

See Her Naked In:

John Carpenter's Body Bags (1993) Bush

Alexandra Tydings

Born: December 15, 1972
Washington, DC
Skin-O-Meter: Great Nudity

After a few small parts, Alexandra Tydings set the screen on fire on the Showtime series *Red Shoe Diaries 7: Burning Up* in 1997. The same year revealed what a true goddess she was as the valley girl "Aphrodite," spilling out onto the small screen syndicated series *Hercules: The Legendary Journeys* and *Xena: Warrior Princess*. Seeing the deep cleavage of her Greek globes makes any man wish her good Tydings.

SKIN-fining Moment:

Red Shoe Diaries "Burning Up" (1994) Alexandra offers up her astonishing ogle-orbs while snoozing, chatting, and then doing some bouncy deep breathing routines. Those are some glad Tydings!

TeleVisions:

Red Shoe Diaries Breasts, Bush, Buns

Aisha Tyler

Born: September 18, 1970
San Francisco, California
Skin-O-Meter: Brief Nudity

Educated in the Ivy League, Aisha Tyler is sure to get audiences' stems stiff. She first made funny bones and other hard objects happy as a host on E!'s *Talk Soup*, but viewers demanded more than a spoonful from this silky ebony temptress. Next, she broke the color barrier on *Friends* with the first recurring role given to an African American. Aisha played a paleontologist who got into a love triangle with Joey and Ross, which is sure to raise more than dinosaur bones. Aisha proved

she's a force to be reckoned with playing Mother Nature in *The Santa Clause 2* (2002). But her natural beauty is more evident on the hit F/X drama *Nip/Tuck*, where she beds one of the plastic surgeons and, upon leaving the sheets, shows off her shitter, which is the shit. No wonder her first name sounds so much like ass.

SKIN-fining Moment:

Nip/Tuck "Manya Mabika" (2004) Aisha rises from bed next to her man, and we get an overhead view of her velvety-smooth chocolate bun-buns.

TeleVisions:

Nip/Tuck Buns

> "The boobs were pretty good—a lot bigger than mine."
>
> —LIV TYLER ON A DOLL PATTERNED AFTER HER *LORD OF THE RINGS* CHARACTER

Liv Tyler

Born: July 1, 1977
Portland, Maine
Skin-O-Meter: Great Nudity

Pouty, doe-eyed Liv Tyler first drove men nuts paired with the wickedly wanton Alicia Silverstone in Aerosmith's "Crazy" video. The two young vixens rode that wild trip to superstardom. Liv's big-screen debut was *Heavy* (1995), but she didn't show her heavy hitters until later that year in a slightly skinful spread in *Playboy*. It wasn't until Bernardo Bertolucci's *Stealing Beauty* (1996) that we got a glance at her sweet beauties onscreen. Since then, Liv has shown little interest in disrobing, although she's cut a sexy figure in fare such as *Armageddon* (1998), *Dr. T and the Women* (2000), and *One Night at*

McCool's (2001). Perhaps best known as Arwen, the elf princess who gets hot for man meat in *The Lord of the Rings* trilogy, this magical enchantress makes Mr. Skin take Liv of his senses.

SKIN-fining Moment:

Stealing Beauty (1:02) Come bask in Liv's left-side love-bubble as she poses outdoors for a painting.

See Her Naked In:

One Night at McCool's (2001) Buns
Stealing Beauty (1996) Breasts, Thong

Hunter Tylo

Born: July 3, 1962
Fort Worth, Texas
Skin-O-Meter: Great Nudity

With her simmering, soul-stirring stare and the glittering promises of heaven-on-earth revealed in her wickedly wide grin, miraculous brunette Hunter Tylo just might be the sexiest born-again Christian in all creation. Just don't expect to see Tylo's terrific twosome and high-end bum show up in *Playboy* any time soon, like not until hell freezes over. Lucky for us unrepentant skinners, before she was a saint, Hunter had a past as a hungry actress who signed on for the cheese horror flick *The Initiation* (1984). The future holy woman's ungodly thick bush is flaunted in a better-than-obligatory shower scene as heavenly Hunter struts across the room in nothing but the glory God gave her.

SKIN-fining Moment:

The Initiation (0:33) A quick shot of full-frontal nudity in the shower, then a nice flash of gash when she gets out and dries herself off. Hole-y Hunter!

See Her Naked In:

The Initiation (1984) FFN

Susan Tyrrell

Born: March 18, 1945
San Francisco, California.
Skin-O-Meter: Great Nudity

With her brazen disregard for convention and her proven willingness to strip to the bare essence for the sake of cinematic art, blonde and boobular tyro Susan Tyrrell could have easily strived for notoriety. Rather than rely on hype and flash, Susan took one demanding and modest character role after another, amassing a body of stellar and true work while leaving behind a revealing legacy of her stellar and true body. Though her best shot at an Oscar came as a blowsy barfly in director John Huston's *Fat City* (1972), Susan's best shots at skinmortality are found in *Tales of Ordinary Madness* (1983). Look for a ripened blonde spread eagle in black lingerie. There will not be one false move in every jiggle of thigh, buttock, and breast.

SKIN-fining Moment:

Tales of Ordinary Madness (0:25)
Nerps, mutt, and rump in (and out of) a sexy lingerie outfit as Ben Gazarra bangs her every which way and loose all over a living room.

See Her Naked In:

Far From Home (1989) Breasts
Flesh+Blood (1985) RB
Tales of Ordinary Madness (1983) Breasts, Bush, Buns
Night Warning (1981) LB
Forbidden Zone (1980) LB
The Killer Inside Me (1976) Breasts
The Steagle (1971) LB
Shootout (1971) RB

Cathy Tyson

Born: June 12, 1965
Liverpool, England, UK
Skin-O-Meter: Brief Nudity

A light-skinned, mixed-race vision of exquisite refinement and feline sensuality, British actress Cathy Tyson is the daughter of a black lawyer from Trinidad and a white English social worker. Too cool for school, Cathy quit college at seventeen and within two years graduated to a position with the Royal Shakespeare Company. But it was in the company of gritty Brit screen star Bob Hoskins as a wistful, jaded, brave, and jilted prostitute in Neil Jordan's *Mona Lisa* (1986) that Cathy achieved everlasting renown. A couple of years later, the same eternal glory was bestowed upon the chest flesh of her body double in director Wes Craven's *Serpent and Rainbow* (1988).

SKIN-fining Moment:

Band of Gold (1995) Cathy's cocoacasabas float freely in the tub, just before she stuffs herself sexily into a black bra and panties.

See Her Naked In:

Serpent and the Rainbow (1988) Body Double—Breasts

TeleVisions:

Band of Gold (mini-series) Breasts

u

Fabiana Udenio

Born: December 21, 1964
Buenos Aires, Argentina
Skin-O-Meter: Brief Nudity

Most skinophiles will recognize chesty Italian import Fabiana Udenio as the seductive villainess Alotta Fagina in the original *Austin Powers* (1997) movie, but eagle-eyed skin scouts may have seen her in any number of Hollywood productions. The former Miss Teen Italy has enjoyed a remarkably steady career as a bit player on countless TV shows—among them *Cheers, Baywatch, NYPD Blue,* and *Babylon 5*—and films, including *Bride of Re-Animator* (1990), *Summer School* (1987), and *The Wedding Planner* (2001). Though she has yet to be cast in a headlining role, Fabiana's smoldering sex appeal and adorable accent have earned her leading-lady status in Mr. Skin's book.

SKIN-fining Moment:

Diplomatic Immunity (1:12) Nice look at Fabiana's fabulous floppers when a horned-up photog rips her blouse open to take pictures.

See Her Naked In:

Austin Powers: International Man of Mystery (1997) Nip Slip RB
Diplomatic Immunity (1991) Breasts
Bride of Re-Animator (1990) LB
Hardbodies 2 (1986) Breasts

Claudia Udy

Born: March 18, 1960
Albuquerque, New Mexico
Skin-O-Meter: Hall of Fame

Claudia Udy put the can in Canada, beginning with the comedy *Heaven Help Us!* (1982). She later crossed the Dominion to doff her décolletage for the first time in *American Nightmare* (1983), then went back again to display her maple leaf in *Joy* (1983). Her boobagerie is visible throughout the decade in *Out of Control* (1985), *Dragonard* (1987), and *Master of Dragon Hill* (1989). Afterward she kept those glass-cutting nips

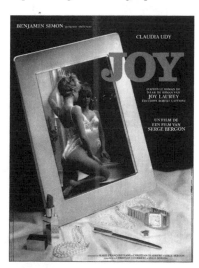

JOY: IN THE EARLY '80S, SEX FILMS USED POSTERS LIKE THIS TO SELL THE IDEA OF "SOPHISTICATION." AND BY "SOPHISTICA-TION," IN THIS CASE, I MEAN "CLAUDIA UDY'S BOOTY."

covered, and her career ended with the fitting title *To the Death* (1993). In her day, though, Udy was an udder delight.

SKIN-fining Moment:

Joy (0:11) Ody's udders are in full view, as well as her udder side, as she gets into the bathtub, then climbs out to lay naked in bed. Udderly marvelous!

See Her Naked In:

Nightforce (1987) FFN
Dragonard (1987) Breasts
Master of Dragonard Hill (1987) FFN
Out of Control (1984) Breasts
Joy (1983) FFN, Buns
American Nightmare (1983) Breasts, Buns

Helene Udy

Born: November 1, 1962
Montreal, Quebec, Canada
Skin-O-Meter: Great Nudity

Canadian film aficionados are well aware of heavenly Helene Udy's skinematic resumé. Sure, she can write and direct, which she proved with *Naked in the Cold Sun* (1997), but Helene's at her best when she's showing breast. In Canadian movie of the week *One Night Only* (1986), Helene made the small screen sizzle by flashing her gelatinous garbanzos. Two years later, she let her blouse bunnies once again bounce freely in the low-budget horror flick *Pin* (1988).

Her most skintastic performance, however, took place in *Sweet Murder* (1990), a Canuck version of *Single White Female* (1992) (which is odd, since it was released two years before the Bridget Fonda flick). As the kooky chick with killer double barrels, Helene gave us boob, booty, and a full-frontal nude shot. Udy-la-la!

SKIN-fining Moment:

Pin (1:03) Ms. Udy shows off two tight li'l boobies in her bedroom.

See Her Naked In:

Sweet Murder (1990) FFN, Buns
Pin (1988) Breasts
One Night Only (1986) Breasts, Buns
Pick-up Summer (1980) Breasts

Tracey Ullman

Born: December 30, 1959
Slough Berkshire, England, UK
Skin-O-Meter: Brief Nudity

Fans of comedy must thank Tracey Ullman for introducing us to *The Simpsons* . . . oh, and she's pretty funny herself. This Briton washed onto these shores in the '80s with her eponymous comedy show on Fox, followed by her HBO series *Tracey Takes On*. Name any type of person, and it's very likely she's played it, even the type of person who would show their bum. We can't say she's shown us *Plenty* (1985), but she's not a complete skinflint either. Tracey takes on mooning, proving she's ready to bare in Robert Altman's fashion farce *Ready to Wear* (1994). Never let it be said that any actress on our roster has been left behind.

SKIN-fining Moment:

Ready to Wear (1:32) Tracey takes off her little black dress to reveal a little black thong and two pleasantly round rump-cheeks.

See Her Naked In:

Ready to Wear (1994) Thong
Household Saints (1993) LB

Liv Ullmann

Born: December 16, 1939
Tokyo, Japan
Skin-O-Meter: Brief Nudity

Liv Ullmann was already well established in her native Sweden when director Ingmar Bergman discovered her on the street in Stockholm. He put her in his classic arthouse hit *Persona* (1966), and soon she was the arthouse Marilyn Monroe. Classically beautiful Liv also made an impression on her director when the cameras weren't rolling. Ullmann and Bergman had an illicit affair, never got married, but did produce a daughter who is genetically predetermined to take over the world with her beauty and brains. Mama ain't half bad herself, of course, as she proved when flashing her funbags in *Shame* (1968). Liv has never made much of a career for herself Stateside, but she remains aware and appreciative of our cultural advances. She revealed on a Norwegian talk show in November 2003 that the only TV shows she watches regularly are *Sex and the City* and *Everybody Loves Raymond*. Hopefully, Liv knows that her American fans are hungry for another sample of her juicy Swedish meatballs.

SKIN-fining Moment:

Shame (0:01) Liv pulls up the shade, illuminating the sunny-side-ups that poke out of her PJs.

See Her Naked In:

Richard's Things (1981) LB
Shame (1968) Breasts
Ung flukt (1959) Breasts, Buns

Sharon Ullrick

Born: March 19, 1947
Dallas, Texas
Skin-O-Meter: Brief Nudity

Sharon Taggart showed promise when she delightfully debuted her charming jugs as Charlene Duggs in *The Last Picture Show* (1971). She let Timothy Bottoms play with her tops, but he didn't get far enough to declare *That's My Bush*. That honor goes to viewers of *The Harrad Experiment* (1973), who get to see Taggart's ta-tas and toybox in technicolor, which likely put a rise in co-star Don's Johnson. This was unfortunately her last pink-ture show before moving on to TV movies such as *Billy: Portrait of a Street Kid* (1977) and reprising her role as Charlene in *The Last Picture Show* sequel *Texasville* (1990). This stoppage of skinnage coincides with the actress's name change to Sharon Ullrick—does this mean there's a Mr. Ullrick keeping her covered up? Come on, dude, Sharon share alike!

SKIN-fining Moment:

The Last Picture Show (0:11) A decent gander at Sharon's Dairy Cannons when she gets topless in Timothy Bottoms's truck for a grope, though she seems to be more trouble than she's worth.

See Her Naked In:

The Harrad Experiment (1973) FFN, Buns
The Last Picture Show (1971) Breasts

Kim Johnston Ulrich

Born: March 24, 1955
Ripon, California
Skin-O-Meter: Brief Nudity

Because Kim Johnston Ulrich works mostly in television, her marvelous milkers are kept pretty well under wraps. Since her turn on *As the World Turns*, she has added her babitude to everything from *Remington Steele* to *3rd Rock from the Sun* and most recently played "Ivy Winthrop Crane" on *Passions*. Though she's had a few theatrical parts, her most skinful role has ironically been on the boob tube. In the TV movie *Blood Ties* (1991), while Kim lay under Harley Venton, censors missed a small slippage of nippage. There's many a slip between cut and a nip . . . as the world moves.

SKIN-fining Moment:

Blood Ties (1:08) Very brief partial bunnage having sex in bed.

See Her Naked In:

Rumpelstiltskin (1995) Buns
Blood Ties (1991) Breasts

Deborah Kara Unger

Born: May 12, 1966
Vancouver, British Columbia, Canada
Skin-O-Meter: Hall of Fame

A fine-featured, delicate, sloe-eyed blonde with tit-enhancing posture, British Columbia's Deborah Kara Unger has never shied away from exuding sexual energy. The Canadian charmer positively vibrates with erotic tension throughout the duration of director and fellow Canuck David Cronenberg's *Crash* (1996). Live-wire highlights include her ass presented for kissing, boobs mauled and lolling on their own, and a selection of close-up beaver shots, including a startling hand-in-the-clam sequence that is positively electrifying. This is shock value at a very high rate of exchange.

SKIN-fining Moment:

Crash (0:45) As James Spader bangs her from behind, we get an amazingly long, leeringly luscious view of Deb's hairy loin.

See Her Naked In:

Stander (2003) Buns
Sunshine (1999) Bush
The Rat Pack (1998) Bush, Buns
Crash (1996) RB, Bush, Buns
Keys to Tulsa (1996) Bush
Highlander III: The Final Dimension (1994) Breasts, Bush, Buns
Whispers in the Dark (1992) LB, Buns

Gabrielle Union

Born: October 29, 1973
Omaha Nebraska
Skin-O-Meter: Brief Nudity

UCLA law student turned model Gabrielle Union made the jump again to acting via single-episode appearances on the hit series *Moesha*, *Malibu Shores*, and *Saved By the Bell: The New Class* in 1996. Movies followed, including the teen smashes *She's All That* (1999), *10 Things I Hate About You* (1999), and *H-E Double Hockey Sticks* (1999). (OK, maybe that last one wasn't much of a smash.) After a lead role on the short-lived series *City of Angels*, Gabrielle returned to the silver screen in such films as *Love & Basketball* (2000), *Bring It On* (2000), and *Bad Boys II* (2003), certifying her place in Hollywood history as a bona fide star. As for a boner-inducing hottie, yes, she's got that covered, too. The state of this Union will be very closely watched!

SKIN-fining Moment:

Bad Boys II (2:17) Nice nip-slip when Gabrielle hits the dirt. That's what I call a perfect union.

See Her Naked In:

Bad Boys II (2003) Nip Slip LB

V

Brenda Vaccaro

Born: November 18, 1939
Brooklyn, New York
Skin-O-Meter: Great Nudity

A much-admired, long-term veteran of the New York stage, raspy brunette Brenda Vaccaro's work in TV and film, though voluminous, has been secondary to her theatrical achievements. Vaccaro is esteemed as a pro's pro among her fellow performers, but she has never accumulated the enthralled fan base of lesser talents who wore less clothing. Brenda might be the fixation of tribute sites galore if she'd left behind a trail of explosive exposure such as her breast-flaunting bedroom taunting of Jon Voight in *Midnight Cowboy* (1969). Her face-gnashing, knocker-mashing stint beneath the thrust of Voight is sufficient for this classy broad to earn her due from Mr. Skin, but then Brenda went the extra mile—and the extra decades—with a surprising (and even more surprisingly sexy) nude scene in *Sonny* (2003). Brenda was sixty-three years old when she shot this latest topless turn, throwing down a challenge to Grandmas everywhere for the title of GILF of the 21st Century.

SKIN-fining Moment:

Midnight Cowboy (1:30) A speedy look at Brenda Vaccaro's Camaro's as she humps Jon Voight.

See Her Naked In:

Sonny (2002) Breasts
House by the Lake (1976) Breasts
Summertree (1971) Breasts
Midnight Cowboy (1969) Breasts

Justina Vail

Kuala Lumpur, Malaysia
Skin-O-Meter: Brief Nudity

We sure like the set of brains on "Dr. Olga Vukavitch," the ravishing Russian played by Justina Vail on UPN's *Seven Days*. Born in Malaysia to British parents and raised in Hong Kong, Justina is all hot! Her screen efforts include the former girlfriend of *Jerry Maguire* (1996), "Beautiful Girl" in *Kiss the Girls* (1997), and an un-Vail-ing performance in the aptly titled *Naked Souls* (1995). Not only are this Brit's boulders visible, she exposes her shepherd's pie and rides one lucky bloke's banger. Who knew Olga could be so volga?

SKIN-fining Moment:

Naked Souls (0:29) If the totally naked and mega-hot Justina Vail ever rides on top of you while sucking on your fingers . . . do what this guy does: just LAY THERE and ENJOY IT!

See Her Naked In:

Naked Souls (1995) FFN

Nancy Valen

Born: December 16, 1970
Hallandale, Florida
Skin-O-Meter: Brief Nudity

As sultry Captain Samantha Thomas, Nancy Valen is one of the most underpraised beauties of the *Baywatch* dynasty. Of course, the problem may be that Nancy's later pursuits focused on family fare. Even then, she was certainly sexy as Detective Angela Archer—moonlighting as The Angel of Death—on the syndicated actioner *Black Scorpion*. But you have to look back to Nancy's early days for a memorable slip of the nip, when she's jumping out of bed as a young co-ed in the debate-team drama *Listen to Me* (1989).

SKIN-fining Moment:

Listen to Me (0:06) Super-quick left breast in bed with her boyfriend when Kirk Cameron comes in and ruins everybody's fun.

See Her Naked In:

Final Embrace (1992) Body Double—Breasts, Bush
Listen to Me (1989) LB

Monique van de Ven

Born: July 28, 1952
Zeeland, Netherlands
Skin-O-Meter: Great Nudity

Monique van de Ven is a Dutch treat, an act-chest of considerable assets, including a svelte body and a willingness to show it off whilst utterly naked. She started her career with a turn in the Paul Verhoeven-directed, Rutger Hauer-starring skin flick *Turkish Delight* (1973), in which she firmly planted her foot in the ass of stardom in the skintastic role of Olga. Monique appeared nude throughout, including a "mixing the pudding" scene that's sure to get your tapioca bubbling. She teamed up again with Verhoeven and Hauer for another starring role in *Keetje Tippel* (1975), which managed to show off every bit of Monique's fantastic flesh yet again. By the mid '80s, though, Monique was growing tired of the Netherlands (though we'd never tire of *her* netherlands) and decided to try her hand in Hollywood like her former Dutch cohorts. Unfortunately, after such disappointments as *Tonight's the Night* (1987), *Paint It Black* (1989), and *The Man Inside* (1990)—oh, to be that man!—Monique returned to the Netherlands where, let's hope, she'll let her tulips bloom onscreen once more.

SKIN-fining Moment:

Turkish Delight (0:54) Rutger Hauer sticks a flower in her ass and then spanks her . . . also nice view of her shrubbery and breasts running away from him.

See Her Naked In:

Iris (1987) Breasts
Brandende liefde (1983) FFN, Buns
Keetje Tippel (1975) FFN, Buns
Turkish Delight (1973) FFN, Buns

Mamie Van Doren

Born: February 6, 1931
Rowena, South Dakota
Skin-O-Meter: Great Nudity

If Jayne Mansfield was the B-movie version of Marilyn Monroe, Mamie Van Doren was the DD-movie version of Jayne Mansfield. And

that's saying a lot. (And twice, at that!) Mamie's family moved from South Dakota to La-La Land shortly after World War II, and it didn't take long for the then-Joan Olander to snag first prize in the Miss Palm Springs beauty contest. Despite her discovery by breast fetishist Howard Hughes, her career didn't take off the way Jane Russell's did, even with a nice turn in the Doris Day laugher *Teacher's Pet* (1958). After becoming the spokeswoman for the bullet bra, she was relegated, thankfully, to sleaze classics like *The Beat Generation* (1959), *The Big Operator* (1959), and *Sex Kittens Go to College* (1960). Mamie dropped out of movies after the '60s (at least for a time) but made her presence known by crashing Hollywood socials wearing notoriously outrageous, more-than-revealing outfits. In 1987 she published her memoirs, *Playing the Field*, a delicious read that detailed her torrid affairs with hundreds of Hollywood stars, from Steve McQueen to, yes, even proto-pansy Rock Hudson. In a cruel twist of fate (or stroke of luck, depending upon whom one asks) Mamie neglected to flash any flesh on film until after the sexual revolution had run its course. Long after. In 2000, at the ripe old age of sixty-nine, Mamie and her mammaries made a memorable appearance on the German television series *Liebe Sünde*. Then a few years later she flashed her flop doodles again in the college-kid comedy *Slackers* (2002)—that makes her seventy-one, for those keeping score at home. And yes, they still look magnificent.

SKIN-fining Moment:

Slackers (0:34) Mamie pulls out her massive, magnificent mammaries so Jason Schwartzman can give them a sponge bath. That's a helluva pair for a 70-year old woman!

See Her Naked In:

Slackers (2002) Breasts

TeleVisions:

Liebe Sünde Breasts

Joyce Van Patten

Born: March 9, 1934
New York, New York
Skin-O-Meter: Brief Nudity

Blonde and green-eyed Joyce Van Patten has a face that can go from an ordinary part of the crowd to a yearning object of desire depending on what the role calls for. The sister of long-time actor Dick Van Patten, Joyce has been employing her versatility and charm since the age of fourteen when she worked her first part on *The Philco Television Playhouse*. That was back in 1948. In the meantime, vivacious Van Patten filled her resumé with historic series such as *The Many Loves of Dobie Gillis*, *The Danny Kaye Show*, *The Don Rickles Show*, and *The Mary Tyler Moore Hour*. Joyce's big-screen presence was less pronounced, but keep a keen eye out for protruding nipples in *Housewife* (1972).

SKIN-fining Moment:

Bone (0:42) Breasts as she fights with Yaphet Kotto on a poker table, punctuated by a bit of butt.

See Her Naked In:

Bone (1972) Breasts, Buns

Alexandra Vandernoot

Born: September 19, 1965
Brussels, Belgium
Skin-O-Meter: Great Nudity

Like Avis is to Hertz, so the Belgians are to the French. "We Try Harder" might well be the national motto, and the sentiment of going the extra distance is certainly evident in the work ethic of Brussels-born career actress Alexandra Vandernoot. American audiences are primarily aware of Alexandra as fair maiden Tessa Noel on the sword-swinging series *Highlander*, but the citizens of France know and fear Alexandra as the upstart maverick who bravely bares what prissy Parisian misses are too chicken to show. Alexandra's daring disrobings in *L'Ange tombe du ciel* (1999), *Charmant garçon* (2000), and *Gangsters* (2002) have French cineastes shaking in their boots—and she'll shiver your timbers, too.

SKIN-fining Moment:

Dilemma *Alexandra displays her Vanderknockers and side buns while lying atop a guy in bed.*

See Her Naked In:

Gangsters (2002) Buns
Charmant garçon (2000) RB
L'Ange tombe du ciel (1999) Breasts, Buns
Strangers (1991) Breasts
Dilemma (1989) Breasts

Vanity

Born: January 4, 1959
Niagra Falls, Ontario, Canada
Skin-O-Meter: Great Nudity

You're so vain, Denise Katrina Matthews! You probably think this bio is about you—and you're right! Former front-woman of the sexplicitly delicious girl group Vanity 6, this *nasty girl* has every reason to be proud. Previously known as Vanity, as she was christened by The Artist Formerly Known As You Know Who, in the '80s Denise was an international sex symbol best known for her bone inducing lyrics, nipple-peeking lingerie and in your face ass (and bare to boot) during performances. Denise went from displaying *A* on stage, directly to movies. She showed her handful of hershey kisses in *Never Too Young to Die*

(1986) and *Action Jackson* (1988) and was her most prideful in *Tanya's Island* (1980), baring *B*-eautiful boobs, buns, and bristly black bush. Lashing out against the seven deadly sins, the former Vanity has become a born-again Christian. After bowing down to his Unholy Purpleness, she'd seem to have plenty of experience on her knees.

SKIN-fining Moment:

52 Pick-Up (0:47) *Vanity shows her can-ities while stripping for Roy Scheider while he takes Polaroids. Long scene. Outstanding!!!*

See Her Naked In:

Action Jackson (1988) Breasts
Never Too Young to Die (1986) Breasts
52 Pick-Up (1986) Breasts
Famous T&A (1982) Breasts
The Best of Sex and Violence (1981) Breasts, Buns
Tanya's Island (1980) FFN, Buns

TeleVisions:

Tales from the Crypt Breasts, Buns

Leonor Varela

Born: December 9, 1972
Santiago, Chile
Skin-O-Meter: Great Nudity

A worldly, cosmopolitan, exotic flair comes naturally to picture-perfect brunette Leonor Varela. Born in South America of Chilean and French parentage, young and lissome Leonor grew up in Costa Rica, Colorado, and France and matured into a woman so sultry that she looks like she could fire up a sauna with her left buttock alone. And still, some culture buffs claimed surprise when gazelle-graceful Leonor, a total unknown at the time, was chosen from a field of thousands to star as the title temptress in the ABC mini-series *Cleopatra* (1999). Any incredulity gave way to drop-jaw idolatry the moment Leonor appeared on set in her flowing,

diaphanous gowns. Co-star Billy Zane was so stricken by the striking multiethnic eroticist that he ended up engaged to marry her.

SKIN-fining Moment:

Pas si grave (0:40) *Varela pops out of the sack to throw on some pristine white panties, but not before she shows teaties and tail.*

See Her Naked In:

Pas si grave (2003) Breasts, Buns
Les Infortunes de la beauté (1999) Breasts, Buns

Valentina Vargas

Born: 1964
Santiago, Chile
Skin-O-Meter: Great Nudity

Latina lass Valentina Vargas works all over the globe, and what globes they are. She first made a great impression on skinophiles by climbing all over Christian Slater in the skinternational production *The Name of the Rose* (1986), getting dirty in both senses of the word. Next she roared in Germany's *The Tigress* (1992), with her pelt in plain view. France's *Chili con carne* (1999) is especially spicy, and Valentina got top billing in the credits and on her co-star. No matter what country she works in, she can still speak the language of skin.

SKIN-fining Moment:

The Name of the Rose (0:44) *Valentina strips down and straps on the man-meat of young monk Christian Slater. Hot, unholy sex and awesome eyefuls of Valentina's boobs, buns and bush.*

See Her Naked In:

Southern Cross (1999) Breasts
Chili con carne (1999) Breasts
Die Tigerin (1992) FFN, Buns
Street of No Return (1989) FFN, Buns
The Name of the Rose (1986) Breasts, Bush, Buns

Indira Varma

Bath, England, UK
Skin-O-Meter: Great Nudity

Indian born (and half Swiss) Indira Varma was always an exotic beauty, but until she took on the role of Maya in *Kama Sutra: A Tale of Love* (1996)—which was also her debut—many of us were in the dark as to the hot charms of Asia. Indira left nothing to the imagination as to why Bollywood is thriving. Better still, unlike the conservative productions that come out of Bombay, *Kama Sutra* lived up to its promise of wanton lust. Indira gave us a feast for the eyes with her breast vindaloo, curry heinie, and poon bread served up spicy and hot. She's gone on to a fine career, starring in the acclaimed BBC series *Canterbury Tales* and *Pride and Prejudice* (2004). But *Kama Sutra* remains a huge hit on video, thanks to director Mira Nair's ability to capture the jealousy and frenzied sexuality of two women who have spent nearly their entire lives together. Plus, we get to see them fondle each other.

SKIN-fining Moment:

Kama Sutra: A Tale of Love (0:15) *Breasts! Butt! Bush! And the best of all bonuses, burgerage from behind while shes being banged!*

See Her Naked In:

Zehn wahnsinnige Tage (1999) RB, Buns
Kama Sutra: A Tale of Love (1996) FFN, Buns

Roberta Vasquez

Born: February 13, 1963
Los Angeles, California
Skin-O-Meter: Great Nudity

After an appearance as the *Playboy* Playmate of the Month in November 1984, mega-mammed Latina Roberta Vasquez plunged right into acting, with a bit part in Cheech & Chong's video *Get Out of My Room* (1985). The role may have been small, but she followed it up with a meatier part in *Picasso Trigger* (1988) alongside fellow Playmates Dona Speir and Hope Marie Carlton. Unfortunately, she kept herself clothed in that one, too. She finally took the gloves off (along with everything else) after hooking up with B-movie filmmaker Andy Sidaris for a series of low-budget action thrillers: *Guns* (1990), *Do or Die* (1991), *Hard Hunted* (1992), and *Fit to Kill* (1993). All films feature lengthy looks at Roberta's round 'n' lovelies, and she shares screen time with similarly scintillating sexpot Julie Strain, among others. Though her mainstream film appearances dried up in the early '90s, you can still give her bodacious bod an extended eyeballing thanks to the many *Playboy* videos available, including *Playmate Playoffs* (1986), *Playmates at Play* (1990), and *21 Playmates Centerfold Collection Volume II* (1996).

SKIN-fining Moment:

Fit to Kill (0:52) *T&A during a torrid bedroom tussle with her man-friend.*

See Her Naked In:

Fit to Kill (1993) Breasts, Thong
Hard Hunted (1992) Breasts
Do or Die (1991) Breasts
Guns (1990) RB
Numerous *Playboy* Videos

Emmanuelle Vaugier

Born: June 23, 1976
Vancouver, British Columbia, Canada
Skin-O-Meter: Brief Nudity

Foxy French Canadian Emmanuelle Vaugier is another of the WB women who occasionally experiments in edipermity. Though she spent the early part of the millennium guesting on such WB series as *Charmed*, *Smallville*, and *One Tree Hill*, she first dabbled on the side of skin, showing how well she's molded in *The Sculptress* (2000), a.k.a. *The Demon Within*. Skip *Suddenly Naked* (2001); it doesn't apply to her. Emmanuelle's breakthrough in breastitude is *40 Days and 40 Nights* (2002). As Josh Hartnett's date, Vaugier gets violent when he fakes an orgasm with her and then tries to hide the unsoiled scumbag. Fake an orgasm with Emmanuelle? Now that's acting!

SKIN-fining Moment:

40 Days and 40 Nights (0:09) *Emmanuelle shows tons of tits (albeit in a multitude of brief flashes, but nonetheless . . .) in this sex scene with Josh Hartnett.*

See Her Naked In:

Call Me: The Rise and Fall of Heidi Fleiss (2004) LB, Buns
40 Days and 40 Nights (2002) Breasts
The Demon Within (2000) Breasts, Thong

Isela Vega

Born: November 5, 1939
Hermosillo, Sonora, Mexico
Skin-O-Meter: Hall of Fame

In what movies has Isela Vega shown her magnificent Mexican mams? Better to ask which ones she hasn't! Her last name means "fertile valley," but it's her peaks she's known for. With over sixty films to her credit, her massive maracas pop out in at least a third of them. She began in comedies such as *SOS Conspiracion Bikini* (1967) and *La Cama* (1969), a.k.a. *The Bed*, has worked with Sam Peckinpah in *Bring Me the Head of Alfredo Garcia* (1974), and continues to make movies today. The last sight of her nude nay-nays was in *Nana* (1985). Bring me the rack of Isela Vega!

SKIN-fining Moment:

Bring Me the Head of Alfredo Garcia (0:48) *Breasts when Kris Kristofferson rips off her shirt. Long scene.*

See Her Naked In:

Nana (1985) Breasts
Amantes del señor de noches (1983)
El Macho bionico (1981) FFN, Buns
Una Gallina muy ponedora (1981) FFN, Buns
Las Mujeres de Jeremías (1980) FFN
Las Tentadoras (1980) FFN
La Pulquería (1980) FFN
La Pecadora (1979) FFN
Oro rojo (1978) FFN
Muñecas de medianoche (1978) Breasts, Buns
Las Apariencias engañan (1978)
Acto de posesión (1977) FFN
Celestina (1976) Breasts
Drum (1976) Breasts
El Hombre de los hongos (1976) Breasts
La India (1975) FFN, Buns
Bring Me the Head of Alfredo Garcia (1974) Breasts
De Noche el deseo hega (1973)
The Deadly Trackers (1973) LB
Las Golfas (1969) Breasts

Paz Vega

**Born: January 2, 1976
Sevilla, Spain
Skin-O-Meter: Great Nudity**

Spanish director Pedro Almodóvar's *Talk to Her* (2002) included a suddenly skinteresting black-and-white silent film within the film that featured a giant, sleeping, naked woman. Arthouse habitués left the theater wondering, "Who was that slumbering seductress? How can I see more of her, when she is awake and moving around and still naked?" The giant object of brunette desire is named Paz Vega. She is the most beautiful screen presence ever to come out of Sevilla, Spain. Her entire, gloriously natural, supple, and gravity-defying body can be seen standing, running, lying down, and writhing on the ground in *Lucía y el sexo* (2001). Bush galore, butt galore, boobs galore; If the local video store's foreign section does not stock this film, an expedition to Europe may be in order.

SKIN-fining Moment:

Sex and Lucia (0:22) Paz's boyfriend strips her naked despite the fact that she's passed out drunk.

See Her Naked In:

El Otro lado de la cama (2002) Breasts
Talk to Her (2002) FFN
Sex and Lucia (2001) FFN, Buns
Zapping (1999) Breasts, Buns

Concha Velasco

**Born: November 29, 1939
Valladolid, Spain
Skin-O-Meter: Great Nudity**

Some names transcend the limitations of conflicting languages, and that is why a discerning man knows before he sees her, from her tag alone, that Concha Velasco is an exotic, international sex symbol. A seriously trained dancer whose first cinematic exposure came in 1954, Concha has reigned on the stage and screen of her native Spain in a career that has outlasted the tenure of a dictator for life, survived the depleted influence of a waning monarchy, and burgeoned with the emergence of a vibrant democracy. In comedies and tragedies, Concha has embodied the vibrant, life-loving soul of her native land, and in *Yo soy Fulana de Tal* (1975), she flashed that vibrant embodiment in a fully nude bathtub frolic.

SKIN-fining Moment:

Yo soy Fulana de Tal (1:16) Concha poses nude for a painting and we see her plucky pair of boobies.

See Her Naked In:

Libertad provisional (1976) Breasts
Esposa y Amante (1976) Breasts, Buns
Yo soy Fulana de Tal (1975) Breasts

Patricia Velasquez

**Born: January 31, 1971
Guajira, Venezuela
Skin-O-Meter: Brief Nudity**

Venezuelan-born model-turned-actress Patricia Velazquez has been showcasing her exotic beauty in fashion and men's mags for years—we're particularly fond of her dripping-wet appearances in the annual *Sports Illustrated Swimsuit Edition*. Her skinematic contributions, however, were unremarkable until her appearance in the blockbuster action-adventure flick *The Mummy* (1999), starring Brendan Fraser. Patricia's cocoa-brown eyes and feline grace were put to excellent use in her role as the Pharoah's adulterous wife, Anck Su Namun. Though she didn't appear in the altogether, she did wear an outfit consisting mostly of a thin coat of gold body paint that'll have you drooling in your lap and crying for your Mummy. A sequel was inevitable, and, lucky for skinophiles, Patricia's role in *The Mummy Returns* (2001) was expanded to include a swimsuit-clad fight sequence with curvy co-star Rachel Weisz. Since she seems to wear less clothing in each film she makes, here's hoping she'll loosen the bandages a tad in her next go-round.

SKIN-fining Moment:

Mindhunters If you're a man-hunter, you can spy some nipple while Pat soaps up in the shower. And I know you can do it.

See Her Naked In:

Mindhunters (2004) RB
Sports Illustrated: '94 Swimsuit Video (1994) Thong

Diane Venora

**Born: August 10, 1952
Hartford, Connecticut
Skin-O-Meter: Brief Nudity**

If you happen to be a single male who is also a troubled or troubling genius, and you are in the market for a mate, you would be wise to ask New York-based stage-and-screen luminary Diane Venora out on a date. The black-haired, pale-complected beauty has portrayed the wife of messed-up jazz giant Charlie Parker in *Bird* (1988), the estranged, pill-popping, sexually active bride of raging copper Al Pacino in *Heat* (1995), and the soon-to-be widow of megalomaniac painter Pablo Picasso in *Surviving Picasso* (1996). Perhaps you'd like to savor a look at Diane's goods before sealing the deal? Then slip into something comfortable and delight in Diane's delectable epidermis as it lights up *Terminal Choice* (1985).

SKIN-fining Moment:

Terminal Choice (0:48) Diane's character indulges in nookie and some right-side rackage comes into view. Since the shot's face-free, though, it could be a Body Double.

See Her Naked In:

Terminal Choice (1985) LB

Brenda Venus

Biloxi, Mississippi
Skin-O-Meter: Brief Nudity

With straight, jet-black hair framing the perfect, pleasing oval of her cherubic and placid face, as pale and deeply lustrous as a pearl, queenly Mississippian Brenda Venus might easily have posed as though rising out of an oyster shell for the Re-naissance painter Botticelli's immortal *Birth of Venus*. Unfortunate for art history class, but fortunate for those eager aesthetes who haunt video-store rental shelves, Brenda was born a few hundred years too late to be hanging in some dusty European museum but just in time for the 1970s explosion in exploitation cinema. Admire this modern masterpiece in *The Psycopath* (1973), *Foxy Brown* (1974), or *The Swashbuckler* (1976).

SKIN-fining Moment:

The Eiger Sanction (1:04) Brenda shows her bodacious booty after peeling off her pants, then some very nice boobs while getting into bed with Clint NORTHwood.

See Her Naked In:

The Eiger Sanction (1975) Breasts, Buns

Maribel Verdú

Born: October 2, 1970
Madrid, Spain
Skin-O-Meter: Hall of Fame

Born in Madrid, Spain, this senorita caliente is already a big-name show stopper in her native country. Unfortunately, even though Maribel Verdú's film *Belle époque* (1992) won an Academy Award for Best Foreign Film, it didn't exactly serve to make her a household name here in the States. Fortunately, that all changed when Maribel took a part in the surprise international sensation *Y tu mamá también*

MR. SKIN'S TOP TEN

Naked Stars from Spain
. . . Bare-celona babes

10. Penelope Cruz

9. Inés Sastre

8. Leonor Watling

7. Soledad Miranda

6. Ariadna Gil

5. Amparo Muñoz

4. Elena Anaya

3. Paz Vega

2. Victoria Abril

1. **Maribel Verdú**

(2001), in which she played the Older Lady joining young, dumb, and full-of-come teenagers Gael Bernal and Diego Luna on a road trip. Naturally, the little venture included a sack-load of hot, hot sex, some of which (most notably the three-way at the end) appeared to have *not* been simulated. And yes, every last inch of Maribel's incredible body is put on complete, plain-as-day display. No wonder the movie won so many awards. For some nice, somewhat tamer shots of Maribel's chi-chis, have a look at *Goya en Burdeos* (1999). For some seriously (some might say hardcore) good stuff, check out *Lovers* (1991), where the delightful muchacha gets downright dirty with Victoria Abril, Spain's other hot mamacita. Now that's the kind of acting we can get behind!

SKIN-fining Moment:

Y tu mamá también (1:34) Breasts . . . then panties come off when the two teenagers get busy with her. One of the hottest menage scenes you'll ever see. Very explicit.

See Her Naked In:

Y tu mamá también (2001) FFN, Buns
Goya en Burdeos (1999) FFN, Buns
Frontera Sur (1998) Bush
El Entusiasmo (1998) RB, Buns
Carreteras secundarias (1997) Breasts, Buns
La Buena estrella (1997) RB, Buns
La Celestina (1996) Breasts, Bush
Huevos de oro (1993) FFN, Buns
Tres palabras (1993) RB
El Beso del sueño (1992) FFN
Belle époque (1992) Nip Slip LB
Lovers: A True Story (1992) Bush
Salsa rosa (1991) Breasts
Sinatra (1988) Breasts, Bush
Soldadito español (1988) FFN
El Aire de un crimen (1988) Breasts
La Estanquera de Vallecas (1987) LB
El Orden cómico (1986) Breasts

Petra Verkaik

Born: November 4, 1966
Los Angeles, California
Skin-O-Meter: Great Nudity

Ah, Petra Verkaik. Red-blooded males everywhere know her as the leggy brunette with a face like an angel and the awe-inspiring rack of a Russ Meyer girl—and every ounce of those DD-cup beauties is natural. It's no small wonder that as of 2003 the bodacious Bunny has made more appearances in *Playboy* than any other centerfold model. But what of her skinematic roles? She's had bit parts in a couple of flicks, including *Pyrates* (1991) and *Rainbow Drive* (1990), and even doffed her bra for a couple of must-see scenes in *The Last Road* (1997), co-starring Amazonian *Penthouse* Pet Julie Strain. One of Petra's sillier, saucier appearances was during an Al Bundy dream sequence on the trashy TV sitcom *Married . . . with Children*—the top-heavy vixen made a cameo as a cover girl for the aptly named *Big Uns* magazine. If you want to see every inch of Petra, however, you can choose from a slew of fleshtastic *Playboy* video titles such as *Sexy Lingerie II* (1990), *Wet & Wild III* (1991), and *Centerfold Fantasies* (1997).

SKIN-fining Moment:

The Last Road (0:18) Petra plies her boyfriend with her bare boo-boos and bunnage.

See Her Naked In:

The Last Road (1997) Breasts, Thong
Centerfold Fantasies (1997) FFN, Buns
Numerous *Playboy* Videos

Kate Vernon

Born: 1961
Canada
Skin-O-Meter: Great Nudity

When your first exposure to the world of entertainment is a role as "Cellmate" in the skin classic *Chained Heat* (1983), then no holes are barred for onscreen nudity. Oddly, Kate Vernon didn't take off her clothes in her debut, but it wasn't long before the mini-mammed blonde was shaking her moneymaker in a sordid selection of sinema's breast. This cutie almost became an architect after high school but decided she'd prefer erecting something a little bit more human, like those skyscrapers in men's pants, and so she went off to Hollywood and built a career. By *Roadhouse 66* (1984) and *Alphabet City* (1984), Kate was already flashing her light fantastics onscreen. Then it was off to the boob tube, dressed in sexy attire, to make the nighttime soap *Falcon Crest* something to crow about. She went from the sweet "Lorraine Prescott" on that show to the bitchy "Benny" on the series *Pretty in Pink*. Back on the big screen Kate was breaking the color barrier in Spike Lee's *Malcolm X* (1992), locking juicy lips with Denzel Washington. But she broke the skin barrier in such titles as *Soft Deceit* (1994), *Dangerous Touch* (1994), and *Bloodknot* (1995), which was her last but most lustful nudity. There's a town in New York called Mount Vernon—Mr. Skin hopes Kate's there because he's flying in for a quickie.

SKIN-fining Moment:

Dangerous Touch (0:29) Nice shot of those natural cups when she rides lucky Lou Diamond Phillips in a convertible.

See Her Naked In:

Bloodknot (1995) Breasts, Bush
Dangerous Touch (1994) Breasts
Soft Deceit (1994) RB
Hostile Takeover (1988) Breasts
Roadhouse 66 (1984) Breasts
Alphabet City (1984) Breasts

Victoria Vetri

Born: September 26, 1944
San Francisco, California
Skin-O-Meter: Great Nudity

In a world where the milk in your fridge usually lasts longer than the average Playmate's career, model/actress Victoria Vetri has succeeded against all odds. The sexpot-cum-starlet first came into the public eye with her 1967 centerfold appearance in *Playboy* (she was voted Playmate of the Year in 1968) and continued her reign with a heaping helping of TV and movie appearances. The small screen was graced with her kittenish beauty via appearances on shows such as *Bonanza*, *The Man from U.N.C.L.E.*, *Hogan's Heroes*, and *Batman*. Her skinematic output boasts not one but two chances to gaze upon her curvaceous charms. She had a prehistorically prurient skinny-dipping scene in *When Dinosaurs Ruled the Earth* (1970) and bared buoyant boobage in *Invasion of the Bee Girls* (1973). The Italian-sired lovely even made an appearance in Roman Polanski's classic horror film *Rosemary's Baby* (1968), playing the ill-fated neighbor to pert-nipped pixie Mia Farrow.

SKIN-fining Moment:

Group Marriage (0:28) Long looks at Vicki's va-vooms and caboose when she climbs into bed with enough guys for each of her inputs.

See Her Naked In:

Invasion of the Bee Girls (1973) Breasts, Buns
Group Marriage (1972) Breasts, Buns
When Dinosaurs Ruled the Earth (1970) Breasts, Bush, Buns

Cerina Vincent

Born: February 7, 1979
Las Vegas, Nevada
Skin-O-Meter: Great Nudity

> "Taking this role was a huge decision for me, and I didn't know whether I could do it. I hadn't done nudity before. I fell in love with the character so much that I'm always naked now. I walk around naked. In fact, I go grocery shopping naked."
>
> —CERINA VINCENT ON *NOT ANOTHER TEEN MOVIE*

Cerina Vincent got her big acting break back in 1999 when she landed the coveted role of Yellow Galaxy Ranger on the hit kiddie series *Power Rangers Lost Galaxy*. The brunette beauty vaulted about the cosmos kicking the crap out of bad-guy aliens whilst simultaneously teaching children all sorts of valuable moral lessons. Fortunately, Cerina seems to have left the kiddie-entertainment business long behind, opting instead for parts in such adult-oriented fare as the sexy soap *Undressed* on MTV, as well as the skin milestone *Not Another Teen Movie* (2001), in which she portrayed the often-naked foreign exchange student Areola. Although she stayed just shy of a full-frontal flash in the flick, Cerina's remarkable rack appears in all its naked glory in every scene she's in. Hey, Hollywood, here's how to save dough on your costume budgets!

SKIN-fining Moment:

Not Another Teen Movie (0:11) Breasts so beautiful that even the subtitles clear the way! Cerina's fun bags take front and center as she chats with the school principal, then we get a quick peek at her lovely rump, and then a few more titty shots! Wow!

See Her Naked In:

Cabin Fever (2002) Breasts
Not Another Teen Movie (2001) Breasts, Buns

Vitamin C

Born: July 27, 1970
Old Bridge, New Jersey
Skin-O-Meter: Brief Nudity

Always take your Vitamin C, says Mr. Skin. The svelte, orange-haired hottie was born Colleen Fitzpatrick (lucky Patrick), and began her career as the nemesis of rotund Ricki Lake in John Water's *Hairspray* (1988). Vitamin C followed her little lungs into a career change as a singer in the British band Eve's Plum. While audiences watered over Vitamin C's plum, her big success came in 1999 with the release of her chart-topping solo album. From here on out the "C" in Vitamin C stood for cinema, as she returned to the big-screen as herself in *Da Hip Hop Witch* (2000), *Scary Movie 2* (2001), *Get Over It* (2001), and the TV series with the funny name, *The Andy Dick Show*. Yes, Vitamin C is good for you, especially when it comes in female form.

SKIN-fining Moment:

Dracula 2000 (0:57) Brief shot of her Vitamin B's on top of Dracula.

See Her Naked In:

Dracula 2000 (2000) Breasts

Darlene Vogel

Born: October 25, 1962
Danbury, Connecticut
Skin-O-Meter: Great Nudity

When a woman is blonde and clear eyed with an easy, dazzling smile, such as seen on the face of actress Darlene Vogel, it's easy to believe everything she says. When Darlene, an alumna of New York's Fashion Institute of Technology, appeared in television commercials and seductively informed us that "milk does a body good," we naturally took what she said as gospel, especially as it was coming from a body with such good milkers. Darlene and her darling dairy spouts rode the milk train to television prominence, first in five years of fitting into bikinis and revealing casual wear as a star attraction of *Pacific Blue*, and later as a slinky fox in form-fitting outfits prowling the stages of *One Life to Live*. When Darlene tosses back her shoulders and flexes her physique, you can be sure that every word of her body language is the God's honest truth.

SKIN-fining Moment:

Ring of Steel (0:15) Darlene bucks atop the baloney pony, plastic love-pillows careening as she climaxes in profile.

See Her Naked In:

Ring of Steel (1994) Breasts
Ski School (1991) Breasts

W

Lindsay Wagner

Born: June 22, 1949
Los Angeles, California
Skin-O-Meter: Brief Nudity

Los Angeles, California, is world renowned as a spawning ground for beautiful, sexually forward women. A pulchritudinous example of the local produce is light-brunette 1970s jiggle sensation Lindsay Wagner. A lean but built specimen of California cool, Lindsay first hit the big money during a guest spot as Jamie Sommers on the TV sensation *The Six Million Dollar Man*. Wagner's character was so richly received that she soon had a series of her own, *The Bionic Woman*. Although she never shed her clothes while within the range of network cameras, Wagner did keep her often erect nipples and bra-free bosom within the frame of action. Adolescent boys of all ages flocked to her fan club.

SKIN-fining Moment:

Two People (1:18) Bionic boobies! Lindsay loses her her shirt while getting lovey dovey in a bedroom with Peter Fonda. Come see her Six Million Dollar Titlets!

See Her Naked In:

Two People (1973) Breasts

Natasha Gregson Wagner

Born: September 29, 1970
Los Angeles, California
Skin-O-Meter: Hall of Fame

Natasha Gregson Wagner is genetically programmed for extreme hotness. The daughter of Natalie Wood and Richard Gregson, stepdaughter of Robert Wagner, and niece of Lana Wood, she also has big-time Hollywood success destined through her pedigree. Natasha debuted in *Dark Horse* (1992) opposite the mega-mam talent Mimi Rogers. Natasha sports a more streamlined pair than Mimi, but she's happy to share. She first bared her sweet half-grapefruit-sized little boobies in the thriller *Dead Beat* (1994), but for better skin by this cute brunette check out her dimly lit sex scenes in *Lost Highway* (1997), *Another Day in Paradise* (1998), and *Modern Vampires* (1999). Natasha's breast skinchievement is a toss up between *First Love, Last Rites* (1997) and *The Way We Are* (1997). The latter gets a heads up, if you know what we mean, for anyone who claims to have an interest in this American pixie. She is more or less naked for the entirety of her small role, including some great butt shots and even a brief frontal while taking a shower, which reveals her ever-so-neatly trimmed little beaver. Good things do come in small packages, and Natasha is one petite powerhouse.

SKIN-fining Moment:

Modern Vampires (0:50) Ferociously sexy servings of Nat's delicious dubloons when she gets it on atop a car with Casper Van Dien.

See Her Naked In:

Modern Vampires (1999) Breasts
Another Day in Paradise (1998) Breasts
Lost Highway (1997) Breasts
First Love, Last Rites (1997) Breasts, Buns
The Way We Are (1997) FFN, Buns
Dead Beat (1994) RB

Corinne Wahl

Born: September 30, 1953
Boston, Massachusetts
Skin-O-Meter: Great Nudity

Just because a star of tape and screen has most often been cast in roles such as Voluptuous Woman and Debutante doesn't mean that she isn't important as a human being, especially when that star is Corinne Wahl. Corinne was a three-time *Penthouse* Pet, which means two things: She's combustibly hot in the body area, and chances are her smoldering smokestacks will show up in the celluloid limelight. The great thing about Corinne's anonymous sexual supporting roles is that they are so obviously and effectively her! Those are her fertile, engulfing hips! That's her downy-soft washboard tummy! The billowy head of auburn tresses? Hers alone! Have we forgotten anything? Just two tits, each as big and round and natural as her skull, but both way softer.

SKIN-fining Moment:

Amazon Women on the Moon (1:13) *A sweet, lengthy look at Corrine's mammoth mounds as she simulates a silly porno movie.*

See Her Naked In:

Screwball Hotel (1988) Buns
Amazon Women on the Moon (1987) Breasts
New York Nights (1984) Breasts
Brainwaves (1982) FFN
C.O.D. (1981) Breasts
Hot T-shirts (1979) Breasts

Sonya Walger

London, England, UK
Skin-O-Meter: Brief Nudity

When an actress is deeply and uniquely sexy, it takes only one role for her allure to penetrate to and permeate the core longing of the collective male libido. Such is the mass yearning aroused by snooty but sensual blonde Sonya Walger, with her businesslike rack pushed forward by perfectly proper posture and her clipped English accent emanating from a pair of pursed, plush lips, as she wholly dominates and out-rates the sniveling little husband to her shining trophy wife on the HBO relationship-disaster show *The Mind of the Married Man*. One craven gawk at Sonya's swinging twins bulging and bursting from their holsters, and any man, married or single, knows why paying the cable bill is priority one.

SKIN-fining Moment:

The Vice (1999) Sonya rides man-rod while seated on a bed and then we get a hot glute shot and a wonderous wallop of her sizable right-side Walger.

TeleVisions:

The Vice RB, Buns

Ally Walker

Born: August 25, 1961
Tullahoma, Tennessee
Skin-O-Meter: Brief Nudity

Ally Walker could probably tell what we're thinking when we watch her, having played forensic psychologist "Dr. Samantha Waters" on TV's *Profiler*. And she shouldn't be surprised—we've been thinking the same thing since first seeing her on the soap *Santa Barbara* in the '80s. We never would have had these thoughts had she stayed a scientist in real life and not been discovered at a restaurant in L.A. This led to shows such as *True Blue* and films such as *Singles* (1992) and *Happy, Texas* (1999). Our thoughts were eventually realized when she skinny dipped in a scene from *Just Looking* (1995). Her full-frontal presence makes a big splash.

SKIN-fining Moment:

Just Looking (1:05) Ally goes skinny dipping, briefly showing her niplets in the water and a glimpse of underwater crotch.

See Her Naked In:

Just Looking (1995) FFN

Polly Walker

Born: May 19, 1966
Cheshire, England, UK
Skin-O-Meter: Great Nudity

A classy English lassie with a full-bodied chassis, Polly Walker is one of those eminently respectable English actresses whose accent is as high-flown as her breasts. Polly has established a solid reputation in such period-piece costume dramas as *Emma* (1996) and *Restoration* (1995). The dimpled brunette's

artistic ass-pirations are broad enough to encompass exploring the full spectrum of her ass in costume-free dramas such as *8½ Women* (1999). The countless wonders of *8½ Women* include Walker walking fully nude to the camera, standing fully nude in a sun-drenched shower, and rotating the spheres of her big, round Brit bum as she slowly spins out of bed and goes to look for some clothes.

SKIN-fining Moment:

8½ Women (1:20) Nice full-frontal shot of Polly in the shower with the old man . . . Voluptuous!

See Her Naked In:

8½ Women (1999) FFN, Buns

Laurie Wallace

Born: August 25, 1975
Baltimore, Maryland
Skin-O-Meter: Great Nudity

A true Ren-skin-sance woman, Laurie Wallace has appeared in everything from A-list Hollywood movies, network television, and *Playboy* magazine to foot fetish videos, smutty mags, and direct-to-video horror flicks, always bringing an air of high-class honey that's hard to find in mentertainment. Laurie is also an absolute goddess and usually cleans the floor with her co-stars' panties (not before getting into them) no matter the level of production. She's dipped her toes in just about every facet of skin-biz, starting with small roles in Hollywood fare like *Wild Things* (1998) and *Holy Man* (1998), quickly moving into Seduction Cinema classics like *Girl Explores Girl* (1998) and the *Erotic Witch Project* series, where her slightly augmented 34Cs get to breathe in the open air for hours. In 1999 she began her association with *Playboy* and hasn't slowed down since, lending her perfect peds to fetish videos like *Too Hot For Shoes!* (2002), *Bondage Therapy* (2002), and *Barefoot Enticements* (2002), appearing in many hardcore videos under the Katie Keane moniker, and wowing surfers with her whoppers on the world wide web at Danni's Hard Drive—Laurie's work ethic always keeps the competition at bay and her clothes far, far away.

MR. SKIN'S TOP TEN

Best Mainstream Sex Scenes
. . . The joy of sex seen

10. **Kim Basinger and Mickey Rourke**
    —*9½ Weeks* 1986 (1:12)

9. **Emma Thompson and Jeff Goldblum**
   —*The Tall Guy* 1990 (0:34)

8. **Maria Schneider and Marlon Brando**
   —*Last Tango in Paris* 1972 (1:16)

7. **Carré Otis and Mickey Rourke**
   —*Wild Orchid* 1990 (1:44)

6. **Jane March and Tony Leung Ka Fai**
   —*The Lover* 1992 (0:54)

5. **Elizabeth Berkley and Kyle MacLachlan**
   —*Showgirls* 1995 (1:24)

4. **Julie Christie and Donald Sutherland**
   —*Don't Look Now* 1973 (0:29)

3. **Sherilyn Fenn and Richard Tyson**
   —*Two Moon Junction* 1988 (1:24)

2. **Hudson Leick and Ryan Alosio**
   —*Denial* 1998 (0:43)

1. **Halle Berry and Billy Bob Thornton**
   —*Monster's Ball* 2001 (1:13)

SKIN-fining Moment:

Witchbabe: Erotic Witch Project 3 (0:16) Breast and a hint of bush as she masturbates in the woods with a feather.

See Her Naked In:

The Erotic Mirror (2002) FFN, Buns
Witchbabe: Erotic Witch Project 3 (2001) FFN

Dee Wallace-Stone

Born: December 14, 1949
Kansas City, Missouri
Skin-O-Meter: Brief Nudity

Dee Wallace-Stone's honey-blonde good looks are a classic all-American mixture of sensual yearning and knowing innocence that makes a tremendous first impression. Dee's is the kind of natural beauty, entitled yet corn-fed, that has fueled the immensely profitable image factories of designers such as Ralph Lauren and Tommy Hilfiger. After one quick sighting of Dee on a 1975 episode of *The Streets of San Francisco*, she was plucked from thousands and placed in contention for ever-lasting fame. She can be seen in such enduring 1970s classics as *The Stepford Wives* (1975) and *The Hills Have Eyes* (1977). Although she would later pop up in *E.T. the Extra-Terrestrial* (1982), Dee peaked in *10* (1979), offering a peek of her USDA prime ass. If she'd shown more, Dee Wallace-Stone might have become Farrah Fawcett. As fate had it, she was relegated to a series of "mom" roles, then faded away.

SKIN-fining Moment:

10 (1:09) Dee displays her derriere a few fleeting times while gathering up her clothes after some Horizontal Hokey-Pokey action with Dudley Moore.

See Her Naked In:

Shadow Play (1985) Breasts
10 (1979) Buns

Jessica Walter

Born: January 31, 1940
Brooklyn, New York
Skin-O-Meter: Brief Nudity

Play Misty for Me (1971) is one of the great hit thrillers of all time, mainly because of Jessica Walter's sexy psycho stalker. It was a true star turn for the stunning brunette with the sexy voice and modest titties. From there, though, Walter made her own strange career path, mixing classy indie films with multiple *Love Boat* appearances. But she's never given a bad performance and always looks supremely sexy— usually while playing an aloof beauty with smoldering sexuality. Jessica's only gotten better over the years, too, as seen in scenes from *The Flamingo Kid* (1984), *PCU* (1994), and *Slums of Beverly Hills* (1998).

SKIN-fining Moment:

Play Misty for Me (0:13) Blue-lit right boo-boo in bed when she's between the sheets with Clint Eastwood.

See Her Naked In:

Play Misty for Me (1971) RB

Julie Walters

Born: February 22, 1950
Birmingham, England, UK
Skin-O-Meter: Great Nudity

One of Britian's most beloved actresses, Julie Walters was nominated for an Oscar for her role as a working-class woman in *Educating Rita* (1983). This led to a few years of international fame and even more character roles. But to get everyone's knickers in a knot, she gave wankers worldwide something to work with by serving up her fish and chips during a full-frontal shower in *She'll Be Wearing Pink Pyjamas* (1984) and again cutting open the corset for *Personal Services* (1987), in which she played a real-life London madam. Nearly twenty years later, and in the wake of her recent success in the *Harry Potter* movie series, Juile returned to her raunchy roots with a strip-down ivory-tickling scene in *Calendar Girls* (2003), giving up the bum and back, and proving that, even at fifty-three years old, she still has that skin spark.

SKIN-fining Moment:

She'll Be Wearing Pink Pyjamas (0:07) Julie's in the middle, sudsing up with some other mature, totally naked matrons in the shower. All three B's for all involved!

See Her Naked In:

Calendar Girls (2003) Buns
Personal Services (1987) LB
She'll Be Wearing Pink Pyjamas (1984) FFN, Buns

Laurie Walters

**Born: January 8, 1947
San Francisco, California
Skin-O-Meter: Great Nudity**

Wispy, thin brunette Laurie Walters started working way ahead of the nudity curve and ended flat-out fully clothed. Though her career arc opposes the commonly seen descent into B-movie booby and bun exposure, fans of willowy Walters can take solace in the fact that their girl was at one time a ground-breaking mound shaker. *The Harrad Experiment* (1973) was considered quite risqué for its time. The film's open-shirt, pants-off policy gave skinema devotees of the day every reason to believe that it was heralding a new age of frank, muff-baring movies. The plot concerned a group of advanced-placement college students who enrolled in a special program where they exchanged their bell bottoms and peasant blouses for bare skin. Laurie's shy poolside prancing is head to foot revealing, front and

back. The lissome lass might have become a skin icon. Unfortunately, she landed a part on *Eight Is Enough*, which pulled her into the TV eye, a locus from which she rarely emerged.

SKIN-fining Moment:

The Harrad Experiment (0:42) She takes off her robe and shows it ALL when going skinny dipping with Don Johnson.

See Her Naked In:

Famous T&A (1982) FFN
Love All Summer (1974) Breasts
The Harrad Experiment (1973) FFN, Buns

Melora Walters

**Born: October 21, 1968
Riyadh, Saudi Arabia
Skin-O-Meter: Great Nudity**

Blonde, with a strong-featured, striking face, solid high tits, and long legs topped by a hot ass, Melora Walters has used her strengths to good advantage. Evidently, wicked Walters couldn't wait for her stint on *Roseanne* to end so she could get some air on her skin. Her ensemble bits in Paul Thomas Anderson's *Boogie Nights* (1997) and *Magnolia* (1999) featured quick bursts of incidental flesh, but Walters writhed in front-and-center blonde abandon as a tits-out lap dancer in *Twenty Bucks* (1993). For much more of Melora, give a gander to her gleeful full sexposure in *Los Locos: Posse Rides Again* (1997). Melora's pussy trots right along with them, hanging out as she breezes across the screen.

SKIN-fining Moment:

Twenty Bucks (0:14) T&A as stripper. Melora gets ready to earn some single dollar bills at a bachelor party.

See Her Naked In:

Cold Mountain (2003) Breasts, Buns
Desert Saints (2002) Breasts

Speaking of Sex (2001) LB, Buns
Magnolia (1999) Breasts
Los Locos: Posse Rides Again (1997) FFN, Buns
Twenty Bucks (1993) Breasts, Buns
America's Deadliest Home Video (1993) Breasts

TeleVisions:

Dream On LB

Jess Walton

**Born: February 18, 1949
Grand Rapids, Michigan
Skin-O-Meter: Great Nudity**

Tall and stately slim-line brunette Jess Walton carries around a TV resumé that reads like an induction sheet for the television arts hall of fame. The Michigan-born, Canadian-raised classic beauty can be enjoyed on reruns of *Gunsmoke*, *Cannon*, *Kojak*, *S.W.A.T.*, *The Streets of San Francisco*, *Starsky and Hutch*, *Ironside*, and *Marcus Welby, M.D.*. After sailing through the '70s at the breezy fore of TV's golden age, Jess blew into a recurring role on daytime standard *The Young and the Restless* at the end of the '80s, where she connived and thrived for more than a decade.

SKIN-fining Moment:

The Peace Killers (0:46) Extensive look at Ms. Walton's watermelons as a disgusting group of thugs tear off her top during a pre-rape rumble.

See Her Naked In:

Monkeys in the Attic (1974) Breasts, Bush, Buns
The Peace Killers (1971) Breasts

Lalla Ward

**Born: June 28, 1951
London, England, UK
Skin-O-Meter: Brief Nudity**

She joined young Kim Catrall in displaying her rosy ass in *Rosebud*

(1975), but Lalla Ward really got our trousers pitching the big tent with her role in *Vampire Circus* (1972). She may have been born as Honourable Lady Sarah Ward, daughter of Lord Bangor, but Lalla's acting career was strictly for the masses. She's a sci-fi legend thanks to her work in *Dr. Who* projects, but Lalla eventually gave up acting in favor of writing and painting.

SKIN-fining Moment:

Rosebud (0:19) Yet another bare bottom comes courtesy of kidnappee Lalla Ward.

See Her Naked In:

Rosebud (1975) Buns

NIGHT SCHOOL: WAIT, I THOUGHT "B" WAS FOR SOMETHING ELSE! A CLASSIC POSTER FROM THE SLASHER ERA, A GOLDEN TIME IN TERMS OF SCREAMING NUBILES TURNING UP NAKED ON SCREEN.

Rachel Ward

Born: September 12, 1957
Cornwell Manor, Oxfordshire, England, UK
Skin-O-Meter: Great Nudity

Big eyes flashing with the pleading of a doe, sinewy flesh coiling and striking with the grace of a serpent, brunette Rachel Ward is a heartbreaker. Although the intense, deeply erotic Englishwoman is stunning to the eyes in a wide range of roles, her thin limbs and large, devil-given breasts are used to best effect in the portrayal of the femme fatale. Rachel is always a danger to the screen, scorching the celluloid even in such seemingly innocuous fare as the early Steve Martin vehicle *Dead Men Don't Wear Plaid* (1982). When she actually drops her top or lifts her sexquisite bum to the footlights, prepare to become a lost cause. Abandon all resistance, ye who enter *Night School* (1981) or wager to remain complacent *Against All Odds* (1984).

SKIN-fining Moment:

Night School (0:29) Quick upper boobage and a nice moment of Rachel's rear-end as some weirdo slathers red paint all over her nude, showering form.

See Her Naked In:

Double Jeopardy (1992) Breasts
Against All Odds (1984) Buns
Night School (1981) Breasts, Buns

Susan Ward

Born: April 15, 1976
Monroe, Louisiana
Skin-O-Meter: Brief Nudity

A smoky and smokin' brunette with sexquisite gem-cut eyes set in a sinsational heart-shaped face, model turned onscreen showstopper Susan Ward has been cast as an ideal of female attraction, and she certainly fits the picture. Susan's flashes of dramatized desire stole their first scenes on the set of daytime dysfunction junction *All My Children*. She soon moved on to hogging all the prurient attention paid to *Malibu Shores* and *Sunset Beach*. Something about Ward's ability to emote in a bikini landed her the assignment to play a perfect walking wet dream in *Shallow Hal* (2001), where she fills out a sports bra and camisole. For a look at the miracles that lie beneath, delve into *The In Crowd* (2000). Susan's perfectly sculpted tits and their pop-out nips are a true revelation.

SKIN-fining Moment:

The In Crowd (0:18) Brief left ta-ta in jeans talking to Lori Heuring.

See Her Naked In:

The In Crowd (2000) Breasts

Arian Waring Ash

Skin-O-Meter: Brief Nudity

With a name like Arian Waring Ash you'd expect this talented newcomer to be an ass-kicker, but instead this comely dark-haired pretty is almost waif-like in her appearance and into making love, not war. She proves that explicitly in the gritty Vietnam drama *Tigerland* (2000), which also offers her sole movie skin—but be patient, she's young and too hot for the clothes to stay on for long. Her debut came in the early '90s TV series *Welcome Freshmen*, and Arian looked welcoming to all comers. She followed that up with the sexy made-for-TV thriller *The Babysitter's Seduction* (1996). She mostly shows up onscreen in bit parts, but, oh, those bits. In *Phone Booth* (2002), she played one of the streetwalkers tempting Colin Farrell in torn stockings, hot pants, and a skimpy bra. Wonder why Farrell didn't get out of that phone booth and into a short-stay hotel to burn red hot with the smoking Ash?

SKIN-fining Moment:

Tigerland (0:08) Breasts and bushish getting banged on the floor by a guy while Colin Farrell watches.

See Her Naked In:

Tigerland (2000) FFN, Buns

TeleVisions:

Going to California

Julie Warner

Born: February 9, 1965
Manhattan, New York
Skin-O-Meter: Great Nudity

What is it about Julie Warner that makes you want to take a second look? Maybe it's her earthy, wholesome beauty, that certain quality of freshness that evokes images of the girl next door. Julie's small-town sensuality makes her perfect for her featured role as the country cutie of Michael J. Fox's dreams in *Doc Hollywood* (1991). Julie gets juices flowing in the first few frames of the flick, emerging from a morning swim wearing only a teeny bikini bottom and a smile. "You can blink now," she says to the flabbergasted Fox who can't take his eyes off her perky, pink-nipped pair. Doc Hollywood's advice? Take two of THOSE and don't call him in the morning! Julie's natural innocence is a cunning contrast against a comedic backdrop. She's a fresh-faced foil in Andrew Dice Clay's *The Diceman Cometh* (1989) (you bet he did!), a jewel among jokesters Chris Farley and David Spade in *Tommy Boy* (1994) (boy oh boy is she sweet), and a skinsational weekending treat with Billy Crystal in *Mr. Saturday Night* (1992). Daydreamy diddlers will be dazzled by Julie's homegrown gorgeousity in *Wedding Bell Blues* (1996) and *The Puppet Master* (1994). Warning: Repeated viewing of Ms. Warner's warm,

magnetic presence can be addictive.

SKIN-fining Moment:

Doc Hollywood (0:15) Primo PG-13 nudity as Julie skinny dips, then bares her juggles in front of Michael J. Fox.

See Her Naked In:

Doc Hollywood (1991) Breasts

T.C. Warner

Born: March 5, 1977
San Francisco, California
Skin-O-Meter: Great Nudity

T.C. Warner, a little slip of a girl, grew up with dreams of directing movies. After earning a bachelor's degree in film, this scholastic sexpot decided to flaunt her fine frame in front of the camera. T.C. played the *Teenage Cutie* in guest spots on *L.A. Law*, *Married . . . with Children*, and *Beverly Hills, 90210* before going all the way to show her T&A in the thriller *The Art of Dying* (1991). T.C.'s most recent racy performance in *Diary of a Sex Addict* (2001) is equally to die for. Warning: Too much gaping at the lusty lass may cause cramping and temporary blindness.

SKIN-fining Moment:

The Art of Dying (0:33) As T.C. takes a shower, we see her sudsy boobs and buns intercut with Kathleen Kinmont's flouncing funbaggage. Unfortunately a psycho trannie ruins the fun by knifing T.C. as she soaps up.

See Her Naked In:

The Art of Dying (1991) Breasts, Buns

Jennifer Warren

Born: August 12, 1941
New York, New York
Skin-O-Meter: Brief Nudity

Growing up in the free-spirited neighborhood of Greenwich Village,

New York, Jennifer Warren has a natural flare for the flip and flamboyant. Jen began her career as a fresh-faced funny lady on the prominently progressive series *The Smothers Brothers Comedy Hour* in the late '60s. Beloved for having both brains and boobiliciousness, she was soon snatched to play in thrillers such as *Sam's Song* (1969) with a young Robert De Niro and *Night Moves* (1975) opposite Gene Hackman. Carefree and curvy, Jen embraces Gene with open arms and an open top, becoming skintimately acquainted onscreen. In her one and only flash of flesh, Warren warmly invites Hackman to taste her succulent suckables, much to his mouthwatering delight. What sweet teats! As Paul Newman's frustrated wife in *Slap Shot* (1977), Jennifer is bewitchingly bitchy. Although she deserves a time-out for hen-pecking her poor hubby, those cashmere-crushed cazoongas and that fur-covered form still make you want to score. Finding a niche in playing the bitch, Jennifer subsequently starred in TV dramas like *Paper Dolls* (1984) and *Confessions of a Married Man* (1983). Mr. Skin triple dares you to find one performance with the juicy Jennifer that isn't simply skintastic!

SKIN-fining Moment:

Night Moves (0:56) Gene Hackman opens Jennifer's shirt and then rubs his meat-hooks all over her fleshy maw-maws.

See Her Naked In:

Night Moves (1975) Breasts

Kiersten Warren

Born: November 4, 1965
Iowa
Skin-O-Meter: Brief Nudity

Iowa-born ingénue Kiersten Warren first rang the randy alarm on *Saved by the Bell: The College Years*. While she continued to share her carrot-topped charisma in small roles in major films such as *Independence Day* (1996), *Duets* (2000), and *The Divine Secrets of the Ya-Ya Sisterhood* (2002), Kiersten was at her biggest and breast undressed baring her perky points in *Painted Hero* (1996) and *Liberty Heights* (1999). With divine Ya-Yas such as Kiersten's, this sister is a guaranteed "yowza!" in every skindeavor.

SKIN-fining Moment:

Painted Hero (0:22) Kiersten lifts her shirt and flashes her poke-em's at Dwight Yoakam.

See Her Naked In:

Liberty Heights (1999) Buns
Painted Hero (1996) Breasts

Lesley Ann Warren

Born: August 16, 1946
New York, New York
Skin-O-Meter: Brief Nudity

Naturally stacked redhead Lesley Ann Warren played the intriguing and covert Dana Lambert on the original *Mission Impossible* spy series, and tracking down hard evidence of her soft realities has been an almost impossible mission itself. Although her '60s-chic high cheekbones and wide, dark, soul-engulfing eyes were confined mostly to the small screen, Warren did bust out of the box for a showy, if sequin-covered, performance as a mobster's hot babe in *Victor/Victoria* (1981). The New York native's one confirmed nip sighting occurred almost ten years earlier. Lesley Ann fished out the natural knockouts, but only for the briefest, slightest peek, in *Where the Eagles Fly* (1972). Anyone who glides by there had better be looking with an eagle eye.

SKIN-fining Moment:

Where the Eagles Fly (0:11) Very brief breast shot when she drops her bath towel.

See Her Naked In:

Where the Eagle Flies (1972) Breasts

Dionne Warwick

Born: December 12, 1940
East Orange, New Jersey
Skin-O-Meter: Brief Nudity

Bronzilicious darling Dionne Warwick is well known as the celebrity spokesperson for the Psychic Friends Network and as the hostess with the most ass on the dance extravaganza *Solid Gold*. In her days before speaking to the dead and disco dancing, Dionne's voice was the favorite choice of lyrical legend Burt Bacharach. Lady D was at the top of the pops for several decades singing Bacharach's hit songs such as "Do You Know the Way to San Jose" and "That's What Friends are For." While Warwick's movie roles were mostly via the boob tube, her one skinematic stint was solid gold. She bared her brown-sugar babies in the little-known flick *Slaves* (1969). With such a sultry sound and delicious chocolate physique, it's easy to be enslaved by Dionne's delightful mojo.

SKIN-fining Moment:

Slaves Forget the Psychic Friends! Dionne shows her sweater friends that's what it's all about, Alfie!

See Her Naked In:

Slaves (1969) Breasts

Felicity Waterman

Skin-O-Meter: Great Nudity

Bubbly brunette Felicity Waterman's cinematic appearances are like an instant shot of sunshine. While many of her parts are small, mighty-mammed Waterman still manages to make people happy with a big splash of sexiness. She was crazy cute as the naughty naval officer on the series *Pensacola: Wings of Gold* and made *Die Hard 2* (1990) even harder with her simple appearance as a sweetly nipped stewardess. Felicity had her biggest and breast role to date in *Unlawful Passage* (1994), with bare boobage so large and in charge it could be illegal. With frontal fleshpots as full and fine as Felicity's, she borders on indecent exposure in every skindeavor.

SKIN-fining Moment:

Unlawful Passage (0:27) Nice view of her boobs whilst having sex on the beach.

See Her Naked In:

Unlawful Passage (1994) Breasts, Thong

Leonor Watling

Born: July 28, 1975
Madrid, Spain
Skin-O-Meter: Great Nudity

A Spanish-born actress with limited work experience west of the Atlantic, impish burning bush Leonor Watling is why all praise must be given to those who import foreign videos and DVDs to these shores. Brunette Leonor's face alone is enough to enchant, with its fresh burst of playful passion, its lips for nibbling, its eyes for silently communicating the need to be lavished in love. And then, as if that is not enough, there are the wondrous Watling tits. Any skin men who were dragged to the art-house on date night to sit through *Talk to Her* (2002) have already sung hosannas to the temple of Leonor. Through most of the film, she pretends to be in a coma—but a coma with no clothes on! For a far more active brand of nude revelry, including the swaying nirvana of a Leonor-on-top boff scene, venture into the skinsational

Son de mar (2001). The film has subtitles, but no one has ever looked away from Leonor long enough to read them.

SKIN-fining Moment:

Son de mar (0:25) Great toplessness as Leonor's boyfriend pulls her blouse down to play with the twins.

See Her Naked In:

Talk to Her (2002) Breasts
Son de mar (2001) FFN, Buns

Alberta Watson

Born: March 6, 1955
Toronto, Ontario, Canada
Skin-O-Meter: Hall of Fame

Perky-nipped Peta Wilson isn't the only forceful female worth yanking about on the series *La Femme Nikita*. Alberta Watson is beautifully bombastic as "Madeline," the ball-busting top banana of the show's secret terrorist tail-kicking corp. Wicked in her desire to banish the baddies, she delights in psychological and sexual manipulation, and cold-blooded, groan-gouging torture. In directives to "Nikita," you'll spy some serious Sapphic chemistry. A little bondage and discipline wanks every time. Watson watchers have been skintensely studying this ballsy beauty's performances since the '70s, when she bared her bouncy B-cups in *Power Play* (1978) and *In Praise of Older Women* (1978). Alberta receives much praise and fluid-filled sprays for performances in skinde-pendent films. Ms. Watson's career took a scandalously skincestuous turn in *Spanking the Monkey* (1994). Playing a tantalizingly twisted mom, bored with a broken leg, she turns her attention to her own son's seed, baring her ripe melons and grassy knoll as the fruit of her loins looks on. Spanktastic! If you've seen Alberta in *The Sweet Hereafter* (1988),

then you know what we're all hereafter: BOOBAGE, BOTTOMS, AND BUSH! Alberta delivers, including a full-frontal fest of *hair-iffic* proportions. Heavenly! Elementary, my dear Watson! You're skinsational in (and out of) everything you touch.

SKIN-fining Moment:

In Praise of Older Women (0:52) The always amiable "A-cup" Alberta Watson has a nice long talk with Tom Berenger while she's sitting in a chair—tits ahoy! Then it's off to bed for more "topless talk."

See Her Naked In:

The Sweet Hereafter (1997) FFN, Buns
Seeds of Doubt (1996) Body Double—Breasts
Spanking the Monkey (1994) FFN
Destiny to Order (1990) Buns
The Keep (1983) Breasts, Bush
In Praise of Older Women (1978) Breasts
Power Play (1978) Breasts

Emily Watson

Born: January 14, 1967
Islington, London, England, UK
Skin-O-Meter: Great Nudity

Look at that funny, poignantly expressive face. You see an expanse of forehead; eyes that protest, cry, beg, and demand all at once; and a mouth that is never far from a wiseacre's grin or a voluptuary's grimace. Emily Watson is one of the most talented and adventurous actresses to come out of England in the past ten years. Her daring portrayal—both muff-baring and soul-baring—of a sexual barterer who bargains for more than she can handle in *Breaking the Waves* (1996) caused the international film-going community to sit up and check its pulse. Nipples pinched and tweaked, bush out, legs splayed, sex that defied categorization as simulation— Emily had arrived at a peak most actresses never acheive.

SKIN-fining Moment:

Breaking the Waves (1:26) Full-frontal nudity lying on a bed trying to seduce the doctor.

See Her Naked In:

Hilary and Jackie (1998) Breasts
Metroland (1997) Breasts
Breaking the Waves (1996) FFN

Naomi Watts

Born: September 28, 1968
Shoreham, England, UK
Skin-O-Meter: Great Nudity

Naomi Watts has got the power! She first got a charge with Nicole Kidman, who she met at a commercial casting call when the two were unknowns. While her Aussie girlfriend shot to fame first, Naomi's lissome form was soon to follow. She debuted in *For Love Alone* (1986). Audiences loved her alone in the film, and she rode that success to the Down Under soap *Home and Away* in 1991. Mr. Skin got a glimpse of Naomi down under in a full-frontal shower scene from *Gross Misconduct* (1993). She also flashed her bouncing buoys without the cover of even a transparent shower curtain. Naomi teamed up with pixie plaything Lori Petty as the one with tits in *Tank Girl* (1995). But it wasn't until perverted director David Lynch cast her in his lesbo wet dream *Mullholland Dr.* (2001) that Noami made jaws drop and crotches rise. She fingered herself and rubbed muffs in a hot Sapphic suck down with Laura Harring. As long as Naomi Watts electrifies the big screen, Mr. Skin will always be turned on.

SKIN-fining Moment:

Mullholland Dr. (2:01) Nymph-like Naomi straddles her red–hot lesbo mama, breasts ahoy, wearing only jean-shorts. She's ready to grind . . . Oooooh yeah!

See Her Naked In:

We Don't Live Here Anymore (2004) Breasts
21 Grams (2003) Breasts
The Outsider (2002) LB
Mulholland Dr. (2001) Breasts
Gross Misconduct (1993) FFN

"My job is not the exhibition of my body. Talking with people and making friends in all nations is my main duty."

—SHAWN WEATHERLY ON WINNING THE 1980 *MISS UNIVERSE* CROWN

Carol Wayne

Born: September 6, 1942
Chicago, Illinois
Died: January 1, 1985
Skin-O-Meter: Great Nudity

Bubbly and breasty with a coquettishly sweet demeanor, Carol Wayne became famous as one of the "Tea Time Ladies" on *The Tonight Show Starring Johnny Carson*. Plumping peters and rocking Johnny's jock in low-cut dresses, Carol's cups of *T* certainly overflowed with skinspiration. Her high-pitched voice and whooping whoppers helped add some much-needed yank to late-night wank banks in the '70s. Carol finally showed Americans what they had all fantasized about in the wee TV hours in *Heartbreakers* (1984). Whether breaking hearts or fattening hard-ons, Carol Wayne is one stacked stunner for the centuries.

SKIN-fining Moment:

Heartbreakers (0:40) After doing a little dance, Carol lets loose her howlingly huge Grand Tetons for Peter Coyote.

See Her Naked In:

Heartbreakers (1984) Breasts

Shawn Weatherly

Born: July 24, 1959
Sumter, South Carolina
Skin-O-Meter: Great Nudity

It wasn't so long ago that if Miss USA or Miss Universe turned up

nude in a magazine or movie, the entire media tilted in a whirl of shame and blame. Lucky for Shawn Weatherly, and lucky for us, times have changed. Nowadays, if a high-legged, high-butted, high-racked, high-haired blonde with pageant-winner looks decides to capitalize on her credentials, we're right there with her. We've supported Shawn's career decisions and artistic visions through her stint on *Baywatch*. We've cheered the towering blonde inferno's fiery topless turn in *Thieves of Fortune* (1989). We've heartily approved of her profile of pressed-breast in *Amityville 1992: It's About Time* (1992). We encourage Shawn's further pursuits in the no-swimsuit competition.

SKIN-fining Moment:

Amityville 1992: It's About Time (0:07) Sweat-drenched casabas as she gets pumped by her husband in bed.

See Her Naked In:

Amityville 1992: It's About Time (1992) Breasts
Thieves of Fortune (1989) Breasts

Sigourney Weaver

Born: October 8, 1949
New York, New York
Skin-O-Meter: Great Nudity

Rare is the skinema fan who is alien to the allure of tall drink of hot water Sigourney Weaver. Sigourney did for cotton panties in *Alien* (1979) what Sharon Stone would do for white scarves in *Basic Instinct*

(1992). She took a lowly staple out of the woman's accessory drawer and elevated it to a fetishistic trigger. Educated at Stanford and Yale, this five-foot-ten-inch thespian is smart enough to know that "if movies are supposed to be about real people, they take off their clothes." The real Weaver's pop top pops up in *Half Moon Street* (1986). She is stark naked in stark light playing a part-time prostitute. To celebrate turning fifty, flab-free Sigourney stripped down to actual bush in *A Map of the World* (2000), showing off a physique that is still capable of blowing out all the candles.

SKIN-fining Moment:

Half Moon Street (0:39) Thrice is nice in this three-parter: jiggling jubblage while riding an exercise bike, foggy fuzzpot and fanny through the shower door, then quick boobs as she towels off.

See Her Naked In:

A Map of the World (2000) Breasts, Bush
Death and the Maiden (1994) Breasts
Half Moon Street (1986) FFN, Buns
One Woman or Two (1984) LB

Chloe Webb

Born: 1960
Greenwich Village, New York
Skin-O-Meter: Great Nudity

If not for Chloe Webb there might not be Courtney Love. The Hole singer has since transcended her baby-doll groupie roots to become a star herself. Still, the physical and behavioral similarities shared by the up-and-coming Courtney and the chaotic, doomed, destructive character Chloe Webb presented as Sid Vicious's girlfriend in *Sid and Nancy* (1986) are creepy, to say the least. In fact, Webb's channeling of a rock 'n' roll casualty is plenty creepy even without the Love connection. At times, if not for the fact that Chloe is lolling in bed with her milky dugs dangling, it would be almost painful to watch. Webb takes the pain away again in *The Belly of an Architect* (1987) and *Tales of the City* (1994). Or was that last one *Tales of Flashed Titty*?

SKIN-fining Moment:

Sid and Nancy (0:44) We see topless Chloe's punk-rocks as she mixes it up with vicious Gary Oldman.

See Her Naked In:

The Belly of an Architect (1987) RB, Buns
Sid and Nancy (1986) Breasts

TeleVisions:

Tales of the City Breasts

Amy Weber

Born: July 2, 1972
Peoria, Illinois
Skin-O-Meter: Great Nudity

She started out on *Saved by the Bell*, but Amy Weber now has a body that makes us *Screech*. She has shown tremendous versatility, and that's just her first starring role in *Forbidden Games* (1995). She's versatile by herself, with partners, and especially in a hot tub gleesome threesome with skin-temporaries Griffen Drew and Gail Harris. Amy's work since then has been much more skin-nocuous, but her voluptuous versatility is still voluminous. On television, there's her recurring role on *Port Charles* and fare such as *Undressed*, *Pacific Blue*, *L.A. Heat* (as "Julia the Nudist"), and her hosting of the reality series *Getaway*. On film, there are bit parts in *Kolobos* (1999), *Crackerjack 3* (2000), and *Joe Dirt* (2001). Amy has said she's taking voice lessons with plans to cut an album. She certainly has the lungs for it.

SKIN-fining Moment:

Forbidden Games (1:04) Nude-uddered Amy brings the bathtub to a boil by leztastically boinking a luscious brunette.

See Her Naked In:

Forbidden Games (1995) Breasts, Buns
Dangerous Seductress (1992) Breasts, Buns

Heather Weeks

UK
Skin-O-Meter: Brief Nudity

Judging from one brief scene in *Left Luggage* (1998), someone evidently did leave their luggage behind, for there are no clothes to be found on Heather Weeks. Not only is there a good shot of Weeks's peaks, Heather's feathers are also visible. Except for those few seconds of her skinny dipping with Laura Fraser, the rest of the film is fairly skin-nocuous. She's had equally tame roles as "Guest" in *Hilary and Jackie* (1998) and "Student" in *The Discovery of Heaven* (2001). The true discovery of heaven will be the day we see Heather's booboliciousness once again. We hope it's any day now; we've been waiting years to see more Weeks.

SKIN-fining Moment:

Left Luggage (0:58) Heather (on the right) hops completely naked into the lake with Laura Fraser, whereupon both British babes show all three of their B-areas as they skinny dip.

See Her Naked In:

Left Luggage (1998) FFN
Twice Upon a Yesterday (1998) LB

Teri Weigel

Born: February 24, 1962
Fort Lauderdale, Florida
Skin-O-Meter: Great Nudity

When she first careened from the heady erotic heights of *Playboy* superstardom to the grittier attractions of XXX notoriety, Teri Weigel was perhaps the most beautiful woman ever to engage in hardcore sex on film. Her plunge as the first Playmate to go hardcore in *Inferno* (1991) was one of the most anticipated crossovers in the history of sexual entertainment. Her fiery lust making was fully compatible with her unmatched, coltish beauty, exceeding all expectations.

SKIN-fining Moment:

Savage Beach (0:33) Ms. Weigel busts out her wide-load torso-torpedos taking her shirt off before hitting the sheets.

See Her Naked In:

Cooking With Porn Stars (2002) Breasts
Inside Out III (1992) Breasts
Innocent Blood (1992) Breasts, Thong
Auntie Lee's Meat Pies (1992) Thong
Predator 2 (1990) FFN
Marked for Death (1990) Breasts
Savage Beach (1989) Breasts
Far From Home (1989) Breasts
The Banker (1989) Breasts
Night Visitor (1989) Breasts
Glitch! (1988) RB, Thong
Cheerleader Camp (1987) Breasts
Numerous *Playboy* Videos
Numerous Adult Movies

Roberta Weiss

Born: September 5, 1958
Winnipeg, Manitoba, Canada
Skin-O-Meter: Great Nudity

Roberta Weiss has made smart choices in her skintastic career. This Canadian cutie has all the brown-eyed girlish gusto of look-alike Laura San Giacomo but with an added aura of exhibitionism resulting in a more boobilicious and bottom-baring body of work. This earthy-looking eyeful made her debut in *Autumn Born* (1979). As a brazen bad girl bound for punishment, Berta bends over for a vigorous fanny whacking, exposing a super shapely rear covered by only teeny white panties. What a spankilicious start! Before meeting her dark destiny with a serial killer in *The Dead Zone* (1983), Weiss's wobblers made the breast out of a scary situation. What a pair to die for! Roberta's peaches are at their succulent sweetest in *Shades of Love: Tangerine Taxi* (1988) and *Cross Country* (1983). Both offer lingering looks at her immensely appetizing areolas. Fruity, mouth-sized fun! She enjoyed a brief stint on Canadian television in *Family Passions,* but randy Roberta hasn't been seen since. If she is *Weiss,* she'll come back to the fans who miss this comely Canuck.

SKIN-fining Moment:

Cross Country (0:59) Breasts lying in bed with two other people.

See Her Naked In:

How to Make Love to a Negro. . . . (1989) Breasts, Buns
Shades of Love: Tangerine Taxi (1988) LB
The Dead Zone (1983) Breasts
Cross Country (1983) Breasts

TeleVisions:

The Hitchhiker Breasts, Buns

Rachel Weisz

Born: March 7, 1971
London, England, UK
Skin-O-Meter: Great Nudity

Rachel Weisz is best known as Brendan Fraser's sexy accessory in *The Mummy* (1999) and *The Mummy Returns* (2001). While Rachel looks hotter than high noon in the Sahara in the flicks, she sadly never unwraps. But Rachel is no newcomer to film—in fact, her earlier performances marked her as a nude-comer. She popped her skin cherry in *Advocates* (1991) with a wet, topless tub scene where her ample bosom waves a carnal hello. Proving an advocate for nudity, she exposed her gorgeous gluteus in the British TV mini-series *Scarlet &*

Black (1993). In *Stealing Beauty* (1996), Rachel's beautifully exposed rack stole Mr. Skin's attention from the young charms of her equally shirtless co-star Liv Tyler. But it was her bottomless strut in the aptly titled *I Want You* (1998) that had Mr. Skin seeing pink. Rachel loves sharing her body to this day and flashed her big white moon in *Enemy at the Gates* (2001). Let's hope Rachel keeps those gates open for a long time.

SKIN-fining Moment:

I Want You (1:15) Nice bush shot after taking off her bikini bottoms. Dark scene.

See Her Naked In:

Enemy at the Gates (2001) Buns
I Want You (1998) RB, Bush
Stealing Beauty (1996) Breasts, Bush
Scarlet & Black (1993) Buns
Advocates (1991) Breasts

Raquel Welch

Born: September 5, 1940
Chicago, Illinois
Skin-O-Meter: Never Nude

Before Raquel Welch became a movie star she was already famous as the '60s most beautifully busty bikini pinup. The five-foot-six-inch top-heavy temptress didn't make a name for herself onscreen until the sci-fi classic *Fantastic Voyage* (1966), in which scientists shrunk her 37-23-35 figure down to microscopic size to enter a man's body. Mr. Skin would like to enter Raquel's body, but at full size. For a sex symbol, Raquel is surprisingly sparse in skinage. Her breast performance may be in a fur bikini fighting off Ray Harryhausen's stop-motion animated dinosaurs in *One Million Years B.C.* (1966). The studio hyped the prehistoric picture as "Raquel Welch in Mankind's First Bikini!" She went on to the role she was born to play, Lust in *Bedazzled* (1967). In *Myra Breckinridge* (1970),

the voluptuous star removed her panties for ogle-eyed old man John Huston, not that viewers got to see anything. But then, Raquel's cleavage shows more boob than even most topless cuties are blessed with.

SKIN-fining Moment:

One Million Years B.C. (0:27) Cavebabe Raquel models mankind's first bikini on a seaside hunting expedition. The suit's made of rawhide, and seeing her in it will turn your hide raw!

Tahnee Welch

Born: December 26, 1961
San Diego, California
Skin-O-Meter: Great Nudity

It can't be easy to go through life as the daughter of the world's ideal big-breasted poster woman Raquel Welch. Life's even harder when mom only passed down about half of her world-conquering rack. Still, Tahnee Welch did her best with what superior bits and bumps did bounce her way from the gene-pool crapshoot. Tahnee's face is a winner, and no losers are born with an ass like the one she sits on. Her skin is flawless and the color of a warm, sweet, stimulating drink. She began her stay in the skinlight playing an alien seductress in *Cocoon* (1985). She did a lot of her most revealing work on the alien shores of Europe. Track down *Der Joker* (1987) for an indicative display of hanky panky, including a close-cropped bare-bottom spanking.

SKIN-fining Moment:

Night Train to Venice (1:18) Tahnee doesn't Welch in this bedroom scene with Hugh Grant. We get a glimpse of the glands she obviously didn't inherit from her mom.

See Her Naked In:

The Criminal Mind (1996) LB
Night Train to Venice (1993) Breasts
L'angelo con la pistola (1992) Breasts
La Bocca (1990) Breasts
Der Joker (1987) LB, Buns
Cocoon (1985) Body Double—Buns

Mary Louise Weller

Skin-O-Meter: Great Nudity

The time of waspish buxom blonde Mary Louise Weller upon the stage of skin was all too brief. But Mary Louise's impact will be long lasting, pounded home anew every time a young skin scout earns his boob-hunter merit badge during his first viewing of the puerile and prurient frat-boy fun classic *Animal House* (1978). Remember that massive,

---

MR. SKIN'S TOP TEN

Best Voyeur Scenes
. . . Hairy pie-ball

10. Melanie Griffith
    —*Body Double* (1984) (0:22)

9. Marie Liljedahl
    —*Inga* (1967) (0:50)

8. Lori Singer
    —*Short Cuts* (1993) (0:47)

7. Hayley Mills
    —*Deadly Strangers* (1974) (1:04)

6. Shannon Elizabeth
    —*American Pie* (1999) (0:44)

5. Priscilla Barnes
    —*Texas Detour* (1977) (1:03)

4. Laura Antonelli
    —*Venus in Furs* (1969) (0:03)

3. Morgan Fairchild
    —*The Seduction* (1982) (0:51)

2. Julie Brown
    —*Bloody Birthday* (1981) (0:13)

1. **Mary Louise Weller**
    —*Animal House* (1978) (0:39)

---

milky-white set of orbicular mammaries that filled the sorority-house window as Mandy Pepperidge stroked herself to orgasmic bliss and John Belushi bugged his eyes outside? That magic rack depended from the chest of Mary Louise Weller. Better to have blazed for one instant and faded away than to have kept your shirt on the whole time.

SKIN-fining Moment:

Animal House (0:39) As John Belushi peeps through her sorority–house window, Mary removes her bra, cups her hubba-bubbas, and slides a hand into her panties.

See Her Naked In:

Forced Vengeance (1982) Breasts, Bush
Animal House (1978) Breasts

Gwen Welles

Born: March 4, 1951
Chatanooga, Tennessee
Died: October 13, 1993
Skin-O-Meter: Great Nudity

She started out with a part on *Ironside,* but Gwen Welles went on to show enough to make even Raymond Burr's character stand up straight. Director Roger Vadim continued his Svengali-like tradition of getting actresses to strip when he cast her heavenly body in *Hellé* (1971), and she was soon showing her red mane in *Hit!* (1973), *Nashville* (1975), and *Between the Lines* (1977). After that, she was barely bare and worked skinconsistently throughout the '80s and '90s until her death in 1993. Now she's entertaining in that great Skin Central in the sky.

SKIN-fining Moment:

Hit! (2:03) Gewn takes off her top and beguiles some girl with her tits before killing her.

See Her Naked In:

Between the Lines (1977) Breasts, Buns
Nashville (1975) Breasts, Buns
Hit! (1973) Breasts
Hellé (1971) FFN

Jennifer Welles

Skin-O-Meter: Brief Nudity

She went on to porn stardom, but nobody should miss Jennifer Welles's amazingly sexy turns in mainstream films. Jennifer first shocked suburban audiences as a magician's assistant in *Is There Sex After Death?* (1970). She then showed off her amazing hourglass figure in the cult thriller *Sugar Cookies* (1973) before grooving in *The Groove Tube* (1974), dancing naked in front of young Chevy Chase. From there, Jennifer ditched the counterculture for the real underground, eventually walking off with an Erotica Award for her performance in *Little Orphan Sammy* (1976).

SKIN-fining Moment:

Sugar Cookies (0:56) Jenny provides some gratuitous skinnage while lying completely naked on a sofa, followed by a complete full-frontal flesh flash as she gets up to put on some clothes.

See Her Naked In:

The Groove Tube (1974) FFN, Buns
Sugar Cookies (1973) FFN
Is There Sex After Death? (1971) FFN, Buns
Numerous Adult Movies

Terri Welles

Born: November 21, 1956
Santa Monica, California
Skin-O-Meter: Great Nudity

Santa Monica stunner Terri Welles first caught the public's fly with a spread in *Playboy* in 1980. Her booby blonde beauty led to her being christened Playmate of the Year in 1991. You can't go wrong with any of Terri's tutelage with *Playboy*. *Playmates: The Early Years* (1992) and *Playmates of the Year: The '80s* (1989) are equally tit-tastic. Welles constantly wages the war of going above and beyond B-pictures, but she managed to lend a big bang to small parts in *The Firm* (1993) and *Ballistic* (1995). This bubbly blondie's most major role came by way of *Looker* (1981), featuring a lingering looky-loo at her humungo hoots. With Terri in toe, you can be sure that all will be well when featuring Welles.

SKIN-fining Moment:

Looker (0:02) Terri shows her topless milk-Welles when prepping for a photo shoot.

See Her Naked In:

Looker (1981) Breasts
Numerous *Playboy* Videos

Julian Wells

Skin-O-Meter: Great Nudity

Blonde and boobilicious Julian Wells is one of the Sapphic stars of Seduction Cinema, the video company responsible for some of the breast softcore skinema around. The mouth-watering Wells, along with gorgeous gal-pal muff munchers like Misty Mundae and Darian Caine, stars in Seduction's spanktastic spoofs, with mostly girl-on-girl action angles. The more mature mama of the brood, Julian plays dominating, grown-up characters convincingly with a wiser woman of the world aplomb, like the sexy psychiatrist pushing the love drug "Euphoria" in *Dr. Jekyll & Mistress Hyde* (2003) or the talk-show hostess with the most-ass "Remis Phildin" in *Who Wants to Be an Erotic Billionaire?* (2002). Jules is devilishly delicious in *Sin Sisters* (2003) as a sadistic carpet-licking kidnapper. Julian takes two schoolgirl sisters (played by real life sisters Misty and Chelsea Mundae) as prisoners of love, forcing the young girls to partake in erotic games for her pleasure and their freedom. With Julian in and out of a silky tiger-striped robe, the ladies are forced to view their ferocious captor's generous jigglies, barely haired beaver, and booming bottom while in captivity. What a perfect petting zoo! Julian gets gorgeously juicy when Chelsea Mundae ferociously licks and sucks her sweet little lips down south. Yummy! Yummy! Yummy! You'll get lust in your tummy! As with any Seduction Cinema pick starring Julian, all's well that ends *Wells*.

SKIN-fining Moment:

Pleasures of a Woman (0:07) Nice shot of Julian's hooters as Syn Dê Vil and Darian Caine double-team her in a most leztastic fashion.

See Her Naked In:

Young and Seductive (2004) FFN
SpiderBabe (2003) Breasts, Bush, Buns
Sin Sisters (2003) FFN, Buns
Sexy American Idle (2003) Breasts, Thong
That 70's Girl (2003) FFN, Buns
Pleasures of a Woman (2002) Breasts, Bush
Who Wants to Be an Erotic Billionaire? (2002) FFN

Ming-Na Wen

Born: November 20, 1963
Coloane Island, Macau
Skin-O-Meter: Brief Nudity

China has a population of a few billion souls, but as long as that huge and teeming nation occasionally pops out a slinky showpiece sensation along the lines of Ming-Na Wen, Mr. Skin says the more the merrier. From her coal-black tresses to her glittering anthracite eyes to the set, sensual secrets of her sumptuous lips to the slim strength packed with such enticing curvature into her tempting and graceful torso, Ming-Na is a poster girl for Asian adoption. Every day they kill girl babies over there in mainland China! Check out high achiever Ming-Na as a network TV doctor on both *Outreach* and *ER*. A Peking adoptee is likely to grow up to be a productive and accomplished member of society! It is every able American male's duty to save a Chinese girl today. Need further convincing? One peek at Ming-Na Wen's cinnamon peaks as she sleeps on her back with the sheet bunched down below her breasts in *One Night Stand* (1997) should seal the deal.

SKIN-fining Moment:

One Night Stand (1:04) A slumbering Ming-Na shows off her lovely egg rolls before Wesley Snipes ruins the view.

See Her Naked In:

One Night Stand (1997) Breasts

Chandra West

Born: December 31, 1970
Edmonton, Alberta, Canada
Skin-O-Meter: Brief Nudity

Someone said, "Go West, young man," and they were probably talking about Chandra West. The great brunette hottie from the Great White North first made a name for herself working the B-movie circuit in sequels such as *Universal Soldier II* (1998) and *Universal Soldier III* (1998). While the busty beauty is universally arousing, camouflage isn't her best color. She started to show her true colors in *The Perfect Son* (2000), who must have had a tight pair of pants watching her T&A. With the skin barrier broken, one would think the pie's the limit for this sexy show-off. Then she upped and left the big screen for the boob tube. It was the breast move of her career, as she landed on the skintillating *NYPD Blue* in a recurring role as a doctor. She's good for what ails you in her moist revealing nudity to date. Let's just say, "Bottoms up!" and enjoy a refreshing drink of Chandra's booty.

SKIN-fining Moment:

NYPD Blue "Keeping Abreast" (2003) Chandra peels down to bed Mark-Paul Gosselar. Nice close-up of her NYPD moon.

See Her Naked In:

The Perfect Son (2000) Breasts, Buns

TeleVisions:

NYPD Blue Nip Slip LB, Buns

Wendi Westbrook

Mt. Pleasant, Texas
Skin-O-Meter: Great Nudity

Whoever thinks that radio is a medium only for the ugly must not know about Wendi Westbrook. The brown-haired hottie began as a DJ on a country station in Dallas, Texas, her smooth sound capturing the attention of fans like a sexy whisper. With a brunette buxomness and face too fetching to be anonymous, Wendi excelled in personal appearances and caught the eyes (and flies) of Miller Beer, who hired this delicious disc jockey to be their pinup poster girl. The city of angels then coaxed this country cutie into working for KHS-FM, Los Angeles. Her vivacious voice became so requested that she replayed nightly shows to an affiliate in Japan and hosted her own nationally syndicated program, *Hitline USA*. Along with her auditory accolades, Wendi delved into the more physical media of film, starring in small productions like *Video Murders* (1988) and *Blame It on the Vodka* (1992). In *Married People, Single Sex* (1993), Wendi is at her wildest, making her private parts public, including a full-frontal flash of her hairy slice of heaven. She followed that hair-raiser with a whacked out turn in the women-in-prison flick *Under Lock and Key* (1995). The beautifully bare Ms. Westbrook was in perfect company, surrounded by a cast of incredibly tasty skincarcerates. What a delicious dish of prison flesh! Wendi's tantalizing tone and booming beauty are a one of a kind, cunning combination of the skinses.

SKIN-fining Moment:

Blame it on the Vodka (0:20) Buns and breasts in the bathroom with Barry, then again banging him in the shower, long scene.

See Her Naked In:

Under Lock and Key (1995) FFN, Buns
Married People, Single Sex (1993) Breasts, Bush, Buns
Blame It on the Vodka (1992) Breasts, Buns

TeleVisions:

Hotline Breasts, Buns

Carrie Westcott

Born: December 12, 1969
Mission Hills, Kansas
Skin-O-Meter: Great Nudity

Any yanker within a hundred-mile wanking distance will agree that Carrie Westcott is an orgiastic, feminine force to be reckoned with. This country cutie posed for *Playboy* in September of 1993 as a ruse to ruffle a former boyfriend's feathers. Ain't revenge sweet? Now this sweet bird of youth has flown on to more skintense horizons. A lovely vision of lustiness, Carrie is at her bumpilicious best when prancing in sex-vexed vids such as *Night Dreams* (1993), *Playboy Wet & Wild: Hot Holiday* (1995), and *No Boys Allowed* (2000) (except for you, of course). For the more closetedly shy, stick-flicking fearfuls of the adult video section, Mr. Skin recommends Westcott's skinematic dive into the mainstream movie *Lover's Leap* (1995). Be careful not to jump out of your pants at the site of her mouth-watering mammoth mammaries and bootilicious backside. Braver men have failed. Since this blonde bombshell's buxom body *Carries* a lot of weight around *Playboy* headquarters, expect to be seeing a lot more of this naughty nighttime temptress.

SKIN-fining Moment:

Lover's Leap (0:02) Carrie canoodles with her dude in the woods. T&A amongst the trees.

See Her Naked In:

L.E.T.H.A.L. Ladies: Return to Savage Beach (1998) Breasts, Buns
Centerfold Fantasies (1997) FFN
Lover's Leap (1995) FFN, Buns
Numerous *Playboy* Videos

TeleVisions:

Erotic Confessions FFN

Virginia Wetherell

Born: May 9, 1943
Farnham, Surrey, England, UK
Skin-O-Meter: Great Nudity

The stunningly statuesque Virginia Wetherell has a certain sinister sexuality, making her a natural to play the heartthrob of the horror set in the '70s. This pale, hauntingly hot mamma of the macabre delved into devilish pursuits with Hammer Films, making horrific classics such as *The Curse of the Crimson Alter* (1968), *Dr. Jekyll and Sister Hyde* (1971), *Demons of the Mind* (1972), and *Dracula* (1973). Before her reign as resident scream queen for Hammer, this British beauty starred in the Edgar Wallace mysteries *Ricochet* (1963) and *The Partner* (1963), had a cameo with Michael Caine in *Alfie* (1966), and appeared in the occasional guest spot on English mindblowers like *Dr. Who* and *No Hiding Place*. Many remember Virginia breast as the untouchable horror-show hottie in *A Clockwork Orange* (1971). Tit bare in tiny panties, this tall temptress is trotted out to test Malcolm McDowell's aversion therapy, with electrifying results. Viddy well, my brothers! Virginia sends shockwaves into the pants of millions in *Demons of the Mind*. While admiring herself in a mirror, she shows peeks of her own peaks, spanktastic ass, and hairiffic furburger. Beastly and beautiful! Still a flaxen-haired vision of vixenism, Virginia made a comeback in Hammer's *Love is the Devil* (1998). Let's hope this trend continues, as Virginia's fans would have a devil of a time letting her go.

SKIN-fining Moment:

A Clockwork Orange (1:23) Amazing upper anatomy as Virgina struts across a stage topless to prove that Malcom McDowell has been brainwashed.

See Her Naked In:

Demons of the Mind (1972) FFN, Buns
A Clockwork Orange (1971) Breasts

Joanne Whalley

Born: August 25, 1964
Salford, Manchester, England, UK
Skin-O-Meter: Brief Nudity

Joanne Whalley, perhaps best known as Joanne Whalley Kilmer, ditched big ego-ed hubby Val Kilmer in February 1997. Whalley watchers are excited to see what this cunning canary can do now that she's flown the coop. Beloved to fans since her enchanting performance as the red-haired, wispy Sorsha in *Willow* (1988), Joanna has a history of playing a wide variety of roles, from the curvaceous crooning nurse in the British serial *The Singing Detective* to the former first lovely lady Jacqueline Kennedy in the series *Jackie Bouvier Kennedy Onassis* to the tasty trouble-making tramp about town in *Scandal* (1989). This curvy chameleon is most colorful when turning toward more skinteresting flesh tones. Although Joanne used a bootilicous body double in *Scandal*, she did bare her perfectly perky pair in *Breathtaking* (2000). They certainly are! From her recent stint as the mature, mammarificly hot mamma in the TV mini *40* (2003) to her groping groupie days as a briefly featured band banger in *Pink Floyd The Wall* (1982), all of Whalley's work is worth a watch. Here's hoping this red-hot, British brick house is here to stay.

SKIN-fining Moment:

Scandal (0:31) BODY DOUBLE: Great shot of some unbelievable buns as she dances with palm leaves, then totally nude as she tries to run away. Unfortunately, most of the skinnage comes courtesy of a body double.

See Her Naked In:

Breathtaking (2000) Breasts, Buns
Scandal (1989) Body Double—FFN, Buns

TeleVisions:

40 LB
A Kind of Loving Breasts

Shannon Whirry

Born: November 7, 1964
Wisconsin
Skin-O-Meter: Hall of Fame

Sumptuously suckadocious breast-bomb Shannon Whirry commenced her career with a (two) bit part in the Steven Seagal action flick *Out for Justice* (1991), but praise be, she quickly moved on to more skinful fare—because this whole-lotta-woman has more than enough skin to share! Since the early 1990s she's suck-cessfully balanced between TV gigs on shows such as *Eden*, *Black Scorpion*, and *Mike Hammer, Private Eye* and such skintastic softcore teat treats as *Animal Instincts* (1992), *Body of Influence* (1993), and *Lady in Waiting* (1994). If you catch sight of naturally super-stacked Shannon on a video sleeve, grab the flick immediately. Then try to keep your mitts off the TV screen!

SKIN-fining Moment:

Me, Myself & Irene (0:21) Just when you thought nobody could compete with Bryan Brown's luck in Full Body Massage, *along comes Jim Carrey, who spies naturally super-knockered Shannon breast feeding her baby and then switches the little sucker with himself, maniacally mouthing this software superstarlet's supremely sumptuous milk-mountain.*

See Her Naked In:

Me, Myself & Irene (2000) RB
Exit (1996) Breasts, Buns
Playback (1996) Buns
Ringer (1996) FFN, Buns

The Granny (1995) Breasts
Private Obsession (1995) FFN, Buns
Dangerous Prey (1995) FFN, Buns
Animal Instincts II (1994) FFN, Buns
Mirror Images II (1994) FFN, Buns
Fatal Pursuit (1994) FFN, Buns
Lady In Waiting (1994) FFN, Buns
Body of Influence (1993) FFN
Animal Instincts (1992) FFN, Buns

Elizabeth Whitcraft

Skin-O-Meter: Great Nudity

The Itty Bitty Titty Committee is proud to add a new inductee to their '80s branch of small-breasted beauties. Elizabeth Whitcraft earned her IBTC status after years of showing her curlicued cuteness and A-sized cupfuls onscreen. Elizabeth began her career in small-scale flicks like *Birdy* (1984) and soon flew the coup to bigger horizons like *Angel Heart* (1987), showing off her big-nipped, lovely little suckables to Mickey Rourke. With all her olive-toned, dark-locked lusciousness, Elizabeth is perfect playing the gorgeous girlfriend of Italian horny studs. She plays the sweet-faced, big-haired, little-breasted bit-o-honey of Joe Pesci's dreams in *Goodfellas* (1990) and the home-wrecking tiny-topped tramp in *Working Girl* (1988). In the latter, Melanie Griffith opens her bedroom door to find Lizzy letting loose her miniscule mams atop a very hairy Alec Baldwin. If Mel only knew . . . tiny-titted gals need love too. Be sure to keep a place in your heart (and your pants) for the wittle bitted Ms. Whitcraft and all the girls of the IBTC.

SKIN-fining Moment:

Angel Heart (0:33) Rourke helps Elizabeth out of her clothes while she attempts to make conversation in bed, and as a result, we're treated to a tasty gander at her big, milky globes. Hoo-zah!

See Her Naked In:

Eden 3 (1993) Breasts
Inside Out II (1992) Breasts
Working Girl (1988) FFN
Angel Heart (1987) Breasts

Vanna White

Born: February 18, 1957
North Myrtle Beach, South Carolina,
Skin-O-Meter: Brief Nudity

Talent is an elusive quality to define, but Vanna White has got it in full-figured spades. How else to account for the long-running success of game show *Wheel of Fortune*? The ever-delectable and deceptively demure Ms. White makes it all look so easy. Speaking nary a word, perched on medium-height heels, she confidently stalks the length of the *Wheel of Fortune* playing board and flips letters to reveal a secret word or phrase. The legions of male fans who are riveted to every twist of Vanna's tidy hips, to every flounce of her full-frontal lobes, to every flip of her flouncy coiffure know that the secret is Vanna herself. Fully clothed, without saying a word, she has mesmerized the male half of a nation. That's talent.

SKIN-fining Moment:

Gypsy Angels (0:40) Can I get an "N," Pat? Alright, I'd like to solve the puzzle . . . Is it "Nipple Slipple?" Hooray!

See Her Naked In:

Gypsy Angels (1980) RB, Thong

Lynn Whitfield

Born: October 15, 1953
Baton Rouge, Louisiana
Skin-O-Meter: Great Nudity

The main reason that more skinthusiasts aren't setting up Web sites devoted to Lynn Whitfield is that she hit the entertainment scene at least ten years too late. If black, stacked, and delicious Lynn had brought her hard-black-lady-with-a-soft-chocolate-center attitude around in the early 1970s, she might be mentioned in the same panting breath as Pam Grier is today. Too bad for skin history, and for Lynn too, that her hydraulic front and rear bumpers didn't pull up for attention until 1981. What she, and we, got were spots on *Hill Street Blues* instead of mass exposure in something like *Foxier Brown than You All Will Ever Be*. But all is not lost. See a double eyeful of what might have been in Lynn's Emmy-grabbing, banana-twirling lead in *The Josephine Baker Story* (1991).

SKIN-fining Moment:

The Josephine Baker Story (0:33) *The coffee-colored cutie bares her bouncing breasts and beautiful butt while doing the Banana Dance.*

See Her Naked In:

A Thin Line Between Love and Hate (1995) Breasts
The Josephine Baker Story (1991) Breasts, Buns

Margaret Whitton

Born: November 30, 1950
Philadelphia, Pennsylvania
Skin-O-Meter: Great Nudity

Margaret Whitton first played with the big boys in *Major League* (1989). Just barely baring her baseballs (her points covered by pasties), her almost nudity was minor compared to the homerun she hit in *Ironweed* (1987). Margaret's garden was a gloriously overgrown full-frontal frenzy! Sweetly seasoned at the time of the film, this then-thirty-seven-year-old eyeful got into the game a bit late but still scored big points for her bush baring and her later grown-up gorgeosity in *The Man Without a Face* (1993) and *Major League II* (1994).

SKIN-fining Moment:

Ironweed (1:19) *Maggie wears stockings, a big white hat, and nothing else as she struts about a yard mams-and-muffshish-first.*

See Her Naked In:

Ironweed (1987) FFN
Secret of My Success (1987) Breasts

Saskia Wickham

Born: January 14, 1967
Holland Park, London, England, UK
Skin-O-Meter: Great Nudity

British TV actress Saskia Wickham spends most of her time on the British boob tube (and my, what boobs they are!) but can be found on the silver screen from time to time. Saskia, the daughter of famed British actor Jeffrey Wickham, made her acting debut in 1975 at age eight on the hit British children's television series *The Villains*. After taking time off for school, she returned to showbiz as the title character in the made-for-BBC-movie *Clarissa* (1991), an eighteenth-century period piece. Her fame continued in her highly popular roles on British TV series *Boon* and *Peak Practice*, on which she played a rural doctor. In 1994 she starred opposite Christian Bale in *Royal Deceit*, a retelling of *Hamlet*. In the film, Saskia can be seen sitting topless outdoors with her long hair covering one breast, romping naked through a barnyard with two equally naked babes, then going for a roll in the hay (quite literally) with Bale. (Bale . . . hay . . . hmmm . . . Did they plan that?) She made a naked return to the small screen while *pregnant*, playing a "mother earth" type who wants to have a natural birth in the British TV movie *William and Mary* (2003).

SKIN-fining Moment:

Royal Deceit (0:13) *Blonde sweetie Saskia shows ass while opening the bath-house door for the other chicks to join her. Then we see her breasts in the wonderfully crowded tub.*

See Her Naked In:

Royal Deceit (1994) Breasts, Buns

Lynda Wiesmeier

Born: May 30, 1963
Washington, D.C.
Skin-O-Meter: Great Nudity

A baby-faced, beach-fresh, feathered-blonde beauty appeals to the male need to be helpful and supportive on many different levels, particularly if the flaxen-tressed fluff top is burdened with a bulky, unmanageable, uncontainable rack of bulbous boobs. When smiling imp Lynda Wiesmeier appears onscreen in *Preppies* (1982), lolling about upon an unmade bed, her modesty shielded by nothing more than a flimsy slip of white panties, chivalrous instincts are aroused in any viewing man worthy of his testosterone. He is gripped by a hard-wired urge to give hands-on assistance and aid Lynda in corralling those large and unwieldy mounds of joy wobbling to and fro upon her chest, a need to help that will only be intensified by leering at Lynda's wildly waving wonders in *Malibu Express* (1985) and *R.S.V.P.* (1984), among many others.

SKIN-fining Moment:

Wheels of Fire (0:24) *Topless ta-tas when thugs throw her on the floor.*

See Her Naked In:

Evil Town (1987) Breasts
Malibu Express (1985) Breasts
R.S.V.P. (1984) FFN, Buns
Red Hot Rock (1984) FFN, Buns
Wheels of Fire (1984) Breasts
Private School (1983) FFN, Buns
Joysticks (1983) Breasts
Preppies (1982) Breasts
Numerous *Playboy* Videos

Mary Charlotte Wilcox

Hamilton, Ontario, Canada
Skin-O-Meter: Great Nudity

It's not every professional actress who is equally adept at assaying roles of unrelenting drama and parts that call for continual and exquisite comedic timing, but then narrow and angular blonde Mary Charlotte Wilcox is not just any professional actress. Few of the laugh seekers who snickered at Mary Charlotte's pitch-perfect performance as the snarky nurse in *Strange Brew: The Adventures of Bob & Doug McKenzie* (1983) or who chuckled and choked on Cheetos while Mary Charlotte cracked wise and took psychic pratfalls as a pivotal part of the ensemble parody perfected by *SCTV Channel* and *SCTV Network 90* had any idea that the animated and expressive blonde had a firm grounding in the serious dramatic arts. But check the records. This same goofy and witty Mary Charlotte Wilcox previously shone as Janice Whitney on *Days of Our Lives*.

SKIN-fining Moment:

Beast of the Yellow Night (0:20) Mary's perkies are pokin' out and red-lit in this love scene with John Ashley. Don't miss that quick flash of ass, either!

See Her Naked In:

Love Me Deadly (1972) Breasts
Beast of the Yellow Night (1971) Breasts, Buns

Valerie Wildman

Miami Beach, Florida
Skin-O-Meter: Brief Nudity

Any parent who is having trouble with a college-age kid who refuses to hold down a part-time job just because he's taking a few auto-shop classes at the local community college should steer the ungrateful slacker's nose in the direction of sweet-smelling, multi-tasking blonde Valerie Wildman. Not only does this svelte and beguiling diva hold down a full-time job as golden-hearted Faye Walker on the long-running soap *Days of Our Lives*, she also has the time and energy to be a stepmother to four kids, counsel young people, work on her Ph.D. in child and adolescent psychology, and run Wildwind Productions, dedicated to creating films and TV projects that "uplift the human

spirit." If the layout student grumbles that Valerie hasn't done anything to uplift him lately, smack the snotnose across the face with a copy of *Inner Sanctum* (1991), and see if he can keep his spirit from rising once Val's clothes drop.

SKIN-fining Moment:

Inner Sanctum (0:11) Wildman is no wild woman—she acts coy as her guy pulls down her nightgown to expose one shy boober.

See Her Naked In:

Inner Sanctum (1991) RB

Donna Wilkes

Born: November 11, 1959
California
Skin-O-Meter: Great Nudity

Mr. Skin worships the skindeavors of all of his featured actresses. Regardless of star status or bra size, no skinematic memory or mammary is too small to be loved. In fact, Mr. Skin immensely adores the under-appreciated heroines of tiny-yet-mighty stature, especially when they are members of the Itty Bitty Titty Committee. Take for example the delightful Donna Wilkes, a charter member of the IBTC since her unforgettable turn as McLean Stevenson's daughter on NBC's legendary '70s sit-bomb *Hello, Larry*. One teeny little dish of fleshy fun, Wilkes's wee willy windbags were always suckably scrumptious onscreen. Topless in *Frye* (1978), those teeny tats stand stiffly at attention as she dances around, locking lips with a gal pal for two tantalizing minutes! Be still my beating hard-on. Miniscule mam munchers will go CRAZY for Donna's cute cupables in *Schizoid* (1980), when she opens the shower door for a lingering peek at her petite pair. Fans will forever cherish the remembrance of Donna's little Debbies. My, what tasty teats!

SKIN-fining Moment:

Fyre (1:13) Donna's the shorter-haired shirtless girl who joins her naked-nippled friend in bed with some older guy. Then she does a little dance and reconvenes with her pal for a bout of bare-titlet lesbotronics.

See Her Naked In:

Schizoid (1980) Breasts, Buns
Fyre (1978) Breasts

Barbara Williams

Vancouver Island, British Columbia, Canada
Skin-O-Meter: Great Nudity

Talent refuses to be contained, particularly the creative gifts of multifaceted, red-tinged brunette Barbara Williams. Students of comedic classics will recognize Barbara's name from the story-writing credits for humorist Pauly Shore's mirth-provoking milestone *Jury Duty* (1995), but authorship is not even half the Barbara Williams story. When Barbara's *E! True Hollywood Story* is written, two central chapters will be the appearance of the firm, full Williams breasts and a shadow of love delta in *Thief of Hearts* (1984), followed by five minutes of *E! True Hollywood* commercials, and a return from the station break that focuses on Barb emerging from a chilly pond in *Oh, What a Night* (1992), her nipples hard as frozen raisins,

BARBARA WILLIAMS LEANS IN FOR SOME STEVEN BAUER LOVIN' IN *THIEF OF HEARTS*.

her thick puff of fuzz dark and distinct beneath soaked and clinging panties. Oh, what a bush!

SKIN-fining Moment:

Thief of Hearts (53:00) Barbara goes starkers with Steven Bauer, delivering unto him her boobaloos, butt, and even a hint of lap-lint.

See Her Naked In:

Oh, What a Night (1992) Breasts, Buns
Thief of Hearts (1984) FFN

Cindy Williams

Born: August 22, 1947
Van Nuys, California
Skin-O-Meter: Never Nude

Plenty of young men's lennies got all squiggy over the sight of Cindy Williams on *Laverne & Shirley*. The character of Shirley Feeney started as a slut on *Happy Days*, but she was a perfect little pixie by the time Cindy landed her weekly series. This, of course, only made her sexier. Cindy's series debuted the same year as her starring role in *The First Nudie Musical* (1976), but fans found she was equally chaste in that film. Fortunately, the advent of home video provided key rewind moments for Cindy's early-on bra-clad appearance in the thriller *The Killing Kind* (1973). She's also sexed up her image in later roles, including some great outfits in *Meet Wally Sparks* (1997) and the sci-fi parody *Spaceship* (1981).

SKIN-fining Moment:

The Killing Kind (0:15) TV's Shirley Feeney peels to her bra and panties, then preens on a bed while a peeping perv peers in on her and pets his pussy (he's holding a cat).

Cynda Williams

Born: 1966
Chicago, Illinois
Skin-O-Meter: Hall of Fame

The secret to a tremendous breast shot in a movie is that the actress on display possesses a tremendous set of breasts. Tremendously blessed Cynda Williams is arguably the best open secret in skinema today, and her frontal miracles are backed up by a sublime behind. Black, stacked, and beautiful, Cynda arched her back and thrust her chest into prominence while writhing beneath Denzel Washington in Spike Lee's *Mo' Better Blues* (1990). She backed up that initial foray into tremendous skinema with the bootylicious wonder of *Wet* (1995). The camera, like a panting animal, zooms close in on Williams's ass and the darker depths of the split between her cheeks as the lubricious orbs rise from a bath and water and suds fall away. All rise for the tremendous assets!

SKIN-fining Moment:

Spirit Lost (0:32) Cynda busts out her tan torso-torpedoes as she pulls her dress down and gets some lovin' from a fella on the floor.

See Her Naked In:

Caught Up (1998) Breasts
Relax . . . It's Just Sex (1998) Breasts
Spirit Lost (1996) Breasts
Machine Gun Blues (1996) Breasts
Fallen Angels: Fearless (1995) Breasts
Condition Red (1995) Breasts, Buns
Wet (1995) Breasts, Buns
Mo' Better Blues (1990) Breasts

TeleVisions:

Fallen Angels RB

Edy Williams

Born: July 9, 1942
Salt Lake City, Utah
Skin-O-Meter: Great Nudity

Booby beauty Edy Williams is breast remembered by Mr. Skin for her part as pretty porn princess "Ashley St. Ives" in the rack-lovin'

Russ Meyer flick *Beyond the Valley of the Dolls* (1970). When this delicious doll whispered, "You're a groovy boy. I'd like to strap you on sometime," a theater full of horn dogs were ready to take her up on her offer. Booming of *breastage*, *bush*, and *buns*, Edy is a breathtaking B-movie mama, flashing her fit frame in flicks such as *Chained Heat* (1983), *Hollywood Hot Tubs* (1984), and *Dr. Alien* (1988). Although Edy began her yen for skin in the early '70s, penises still pound over this vixenish Venus's most recent efforts. Still sporty in her late forties, Williams flashed her still-fantastic plastic in *Bad Girls from Mars* (1990). Be you man or Martian, a skinematic scoop of Edy is guaranteed to give you nice dreams.

SKIN-fining Moment:

Chained Heat (0:30) Edy exhibits a nice full-frontal flesh-flash while giving Marcia Karr a hand in the shower . . . It's Lez-Tastic!

See Her Naked In:

Bad Girls From Mars (1990) Breasts
Nudity Required (1989) Breasts
Rented Lips (1988) Breasts
Dr. Alien (1988) Breasts
Hellhole (1985) Breasts
Hollywood Hot Tubs (1984) Breasts
Chained Heat (1983) FFN
Famous T&A (1982) Breasts, Buns
The Best of Sex and Violence (1981) Breasts
An Almost Perfect Affair (1979) Breasts, Buns
Peccati in famiglia (1975) FFN, Buns
Dr. Minx (1975) Breasts

JoBeth Williams

Born: December 6, 1948
Houston, Texas
Skin-O-Meter: Great Nudity

Moms and female attorneys are usually not thought of as the sexiest archetypes alive, but dark-haired and frankly attractive actress JoBeth

Williams reminds the skin legions to keep an open mind. After spending several years developing her smoldering stare on daytime soap operas, JoBeth was prepared to take her heat to the big screen. As a naked lawyer, Williams's small, up-swinging breasts and narrow nates provided much-welcome sexual relief in the divorce drama *Kramer vs. Kramer* (1979). The unclothed counselor further reminded viewers that lasses who wear glasses can be instantly hot if they just drop their tops. JoBeth made an indelible mark as the hot mama whose panties twist in a spooky knot in the supernatural thriller *Poltergeist* (1982). Jimmy! Can your mom come out and play?

SKIN-fining Moment:

Kramer vs. Kramer (0:45) Hot and hilarious T&A when JoBeth gets discovered naked in a hallway by a clueless kid who asks if she likes fried chicken.

See Her Naked In:

Chantilly Lace (1993) Breasts
Teachers (1984) Breasts
Kramer vs. Kramer (1979) Breasts, Buns

Kelli Williams

Born: June 8, 1970
Los Angeles, California
Skin-O-Meter: Brief Nudity

When your daddy is a super Beverly Hills plastic surgeon and Mommy is super TV star Shannon Wilcox of *Dallas* and you're a pert-bottomed, plump-lipped nymph with poise and a practiced pout, two things can be assumed about your future: You will always look as good as is medically possible and, as in the case of Kelli Williams, a career in some aspect of showbiz is there for you if you really, really want it and work for it really, really hard, twice as hard as an outsider who doesn't have to prove she's not just being

given a job on the merits of being Mommy's little performing prodigy. A dirty blonde so shady as to verge on brunette, sultry and prepossessed Kelli perfected her winning smile while shooting TV commercials as a baby. She went to high school with the likes of Tori Spelling and Monica Lewinsky and has been popping up in films and TV since the dawn of the 1990s. Her most lasting impressions so far have been made as snarly, darling lawyer Lindsay Dole on the legal-beagle drama *The Practice*.

SKIN-fining Moment:

E=mc2 (0:54) Fast right juggle in bed with Jeremy Piven.

See Her Naked In:

E=mc2 (1996) RB

Kimberly Williams

Born: September 14, 1971
Rye, New York
Skin-O-Meter: Brief Nudity

Wholesome, pretty brunettes whose pursed lips and twinkling eyes reflect their anticipation that life will bring them a never-ending stream of sweetness and light are sexy too. Doubt that a goody-goody can inspire good-bad thoughts of nasty-clean fun? Rent against character and check out the Steve Martin career-saver *Father of the Bride* (1991). Try not to covet the covered loveliness of Steve's daughter, the bride-to-be, Kimberly Williams. The sugary sexiness of Kimberly's dimpled smile, her light as spun glass sylphlike form, that tidy little ass on her. Who wouldn't want to marry this chick, just to get her in a room alone with her clothes off? Well, no reason to resort to matrimony. Daddy's girl Kimberly spills her boobies during a sheet-covered bed-top boff in *Elephant Juice* (1999). So there're the headlights, how about some caboose?

SKIN-fining Moment:

Elephant Juice (0:43) Petite Kimmy pops out her surprisingly sizable milk-pumps while her guy dines at the Y. Nice overhead shot of them in bed.

See Her Naked In:

Elephant Juice (1999) Breasts

Malinda Williams

Born: December 3, 1975
Elizabeth, New Jersey
Skin-O-Meter: Brief Nudity

A stone-soul fox with perfectly paired pillow lips like two sweet, ripe, juice-dripping dates; eyes dark and simmering like pools of bitter-sweet chocolate; rounded, full, and high cheeks that make gazing at her face a preview of the mesmerizing symmetry to be appreciated while gazing upon the high cushions of her rear buns. Then there's that smile that bursts from the mocha sky of her face like a sparkling, white sun and a chest capable of containing the hopes and wishes of an entire race—the male race. New Jersey-born Malinda Williams didn't need to go through all the trouble of attending New York's Actors Conservatory, but the fact that she did makes her character Tracy "Bird" Van Adams on the Showtime family drama *Soul Food* even more of an inspiration.

SKIN-fining Moment:

Soul Food "Help" (2002) Malinda's brown bombers bounce bewitchingly as she bones Darrin Dewitt Henson in bed.

TeleVisions:

Soul Food RB

Michelle Williams

Born: September 9, 1980
Kalispell, Montana
Skin-O-Meter: Great Nudity

One of God's greatest gifts to male-kind is the cherubic blonde ingénue, she of the straight-staring, wonder-brimming eyes and plush, parted lips, open as if taking in a sigh of singular sensual surprise. The miracle of a baby-face heartthrob in the mold of preternaturally fair Michelle Williams is that while the body matures into the action-packed curves of a grown woman, the angel mug retains the libido-inspiring innocence of a recent virgin. Michelle's mien of uncertain cherry first surfaced at the start of a five-season courtship as one of the impossible *Dawson's Creek* cuties. Soon Michelle's nips had popped hard under the mam-handling of Chloë Sevigny in *If These Walls Could Talk 2* (2000), and she'd shared a dirty-minded bath with experienced nymph Anna Friel in *Me Without You* (2001). Now Michelle's wide-eyed wonder is the awe of a newfound joy in erotic explorations.

SKIN-fining Moment:

If These Walls Could Talk 2 (0:57) A great view of her "Dawson's Peaks" when Chloë Sevigny lezbonically pushes up Michelle's shirt and gives them a nice squeeze.

See Her Naked In:

Me Without You (2001) Breasts
If These Walls Could Talk 2 (2000) Breasts

Olivia Williams

Born: January 1, 1968
Camden Town, North London,
England, UK
Skin-O-Meter: Great Nudity

The lazy-lidded insouciance of her impertinently sensuous stare, her satiny pale skin, her raven-dark hair (although at times bleached blonde), the rose-nipped throw pillows tossed so casually on her breastplate, all of this combines to make England's Olivia Williams a hot prospect on the skin-sighting scene. In the eerie thriller *The Sixth Sense* (1999), Olivia exuded the frustrated longing of a ripe-bodied beauty deprived of her cherished love. Olivia bursts through her erotic constraints in the gripping, slipping, and groping bed play of *The Postman* (1997). She tosses all caution and her two chest ornaments to the sun-drenched breeze in *Dead Babies* (2000). Infants of all ages are given a glimpse of what makes life worth living.

SKIN-fining Moment:

The Postman (1997) Olivia sheds her threads (displaying a sweet rump) and beds Kevin Costner, baring her breasts all the while.

See Her Naked In:

The Heart of Me (2002) RB
Mood Swingers (2000) Breasts
The Postman (1997) Breasts, Buns

Sasha Williams

Oakville, Ontario, Canada
Skin-O-Meter: Great Nudity

Hollywood should give itself an award for bringing together two generations of males and uniting fathers and sons in their appreciation of a single ideal, one that has been presented from a pair of wholly divergent angles, that ideal being metallic-toned brunette Sasha Williams. Imagine a young dad sitting patiently with his preadolescent boy as the kid watches, for the thousandth time, a replay of *Power Rangers Lightspeed Rescue*. The pop sits stoically, wanting his child to have every happiness but wondering how much more of this toddler entertainment he can take before his brain bakes. "If only some of these female rangers, like that yellow one for instance, were available to be perused in the nude. Then I would suffer a little less." Well, Hollywood has come through again, because the Yellow Lightspeed Ranger is played by Sasha Williams, the same Sasha Williams who will wholly entrance Daddy with her enticing nudity in *DarkWolf* (2003).

SKIN-fining Moment:

DarkWolf (2003) Wacky soft-Sapphic, body-painted, crotch-patched photo shoot, Sasha has the dark hair. Andrea Bogart is the blonde. Ah-whoo!

See Her Naked In:

DarkWolf (2003) Breasts, Buns

Wendy O. Williams

Born: May 28, 1949
Rochester, New York
Died: April 6, 1998
Skin-O-Meter: Great Nudity

The hardest-rocking raunch 'n' roller in showbiz, Wendy O. Williams claimed her fame by thrashing onstage wearing little more than electrical tape, shaving cream, and a Mohawk haircut. Walking multiple tightropes that combined punk, speed metal, performance art, and schlocky shock entertainment, Williams was loud, brash, and reviled as much as she was loved. In the early 1980s Williams graduated from seedy New York City live sex shows to front a band of mayhem rockers. The Plasmatics were known as much for blowing up crap onstage

SCHOOL OF HARD KNOCKERS: WENDY O. WILLIAMS (CENTER, IN BLACK UNDIES) AND THE GANG IN *REFORM SCHOOL GIRLS*.

as they were for their crude, high-volume music. Aside from creating a screeching singing sensation, Williams left an impression on film. For hard-R breast action, choose *Reform School Girls* (1986). Harder pleasures are packaged in *Candy Goes to Hollywood* (1979). Unfortunately, rock and movie stardom is fleeting. Wendy, born in 1949, was at least a generation older than her core audience, which dwindled and left her alone. She took her own life in 1998.

SKIN-fining Moment:

Reform School Girls (0:26) Flashes of plastic sacks and seat-meat in the shower room as bleached-blonde Wendy hangs with her gang.

See Her Naked In:

Reform School Girls (1986) Breasts, Bush, Buns
Candy Goes to Hollywood (1979) FFN, Buns
Numerous Adult Movies

Bridgette Wilson

Born: September 25, 1973
Gold Beach, Oregon
Skin-O-Meter: Brief Nudity

Although she has mostly played lesser roles and is better known as the love muffin of tennis ace Pete Sampras, Oregon-born natural beauty Bridgette Wilson possesses the raw materials for skinmortality: A generous set of lips, a vulnerable yet saucy cast to her eyes, a full-bodied mane of shadowy blondness, skin as pure and delicate as angel's breath, and a willingness to engage in the equivalent of a one-woman wet-blouse contest while inflicting exquisite discipline upon Adam Sandler in *Billy Madison* (1995). Bridgette's undercover charms can be seen in *The Real Blonde* (1997), an indie frolic that exposes Bridgette as a comic actress capable of getting a laugh and flashing her incredible nipples and cleavage at the same time.

SKIN-fining Moment:

The Real Blonde (1:20) Brief right boobery as Bridgette takes part in a photo shoot.

See Her Naked In:

The Real Blonde (1997) RB

Debra Wilson

Born: April 26, 1970
South Ozone Park, Queens, New York
Skin-O-Meter: Brief Nudity

When a woman can be both fine of fanny and funny as five straight fart jokes, she is a valuable addition to any dinner party, even if that dinner is a can of cold beans in front of the TV set watching black, delirious, and delicious Debra Wilson cracking wise and wild on *Mad TV*, as well as cracking that bootilicious butt. Debra's signature characters on the raucous and riotous ensemble comedy-skit series include Malina, Bunifa, and Tovah. Mouthy and magically agile of face, wondrous lady Wilson is equally adept at wrenching laughs as a fast-talking pimp on the stroll and as a sweet and sibilant, sugar-honey trophy wife. During a 1999 nightgown-clad *Mad* episode, Debra's impressive nipples were perfectly expert at making a pair of eye-popping impressions. But she really hit viewers' funny boners with her earth-quaking sex scene in *Skin Deep* (2003). Debra shakes, rattles, and rolls out of her black bra while on top of her love stud. Her shoulder boulders avalanche, and any man would die to be smothered in her big rocks. But things get even hairier later when Debra's stalking her kitchen in a transparent teddy that exposes her bare beaver. That's a plush toy no one would grow tired of.

SKIN-fining Moment:

Skin Deep (0:03) Debra roughly rides her fella with the force of hurricane, and her humungous, all-natural right whopper swings into view.

See Her Naked In:

Skin Deep (2003) RB, Bush

Kristen Wilson

Born: 1969
Chelmsford, Massachusetts
Skin-O-Meter: Great Nudity

The fact that the animals spoke to African American laugh rioter Eddie Murphy in *Dr. Dolittle* (1998) and *Dr. Dolittle 2* (2001) was relatively easy to accept. What stumped credibility was that Eddie's character was blessed with an angelic vision of sensual loveliness for a wife and that such a hot, wholesome, love-inspiring woman would stick with a wacko who talks to animals. It is a testament to the thespian superiority of mocha-light beauty Kristen Wilson that audiences, rather than simply toss up their hands in disbelief, found themselves enchanted and aroused by her dutiful and bootiful depiction of wifely splendor. Rather than leave the initial *Dolittle* in exasperated disgust, paying customers instead exited the theater looking forward to seeing Kristen again in the sequel. To watch a side of Kristen that wouldn't quite fit the family-lady image of the doctor's wife, check out the naked voodoo in *Ritual* (2001).

SKIN-fining Moment:

Ritual (0:26) Ding DONG! Kristen answers the door sans a stitch of clothing, then bares her caboose when she lets her pal inside.

See Her Naked In:

Ritual (2001) Buns

Peta Wilson

Born: November 18, 1970
Sydney, New South Wales, Australia
Skin-O-Meter: Great Nudity

Although born in Australia, flaxen vixen Peta Wilson was an Army brat who spent her childhood years in Papua, New Guinea. While coming of age in that appropriately exotic locale, Peta developed her killer body as a competitive athlete. She finally stormed Hollywood in 1997 as the USA Network's five-foot-ten, ferociously carnal *La Femme Nikita*. The series, based on the cult French film starring Anne Parillaud, follows druggie gang-banger Peta after she's recruited by the government and trained to be a creatively lethal assassin. After scorching TV screens for a few seasons, Peta absolutely ignited the berserk lipstick-lesbian thriller *Mercy* (1999). After exhibiting what ranks as one of *the* finest asses ever photographed in a sick—but insanely arousing—scene where she prostitutes herself by pretending to get shot in the head, kink-fueled Peta literally hurls her body at detective Ellen Barkin and sets off a series of Sapphic encounters that show absolutely no *Mercy* when it comes to heat.

SKIN-fining Moment:

Mercy (0:46) Ass-tastic back nudity followed by first-rate full-frontalage when Peta dances in the window as Ellen Barkin watches.

See Her Naked In:

Mercy (2000) Breasts, Bush, Buns
The Sadness of Sex (1995) Breasts
Loser (1991) RB

TeleVisions:

La Femme Nikita Buns
Strangers Breasts, Buns

Reagan Wilson

Born: March 6, 1947
Torrance, California
Skin-O-Meter: Brief Nudity

Despite the reported fixation of tiny emperor Napoleon Bonaparte upon the aroma of unwashed womanly parts, most men would agree that cleanliness is next to sexiness, especially when a rack-heavy, alabaster-complected seductress is lolling breasts out and breathless in a sudsy tub, waiting to scrub and be scrubbed by any guy who happens along, which is precisely the scenario presented by comely Reagan Wilson in the primeval gore thriller *Blood Mania* (1970). Reagan and her soaring shelf would later be cast in *Running with the Devil* (1973), but her tub dallying in *Mania* remains Satan's go-to scene when he wants to get the blood in his bones boiling.

SKIN-fining Moment:

Blood Mania (0:07) A flash of ass and some nice looks at her rack in the bathtub with Peter Carpenter. We're guessing that "Getting Clean" wasn't the only thing he was thinking about, there . . .

See Her Naked In:

Blood Mania (1970) Breasts, Buns

Sheree J. Wilson

Born: December 12, 1958
Rochester, Minnesota
Skin-O-Meter: Brief Nudity

It's no surprise that picture perfect Sheree J. Wilson found her way into the spotlight, because this Minnesota muffin has the glamor goods locked down and is not too shabby in the acting department either. Mistaken as a model while working behind the scenes on a photo shoot, Sheree spent three years plying her petite frame and classic beauty in numerous fashion mags—eventually moving into film

and television work, where she's made a luscious addition to several made-for-TV movies and series. Her first taste of Tinseltown came with sassy, sexy stints in 1980s B-movies like *Crimewave* (1984) and *Fraternity Vacation* (1985), in the latter playing a big-brained but short-bikinied beach babe who's the object of everyone's sandy sex drive. Once television producers got a glimpse of her all-American good looks and energetic attitude, Sheree became a staple in homes across the nation on *Dallas* for five seasons and kept it in Texas for her next role on *Walker, Texas Ranger*, as the strong and sensual love interest to high kicker Chuck Norris. But for a peek at her own prairie puppies, click out of primetime and onto Showtime for the made-for-cable thriller *Past Tense* (1994).

SKIN-fining Moment:

Past Tense (1:00) Sheree wears a vest that can't suppress her left breast in front of Scott Glenn.

See Her Naked In:

Past Tense (1994) LB

Penelope Wilton

Born: June 3, 1946
Scarborough, England, UK
Skin-O-Meter: Brief Nudity

As a longtime veteran of the British film scene, Penelope Wilton has done it all. She's snagged bit parts in made-for-TV movies such as *An Affair of Honour* (1972) and *Mrs. Warren's Profession* (1972) and tackled meatier roles in productions of Shakespeare's *King Lear* (1982) and *Othello* (1981). Only recently, however, has the seasoned saucepot come to her senses and started loosening the corset strings. She recently appeared as one of several small-town matrons who pose in the buff for charity in the inspired-by-a-true-heartwarming-story flick

Calendar Girls (2003). If that ain't enough, she also treated viewers to a nipple-baring shower scene as Judi Dench's late-blooming lezzie lover in the well-reviewed biopic *Iris* (2001), also starring thick-bottomed thespian Kate Winslet. It may have taken a while for this peach to ripen, but you've gotta hand it to Wilton for keeping it juicy.

SKIN-fining Moment:

Iris (0:55) A quick shot of Penelope's left lactoid as she washes Judi Dench's back in the shower. Apparently Judi's a dirty girl.

See Her Naked In:

Calendar Girls (2003) LB, Buns
Iris (2001) LB

Barbara Windsor

**Born: August 6, 1937
Shoreditch, London, England, UK
Skin-O-Meter: Brief Nudity**

Fans of *Carry On*, the long-running and infamous British movie series, are well-acquainted with the comedic, curvaceous charms of Barbara Windsor. She's best known for her role as the airheaded and ample Daphne Honeybutt, a role Windsor was without question born to play. She teased and tarted her way through more than a dozen *Carry On* films, showing true (yet criminally brief) skin in *Carry On Camping* (1969) and *Carry On Dick* (1974). Windsor's most celebrated (and likewise fleeting) mam flashing appears in an unrelated flick, *Not Now Darling* (1973). Though she's never appeared as nudie cutie as skin fans would like and has been buttoned-up in recent years, Windsor is one luscious limey whose lascivious legend is not soon forgotten.

SKIN-fining Moment:

Carry on Abroad (0:25) Babs showers and shows us what she's got in the seat department. Carry on stroking.

See Her Naked In:

Carry On Dick (1974) Breasts
Carry On Girls (1973) LB
Not Now Darling (1973) RB
Carry On Abroad (1972) Breasts, Buns
Carry On Henry (1971) Buns
Carry On Again Doctor (1969) Buns
Carry On Camping (1969) Breasts, Buns

Romy Windsor

Skin-O-Meter: Great Nudity

Raven-haired Romy Windsor has had few leading roles—her appearances in the lupine schlockfests *The Howling IV: The Original Nightmare* (1988) and *The Howling: New Moon Rising* (1995) notwithstanding—but she's done fairly well for herself as a bit player. Her career has none-too-auspicious roots in the screwball sex comedy *Up the Creek* (1984) but has grown somewhat more respectable (if way less revealing) with her small roles in better-known films such as John Woo's *Face/Off* (1997) and the artsy-fartsy costume drama *The House of Usher* (1988). She's also made television appearances on the *The X Files* and *Nash Bridges*, among others. Sadly, none of these appearances have been nude.

SKIN-fining Moment:

Thief of Hearts (0:12) She's all raw-n-stuff on the bed and she gives us her bumps and even some poontang when she gets up.

See Her Naked In:

Thief of Hearts (1984) FFN

Debra Winger

**Born: May 17, 1955
Cleveland, Ohio
Skin-O-Meter: Great Nudity**

Debra Winger has a genteel beauty and a clutch of Oscar nominations from movies big on social

LOVE! SET! SNATCH! DEBRA WINGER IN *MIKE'S MURDER.*

commentary that she did between the late 1970s and the mid-1980s. Somehow those qualifications have combined to obscure the fact that Winger also commands a supple torso and a face that mixes longing beauty and lusty, playful joy. Debra's best formative-period ride came in *An Officer and a Gentleman* (1982). She saddled up and sent her ass and tits in motion while mounting Richard Gere cowgirl style. As the actress's body of work matured, so did her body, as in *Mike's Murder* (1984). Fully grown, at the peak of her powers, Winger is naked often and with commendable variety in *The Sheltering Sky* (1990). All spots of interest are highlighted—from boobs to buns to bush.

SKIN-fining Moment:

An Officer and a Gentleman (1:06) Adorable buns and breasts as she makes love to Richard Gere.

See Her Naked In:

Wilder Napalm (1993) LB
A Dangerous Woman (1993) Bush
The Sheltering Sky (1990) Breasts, Bush, Buns
Mike's Murder (1984) Nip Slip LB
An Officer and a Gentleman (1982) Breasts, Buns
Slumber Party '57 (1977) Breasts

K.C. Winkler

**Born: 1956
Ontario, California
Skin-O-Meter: Great Nudity**

How did frosty-haired sex kitten K.C. Winkler come to inhabit such a bodaciously flab-free and fabulous body? The answer is that she spent years as "Body by Jake" Steinfeld's primary prop and shimmying shill. An infomercial does no good without ab-crunching K.C. dripping sex appeal like sweat in her skimpy, clinging workout togs as she demonstrates the bun-tightening, tummy-defining, rack-stretching techniques of the Body by Jake regimen. Is it exercise that Jake is selling, or sexercise? No such confusion exists in K.C.'s two best sexploitation stints. *H.O.T.S.* (1979) is a basic excuse for well-hung ladies to flail their dangling chest parts, and is there any doubt about what will be bouncing into view in *The Happy Hooker Goes to Hollywood* (1980)?

SKIN-fining Moment:

The Happy Hooker Goes Hollywood (0:44) Nice rack shot when playing pool with Susan Kiger.

See Her Naked In:

The Happy Hooker Goes Hollywood (1980) Breasts
H.O.T.S. (1979) FFN

Mare Winningham

Born: May 16, 1959
Phoenix, Arizona
Skin-O-Meter: Brief Nudity

Largely overlooked by the skinlight, Mare Winningham was a singing, song-writing, seriously acting icon of the 1980s. Loosely affiliated with the widely exposed group of post-boomer acting kids known as the Brat Pack, Mare was the first of that bunch to receive an Oscar nomination. She picked up the nod for her career-peak performance in *Georgia* (1995). Winningham did all her own vocals in the film, in which she plays a famous folk singer. Mare might be more famous today if she'd peppered her career with more peeks like the ones in *One Trick Pony* (1980). Appearing as an ingénue across from crusty folk singer Paul Simon, the young Mare is squeaky clean for all to see in a splashy bathtub scene.

SKIN-fining Moment:

One Trick Pony (0:15) An extended look at Mare's pears as she shares a bathtub with Paul Simon.

See Her Naked In:

Threshold (1981) FFN
One Trick Pony (1980) Breasts

Kitty Winn

Born: February 21, 1944
Washington D.C.
Skin-O-Meter: Great Nudity

Early in her career, Kitty Winn was wowing 'em onstage, earning rave reviews for her debut Broadway performance in Anton Chekov's *Three Sisters* and her later appearance in *Hamlet* for New York's Shakespeare in the Park. She is best remembered, however, for her role as Linda Blair's cute, concerned nanny in William Friedkin's horror classic *The Exorcist* (1973). She reprised that role in the not-so-great follow-up *Exorcist II: The Heretic* (1977) but also carved out a decent career for herself with appearances on TV shows such as *Kojak* and in the films *They Might Be Giants* (1971) and *The Last Hurrah* (1977). Her brief but noteworthy career wound down towards the end of the '70s, her last role being the lead in the lackluster thriller *Mirrors* (1978).

SKIN-fining Moment:

Panic in Needle Park (0:42) Kitty's pale pair makes an appearance as she gets out of Pacino's bed.

See Her Naked In:

Panic in Needle Park (1971) Breasts

Beth Winslet

Born: April 30, 1978
Reading, Berkshire County, England, UK
Skin-O-Meter: Brief Nudity

Big sisters can be a burden, especially when they carry around the bulging bosom and sensual, swelling hips of an earth goddess prototype such as English actress Kate Winslet. What's a little sister to do? Well, if she's Kate's younger sibling Beth Winslet, the family competition for who can monopolize the most attention should extend to the revealingly big screen of world cinema. So what if bully Kate drew all the world's stares as a star-crossed lover in the international blockbuster *Titanic* (1997)? Sly and spry Beth stole all eyes back with her fleshy flashes in *The Scold's Bridle* (1998). But wait. Not to be outdone, older, slyer Kate has trumped Beth's flash with full-on total frontal nudity in *Holy Smoke* (1999). The lesson to be learned, little sister, is that you simply must try harder.

SKIN-fining Moment:

The Scold's Bridle (1:08) Beth leans back and her bare bo-bo's wobble in and out of view. She could learn a thing (and two!) about getting nude from her sister Kate!

See Her Naked In:

The Scold's Bridle (1998) Breasts

Kate Winslet

Born: October 5, 1975
Reading Berkshire England, UK
Skin-O-Meter: Hall of Fame

Full bodied and light brunette, with a proud sensualist's craving eyes and thick, savoring lips, British-bred thespian Kate Winslet is a purveyor of passion presented in an attempt to communicate and arouse emotional purity. Wondrous, adventurous Winslet is willing to exploit every weapon in her arsenal to express the inner truths that run beneath our surface coverings. Again and again, she discards her surface clothing and uncovers her splendid and true self, stripped to the essence of skin and fuzz. Exult with courageous Kate as her furry flag and billowy pair waft in pursuit of unflagging authenticity in *Jude* (1996) and *Holy Smoke* (1999) and as her titans of truth grace the mass-entertainment blockbuster that is *Titanic* (1997).

SKIN-fining Moment:

Titanic (1:25) Awesomely buoyant buns and boobs while posing for Leonardo DiCaprio, Sketch Artist and Lucky Bastard.

See Her Naked In:

Iris (2001) FFN, Buns
Quills (2000) Breasts
Holy Smoke (1999) FFN
Hideous Kinky (1998) Breasts
Titanic (1997) Breasts, Buns
Jude (1996) FFN
Heavenly Creatures (1994) Breasts

Alexus Winston

Born: February 20, 1978
Los Angeles, California
Skin-O-Meter: Great Nudity

Luscious L.A. glamour goddess Alexus Winston began her rise to skin stardom as the Miss November *Penthouse* Pet in 1997 and has since become one of the magazine's most requested supernudes, strutting her stuff and spreading her charm in several issues, where her striking emerald eyes and quarter-bouncing tight frame have made her a steady staple in the American male diet. It's no surprise that she's programmed her best bits and bytes into a lucrative Web modeling career, where she can be found in fine form on her own site or in computer-crashing spreads on Danni Ashe's site, including hot cyber scenes with Asia Carrera and Aimee Sweet. In fact, her hot factor is so high she's making moves into the mainstream as well, serving as pitchwoman for a brand of Horny Goat Weed, as well as a stint as correspondent for E! Entertainment Television's *Wild On . . .* series. But if Alexus's PG-rated fare is too tame for tawdry tastes, she also appeared minus the miniskirt in some low budget productions like *Survivors Exposed* (2001) and *Bare Wench Project 2: Scared Topless* (2001), where she returned to her raunchy roots in roles better suited to wearing no suit at all.

SKIN-fining Moment:

The Bare Wench Project 2: Scared Topless (0:27) Alexus's boobs come into view as she performs a little picnic-blanket hanky-panky on Juliet Cariaga.

See Her Naked In:

Survivors Exposed (2001) FFN
The Bare Wench Project 2: Scared Topless (2001) FFN

Reese Witherspoon

Born: March 22, 1976
Baton Rouge, Louisiana
Skin-O-Meter: Great Nudity

Cute as a button, but capable of playing as devious as a python, effervescent Tennessee-bred blonde Reese Witherspoon has brought an inner core of sensual bubbling to almost every role she has played. As Tracy Flick, the sexually manipulative bundle of blonde ambition in *Election* (1999), Reese, while fully clothed, left no doubt that her character could melt the inhibitions of a most-upstanding community member and reduce him to little more than *Erection*. Naked, this example of southern sass is even more devastating to staid thinking. Just try to keep a pure thought through the highlight of *Twilight* (1998). Reese's upturned breasts sit as cute and perky as her pert nose while a dude nibbles from nips to a descending path that leads his head down below frame. The viewer is left with Reese's head-spinning grin of sexy satisfaction.

SKIN-fining Moment:

Twilight (0:02) A nice look at topless Reese's pieces, lying in bed talking to Jeff. Sweet Home Ala-Booby!

See Her Naked In:

Twilight (1998) Breasts

Alicia Witt

Born: August 21, 1975
Worcester, Massachusetts
Skin-O-Meter: Brief Nudity

Red hair, bite-sized strawberry nips, and a complexion like the flowing white light of heaven don't guarantee success as a movie star. Such stellar attributes do, however, ensure that onscreen imp Alicia Witt will be wondered about and worshiped by legions of mesmerized skinfidels until skindom come. Hopefully it won't take that long for Alicia to peel off with some meaningfully revelatory footage. To date, her most-nude tumble was portraying a bratty, slightly slutty movie exec on an episode of The Sopranos. Alicia's character screws, then screws over, a member of the Soprano crew. She's not nearly naked enough in doing so. The enticing fire head has tripped about in lingerie in Playing Mona Lisa (2000) and Two Weeks Notice (2002) and modeled electrical-tape pasties in Four Rooms (1995). When will the heavens part and show us the unadorned miracle of Witt?

SKIN-fining Moment:

The Sopranos "D-Girl" (2000) Flame-maned Alicia's milky–white right diary-dumpling slips out of her robe while she rides Michael Imperioli's meat–gat in a hotel room.

TeleVisions:

The Sopranos RB, Buns

Kathryn Witt

Born: November 30, 1950
Miami, Florida
Skin-O-Meter: Brief Nudity

Brunette beauty Kathryn Witt kicked her career off with a bang, scoring a small part alongside Hollywood heavyweights James Caan and Alan Arkin in the cop comedy *Freebie and the Bean* (1974). From there, she snagged another small role alongside one of the greats, appearing with Dustin Hoffman in the critically acclaimed biopic *Lenny* (1974). While she still appeared in films now and then—including the classic Playmate-done-wrong pic *Star 80* (1983)—the lean-hipped lass mostly displayed her talents (if not her naughty bits) on the boob tube, appearing in everything from the Connie Sellecca stewardess adventure series *Flying High* to the goofy hidden treasure caper *Masserati and the Brain* (1982). Her only lead role was opposite an ancient, carnivorous lizard man in the horror flick *Demon of Paradise* (1987). Fans last spied the silken-haired sexpot in a bit part in the Oscar-winning Tom Hanks weepie *Philadelphia* (1983). While Hanks's portrayal of a man suffering from AIDS had 'em sobbing in the aisles, it's the thought of never seeing winsome Witt on the silver screen again that gets Mr. Skin all choked up.

SKIN-fining Moment:

Lenny (0:43) A great look at Witt's tits as she prepares to have lesbi-sex with Valerie Perrine.

See Her Naked In:

Lenny (1974) Breasts
Freebie and the Bean (1974) Buns

Karen Witter

Born: December 13, 1961
Long Beach, California
Skin-O-Meter: Great Nudity

Some women deserve to be kicked out of bed simply to enjoy the twist and bounce of their buttocks as they waltz away from the duvet. Such an awe-inspiring, compact, and tidy ass is attached to blonde, limber, lean lass Karen Witter as she walks with proud dignity and wiggling heinie after doing sheet stunts in *Another Chance* (1989). Though Karen's California-blonde face is as pretty and breezy as the mugs seen on the models in ads for breath freshener, her room-lighting eyes dim to faded memories in the overwhelming glow of those two taut, tight, palm-sized nether globes. For auxiliary views of the illuminating vision that is Karen Witter, switch on *Midnight* (1989).

SKIN-fining Moment:

Midnight (0:32) Karen leans down hard on her loverman and we see her smushed witter-titters, plus one quick slip of left nip.

See Her Naked In:

Midnight (1989) LB
Another Chance (1989) Breasts, Buns
Numerous Playboy Videos

TeleVisions:

Bedtime Breasts, Buns

Annie Wood

Born: 1971
Los Angeles, California
Skin-O-Meter: Great Nudity

Though her short-lived game show *Bzzz!* (which the sexy screwball both hosted and produced) did little to rouse audiences, B-movie veteran Annie Wood has since strutted her perky blonde stuff through a number of higher-profile projects. She's made several appearances on the Ted Danson sitcom *Becker*, playing a trashy and flashy single mom, and has tackled other appealingly raunchy small-screen roles as a crack ho, a stripper, and even Jessica Hahn, the latter in the TV movie *Fall from Grace* (1990). Wood has an appealingly cute-yet-sexy look and a set of pipes to match—listen up for her voice-over work in Baskin Robbins commercials and get an earful of sexy sass.

SKIN-fining Moment:

Cellblock Sisters: Banished Behind Bars (0:15) Annie'll give ya Wood all right! Get a load of her jail-bound jubblies in this smokin' sex scene.

See Her Naked In:

Cellblock Sisters: Banished Behind Bars (1996) Breasts
Inside Out IV (1992) LB

TeleVisions:

Love Street Breasts, Bush, Buns

Cynthia Wood

Born: September 25, 1950
Burbank, California
Skin-O-Meter: Brief Nudity

If ever a sweet, young hardbody would appear as a hot-pants honey, dancing her way through an epic and historic filmic achievement in a teasingly revealing cowgirl outfit, and then if that body would return twenty-something years later to drop the skimpy cowgirl top and impress her floating wonders and standup nipples on a hang-jawed audience, would that that body would be the body of Cynthia Wood. Upon its initial release, director Francis Ford Coppola's *Apocalypse Now* (1979) blew cinema fans away with its dark visions and haunting metaphors and also with the boogaloo buns and boobies of fair blonde sensual bundle Cynthia Wood, onstage and on the verge of nudity to entertain a seething mob of sex-starved troops. Imagine the surprise of the teased G.I.s when more than two decades later Francis Ford revealed he had been holding back, issuing a new director's cut, *Apocalypse Now Redux* (2001), a far more revealing show that is again stolen by the jutting flesh ledge of Cynthia Wood, this time with breasts out in the clear light of day, two grand installments of soldiers' pay.

SKIN-fining Moment:

Apocalypse Now Redux (1:28)
Cynthia services service man Sam

Bottoms and shows her top in a helicopter. It's a real Teat Offensive.

See Her Naked In:

Apocalypse Now Redux (2001) Breasts
Van Nuys Blvd. (1979) Breasts

Janet Wood

Skin-O-Meter: Great Nudity

In *Up!* (1976), one of the raunchier of Russ Meyer's mega-jugs marathons, Janet Wood shows plenty o' boob (and more) in a sea of boundless, blessed bosom. Although not as invested with the usual chestedness of most of Meyer's anti-ingénues, Wood can still raise wood in any of her, ahem, titillating roles. Following along with this theme of boobs, bush, and B-movies, Mr. Skin now adds bikers: Check out more of J-Wo in Roger Corman's classic *Angels Hard as They Come* (1971). This is the ultimate nexus of all things B-movie, with healthy doses of Janet dancing topless, not to mention hippies, bikers, bad dialogue, and Wood at her breast, er, best in a rather rough and tumble bodice-ripping style scene.

SKIN-fining Moment:

Angels Hard as They Come (1:10)
Janet does a lengthy topless dance with Neva Davis for an obviously enthralled group of fellers.

See Her Naked In:

Slumber Party '57 (1977) Breasts
Up! (1976) FFN
The Centerfold Girls (1974) Breasts
G.I. Executioner (1973) Breasts, Buns
Angels Hard as They Come (1971) Breasts

Lana Wood

Born: March 1, 1946
Santa Monica, California
Skin-O-Meter: Great Nudity

A picture-perfect brunette with willing, wide brown eyes set in a wavy frame of amber-brown hair, Lana Wood had the bountiful heaven-leavened mams and stellar Hollywood lineage (she is the younger sister of eternal starlet Natalie Wood) that make for greatness. Lana's big top started very near the top as Plenty O'Toole, beguiling Sean Connery's James Bond in *Diamonds Are Forever* (1971). The best plot twist in *Diamonds* had Lana's big guns forever spilling from their low-cut holsters. Ten years later, the expanses of breast flesh would cascade gloriously down Wood's chest, accessorized with nipples the size of small pancakes, in *Demon Rage* (1981). *Demon* also featured the raging left third of Lana's pubic triangle.

SKIN-fining Moment:

Demon Rage (0:09) The Demon, which is evidently a pulsating pink light, pulls the bedsheet off of Lana, revealing her massive melons and even a touch of muff! Thank you, Mr. Demon!

See Her Naked In:

Demon Rage (1981) Breasts, Bush
Grayeagle (1978) RB
A Place Called Today (1972) Breasts

Natalie Wood

Born: July 20, 1938
San Francisco, California
Died: November 29, 1981
Skin-O-Meter: Never Nude

She could have been America's sweetheart, except there was something naughty in the impish mischief of her devilish good looks. She played a little more tart than sweet. The always sexy, never virginal Natalie Wood started as a child actress in the 1950s. She stepped into her bad-girl stride as carnally knowledgeable juvenile delinquents in *Rebel without a Cause*

(1955) and *West Side Story* (1961). Although she continued to excel in roles that stretched the boundaries of Hollywood content, and she never lost an iota of her core-deep sex appeal, the closest Natalie ever came to full-frontal disclosure was in *Bob & Carol & Ted & Alice* (1969). The picture tackled the risqué topic of mate swapping and featured racy sequences of Natalie in bra and panties or bikini. Tragically, November 29, 1981, will forever live as the day Natalie Wood's life was cut short, along with the abiding hopes of millions of her fans.

SKIN-fining Moment:

Bob & Carol & Ted & Alice (1:13) Nat shakes her hips and does the most impishly sexy strip down to pink bra- and-panties for Elliot Gould. You'll get Wood all right!

Bambi Woods

Died: 1986
Skin-O-Meter: Great Nudity

Blonde, improbably wholesome looking, with beautiful, downy-soft breasts, Bambi Woods was the star and prime selling point of one of the best-grossing porn flicks of all time. The marketing geniuses behind *Debbie Does Dallas* (1978) did nothing to dispel the myth that Bambi had been a real-life member of the renowned Dallas Cowboys Cheerleaders. A story that is probably closer to actual events is that Woods tried out for the squad but was cut. She has achieved an immortality beyond what any mere cheerleader could dream of. In the original *Debbie* and its two sequels (1981 and 1985), Woods managed to be both wanton and virginal, appearing sweet and innocent while her body shined with a sheen of sex sweat and misplaced bodily fluids. If a person was determined to watch only one porno in his lifetime, the

original *Dallas* would make him regret that limiting decision.

SKIN-fining Moment:

Debbie Does Dallas (1:18) This Bambi is a different kind of dear, but she definitely supplies Woods. Cheer for her here as she tests a male player's meat- bat in a sporting–goods store. He hits a home run.

See Her Naked In:

Debbie Does Dallas (1978) FFN, Buns
Numerous Adult Movies

Barbara Alyn Woods

Skin-O-Meter: Great Nudity

Television has a way of distorting reality. Barbara Alyn Woods probably achieved her broadest fame as the mom on the network family laugh fest *Honey, I Shrunk the Kids* between the years 1997 to 2000. But look at the smirking mischief in Barbara's saucy stare. Let your gaze drift down past the pert set of her plush and pliable lips and rest upon the soft protrusion of her rising cleavage. Don't feel like shrinking, do you? To expand into a fuller consciousness of Barbara's appeal, grow with her snake-handling topless dancer in *Striptease* (1996), stretch out and enjoy wonderful Woods as the flesh-baring hostess of the Playboy Channel *Fantasy Island* knock-off *Eden*, and be a big boy as Barbara Alyn bares big-as-life buns and boobs in *Inside Out* (1992).

SKIN-fining Moment:

Dance With Death (0:17) Babs seems a bit nervous as she strips during an amateur contest. Look at her nice, natural boobs: she's got nothing to worry about!

See Her Naked In:

Striptease (1996) Breasts, Thong
Dead Weekend (1995) Breasts
Eden 6 (1994) Breasts, Buns
Eden 5 (1993) Breasts, Buns

Eden 3 (1993) Breasts, Buns
Flesh and Bone (1993) Buns
The Waterdance (1992) Thong
The Terror Within II (1992) Breasts, Buns
Eden (1992) Breasts, Buns
Inside Out (1992) Breasts, Buns
Dance With Death (1991) Breasts, Thong

TeleVisions:

Dream On Breasts, Buns

Natalia Wörner

Born: September 7, 1967
Stuttgart, Germany
Skin-O-Meter: Hall of Fame

Before getting her start in acting, Natalia Wörner was a successful international model working in Paris, Milan, New York, Zurich, and Vienna. Not very well known in America, Natalia has been a house- hold name in Europe since her debut in the German film *Thea und Nat* (1992). Equally at ease in comedies, dramas, thrillers, and horror movies, she also seems quite comfortable appearing onscreen in the furry-muffed buff. Her magnificently untamed bush and gloriously proportioned gazongas are in full gratuitious display before, during, and after a shower (her very first skin scene!) in *Die Sieger* (1994). Later that same year she showed some flesh opposite Gerard Depardieu in *La Machine* (1994). For the best bang for your foreign film buck, check out the very nearly explicit sex scenes in *Der Elefant vergißt nie* (1995), which only runs twenty-nine minutes, so there's no waiting around for the good parts!

SKIN-fining Moment:

Die Sieger (0:13) Completely muff- tastic full-frontal wonder from Natalia as she enters a hot tub behind a steamy glass partition.

See Her Naked In:

Liebe und Verlangen (2003) Breasts, Bush, Buns

Der Seerosenteich (2002) Breasts, Buns
Liebe unter Verdacht (2002) Breasts, Buns
Klassentreffen—Mordfall unter Freunden
    (2001) LB, Buns
Verbotene Küsse (2001) Breasts, Bush, Buns
Der Handymörder (1998) LB
Zur Zeit zu zweit (1998) RB
Spiel um dein Leben (1997) Breasts
Der Rosenmörder (1997) Breasts, Buns
Irren ist männlich (1996)
Der Elefant vergißt nie (1995) Breasts, Buns
Kinder der Nacht (1995) FFN, Buns
Unter Druck (1995) LB
Um die 30 (1995) RB
Die Sieger (1994) FFN
La Machine (1994) Breasts

Mary Woronov

Born: December 8, 1943
Palm Beach, Florida
Skin-O-Meter: Hall of Fame

Sultry, tall, brunette, cutting-edge culture icon Mary Woronov is similar to cult drag star Divine, except that Mary is really a woman. In the 1960s she sampled a strong taste of fame and anti-fame when she was hanging around artist Andy Warhol and the creative misfits who populated his famous Factory. Her proximity to the basic sensationalism of such Warhol films as *Trash* and *Flesh* taught Mary that art could be achieved in low places and that almost any movie can be improved if a lanky, brooding, dark-haired woman takes off her clothes and teases her nipples to erection. It is also beneficial if she makes out with another naked chick or if she stands and flexes her exposed ass muscles at the camera. See the formula worked to perfection in *Sugar Cookies* (1973), *Death Race 2000* (1975), *Eating Raoul* (1982), and *Angel of H.E.A.T.* (1982).

SKIN-fining Moment:

Eating Raoul (0:48) Ms. Woronov shows her wobblies as she struggles with Ed Begly Jr. and again when

Robert Beltran counts cash on her stomach.

See Her Naked In:

*Scenes From the Class Struggle in Beverly
    Hills* (1989) Breasts
Angel of H.E.A.T. (1982) FFN
Eating Raoul (1982) Breasts, Buns
Death Race 2000 (1975) Breasts, Bush
Sugar Cookies (1973) FFN, Buns
Kemek (1970)

Fay Wray

Born: September 15, 1907
Near Cardston, Alberta, Canada
Died: August 8, 2004
Skin-O-Meter: Brief Nudity

A direct line can be traced from the black-and-white histrionics of waifish flapper babe of yore Fay Wray and the full-color scream queens of today's gore and horror extravaganzas. When Fay Wray wailed and wilted in the grasp of the big title ape in *King Kong* (1933), she had already been emoting up a storm in silent films for at least a decade. How was she to know that the combination of a very attractive woman in peril, a skimpy outfit, and a slip of nip would turn out to be such a successful and long-running Hollywood formula? And how was she to know that her brief bobbling of boob into the never-blinking eye of the camera lens would have the unblinking attention of skinthusiasts down through the ages? Check out *King Kong*, and go a little ape.

SKIN-fining Moment:

King Kong (1:12) Fay is way hot—so much so that she has to be dunked in the drink where her demure dumplings get cooled off alongside Bruce Cabot. Her right rack-flesh will put a monster in your pants.

See Her Naked In:

King Kong (1933) Nip Slip RB

Robin Wright Penn

Born: April 8, 1966
Dallas, Texas
Skin-O-Meter: Great Nudity

Robin Wright Penn's name is preceded by "and introducing" in the blockbuster film *The Princess Bride* (1987). While that movie made her a star, Robin's real debut was in the less mainstream *Hollywood Vice Squad* (1986). Either way, men around the world were happy to have the Texas native strut her stuff on the big screen. She was nominated for a Golden Globe as Jenny in *Forrest Gump* (1994), but if you want to see her golden globes, check out *State of Grace* (1990). Robin's milky-white bobbins are seen fleetingly, and, though it marks her skin debut, she went on to bigger and breastier things. Robin showed off her assets in *Denial* (1991) and the aforementioned *Forrest Gump*. In real life, she married hothead Sean Penn, who doesn't mind sharing his bounty with the public. Robin truly flies in *Moll Flanders* (1996), which offers a lingering look at her luscious lungs. That's a Penn we'd like to get our hands on and write something erotic!

SKIN-fining Moment:

State of Grace (0:38) Raw Robin rack as she accepts Sean's Penn-is while they're both standing up.

See Her Naked In:

Loved (1997) Breasts, Buns
Moll Flanders (1996) Breasts
Forrest Gump (1994) Breasts, Buns
Denial (1991) Buns
State of Grace (1990) Breasts

Jenny Wright

Born: March 23, 1962
New York, New York
Skin-O-Meter: Great Nudity

A natural blonde with a brunette soul, Jenny Wright could play anything from a vampire (in *Near Dark* [1987]) to a brothel owner (in *Young Guns II* [1990]) with equal aplomb. With her goo-goo-doll green eyes and a baby-doll mouth that seems always to have just finished sucking her thumb, Wright has the bruised purity of a sinfully hot angel who has discovered, somewhat against her will, the thrill of being bad. Her chest pillows and her seat cushions perfectly complement the soft swellings of her lips and high, round cheeks. Hers are the full profile breasts dangling in *Pink Floyd the Wall* (1982). That hefty side of jug in *The Wild Life* (1984) is hers as well. And don't forget to credit her for the split cheeks of *Young Guns II*. With equipment this good, Jenny couldn't help but seem a bit bad.

SKIN-fining Moment:

Pink Floyd the Wall (0:42) A sexy look at Jenny's bouncing jugs as she enjoys some backstage debauchery.

See Her Naked In:

The Lawnmower Man (1992) RB
Young Guns II (1990) Buns
The Wild Life (1984) Breasts
World According to Garp (1982) Breasts
Pink Floyd the Wall (1982) Breasts

"If all is going well in my life, sex with my boyfriend or a beautiful man. And if all is not going well— sex with myself."

—KARI WUHRER ON HOW SHE UNWINDS

Vivian Wu

Born: 1966
Shanghai, China
Skin-O-Meter: Great Nudity

Imperiously demure, exhibiting an impassive beauty, her womanly emotions fully contained by a porcelain-perfect complexion, Chinese-born actress Vivian Wu has almost always adhered to her homeland's archetypal notion of female grace. She played to stereotype in such Asian-themed blockbusters as *The Last Emperor* (1987), *The Joy Luck Club* (1993), and *The Teenage Mutant Ninja Turtles III* (1993). But there is one outstanding exception to Vivian's rule of staid appearances. That joyous aberration is *The Pillow Book* (1995). In Asian culture, pillow books are tomes compiling erotic writings. In the movie, Vivian's slender, naked body is used as the manuscript upon which these sensual stories are written and then played out. Almost every inch of her skin, including that moist strip of flesh stretching from her heavenly portal to her excretory porthole, is shown off from every available angle. Tradition will never be the same.

SKIN-fining Moment:

The Pillow Book (0:59) Vivian gets topless and shows her Wu-Wu's.

See Her Naked In:

The Pillow Book (1995) FFN, Buns

Kari Wuhrer

Born: April 28, 1967
Brookfield, Connecticut
Skin-O-Meter: Hall of Fame

The story of Kari Wuhrer is one of a meteoric rise to B-movie glory and full nudity. Kari was spotted as a fourteen-year-old punk rocker by talent scouts from the Ford modeling agency. Modeling exposure led her to talent scouts from MTV. The wide audience gained by being a VJ allowed Kari to leap into the movie-starlet role. Luckily, the statuesque and stacked brunette (sometimes a blonde) didn't jump as high as former MTV drudges Jon Stewart and Adam Sandler, or she wouldn't be naked so often. Kari is stuck in the naked circle of career limbo. She aired her bush in *Boulevard* (1994); she aired it some more in *Luscious* (1997); and she kept the trim just out of sight in *Spider's Web* (2001). It's a great bush. All the parts that go with it are great, too.

SKIN-fining Moment:

***Luscious (0:04)** Full-frontal fun taking off her robe and posing for Stephen Shellen. Long scene. Unfucking believable!!!*

See Her Naked In:

King of the Ants (2003) FFN, Buns
Spider's Web (2001) Breasts, Buns
Lip Service (2000) Thong
Poison (2000) Breasts, Thong
Ivory Tower (1999) Buns
Kate's Addiction (1999) LB, Thong
Phoenix (1998) Breasts, Buns
Luscious (1997) FFN, Buns
Sex and the Other Man (1997) FFN, Buns
Beyond Desire (1996) Breasts, Buns
An Occasional Hell (1996) Breasts, Thong
Terminal Justice (1995) Breasts
Hot Blooded (1995) RB
The Crossing Guard (1995) Breasts, Thong
Boulevard (1994) FFN, Buns
Sensation (1994) FFN, Buns

Jane Wyatt

Born: August 12, 1911
Campgaw, New Jersey
Skin-O-Meter: Brief Nudity

Jane Wyatt is a Jersey girl, a high society piece of ass who gave up the bluebloods to make red-blooded men's arteries (among other things) harden with her provocative stage, film, and TV work. Though moist famous as the prim and proper wife and mother on *Father Knows Best*, Jane had a less conventional side. She appeared opposite Gregory Peck in the searing indictment of anti-Semitism *Gentlemen's Agreement* (1947), but an ever more radical exposure occurred earlier in her career. In the story of paradise found *Lost Horizon* (1937), Jane reveals why this Shangri-La was truly heaven. In a pre-Hayes Code flash of skin, Jane took a skinny dip into the water and made audiences' laps wet. When it comes to making viewers happy, Jane says, *Wyatt not!*

SKIN-fining Moment:

Lost Horizon (1937) Father knows breast? Jane's character indulges in a shocking-for-1937 skinny dip. We get a long-shot of somebody's boobs, buns, and bush. Could be Jane, could be a Body Double. Still: 1937!

See Her Naked In:

Lost Horizon (1937) Body Double—FFN, Buns/Her—Buns

Dana Wynter

Born: June 8, 1931
Berlin, Germany
Skin-O-Meter: Brief Nudity

The daughter of a hotshot surgeon, Apache-eyed, whippet-thin brunette Dana Wynter was born in Berlin, Germany, slightly before the rise of the Nazis and was lucky enough to grow up in London, England. Bright and scholarly, Dana only took to theatrics as a break from her pre-med studies, but medicine would just have to wait when Dana discovered a higher calling, that of a big Hollywood movie celebrity. Receiving star billing for features that started with *Lady Godiva Rides Again* (1951) and moved up through *Invasion of the Body Snatchers* (1956) and *Airport* (1970), Wynter's wild and wonderful ride was crowned with a regal slip of nip during a bed-top grapple beneath a huffing honkie in *If He Hollers, Let Him Go!* (1968).

SKIN-fining Moment:

If He Hollers, Let Him Go! (0:43) Lightning, quick left-side nip-slip as Dana makes out with Kevin McCarthy in bed.

See Her Naked In:

If He Hollers, Let Him Go! (1968) LB

Sarah Wynter

Born: February 15, 1973
Newcastle, Australia
Skin-O-Meter: Great Nudity

With a timeless beauty and strong, sensual presence, Sarah Wynter could warm up the farthest reaches of space—but we'll settle for the space between commercials she's filled on the second season of television's *24* as wealthy legal eagle Kate Warner. And by the looks of it, this Wynter is certainly heating up as she inches closer to Hollywood stardom, mixing up a powerful potion of drop-dead gorgeous and pistol-whip smarts that inebriates more than any libation. But Sarah is certainly due the spoils of skin, since she's opened the pouch and kicked out the koalas more than once on her path to A-list royalty. Catching the acting bug in her native Australia, she got a late start Stateside but regardless has managed to grab some impressive television and movie roles—most of which have allowed her to leave her clothes way down under. Her first Stateside break came in the form of the series premiere of *Sex and the City*, which led to some forgettable but lip-lickable parts in Hollywood fodder like *Species II* (1998), *The 6th Day* (2000), and *Bride of the Wind* (2001), all for which her barbies were turned on full blast and proved to be no shrimps. Sarah Wynter is proving to be Australian for skin.

SKIN-fining Moment:

Species II (0:38) Check out Sarah's sweet skinsacks as she drops her nightgown and climbs atop some guy.

See Her Naked In:

Bride of the Wind (2001) Breasts
The 6th Day (2000) LB, Buns
Species II (1998) Breasts

Amanda Wyss

Born: November 24, 1960
Manhattan Beach, California
Skin-O-Meter: Brief Nudity

Blonde and fair of skin, her pouting lips and hooded eyes signifying the promise of and hope for sensual satiation, Manhattan Beach, California, native Amanda Wyss didn't have far to travel in her quest to take Hollywood by storm. Hardly in her twenties, her brazen, fresh-faced insouciance earned her a slot in the esteemed ensemble that banded together to make *Fast Times at Ridgemont High* (1982). With no time to look back, Amanda played a crucial role in all-time teen-terror delight *A Nightmare on Elm Street* (1984), was kid-at-heart Bridget Cagney to Sharon Gless's grownup detective on the cop TV long-runner *Cagney & Lacey*, and bared her grownup breasts in *Deadly Innocents* (1990), a lethal allure that she has yet to match.

SKIN-fining Moment:

Deadly Innocents (1:29) Ripe right rackage as Amanda settles into the sack with a male member of the species.

See Her Naked In:

Deadly Innocents (1990) Breasts

y

Missy Yager

Skin-O-Meter: Brief Nudity

Some jobs demand more propriety than others, and a career in the scholastic sector is unthinkable to any aspirant who is not entirely upstanding and staid. Brunette, intensely earnest, and blue-eyed Missy Yager projects a solidity of character that would reassure any parent that their child was in stable, responsible hands, which is perhaps part of why Missy is so effective in her academic role on the Fox high-school melodrama *Boston Public*. Another aspect of the Yager appeal, which has enchanted and entranced on shows as diverse as *JAG*, *Six Feet Under*, and *NYPD Blue*, is the nagging suspicion that she arouses in the fathers of her students that some secret aspect of her past is not quite savory.

SKIN-fining Moment:

Interview with the Vampire (0:50) *Brief full-frontal shot through a cracked-open door while Missy bathes herself as Kirsten Dunst contemplates the possibility of having a suck.*

See Her Naked In:

Dead Man Walking (1996) Buns
Interview with the Vampire (1994) FFN

Cassie Yates

Born: March 2, 1951
Macon, Georgia
Skin-O-Meter: Great Nudity

As the 1970s spilled into the early '80s, a golden age was created for curly-headed blondes with dimpled imp grins who were willing to show their mouth-watering mouthfuls while performing in necessarily nude scenes that added a cachet of edgy immediacy to movies that mattered, such as the Vietnam revenge drama *Rolling Thunder* (1977), *Convoy* (1978), a Sam Peckinpah tribute to the embattled American trucker, and *The Osterman Weekend* (1983), a dissection of political corruption and manipulation at the highest levels, also directed by Peckinpah. Aside from a commitment to commentary on societal ills in a beleaguered democracy, each of these three films also shares a slice of nudity from dimpled imp towhead Cassie Yates, who would bask in this meaningful glory at the tail end of the 1980s, where she reigned as Sarah Curtis on archetypal nighttime soap *Dynasty*.

SKIN-fining Moment:

Rolling Thunder (1:31) *Ta-ta's when she takes her shirt off for Tommy Lee Jones.*

See Her Naked In:

The Osterman Weekend (1983) Breasts
Convoy (1978) LB
Rolling Thunder (1977) Breasts

Kim Yates

Born: June 6, 1969
Elizabeth, New Jersey
Skin-O-Meter: Great Nudity

Being successful in life as a sexy blonde comes down to this: When fate hands you coals, turn them into a smoldering career as the sizzling sexpot in a long series of hard-R erotic thrillers. Thus when the TV production *Maui Heat* failed to catch fire for bra-bursting blonde Kim Yates, she quickly turned to plan B-movie. Light up your life with smoke-free visual incendiaries in such burning-bush fare as *Loveblind* (1999). Actually, the New Jersey-born Yates's garden state seems to have very little foliage on it. It sure is nice to be afforded the footage with which to make that observation. Kim has a stack of credits; she's stacked in all of them, usually with open rack and often featuring a boff grapple that we dare you to swear is faked.

SKIN-fining Moment:

Secret Pleasures (0:39) *Kim's pleasures aren't secret at all here, as she lays all the good bare before, during, and after copulating with her boyfriend on a couch. FFN, buns.*

See Her Naked In:

Hard as Nails (2001) Breasts
Timegate: Tales of the Saddle Tramps (1999) FFN, Buns
Loveblind (1999) FFN, Buns
Secret Pleasures (1999) FFN, Buns

Alien Files (1999) FFN, Buns
Intimate Nights (1998) FFN, Buns
Striking Resemblance (1997) FFN, Buns, Thong
Dangerous Invitation (1998) FFN
Teach Me Tonight (1997) FFN, Buns
The Price of Desire (1996) FFN, Buns
Maui Heat (1996) FFN, Buns

TeleVisions:

Beverly Hills Bordello FFN, Buns
Erotic Confessions Breasts, Bush, Buns
Nightcap FFN, Buns
Pleasure Zone FFN, Buns

Carrie Jean Yazel

**Born: November 30, 1969
Huntington Beach, California
Skin-O-Meter: Brief Nudity**

Carrie Jean Yazel did what any curvy California girl worth her weight in sunscreen and boobage should do by posing without her clothing. As a *Playboy* Playmate in May 1991, Carrie caught the flies of Hollywood execs, who cast this flesh-packed fox in *Death Becomes Her* (1992), *The Settlement* (1999), and *Mr. Baseball* (1992). After guest starring on the sexplicit *Silk Stalkings*, Carrie hit a home run by unveiling her bubbling breastage on the Showtime series *Compromising Situations*. Rest assured that this blonde beauty doesn't compromise when it comes to flaunting her fetching figure onscreen. From her *Playboy* vids to her butt baring in *Death Becomes Her*, any of Carrie's onscreen sexcapades are a major source of skinspiration.

SKIN-fining Moment:

Death Becomes Her (0:28) Just a fleeting flash of Carrie Jean's ass in the mirror when she ducks out of the camera's eye. It's quick, but damn is that a nice can!

See Her Naked In:

Death Becomes Her (1992) Buns
Numerous *Playboy* Videos

TeleVisions:

Compromising Situations Breasts

Rachel York

**Born: August 7, 1971
Orlando, Florida
Skin-O-Meter: Brief Nudity**

Suggestion: If you ever find yourself browsing the MrSkin.com archives and come across Rachel York's bedspring-breaking scene with George Segal in *Taking the Heat* (1993), click through it reeeal slow. You can thank Mr. Skin later for fogging up your monitor. This is one steamy sex scene and probably the most acrobatic that York's breasts have ever been on camera. Unfortunately, Rachel's silver-screen skin-baring history is all too brief, as she is far more likely to be seen high kicking those luscious legs on Broadway. York has strutted her fine stuff in such favorites as *Victor/Victoria*, *Les Miserables*, and *The Scarlet Pimpernel*.

MR. SKIN'S TOP TEN

Classic Movie Stars I Wish Got Naked
. . . No nudes is bad news

10. Mae West
9. Kim Novak
8. Lauren Bacall
7. Eva Marie Saint
6. Rita Hayworth
5. Donna Reed
4. Ava Gardner
3. Jane Russell
2. Raquel Welch
1. **Grace Kelly**

SKIN-fining Moment:

Taking the Heat (0:22) Bouncing breasts while on top of George Segal during sex. Long scene.

See Her Naked In:

Taking the Heat (1993) Breasts

Susannah York

**Born: January 9, 1941
London, England, UK
Skin-O-Meter: Great Nudity**

British-bred serious thespian Susannah York was one of the first ladies of film to put the "gland" in England. It's time to jostle the mammary. With her pouting lips, modish short hairdo, boyish hips, and teeny pencil-eraser nips, Susannah was perfectly presented as one half of a lesbian couple in *The Killing of Sister George* (1968). For its day, the picture's muff-munching themes and graphic titty nudity were considered quite risqué. Even contemporary audiences can expect an electric thrill as York models her lacy black lingerie, then decides the bra is simply far too confining. Susannah's oversized eyes slightly avert themselves as a lady love licks and tweaks her nipples to a state of straining urgency. All other eyes will be riveted to those two spots.

SKIN-fining Moment:

The Killing of Sister George (2:07) A nice look at Suzannah's shirt-jammers as the older Beryl Reid puts some sly titty-sucking lesbi-moves on her in bed.

See Her Naked In:

The Silent Partner (1979) RB
The Shout (1978) Breasts, Buns
The Adventures of Eliza Fraser (1976) Breasts
Images (1972) FFN, Buns
The Killing of Sister George (1968) Breasts

Dey Young

Born: July 28, 1955
Bloomfield Hills, Michigan
Skin-O-Meter: Brief Nudity

When Dey Young was a wee miss fresh out of Michigan, she starred as the lusty leading lady in the rockstravaganza *Rock 'n' Roll High School* (1979). As if rockin' and rollin' and what not with the Ramones weren't enough for any young starlet in a lifetime, Dey continued to shake the charms between her arms as a successful character actress in funky flicks such as *Strange Behavior* (1981), *The Mod Squad* (1999), and *The Serpent and the Rainbow* (1988). While any of Young's brief yet boobilicious appearances are sufficient to get pant pythons a-pounding', Dey is breast undressed in *Conflict of Interest* (1993). Even in the background, Dey is always un-Dey-niably noticed.

SKIN-fining Moment:

Conflict of Interest (0:30) Brief breasts in this dark scene with Christopher McDonald.

See Her Naked In:

Conflict of Interest (1993) Breasts

Karen Young

Born: September 29, 1988
Pennsylvania
Skin-O-Meter: Great Nudity

With a face that specializes in the erotic embodiment of agonized ecstasy, Karen Young doesn't land a ton of sex-bunny roles. The edgy parts she is drawn to, however, expose her edgy parts and have long drawn an audience of skin cognoscenti. In her early twenties, young and full of tit, with a finely creased, buoyant speck of an ass, Karen showed all her goods in *Handgun* (1983) and showed a gutsy way of handling a pistol as well. Take a glance at her presentation of unfulfilled rack in the anti-romance *The Wife* (1996). Focus extensive scrutiny on Karen's pearly-white skin and puckering pink nipples in *Mercy* (1999), a spooky delve into the darker aspects of sex that includes S/M costuming and kinky bondage balling. Young keeps getting better as she grows older.

SKIN-fining Moment:

Mercy (1:24) Orange muff time! Karen gives up a brief shot of lower frontal nudity in bed with Julian Sands, then some brief hooterdom. Nice work.

See Her Naked In:

Mercy (2000) FFN
The Wife (1996) Breasts
Night Game (1989) RB
Criminal Law (1988) Breasts, Buns
Handgun (1983) Breasts, Buns

> "Being a blonde makes you very ruthless, insane, and self-centered."
>
> —SEAN YOUNG

Sean Young

Born: November 20, 1959
Louisville, Kentucky
Skin-O-Meter: Hall of Fame

She's kooky and she's classy. It's the Sean Young conundrum. A *conundrum* is a type of mystery, an intricate and difficult problem with no clear-cut answer. Such is the middle name of Sean "Conundrum" Young. Brunette and slim with form-fitted ass cheeks and easy-swinging udders, she's exciting to look at and hard to forget. But her onscreen fireworks have often been upstaged by offscreen meltdowns. There was the restraining order filed by James Woods after a terminated affair. There was the spectacle of Sean parading around in a cat suit, crying that she'd been robbed of the Catwoman role in *Batman Returns* (1992). And now there is a career curve in flux that creates an influx of breast and derriere curves. *Control* (2001) boasts tits and fully naked fake love-making. *Out of Control* (1998) places a camera up Sean's ass crease and slips in a peek of pubes. And that is only the tip of the furburger. It's crazy. Who can figure it out?

SKIN-fining Moment:

Love Crimes (1:01) It looks like a quick nip slip when Sean hits the bathtub, but when Bergin snaps a Polaroid of her nakedness she stands up and shows everything!

See Her Naked In:

Seduced by a Thief (2001) Breasts
Threat of Exposure (2001) RB, Thong
Out of Control (1998) FFN, Buns
Motel Blue (1997) Body Double—Breasts, Buns
Men (1997) FFN, Buns
Dr. Jekyll and Ms. Hyde (1995) Breasts
Mirage (1995) FFN, Thong
Even Cowgirls Get the Blues (1994) Breasts
Fatal Instinct (1993 Thong
Forever (1992) Breasts
Blue Ice (1992) Breasts, Buns
Sketch Artist (1992) RB
A Kiss Before Dying (1991) Breasts
Love Crimes (1991) FFN, Buns
Fire Birds (1990) RB
The Boost (1988) Breasts, Buns
No Way Out (1987) Breasts

Z

Zabou

Born: October 30, 1959
Paris, France
Skin-O-Meter: Brief Nudity

Before grade school, Zabou, who is the offspring of noted French actor Jean-Claude Drouot, started acting at her daddy's knees on his hit series *Thierry la Fronde*—well, it was a smash in France. Well, she's all grown up and making an even bigger impact in her native land's notorious sinema. The svelte, small-breasted pixie has been in such films as *Le Beauf* (1987), *Crimes et jardins* (1991), and *La Grande fille* (1994). Surprisingly, in spite of her countless appearances on the sensual screen of her beloved and frisky homeland, Zabou has been, relatively speaking, a bit on the skingy side. She didn't flash her petite pair until *The Perils of Gwendoline in the Land of the Yik Yak* (1984) opposite the equally naked Tawny Kitaen. There are ample looks at both actresses' mesmerizing chest flesh, plus it's kinky with naked bondage and other pants-raising activities. Zabou next lent her naked chest to American actress Sigourney Weaver's film *One Woman or Two* (1985). During the scene in question, Zabou is showing her hooters to none other than Gérard Depardieu. It's good to be French. She went on to bare her breastages yet again in *Le Complexe du kangourou* (1986) and *Moitié-moitié* (1989).

SKIN-fining Moment:

The Perils of Gwendoline in the Land of the Yik Yak (0:40) Nice look at Zabou's zaboobs as she removes her shirt in the rain.

See Her Naked In:

Moitié-moitié (1989) RB
La Travestie (1988)
Le Complexe du kangourou (1986) Breasts
One Woman or Two (1984) Breasts
The Perils of Gwendoline in the Land of the Yik Yak (1984) Breasts, Thong

---

"Nobody ever really thought I could do anything except look sexy on a poster and go shopping."

—PIA ZADORA

Pia Zadora

Born: May 4, 1954
Hoboken, New Jersey
Skin-O-Meter: Great Nudity

Impish and baby-faced, with a prepubescent pout and a hefty pair of grown-up titties, Pia Zadora is most famous for being Pia Zadora, and that's not fair. The prettiest little shag haircut ever to bop out of Hoboken, New Jersey, just can't get out from under the shadow of her own life. No one cares that she was on Broadway at eight, stomping the floorboards opposite living legend Tallulah Bankhead. The hit-single duets with the likes of Lou Christie and Jermaine Jackson are long forgotten. All anyone recalls is the marriage to a corporate raider twice her age and the scandal when her geezer hubby was suspected of buying Golden Globe votes for his darling Zadora. But what about those baby-soft boobies and that split loaf of sweet seat meat as immortalized in *Butterfly* (1981) ? It is a shame to let such beauty lapse from memory.

SKIN-fining Moment:

Butterfly (0:35) Pia steams up a tub toplessly as Stacy Keach sudses up her suckables from behind.

See Her Naked In:

The Lonely Lady (1983) Breasts, Buns
Nevada Heat (1982) RB, Buns
Butterfly (1981) Breasts, Buns

Roxana Zal

Born: November 8, 1969
California
Skin-O-Meter: Brief Nudity

The emotional push and pull of teenage angst can in large part be attributed to the conflict caused by a young lady's awakening sexuality. No chronicler of budding womanhood has held that cusp of agony and ecstasy so exquisitely as Roxana Zal. With the direct, questioning stare of her large, dark eyes, the impertinent thrust of her fetchingly slight underbite, and the restless rumblings of fresh flesh sprouting beneath her sweater, Roxana specialized in playing the daughter on the verge of a nervous breakthrough. In such dramas of postpubescence as *Adventures of Pollyanna* (1982), *Testament* (1983), and *Table for Five* (1983), Zal shone as the girl who would one day grow up to show her tits on film.

SKIN-fining Moment:

Red Line (0:50) Nice look at Roxana's rack as she emerges from the bathroom wearing nothing but black panties.

See Her Naked In:

3-Way (2004) Breasts
Butterfly Legend (1999) Breasts
Strip 'n Run (1998) Breasts
Red Line (1996) Breasts

Lisa Zane

Born: April 5, 1961
Chicago, Illinois
Skin-O-Meter: Brief Nudity

Brunette tinderbox Lisa Zane has secured herself a stream of residual checks with steady and plentiful appearances on network dramas, including recurring roles on the huge hits *ER* and *L.A. Law*. Compact, but plush of butt, with a wide mouth and openly provocative eyes set in a heart-shaped face, small and perky up top, there was a time when Lisa was not so secure. During those days of possibility she might strip down to soap and suds for a tight-squeeze shower-stall dalliance as she did in *Pucker up and Bark Like a Dog* (1989). She might pucker up and soulfully suck face with a stunning blonde of her own gender, as she did in *Terrified*

(1995). She might even go entirely cowboy in a girl-on-top sex romp with her tid-bit titties flouncing and her beaver flashing, as she did in *Bad Influence* (1999). A little insecurity could go a long way.

SKIN-fining Moment:

Pucker Up and Bark Like a Dog (0:52) Breasts in the shower and then in bed with her boyfriend. Zane-y!

See Her Naked In:

Unveiled (1993) Nip Slip LB
Bad Influence (1990) Breasts, Bush
Pucker Up and Bark Like a Dog (1989) Breasts

Lora Zane

Skin-O-Meter: Brief Nudity

Lora Zane is a waif-like beauty with luminous eyes, dark hair, and the small sweater wings of a fairy goddess. She's breast up close and personal, which explains her work on the stage. But Lora has also graced the boob tube with some sexy guest spots on various series such as *Married . . . with Children*, *Renegade*, and *Silk Stalkings*. She made her film debut in *Men Don't Leave* (1990), which is an odd choice for the openly lesbian thespian—at least that's the scuttlebutt, according to various Hollywood rags. Lora is a hard one to find onscreen, but in *Live Nude Girls* (1995) her time onscreen will get audiences hard . . . very hard. In a movie with exceptional nudity from such sweet tarts as Olivia d'Abo and Dana Delany, Lora still managed to express her sensual self in a very tasty fashion. She explored a fantasy of flour being patted over her mini-mams, which is sure to make viewers' dough rise. Lora didn't appear in another movie until *Under the Influence* (2002), a sexy thriller that somehow never utilized Lora's udderly hot under-things.

She's been off the radar since then, but Mr. Skin would sure love to get under her influence again sometime soon.

SKIN-fining Moment:

Live Nude Girls (0:05) Lora lies on a table in a fantasy, with her bare sugar-sacks being covered with flour. In-Zane!

See Her Naked In:

Live Nude Girls (1995) Breasts

Victoria Zdrok

Born: March 3, 1973
Kiev, Ukraine
Skin-O-Meter: Great Nudity

Brains may be good, as far as they go, but if an aspiring immigrant girl really wants to jump to the upper echelons of the American lifestyle, she should follow the example of Ukranian-born, azure-gazing blonde Victoria Zdrok. Victoria has moved through this life in the kind of super-built body that caused *Playboy* magazine scouts to yank her out of a psychology convention and open for her the door to the rewards and riches attendant with being crowned Playmate of the Month for October 1994. A Ph.D. in clinical psychology, Victoria has been smart enough to remain one of the hottest ladies in the land for a long, long time, ascending to the position of *Penthouse* magazine's Pet of the Year in 2004.

SKIN-fining Moment:

Playboy Celebrity Centerfold: Patti Davis (0:46) Vic poses outside, presenting us with her buxom boulders, fluffy tuft, and Zdrok-Zdrok-hard heinie.

See Her Naked In:

Temptations (2003) FFN, Buns
Playboy Celebrity Centerfold: Patti Davis (1994) FFN, Buns

Renée Zellweger

Born: April 25, 1969
Katy, Texas
Skin-O-Meter: Never Nude

Born in Texas of Swiss/Norwegian parents, Renée Zellweger was destined to be big and beautiful. She does not disappoint. The pretty blonde with the squinty eyes and permanently pouting mouth is a turn-on who turned out to be one of the most successful actresses in Hollywood. But her beginnings are humble, like her juicy melons, and she first auditioned for movie roles in her native Lone Star State. She got bit parts in *Reality Bites* (1994) and *Empire Records* (1995), but it was the local low-budget flicks that launched her into stardom. Critics were wowed by her damsel-in-distress role in *Return of the Texas Chainsaw Massacre* (1994), opposite fellow Texan up-and-comer Matthew McConaughey, and *Love and a .45* (1994). It was in the latter that viewers got their first and, frankly, only look at Renée's lovely body. She didn't flash the breast bits but got leggy in her silky panties, was cheeky rolling about in a bedroom scene, and flapped her floppers in a wet baby-T. That led to her being cast as co-star to Tom Cruise in the mega-hit *Jerry Maguire* (1996). While she didn't show us the honey, Renée was still charming in a girl-next-door-that-we'd-love-to-bang kind of a way. Mr. Skin isn't the only one who feels that way. After appearing with Jim Carrey in the comedy *Me, Myself & Irene* (2000), the two were engaged to be married. Luckily that broke off, and randy Renée is a free-range chicken ready to pluck. She put on some pounds and squeezed into a Playboy Bunny suit for her next smash hit, *Bridget Jones's Diary* (2001), and then lost it for a sleek and sensual turn as a femme fatale in the blockbuster musical *Chicago* (2002). Oscar gold swooned for her performance in *Cold Mountain* (2003), but Mr. Skin just hopes that she finally flashes those mouth-watering hills of hers before they become cold mountains.

SKIN-fining Moment:

Love and a .45 (0:13) Check peck! Renée lies in bed with Gil Bellows, then rolls over to reveal her thong undies.

Leslie Harter Zemeckis

Skin-O-Meter: Great Nudity

If you recognize Leslie Harter Zemeckis, it's because she's shown her fetching face and form on many a sexy series. Leslie made us feel funny inside with her curvy cans and obtuse caboose in guest appearances on *Caroline in the City*, *Silk Stalkings*, and *Beverly Hills, 90210*. It's easy to want to follow this fox around town after seeing her at her best undressed in flesh flicks such as *Damien's Seed* (1996), *Life As a Gigolo* (1998), and *The Sexperiment* (1998). Conduct your own sexperiment by catching Zemeckis during any of her skinematic stylings onscreen.

SKIN-fining Moment:

Damien's Seed (0:56) Electrifying eyefuls of Leslie's garters and swell-sized powerfully puffy-nipped natural-sacks as she boinks a dude and then basks bare-boobedly in the dewey afterglow.

See Her Naked In:

Sacrifice (2000) LB
Life of a Gigolo (1998) FFN, Buns
The Sexperiment (1998) Breasts, Bush, Buns
Damien's Seed (1996) Breasts

TeleVisions:

Women: Stories of Passion Breasts, Buns

Patricia Zentilli

Born: November 27, 1970
Kingston, Ontario, Canada
Skin-O-Meter: Brief Nudity

If cable TV has done nothing else, it has kept legions of married men and junior-high Lotharios out of the drive-in theaters and downtown grindhouses. As recently as one generation back, the inquisitive male of the species was forced to venture from his home and endure indignities such as bad weather, face-sucking teenagers, and seat-hopping pederasts for the simple pleasure of witnessing casual and essential nudity in a dramatic presentation. Now he need only possess a satellite dish or premium cable and no parental or spousal controls, and he is rewarded with the likes of platinum-tressed gem Patricia Zentilli, a vibrant and unbridled thespian who appears to specialize in emoting while nakedly enduring shower spray and portraying the raw moments of a porn starlet's workday, all fed direct to the home screen on Sci-fi's *Lexx* and Showtime's *Street Time*.

SKIN-fining Moment:

Lexx "Wake the Dead" (1999) Patricia soaps up in a coed space shower, showing off her cosmic casabas and full moon.

TeleVisions:

Lexx Breasts, Buns
Street Time Breasts

Catherine Zeta-Jones

Born: September 25, 1969
Swansea, West Glamorgan, Wales, UK
Skin-O-Meter: Great Nudity

With hair as black as night framing a classic beauty of striking angular cheekbones, searing brown eyes, and passion-pulsing lips, Catherine Zeta-Jones exhibits the striking Latin passion and sensuality as shaded in a Valasquez portrait. But unlike the seventeenth-century noblewomen of Madrid who sat for the Spanish master, Zeta-Jones is Welsh, and her sizzling onscreen sexuality has taken America by storm. It is not because Catherine exposed her breastly contours and erectile nipples to camera light that she is one of the world's biggest movie stars today. Those fleeting flashes of chest-flesh past do, however, make viewing Zeta-Jones slithering in a skintight burglar's outfit in *Entrapment* (1999) just a mite sexier.

SKIN-fining Moment:

Les Mille et une nuits (0:50) CZJ shows her ample breastage as she falls from the sky, then a quick look at her hind quarters as she lands in an old guy's lap. Force of habit, I guess . . .

MR. SKIN'S TOP TEN

Greatest Movies Ever Made

. . . Masterpiece (of ass) theatre

10. *Sirens* 1994 (Australia)
9. *La Belle noiseuse* 1992 (France)
8. *Dancing at the Blue Iguana* 2000 (USA)
7. *Salon Kitty* 1976 (Italy)
6. *Full Body Massage* 1995 (USA)
5. *Games Girls Play* 1974 (UK)
4. *Prison Girls* 1972 (USA)
3. *Two Moon Junction* 1988 (USA)
2. *Up!* 1976 (USA)
1. ***Showgirls* 1995 (USA)**

See Her Naked In:

The Mask of Zorro (1998) Nip Slip RB
Katharina die Große (1995) Buns
Out of the Blue (BBC-TV) (1991) Breasts
Les Mille et une nuits (1990) Breasts, Buns

Nikki Schieler Ziering

Born: August 9, 1971
Norwalk, California
Skin-O-Meter: Great Nudity

Imagine if the finest blue-eyed, hungry-mouthed, huge-boobed blonde beauties who populate the pages of a magazine such as *Playboy*, particularly the centerfold pages of that esteemed publication's September 1997 issue, could be made to order in a flesh-and-blood version that would then join the rest of us in real life as a cleavage-carting fixture in gonadally mesmerizing feature entertainments of tube and screen, such as *American Wedding* (2003). But wait, what we describe is, indeed, reality. Fantastically foxy blonde Nikki Schieler Ziering is all the proof necessary that we live in the best of all possible universes. Upgrade your existence with Schieler Ziering reruns of *Silk Stalkings*, *V.I.P.*, and *Pacific Blue*, or simply turn back the hands of time and let the clock stick at Nikki's bachelor-party debauchery in *American Wedding*.

SKIN-fining Moment:

American Wedding (0:44) Hat trick three-parter! Darling Nikki, leather-clad as a "bad cop" stripper, shows off her silicone sweater treats at the bachelor party. Cuff me, please.

See Her Naked In:

American Wedding (2003) Breasts
Numerous *Playboy* Videos

Daphne Zuniga

Born: October 28, 1962
Berkeley, California
Skin-O-Meter: Great Nudity

With a look that is kind, sensual, sensitive, and caring, dark-haired beauty Daphne Zuniga combines the best traits of a beloved pet puppy and a movie-star-quality lust object. Though her lasting impressions seem to be destined for the TV screen, particularly on the bed-hopping marathon *Melrose Place*, Daphne was once a force to reckon with on the big screen. She seduced the outer galaxies as Druish Princess Vespa in director Mel Brooks's screwy *Spaceballs* (1987). Augmenting her rites of interplanetary seduction, delicious Daphne cracked a tight butt smile while tugging up her panties in the teen slasher pic *The Initiation* (1984), cowered totally naked from a pursuing menace in *Last Rites* (1988), and let her ass luxuriate in a shadowy, long-running, bed-top shot in *Staying Together* (1989). For someone so nice, Daphne sure is cheeky.

SKIN-fining Moment:

Staying Together (0:59) An extremely long visit with Daphne's dimpled derriere as she receives some bedtime action.

See Her Naked In:

Staying Together (1989) Buns
Last Rites (1988) LB, Buns
The Initiation (1984) Buns

Elsa Zylberstein

Born: October 16, 1969
Paris, France
Skin-O-Meter: Great Nudity

Perhaps it is true that the ladies from France wear no underpants. Evidence of a pantie-free society is offered by the unclad, white-as-naked-day butt of raven-haired Parisian coquette Elsa Zylberstein. Elsa's sweetly symmetrical couch cushions make a show of unity in *Lautrec* (1998) and *Un Ange* (2001), a pair of elevated cultural offerings from the land of liberty, fraternity, and derriere. A shadowy pinch of muff in *Metroland* (1997) lends further credence to the ladies of ooh-la-la land eschewing the wisp of satin or cotton at the crotch. But let's talk tits. Elsa possesses big natural ones and a face just as downy soft and enveloping as her formidable cleavage. Both are featured in close-ups in almost all her films. How can she be faulted if her panties are only an afterthought?

SKIN-fining Moment:

Metroland (0:51) Fresh from sex, Elsa shows off her upper-orbs while chatting in the sack with Christian Bale.

See Her Naked In:

Monsieur N. (2003) Breasts
Un Ange (2001) Breasts, Buns
Lautrec (1998) Breasts, Buns
L'Homme est une femme comme les autres (1998) Breasts
Metroland (1997) Breasts
Tenue correcte exigée (1997) Breasts, Buns
Farinelli (1994) Breasts
Van Gogh (1991) Breasts, Bush, Buns

Anatomy Awards

Every spring, Mr. Skin announces the winners of the Anatomy Awards—his picks for the finest skinchievements in the nudity arts and sciences that took place during the previous year. After revealing the randy recipients on The Howard Stern Show, the complete list of the victorious vixens and fleshy films is posted on MrSkin.com. The following pages compile the entire history of Mr. Skin's Anatomy Awards.

2004 Anatomy Awards

Best Wet T-shirt—Carmen Electra, *My Boss's Daughter*
Debut Nude Scene—Christina Ricci, *Prozac Nation*
Best Network TV Nudity—Charlotte Ross, *NYPD Blue*
Best Talk Show Outfit—Cameron Diaz, *The Tonight Show*
Best Nudity by a Former Child Star—Justine Bateman, *Out of Order*
Best Nudity by a Dead Chick—Jessica Karr, *Bad Boys II*
Best Bikini—Demi Moore, *Charlie's Angeles: Full Throttle*
Best Bondage Scene—Chloe Hunter, *Spun*
Best Bunnage—Kristanna Loken, *Terminator 3: Rise of the Machines*
Best Nip Slip—(Tie) Jennifer Love Hewitt, *The Tuxedo* and Mandy Moore, *How to Deal*
Best Breasts (Real Funbags)—Ludivine Sagnier, *The Swimming Pool*
Best Breasts (Phony Funbags)—Nikki Schieler Ziering, *American Wedding*
Best Furburgerage—Mary Louise Parker, *Angels in America*
Best B-movie—*SpiderBabe*
Best Over 50 Nude Scene—Diane Keaton, *Something's Gotta Give*
Best Retro DVD Nudity Release in 2003—*The Woman in Red* (1984)
Best KY Jelly Wrestling Scene—Lisa Donatz and Corinne Kingsbury, *Old School*
Breast Picture (Best Movie for Nudity—*In the Cut*
Lifetime SKINchievement Award—Mimi Rogers

2003 Anatomy Awards

Best Funbags—Heather Graham, *Killing Me Softly*
Best Lesbo Scene—Rebecca Romijn-Stamos and Rie Rasmussen, *Femme Fatale*
Best Nip-slip (Unintentional Nippage)—Christina Aguilera, *MTV Diary*
Best Lip-Slip (Unintentional Nippage)—Kelly Hu, *The Scorpion King*
Best Geriatric Jugs—Mamie Van Doren, *Slackers*
Best Bikini Scene—Eliza Dushku, *The New Guy*
Best Ass—Nicole Kidman, *Birthday Girl*
Best Sex Scene—Selma Blair, *Storytelling*
Best Panty Flash—Liv Tyler, *One Night at McCool's*
Best Crotch Patch—Angie Everhart, *Sexual Predator*
Best Furburgerage—Emily Mortimer, *Lovely & Amazing*
Best Pokiosity—Kirsten Dunst, *Spiderman*
Scariest Nude Scene—Kathy Bates, *About Schmidt*
Best Movie for Nudity—*Frida*
Lifetime SKINchievement Award—Jacqueline Bisset

2002 Anatomy Awards

Best Breasts:
B Cup Division—Penelope Cruz, *Captain Corelli's Mandolin*
C Cup Division—Angelina Jolie, *Original Sin*
D Cup Division—Jennifer Tilly, *Dancing at the Blue Iguana*

Best Nude Debut—Rachel Miner, *Buffy*

Best Lesbo Scene—Piper Perabo and Jessica Pare, *Lost and Delirious* (00:28:40)

Best Nip-slip (Unintentional Nippage)—Nicole Kidman, *Moulin Rouge*

George W. Bush Award (Best Bush Shot)—Laura Linney, *Maze*

Best Sex Scene—Halle Berry and Billy Bob Thorton, *Monster's Ball*

Best Nudity by an Old Broad—Farrah Fawcett, *Dr. T and the Women*

Devastating Dumper Award (Best Ass)—Daryl Hannah, *Dancing at the Blue Iguana*

Best Use of a Lollipop—Alisha Klass, *Center of the World*

Best Nudity by a Foreign Babe—Alex Kingston, *Essex Boys*

Best Close-up Crotch View—Bijou Phillips, *Bully*

Best Topless Ping-Pong Scene—Odessa Munroe and Tracy Trueman, *Saving Silverman*

Breast Picture (Best Movie for Nudity)—*Dancing at the Blue Iguana*

Lifetime SKINchievement Award—Angie Dickinson

2001 Anatomy Awards

Best Breasts:
B Cup Division—Amy Smart, *Road Trip*
C Cup Division—Katie Holmes, *The Gift*
D Cup Division—Jennifer Connelly, *Waking the Dead*

Best Debut Nude Scene—Amanda Peet, *The Whole Nine Yards*

Best Lesbo Scene—Michelle Williams and Chloë Sevigny, *If These Walls Could Talk 2*

All Deliveries in Rear (Best Butt Shot)—Peta Wilson, *Mercy*

Apple Doesn't Fall Far From the Tree Award (2nd Generation Nudity)—Kate Hudson, *Almost Famous*

George W. Bush Award (Best Bush Shot)—Kate Winslet, *Holy Smoke*

Best Full Frontal by a TV Star—Alex Kingston, *Essex Boys*

Kathy Bates Award (Actress That Should Have Left Her Clothes On)—Ella Mitchell, *Big Momma's House*

Best Over 50 Nude Scene—Barbara Hershey, *Drowning on Dry Land*

Best Striptease—Shannon Elizabeth, *Dish Dogs*

Best Nudity by a Dead Chick—Catherine Sutherland, *The Cell*

Best Skinny Dip—Charlize Theron, *Reindeer Games*

Breast Picture (Best Movie for Nudity)—*8½ Women*

Best TV Show for Nudity—*Sex and the City*

Wildest Sex Scene—Ménage à trois scene, *American Psycho*

Best Nudity by a Foreign Babe—Laetitia Casta, *La Bicyclette Bleue*

Lifetime SKIN chievement Award—Sharon Stone

2000 Anatomy Award Winners

Best Skin Flick (Theater)—*American Pie*

Best Skin Flick (DVD)—*Jaded*

Best Made-for-Cable Movie—*Introducing Dorothy Dandridge*

Best Breasts (Real)—Diane Lane, *A Walk on the Moon*

Best Breast (Phony)—Shannon Elizabeth, *American Pie*

Best Buns—Nicole Kidman, *Eyes Wide Shut*

Nice Beaver—Elizabeth Perkins, *I'm Losing You*

Best Nude Scene by a Chick with a Famous Dad—Alison Eastwood, *Friends & Lovers*

Hottest Star—Angelina Jolie, *Pushing Tin*

Best Bikini—Ali Larter, *Varsity Blues*

Best Lesbo Kiss—Sarah Michelle Gellar and Selma Blair, *Cruel Intentions*

Biggest Natural Funbags—Aida Turturro, *Illuminata*

Best Debut Nude Scene—Tara Reid, *Body Shots*

Best Nudity in a Chick Flick—*Illuminata*

Best Over 40 Nude Scene—Rene Russo, *The Thomas Crown Affair*

Best Over 50 Nude Scene—Patti LuPone, *Summer of Sam*

Hottest Teacher Who Also Works at a Strip Joint—Tonie Perensky, *Varsity Blues*

Best Nudity in a PG Movie—Sharon Stone, *The Muse*

Hottest Foreign Babe—Kate Winslet, *Hideous Kinky*

Best Documentary—*The Mating Habits of the Earthbound Humans*

Best Wet T-shirt—Keri Russell, *Eight Days a Week*

Mr. Skin's Lifetime SKINchievement Award—Phoebe Cates, *Paradise '81*

Video Resources

Mr. Skin's Skincyclopedia would have been impossible without the assistance and heroic efforts of the following video companies. When you want to buy one (or more) of the movies I've reviewed (and countless others), here are the outlets on which you can (and should) rely.

Anchor Bay Entertainment
anchorbayentertainment.com

Ardustry
ardustry.com

Blue Underground
blue-underground.com

Brain Damage
braindamagefilms.com

Central Park Media
centralparkmedia.com

Columbia TriStar
sonypictures.com

Elite Entertainment
elitedisc.com

Facets Multimedia
facets.org/asticat

First Look
firstlookmedia.com

First Run Features
Firstrunfeatures.com

Fox Home Entertainment
foxhome.com

Koch
Kochentertainment.com

Life Size Entertainment
lser.net

Media Blasters
media-blasters.com

MGM Home Video
mgm.com/video.do

MTI
edbaran.com/mti
    homevideo/index.htm

Music Video Distributors
musicvideodistributors.com

New Line
newline.com

New Yorker Films
newyorkfilms.com

Panik House Entertainment
panikhouse.com

Paramount
paramount.com

Pathfinder Pictures
pathfinderpictures.com

Playboy
playboy.com

Retro Media
retromedia.org

Seduction Cinema
seductioncinema.com

Something Weird Video
somethingweird.com

Synapse Films
synapse-films.com

Sub Rosa
b-movie.com

TLA Releasing
tlavideo.com

Troma
troma.com

Vanguard
vanguardcinema.com

Velocity
thinkfilmcompany.com

Ventura Distribution
venturadistribution.com

Wellspring
wellspring.com/homevideo/

Wicked Pixel Films
wickedpixel.com

Xenon
xenonpictures.com

Skindex